Hidden Rockies

The Adventurer's Guide

Published by: Ulysses Press
3286 Adeline Street, Suite 1
Berkeley, CA 94703

Library of Congress Catalog Card Number 94-60060
ISBN 1-56975-000-9

Printed in the U.S.A. by R. R. Donnelley & Sons

10 9 8 7 6 5 4 3 2 1

Managing Editor: Claire Chun
Project Director: Ellen Nidy
Editorial Associates: Doug Lloyd, Jennifer Wilkoff, Mark Rosen, Lee Micheaux
Proof Reader: Kate Baldus
Cartographer: Bruce Appleyard/GeoGraphics, Berkeley, CA
Cover Design: Design Works, Leslie Henriques
Index: Sayre Van Young
Cover Photography: Front cover photo by Kerrick James; back cover photo by R. Dahlquist/SuperStock
Color Separation: Twin Age Limited, Hong Kong

Distributed in the United States by Publishers Group West, in Canada by Raincoast Books, and in Great Britain and Europe by World Leisure Marketing

Hidden Rockies

The Adventurer's Guide

John Gottberg   Richard Harris

Editor
Fran Haselsteiner

Illustrator
Doug McCarthy

Ulysses Press   Berkeley, CA

Contents

CHAPTER ONE
The Rocky Mountains 1
Why 1
The Story of the Rocky Mountains 4
Where to Go 16
When to Go 19
How to Deal With . . . 29
Sporting Life 37

CHAPTER TWO
Denver and the Front Range 43
Denver 44
West of Denver 55
North of Denver 64
Colorado Springs Area 75
Pikes Peak Area 83
Pueblo-Walsenburg-Trinidad Area 93
Sporting Life 96
Transportation 102

CHAPTER THREE
Northern Colorado Rockies 105
Winter Park–Grand Lake Area 106
Breckenridge–South Park Area 111
Vail-Leadville Area 117
Aspen Area 126
Glenwood Springs Area 132
Steamboat Springs Area 137
Sporting Life 142
Transportation 151

CHAPTER FOUR
Southern Colorado Rockies 155
Alamosa Area 158
Gunnison–Crested Butte Area 163
Grand Junction Area 172
Durango and San Juan Skyway Area 178
Sporting Life 196
Transportation 207

CHAPTER FIVE
Utah Rockies 211
Vernal Area 212
North of Salt Lake City 217
Salt Lake City 223
South of Salt Lake City 231
Sporting Life 241
Transportation 245

CHAPTER SIX
Southern Wyoming Rockies 249
Cheyenne-Laramie Area 250
Rock Springs–Green River Area 259
Casper Area 265
Lander Area 272
Sporting Life 278
Transportation 282

CHAPTER SEVEN
Yellowstone and Jackson Hole 285
Jackson Hole 286
Grand Teton National Park 295
Yellowstone National Park 299
Yellowstone Gateway Communities 313
Sporting Life 316
Transportation 325

CHAPTER EIGHT
Northern Wyoming Rockies 329
Cody Area 330
Big Horn Country 339
Sheridan Area 347
Northeastern Wyoming 353
Sporting Life 358
Transportation 365

CHAPTER NINE
Southwestern Idaho Rockies 367
Boise Area 368
Treasure Valley 380
Hells Canyon and the McCall Area 382
Boise County and the Boise Basin 389
Mountain Home and Owyhee County 392
Sporting Life 395
Transportation 401

CHAPTER TEN
Southeastern Idaho Rockies 405
Twin Falls Area 406
Sun Valley Area 414
The Sawtooths and Upper Salmon 420
Pocatello Area 425
Bear River Country 430
Idaho Falls 434
The Swan and Teton Valleys 437
Henry's Fork 440
Sporting Life 442
Transportation 451

CHAPTER ELEVEN
Northern Idaho Rockies 455
Lewiston-Moscow Area 456
Coeur d'Alene Area 466
Sporting Life 475
Transportation 480

CHAPTER TWELVE
Western Montana Rockies 483
Missoula 484
Bitterroot Valley 490
Flathead Indian Reservation and Lake 494
Flathead Valley 499
Glacier National Park 504
Sporting Life 510
Transportation 516

CHAPTER THIRTEEN
Southern Montana Rockies 519
Helena Area 520
Butte Area 527
Dillon Area 533
Alder Gulch 538
Bozeman Area 540
Park and Sweet Grass Counties 548
Sporting Life 552
Transportation 558

CHAPTER FOURTEEN
Montana East of the Rockies 561
Billings Area 562
The Big Horns and Beyond 570
The Lower Yellowstone Valley 574
Great Falls Area 577
The Hi-Line 584
The Heartland 588
Sporting Life 590
Transportation 595

Index 599
About the Authors 626

MAPS

The Rockies 3
Colorado Front Range 45
Downtown Denver 49
Denver Area 59
Northern Colorado 107
Southern Colorado 157
Northern Utah 213
Salt Lake City 225
Southern Wyoming 251
Yellowstone & Jackson Hole 287
Northern Wyoming 331
Southwest Idaho 369
Southeast Idaho 407
Northern Idaho 457
Western Montana 485
Southern Montana 521
Eastern Montana 563

SPECIAL FEATURES

The Meaning of Mountains	12
Colorado's Golden Glow	86
Melting Dreams and Mountain Bikes	120
Colorado's Native American Heritage	180
In the Land of Latter-Day Saints	236
Wagon Trains on the Oregon Trail	266
Winter Wonderland	319
Spirit of the Old West: "Buffalo Bill" Cody	337
An Eagle's-Eye View of the Snake River	379
Heaven for Fly-Fishermen	443
I Will Fight No More, Forever	461
Beware the Bear	509
Ghost Towns	541
Charles M. Russell: The Cowboy Artist	583

Notes from the Publisher

Throughout the text, hidden beaches, locales, special features, remote regions and little-known spots are marked with a star (★).

* * *

An alert, adventurous reader is as important as a travel writer in keeping a guidebook up-to-date and accurate. So if you happen upon a great restaurant, discover a hidden locale or (heaven forbid) find an error in the text, we'd appreciate hearing from you. Just write to:

Ulysses Press
3286 Adeline Street Suite 1
Berkeley, CA 94703

* * *

It is our desire as publishers to create guidebooks that are responsible as well as informative. The danger of exploring hidden locales is that they will no longer be secluded.

We hope that our guidebooks treat the people, country, and land we visit with respect. We ask that our readers do the same.

CHAPTER ONE

The Rocky Mountains

The Why, Where, When and How of Traveling in the Rockies

Why

The explosive spoutings of Yellowstone's Old Faithful Geyser, the sweeping panoramic view from the summit of Pikes Peak, the splashes of aspen gold across the mountainsides in autumn and the stately Victorian mansions built by gold and silver barons in dozens of small towns—these are just a few of the sights you'll experience while touring the Rocky Mountains and treasure for years to come.

The Rockies form a vast, varied, supremely rugged landscape that surrounds the traveler with constant reminders of the majestic power of nature in the raw at any time of year: winter snowdrifts 25 feet deep covering mountainsides nearly to the treetops; spring waterfalls plunging down sheer canyon walls, summer thunderstorms whose awesome fury gives life to fragile meadows of alpine wildflowers; and autumn leaves in flaming hues that dance in defiance of bitter arctic storms to come.

History, too, is everywhere you look though even today the land remains mostly untamed. Abandoned gold and silver mines that once yielded untold wealth dot the mountainsides above ghost towns that flourished and vanished in a few short decades, mute testimony to humankind's puny attempts at conquering the power of the wilderness. Railroad beds, their tracks ripped up long ago for scrap metal, reach mountain heights and canyon depths, amazing us with their builders' achievement and folly. Artifacts and remnants of the original Native American tribes who traveled these mountains for millennia hint at ways to live in harmony with the forces of nature.

Today, the Rockies provide unparalleled opportunities for outdoor adventuring of all kinds. Downhill and cross-country skiing, mountain biking, backpacking, boating, trout fishing, horseback riding—the region offers something for every vacationer who wants to spice up his or her trip with once-in-a-lifetime thrills.

Hidden Rockies is designed to help you explore the mountainous regions of Colorado, Utah, Wyoming, Idaho and Montana. It covers popular, "must-see" places, offering advice on how best to enjoy them. It also tells you about many off-the-beaten-path spots, the kind you would find by talking with folks at the local café or with someone who has lived in the area all of his or her life. It describes the region's history, its natural areas and its residents, both human and animal. It suggests places to eat, to lodge, to play, to camp. Taking into account varying interests, budgets and tastes, it provides the information you need whether your vacation style involves backpacking, golf, museum browsing, shopping or all of the above.

This book covers the Rocky Mountain regions of five states. Colorado, the most populous part, has the highest concentration of "Fourteeners"—mountain peaks reaching elevations of more than 14,000 feet above sea level. Utah's Rockies, limited to two ranges that are perpendicular to each other, shelter the Great Salt Lake and the homeland of the Mormons. Wyoming boasts Yellowstone and Grand Teton national parks. The Oregon Trail extends through both Wyoming and Idaho; Idaho also is the home of Hells Canyon, deeper than the Grand Canyon, and renowned whitewater rafting and flyfishing. Montana has Glacier National Park, Little Bighorn Battlefield and vast stretches of "Big Sky" country. Owing to space limitations, this book does not include the part of the Rocky Mountains that extends from the Colorado state line south into New Mexico, encompassing Taos and Santa Fe. The New Mexico Rockies receive extensive coverage in this book's companion volume, *Hidden Southwest*.

The traveling part of the book begins in Chapter Two with Denver, the region's largest city and main transportation hub, and includes the towns and cities of Colorado's Front Range as well as the nearby mountains. Chapter Three heads west into the heart of the Colorado Rockies, home of such world-class ski resorts as Aspen, Vail, Breckenridge and Steamboat Springs. Chapter Four covers the southern part of Colorado from the Great Sand Dunes to the San Juan Skyway, the most spectacular scenic route in a state that's full of great roadside views.

Chapter Five looks at the Rocky Mountains in the northeast quadrant of Utah. In this chapter you'll find complete information on Flaming Gorge National Recreation Area and the Great Salt Lake, as well as the religious sights of Salt Lake City, the largest city on the western slope of the Rockies. This chapter also takes you to lesser-known areas in the Wasatch and Uinta mountains with their grand-scale canyons and wilderness areas. For other mountain areas in the southern part of the state, you'll want to refer to *Hidden Southwest*.

Chapters Six through Eight explore Wyoming. Chapter Six takes you through the eloquent emptiness of southern Wyoming, following the tracks of the pioneers along the Oregon Trail to the magnificent Wind River Range. Chapter Seven visits Yellowstone National Park, the world's preeminent thermal wonderland, plus the spectacular mountain scenery of nearby Grand Teton National Park and the booming Old West town of Jackson. Chapter Eight spans the rest of northern Wyoming from Cody, "rodeo capital of the world," through the Big Horn Mountains to Devils Tower National Monument.

Chapters Nine through Eleven focus on Idaho. Chapter Nine begins in Boise, the surprising state capital, and takes in the remarkable Snake River chasm of Hells Canyon. Chapter Ten heads east to the resort area of Sun Valley and the Sawtooth National Recreation Area, and follows the ever-changing Snake through southeastern Idaho. Chapter Eleven visits the pristine lakes and remote rivers of the northern Panhandle.

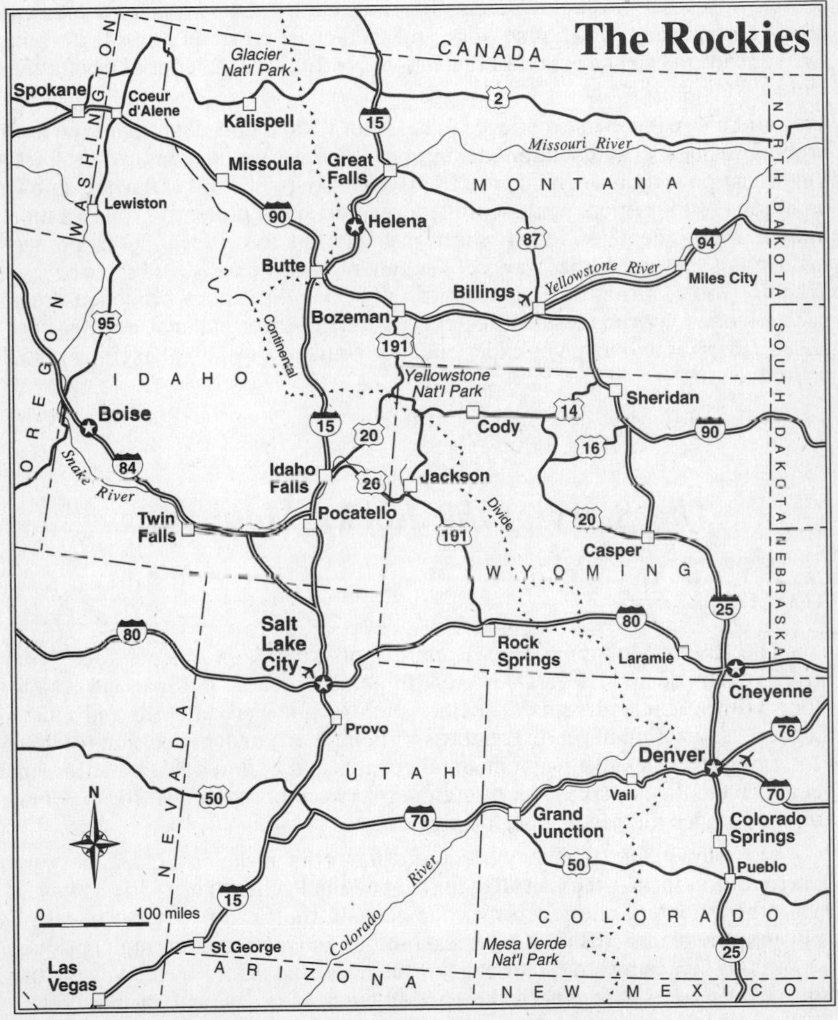

Chapters Twelve through Fourteen cover Montana. Chapter Twelve surveys western Montana, including glorious Glacier National Park, the National Bison Range and the beautiful Flathead Lake area. Chapter Thirteen delves into the rich heritage of southern Montana's most famous mining towns, past and present. Chapter Fourteen focuses on the seemingly endless plains of eastern Montana, a region dominated by the Missouri and Yellowstone rivers and including Bighorn Canyon National Recreation Area and Little Bighorn Battlefield National Monument.

What you choose to see and do is up to you. The old cliché that "there is something for everyone" pretty well rings true in the Rocky Mountains. In this book you'll find free campgrounds with hiking trails and fantastic views as well as several plush playgrounds for the wealthy and well known. You can take a chairlift to a high alpine ridge and then coast down on a mountain bike. Or check into a bed and breakfast that has delightful little galleries and boutiques within walking distance.

There's so much to experience in the Rocky Mountain states that even most lifelong residents can count on making new discoveries once in a while. First-time vacation visitors are hard pressed just to make brief stops at the best-known highlights of the region, while seasoned travelers often prefer to explore a more limited area in depth and then return on later trips to different spots, perhaps in different seasons. Either way, people generally come back, and often to stay. Whether you're a first-time visitor setting out on your Rocky Mountain dream vacation or a long-time resident searching for that proverbial undiscovered spot, *Hidden Rockies* will help you experience for yourself a wealth of exciting places and adventures.

The Story of the Rocky Mountains

GEOLOGY

The Rocky Mountains consist mainly of granite, an igneous rock. That means it is made up of several different minerals—quartz, feldspar and granite, along with traces and veins of metals such as gold, silver, lead and zinc—blended deep within the earth countless millennia ago under conditions of great heat. Long after the other major mountain chains in the United States had already been formed, the massive layer of granite that would become the Rocky Mountains lay under the sandy floor of a great sea.

Very slowly, inexorably, two tectonic plates that make up most of the North American continent—the Canadian Shield and the Pacific Plate—drifted toward each other, floating on molten rock far beneath the earth's surface. In a slow collision, the plates crushed against each other and started to crumple, pushing the granite layer upward. Dinosaurs, which were abundant in the area at that time, would have experienced the phenomenon as occasional earthquakes.

Sixty million years ago, around the time dinosaurs became extinct, the granite mass cracked through the red sandstone surface that had been beaches and marshy wetlands. In many places along the edges of the uplift, the fractured sandstone was thrust skyward to create the spires and hogback formations that characterize the Front Range of the central Rockies today. The collision of tectonic plates and the uplifting of the granite rock continues even now, though the process is so slow that the mountains have gained only a few inches in height during the time humankind has walked the earth.

The mountains as we see them today were shaped by glaciers. A series of ice ages, the last of which ended 10,000 years ago—a mere eyeblink in geological time—covered the high country in accumulations of snow and ice. These glaciers flowed down the mountainsides slowly, in solid frozen rivers that gouged deep valleys called moraines, creating steep mountain faces and marking the courses for the turbulent rivers that would slice canyons hundreds of feet deep.

The lofty mountains attract storm clouds like a magnet, making for rainfall and snowfall many times greater than in the deserts and arid prairies at their feet. Runoff from the melting snowpack in spring and the thunderstorms of summer gives birth to most of the great rivers of the West, including the Colorado, Rio Grande, Arkansas, Platte, Snake, Yellowstone and Missouri. It is the rivers that give significance to the Continental Divide, the dotted line on maps that meanders through the wilderness connecting the highest mountain passes.

All precipitation that falls east of the Continental Divide flows eventually to the Gulf of Mexico or the Atlantic Ocean (or, near Glacier National Park, to Hudson Bay), while west of the Divide it flows to the Pacific. In some places, such as Wyoming's Great Divide Basin, the backbone of the continent is marked by nothing more spectacular than a point-of-interest sign at a roadside rest area. In others, crossing the Continental Divide means climbing a switchback road up a wall of granite to the summit of a pass more than two miles above sea level.

Volcanism has had a profound effect in parts of the Rockies. The earth remains especially restless in and around Yellowstone National Park, which encompasses a giant ancient caldera. Geysers, hot springs, fumaroles and boiling mud appear here in greater concentrations than anywhere else on earth, and the area weathers more earthquakes than anywhere in the lower 48 states outside of California. Central Idaho southwest of Yellowstone is a vast and porous lava plain that was active until only about 2000 years ago. Hot springs throughout the northern Rockies are reminders that volcanism remains a force.

HISTORY

NATIVE PEOPLE Native Americans touched the Rockies lightly and with reverence. The people of the mountains—Utes in Colorado and Utah, Shoshone in Wyoming and southern Idaho, Nez Perce and Coeur d'Alene in northern Idaho, Flathead and Blackfoot in Montana—lived as nomads, huddling around fires in bison-leather tents through thousands of long, brutal winters along the foothills of the Rockies, waiting to follow the spring snowmelt into hidden canyons and ancient forests of the high country. The Native American population of the Rockies was never large. The Ute, for instance, laid claim to virtually all the mountain country of Colorado yet numbered only about as many as the year-round residents of Aspen today. With such a vast territory to roam, the mountain tribes rarely came into conflict. In fact, they rarely encountered one another except on purpose, in intertribal powwows held at traditional times and places for purposes of trade, social contests, spiritual ceremonies and political diplomacy.

Warfare among the tribes took place mainly along the eastern edge of the mountains, where Plains Indians such as the Arapaho, Crow and Cheyenne would send hunting parties into the rich high-country valleys of the mountain people. Before the arrival of whites, intertribal battles bore little resemblance to the bloodbaths that would come later. War parties were generally small and had no firearms, steel or horses. The limited supply of arrows a warrior could carry did not last long in battle, and it was better to save them for hunting if possible, since each handmade arrow represented many hours of work.

At least two non-Indian influences—horses and guns—began to change the tribes' way of life long before the first white man set foot in the central and northern Rockies at the beginning of the 19th century. Horses first came into Indian hands in northern New Mexico in 1680, when Pueblo people revolted against their Spanish oppressors, looting and burning every settler's home. Navajo and Apache groups agreed to help the Pueblos drive out the Spaniards; in exchange, they could keep all the livestock they could round up from the Spanish ranches and farms—including thousands of horses. Many more horses driven off from the ranches were never captured but instead went wild to spawn the herds of mustangs that inhabit remote areas of all five Rocky Mountain states even today. As neighbors of the Navajo, the Ute people got their first horses around 1700, and within the next 60 years virtually every tribe in the Rocky Mountain West had bought, captured or stolen enough horses to breed its own herd. Horses let the Indians travel much farther and faster, bringing more frequent contact—whether friendly or hostile—between tribes.

Guns spread more slowly among Native Americans. In the British and French settlements along America's east coast, armies of both colonial powers gave rifles to tribes that helped fight the Seven Years War (1756–63). Guns meant power to conquer other tribes. Fur traders on what was then the American frontier found that the self-defense needs of the tribes made guns extremely valuable as items of exchange, as well as empowering the tribes to hunt more efficiently and trade larger quantities of valuable furs for more guns. As a tribe got guns by trading with whites from the east, it often turned them against rival tribes to the west in order to expand its hunting territory. In this way, firearms often made their way westward ahead of the first white explorers.

EXPLORERS AND MOUNTAIN MEN A vast area of North America, from the Mississippi River to the Pacific Northwest coast, including all of the central and northern Rockies, was claimed as Spanish territory in 1769, even though no Spanish settlement was ever established beyond the port city of New Orleans. France acquired the Louisiana Territory from Spain by treaty in 1800, but except for small trading expeditions up the river, the French found it impossible to occupy, or even explore and map, the territory. In 1803 they sold it to the United

States for $12 million. Two years later, the first French trappers and traders reached the Rocky Mountains; they had been in the wilderness so long that they did not know the region had been sold to America. Nor did it matter much, since virtually all the estimated 150 French frontiersmen who went West found homes among the tribes and never returned to civilization.

No American expedition reached the Rocky Mountains until the summer of 1805, when 45 men led by Captain Meriwether Lewis and William Clark made their way up the Missouri River and across Montana and Idaho. They found willing guides in Shoshone interpreter Sacajawea and her French fur-trader husband, who led them all the way to the mouth of the Columbia River on the Pacific coast.

Before the Lewis and Clark party returned, the U.S. government sent another expedition under the leadership of Captain Zebulon Pike to trace the Arkansas River to its source. After seeing (and failing in attempts to climb) the peak that would later bear his name, Pike was arrested as a spy by the Mexican army and imprisoned in Santa Fe. He was released only after making an unauthorized agreement that henceforth the Arkansas River would be recognized as the border between U.S. and Mexican territory—an agreement that would last in the Rocky Mountain region for the next 43 years.

On Lewis and Clark's return trip in 1806, expedition member John Colter left the party to seek his fortune as a trapper and trader on the new frontier. He returned to St. Louis, Missouri, four years later with stories of boiling springs and smoke spewing from the earth: He was the first white man to see the strange landscape that would become Yellowstone National Park. Although most people dismissed Colter's tales as the product of an imagination gone mad in the wilderness, no one ignored the fact that he had also brought back a fortune in beaver pelts.

In 1811, less than a year after Colter's return from the wilderness, John Jacob Astor's American Fur Company sent its first expedition into the Rockies. As large international fur-trading companies established trading posts along the eastern edge of the Rockies, hundreds of freelance adventurers set off to probe deeper into the mountains in search of pelts. These "mountain men," as they were called—men like Jim Bridger, Jedediah Smith, David Jackson, Jeremiah "Liver Eatin'" Johnston and Thomas "Broken Hand" Fitzpatrick—explored virtually every valley in the Rockies during the next 30 years, bringing back more than half a million beaver pelts each year. In order to kill animals in such phenomenal numbers, the mountain men not only set their own traps but also traded gunpowder and bullets to the Indians for more furs. By the 1840s, beavers had become nearly extinct in the Rockies. The last of the old-time fur trappers either became guides for army expeditions and pioneer wagon trains or established their own trading posts, where they continued to sell ammunition to the tribes—a practice that would soon become controversial and then illegal.

PIONEERS AND PROSPECTORS The first wagon train crossed the Continental Divide in 1842. It was made up of 100 frontier families from Iowa, Kentucky, Illinois and Missouri, traveling in Conestoga wagons with a herd of cattle, bound for Oregon's fertile Willamette Valley. The route they blazed, which came to be known as the Oregon Trail, would be used by virtually all pioneers en route to the western territories for the next 27 years. From 1842 to 1847, about 5000 people made the journey west—a mere trickle compared to the great migration to come. Although pioneers passed along the trail in growing numbers each year, they all continued to the West Coast. Hardly anyone stayed to settle in the Rockies until 1848, when about 5000 Mormons followed the Oregon Trail and then turned south to establish Salt Lake City, the oldest permanent civilian settlement in the Rocky Mountain region. The following year, gold was discovered in California, and the floodgates of western migration opened wide. Between 1849 and 1869, about 350,000 people made the arduous journey across the Great Divide to the far West.

Settlement came suddenly to Colorado in 1859, when gold was discovered in several areas of the high mountains west of present-day Denver, touching off the "Pikes Peak or Bust" gold rush. People flocked to gold and silver boom towns such as Central City and Leadville, as well as the Front Range towns of Denver and Colorado City (now part of Colorado Springs) in such numbers that Colorado—a region that previously had been inhabited only by Native Americans and fur traders—was declared a territory in 1862, just three years after the gold rush began. Fourteen years later, on the centennial of the Declaration of Independence, it became a state, giving rise to the nickname, "the Centennial State."

The years following the Civil War saw the construction of four major railroads. The first, the Union Pacific, made its way across the desert of the Great Divide Basin in southern Wyoming to meet the Central Pacific railroad from San Francisco just north of the Great Salt Lake in 1869, forming the first transcontinental railroad and bringing the era of the covered wagon to an end. Other main routes came soon after—the Northern Pacific, which followed a winding route through the Montana Rockies en route to Portland, Oregon, and the Santa Fe Railway, which followed the old Santa Fe Trail through Trinidad, Colorado, on its way to New Mexico Territory. The cities of Cheyenne, Wyoming, and Billings and Missoula, Montana, sprang up along the main transcontinental routes. Shorter railroad lines soon linked these main rail arteries to the region's major cities, Denver and Salt Lake City, and within a few more years a network of narrow-gauge railroads connected these and other cities with mining towns throughout the mountains.

At the same time that bison were being exterminated to feed railroad work crews, leaving boundless empty grazing land, the new transportation network made cattle and sheep ranching feasible in the Rockies. Beginning in the mid-1870s, vast cattle ranches that measured in the millions of acres were established in Wyoming and eastern Montana under absentee ownership, often British. These ranches thrived, employing thousands of cowboys and earning their owners bigger profits, in many cases, than the gold and silver mines had ever yielded. On some of the ranches, cattle came to number in the millions—on paper, at least. The unfenced rangeland was so big that actually counting the cattle—let alone rounding them up and branding them—was impossible.

The demand for more land for railroads, ranches and mines inevitably led to conflict between the settlers and the native Indian landholders. Major conflicts erupted in the 1860s and 1870s in eastern Colorado, the Tongue River country of northern Wyoming and southern Montana, and the Idaho Panhandle. Four hundred Shoshone were wiped out in Idaho's Battle of Bear River; two hundred Cheyenne were slain in Colorado's Sand Creek Massacre in 1864; 260 U.S. cavalry were annihilated by Crow and Cheyenne at Montana's Battle of Little Bighorn ("Custer's Last Stand") in 1876. Eventually, all tribes were subjugated and restricted to reservations.

THE DECLINE OF THE OLD WEST The end of the great ranches came in the brutal winter 1887–88, when a single blizzard heaped snow higher than the cattle's heads and was followed by weeks of record cold temperatures. When the spring thaw came, few cattle could be found alive. Many ranch owners went bankrupt, leaving the former ranches unsupervised. Newcomers rushed in to seize pieces of the abandoned lands. Many started their own ranches on a more modest scale. Others, however, raised sheep, which ruined the rangeland for cattle. Still others, known as "grangers," started dry-land farms and were universally hated by ranchers because they fenced open rangeland and built roads.

Legal title to lands that had been part of bankrupt ranches was vague at best, so violent clashes erupted among cowboys, sheepmen and grangers. The lawlessness was made worse when some cowboys from the early ranches turned to crime after losing their jobs, forming outlaw bands that lived by armed robbery. Rampant lawlessness continued into the early years of the 20th century. Eventually, when landholders had occupied their ranches and farms long enough to file for legal title under the law of adverse possession, the violence faded.

The mining districts of the Rockies continued to flourish until 1893, when the U.S. Congress ended silver subsidies, bringing about a collapse in the market. Towns that depended mainly on silver mining, such as Aspen and Leadville, Colorado, were all but abandoned within a few years. Many miners moved to the newfound goldfields of Cripple Creek, Colorado, site of the last major gold boom in the Rockies, which quickly grew to become one of the largest cities in the Rocky Mountain region. Here, too, violence became commonplace as labor union organizers battled against enforcers hired by the mine owners. Dynamite was the weapon of choice. The gold-mining industry prospered until 1933, when it, too, came to an abrupt end as a change in federal law ruined the market for the precious metal. Copper created Butte, Montana, a city of 100,000 people at the turn of the 20th century; Butte's open-pit mines remain productive today.

MODERN TIMES Railroads made it easy for vacationers to visit the Rocky Mountains. Yellowstone became the world's first national park in 1872. Tourism came to the Pikes Peak and Glenwood Springs areas around 1885 and to Estes Park around 1900. In those days, however, the Rockies were much more remote than the African veldt or the Australian outback is today—the exclusive province of adventurers, tycoons and wealthy dilettantes. It was not until the 1920s, when many Americans bought automobiles and the first main highways were paved, that tourists began heading for the Rockies in large numbers. Ever since, tourism has been central to the economies of all Rocky Mountain states and has increased steadily. Tourism got a major mid-century boost with the development of Sun Valley, Aspen, Vail, Jackson Hole and a host of other ski resorts that created a second tourist season in the winter and brought millions of additional visitors to the region. These winter-season resorts, in turn, began to experiment with other kinds of facilities designed to stimulate the local economy during the roughly seven months of the year when the ski slopes were closed. Conference centers, golf courses and alpine slides popped up in every ski town. Finally, in the early 1980s, a single stunt—an impromptu race up a jeep road and over a mountain pass from Crested Butte to Aspen on battered old bicycles—spawned the mountain-bike industry, which has since transformed summer sports in many areas of the Rockies, providing an ideal way to experience the mountain magnificence around resort towns in the summertime.

But as enticing to tourists as the wild, pristine Rocky Mountain environment has proven to be, other forces that are less ecologically benign have arisen. The energy boom started in the 1920s with the discovery of large oil and gas deposits in the wastelands of central Wyoming, and it may have been an ill omen that the land at the center of the oilfields, known as the Teapot Dome, almost immediately became the namesake of one of history's worst government corruption scandals. Public officials went to jail, but development went on. Coal mining grew to become a huge industry in some parts of the Rockies, while along Colorado's western slope discoveries of uranium and oil shale touched off new waves of prospecting and mining operations.

With the late 1960s and early 1970s, population growth and development came to Colorado's Front Range in a big way, making it one of the fastest-growing areas in the United States. Many communities doubled in size in a year, then doubled again the next year. With this rampant development came skyrocketing prices for land in the nearby mountains, and soon formerly remote areas were being filled with paved roads, vacation homes and condominiums.

Saving the natural landscape from real-estate development and other forms of economic exploitation has become a primary concern in Colorado. In recent years, some of the nation's strictest environmental laws, including the only statewide ban on timber clear-cutting in National Forest lands, have been implemented. Tension between developers and conservationists remains a polarizing reality in Colorado, however. Other Rocky Mountain states, particularly Idaho and Montana, which only now are attracting national attention as among the last best places for modern-day pioneers to settle, look to Colorado as both a good and bad example in planning their own destinies.

FLORA

Altitude makes all the difference when it comes to plant life in the Rocky Mountain states. At lower elevations—"low" in this region meaning about a mile above sea level—the environment consists of arid prairies with vegetation so sparse that it takes from 25 to 40 acres to graze a single cow. The reason is that the Rocky Mountains cast a "rain shadow"; as weather patterns move from west to east, clouds dump most of their rain or snow on the high, cool mountains, leaving little moisture to fall on the prairies. The closer the land is to the base of the mountains, the drier it is, with natural vegetation that consists mainly of thin veneers of grass punctuated by prickly pear cactus. In some areas, especially northeastern Colorado and southern Idaho, farmers have transformed this seeming wasteland into fields of wheat, potatoes, sugar beets and other crops made possible by irrigation wells that tap into huge underground aquifers fed by the moisture that falls in the mountains and then seeps into the earth.

The foothills along the eastern edge of the Rockies are even drier than the prairies, since they are not only in the mountains' rain shadow but also steep enough so that whatever rain does fall quickly spills away like water off a duck's back. The foothills are just high enough, however, that cooler temperatures let snow melt more slowly, seeping into the top layer of earth to sustain scrub, small trees that may reach a mature height of only five or six feet. The most common scrub tree in the foothills is Gambel oak (commonly called scrub oak), a diminutive cousin of the stately oak trees found in lowland forests of the eastern United States. Other scrub trees include juniper and, in the southern foothills, piñon.

Mountain forests, too, change with elevation, forming three distinct bands. On the lower slopes of the mountains, ponderosa pine stand 50 feet tall and more. Douglas fir and blue spruce dominate the higher reaches of the mountains. Between the two bands of evergreen forest, shimmering stands of aspen trees fill the mountainsides and paint them bright yellow in early October. The aspen, perhaps the most intriguing and distinctive tree in the Rockies, is what forestry experts call an "opportunistic species": Stands grow wherever clearings appear in the evergreen woods—usually because of forest fires or pine beetle infestations. Gradually, over a span of centuries, the taller evergreens will crowd out old aspen stands as new ones appear elsewhere. The aspen is a delicate tree that cannot tolerate high- or low-altitude extremes. Attempts to use aspens for landscaping in lower places like Denver and Colorado Springs almost always end in failure.

The upper boundary of the deep green forests of spirelike Douglas fir is known as "timberline," the elevation above which temperatures drop below freezing at night year-round and trees can't grow. Timberline is around 10,500 to 11,000 feet in the southern Colorado Rockies and lower the farther north you go—around 6000 feet in Glacier National Park. Above timberline lies the alpine tundra, a delicate world of short grasses and other green plants rooted in permafrost, where tiny flowers appear for brief moments each summer. At the highest elevations—14,000-foot mountain summits in Colorado, 10,000 feet near the Canadian border—summer freezing prevents even the small plants of the tundra from growing. Up there, clinging to the granite cliffs and boulders, grows lichen, a symbiotic combination of two plants that survive in partnership: a type of moss forms a leathery, sheltering shell that protects an alga, which in turn provides nutrients by photosynthesis to feed the moss. This ingenious arrangement is perhaps the ultimate tribute to life's amazing capacity for adapting to even the harshest environments.

FAUNA

One of the Rocky Mountain region's greatest attractions is its abundance of wildlife. You are most likely to get a good look at large animals in national

(Text continued on page 14.)

The Meaning of Mountains

Native Americans saw Pikes Peak as a stairway to heaven. Holy men of the Cheyenne and Arapaho tribes climbed the great mountain in search of visions, believing that the summit formed a gate to another world where gods or spirits lived. The gods could use the same doorway to enter the human world. That was why the land below the mountain—including the healing mineral springs of Manitou and the fantastic redrock sentinels of the Garden of the Gods—was considered holy ground. Indians picked it as the ideal site for intertribal powwows because to wage war in sight of the gods was unthinkable.

At least that's the local legend in the Pikes Peak region. Nobody really knows much about what the native peoples along the Front Range believed. Within a few years after the first white settlers arrived, the Indians were gone, leaving early-day tour guides and promoters free to concoct whatever old Indian legends they wished. The fact that this Pikes Peak legend has been passed along by word of mouth for more than a century suggests that it contains a kind of truth. The mountain is a sacred place. We, locals and visitors alike, can feel its power for ourselves.

Frank Waters, who is widely considered to be the greatest writer of the American Southwest, was born and raised within view of Pikes Peak in Colorado Springs. Noting that "there exists for each of us a psychological archetype, or a Guru, manifested as a physical mountain," he wrote extensively about the role of sacred mountains revered by many cultures around the world. Mountains have been revered by the Celts of the British Isles, the Buddhists in India and Tibet, the Taoists in China, the *Shugendo* sect in Japan, the Aztecs in ancient Mexico and the Navajo of the American Southwest.

It may well be that the Rocky Mountains hold such fascination for vacationers today precisely because of the spiritual significance of mountains ingrained in human consciousness since ancient times. Confronted with even a single mountain peak, a pyramid of granite weighing literally *trillions* of tons, standing more than a mile high from base to summit, what human can resist being swept away by awe?

Mysticism aside, there's no question that the presence of mountains transforms a person's sense of place. In flat places such as Wichita, Dallas or even New York City, we can go for days or even years without a glimpse of the natural world. But in the Rocky Mountain West, though, where the horizon is always shaped by mountains, nature is a constant presence. Out our motel windows, in a gap between city skyscrapers in the rear-view mirror on the freeway, a hundred times a day we catch glimpses of the ever-present alpine wilderness—hard to reach, perhaps, but impossible to ignore.

The visible presence of wilderness that mountains offer may be more valuable in today's postindustrial society than ever before, for wilderness mirrors the core of human nature. It reminds us of a time, not so long ago in the context of a mountain's age, when the quest for warmth, food and shelter preoccupied humankind on a daily basis and such things as money, machinery and written language lay far beyond the reach of imagination. It reminds us that the primeval place from which our earliest ancestors emerged was not bleak and comfortless or static, but a living world of life and death, dancing light and running water, forest fires and avalanches and other furious acts of God balanced by warm sunshine and meadows of wildflowers and other beauties of nature. Mountains remind us that this world need not be lost to us.

Perhaps this ancient connection is the reason wilderness issues stir such heated controversy today. The American political system quite often becomes a battleground between those who value harmony with nature and those who view nature as raw material to be conquered and exploited. Between 1964 and 1979, the federal government placed more than six million acres of roadless lands in the American West under permanent protection as wilderness areas. But from 1980 and 1992, a presidential moratorium blocked creation of new wilderness areas and expanded timber clear-cutting in the national forests to unprecedented levels.

Environmentalists responded by using the Endangered Species Act to protect vast tracts of mountain forest as habitat for two rare subspecies of spotted owls and an elusive little weasel known as the pine marten. The clash between timber interests and "preservationists" swept the western states, growing heated and sometimes violent. Then the political pendulum swung back. The U.S. Congress passed the Wilderness Act of 1993, granting wilderness-area status to more than half of the remaining unprotected roadless land in the West, mostly in the Rocky Mountains. State governments and federal courts halted timber cutting throughout much of the Rocky Mountain region. But by 1995, bills to abolish both the National Forest system and the Endangered Species Act were receiving serious consideration in the U.S. Congress. The question of protecting wilderness versus exploiting it is likely to continue as one of the great issues of our lifetime.

Mountains: They're too heavy to move and too big to ignore, so we might as well make friends with them. The Rocky Mountain states—Colorado, Utah, Wyoming, Idaho and Montana—contain 47 national forests, 26 national parks and monuments, 22 national wildlife refuges and 40 federal Bureau of Land Management scenic areas, more than any other region of the country. Take a weekend or a lifetime to explore some of them and experience for yourself the mystical spirit of the mountains.

parks, where long-standing prohibitions against hunting have helped them lose their fear of humans. Wildlife populations are about the same in national forests, but sightings are much less common because animals generally keep their distance from roads, trails and any human scent.

The eastern foothills, high plains and mountain parks (not the kind with rangers, but flat grasslands surrounded by mountain ranges) are a favorite habitat of jackrabbits, coyotes and pronghorn antelope, as well as prairie birds such as hawks, grouse and pheasants. Coyote populations are on the increase just about everywhere in the West. They are commonly seen not only in open grasslands but also on the outskirts of urban areas, including the suburbs of Denver. Intelligent and curious, coyotes can often be spotted observing humans from a distance. They are rarely dangerous to humans, though they may sometimes attack small pets.

Pronghorn antelope, once hunted nearly to extinction and until recently listed as a threatened species under the federal Endangered Species Act, have multiplied to the point that they are now a common sight on the high plains. They are most common in northeastern and central Wyoming, from the Black Hills to the Great Divide Basin. Although these tan, black and white deerlike creatures with short legs and large heads are commonly called antelope, they are not related to the true antelope of Africa and Asia. In fact, they are not related to any other living species.

American bison, more often called buffalo although they are unrelated to Asian buffalo, once roamed throughout the Rocky Mountains. Today they are found only on buffalo ranches, a growing industry along the Front Range, and in a few protected areas like Yellowstone National Park, the National Bison Range in Montana, and Antelope Island in Utah's Great Salt Lake.

There are also rattlesnakes in the foothills and high plains. The good news is that they rarely venture into the mountains. Snakes and other reptiles are cold blooded and cannot function in low temperatures, so they are hardly ever found at elevations above about 7000 feet. When hiking at lower elevations, walk loudly and never put your hand or foot where you can't see it.

Deer, mountain lions and bobcats inhabit the western plateaus and, in smaller numbers, the eastern foothills. While mule deer and white-tailed deer may be spotted anywhere in the mountains, they prefer to graze in areas where scrub oak grows. Mountain lions hunt deer and prefer areas with high rocks, where they can spot both dangers and prey a long way away. Since mountain lions are nocturnal and reclusive, it's a stroke of luck to glimpse one darting across the road in your headlights at night. They have not been known to attack humans in the Rockies, though several recent incidents in California have proved that they can be dangerous. Wild horses also graze the remote plateaus and mesas on the west side of the Rockies, especially in western Colorado, near Bighorn Canyon on the Wyoming-Montana border, and on Idaho's Owyhee Plateau.

In forests and meadows of the central Rockies, common small mammals include squirrels, chipmunks, raccoons, porcupines and skunks. Large animals include elk and black bears. Since elk prefer high mountain meadows in the warm months, they are usually seen outside of national parks by serious hikers who venture deep into the wilderness. Sightings are more common in winter, when they descend to lower elevations where grass is easier to reach under the snow. In some areas, usually marked by signs and sometimes observation areas, herds of elk can often be spotted from the road in winter; they are especially common in the Mammoth Hot Springs area of Yellowstone National Park. Moose are found in the northern Rockies of Wyoming, Idaho and Montana. Most frequently found in marshy areas around dawn or dusk, these herbivores are hard to spot because of their ability to blend into forest surroundings.

As for black bears, they are elusive but more common than most hikers realize. In times of drought, when food becomes scarce, it's not unusual for a bear to raid trash cans along the fringes of civilization. Black bears rarely attack people, but they are unpredictable and can be dangerous because of their size. Most injuries involving bears happen because campers store their food inside tents with them at night. When camping in the forest, one should leave all food inside a closed vehicle or suspended from a tree limb. Grizzly bears, larger and more aggressive cousins of black bears, live in the backcountry of Yellowstone and Glacier national parks and adjacent wilderness areas but are extinct in almost all other parts of the region. Several unconfirmed sightings have been reported in the San Juan Mountains of southwestern Colorado in recent years.

Wolves were also extinct in most of the U.S. Rockies until 1995, when in a highly controversial move the first timberwolves were reintroduced to the backcountry of Yellowstone National Park and Idaho's Frank Church–River of No Return Wilderness. A few unconfirmed sightings have provided evidence to support claims that wolves were also reintroduced surreptitiously to the San Juans by radical environmentalists in the late 1980s.

Beavers once inhabited virtually every stream in the Rockies. Trapped by the millions for their pelts in the early 19th century, these largest of North American rodents once stood on the brink of extinction. In more recent times, they have too often been considered pests because their habit of damming streams (to create ponds surrounding their dome-shaped sticks-and-mud lodges) floods the most desirable areas of mountain valleys. Landowners persisted for many years in poisoning the beavers or dynamiting their dams and putting up low electric fences to keep them away. Now a protected species in all Rocky Mountain states, beavers seem to be making a slow comeback. It's not unusual to discover beaver ponds on backcountry streams, and if you watch a pond near sunset, you may get a look at the animals themselves.

Above timberline, Rocky Mountain bighorn sheep are common and easy to spot in alpine meadows. Herds of ewes are protected by a single ram, while other males lead a solitary existence elsewhere until mating season, when the high crags echo with the crash of horns as young rams challenge their elders for dominance over the female herd. In areas with vehicular traffic, such as Pikes Peak, Mount Evans and Rocky Mountain National Park's Trail Ridge Road, the sheep vanished in the 1950s because the rams were so distracted by the noise of cars that they became impotent. New herds were brought from the Collegiate Range in central Colorado, which had become overpopulated with the sheep, and they have made a successful comeback, particularly on Pikes Peak. Mountain goats—shaggy, snow white and solitary—may also be seen in some high mountain areas, especially Rocky Mountain and Glacier national parks and Idaho's Sawtooth National Recreation Area. The smaller animals most commonly seen above timberline are golden marmots, large, chubby rodents nicknamed "whistlepigs" because they communicate with shrill whistles. Smaller rodents called picas colonize high-altitude rock piles, where swarms of hundreds are sometimes seen.

Where to Go

The Rocky Mountains are truly vast. They cover roughly 400,000 square miles, an expanse equivalent to the combined areas of California and Texas, the two largest states in the contiguous United States. Most residents of the Rocky Mountain states have not explored the entire region, and any attempt to visit all areas described in this book during a single vacation is doomed from the outset. If you try to "see it all" in a single trip, you may find yourself so focused on covering large distances that you sacrifice quiet moments to appreciate the natural beauty you came to see. Deciding what to see and where to go is a tough choice. The good news is, no matter how many times you visit, there will always be more places to discover the next time you come.

Many travelers begin their Rocky Mountain adventures in the **Colorado Front Range**, the most developed area in the Rocky Mountain states, where the greatest concentration of the region's residents live. The 200-mile-long Front Range corridor encompasses the sprawling megalopolis of Denver and its suburbs, the booming university towns of Boulder and Fort Collins, the old-time tourist town-turned-modern city of Colorado Springs and the former steel-mill city of Pueblo. Viewed from any of these cities, lofty mountain splendor fills the western horizon, and a drive of an hour or less will take you deep into a world of spectacular canyons, forests and peaks. Highlights include two of the longest-established tourist zones in the West—Estes Park/Rocky Mountain National Park and Manitou Springs/Pikes Peak—as well as once-prosperous gold-boom towns such as Cripple Creek and Central City. The mines shut down long ago, but visitors flock to saloons where the Old West lives on—financed by slot machines and video poker.

Northern Colorado is ski country. Most of the state's world-renowned ski resorts, including Aspen, Vail, Steamboat Springs and Breckenridge, cluster in the heart of the central Rockies, easily reached via Route 70. This is the only major area of the Rocky Mountains where more vacationers come in winter than in summer. Millions of ski enthusiasts each year pay top dollar for lodging and lift tickets to experience the thrill of plunging thousands of feet down mountain slopes, while others put on cross-country skis to discover budget-priced exhilaration and the natural beauty of winter in the high country. Summer brings off-season bargains at northern Colorado's luxury megaresorts, as most ski areas keep chairlifts running, offering an amazingly easy way to climb mountains.

One of Colorado's fastest-growing tourist areas today, Glenwood Springs, invites you to hike or bike on the newly created Glenwood Canyon Trail, then relax in one of the region's largest hot-springs pools.

Southern Colorado has its own character, quite different from the grand-scale tourism and development found in the northern part of the state. Even Durango, the main base for touring the southern Colorado Rockies, is surprisingly low key. Mesa Verde National Park, the Durango & Silverton Narrow-Gauge Railroad and the San Juan Skyway top the list of Durango-area attractions. Southern Colorado also boasts some of the most remote Rocky Mountain ski-resort towns, notably Telluride and Crested Butte. Travelers in search of hidden Colorado will find it in some of the state's least-visited and most remarkable places—the San Luis Valley, the Colorado River canyonlands around Grand Junction and the vast island in the sky that is Grand Mesa.

Visitors to **Utah** will discover another side of the Rockies—in more ways than one. Among the well-kept secrets here in the westernmost part of the central Rockies are outstanding ski resorts such as Snowbird and Park City, lush canyons and spectacular wilderness hiking areas. They are within a short drive of Salt Lake City and other towns in the fertile valley that lies between the mountains and the Great Salt Lake. Here, too, visitors can get a close-up look at the unique subculture shaped by the Church of Jesus Christ of Latter-day Saints (the Mormons), the largest religious sect that has ever originated in the United States.

Most travelers' first impression of **southern Wyoming** is that of a stark and desolate wasteland. They may be right—until they get far enough off the freeway to poke around in the hidden backcountry and discover how exquisite a wasteland can be. Little-known places waiting to be explored include Vedauwoo Recreation Area and the Snowy Range. If you're heading for Jackson and Yellowstone National Park, don't pass up the chance to trace the historic Oregon Trail and follow the Wind River Range, one of Wyoming's most splendid expanses of mountain wilderness.

Wyoming's northwestern corner is encompassed by **Yellowstone National Park and Jackson Hole**. The world's first national park and undoubtedly its most famous, Yellowstone is a remarkable thermal wonderland of more than 10,000 geysers, hot springs and boiling mud caldrons, as well as impressive canyons, waterfalls and high-elevation lakes, all on the crest of an ancient volcanic crater. It also has perhaps the Rockies' most varied and accessible wildlife, from elk and moose to bison and grizzly bears. Its neighbor to the south, Grand Teton National Park, preserves some of North America's most spectacular mountain scenery. The main gateway town of Jackson, which wears its Old West facade as well as any community in the Rockies, is at the heart of a beautiful and historic valley called Jackson Hole, well known to 19th-century mountain men.

Moving east from Yellowstone across the rest of **northern Wyoming**, travelers pass through such tried-and-true capitals of cowboy culture as rodeo-crazy Cody, named for its inimitable founder, "Buffalo Bill," and the ranching center of Sheridan. The lofty Big Horn Mountains—which contain some of America's oldest "dude ranches" as well as such mysterious ancient sites as Medicine Wheel National Historic Landmark—divide this grassland region into two riverine basins. To the west, the Big Horn Basin is climaxed by the hot springs of Thermopolis and the age-old strata of Bighorn Canyon National Recreation Area on the Montana border. To the east, the Powder River Basin stretches from Hole-in-the-Wall, once the hideout of notorious outlaw Butch Cassidy and his Wild Bunch, across the coal-mining country around Gillette to Devils Tower National Monument, which rises like a petrified tree stump at the western edge of the Black Hills.

Idaho is a state of rivers—there's more raft-ready whitewater here than anywhere in the United States outside of Alaska—and **southwestern Idaho** is a case in point. All summer long, townspeople float the Boise River through Boise, the rapidly growing state capital and largest city in the northern Rockies, located where the Great Basin meets the Snake River Plain and the Rocky Mountain foothills. Arcing around Boise, the Snake courses through the Snake River Birds of Prey National Conservation Area, home of North America's highest concentration of raptors; irrigates the fertile Treasure Valley; then roars through Hells Canyon National Recreation Area, which encompasses the deepest gorge on the continent. The resort town of McCall is the gateway to the Frank Church–River of No Return Wilderness surrounding the Salmon River, and the Bruneau Dunes are America's tallest sand dunes.

The geological drama reaches even greater extremes in **southeastern Idaho**. Although the Snake, which crosses the region from east to west, is frequently dammed, its reservoirs nourishing Idaho's famous potato fields, the river's natural creations are more prominent: Horseshoe-shaped Shoshone Falls are higher than Niagara, and the Thousand Springs burst from sheer canyon walls. Nearby ice caves contrast with steaming hot springs. Idaho's tallest mountain, 12,662-foot Borah Peak, looms over a vast central lava plain best seen at Craters of the Moon National Monument. Hagerman Fossil Beds National Monument and City of Rocks National Reserve are also fascinating. The region's common treads are the wagon ruts of the Oregon Trail tracing the banks of the Snake. North of the Snake River Plain are the world-famous resort area of Sun Valley and the Sawtooth National Recreation Area, encompassing high, craggy peaks and the headwaters of the wilderness Salmon River, the broadest river system within any one state outside of Alaska.

Pristine lakes and wild-and-scenic rivers are trademarks of the **northern Idaho** Panhandle. The nationally acclaimed resort town of Coeur d'Alene rests on the shore of an evergreen-shrouded lake of the same name. An easy drive away are deep blue Lake Pend Oreille and remote Priest Lake. The historic Lewis and Clark Trail follows the Lochsa and Clearwater rivers through the Panhandle, and Nez Perce National Historical Park memorializes dozens of sites associated with a remarkable native tribe. Here, too, are the rolling hills of the grain-rich Palouse country, stands of giant old-growth cedar and pine, and some of the nation's most productive and historic silver mines and their adjacent communities.

Western Montana is the home of Glacier National Park, which stakes a deserving claim to being the "roof of the Rockies." Straddling the Continental Divide on the Canadian border, this vast region of chiseled peaks and broad valleys, of deep blue lakes and racing rivers, has a watershed that flows in not two but three directions: to the Pacific Ocean, the Gulf of Mexico and Hudson Bay. The park boasts hundreds of miles of trails and thousands of large animals. South and west of Glacier Park, waves of mountain ranges shelter the likes of Flathead Lake, the largest natural freshwater lake west of the Mississippi River; the National Bison Range, within the Flathead Indian Reservation; the university city of Missoula; and the lovely Bitterroot Valley, flanked on either side by steep ridges.

Southern Montana is mining country, past and present. Gold-rush history lives on in ghost towns like Bannack, established as the first territorial capital after ore was discovered here in 1862, and Virginia City, which tourism has kept alive and well and far more law abiding than it was in the 19th century. The main street of the charming state capital, Helena, is still known as Last Chance Gulch. Butte, whose copper mines once earned it the label "the richest hill on earth," has a stately and historic hillside downtown that is more reminiscent of old San Francisco than of any other city in the Rockies. Sophisticated Bozeman has burgeoned as a gateway to Yellowstone National Park, less than two hours' drive south. Scenic attractions range from the subterranean network of Lewis and Clark Caverns to the gaping cliffs of the Gates of the Mountains Wilderness on the Missouri River.

Eastern Montana has earned the state's "Big Sky" nickname. The vast prairies that extend east from the crest of the Rockies once were the domain of Plains Indians, who hunted bison, deer and pronghorn antelope by the thousands. Eons before them, this area was a veritable Jurassic Park. Today dinosaur digs, ancient buffalo jumps and tribal reservations are among the region's highlights, along with the huge Charles M. Russell National Wildlife Refuge, which flanks serpentine Fort Peck Lake on the Missouri River, just east of the historic inland steamboat port of Fort Benton. Montana's largest city, Billings, located on the broad Yellowstone River, is a gateway to Bighorn Canyon National Recreation Area, Little Bighorn Battlefield National Monument and the mountain town of Red Lodge, at the foot of the spectacular Beartooth Highway to Yellowstone Park.

When to Go

SEASONS

Though it may sound romantic, springtime in the Rockies is less than appealing in reality. Cold winds, occasional avalanches, brown vegetation and plenty of mud are a few of the reasons that most people in the tourist business here shut down their shops and motels in April and take their own vacations to more southerly climes. Just about any other time of year, however, the climate is ideal for one kind of outdoor recreation or another, giving rise to the Rocky Mountain region's distinctive summer-and-winter double tourist season.

The traditional summer tourist season, which runs from Memorial Day to Labor Day, is characterized by cool nights, mild days, colorful wildflowers and sudden, brief afternoon rainstorms. In most parts of the Rockies, it's a good idea to start outdoor activities early and carry ponchos or waterproof tarps on all-day hikes, since rain is almost inevitable in the afternoon. In a common, peculiar phenomenon, wind currents called "waves" can carry precipitation for long distances from clouds hidden behind the mountains, causing "sun showers." Old-timers say that if it rains while the sun is shining, it will rain again tomorrow. This adage almost always holds true—but then, if it doesn't rain in the sunshine, it's still likely to rain tomorrow. The good news is, summer rains rarely last more than an hour, and skies generally clear well before sunset.

East of the Continental Divide and along the Front Range, clouds typically build in the early afternoon and then burst into thunder, lightning and sometimes hail. In mountain areas west of the Continental Divide, storms tend to be smaller, more scattered and much more frequent. In the San Juan Mountains of southwestern Colorado, it's not unusual to encounter five or six brief rainstorms in a single day. An exception to this rule is Idaho's Snake River Plain, which can be barbarously hot and dry in midsummer, its 90° to 100°F temperatures only rarely broken by thunderstorms, which tend not to descend from the adjacent foothills.

Above timberline (about 10,500 feet above sea level in Colorado, lower in the northern Rockies), temperatures fall below freezing at night all summer and typically reach only 40° to 50°F at midday. It is not unusual for high mountain roads such as the Pikes Peak Highway, Rocky Mountain National Park's Trail Ridge Road and Glacier National Park's Going-to-the-Sun Road to be closed by blizzards even in August, sometimes stranding motorists for an hour or two before snowplows clear the road.

Early fall—around the end of September—is one of the most delightful times to visit the Rockies, as the turning of the aspens paints the mountainsides in yellow with splashes of orange and red, brilliant against a deep green background of evergreen forests. Mountain highways tend to be crowded with carloads of leaf-gawkers on weekends but not on weekdays, while hiking and biking traffic on forest trails is much lighter than during the summer. The weather is generally dry and cool in early fall, making it a great time to take a long wilderness hike or mountain-bike excursion. The first light snowfall can be expected in the high country around the first week of October (national parks usually close about this time) and along the Front Range around the third week; the first heavy snow typically comes around Halloween. November is hunting season, a good time to stay out of the mountains unless you're armed and dangerous.

The official ski season in the Rockies runs from Thanksgiving through March, the period in which all ski areas expect a reliable snow base and within which all ski events and package tours are scheduled. If you're planning ahead for a major ski vacation, you'll want to schedule it between those dates, too. In reality, snowfall amounts, as well as winter temperatures in the mountains, can vary a lot from year to year, so the actual dates of operation at various ski areas are somewhat unpredictible. These days, the huge artificial snowmaking capacity of most ski areas almost always assures a Thanksgiving opening day. While snowmaking usually ceases after March when advance-reservation business slows down, skiing continues until spring temperatures rise enough to erode the snow base. In some years, at some ski areas, late-season skiing may continue well into April. Uncrowded ski trails, discount lift tickets and lots of sunshine make the late season a favorite time for many local ski enthusiasts.

CALENDAR OF EVENTS

JANUARY

Denver and the Front Range: The **National Western Stock Show and Rodeo**, the world's largest livestock show, features top-name country-and-western music concerts and a parade through the streets of Denver.

Northern Colorado: **Ullrfest** in Breckenridge honors the Norse god of snow with a parade, fireworks, torchlight skiing and cross-country ski competitions. Aspen's five-day **Winterskol** features a parade, torchlight skiing, fireworks and skydiving.

Utah: The **Sundance Film Festival** at Sundance Resort east of Provo is the most prestigious independent filmmakers' event in the United States. The **Utah Winter Games** are spread among several ski areas in the Utah Rockies. Street celebrations and games mark Ogden's **Hof Winter Carnival**.

Southwestern Idaho: The ten-day **McCall Winter Carnival** is highlighted by its world-class ice-sculpting contest near the shores of Payette Lake; there are also snowmobile and ski races, parades, fireworks and an evening ball.

Northern Idaho: The **Sandpoint Winter Carnival** includes ten days of festivities near Lake Pend Oreille, including snow sculptures, snowshoe softball, a torchlight parade and a Christmas tree–burning ritual.

Southern Montana: Bozeman's **Montana Winter Fair** is a week-long event that includes livestock shows, sheep-shearing and draft horse–pulling contests, cooking and crafts competitions.

FEBRUARY

Northern Colorado: The week-long **Steamboat Springs Winter Carnival** includes ski races, contests and street celebrations.

Utah: Park City is the site of the **Jans Handicapped Ski Challenge**. The following week, Salt Lake City hosts the **Utah Special Olympics Winter Games**.

Northern Idaho: Some of the world's best-known musicians are featured at the four-day **Lionel Hampton Jazz Festival** on the University of Idaho campus in Moscow.

Western Montana: The **Whitefish Winter Carnival** includes parades, fireworks and a formal ball, plus torchlight skiing and races on The Big Mountain. The 500-mile **Race to the Sky Dog Sled Race** from Helena to Holland Lake is exceeded in length in the United States only by Alaska's Iditarod.

MARCH

Denver and the Front Range: Denver's **St. Patrick's Day Parade**, the second largest in the nation, features more than 5000 horses as well as floats and marching bands.

Southern Colorado: The **Monte Vista Crane Festival** celebrates the migration of sandhill and whooping cranes with art shows, naturalist speakers and bus tours of Rio Grande Wildlife Refuge.

Utah: Salt Lake City has a **St. Patrick's Day Parade**.

Northern Idaho: The **Moscow Mardi Gras and Beaux Arts Ball** includes a Mardi Gras parade and celebrity bands.

Western Montana: In Missoula, the **International Wildlife Film Festival** screens videos from around the world for a full week and offers workshops, lectures and seminars.

Southern Montana: As many as 50,000 people are Irish for two days around **St. Patrick's Day** in Butte.

Montana East of the Rockies: The four-day **C. M. Russell Auction of Original Art** in Great Falls is widely regarded as the nation's largest and finest auction of original western art of the 19th and 20th centuries.

APRIL

Denver and the Front Range: Thousands attend the spectacular **Easter Sunrise Pageant** at Garden of the Gods in Colorado Springs.

Utah: Park City celebrates the season with a big **Easter Egg Hunt**.

Yellowstone and Jackson Hole: Competitors in Teton Village's **Pole, Pedal and Paddle Races** ski down Rendezvous Peak, bicycle to the Snake River and kayak or canoe to the finish line.

Northern Idaho: Garden tours and an arts and crafts fair highlight Lewiston's **Dogwood Festival**, a ten-day rite of spring that includes a rodeo, concerts and plays.

MAY

Denver and the Front Range: **Cinco de Mayo**, Mexico's commemoration of the 1882 defeat of French troops at the Battle of Puebla, is observed in Denver with fiestas downtown and along Santa Fe Drive. **Territory Days** celebrates the bygone era when Colorado Springs' Old Colorado City Historic District was the territorial capital.

Southern Colorado: Durango's **Iron Horse Bicycle Classic**, a grueling three-day series of bike races on local roads and trails, draws more than 2000 competitors from around the world.

Yellowstone and Jackson Hole: The **Elk Antler Auction** in Jackson raises money for Scouts and the National Elk Refuge.

Southwestern Idaho: Payette couples its **Apple Blossom Festival**, including a parade, carnival and crafts show, with the **Great Payette Balloon Classic** of colorful hot-air craft.

Southeastern Idaho: **Western Days** in Twin Falls offers a full week of events, including a parade, dances, a barbecue, a chili cook-off and an Old West shoot-out. The high point of **Hagerman Fossil Days** is the opportunity to tour remote reaches of Hagerman Fossil Beds National Monument.

Northern Idaho: A parade kicks off the **Riggins Rodeo**, staged within a natural stadium contained by steep Salmon River canyon walls. **Fred Murphy Days** in Coeur d'Alene includes a parade, street dances, food booths, a juggling competition and the Coeur d'Alene Marathon.

Montana East of the Rockies: Billings hosts the **All Nations Indian Rodeo Championships** over three days at the end of the month. Miles City's **Bucking Horse Sale** features three days of bucking-bronc riding, thoroughbred and wild-horse racing, street dances and a parade.

JUNE

Denver and the Front Range: In Boulder, the **Colorado Freedom Festival** presents art, music, dance, speakers, carnival rides and kids' events built around a theme of world peace. The **Greeley Independence Stampede** fills two weeks leading up to July 4th with family fun, including foot races, fireworks, parades, street breakfasts and the world's largest Fourth of July rodeo.

Northern Colorado: Salida's **FIBArk Boat Race** is the oldest, longest and most famous kayak race anywhere; the four-day event also includes raft, foot and bike races, live entertainment and a parade. Late June marks the start of the nine-week **Aspen Music Festival**, the premier music festival in the United States, with opera, jazz, classical and chamber-music performances daily for nine weeks. Glenwood Springs' **Strawberry Days**, Colorado's oldest town celebration, lasts for a full week and includes a rodeo, a talent show, live entertainment and a parade.

Southern Colorado: The **Telluride Bluegrass Festival**, the granddaddy of Telluride festivals, fills the town with big-name musicians and enormous crowds of festival-goers.

Utah: Fort Duchesne is the site of the **Ute Indian Powwow**. Salt Lake City hosts the **Utah Arts Festival**.

Southern Wyoming: The highlight of Encampment's **Woodchoppers Jamboree** is a series of contests for the Rocky Mountain Champion Lumberjack title. Fort Washakie is the site of the **Indian Days Powwow**.

Northern Wyoming: The 19th century is recalled during **Bozeman Trail Days**, a living-history program held at Fort Kearny and various locations in Sheridan and Buffalo. Late in the month, about 300 Native American dancers participate in traditional costume at the **Plains Indian Powwow** in Cody; onlookers are invited to take part in some of the dances.

Southwestern Idaho: The **Boise River Festival**, Boise's top annual event, includes elaborate day and night parades, outdoor concerts by national acts, an air show, a hot-air balloon fest and sports events centered around the river and its parks. Weiser hosts the **National Old-Time Fiddlers Contest**, during which the best country fiddlers in America play in competition and informal jam sessions.

Southeastern Idaho: At the **Massacre Rocks Rendezvous**, at Massacre Rocks State Park, and the **Fort Henry Mountain Man Rendezvous**, at Henry's Lake State Park, events such as knife throwing and black-powder shoots enhance an 1830s atmosphere of fur trappers' camps, teepee villages and traders' rows.

Northern Idaho: Sandpoint's **Timberfest**, a celebration of the logging industry, includes competitions in axe throwing, pole climbing and log rolling.

Southern Montana: Montana State University in Bozeman is the site of the **College National Finals Rodeo**, five nights of competition for college scholarships between rodeo riders from schools around the country.

Montana East of the Rockies: The highlight of **Little Big Horn Days** in Hardin is a full-scale reenactment of Custer's Last Stand.

JULY

Denver and the Front Range: An **Old Fashioned Fourth of July** with live music, a picnic and demonstrations of traditional skills from quilting to blacksmithing is held in Denver's Four Mile Historic Park. Later in the month, the **Denver Black Arts Festival** presents creations by African American artists and artisans. The renowned **Central City Opera Festival** begins, with three operas in English presented in rotation through August. Boulder fairly bursts with live cultural performances—the overlapping **Colorado Dance Festival**, **Colorado Music Festival** and **Colorado Shakespeare Festival**.

Southern Colorado: In Crested Butte, a five-day **Mountain Man Rendezvous** features period costumes, rough-and-tumble contests and music. In Grand Junction, **Dinosaur Days** presents a dinosaur parade and paleontology lectures, and the public is invited to help dig for fossils.

Utah: The **Railroaders Festival** at Golden Spike National Historic Site commemorates the completion of the first transcontinental railroad with puffing steam engines, a reenactment of the driving of the golden spike and a buffalo-chip-throwing contest. **Pioneer Day** commemorates the founding of Salt Lake City and the selection of the site for the Mormon Temple in 1847; the state's most important secular holiday, it is celebrated in all Utah communities.

Southern Wyoming: **Cheyenne Frontier Days**, the world's largest outdoor rodeo, held annually since 1897, features free pancake breakfasts, chuck-wagon races, free entertainment and carnival rides, staged Old West gunfights, Native American dancers and country music concerts. Wyoming's oldest **Fourth of July** celebration, and one of the largest, is held at South Park City. **Traditional Sun Dances** are held on the Wind River Indian Reservation for three days in mid-July.

Yellowstone and Jackson Hole: The eight-week **Grand Teton Music Festival** at Teton Village is in full force, with concerts by the likes of the Moscow String Quartet and members of the New York Philharmonic Orchestra. Jackson is busy with its **Cowboy Poetry Gathering**, **Teton Country Fair** and **Mountain Arts Rendezvous**.

Northern Wyoming: The biggest rodeo of the year in Cody, the self-proclaimed "rodeo capital of the world," is the **Cody Stampede**; festivities include four rodeo sessions, two parades, country-and-western dances, art shows and Fourth of July fireworks. Sheridan's biggest annual festival is **Sheridan WYO Days**, including a parade and one of the oldest rodeos in the United States. Soon thereafter, **All American Indian Days** draw tribes from throughout North America to Sheridan. The world's largest rodeo, in terms of number of competitors, is the **National High School Finals Rodeo** in Gillette at the end of the month.

Southwestern Idaho: Nampa's **Snake River Stampede** is one of the top 25 rodeos in the country; there are also parades and nightly concerts by leading country-and-western stars. The **McCall Summer Music Festival** features folk- and world-music performers from throughout the Northwest.

Southeastern Idaho: The **Sun Valley Music Festival** kicks off two weeks of performances by classical and jazz musicians from throughout the country. Besides July 4 fireworks, **Salmon River Days** in Salmon includes kayak and raft races, a rodeo, a triathlon, parade and staged bank robbery. Montpelier's **Oregon Trail Rendezvous Pageant** takes place on the trail itself, with actors reenacting the drama of the pioneer movement west.

Northern Idaho: Coeur d'Alene's **Art on the Green** is a three-day weekend of arts, crafts and dance festivals. The **Festival at Sandpoint**, which extends to mid-August, is an evening series of classical, pop, jazz and ragtime concerts along the shore of Lake Pend Oreille.

Western Montana: July is powwow time. On the Flathead Indian Reservation, the **Arlee Powwow**, on the Jocko River north of Missoula, features Salish and Kootenai dancing, stick games, horse racing and a rodeo. The **Standing Arrow Powwow**, at Elmo on Flathead Lake, is highlighted by Kootenai dancing. At Browning on the Blackfeet Indian Reservation, **North American Indian Days** focus on the dancing, singing, drumming and games of this Plains Indian tribe; there's a parade and a rodeo. Also in July, the **Flathead Festival** offers two weeks of classical, jazz, New Age, opera and other musical concerts spread across the Flathead Valley from Bigfork to Whitefish.

Southern Montana: The quiet streets of Bannack State Park, west of Dillon, come to life for **Bannack Days**, featuring pioneer craft demonstrations and activities that include horse-and-buggy rides, black-powder shooting and panning for gold.

Montana East of the Rockies: The granddaddy of all Montana rodeos is the **Wild Horse Stampede** at Wolf Point on the Fort Peck Indian Reservation; evolved from traditional powwows and bucking contests, it features wild-horse races and other events. On the Northern Cheyenne Indian Reservation at Lame Deer, the **Northern Cheyenne Powwow** on the July 4 weekend features parades, dancing, drumming, singing and feasting.

AUGUST

Denver and the Front Range: Fort Collins' big local festival, **New West Fest**, features food, music, arts and crafts and contests. In Colorado Springs, the **Pikes Peak or Bust Rodeo** kicks off with a street breakfast and parade. Pueblo is the site of the **Colorado State Fair**.

Northern Colorado: Hundreds of fine American wines, as well as cuisine from Colorado's top chefs, are available for sampling at Winter Park's **Rocky Mountain Wine and Food Festival**. Celebrities flock to Vail for the **Jerry Ford Invitational Golf Tournament**. Leadville celebrates **Boom Days** with a parade, carnival, street fair, 22-mile burro pack race and mine-drilling contests. Musicians come from all over the United States and Europe to participate in the three-day **Central City Jazz Festival**.

Southern Colorado: Telluride events include the **Telluride Chamber Music Festival** and the **Telluride Jazz Celebration**.

Utah: Visual and performing arts are showcased in the **Park City Arts Festival**.

Southern Wyoming: Casper hosts the **Central Wyoming Fair**. Later in the month, the **Wyoming State Fair** in Douglas features livestock shows, arts and crafts, a rodeo and big-name country-music concerts. The **Fort Bridger Rendezvous**, the state's largest gathering of modern-day mountain men, is held on Labor Day weekend at Fort Bridger State Historic Site. The **Green River Rendezvous** near Pinedale is another large mountain-man gathering.

Northern Wyoming: The colorful **Gift of the Waters Pageant** in Thermopolis honors Chief Washakie and the U.S. government for their foresight in protecting the healing waters of Thermopolis Hot Springs in 1896.

Southwestern Idaho: Horses and riders reenact a fording of the Snake River by a pioneer wagon train during **Three Island Crossing**, a weekend-long event on a portion of the original Oregon Trail at Glenns Ferry; there's also a parade, crafts exhibits, an Old West shootout and a barbecue. The **Western Idaho Fair** in Boise is the state's biggest fair, featuring carnival rides, agricultural exhibits, food booths and big-name country and pop entertainers.

Southeastern Idaho: The **Shoshone-Bannock Indian Festival** at Fort Hall features dances and games in traditional native costume and the All-Indian Old Timers Rodeo. Rexburg's **Idaho International Folk Dance Festival** draws dance troupes from around the world for eight days of traditional dancing and music, kicked off by a colorful street fair. During **Pierre's Days/Cultural Arts Rendezvous** in Driggs, 1830s mountain men's rendezvous are reenacted with such tongue-in-cheek events as the John Colter Indian Escape Dash and the Mr. Pierre Tall Tale Contest. There's a **Northern Rockies Folk Festival** at Hailey.

Northern Idaho: Coeur d'Alene Indians make a pilgrimage to Cataldo's Old Mission State Park for **The Coming of the Black Robes**, a traditional religious ceremony open to the public.

Western Montana: The five-day **Northwest Montana Fair** in Kalispell highlights the August calendar.

Southern Montana: The **Sweet Pea Festival of the Arts** in Bozeman attracts big-name national and regional musicians for rock and jazz concerts; there are also a parade, arts and crafts, sporting events and a climactic ball.

Montana East of the Rockies: Crow Agency, on the Crow Indian Reservation, becomes the "teepee capital of the world" for five days during the **Crow Fair and Powwow**, when hundreds of tepees rise from the banks of the Little Bighorn River; events include parades, rodeos, dancing, singing, feasting and horse races.

Wadopana Powwow is celebrated at Wolf Point on the Fort Peck Indian Reservation. In Red Lodge, the nine-day **Festival of Nations** pays homage to immigrants from many countries who built the old mining town; highlights include traditional dances, craft demonstrations, an international cooking pavilion and a parade. Lewistown's **Montana Cowboy Poetry Gathering** is two days of authentic rhymes and recitations, music and dance.

SEPTEMBER

Denver and the Front Range: **Oktoberfest** is celebrated in mid-September in Denver's Larimer Square as well as in Golden and Pueblo. The **Colorado Springs Hot-Air Balloon Classic** features more than 100 balloons.

Northern Colorado: **Vailfest** livens up the Vail Valley with food, entertainment and children's activities. Steamboat Springs hosts the **Steamboat Vintage Auto Race and Concours d'Elegance** on Labor Day Weekend.

Southern Colorado: Twenty-one southwestern Colorado communities join together to stage the spectacular **Colorfest**, with more than 70 special events plus hikes, jeep trips and auto tours to see the fall colors. The **Telluride Hang Gliding Festival** is the world's largest and most spectacular hang-gliding event.

Utah: The **Utah State Fair** is held in Salt Lake City. The city also hosts an annual **Greek Festival** around the same time.

Yellowstone and Jackson Hole: The **Jackson Hole Fall Arts Festival**, with most events in Jackson, extends through the last half of September and includes the all-day Western Art Symposium.

Southwestern Idaho: Artists from all over the United States display their works during Boise's **Art in the Park**, a three-day event featuring music, food and kids' events.

Southeastern Idaho: Country stars appear at the **Eastern Idaho State Fair** in Blackfoot. Near Sun Valley, the **Ketchum Wagon Days Celebration** is highlighted by the largest nonmotorized parade in the West, a procession of giant ore wagons used in past mining days; other events include band concerts, dances, a carnival and a car auction.

Northern Idaho: The **Lewiston Roundup** features a top-class rodeo and a cowboy breakfast. In Orofino, the **Clearwater County Fair and Lumberjack Days** includes a parade, a carnival and a logging competition that attracts timbermen from all over the world.

Western Montana: Libby's **Nordicfest** is a three-day celebration of the logging town's Scandinavian heritage, featuring traditional crafts, food, dancing and sporting events.

Montana East of the Rockies: In Laurel, west of Billings, **Herbstfest** is a traditional Russian-German harvest festival with music, dancing, drinking and feasting.

OCTOBER

Denver and the Front Range: The three-day **Colorado Performing Arts Festival** in Denver presents free music, dance and theater events. Later in the month, the city hosts the **Denver International Film Festival** and the **Denver International Open House Arts Weekend**.

Southern Colorado: Durango is the scene of the **Western Arts, Film and Cowboy Poetry Gathering**.

Southwestern Idaho: The **Renaissance Faire** in Boise is appropriately sited at the medieval-looking Old Idaho Penitentiary and the adjacent Idaho Botanical Garden.

Northern Idaho: The **Idaho State Draft Horse International** in Sandpoint offers exhibits and contests demonstrating the speed and strength of such great working horses as the Clydesdale and the Percheron.

Western Montana: The **Flathead International Balloon Festival** adds a splash of color to the Flathead Valley skies.

NOVEMBER

Denver and the Front Range: Beginning around Thanksgiving and lasting through the National Western Stock Show in January, downtown Denver's city and county buildings are festooned with the **World's Largest Christmas Lighting Display**.

Utah: Mormons mark the Christmas season with a spectacular **Christmas Lights Display** at Salt Lake City's Temple Square.

Southwestern Idaho: Boise, "the City of Trees," observes a **Festival of Trees** over Thanksgiving weekend with a display of lavishly decorated Christmas trees and holiday wreaths.

Southeastern Idaho: Preston's **Idaho Festival of Lights** begins with a Veterans Day parade and continues until Christmas with parades and a musical show; the town's lighting display is considered the state's best.

Southern Montana: About 400 bald eagles congregate on the Missouri River near Helena between early November and mid-December to feed on spawning salmon; during this **Bald Eagle Migration**, a visitors center offers hands-on displays and viewing telescopes.

DECEMBER

Denver and the Front Range: Denver's holiday-season traditions include the **Larimer Square Christmas Walk**, re-creating the ambience of a traditional Victorian Christmas, and the downtown **Parade of Lights**, an illuminated nighttime parade with floats and marching bands. Pueblo also has a nighttime **Christmas Parade of Lights**, as well as a traditional Mexican-style **Las Posadas** procession.

Utah: A Christmas Eve **Torchlight Parade** is held at the Park City ski area.

Yellowstone and Jackson Hole: **National Elk Refuge Sleigh Rides** begin in December and extend into March.

Western Montana: **Christmas in Bigfork** is a month-long observance that features colorful lighting displays, caroling, sleigh rides and a variety of special holiday events.

How to Deal With . . .

VISITOR INFORMATION

For free visitor information packages including maps and current details on special events, accommodations and camping, contact the **Colorado Tourism Board** (1625 Broadway, Suite 1700, Denver, CO 80202; 800-433-2656), the **Utah Travel Council** (Council Hall/Capitol Hill, Salt Lake City, UT 84114; 801-538-1030, fax 801-538-1399), the **Wyoming Division of Tourism** (Route 25 at College Drive, Cheyenne, WY 82002; 307-777-7777), **Travel Montana** (1424 9th Avenue, Helena, MT 59620; 406-444-2654, 800-847-4868) or the **Idaho Travel Council** (700 West State Street, Boise, ID 83720; 800-635-7820). In addition, most towns have chambers of commerce or visitor information centers. Tourist information centers are usually not open on weekends.

PACKING

The old adage that you should take along twice as much money and half as much stuff as you think you'll need is sound advice as far as it goes. Bear in mind, though, that in the more remote reaches of the Rockies you might come across a store selling something more substantial than beef jerky and country-and-western cassettes . . . well . . . every once in a while.

Westerners are casual in their dress and expect the same of visitors. Once you leave the Denver metropolitan area, restaurants with dress codes are few and far between, though major resort towns such as Vail, Aspen and Sun Valley cater to such upmarket vacationers that you may want to wear sport clothes a little more chic than a plaid flannel shirt and old Levi's. Then again, you may not. They'll never know whether you're an eccentric billionaire. These three ski areas in particular seem to fancy themselves the Paris, Milan and Rome of winter sportswear; otherwise, hardly anybody comes to the Rocky Mountains to show off their clothes.

When packing clothes, plan to dress in layers. Temperatures can turn hot or cold in a flash. During the course of a single summer day in the mountains, you can expect to start with a heavy jacket, a sweater or flannel shirt and a pair of jeans, peeling down to a T-shirt and shorts as the day warms up, then putting the extra layers back on as the late-afternoon shadows set in.

Other essentials to pack or buy along the way include a good sunscreen and high-quality sunglasses. Cool temperatures often lull newcomers into forgetting that thin high-altitude air filters out far less of the sun's ultraviolet rays; above timberline, exposed skin will sunburn faster than it would on a Florida beach. If you are planning to camp in the mountains during the summer months, you'll be glad you brought mosquito repellent. Umbrellas are considered an oddity in the western states. You'll hardly ever see one, and you'll get funny looks from the locals if you carry one. The approved means of keeping chilly afternoon rain from running down the back of your neck is a cowboy hat.

For outdoor activities, tough-soled hiking boots are more comfortable than running shoes on rocky terrain. Even RV travelers and those who prefer to spend most nights in motels may want to take along a backpacking tent and sleeping bag when the urge to stay out under star-spangled western skies becomes irresistible. A canteen, first-aid kit, flashlight and other routine camping gear are also likely to come in handy. Both cross-country and downhill ski rentals are available everywhere you look during the winter, though serious skiers may find that the quality and condition of rental skis leave something to be desired. In the summer, mountain bikes can be rented in just about any small town in the Colorado Rockies and are widely available as well in Utah, Idaho and Montana. Other outdoor-recreation equipment—kayaks, fishing tackle, golf clubs and gold pans—generally cannot be rented, so you'll want to bring the right gear for your special sporting passion.

A camera, of course, is essential for capturing your travel experience; of equal importance is a good pair of binoculars, which let you explore distant landscapes from scenic overlooks and bring wildlife up close. And don't, for heaven's sake, forget your copy of *Hidden Rockies*.

HOTELS

Lodgings in the Rockies run the gamut from tiny one-room cabins to luxury hotels that blend traditional alpine-lodge ambience with contemporary elegance. Bed and breakfasts can be found in almost all Rocky Mountain towns you're likely to visit—not only chic destinations like Aspen, Colorado, and Jackson, Wyoming, but also such off-the-beaten-path places as Creede and Rawlins, Coeur d'Alene and Bigfork. They come in all types, sizes and price ranges. Typical of the genre are lovingly restored Victorian-era mansions comfortably furnished with period decor, usually with fewer than a dozen rooms. Some bed and breakfasts, however, are guest cottages or rooms in nice suburban homes, while others are larger establishments, approaching motel size, of the type sometimes referred to as country inns.

The abundance of motels in towns along all major highway routes presents a range of choices, from name-brand motor inns to traditional mom-and-pop establishments that have endured for the half century since motels were invented. While rather ordinary motels in the vicinity of major tourist destinations can be pricey, lodging in small towns away from major resorts and interstate routes can offer friendliness, quiet and comfort at ridiculously affordable rates.

At the other end of the price spectrum, peak-season rates at leading ski resorts can be incredibly costly. To save money, consider staying in more affordable lodging as much as an hour away and commuting to the ski slopes during the day, or plan your vacation during "shoulder seasons," before and after the peak seasons. Even though the summer is a lively time in many ski towns, accommodations are in surplus and room rates often drop to less than half the winter rates.

In some parts of the Rockies, particularly Colorado and Utah, you'll find lavishly restored historic hotels that date back to the gold-boom days of the late

19th century. Many combine affordable rates with plenty of antique decor and authentic personality. Most national parks in the region have lodges that offer distinctive accommodations at midrange rates; some, like the Old Faithful Inn at Yellowstone National Park and the Glacier Park Lodge at East Glacier Park, Montana, rank high among the region's most memorable historic inns. These and other National Park lodges are among the most sought-after accommodations in the Rockies region, so travelers need to make reservations several months in advance.

Guest ranches are located throughout the Rocky Mountain region. Horseback riding is the common theme of all; some offer luxury lodging, spa facilities and a full range of activities that may include fishing, boating, swimming and even tennis. Others operate as working ranches, providing lodging in comfortably rustic cabins and offering the opportunity to participate in roundups and other ranching activities. Rates at most guest ranches are comparatively expensive but include all meals and use of recreational facilities. Most guest ranches have minimum-stay requirements ranging from three days to a week.

Whatever your preference and budget, you can probably find something to suit your taste with the help of this book. Remember, rooms can be scarce and prices may rise during peak season, which is summer throughout most of the region and winter in ski resorts. Travelers planning to visit a place in peak season should either make advance reservations or arrive early in the day, before the "No Vacancy" signs start lighting up.

Lodging prices listed in this book are high-season rates. If you're looking for off-season bargains, it's good to inquire. *Budget* lodgings generally run less than $50 per night for two people and are satisfactory and clean but modest. *Moderate* hotels range from $50 to $90; what they have to offer in the way of luxury will depend on where they are located, but they generally offer larger rooms and more attractive surroundings than budget lodgings. At *deluxe*-priced accomodations, you can expect to spend between $90 and $130 for a homey bed and breakfast or a double in a hotel or resort. In hotels of this price you'll generally find spacious rooms, a fashionable lobby, a restaurant and often a bar or nightclub. *Ultra-deluxe* facilities, priced above $130, are the finest in the region, offering all the amenities of a deluxe hotel plus plenty of extras.

Room rates vary as much with locale as with quality. Some of the trendier destinations have no rooms at all in the budget price range. In other communities—those where rates are set with truck drivers in mind and those in out-of-the-way small towns—every motel falls into the budget category, even though accommodations may range from $19.95 at rundown, spartan places to $45 or so at the classiest motor inn in town. The price categories listed in this book are relative, designed to show you where to get the most out of your travel budget, however large or small it may be.

RESTAURANTS

Fine dining in the Rockies tends to focus on the region's traditional cuisine—beef and trout. In Colorado you can also count on finding Mexican restaurants in just about every town you come to, and in Utah the same is true of Chinese restaurants. Competition for restaurant business is fierce in the more exclusive resort areas, such as Aspen, Vail, Jackson and Sun Valley, and it's there you'll find menus featuring everything from duck *à l'orange* to grilled elk. In Denver and some other areas of Colorado, buffalo meat is an emerging as a specialty thanks to a growing number of ranches that have turned to raising this tasty, lean, low-cholesterol alternative to beef. If your idea of an ideal vacation includes savoring epicurean delights, then by all means seize opportunities whenever they arise. When traveling in the Rockies, you can go for days between gourmet meals.

Restaurants listed in this book generally offer lunch and dinner unless otherwise noted. Dinner entrées at *budget* restaurants usually cost $8 or less. The ambience is informal, service usually speedy and the crowd often a local one. *Moderate*-priced restaurant entrées range between $8 and $16 at dinner; surroundings are casual but pleasant; the menu offers more variety and the pace is usually slower than at budget restaurants. *Deluxe* establishments tab their entrées from $16 to $24; cuisines may be simple or sophisticated, depending on the location, but the decor is plusher and the service more personalized than at moderate-priced restaurants. *Ultra-deluxe* dining rooms, where entrées begin at $24, are often the gourmet places; here cooking has become a fine art and the service should be impeccable.

Some restaurants change hands often and are occasionally closed in low seasons. Efforts have been made in this book to include places with established reputations for good eating. Compared to evening dinners, breakfast and lunch menus vary less in price from restaurant to restaurant.

DRIVING THE ROCKIES

Some first-time visitors to the Rockies wonder why so many mountain roads do not have guard rails to separate motorists from thousand-foot dropoffs. The fact is, highway safety studies have found that far fewer accidents occur where there are no guard rails. Statistically, edgy, winding mountain roads are much safer than straight, fast interstate highways. Unpaved roads are another story. While many are wide and well graded, weather conditions or the wear and tear of heavy seasonal use can create unexpected road hazards. Some U.S. Forest Service and Bureau of Land Management roads are designated for four-wheel-drive or high-clearance vehicles only. If you see a sign indicating four-wheel-drive only, believe it. These roads can be very dangerous in a standard passenger car without the high ground clearance and extra traction afforded by four-wheel drive—and there may be no safe place to turn around if you get stuck.

Some side roads will take you far from civilization, so be sure to have a full radiator and tank of gas. Carry spare fuel, water and food. Should you become stuck, local people are usually helpful about offering assistance to stranded vehicles, but in case no one else is around, for extended backcountry driving a CB radio or car phone would not be a bad idea.

In the winter months, mountain passes frequently become snowpacked, and under these conditions tire chains are required by law in most Rocky Mountain states, even on main highways. State patrol officers will make you turn back if your car is not equipped with chains, so make sure you have them. At the very least, studded tires—legal in this region from November to April—are recommended. In winter it is wise to travel with a shovel and blankets in your car.

If your car does not seem to run well at high elevations, you should probably have the carburetor adjusted at the next service station. The air at Rocky Mountain altitudes is "thin"—that is, it contains considerably less oxygen in a given volume than air at lower altitudes. The carburetor or fuel injection unit should be set leaner to achieve an efficient fuel-to-air mixture. Another common problem when climbing mountain passes is vaporlock, a condition in which low atmospheric pressure combined with high engine temperatures causes gasoline to evaporate in the fuel lines, making bubbles that prevent the fuel pump from functioning. The result is that your car's engine coughs and soon stops dead. If this occurs, pull over to the side of the road and wait until the fuel system cools down. A damp rag held against the fuel line will speed up the process and get you back on the road more quickly.

You can get full information on statewide road conditions at any time of year by calling the following numbers: in Colorado, 303-639-1234 (for the Front Range and eastern plains) or 303-639-1111 (for the Rockies and western slope); in Utah, 800-752-7600; in Wyoming, 307-635-9966; in Idaho, 208-336-6000; in Montana, 800-226-7623.

TRAVELING WITH CHILDREN

Any place that has wild animals, cowboys and Indians, rocks to climb and limitless room to run is bound to be a hit with youngsters. Plenty of family adventures are available in the Rockies, from manmade attractions to experiences in the wilderness. A few simple guidelines will help make traveling with children a pleasure.

Book reservations in advance, making sure that the places you stay accept children. Many bed and breakfasts do not. If you need a crib or extra cot, arrange for it ahead of time. A travel agent can be of help here, as well as with almost all other travel plans.

If you are traveling by air, try to reserve bulkhead seats where there is plenty of room. Take along extras you may need such as diapers, changes of clothing, snacks, toys and small games. When traveling by car, be sure to take along the extras, too. Make sure you have plenty of water and juices to drink; dehydration can be a subtle but serious problem. Most towns have all-night convenience stores that carry diapers, baby food, snacks and other essentials; national parks and some state parks also have such stores, though they usually close early.

A first-aid kit is a must for any trip. Along with adhesive bandages, antiseptic cream and something to stop itching, include any medicines your pediatrician might recommend to treat allergies, colds, diarrhea or any chronic problems your child may have. Mountain sunshine is intense, so take extra care for the first few days. Children's skin is usually more tender than adult skin, and severe sunburn can happen before you realize. A hat is a good idea, along with a reliable sunblock.

Many national parks and monuments offer special activities designed just for children. Visitors center film presentations and rangers' campfire slide shows can help inform children about the natural history of the Rockies and head off some questions. Still, kids tend to find a lot more things to wonder about than adults have answers for. To be as prepared as possible, seize every opportunity to learn more—particularly about wildlife, a constant curiosity for young minds.

TRAVELING WITH PETS

The Rockies are big dog country, and you'll probably notice more recreationers traveling with their pets than in other regions. Pets are permitted on leashes in virtually all campgrounds. But few bed and breakfasts or guest ranches will accept them, and more run-of-the-mill motels, particularly in Colorado tourist areas, seem to be adopting "No Pets" policies each year. Otherwise, the main limitation of traveling with a canine companion is that national parks and monuments prohibit pets on trails or in the backcountry. You are supposed to walk your dog on the roadside, then leave it in the car while you hike in the woods. Make sure the dog gets adequate ventilation and water. Fortunately, dogs are free to run everywhere in national forests, and leashes are required only in designated camping and picnic areas.

Wildlife can pose special hazards for pets in the backcountry. At lower elevations in the plains and foothills, campers should not leave a cat or small dog outside at night because coyotes may attack it. In remote forest areas, it's especially important to keep an eye on your dog at all times. Bears are upset by dogs barking at them and may attack even very large dogs. Porcupines, common in pine forests, are tempting to chase and slow enough to catch; if your dog *does* catch one, a mouthful of quills means painfully pulling them out one by one with a pair of pliers or making an emergency visit to a veterinary clinic in the nearest town.

BEING AN OLDER TRAVELER

The Rocky Mountain West is a hospitable place for older vacationers, many of whom migrate from hotter climates to enjoy the cool summers. Persons 62 and older can save considerable money with a Golden Age Passport, which allows free admission to national parks and monuments. Apply for one in person at any national-park unit that charges an entrance fee. The passports are also good for a 50 percent discount on fees at most national-forest campgrounds. Many private sightseeing attractions also offer significant discounts for seniors.

The **American Association of Retired Persons** (AARP) (3200 East Carson Street, Lakewood, CA 90712; 310-496-2277) offers membership to anyone 50 and over. AARP's benefits include travel discounts with a number of firms.

Elderhostel (75 Federal Street, Boston, MA 02110; 617-426-7788) offers all-inclusive packages with educational courses at colleges and universities. In the Rocky Mountain region, Elderhostel courses are available in numerous locations including Boulder, Gunnison and Durango, Colorado; Logan and Salt Lake City, Utah; and Laramie, Wyoming.

Be extra careful with your health. High altitude is the biggest risk factor. Since many driving routes through the Rockies cross mountain passes at 10,000 to 12,000 feet above sea level, it's advisable to ask your physician if high altitude is a problem for you. People with heart problems are commonly advised to avoid all physical exertion above 10,000 feet, and those with respiratory conditions such as emphysema may not be able to visit high altitudes at all. In the changeable climate of the Rockies, seniors are more at risk of suffering hypothermia. Many tourist destinations in the region are a long way from any hospital or other health-care facility.

In addition to the medications you ordinarily use, it's a good idea to bring along your prescriptions in case you need replacements. Consider carrying a medical record with you, including your history and current medical status as well as your doctor's name, phone number and address. Make sure that your insurance covers you while you are away from home.

BEING A TRAVELER WITH DISABILITIES

Colorado and, to a lesser extent, other states in the Rocky Mountain region are striving to make public areas fully accessible to persons with disabilities. Parking spaces and restroom facilities for the physically challenged are provided according to both state law and national-park regulations. National parks and monuments also post signs that tell which trails are wheelchair accessible. Some recreation areas even have Braille nature trails with marked points of interest appealing to the senses of touch and smell.

Golden Access Passports, good for free admission to all national parks and monuments as well as discounts at most federal public campgrounds, are available at no charge to persons who are blind or have a permanent disability. You may apply in person at any national park unit that charges an entrance fee.

Information sources for travelers with disabilities include the **Society for the Advancement of Travel for the Handicapped** (347 5th Avenue, Suite 610, New York, NY 10016; 212-447-7284), the **Travel Information Center** (215-456-9600) and **Mobility International USA** (P.O. Box 10767, Eugene, OR 97440; 503-343-1284). For general travel advice, contact **Travelin' Talk** (P.O. Box 3534, Clarksville, TN 37043; 615-552-6670), a networking organization.

BEING A FOREIGN TRAVELER

PASSPORTS AND VISAS Most foreign visitors, other than Canadian citizens, need a passport and tourist visa to enter the United States. Contact your nearest U.S. embassy or consulate well in advance to obtain a visa and to check on any other entry requirements.

CUSTOMS REQUIREMENTS Foreign travelers are allowed to carry in up to 200 cigarettes (or 100 cigars) and $400 worth of duty-free gifts, which may include one liter of alcohol (for travelers age 21 or over). You may bring in any amount of currency but must fill out a form if you bring in more than U.S.$10,000. Carry any prescription drugs in clearly marked containers. You may have to produce a written prescription or doctor's statement for the customs officer. Meat or meat products, seeds, plants, fruits and narcotics are not allowed to be brought into the United States, and there is a long list of other contraband items, from live birds and snakes to switchblade knives, which vacation travelers hardly ever carry along. Contact the **United States Customs Service** (1301 Constitution Avenue Northwest, Washington, DC 20229; 202-566-8195) for further information.

DRIVING If you plan to rent a car, you should obtain an international driver's license before arriving in the United States. Some car-rental agencies require both a foreign license and an international driver's license. Virtually all agencies require a lessee to be at least 25 years of age and to present a major credit card.

CURRENCY U.S. money is based on the dollar. Bills generally come in denominations of $1, $5, $10, $20, $50 and $100. Every dollar is divided into 100 cents. Coins are the penny (one cent), nickel (five cents), dime (ten cents) and quarter (25 cents). Half-dollar and dollar coins exist but are rarely used. You may not use foreign currency to purchase goods and services in the United States. Consider buying travelers checks in dollar amounts. You may also use credit cards affiliated with an American company such as Interbank, Barclay Card, VISA and American Express.

ELECTRICITY AND ELECTRONICS Electric outlets use currents of 110 volts, 60 cycles. For appliances made for other electrical systems, you need a transformer or other adapter. Travelers who use laptop computers for telecommunication should be aware that modem configurations for U.S. telephone systems may be different from their European counterparts. Similarly, the U.S. format for videotapes is different from that in Europe; U.S. Park Service visitor centers and other stores that sell souvenir videos often have them available in European format.

WEIGHTS AND MEASURES The United States uses the English system of weights and measures. American units and their metric equivalents are: 1 inch = 2.5 centimeters; 1 foot (12 inches) = 0.3 meter; 1 yard (3 feet) = 0.9 meter; 1 mile (5280 feet) = 1.6 kilometers; 1 ounce = 28 grams; 1 pound (16 ounces) = 0.45 kilogram; 1 quart (liquid) = 0.9 liter.

The Sporting Life

CAMPING

RV or tent camping is a great way to tour the Rockies during the summer months. Besides saving substantial sums of money, campers enjoy the freedom to watch sunsets from beautiful places, spend nights under spectacularly starry skies and wake up to find themselves in lovely surroundings that few hotels can match.

Most towns have commercial RV parks of some sort, and long-term mobile home parks often rent spaces to RVers by the night. But unless you absolutely need cable television, none of these places can compete with the wide array of public campgrounds available in national and state parks, monuments and forests. Federal campground sites are typically less developed: You won't find electric, water or sewer hookups in campgrounds at national forests, national monuments or national recreation areas (with the exception of one campground on the Wyoming side of Bighorn Canyon National Recreation Area). As for national parks, there are more than 300 hookups in Yellowstone, more than 200 each in Grand Teton and Glacier. The campground at Mesa Verde has some sites with full hookups, but Rocky Mountain National Park, with five large campgrounds totaling almost 600 sites, has none. In Colorado, only a few state park campgrounds at major recreation lakes near cities have hookups; most do not, and the same is true for Utah, Wyoming and Montana state parks. Idaho is the best adapted for RVs: Half of its 22 state parks offer hookups. The largest public campgrounds, such as those in national parks, offer tent camping loops separate from RV loops, as well as hike-in backcountry camping by permit. There is no charge in national forests for primitive camping.

You won't find much in the way of sophisticated reservation systems in the Rockies. In July and August, the largest campgrounds in Rocky Mountain, Yellowstone and Grand Teton national parks require reservations through **MISTIX** (800-365-2267; credit card required); reservations are not accepted at Glacier National Park, nor are they taken for most Yellowstone and Grand Teton campgrounds. The general rule in public campgrounds is still first-come, first-served, even though they fill up practically every night during peak season. For campers, this means traveling in the morning and reaching your intended campground by early afternoon—or, during peak season at Yellowstone, by late morning. In many areas, campers may find it more convenient to keep a single location for as much as a week and explore surrounding areas on daytrips. In a few resort areas where housing is very expensive, particularly Aspen, don't expect to find a campsite no matter how early in the day you arrive; students working seasonal jobs and other long-term visitors monopolize the public campgrounds all summer, trading locations every two weeks to avoid maximum-stay limitations.

For a listing of state parks with camping facilities and reservation information, contact **Division of Parks and Outdoor Recreation** (1313 Sherman Street, Room 618, Denver, CO 80203; 303-866-3437), **Utah Division of Parks and Recreation** (1636 West North Temple Street, Suite 116, Salt Lake City,

UT 84116; 801-538-7220), **Wyoming Division of Parks & Historic Sites** (Barrett Building, 2301 Central Avenue, Cheyenne, WY 82002; 307-777-6323), **Idaho State Parks & Recreation** (5657 Warm Springs Avenue, Boise, ID 83712; 208-334-4199) and **Montana Department of Fish, Wildlife & Parks** (1420 East 6th Avenue, Helena, MT 59620; 406-444-2535).

Information on camping in national forests is available by calling 800-280-CAMP, or from U.S. Forest Service regional offices. Colorado and Wyoming: **U.S. Forest Service—Rocky Mountain Region** (P.O. Box 25127, Lakewood, CO 80225; 303-236-9431). Utah and southern Idaho: **U.S. Forest Service—Intermountain Region** (2501 Wall Avenue, Ogden, UT 84401; 801-625-5306). Montana and northern Idaho: **U.S. Forest Service-Northern Region** (P.O. Box 7669, Missoula, MT 59807; 406-329-3511). Information on camping at national parks and monuments is available from the **National Park Service—Rocky Mountain Regional Headquarters** (P.O. Box 25287, Denver, CO 80225; 303-969-2000).

WILDERNESS AREAS AND PERMITS

The passage of the Wilderness Act of 1993 represented a major expansion of federal wilderness protection. Today, more than one billion acres of national-forest and Bureau of Land Management (BLM) land in the Rocky Mountain states has been designated as wilderness. To be considered for federal wilderness protection, an area must consist of at least five contiguous square miles without a road of any kind. At the time it has been declared a wilderness area, the land is limited to uses that existed as of that date. Since most wilderness areas in the Rockies were created quite recently—from 1978 to 1980 and in 1993—it is generally the highest peaks, where roads are few and far between, that qualify for wilderness status. Besides protecting ancient forests from timber cutting by newly developed methods like skylining or helicopter airlifting, federal wilderness designation prohibits all mechanized transportation—no jeeps, motorcycles or all-terrain vehicles and, after years of heated controversy, no mountain bikes. Wilderness areas usually have well-developed trail networks for hiking, cross-country skiing and pack trips using horses or llamas.

You no longer need a permit to hike or camp in BLM wilderness areas, but plan to stop at a ranger station anyway for trail maps and advice on current conditions and fire regulations. Tent camping is allowed without restriction in wilderness areas and almost all other backcountry areas of national forests, except where posted signs prohibit it. Throughout the national forests in dry season and in certain wilderness areas at all times, regulations may prohibit campfires and sometimes ban cigarette smoking, with stiff enforcement penalties.

For backcountry hiking in most national parks and monuments, you must first obtain a permit from the ranger at the front desk in the visitors center. The permit procedure is simple and free. It helps park administrators measure the impact of hiking on sensitive ecosystems and distribute use evenly among the major trails.

BOATING AND RAFTING

Many large artificial lakes in and around the Rockies are administered as state parks, while others are national recreation areas, some of them supervised by the U.S. Army Corps of Engineers. Federal boating safety regulations may vary slightly from state regulations. Indian reservations have separate rules for boating on tribal lakes. More significant than any differences between federal, state and tribal regulations are the local rules in force for any particular lake, which are posted near boat ramps. Ask for applicable boating regulations at a local marina or fishing supply store or use the addresses and phone numbers listed in "Parks" or other sections of each chapter in this book to contact the headquarters for lakes where you plan to use a boat.

Boats, from small motorized skiffs to big, fast bass boats and sometimes even houseboats, can be rented by the half-day, day, week or longer at marinas on many of the larger lakes. At most marinas, you can get a boat on short notice if you come on a weekday, since much of their business comes from local weekend recreation.

River rafting is a very popular sport in many areas of the Rockies, notably the Arkansas River (the most-used whitewater recreation river in the United States) between Salida and Cañon City, Colorado; the Roaring Fork River between Aspen and Glenwood Springs; the Payette River north of Boise; the Flathead River near West Glacier Park; and, for week-long backcountry float trips, the Yampa River in Dinosaur National Monument, the Snake River through Hells Canyon National Recreation Area along the Idaho-Oregon border and the Salmon River through the Frank Church–River of No Return Wilderness in central Idaho. Independent rafters are welcome, but because of the bulky equipment and specialized knowledge of river hazards involved, most adventurous souls stick with group tours offered by the many rafting companies located throughout the region. State and federal regulations require rafters, as well as people using canoes, kayaks, sailboards or inner tubes, to wear life jackets.

FISH AND FISHING

The Rocky Mountains are justly famous for the fishing to be found in their alpine lakes and streams. Colorado alone boasts 7000 miles of streams and more than 2100 lakes. The more accessible a shoreline is, the more anglers you're likely to find there, especially during the summer months. You can beat the crowds by hiking a few miles into the backcountry or, to some extent, by planning your fishing days during the week.

Fish hatcheries in all the Rocky Mountain states keep busy stocking streams with trout, particularly rainbows, the West's most popular game fish. In Colorado, for instance, 22 million rainbow trout are stocked annually. Many coldwater mountain lakes also offer fishing for cutthroat and other trout, kokanee salmon, mountain whitefish and arctic grayling. In the Snake River and its tributaries, the autumn spawning run of anadromous steelhead trout is the highlight of the angler's year; spawning salmon, however, have become rare this far inland. Catch-and-release flyfishing is the rule in some popular areas, allowing more anglers a chance at bigger fish. Be sure to inquire locally about eating the fish you catch, since some seemingly remote streams and rivers have been contaminated by old mines and mills.

The larger reservoirs, especially those located at lower elevations, offer an assortment of sport fish, including carp, crappie, channel catfish, largemouth bass, smallmouth bass, white bass, bluegill, bullhead, perch, walleye and northern pike.

For copies of state fishing regulations, inquire at a local fishing supply or marina, or contact the **Colorado Division of Wildlife** (6060 Broadway, Denver, CO 80216; 303-297-1192), the **Utah Division of Wildlife Resources** (1596 West North Temple Street, Salt Lake City, UT 84116; 801-538-4700), the **Wyoming Game and Fish Department** (5400 Bishop Boulevard, Cheyenne, WY 82006; 307-777-4601), the **Idaho Department of Fish and Game** (600 South Walnut Street, Boise, ID 83701; 208-334-3700) or the **Montana Department of Fish, Wildlife & Parks** (1420 East 6th Avenue, Helena, MT 59620; 406-444-2535).

State fishing licenses are required for fishing in national parks, national forests and national recreation areas, but not at Yellowstone National Park, which has its own seven-day fishing regulations, or on Indian reservations, where daily permits are sold by the tribal governments.

Nonresidents may pay $50 for a one-year fishing license in any one state, three to five times the resident fee. But less costly, short-term licenses (for ten days or less) are also available to nonresident visitors. Nonresident children normally fish free with a licensed adult. High-lake and stream fishing seasons normally begin in late spring and run through the fall; lower-elevation lakes and reservoirs may be open year-round for fishing.

WINTER SPORTS

Each of the Rocky Mountain states has a winter "hotline," updated daily with current weather and snow conditions at downhill ski resorts throughout the state. In Colorado, call 303-831-7669; in Utah, 801-521-8102; in Wyoming, 800-225-5996; in Idaho, 800-635-7820; in Montana, 406-444-2654. You should also call for road conditions; see "Driving the Rockies," above.

All state parks and recreation departments (see the listing under "Camping," above) administer snow park areas that provide cross-country skiers and snowmobilers with access to extensive networks of groomed trails. The fee charged for season parking is much less than the fine you must pay if you park without a permit.

GUIDES AND OUTFITTERS

The best way to assure the reliability of the folks guiding you into the wilderness by horse, raft or cross-country skis is to choose someone who has met the standards of a statewide organization of their peers. For membership lists, contact the **Colorado Guides and Outfitters Association** (P.O. Box 31438, Aurora, CO 80041; 303-751-9274), **Utah Guides and Outfitters** (3031 South, 500 East, Salt Lake City, UT 84106; 801-466-1912), **Wyoming State Outfitters and Professional Guides Board** (1750 Westland Road, Cheyenne, WY 82002; 307-777-5323), the **Idaho Outfitters and Guides Association** (P.O. Box 95, Boise, ID 83701; 208-342-1919) and the **Montana Outfitters and Guides Association** (P.O. Box 1248, Helena, MT 59624; 406-449-3578).

CHAPTER TWO

Denver and the Front Range

Of the seven million people who live in the Rocky Mountain states, nearly half make their homes in the 200-mile corridor commonly called the Colorado Front Range, which runs along the foothills of the Rockies from Denver north to Fort Collins and south to Pueblo.

Most visitors from out of state, whether they arrive by car, plane or train, begin their explorations of the Rocky Mountains in Denver. It has the biggest museums, the best shopping malls and the most restaurants in the five-state region. But let's face it: People come to the Rockies to find natural beauty on a grand scale, and Denver, with its often overwhelming traffic and air pollution, is not the best place to look for it.

Fortunately, in the mountains just beyond the edge of the city you'll find towering mountain peaks, old mining towns and plenty of scenery and history. Denver, Boulder, Colorado Springs and most of the area's county governments have cooperated to set aside vast expanses of mountain parklands, protecting their skylines from both mining exploitation and subdivision development. The Front Range has more than 400 open-space parks in all. Many are completely inaccessible, while others provide unparalleled recreational opportunities.

Two other areas along the Front Range—Rocky Mountain National Park, adjoining the town of Estes Park, and the Pikes Peak area around Colorado Springs—are old-timers when it comes to tourism. Sightseeing attractions have been in continuous operation since the beginning of the 20th century, when Aspen and Durango were forgotten, nearly abandoned mining towns and Vail had not yet been imagined. Tourism on the Front Range took on an additional aspect in 1991, when the state legislature legalized limited-stakes casino gambling to stimulate the economies of three famous but crumbling and nearly abandoned Front Range cities of the gold-mining era—Central City, Black Hawk and Cripple Creek.

The first exploration of the Front Range by whites took place in 1810, when Captain Zebulon Pike followed the Arkansas River westward to the foot of the mountain that would later be named after him. After a failed attempt to climb the peak, Pike headed south along the Front Range and was arrested as a spy near present-day Pueblo soon after crossing the Arkansas River, the northern border of the 200-year-old Spanish colony of New Mexico. After his release from a Santa Fe prison, Pike returned to the United States and published his journal, which became a popular bestseller of its day. In the next 50 years, however, only U.S. Army cartography expeditions and a handful of mountain men ventured into the Rockies.

Both Denver and Colorado City got their start as supply points for the "Pikes Peak or Bust" gold rush, which started in 1859. Colorado City was later absorbed by Colorado Springs, which was founded in 1872 as a tourist resort town. A succession of gold strikes, culminating in the Cripple Creek gold boom of the 1890s, brought explosive population growth to the Front Range. In the long run, however, the farmlands around Boulder, Fort Collins, Greeley and other northern communities have proven to be a resource more enduring than gold. North of Denver, the main cash crop is sugar beets, and its fastest-growing industry is bison ranching.

Severe weather is the exception, not the rule, in the Front Range. Its climate is cool and dry, and its cities boast more than 300 days of sunshine a year. All the towns discussed in this chapter can be reached year-round without crossing a mountain pass that might require tire chains, all are within one hour's drive of Route 25 and most can be visited on daytrips from Denver.

Denver

With a population of almost two million, the Denver metropolitan area is by far the largest population center in the Rocky Mountain West. Although the freeways may be daunting, the suburban sprawl awesome in its extent and the mountains obscured by smog, Denver is actually a fun and easy place to visit. Most of the major points of interest are clustered in the downtown area, within walking distance of one another.

A good landmark from which to start exploring downtown Denver is the **Colorado State Capitol** (Sherman Avenue between 14th and East Colfax avenues; 303-866-2604), conventional in design but with a gleaming dome gilded with 303 ounces of 24-carat gold from the mines of Colorado. Free tours start on the half hour, weekdays only, and go all the way up into the dome, 180 feet above the ground floor.

Stone lions flank the front door of the **Molly Brown House** (1340 Pennsylvania Street; 303-832-1421; admission), three blocks east of the capitol building. The mansion belonged to Leadville Johnny Brown, who struck it rich in the goldfields, and his wife, Molly, who achieved local fame as a survivor of the *Titanic* disaster. Their story became a hit Broadway musical and movie, *The*

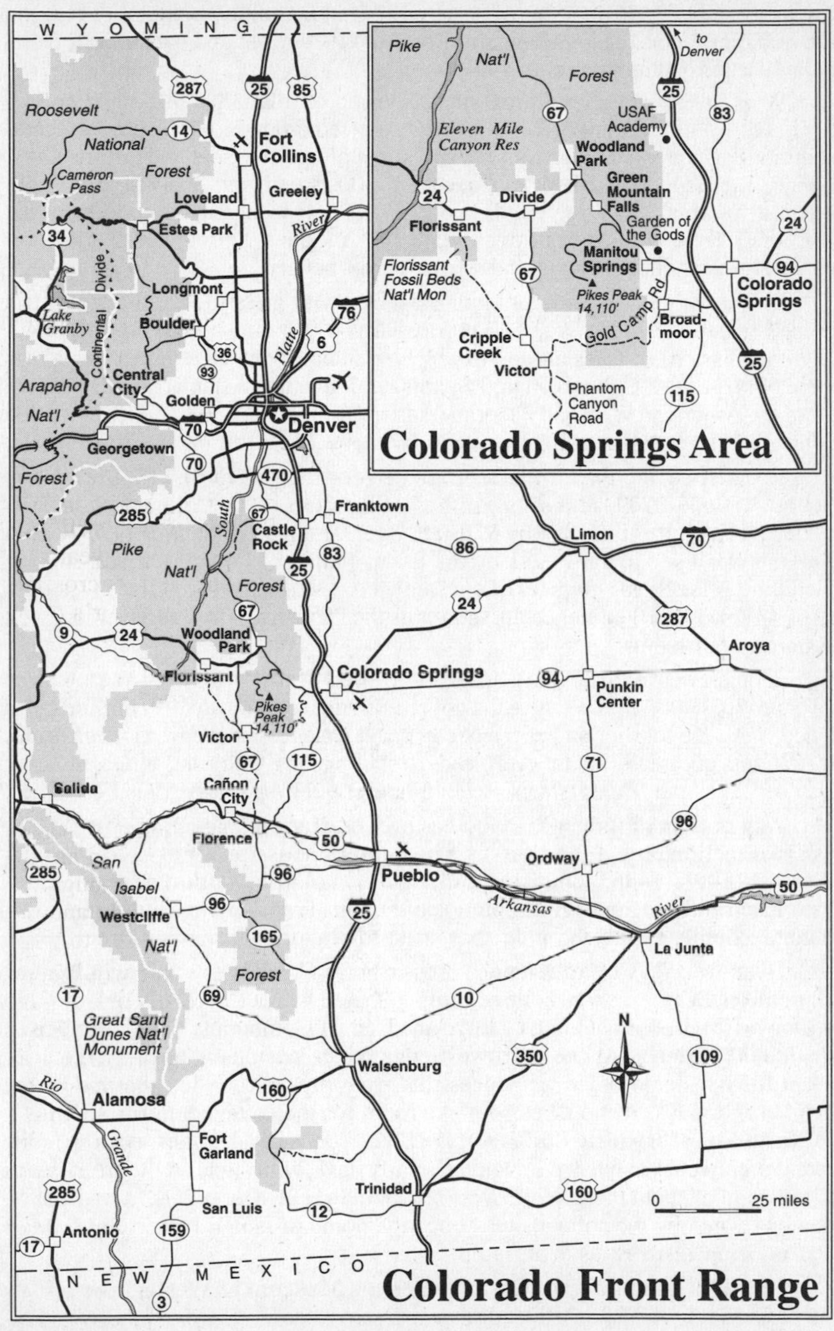
Colorado Springs Area
Colorado Front Range
Pike
Nat'l
Forest
to Denver
USAF Academy
Eleven Mile Canyon Res
Woodland Park
Green Mountain Falls
Divide
Florissant
Garden of the Gods
Manitou Springs
Colorado Springs
Florissant Fossil Beds Nat'l Mon
Pikes Peak 14,110'
Gold Camp Rd
Broadmoor
Cripple Creek
Victor
Phantom Canyon Road
W Y O M I N G
Roosevelt
National
Forest
Cameron Pass
Fort Collins
Greeley
Loveland
Estes Park
River
Continental Divide
Lake Granby
Longmont
Boulder
Platte
Arapaho
Nat'l
Central City
Golden
Denver
Georgetown
Forest
South
Franktown
Castle Rock
Limon
Pike
Nat'l
Forest
Woodland Park
Florissant
Colorado Springs
Aroya
Punkin Center
Pikes Peak 14,110'
Victor
Salida
Cañon City
Florence
Pueblo
Ordway
San
Isabel
Westcliffe
Nat'l
Forest
Arkansas
River
La Junta
Great Sand Dunes Nat'l Monument
N
Rio
Grande
Alamosa
Walsenburg
Fort Garland
Trinidad
San Luis
Antonio
0
25 miles
N E W M E X I C O

Unsinkable Molly Brown. Now restored to its turn-of-the-century glory, the house radiates conspicuous consumption from its gold-leafed parlor ceilings to its lavish third-floor ballroom.

West of the capitol building stand a group of municipal buildings collectively known as the **Denver Civic Center**, erected around a Greek amphitheater commonly frequented by picnickers and street preachers. Southeast of the Civic Center, the **Colorado History Museum** (1300 Broadway; 303-866-3681; admission) presents changing exhibits on the state's heritage assembled from the museum's large collection of documents and antiques. Permanent displays include Plains Indian artifacts and Mesa Verde pottery.

The six-story free-form building gleaming with glass tiles at the south end of the Civic Center is the **Denver Art Museum** (100 West 14th Avenue; 303-640-2793; admission). It takes all day to see everything in this huge museum. Wings are devoted to pre-Columbian and Spanish colonial art, Asian art, 19th-century art of the American West and decorative arts, among others. The museum's pride is an American Indian collection, said by many to be the finest in the world.

Located behind the art museum, the **Byers-Evans House** (1310 Bannock Street; 303-623-0709; admission) is the headquarters of the Colorado State Historical Society. Built in 1883 by William Byers, founder of the *Rocky Mountain News*, it was lived in until 1981 by the Evans family of Denver philanthropists, including Anne Evans, founder of the Denver Art Museum. The house is restored to pre–World War I opulence and contains the Denver History Museum as well as family heirlooms.

A block west of the Civic Center, the **United States Mint** (320 West Colfax Avenue; 303-844-3582) is where the government makes more than 30 million coins a day. Take the tour for an experience in small change that even Las Vegas can't match. Just in case the nation ever needs to start making gold coins again, the mint also serves as the United States' second-largest gold repository after Fort Knox.

Any present or former kid who has ever dreamed of becoming a firefighter can fuel that fantasy at the **Denver Firefighters Museum** (★) (1326 Tremont Place; 303-892-1436; admission), in Denver's old fire station near the mint. You'll see antique fire engines, photos of famous fires and the firefighters' dormitory, complete with the pole they used to slide down.

Head west on Colfax Avenue across Cherry Creek to the **Auraria Higher Education Center**, a large college campus shared by the University of Colorado at Denver, Metropolitan State College and Denver Community College and used by 30,000 students. At the northwest edge of the campus is a shady block of beautifully restored older residences that were preserved when the rest of the neighborhood was demolished to make room for the college buildings. Known as **Ninth Street Historic Park** (★), the block contains 14 homes, each in a different architectural style from Denver's early days, with signs on the front lawns to tell visitors about them. Northwest of Ninth Street Historic Park, a small 1911 duplex owned by the colleges was once the home of Israeli leader Golda Meir and is being restored as a museum.

Four blocks north of the Civic Center, the **Museum of Western Art** (1727 Tremont Place; 303-296-1880; admission), across the street from the Brown Palace Hotel, exhibits more than 100 paintings by Thomas Moran, Charles Russell, Frederic Remington, Thomas Hart Benton, Georgia O'Keeffe, and many others. In earlier days, the red-brick 1880 Victorian building that now houses the museum was a bordello and casino.

Skyscrapers turn the downtown streets into echoing canyons through which streams of humanity flow. The pedestrians-only **16th Street Mall**, the most people-friendly route through the heart of the city, starts at Broadway two blocks north of the Civic Center and runs northwest for the entire one-mile length of downtown. Cafés and shops line the mall, and free frequent shuttle buses run from one end to the other. Points of interest along the way include the **Paramount Theatre** (1621 Glenarm Place; 303-534-8336), the city's only surviving motion-picture palace, now used for plays, rock concerts and Denver Chamber Orchestra performances, as well as several blocks of department stores and refurbished commercial buildings that date back to the late 1800s. The **D & F Tower** (1601 Arapaho Street), now dwarfed by skyscrapers nearby, was the tallest building west of the Mississippi when it was completed in 1909 as part of the Daniels & Fisher department store (which later merged with the May Company to create Denver's leading department store, May D & F). The tower is not presently open to the public.

At the northwest end of the 16th Street Mall is Writer Square, a modern development that integrates retail, office and living space. It is the gateway to the **Lower Downtown Historic District**, usually referred to as "the LoDo." The area of historic buildings from the late 1800s starts at **Larimer Square**, Denver's oldest commercial block. Restored in 1964, it was one of the first officially designated historic districts in the United States. Today, Larimer Square is filled with restaurants and unique shops. The LoDo Historic District continues for about six blocks to grand old **Union Station** (1701 Wynkoop Street), still used by Amtrak and ski-train passengers.

Elsewhere in the downtown area, the **Black American West Museum** (★) (3091 California Street; 303-292-2566; admission) traces the roles African American pioneers, cowboys, miners, soldiers and politicians played in settling the West. The museum is housed in the former office and residence of Dr. Justina Ford, a black woman physician who practiced in Denver for 50 years.

The **Trianon Museum and Art Gallery** (335 14th Street; 303-623-0739; admission) contains French paintings from the 16th through 18th centuries as well as Asian art and a large gun collection.

The **Turner Museum** (733 Downing Street; 303-832-0924; admission) is a private collection of prints by English Impressionist artist J.M.W. Turner and American landscape painter Thomas Moran. Tours are by appointment and can include a formal high tea.

Located just off Route 25 at the 7th Street exit, on the other side of the freeway from Mile High Stadium, is the **Children's Museum of Denver** (2121 Children's Museum Drive; 303-433-7444; admission). Exhibits include a room where kids can "swim" through thousands of plastic balls, a transparent house that shows how plumbing and wiring work and a child-size supermarket.

About three and a half miles east of downtown, off Colorado Boulevard between 17th and 23rd avenues, is Denver's large **City Park**. There, the **Denver Museum of Natural History** (2001 Colorado Boulevard; 303-322-7009; admission) displays everything from skeletons of dinosaurs and a great blue whale to a life-size Navajo hogan and Eskimo igloo, plus dioramas of wildlife from the plains and mountains of Colorado as well as other continents. The museum's gold collection features the largest gold nugget ever found in Colorado, weighing eight and a half pounds. Attached to the museum, **Gates Planetarium** (303-370-6487; admission), alternates astronomy presentations and laser light shows throughout the day, and an **IMAX Theater** (303-370-6300; admission) shows thrill-a-minute films on a wraparound screen. In another part of City Park, the **Denver Zoo** (303-331-4110; admission) has more than 1700 animals from around the world, some caged and others in open habitats.

Just across the street from the west boundary of City Park, the **Denver Museum of Miniatures, Dolls and Toys** (★) (1880 Gaylord Street; 303-322-1053; admission) exhibits some of the largest and most lavish dollhouses ever created, including reproductions in miniature of Molly Brown's mountain shack near Leadville, an adobe Indian pueblo and a mansion complete with working electric lights.

About a mile southwest of City Park is **Cheesman Park**, home of the **Denver Botanic Gardens** (1005 York Street; 303-331-4000; admission), with its array of indoor and outdoor environments including a Japanese garden, a habitat for nesting birds, a "Plants of the Bible" garden and a re-creation of a tropical rainforest. Of special interest is the alpine rock garden, which contains more than 3500 species of high-mountain plants from around the world.

The oldest building in Denver is the former stagecoach station at **Four-Mile Historic Park** (★) (715 South Forest Street; 303-399-1859; admission). The station, which was in the middle of nowhere when it was built in 1860, is now surrounded by the affluent southeast Denver neighborhood of Glendale. Volunteers in period costume show visitors around the main travelers' inn as well as the barn and other outbuildings, some of which have been reconstructed with 19th-century tools and construction methods. Farm animals and peacocks wander through the 14-acre park. Traditional beekeeping techniques are demonstrated with active hives in a bee house.

DENVER HOTELS

Although rates for lodging in downtown Denver tend to be very expensive, those traveling on minimal funds can find budget-priced beds at the **Denver International Youth Hostel** (630 East 6th Avenue; 303-832-9996), a large AYH-affiliated hostel offering separate dormitory-style accommodations for men and women. There is a curfew, and guests must furnish their own sheets or rent them, but both the location and the price are hard to beat. For low-budget private rooms with basic beds and bare walls, check out the **YMCA** (25 East 6th Street; 303-861-8300). Though some areas are for men only, a new annex offers coed accommodations.

Toward the other end of the lodging spectrum, the ultra-deluxe **Brown Palace Hotel** (321 17th Street; 303-297-3111, 800-321-2599, fax 303-293-9204) has enjoyed a reputation as Denver's finest hotel ever since it was built in 1892, when cattle barons and railroad tycoons made this their home away from home. In those days, the seven-story red stone structure with its distinctive triangular shape dominated the downtown skyline; today, the 232-room hotel still stands proud among the steel-and-glass faces of neighboring skyscrapers. A lofty, six-story-high stained-glass atrium makes the hotel far more impressive inside than out. Guest rooms are individually decorated in a variety of styles spanning the lifetime of the hotel: gracious Victorian, lively art deco and bright contemporary.

The architect of the Brown Palace also designed the smaller, 81-room **Oxford Hotel** (1600 17th Street; 303-628-5400, 800-228-5838, fax 303-628-5413), located in the LoDo historic district. It prospered for decades as the grand hotel closest to Union Station. In the 1930s a top-to-bottom renovation transformed

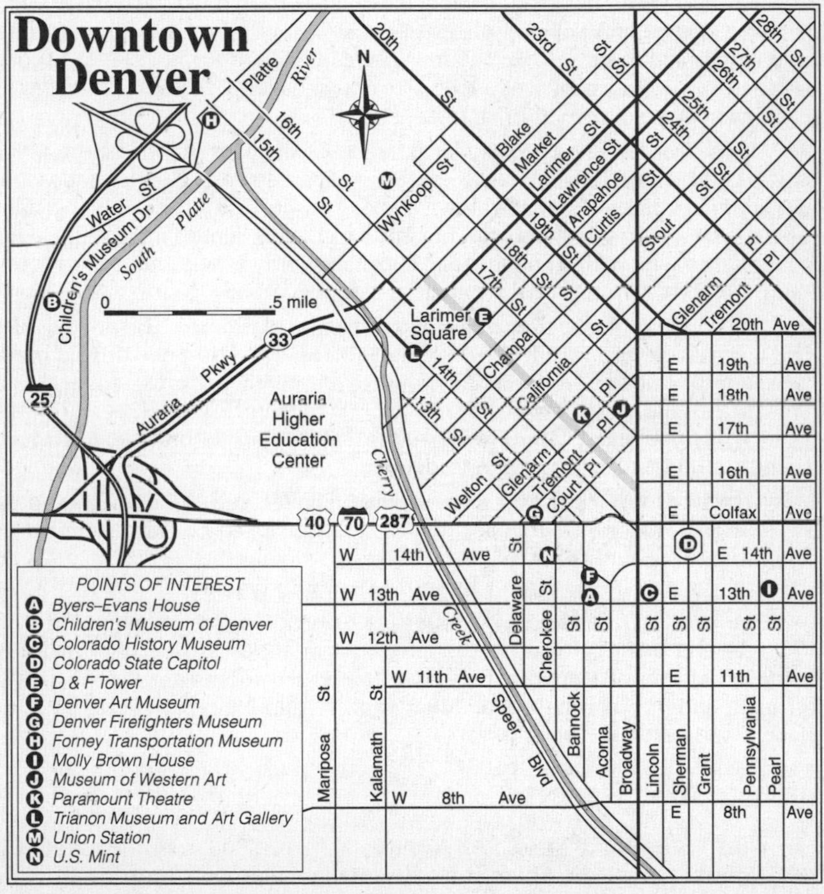

it into an art deco masterpiece. The hotel deteriorated with the decline of train travel and finally was closed down for restoration in 1979. Today, the sterling-silver chandeliers have been stripped of layers of paint and faithful copies of the original carpets grace the hotel's corridors after a $12 million effort that restored the glory of this elegant small hotel. Rooms have dark wood antique furnishings and soft-hued floral patterns; some have canopied beds and fireplaces. Deluxe to ultra-deluxe.

You wouldn't know it from its plain-jane exterior, but the little **Cambridge Hotel** (1560 Sherman Street; 303-831-1252, 800-877-1252) is one of the best bets in the downtown area for low-profile luxury. Just half a block from the capitol, the Cambridge offers 27 guest accommodations—all suites—ranging from parlor-style to two-bedrooms. Each is individually decorated in a wildly unique style: Oriental, French traditional, English-country manor or futuristic. Deluxe to ultra-deluxe.

Loews Giorgio Hotel (4150 East Mississippi Avenue; 303-782-9300, fax 303-758-6542) is an Italian-style hotel ten minutes from downtown in the Glendale area. Palms and hanging plants give the atrium lobby a tropical feeling; the columns and murals evoke an atmosphere of ancient Rome. The 187 rooms have balconies and a choice of a king-size or two queen-size beds. Deluxe room rates include a continental breakfast.

One of Denver's best bed and breakfasts is **Castle Marne** (1572 Race Street; 303-331-0621, fax 303-331-0623), an 1889 Richardsonian Romanesque stone mansion five minutes from downtown. Among the curiosities found in this nine-room inn are the first indoor bathroom in Denver and a sunroom jacuzzi. Rooms are furnished with period antiques and decorated with vintage and local artwork. Rates are deluxe to ultra-deluxe and include a complete gourmet breakfast.

Located four blocks from downtown in Denver's Clement Historic District, the **Queen Anne Inn B & B** (2147 Tremont Place; 303-296-6666, fax 303-296-2151) consists of two Victorian-era houses with porches, turrets, sundeck, hot tub, gardens and patio. Two of the 14 guest rooms have fireplaces and all are distinctively decorated with flowery motifs and four-poster brass beds to create a romantic ambience. Moderate to deluxe.

Merritt House (941 East 17th Avenue; phone/fax 303-861-5230), in the Swallow Hill Historic District near the capitol, is a ten-room Queen Anne mansion furnished in turn-of-the-century antiques. Among the special features are a private jacuzzi in each guest room. Moderate to deluxe.

The brownstone **Holiday Chalet** (1820 East Colfax Avenue; 303-321-9975, fax 303-377-6556) was originally built in 1896 as the Bohm mansion, residence of one of Denver's first jewelers. Its ten rooms are furnished with heirloom antiques and have individual kitchens and baths. Moderate rates include a self-serve breakfast.

DENVER RESTAURANTS

Cliff Young's (700 East 17th Avenue; 303-831-8900) tops the list of Denver's finest restaurants. Situated in a restored downtown storefront from the early 1900s, the restaurant is divided into several dining areas, one of which is the Amethyst Room, perhaps the most elegant dining room in Denver. The creative menu spotlights American nouvelle cuisine with such selections as a carpaccio of free-range veal and buffalo appetizer, lamb chops with shiitake mushroom caps, and medallions of pheasant. Deluxe.

The **Wynkoop Brewing Company** (1634 18th Street; 303-297-2700) is Colorado's oldest brewpub (a genre that has recently become ubiquitous in the Denver-Boulder area). Located in an old warehouse in the LoDo district, the establishment brews its own beer—more beer, they claim, than any other brewpub in the country—and serves it in a traditional tavern atmosphere along with English and Scottish food selections, such as shepherd's pie and black-and-tan dessert. Moderate.

Many Denver gourmands contend that the **Imperial Chinese** (1 Broadway; 303-698-2800) is the best Chinese restaurant in the Rocky Mountain region. It certainly has the most elaborate decor, from the papier-mâché lions that guard the front entrance to the high-style Hong Kong glitz of the dining area. Seafood is the specialty. Try the Dungeness crab in hot Szechuan spices and scallops stir-fried with oriental vegetables. Deluxe.

Strings (1700 Humboldt Street; 303-831-7310) serves imaginative contemporary cuisine à la carte and offers patio dining. Sample dishes include *penne bagutta* (a homemade pasta), steamed oysters and *champagne beurre blanc*. The clientele presents a striking cross section of Denverites—on any evening you're likely to see diners wearing everything from T-shirts to tuxedos. Deluxe.

In the mood for something exotic? Try **India's** (3333 South Tamarac Drive; 303-755-4284). A big tandoor oven forms the centerpiece in this casually elegant neighborhood restaurant. Tandoori cookery involves heating such an oven to more than 700°F and cooking the savory meat and fish entrées until precisely the right moment. Outstanding vegetarian dishes are also available. Moderate.

An amazingly good Italian restaurant is **O Sole Mio** (5501 East Colfax Avenue; 303-329-6139). The decor is nothing special, but the attentive hospitality makes you feel right at home. The menu, which changes daily, features innovative northern Italian dishes. Besides conventional pasta and veal dishes, you'll often find menu specials that feature duck, quail or seafood. There is also a fair selection of vegetarian dishes. Moderate.

The **Denver Salad Company** (2700 South Colorado Boulevard; 303-691-2050) has a 70-item salad bar plus soups, homemade muffins, pasta, baked potatoes, cakes and puddings. The no-nonsense ambience features touches of Eurotech decor. Budget.

In part of the historic building that was once Denver's grand Paramount Theatre, rescued from demolition with all artwork and original gilding still intact, **Paramount Café** (511 16th Street; 303-893-2000) is a lively bar and grill specializing in buffalo burgers and teriyaki chicken. Dining is either inside or on the patio. Budget.

A good low-priced eatery on 16th Street Mall is **Goldies Delicatessen** (511 16th Street; 303-623-6007), a traditional New York–style deli open for lunch only. Here's where you can get lox and bagels or kosher pastrami on dill rye to eat there or take out for a picnic in the mountains (something you can't do in New York). Budget.

Mataam Fez (4609 East Colfax Avenue; 303-399-9282) serves Moroccan food in a sumptuous Arabian Nights atmosphere with tented ceiling and decor from Morocco. Diners are seated on the floor on pillows and leather puffs. The five-course prix fixe meal includes a choice of entrées such as Cornish game hen in a sauce of honey and almonds or shrimp pel-pel, plus soup, salad, appetizer and fresh-fruit dessert. Deluxe.

The **Denver Buffalo Company** (1109 Lincoln Street; 303-832-0880) is an all-American steak-and-potatoes restaurant with a difference: only buffalo meat is served. (There are also a few vegetarian and fish entreés.) Try the cowboy filet—buffalo pan-seared with peppers, onions and southwestern spices. The restaurant raises its own buffalo on a ranch outside the city and has a gift shop that sells buffalo products. The decor features ranch memorabilia and bison motifs. Prices range from moderate to ultra-deluxe.

The quaint, Old World–style **Little Russian Cafe** (1424-H Larimer Street; 303-595-8600) on Larimer Square features authentic Russian food. Favorites are beef stroganoff and *pelmeni*, beef dumplings. Also available are European wines and beers and plenty of vodka. Patio dining is available in summer. Moderate.

DENVER SHOPPING

As the largest city in the Rocky Mountain states, Denver caters to many people who live in small ranch, mining and oil communities and come to "the big city," often traveling hundreds of miles, for special-occasion shopping sprees. Nowhere is this phenomenon more vividly apparent than along the **16th Street Mall**, a major downtown street that has been closed to traffic for its entire one-mile length. Amid fashion boutiques, Parisian-style sidewalk cafés, numerous sporting goods shops and outdoorsy clothiers, 16th Street still has some of Denver's longest-established retail stores—for instance, **Joslin's** (16th Street Mall at Curtis Street; 303-534-0441), Denver's oldest department store; **May D & F** (16th Street and Tremont Place; 303-620-7500), headquarters of a chain that got its start in Leadville during the gold boom; and **Miller Stockman** (1600 California Street; 303-825-5339), which has been selling western accessories at this location since 1918. Near the northwest end of 16th Street Mall are **Tabor Center** (16th and Lawrence streets; 303-534-2141), a two-block-long, three-story atrium containing 65 upscale stores, and the **Bridge Market**, where vendors sell such wares as T-shirts, imports, paintings and electronic novelties from pushcarts.

Larimer Street, at the northwest end of 16th Street Mall just past Tabor Center, was Denver's original main street. It had deteriorated into the city's skid row by the 1960s, when a massive urban-renewal effort transformed it into a showpiece historic district of red-brick Victorian restorations. Two shopping blocks, Writer's Square (15th and Larimer streets) and **Larimer Square** (14th and Larimer streets), offer an ever-changing kaleidoscope of specialty stores ideal for gift shopping. The award-winning custom-designed jewelry of goldmith **John Atencio** (1512 Larimer Street; 303-534-4277) is representative of the elegant offerings to be found in Writer's Square. In Larimer Square, check out **Colorado Sampler** (1421 Larimer Street; 303-629-0487) and **Earth Works, Ltd.** (1421-B Larimer Square; 303-825-3390); both carry wide arrays of made-in-Colorado arts and crafts.

Just south of downtown, **Gart Bros. Sports Castle** (10th Avenue and Broadway; 303-861-1122) is the world's largest sporting goods store. It has its own tennis court and ski mountain, and shoppers can ride around the huge store on golf carts.

The reigning queen of metropolitan Denver shopping malls is the **Cherry Creek Shopping Center** (3000 East 1st Avenue; 303-388-3900), located at University Avenue southeast of downtown. This one-million-square-foot indoor mall features such upscale chain department stores as Saks Fifth Avenue, Neiman Marcus and Lord & Taylor, along with more than 130 specialty shops and restaurants. The adjoining **Cherry Creek North** area along 3rd Avenue features one of the city's highest concentrations of fine-art galleries, such as **PISMO** (2727 East 3rd Avenue; 303-333-7724), specializing in works made with natural materials such as shells, fossils and minerals; **Show of Hands Gallery** (2610 East 3rd Avenue), showing hand-dyed silks, stained glass and other creations by Colorado artisans; and the **Canyon Road Gallery** (257 Fillmore Street; 303-321-4139), featuring Native American and southwestern art from Santa Fe. But the *sine qua non* for browsing in the Cherry Creek area is the **Tattered Cover Book Store** (2955 East 1st Avenue; 303-322-7727), the largest independent bookstore in the United States. The shelves of the huge, four-story store display an astonishing 400,000 volumes.

Most antique dealers in Colorado import their wares from the Midwest. To the extent that there are any authentic Colorado antiques to be found, the place to look for them is the Antique Mall of Lakewood (9635 West Colfax Avenue, Lakewood; 303-238-6940), several miles west of downtown Denver. The mall provides showroom space for more than 200 antique dealers under one roof. Another big antique shopping center is the **Antique Guild** (1298 South Broadway; 303-722-3359), where nearly 250 dealers show their wares.

DENVER NIGHTLIFE

Denver is the region's major center for the performing arts. Theater productions are presented at the Helen Bonfils Theater (Denver Center for the Performing Arts, 1245 Champa Street; 303-893-4100), which encompasses four separate theaters and is associated with the National Theatre Conservatory. Musical performances are presented at the Denver Center for the Performing Arts by the **Colorado Symphony Orchestra** (303-986-8742), the **Denver Chamber Orchestra** (303-825-4911), **Opera Colorado** (303-778-6464) and the **Colorado Ballet** (303-298-0677). For a complete rundown on current performances, call 303-893-4000.

As for nightclubs, Denver has plenty of them. You'll find country-and-western music nightly at the **Grizzly Rose Saloon & Dance Hall** (5450 North Valley Highway; 303-295-1330), the kind of place where Wednesday is known as "Strut-Your-Stuff-in-Jeans Night," meaning that women wearing jeans get free wine. Cover. At the other end of the cowboy dance-club spectrum, **Charlie's** (900 East Colfax Avenue; 303-839-8890) offers country-and-western deejay dancing for a predominantly gay crowd nightly.

Comedy Works (1226 15th Street; 303-595-3637) features nationally known standup comics Wednesday through Sunday and has an open-mike night on Tuesdays. **Comedy Sports** (1634 18th Street; 303-860-9782), downstairs from the Wynkoop Brewing Company brewpub, offers tag-team improvisational comedy Thursday, Friday and Saturday nights. Cover at both clubs.

Mercury Café (2199 California Street; 303-294-9281) offers jazz Tuesday through Sunday, an open stage for drumming and storytelling on Wednesdays and poetry readings and performance art on Fridays. **El Chapultapec** (1962 Market Street; 303-295-9126) also features live jazz nightly. Cover at both clubs.

Rock Island (Wazee and 15th streets; 303-572-7625) is a popular club for alternative dance music, hip-hop to slammin'. Cover. Alternative dance music is featured on Wednesday evenings at the eclectic **Jimmy's Grille** (320 South Birch Street; 303-322-5334), which also offers live blues on Mondays and reggae on Thursday, Friday and Saturday nights. There's a cover on reggae nights.

DENVER PARKS

Barr Lake State Park—This artificial lake was originally part of Denver's sewer drainage system. Abandoned after a flooding South Platte River washed it out in 1965, the lake became lush, exceptionally fertile wetlands. Thirty years later, it provides habitat for about 300 bird species and is the favorite birdwatching spot in the Denver area. A nine-mile hiking and biking trail encircles the lake, and wakeless boating is permitted.

Facilities: Trails, nature center, boat ramp; day-use fee, $3; information, 303-659-6005. *Fishing:* Good for crappie, bass and catfish.

Getting there: Take Route 76 for 23 miles northeast of downtown Denver, past the reservoir, to Bromley Lane (Brighton, Exit 23). Head east and follow Piccadilly Road to the park entrance.

Chatfield State Recreation Area—The Denver area's most popular recreational lake is shared by sailboats, windsurfers, waterskiers, fishermen, scuba divers and swimmers. It gets very crowded on sunny summer weekends. It also offers 24 miles of horseback and hiking trails through the surrounding foothills. It is the starting point for the Denver Greenways Trail, a paved biking and jogging trail that follows the South Platte River for more than 20 miles to downtown Denver. Great blue herons are abundant in the area, as are birdwatchers.

Facilities: Picnic area, restrooms, marina, nature trails, arboretum, horse rentals, groceries, boat ramp, boat rentals; day-use fee, $3; information, 303-791-7275. *Swimming:* Permitted. *Fishing:* Fair to good for perch, crappie, bass, bullhead, bluegill and catfish.

Camping: There are 153 RV/tent sites (all with full hookups); $7 to $10 per night.

Getting there: Located 25 miles southwest of downtown Denver in suburban Littleton. Take Wadsworth Boulevard or Route 470 to Route 121, which goes south through the park.

Roxborough State Park—This natural area is dominated by a series of hogback ridges thrust through the earth's crust by the same seismic upheavals that created Red Rocks west of Denver and the Garden of the Gods at Colorado Springs. Trails wind through the canyons between the rock ridges.

Facilities: Visitors center, restrooms, hiking, biking and cross-country skiing trails; day-use fee, $3; information, 303-973-3959.

Getting there: Located seven miles south of Chatfield State Recreation Area on Roxborough Park Road.

Cherry Creek State Recreation Area—The nearest large lake to Denver, now surrounded by suburbs on three sides, gets unbelievably crowded on weekends as tens of thousands of locals descend on Cherry Creek Reservoir for windsurfing, waterskiing, sailing, fishing, swimming and sunbathing at the small, sandy beach.

Facilities: Picnic areas, restrooms, hiking and horseback trails, marina, boat rentals, boat ramps, swimming beach; day-use fee, $3; information, 303-699-3860. *Swimming:* Permitted. *Fishing:* Good for walleye, perch, crappie, largemouth bass, catfish, pike and bluegill.

Camping: There are 102 RV/tent sites (no hookups); $7 to $10 per night.

Getting there: Located one mile south of Route 225 on Parker Road.

Castlewood Canyon State Park (★)—About 20 miles upstream from Cherry Creek Reservoir is the site of an early reservoir that provided water for Denver until the dam was destroyed by a flood in 1933. Today, the canyon where the lakebed used to be is thickly wooded with pine, fir, aspen and scrub oak protected by sheer sandstone cliffs. Relatively few visitors come to this idyllic area. Hidden as it is in the midst of dry, featureless prairie, you don't see the creek and woodlands until you reach the canyon rim. Birdwatching and hiking are the main attractions.

Facilities: Picnic area, restrooms, visitors center, nature trails; day use fee, $3; information, 303-688-5242.

Getting there: Located 27 miles southeast of downtown Denver off Route 83. From Franktown, take Route 86 west for a quarter-mile, then County Road 51 south for three miles.

West of Denver

The western suburbs of the greater Denver area collide with mountain forests and rock cliffs no more than 20 miles from the state capitol downtown. Thanks to this proximity, Denver's municipal government has acquired areas outside the city over the years to create the Denver Mountain Parks System. These and other points of interest on the slopes just west of Denver make for memorable daytrips—and a complete change of pace from the city below.

Red Rocks Park (Hogback Road, Morrison; 303-640-2637) is located along the sandstone escarpment above the town of Morrison. To get there, take Route 285 west from Route 25 through Englewood, the major suburb on the south side of downtown Denver. Turn north on Route 8. The park is best known as the site of **Red Rocks Amphitheater**, one of the most important concert venues in the Rockies. Bruce Springsteen, U-2 and the Beatles (on their first U.S. tour!) are among the performers who have stood on the stage. You can stand there too, unless preparations are being made for a concert that night. The acoustics of the natural amphitheater surrounded by sandstone cliffs are so perfect that a person standing at the back of the 8000 seats can hear a ping-pong ball drop on the concrete stage—without a microphone. Also in the 2700-acre park is **Dinosaur Ridge**, where visitors can see a working fossil dig and the actual footprints of a *Tyrannosaurus rex*.

Ten miles up Bear Creek Canyon on serpentine Route 74 is **Evergreen**, a former ranching town next to an artificial lake at the foot of Mount Evans. The village is now the center of an exclusive bedroom community set among ponderosa pines and sandwiched between the Red Rocks Park backcountry on the east and the 4000-acre Mount Evans State Wildlife Area on the west. The **Hiwan Homestead Museum** (4208 South Timberville Drive, Evergreen; 303-674-6262) preserves a rustic mansion in a narrow valley. The antique furnishings and decor of the interior span a 50-year period from 1889 to 1930. Exhibits tell about Evergreen's early settlers. The neighborhood of custom homes on five-acre lots surrounding the museum were once part of the ranch.

Five miles north of Evergreen on Route 74, the town of **Bergen Park** is the starting point of the road up Mount Evans. Bergen Park is only three miles from busy Route 70 (Exit 252). At Exit 253, a mile east on the interstate, is **Genessee Park**, a Denver mountain park, where a city-owned bison herd has roamed since 1914.

From Bergen Park, Route 103 climbs laterally across the steep north face of the mountain for 19 miles among aspen groves and tall fir forests to picture-perfect **Echo Lake**, just below timberline, where the paved **Mount Evans Road** (Route 5) turns off for its ascent to the 14,264-foot summit. Open only during the summer months, the 14-mile-long road over alpine tundra is the highest auto route in the Rocky Mountains, reaching 164 feet higher than the summit of Pikes Peak. In fact, Mount Evans is only 169 feet shorter than Mount Elbert, the highest mountain in Colorado. Adventuresome visitors may wish to forgo the drive up the last steep, twisting mile to the summit, park at **Summit Lake** and climb the trail up the last 600 vertical feet of the mountain. Take your time, though. Strenuous exercise can bring on altitude sickness in the thin atmosphere, with symptoms of dizziness, fainting or nausea. Thunderstorms can also pose a hazard: more people are struck by lightning on Mount Evans than anyplace else in the state.

From Echo Lake, Route 103 continues for another 14 miles down Chicago Creek Canyon and returns to Route 70 at **Idaho Springs**. The springs for which the town was named feed a greenhouse swimming pool, individual tubs and a vapor pool at the **Indian Springs Spa** (302 Soda Creek Road, Idaho Springs;

303-567-2191; admission). The spa's unique feature is Club Mud, a pool where you can immerse your whole body in warm, earthy ooze.

Idaho Springs, founded as the site of the first important gold strike in the Colorado Rockies, grew up as the hub of the silver district that included Black Hawk and Central City. The downtown **historic district** along Miner Street between 13th and 17th avenues is lined with ornate Victorian buildings, some of them dating back to the 1850s.

Several sights recall the old mining days. The **Phoenix Gold Mine** (Trail Creek Road, Idaho Springs; 303-567-0422; admission) offers tours of a family-owned gold mine that still operates on a small scale and utilizes traditional mining methods.

For a different slant on mining, visit the **Edgar Mine** (★) (Dry Gulch, Idaho Springs; 303-567-2911; admission), an 1870s shaft that the Colorado School of Mines in Golden has revived as an underground research and instruction facility where visitors can take a peek at the latest in mining technology. It is used for classes during the school year and offers public tours during summer vacation.

Most of the gold ore mined in the area was refined at the **Argo Mill and Museum** (2317 Riverside Drive, Idaho Springs; 303-567-2421; admission). Thoroughly commercialized today, the historic mill offers gold panning, curios and staged shootouts.

A mile west of town at Exit 238 from Route 70, the paved 12-mile Fall River Road leads to the ghost town of **Alice** (★), which dates back to the 1860s and was the site of the richest gold mine in the area. A 1915 schoolhouse and a scattering of old log cabins remain. Above the town site at the end of a half-mile walking trail, **St. Mary's Lake** shimmers at the foot of **St. Mary's Glacier**, one of the few true glaciers in Colorado, on the slope of Mount Kingston (12,136 feet).

Other old mining towns along Route 25 in the Idaho Springs vicinity—especially **Empire** and **Georgetown**—combine historic districts showcasing their mining-era heritage with modern residential development.

From the Idaho Springs vicinity, the nine-mile **Oh My God Road** (★) winds up through Virginia Canyon to Central City. It is unpaved but well maintained and can easily be driven in a passenger car. Along the way are hundreds of old mines and the ghost town of **Russell Gulch**, which got its start in the 1860s and grew to a peak population of 2500, mostly immigrant miners from the Italian and Austrian Alps. For motorists who are timid about mountain driving, an easier, paved road—Route 119—goes through Clear Creek Canyon to Central City from Exit 244 on Route 70, three miles east of Idaho Springs.

Central City, one of Colorado's preeminent historic mining towns, has a population of 300 today but was the largest city in the territory around the time of the U.S. Civil War: in the early 1860s Central City had 15,000 residents, well over Denver's 6000. It became the cultural center of the Colorado Rockies as well, with a theater district that included the grandest opera house in the West. When Colorado became a state in 1876, Central City was one of the top choices for the state capital and lost the honor by a close vote. But the richest gold and silver ore ran out by 1880, and creeping unemployment brought about the city's agonizingly slow abandonment over a period of 50 years.

The restoration of the opera house and an elegant hotel during the 1930s focused attention once more on the picturesque old town of Victorian brick buildings adorned with fluted columns and fanciful stonework that loom like wraiths out of a not-so-ancient past. Although tourists have crowded the streets of Central City for decades, an economy based on seasonal curio shops and luncheon restaurants could not generate the kind of money needed to keep most of the old buildings from deteriorating. In 1990, Coloradoans voted to legalize $5-limit casino gambling in Central City and Black Hawk as well as Cripple Creek, with the provision that casinos could be operated only in existing historic buildings. Given Central City's location, half an hour's drive from a city of a million people, it's no wonder that the casino idea has succeeded enormously in bringing money to the town and fixing up every building in sight. The controversial change also has obscured much of Central City's unique historical character behind a veneer of glitz, clamor and greed, and it has driven most old-timers to sell out and leave town.

History is still there, however—if you look for it. The **Opera House** (200 Eureka Street, Central City; 303-279-3200; admission) has crystal chandeliers and elaborate wall murals. Although it was open for only about five years at the end of the mining boom, since its restoration in the 1930s it has been, and continues to be, the most popular place to see opera in Colorado.

Next door to the opera, the **Teller House** (120 Eureka Street, Central City; 303-582-3200; admission) was built in 1872 as a boardinghouse for miners, but when the sidewalk in front of the hotel was paved with silver ingots to welcome visiting President Ulysses S. Grant, it began to gain its reputation as the city's elegant hostelry. When silver baron and U.S. Senator Horace Tabor turned one floor of the hotel into a lavish suite for his mistress, Black Hawk divorcee Elizabeth "Baby Doe" (who would become his second wife and a legendary figure in Colorado history), he refurbished the hotel in grand style, redecorating in opulent French-provincial style and lining the walls with 12-foot-tall diamond dust mirrors imported from Italy and brought from the East Coast by wagon. When University of Denver students began restoration efforts in 1932, they found the mirrors still in place and part of the abandoned hotel in use as a chicken coop.

Today, the Teller House is owned by a Swiss investment group that has converted much of it into Central City's most lavish gambling casino, but visitors can still see the Baby Doe suite on guided tours and the famous "Face on the Barroom Floor" in the casino bar. The claim is often heard that this haunting portrait was the subject of H. Antoine D'Arcy's tragic 19th-century poem of the same name, but in fact it was the poem that inspired Colorado artist Herndon Davis, who restored the hotel's murals during the 1930s, to paint his wife's face on the floorboards.

Across from the Teller House, the **Thomas-Billings Home** (109 Eureka Street, Central City; 303-582-3435; admission) was boarded up in 1917 and, like a huge time capsule, remained untouched until new owners reopened it 70 years later. Restored with original furnishings and period decor, the house op-

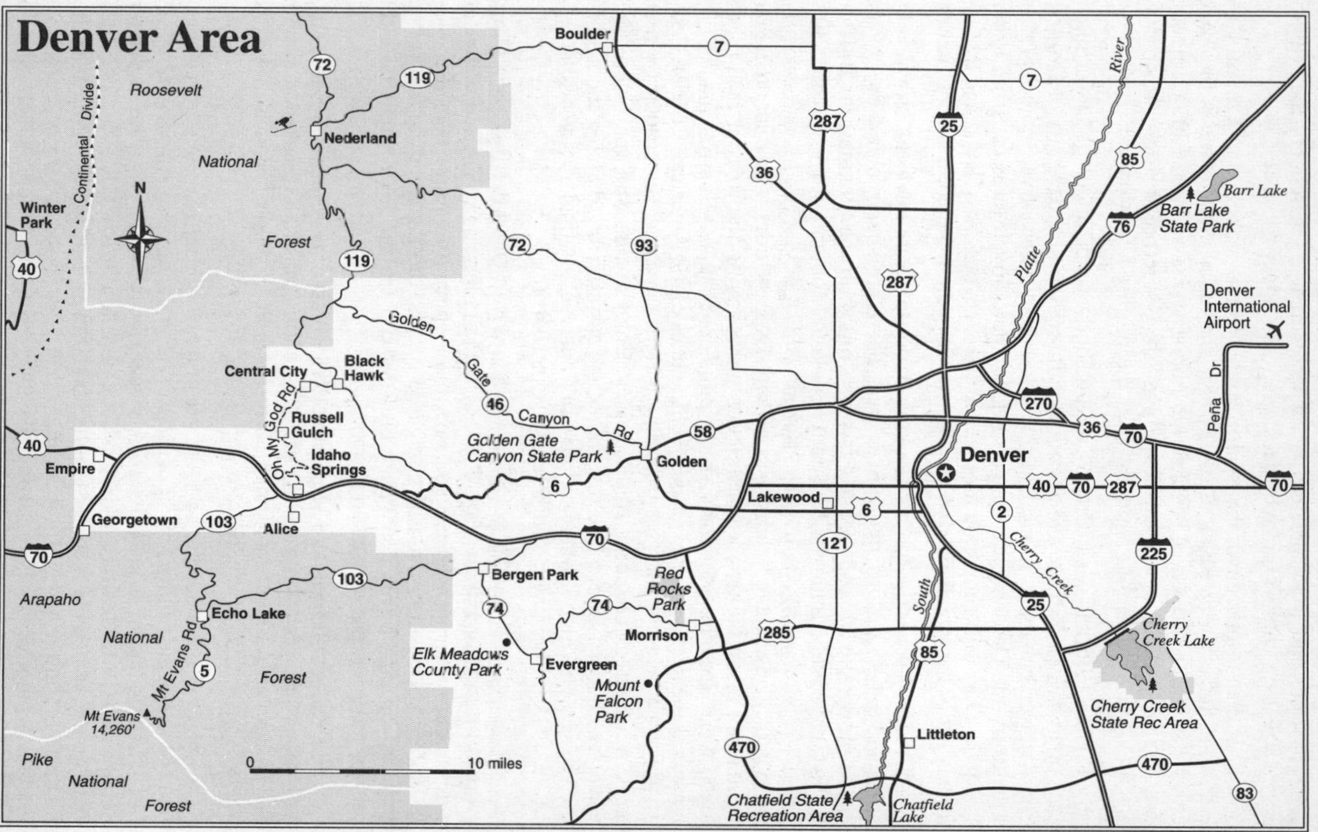
Denver Area
Boulder
Roosevelt
National
Forest
Continental Divide
Nederland
Winter Park
N
Central City
Black Hawk
Russell Gulch
Oh My God Rd
Idaho Springs
Empire
Georgetown
Alice
Golden Gate Canyon Rd
Golden Gate Canyon State Park
Golden
Lakewood
Denver
Denver International Airport
Peña Dr
Barr Lake
Barr Lake State Park
Platte River
South
Cherry Creek
Cherry Creek Lake
Cherry Creek State Rec Area
Bergen Park
Red Rocks Park
Morrison
Echo Lake
Elk Meadows County Park
Evergreen
Mount Falcon Park
Arapaho
National
Forest
Mt Evans Rd
Mt Evans 14,260'
Pike
National
Forest
0
10 miles
Littleton
Chatfield State Recreation Area
Chatfield Lake

erates as a museum. Since the original owners were local merchants, the exhibits emphasize 19th-century product packaging and advertisements.

Less than a mile down the road from the eastern outskirts of Central City is the smaller town of **Black Hawk**, where the main sight to see is the **Lace House** (161 Main Street; 303-582-5211; admission), a restored 1863 Carpenter Gothic-style gabled home known locally as "the Gingerbread House." Its rooms are filled with household antiques from the mining-boom period.

Route 119/6, the Clear Creek Canyon Highway, parallels the newer interstate highway at a distance and goes downhill for 20 miles to the city of **Golden**. For a slower but more scenic and much less busy alternative, motorists may wish to try the Golden Gate Canyon Road (Route 46). It turns off from Route 119 at the Dory Hill campground, seven miles north of Black Hawk, and threads its way out of the mountains through a narrow canyon to the north side of Golden.

Golden is set at the foot of **Lookout Mountain**, the low peak crowned by broadcast towers serving the Denver area. There are spectacular views of the city from the paved road that winds seven miles up the mountain to **Buffalo Bill's Grave and Memorial Museum** (Lookout Mountain Road, Golden; 303-526-0747; admission). William F. "Buffalo Bill" Cody began his career on the prairies of Kansas and Nebraska as a Pony Express rider, army scout, Indian fighter and bison hunter for construction crews laying the first railroad tracks to the West. Stretching the truth a little, dime novelist Ned Buntline made Cody famous as the hero of numerous best-selling tales of the American frontier. Cody cashed in on his reputation by producing a Wild West spectacular that featured a cast of hundreds including Annie Oakley, Chief Sitting Bull and several live bison. The hugely successful show toured the eastern United States and Europe for 30 years but finally collapsed into bankruptcy. Cody died a 70-year-old pauper in 1917 while staying with relatives in Denver.

Golden is best known for its largest employer, the **Adolph Coors Company** (13th and Ford streets; 303-277-2337). First brewed in 1873 and still made with mountain spring water, Coors Beer has a special mystique that lingers on from the days when it could be purchased only in the Rocky Mountain states. Visitors can take a free tour of the brewery and see the huge vats where the beer is made. There is a tasting room.

The **Colorado Railroad Museum** (17155 West 46th Avenue, Golden; 303-279-4591) provides an overview of 19th-century railroad development with maps, memorabilia and more than 50 locomotives, carriages and trolley cars. There is also a large model-train collection on display.

Since 1871, Golden has been the site of one of the nation's leading colleges for geologists, the Colorado School of Mines. For the largest exhibit of minerals, fossils, gems and ores to be found anywhere in the state, visit the **Colorado School of Mines Geology Museum** (16th and Maple streets; 303-273-3823). Also on the campus is the **U.S. Geological Survey National Earthquake Information Center** (1711 Illinois Street; 303-273-8500), where seismographs monitor earthquake activity throughout the world. Free tours, which must be arranged in advance, are available on weekdays.

WEST OF DENVER HOTELS

The Peck House (83 Sunny Avenue, Empire; 303-569-9870, fax 303-569-2743) originally opened its doors as a stagecoach stop in 1862 and has been in continuous operation longer than any other hotel in Colorado. The parlor and all 11 guest rooms are so sumptuously decorated in Victorian-era antiques that the Peck House won the Governor's Award for Historic Restoration in 1993. The moderate rates include a continental breakfast.

A red-and-white Victorian Cape Cod home in the Georgetown Historic District, **The Hardy House B & B Inn** (605 Brownell Street, Georgetown; 303-569-3388) was originally built in 1880 by the local blacksmith. Today, the inn offers five guest rooms with private baths and period decor. There is a fireplace in the sitting room and a hot tub on the sundeck out back. Deluxe rates include an elegant candlelight breakfast.

Built by the founder of the Coors brewery in 1928, **Alpendorf on the Lake** (P.O. Box 819, Georgetown, CO 80444; 303-569-2681) consists of a two-bedroom chalet, a three-bedroom chalet and two rustic cabins without plumbing, all on the shore of a private lake on Guanella Pass, 13 miles above Georgetown. All lodgings have fireplaces and are furnished with an eclectic assortment of well-used furniture. The secluded lake is ideal for sailboating, canoeing and trout fishing, and the surrounding national has an abundance of hiking trails and possibilities for cross-country skiing. Rates are deluxe for the chalets and moderate for the cabins.

The Central City–Black Hawk area has practically nothing to offer in the way of accommodations. There are two deluxe-priced guest suites furnished in country southwestern pieces at the **Winfield Scott Guest Quarters** (210 Hooper Street, Central City; 303-582-3433) on the hillside above Central City; and three small, rather plain moderate-priced rooms in the **Shamrock Inn** (351 Gregory Street, Black Hawk; 303-582-5513) and not much else. That will change with the completion of the huge new **Harvey's Casino Hotel and Resort**, under construction in Central City.

Ramada Hotel–Denver West (14707 West Colfax Avenue, Golden; 303-279-7611, 800-729-2830, fax 303-278-1651), a modern 225-room hotel, is ideally located as a base for exploring areas west of Denver. The rooms are spacious and the furnishings are exactly what you'd expect from a first-class corporate motor inn—short on personality but otherwise flawless. The indoor recreation center, including a swimming pool, whirlpool spa, exercise room, miniature golf, ping-pong, and video games, makes it a good choice for families. Moderate.

Originally built in the early 1900s as a private mansion, the deluxe **Table Mountain Inn** (1310 Washington Avenue, Golden; 303-277-9898, 800-762-9898, fax 303-271-0298) was so extensively remodeled in 1992 that its original character is concealed by a no-expense-spared coat of Santa Fe style. Most of the 32 rooms have balconies or patios with views of the foothills, and some suites have jacuzzis.

WEST OF DENVER RESTAURANTS

If you've never seen a buckskin-clad waitperson open a champagne bottle with a tomahawk, you'll have a chance to witness this spectacle at **The Fort**

(19192 Route 8, Morrison; 303-697-4771). Designed in southwestern adobe style after Bent's Fort, the first trading post in Colorado, The Fort has a lovely setting near Red Rocks Park, an Indian teepee out front, a picturesque courtyard and round *horno*-style fireplaces. It serves more buffalo meat than any other restaurant, along with such other frontier delicacies as rattlesnake, roast buffalo marrow bone, and Rocky Mountain oysters (which, it should be mentioned, are not really oysters at all). Deluxe.

Buffalo Bar and Restaurant (1617 Miner Street, Idaho Springs; 303-567-2729) has a bar that dates back to 1860, a museumlike assemblage of antiques and memorabilia, and great views of Bridal Veil Falls from the back dining rooms. The menu is eclectic, specializing in buffalo and also featuring an assortment of salads and sandwiches, Italian and Mexican selections and smoked baby back ribs. Moderate.

Emily's Fine Dining Parlors (131 Main Street; 303-582-1171), located in Harrah's Glory Hole Casino, is one of the few restaurants in Central City that rises above fast-food quality and ambience. The restaurant's Victorian decor and antique furniture, including marble-top tables, create an intimate feeling. The menu includes prime rib, seafood, pasta and poultry dishes. Emily's takes special pride in its desserts, such as a scrumptious mud pie. Deluxe.

The **Black Forest Inn** (Black Hawk; 303-279-9971) was a centerpiece of the Central City–Black Hawk District long before the first casino opened. In fact, Denverites have been driving out here since 1958 to enjoy the finest German food in Colorado. The atmosphere is as Bavarian as cuckoo clocks and oom-pah bands, and so is the dinner menu, which includes beautiful presentations of wienerschnitzel, sauerbraten and other authentic German specialties. The lunch menu offers more regular American fare. Moderate to deluxe.

In the Golden foothills, **Briarwood Inn** (1630 Eighth Street, Golden; 303-279-3121) is considered one of the finest restaurants in the Denver area. It features Continental dining, candlelight, polished silver, fine china and lavish European-country decor. The menu offers prime rib, lobster, Dover sole and beef Wellington; all entrées include appetizers and dessert. Ultra-deluxe.

El Rancho Lodge and Restaurant (29260 Route 40, Golden; 303-526-0661), a historic mountain lodge, has been a favorite special-occasion restaurant for generations of Front Range residents. Diners enjoy a spectacular Continental Divide view. Primarily a steakhouse, El Rancho also serves prime rib and trout. Ice-cream sundaes are included with all dinners. Moderate.

WEST OF DENVER SHOPPING

When it comes to shopping, the small towns west of Denver are in the shadow of the big city and offer less than you would find in similar-sized communities on the other side of the Continental Divide.

Red Men Hall (125 West Park Avenue; 303-569-3243), in the tiny town of Empire between Central City and Georgetown, has been in operation since 1898 and now sells museum-quality American Indian paintings, sculpture, lithographs, pottery, jewelry, kachinas and baskets.

In Golden, **Heritage Square** (Route 40; 303-279-2789) is a combination shopping center and theme park with an Old West motif. You can, if you wish, browse through gift shops with an ersatz old-fashioned flavor while the kids get their thrills on the alpine slide and go-cart racetrack or try bungee jumping.

WEST OF DENVER NIGHTLIFE

Gambling casinos are the sole entertainment—indeed, the only industry of any kind—in Central City (15 casinos) and Black Hawk (20 casinos). The betting limit is $5 at all casinos; only blackjack and poker tables are permitted, along with mechanical "one-armed bandits" and video gaming including poker, blackjack and keno machines.

WEST OF DENVER PARKS

Red Rocks Park—Seventy-million-year-old splinters of sandstone broke through the earth's surface in the upheavals that created the Front Range to form 400-foot-tall rock formations shaped like the prows of sinking ships. Two of them wrap around a 9000-seat natural amphitheater that serves as one of the nation's most unique rock and country concert venues. Although the amphitheater is the main sightseeing highlight, the surrounding 600-acre Denver Mountain Park offers paved roads to picnic spots and hiking trails through foothills covered with scrub oak and rock monoliths. Rock climbing is prohibited.

Facilities: Picnic areas, restrooms, store; information, 303-640-2637.

Getting there: The park is located near the town of Morrison. From Route 70, take Exit 259 and follow Route 26 south to the well-marked park road. It can also be reached via Route 74.

Elk Meadows County Park and **Dedisse Park**—Elk Meadows, a Jefferson County Open Space Park, adjoins Bergen Peak State Wildlife Area on one side and Dedisse Park, part of the Denver Mountain Parks system, on the other. An easy six-mile trail that loops through varied terrain—meadows, sunny mountain slopes and dark forest nooks—is a favorite of joggers and mountain bikers. There are plenty of benches at scenic overlooks, and longer trails climb into the wildlife area and wind south toward Dedisse Park, which has more well-worn hiking trails as well as picnic sites with stone fireplaces and shelters built in the 1930s by the WPA.

Facilities: Trails; picnic areas and restrooms at Dedisse Park; information, 303-697-4545.

Getting there: Parking area and trailhead located along the west side of Route 74 about three miles north of Evergreen.

Golden Gate Canyon State Park—This 14,000-acre expanse of mountain meadows and canyons is the largest of the many state, county and municipal mountain parks along the Front Range. It has more than 60 miles of hiking and horseback trails, many of which are groomed for cross-country skiing in winter. Panorama Point offers a spectacular view of the Continental Divide. The visitors center has interpretive exhibits on plant and animal life and geology. Parking spaces can be hard to find on summer weekends.

Facilities: Picnic areas, restrooms, hiking trails, visitors center; day-use fee, $3; information, 303-592-1502. *Fishing:* Good for rainbow trout.

Camping: There are 164 RV/tent sites (no hookups); $7 to $10 per night; reservations, 303-470-1144 or 800-678-2267.

Getting there: From Golden, take Washington Avenue north for one and a half miles; then turn west on Golden Gate Canyon Road. This paved road runs for about 15 miles through the park and comes out on Route 119 between Central City and Nederland.

North of Denver

North of Denver, a string of prosperous small cities flourishes amid lakes and sugar-beet fields at the foot of the Rockies. Boulder and Fort Collins revolve around the campuses of Colorado's two largest universities. Neither they nor the area's other towns, like Loveland and Greeley, are geared toward tourism, though each of these communities has its own distinctive charm. In contrast, tourist hospitality is the sole industry in Estes Park, the town just outside the entrance to Rocky Mountain National Park. Incomparable mountain splendor within easy daytrip distance of most Front Range cities—a 30-mile drive from either Boulder or Loveland and just 55 miles from Denver—makes Rocky Mountain National Park the most popular sightseeing attraction in Colorado.

From Denver, the most direct route to Estes Park and Rocky Mountain National Park is through **Boulder**, the home of the main campus of the **University of Colorado**. The university sprawls across the south side of town, bounded by Foothills Parkway on the east and Broadway on the west. The easiest access is from 26th Street (Route 36, the main highway from Denver). At the heart of the campus, broad green quadrangles are shaded by century-old fir trees and flanked by massive stone buildings with Mediterranean-style red tile roofs. One main visitors attraction on the campus is the **University of Colorado Museum** (Henderson Building, 15th Street and Broadway; 303-492-6165), which displays a full range of collections from dinosaur fossils to plant specimens, including a treasure trove of southwestern artifacts. Also of interest on campus is **Fiske Planetarium** (Regent Drive; 303-492-5001; admission), whose Zeiss star projector, one of the largest in the world, accurately simulates more than 3000 celestial bodies. Public star shows are presented on weekend evenings and Sunday afternoons.

The best show in Boulder is along **Pearl Street Mall**, downtown between 11th and 15th streets. In the 1970s, Boulder's main downtown street was the model for the kind of cute, café-lined, pedestrians-only historic district that has since sprung up in urban-renewal zones all over America. But the feel of Pearl Street remains unique thanks in large part to its street performers. Almost any day of the year finds folksingers playing for handouts beside the fountains and sculptures. On sunny summer weekends the mall is often completely lined with musicians, magicians, mimes and even acrobats performing in a dizzying impromptu circus.

Visitors are welcome to take a self-guided tour of the **National Center for Atmospheric Research** (1850 Table Mesa Drive, Boulder; 303-492-1174). The red sandstone building, set at the foot of the huge, slanted cliffs called the Flatirons on the southwest outskirts of the city, was designed by I. M. Pei, whom many consider to be America's finest living architect. Inside, exhibits cover everything from thunderstorms to global warming and offer a close-up look at the surface of the sun. Visitors can see two Cray supercomputers, whose speed of up to a billion calculations per second makes them the world's fastest computers at the time of this writing.

Two of Boulder's most unusual manufacturing firms strive to attract visitors. **Celestial Seasonings** (4600 Sleepytime Drive; 303-530-5300), which produces herb teas, offers weekday factory tours revealing how its teas are invented, blended and packaged. **Leanin' Tree** (★) (6055 Longbow Drive; 303-530-1442), the leading publisher of western greeting cards, has a free museum of western art containing the originals of paintings reproduced on their cards as well as other cowboy paintings and sculptures.

For the best view of the Boulder area, take the paved, serpentine Flagstaff Mountain Road about three miles to a 7000-foot summit overlooking the city. Before entering wild Boulder Mountain Park with its dramatic cliffs and canyons, the road goes through **Chautauqua Park** (900 Baseline Road; 303-422-3282). At the center of this large, grassy foothills park is a big, whitewashed wood community center that was built in 1898 and, like its namesake at Lake Chautauqua, New York, has been used for summer conferences, lectures and concerts ever since.

Another scenic mountain drive from Boulder is Route 119, which winds for 16 miles up **Boulder Canyon**. Midway up the canyon, the creek plunges over **Boulder Falls**, a pretty spot any time and most spectacular during the spring runoff. At Nederland, near the upper end of the canyon, motorists can join the **Peak to Peak Highway** (Route 72 North and Route 119 South) and follow it 15 miles south to Central City or 42 miles north to Estes Park and the entrance to Rocky Mountain National Park. While this is not the most direct route from Boulder to the national park, much less the fastest, it is certainly the most scenic.

The most direct route from Route 25 to Estes Park and Rocky Mountain National Park is through the arts-oriented community of **Loveland**. Visitors can watch bronze sculptures being poured at either of the town's two art foundries, **Art Castings** (511 8th Street Southeast; 970-667-1114) and **Loveland Sculpture Works** (205 12th Street Southwest; 970-667-0991), and see some of the results on exhibit in the city-owned **Benson Park Sculpture Garden** (29th Street at Aspen Drive; 970-663-2940). Much of the **Loveland Museum and Gallery** (5th Street at Lincoln Avenue; 970-667-6070) is given over to showing the works of local artists. The museum also features a 2000-square-foot relief map of **Big Thompson Canyon**. You can see the lower portion of the canyon for yourself by taking Route 34 west toward Estes Park, a distance of 30 miles. If the name rings a bell, it is probably because the long, narrow canyon gained national notoriety in 1977 as the scene of one of Colorado's most terrible disasters, a huge flash flood in which scores of campers drowned.

Before heading into the mountains, travelers may wish to take a detour from Loveland 13 miles east to **Greeley** for a dose of history straight out of Colorado's richest farm country. The city was named for *New York Tribune* publisher Horace Greeley, who is often credited with coining the slogan, "Go West, young man, go West." (Actually, the words were written by journalist John Babson Lane, but Greeley printed them.) Horace Greeley used his newspaper to recruit members for a Utopian farming cooperative, the Union Colony, which, under the leadership of the *Tribune*'s agriculture editor, Nathan Meeker, founded the town in 1870.

For a look at the early years of the Union Colony, visit the **1870 Meeker House Museum** (1324 9th Avenue, Greeley; 970-350-9220; admission), the original two-story adobe house built by the colony's leader and furnished with articles belonging to him and his family. More about the colony, including lots of documents and photographs, can be found nearby at the **Greeley Municipal Museum** (919 7th Street; 970-350-9220; admission).

While **Centennial Village** (1475 A Street, Greeley; 970-350-9220; admission) officially got its name because it was opened on the 100th anniversary of Colorado statehood in 1976, it also recalls James A. Michener's fictionalized history of the region, *Centennial*. Michener, who lived here while researching and writing the book, used Greeley as the model for his fictitious town of Centennial. The village is actually a large, grassy park where historic buildings have been collected from throughout the northeastern plains and arranged in a chronology of 60 years of settlement. Included, among other structures, are an Indian tepee, a homesteader's sod house, a whitewashed one-room schoolhouse, a Victorian residence, a firehouse and a blacksmith's shop.

Twelve miles north of Loveland via Route 25, **Fort Collins** is the site of Colorado State University, which includes the state's agricultural, forestry and veterinary schools. The town's original commercial district, which dates back to the 1870s, has been refurbished as the **Historic Old Town District**, a pretty town square lined with galleries, specialty shops and cafés, on Mountain Avenue between Remington Street and North College Avenue.

The **Fort Collins Museum** (200 Matthews Street, Fort Collins; 970-221-6738) displays artifacts from the city's early years as a fur trappers' outpost and a U.S. cavalry fort protecting pioneers on the Overland Trail. Outside the main museum are two cabins—one of them is the oldest log cabin in the state—and a one-room schoolhouse, both relocated from elsewhere in the county.

Nearby, the 1879 Victorian **Avery House** (328 West Mountain Avenue, Fort Collins; 970-221-0533), one of the city's grandest mansions, has been restored and furnished with antiques of the period. Public tours are offered twice weekly, on Wednesday and Sunday afternoons.

The Fort Collins Municipal Railway (admission), the last of the old-time streetcars that provided public transportation in most Colorado cities from the 1930s through the 1950s, operates only on weekends and holidays from May through October. It travels a route between Historic Old Town and the **City Park** at Roosevelt Avenue and Oak Street.

Free tours are offered at the **Anheuser Busch Brewery** (2531 Busch Drive, Fort Collins; 970-490-4691). More modern and high-tech than the Coors brewery in Golden but lacking Coors' ties to Colorado tradition, the Anheuser Busch facility is worth a visit primarily because of its mascot Clydesdale team. The horses perform once a day, and all tours include a walk through their barn.

East of town on the other side of the interstate is Fort Collins' most unique sight, the **Swetsville Zoo** (Harmony Road; 970-484-9509). The "animals" in the park are more than 70 life-size sculptures made from junkyard pieces of cars and farm machinery.

Of the cities along the northern Colorado Front Range, Fort Collins is the only one not on a direct route to Rocky Mountain National Park. Instead, motorists who head west into the mountains from Fort Collins on Route 14 discover a less-traveled highway that runs north of the national park through the **Poudre River Canyon**, snaking along the Cache La Poudre River past campgrounds, picnic areas and fishing spots and through a long tunnel on its way up to the summit of **Cameron Pass** (10,276 feet). Turnouts on both sides of the pass afford dramatic views of the 2000-foot cliff faces of the **Nokhu Crags**, which mark the northwest corner of Rocky Mountain National Park. The area is mountain wilderness so rugged that even though the park boundary is less than five miles away from Cameron Pass, it is impossible to reach by road. The distance from Fort Collins to Cameron Pass is 68 miles.

Though it's on a direct route to Rocky Mountain National Park and just 30 miles from Boulder, Longmont or Loveland, **Estes Park** is a world apart. Estes Park has thrived as a tourist town ever since the park opened in 1915, and today it feels a little quaint with its old-fashioned curio shops full of ersatz Indian items, Asian-made Colorado ashtrays and souvenir rocks. Since there is no food or lodging within the national park, Estes Park is the place for non-campers who wish to spend more than a single day there. Visitors can ride the **Aerial Tramway** (420 East Riverside Drive; 970-586-3675; admission) up 1200 feet from the middle of town to the top of Prospect Mountain for an overview of Estes Park, Lake Estes and the Big Thompson River.

Perhaps the most unique sight in Estes Park is the grand old **Stanley Hotel** (333 Wonderview Avenue; 970-586-3371). Even if you're not planning to stay there, stroll the lobby and grounds of this elegant, historic resort hotel. It was built in 1909, six years before the national park opened, by the man who invented the steam-powered automobile, the Stanley Steamer. The hotel is said to have inspired Stephen King's breakthrough novel, *The Shining*.

An original Stanley Steamer is on display in the **Estes Park Area Historical Museum** (200 4th Street, Estes Park; 970-586-6256; admission), along with a 19th-century settler's log cabin, the original Rocky Mountain National

Park headquarters building and exhibits on the town's history, including kitsch from the early years of tourism.

The free **MacGregor Ranch Museum** (Devil's Gulch Road, Estes Park; 970-586-3749) preserves the homestead of one of the Estes Park region's first settlers, Alexander MacGregor, who led the legal battle against a British earl who claimed all the area's land in the 1870s. Besides a complete documentary record of the land dispute, the museum has antique furnishings, ranch implements and a sizable collection of western paintings.

A best-selling mystery novel of the 1920s, *Seven Keys to Baldpate*, inspired another historic Estes Park hotel. Gordon and Charles Mace, who built it in 1917, named it the Baldpate Inn after the novel. Later, attorney Clarence Darrow started a tradition by declaring that each guest should contribute a key to the hotel. Over the years the collection grew to become the world's largest. The more than 20,000 keys in the free **Baldpate Inn Key Room** (★) (Route 7; 970-586-6151) include keys to Mozart's wine cellar, Jack Benny's dressing room and the Pentagon. The inn is eight miles south of Estes Park on Route 7.

Close by on the same highway, the free **Enos Mills Cabin and Nature Study Area** (Route 7, Estes Park; 970-586-4706) was the 1885 homestead of the naturalist who persuaded Congress to create Rocky Mountain National Park. The old cabin, where Mills' writings and photographs are on display, sits within a 200-acre preserve laced with nature trails.

The 19 miles of Route 7 from Estes Park south to Raymond are part of the **Peak to Peak Highway**, which continues as Route 72 for another 37 miles through Nederland, at the upper end of Boulder Canyon, to Central City. The Route 7 portion skirts the Rocky Mountain National Park boundary, passing between two of the area's highest mountains, **Mount Meeker** (13,911 feet) and **Longs Peak** (14,256 feet). The latter marks the southeast corner of Rocky Mountain National Park.

While all the mountains that flank Colorado's busy Route 25 corridor are commonly referred to as the Front Range, the actual mountain range of that name runs through **Rocky Mountain National Park** (Estes Park; 970-586-1333; admission). The most popular tourist spot in Colorado, the national park is where the Continental Divide reaches closest to the eastern Colorado plains. It encompasses some of the highest, most rugged terrain in the Rockies. During the summer months, expect long lines of cars at the main park entrance on Route 36 just west of Estes Park. Every place that is accessible by car in the east side of the park is crowded at all times in tourist season and on weekends all year. Relatively few visitors wander far from the roadways, however, and with 76 mountain summits above 12,000 feet in elevation, the possibilities for exploring the wilderness on foot or horseback are practically endless.

As soon as you enter the park, you find yourself facing a fork in the road. A left turn takes you to **Moraine Park**, where the Big Thompson River meanders through a broad, grassy valley gouged by ancient glaciers and surrounded by mountain crags. The rustic **Moraine Park Museum** has exhibits that explain the natural history of Rocky Mountain National Park. The road climbs for ten miles, following Glacier Creek and passing numerous marked trailheads, to

Bear Lake, a classic mountain lake surrounded by a paved nature trail and, most of the time, hundreds or even thousands of sightseers. It is typical of dozens of other fair-size natural lakes in the park, most of them accessible only by hiking or horseback trails. While motorists can drive their cars to Bear Lake and join others in a desperate search for parking spaces, an easier and more scenic option is to take one of the shuttle buses that run frequently from the Moraine Park Museum and stop at each trailhead on the way to the lake.

Take the right-hand fork inside the park entrance to drive up **Trail Ridge Road**, the highest continuous automobile road in North America. Completed in 1932, the 45-mile-long paved road traces an old Ute Indian migration route along a ridge high above timberline, paralleling the jagged, impassable rock-and-ice wall of the Continental Divide. Just beyond the highest point on the road (12,183 feet), the **Alpine Visitors Center** stands on the windswept brink of rocky cliffs where snowdrifts remain year-round. It has snacks, souvenirs, and an observation deck. While most people turn around at the visitors center and return the way they came, the road continues over the Continental Divide to the town of Grand Lake at the park's west entrance (see "Winter Park–Grand Lake Area" in Chapter Three, "Northern Colorado Rockies"). Oddly enough, Milner Pass, where Trail Ridge Road crosses the Great Divide, is about 1200 feet *lower* than the Alpine Visitors Center.

Because they have enjoyed protection from hunters for more than 75 years in Rocky Mountain National Park, wildlife both large and small is abundant and not too shy. You are more likely to see elk here than anywhere else in Colorado. Watch for them in high, distant meadows in the summer and in the lowlands of Moraine Park during the cold months. Bighorn sheep, mountain goats, bald eagles, peregrine falcons and black bears are just a few of the animals you may spot. Be sure to bring binoculars and a loaded camera.

NORTH OF DENVER HOTELS

Built in 1908, the **Hotel Boulderado** (2115 13th Street, Boulder; 303-442-4344, 800-433-4344, fax 303-442-4378) has been painstakingly restored to the grandeur of earlier times, when such celebrities as Bat Masterson, Ethel Barrymore and Douglas Fairbanks Jr., stayed here. Rich woodwork and overstuffed antique armchairs and sofas grace the lobby under a two-story-high stained-glass canopy. The 160 rooms also feature antique furnishings and flowery period decor as well as such amenities as fresh flowers daily. Deluxe.

A few blocks east of the pedestrians-only part of downtown, the **Pearl Street Inn** (1820 Pearl Street, Boulder; 303-444-5584, fax 303-444-6494) offers seven antique-decorated rooms, all with private baths, fireplaces and private entrances, surrounding a peaceful central courtyard. Some rooms are in the historic main house; others are in a contemporary annex built in 1985. Deluxe rates include a full breakfast.

Another Victorian-era home turned bed and breakfast in the downtown area, the **Briar Rose** (2151 Arapahoe Avenue, Boulder; 303-442-3007) has nine guest rooms—five in the main 1890-vintage house and four more in a separate guest house. Some rooms have fireplaces, others have balconies or private patios, and all have queen-size beds with feather comforters. A gourmet continental breakfast is served sitdown-style. Deluxe.

While lodging rates in Boulder tend to run higher than in most communities in the state, affordable accommodations can be found at the **Foot of the Mountain Motel** (200 Arapahoe Avenue; 303-442-5688), The 18 guest rooms are in rustic cabins dating back to 1930. They have been nicely renovated and feature all the conveniences of a modern midrange motel. Moderate.

Lodgings in Fort Collins generally can't compare with those in Boulder for history or charm but are much less expensive. Try the **Mulberry Inn** (4333 East Mulberry Street; 970-493-9000, 800-234-5548), which has 120 motel-style rooms, all with queen-size beds and standard amenities. In addition, some rooms have jacuzzis, and suites have private sundecks. Rooms are in the budget range, suites in the moderate range.

The **Grand Heritage Stanley Hotel** (333 Wonderview Avenue, Estes Park; 970-586-3371, 800-762-5437) was built as a resort in 1909 by inventor F. O. Stanley (one of his Stanley Steamers, a steam-powered touring automobile, is on display in the lobby). Most of the 92 guest rooms in this hillside hotel have views of the Continental Divide or Lake Estes. All of the rooms are refurbished with period furnishings and decor. Facilities include a swimming pool, hot tub and volleyball court. The hotel has hosted guests as diverse as the Emperor of Japan and Bob Dylan and inspired Stephen King's novel, *The Shining*. Rates fall in the deluxe range.

Built in 1917, the **Baldpate Inn** (4900 South Route 7, Estes Park; 970-586-6151) took its name from a best-selling mystery novel of the time called *Seven Keys to Baldpate*, which inspired its huge, world-famous key collection. Autographed photos of celebrities who have been guests there are also on display. The 12 guest rooms and three individual cabins are rather small but nicely furnished with antiques and handmade quilts. Set at an elevation of 9000 feet, the inn commands a grand view of the valley below. Moderate.

Built on land that formerly belonged to the Irish Earl of Dunraven, **Tiny Town Cottages** (830 Moraine Road, Estes Park; phone/fax 970-586-4249) has 20 cozy cottages set on the banks of a river stocked for trout fishing. The cottages feature queen- or king-size beds, kitchens and fireplaces. Rates include a continental breakfast. Moderate.

NORTH OF DENVER RESTAURANTS

Boulder's ultimate fine-dining establishment is the **Flagstaff House Restaurant** (1138 Flagstaff Road; 303-442-4640) on Mount Flagstaff 1000 feet above town. Floor-to-ceiling walls of glass give diners an unparalleled view, especially after dark, when dinner is served by candlelight and the city's lights along the Front Range have full impact. Dining is formal (no T-shirts or shorts, please), and the menu changes frequently. A typical dinner might include an appetizer of ahi tuna sushi, a main course of spicy elk dumplings and, for dessert, an edible milk-chocolate box filled with raspberry mousse. Ultra-deluxe.

Two Bitts Bistro and More (1155 Canyon Road, Boulder; 303-442-8400) serves gourmet southwestern cuisine in a New Mexico–style setting with Santa Fe–style decor. The menu, which focuses on unique dishes, changes monthly. A recent menu offered an appetizer of poached sea scallops, entrées like sesame salmon with jasmine rice and a tofu piccata, and a crushed pink-peppercorn lemon tart. The restaurant also serves pizzas baked in a brick oven. Deluxe.

The menu is predictably all-American at **Teddy Roosevelt's American Grille** (Hotel Boulderado, 2115 13th Street, Boulder; 303-442-4560), in a rustic atmosphere decorated with memorabilia from the turn of the century. The restaurant was the original dining room of the Hotel Boulderado when President Theodore Roosevelt stayed there, and it is the favorite fine restaurant on Pearl Street Mall. Prime rib is the house specialty; the restaurant also offers steak, pasta, seafood and chicken dishes, sandwiches and salads. The most imaginative menu items are the desserts, such as a Bailey's pear mousse. Budget to deluxe.

Waitresses on roller skates serve up cheeseburgers, fries and hefty portions of meatloaf and chicken-fried steak at the **L.A. Diner** (1955 28th Street, Boulder; 303-447-1997). Shiny and high camp, this '50s-style nostalgia palace features a jukebox full of seminal rock-and-roll classics that had already become oldies-but-goodies before most of the diner's college-student patrons were born. Budget.

Boulder has a great selection of ethnic restaurants. One of the more unusual international eateries in town is **Narayan's Nepal Restaurant** (921 Pearl Street; 303-447-2816), a storefront restaurant decorated with Nepalese artifacts at the west end of Pearl Street Mall. Lamb curry, the house specialty, shares the menu with unusual chicken and pork dishes as well as a wide selection of vegetarian choices. Moderate.

In Fort Collins, a good place for dinner is **Cuisine! Cuisine!** (130 South Mason Street; 970-221-0399), a cozy Continental restaurant with candles, lace curtains and turn-of-the-century decor. The menu presents a tempting array of choices, with appetizers such as mussels, smoked salmon and veal sweetbreads; a roasted red-pepper salad; entrées including lamb chops with rosemary sauce and several seafood choices, plus homemade desserts and a long wine list. Moderate.

The **Silver Grill Cafe** (218 Walnut Street; 970-484-4656) has been a fixture in Fort Collins' Old Town Historic District for more than 60 years. The café serves no-nonsense breakfasts from biscuits and gravy to steak and eggs. The lunch menu features daily grill specials and a choice of sandwiches. Refurbished in the recent gentrification of Old Town, the café still makes you feel as if you've stepped into an earlier era. Budget.

The **Fawn Brook Inn** (Allenspark; 303-747-2556), four miles south of Estes Park, has a reputation for the finest dining in the vicinity. Open Friday, Saturday and Sunday only, this mountain lodge south of town offers a changing selection of wild-game dishes, veal, duck and seafood traditionally prepared in Continental style. The contrast of the rugged setting and rustic old lodge with the elegant presentation and service makes the Fawn Brook Inn extra-special. Ultra-deluxe.

For a more affordable feast, head for **Nicky's** (1350 Fall River Road, Estes Park; 970-586-5376), an eclectic American-Greek-Italian restaurant specializing in prime-rib dinners in a clean, contemporary family-dining atmosphere. Entrées range from spinach pie to lasagna, with ice cream, fruit pie or cheesecake for dessert. Moderate.

Even more eclectic is the **Gazebo Restaurant** (225 Park Lane; 970-586-9564), next to Bond Park in downtown Estes Park. The international menu features specialties from Italy, Afghanistan, the Caribbean and Mexico among its 48 entrées. The environment is formal, with white-linen service for both lunch and dinner, and the decor is bursting with silk flowers and floral prints. Deluxe.

Giant breakfast burritos are the claim to fame at **Ed's Cantina & Grill** (362 East Elkhorn Avenue, Estes Park; 970-586-2919), which also serves an assortment of burgers and Mexican favorites for lunch and dinner among baseball memorabilia and beer signs. Budget.

NORTH OF DENVER SHOPPING

Pearl Street Mall, Boulder's pedestrians-only downtown main street, is so full of life that shopping is almost incidental. Many of the numerous small shops that line the street specialize in arts, crafts and unique gift items. **Art Mart** (1222 Pearl Street; 303-443-8248) exhibits the works of more than 200 Boulder-area artisans in all media. Across the street, **Art Source International** (1237 Pearl Street; 303-444-4080) is Colorado's largest dealer in historic photographs and 19th-century prints and maps. Good selections of local arts and crafts can be found at both the **Boulder Arts & Crafts Cooperative** (1421 Pearl Street; 303-443-3683) and **Handmade in Colorado** (1426 Pearl Street; 303-938-8394). For shoppers whose tastes run to the exotic, **Traders of the Lost Art** (1429 Pearl Street; 303-440-9664) has clothing and one-of-a-kind imports from South America, Asia and Africa. **Ecology House** (1441 Pearl Street; 303-444-7023) features gift items, both practical and whimsical, designed with environmentalists in mind.

Antique dealers dominate the main street of tiny **Niwot**, midway between Boulder and Longmont on Route 119.

In Fort Collins, the triangular **Old Town Square** (Mountain Avenue at College Avenue) has a handful of galleries offering local crafts and fine art.

Estes Park, where the tourism industry has thrived for more than a century, has every kind of gift and curio shop imaginable. There are clusters of arts and crafts retailers such as the **Old Church Shops** (157 West Elkhorn Avenue), as well as more sophisticated galleries such as the **Art Center of Estes Park** (Wonderview Avenue and Route 134; 970-586-5882), which offers art classes and painting trips.

One of the oldest and most beloved stores in the Estes Park area—and still one of the best—is the **Charles Eagle Plume Gallery of Native American Arts** (Route 7, Estes Park; 970-586-4710) ten miles south of town. Started in the 1930s by Charles Perkins (a native Coloradoan who was so proud to be one-fourth Blackfoot Indian that he changed his last name to reflect his heritage), it was one of the first stores in America to deal exclusively in Native American collectibles. The store continues to uphold his reverence for Indian arts and traditions: it contains one of the world's finest private collections of Plains Indian artifacts and offers high-quality tourist-trade goods and collectibles for sale.

NORTH OF DENVER NIGHTLIFE

The University of Colorado sponsors a full range of events, most of them open to the public. Check the Boulder *Daily Camera*'s Friday edition or any of the many bulletin boards around town for current happenings.

University students dominate the Boulder bar scene. A popular, eclectic hangout is the **West End Tavern** (926 Pearl Street; 303-444-3535), which features alternative music on Tuesday, jazz on Wednesday, comedy on Saturday and a deejay on other nights. Cover. The **Walnut Brewery** (1123 Walnut Street; 303-447-1345), one of the town's many brewpubs, has live jazz and blues on Friday and Saturday nights. **Tulagi** (1129 13th Street; 303-442-1369), a longtime favorite student beer joint, has local dance music four or five nights a week. **The Sink** (1165 13th Street; 303-444-7465) serves up pizza, burgers, beer and, on weekends, live reggae or rock.

Fox Theatre (1135 13th Street, Boulder; 303-447-0095), a 625-seat showcase concert club, features a variety of local and national acts, from jazz and folk to contemporary and alternative music nightly. Cover.

In Fort Collins, **Fort Ram** (450 North Linden Street; 970-482-5026) is a top student dance club that boasts the largest dancefloor in northern Colorado. Music (deejays, with some live bands) ranges from Top-40, alternative and hip-hop to "retro"—meaning, in current student parlance, oldies from the 1980s.

The name tells you everything you need to know about the **Barleen Family Country Music Dinner Theater** (1110 Woodstock Drive, Estes Park; 970-586-5749), one of the town's favorite entertainment spots. For a rowdier scene, check out **Lonigan's Saloon** (110 West Elkhorn Avenue; 970-586-4346), with live acoustic music on Tuesday and loud rock for dancing on Friday and Saturday.

NORTH OF DENVER PARKS

Rocky Mountain National Park—One of the premier areas in the U.S. National Park System, this 266,957-acre mountain recreation area reaches from meadows at 8000-foot elevation into the high mountains, containing 107 peaks over 12,000 feet. Easy access from Denver and other Front Range cities makes this one of the most crowded summertime destinations in Colorado.

Facilities: Picnic areas, restrooms, visitors centers, campfire programs, cafeteria, horse stables, shuttle buses, hiking trails (355 miles of them); day-use fee, $5; information, 970-586-1206. *Fishing:* Permitted for trout in backcountry lakes and streams.

Camping: Permitted in five public campgrounds totaling 586 sites (no hookups); $10 per night. In July and August, reservations are required for the two largest campgrounds, Glacier Basin and Moraine Park (MISTIX, 800-365-2267; credit card required). A limited number of backcountry campsites are available by permit.

Getting there: The main east entrance is three miles west of Estes Park on Route 34/36. The west entrance is about two miles north of Grand Lake on Route 34.

Boulder Mountain Park—Little by little, Boulder taxpayers' dollars have purchased the mountains that flank the west side of the city in order to protect this dramatic stretch of the Front Range from development. The park includes the huge slanted expanse of granite cliffs known as the Flatirons as well as Flagstaff Mountain, where a three-mile switchback winds to the 1600-foot summit—a great spot for watching stars, the lights of Boulder or the breaking dawn. Several hiking trails start from Sunrise Circle Amphitheater.

Facilities: Picnic areas, restrooms, hiking trails; day-use fee, $5; information, 303-441-3400.

Getting there: Follow Baseline Road west from Boulder; it becomes Flagstaff Mountain Road as it winds its way up to the trailhead and the summit.

Eldorado Canyon State Park—Rock climbers come from as far away as Europe to challenge the sheer, vertical 850-foot sandstone cliffs that enclose Eldorado Canyon. There are picnic areas along the creek at the canyon's bottom and ten miles of trails for hiking and mountain biking.

Facilities: Picnic areas, restrooms, hiking trails; day-use fee, $3; information, 303-494-3943. *Fishing:* Rainbow trout is the main catch.

Getting there: Located eight miles southwest of Boulder on Route 170, above the village of Eldorado Springs.

Horsetooth Reservoir and **Horsetooth Mountain Park**—Long, narrow Horsetooth Reservoir hugs the foothills due west of Fort Collins. The lake is a popular, often crowded water-sports area used for waterskiing, boating, windsurfing and swimming. A paved county road runs along the eastern shore, which is often lined with anglers. The lake is flanked on the west by the Lory State Park and Horsetooth Mountain Park.

Facilities: Picnic areas, restrooms, boat ramp, marinas, hiking trails; day-use fee, $5; information, 970-679-4570. *Swimming:* Permitted. *Fishing:* Good for walleye, bass, bluegill and rainbow trout.

Camping: There are 115 RV sites (water and electric hookups) and 100 tent sites around the lake; $7 to $10 per night.

Getting there: From Bellvue, ten miles west of Fort Collins, County Road 23 heads south along the eastern shore of the lake.

Lory State Park—An unpaved road and 30 miles of hiking, mountain-biking and horseback-riding trails wind among Lory State Park's arid foothills, grasslands and up-thrust rock formations. Deer are abundant. A jeep trail, ideal for mountain biking, runs from the state park across the east face of nearby Horsetooth Mountain, named for its crowning rock formation, which some say resembles a horse's bicuspid.

Facilities: Picnic areas, restrooms, hiking trails, double diamond horse stable with rentals; day-use fee, $3; information, 970-493-1623. *Fishing:* Good for walleye, largemouth and smallmouth bass, bluegill and rainbow trout.

Camping: There are six hike-in backcountry tent sites; $2 per night.

Getting there: Shortly before reaching Horsetooth Reservoir, County Road 25G branches off westward to Lory State Park.

Roosevelt National Forest—This 788,000-acre forest spans the eastern slope of the Rockies from Central City to the Wyoming state line and wraps around three sides of Rocky Mountain National Park. Its most distinctive feature is a series of deep gorges, including Big Thompson Canyon and Poudre River Canyon, both accessible by paved highway. Two National Forest wilderness areas—Indian Peaks Wilderness and Comanche Peak Wilderness—adjoin Rocky Mountain National Park; there are also two other, smaller wilderness areas—the Rawah Wilderness and the Cache La Poudre Wilderness.

Facilities: Picnic areas, hiking trails, jeep trails; information, 970-498-1100. *Fishing:* Good for rainbow and other trout species.

Camping: Twenty-six campgrounds offer a total of 685 RV/tent sites (two campgrounds have electric hookups), most of them in the Poudre River Canyon west of Fort Collins; $5 to $10 per night.

Getting there: The forest's main recreational access is up the Poudre River Canyon on Route 14. There is also access to lakes and campgrounds from Route 72 between Raymond and Central City.

Colorado Springs Area

"Pikes Peak or Bust!" was the rallying cry that carried more than 100,000 pioneers west in 1859, pursuing rumors of gold strikes deep in the unexplored wilderness of the Colorado Rockies. As they crossed the Great Plains in wagons or on foot with handcarts, Pikes Peak was the first mountain peak to break the skyline, announcing the end of the two-month journey. The huge mountain marked the gateway to the land where veins of gold and silver lay waiting to be claimed. Colorado City, at the foot of Pikes Peak, marked the start of a road many gold seekers took on their way to South Park and Leadville, and formed the nucleus of modern Colorado Springs.

In 1872, railroad builder William Jackson Palmer ran 60 miles of track south from Denver, then founded Colorado Springs so people would have someplace to go on his railroad. The city's name is a synthesis of Colorado City and Manitou Springs, already a famous spa. There never were any springs in Colorado Springs.

As it grew into an exclusive resort, Colorado Springs was nicknamed "Little London" for its popularity with British nobility. Later still, it came to be known as "Newport in the Rockies" for its elegant mansions. From the 1890s to the 1960s, Colorado Springs was one of the wealthiest communities per capita in the country, the Aspen of another time.

Today, **Colorado Springs** is by far the largest community in the Pikes Peak area—in fact, the second-largest city in Colorado and the third largest in the Rocky Mountain West. The population of Colorado Springs quadrupled between 1969 and 1972 as military personnel returning from Vietnam were discharged from the army at Fort Carson south of town. Electronics firms built plants on the north side. Suburbs and shopping malls sprawled farther and farther out across the eastern plains. But the old-time tourist towns in the hills and canyons along the west edge of the city, seemingly oblivious to the metropolis bustling along on the other side of the freeway, have changed hardly at all in two generations.

It is possible to see all the major sights of the Pikes Peak area without going into the downtown or east-side areas of Colorado Springs. Visitors who take the time to explore these parts of town, however, can find a few unique places. **The Colorado Springs Pioneers Museum** (215 South Tejon Street; 719-578-6650), in the old county courthouse across the street from the present courthouse and jail at the south end of downtown, has two floors of exhibits ranging from antique Van Briggle pottery to firearms. The restored courtroom upstairs dates back to 1903 and has been used as a set for motion pictures and the "Perry Mason" television series.

One mile north of downtown, adjacent to the Colorado College campus, is the **Colorado Springs Fine Arts Center** (30 West Dale Street, Colorado Springs; 719-634-5581; admission). The building is said to be the finest example of an odd architectural style called "Pueblo Deco"—a 1930s art deco variation inspired by the Indian architecture of New Mexico. The permanent exhibits also have a southwestern flavor, with Pueblo and Navajo Indian collections and a replica of a *penitente* chapel.

East of downtown, the **U.S. Olympic Training Center** (1750 East Boulder Street, Colorado Springs; 719-578-4644) occupies a former U.S. Air Force base that was abandoned as the city grew to surround it. Each year, more than 15,000 Olympic hopefuls attend training camps at the 37-acre complex. Regularly scheduled tours take visitors through the athletic facilities.

Of the numerous special-interest museums in Colorado Springs, none is more offbeat than the **Tesla Museum** (★) (2220 East Bijou Street; 719-475-0918; admission). Nikolai Tesla, inventor of alternating current, the electric motor and the Tesla coil, saw his reputation destroyed in a vicious publicity war with his rival, Thomas Edison. He moved to Colorado Springs to conduct experiments with lightning in search of a way to transmit electricity without wires. Although his original laboratory is long gone, some of his sensational scientific demonstrations, such as how one million volts of electricity can flow through the human body harmlessly, are re-created daily by the museum staff.

Colorado City, founded in 1859 during the Pikes Peak gold rush, was the first town in the Pikes Peak area. Now part of Colorado Springs's west side, the old wooden storefronts and red-brick Victorian office buildings along the main street of **Old Colorado City** were refurbished in the 1970s and 1980s and reborn as a historic district of cafés and cute shops. Located on West Colorado Avenue between 24th and 31st streets (take Cimarron Street/Route 24 west from Route 24 and turn left on 26th Street), Old Colorado City is a centrally located starting point for touring the major tourist attractions of the Colorado Springs area.

On the city's northwestern outskirts lies the **Garden of the Gods**. (One route into the park is north from Old Colorado City on 31st Street; others are from Manitou Springs and the Garden of the Gods Road exit from Route 25 north of Colorado Springs.) The 1350-acre city park is filled with orange sandstone spires and monoliths and bordered by an escarpment of pink alabaster. Take a hike or just drive through the park on paved roads to see Balanced Rock, Steamboat Rock and the Kissing Camels, some of the most photographed rock formations in the West.

Near the north entrance to the Garden of the Gods is **White House Ranch Living History Site** (Gateway Road, Colorado Springs; 719-578-6777; admission). This city-operated living museum re-creates early-day farms of the Pikes Peak area. Buildings include a 1868 homestead, a 1895 ranch house, and a bigger 1907 home. Guides in period costume enact old-time lifestyles, and the fields and pastures of the ranch are worked by means of traditional 19th-century farming methods.

Nearby, **Glen Eyrie** (★) (3820 North 30th Street, Colorado Springs; 719-598-1212) was the mansion of Colorado Springs's founder, Denver and Rio Grande Railroad tycoon William Jackson Palmer. When it was built in 1904, the 67-room Tudor-style castle with its 700 acres of grounds was the largest and most expensive home west of the Mississippi. It had its own steam-powered electrical generator and a four-story elevator. A mile-long chimney tunnel that carried smoke from the mansion's 24 fireplaces far up the canyon reveals the dislike of smoke and soot that Palmer developed during his years as a railroad builder. The same aversion prompted him to include the nation's first air-pollution laws in the original Colorado Springs city charter. Glen Eyrie is now the headquarters of a Christian youth group called the Navigators. Call for current information on tours of the estate.

After driving through the Garden of the Gods, many visitors continue north via Route 25 for about ten miles to the **United States Air Force Academy** (Route 25 North, Colorado Springs; 719-472-2025), where college-age cadets train to become career officers in a rigorous four-year program. With more than one million visitors a year, the academy is the most-visited tourist attraction in the Pikes Peak area. The buildings of greatest interest to visitors include the Barry Goldwater Visitors Center, the planetarium, the athletic field house, and the cadet chapel with its 17 futuristic spires. On weekdays during the school year, visitors are welcome to watch the noon formation (it's actually at 12:30), in which 4400 cadets assemble in rank and file on the central parade ground before marching to lunch.

Between the Garden of the Gods and the Air Force Academy, the **Pro Rodeo Hall of Fame and American Cowboy Museum** (101 Pro Rodeo Drive, Colorado Springs; 719-593-8847; admission) presents short films on rodeo riding and the more mundane work of punching cattle. The highlight of the museum, the Pro Rodeo Hall of Fame commemorates legendary bronco and Brahma riders. During the summer months, rodeo demonstrations are held daily in the outdoor arena.

A visit to the **Western Museum of Mining & Industry** (125 Gleneagle Drive, Colorado Springs; 719-488-0880; admission), near the Air Force Academy's north gate, can enhance travelers' understanding and appreciation of the gold mines they will see in the Cripple Creek area and other parts of Colorado.

Exhibits demonstrate the complete process of gold mining, from prospecting through drilling and blasting to refining the ore.

To tour the sights of the Broadmoor area on the southwest edge of Colorado Springs, start from Old Colorado City or Route 24 West and take 21st Street south. Near the intersection of 21st Street and Route 24 is a cluster of commercial tourist attractions, including the **Hall of Presidents Wax Museum** (1050 South 21st Street, Colorado Springs; 719-635-3553; admission), with more than 130 life-size replicas of U.S. presidents, first ladies, and other historical figures, and **Ghost Town Museum** (400 South 21st Street, Colorado Springs; 719-634-0696; admission), which contains Old West antiques and re-creations of frontier buildings. Across the parking lot from Ghost Town Museum is **Van Briggle Art Pottery** (600 South 21st Street, Colorado Springs; 719-633-4080). The legacy of famed ceramic artist Artus Van Briggle, the sculptural and free-form pottery is made in various styles, including some art-deco designs from the '30s. The free tour shows how artisans throw clay on potters' wheels, shape it, glaze it and fire it. Visitors can buy the pottery at the showroom. Van Briggle's is in the old railroad roundhouse where ore trains from Cripple Creek turned around. Across the street, a tall smokestack is all that's left of the old mill where gold was refined and cast into bars.

Continue south on 21st Street for about two miles, past Cheyenne Boulevard and Cheyenne Road, to reach the extensive resort complex of the **Broadmoor Hotel** (1 Lake Avenue, Colorado Springs; 719-634-7711). Even if the ultra-deluxe rates discourage you from staying there, stop in to see this magnificent hotel, ranked as the finest resort west of the Mississippi during the 1920s. The pink Italian Renaissance hotel, with its Mediterranean tile roof and multilevel lobby a fantasy of polished Colorado marble, is located on the shore of its own idyllic private lake. It has its own zoo and boasts two of the state's finest golf courses. At the south end of the lake is a building that houses two indoor ice-skating rinks—one open to the public year-round, the other reserved for the use of Olympic hopefuls. The free **World Figure Skating Hall of Fame & Museum** (20 1st Street, Colorado Springs; 719-635-5200), memorializes champion skaters who trained at the Broadmoor, including Peggy Fleming and Sonja Henie.

The tennis club, spa and other facilities that surround the hotel itself are just the tip of the iceberg. Past the golf course and up the side of Cheyenne Mountain, the Broadmoor has not only its own ski slopes but also its own zoo. The **Cheyenne Mountain Zoo** (4250 Cheyenne Mountain Zoo Road, Colorado Springs; 719-475-9555; admission), perched midway up the mountainside, has the most spectacular location of any zoo we've seen. Today the zoo has more than 500 animals, including an impressive herd of giraffes.

The paved road through the zoo continues in a series of steep switchbacks up the mountain to the **Will Rogers Shrine of the Sun**. The four-story stone tower, which commands perhaps the finest possible view of the Colorado Springs area, was originally conceived as Cripple Creek gold tycoon and Broadmoor founder Spencer Penrose's monumental tomb. Before it was completed, humorist Will Rogers, a friend of Penrose's, died in a plane crash, and the tower was dedicated to him. Penrose and his wife (but not Will Rogers) are buried under the floor of the small room in the base of the shrine, making him perhaps the only man in history to successfully promote his own grave as a tourist attraction.

From the Broadmoor area, head west on either Cheyenne Boulevard or Cheyenne Road; they merge and less than a mile later divide again at the mouth of Cheyenne Canyon. **Seven Falls** (2850 South Cheyenne Canyon Road, Colorado Springs; 719-632-0765; admission), in the south fork of the canyon, is one of the region's oldest commercial tourist attractions. South Cheyenne Creek tumbles into this box canyon down a near-vertical granite cliff in a stairstep series of waterfalls—count 'em, seven—for a total drop of about 300 feet. It is not possible to see all the falls from the bottom of the canyon. Stairways go up the cliff beside the falls, and another goes to a lookout point from which all can be seen. An incline elevator also goes up to the lookout. At night, colored floodlights illuminate the cliffs for a mile down the canyon, all the way to the tollgate.

Drivers who turn right instead of left at the Seven Falls turnoff find themselves in **North Cheyenne Canyon**, which is quite different from South Cheyenne Canyon. For one thing, it's free. Like the Garden of the Gods, North Cheyenne Canyon is a Colorado Springs city park. And as in the Garden of the Gods, you're likely to see expert rock climbers challenging the 400-foot-high granite walls in the middle part of the canyon. The paved road twists, steeply in places, to **Helen Hunt Falls**, a classic mountain waterfall that looks exactly like the one on Coors Beer labels.

Not far past the falls, the North Cheyenne Canyon road joins the narrow, unpaved **Gold Camp Road**. Originally the track bed for the Cripple Creek Short Line narrow-gauge railroad, which carried ore down from the goldfields at the turn of the century, the road runs through Pike National Forest around the south side of Pikes Peak for 36 slow miles to return to the pavement near Victor. For a shorter trip—and one affording some of the most spectacular views—return via North Cheyenne Canyon to Colorado Springs. The eight-mile trip follows the rim of the canyon, goes through two railroad tunnels and traverses the mountainside high above the city. Despite appearances, there *is* room for two vehicles to pass each other.

The Gold Camp Road comes back to town on 26th Street, across Route 24 from the Old Colorado City area. The road descends from the mountainside into **Bear Creek Regional Park**. The solar-heated **Bear Creek Nature Center** (245 Bear Creek Road, Colorado Springs; 719-520-6387), at the northwest side of the park, has exhibits on the wildlife of the park's foothills and streamside forests, which can be explored on a network of nature trails.

COLORADO SPRINGS AREA HOTELS

The cheapest beds in the region are at the **Garden of the Gods Youth Hostel** (3704 West Colorado Avenue, Colorado Springs; 719-475-9450), located near the south entrance to the Garden of the Gods. The AYH-affiliated hostel, part of the large, crowded Garden of the Gods campground, consists of 12 spartan dormitory cabins with four bunk beds each. Guests share the campground's restroom and shower facilities. Budget.

For low-priced accommodations with a touch of antique atmosphere, check out the **Buffalo Lodge** (3700 West Colorado Avenue; 719-634-2851), on the boundary between Colorado Springs and Manitou Springs. The venerable old lodge has 20 small, threadbare creekside motel rooms with dark and dreary wood paneling plus a large, beautifully rustic lobby right out of a century past. Budget.

There are also a number of older, budget-priced motels along West Colorado Avenue between Old Colorado City and Manitou Springs, relics from the pre-freeway era when this street was the main highway to Pikes Peak and points west. A good bet in this area is the **Garden of the Gods Motel** (2922 West Colorado Avenue; 719-636-5271), a two-story motel offering the most ordinary rooms imaginable and an indoor heated swimming pool within easy walking distance of Old Colorado City. Budget to moderate.

Located in the residential part of historic Old Colorado City, the **Holden House Bed and Breakfast Inn** (1102 West Pikes Peak Avenue, Colorado Springs; phone/fax 719-471-3980) has six guest rooms and suites in a Victorian-era Colonial revival home and carriage house. Some suites feature fireplaces and Roman marble tubs large enough for two. Moderate.

The finest bed and breakfast in downtown Colorado Springs is the **Hearthstone Inn** (506 North Cascade Avenue; 719-473-4413, 800-521-1885, fax 719-473-1322), an 1885 Victorian mansion built by a paper bag tycoon. The innkeepers annexed the neighboring building, built in 1885 as a tuberculosis sanatorium, and extensively remodeled both buildings to create an antique-filled 25-room hostelry that glows with warm elegance. Rates range from moderate to deluxe and include a full breakfast.

The **Broadmoor Hotel** (1 Lake Avenue, Colorado Springs; 719-634-7711, 800-634-7711, fax 719-577-5779) has traditionally been considered the finest resort hotel in the Rocky Mountains. Instead of slipping into decay like so many other grand hotels, for decades the Broadmoor has been pursuing an expansion program designed to keep up with the finest new resorts worldwide. Three hotel annexes have brought the total number of rooms to 700. Rooms in both the old and new parts of the hotel were recently redecorated with antiques, and the hotel's common areas are filled with original paintings by Toulouse-Lautrec and Maxfield Parrish as well as priceless oriental artworks. Among the Broadmoor's recreational facilities are three golf courses, three swimming pools, 16 tennis courts, a spa, stables, a hot-air balloon and a shooting range. Ultra-deluxe.

The historic **Outlook Lodge** (Route 24, Green Mountain Falls; 719-684-2303) was originally built in 1889 as the parsonage for a church and has been a hotel since the 1920s. The wraparound house with veranda is situated near a lake in a quiet little mountain community five miles west of Manitou Springs on the side of Pikes Peak. Each of the eight guest rooms is different. All have antique and period furnishings, and most have private baths. Moderate rates include a full breakfast.

For gay-friendly accommodations in the vicinity of Colorado Springs (a city that has gained a homophobic reputation in recent years), contact the **Pikes Peak Paradise B & B** (P.O. Box 5760, Woodland Park, CO 80866; 800-354-0985, fax 719-687-9008). This five-bedroom inn on a dirt backroad in the ponderosa pine forest 25 minutes west of the city resembles a southern mansion and offers a romantic atmosphere with plenty of privacy. Amenities include a sundeck and hot tub. Clientele is 50 percent gay, 50 percent straight. Moderate.

COLORADO SPRINGS AREA RESTAURANTS

Giuseppe's Depot (10 South Sierra Madre Street; 719-635-3111) is a Colorado Springs classic. You'll find great pizzas and huge submarine sandwiches here, alongside more sophisticated fare such as rib-eye steaks, lasagna and snow crab, Key-lime pie and Kahlúa chocolate mousse as well as a good selection of wines. Windows overlook the railroad yards, where coal trains still rumble by. Budget to moderate.

Another old-time downtown favorite is **Michelle's** (122 North Tejon Street, Colorado Springs; 719-633-5086), a candy shop, soda fountain and café operated by a Greek family since 1950. The front part of the café is a shop displaying candies made on the premises. In the back part, people gorge themselves on big, elaborate concoctions of homemade ice cream. Though fewer than one out of ten patrons actually comes here to eat, there is a limited but tasty lunch and dinner menu ranging from cheeseburgers to Greek hero sandwiches. Budget.

The **Mountain View Dining Room** (Cheyenne Mountain Conference Resort, 3225 Broadmoor Valley Road, Colorado Springs; 719-576-4600), serves buffet-style gourmet dinners featuring six hot entrées plus vegetables, potatoes and rice as well as an array of desserts including six different cakes and pies plus ice cream, brownies and petits fours—all you can eat at a fixed price. The view takes in not only the mountains but also the distant glow of Colorado Spring's city lights. It's perfect by candlelight. Deluxe.

If down-home food—and lots of it—sounds good to you, check out the **Hungry Farmer** (575 Garden of the Gods Road, Colorado Springs; 719-598-7622), a huge restaurant on the north side of town that was designed to resemble a barn. Waitpersons wear overalls, and the decor is way cuter than any real farmyard ever was. A bottomless bucket of thick, hearty soup, homemade oatmeal muffins and cinnamon rolls come with all meals. Entrées include seafood, steaks, ribs, fried chicken and liver and onions. Moderate.

The Pampered Palate (2625 West Colorado Avenue, Colorado Springs; 719-632-9299), a small restaurant with 15 tables in a turn-of-the-century house, changes its main menu monthly and its dessert menu daily, offering an intriguing choice of dishes from Asia, Spain, France and Oregon, the chef's original home. This is the best restaurant in Colorado City's historic district. Moderate.

COLORADO SPRINGS AREA SHOPPING

Despite high-volume tourism, Colorado Springs and the Pikes Peak area have never developed the high-priced, arts-oriented retail shops that characterize so many Colorado resort areas.

Recently in Colorado Springs, **Old Colorado City**, a formerly rundown three-block area along Colorado Avenue, has blossomed into new life with an array of artisans' shops. **Simpich Character Dolls** (2413 West Colorado Avenue; 719-636-3272) is both factory and gallery for these unique, individually made collectible dolls, which are sold nationwide; factory tours are available. Artist Michael Garman, famous in the world of cowboy art for his finely detailed sculptural miniatures of Old West street scenes, had his factorylike studio in Old Colorado City long before the neighborhood became trendy; today, his works are on display in the big **Michael Garman Gallery** (2416 West Colorado Avenue; 719-471-9391).

COLORADO SPRINGS AREA NIGHTLIFE

Jeff Valdez' Comedy Corner (1305 North Academy Boulevard; 719-591-0707) is Colorado Springs' top comedy club and features adult humor. The top singles dance club is **Meadow Muffins** (2432 West Colorado Avenue; 719-633-0583), a perennial favorite even though it presents deejay dance music only. A lively alternative dance club that does have live bands is the student-oriented **The Club House Underground Pub** (130 East Kiowa Street; 719-633-0590).

For adults, the classic Colorado Springs hangout is the **Golden Bee** (Broadmoor Hotel, 1 Lake Avenue; 719-634-7711). A sing-along ragtime piano player encourages a party atmosphere; the crowd is a mix of the Broadmoor's well-heeled guests and Colorado Springs locals who come here for fun. This is where you can watch sophisticated women dripping in diamonds, lawyers and bankers competing to see who can chug a "yard" of beer (a three-foot-tall carafe) the fastest.

A long-established gay-friendly club is the **Hide N'Seek** (512 West Colorado Avenue, Colorado Springs; 719-634-9303), featuring deejay dance music. The dark, warehouselike club has one of the town's largest dancefloors.

COLORADO SPRINGS AREA PARKS

Bear Creek Regional Park and **Bear Creek Canyon Park**—Birdwatchers, equestrians and joggers meet on this network of trails among the scrub oak foothills on the west side of Colorado Springs. The visitors center, an experimental solar-powered structure, contains exhibits on bird and animal life found within the park boundaries, as well as live animals and relief maps of the park and the Pikes Peak area. While the west half of the park is rugged and wild, the east half has neat lawns, tennis courts and soccer and football fields. Bear Creek Canyon Park, adjoining the west side of Bear Creek Wilderness Park and continuing south to Gold Camp Road, follows the creek for about two miles and offers numerous parking areas and picnic sites. The area is especially beautiful in autumn, when the forest along the creek bursts into a riot of reds, oranges and golds.

Facilities: Picnic areas, restrooms, visitors center, game fields, nature trails; information, 719-520-6387.

Getting there: Located south of Route 24 between 21st Street and 26th Street, which becomes Bear Creek Canyon Road and joins the Gold Camp Road.

Pikes Peak Area

Besides the huge granite massif that dominates the skyline west of Colorado Springs, the Pikes Peak region includes an assortment of towns and scenic routes that surround the mountain on all sides. Manitou Springs, the quaint old tourist town at the foot of Pikes Peak's east face, is the natural starting point for exploring the town and the region. From there, the main highway skirts the north side of the mountain, following an old railroad route known as Ute Pass (though it is not a true pass because it has no summit). Other former railroad routes—the Gold Camp Road from Colorado Springs and the Phantom Canyon Road from Cañon City—provide access to the rugged forest and canyon country on the south side of the Peak. On the west side, the Cripple Creek District was once the richest gold field in the Rockies, supporting a city that ranked as one of the region's largest at the turn of the century—long since abandoned but recently revived as a gambling center. Allow at least four days to explore all sides of Pikes Peak, beginning with an ascent to the summit.

Pikes Peak (14,110 feet) is not the highest mountain in the Colorado Rockies (Mount Elbert, between Leadville and Aspen, is 323 feet higher). It is not even the highest mountain with a road to the top. (Mount Evans, west of Denver, is 154 feet higher.) But Pikes Peak is certainly the most famous mountain in the Rockies. To early pioneers and prospectors its name was synonymous with gold, for the massive, solitary mountain marked the gateway to the goldfields around Fairplay and Leadville—though it was not found on its slopes until about 35 years after the Pikes Peak gold rush.

Pikes Peak was also the first major tourist attraction in Colorado. When Captain Zebulon Pike, the explorer for whom the mountain was named, failed to reach the summit on his 1810 expedition, undertaken to map the southern reaches of the Louisiana Purchase and the Mexican border, he declared that the mountain would never be climbed. But by the 1870s, thousands of visitors were climbing Pikes Peak on foot, on muleback and by horse-drawn carriage. A fancy resort hotel at the 11,000-foot level on the west side of the peak, its ruins now lost beneath the surface of a city reservoir, did a thriving business for decades. Cog railway tracks reached the summit in 1891, and two years later, Katherine Lee Bates wrote the lyrics to "America the Beautiful" on top of the peak.

In 1916, when gold-refinery tycoon and philanthropist Spencer Penrose converted the old carriage road up the peak to a graded automobile toll road, the assault on Captain Pike's "unclimbable" mountain began in earnest. Now, more than 250,000 people reach the summit of Pikes Peak each summer.

The **Pikes Peak Highway** (719-684-9138; admission) turns off from Route 24 at the tiny town of Cascade, three miles west of Manitou Springs. The road is 19 miles long, paved with blacktop for the first seven miles and gravel for the last 12. It takes about two hours to drive to the summit. Only on the switchback climb from the house at Glen Cove to the top ridge is the road edgy enough to make inexperienced mountain drivers wish there were guard rails. Accidents are rare, but breakdowns are common since some vehicles need fuel-system adjustments to run at such high altitudes. Motorists who are inexperienced at mountain driving would be well advised to take the cog train instead, which ascends the east face of the mountain at a straight, steep angle from Manitou Springs.

The Pikes Peak summit has a large curio shop, snack bar and observation deck. From the top, on a clear day, you can see most of Colorado, from the Continental Divide to the boundaries of Kansas, Oklahoma and New Mexico. The eastern horizon is about 175 miles away. While on the summit, keep in mind that there is not much oxygen at 14,000 feet. Excessive exercise can cause altitude sickness—dizziness, nausea, fainting. Alcoholic beverages, which have a much more powerful effect at high altitudes, should be avoided. Another high-altitude effect many people experience is sleepiness on the way down the mountain.

About two miles west of Old Colorado City, Manitou Springs is the actual site of the 26 mineral springs for which Colorado Springs was named. Beginning in the 1870s, people from the East and even Europe began to flock to Manitou Springs for the dry mountain climate and the healing waters, which were thought to cure everything from tuberculosis to polio. In those days, the circular building in the center of town was a fashionable spa, and a geyser spurted at regular intervals on Manitou Avenue. Most of the springs have been capped or clogged by mineral deposits, though a few still trickle fizzy mineral water by the roadside. A small exhibit case in the **Manitou Springs City Hall** (606 Manitou Avenue; 719-685-5481) shows each spring's location, status and mineral content.

Today, a number of old-time attractions live on in this quaintly old-fashioned tourist town. Up the hill, easier to reach from the Route 24 bypass than from the town itself, the **Cave of the Winds** (Cave of the Winds Road, Manitou Springs; 719-685-5444; admission) has been one of the Pikes Peak area's top commercial sites for more than a century. The cave is long, narrow and twisting, with plenty of stalactites, stalagmites, crystal formations and colored lights.

Just down the highway from the cave, the **Manitou Cliff Dwellings Museum** (Route 24, Manitou Springs; 719-685-5242; admission) is a group of Anasazi cliff dwellings that were found in a canyon near Dolores in southwestern Colorado and moved to a sandstone cliff above Manitou Springs in the 1920s. It probably made sense at the time, when few travelers could reach the area of Dolores and Mesa Verde. Today, the most remarkable fact about these reconstructed cliff dwellings is that they were disassembled into tens of thousands of individual stones, each marked for position, and reassembled 300 miles away.

The best Manitou Springs tourist attractions are on Ruxton Avenue, which leads south up a canyon from the center of town. **Miramont Castle** (★) (9 Capitol Hill Avenue, Manitou Springs; 719-685-1011; admission) is a restored 1895 stone mansion built by a wealthy French priest who had come to Manitou Springs to seek a cure for his tuberculosis. It was opened to the public as a museum in the late 1970s. A fantasyland of eclectic architecture, the castle incorporates nine different styles—among them Romanesque, Gothic, Tudor and Byzantine. Some rooms have been restored with period furnishings, while others house miscellaneous collections such as dolls and toy trains.

At the end of Ruxton Avenue is the depot for the **Pikes Peak Cog Railway** (515 Ruxton Avenue, Manitou Springs; 719-685-5401; admission), certainly the easiest way to climb the peak. The railroad, the highest in the United States, uses Swiss-made two-car diesel trains to climb the otherwise-inaccessible west face of Pikes Peak. The trains run from May through October, twice daily during the spring and fall, as many as eight times a day during peak season. The round trip takes between three and four hours, climbing grades as steep as 26 percent. Reservations are essential.

In addition to the interpretive exhibits at the visitors center on Pikes Peak's summit, two new small museums tell more about the mountain and its history. The **Pikes Peak Auto Hill Climb Race Car Museum** (135 Manitou Avenue, Manitou Springs; 719-685-4400; admission) traces the traditional Fourth of July road race to the summit, presents video views of what driving in the race is like, and displays some of the cars that have raced up the peak in past years. In the bedroom community of Woodland Park, up Route 24 on the way to Cripple Creek, a rustic cabin houses the free **Pikes Peak Museum** (720 West Route 24, Woodland Park; 719-687-3041), which offers exhibits on railroads, Indians, wildlife and other aspects of Pikes Peak history.

No tour of the Pikes Peak region is complete without a visit to the **Cripple Creek–Victor Historic District**, located at 9600 feet above sea level on the west slope of Pikes Peak, about an hour's drive from Colorado Springs. To get there, take Route 24 west for 25 miles to the crossroads town of Divide, then Route 67 south for 18 miles. In the summer tourist season and on weekends year-round, expect long lines of traffic at the one-lane, stoplight-controlled tunnel on Route 67.

The town of **Cripple Creek** was founded in 1891 after a local rancher spotted gold nuggets in the mountain stream of the same name. The discovery touched off the last great gold rush in the lower-48 United States, and by 1900, the Cripple Creek–Victor metropolitan area had become the largest city in Colorado, with a population of more than 60,000 including nearby Victor and several smaller settlements. The district boasted 150 saloons, 91 lawyers, and 15 newspapers. The mines of the Cripple Creek district produced some 625 tons of gold, worth more than eight billion dollars at today's gold prices.

Twenty years after the town was founded, most of the mines in the Cripple Creek district had closed down. Little by little, the 100 or so blocks of residential neighborhoods vanished as the few remaining residents tore down abandoned buildings for firewood until only bare, grassy hillsides remained. A stark reminder of the transitory nature of mortals' works and wealth set against a background of Pikes Peak's massive, timeless crags, Cripple Creek gradually developed a low-key tourism economy, and by the late 1960s a number of shops had opened along main street to sell arts and crafts, antiques and curios.

In 1991, the Colorado legislature legalized casino gambling in Cripple Creek. The idea was to generate money to preserve the historic buildings, many of which were crumbling away with neglect. When the casinos opened in 1993, the interior of every building on Bennett Avenue had been spruced up with pseudo-Victorian glitz. Slot machines and blackjack tables had displaced almost every other business in town, and huge tracts of vacant land had become parking lots. How gambling will ultimately reshape Cripple Creek's character is any-

(Text continued on page 88.)

Colorado's Golden Glow

Colorado was settled later than any of its neighboring states because mountain winters made it a hard place to survive in. But rumors of gold turned the eastern slope of the Colorado Rockies into the region's main population center almost overnight. A trickle of prospectors started arriving in the territory in 1849, a year after the discovery of gold at Sutter's Mill in California proved that gold existed in U.S. territory.

The gold find that touched off the 1858 "Pikes Peak or Bust" gold rush turned out to be a bust—a discovery of about $200 worth of gold flakes in **Cherry Creek**, where no more gold has been seen since. Large numbers of gold hunters made their way to Colorado's Front Range, chasing exaggerated reports of the find. Many newcomers starved that winter.

But the following May saw the first of a seemingly endless string of fabulous finds in the canyon country along the route of present-day Route 70. **Idaho Springs**, **Central City** and **Georgetown** boom towns appeared ever deeper in the forbidding mountains. By 1861, two years after the first find, claims had been staked along every foot of Clear Creek's banks, and the gold fields of Colorado were producing 150,000 ounces of gold a year (worth about $60 million today).

Gold hunters poked into every canyon and creek of the Rocky Mountain labyrinth. Wherever a trace of "color" was found, a gold camp would appear. If the discovery proved significant enough to become a mine, the camp would instantly become a town complete with shops, saloons, hotels, newspapers and lots of lawyers.

The gold rush lasted for only a few years. By the end of the Civil War in 1865, Colorado's gold production was already declining. By 1868, it had dwindled to almost nothing, leaving the miners to scramble after lesser minerals like silver, lead and even coal. In all, the "Pikes Peak or Bust" gold rush produced about one-sixteenth the amount of gold that came from California during the same years.

In the 1870s, gold continued to lure prospectors into the mountains, from **Leadville** to the **San Juan Mountains** of southwestern Colorado, but once there, most would-be gold hunters found that the real fortunes were being made in silver and more mundane metals such as zinc and lead. It was a common to hear about newcomers buying fraudulent "salted gold mines"—in which a small amount of gold was fired into an exposed wall with a shotgun to falsify assays—who dug a little farther and found rich silver lodes. But the greatest gold find in Colorado was yet to come.

Cowboy Bob Womack found the first nuggets of gold in a stream called Cripple Creek on the back side of Pikes Peak in 1879, but it took 11 years for him to convince anyone that his find was genuine. By the time he finally found a backer and proved his gold find, he had become known as "Crazy Bob," and his credibility was so low that he sold his interest for only $500; within the next year, it produced more than $200,000 in gold ore. Womack is memorialized today by the Cripple Creek casino named after him.

Gold mining was rarely a profitable business. Of nearly 100,000 people who flocked to the Cripple Creek gold fields, 28 became millionaires from their gold claims. Only one was a professional prospector and none were miners; most were shopkeepers, construction workers, lawyers, pharmacists and real estate agents. All made their millions by selling their claims to mining corporations, which rarely recovered as much gold as they paid for the claims.

The main reason mining companies were interested in Colorado gold at all was that it was easy to sell stock in gold mines. The United States was on the gold standard in those days, meaning that the nation's economy could expand only as fast as gold was produced. Because even a money-losing mine was good for the national economy, eastern politicians poured money into gold production. Of the 5000 exploratory holes that were dug in Cripple Creek, 700 became working mines. Yet more than 12,000 mining corporations were selling stock on the now-defunct Colorado Springs stock exchange.

In 1933, the United States went off the gold standard but still regulated gold prices at levels too low for profitable mining. Nearly all gold mines in Colorado shut down. Gold prices were deregulated in 1976 and instantly jumped from $35 an ounce to around $400 an ounce. But because of the huge equipment investments required, few mines have been reopened. Instead, gold companies use high-tech cyanide leaching methods to extract more gold from old mines and refinery slag heaps.

A lot of old-time Coloradoans believe the legendary gold veins of the Cripple Creek District were a mere offshoot of an immense mother lode hidden deep beneath the Pikes Peak massif. Amateur and professional geologists have been debating this theory's likelihood for decades, since tunneling beneath the mountain to find out would be so enormously costly that nobody is likely to do it. Even scoffers agree that there is probably more gold under the hills of Cripple Creek today than the $412,974,848 worth of ore (that's about 1,200,000 ounces of gold, worth something like $5 billion today) mined there between 1890 and 1950. Today, fortune seekers are more likely to play the Colorado lottery (the odds are better), and mining companies are content to leave most of Colorado's remaining gold in the ground—for now.

body's guess. Meanwhile, wild donkeys, great-grandchildren of beasts that pulled ore carts in the old days, still wander the streets, and several tourist attractions from the pre-casino days continue to operate.

The two-story **Cripple Creek District Museum** (Bennett Avenue, Cripple Creek; 719-689-2634; admission), at the east end of town, offers a look at the mining district's heyday, including its seamy or otherwise unpleasant aspects: fast money, deadly epidemics, labor violence, gambling and prostitution. One of the most interesting exhibits is a model showing the vast underground network, many miles of tunnels reaching thousands of feet into the earth, in just one of the district's 500 gold mines.

Near the museum, the **Cripple Creek and Victor Narrow Gauge Railroad** (520 East Carr Street, Cripple Creek; 719-689-2640; admission) takes passengers on a 45-minute narrated trip through the goldfields in open railcars pulled by an old-time steam locomotive. The old mines and other abandoned buildings along the way are off-limits to sightseers these days. A mining company is recovering gold from the low-grade ore found in mine tailings through a highly toxic cyanide leaching process.

About a mile out of town, the **Molly Kathleen Gold Mine** (Route 67, Cripple Creek; 719-689-2465; admission) offers tours into a gold mine. An elevator drops visitors down a shaft to a tunnel 1000 feet underground to see where miners blasted and drilled along a gold vein. Everyone who takes the tour receives a sample of gold ore. Open May through October.

Seven miles south of Cripple Creek, at the other end of the mining district, lies **Victor**. By some legislative whim, gambling was legalized in Cripple Creek but not in Victor, so visitors to the smaller near–ghost town can get a good idea of what Cripple Creek was like before casinos. Victor's main attraction is the **Victor–Lowell Thomas Museum** (3rd Street; 719-689-3211; admission), the small house where the journalist-adventurer lived during his boyhood. Thomas began his distinguished career as a cub reporter on the *Victor Record*. The newspaper building is still standing.

From the west end of Bennett Avenue in Cripple Creek, unpaved County Road 1 passes the perfect little volcanic cone of **Mount Pisgah** and runs through ranchland for about 20 miles and intersects Route 24 at Florissant, eight miles west of the main Cripple Creek turnoff at Divide. The road past Mount Pisgah takes motorists to **Florissant Fossil Beds National Monument** (★) (Florissant; 719-748-3253), a 6000-acre expanse where volcanic ash covered a sequoia forest 35 million years ago, preserving plants, insects, fish and a few birds and mammals of the Eocene era. The monument's most striking feature is a forest of giant petrified tree stumps. Equally interesting is the visitors center's display of remarkably detailed small fossils found in the monument.

It is possible to make a loop tour and see the Cripple Creek district and the Royal Gorge in the same day by taking the steep, narrow, unpaved and spectacularly scenic road that starts near Victor and winds between the reddish granite walls of **Phantom Canyon** to reach Route 50 at Florence, a few miles east of Cañon City. The 35-mile drive takes about two and a half hours. Like the Gold Camp Road, the Phantom Canyon Road was originally a narrow-gauge railroad route. In their haste to build the first railroad to the Cripple Creek district in 1893, the engineers cut a few corners, and on the second Florence-to-Cripple Creek run the train tumbled off a trestle into the canyon. By the time the tracks were reopened, the Midland Railroad route from Colorado Springs had won the race to the goldfields.

Cañon City, a quiet ranching town on the Arkansas River, is named for the geological wonder that has become its claim to fame and fortune. The **Royal Gorge** (719-275-7507; admission) is owned by the municipal government, and visitor admission fees provide the town's main source of revenue. The gorge is one of the deepest canyons in Colorado, 1053 feet from the rim to the Arkansas River at the bottom. Visitors can descend to river level on an incline railway or glide across the gorge on an aerial tramway. The canyon's main attraction, however, is the world's highest suspension bridge, built in 1929. Clatter across it by car or simply walk out to the middle for a swaying, dizzying view of the gorge.

Just outside the Royal Gorge entrance gate is **Buckskin Joe** (County Road 3A, Cañon City; 719-275-5149; admission), a movie-set town of pioneer buildings collected from around the state and placed below the stunning backdrop of the Sangre de Cristo Range. When not in use as a film location, Buckskin Joe does a roaring business as a stagecoaches-and-shootouts tourist theme park.

Motorists who enjoy mountain driving should not miss **Skyline Drive**, a three-mile scenic detour on the way back from Royal Gorge to Cañon City. Built in 1915 by an automobile club to prove the feasibility of asphalt highways, it was the first paved road west of the Mississippi. The narrow one-way road runs above the town along the top of a hogback ridge with 800-foot dropoffs on both sides.

The **Colorado Territorial Prison Museum** (201 North 1st Street, Cañon City; 719-269-3015; admission) was in use as a state maximum-security facility until the late 1970s, when the Colorado Supreme Court ruled that to confine prisoners there was "cruel and unusual punishment." Since then, the old stone prison has been opened to the public, providing a close-up look at the section where women prisoners were held.

The most direct route between Cañon City and Colorado Springs is Route 115, which runs along the perimeter of a military reserve used for maneuvers by the mechanized infantry forces at Fort Carson army base. The 42-mile trip takes less than an hour. Along the way, nine miles outside of Colorado Springs, an iron sculpture of a beetle larger than a man marks the entrance to the private, eccentric little **May Natural History Museum** (Route 115, Colorado Springs; 719-576-0450; admission). The museum contains more than 7000 mounted insects of the tropics, some of them brightly colored and others incredibly large.

To reach Route 25 from Cañon City, take Route 50 east for 39 miles to Pueblo.

PIKES PEAK AREA HOTELS

Manitou Springs is full of little ma-and-pa motels, cottages and guest houses dating back to the early 20th century, when this little town in the shadow of Pikes Peak was one of the most popular tourist resorts in the Rockies. Some are rundown and only marginally acceptable by modern standards; most are remarkably affordable. One of the nicer old cabin compounds is **Town-n-Country Cottages** (123 Crystal Park Road; 719-685-5427), which has ten recently renovated Spanish-style one- to three-room cabins with full baths and furnished kitchens. The four-acre grounds have an outdoor swimming pool, a hot tub, barbecue grills, a laundromat, a game room and a children's playground. A stream runs through the property, and there is easy access to hiking trails. Moderate.

Situated in the middle of the Manitou Springs Historic District, the **Two Sisters Inn** (10 Otoe Place; 719-685-9684) offers five guest rooms in a charming Victorian bungalow that was originally a boardinghouse for the town's schoolteachers. The atmosphere here is light and airy, and fresh flowers are everywhere. Works by local artists are on exhibit in the lobby, and the parlor has a large fireplace and antique piano. Rates include a gourmet three-course breakfast, formally served with crystal and silver. Moderate.

Built in 1871, the **Red Crags B & B** (302 El Paso Boulevard, Manitou Springs; 719-685-1920, fax 719-685-1073) was a favorite vacation spot of President Theodore Roosevelt. The six guest rooms and suites, which were renovated in 1991, feature Victorian-era antique decor. The private patio has a Pikes Peak view and a jacuzzi. The landscaping of the two-acre grounds includes a duck pond and herb gardens. Deluxe rates include a full breakfast.

The **Imperial Hotel** (123 North 3rd Street; 719-689-2922, 800-235-2922) was Cripple Creek's most elegant hotel when it was built in 1896 at the peak of the gold boom. When the city was largely abandoned, the hotel kept its doors open by presenting authentic Victorian melodramas that have been imitated throughout the West. While the melodrama is still presented nightly for most of the year, the big draw these days is gambling. The Imperial's casino occupies drawing rooms on three floors of the hotel. Most of the 29 guest rooms and suites have been remodeled with original period oil paintings and antique or period furnishings; 11 have private baths. Rates, including a continental breakfast, are moderate.

In the heart of the historic mining district but several miles away from the gambling action, the **Victor Hotel** (4th Street at Victor Avenue, Victor; 719-689-3553, fax 719-689-3979) was built in 1892 as a bank with hotel rooms upstairs. Now entirely a hotel, it features original woodwork and furnishings in its lobby and 30 rooms with period furnishings. The original Otis birdcage elevator, the first elevator in the Cripple Creek district when it was installed in 1899, is still in use. Moderate.

For Cañon City visitors, a good place to spend the night is the modern **Cañon Inn** (Route 50 at Dozier Street; 719-275-8676, fax 719-275-8675). Located six miles from Royal Gorge, this motor inn has 152 contemporary, oversized rooms with all standard amenities. Facilities include six indoor hot tubs and an outdoor heated swimming pool. Moderate.

PIKES PEAK AREA RESTAURANTS

A long-standing favorite for fine dining in Manitou Springs is the **Craftwood Inn** (404 El Paso Boulevard; 719-685-9000), with its romantic ambience in a lovely 1912 Tudor-style home that was once a woodcrafter's studio and shop. The à la carte menu specializes in wild game—caribou, elk, pheasant, venison, quail, duck, rabbit, antelope and Colorado mountain bass—but also has some excellent vegetarian dishes, plus unique desserts such as white chocolate ravioli and jalapeño white-chocolate mousse. The owner is a connoisseur of wines, so the wine list contains some of the most expensive selections found anywhere. Deluxe.

Vegetarian world cuisine is the focus of the **Adams Mountain Café** (110 Cañon Avenue, Manitou Springs; 719-685-1430). The restaurant-coffee shop maintains a friendly, casual atmosphere amid Victorian antique furnishings. Typical of the international no-meat offerings is orzo Mediterranean—orzo pasta with broccoli, sun-dried tomatoes, onions, cucumbers, dill and garlic. White poultry and shrimp are also served. Desserts such as almond strawberry shortcake and a list of fine wines, beers and gourmet coffees round out the menu. Moderate.

The **Old Chicago Casino** (419 East Bennett Avenue, Cripple Creek; 719-689-7880), a location of the Old Chicago Pizza chain found up and down the Front Range, is the major restaurant in Cripple Creek today. The Old Chicago has been designed to accommodate diners and slot machines in the same space—with the result that bus-tour groups tend to descend on it at conventional lunch hours. The menu includes hamburgers, turkey, lasagna and other standard fare, as well as 110 brands of beer, but the best deal in town is the all-you-can-eat pizza, soup and salad bar. Budget.

Zeke's (108 South 3rd Street, Victor; 719-689-2109) is the oldest continuously operating business in the Cripple Creek district; the owners' ancestors started their first restaurant in Victor in 1888, even before the start of the gold boom, and moved to the present location in 1899. The walls are of old red bricks and the tables, each different, are wooden and old. The menu ranges from hamburgers and hot dogs to full meals such as pork steak with mashed potatoes and mixed vegetables. The chili is said to be world famous—that is, Lowell Thomas once praised it in a newspaper column. Budget.

In Cañon City, fine dining is found at **Merlino's Belvedere** (1330 Elm Avenue; 719-275-5558), operated by an Italian family of long-time residents. The emphasis is on Italian food—veal parmesan, fettuccine—but the menu also includes salmon, shrimp, trout, prime rib, filet mignon and great desserts. Also featured are ciders made by the Merlino family and sold throughout the region. Moderate prices.

PIKES PEAK AREA SHOPPING

The region supports a fair number of artists and craftspeople, found in highest concentration in Manitou Springs, adjoining the western city limit of Colorado Springs along Manitou Avenue (Business Route 24). You can see a representative sampling of local arts and crafts at the **Commonwheel Artists Co-op** (102 Cañon Avenue; 719-685-1008), one of the region's longest-established co-op galleries. The newer **Manitou Art Center** (513 Manitou Avenue; 719-685-1861) houses galleries, shops and studios featuring local artists' works in all media.

PIKES PEAK AREA NIGHTLIFE

The top nighttime tourist attraction in the Colorado Springs area is **Laser Canyon** (Cave of the Winds, Manitou Springs; 719-685-5444; admission). You may have seen laser light shows before; you may even have seen better ones—this program seems a bit "dumbed down" for mass appeal with an uncomfortable mix of educational lecture, flag-waving old-time pop songs and a too-brief taste of hard rock—but this is probably the only place where you'll see computer-animated laser imaging projected onto an 800-foot-high limestone canyon wall. Spectacular.

On the other side of Pikes Peak, Cripple Creek is one of the three historic mining towns where casino gambling ($5-per-bet limit) is legal. All of its 25 gambling casinos are located along three blocks of Bennett Avenue.

PIKES PEAK AREA PARKS

Pike National Forest—This forest, which includes all of Pikes Peak as well as the Rampart Range between Colorado Springs and Denver including the roadless Lost Creek Wilderness, encompasses more than 1,100,000 acres of pine, aspen and fir forests and alpine tundra. More visitors use it for recreation than any other national forest in Colorado. In the winter, the U.S. Forest Service operates a small downhill ski area beside the Pikes Peak Highway; cross-country skiing is also popular on trails near Colorado Springs.

Facilities: Picnic areas, restrooms, hiking trails, jeep and bike trails, ski area; information, 719-545-8737.

Camping: There are 56 campgrounds with a total of more than 900 RV/tent sites (no hookups); $3 to $10 per night.

Getting there: Primary access to Pike National Forest is via the Pikes Peak Highway, the Gold Camp Road between Colorado Springs and Cripple Creek, and the Rampart Range Road between Colorado Springs and Sedalia.

Meuller State Park and Wildlife Area—This 12,000-acre mountain park provides camping in the vicinity of Cripple Creek. It also has an 85-mile network of hiking trails through a variety of habitats ranging from aspen and conifer forests to spectacular rock formations and open meadows ablaze with windflowers. Abundant wildlife includes deer, elk, wild turkeys, bears and bighorn sheep.

Facilities: Picnic areas, restrooms, showers, hiking trails, ice-skating pond; day-use fee, $3; information, 719-687-2366. *Fishing:* Good for rainbow trout in Fourmile Creek.

Camping: There are 12 walk-in tent sites, $7 per night; and 78 RV/tent sites with electrical hookups, $10 per night.

Getting there: It's located three and a half miles west of Divide off of Route 67.

Pueblo-Walsenburg-Trinidad Area

Motorists heading south from the Colorado Springs area on Route 25 will find a landscape so vast and empty that it strikes a startling contrast to the busy, heavily populated Front Range corridor of northern Colorado. There are only three towns on the 140-mile route from Colorado Springs to the New Mexico state line, and none of them is generally regarded as a tourist destination. Those who prefer to avoid the interstate and stick to secondary highways will discover leisurely, scenic backroads along the base of the Sangre de Cristo Range.

Pueblo is Colorado's third-largest city; it was the second largest before Colorado Spring's prodigious growth spurt in the early 1970s. The city thrived because in 1875 the Colorado Fuel and Iron Company (later CF&I Steel), which dominated coal mining in Colorado for generations, chose this location as the site of its huge steel mill. Today it is the only Front Range city with a declining population. Except for specialty steel manufacturing on a very small scale, the mill has not operated since 1982. The mill's smokestacks stand abandoned now, and nothing moves in the network of conveyors and catwalks that link the buildings and coke ovens on the east side of Route 25. The shutdown improved air quality, but the economy has not yet fully recovered.

Certainly Pueblo's top sightseeing highlight is **Rosemont** (419 West 14th Street; 719-545-5290; admission). This three-story, 37-room stone mansion, one of the grandest in Colorado, was built for a banker in 1893. On display in the servants' quarters, the McClelland Collection of curiosities from around the world strikes a fun-loving counterpoint to the opulence of Rosemont's polished wood-and-marble interiors. Look for the rose motif, which appears somewhere in each room of the home.

At the northeast end of Pueblo's historic district, the modern **Sangre de Cristo Arts and Conference Center** (210 North Santa Fe Avenue; 719-543-0130) has three galleries that show changing exhibits, works by regional artists and shows on national tour, as well as a permanent collection of western art. There are also a children's museum and a theater that presents local theater and dance productions.

Perhaps the most unique sight in Pueblo, even more astonishing than the abandoned steel mill, is the **Pueblo Levee Mural Project**. Sixty feet high and four and a half miles long, the levee that conducts the Arkansas River through Pueblo was a graffiti-riddled eyesore until 1980, when the city began inviting individuals and organizations to paint sections of a continuous mural along the levee every Cinco de Mayo, recycling surplus paint that has been collected as toxic waste. The result is one of the largest community-participation artworks ever made—and it's growing longer each year.

Aside from the lake and trails of Lathrop State Park, **Walsenburg** has little but fuel and fast food to entice travelers off the interstate. But the massive stonework of its old courthouse, high school and other buildings, quarried locally in the early 20th century, when Walsenburg was an important railroad junction, gives this unpretentious little town far from anyplace else a rare feeling of permanence.

Southwest from Walsenburg, the **Highway of Legends Scenic Byway** (Route 12) loops around the back side of the Spanish Peaks and returns to the interstate at Trinidad. The **Spanish Peaks** (12,683 feet and 13,626 feet) are the easternmost mountains in the Rockies except for Pikes Peak. The 82-mile paved highway reaches only 9941 feet in elevation as it passes between the Spanish Peaks and the Sangre de Cristos. Along the route lie lakes like mirrors, crumbled adobe ruins, abandoned mines and mills, modern vacation cabins, some of Colorado's most colorful fields of wildflowers and the strange natural formations called the **Great Dikes**, hundreds of narrow rock walls up to 100 feet high and 14 miles long. At Stonewall Gap, the road goes through a natural gateway in the dikes.

Located in the foothills and canyons below Raton Pass, the low, often stormy summit that marks Colorado's boundary with New Mexico, **Trinidad** got its start in the 1830s as a way station on the Santa Fe Trail and became a busy railhead for shipping coal from area mines. The center of town, now preserved as the **Corazon de Trinidad National Historic District**, presents a distinctive blend of New Mexican adobe construction with Colorado's Victorian architecture.

PUEBLO-WALSENBURG-TRINIDAD AREA HOTELS

A veranda, a winding staircase, inlaid wood floors and stained glass are among the elegant architectural features of the **Abriendo Inn** (300 West Abriendo Avenue; 719-544-2703, fax 719-542-4114), a 1906 foursquare-style brick mansion built by Pueblo brewery owner Martin Walter. It is centrally located in Pueblo's historic district. Each of the ten rooms is individually decorated with Victorian and Asian antiques. Moderate rates include a full gourmet breakfast.

The **Inn at Pueblo West** (201 South McCulloch Boulevard, Pueblo; 719-547-2111), a Best Western affiliate, is an attractive Spanish-style 80-room resort hotel located eight miles west of the city. Guest rooms are exceptionally spacious and feature bright, contemporary decor. Guests enjoy the use of tennis courts on the inn grounds and a golf course nearby. Deluxe.

Travelers won't be disappointed with the spacious, contemporary rooms at the 55-unit **Country Club Inn** (900 West Adams Street, Trinidad; phone/fax 719-846-2215, 800-955-2215). This motor inn with its hillside location commands a view of Trinidad and the interstate. Many of the bright, spacious rooms overlook the municipal golf course. It has an outdoor swimming pool, a jacuzzi and an exercise room. Moderate.

PUEBLO-WALSENBURG-TRINIDAD AREA RESTAURANTS

You'll find Continental cuisine at affordable prices at **La Renaissance** (217 East Routt Avenue, Pueblo; 719-543-6367), which has been operating in a converted 1886 church since the early 1970s. High ceilings and stained glass add a touch of class to the casual ambience. Specialties include baby back ribs and slow-roasted prime rib. Moderate.

Ianne's Whisky Ridge (4333 Thatcher Avenue, Pueblo; 719-564-8551) is a good Italian restaurant with white linen tablecloths and a seductive menu featuring such selections as pasta primavera, chicken piccata, veal marsala, linguini, scampi, calamari and escargot. Dinner only; moderate.

PUEBLO-WALSENBURG-TRINIDAD AREA NIGHTLIFE

Pepper's Nite Club (4109 Club Manor Drive, Pueblo; 719-542-8629), bills itself as the hottest nightclub between Denver and Albuquerque, although not everyone would agree. The club features mainly recorded music with occasional live bands. The sound is '50s, '60s and '70s pop except on Thursday, College Night, when techno-alternative music is the main attraction. Nationally known comedy acts are featured on Saturday nights. Cover.

PUEBLO-WALSENBURG-TRINIDAD AREA PARKS

Lake Pueblo State Recreation Area—Surrounded by arid prairie and limestone cliffs, with mountain views to the west, windswept Pueblo Reservoir is a favorite sailing and windsurfing lake. Swimming is prohibited in the lake but permitted in the Rock Canyon area below Pueblo Dam. The recreation area also takes in a wide strip of wild land around the lake, providing habitat for coyotes, deer, wild turkeys and many other denizens of the high plains. This backcountry is accessible via a number of hiking and horse trails.

Facilities: Picnic area, restrooms, boat ramps, marinas, cruise boat, visitors center, trails, day-use fee, $3; information, 719-561-9320. *Swimming:* Permitted below the dam. *Fishing:* Good for bass, carp, catfish and other lake species.

Camping: There are 221 RV/tent sites (no hookups); $7 to $10 per night. They are usually full on weekends; call 800-678-2267 for reservations.

Getting there: Located four miles west of the city, with access from Route 50 at the town of Pueblo West via Nichols Road or McCulloch Boulevard; also accessible from Route 96.

San Isabel National Forest—Extending as far north as Buena Vista in South Park and south to within a few miles of the New Mexico state line, this long, narrow strip of national forest contains the Sangre de Cristo Range, the Wet Mountains and the Spanish Peaks. Much of the forest is hard to reach because the Sangre de Cristos are so steep that not even jeep trails climb them. The Sangre de Cristo Wilderness, reaching from the north end of the range as far south as the Great Sand Dunes, encompasses 226,000 acres. It was the largest of the wilderness areas created by the 1993 Wilderness Act.

Facilities: Hiking trails; downhill skiing at Conquistador Ski Area; day-use fee, $3; information, 719-545-8737.

Camping: There are 48 campgrounds with a total of 1011 RV/tent sites (one campground has electrical hookups); $7 to $12 per night.

Getting there: The easiest access to the Sangre de Cristo portion of San Isabel National Forest is via several unpaved roads that run west from Westcliffe into the mountains. Wet Mountain access is via Route 165. Access to the Spanish Peaks unit of the forest is via the Highway of Legends Scenic Byway (Route 12) from Trinidad.

Lathrop State Park—The park's twin lakes, Martin Lake and Horseshoe Lake, are quite small, but that doesn't stop Walsenburg-area residents from flocking here for waterskiing, sailboarding and fishing. A hiking trail wanders among rock formations on its way up to a hogback ridge, and the campground offers a view across Martin Lake to the Spanish Peaks. Its convenience to Route 25 makes Lathrop State Park a welcome oasis on a long, desolate highway drive.

Facilities: Picnic area, restrooms, showers, visitors center, boat ramp, hiking and bike trails, golf course; day-use fee, $3; information, 719-738-2376. *Swimming:* Permitted. *Fishing:* Good for rainbow trout, bass, catfish, walleye and tiger muskie.

Camping: 97 RV/tent sites (most with hookups); $6 to $10 per night.

Getting there: Located off Route 160, three miles west of Walsenburg.

Trinidad State Recreation Area—Trinidad Lake, which hides old coal mines in its depths, offers fishing, boating and windsurfing in the pretty Purgatoire River Valley above the town of Trinidad. Nine miles of backcountry hiking trails within the park take you among hills studded with piñon and juniper. They connect with a vast network of jeep roads and trails into the surrounding San Isabel National Forest.

Facilities: Picnic area, restrooms, boat ramp, hiking trails; day-use fee, $3; information, 719-846-6951. *Fishing:* Good for rainbow trout, walleye, largemouth bass, channel catfish and bullheads.

Camping: 62 RV/tent sites (most with hookups); $7 to $10 per night.

Getting there: Located four miles west of Trinidad on Route 12.

The Sporting Life

FISHING

Most fishing along the Front Range is in warm-water reservoirs such as Cherry Creek Lake and Chatfield Lake near Denver, Horsetooth Reservoir near Fort Collins, Pueblo Reservoir near Pueblo and Trinidad Lake near Trinidad. The catch in these lakes can include largemouth bass, channel catfish, pike, bluegill, carp, bullhead, perch and crappie.

BOATING, WINDSURFING AND WATERSKIING

Sailboats, power boats, fishing boats and pontoon boats, as well as sailboards and jet skis, are rented at **Cherry Creek Marina** (303-779-6144) for use on Cherry Creek Reservoir south of Denver. Rentals are also available at **Chatfield Marina** (303-791-7547) on Chatfield Reservoir.

RIVER RAFTING

Gentle river rafting is available right in Denver at **Platte River Rafting** (2200 7th Street; 303-477-0379). The Arkansas River above Cañon City, including but not limited to the Royal Gorge, is the busiest whitewater-rafting river in the state. More than 40 rafting companies use it. Among them are Cañon City's **Arkansas River Outfitters** (719-275-3229), **Brown's Royal Gorge Rafting Tours** (719-275-5161), **Royal Gorge River Adventures** (719-269-3700) and **Sierra Outfitters** (719-275-0128).

BALLOONING

Life Cycle Balloon Adventures (2540 South Steele Street, Denver; 303-759-3907) offers daily champagne flights along the Front Range. North of Denver, **Air Boulder** (3345 15th Street, Boulder; 303-442-5253) conducts sunrise balloon flights followed by a champagne picnic breakfast.

SKIING

The mountains along the Front Range have no large ski resorts. Since winter storms that approach from the west dump most of their snow along the Continental Divide, snowfalls along the Front Range are unreliable, and often temperatures are not low enough to hold a base of artificial snow.

WEST OF DENVER Major ski areas within easy daytrip distance of the Denver area, including Loveland Basin–Loveland Valley, Arapaho Basin, Copper Mountain Resort, Keystone and Winter Park, are described in Chapter Three, "Northern Colorado Rockies."

NORTH OF DENVER **Eldora Mountain Resort** (Nederland; 303-440-8700), near the upper end of Boulder Canyon, may be modest in size as Colorado ski areas go, but with five chairlifts and a vertical drop of 1400 feet, it is the largest ski area in the Front Range. The slopes are often packed with students from the University of Colorado, a short drive away. Open December through March.

The region's best cross country skiing trails are found within **Rocky Mountain National Park.**

PIKES PEAK AREA The Forest Service operates a small ski hill with a T-bar lift, open only when natural snowfall permits, about eight miles up the Pikes Peak Highway. For real downhill skiing, though, the ski areas closest to the area are Breckenridge, 150 miles away (see Chapter Three, "Northern Colorado Rockies") and Monarch, 120 miles away (See Chapter Four, "Southern Colorado Rockies").

The best cross-country skiing is found at **The Crags** and **Meuller State Park**, both off Route 68 on the west side of Pikes Peak en route to Cripple Creek.

SKI RENTALS Downhill and cross-country ski rentals, as well as snowboard rentals are available in Denver at many locations, including **Breeze Ski Rentals** (405 Urban Street #205, Lakewood; central reservations: 303-980-1223), with seven locations in the greater Denver area, and Sports Rent (560 South Holly Street, Denver; 303-320-0222). Cross-country skis and guided tours within Rocky Mountain National Park are available at **Colorado Wilderness Sports** (3587 East Elkhorn Avenue, Estes Park; 970-586-6548).

In Colorado Springs, nordic ski rentals are available at **Mountain Chalet** (226 North Tejon Street; 719-633-0732).

ICE SKATING

Evergreen Lake (303-674-2677), just west of the town of Evergreen, is one of the most popular outdoor ice-skating spots in the state. Skate rentals are available at the lake. Fort Collins has a fine indoor ice rink, open year-round, at the **Edora Pool Ice Center** (1801 Riverside Drive; 970-221-6679). Colorado Springs has a downtown skating rink under an atrium at the **Plaza Ice Chalet** (111 South Tejon Street; 719-633-2423). **The Broadmoor Ice Arena** (Broadmoor Hotel, Colorado Springs; 719-634-7711) is open to the public for limited hours; this is where many Olympic gold-medal winners such as Peggy Fleming trained under Broadmoor Hotel sponsorship.

GOLF

DENVER Denver has 40 golf courses. Those open to the general public include **City Park Golf Course** (East 25th Avenue at York Street; 303-295-4420), the **Harvard Gulch Golf Course** (East Iliff Street at South Clarkson Street; 303-698-4078), **Kennedy Golf Course** (10500 East Hampden Avenue; 303-751-0311), **Overland Park Golf Course** (South Santa Fe Drive at Jewell Street; 303-698-4975), **Wellshire Country Club** (3333 South Colorado Boulevard; 303-692-5636), **Park Hill Golf Course** (Colorado Boulevard at 35th Avenue; 303-333-5411) and the beautiful **Arrowhead Golf Club** (10850 West Sundown Trail, Littleton; 303-973-9614) in Roxborough State Park.

WEST OF DENVER In the mountains within an hour's drive west of Denver are Evergreen's nine-hole **Evergreen Golf Course** (29614 Upper Bear Creek Road; 303-674-4128) and the **Hiwan Golf Club** (303-674-3366; prior arrangements necessary), one of the region's finest golf courses.

NORTH OF DENVER In Boulder, there are the **Lake Valley Golf Course** (Route 36 at Neva Road; 970-442-7851) and the beautiful **Flatirons Golf Course** (5706 Arapahoe Avenue; 970-442-7851). Fort Collins has the **Collindale Golf Course** (1441 East Horsetooth Road; 970-221-6651). In Estes Park there's the **Estes Park Golf Club** (1080 South St. Vrain Avenue; 970-586-8146) and the nine-hole **Lake Estes Executive Course** (690 Big Thompson Avenue; 970-586-8176).

COLORADO SPRINGS AREA Public courses in Colorado Springs include the **Patty Jewett Golf Course** (900 East Española Street; 719-578-6825), **Pine Creek Golf Club** (9850 Divot Trail; 719-594-9999) and **Valley Hi Municipal Golf Course** (610 South Chelton Road; 719-578-6351).

PIKES PEAK AREA In Cañon City, the **Shadow Hills Country Club Golf Course** (1232 County Road 143; 719-275-0603) is open to the public on weekdays, members-only until 3 p.m. on weekends.

PUEBLO-WALSENBURG-TRINIDAD AREA Pueblo has the **Walking Stick Golf Course** (4301 Walking Stick Boulevard; 719-584-3400), **City Park Golf**

Course (3900 Thatcher Avenue; 719-561-4946) and **Pueblo West Golf Club** (Route 50 at McCullock Boulevard; 719-547-2280).

TENNIS

Denver has courts at **City Park** (23rd and York streets) and **Washington Park** (East Louisiana Avenue at South Humboldt Street). For a complete listing, call Denver Parks and Recreation (303-964-2522). In Boulder, look for courts at **Chautauqua Park** (9th Street at Baseline Road) and the **North Boulder Recreation Center** (3170 North Broadway; 303-441-3444). Fort Collins has courts at **Warren Park** (Lemay Street at Horsetooth Road). Estes Park has municipal courts at **Stanley Park** (Community Drive). Colorado Springs has public tennis courts at **Monument Valley Park** (Monument Creek; 719-578-6636), **Bear Creek Regional Park** (21st Street at Argus) and **Memorial Park** (East Pikes Peak Avenue at Hancock Street; 719-578-6676).

HORSEBACK RIDING

DENVER In the Denver area, horseback-riding tours are available at **Stockton's Plum Creek Stables** (7479 West Titan Road, Littleton; 303-791-1966).

NORTH OF DENVER Near Boulder, horses can be rented at **Bar-A Stables** (6000 West Coal Creek Drive, Superior; 303-499-4464). In Fort Collins, rentals are available at **Double Diamond Stables** (Lory State Park; 970-224-4200) for riding on trails within the park. The Estes Park area has a plethora of riding stables, including **Cowpoke Corner Corral** (YMCA Road, Estes Park; 970-586-5980), **Elkhorn Stables** (650 West Elkhorn Avenue, Estes Park; 970-586-3291), **Moraine Park Stables** (Rocky Mountain National Park; 970-586-2327) and **National Park Village Stables** (Fall River Road, Rocky Mountain National Park; 970-586-5890).

COLORADO SPRINGS AREA Horses for riding in the Garden of the Gods may be rented at **Academy Riding Stables** (4 El Paso Boulevard, Colorado Springs; 719-633-5667).

PIKES PEAK AREA Near Cañon City, public stables are located on **Indian Springs Ranch** (Indian Springs; 719-372-3907).

BICYCLING

DENVER Denver has an extensive urban trail system. Though shared with hikers, joggers and equestrians, the more than 100 miles of trails that reach out from the city as far as Chatfield and Cherry Creek state recreation areas are smooth, fairly level and perfect for cycling. Detailed trail maps are available from the **Colorado Division of Parks and Outdoor Recreation** (1313 Sherman Street #618, Denver; 303-866-3437).

WEST OF DENVER **Elk Meadows County Park** (Evergreen; 303-278-5925) north of Evergreen has six miles of trails through varied terrain that are used by hundreds of mountain bikers daily (mostly local residents).

NORTH OF DENVER The **Boulder Creekpath** forms the main artery of a 50-mile bicycle trail system throughout the Boulder area.

PIKES PEAK AREA Several multiple-use trails off **Gold Camp Road** above the junction with North Cheyenne Canyon Road are popular for mountain biking. A great area for dirt-road bike touring is the **Rampart Range Road** between the Garden of the Gods and the mountain town of Woodland Park. West of Cañon City, the three-mile **Tunnel Drive**, which leads to an overlook near Royal Gorge, has been closed to motor vehicles and is now a popular bike route.

PUEBLO-WALSENBURG-TRINIDAD AREA The **Pueblo Greenway** offers 30 miles of multiple-use trails suitable for biking along the Arkansas River, from Lake Pueblo east through Pueblo.

BIKE RENTALS Oddly, it is difficult to find bicycles for rent in Denver, though mountain-bike rentals are a big industry in many other areas of the state. You can rent both touring bikes and mountain bikes in Boulder at **Cycle Logic** (2525 Arapahoe Avenue; 303-443-0061) and **University Bicycles** (839 Pearl Street; 303-444-4196). **Eldora Mountain Resort** (Nederland; 303-440-8700) also rents mountain bikes. In Colorado Springs, mountain bikes are for rent at **Criterium Bike Shop** (826 North Tejon Street; 719-475-0149).

HIKING

All distances listed for hiking trails are one-way unless otherwise noted.

DENVER **Roxborough State Park** near Littleton, a southwestern suburb of Denver, has a network of trails through the canyons formed between tall sandstone ridges. Although the longest trails run for only a mile or so one way, they interconnect to create hikes of up to eight miles. **Castlewood Canyon State Park** has a number of interconnected trails totaling about four miles through a green canyon carved into the prairie near Franktown, a southeastern suburb.

WEST OF DENVER Nearly ten miles of trails meander among the eroded sandstone formations of Morrison's **Red Rocks State Park**. In the Evergreen area, **Elk Meadows County Park** has an easy six-mile loop trail through mountain meadows and ponderosa-covered mountainsides shared by hikers, joggers and bikers.

Golden Gate Canyon State Park, which lies between Golden and Central City, offers more than 80 miles of hiking trails through dramatic canyon country. Arapaho National Forest in the vicinity of Idaho Springs and Georgetown has a truly vast trail network. Among the best trails are the four-mile **Chicago Lakes Trail** from Echo Lake on the Mount Evans Highway, the 12-mile climb from the Echo Lake trailhead to the summit of **Mount Evans** (12 miles) and the five-mile trail to the twin summits of **Grays Peak and Torreys Peak** from the trailhead on Stevens Gulch Road west of Georgetown. One of the easiest ways to climb to the summit of a 14,000-foot mountain is to hike the **Mount Bierstadt Trail** (2.5 miles) from Guanella Pass above Georgetown.

NORTH OF DENVER The mountains on Boulder's western edge, including Boulder Mountain Park, offer some of the most accessible hiking trails in the Front

Range. Major trailheads at Chautauqua Park and at Sunrise Amphitheater on Flagstaff Mountain provide access to such backcountry routes as the **Enchanted Mesa Trail** (3 miles) and longer trails leading to the Flatirons. There is also good hiking just outside the city in Sunshine Canyon, at the west end of Mapleton Street.

In the Poudre River Canyon west of Fort Collins, the **Greyrock Trail** (3 miles) makes a steep climb to a spectacular viewpoint overlooking the canyon and the lofty mountain ranges to the west.

Rangers estimate that only 15 percent of visitors to Rocky Mountain National Park venture more than a quarter-mile from their cars. Considering how many people visit the park on a typical summer day, this still means that the main trails see heavy use. You may never find solitude, but you will find hundreds of miles of alpine trails through mountain scenery as spectacular as any you can imagine. Among the great trails in the national park are the fairly easy **Bridal Veil Falls Trail** (6 miles), near the north boundary of the park; the hike from the **Flattop Trail** starting at Bear Lake on the **Fern Lake Trail** (a total one-way hike of about 6 miles); and the climb to the summit of Longs Peak by either the more popular **East Longs Peak Trail** (8 miles) or the longer, less crowded **North Longs Peak Trail** (9 miles), which merges with the East Longs Peak Trail about three miles below the summit.

COLORADO SPRINGS AREA On the southwestern edge of Colorado Springs, North Cheyenne Canyon has several outstanding, easy-to-reach trails. The **Mount Cutler Trail** (1.75 miles) climbs 500 feet from the middle part of the canyon up to the ridge between North and South Cheyenne canyons for a view of Seven Falls; the **Columbine Trail** (5 miles) runs the length of the canyon from its lower end to Helen Hunt Falls.

PIKES PEAK AREA The ultimate Colorado Springs–area hike is the **Barr Trail** (17 miles) from Manitou Springs to the summit of Pikes Peak. The first three miles of the trail, from the Pikes Peak Cog Railway parking lot on Ruxton Avenue to the top of Mount Manitou, is the steepest portion. From there it's an easy ridgeline walk to Barr Camp at timberline on the east face of Pikes Peak. The last few miles of switchbacks, up rocky alpine slopes, are difficult not so much because the trail is steep as because the air is thin. There is also a short trail up Pikes Peak from The Crags, a National Forest campground on a marked dirt road off Route 67 on the west face of the peak near Cripple Creek.

Near Cripple Creek, Meuller State Park has a 85-mile network of hiking trails, ranging from the easy, spectacular **Outlook Ridge Trail** (2 miles) to the long, strenuous **Four Mile Overlook Trail** (9 miles), which commands dramatic views of remote Four Mile Canyon.

PUEBLO-WALSENBURG-TRINIDAD AREA In San Isabel National Forest, the short, steep **West Spanish Peak Trail** (3 miles) to the 13,626-foot summit west of Trinidad is one of several outstanding trails among the Spanish Peaks. A longer but easier trail, the **Wahatoya Trail** (10 miles), climbs over the saddle between the two peaks; the distance from the trailhead on Huahatolla Valley Road to the upper ridge is four miles, and from there it is possible to leave the established trail and scramble across rocky alpine terrain to the summit of **East Spanish Peak**.

Transportation

BY CAR

Every place described in this chapter is within about an hour's drive from **Route 25**, which traces the edge of the Rockies northward to Fort Collins and Cheyenne, Wyoming, and southward to Colorado Springs, Pueblo and Trinidad. Route 25 intersects east-west **Route 70** in Denver. Following Route 70 West will take you to Idaho Springs, Georgetown and Central City.

Boulder is reached via **Route 36**, which runs northwest from Denver. This highway continues into the mountains, ending in Estes Park.

BY AIR

The state-of-the-art **Denver International Airport** (known as "DIA"), completed in October 1993, ranks as the world's largest airport, covering an area of 53 square miles—twice the size of Manhattan. At $5 billion, it is the most expensive airport ever built, yet it actually handles fewer flights than the old airport it replaced did.

Denver International Airport is served by America West, American Airlines, Continental Airlines, Delta Air Lines, Great Lakes Airlines, Mexicana, Trans World Airlines, United Airlines and USAir, as well as the commuter carriers Mesa Airlines, Continental Express and United Express.

Airport transportation from Denver International Airport is by taxi or shuttle. The **Airporter** (303-321-3222) runs shuttle vans from the airport to downtown hotels every 15 minutes and to southeast Denver hotels every 30 minutes. The **RTD** (303-299-6000) regional bus system offers low-cost hourly bus service to and from the airport.

Boulder has no commercial air service; the **Airporter** (303-321-3222) runs hourly shuttle vans between Boulder and the Denver airport. **RTD** buses also go to the Denver airport from Boulder. Estes Park also has no airport. **Charles Tour and Travel Services** (970-586-5151, 800-950-3274) operates shuttle vans to the Denver airport.

Continental Express flies to the **Fort Collins–Loveland Municipal Airport**. Area residents take one of these commercial flights to Denver and then make connections with interstate or international flights.

Colorado Springs Airport is served by America West, American Airlines, Continental Airlines, Delta Airlines, Mesa Airlines and Trans World Airlines. **Airport Shuttle Service** (719-578-5232) shuttles air passengers to and from major hotels. **Colorado Springs Transit** (719-475-9733) provides low-cost bus service to and from the airport.

The **Pueblo Memorial Airport** has America West, Continental Express and Trans World Airlines flights; both **City Cab** (719-543-2525) and **City Bus** provide airport ground transportation.

BY TRAIN

Amtrak's "Zephyr" stops at Union Station (707 17th Street, Denver; 303-534-2812, 800-872-7245) on its run between Chicago and San Francisco. The portion of the route that crosses the Rockies between Denver and Glenwood Springs is one of the most spectacular rides on the Amtrak system. Another Amtrak train, the "Southwest Limited," cuts across southeastern Colorado with stops in Trinidad and La Junta, a farming community east of Pueblo, on its route between Chicago and Los Angeles. Call for schedule information and reservations on either train.

BY BUS

Greyhound Bus Lines serves Denver (1055 19th Street; 303-292-6111) as well as Fort Collins (Route 501 at Riverside Avenue; 970-221-1327).

RTD (Regional Transportation District; 970-299-6000) buses connect Denver with Boulder, Nederland and Longmont.

TNM&O Coaches, a Greyhound affiliate, provides service to Colorado Springs (120 South Weber Street; 719-635-1505), Pueblo (116 North Main Street; 719-544-6295) and Trinidad (639 West Main Street; 719-846-7271).

CAR RENTALS

Among the many car-rental agencies at or near the Denver and Colorado Springs airports are **A-Courtesy Rent A Car** (800-441-1816), **Alamo Rent A Car** (800-327-9633), **Avis Rent A Car** (800-331-1212), **Budget Rent A Car** (800-527-0700), **Dollar Rent A Car** (800-800-4000), **Enterprise Rent A Car** (800-325-8007), **Hertz Rent A Car** (800-654-3131) and **National Interrent** (800-328-4567). Motor homes and RVs are for rent at **Cruise America** (8950 North Federal Boulevard, Denver; 800-327-7799).

In Pueblo's airport, try **Avis Rent A Car** (800-331-1212), **Budget Rent A Car** (800-527-0700) and **Hertz Rent A Car** (800-654-3131).

PUBLIC TRANSPORTATION

RTD (Regional Transportation District) (303-299-6000) provides bus service throughout the Denver, Evergreen, Boulder and Longmont areas. Public buses in Fort Collins are operated by **Transfort** (970-221-6620). Greeley also has public bus service, called simply **The Bus** (970-353-2812). Colorado Springs municipal buses are operated by **Colorado Springs Transit** (719-475-9733). Pueblo public transportation is provided by **City Bus** (719-542-4306).

TAXIS

Major cab companies that serve the greater Denver area include **Metro Taxi** (303-333-3333), **Yellow Cab** (303-777-7777) and **Zone Cab** (303-444-8888). In Boulder, **Boulder Yellow Cab** (303-442-2277) provides taxi service. In Fort Collins, it's **Shamrock Yellow Cab** (970-224-2222). **Yellow Cab** (719-634-5000) is the local taxi company in Colorado Springs.

CHAPTER THREE

Northern Colorado Rockies

Snow—lots of it—covers the mountains of northern Colorado for about half the year. This area has a higher average elevation and more mountain peaks over 14,000 feet high than any other part of the Rockies south of the Canadian border, and the lofty summits attract snowstorms like a magnet. Aspen, for instance, receives an average annual snowfall of 300 inches; Vail averages 335 inches, Winter Park 353 inches, and Arapahoe Basin 360 inches. That's 30 *feet* of snow.

Almost all the most famous ski resorts in Colorado—Aspen, Vail, Breckenridge and Steamboat Springs, along with less-trendy local favorites like Winter Park, Arapahoe Basin, Loveland Basin, Keystone, Copper Mountain and Sunlight—share one thing in common. Like most of the other places described in this chapter, they lie within an hour's drive from Route 70.

The 148-mile stretch of freeway from the eastern edge of the mountains at Denver to the western edge at Glenwood Springs is the crowning achievement of the interstate highway system. The opening of the Eisenhower Memorial Tunnel in 1973, carrying traffic underneath the Continental Divide, and then the completion in 1993 of the Glenwood Canyon Project, the state of the art in environmentally friendly freeways, transformed Route 70 from a steep, nerve-wracking route that was often closed in winter into a busy, high-speed four-lane transcontinental truck corridor through the central Rockies, bringing every town in northern Colorado within an easy morning's drive from Denver.

Echoes of the past still linger among the peaks and gorges of the northern Colorado Rockies. Following the "Pikes Peak or Bust" gold rush of the 1860s, prospectors by the thousands scoured every creek and gulch in the high country for nuggets that might lead the way to a vein of gold. Some found it. More often, flashes of gold lured them to lodes of silver instead. Money poured out of the mountains. Communities like Leadville, Breckenridge and Aspen appeared overnight and blossomed into cities.

Then fundamental changes in the American economy ruined the precious-metals market, and the silver-lined Victorian-style towns of the high Rockies faded into oblivion. Many of them died, leaving stone chimneys, crumbling red-brick walls, slag heaps, dilapidated mine buildings and big rusted pieces of gnarled machinery strewn about the landscape against backdrops of forbidding granite peaks. Others clung to narrow ledges of survival for generations.

After half a century, Lady Luck blew another kiss to some of the region's old mining towns, in a form more unlikely than gold: downhill snow skiing, then as esoteric as bungee jumping or hang gliding today, became the most popular thrill sport in America. Steep, rugged mountain slopes and snow accumulations of up to 20 feet had always made the Rockies a forbidding place to spend the winter; now they revealed themselves as assets more valuable than silver or gold.

Today, with improved highway access, Aspen has far surpassed its gold-rush opulence. A pristine wooded valley has been transformed into Vail, the world's largest ski resort. Glenwood Springs, a long-neglected turn-of-the-century spa, has emerged as the latest recreation boom town. And Leadville, full of history but lacking tourism development, endures. With its fairytale alpine towns perched on the rooftop of America, this region is where most visitors come to bring their Rocky Mountain daydreams to vibrant life.

Winter Park–Grand Lake Area

Leaving Route 70 at Empire (Exit 233), Route 40 will take you up a sweeping series of switchbacks to the top of 11,315-foot **Berthoud Pass** and then twist down the other side of the Continental Divide into **Winter Park**, one of Colorado's most popular ski areas and one of the closest to Denver, just 67 miles away. If you're looking for a unique ski weekend and want to avoid the heavy ski-season traffic on Berthoud Pass, make reservations early for the **Winter Park Ski Train** (303-296-4754). Running from Denver's Union Station only on ski-season weekends, the train carries passengers on a scenic two-hour trip through areas that are inaccessible by road in winter. In the summer, the ski slopes at Winter Park offer chairlift rides and an **alpine slide** (970-726-5514).

With no old town to serve as a nucleus for the community, Winter Park has sprawled into a characterless town of condominiums and shopping centers where sporting goods stores are the specialty. Once virtually deserted outside of ski season, Winter Park has recently gained renown as a mountain-bike mecca thanks to its 500-mile bike trail network, one of the largest in the state. Music festivals and Saturday-night rodeos also enliven the summer season.

North of Winter Park, the highway becomes straight and level as it crosses **Middle Park**, one of Colorado's three broad "parks"—high, grassy plains that form bowls in the surrounding mountains. North Park lies straight ahead, while

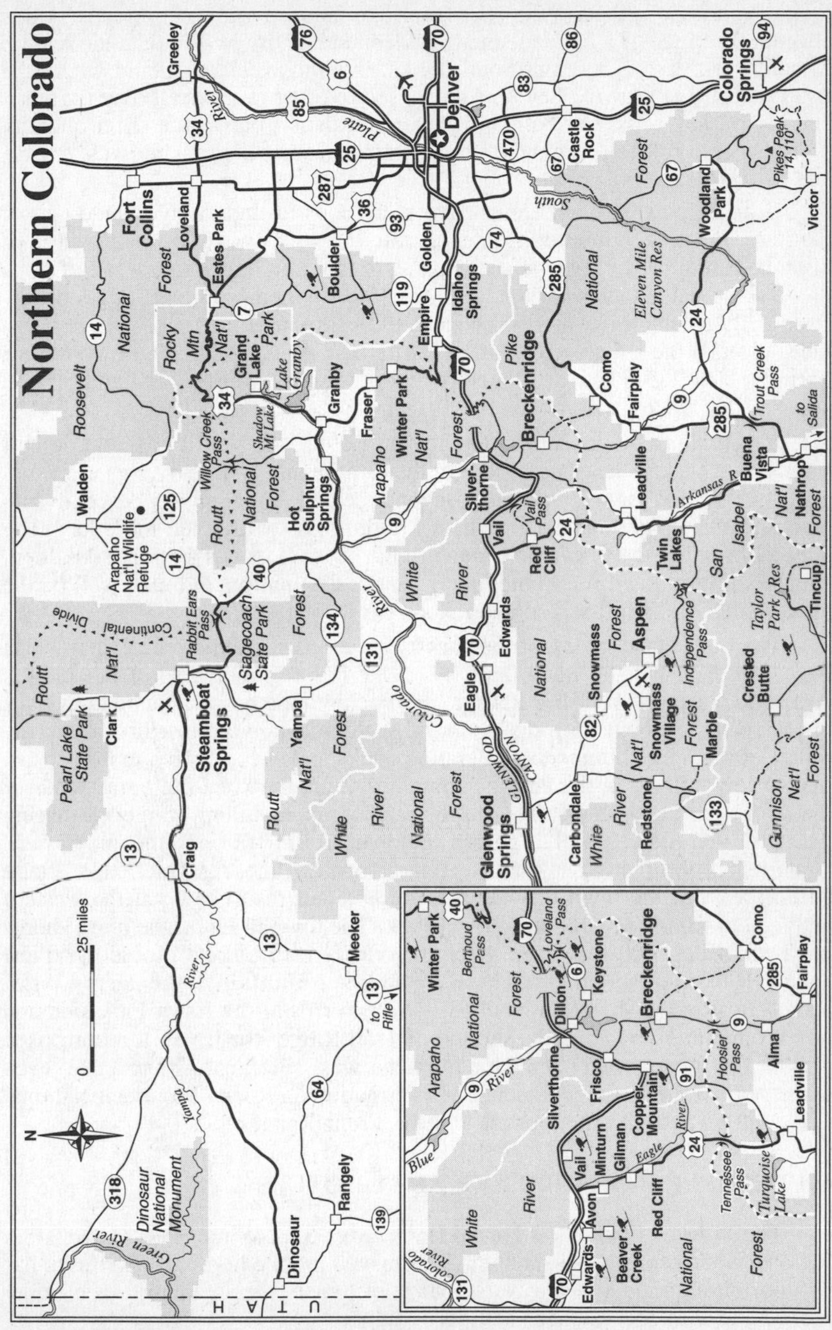
Northern Colorado
25 miles
Greeley
Fort Collins
Loveland
Estes Park
Boulder
Golden
Denver
Idaho Springs
Empire
Castle Rock
Colorado Springs
Woodland Park
Victor
Pikes Peak 14,110'
Eleven Mile Canyon Res
Walden
Arapaho Nat'l Wildlife Refuge
Rabbit Ears Pass
Willow Creek Pass
Grand Lake
Lake Granby
Shadow Mt Lake
Granby
Fraser
Winter Park
Hot Sulphur Springs
Stagecoach State Park
Steamboat Springs
Clark
Pearl Lake State Park
Yampa
Craig
Meeker
to Rifle
Rangely
Dinosaur
Dinosaur National Monument
Green River
Yampa River
UTAH
Continental Divide
Rocky Mtn Nat'l Park
Roosevelt National Forest
Routt National Forest
Arapaho Nat'l Forest
White River National Forest
Pike National Forest
San Isabel Nat'l Forest
Gunnison Nat'l Forest
Silverthorne
Breckenridge
Como
Fairplay
Vail
Vail Pass
Red Cliff
Leadville
Twin Lakes
Buena Vista
Nathrop
to Salida
Trout Creek Pass
Arkansas R.
Edwards
Eagle
Glenwood Springs
Glenwood Canyon
Colorado River
South Platte River
Carbondale
Redstone
Marble
Snowmass
Snowmass Village
Aspen
Independence Pass
Crested Butte
Taylor Park Res
Tincup
Arapaho National Forest
Berthoud Pass
Loveland Pass
Keystone
Dillon
Frisco
Copper Mountain
Hoosier Pass
Alma
Minturn
Gilman
Eagle River
Avon
Beaver Creek
Tennessee Pass
Turquoise Lake
Blue River
White River National Forest

South Park is described in the "Breckenridge–South Park" section later in this chapter. The idea of a huge mountain park sounds more idyllic than the reality. Middle Park, like North and South Parks, is windswept ranchland where the main industry is growing hay for sale as feed to other ranches all over the state. Haystacks, hay rolls, hay bails in heaps taller than a barn—the sheer quantity of hay visible from the highway is impressive. The park's ranch towns, **Fraser** and **Granby**, are not.

Granby, however, is an important crossroads in this rarely visited part of the state. If you continue on Route 40 as it veers westward in the direction of distant Steamboat Springs, you soon come to Hot Sulphur Springs, site of a spa of the same name that was popular in the 1920s, when trainloads of people arrived daily to take the waters. The spa's old bathhouse has fallen into decrepitude, though the owners of **Hot Sulphur Springs** (Route 40, Hot Sulphur Springs; 970-725-3306) still operate an outdoor swimming pool and private sweat baths fed by the smelly 104°F water.

If you continue north from Granby on Route 125, you'll cross the Rabbit Ears Range back to the eastern slope of the Continental Divide over gentle, pine-clad 9621-foot Willow Creek Pass. Beyond the pass, the highway descends into **North Park**, bigger and broader than Middle Park, with even more hay. The only town in North Park large enough to have a café or gas station is **Walden**, which is not on the direct route to any tourist destination and may well be the least-visited town in the Colorado Rockies.

The only place in any of the parks where you can experience what North Park, Middle Park and South Park were like before the arrival of ranching is **Arapaho National Wildlife Refuge** (★), occupying a broad area on both sides of the road for about 15 miles south of Walden. Many ponds throughout the refuge attract large numbers of migrating ducks and geese, which in turn attract quite a few hunters in the fall; in summer, though, the knee-high grasslands of the refuge are home to nearly 300 species of birds, including songbirds darting wherever you look as well as grouse and quail trotting through the underbrush. Upon reaching the highway intersection at Granby, most travelers take Route 34 northeast to the town of **Grand Lake**, a small resort town at the western entrance to Rocky Mountain National Park. The town is set on the north shores of 12-mile-long, 400-foot-deep, glacier-carved **Grand Lake**, Colorado's largest natural lake, and the larger, manmade **Shadow Mountain Lake** nearby. Most visitors to Rocky Mountain National Park enter from the Estes Park side and turn around after reaching the summit of Trail Ridge Road; you'll be surprised at how few people enter the park from the west side near Grand Lake, even at the peak of the summer season. For information on Rocky Mountain National Park, see Chapter Two, "Denver and the Front Range."

WINTER PARK–GRAND LAKE AREA HOTELS

The **Winter Park AYH Hostel** (P.O. Box 3323, Winter Park, CO 80482; 970-726-5356) consists of six humbly furnished mobile homes. Each trailer has two dormitory rooms with two to four bunks each. Occupants of each trailer share bathroom and kitchen facilities. Budget.

Winter Park offers a vast array of accommodations in all price ranges. The town is packed to capacity on winter weekends but has an abundance of lodging at other times. As at many ski resorts, room rates tend to be expensive in winter but drop by as much as 50 percent in summer. Among the several luxury ski lodges there, the **Iron Horse Resort** (P.O. Box 1286, Winter Park, CO 80482; 970-726-8851, 800-621-8190) stands out because of its easy access to the main trail between the Winter Park and Mary Jane ski areas, affording from-your-doorstep skiing in winter and boundless biking or jogging possibilities in summer. It also has an indoor-outdoor pool and four open-air hot tubs. The 120 rooms and suites in this modern lodge have fireplaces, balconies and kitchenettes with microwave ovens. Rooms are done in cheerfully contemporary southwestern decor. Ultra-deluxe.

Affordability and Old World ambience combine at **Gasthaus Eichler** (78786 Route 40, Winter Park; 970-726-5133, 800-543-3899), an exact replica of a charming little alpine inn in Germany. The 15 cozy rooms have down comforters on the beds, lace curtains on the windows and a host of other homey touches. Moderate.

Winter Park has a number of small, two- or three-room bed and breakfasts close to the ski slopes. All are in modern homes since there's little historic architecture in the area. Representative of the type is the wonderful little **Aspen Rose** (244 Forest Trail Road; 970-726-5039). Operated during ski season and the spring and fall shoulder seasons, the Aspen Rose offers four guest rooms lovingly decorated with European country furnishings and flowery wallpaper. Moderate.

Winter Park also has many rental condominiums. For information and reservations, call **Winter Park Central Reservations** (970-726-5587, 303-447-0588, 800-453-2525).

Although Granby itself is a cattle-shipping town with little to interest visitors aside from a sprinkling of budget-priced independent motels, a number of ranches in the area have evolved into first-class dude ranches. Located seven miles west of Granby, **Drowsy Water Ranch** (Route 40, Granby; 970-725-3456, 800-845-2292) specializes in horseback riding, from beginners' lessons to all-day pack trips. The ranch also has a swimming pool, a hot tub and fishing ponds. Accommodations are in nine cabins and eight guest rooms in the main lodge, originally built as a ranch house in the 1920s and recently renovated. While this is by no means the most expensive guest ranch in the Granby area, rates are in the ultra-deluxe range, and minimum-stay requirements apply in midsummer.

The **Grand Lake Lodge** (15500 Route 34, Grand Lake; 970-627-3967), a historic mountain lodge built in 1925, offers fabulous views of Grand Lake and Shadow Mountain Lake from its hillside vantage point. Amenities include an outdoor swimming pool overlooking the valley below and a huge lobby fireplace to chase away the evening chill. Accommodations are in 66 rustic two-room cabins, some with kitchenettes. Moderate.

Built from rough-hewn logs and local stone, **Shadowcliff Lodge** (P.O. Box 658, Grand Lake, CO 80447; 970-627-9220) overlooks Grand Lake from an even more spectacular location at the top of a cliff. While there are three individual cabins with kitchenettes and fireplaces (bring your own sheets), most accommodations are in the 19 lodge rooms containing four to eight bunk beds each and in youth hostel–style dorms. Budget.

WINTER PARK–GRAND LAKE AREA RESTAURANTS

Winter Park specializes in food with a German accent. For one of the finest dinners in town, make reservations at the **Gasthaus Eichler** (Route 40; 970-726-5133). Situated on the ground floor of the small inn of the same name, the dining room has a distinctly Old World feeling and serves the most authentic *rindsrouladen*, *jägerschnitzel* and *kassler rippchen* in the Colorado ski country. Closed in summer. Deluxe.

The café-style **Carver Brothers Bakery** (behind Cooper Creek Square, Winter Park; 970-726-8202) serves pastries, gourmet coffee, full breakfasts and, for lunch, soups, salads and submarine sandwiches. For dinner, served during ski season only, you can choose from a menu including steaks, chicken and veal prepared in a variety of ways, as well as pastas. Budget to moderate.

In Grand Lake, the **Grand Lake Lodge Restaurant** (Route 34; 970-627-3967) lets you enjoy a fantastic view of Grand Lake and Shadow Mountain Lake along with your breakfast buffet, pasta luncheon special or elegant dinner. Nightly chef's specials include fish, lamb, wild-game entrées and steaks. Moderate.

In a restored 90-year-old historic lodge with a whitewater view of the Blue River, **The Rapids Restaurant** (209 Rapids Lane, Grand Lake; 970-627-3707) features gourmet Italian cuisine like spaghetti with sausage, fettuccine Alfredo and scampi. All meals are served with an appetizer tray of boiled shrimp, beef pâté and salmon mousse, a caesar salad, and sorbet for dessert. Deluxe.

A long-established local favorite in Grand Lake, the **Mountain Inn** (612 Grand Avenue; 970-627-3385) is in a cozy old knotty-pine log inn warmed by a big wood-burning stove. Choose from a charbroiled New York strip steak, a beef kebab, trout amandine or barbecued chicken. All meals are served with soup, salad, biscuits and ice cream. Moderate.

Fine dining is surprisingly affordable at **Caroline's Cuisine** (9921 Route 34, Grand Lake; 970-627-9404). This casually elegant restaurant in the round alongside the headwaters of the Colorado River, north of Grand Lake, is worth the drive for its imaginative presentations of shellfish, duck and veal as well as roast beef, filet mignon and pasta dishes. Moderate to deluxe.

WINTER PARK–GRAND LAKE AREA SHOPPING

This is not an area for recreational shopping, unless you're interested in sporting goods, available in abundance at Winter Park's shopping centers. For souvenirs, the **West Portal Galleria**, at the base of Winter Park Mountain, has T-shirts and other inexpensive curios.

In Grand Lake, an attractive shop on the lakefront boardwalk is the long-established **Gallery of Western Art** (1114 Grand Avenue; 970-627-3339), featuring Native American art, designer jewelry and southwestern fashions.

WINTER PARK–GRAND LAKE AREA NIGHTLIFE

In ski season you'll find live music most evenings at a number of lively après-ski bars. In Winter Park these include **The Slope** (Route 40; 970-726-5727), **The Derailer** (Winter Park Resort; 970-726-5514) and **Stampede** (Cooper Creek Square; 970-726-9433). The most popular partying bar in the valley is the **Crooked Creek Saloon** (Route 40, Fraser; 970-726-9250), a rock-and-roll roadhouse in nearby Fraser where mountain bikers meet the local cowboys, get rowdy and remain so until 2 a.m.

The repertory group at the **Theatre in Grand Lake** (Grand Avenue; 970-627-8971) presents five light, contemporary plays nightly throughout the summer. Otherwise, when it comes to nightlife, Grand Lake is on the slow side. But you'll find a western atmosphere and live country bands on weekends at the **Lariat Saloon** (1121 Grand Avenue; 970-627-9965) and down the street at the historic **Stagecoach Inn** (920 Grand Avenue; 970-627-9932).

WINTER PARK–GRAND LAKE AREA PARKS

Arapaho National Recreation Area—The recreational area surrounds Lake Granby, the largest of the recreational lakes in the Grand Lake area, as well as Shadow Mountain Lake, Willow Creek Reservoir and the smaller, more remote Monarch Lake, Strawberry Lake and Meadow Creek Reservoir. It also provides trailhead access to the Indian Peaks Wilderness in Arapaho National Forest on the Roaring Fork, Cascade Creek, Columbine Lake and other high-country trails.

Facilities: Picnic areas, restrooms, boat ramps, marina, mountain-biking and hiking trails; information, 970-887-3331. *Fishing:* Good for rainbow trout, Snake River cutthroat and kokanee salmon. Mackinaw upwards of 30 pounds have been pulled from the depths of Lake Granby.

Camping: Twenty campgrounds offer a total of 602 RV/tent sites (no hookups); $8 to $10 per night.

Getting there: The main access roads turn off Route 34 westward to Willow Creek Reservoir and eastward to Lake Granby five miles north of Granby.

Breckenridge–South Park Area

Continuing westward on Route 70, about 60 miles west of Denver, you reach the **Eisenhower Memorial Tunnel**, a 9000-foot tunnel carved through a formerly impassable ridgeline on the Continental Divide. When it was opened in 1973, the tunnel streamlined travel on Route 70, which had previously been routed over 11,992-foot **Loveland Pass** to the south. You can still take paved Route 6 over the old pass, now a relatively traffic-free scenic route. Along the old route, three ski areas—**Loveland Basin–Loveland Valley** (303-569-3203), on the east side of the Continental Divide; **Arapahoe Basin** (970-468-0718), on the west side; and **Keystone Resort** (970-468-4300), midway between the pass and Dillon Reservoir—rank as the busiest slopes in Colorado. Keystone operates a chairlift for hikers and sightseers during the summer.

Route 70 and the Loveland Pass Road merge again at the foot of the pass beside **Dillon Reservoir**. The west shore of the reservoir has grown into a rather bland, conformist sprawl of townhouses and shopping centers making up the communities of Dillon, Silverthorne and Frisco.

From Frisco, take Route 9 south for ten miles to reach the town and ski area of **Breckenridge**. If ever a mountain town was at risk of becoming "another Aspen," in both the best and worst senses of the term, it is Breckenridge. It is the closest major ski resort to the fast-growing Colorado Springs area, less than two hours' drive away. It is even closer to Denver—not quite as close as Winter Park, Arapaho Basin, Loveland Basin, Copper Mountain or Keystone—but the town's personality makes the longer drive worth it for many Denverites. As a result, it sometimes gets very crowded. From Thanksgiving through the end of March, skiers descend on Breckenridge in astonishing numbers every weekend, packing the miles of parking lots that lie between the streets of town and the ski slopes, creating long lift lines and bumper-to-bumper traffic up and down Main Street.

If at all possible, plan your ski trip to Breckenridge during the week, when overcrowding is not a problem, in order to really enjoy your stay. This former gold- and silver-mining town of stately old Victorian homes painted in wild color combinations, often refurbished with Tyrolean-style decorative trim, seems to be the community of choice for ski instructors, restauranteurs, innkeepers and others who choose to relocate from the Alps to the Rockies. At any time of year German and the Scandinavian languages are commonly heard on the streets and in the coffee shops.

Breckenridge has a kind of theme-park quality in the summer months, when the ski mountains are transformed into thrill rides. The **SuperChair** (970-453-5000; admission) chairlift runs to the top of the Peak 8 ski slope, providing easy access to trails through 11,000-foot-high alpine meadows for hiking, mountain biking and horseback riding (there is a rental stable on Peak 8). When you're ready to head back down the mountain, consider the **Super Slide** (admission). Adults and children alike plunge down the mountainside on wheeled sleds via a fiberglass chute, at speeds of up to 40 miles per hour—it's like riding a roller coaster that's entirely downhill. And if that's not enough family fun for one day, at the foot of Peak 8 is **Amaze'n Breckenridge** (970-453-7262; admission), Colorado's largest human maze, covering 10,000 square feet and containing more than a mile of passageways; an observation deck above gives you the opportunity to giggle at family members as they get themselves hopelessly lost.

As you continue south from Breckenridge on Route 9, you face a series of sudden, tight switchback curves that makes its way up a steep mountain slope to the summit of 11,541-foot Hoosier Pass on the Continental Divide.

A scenic unpaved alternative to the highway over Hoosier Pass is the **Boreas Pass Road** (★), a wide and well-maintained gravel road that follows an old narrow-gauge railroad route as it gradually climbs above timberline to cross the Continental Divide at an elevation of 11,482 feet. Remains of old ranches and railroad buildings dot the roadside on this spectacular drive, which brings you out at the ghost town of **Como**, northeast of Fairplay on Route 285.

A few miles south of Hoosier Pass, at the tiny town of Alma, take unpaved County Road 8 and then Forest Road 415 for a total distance of about six miles to the **Bristlecone Pine Scenic Area** (★), one of several alpine areas in Colorado where these stunted, slow-growing trees are twisted by the wind into fantastic and grotesque shapes. The trees are some of the oldest living organisms on earth. Some have been determined to be almost 5000 years old—twice as old as California's giant redwoods.

A favorite jeep route in the South Park region, the **Mosquito Pass Road** (★) lumbers from Alma over a 13,188-foot pass, then descends into Leadville. The first seven miles of the road, past the remains of old mines and the ghost town of **Park City**, are usually fine for passenger cars; the last three miles to the pass summit are steep and rocky and can be negotiated only by high-clearance, four-wheel-drive vehicles.

The next town down Route 9, Fairplay is the site of **South Park City** (719-836-2387), an open-air museum that gives visitors glimpses into the details of everyday life during the gold-rush era. More than 30 buildings have been moved here from abandoned mining towns in the area and filled with antiques and artifacts of the time to create the quintessential Colorado ghost town. This is not one of those movie-set/tourist-trap assemblages of old western buildings; it's well worth visiting for the powerful sense of the past it evokes.

Buena Vista, ranch center for South Park and home of the Colorado State Reformatory, may not look like much, but its setting, where the high plains of South Park meet the solid wall of the **Collegiate Peaks**, defies comparison. Colorado's greatest concentration of 14,000-foot peaks stands in a row just west of Buena Vista. In the southernmost of the Collegiate Peaks is **Mount Princeton Hot Springs** (15870 County Road 162, Nathrop; 719-395-2447), where geothermal swimming pools are open to the public. Directions to Nathrop are in "Breckenridge–South Park Area Hotels," below.

Despite its windswept emptiness, South Park is an important crossroads for motorists touring Colorado. From Buena Vista, Route 24 heads east to Cripple Creek and Colorado Springs. From Salida, a small town south of Buena Vista where the main industry is whitewater rafting, Route 50 follows the Arkansas River east down a long canyon to Cañon City and Pueblo, and west over Monarch Pass to the Gunnison, while Route 285 continues south across the San Luis Valley.

BRECKENRIDGE–SOUTH PARK AREA HOTELS

The lowest-cost accommodations in the area are at **Alpen Hütte** (471 Rainbow Drive, Silverthorne; 970-468-6336), an unaffilliated hostel with 66 beds in nine spartan dormitory rooms with shared baths. The lounge area has a fireplace, and there are a reading room and a game room. Though the town of Silverthorne lacks character, a free shuttle bus runs to Breckenridge and several ski areas. Budget.

Among the upscale ski lodges in Breckenridge, it's hard to beat **The Lodge at Breckenridge Spa** (112 Overlook Drive; 970-453-9300, 800-736-1607, fax 970-453-0625), located high on a mountainside. The lodge's guest-room balconies and picture windows offer some of the most majestic mountain views you're ever likely to experience from the comfort of a luxury suite. The 45 suites, each with a kitchen and sitting room, are individually decorated in contemporary western, southwestern and European themes. The lodge has landscaped gardens and a complete spa. Ultra-deluxe.

A wide range of modern accommodations can be found at **The Village at Breckenridge** (655 South Park Street, Breckenridge; 970-453-2000, 800-800-7829, fax 970-453-3116), a huge 11-building complex that sprawls around the Peak 9 chairlift. A single reservation desk offers rooms in what is virtually a hotel shopping mall consisting of the Village Hotel (standard rooms), the Liftside Inn (studio suites), the Hotel Breckenridge (full suites), the Plaza Condominiums (standard condos) and the Châteaux (deluxe condos). Besides lodging, The Village at Breckenridge complex contains ten restaurants, a full range of shops and two health clubs with swimming pools, hot tubs, saunas, exercise rooms and racquetball courts. Ultra-deluxe.

A perennial favorite among Breckenridge's many bed and breakfasts is the **Fireside Inn** (114 North French Street; 970-453-6456), a historic 1879 home where lodgings include four private rooms decorated with antiques, including a lavish Victorian-style suite, as well as five youth-hostel dorm rooms. You meet the most fascinating assortment of people around the fireplace and the hot tub, since rates year-round (including continental breakfast in summer) range all the way from budget to ultra-deluxe.

The **Cotten House Bed and Breakfast** (102 South French Street, Breckenridge; 970-453-5509) offers three guest rooms individually decorated in Victorian, Old West and southwestern styles, in a restored 1886 home two blocks from the restaurants and shops of Main Street. A full menu breakfast is included in the moderate room rate.

Open only during the summer months, the **Trout City Inn** (Route 24/285, Buena Vista; 719-395-8433) is located on 9346-foot Trout Creek Pass eight miles east of Buena Vista. A century-old narrow-gauge train station and two old-time railroad cars have been refurbished to create four guest accommodations so authentically decorated in elegant Victorian fashion and in such a remote location that they're the next-best thing to a time machine. A full breakfast is included in the moderate rates.

Nestled among the evergreens at the foot of the dramatic Chalk Cliffs, **Mount Princeton Hot Springs Resort** (★) (15870 County Road 162, Nathrop; 719-395-2447) has been the site of one hotel after another since 1870. Today, a modern lodge and adjacent motel offer pleasant, spacious accommodations, a dining room and a spacious sun deck. Four of the largest among many hot springs in the vicinity feed the resort's three outdoor swimming pools and two private hot tubs. To find this secluded resort, drive eight miles south from Buena Vista on Route 285 to Nathrop and turn west on the well-marked county road; the resort is five miles up the unpaved road. Deluxe.

The Poor Farm Country Inn (8495 County Road 160, Salida; 719-539-3818), situated on the bank of the Arkansas River, actually once served as the county poor farm, where, for more than 50 years, indigents were sent to work for room and board. Today, it has been refurbished in light, contemporary style as a combination hostel–bed-and-breakfast inn, with a 12-bed dormitory on the top floor and five individual guest rooms—some with shared baths, others private—on the second floor. The countryside location offers trout fishing and great mountain views. Budget to moderate.

BRECKENRIDGE–SOUTH PARK AREA RESTAURANTS

Breckenridge has more than 50 restaurants, each one apparently trying to be as different as possible from the others. Northern Italian cuisine is featured at the **St. Bernard Inn** (103 South Main Street; 970-453-2572), housed in a warmly restored Victorian-era building with its original tin roof. The restaurant serves its own pasta daily as well as fresh seafood in creamy sauces. For dessert, try the tiramisu. Moderate.

In an 1893 building decorated with authentic photographs of Breckenridge during the mining era, **The Prospector** (130 South Main Street; 970-453-6858) serves good old-fashioned home-style cooking. Menu choices include meat loaf, homemade soups, pork roast and fried chicken. Breakfast specialties include *huevos rancheros* made with the hottest chili in town. Budget to moderate.

Down the street, **Poirrier's Cajun Café** (224 South Main Street, Breckenridge; 970-453-1877) serves Cajun and Creole cuisine in an atmosphere of southern hospitality. The menu includes blackened catfish, grilled shrimp, crawfish in gravy and the chef's award-winning bread pudding. Moderate.

The Blue Moose (540 South Main Street, Breckenridge; 970-453-4859), specializing in salads and vegetarian dishes, also offers burgers, fish and steaks. Dine inside or on the open deck with a great view of the Ten Mile Range. Budget.

You can feast on sushi flown in fresh from the West Coast and Japan in the historical ambience of a Victorian home at **Jacksan's Sushi House** (318 North Main Street, Breckenridge; 970-453-1880). Besides 47 kinds of sushi, the menu features such delicacies as fried oysters, octopus sunomono salad and vegetable tempura. Moderate.

The restaurant choice in South Park is more limited but far from hopeless. The hands-down favorite in Buena Vista is **Casa Del Sol** (303 Route 24; 719-395-8810), an outstanding Mexican restaurant that features dishes made from regional recipes collected throughout Mexico, from seafood quesadillas to *enchiladas suizas* and *pollo en mole*. Mexican guitar music, kachina and chile ristra decor and summer outdoor dining add spice to the homey atmosphere. Moderate.

In Salida, try **Country Bounty** (413 West Rainbow Boulevard; 719-539-3546) for huge portions of home cookin'. This family-style restaurant features a long and varied menu that ranges from fresh-caught Arkansas River trout, homemade soups and Mexican combination plates to specialties such as almond chicken Shanghai in a sesame-ginger sauce. The ambience is more like a gift shop than a restaurant, with country crafts, Indian jewelry and curios—all with price tags—wherever you look. Budget to moderate.

BRECKENRIDGE–SOUTH PARK AREA SHOPPING

While sporting goods shops dominate the historic main street and adjacent modern shopping centers of Breckenridge, there is also a small but stylish collection of art galleries. Established for more than 25 years, **Breckenridge Galleries** (124 South Main Street; 970-453-2592) features original artwork from the Rocky Mountain region with an emphasis on landscapes and western-theme paintings and sculptures. **Silver Shadows Gallery** (Four Seasons Plaza, 411 South Main Street; 970-453-4938) carries fine prints, Native American rugs and southwestern art. **Images of Colorado** (Four Seasons Plaza, 411 South Main Street; 970-453-2219) offers beautiful mounted Colorado landscape photographs. Jewelry, pottery, wooden toys, antler art and gourmet food are among the affordably priced handmade gift items at **Homegrown Creations** (109 North Main Street; 970-453-1025).

BRECKENRIDGE–SOUTH PARK AREA NIGHTLIFE

Many of the hottest nightspots in Summit County are not in Breckenridge but in Keystone. The rowdy **Snake River Saloon** (23074 Route 6; 970-468-2788), has live rock-and-roll nightly in ski season and Thursday through Saturday year-round. For something a little more mellow, enjoy a game of bridge, chess or backgammon in front of the 15-foot fireplace in the **Tenderfoot Lounge** (Keystone Lodge; 970-468-2316).

The **Breckenridge Brewery & Pub** (600 South Main Street; 970-453-1550), a lively, youth-oriented aprés-ski brewpub, is one of the most happening places in Breckenridge these days, as is **Tiffany's** (Beaver Run Resort; 970-453-6000 ext. 7914), a disco dance club at the base of Peak 9. **Downstairs at Eric's** (111 South Main Street; 970-453-1401) features live rock music.

The **Backstage Theater** (Bell Tower Mall, 605 South Park Street, Breckenridge; 970-453-0199) presents plays several nights a week during the summer and ski seasons.

BRECKENRIDGE–SOUTH PARK AREA PARKS

Dillon Reservoir—Proximity to Route 70 and explosive real estate development in the Silverthorne and Frisco areas have made this large, scenic reservoir surrounded by wooded mountain slopes one of the most popular recreational lakes in the state. Most of the north shore is developed, while the south shore is a series of wooded peninsulas offering secluded campgrounds.

Facilities: Boat ramps, marinas; information, 970-468-5400; restrooms in campgrounds only. *Fishing:* Good for rainbow trout, brown trout, cutthroat and kokanee salmon.

Camping: Four campgrounds operated by the U.S. Forest Service on Dillon Reservoir offer 380 RV/tent sites (no hookups); $8 to $10 per night.

Getting there: Located just off Route 70 at Exits 203 (Frisco) and 205 (Silverthorne/Dillon). Paved roads encircle the lake, providing access to campgrounds and boat ramps.

Vail-Leadville Area

Beyond the busy pseudosuburban zone of Silverthorne and Frisco on the shore of Dillon Reservoir, Route 70 West passes Copper Mountain Ski Area and climbs in a few miles to **Vail Pass** (10,666 feet). The summit is not a lofty ridge but rather an expanse of mountain meadows that's not much to look at. If you're seeking alpine majesty, take **Shrine Pass Road** (★), just west of the Vail Pass summit. Open in summer only and normally suitable for passenger cars, the unpaved road crests the 11,089-foot pass to the west in about four miles, then descends through a scenic canyon to the tiny mining town of Redstone on Route 24 between Leadville and Vail.

From Vail Pass, the interstate descends into the **Vail Valley**, site of America's largest ski resort. Vail is still a young town. Taking its name from the pass to the east, which had unglamorously been named for a Depression-era state highway engineer, the resort was built in secrecy within a single year and unveiled to the public in 1962. Lacking the historical patina of towns like Aspen, Crested Butte and Breckenridge, Vail gained a reputation as a snow swept, artificially Swiss theme-park sort of place that mocked the "real" Colorado. But Vail's image has mellowed with age as the saplings planted in 1962 have grown into a forest of shade trees enfolding each street and pathway. The windowboxes of Vail Village still contain plastic flowers in ski season, but real ones are substituted in summer. Development has kept expanding westward down the valley to include **Avon** and the newest resort, **Beaver Creek**, below the gleaming slopes of a ski megaresort covering 15 square miles with 25 chairlifts and gondolas and 182 named trails. Although winter visitors may marvel at the astonishing lattice of trails that spans Vail Mountain, the real appeal of this ski area lies hidden behind the mountain's top ridge. The Back Bowls of Vail are every deep-powder skier's fantasy, the most remote and expansive mountain skiing that can be reached by ski lift anywhere in the world.

In the summer months, gondolas and chairlifts carry picnickers, hikers and mountain bikers to the tops of the ski mountains from several points. The **Vista Bahn Express Lift** (970-476-5601; admission) runs from Vail Village up to Mid-Vail, below the summit of Vail Mountain, while about a mile to the west, **Lionshead Gondola** (970-476-5601; admission) runs up to Eagle's Nest Ridge. Several miles west in Beaver Creek, the **Centennial Express Chairlift** (970-949-5750; admission) runs to Spruce Saddle, high on Beaver Creek Mountain.

The **Colorado Ski Museum and Ski Hall of Fame** (Route 70, Exit 176, Vail; 970-476-1876; admission) traces the history of Colorado skiing with videos and exhibits, including one that demonstrates the evolution of ski equipment from the improbably long, heavy wooden skis of a century ago to the latest in fast, nimble fiberglass skis and high-tech boots.

The **Betty Ford Alpine Gardens** (South Frontage Road, Vail; 970-476-0103; free), adjacent to the Gerald R. Ford Amphitheater just east of town, sparkle in summer with tiny, bright blossoms unique to the fragile alpine environment. The Alpine Gardens are the world's highest public gardens. There is also a children's playground and a broad park lawn for picnicking.

Nearby, the **Vail Nature Center** (75 South Frontage Road, Vail; 970-479-2291) preserves an unspoiled seven-acre sample of the Vail Valley's natural environment and has a visitors center in a restored farmhouse, one of the oldest remaining buildings in the Vail Valley. The nature trails are groomed in winter for cross-country skiing.

If you're headed for Leadville from Denver, Route 91 exits from the interstate at **Copper Mountain Ski Area** (Route 70, Copper Mountain; 970-968-2882, 800-458-8386). The most curious spot on this 25-mile shortcut is the **Climax Molybdenum Mine**, a massive operation that produced most of the world's supply of molybdenum, a metal used in stainless-steel alloys. The mine shut down in 1980 because of the decline in American steel production and the development of synthetic substitutes. Climax, the company town for the mine workers, has joined the new generation of ghost towns.

Whichever route you take to **Leadville**, the trip is bound to be easier than it was for the people who started a mining camp on this site in 1860 during the Pikes Peak gold rush. Early prospectors followed a narrow track around Pikes Peak and across wind-blasted South Park to reach this inhospitable place at an elevation of more than 10,000 feet, surrounded by the Gore, Mosquito and Sawatch mountain ranges. Many came on foot, transporting their worldly possessions in wheelbarrows. Within 20 years, Leadville grew to be the second-ranking city in Colorado, with a population nine times as large as it is today.

Above all, there were Horace Tabor and Baby Doe, whose story epitomizes the euphoria and tragedy of Colorado's mining past. A confidence man sold Tabor a "worthless" mine that had been salted with a few ounces of gold buckshot. Tabor dug just a few feet and struck the richest silver lode in Colorado history. Tabor renamed his mine The Matchless. After he was elected to the U.S. Senate, Tabor married his mistress, Elizabeth "Baby Doe" McCourt. Together they proceeded to spend Tabor's money lavishly. But then . . . the price of silver collapsed—along with Horace and Baby Doe Tabor's fortunes. Tabor was working for the post office when he died six years later. Penniless, Baby Doe clung to the Matchless Mine for 36 years, hoping the price of silver would recover, living in an adjacent one-room cabin where she was discovered one winter morning during the worst days of the Great Depression, wrapped in newspapers for warmth, frozen. You can visit the **Matchless Mine** (East 7th Street; admission) and Baby Doe's cabin, located one mile east of town on a well-marked road.

With its red velvet seats and ornately hand-painted stage backdrops, the **Tabor Opera House** (308 Harrison Street; 719-486-3900; admission) was the most elegant theater between St. Louis and San Francisco when Horace Tabor built it in 1879. Miners paid large sums to see world-class operas, theatrical presentations and vaudeville shows on this stage. Today, visitors can wander through the opera house on a self-guided tour.

For more about Leadville's history, visit the **Healy House and Dexter Cabin** (912 Harrison Avenue; 719-486-0487; admission). Operated by the Colorado Historical Society, the two very different homes—one an early prospector's cabin and the other an ornate Victorian mansion—house a museum of gold-rush and boom-town memorabilia. The most unique part is the cabin, which an early-day mining millionaire converted into a private poker club. It still looks rustic on the outside but was luxuriously appointed inside with richly polished woodwork.

The **Heritage Museum** (9th Street at Harrison Avenue; 719-486-1878; admission), housed in Leadville's historic 1904 Carnegie Library building, recreates the town's early days in a series ofs dioramas and exhibits everything from Victorian-era furnishings to memorabilia of the 10th Mountain Division and contemporary paintings by local artists.

The most unusual of Leadville's several historical museums is the **National Mining Hall of Fame and Museum** (120 West 9th Street, Leadville; 719-486-1229; admission), which contains an amazingly realistic full-size reconstruction of a hard-rock mine, as well as a collection of gold nuggets and an exhibit that details the roles mining has played in shaping America's history and economy.

The **Leadville, Colorado & Southern Railroad** (326 East 7th Street, Leadville; 719-486-3936) offers three-hour round trips between Leadville and Climax twice daily in summer and on weekends during fall colors. Though the trains are of '30s to '50s vintage, the guide's narration focuses on the early boom days of the Leadville area, pointing out abandoned gold and silver mines along the way.

Fifteen miles south of Leadville on Route 24, the Twin Lakes turnoff (Route 82) offers a shortcut from the Front Range cities to Aspen—over 12,095-foot Independence Pass, the highest Rocky Mountain pass that can be reached on a paved road.

VAIL–LEADVILLE AREA HOTELS

Virtually all accommodations in Vail Village are very expensive, so you might as well go for the best, right? The reigning lodge in the village is **Sonnenalp** (20 Vail Road; 970-476-5081, 800-654-8312, fax 970-476-1639), actually three inns—the Bavaria Haus, Austria Haus and Swiss Chalet—under unified management, separated by other lodges in a two-block span along Gore Creek near the center of Vail Village. Though Sonnenalp has 180 guest rooms and suites, the decentralized arrangement preserves the feel of a small European-style country inn. Rooms feature furnishings imported from Germany. Rates are ultra-deluxe.

Gasthof Gramshammer (231 East Gore Creek Drive; 970-476-8816, fax 970-476-8816) is another European-style lodge that radiates that *Sound of Music*

(Text continued on page 122.)

Melting Dreams and Mountain Bikes

The most amazing structure ever built in Leadville was not the ornate Tabor Opera House or the mansion of a silver baron. It was the Leadville Ice Palace, an attraction no traveler now living has ever seen.

Out-of-work miners quarried 5000 tons of ice blocks from frozen lakes to build Leadville's Ice Palace. Larger than the ice palaces that had been built for exhibitions in Moscow, Montreal and St. Paul, it boasted a facade 420 feet long and contained a skating rink, a dining room and two ballrooms. Like a Walt Disney castle in crystal, it had medieval ramparts, turrets and pointed towers from which colorful pennants fluttered. Denver socialites and politicians arrived by horse-drawn sleigh to attend galas, making grand entrances through the palace's huge arched gateway.

Construction of the Ice Palace began on November 28, 1895, a year and a half after the U.S. Congress had repealed a law subsidizing silver production and thus destroyed the economies of Colorado's silver-mining towns. Leadville's business leaders, believing the economic downturn to be temporary, had pooled contributions and hired the town's unemployed workers to build the ice palace. Their idea was that the miners would spend the money with local merchants, and then sightseers would bring tourism dollars to town, keeping Leadville's economy afloat until the silver market revived. According to the plan, the town would build a new Ice Palace each winter. But the Ice Palace began to melt the following March and was closed on March 28, 1896, never to be replicated. By the following winter, most workers and business owners had abandoned Leadville.

The Leadville Ice Palace symbolizes the challenge that has faced virtually every Colorado mountain town during the 20th century: How can local residents create prosperity in a place that has no industry, no agriculture and no commercial significance? But today the city fathers who concocted the Ice Palace scheme would feel prophetic indeed if they could see what has become of another, somewhat smaller silver-mining town just 28 miles away from Leadville as the crow flies, on the other side of Colorado's highest mountain. In Aspen, celebrities prowl the main street armed with charge cards that know no credit limits. A typical condominium unit goes for the same price as seven tons of pure silver ingots. And all because of the same natural resource Leadville tapped briefly a century ago—extreme winter weather.

Since 1950, skiing has brought enormous wealth to such near–ghost towns as Breckenridge, Crested Butte and Telluride, just as it has created whole new megaresort communities like Vail and Winter Park. Yet no ski-town entrepreneur can ever quite dismiss the image of the Ice Palace in March . . . melting. Colorado weather is never "normal"; like a gold or silver vein, winter defies prediction. Locals still recall the Great Snow Drought of 1975, a winter so warm that snow-making equipment could not keep the ski slopes operating. Aspen and Vail were declared federal disaster areas. Hundreds of bankruptcies resulted.

Since then, year-round diversification—stimulating tourism during the roughly seven months of the year when there is little or no snow—has become the goal of every ski town. Summer cultural events, from the highbrow Aspen Music Festival to the rowdy, funky Telluride Bluegrass Festival, compete for summer vacationers' attention on virtually every summer weekend. Ski lifts and gondolas now run all summer, carrying visitors high above timberline where they find hiking trails, horse stables and even fancy restaurants. Other attractions, from slot machines to steam trains, also spell resurrection for many mountain towns.

Since the invention of the mountain bike in the early 1980s, cycling has become the biggest boost to summer tourism. Indeed, entrepreneurs are discovering that mountain bikes and skis have a lot of similarities. Like skiing, mountain biking offers a choice of a free trip up and down forest trails or, for the price of a gondola ticket, an ultimate downhill thrill. Like skiing, mountain biking means a brisk business in equipment rentals that doubles the income of shops that rent skis in winter.

Now mountain towns from Winter Park to Crested Butte are cashing in on the mountain-bike craze by building elaborate trail networks specifically for off-road cycling. But the greatest achievement in bike trails so far is the Glenwood Canyon Bike Trail. Part of a landmark highway project, this easy paved trail offers first-time mountain bikers a painlessly spectacular introduction to the sport. It has transformed Glenwood Springs into a prototype for a new breed of mountain town, where bike rentals mean even bigger business than ski rentals.

Ski lifts? Concerts? Casinos? Bicycles? To visitors they may seem unlikely foundations for an economy, but the old-timers of Leadville and Aspen, not to mention the former residents of the dozens of forgotten ghost towns that dot the remote canyons and wind-blasted slopes nearby, would have understood perfectly. In these mountains, the illusive and transitory thing called wealth is where you find it.

charm that is distinctive to Vail. In fact, this 27-room inn, one of the first lodges in Vail, set the style for much of the architecture and decor in Vail Village. Guest rooms range from standard hotel rooms to two-bedroom suites with full kitchens, and all have fireplaces. Winter rates are in the ultra-deluxe range with a one-week minimum stay.

The Lodge at Vail (174 East Gore Creek Drive, Vail; 970-476-5011, 800-331-5634, fax 970-476-7425) is the longest-established American-style luxury resort hotel in Vail Village. Guest rooms, each with a private balcony, are richly appointed in gleaming mahogany and marble. Facilities include a heated swimming pool, jacuzzis, a sauna, a workout room and tennis courts. Rates are in the ultra-deluxe range year-round.

Low-cost lodging—in Vail? Actually, **The Roost Lodge** (1783 North Frontage Road; 970-476-5451) is in West Vail, on the other side of the interstate from Vail Village and the ski slopes; shuttle buses run hourly. This 72-unit, family-run A-frame lodge offers clean, basic rooms plus swimming pool, jacuzzi, sauna and continental breakfast, all for moderate rates in winter.

The finest hotel in the Vail Valley may be **The Lodge at Cordillera** (P.O. Box 1110, Edwards, CO 81632; 970-926-2200, 800-877-3529), a European-style mountain lodge secluded in 3200 acres of private forest about three miles from Beaver Creek Resort. Designed by Belgian architects, the lodge is as eclectic as it is elegant, featuring Chinese slate roofs, Spanish wrought-iron filigree, handmade French furnishings and natural wood and stonework from the Colorado Rockies. Rooms feature balconies and queen- or king-size beds with down quilts, and many have fireplaces. The European-style spa has hydrotherapy tubs, a full range of exercise machines, two swimming pools, jacuzzis, a sauna and a steam room. On the grounds are an 18-hole golf course, tennis courts and miles of mountain-bike trails. Ultra-deluxe.

En route to Leadville, **Copper Mountain Resort** (P.O. Box 3001, Copper Mountain, CO 80443; 970-968-2318, 800-458-8386, fax 970-968-2308) offers a range of hotel- and condominium-style accommodations in several buildings clustered around the foot of the ski slopes. While lodgings vary in size and amenities (higher-priced units have kitchens, fireplaces and balconies), the mildly southwestern decor is fairly uniform throughout. Guests have complimentary privileges at the Copper Mountain Athletic Club, where facilities include an indoor swimming pool, hot tubs, saunas, exercise rooms and tennis and racquetball courts. Ultra-deluxe.

The historic **Delaware Hotel** (700 Harrison Avenue, Leadville; 719-486-1418, 800-748-2004), dating back to 1886, was reopened on its 100th birthday after a beautiful restoration to its original gold-boom opulence. The 36 guest rooms feature brass beds with cozy down quilts and lace curtains. Crystal chandeliers and Victorian antique furniture grace the lobby. Moderate.

The **Leadville Country Inn** (127 East 8th Street, Leadville; 719-486-2354, 800-748-2354), a Queen Anne–style Victorian mansion built in 1893, has nine guest rooms, some in the main house and others out back in the carriage house, with restored polished wood trim, brass beds and claw-foot tubs. A full gourmet breakfast is included in the moderate room rate.

Club Lead (500 East 7th Street, Leadville; 719-486-2202) is an unaffiliated youth hostel with five six-bunk dorm rooms as well as five private rooms with queen-size beds. There is a hot tub. Budget.

VAIL–LEADVILLE AREA RESTAURANTS

Candlelight dining and French cuisine make **The Left Bank** (Sitzmark, Vail Village; 970-476-3696) an excellent choice for fine dining in Vail. Established in 1970 by a top French chef, the restaurant is decorated with family heirlooms and paintings enhanced by a pretty view of Gore Creek. Bouillabaisse is a house specialty, along with rack of lamb, duck à l'orange and homemade pâté de foie gras, and the wine list offers more than 400 selections. Deluxe.

Michael's American Bistro (Vail Gateway Plaza, 12 South Frontage Road; 970-476-5353), on the second floor of Vail's largest enclosed mall, under an atrium overlooking the shops below, doubles as a gallery for international photographers and painters. House specialties include a European-style pizza baked in a wood-fired oven and a gingery tuna pepper steak served with garlic mashed potatoes. The menu also features grilled seafood and wild game; the wine list is one of the largest in Vail. Deluxe.

For cheap eats, Vail-style, the place to go is **DJ's Classic Diner** (616 West Lionshead Circle, Vail; 970-476-2336), open 24 hours a day during ski season, shorter hours off-season. As the name promises, this is an improbably downhome little counter-service restaurant where your waitperson is likely to also be the cook and dishwasher. The menu includes pasta, burritos, blintzes, omelettes and dessert crêpes, as well as wine and beer. Portions are big, prices are budget.

Don't be fooled by the funky name: **Beano's Cabin** (Larkspur Bowl, Beaver Creek; 970-349-9090) is the most exclusive restaurant in the Vail Valley. Guests arrive by Sno-Cat–drawn sleigh in winter (horseback or horse-drawn wagon in summer) at this elegantly rustic hunting lodge decorated with pioneer paraphernalia, secluded in the Larkspur Bowl on Beaver Creek Mountain. The prix-fixe menu, which changes daily, features a six-course dinner with a choice of eight entrées, including lamb, beef, poultry and seafood dishes as well as special gourmet pizzas. Dinner only; reservations essential. Ultra-deluxe.

Also in the Beaver Creek area, the family-oriented **Cassidy's Hole in the Wall** (82 East Beaver Creek Boulevard, Avon; 970-949-9449) started as a barbecue place. It still offers a full rack of barbecued baby back ribs but has expanded its menu to include more than 80 items, including burgers, Mexican food and Rocky Mountain oysters. The decor is Old West–saloon style (later in the evening it turns into a cowboy dance club). Budget to deluxe.

In contrast to Vail's highly competitive haute cuisine scene, Leadville eateries seem to have trouble keeping their doors open for more than a single season. The old standby for fine dining in the area, **The Prospector** (Route 91; 719-486-2117), is three miles north of town in a rustic-looking lodge with rust-coated mining equipment strewn in the yard. The menu features a fairly standard selection of steak, seafood and chicken entrées along with a salad bar and homemade soup. The portions are huge and the cooking is just like Mom's. Moderate.

Speaking of Mom, check out **Mom's Place** (612 Harrison Avenue, Leadville; 719-486-1108), where the specialty is burgers—not only giant two-fisted bacon cheeseburgers but also ground-turkey burgers and vegetarian black-bean burgers. There's also pizza and a breakfast menu. Budget.

Leadville has had a large Hispanic population throughout its history as a mining town, but until recently most Spanish-speaking residents lived in a separate municipality called Stringtown, adjacent to Leadville's southern city limit. Annexed to Leadville in the late '70s, Stringtown still retains its own ethnic identity—and some of the tastiest and most atmospheric no-frills Mexican restaurants in the Rockies. A long-time favorite is **La Cantina** (1942 Route 24 South; 719-486-9927). Seating is in big wooden booths scarred by time. Mexican jukebox music plays in the background. Enchiladas, tamales and Mexican beer are among the specialties of the house. Budget.

VAIL-LEADVILLE AREA SHOPPING

Many of Colorado's most exclusive art galleries are located in Vail. The place to start browsing is **Knox Galleries** (Village Inn Plaza, 100 East Meadow Drive; 970-476-5171), which is remarkable for its life-size bronze sculptures of people placed around the plaza in front of the gallery. In the same block are **Claggett/Rey Gallery** (Village Inn Plaza, 100 East Meadow Drive; 970-476-9350), featuring traditional and western paintings and bronze sculptures; **Olla Podrida** (Village Inn Plaza, 100 East Meadow Drive; 970-476-6919), exhibiting 19th-century American folk art and contemporary art by local painters with national reputations; and **Vail Fine Art Gallery** (141 East Meadow Drive; 970-476-2900), with an array of regional and international paintings and prints including works by Renoir, Picasso, Warhol and Chagall.

Fine jewelry is another Vail specialty. Take a look at the contemporary variations on southwestern styling at **Gore Creek Gold** (183 East Gore Creek Drive; 970-476-0900); the fun pieces in sterling and semiprecious stones at **Karats by the Fountain** (201 East Gore Creek Drive; 970-476-4766); the imaginative variations on traditional designs in gold and diamonds at **Currents** (285 Bridge Street; 970-476-3322); and the unusual, eye-catching inlaid stone jewelry at **Gotthelf's** (196 Gore Creek Drive; 970-476-1778). Authentic western collectibles are featured at the **Battle Mountain Trading Post** (Vail Gateway; 970-479-0288).

Leadville has a handful of unpretentious galleries featuring the work of local artists, such as the **Little Cottage Gallery** (108 West 8th Street; 719-486-2411). A number of antique shops specialize in mining-era memorabilia, notably **Sweet Betsy's from Pike** (122 East 7th Street; 719-486-2116). The most unusual gift items to be found around Leadville are mineral specimens and mining artifacts, found at a number of shops including **The Mining Gallery** (711 Harrison Street; 719-486-0622), in the Tabor Grand Hotel.

VAIL-LEADVILLE AREA NIGHTLIFE

The Vail Valley supports a nightclub scene that runs the gamut from sedate to rowdy. In Vail, **The Club** (304 Bridge Street; 970-479-0556) features rock music live and loud Tuesday through Saturday. **Garton's** (Crossroads Center; 970-479-0607) offers something for everybody—disco on Sunday, comedy on Monday, country-and-western on Tuesday, poetry on Friday and rock music on the other nights. **Louie's** (227 Wall Street; 970-479-9008) has live jazz Thursday through Saturday. **Mickey's** (The Lodge at Vail, 174 East Gore Creek Road; 970-476-5011) features a mellow atmosphere and stylings from the Piano Man, a local fixture for more than 20 years. You'll find a hot disco environment at **Sheika's** (Gasthof Gramshammer, 231 East Gore Creek Drive; 970-476-1515). Pool tables and country music—sometimes live, more often recorded—are found at the **Sundance Saloon** (675 Lionshead Place; 970-476-3453) and the **Jackalope Cantina** (2161 North Frontage Road, West Vail; 970-476-4314).

Leadville's historic old saloons tend to be a tad less sophisticated than Vail's chic nightspots, but at least a beer costs a lot less. Saturday night on the town means bars with pool tables, country-and-western on the jukebox, and sometimes barroom brawls straight out of the cowboy movies. If this sounds like your idea of a good time, head for the **Pastime Saloon** (120 West 2nd Street; 719-486-9986), **Silver Dollar Saloon** (315 Harrison Street; 719-486-9914) or **Scarlet Tavern** (326 Harrison Street; 719-486-9901).

VAIL-LEADVILLE AREA PARKS

Turquoise Lake—One of the most beautifully situated recreational lakes in Colorado, this large reservoir just west of Leadville is managed by San Isabel National Forest. A hilly, paved 19-mile loop road encircles the lake at a distance, while more than a dozen access roads lead to secluded campgrounds, picnic areas and fishing spots along the shore. A foot trail meanders among the pines all the way around the lake, hugging the shoreline out of sight of the main road.

Facilities: Picnic areas, restrooms, boat ramp, hiking trail; information, 719-486-0752. *Fishing:* Good for native and Snake River cutthroat, rainbow trout, lake trout and kokanee.

Camping: Eight campgrounds around the lake have a total of 269 RV/tent sites (no hookups); $9.50 to $12 per night.

Getting there: Located five miles west of Leadville via Turquoise Lake Road (6th Street).

White River National Forest—Three large wilderness areas surround the Vail and Leadville area. The Eagle's Nest Wilderness, a spectacular area of serrated mountain ridges and glacial valleys, lies just north of Vail Pass. Lakes, waterfalls and wetlands characterize the lofty Holy Cross Wilderness south of Vail. Colorado's second-highest peak, 14,421-foot Mount Massive, is the centerpiece of the Mount Massive Wilderness, which extends from Leadville west to Independence Pass.

Facilities: Hiking trails; information, 970-945-2521. *Fishing:* Good for native and stocked trout in many lakes and streams, particularly in the Holy Cross Wilderness.

Camping: Most campgrounds in the area are around Turquoise Lake (see above). There are several small National Forest campgrounds, each with about a dozen sites (no hookups), along Route 24 and the eastern boundary of the Holy Cross Wilderness, with fees of $6 per night.

Getting there: Access to the Eagle's Nest Wilderness is from a trailhead east of the summit of Vail Pass as well as several dead-end hikes lower in the Vail Valley. The main trailheads for the Holy Cross Wilderness are on Forest Roads 707 and 703, which turn off Route 24 between Minturn and Red Cliff. Main trailheads for the Mount Massive Wilderness are on Forest Roads 105 and 110, which branch off the Turquoise Lake Road west of Leadville.

Aspen Area

From Twin Lakes south of Leadville, Route 82 follows the North Fork of Lake Creek around the south slope of 14,433-foot Mount Elbert, the highest mountain in Colorado, and then climbs by switchbacks up the granite spine of the Sawatch Range to cross the Continental Divide over 12,095-foot **Independence Pass**. At the pass summit, where tiny flowers spangle the permafrost tundra in midsummer, you get an incomparable panoramic view of the vast, high mountain wilderness that forms the heart of the central Rockies. A Y-shaped chain of mountains extends 30 miles northward to Vail, 30 miles southward to Salida and 50 miles westward to Redstone, dominated by 20 peaks over 14,000 feet high. Aspen nestles in the notch of the Y, sheltered by a natural fortress of alpine pinnacles that protect it from everyday reality.

Snow banks up to 16 feet deep close Independence Pass in the winter, so the only way to drive to Aspen then is via the fast four-lane segment of Route 82 that links the town with Glenwood Springs and Route 70. This approach creates a much different impression of Aspen, taking you past the suburban rows of custom and tract homes that have all but swallowed the town of **Carbondale**, where many Aspen locals actually live, and from which they daily commute 30 miles to work through a landscape thick with recently constructed homes and condominiums. By the time you pass the sprawling industrial and warehouse district and big, busy airport and reach the town of Aspen itself, you may feel as if you've reached the downtown area of a fair-sized city.

Aspen! In every small town in the Rockies preservationists worry that their corner of the world will become another one, while developers fantasize about being the next one. **Aspen** has served as the prototype for redevelopment of old mountain villages for a half century, yet there's still only one Aspen—the ultimate ski resort and one of the most expensive places on earth.

Aspen's new ski slopes built after World War II drew worldwide attention in 1950, when Aspen hosted the World Alpine Ski Championships. Walter Paepke, the Chicago cardboard-box tycoon who was the original investor in Aspen's ski slopes, recognized early that it takes more than snow to make a world-class resort. In fact, he envisioned Aspen primarily as a conference center and secondarily as a ski resort. Paepke restored and reopened the Hotel Jerome and Wheeler Opera House, gave local residents free paint to spruce up their homes, then sponsored Aspen's first major cultural event—a celebration of the bicentennial of Goethe's birth—and brought in an all-star cast of great minds and talents including Albert Schweitzer, Thornton Wilder, Arthur Rubinstein and the Minneapolis Symphony Orchestra. The event became the forerunner of the Aspen Music Festival and School as well as the Aspen Institute of Humanistic Studies.

The late '50s and early '60s saw other rundown old mining towns throughout the Rockies blossom into winter megaresorts, but none has ever matched Aspen's image for glamour. A vacation home in Aspen has become an ultimate status symbol. The Aspen Skiing Company has been bought by Twentieth Century Fox. Aspen now has more movie stars than Yellowstone has bears, and the police have come to take their job—keeping the riffraff out—very seriously. The wild Aspen lifestyle probably still exists, but it's in the hot tubs of huge houses up private lanes protected by armed guards. The closest most visitors are likely to get to it is a glimpse of a celebrity in a restaurant or supermarket.

As for the town's Victorian past, most historic buildings of downtown Aspen have been preserved, though they have been engulfed by more contemporary structures and renovated beyond recognition. The most impressive older building, and still the tallest building in town, is the **Wheeler Opera House** (320 East Hyman Avenue; 970-920-5770), one of Colorado's finest opera houses when it opened in 1888. Today it serves as Aspen's principal indoor stage, hosting concerts, theater performances, opera, ballet, big bands and classical artists almost every night of the year. Guided tours are available by request during the day.

Jerome B. Wheeler, a partner in Macy's department store in New York City and the town's founding father, lived in the beautiful 1888 Queen Anne–style Victorian mansion that now houses the **Wheeler-Stallard House Museum** (620 West Bleeker Street; 970-925-3721; admission). Open afternoons only, the museum traces Aspen's history from silver boom to bust and back to its current status as one of the world's premier resorts. Also in the Wheeler-Stallard House is the **Aspen County Historical Archives**, a treasure trove of historical photos, century-old newspapers and historical documents.

Oddly enough, the **Aspen Art Museum** (590 North Mill Street; 970-925-8050; admission) has no permanent collection. Instead, this large brick Victorian-era building, originally the town's power plant, provides public visual arts space for rotating painting, sculpture, architecture and design exhibitions.

The essence of downtown Aspen is its array of expensive galleries, sportswear shops and restaurants; yet less than a mile away from downtown lies roadless wilderness. One way to reach the high mountains is to take the **Silver Queen Gondola** (Aspen Mountain; 970-925-1220) to the 11,212-foot summit of Aspen Mountain. It operates in both winter and summer. In summer, the gondola provides easy access to high-country trails, as well as to the mountaintop Sundeck Restaurant, where Aspen Music School students perform regularly.

A very popular spot nearby is **Maroon Lake**, a beautiful mountain lake set at the foot of North and South Maroon Peaks and Pyramid Peak, all over 14,000 feet in elevation. Defoliated by too many visitors, the lake is closed to motor-vehicle traffic during the summer season (mid-June through Labor Day) except for overnight campers with hard-to-get U.S. Forest Service permits. Shuttle buses operated by **Roaring Fork Transit Agency** (Aspen; 970-925-8484; fee) run frequently from the T-Lazy-7 Ranch, partway up Maroon Creek Road. The last bus leaves the lake in late afternoon. Maroon Lake is the trailhead for a vast network of foot and horse trails in the **Maroon Bells–Snowmass Wilderness**. There are also easy, scenic trails around the lake and along the creek.

Today only nine abandoned and tumbled buildings remain of the town of **Ashcroft**, which in the 1880s boasted a population larger than Aspen's. To reach the picturesque old townsite, drive 12 miles south of town on Castle Creek Road. Midway between Aspen and Ashcroft is the turnoff for the Conundrum Creek trailhead. From there it is a long but gentle nine-mile walk from the trailhead to **Conundrum Hot Springs** (★), a pair of idyllic hot-spring pools, three feet and four feet deep, with water temperatures that fluctuate from 99° to 103°F. Overnight camping is permitted in designated backcountry campsites.

ASPEN AREA HOTELS

If you have to ask about room rates, overnighting in Aspen is probably a bad idea. Just about every private room in the area is priced in the ultra-deluxe range during ski season, though a few plummet into the deluxe range off-season.

The original class act in town is the **Hotel Jerome** (330 East Main Street, Aspen; 970-920-1000, 800-331-7213, fax 970-920-1040). Originally built by local silver tycoon Jerome B. Wheeler in 1889 with the intention of surpassing even the finest New York hotels, the Jerome was restored in 1950 as the centerpiece of the newly opened ski resort. Since then, the management has added to the decor year by year with museumlike care. Fine Victorian antiques grace not only the common areas but also the 89 guest rooms and suites, each of which is uniquely furnished and decorated. The spacious bathrooms are done in white marble and feature jacuzzi tubs large enough for two. Ultra-deluxe.

While the Jerome vied with the best New York hotels of the late 19th century, the **Ritz-Carlton Hotel** (315 East Dean Street; 970-920-3300) is designed to rival the great hotels of today. Despite its size, the red-brick exterior of this 257-room hotel merges gently into downtown Aspen's remaining Victorian-era architecture. The lobby, a wonderland of fine art and classic luxury, makes an ideal place to loiter and watch for movie stars. The rooms, like everything else in the hotel, feel larger than life, with rich carpeting, flowery upholstery and giant marble-clad bathrooms. Rates are . . . need you ask?

For well-heeled travelers who shudder at the term *resort hotel*, there's the wonderful **Hotel Lenado** (200 South Aspen Street; 970-925-6246, 800-321-3457, fax 970-925-3840) a small, elegant European-style luxury hotel situated in the heart of downtown Aspen. The 19 guest rooms are done entirely in various kinds of wood (*lenado* means "wooded" in Spanish), from the polished wood floors, ceilings and wall paneling to the bentwood beds and sofas. The lobby area features a vaulted ceiling, a two-story-high fireplace and a profusion of windows that lets you view the town streets from the stairway. The common areas also include a library, a bar and a hot tub. A gourmet breakfast is included in the room rate—ultra-deluxe.

Among Aspen's many bed and breakfasts, **Sardy House** (128 East Main Street; 970-920-2525, 800-321-3457, fax 970-925-3840) boasts the most historic old building. Originally built as a private residence in 1892, this red-brick mansion was one of the first Victorian-style homes in Aspen. Exceptional care is evident in the decor and furnishings, which seamlessly blend period antiques with modern items to create a distinctive feel of opulence that transcends time. The 20 guest rooms have jacuzzis; a hot tub, sauna and swimming pool are behind the main house. Rates, including a full menu breakfast, are ultra-deluxe.

The closest thing in Aspen to low-cost lodging is the **St. Moritz Lodge** (334 West Hyman Avenue; 970-925-3220)—part unaffiliated youth hostel and part hotel, with 12 small dorm rooms sharing communal bathroom facilities and 13 small, deluxe-priced standard rooms including private baths. There's a fireplace in the lobby and a jacuzzi, a sauna and an outdoor swimming pool. Dormitory beds are in the budget range all year.

The **Alpine Lodge** (1240 East Cooper Street; 970-925-7351), a Bavarian-style house that dates back to the turn of the century and has operated as a ski lodge since the 1950s, is reputed to be the best lodging bargain in Aspen. The main lodge contains seven compact guest rooms, some with private bath, and there are four rustic cabins. Moderate to deluxe.

Room rates in nearby Snowmass run slightly lower than in Aspen. Representative of these somewhat affordable lodgings is the 44-room **Snowmass Inn** (Daly Lane, Snowmass Village; 970-923-4202), a modern four-story ski lodge with crazily compact rooms: each has a wall bed that is stored during the day and pulled out at night, and there's a sofa bed, too, so four people can share a room, albeit in cramped quarters. The lodge has a lobby fireplace, heated swimming pool, jacuzzi and sauna. Deluxe to ultra-deluxe.

ASPEN AREA RESTAURANTS

"Aspen Nouveau" may best describe the cuisine at **Piñons** (105 South Mill Street, Aspen; 970-920-2021), which is widely considered the best restaurant in town. It is certainly one of the most innovative restaurants anywhere. The constantly evolving menu features such specialties as an appetizer of lobster strudel with morel and chanterelle mushrooms and an entrée of sauteed ahi breaded with crushed macadamia nuts. The decor is a light, airy takeoff on western ranch-house style, with log pillars, leather-wrapped banisters and window shutters fashioned from willow twigs. Ultra-deluxe.

The Restaurant at the Little Nell (675 East Durant Avenue; 970-920-4600), located in a stylish luxury ski lodge near the foot of the Aspen Mountain gondola, characterizes its food as "American alpine cuisine," which apparently means originality and innovation: highly improbable combinations of many fresh ingredients that result in surprisingly delicious dishes. For example, there's a casserole of grilled elk and filet mignon with carmelized onions, apples, sweet potato crisps and sun-dried cherries. If that doesn't suit, try the roast rack of lamb served with peanut-vegetable rice, tortilla salad and a sauce of roasted tomatoes and ancho peppers. Desserts include warm chocolate cake with vanilla-bean ice cream and warm apple-blackberry tarts with cinnamon Caldados ice cream. Ultra-deluxe.

For a more affordable full dinner, try **The Grove** (525 East Cooper Avenue, Aspen; 970-925-6162), also near the gondola. This casual spot offers fairly conventional meals such as pasta, chicken and steak. The most popular entrée is Rocky Mountain trout. They also offer a wide selection of breakfast dishes and lunch sandwiches and salads. Budget to moderate.

Cache Cache (205 South Mill Street, Aspen; 970-925-3835) brings Aspen-style culinary innovation to French-country cooking in a casual bistro setting that glows with pastel hues and art deco touches. Try the osso buco on risotto cake or the free-range chicken Provençal. Moderate to deluxe.

Bentley's at the Wheeler (328 East Hyman Avenue, Aspen; 970-920-2240), an old-fashioned English pub located in the Wheeler Opera House and decorated with Victorian antiques (including a handcrafted hardwood bar that was originally a British bank counter), features traditional fish-and-chips as well as other fresh fish dishes, pasta and homemade cheesecake. Moderate.

Chinese food, found in almost all Colorado towns, is a rarity in Aspen's highly competitive restaurant scene. One delightful exception is **Asia** (132 West Main Street; 970-925-5433), housed in an elegant Victorian mansion. The lengthy menu features Cantonese, Hunan, Mandarin and Szechuan selections. Specialties include crab Rangoon and crispy Peking duck. Moderate.

Out of town, a fine dining favorite is the **Pine Creek Cookhouse** (11399 Castle Creek Road, Ashcroft; 970-925-1044), an elegantly rustic log cabin decorated in old-fashioned ski-lodge style 12 miles from Ashcroft near the ghost town of Ashcroft. You can drive there in summer, but in winter the trip itself is a wonderful part of this exceptional dining experience: starting at the nordic ski center on Castle Creek Road, you can either follow a guide on a 20-minute cross-country ski trek in the moonlight or ride to the restaurant in a horse-drawn sleigh. The menu is limited to three entrées, which are different every night. Ultra-deluxe.

No survey of Aspen dining would dare omit the legendary **Woody Creek Tavern** (2 Woody Creek Plaza, Woody Creek; 970-923-4585), located on Woody Creek Road, six miles down-valley from Aspen. Made famous in the 1970s by *Rolling Stone* journalist Hunter Thompson, still a regular here, it attracts resident celebrities like musician Don Henley of the Eagles and "Miami Vice" veteran Don Johnson. Its pool tables, burgers 'n' beer and self-consciously funky ambience offer a welcome change of pace when Aspen chic starts to cloy. Budget to moderate.

ASPEN AREA SHOPPING

Shopping, of course, is a big part of what Aspen is all about. The array of beautiful clothing, jewelry, art and gift items is staggering, and the price tags are mind numbing. If you like to window-shop, you could easily spend your whole vacation right here. If you like to shop for keeps, you could spend your life savings.

Solidly in the realm of fine contemporary visual arts are the **Barney Wyckoff Gallery** (312 East Hyman Avenue; 970-925-8274) and **Aspen Grove Fine Arts** (525 East Cooper Avenue, upstairs; 970-925-5151). For something a bit more traditional, visit **Galerie Du Bois** (407 East Hyman Avenue, upstairs; 970-925-5525), an ornate salon showing gilt-framed works by French post-Impressionist painters. The **Huntsman Gallery of Fine Art** (521 East Hyman Avenue; 970-920-1910), showing a full range of nationally known traditional painters, is Aspen's largest gallery.

Just for fun, poke your head into **Angels Can Fly** (301 East Hopkins Avenue; 970-925-8660), a gallery celebrating humor in comical arts and crafts and zany jewelry. Humor also meets art at the **Art Tee Gallery** (401 East Hyman Avenue; 970-920-2648), where original "wearable art" T-shirts are displayed on the walls like paintings.

For a completely different concept in wearable art, check out **Cheeks** (420 Hyman Avenue; 970-925-3634) and **The Freudian Slip** (416 South Hunter Street; 970-925-4427), both of which deal in lingerie as elegant as it is naughty. Experienced perfume designers can help you custom-blend your own fragrance from 380 different aromatic oils at **Ëssense Natural** (520 East Durant Street; 970-544-0544). And the **Margaux Baum Gallery** (610 East Hyman Avenue; 970-925-6068) specializes in erotic art.

Last, perhaps, but far from least, you'll find end-of-the-season leftovers from many of Aspen's finest boutiques, along with celebrity cast-off clothing, at the oldest secondhand store in town, **Gracy's** (202 East Main Street; 970-925-5131).

ASPEN AREA NIGHTLIFE

Summer brings a full schedule of cultural events to Aspen. Drawing some of the country's most talented musicians and enthusiastic audiences, the two-month-long **Aspen Music Festival** (970-925-3254) offers daily performances in its tent theater on Gillespie Street at the northwest edge of town. Held every summer since the early 1950s, the festival draws the world's top students and leading virtuosos in a broad range of musical styles, from classical to jazz and avant-garde. More very lively arts: **Theatre in the Park** (Art Park; 970-925-9313), a two-month series of contemporary plays; the six-week **DanceAspen** (970-925-7718) festival; and the week-long **Aspen Filmfest** (610 East Bleeker Street; 970-925-6882). The **Wheeler Opera House** (320 East Hyman Avenue; 970-920-5770) presents live concerts, plays and dance programs almost every night year-round.

Aspen's nightclub scene is built to accommodate elbow-to-elbow après-ski crowds during the winter season. In summer, most clubs continue to present live music at least on Friday and Saturday evenings. The **Flying Dog Brew Pub** (424 East Cooper Street; 970-925-7464) has contemporary rock music and a young crowd. **Legends of Aspen** (325 East Main Street; 970-925-5860), another young, loud bar, features live rock music on some nights and sports on big-screen TV on other nights. **Shooters Saloon** (220 South Galena Street; 970-925-4567), Aspen's only country-and-western dance club, features nationally known live bands on weekends.

For a more sophisticated scene, there is **Mezzaluna** (600 East Cooper Street; 970-925-5882), which has a reputation as the best club in town for celebrity-gawking. Both the **Ritz-Carlton Lobby Lounge** (315 East Dean Street; 970-920-3300) and the **Bar at the Little Nell** (675 East Durant Avenue; 970-920-4600) feature live soft jazz Tuesday through Sunday evenings.

ASPEN AREA PARKS

White River National Forest—This two-and-a-quarter-million-acre forest is Colorado's largest. Of its eight designated wilderness areas, two—the Hunter-Fryingpan Wilderness and the Maroon Bells–Snowmass Wilderness—flank the town of Aspen. The main trailheads that provide access into the wilderness areas are at Maroon Lake, at Ashcroft and near the summit of Independence Pass. The Maroon Bells–Snowmass Wilderness is one of the most heavily used wilderness areas in Colorado, and human impact on the delicate alpine ecosystem has become a serious problem. By contrast, the Hunter-Fryingpan Wilderness offers plenty of pristine solitude.

Facilities: Jeep, hiking and horse trails. *Fishing:* Good for trout, particularly in mountain lakes in the Hunter-Fryingpan Wilderness.

Camping: Permitted in designated areas only, in eight campgrounds totaling 183 RV/tent sites (no hookups); $6 to $8 per night.

Getting there: Forest access from Aspen is via Route 82 East (Independence Pass), Castle Creek Road and Maroon Creek Road.

Glenwood Springs Area

In 1993 construction was completed on the formerly narrow and winding 12-mile stretch of Route 70 through **Glenwood Canyon**, the last portion of the road to become a four-lane divided highway. Thanks to imaginative engineering, half a billion taxpayer dollars and Colorado's tough, controversial environmental laws, Glenwood Canyon is today the most beautiful scenic area on any U.S. interstate highway. The roadways, terraced up the canyon walls with eastbound and westbound lanes at different levels, stand on concrete pillars up to 80 feet tall to minimize impact on the environment. In the few places where rock cuts or blasting were necessary, the rock was resculpted to make the surface look natural. Contractors were fined for *any* shrubs or trees they destroyed while building the road, the amounts ranging from $35 for a raspberry bush to more than $22,000 for a Douglas fir. A 4000-foot tunnel conceals the freeway from sight of hikers on the Hanging Lake Trail, the most popular recreational spot in the canyon.

At the bottom of the 1800-foot-deep gorge, well below the din of the interstate, the paved **Glenwood Canyon Trail** takes walkers, joggers, cyclists and even rollerbladers along the bank of the Colorado River. Hiking trails start at three rest areas along the way. The most spectacular is the steep 1.2-mile trail that climbs to **Hanging Lake**, where waterfalls feed a gem-blue pool on a narrow terrace 930 feet up the canyon's sheer granite wall. Formerly one of the "hidden" wonders of the Rockies, Hanging Lake Trail has become the single most popular hiking trail in Colorado since completion of the Glenwood Canyon Project. The trail starts from Sixth Street on the east side of Glenwood Springs, near the Yampah Vapor Caves. The Hanging Lake trailhead is ten miles from town. The entire Glenwood Canyon Trail is 20 miles long, paved all the way.

Glenwood Springs has had a roller-coaster career as a resort town since the 1880s, when Aspen silver tycoon Jerome B. Wheeler built a hot-springs spa there. He hoped to attract wealthy easterners and Europeans, but the resort soon became a rough-edged playground for the wealthier denizens of nearby mining towns like Aspen and Leadville. Alongside the grand Colorado Hotel, the elegant bathhouse and the polo field stood some of the finest gambling casinos in the West and no fewer than 22 saloons.

Glenwood Springs' popularity waned by the 1920s, though in the '30s it gained notoriety as a mountain hideaway for Al Capone and other gangsters. Until as recently as the 1970s it remained a low-budget party town where college students flocked on weekends. The recreation boom that transformed other nearby towns pretty much bypassed Glenwood Springs until the past few years, when the wave of big-money tourism that poured out of Aspen to create such upscale bedroom communities as Carbondale finally washed over Glenwood Springs like a fresh coat of paint. Now a popular weekend destination for Denverites as well as an easy daytrip from Vail, Glenwood Springs is once again one of Colorado's liveliest mountain towns.

One memento of Glenwood Springs' colorful past is **Doc Holliday's Grave** in Linwood Cemetery, reached by foot trail from Cemetery Road, two blocks east of the Chamber of Commerce, which is located along Route 82. Holliday, a dentist from Virginia, had moved West to seek a cure for tuberculosis. Making his way as a professional gambler, he gained national notoriety as the subject of a best-selling paperback book, *My Friend, Doc Holliday*, written by lawman Wyatt Earp. Following the legendary gunfight at the OK Corral in Tombstone, Arizona, Holliday moved to Glenwood Springs, where he spent the last year of his life and then succumbed to tuberculosis. Also buried in the same cemetery is Kid Curry (a.k.a. Harvey Logan), a member of Butch Cassidy's gang.

More recollections of Glenwood Springs' early days can be found at the **Frontier Historical Museum** (1001 Colorado Avenue, Glenwood Springs; 970-945-4448; admission), where you can see a generous sampling of Victorian-era mine-camp elegance, including the marriage bed shared by silver tycoon and scandal-ridden senator Horace Tabor and his mistress-turned-wife, Baby Doe. There are also Native American artifacts and a walk-through replica of a coal mine.

The center of the action is **Glenwood Hot Springs** (401 North River Street, Glenwood Springs; 970-945-7131; admission), with the world's largest hot-spring pool: it's two blocks long, holds 1000 bathers and has a water slide. There is also a smaller, hot-tub-temperature (104°F) therapeutic pool. Lockers and towels are provided, and a shop beside the locker rooms sells bathing suits. Although the pools are outdoors, they are open until 10 p.m. in winter and summer.

A short distance from the hot springs is **Yampah Vapor Caves** (709 East 6th Street, Glenwood Springs; 970-945-0667; admission), geothermally heated steam baths in three natural caves—two for men and one, the largest, for women. The Ute Indians are said to have revered the caves for their healing powers. The recently renovated vapor caves now feature soft, spacey music; additional amenities include massages and individual hot tubs.

For a fascinating daytrip from Glenwood Springs, take Route 82 south for 12 miles to Carbondale and then fork left on Route 133, which goes around the twin 14,000-foot red-hued mountain peaks known as the Maroon Bells on the non-Aspen side. Seventeen miles down this road lies the tiny village of **Redstone** (★), originally a turn-of-the-century coal-mining town and now one of the most secluded luxury resort areas in Colorado. The sight that makes the trip worthwhile is **Redstone Castle** (58 Redstone Boulevard; 970-963-3463). Built by the founder of Colorado Fuel & Iron, which operated the big steel mill at Pueblo and controlled most of the state's coal mines, the 42-room castle is one of the most remarkable architectural achievements of Colorado's early days. The massive red sandstone mansion was abandoned after only a few years of occupancy when the owner lost everything in a corporate takeover. It has recently been restored in lavishly authentic fashion. Now operated as a bed and breakfast, the castle welcomes sightseers.

About five miles southeast of Redstone on a well-marked, exceptionally scenic back road is the even smaller village of **Marble** (★), site of a huge abandoned marble mill, still surrounded by broken slabs and columns of gleaming white marble scattered all about.

GLENWOOD SPRINGS AREA HOTELS

The AYH-affiliated **Glenwood Springs Hostel** (1021 Grand Avenue, Glenwood Springs; 970-945-8545) offers 24 dormitory beds, along with kitchen and laundry facilities and shared baths, as well as a photographers' darkroom and book and record library. Budget.

One of the first grand hotels in the Rockies, the **Hotel Colorado** (526 Pine Street, Glenwood Springs; 970-945-6511, 800-544-3998, fax 970-945-7030) celebrated its 100th birthday in 1993. Modeled after the Villa de Medici and built of native sandstone and Roman brick, the formerly opulent Italianate-style hotel once welcomed President William Taft and was a favorite haunt of Theodore Roosevelt's during his presidency. The landscaped courtyard is inviting, the lobby is truly vast, and each of the 126 rooms and suites is individually decorated in restful, muted hues. Moderate.

Hot Springs Lodge (415 6th Street, Glenwood Springs; 970-945-6571, 800-537-7946, fax 970-945-6683) is right across the street from Glenwood's famed hot-spring pools. The decor is contemporary, and though some may find the color scheme—a clash of pinks and blues—unsettling, the 107 guest rooms are bright and exceptionally spacious, offering a choice of two queen-size beds or one king-size, and most have balconies. Moderate.

The classiest accommodations in town today are at the **Hotel Denver** (402 7th Street, Glenwood Springs; 970-945-6565, fax 970-945-2204), across the street from the Amtrak station and a short walk from the hot springs. Built in 1906, the hotel has been completely renovated in art deco–revival style. The lobby is under a three-story atrium. The rooms are spacious and modern. Deluxe.

The **Kaiser House** (932 Cooper Avenue; 970-945-8827, fax 970-945-8826), a seven-unit bed and breakfast in a turn-of-the-century three-story Victorian residence, is within a few blocks' walk of the hot springs and the shops and restaurants of downtown Glenwood Springs. The house, completely renovated in contemporary style, has a parlor fireplace and an outdoor hot tub, and there's a resident masseuse. The full gourmet breakfast, featuring such delicacies as nutty waffles and fresh vegetable quiche, is probably the best in town. Moderate.

Adducci's Inn Bed & Breakfast (1023 Grand Avenue, Glenwood Springs; 970-945-9341) is another antique-decorated B & B in an older downtown residence, this one built in 1900. More budget-oriented than the Kaiser House, Adducci's Inn offers five simple, pleasant rooms. Each room has a private WC, but showers are down the hall. There's a hot tub. Budget.

In the hideaway community of Redstone, the **Cleveholm Manor** (58 Redstone Boulevard; 970-963-3463, 800-643-4837) has been nicknamed "Redstone Castle" since the turn of the century, when it was the home of Colorado's leading coal and steel baron. Today the castle has been restored to the opulence of that era with museum-quality antiques including chandeliers and velvet-upholstered furnishings. It operates as a bed and breakfast with eight rooms and suites priced in the ultra-deluxe range as well as eight more modest rooms, once servants' quarters, which share bathrooms and rent in the moderate range.

GLENWOOD SPRINGS AREA RESTAURANTS

In contrast to the high cost of eating in Aspen, Glenwood Springs presents an array of good restaurants for every culinary preference at surprisingly low prices.

Centrally located downtown, **The Loft** (720 Grand Avenue; 970-945-6808) is a long-time local favorite. The big, brick-walled restaurant is on the second floor, and the nonsmoking section has picture windows overlooking the main street of town. The menu features steaks, seafood and Mexican food, plus the house dessert specialty, mud pie. Budget.

Across the street, the **Italian Underground** (715 Grand Avenue; 970-945-6422) is located in the basement of the historic Silver Club Building, originally a turn-of-the-century gambling hall. Northern Italian food, pizzas and ice cream are all homemade. Budget.

The **19th Street Diner** (1908 Grand Avenue, Glenwood Springs; 970-945-9133) is an authentic '50s-style local hangout decorated entirely in black and white. The large menu features a little of everything, from hamburgers with fries, chicken-fried steak with mashed potatoes and gravy, to fajitas, *huevos rancheros* and fettucine. Budget.

Big, crackling fireplaces in each of two separate dining areas set the tone for **The Fireside** (51701 Route 6, Glenwood Springs; 970-945-6613), a quiet, friendly, family-style restaurant that serves some of the best home-style food in the area. While the menu features a full selection of steak, seafood and chicken entrées, the house specialty is baby back pork ribs smoked over apple wood. The restaurant also offers a good salad bar, homemade soups and a luncheon buffet. Moderate.

The elegant Victorian-style **Sopris Restaurant** (7215 Route 82, Glenwood Springs; 970-945-7771) is widely considered the best in the Glenwood Springs area. Fresh flowers and candlelight set the mood. For starters, there are salads topped with raspberry vinaigrette and appetizers like escargot and snow crab claws. Entrées include veal, rack of lamb, fresh Miami stone crab and vegetarian dishes. Moderate to deluxe.

Buffalo Valley (3637 Route 82, Glenwood Springs; 970-945-5297), located in a building that used to be a local historical museum, has a saloonlike atmosphere featuring the largest dancefloor in the state and a bar inlaid with 1000 silver dollars. Beef dominates the menu in the form of steak, prime rib and barbecued ribs, and there is a large, elaborate salad bar. Budget to deluxe.

GLENWOOD SPRINGS AREA NIGHTLIFE

It's a good thing the hot springs stay open until 10 p.m., because Glenwood Springs does not have an overabundance of other nightlife. The local rock-and-roll hot spot, featuring live bands nightly, is **Mother O'Leary's** (914 Grand Avenue, Glenwood Springs; 970-945-4078).

GLENWOOD SPRINGS AREA PARKS

Rifle Falls State Park—A 45-minute drive from Glenwood Springs, Rifle Falls is hidden in a shale canyon in northwestern Colorado's dry plateau country. Rifle Creek splits into several cascades that spill side by side into the canyon, creating an oasis lush with ferns, mosses and wildflowers. Among the falls and along the canyon wall are marked entrances to several small caves that are easy to explore with a flashlight.

Facilities: Picnic area, restrooms, nature trail; day-use fee, $3; information, 970-625-1607.

Camping: There are 18 RV/tent sites (no hookups); $6 per night. Additional camping can be found a few miles farther up the same road at Rifle Gap

State Park and several small campgrounds with hookups in White River National Forest; $10 per night.

Getting there: Located on Route 325 15 miles north of the town of Rifle, which is 27 miles west of Glenwood Springs on Route 70.

Steamboat Springs Area

As you approach **Steamboat Springs** down the long, sweeping curve of Route 40's steep descent from the summit of 9426-foot Rabbit Ears Pass, the first thing you see is a hillside completely covered with condominiums that fill up on winter weekends. Thriving on the recreation industry, Steamboat Springs has a hip, sporty subculture. It often seems as if everyone in town rides a mountain bike—at the same time. Yet unlike other famous-name ski resorts like Aspen, Breckenridge or Telluride, Steamboat was not a boom-and-bust mining town, and it was never abandoned. Instead, this former rough-and-ready ranching center still retains a bit of its original character. The downtown area is preserved as the **Steamboat Springs Historic District**. Its storefronts have a look of western small-town Americana with a fresh coat of paint. Unlike almost all other ski towns mentioned in this chapter, Steamboat Springs is low enough (6000 feet) in elevation so that its streets are usually free of snow and ice. The commercial area known as Steamboat Village, around the base of the ski area, is 900 feet higher and stays snowpacked most of the winter.

North of town, the lower slope of **Steamboat Ski Area** (2305 Mount Werner Circle, Steamboat Springs; 970-879-6111) rises from the jumble of condominiums and ski lodges. Viewing it from below, you can't see a hint of the ski area's true extent. Above the midpoint, a long ridgeline leads back to a maze of slopes and trails spanning the faces of four mountains. The Thunderhead Chairlift and more expensive Silver Bullet Gondola run all summer, carrying mountain bikers to the ski area's mountain-bike trail network, which joins longer trails in adjoining Routt National Forest.

Eight miles north of town, **Strawberry Park Hot Springs** (★) (Strawberry Park Road; 970-879-0342; admission) is one of the most idyllic hot springs in Colorado. Water from several scalding hot springs mixes with chilly creek water in a series of six hot-tub-depth rock pools. This site used to be a closely guarded secret spot where locals went to bathe nude, but so many people have discovered it over the years that now bathing suits are required during daylight hours, though they are still optional after dark. There are a few rustic cabins and campsites available for rent.

Another picture-perfect spot just beyond the edge of Steamboat Springs is **Fish Creek Falls**, a popular picnic spot four miles east of town on the road of the same name. The falls plunge 200 feet into a canyon. A short trail leads down to a picnic area in the canyon, and a bridge provides a great view of the falls. Another short, steep trail leads to an overlook above the falls.

South of Steamboat Springs stand the Flat Tops, a rugged range of 11,000-foot plateaus. Few visitors venture far into the **Flat Tops Wilderness**, a wonderland of alpine meadows, tundra and lakes protected by volcanic cliffs, where elk and black bear are more commonly seen than humans. Access to the wilderness is from nine trailheads along the 82-mile **Flat Tops Trail Scenic Byway** (★), which runs from Yampa (27 miles south of Steamboat Springs on Route 131) west to Meeker (41 miles north of Route 25 on Route 13). The route is paved for 42 miles, and the rest is a wide, smooth gravel road skirting the northern boundary of the wilderness area.

West of Steamboat Springs lies one of the emptiest parts of Colorado, an arid stretch of shale badlands. The main point of interest in this part of the state is **Dinosaur National Monument**, which straddles the Colorado-Utah state line. (see the Vernal section of Chapter Five, "Utah Rockies," for information). The Colorado side of the park is wild canyon country that includes 44 miles of the Green River, 48 miles of the Yampa and the two rivers' confluence. There are no roads and only a few two-track jeep trails through the northern backcountry of the park; the main access is by river raft. Taking a marked turnoff from Route 318, motorists can reach the launch point for trips down the Green River. From there it's an easy hike to an overlook view of the **Gates of Lodore** (★), dramatic quartzite cliffs that rise suddenly to an elevation of 2300 feet above the river. Plunging through the Canyon of Lodore, the water pounds over Disaster Falls and gushes through Hell's Half Mile before slowing to mirrorlike serenity as it makes its way through python bends that shelter sandy beaches nearing the raft pullout point at **Echo Park** (★), near the south side of the national monument. A paved scenic road that starts just east of the town of Dinosaur, three miles from the state line, runs 25 miles through slickrock country to an overlook that offers an awe-inspiring view of Echo Park. From this paved park road, a 14-mile unpaved side road bounces its way to the riverbank tent campground at Echo Park itself.

STEAMBOAT SPRINGS AREA HOTELS

The **Rabbit Ears Motel** (201 Lincoln Avenue, Steamboat Springs; 970-879-1150, 800-828-7702) has 65 standard motel rooms recently refurbished in bright colors and an array of thoughtful little appliances such as coffeemakers and clock radios. The prices are among the lowest in town, and if that's not enough, guests receive a discount at the Steamboat Springs Health and Recreation hot-springs spa across the street. Moderate.

Homey and historic, the little **Harbor Hotel** (703 Lincoln Avenue, Steamboat Springs; 970-879-1522, 800-543-8888, fax 970-879-1737) has been in operation for more than 50 years. Of the 62 guest rooms, only 15 are in the old hotel, and these feature Victorian-period furnishings and decor. Two recent annexes contain standard motel rooms and condominiums with full kitchens. Facilities include jacuzzis and a sauna. Deluxe.

Located downtown, a short shuttle bus trip from the ski slopes, the **Steamboat Bed & Breakfast** (442 Pine Street, Steamboat Springs; 970-879-5724) was originally built in 1891 as the town's first church. Partly gutted by fire, it was completely renovated into a comfortable little inn. The six guest rooms are furnished with antiques and period reproductions. Facilities include fireplaces, a hot tub and an outdoor deck overlooking meticulously landscaped gardens. Rates, including a full breakfast, are moderate.

Set on a hillside between downtown and the ski area, the **Overlook Lodge** (1000 High Point Drive, Steamboat Springs; 970-879-2900, 800-752-5666) offers views from most guest rooms as majestic as the name suggests. Besides the 117 plain, pleasant guest rooms and suites, the lodge offers a full complement of facilities including a heated indoor pool, saunas, jacuzzis, tennis courts and a miniature golf course. Ultra-deluxe.

Among the many guest ranches in the Steamboat Springs area, **The Home Ranch** (54880 County Road 129, Clark; 970-879-1780, 800-223-7094, fax 970-879-1795), located 19 miles up the road to Steamboat Lake, stands out as the most luxurious. Some of the 13 guest units are in the main ranch house, while others are in modern, beautifully appointed cabins a short walk away. Each cabin has its own jacuzzi. Riding and flyfishing lessons are offered, as are treks into the Mount Zirkel Wilderness, and there are a swimming pool and a sauna. The ranch stays open year-round and offers 25 miles of groomed cross-country ski trails in winter. Ultra-deluxe.

A number of resorts dot the area around Steamboat Lake and Hahn Peak. The one with the most atmosphere is **The Inn at Steamboat Lake** (61276 County Road 129, Clark; 970-879-3906, 800-934-7829). Newly built in 1990 in classic style, this eight-room bed-and-breakfast inn has a huge porch and wraparound balcony complete with hot tub overlooking the lake. Rooms are wood-paneled and spacious with contemporary furnishings. Deluxe.

STEAMBOAT SPRINGS AREA RESTAURANTS

For the ultimate in Steamboat Springs dining, take a gondola ride to the top of Thunderbird Peak and **Hazie's** (Thunderhead Terminal, Silver Bullet Gondola; 970-879-6111), where china, sterling silver and crystal catch the soft glow of candlelight in a spectacular setting overlooking the town. Fixed-price four-course dinners offer a choice of seafood, chicken, beef and veal entrées plus appetizers, soup, salad and a dessert cart. The gondola ride and live music are included in the dinner price. Ultra-deluxe.

La Montaña (2500 Village Drive, Steamboat Springs; 970-879-5800), an exceptional southwestern restaurant located in a shopping center at the foot of the ski slopes near the gondola, serves intriguing variations on traditional New Mexico and Tex-Mex cuisine. Elk meat, a specialty here, turns up in a variety of forms—elk loin with pecans, elk fajitas and braided elk sausage—but you'll also find mesquite-grilled lamb and chorizo sausages as well as *chile rellenos* and other favorites. The thoroughly modern decor features art photographs and abundant greenery in a sunny atrium. Moderate to deluxe.

A very popular Mexican restaurant at the ski slopes, **Dos Amigos** (Ski Time Square, Steamboat Springs; 970-879-4270) is known for such house specialties as *chile rellenos* stuffed with Monterey jack cheese and a wide range of enchilada choices, including spinach and mushroom enchiladas, *vegetarino del cocinero* (fresh vegetable enchiladas) and *enchiladas pescador* (seafood enchiladas) with blue-corn tortillas. Adobe-style stucco walls, old-time photos and lots of plants enhance the casual ambience. Budget.

Antare's (57½ 8th Street, Steamboat Springs; 970-879-9939), located in a 1906 building, cultivates an air of casual elegance with polished hardwood floors, parquet tables and an antique bar in the lounge. Its "new American" cuisine highlights eclectic blends of regional and ethnic recipes adapted to contemporary tastes. Among the entrées are Maine lobster in mushroom sauce on a bed of chili-pepper linguine; lamb chops with a chutney of melon, mint and chili; and tender veal with a chardonnay and watercress sauce. Moderate to deluxe.

A local downtown favorite for breakfast or lunch, **Winona's** (617 South Lincoln Avenue, Steamboat Springs; 970-879-2483) serves traditional American food for breakfast, lunch and dinner as well as specialty coffees. This casual café doubles as a bakery, so house specialties include homemade muffins, scones, cinnamon rolls and scones. Other breakfast choices include Belgian waffles, eggs Benedict and *huevos rancheros*. Lunch features design-your-own hoagie sandwiches, homemade soups and salads. Budget.

STEAMBOAT SPRINGS AREA SHOPPING

In Steamboat Springs you'll find western women's fashions at **Audacity** (435 Lincoln Avenue; 970-879-3822), western crafts and collectibles at **Art Quest** (511 Lincoln Avenue; 970-879-1989), Indian jewelry at **Steamboat Custom Jewelers** (837 Lincoln Avenue; 970-879-6332), western-style interior decor at **Bunkhouse Interiors** (908 Lincoln Avenue; 970-879-6802), western paintings at the **Garrett Gallery** (912 Lincoln Avenue; 970-879-8003) and western-style leather goods at **Old Town Leather, Etc.** (929 Lincoln Avenue; 970-879-3558). One of the most intriguing places to browse is the **Fair Exchange Company** (54 9th Street; 970-879-3511), a long-established secondhand store that carries everything from used skis and military surplus camping gear to natural-fiber consignment clothing, as well as a scattering of ranch country antiques.

STEAMBOAT SPRINGS AREA NIGHTLIFE

Live rock and reggae are featured at **Heavenly Daze** (Ski Time Square, Steamboat Springs; 970-879-8080), a vast, 4000-square-foot brewpub at the foot of the ski mountain. In the same shopping center, **The Tugboat** (970-879-7070) has been serving up televised sports on weekdays and live rock and blues on weekends since 1973. Live rock music by the ski slopes can also be found at **The Inferno** (2305 Mt. Werner Circle; 970-879-5111), the most notorious singles bar in town, where drink prices change constantly, determined by the spin of a "shot wheel." Two-steppers will find the region's hottest country-and-western bands and a huge dancefloor, plus dance lessons on weeknights, at **The Saloon at Steamboat** (Sundance Plaza, Steamboat Springs; 970-879-6303).

STEAMBOAT SPRINGS AREA PARKS

Stagecoach State Park—Stagecoach Reservoir on the Yampa River is the closest recreational lake to Steamboat Springs and provides the most convenient public camping for visitors to the area. The lake is surrounded by hilly native grasslands with distant views of the mountains around Steamboat Springs. Waterskiing and fishing are the main activities, and a hiking trail traces the entire undeveloped south shoreline.

Facilities: Picnic areas, restrooms, boat ramp, marina, phones, hiking trail, groceries; day-use fee, $3; information, 970-736-2436. *Fishing:* Good for rainbow trout and Snake River cutthroat.

Camping: Permitted in 92 RV/tent sites (62 sites have electrical hookups); $10 per night.

Getting there: Located 16 miles south of Steamboat Springs via Route 131 and County Road 14.

Steamboat Lake and **Pearl Lake State Parks**—Located on the pine-clad slopes of Hahn Peak near the Continental Divide, Steamboat Lake State Park is a popular recreational area for fishing, boating, windsurfing and waterskiing. Smaller, older Pearl Lake State Park, two miles away, is also administered by the Steamboat Lake State Park office. Pearl Lake is set aside for wakeless boating and fly and lure fishing.

Facilities: Picnic areas, restrooms, boat ramps, marina, waterski course, nature trail; day-use fee, $3; information, 970-879-3922. *Fishing:* Good for rainbow trout in Steamboat Lake and cutthroat in Pearl Lake.

Camping: There are 183 RV/tent campsites (no hookups) at Steamboat Lake; $6 per night. Pearl Lake has 39 sites for tents and self-contained RVs (no hookups); $6 per night.

Getting there: Both parks are located 24 miles north of Steamboat Springs on paved County Road 129.

Routt National Forest—This 1,127,000-acre expanse of forest and high grasslands virtually surrounds Steamboat Springs. It includes the Mount Zirkel Wilderness, one of the first wilderness areas created in Colorado, with its steep, rugged bare granite pinnacles and lush valleys along the Elk and Encampment rivers. Also within the Routt National Forest boundaries are parts of the Flat Tops Wilderness and the Never Summer Wilderness.

Facilities: Picnic areas, restrooms, hiking trails; information, 970-879-1722. *Fishing:* Good for several trout species in streams and alpine lakes.

Camping: Forty-two campgrounds offer a total of 523 campsites (no hookups), mostly in the Rabbit Ears Pass area and along the Elk River; free to $6 per night.

Getting there: The Rabbit Ears Pass area is on Route 40 southeast of Steamboat Springs. Other forest-access routes include Route 16 west from Yampa, which climbs to the Flat Tops where several trails lead into the Flat Tops Wilderness, and Forest Road 400, which follows the Elk River east from the main road to Steamboat Lake, ending in the main trailhead for the Mount Zirkel Wilderness.

The Sporting Life

RIVER RAFTING, KAYAKING AND CANOEING

BRECKENRIDGE–SOUTH PARK AREA The Salida area, on the southern edge of South Park near the headwaters of the Arkansas River, is one of the top whitewater rafting areas in Colorado. Nearly 100 tour operators operate there, including **Rocky Mountain Tours** (12847 South Route 285/24, Buena Vista; 719-395-4101), **Dvorak Kayaking & Rafting Expeditions** (17921 Route 285, Nathrop; 719-539-6851), **Canyon Marine** (129 West Rainbow Boulevard, Salida; 719-539-7476) and **Moondance River Expeditions, Ltd.** (310 West 1st Street, Salida; 719-539-2113).

VAIL-LEADVILLE AREA In the Vail area, there is whitewater rafting during the spring runoff (May to mid-July) on the **Eagle River**. Trips are offered by **Timberline Tours** (Vail; 970-476-1414) and **Raftmeister** (Lionshead, Vail; 970-476-7238).

ASPEN AREA In Aspen, whitewater raft trips on the Roaring Fork River are operated by **Aspen Whitewater Rafters** (555 East Durant Street; 970-925-5405), **Colorado Riff Raft** (555 East Durant Street; 970-925-5405) and **Blazing Paddles** (407 East Hyman Avenue; 970-925-5651). The **Aspen Kayak School** (P.O. Box 1520, Aspen, CO 81611; 970-925-4433) offers classes on the Roaring Fork River, from one-day and weekend classes to full week-long courses. Guided canoe trips on the Roaring Fork River are available from **Snowmass Whitewater** (Snowmass; 970-925-7238).

GLENWOOD SPRINGS AREA In Glenwood Springs, raft trips both through Glenwood Canyon on the Colorado River and down the Roaring Fork River are offered by **Rock Garden Rafting** (1308 County Road 129; 970-945-6737) and **Whitewater Rafting** (51100 Route 6/24; 970-945-8477).

STEAMBOAT SPRINGS AREA Raft trips both on the Yampa River around Steamboat Springs and on the wilder reaches of the Snake and Yampa rivers in Dinosaur National Monument can be arranged through **Buggywhip's Fish & Float Service** (435 Lincoln Avenue, Steamboat Springs; 970-879-8033) or **Adventures Wild Rafting** (P.O. Box 774832, Steamboat Springs, CO 80477; 970-879-8747).

BALLOONING AND GLIDING

VAIL-LEADVILLE AREA In Vail, **Camelot Balloons** (970-476-4743), **AeroVail** (970-476-7622) and **Mountain Balloon Adventures** (970-476-2353) offer hot-air-balloon rides complete with champagne.

ASPEN AREA **Aspen Balloon Adventures** (970-923-5749) and **Unicorn Balloon Company** (970-925-5752) offer hot-air-balloon flights over the Aspen area, while **Gliders of Aspen, Inc.** (Aspen Airport; 970-925-3694) offers glider lessons and introductory flights above some of the most spectacular terrain in the Rockies. Aspen is also the only place in Colorado where you can experience paragliding, a hybrid between skydiving and hang gliding that involves leaping off a mountaintop with a steerable rectangular parachute. Call the **Aspen Paragliding School** (417 South Spring Street, Aspen; 970-925-7625).

STEAMBOAT SPRINGS AREA In Steamboat Springs, balloon trips are offered by **Balloons over Steamboat** (970-879-3298), **Pegasus Balloon Tours** (970-879-9191) and **Aero Sports** (970-879-7433).

DOWNHILL SKIING

WINTER PARK–GRAND LAKE AREA **Winter Park Resort** (Winter Park; 970-726-5514) is a large ski area covering four mountains with a vertical drop of 3060 feet. Even though Winter Park has 20 chairlifts with a total capacity of 30,600 skiers an hour, it is often crowded, especially on weekends, because of its nearness to Denver. The majority of the ski trails are rated intermediate. An alternative is the new, smaller **SilverCreek Ski Area** (Route 40, SilverCreek; 970-887-3384) near Granby, north of Winter Park. With a vertical drop of 1000 feet and three chairlifts, SilverCreek offers a fair selection of trails from beginner to advanced. Both ski areas are open Thanksgiving through March.

North of Winter Park near the small ranching center of Fraser, you can rent a giant inner tube and bounce down steep, powdery slopes at the **Fraser Valley Tubing Hill** (Route 40, Fraser; 970-726-5954).

BRECKENRIDGE–SOUTH PARK AREA Several major downhill ski areas are located along the Loveland Pass Road (Route 6), which diverges from Route 70 just east of the Eisenhower Memorial Tunnel and rejoins the interstate at Silverthorne. **Loveland Basin and Loveland Ski Valley** (Route 6; 303-569-3203), just off the interstate and 12 miles from Georgetown, receive the second-highest snowfall in the Colorado Rockies—375 inches in an average year. With eight chairlifts and a vertical drop of 1520 feet, this moderate-size ski area offers 25 percent beginner, 48 percent intermediate and 27 percent advanced slopes. Its proximity to Denver, plus a complete absence of lodging at the slopes, means Loveland Basin and Valley is used mainly by Denverites; it is very crowded on weekends but nearly empty on weekdays. The slopes are open from mid-November to early April.

On the other side of 11,992-foot Loveland Pass, **Arapahoe Basin** (Route 6; 970-468-0718) is America's highest ski area; the highest lift reaches an elevation of 12,450 feet above sea level. With five chairlifts and a vertical drop of 1670 feet, "A-Basin" (as Coloradoans have nicknamed it) may not be among the region's largest ski areas, but it is certainly one of the most dramatic. The slope is so steep it looks almost like a sheer, snowpacked cliff, and 90 percent of the terrain is rated intermediate to advanced. The mogul fields at Arapahoe Basin are legendary. A-Basin is open from mid-November to early April.

Keystone Resort (Route 6; 970-468-4300) doesn't look like much from the road; steep, tree-covered slopes conceal most of the ski trails higher up the mountain and on its back side, accessible on two gondolas and four chairlifts. The vertical drop is 2580 feet. Only 8 percent of the ski area is suitable for beginners, while 55 percent is rated intermediate and 37 percent expert. Operated by the same management as Arapahoe Basin, Keystone is open from mid-November to late April.

The most impressive ski slopes in these parts are at **Breckenridge Ski Area** (Breckenridge; 970-453-5000). Breckenridge covers three mountains with an interconnected trail network that offers a vertical drop of 3400 feet. About 20 percent of the trails are rated for beginners, 30 percent intermediate and 50 percent advanced and expert. The back bowl of Peak 8 offers the highest-altitude inbounds skiing in the world. The season runs from Thanksgiving to mid-March.

VAIL-LEADVILLE AREA The Vail Valley reigns as the world's largest ski development, with a total lift capacity of more than 61,000 skiers per hour. There are three separate base areas. **Vail Ski Area** (Vail; 970-476-3239) alone spans seven miles of mountainside, served by one gondola and 18 chairlifts. The vertical drop is 3250 feet. The front side of the mountain is well balanced for all skill levels, with about 33 percent beginner trails, 33 percent intermediate and 33 percent advanced. The much larger bowl area on the back side of the mountain is 36 percent intermediate, 64 percent advanced. Just west of Vail, the **Beaver Creek Ski Area** (Avon; 970-949-5750) surpasses Vail in height, with a vertical drop of 3340 feet. Its ten chairlifts have about half the capacity of the larger ski area next door. Its trails are challenging, with 43 percent of them rated advanced or expert. Finally, there's **Arrowhead Ski Area** (676 Sawatch Drive, Edwards; 970-926-3029), a small area just west of Beaver Creek on the lower slope of the same mountain. The vertical drop is 1714 feet. There are two chairlifts, and the trails are well balanced for all ski levels—30 percent beginner, 50 percent intermediate and 20 percent advanced. The season at all three Vail Valley ski areas runs from Thanksgiving through March.

Leadville's little-known downhill ski area, located ten miles north of town on Tennessee Pass, is **Ski Cooper** (Route 24; 719-486-2277). It has two chairlifts and a vertical drop of 1200 feet. Trails are 30 percent beginner, 40 percent intermediate and 30 percent advanced. Open Thanksgiving through early April.

ASPEN AREA Aspen has four ski mountains in a row, all under the same management—Aspen Mountain, Aspen Highlands, Tiehack and Snowmass (970-925-1220 for all four ski areas). You can buy a lift ticket for any of the mountains or a comprehensive ticket for all four. **Aspen Mountain**, the original Aspen ski area, sprawls in plain view just a few blocks from the center of town. It has a vertical drop of 3267 feet with a challenging array of ski trails—35 percent intermediate, 35 percent advanced and 30 percent expert—and is served by a gondola and seven chairlifts. **Aspen Highlands** is about the same size as Aspen Mountain, and taller, with a vertical drop of 3800 feet. Although most of the ski area is not visible from below, nine chairlifts carry skiers up to the higher reaches of the ski area and a number of challenging ski trails. The area is 23 percent beginner, 48 percent intermediate and 29 percent advanced and expert. **Tiehack/Buttermilk**, the smallest of the Aspen ski mountains, is a good midsize ski area in its own right, with six chairlifts and a vertical drop of 2030 feet. Its trails are balanced for all skill levels—35 percent beginner, 39 percent intermediate and 26 percent advanced. **Snowmass** is the largest of the Aspen ski areas, nearly as large in area and lift capacity as all the other three combined. Its vertical drop is 3615 feet. It has 15 chairlifts. Its trails are 9 percent beginner, 51 percent intermediate, 18 percent advanced and 22 percent expert. The season for all Aspen ski areas runs from Thanksgiving through the end of March.

GLENWOOD SPRINGS AREA Downhill skiing in the Glenwood Springs area is at the relatively small **Ski Sunlight** (10901 Four Mile Road, Glenwood Springs; 970-945-7491). Although this ski area has only three chairlifts, its trails—20 percent beginner, 58 percent intermediate and 22 percent advanced—offer a fairly impressive vertical drop of 2020 feet. The season is from Thanksgiving through mid-March.

STEAMBOAT SPRINGS AREA **Steamboat Ski Area** (2305 Mount Werner Circle, Steamboat Springs; 970-879-6111) ranks third among Colorado ski areas, after Vail and Aspen. From its deceptively compact base, the big 18-passenger gondola and 17 chairlifts carry skiers up a long ridgeline to trails that cover four mountainsides. The vertical drop is 3488 feet. The trails are 15 percent beginners, 54 percent intermediate and 31 percent advanced.

SKI RENTALS Among the many ski-rental shops in Winter Park are **Sport Stalker** (Cooper Creek Square; 970-726-8873) and **Flanagan's Ski Rentals** (Route 40; 970-726-4412); both rent cross-country and downhill skis as well as snowboards. In Grand Lake, **Never Summer Mountain Products** (919 Grand Avenue; 970-627-3642) rents cross-country skis.

The Breckenridge–South Park area has an overwhelming number of ski-rental shops. For downhill skis, snowboards and cross-country skis, check out **Wilderness Sports** (171 Route 9, Silverthorne; 970-468-8519), **Virgin Islands Ski Rental** (Summit Place Shopping Center, Silverthorne; 970-468-6655), **Mountain View Sports** (22869 Route 6, Keystone; 970-468-0396) and **Rebel Sports** (111 Ski Hill Road, Breckenridge; 970-453-2565). You'll find nordic equipment at **Mountain Outfitters** (112 South Ridge Street, Breckenridge; 970-453-2201).

Downhill skis and snowboards are for rent at many Vail-Leadville area shops, including **Base Mountain Sports** (492 East Lionshead Circle, Vail; 970-476-3689) and **American Ski Exchange** (225 Wall Street, Vail; 970-476-1477). For both nordic and alpine equipment, visit **Christy Sports, Ltd.** (293 Bridge Street, Vail, 970-476-2244; and 182 Avon Road, Avon, 970-949-0241) or **Bill's Sport Shop** (225 Harrison Avenue, Leadville; 719-486-0739).

Among the myriad ski-rental places in the Aspen area are **Aspen Sports** (408 East Cooper Avenue Mall, Aspen, 970-925-6331; 303 East Durant Avenue, Aspen, 970-925-6332; Snowmass Village Mall, Snowmass Village, 970-923-6111; and Snowmass Center, Snowmass Village, 970-923-3566); **Pomeroy Sports** (614 East Durant Avenue, Aspen; 970-925-7875); and **Incline Ski Shop** (Snowmass Village Mall, Snowmass Village; 970-923-4726). All stores rent downhill and cross-country skis; most rent snowboards, too.

For downhill and cross-country skis as well as snowboards, visit **Ski Sunlight Ski Shop** (1315 Grand Avenue, Glenwood Springs; 970-945-9425).

In Steamboat Springs, downhill skis are for rent at **Sport Stalker** (Ski Time Square; 970-879-2445). Both alpine and nordic equipment are available at **Ski Haus International** (Pine Grove Road; 970-879-0385) and **Straightline Sports** (744 Lincoln Avenue; 970-879-7568).

CROSS-COUNTRY SKIING

WINTER PARK–GRAND LAKE AREA Cross-country ski trails are found around Winter Park at **Idlewild Cross-Country Center** (Route 40, Winter Park; 970-726-5564) and **Devil's Thumb Ranch** (County Road 83, Fraser; 970-726-8231), and in Granby at **SilverCreek Nordic Center** (Route 40, SilverCreek; 970-887-3384). At Grand Lake, cross-country skiing trails are found at the **Grand Lake Ski Touring Center** (Grand Lake Golf Course; 970-627-8008) and throughout Rocky Mountain National Park.

BRECKENRIDGE–SOUTH PARK AREA For cross-country skiers there are groomed trail systems at the **Frisco Nordic Center** (Frisco; 303-668-0866), **Keystone Cross-Country Center** (Keystone; 970-468-4275) and **Breckenridge Nordic Ski Center** (1200 Ski Hill Road, Breckenridge; 970-453-6855).

VAIL-LEADVILLE AREA Groomed cross-country ski trail networks are at **Vail Nordic Center** (1778 Vail Valley Drive, Vail; 970-476-8366), **Vail Nature Center** (75 South Frontage Road, Vail; 970-479-2291), **Golden Peak Center** (Vail Golf Course, Vail; 970-476-3239 ext. 4390), **McCoy Park** (Beaver Creek, Avon; 303-845-5313) and the exclusive **Cordillera Nordic Ski Trail System** (The Lodge at Cordillera, Edwards; 970-926-2200). The **Shrine Pass Road**, which starts at Vail Pass, is also among the area's best cross-country ski trails. **Ski Cooper** (Route 24, Leadville; 719-486-2277) also has a nordic ski center with groomed trails.

The **Tenth Mountain Trail Association Hut System** provides a network of more than 250 miles of trails, with mountain huts (reservations required), linking Vail, Leadville and Aspen. For maps, organized tour information and hut reservations, contact Tenth Mountain Trail Association (1280 Ute Avenue, Aspen; 970-925-5775).

ASPEN AREA Groomed cross-country trails are found at the **Aspen Cross-Country Ski Center** (39551 West Route 82; 970-925-2145) and **Ashcroft Ski Touring Center** (Castle Creek Road; 970-925-1971).

GLENWOOD SPRINGS AREA **Ski Sunlight Nordic Center** (10901 Four Mile Road, Glenwood Springs; 970-945-7491) has miles of groomed cross-country trails, including several that are accessed by chairlifts.

STEAMBOAT SPRINGS AREA For cross-country skiers, the favorite area near Steamboat Springs is the maze of roads and trails from the vicinity of **Rabbit Ears Pass** in Routt National Forest. **Hahn Peak** is another popular cross-country area. There are groomed nordic trails at **Steamboat Ski Touring Center** (Mount Werner Road, Steamboat Springs; 970-879-8180) and the small **Howelsen Hill Ski Area** (Steamboat Springs; 970-879-8499).

For information on renting equipment, see the ski-rental section in "Downhill Skiing" above.

GOLF

WINTER PARK–GRAND LAKE AREA Near Winter Park, the **Pole Creek Golf Club** (Route 140; 970-726-8847) is the only golf course in Middle Park. **The Grand Lake Golf Course** (Grand Lake; 970-627-8008) is nearly 8500 feet above sea level.

BRECKENRIDGE–SOUTH PARK AREA Golf courses in the area include the **Eagle's Nest Golf Club** (305 Golden Eagle Road, Silverthorne; 970-468-0681), the **Keystone Ranch Golf Club** (1437 County Road 150, Keystone; 970-468-4250) and the **Breckenridge Golf Club** (200 Clubhouse Drive, Breckenridge; 970-453-9104).

VAIL-LEADVILLE AREA Public golf courses in the Vail Valley include the **Vail Golf Course** (1778 Vail Valley Drive, Vail; 970-479-2260), the **Eagle-Vail Golf Course** (646 Eagle Road, Avon; 970-949-5267) and the **Beaver Creek Golf Course and Pro Shop** (75 Offerson Road, Beaver Creek; 970-845-5775). Also in the area are the **Copper Creek Golf Club** (104 Wheeler Place, Copper Mountain; 970-968-2339) and the nine-hole **Mount Massive Golf Course** (259 County Road 5, Leadville; 719-486-2176), at 10,200 feet the world's highest golf course.

ASPEN AREA In Aspen, there's the municipal **Aspen Golf Course** (22475 West Route 82; 970-925-2145) as well as the more expensive, privately owned golf course at the **Snowmass Lodge and Club** (239 Snowmass Club Circle, Snowmass Village; 970-923-3148), which is open to the public on a limited basis.

GLENWOOD SPRINGS AREA Glenwood Springs has only a nine-hole executive golf course—the **Glenwood Springs Golf Club** (193 Sunny Acres Road; 970-945-7086). A short drive down the interstate, the **Rifle Creek Golf Course** (3004 Route 325, Rifle; 970-625-1093) is said to be one of the best in the state.

STEAMBOAT SPRINGS AREA Steamboat Springs also has a nine-hole course—the **Steamboat Golf Club** (Route 40; 970-879-4295), as well as the very expensive **Sheraton Steamboat Golf Club** (Clubhouse Drive; 970-879-2220), designed by Robert Trent Jones, Jr.

TENNIS

Public courts are up the highway from Winter Park at the **Fraser Town Hall** (Route 40; 970-726-5562). In Grand Lake, there are free public tennis courts at the **Grand Lake Golf Course** (970-627-8328). In Breckenridge, there are indoor and outdoor public tennis courts at the **Breckenridge Recreation Center** (880 Airport Road; 970-453-1734; fee) and in municipal **Carter Park** on High Street. There are also municipal courts in Dillon's **Town Park** (reservations, 970-468-2403). Vail has 24 public tennis courts, located in **Ford Park** on South Frontage Road and in the **Gold Peak**, **Lionshead** and **Booth Creek** town parks. In Aspen, tennis courts are open to the public for a fee at **Snowmass Lodge and Tennis Garden** (Snowmass Village; 970-923-5600 ext. 122). Steamboat Springs tennis courts are located at the **Steamboat Springs Health and Recreation Association** (136 Lincoln Avenue; 970-879-1828).

HORSEBACK RIDING

WINTER PARK–GRAND LAKE AREA In the Grand Lake area, you can rent horses for trail rides in Rocky Mountain National Park at **Sombrero Stables** (304 West Portal Road, Grand Lake; 970-627-3514).

BRECKENRIDGE–SOUTH PARK AREA In Breckenridge, horses are for rent above the Alpine Slide parking area on Peak 8 at **Breckenridge Stables** (970-453-4438). Rentals and organized trail rides are also available in nearby Silverthorne at **Eagle's Nest Equestrian Center** (Route 9; 970-468-0677).

VAIL-LEADVILLE AREA In Vail, most horseback riding is in the form of guided rides and pack trips. Outfitters include **Beaver Creek Stables** (Beaver Creek Resort, Avon; 970-845-7770) and **Spraddle Creek Ranch** (100 North Frontage Road East, Vail; 970-476-6941). **Leadville Stables** (181 North Route 91, Leadville; 719-486-1497) and **Pa and Ma's Guest Ranch** (East Tennessee Road, Leadville; 719-486-3900) rent horses and offer guided trail rides.

ASPEN AREA In Aspen, **T-Lazy-7: The Ranch** (970-925-4614, 970-925-7140) offers horse rentals, guided rides, pack trips, hay rides, sleigh rides, stagecoach rides, and special Tennessee Walker day rides. **Snowmass Stables** (P.O. Box 6088, Snowmass Village, CO 81615; 970-923-3075) offers riding lessons, guided trail rides, wilderness pack trips and backcountry fishing expeditions, as well as hay-wagon dinner rides and weekly rodeos. **Brush Creek Stables** (P.O. Box 5621, Snowmass Village, CO 81615; 970-923-4252) also has trail rides and pack trips. The **Rocky Mountain Cattle Moo-vers, Inc.** (P.O. Box 457, Carbondale, CO 81623; 970-963-9666) takes city slickers on day-long cattle drives including a steak lunch.

STEAMBOAT SPRINGS AREA A number of stables and guest ranches that rent horses to the public are located along the road from Steamboat Springs to Steamboat Lake. They include **Glen Eden Stables** (61276 County Road 129, Steamboat Springs; 970-879-3864), **Sunset Ranch** (42850 County Road 129, Steamboat Springs; 970-879-0954) and **Steamboat Lake Outfitters** (Steamboat Lake; 970-879-4404).

BICYCLING

WINTER PARK–GRAND LAKE AREA The **Winter Park Mountain Bike Trail System** includes 500 miles of designated trails, eight major loop trips and access to hundreds of miles of logging roads in Arapaho National Forest north of Winter Park. The Grand Lake area has an extensive network of multiple-use trails that are ideal for mountain biking in surrounding areas of Arapaho National Forest.

BRECKENRIDGE–SOUTH PARK AREA The favorite mountain-bike trail in the Breckenridge area is the **Peaks Trail** (9 miles), which runs between Breckenridge and Frisco along the Ten Mile Range. Breckenridge and Keystone chairlifts carry mountain bikers to summer trails high on the ski mountains. In the Fairplay area, mountain bikers use the 35 miles of marked trails in the **Fairplay State Snowmobile Trail System**, two and a half miles north of town on Forest Road 659.

VAIL-LEADVILLE AREA In the Vail area mountain bikes can be rented at Eagle's Nest above the **Lionshead Gondola** for riding on the upper ski trails. For road-bike touring, the **Vail Pass Bikeway** parallels the interstate over Vail Pass. The first half of the 40-mile trip is a grueling climb to the pass summit; from there, it's an unforgettable coast down the mountain in either direction—to Frisco or to Vail. In recent years a growing number of mountain bikers have been discovering the old mining roads that surround Leadville. A number of four-wheel-drive roads, including the spectacular climb over **Mosquito Pass**, also offer mountain-biking challenges.

ASPEN AREA In the Aspen area, you'll find the rugged trail where mountain biking got its start in the early 1980s—the **Pearl Pass Road**, which climbs from Ashcroft over the 12,700-foot pass and descends to Crested Butte. Easier trails are also found throughout the area. For steep road touring, try the **Maroon Lake Road**, closed to private motor vehicles in the summer months but open to cyclists.

GLENWOOD SPRINGS AREA The *sine qua non* bike ride in the Glenwood Springs area is the paved **Glenwood Canyon Trail**, suitable for both mountain bikes and ten-speed touring bikes.

STEAMBOAT SPRINGS AREA The most popular backcountry mountain-biking area around Steamboat Springs is the extensive National Forest trail network accessed from trailheads at **Rabbit Ears Pass** on Route 40 southeast of town. For an easier ride, take the paved five-mile **Yampa River Trail** between Steamboat Village and downtown Steamboat Springs; you can continue on a good dirt road that follows the Yampa River for nine miles south of town.

BIKE RENTALS In Winter Park, you can rent a mountain bike at **Winter Park Sports Shop** (King's Crossing Shopping Center; 970-726-5554) or **Ski Depot Sports** (Park Plaza Shopping Center; 970-726-8055). In Grand Lake, rent them at **Rocky Mountain Sports** (711 Grand Avenue; 970-627-8124).

Rent a mountain bike in Breckenridge at **Kodi Rafting & Bikes** (Bell Tower Shops; 970-453-2194) or at the equipment-rental shop at the base of Peak 8 at **Breckenridge Ski Resort** (970-453-5000).

Mountain bikes, as well as rollerblades, can be rented in Vail at **Buzz's Bikes & Blades** (Sonnenalp Hotel; 970-476-3320) or **Christy Sports** (293 Bridge Street, 970-476-2244; and 182 Avon Road, Avon, 970-949-0241). In Leadville, mountain bikes are for rent at **10th Mountain Sports** (500 East 7th Street; 719-486-2202) and **Bill's Sport Shop** (225 Harrison Avenue; 719-486-0739).

In Aspen, you can rent mountain bikes by the hour, day, week or month at **Ajax Bike & Sports** (635 East Hyman Street; 970-925-7662); they also rent rollerblades. Mountain-bike rentals are also available at **Aspen Velo Bike Shop** (465 North Mill; 970-925-1465) and at Aspen's oldest bicycle tour outfitters, **Timberline Bicycle Tours** (Silver Queen Gondola; 970-925-5773), which also offers three- and five-day hut-to-hut tours between Aspen and Vail. **Aspen Bike Tours** (434 East Cooper Street; 970-920-4059) not only rents bikes but also offers a shuttle service to transport you to trailheads or to the top of the pass for a once-in-a-lifetime downhill coast.

Bicycles are for rent in Glenwood Springs at **Alpine Bicycles** (51027 Route 6; 970-945-6434) and **BSR Sports** (109 6th Street; 970-945-7317).

Steamboat Springs bike-rental shops include **Sore Saddle Cyclery** (1136 Yampa Street; 970-879-1675) and **Ski Haus International** (1450 South Lincoln Avenue; 970-879-0385).

HIKING

All distances listed for hiking trails are one-way unless otherwise noted.

WINTER PARK–GRAND LAKE AREA In the Grand Lake area you'll find trailheads for several spectacular, uncrowded trails on the west side of Rocky Mountain National Park. Among the prettiest is the 3.5-mile **Cascade Falls Trail**, which starts near the park visitors center just north of Grand Lake and makes an easy 300-foot ascent to the waterfalls. Farther north in the park, the **Lulu City Trail** (3 miles) leads to old mines and the ghost town of Lulu City. Nearby, the challenging **Timber Lake Trail** (5 miles) climbs more than 2000 feet from marshy meadows to alpine lakes and tundra.

BRECKENRIDGE–SOUTH PARK AREA Above Breckenridge, Blue Lakes Road near the summit of Hoosier Pass leads to the 2.5-mile hiking trail that leads to the summit of 14,264-foot **Quandary Peak**. Farther south in the Collegiate Peaks, a longer and more challenging ascent that requires no special equipment is the 8.5-mile trail that goes to the summit of **Mount Harvard** (14,420 feet). The upper portion of the climb follows the Colorado Trail, which runs 420 miles from Denver to Durango.

VAIL-LEADVILLE AREA Near Vail, the **Booth Lake Trail** climbs from a trailhead parking lot beside Route 70 for two miles to 60-foot-high Booth Creek Falls and then climbs for four more miles to Booth Lake in the Eagle's Nest Wilderness. A six-mile trail from the end of Forest Road 707 near Minturn climbs to the 14,003-foot summit of **Mount of the Holy Cross** in the heart of the Holy Cross Wilderness. Another six-mile hike of comparable difficulty starts from the Elbert Creek campground near Turquoise Lake west of Leadville and climbs to the 14,421-foot summit of **Mount Massive**, following the Colorado Trail for the first part of the way.

ASPEN AREA In the Aspen area, the popular **East Maroon Creek Trail** from Maroon Lake goes for 8.5 miles to the top of 11,280-foot East Maroon Pass; you can walk as far as you like and return to the lake by the same route.

You may wish to plan an expedition with **Town Taxi** (Aspen; 970-349-5543), on which you take the 13-mile, seven- to ten-hour hike from Maroon Lake over East Maroon Pass to the ghost town of Gothic; then a shuttle picks you up, takes you to Crested Butte (see Chapter Four, "Southern Colorado Rockies") for the night and returns you to Aspen the next day. You can arrange for your lodging, or they can help you make arrangements as part of the package. Another classic Aspen-area hike is the nine-mile **Conundrum Creek Trail** to Conundrum Hot Springs, starting from Castle Creek Road.

GLENWOOD SPRINGS AREA Besides the **Hanging Lake Trail**, the most popular hiking trail in Colorado, a number of lesser-known trails start from the paved Glenwood Canyon Trail and climb to the upper reaches of the canyon. Among them are **No Name Trail** and **Grizzly Creek Trail**, each about two miles long. From the end of 8th Street in town, the well-marked 1.5-mile trail up Lookout Mountain offers spectacular views of the town and the Roaring Fork Valley.

STEAMBOAT SPRINGS AREA One of the first wilderness areas in Colorado, the Mount Zirkel Wilderness northeast of Steamboat Springs has an extensive trail network that can be accessed from the Slavonia trailhead at the end of Forest Road 400, which turns off County Road 129 south of Steamboat Lake. A magnificent day hike from this trailhead is the **Gilpin Lake Trail** (4 miles), a moderate hike to a 10,000-foot alpine lake.

Transportation

BY CAR

All major areas described in this chapter lie within an hour's drive of **Route 70**. To reach Winter Park, take **Route 40** north from the Empire exit; turn off on **Route 34** at Granby to reach Grand Lake. For Breckenridge, turn off south on **Route 9** at Frisco. Leadville can be reached either from the Copper Mountain exit via **Route 91** or from Vail via **Route 24**. Aspen can be reached via **Route 82** either from the east over Independence Pass from Leadville (closed in winter) or from Glenwood Springs to the west. Three highways—Route 40 from Winter Park; Route 9 north from Silverthorne; or **Route 131** north from Wolcott, at the west end of the Vail Valley—lead to Steamboat Springs.

BY AIR

American Airlines and America West Airlines offer direct flights to the **Vail–Beaver Creek Jet Center**. United Express and Continental Express both have frequent flights from Denver International Airport to Aspen's **Pitkin County Airport**, and both airlines offer a few flights from other U.S. cities. Located about 25 miles west of Steamboat Springs in the town of Hayden, the **Yampa Valley Regional Airport** has commuter service from Denver on Continental Express.

BY TRAIN

The **Rio Grande Ski Train** (303-296-4754) runs directly from Denver to Winter Park on winter weekends. **Amtrak** (800-872-7245) offers passenger service to Glenwood Springs on the "California Zephyr" or the "Desert Wind." Both trains follow the same route through the Rockies between Denver and Salt Lake City.

BY BUS

Greyhound offers bus service to Winter Park (Vasquez Road; 303-292-6111), Vail (Vail Transportation Center; 970-476-5137), Aspen (Rubey Park Transportation Center; 970-625-3980), Glenwood Springs (West 6th Street at Laurel Street; 970-945-8501) and Steamboat Springs (30060 West Route 40; 970-879-0866).

CAR RENTALS

Car rentals are available from **Hertz Rent A Car** (800-654-3131) at the Vail–Beaver Creek Jet Center in Eagle.

In Aspen, you'll find **Alamo Rent A Car** (800-327-9633), **Eagle Rent A Car** (800-282-2128), **Thrifty Car Rental** (800-367-2277), **National Interrent** (800-328-4567) and other car-rental desks at the Pitkin County Airport. Four-wheel-drive vehicles are available at **Rocky Mountain Rent A Car** (Aspen; 800-525-2880).

Avis Rent A Car (800-331-1212), **Budget Rent A Car** (800-527-0700) and **Hertz Rent A Car** (800-654-3131) are located at the Yampa Valley Regional Airport.

PUBLIC TRANSPORTATION

The **Ski Lift** (970-390-5438) provides shuttle service between the hotels and ski slopes of Winter Park.

The **Town Trolley** (970-453-2251) provides shuttle service around Breckenridge, while the free **Summit Stage** (970-453-1241) carries passengers throughout the area of Frisco, Dillon, Silverthorne/Keystone, Copper Mountain and Breckenridge.

Free municipal shuttle service operates constantly throughout Vail Village, Lionshead and West Vail about once every five minutes. **Shuttle service** (970-949-1938) is also available, but not free, to the Avon–Beaver Creek area. The **Leadville Transit Department** (800 Harrison Avenue, Leadville; 719-486-2090) runs morning and evening shuttle service to Vail and Breckenridge, where many Leadville residents work.

Aspen's **Roaring Fork Transit Authority** (20101 West Route 82; 970-920-1905) offers free shuttle service in Aspen and runs commuter buses to Snowmass, Basalt, Carbondale and Glenwood Springs.

Steamboat Springs Transit (970-879-3717) operates regularly scheduled shuttle service between downtown Steamboat Springs and the ski area.

TAXIS

Home James Taxi Service (970-726-5060) provides taxi service in the Winter Park area. In Breckenridge, call **Around Town Taxi** (970-453-8294). **Vail Valley Taxi** (970-476-8294) serves the Vail area. Local transportation in Aspen is provided by **Town Taxi** (970-349-5543). **Aspen Limo** (970-925-1234, 800-222-2112) offers scheduled shuttle service to Aspen's Pitkin County Airport, the Glenwood Springs Amtrak station, the Vail Transportation Center and Denver International Airport, all twice daily in the winter and summer seasons and once daily in the off-season. Cab service in Glenwood Springs is provided by **Yellow Cab** (970-945-2225). **Steamboat Taxi** (970-879-3335) and **Alpine Taxi** (970-879-8294) serve Steamboat Springs.

CHAPTER FOUR

Southern Colorado Rockies

From their headwaters just 25 miles apart on opposite sides of Monarch Pass, the Arkansas and Gunnison rivers carve canyons east and west through the mountains. They divide busy, prosperous northern Colorado from less populated, more relaxed southern Colorado.

Southern Colorado is a region of dramatic contrasts. A half-day drive can sweep you from flat desert valleys, where immense sand dunes give sensuous curves to the skyline, up to the Continental Divide over a notoriously steep mountain pass and down again into the land of the ancient Anasazi cliff dwellers. Or through sparkling forests of aspen trees to old mining towns recently revived, repainted, bursting with new life in the heart of the largest, most remote mountain range in Colorado. Or from a canyon so steep and deep that sunlight touches the bottom only briefly to a vast, solitary volcanic island of pristine lakes and Douglas-fir forests 10,000 feet above sea level.

In southern Colorado, food, dress, language and religion have a distinctive character. The region was part of Mexico until 1848. Place names—Alamosa, Rio Grande, Del Norte, Monte Vista—are present-day remnants of its Spanish colonial heritage. The San Juan Mountains, which marked the western edge of the Spanish domain, were the heart of the Ute Indian Nation until 1873, when gold was found in them thar hills and the Utes were evicted. The last Native American nation in Colorado lies south of Durango. Many present-day residents, both Hispanic and Indian, trace their kinship to the land back through the centuries, before the first Anglo explorers set foot in Colorado.

The areas described in this chapter surround the four sides of the San Juan Mountains, the central geological feature of southern Colorado. Often compared to the Swiss Alps, the San Juans cover more area than any other mountain range in the Colorado Rockies. Most of the San Juan Mountains is uninhabited. There are only six populated towns in 10,000 square miles of remote wilderness.

The Alamosa area encompasses the San Luis Valley, a broad basin of sagebrush desert completely surrounded by 13,000-foot mountains. The valley's major attractions are the Great Sand Dunes and the Cumbres and Toltec Scenic Railroad. Birders flock to watch migrating cranes and eagles at two wetland areas in the valley, while history buffs and theatergoers alike make their way to the born-again boomtown of Creede, nestled in the eastern San Juan Mountains.

To the west, the Gunnison–Crested Butte area styles itself as a sports lover's paradise. Blue Mesa Reservoir, Colorado's largest lake, is the centerpiece of Curecanti National Recreation Area, used for everything from trout fishing to windsurfing. Crested Butte, a friendly little ski town in the winter, becomes the world's headquarters of mountain biking in summer. The West Elk Wilderness near Gunnison and Crested Butte is one of the state's least-known great hiking areas. For those visitors whose favorite outdoor sport is sightseeing, there is the awesome Black Canyon of the Gunnison, and for those who love to drive through superb landscape, there's the road up to tiny Lake City, hidden deep in the San Juans.

At the western extremity of the Colorado Rockies, the Grand Junction area rewards those who venture off the interstate with some scenic surprises. Colorado National Monument offers a sample of the spectacular canyon country that flanks the Colorado River, enticing the adventuresome to explore further. Visitors can hike to active dinosaur fossil digs and peek into a working paleontology lab. Then there's the crowning glory of the valley—Grand Mesa, the world's largest flat-topped mountain. Contrast with the desert below intensifies the strangeness of the dark forests and icy lakes on top.

The Durango and San Juan Skyway area, in the southwestern sector of the state, offers what many consider to be the ultimate Colorado vacation experience. Within the radius of an hour's drive from Durango are Mesa Verde National Park, the Ute Indian Reservations, Navajo Lake and Vallecito Reservoir and several trailheads into the vast, roadless San Juan Wilderness. Many visitors prefer to see the San Juans in comfort, by riding the Durango & Silverton Narrow-Gauge Railroad or by driving the San Juan Skyway, a 200-mile scenic route that links three remarkably rejuvenated historic towns—Telluride, Ouray and Silverton. The San Juan Skyway ranks as one of America's most spectacular scenic highways.

A tourist boom in the past decade or so has elevated the Durango and San Juan Skyway area to new heights of prosperity, unprecedented even at the peak of the gold-mining era. Most gold, silver and coal mines have shut down, as have most timber clearcutting operations. All the region's bean farms, sheep ranches and apple orchards have small importance compared to the economic impact of tourism. Towns like Durango and Telluride blend the patina of history with the glow of success as travelers come in growing numbers each year.

When it comes to tourism, the rest of southern Colorado is largely undiscovered territory. Although places like Alamosa, Gunnison and Grand Junction cannot offer much in the way of elegant hotel rooms or trendy dining establishments, those who venture off the beaten track will experience the outdoors in all its glory. Rivers, alpine lakes, jeep roads and foot trails leading ever deeper into the domain of the beaver, the bear, the elk, the cougar; to stark canyons, wildflower meadows and ghost towns sagging in the shadows of snow-capped mountain summits—the possibilities are limitless.

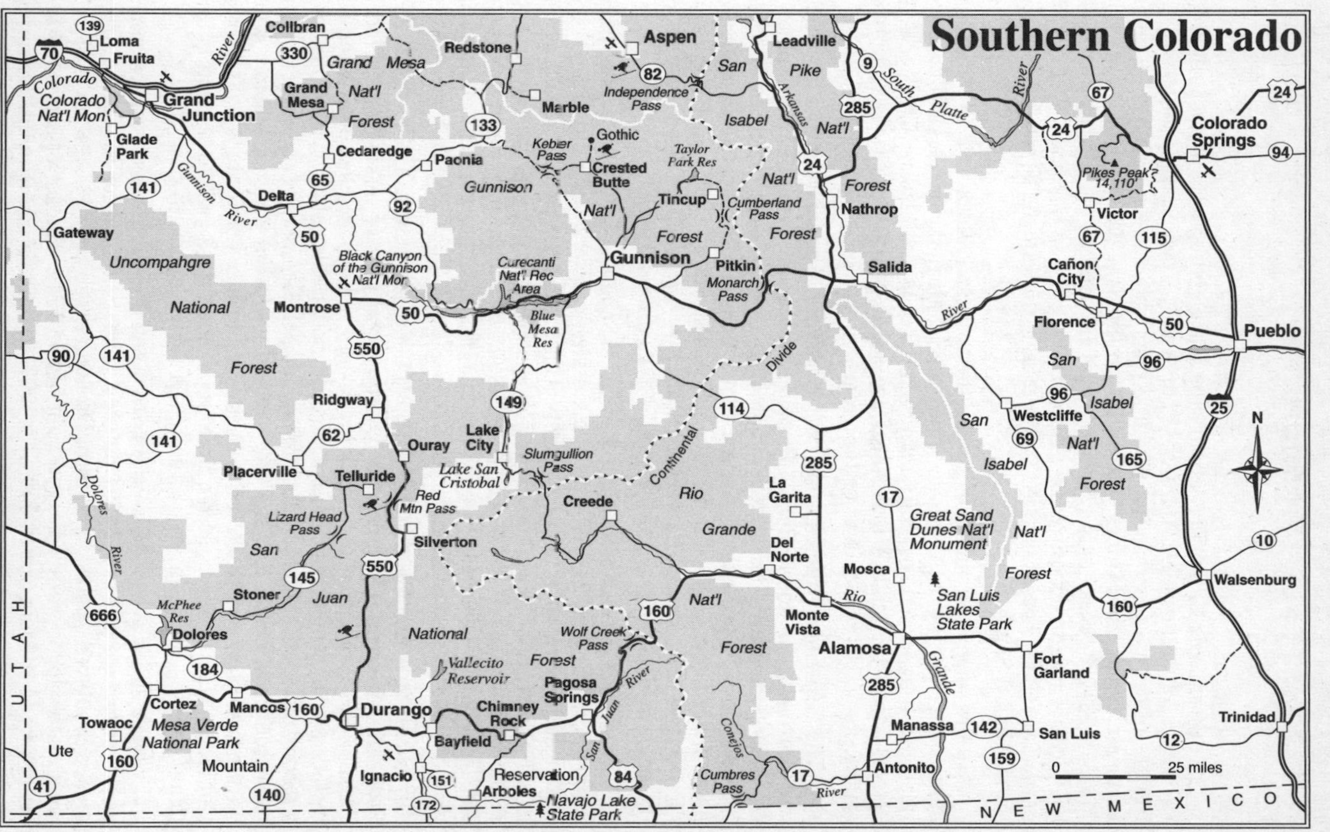
Southern Colorado
Colorado Springs
Pueblo
Walsenburg
Trinidad
Pikes Peak 14,110'
Victor
Cañon City
Florence
Westcliffe
Fort Garland
San Luis
Leadville
Nathrop
Salida
Mosca
Alamosa
Manassa
Antonito
Great Sand Dunes Nat'l Monument
San Luis Lakes State Park
Aspen
Independence Pass
Taylor Park Res
Cumberland Pass
Tincup
Pitkin
Monarch Pass
Gunnison
Crested Butte
Gothic
La Garita
Del Norte
Monte Vista
Continental Divide
Creede
Wolf Creek Pass
Pagosa Springs
Cumbres Pass
Conejos
Navajo Lake State Park
Marble
Kebler Pass
Redstone
Paonia
Curecanti Nat'l Rec Area
Blue Mesa Res
Slumgullion Pass
Lake City
Lake San Cristobal
Silverton
Chimney Rock
Vallecito Reservoir
Arboles
Reservation
Cedaredge
Black Canyon of the Gunnison Nat'l Mon
Ouray
Red Mtn Pass
Ridgway
Telluride
Durango
Bayfield
Ignacio
Collbran
Grand Mesa
Delta
Montrose
Placerville
Lizard Head Pass
Stoner
Mancos
Loma
Fruita
Grand Junction
Glade Park
Colorado Nat'l Mon
Gateway
Uncompahgre National Forest
Dolores
McPhee Res
Cortez
Mesa Verde National Park
Towaoc
Ute Mountain
Gunnison River
Dolores River
Colorado River
San Juan River
Rio Grande
Arkansas
South Platte River
San Isabel Nat'l Forest
Pike Nat'l Forest
Gunnison Nat'l Forest
Rio Grande Nat'l Forest
San Juan National Forest
Grand Mesa Nat'l Forest
0
25 miles
UTAH
NEW MEXICO
N

Alamosa Area

The San Luis Valley is probably the least-visited area in the Colorado Rockies, and unremarkable **Alamosa**, in the valley's center, is the largest town. But one of the most extraordinary natural phenomena in the state lies 36 miles northeast. **Great Sand Dunes National Monument** (11999 Route 150, Mosca; 719-378-2312; admission) is a 50-square-mile expanse of shifting sand, carried by windstorms and deposited over millions of years in this notch at the foot of the Sangre de Cristo Range. At 900 feet high, they are the largest sand dunes in the United States.

In the summer months, visitors by the thousands flock here to climb the dunes or just play on the half-mile-wide "beach" along the broad, shallow, constantly shifting streams of chilly mountain water where Medano Creek makes its way across the sand. A four-wheel-drive road provides access to primitive campgrounds in remote areas of the dunes.

The **San Luis Valley**, an oval of flat land 120 miles long and 60 miles wide surrounded by soaring mountain peaks, was settled in the 1800s by Spanish colonists from nearby Taos. Most people of the valley, descendants of Spanish New Mexican pioneers, live on truck farms along the Rio Grande or in small, poor villages near the foot of the mountains. The valley's inhospitable climate discourages newcomers. Alamosa's winter low temperatures often register as the coldest in Colorado, and the wind blows all year long.

Off Route 160 east of the turnoff to Great Sand Dunes, **Fort Garland Museum** (Fort Garland; 719-379-3512; admission) preserves the old U.S. Army fort established in 1858, shortly after the United States won the territory at the end of the Mexican War. Active for 25 years, the fort was the final command in the military career of Colonel Kit Carson, the Southwest's most notorious Indian fighter. The buildings house exhibits of 19th-century military uniforms, weapons and everyday items.

South of Fort Garland, little **San Luis** is the oldest town in Colorado. The **San Luis Museum, Cultural and Commercial Center** (402 Church Place; 719-672-3611) presents the folk art and history of the valley's people. Exhibits include an outstanding collection of carved wooden saints, known as *bultos*, and a reconstruction of a traditional *penitente* chapel. Beginning at a trailhead near the junction of Routes 159 and 142 in San Luis, a one-and-one-quarter-mile walking trail leads up past a series of life-size bronze statues by local sculptor Humberto Maestas depicting the **Stations of the Cross** (★). At the path's terminus, the top of the mesa, a Crucifixion scene looms over the valley.

A few miles away, the even smaller town of **Manassa** is locally famous as the birthplace of boxer Jack Dempsey, who as a teenager fought for prize money in mining-camp saloons from Durango to the Cripple Creek district and went on to win the world's heavyweight title in 1919. The **Jack Dempsey Museum** (★) (401 Main Street; 719-843-5207) exhibits a collection of Dempsey mementos contributed by residents.

At the southwestern edge of the valley, **Antonito** is the northern terminus of the **Cumbres and Toltec Scenic Railroad** (719-376-5483). Two separate narrow-gauge steam trains run each morning from Antonito, Colorado, and Chama, New Mexico, climbing by sweeping loops through forests of aspen up to Osier, a mountain ghost town that is inaccessible by car. In the afternoon, passengers can return along the same route or, for a higher fare, continue all the way to Chama and take a van back in the evening. The 64-mile Antonito-to-Chama trip is America's longest and highest narrow-gauge steam train route operating today. Motorists can take a scenic drive different from, but comparable to, the train route by taking paved Route 17 over La Manga Pass (10,230 feet) to the summit of **Cumbres Pass** (10,022 feet), where the narrow-gauge tracks parallel the road for several miles. The ghost town of Cumbres, near the summit of the pass, was home to railroad workers who kept the trains running year-round back in the 1880s.

Motorists going west toward Wolf Creek Pass and Durango on Route 160 pass through the towns of **Monte Vista** and **Del Norte**. Monte Vista is best known for the **Monte Vista National Wildlife Refuge** (Route 15; 719-589-4021), well known among birders as a stopover for as many as 20,000 sandhill and whooping cranes migrating south to New Mexico in October and November. Bald eagles and thousands of ducks spend the winter months in these wetlands. Del Norte's **Rio Grande County Museum** (580 Oak Street; 719-657-2847; admission) focuses on the multicultural history of Native Americans, Spanish settlers and Anglo trappers and traders along the upper Rio Grande.

Following the Rio Grande toward its source high in the mountains by way of paved Route 149 brings travelers to **Creede**, one of several spectacularly situated, spruced-up old mining towns turned mountain hideaways in the San Juans. Others include Lake City, Telluride, Ouray and Silverton, covered elsewhere in this chapter; Creede is the only one east of the Continental Divide. Founded in 1889 upon the discovery of the richest silver lode in Colorado, Creede is also remembered in history as one of the wildest western boomtowns. Such legendary characters as the James Gang, "Calamity Jane" Canary, "Poker Annie" Tubbs, con artist "Soapy" Smith and lawman Bat Masterson passed through Creede during its heyday. The boom lasted for only four years, but unlike other similar mine camps, Creede was never completely abandoned. A self-guided auto tour takes visitors to the steep, narrow canyon above town and several of the mines on which Creede's fortunes rose and fell a century ago. A magnificent scenic drive, the 48-mile **Silver Thread Scenic Byway** (Route 149) climbs from Creede past the Rio Grande headwaters and over Slumgullion Pass to the even smaller old town of Lake City (see "Gunnison–Crested Butte Area"). Creede is also home to the finest summer repertory theater in southern Colorado.

ALAMOSA AREA HOTELS

Alamosa's hotel and restaurant selection is on the slim side. A welcome find is the **Cottonwood Inn Bed & Breakfast & Gallery** (123 San Juan Avenue; 719-589-3882), a big pink-and-gray Victorian several blocks from the main highway in a quiet, shady neighborhood. It has six antique-furnished rooms and suites at rates that range from moderate to deluxe. The common areas feature changing exhibits by local artists.

The **Alamosa Lamplighter Motel** (425 Main Street, Alamosa; 719-589-6636, 800-359-2138, fax 719-589-3831) is actually two motels under the same management but several blocks apart, with a total of 70 guest rooms. The rooms, which are about as conventional as motel rooms get, are a bargain when you consider that the rent includes the use of the indoor swimming pool and sauna at the main motel and the jacuzzi in the annex. There is also a restaurant on the premises. Budget.

The most luxurious accommodations in the San Luis Valley are at the **Great Sand Dunes Country Inn at Zapata Ranch** (5303 Route 150, Mosca; 719-378-2356, 800-284-9213, fax 719-378-2428), just three miles from the national monument entrance. Seclusion is part of the allure of this log building complex dating back to the 1880s. The inn doesn't provide phones, television sets or newspapers, but it does have a golf course, pool, jacuzzi, mountain bikes and miles of hiking trails, along with majestic views of the Great Sand Dunes. Fourteen guest rooms feature handmade pine furniture, Indian-design fabrics and Mexican tile bathrooms, adding up to a feel of rustic elegance. The inn's greatest pride is its bison herd—one of the largest in existence anywhere—that grazes on Zapata Ranch's 100,000 acres. Daily tours take guests close to the mighty beasts. Ultra-deluxe.

Travelers can spend the night in a nunnery at **El Convento Bed & Breakfast** (512 Church Place, San Luis; 719-672-4223). Set in the center of a small village that dates back to the Spanish colonial era, this historic building served as a Catholic school and convent before the church decided to remodel it and open it to the public as a bed and breakfast. The four rooms are decorated in authentic southwestern style, with handcrafted furniture and *horno* fireplaces. Moderate prices.

At the other end of the valley, the **Best Western Movie Manor Motel** (2830 West Route 160, Monte Vista; 719-852-5921, 800-771-9468, fax 719-852-0122) harks back to the 1950s and the height of America's infatuation with automobiles. In all 60 units of this otherwise-ordinary motel, big picture windows look out onto the big screen of the Star Drive-In Theater next door. The movie soundtrack plays through speakers installed in each room. Although the drive-in operates during the summer months only, the motel is open year-round. Moderate.

Creede has a few small bed and breakfasts in the upstairs rooms of refurbished historic buildings on the main street near the repertory theater. The **Creede Hotel** (Creede Avenue; 719-658-2608) has been in operation for more than a century and was the only lodging in town until 1992. The five guest rooms are rather sparsely furnished with mining-era antiques. Two other buildings have recently been renovated and opened as bed and breakfasts. **The Old Firehouse No. 1 B & B** (Creede Avenue; 719-658-0212), decorated with firefighting memorabilia and historic photos of old-time Creede, has four guest rooms and a sitting room with a library and games. On the ground floor is an old-fashioned soda fountain. Across the street, **Blessings** (Creede Avenue; 719-658-0215) offers four antique-filled rooms with private baths. Room rates at all three bed and breakfasts are in the moderate range.

ALAMOSA AREA RESTAURANTS

In Alamosa, you can get breakfast all day—until the 2 p.m. closing hour—at **Bauer's Campus Pancake House and Restaurant** (435 Poncha Avenue; 719-589-4202), which caters to the students at Adams State College. Giant cinnamon rolls are the most popular item on the menu. The restaurant also serves weekday lunch specials and Sunday-noon dinners. Budget.

A quiet little place to dine by candlelight is **Lara's Soft Spoken Restaurant** (801 State Avenue, Alamosa; 719-589-6769), featuring homemade Italian entrées along with steaks, shrimp and lobster and Mexican combination plates. The salad bar is popular at lunch time. Budget to moderate.

Enchiladas and hot chili stew are everyday fare for many local people in the San Luis Valley. Mexican restaurants in the area serve good, spicy food at low prices in a simple atmosphere. One such restaurant, **El Charro Café** (421 6th Street, Alamosa; 719-589-2262), has been run by the same family for more than 50 years. Budget; no alcohol. Diners who prefer their Mexican food with margaritas or imported beer might try **Alberto's** (1019 6th Street, Alamosa; 719-589-0277), where a house specialty is *chile rellenos*—green chili peppers stuffed with cheese. The decor features touches of Old Mexico. Budget.

For fine dining in the San Luis Valley, the top choice is the **Great Sand Dunes Country Inn at Zapata Ranch** (5303 Route 150, Mosca; 719-378-2356). Since Zapata Ranch raises bison, the restaurant's specialty is bison steaks and roasts. Patrons can also opt for pasta, seafood or vegetarian dishes. The small restaurant commands a majestic view of the Great Sand Dunes. Moderate.

In San Luis, just about the only place to eat is a good one—**Emma's Hacienda** (719-672-9902). The same family has been operating this tiny restaurant for almost 50 years, and it's as homey as any restaurant around. The menu features traditional regional fare, from chicken and cheese enchiladas to green chili burgers. Budget.

In Creede, the place to eat is the **Creede Hotel Dining Room** (Creede Avenue; 719-658-2608). This little restaurant on the ground floor of a frontier Victorian-style bed and breakfast near the repertory theater serves a full menu of homemade entrées each evening. The emphasis is on Italian food, with house specialties including fettuccine Alfredo and chicken marinara as well as lamb chops from the San Luis Valley cooked with lemon and dill. Can you resist the pecan brandy apple pie? Make reservations well in advance for theater nights. Breakfast and lunch are served daily. Moderate.

Eighteen miles southwest of Creede, a rustic-elegant restaurant stands secluded in the heart of Rio Grande National Forest. The **Bristol Inn** (Route 149, Creede; 719-658-2455) serves lobster, roast beef and quail with a Continental flair. It is busiest around noon on Sundays, when the inn's buffet brunch provides a tantalizing excuse for people all over southern Colorado to go for a drive in the mountains. Moderate to deluxe; reservations required.

ALAMOSA AREA SHOPPING

A fair number of contemporary artists and craftspeople make their homes in the San Luis Valley, where the cost of living is low. While most sell their work in other localities, some also show at galleries in Alamosa. **Firedworks Gallery** (608 Main Street; 719-589-6064) exhibits paintings, pottery and weavings by the studio-gallery's owners and other area artists. A block down the street, **Gallery West** (718 Main Street; 719-589-2275) features paintings, sculptures, graphics, ceramics and fiber art by San Luis Valley artists.

A good place to shop for local arts and crafts is **Centro Artesano** (512 Church Place, San Luis). This little gallery run by the Catholic church shares the building with El Convento Bed & Breakfast, providing exhibit space for the valley's traditional artisans.

Another church-sponsored gallery, the **San Juan Art Center**, is located in the Chapel of San Juan Bautista in the small village of La Garita, eight miles off Route 285 at the foot of the mountains on the northwest side of the San Luis Valley. Open in summer only.

Creede has a mini-arts district on its main street near the repertory theater. Studio-galleries include **Rare Things** (Creede Avenue; 719-658-2376), **Abbey Lane Gallery** (Creede Avenue; 719-658-2736) and the **Quiller Gallery** (Creede Avenue; 719-658-2741). Latin American folk art is featured at **Captive Inca** (Creede Avenue; 719-658-2662).

ALAMOSA AREA NIGHTLIFE

Alamosa's nightlife is pretty much limited to the lounges of the two biggest motor inns—**Fillys at the Holiday Inn** (333 Santa Fe Avenue; 719-589-5833) and the **Alamosa Inn Restaurant and Lounge** (1901 Main Avenue; 719-589-4943). Both feature live music nightly.

Culture in the Rockies pops up in some of the most unlikely places. The **Creede Repertory Theater** (160 Creede Avenue, Creede; 719-658-2540) has been staging plays in the remote mining town seasonally for almost 30 years. It has gained a reputation as the top summer-stock company in the southern Colorado Rockies. Theater professionals from coast to coast vie for roles in a schedule of plays ranging from Shakespearean tragedies to Broadway musicals. Order tickets well in advance; contact CRT Box Office, P.O. Box 269, Creede, CO 81130.

ALAMOSA AREA PARKS

San Luis Lakes State Park—Shallow, natural San Luis Lake, just west of the Great Sand Dunes, is a locally popular spot for waterskiing, fishing, sailing and windsurfing. The north portion of the lake, as well as the wetlands and smaller Head Lake, are off-limits to boats but laced with wide, level trails for nature lovers to observe wildlife such as migrating whooping cranes and bald eagles, as well as native waterfowl, songbirds, coyotes and pronghorns. The park adjoins the second-largest bison ranch in the United States.

Facilities: Picnic areas with tables, restrooms, boat ramp, wildlife-area trails; day-use fee, $3; information, 719-378-2020. *Swimming:* Permitted. *Fishing:* Excellent year-round for trout.

Camping: There are 51 RV/tent sites with electric hookups, tables and fireplaces, drinking water, showers and laundry facilities; $9 to $10 per night.

Getting there: Located ten miles east of Mosca on Six Mile Lane.

Rio Grande National Forest—This horseshoe-shaped, two-million-acre national forest surrounds the San Luis Valley. The eastern part, which runs along the western slope of the Sangre de Cristo Range, is virtually roadless. Much of it has recently been designated the Southern Sangre de Cristo Wilderness. Most trails are only a few miles long, following gulches up the slope of the high, jagged, unbroken wall of 13,000-foot peaks. The other side, covering the eastern slope of the San Juans, offers boundless hiking possibilities in the vast Weminuche Wilderness and the smaller La Garita Wilderness, both in the vicinity of Creede. Forest roads off the paved Silver Thread Scenic Byway (Route 149) provide access to campgrounds and natural and artificial lakes in the high country.

Facilities: Boat ramps at Rio Grande Reservoir, Mix Lake, Cross Creek and Big Meadows campgrounds; picnic areas with tables and restrooms at Hayden Creek, Spring Creek, Big Springs, Columbine and Natural Arch; archery range at Rock Creek Recreation Area. For more information, call 719-852-5941 *Fishing:* Good for trout in Rio Grande Reservoir, Tucker Ponds, Poso Creek and many other lakes and creeks; the upper Conejos River is famous for rainbow trout and kokanee salmon.

Camping: There are 43 campgrounds with a total of 705 RV/tent sites. Most have drinking water but none has hookups. Most sites are $7 per night.

Getting there: Main access roads to the national forest are Route 160 below Wolf Creek Pass, the Silver Thread Scenic Byway (Route 149) beyond Creede and Route 17 over La Manga and Cumbres passes.

Gunnison–Crested Butte Area

In the summer, many visitors to the Gunnison area come for the fishing, as well as other water sports, on Blue Mesa Reservoir, Colorado's largest reservoir. In nearby Crested Butte, mountain biking is the most popular summer sport. **Gunnison National Forest** surrounds Gunnison and Crested Butte with jeep roads to old mining camps and a network of foot trails that could keep a hiker busy all summer. In the winter, Crested Butte enjoys a wealthier lifestyle as a famous ski resort.

Motorists reach the Gunnison area on Route 50 from Cañon City and Salida up a series of switchbacks to the summit of **Monarch Pass** (11,846 feet)—a hard pull for those who are headed for Curecanti National Recreation Area with boats in tow. The town of **Gunnison** is situated among dry hills beside a raging whitewater stretch of the Gunnison River. Nearby, the **Pioneer Museum** (Route 50;

970-641-4530; admission) occupies several buildings, including Gunnison's original one-room schoolhouse. On exhibit are a restored narrow-gauge steam train, early-day automobiles and assorted collections of arrowheads, rocks, farming tools and other memorabilia dating as far back as 1874, when Gunnison was founded as a transportation and supply center for mining camps in the surrounding mountains.

A few miles west of Gunnison, **Curecanti National Recreation Area** (Route 50; 970-641-0406) encompasses the three basins of 20-mile-long Blue Mesa Reservoir, the largest manmade lake in Colorado, as well as the smaller and more secluded Morrow Point Reservoir and long, narrow Crystal Lake, which winds through the upper part of the Gunnison River Gorge. During the summer, the National Park Service operates daily boat cruises with naturalist guides on Morrow Point Reservoir (reservations required; 970-641-0402).

Downriver from Curecanti National Recreation Area, beyond the dam that impounds Crystal Lake, lies **Black Canyon of the Gunnison National Monument** (Montrose; 970-249-7036), which contains the most spectacular 12 miles of the Gunnison River Gorge. The canyon's dark gray cliffs of schist and gneiss, almost 3000 feet deep, rise so steeply that in some places the canyon is deeper than its width from rim to rim. The south rim, easily accessible from Route 50 via a paved park road, has a large campground, a visitors center and numerous overlooks and short hiking trails. The more remote north rim can be reached only by a long unpaved road from the little town of Crawford on Route 92.

A few miles west of Black Canyon of the Gunnison, in the farming community of **Montrose**, is the **Ute Indian Museum** (970-249-3098). Landscaped with columbines of many colors, the museum occupies land that was once the farm of Chief Ouray, the great statesman of the Ute people. He is remembered for negotiating an 1873 treaty with the U.S. government that established a Ute homeland in the San Juan Mountains. Soon after Ouray's death in 1880, the treaty was broken and his people were forced into the badlands of Utah to make way for gold prospectors. Visitors to the museum can see beaded costumes and artifacts, photographs of Ouray and other Ute leaders and a bigger-than-life copy of the broken treaty. **Chipeta Park**, a grassy expanse adjoining the museum, is named for Chief Ouray's wife.

Motorists who travel south from Curecanti National Recreation Area on Route 149 climb through arid foothills toward the distant mountains of the Big Blue Wilderness, enter the red-cliff gorge of the Lake Fork of the Gunnison River and eventually reach **Lake City**. This tiny village is the Hinsdale County seat and, in fact, the only town in the county, which otherwise consists of National Forest land. Lake City is best known as the home of Colorado's most macabre historical figure, Alferd Packer, who was convicted of murdering—and eating —five prospectors who had hired him as a guide in 1874. Cannibal jokes have had a place in Colorado heritage ever since.

The paved 48-mile portion of Route 149 between Lake City and Creede is known as the **Silver Thread Scenic Byway**. It's a pleasant route: Most of it meanders gently through lush green mountain meadows where streams flow together to form the headwaters of the Rio Grande. About three miles south of Lake City is the town's namesake, **Lake San Cristobal**, the second-largest natural body of water in Colorado. It was formed a mere eight centuries ago when a huge mudslide slipped down the slopes below Slumgullion Pass to block the valley and dam the river. The magnitude of the Slumgullion Slide is best appreciated from the overlook near the top of the 11,361-foot pass on Route 149. The short, steep climb from Lake City to Slumgullion Pass is the only difficult part of the drive on the byway.

Lake City is also the starting point for another National Forest scenic route, the **Alpine Loop Backcountry Byway** (★). This narrow, unpaved 63-mile mountain road is very rocky and steep in places, suitable only for four-wheel-drive vehicles and mountain bikes. Passenger cars can take the first stage of the loop, Engineer Pass Road, as far as the site of **Capitol City**. Local ore processor George T. Lee, who founded the town, believed it was destined to become the state capital, but today the site contains only scattered traces of the lavish governor's mansion that Lee built there soon after Colorado attained statehood.

From Capitol City the road deteriorates quickly as it climbs to the 12,800-foot summit of Engineer Pass and descends the wind-blasted south face of Engineer Peak to the early-day mining district of **Mineral Point** and **Animas Forks**, strewn with rusty mementos of past prosperity. Other roads link the historic mining district with Ouray and Silverton. To return to Lake City, take the road from Animas Forks west over Cinnamon Pass (12,620 feet). The return route passes the site of **Sherman**, which was destroyed when a dirt dam burst upriver. Little remains of the town. The road between Sherman and Lake San Cristobal is easily passable by passenger car.

The historic district of **Crested Butte** began in 1879 as a way station on the road between Gunnison and Aspen. It became a mining town when Colorado Fuel & Iron, the Rockefeller family's steel company, discovered large deposits of coal there. Coal mining continued in Crested Butte until the 1950s, saving the beautiful frontier Victorian town from the decay and abandonment that erased so many other Colorado mining towns from the map. Ski-resort development came within a few years after the mines closed. The historic district retains a lot of authenticity and old-time charm beneath new coats of paint. Across the valley, not quite adjoining the old town, is **Mount Crested Butte**, a development of custom homes and luxury condominiums that stands in dramatic contrast to the old town. Among the modern town's part-time residents is former President Gerald Ford, who put Crested Butte in the news during his brief administration in the mid-1970s.

Mountain bikes seem to outnumber cars for most of the summer around Crested Butte. To find out why, one need only look at a Gunnison National Forest map (get one from the ranger station at 216 North Colorado Street, Gunnison; 970-641-0471 or any of several Crested Butte cycle shops) and marvel at the array of dirt roads and jeep trails that lead into the surrounding mountains.

One of the most spectacular routes that is accessible by passenger car is the unpaved **Kebler Pass Road**, which starts at the west end of White Rock Avenue in Crested Butte and goes 31 miles over Kebler Pass (10,000 feet) to Paonia Reservoir. Following an abandoned railroad bed, the road offers panoramic views of the high peaks of the West Elk Wilderness and provides access to aspen forests, alpine meadows and fishing lakes such as **Lost Lake** and **Lake Irwin**.

Some of Colorado's most picturesque old mining towns can be found in the Sawatch Range east of Gunnison and Crested Butte. Eight miles north of Crested Butte on unpaved Forest Road 317 is the site of **Gothic**, a gold-prospecting town that boomed between 1879 and 1881 to 4000 people and 400 buildings—mostly boardinghouses, saloons and bordellos. Unfortunately, none of the eager prospectors who swarmed over the mountainsides around Gothic ever found gold in sufficient quantities to mine, and the town was abandoned in a few years. For the past 60 years, the townsite has been owned by the **Rocky Mountain Biological Laboratory** (970-349-7231), which conducts environmental studies there. A number of the old buildings remain standing along the main road, and there are campgrounds nearby. Guides from the laboratory lead flora and fauna tours around Gothic several days a week.

Other old mining towns in varying states of repair lie secluded in the mountains east of Gunnison and Crested Butte. Pitkin, a notoriously lawless silver-mining town of 1500 people, lasted less than 20 years—from 1879 to 1898—before the mines played out and a rash of fires destroyed the business district. Yet the town was never entirely abandoned; as of the 1990 census, it had a full-time population of 58. Along the paved road to Pitkin, which turns off Route 50 about 12 miles east of Gunnison, lie the ruins of **Ohio City**, a more enduring gold and silver town where mining continued until World War II. A few scattered structures there have been kept up as summer homes.

A mile or so past Pitkin, a rocky dirt road branches off and climbs an old railroad grade for ten miles to the west portal of the **Alpine Tunnel** (★). It took 18 months for a work crew of 400 men to dig this 1771-foot tunnel through the sheer wall of granite that is the crest of the Sawatch Range. In its day—from 1881 to 1910—the tunnel was recognized as an engineering masterpiece, especially since the monumental amount of heavy labor was done in the rarefied air 11,500 feet above sea level. Today, the scope of the accomplishment remains evident even though both portals of the tunnel have collapsed. Nearby are the ruins of Woodstock, where railroad workers lived until 1884, when it was wiped out by an avalanche.

Visitors traveling in high-clearance vehicles can continue on the unpaved road from Pitkin over 12,000-foot Cumberland Pass to **Tincup** (★), one of the most remote mountain communities in the state. Like Pitkin, Tincup earned a reputation in the early mining days as a wide-open, violent town. With a population of 3000, it had 20 saloons and four graveyards. Abandoned in 1918, Tincup was all but forgotten until the 1950s, when radio host Pete Smythe started broadcasting his popular talk show from "East Tincup" (meaning Denver) and rekindled interest in the old ghost town. Now Tincup has a country store, a church and a cluster of summer homes. The original town is preserved as a historic district.

GUNNISON–CRESTED BUTTE AREA HOTELS

For affordable elegance in Gunnison, the best bet is the **Mary Lawrence Inn** (601 North Taylor Street; 970-641-3343). This four-unit bed and breakfast, located in a two-story 1885 former rooming house built in 1885 and situated on a tree-shaded side street, has lovingly decorated theme rooms—southwestern Indian, Victorian, flowery and downright cute. A gourmet breakfast is included in the moderate room rate.

Most of your other lodging choices in Gunnison are the standard-issue motels and motor inns lying along Tomichi Avenue (Route 50). They range from budget-rate independent places such as the plain-and-simple 24-unit **ABC Motel** (212 East Tomichi Avenue; 970-641-2400) to the moderate-priced luxury of the southwestern-style, 48-unit **Best Western Tomichi Village** (Route 50 East; 970-641-1131, 800-528-1234).

One of the nicer guest ranches in the Gunnison–Crested Butte area is **Waunita Hot Springs Ranch** (8007 County Road 887, Gunnison; 970-641-1266). Set among the pines at 9000 feet in the mountains 27 miles northeast of Gunnison, the ranch has a picture-perfect hot-spring pool. No nude bathing here—the staff is cheerfully Christian and holds nondenominational church services on Sunday. The rooms are simple, with wood paneling and wildlife motifs; designed for families and groups, many have bunk beds. The lodge is heated geothermally with water from the springs. The family-oriented ranch has a petting farm and group activities that include fishing, hiking, horseback riding, river trips, hayrides and four-wheel-drive excursions. Rates are moderate and include all meals. Open in the summer only.

The tiny hideaway town of Lake City offers a fine selection of vacation accommodations. Foremost among them is **Crystal Lodge** (Route 149 South; 970-944-2201), secluded in fir-and-aspen forest on the Lake Fork of the Gunnison River near Lake San Cristobal. The lodge offers 14 simple, wood-paneled guest rooms, including five with full kitchens and four housekeeping cabins. The dining room serves the best gourmet meals in town. Amenities include a heated outdoor pool and a sundeck with a spectacular view of nearby Crystal Peak. Moderate to deluxe.

A long-established riverbank cabin complex, **Texan Resort** (Route 149 South, Lake City; 970-944-2246), nestled at the base of a maroon-colored canyon wall, has 15 housekeeping cabins with full kitchen facilities as well as outdoor barbecue grills. It's an easy walk to a 65-foot waterfall nearby. Moderate.

For travelers who prefer to stay in town, the **Cinnamon Inn Bed & Breakfast** (426 Gunnison Avenue, Lake City; 970-944-2641) has four guest rooms, including a luxury suite, in an 1878 two-story Victorian residence that belonged to the town jeweler in Lake City's heyday. Each room is individually decorated with period furnishings. A gallery on the premises exhibits works by local artists. A full gourmet breakfast is included in the deluxe room rates.

Luxurious lodging is not why people come to **Irwin Lodge** (P.O. Box 457, Crested Butte, CO 81224; 970-349-5308); isolation is. Situated in the Elk Mountains at 10,700 feet and overlooking Lake Irwin, the lodge is reached via ten miles of unpaved forest roads (transportation is provided from Crested Butte). The barnlike lodge has 24 very simple, spacious rooms with queen-size beds and foldout couches. The rooms open off the long, narrow common room with its 30-foot ceiling. Although snow closes the road to the lodge for about five months of the year, the lodge stays open as a very exclusive ski resort. Summer rates for bed and breakfast are in the deluxe price range, while winter rates including all meals, skiing and transportation are ultra-deluxe (three-night minimum stay).

Several modern ski lodges and condominium complexes lie at the foot of the Mount Crested Butte ski area. The largest of the lodges, the **Grand Butte Hotel** (Emmons Road, Mount Crested Butte; 970-349-4000, 800-642-4422, fax 970-349-6332), offers 262 bright, contemporary guest rooms and suites with whirlpool baths as well as balconies, refrigerators, queen-size beds and fold-out sofas. The lodge has an indoor swimming pool, a sauna and a spa. Ultra-deluxe. Nearby, the **Nordic Inn** (14 Treasury Road; 970-349-5542) offers cozy, ski-from-your-doorstep lodging, with 27 guest units in a distinctive Scandinavian-style lodge. After a day on the slopes, guests relax around the large fireplace that dominates the lobby or soak in the hot tub. Ultra-deluxe.

Condominium rentals at Mount Crested Butte are available through **Crested Butte Accommodations** (800-821-3718).

Lodgings are generally smaller and more homelike in the old town of Crested Butte, about three miles from the slopes. In the winter, shuttle buses run constantly from town to the ski area. In fact, staying in town offers a wider selection of restaurants and nightlife within walking distance. One good choice is the **Crested Butte Club** (512 2nd Street; 970-349-6655, 800-782-6037), a seven-room bed and breakfast in a frontier-style building with a false facade on the town's main street. The rooms are large and lavishly decorated in Victorian style, with flowery furniture, old-fashioned fireplaces and copper bathtubs, as well as such modern amenities as four-poster waterbeds. This bed and breakfast is also a health club, so guests have access to a lap pool, steam rooms, weights and exercise machines, as well as aerobic and fitness classes. Deluxe.

The **Claim Jumper** (704 Whiterock, Crested Butte; 970-349-6471), probably the most eccentric bed and breakfast in town, seems to have been designed for wealthy college students. The decor—satirical taxidermy and creative clutter that includes a jukebox, a man-eating fish and an in-room putting green—exudes a slightly warped sense of humor, making this four-unit inn a place travelers either love or hate. Each room has its own theme—cowboys, gold miners, sailing ships or sports. Moderate to deluxe.

Accommodations in Crested Butte can be hard to find during the winter months. Travelers can save a lot of calls in search of a vacancy by telephoning **Mount Crested Butte Central Reservations** (800-544-8448) or the **Crested Butte Chamber of Commerce** (970-349-6438).

GUNNISON–CRESTED BUTTE AREA RESTAURANTS

The established favorite for fine dining in Gunnison is the **Cattlemen Inn** (301 West Tomichi Avenue; 970-641-1061). The decor is ranch-style, and the menu offers a full assortment of hand-cut steaks, from sirloin and rib eye to T-bone and filet mignon, as well as chicken and seafood entrées. Prices are moderate to deluxe.

The Trough (Route 50, Gunnison; 970-641-3724), west of Gunnison on the way to Curecanti National Recreation Area, serves steak and seafood favorites in a relaxed, casual environment of natural wood and dim lighting. Swordfish, salmon and catch-of-the-day specials make this the best place in the area to satisfy a craving for fish. Moderate.

Budget-priced meals, from chicken-fried steak to chimichangas, can be found at the **Sundae Shoppe Restaurant** (901 West Tomichi Avenue, Gunnison; 970-641-5051). The restaurant exhibits local arts and crafts, including a kitsch collage of handmade clocks with faces depicting unicorns, owls, Elvis and the pope, to name just a few. As the name suggests, the restaurant doubles as a soda fountain and offers a tantalizing array of banana splits, hot-fudge sundaes, chocolate malts and homemade pies.

The cuisine scene is considerably more interesting in Crested Butte. For starters, the little resort town boasts more French cuisine than the rest of southern Colorado put together. Top of the line is **Le Bosquet** (201 Elk Avenue; 970-349-5808), a small French restaurant decorated in pink hues, lace and photos of French provincial life. The menu features such entrées as elk medallions in cabernet sauce and grilled duck breast in raspberry-mint sauce. Deluxe.

Another French restaurant, **Soupçon** (127 Elk Avenue, Crested Butte; 970-349-5448)—pronounced "soup's on"—has a more rustic ambience—it's in a historic log cabin in the alley behind Kochevar's Bar. The frontier feel of the restaurant sets off the sheer elegance of the cuisine. The gourmet menu, which changes daily, typically features fresh fish and lamb entrées. Classic appetizers include escargot, caviar and duckling mousse. Deluxe.

Karolina's Kitchen (127 Elk Avenue, Crested Butte; 970-349-6756), adjoining Kochevar's Bar, serves assorted soups, salads, sandwiches and steaks in a historic building that once served as Crested Butte's blacksmith shop. Vintage photographs and fragments of old-time machinery and equipment, including a moonshine still, decorate the wall. Moderate.

The two-story **Timberline** (21 Elk Avenue, Crested Butte; 970-349-9831) features a variety of creative Continental dishes, from venison medallions to herb-seasoned pasta in butter sauce and smoked trout. Framed food and wine posters complement the pink-and-gray decor. Deluxe.

The **Slogar Bar & Restaurant** (517 2nd Street, Crested Butte; 970-349-5765) in a picturesque Old West false-front building, serves delicious home-style fried chicken with all the fixin's—cole slaw, fresh vegetables, mashed potatoes and flaky biscuits. Dinner only; moderate.

The **Wooden Nickel** (222 Elk Avenue; 970-349-6350) is the oldest restaurant in the Crested Butte historic district.The original restaurant on the site had been in business for 56 years when it burned to the ground in 1985, so the same owners built this modern restaurant on the same spot. The decor is a clutter of antiques and oddities, including an intricate wooden ship over the fireplace and a number of deer heads. The menu offers just about anything people are likely to crave after a day on the ski slopes, from jalapeño cheese potato skins to steak and lobster. Moderate.

An affordable and often lively place for breakfast or lunch is the **Paradise Cafe** (303 Elk Avenue, Crested Butte; 970-349-6233). The small restaurant, which occupies part of the large, tourist-oriented general store known as the Company Store, has eclectic decor reminiscent of the South Seas and offers a menu of health-conscious breakfasts and overstuffed deli sandwiches. Budget.

For Mexican food in Crested Butte, it's **Donita's Cantina** (330 Elk Avenue; 970-349-6674). This cozy restaurant and lounge, built around a big rock fireplace, features not only predictable taco-and-burrito fare but also such unconventional options as spinach enchiladas. Portions are large and prices are moderate.

GUNNISON–CRESTED BUTTE AREA SHOPPING

Shopping possibilities in Gunnison are limited for the most part to hunting and fishing supplies. The town has one art gallery, **The Great Wall** (125 North Main Street; 970-641-4680), specializing in limited-edition southwestern lithographs. The **Gunnison Rockery** (107 North Main Street; 970-641-1503) carries Indian-style jewelry, decorative rocks and other souvenir items.

Crested Butte offers a larger range of shops and galleries. **Paragon Art Gallery** (132 Elk Avenue; 970-349-6484) shows works by craftspeople and local artists. Other studios and galleries include the **Goodman Gallery** (408 3rd Street; 970-349-5470), which highlights artwork with southwestern and nature motifs.

In Crested Butte, another good bet for gifts is the **Rocky Mountain Chocolate Factory** (314 Elk Avenue; 970-349-0933), which creates attractive gift baskets of handmade chocolates and cookies.

GUNNISON–CRESTED BUTTE AREA NIGHTLIFE

Surprisingly, for a college town Gunnison is practically devoid of nightlife. **The Trough** (Route 50; 970-641-3724), with its dancefloor and live rock bands Thursday, Friday and Saturday nights, is as good as it gets.

Up the hill in Crested Butte, rowdy après-ski clubs line the main street and rock on all year long. **Kochevar's Bar** (127 Elk Avenue; 970-349-6745) retains the feel of an Old West saloon. Pool tables and hot bands keep the place lively well past midnight. A block down the street, the **Idle Spur** (226 Elk Avenue; 970-349-5026) is a spacious bar and restaurant with a large stone fireplace in the middle. Rock bands play in the back room on Thursday, Friday and Saturday nights. A bit more upscale, the **Wooden Nickel** (222 Elk Avenue; 970-349-6350) gradually metamorphoses from restaurant to rock-and-roll bar as the evening wears on.

Well-heeled après-ski revelers gather for happy hour at **The Rafters** (Ski Area Central, Mount Crested Butte; 970-349-2298) and party on into the night once the live rock bands get warmed up. For mellower surroundings at the foot of the ski slopes, visit the **Dugout Lounge** (Mount Crested Butte; 970-349-4041) in the Grand Butte Hotel. Both places are packed elbow-to-elbow during ski season but are pretty dead during the summer months.

GUNNISON–CRESTED BUTTE AREA PARKS

Gunnison National Forest—This 1.7 million-acre forest contains 27 mountain peaks over 12,000 feet high. The forest surrounds the towns of Gunnison and Crested Butte, reaching south to include Slumgullion Pass and the mountains above Lake City. On the north, it borders three other national forests—Grand Mesa, White River and San Isabel—in the highest and most remote part of the Colorado Rockies. The West Elk Wilderness, an expanse of granite peaks and alpine ridges southwest of Crested Butte, is a popular backpacking area. East of Gunnison and Crested Butte, the Sawatch Range was a major mining district in the late 19th century. Today, unpaved forest roads and jeep trails lead back to ghost towns and hidden fishing lakes throughout the district. A bowl in the mountains east of Crested Butte forms the spectacular setting for **Taylor Park Reservoir**, a popular boating and fishing lake.

Facilities: Boat ramps at Taylor Park and Spring Creek reservoirs; picnic areas with tables in Taylor Canyon; information, 970-641-0471. *Fishing:* Good for trout in Taylor Park Reservoir, Spring Creek Reservoir, Lake Irwin, Lost Lake and many smaller lakes and streams.

Camping: There are 26 campgrounds with a total of 376 RV/tent sites (no hookups); most have drinking water; $5 to $12 per night.

Getting there: Paved routes that provide access to the national forest include Taylor Canyon (Forest Road 742), from Route 135 north of Gunnison to Taylor Park Reservoir; and Quartz Creek (76 Road) from Route 50 east of Gunnison to the ghost town of Pitkin. The unpaved Kebler Pass Road winds through alpine lake country to connect Route 135 at Crested Butte with Route 133 near Paonia to form the West Elk Scenic Loop.

Curecanti National Recreation Area—Colorado's largest lake, Blue Mesa Reservoir, is the centerpiece of this boating and fishing area, which also encompasses two smaller reservoirs, Morrow Point Reservoir and Crystal Lake. Blue Mesa Reservoir is used for waterskiing and speedboating; boating on both of the smaller lakes, which have no boat ramps, is limited to hand-carried craft. An area of Blue Mesa Reservoir called the Bay of Chickens is a favorite windsurfing area. The recreation area also includes many miles of backcountry in the foothills around the lakes.

Facilities: Restrooms, picnic areas, boat ramps, marinas, groceries, hiking trails; information, 970-641-2337. *Swimming:* Very cold. *Fishing:* Good for rainbow, brook, brown and mackinaw trout and kokanee salmon.

Camping: Permitted in eight campgrounds totaling 352 RV/tent sites (no hookups); $8 to $9 per night.

Getting there: Located along Route 50 from about 5 to 25 miles west of Gunnison; there are numerous turnoffs to areas of the lakeshore.

Grand Junction Area

The Colorado River pours from a mountain canyon into the Grand Valley, where fruit orchards line its banks and fill the valley with blossoms in the spring. **Grand Junction**, the largest city in Colorado west of the Continental Divide, was named for its location—where the Colorado River (once known as the Grand River) and the Gunnison River meet.

Grand Junction is a long, narrow city, bounded by the interstate on the north and the river on the south. Venturing off the main thoroughfares into the downtown area, you will find a graceful neighborhood of older homes harking back to the more prosperous era when Grand Junction was a major railroad center. Follow Main Street as it meanders from 2nd Street to 7th Street through the **Downtown Shopping Park**. This city center, imaginatively redeveloped back in 1963, combines the amenities of a pedestrian mall with a single traffic lane that curves between too few parking spaces. The city's **Art on the Corner** program, initiated in 1989, has transformed the five-block shopping park into an outdoor sculpture gallery. Under the program, artists from all over Colorado loan their sculptures to the city for one year. At any given time more than 30 works of art wait along the downtown sidewalks to be seen, touched and admired. All are for sale.

The Grand Valley is one of the major dinosaur fossil areas on earth, and the centerpiece of downtown Grand Junction is **Dinosaur Valley** (4th and Main streets; 970-243-3466; admission), a division of the Museum of Western Colorado. This unique museum, which features dinosaur skeletons and realistic, half-sized animated models, is housed in a former department store. One of the display windows contains a casting of the huge legbone of what was the world's largest dinosaur skeleton when it was discovered near Grand Junction in 1900. Through another display window passersby can watch paleontologists at work in the museum's fossil laboratory.

The main location of the **Museum of Western Colorado** (4th Street and Ute Avenue, Grand Junction; 970-242-0971; admission), the largest museum between Denver and Salt Lake City, features a timeline exhibit that traces regional history from 1880 to the present. Two blocks from Dinosaur Valley, the museum also displays Native American artifacts, flora and fauna and historical documents and photographs.

A third unit of the Museum of Western Colorado is **Cross Orchards Historic Site** (3073 F [Patterson] Road, Grand Junction; 970-434-9814). Traditional farm life of the early 1900s is re-created at this open-air museum, originally the headquarters of one of Colorado's largest apple orchards. A portion of the orchard, along with the summer house, workers' bunkhouse, blacksmith shop, barn and packing house, is open to the public. Other exhibits include railroad memorabilia and a collection of road-building machinery. Living-history demonstrations are held daily from mid-April through October; special events include workshops where students learn traditional farming methods using teams of draft horses, antique appraisal sessions and classes on making cornhusk dolls.

The Museum of Western Colorado operates **Little Park Desert Preserve**, on Grand Junction's southern city limits. The 1200-acre wilderness area has trails for hiking and mountain biking. The museum also conducts ongoing fossil digs at **Riggs Hill** and **Dinosaur Hill**, situated near the west and east entrances of Colorado National Monument, as well as at **Rabbit Valley**, 24 miles west of town. All three digs have self-guided walking trails that are open to visitors.

The Grand Valley is wider than the Grand Canyon and nearly half as deep. Orange sandstone cliffs form a wall 2000 feet high along its south side, and from the top rim of the cliffs above Grand Junction you can see that they form one side of a canyon carved by the Colorado River. On its far side, 14 miles away, stands its other wall—the inaccessible, purple-gray Book Cliffs. **Colorado National Monument** (Fruita; 970-858-3617; admission) encompasses 32 square miles of the south rim between Grand Junction and the smaller town of Fruita nearby, providing a small sample of the cliffs and side canyons that enclose the Grand Valley. What makes this particular segment of the rim special is that you can reach it in a passenger car. The 23-mile **Rim Rock Drive** offers more than a dozen scenic view points, some overlooking the orchards, towns and farmlands of the valley, others affording glimpses of secluded side canyons. For most travelers, the dramatic one-hour drive through the national monument alone is worth the price of admission.

Above the cliffs and canyons of Colorado National Monument stretches the broad expanse of Piñon Mesa. You can easily see part of the mesa top by following either of two paved roads that lead from the back entrances of Colorado National Monument up into **Glade Park** (★). The roads pass through cool, dreamlike ranchlands to intersect at the Glade Park General Store, the pastoral setting providing a dramatic contrast to the desertlike landscapes below. About eight miles west of the store on a well-marked, unpaved road is the mesa's top sightseeing highlight, **Miracle Rock**, a balanced rock teetering on the edge of a cliff and said by some to be the largest of its kind on earth. Nearby **Little Dolores Falls** has a little-known campground.

Rattlesnake Canyon (★) may be one of the best-kept secrets in the "Hidden Rockies." Huge natural arches of beige and red sandstone, some with spans of more than 100 feet, line the eastern rim of the canyon. The turnoff for the canyon is just outside the back entrance to Colorado National Monument, off West Glade Park Road. You need four-wheel-drive to reach the trailhead in the Black Ridge Wilderness. Caution: The clay surface of the road to the canyon gets so slippery when wet that even four-wheel-drive vehicles can't travel on it.

There is plenty of spectacular canyon scenery to be found in the uninhabited public lands along the cliffs at the base of the Uncompahgre Plateau for 65 miles south and east of Grand Junction. Little-known canyons can be reached on unpaved ranch roads off Route 50 between Grand Junction and Montrose. For instance, **Dominguez Canyon** (★), on the Gunnison River, offers 20 miles of hidden canyonlands with a marvelous range of environments—from desert to riverbank beaches, from cottonwood forests to waterfalls that plummet down sheer sandstone cliffs. A campground and wilderness trailhead are accessible by car.

For more information on Rattlesnake Canyon or Dominguez Canyon, contact the Bureau of Land Management, Grand Junction District Office (2815 H Road, Grand Junction, CO 81506; 970-244-3050).

First-time visitors to **Grand Mesa**, east of Grand Junction, often expect to find dry, scrubby terrain like that of Mesa Verde and other western Colorado mesas. They are surprised to discover instead a cool mountain landscape of Douglas-fir trees studded with lakes like blue sapphires at elevations of more than 10,000 feet above sea level and a mile above the Grand Valley. Motorists who take the paved, 55-mile **Grand Mesa Scenic Byway** (Route 65) over the mesa top between Routes 50 and 70 feel as if they are climbing the steep, aspen-covered slopes of a mountain the size of Pikes Peak or Mount Evans—except that Grand Mesa's summit looks as if it had been neatly sliced off at timberline to create the world's largest flat-topped mountain. Grand Mesa's unique landscape was formed by an ancient lava flow that protected the softer layers of sandstone and shale beneath as the surrounding terrain eroded away. The mesa top, with its gently rolling, low hills, more than 300 lakes and innumerable streams, is a favorite destination for anglers in summer and cross-country skiers in winter. Despite a handful of rustic resort lodges, most of the mesa seems practically untouched by humankind. Two graded, unpaved roads, Land's End Road and Trickle Park Road, branch off the Grand Mesa Scenic Byway and lead deep into the forest.

GRAND JUNCTION AREA HOTELS

Grand Junction, the only major town on an otherwise-empty 200-mile stretch of Route 70, has about 30 motels with a total of more than 2000 guest rooms. For exceptional accommodations in town, reserve one of the four bold-colored, period-decorated guest rooms at the **Gate House** (2502 North 1st Street; 970-242-6105). The inn was originally a gatehouse of the turn-of-the-century Cleveholm Manor (now also a bed and breakfast) in Redstone, Colorado. The red sandstone gatehouse was disassembled in the 1940s and transported block by massive block over a distance of 120 miles to its present location. Room rates, in the moderate range, are a fraction of what comparable accommodations cost elsewhere in southern Colorado.

Most national motor-inn chains are represented in Grand Junction. From the budget **Value Lodge** (104 White Avenue; 970-242-0651) to the moderate-priced **Grand Junction Hilton** (743 Horizon Drive; 970-241-8888, 800-445-8667, fax 970-242-7266), room rates here are some of the lowest in the state.

There are several forest lodges atop Grand Mesa, all of them small and secluded. **Alexander Lake Lodge** (Grand Mesa; 970-856-6700) has six rustic cabins, some with kitchens, and a main lodge with a dining room and a huge fireplace built from 200 tons of stone. The lodge also has a small grocery and fishing supply store. Rates are moderate. **Spruce Lodge** (Grand Mesa; 970-856-3210) has 14 cabins, all with kitchens, and a restaurant and bar. Both of these are open year-round and fill up with cross-country skiers in winter. **Grand Mesa Lodge** (Grand Mesa; 970-856-3250), open mid-May through October only, has

16 units including both housekeeping cabins and motel-style duplex units on Island Lake, the largest lake on Grand Mesa. There is a grocery store on the premises but no restaurant. Boat rentals are available. Moderate.

GRAND JUNCTION AREA RESTAURANTS

Locals agree that the best restaurant in Grand Junction is **Sweetwaters** (336 Main Street; 970-243-3900). This stylish northern Italian eatery on the Main Street Mall features veal scaloppine and an array of pasta dishes, as well as daily fresh seafood specials. Picture windows afford a view of the sculpture-studded pedestrians-only street scene outside. Moderate.

Nearby, Grand Junction's only Japanese restaurant and sushi bar, **Suehiro Japanese Restaurant** (541 Main Street; 970-245-9548), serves authentic, traditional dishes including tempura, sukiyaki and beef or chicken teriyaki, accompanied by sake, plum wine or Asian beer. Moderate.

Grand Junction's abundance of Chinese restaurants along North Avenue includes the long-established **Far East Restaurant** (1530 North Avenue; 970-242-8131), a spacious tri-level place that specializes in Szechuan and Cantonese cuisine, including an array of seafood entrées such as Australian lobster tail and Alaska king crab. Moderate.

Creative twists on New Mexican food are featured at **W. W. Peppers** (759 Horizon Drive; 970-245-9251). Specialties include chimichangas and crabmeat enchiladas. Steaks and more conventional seafood dishes are also served. The decor strives for the look of contemporary Santa Fe. Budget to moderate.

For just plain good food at the lowest prices in town, try **Starvin' Arvin's** (752 Horizon Drive; 970-241-0430). Particularly known as a breakfast spot—the hotcake stacks are formidable and the biscuits and gravy are legendary among I-70 truckers—the restaurant also serves sandwiches and dinner specials. The decor focuses on the owner's snapshots of people rafting, biking and generally enjoying the outdoors in the Grand Junction area. Budget.

GRAND JUNCTION AREA SHOPPING

As Grand Junction's more practical stores have abandoned the downtown area for the North Avenue commercial strip just a few blocks away, the smaller storefronts of Main Street Mall have reopened as modest galleries, boutiques and antique shops.

For the largest selection of dinosaur-motif gift items you're likely to find anywhere, check out the gift shop at **Dinosaur Valley** (362 Main Street; 970-243-3466). **Quilt Junction** (412 Main Street; 970-245-6700) features locally made quilts as well as a large selection of souvenirs such as T-shirts, coffee mugs and lots of cat-motif gift items; sharing the same building and phone, Gallery 412 exhibits art photographs. **Sunspinner Hand Crafts** (454 Main Street; 970-245-5529) has jewelry and assorted works in glass, pottery and wood handmade by local artisans. The best antique shopping in town is at **Haggle of Vendors Emporium** (510 Main Street; 970-245-1404).

GRAND JUNCTION AREA NIGHTLIFE

A country-and-western atmosphere pervades Grand Junction's after-dark entertainment scene. The top dance club in town is **The Rose** (2993 North Avenue; 970-245-0606). Spacious and neo-Victorian, it offers live country music seven nights a week. **Cahoots** (490 28¼ Road; 970-241-2282) has live rock-and-roll and lively weekend dance crowds.

GRAND JUNCTION AREA PARKS

Grand Mesa National Forest—This 360,000-acre reserve encompasses the world's largest flat-topped mountain, a vast expanse of lakes, lava fields and Douglas-fir forest ranging between 10,000 and 11,000 feet above sea level. Although this forest has no federally designated wilderness area, roads into the central part are for four-wheel-drive vehicles, and much of the eastern half of the mesa is accessible only by hiking and horse trails. The Land O Lakes area, on the western part of the mesa, has more than 300 lakes, many of them connected by a maze of streams and creeks that are legendary among trout fishermen. At the western tip of the mesa, Land's End overlooks the Grand Valley a mile below.

Facilities: There are five picnic areas, all with tables, drinking water and restrooms, ski area; information, 970-242-8211. *Fishing:* Excellent for rainbow, cutthroat and brook trout.

Camping: Grand Mesa has 18 National Forest campgrounds for tents and RVs (no hookups). Those along or near the paved Grand Mesa Scenic Byway include Jumbo (27 sites), Spruce Grove (16 sites), Island Lake (42 sites), Valley View (8 sites), Little Bear (40 sites), Carp Lake (20 sites) and Ward Lake (26 sites). The nightly fee at any of them is $7. More campgrounds are reached via the unpaved Trickle Park Road, which starts near Valley View campground and runs east from the scenic byway for about 14 miles.

Getting there: The main access to Grand Mesa National Forest is via the Grand Mesa Scenic Byway (Route 65). The 55-mile scenic road runs between Cedaredge, a small town 15 miles off Route 50 near Delta, and the Island Acres/Mesa exit from Route 70, about 15 miles east of Grand Junction.

Uncompahgre National Forest—Two separate areas make up Uncompahgre National Forest. The rolling juniper-and-pine-forest terrain of the Uncompahgre Plateau, a vast, uninhabited island in the sky 9000 feet above sea level, extends south of the Grand and Gunnison valleys for 65 miles, from the Grand Junction area to the Montrose area. The Plateau Unit, which has neither high mountains nor significant bodies of water, is not widely used for recreation. If it's solitude you want, this is a good place to look for it. Uncompahgre National Forest also includes the northern part of the San Juan Mountains around Telluride, Ouray and Lake City, described elsewhere in this chapter.

Facilities: None; information, 970-874-6600.

Camping: The Uncompahgre Plateau has four small campgrounds without hookups for tents and RVs. The only one with water is Divide Fork campground (11 sites; $7 per night), on Divide Road south of Grand Junction. Columbine (6 sites;

no fee) is southwest of Delta. Antone Spring (8 sites; $7 per night) and Iron Spring (7 sites; $7 per night) are southwest of Montrose.

Getting there: There is no paved road access. Divide Road, a wide, graded forest road, climbs to the north end of the plateau from Route 141 south of Grand Junction, runs its length and descends to Montrose. The Delta-Nucla Road, another graded dirt road, climbs southwest from Delta to join Divide Road.

Island Acres State Park—Originally a large island in the Colorado River used as a landmark and encampment site by Ute Indians and mountain men, Island Acres was later planted with peach orchards. In 1967, the State of Colorado converted the island into a recreation area by building a dike to link it with the riverbank, leaving four lakes for swimming, fishing and nonmotorized boating.

Facilities: Picnic areas with tables, drinking water and restrooms, nature trail (.75 mile); day-use fee, $3; information, 970-464-0548. *Swimming:* Permitted. *Fishing:* Good for rainbow trout in spring and fall and for catfish, bluegill and carp year-round; ice fishing in winter.

Camping: There are 32 RV/tent sites (no hookups); $9 per night; dump station for RVs.

Getting there: Located 15 miles east of Grand Junction on Route 70 at the exit for the Grand Mesa Scenic Byway.

Vega State Park—The largest body of water in the Grand Valley area, two-mile-long Vega Reservoir is a local favorite for waterskiing, windsurfing and jet skiing. Abundant wildflowers and the subalpine beauty of its mountain setting attract nature lovers to the lake's shore. The park affords access to Grand Mesa trails for hikers, mountain bikers and four-wheel-drive vehicles.

Facilities: Picnic areas with tables, drinking water, restrooms, nature trail (1 mile), boat ramps; day-use fee, $3; information, 970-487-3407. *Fishing:* Good for trout in spring and fall; a very popular ice-fishing spot in winter.

Camping: There are 109 RV/tent sites (no hookups), $6 per night; dump station for RVs. Site reservations can be made through the Colorado Division of Parks and Outdoor Recreation (303-470-1144 in Denver or 800-678-2267).

Getting there: Exit Route 70 at Island Acres State Park and follow Route 330 east through the town of Collbran to the park, a distance of about 35 miles.

Highline Lake State Park—Surrounding two lakes amid Grand Valley farmland near Fruita, this park provides a full range of water recreation. Highline Lake, a 160-acre manmade reservoir, is used for waterskiing, jet skiing and windsurfing; it also offers an overlook where birders watch the many species of migratory birds that use the lake as a rest stop. Boating on the smaller Mack Mesa Lake is limited to hand-propelled and electric craft, and there is a wheelchair-accessible fishing pier.

Facilities: Picnic area with tables and water, restrooms, boat ramp, phone; day-use fee, $3; information, 970-858-7208. *Swimming:* Permitted. *Fishing:* Highline Lake has good warm-water fishing for catfish and crappie. Mack Mesa Lake offers excellent early-season trout fishing.

Camping: There are 25 RV/tent sites (no hookups); $7 per night; showers.

Getting there: Located seven miles northwest of Loma near Route 139.

Durango and San Juan Skyway Area

Durango is the largest town in southwestern Colorado and the natural hub for exploring the Four Corners area. The San Juans, the most spectacular mountains in the central Rockies, dominate the region's skyline wherever you go. The Durango area is a full day's drive from any major population center, giving it an off-the-beaten-path feel.

Durango boasts two immensely popular tourist attractions—Mesa Verde National Park and the narrow-gauge railroad to Silverton. The town also serves as a base camp for the many thousands of outdoor enthusiasts who each year venture into the San Juan Mountains by car, jeep or mountain bike or on horseback or foot to gaze with awe upon a panorama of unvanquished mountain crags that has often been likened to the Swiss Alps.

Motorists coming from the eastern slope on Route 160 reach the Durango area by way of **Wolf Creek Pass** (10,850 feet), one of the highest and steepest passes on any U.S. highway. At the foot of the winding descent down the west side of the pass lies **Pagosa Springs**, a likeable little town named for the steamy, slightly sulfurous **Great Pagosa Hot Springs** (admission) located behind the visitors information center in the middle of town; look for the huge beehive-shaped cone of mineral deposits where the hot water emerges from underground.

The history of the hot springs and the area's Ute Indian inhabitants and early settlers is recalled in displays at the **San Juan Historical Society Pioneer Museum** (1st and Pagosa streets, Pagosa Springs; 970-264-4424). Two miles west of town is the **Fred Harman Art Museum** (Route 160, Pagosa Springs; 970-731-5785), exhibiting collected works by the late Pagosa Springs artist whose cowboy comic strip, "Red Ryder," was syndicated worldwide in the 1950s.

Between Pagosa Springs and Durango, three miles off Route 160 on the road to Navajo Lake, the **Chimney Rock Archaeological Area** (Route 151; 970-264-2268; admission) is open to visitors from mid-May to mid-September by guided tour only; the rest of the year, only group reservations are offered. Nine hundred years ago, this ancient Anasazi pueblo site was the most distant "outlier," or colony, of the huge Native American city at Chaco Canyon in New Mexico. Archaeologists believe that mostly single men lived at the Chimney Rock pueblo, which served as both a ceremonial center and a lumber camp from which logs were floated down the Piedra River for use as roof beams in Chaco Canyon.

South of Pagosa Springs, Durango and Mesa Verde are the adjoining **Southern Ute and Mountain Ute reservations**, the only Native American lands in Colorado. In addition to **Navajo Lake** and the **Ute Mountain Casino** in Towaoc, visitor attractions on the Ute reservations include the **Southern Ute Indian Cultural Center** (Ignacio; 970-563-4531; admission), the only tribally owned and operated Native American museum in Colorado, with exhibits of Ute beadwork, leatherwork and other arts and crafts as well as ancient Anasazi artifacts found on the reservation; and the **Ute Mountain Tribal Park** (Towaoc; 970-565-3751 ext. 282), a remote group of Anasazi pueblo and cliff-dwelling ruins that can be visited only with an Indian guide on a fairly strenuous hike or mountain-bike tour.

Routes 501 and 240 make for a pretty back-road trip between Bayfield and Durango through sheep-ranching country. Many of the sheepherders in this area are Basques who retain their unique language and many traditions brought from the Pyrenees between Spain and France.

Durango got its start in 1880 as a smelter town where gold and silver ore from the mining camps in the San Juan Mountains was refined. Within two years the boom town rivaled Denver as the richest city in Colorado. Although the gold-mining era ended, the town slid into poverty and many structures in Durango were abandoned, the solidly built, elaborately ornamented red-brick buildings downtown endured through the decades. Good times began returning to Durango in the mid-1950s, when Fort Lewis College was established there and the popularity of nearby Mesa Verde National Park began to grow and boosted the local economy. When the Durango & Silverton Narrow-Gauge Railroad was revived in 1981, the town saw a surge of tourism that lifted it to a new level of prosperity. Today, Durango throbs with youthful exuberance thanks to the college students who make up a sizable part of its population. The town also has far more than its share of latter-day mountain men, old and young, who live in the wilderness of the San Juans, at least during the warm months, and come into town for supplies and celebrations.

Each morning from May through October, the **Durango & Silverton Narrow-Gauge Railroad** (479 Main Avenue, Durango; 970-247-2733; admission) fills Durango's downtown historic district with steam and tumult as it loads passengers for the 45-mile trip to Silverton in the heart of the San Juan Mountains. Though steam locomotives pull sightseeing trains through many parts of the West these days, the Durango & Silverton trip, with its trestles hundreds of feet above the Animas River and its thrilling climb along a narrow shelf cut into the sheer Animas River Canyon wall, remains unsurpassed. The trip to Silverton takes three hours. Passengers have a three-hour stay, plenty of time for lunch and shopping. The two-hour return trip arrives in Durango at dinnertime. Passengers can choose to spend one or more nights in Silverton before returning to Durango. One-way tickets allow backpackers to get off the train at the Needleton or Elk Park trailhead and trek into the Weminuche Wilderness. The Durango & Silverton Narrow-Gauge Railroad is one of the most popular tourist attractions in Colorado, carrying more than 200,000 passengers a year; reservations are essential and should be made at least a month in advance.

SAN JUAN SKYWAY LOOP TRIP To experience the San Juans by car, drive the 231-mile **San Juan Skyway**, which follows paved Routes 160, 184, 145, 62 and 550 to form a loop beginning and ending in Durango. The route is clearly marked with "Scenic Byway" signs. In fact, the San Juan Skyway was one of the first routes selected under a 1988 federal law directing the National Forest Service to designate the most scenic driving routes in national forests as scenic byways. But you don't really need special road signs to tell you that you're on one of America's most spectacular drives.

We recommend traveling the San Juan Skyway clockwise, as described later, mainly because drivers unaccustomed to edgy mountain roads will find that the road that climbs south from Ouray is much easier to drive uphill than downhill.

(Text continued on page 182.)

Colorado's Native American Heritage

Anywhere you go in Colorado, particularly in the southwestern part of the state, you'll find reminders of the native people who used to roam the region's mountains, mesas and prairies. In the glass cases of Denver's big art, history and natural-history museums, as well as small-town historical museums across the state, you'll see 19th-century native artifacts. And you'll find souvenir stores everywhere selling turquoise-and-silver Indian-made jewelry, as well as pottery, beadwork and other arts and crafts. It's enough to make one wonder why visitors so rarely see a living Native American in Colorado.

The sad truth is that Colorado was settled at the height of the U.S. government's military campaigns against Native Americans. With few exceptions native peoples were either relocated or exterminated within a few years after Colorado became a state.

By the time the first Anglo explorers set foot in Colorado, the most permanent and sophisticated people who had inhabited the region were long gone. The **Anasazi** (a Navajo name meaning "ancient enemies") began growing corn and building permanent houses around A.D. 800. They built monumental cliff dwellings and pueblos such as the ones visitors see today at Mesa Verde National Park, the Anasazi Heritage Center near Dolores and the Ute Mountain Tribal Park. They accomplished impressive feats of astronomy and architecture, and they established trade networks that reached all the way to the Toltec cities of central Mexico.

Around A.D. 1250 the Anasazi suddenly abandoned the region, moving south into New Mexico, where their descendants now live at Acoma Pueblo near Grants. Why they left the communities where their people had lived for more than 400 years remains one of the most puzzling questions in American archaeology.

For centuries, the nomadic **Cheyenne** and **Arapaho** tribes followed the bison herds across the plains of northeastern Colorado, as they had since the dawn of memory. In 1851, the Cheyenne and Arapaho people signed the Fort Laramie Treaty, granting them spacious reservation lands along the Front Range, including the land where Denver now lies. Ten years later, as the first settlers began homesteading in that area, the government canceled the treaty and relocated the tribes to an arid reservation near Las Animas in southeastern Colorado. Starvation set in, and parties of men left the reservation to scour the countryside for food, alarming the Anglo settlers, many of whom could not communicate with the native people and feared them. In a solitary instance, a farm family south of Denver was killed by a small party of warriors.

Colonel John Chivington of the Colorado National Guard took punitive attack against the Cheyenne and Arapaho people in November 1864, leading a cavalry company in a dawn raid on a reservation village and killing 123 people, mostly women and children. News of the raid, which is now remembered as the Sand Creek Massacre, was received with mixed emotions. Chivington was awarded a medal of honor by the territorial governor and hailed as a hero by some settlers, but he was simultaneously court-martialed by the U.S. Army and drummed out of military service. The Cheyenne and Arapaho people were relocated to reservations in Nebraska and South Dakota, but renegade Cheyenne "dog soldiers" terrorized the Colorado plains for five years before their leader, Tall Bull, was killed in a battle with the cavalry. Buffalo Bill Cody, then a 23-year-old army scout, was inaccurately given credit for killing Tall Bull in a bestselling dime novel that established Cody's reputation as an Indian fighter.

Meanwhile, Kit Carson, another legendary Indian fighter, led actions in the southeastern plains against small, elusive parties of **Comanche**, **Kiowa** and **Prairie Apache** warriors who had been driven from their homelands in West Texas. There was no major, decisive battle. Little by little, the renegades were confined to reservation lands in Oklahoma—or killed.

The Rocky Mountains of Colorado were the domain of the nomadic **Ute** people, who wintered in the canyonlands of southwestern Colorado and Utah and, in summer, roamed the high forests and alpine meadows along the Continental Divide. In 1868, the U.S. government made a treaty with the Ute people, granting them a magnificent 6000-square-mile reservation that contained all of the San Juan Mountains, including the sites of present-day Durango, Silverton, Ouray, Telluride and Montrose. Their leader, Chief Ouray, settled down on a farm that is now the site of Ute Indian Museum and Chipeta Park near Montrose and became one of the most eloquent spokespersons and negotiators for the Native American cause.

But five years later, in 1873, soon after gold was discovered in the San Juans, the government rescinded the treaty, and the Utes were forced to move—some to a reservation south of Vernal, Utah, others to the narrow bands of piñon-covered hills and mesas that lie between the desert and Sleeping Ute Mountain on the southern fringe of their former homeland. The Southern Ute and Ute Mountain reservations are now the only Native American lands in Colorado.

(If we had to choose either the Dolores-Telluride leg of the trip or the Ouray-Silverton leg as a one-way route between Durango and the Gunnison or Grand Junction area, it would be a hard decision indeed; the whole loop route is filled with variety and scenic beauty on a grand scale. However, the segment between Ouray and Silverton has what is probably the most breathtaking scenery.)

First, drive west from Durango on Route 160 to **Mancos**, the small town near the turnoff to **Mesa Verde National Park** (970-529-4465; admission). The national park protects one of the greatest wonders of pre-Columbian America—a community of castlelike stone pueblos built in niches high up the sheer cliffs of the mesa. Mesa Verde is the northernmost site of the ancient Anasazis, whose civilization dominated the Southwest for centuries and who evolved into the Pueblo Indians of modern New Mexico.

The main ruins area at Mesa Verde is below the rim of Chapin Mesa, 21 miles from the park entrance. There is an archaeology museum at the starting point of the two six-mile loop drives that take motorists and cyclists along canyon rims to sites such as Cliff Palace and Balcony House. Exploring the largest ruins involves some climbing on ladders and narrow trails. An unpaved road from Far View Visitors Center leads to a more remote pueblo site on Wetherill Mesa. Keep your eyes peeled for deer and wild horses. The park is open year-round, weather permitting. For more information on Mesa Verde and other ancient ruins in the Four Corners area, see this guidebook's companion volume, *Hidden Southwest*.

From Mancos, go northwest on Route 184 to **Dolores**. Compared to other towns along the San Juan Skyway, Dolores seems so low-key that you may wonder whether anybody lives there. In truth, things have livened up a lot since the completion of **McPhee Reservoir**, just west of town, boosted the bait-and-tackle business. Near the lake is the Bureau of Land Management's **Anasazi Heritage Center** (Route 184, Dolores; 970-882-4811), which displays Pueblo Indian artifacts from the classic period (11th to 13th centuries) that were found in canyons now flooded by the reservoir. Nearby are two partially excavated Anasazi pueblo sites. In the town of Dolores you can see **Galloping Goose #5**, a gasoline-powered hybrid—part Buick passenger bus and part boxcar—that carried passengers on the narrow-gauge trail routes of the San Juans from 1931 to 1951.

Follow Route 145 north from Dolores. At the tiny community of Stoner a side road turns off to follow the **West Fork of the Dolores River**, a popular fishing area. Unpaved forest roads provide access to the aspen-covered plateau above the rim of Dolores Canyon. Route 145, the main highway up the East Fork of the river, is equally scenic. Past Stoner, the highway begins its long climb into the high mountains and ultimately to the summit of **Lizard Head Pass** (10,222 feet), where there is a trailhead for a hiking trail to the top ridgeline of Lizard Head Peak, the mountain with the 400-foot spire of granite on top. Rock climbers rate the monolith as one of the most difficult technical ascents on earth.

No other ski town in Colorado is as far from a major city as **Telluride**. This fact alone has made the town irresistible to skiers who want to *really* escape the outside world. In fact, only Aspen, in its glitzier way, can rival Telluride for away-from-it-allness. But when it comes to mountain scenery, Telluride, set in a basin surrounded by peaks over 13,000 feet high, actually has Aspen beat. Out past the end of 1st Street, Ingram Falls plunges hundreds of feet down craggy cliffs that stand like castle walls. All around, snow-capped mountain turrets protect the town and its residents from the outside world.

Telluride was founded in 1875 as a gold-mining camp. The town's rebirth started in 1971, when plans to build a ski area there were unveiled. Even before the first ski lift was running, a motley assortment of ski bums, trust-fund babies, realtors, lawyers and Aspen dropouts had moved into the near-deserted old mining town to buy up abandoned buildings for back taxes. Many of the newcomers had seen resort money swallow the souls of other historic Colorado gold-rush towns, so the new city fathers promptly adopted rigid preservation laws. Today, the historic district is free of new buildings, and turn-of-the-century structures have been refurbished instead of replaced. Historic landmark buildings include the **Sheridan Opera House**, where Sarah Bernhardt once performed and William Jennings Bryan made a speech, and the **Bank of Telluride**, the first bank Butch Cassidy ever robbed. The bygone glory of the gold era is recalled at the **San Miguel County Historical Museum** (317 North 1st Street; 970-728-3344). Stop in to find out about the days when Telluride supported 26 saloons and 12 houses of ill repute and the miners returned home on winter days by sledding on shovels from the mines down the mountainside to town. Today, the 300-inch annual snowfall makes Telluride a skiers' mecca.

During the summer, Telluride is the festival capital of Colorado. In the mid-1970s, residents hatched a plan to boost the local economy during the no-snow season by hosting the Telluride Bluegrass Festival. It drew huge crowds, and spinoffs in the form of a jazz festival and a film festival came quickly. Today, all three have attained international stature, and other festivals completely fill the town's calendar from mid-May through September except for one weekend in July, when the annual Telluride Nothing Festival packs 'em in.

Summer visitors to Telluride can ride a **ski-slope chairlift** (admission) to the top of the ridge 2000 feet above town or drive up to the old **Idarado Mine and Mill**, the town's biggest employer for more than 50 years in the late 19th and early 20th centuries. Nearby, **Bridal Veil Falls** has the longest vertical drop of any waterfall in Colorado—365 feet.

North of Telluride, Route 145 descends from the mountains. To continue on the San Juan Skyway loop route, turn east on Route 62 at Placerville and then south on Route 550 at Ridgway. Route 550 goes all the way back to Durango. The highway reenters the mountains through the Uncompahgre River Canyon, whose maroon walls rise so steeply that mountain streams plunge over the rim and fall hundreds of feet before splashing against the cliffs. The deepest part of the canyon is the dramatic setting for the village of **Ouray**.

With neither a ski area nor a railroad, Ouray has been spared the kind of industrial tourism that has swallowed other Colorado mining towns whole. The town's slightly old-fashioned charm is as authentic as can be. Most buildings in town date back to the turn of the century and before. Some have been refurbished and painted in rainbow color schemes; others, such as the shell of the grand old Ouray Hotel, built in 1887 and closed in 1964, stand vacant. Main Street has endured good and bad times, and local businesses keep on keeping the spirit of small-town Colorado alive.

Ouray's special claim to fame is its hot springs. At the northern edge of town, the municipal **Ouray Hot Springs Pool** (Route 550; 970-325-4347; admission) has an Olympic-size swimming pool and a smaller, hotter (104°F) pool. Other options include **Wiesbaden Hot Springs Spa** (625 5th Street, Ouray; 970-325-4347) and **Orvis Hot Springs** (1585 County Road 3, Ridgway; 970-626-5324; admission).

Waterfalls are another Ouray specialty. A dozen or more of them plummet down the cliffs surrounding the town. The most accessible is **Lower Cascade Falls**, reached by a half-mile trail that starts a few blocks uphill from Main Street. Farther up the cliffs, the same stream takes an earlier and even longer fall at Upper Cascade Falls, reached by a steep trail two and a half miles long that begins at the natural amphitheater south of town. The most spectacular of Ouray's waterfalls is **Box Canyon Falls and Park** (Route 550 South, Ouray; 970-323-4464; admission). The 285-foot-high falls have sliced a canyon so narrow that visitors who walk into its misty depths along the narrow boardwalks and turn-of-the-century steel bridge feel as if they're in a cave filled to overflowing with the noise and spray of down-rushing water.

Ouray is also an excellent base for exploring old mining roads by mountain bike or four-wheel-drive vehicle. **Engineer Pass Road** (★) leads to the early-day mining district around Mineral Point and Animas Forks, one of Colorado's best ghost towns, to join the **Alpine Loop Scenic Byway**. From there other jeep roads go to Lake City and Silverton.

An easier way to explore the Ouray district's mining heritage is to tour the **Bachelor-Syracuse Mine** (County Road 14, Ouray; 970-325-4500; admission). Mine carts take visitors two-thirds of a mile into the mountain to see where hard-rock miners followed veins of gold and silver ore for a hundred years before the mine ceased operations in 1984.

South of Ouray, the highway climbs steep cliffs in a sweeping series of switchbacks and finally reaches the summit of **Red Mountain Pass** (11,008 feet), the highest point on the San Juan Skyway. Well above timberline, this part of the route offers the most spectacular views of the remote Needle Mountains in the Weminuche Wilderness to the east. Long before the Forest Service dubbed it part of the San Juan Skyway, the stretch of Route 550 between Ouray and Silverton was known as the **Million Dollar Highway**. Some say the name came from the high cost of building the road back in the days when a million dollars was a lot of money for road construction, while others say the road's foundation, built with mine tailings, contains $1 million worth of gold ore. It may well be the most scenic 23 miles of highway in America.

Silverton was founded in 1874 as the center of what would prove to be one of the wealthiest mining districts in southwestern Colorado. Large deposits of gold, silver, copper and lead were located here, but the town could be reached only by crossing high mountain passes, so only limited amounts of ore could be shipped out until the **Denver & Rio Grande Railroad** (now the Durango & Silverton Narrow-Gauge Railroad) reached the town in 1882. As Silverton boomed to a population of 4000 in the next few years, it saw the construction of elegant false-front Victorian buildings along Main Street. The boom faded slowly, until finally the last of the mines closed during World War II. Nearly abandoned, the town became nothing more than a roadside curiosity on Route 550. Motion-picture companies occasionally slapped fresh coats of paint on the old buildings and used Main Street as an Old West location. The revival of the Durango & Silverton Narrow-Gauge Railroad as a scenic train for tourists brought a new wave of prosperity to Silverton.

Besides allowing you to stroll the streets and browse through the town during off-hours, driving to Silverton lets you explore back roads in the surrounding national forest. A short distance north of town, Main Street becomes Forest Road 586. The pavement soon ends, but the road continues past the scattered remains of the old mining towns of Howardsville and Eureka. It is passable without four-wheel-drive as far as **Animas Forks** (★), one of the most picturesque ghost towns in the San Juans thanks to its dramatic timberline setting. Beyond that, rough roads suited only for four-wheel-drive vehicles and mountain bikes climb to join the **Alpine Loop Backcountry Byway** (★) in the heart of the San Juans.

Descending toward Durango down the Animas River Canyon, Route 550 passes the ski resort of **Purgatory** (Route 550, Durango; 970-247-9000). In the summer months, the ski lift (admission) carries thrill seekers up the slopes to careen down an **alpine slide** on vehicles that look like a cross between a sled and a skateboard.

The perfect ending to a tour of the San Juan Skyway is a relaxing dip in **Trimble Hot Springs** (6475 County Road 203, Durango; 970-247-0111; admission). The original resort on the site was built in 1883. Recently rebuilt and reopened, the present hot springs have an Olympic-size swimming pool and a smaller, hotter pool; the water comes from underground at 119°F and is diluted to 104° before being piped into the pool.

DURANGO AND SAN JUAN SKYWAY AREA HOTELS

In Pagosa Springs, the classicst place to stay is three and a half miles west of town at the 100-room **Pagosa Lodge** (Route 160; 970-731-4141, 800-523-7704). The lodge is on a private lake in a resort community of custom-built vacation homes and condominiums with a golf course, tennis courts and a swimming pool, all under a spectacular mountain skyline. Touches of southwestern decor and furnishings as tasteful as they are durable brighten the rather condominial guest rooms. Moderate year-round.

Guests can soak in hot-spring pools at the **Oak Ridge Motor Inn** (158 Light Plant Road, Pagosa Springs; 970-264-4173), a conventional mid-range motor inn where the moderate-priced rooms have air-conditioning and offer a choice of two double beds or one queen-size, or at the nearby, budget-priced, no-frills **Spa Motel** (317 Hot Springs Boulevard, Pagosa Springs; 970-264-5910, 800-832-5523), where the rooms are tidy, well lit and close to the pool.

Our favorite Pagosa Springs accommodations are at a unique landmark bed and breakfast known among locals as "the castle." The 10,000-square-foot **Echo Manor Inn** (3366 Route 84; 970-264-5646) was a typical Queen Anne–style residence until a previous owner—inspired by a visit to Disneyland, so the story goes—started building on towers, gables and sprawling additions, creating an architectural curiosity of such mammoth proportions that cars often stop on the highway to take snapshots. Nine guest rooms, each individually decorated in country style with antiques and a handmade quilt, range from budget to moderate, and there is a deluxe-priced three-bedroom suite with a kitchen and fireplace.

The shores of Vallecito Reservoir, northeast of Durango, are lined with cabins, most of them in small rental cabin compounds referred to as lodges. For instance, try **Circle S Lodge** (18022 County Road 501, Bayfield; 970-884-2473), situated at the north end of the lake near the edge of the Weminuche Wilderness. The seven cabins are spacious enough to accommodate up to nine people and have carpeting, kitchens and fireplaces. Rates are moderate. Farther along the east shore of the lake, two miles past the end of the pavement, **Elk Point Lodge** (21730 County Road 501, Bayfield; 970-884-2482) offers nine cabins, most with fireplaces, and also rents horses and boats. The cabins vary in size and range in price from budget to deluxe.

At the top of the list of Durango's restored historic lodgings is **The Strater Hotel** (699 Main Avenue; 970-247-4431, 800-247-4431, fax 970-259-2208), which has been in continuous operation since 1887, when it was one of the most luxurious hotels in the West. Beautifully maintained, the interior of the five-story hotel now glows with a soft patina of authentic frontier elegance. Twelve-foot-high mirrors and gold-papered walls brighten the lobby, where a big writing desk looks out upon Main Avenue. Since the second coming of the railroad brought prosperity back to Durango, the guest rooms have been refurbished to grand-hotel quality with flowery carpets and ornate 100-year-old walnut furnishings. Deluxe.

A block down the street stands Durango's other historic landmark hostelry, the **General Palmer Hotel** (567 Main Avenue; 970-247-4747, 800-523-3358, fax 970-247-1332). The hotel's namesake, Denver & Rio Grande Railroad owner William Jackson Palmer, founded the town of Durango, as well as other Colorado towns including Colorado Springs. The hotel, which dates back to 1898, was recently restored with period antiques and reproductions. It looks brighter and shinier than the Strater though somehow less genuinely old. The long, narrow lobby has brass fittings, dark wood trim, pink wallpaper, overstuffed armchairs, loveseats, rocking chairs and carpeting in Victorian floral patterns. Rooms are individually decorated. Deluxe.

The **Jarvis Suite Hotel** (125 West 10th Street, Durango; 970-259-6190), in a former theater listed on the National Register of Historic Places, offers 22 sunny, modern suites, each with a fully equipped kitchen. The location, within easy walking distance of the railroad station and all downtown galleries and restaurants, is ideal. Moderate to deluxe.

For a low-priced Victorian atmosphere, try the **Central Hotel and Hostel** (975 Main Avenue, Durango; 970-247-0330). This 1892 hotel, now somewhat rundown and musty, has both dormitory accommodations and very plain private rooms that echo Durango's down-to-earth past. It is upstairs from a downtown pool hall known as the El Rancho Tavern, where Jack Dempsey won $50 in a prizefight in 1915, four years before he won the world's heavyweight championship title; the event is commemorated in a mural painted on the side of the building. Budget.

Durango also has more than 20 bed-and-breakfast inns. In the historic residential neighborhood adjoining downtown, just five blocks from the narrow-gauge railroad station, the **Gable House** (805 East 5th Avenue; 970-247-4982) has antique-furnished guest rooms, each with its own private entrance, in a large, three-story Queen Anne Victorian home with a beautifully landscaped yard. The inn is open during the summer months only. Moderate.

The **Leland House Bed & Breakfast Suites** (721 East 2nd Avenue, Durango; 970-385-1920), another older (circa 1927) home in the downtown area, has one deluxe-rate one-bedroom suite with full kitchen and living room and a plainer moderate-priced single room with kitchenette and private bath, both decorated with pre-Depression antiques from around Colorado.

Away from downtown, Durango-area bed and breakfasts tend to be modern, luxurious and located in spectacular settings. Consider, for example, the **River House Bed & Breakfast** (495 Animas View Drive; 970-247-4775), which overlooks the Animas River from a county road just north of town. As late sleepers soon discover, the narrow-gauge train steams right past the house a little before nine each morning. Gourmet breakfasts are served in a sunny 928-square-foot atrium with a waterfall. Other features include a living room with fireplace and wet bar, a snooker table, a sauna and an exercise room. Some of the individually decorated guest rooms have skylights or clawfoot tubs, and one is entirely lined with shelves of books. Moderate.

Eleven miles southeast of Durango, on a county road a mile from the highway to Ignacio on the Southern Ute Reservation, **Penny's Place Bed & Breakfast** (1041 County Road 307, Durango; 970-247-8928) is a modern home with a glass-roofed solarium over the hot tub, a fireplace and a deck looking out on the La Plata Mountains. A spiral staircase leads up to the master suite, which even has its own laundry facilities. Other guest rooms offer a choice of a four-poster bed or a queen-size brass bed. Moderate.

The largest hotel in Durango, with 154 guest rooms, the **Red Lion Inn** (501 Camino del Rio; 970-259-6580, 800-547-8010, fax 970-259-4398) feels more like a big-city business travelers' hotel than a vacation retreat. Rooms are colorful, contemporary and extraordinarily spacious. The motor inn has an indoor swimming pool, a spa and an exercise room. Deluxe.

Farther from downtown—but more convenient to the ski slopes at Purgatory—the **Iron Horse Inn** (5800 North Main Avenue; 970-259-1010, 800-748-2990, fax 970-385-4791) is Durango's other large, upscale motor inn. Each of the 140 guest accommodations is a suite with a loft bedroom and a fireplace. An indoor swimming pool, a sauna and a whirlpool are on the premises. Rooms facing the railroad tracks are more desirable; the steam train comes by only twice a day, while the highway keeps on rolling all night long with big trucks roaring slowly up the canyon. Moderate to deluxe.

For those who prefer more conventional roadside lodging, the three-mile-long commercial strip along Route 550 on the northern outskirts of Durango is lined with standard highwayside motels. There are enough choices that travelers should be able to spot a few "vacancy" signs even during peak season. While in-season rates for private rooms aren't cheap anywhere in Durango, budget-to-moderate rates can be found at well-maintained independent motels such as the **Caboose Motel** (3363 Main Avenue; 970-247-1191) and the **Alpine Motel** (3515 North Main Avenue; 970-247-4042). Rates at these and other motels in the area drop by 50 percent or more in the winter—a great bargain for skiers at nearby Purgatory.

Several of the finest guest ranches in the state are located in the vicinity of Durango. **Colorado Trails Ranch** (P.O. Box 848, Durango, CO 81302; 970-247-5055), near Vallecito Reservoir, boasts one of the finest western and English-style riding instruction programs offered anywhere. It also has a western village complete with opera house and trading post. The family-oriented ranch offers activity programs organized by age group and supervised by full-time counselors. Other amenities include a heated swimming pool, tennis courts, a fishing pond and archery, rifle target and trap ranges. Guest accommodations are in individual cabins with modern furnishings, carpeting and private baths. Deluxe rates include all meals. Open in the summer only.

Perhaps the ultimate resort ranch experience in southern Colorado is to be found at **Tall Timber** (P.O. Box 90, Durango, CO 81302; 970-259-4813). With just ten modern, split-level suites in duplexes secluded in a shimmering forest of aspens, the resort is so exclusive that it can't be reached by road—only by the narrow-gauge train or helicopter. The suites have high vaulted ceilings, loft bedrooms and marble baths. Among the resort's amenities are a riding stable, a nine-hole golf course, tennis courts, a solar-heated swimming pool, an exercise room and a riverside jacuzzi. San Juan National Forest surrounds the lodge and offers boundless opportunities for hiking and fishing. Rates, as you might expect, are way up in the ultra-deluxe range—as much as $750 a night with a three-night minimum stay. Meals are included in the rate.

The only lodging in Mesa Verde National Park is at **Far View Lodge** (970-529-4421) on the summit of Navajo Hill, commanding a spectacular panoramic view out over the valleys that lie to the south, clear to the huge rock formation known as Shiprock in New Mexico and the Lukachukai Mountains in the Navajo lands of Arizona. The lodge's 150 rooms are in duplex and four-plex units scattered across juniper-covered hillsides. The spacious rooms are decorated in Anasazi motifs and have private sun porches. Open mid-April to mid-October. Moderate.

Telluride's grand old hotel, the red-brick three-story **New Sheridan Hotel** (231 West Colorado Avenue; 970-728-4351, fax 970-728-5024), operated for 30 years—from 1895 to 1925—and then stood abandoned for more than a half century. Thanks to a meticulous restoration completed in 1977, the hotel's lobby and guest rooms have recaptured the glory of bygone days with rich, warm period decor. The 23 guest accommodations vary in size from rather small rooms with shared baths to larger rooms with private baths and a single opulent suite with impressive views of the town and the mountains. Room rates vary wildly, from the ultra-deluxe range with a five-night minimum stay during peak ski season to the budget range with no minimum stay on summer weeknights.

A great Telluride bed and breakfast is **San Sophia** (330 West Pacific Avenue; 970-728-3001). Although situated in the historic district, San Sophia is of recent vintage, designed and built as an inn, with gabled dormers and a central tower. The 16 guest rooms, each named after a gold mine, have soothing pastel interiors appointed with brass beds, etched mirrors, stained-glass windows and extra-large bathtubs. A full breakfast and afternoon wine and hors d'oeuvres are included in the rates, which are ultra-deluxe.

Another Telluride bed and breakfast, **Pennington's Mountain Village** (100 Pennington Court; 970-728-5337, 800-543-1437), ranks as one of the most luxurious and expensive B & Bs in Colorado. It is located by the 12th fairway of the golf course in Telluride Mountain Village, the newly built area on the mesa five miles from the historic district. The inn's ridgeline site affords spectacular panoramic views from every window and balcony. A magnificent circular staircase leads up to 12 guest rooms, each with its own whirlpool bath and private deck. The rooms are decorated in French country style. Common areas include a sunken library and sitting room with a big fireplace and a game room with a pool table. Ultra-deluxe.

Although Telluride lodging tends to be very expensive in peak season, there is one affordable hostelry in town—the **Oak Street Inn** (134 North Oak Street; 970-728-3383). This hostel, situated in a building that was originally a Methodist church and affiliated with American Youth Hostels (AYH), provides very plain private rooms at budget rates and also has six-bed dormitory rooms at youth hostel prices. All rooms have shared baths. The best features are the coed sauna and the upstairs TV lounge where a young, enthusiastic crowd often hangs out.

Ouray offers affordable luxury in lodging along the San Juan Skyway. Even during the peak summer season, rates here are less than they would be for comparable accommodations in Telluride. In winter, skiers can actually save hundreds of dollars on lodging by staying in Ouray and driving an hour to Telluride Ski Area. Many Ouray inns participate in a continuing co-promotion campaign that gives visitors who stay there during the winter discounts on Telluride lift tickets and free admission to Ouray's municipal hot springs.

Ouray's original landmark hostelry, the Beaumont Hotel (circa 1887), kept its doors open until 1964, then closed them for good. The shell of the elegant old building still dominates Main Street, and maybe someday investors will come along to restore it. In the meantime, two smaller historic hotels operate in town. Back in the 1880s, the **St. Elmo Hotel** (426 Main Street; 970-325-4951) was a low-rent boardinghouse for mine laborers' families, but times have changed. Today, this intimate nine-room hotel is full of antiques and period reproductions, stained glass, polished wood and brass trim. Guest rooms, each one individually decorated, have brass beds, lace curtains and ornate mining-era wallpaper. Moderate.

The **Historic Western Hotel Bed-and-Breakfast** (210 7th Avenue; 970-325-4645) opened as a hotel in 1891 and operated as a boardinghouse for mine workers until World War II. Closed but never quite abandoned—it served for a while as office space and a local museum—the three-story wood-frame hotel with its grandiose whitewashed facade is mostly original, refurbished but not rebuilt. The period antiques that grace the 14 small guest rooms and the common areas are genuine but not fancy; they speak with eloquence of daily life in the Old West. Most rooms have shared baths. Moderate.

Box Canyon Lodge & Hot Springs (45 3rd Avenue, Ouray; 970-325-4981) is essentially a standard midrange motel with a spectacularly scenic location and one other distinction: It has outdoor hot tubs fed by natural mineral springs located on the property. The clean, modern guest rooms hint at European sensibilities in their decor and furnishings, and rates are moderate. There are also two luxury suites with fireplaces and fully equipped kitchens.

A different kind of hot-spring experience awaits at the **Wiesbaden Hot Springs Spa and Lodgings** (625 5th Street, Ouray; 970-325-4347). Originally started as Mother Buchanan's Bathhouse in 1879 and later used as a hospital, the place was converted into a European-style spa in the late 1970s. The lodgings are small, conventional motel rooms, apartments and cottages, most of them redecorated with Old World antiques. Guests have full use of the spa facilities, which include a natural vapor cave, a sauna and soaking pool, an outdoor swimming pool and a fully equipped exercise room. Moderate to deluxe.

In Silverton, the historic landmark hotel is the 40-room **Grand Imperial Hotel** (1219 Greene Street; 970-387-5527). Its understated elegance shows in the lobby with its leather-upholstered sofas and in the rooms with their brass beds, crystal chandeliers and oak bathroom fittings. Rates are moderate. The Old West–style saloon on the main floor is open only during daytime hours when the train is in town. The hotel itself is open only from mid-March through September.

There are also a number of smaller, bed-and-breakfast-style lodgings around Silverton. **Smedley's** (1314 Greene Street; 970-387-5423) has just three suites above an ice-cream parlor. The guest suites have period furniture and full kitchens at moderate prices. Nearby and under the same management is the **Wingate House** (1045 Snowden Street; 970-387-5423), an ornate mansard-roofed Victorian home filled with floral patterns and lace. The four antique-furnished guest rooms share two baths. The same innkeepers operate the **Teller House Hotel** (1250 Greene Street; 970-387-5423), a former miners' boardinghouse that is now an AYH hostel offering both dormitory facilities and simple, budget-priced private rooms.

North of Durango, just three miles from Purgatory Ski Area, is the 325-unit **Tamarron Resort** (Route 550, Purgatory; 970-259-2000, 800-678-1000, fax 970-259-0745). Built for $50 million in the early 1970s, Tamarron has become known as one of the state's top resorts, with a golf course that ranks among the best in the Rocky Mountain region. The resort also offers tennis courts, nature trails, riding stables, an indoor-outdoor pool and exercise rooms, as well as easy access to the ski slopes and miles of groomed ski trails. Guest rooms, decorated in pastel hues and southwestern patterns, are on the small side but still include king-size beds and kitchenettes. Three-bedroom condominiums are also available. Ultra-deluxe.

DURANGO AND SAN JUAN SKYWAY AREA RESTAURANTS

Besides the array of family-style restaurants and familiar fast-food places along the three-mile-long Route 550 commercial strip on the northern outskirts of Durango, you'll find a good selection of places to eat in the downtown historic district. In a turn-of-the-century red-brick building next to the narrow-gauge train station, the **Palace Grill** (1 Depot Place; 970-247-2018) offers mesquite-grilled chicken breast and a variety of other dishes such as honey duck and brandy pepper steak in an elegant Victorian-style ambience. Moderate to deluxe.

Family dining meets 19th-century elegance in the stately old Strater Hotel at **Henry's at the Strater** (699 Main Avenue, Durango; 970-247-4431), with its Tiffany lightshades, ornate moldings and trim and red leatherette booths. The menu presents standard steak, chicken, fish and pasta entrées, and there is a prime-rib buffet with a 25-item salad bar. Moderate.

Francisco's Restaurante y Cantina (619 Main Avenue; 970-247-4098), established in 1968 by a family from northern New Mexico, is one of the best Mexican restaurants in Colorado and certainly the most popular restaurant in Durango, with seating for 250 people amid a labyrinth of adobe walls and Santa Fe–style decor. Try the enchiladas Durango, beef wrapped in blue-corn tortillas and smothered in green chili. Besides Mexican food, entrées include steak, chicken, trout and lobster. Budget to moderate.

Downtown Durango has more than its share of breakfast places, all designed to entice visitors before they board the narrow-gauge train. The unpretentious-looking **Carvers' Bakery and Brewpub** (1022 Main Avenue; 970-259-2545) serves healthy breakfast specials such as granola pancakes. For dinner try the fajitas—beef or chicken fried in tequila salsa with green chili and onions, served with black beans, black olives and sour cream. Vegetarian entrées are also featured, and four varieties of home-brewed beer are available. Budget.

In Mancos, a good place to stop and eat after visiting Mesa Verde is **Candy's Country Cafe** (121 Railroad Avenue; 970-533-7941). This little diner—nine tables and a lunch counter in a concrete-block building—serves up hefty helpings of good down-home food, from "wagon wheels and axle grease" (biscuits and gravy) to "pigbutt" (ham steak). Budget.

The sleepy little town of Dolores boasts one of the finest restaurants along the San Juan Skyway, the **Old Germany Restaurant & Lounge** (200 South 8th Street; 970-882-7549). In a renovated turn-of-the-century home, the restaurant is decorated with memorabilia imported from Bavaria, including 800-year-old antiques. The food is also authentically Bavarian. Savor a delicacy such as *Paprikaschnitzel* sausage or sauerbraten with German potato salad. Budget to moderate.

Telluride has about two dozen restaurants, many of which are designed for an upscale resort clientele. Poshest of them all is **La Marmotte** (150 West San Juan Avenue; 970-728-6232), where Continental cuisine and fine wines are served in an intimate environment that looks much like an old wine cellar but in fact was once the town icehouse. Deluxe.

One of the liveliest restaurants in Telluride is the **Floradora Saloon** (103 West Colorado Avenue; 970-728-3888), specializing in beef and offering a large salad bar as well. The Old West saloon atmosphere makes the Floradora a perfect après-ski spot. Moderate.

Two blocks down the main street, **Eddie's** (300 West Colorado Avenue, Telluride; 970-728-5335) serves gourmet pizzas, pasta and overstuffed sandwiches on an outdoor deck with one of the best views in town. Budget.

In Ouray, a good place to dine is **Pricco's Restaurant** (736 Main Street; 970-325-4040). Victorian woodwork complements the exposed brick interior of the restaurant. The specialty of the house is a surf-and-turf plate of shrimp scampi and rib-eye steak. Moderate. The **Piñon Restaurant** (737 Main Street; 970-325-4334) is a modern little café with a tavern upstairs. Try the vegetarian burrito, stuffed with black beans, zucchini, carrots, onions and celery, or the trout with piñon nuts. Moderate.

In Silverton, the **French Bakery Restaurant** (1250 Greene Street; 970-387-5423) in the Teller House Hotel tantalizes guests and passersby alike with the wafting smell of baking bread. It serves omelettes and croissants, sandwiches, soups and full dinners. Its location near the narrow-gauge train depot makes it a lunchtime favorite. Moderate.

Another good place for breakfast, lunch or dinner is the **Pickle Barrel** (1304 Greene Street, Silverton; 970-387-5713), which was operating as a restaurant long before the railroad started running again. In a building that dates back to 1880 and was originally a general store, the restaurant serves sandwiches, steak and trout. Moderate.

DURANGO AND SAN JUAN SKYWAY AREA SHOPPING

At first glance, Main Avenue in Durango's nine-block downtown historic district seems to consist entirely of sporting goods stores. Look closer and you'll find that there are also a lot of factory outlet stores.

The tourism boom that has turned once-sleepy little Durango into prime retail space has also spawned a growing number of art galleries. They exhibit Native American traditional arts as well as works by area artists and craftspeople reflecting the full range of visual and spiritual imagery to be found in the Four Corners area. The largest gallery in town, **Toh-Atin** (145 West 9th Street; 970-247-8277), with a second location, **Toh-Atin's Art on Main** (865 Main Avenue; 970-247-4540), just around the corner, offers high-quality Native American arts and crafts from around the Southwest, including fine selections of both replica Anasazi pottery and authentic modern Pueblo pottery. **Zhoni Indian Arts** (777 Main Avenue; 970-247-2991) also has a selection of collector-quality Native American art and artifacts, while the **New West Gallery** (747 Main Avenue; 970-259-5777) displays sculptures and paintings of Native American subjects as well as an overwhelming selection of turquoise-and-silver jewelry.

Among the dozen or so contemporary galleries in Durango, two of note are **Piedra's Gallery** (846 Main Avenue; 970-247-9395) and **Termar Gallery** (780 Main Avenue; 970-247-3728). With works by many of the best-known southwestern artists, Termar offers the next-best thing to a shopping spree in Santa Fe.

Railroad memorabilia and rare books can be found in Durango at **Southwest Book Trader** (175 East 5th Street; 970-247-8479). Former Presidents Ronald Reagan and George Bush are among the distinguished clientele of **O'Farrell Hat Company** (598 Main Avenue; 970-259-2517), where custom-fitted hats are made the old-fashioned way, by hand.

Telluride has plenty of T-shirt shops and pricey sporting goods stores. It also has a handful of quite upmarket art galleries. As in Durango, the galleries in Telluride feature predominantly Native American arts and Santa Fe– and Taos-style paintings and sculptures, including some pieces that cost as much as a car.

In Ridgway you'll find American Indian and Mexican art, historic photographs by Edward S. Curtis and others, folk art, pottery and hand-loomed textiles at **Los Pinos Antiques** (525 Clinton Street; 970-626-5021).

Souvenir shopping in Ouray offers few surprises but an intriguing ambience. Some of the stores along Main Street look as if they haven't changed in 50 years. Check out, for example, **Big Horn Mercantile** (609 Main Street; 970-325-4257).

Silverton's main industry is curio shops, which cluster along Greene Street between 11th and 14th streets. None stands out. You can also find San Juan Mountains guidebooks and maps as well as hiking and camping gear. **Silverton Mountain Pottery** (Blair Street) has original stoneware handmade in Silverton from local clay.

DURANGO AND SAN JUAN SKYWAY AREA NIGHTLIFE

In Durango, the **Diamond Circle Theatre** (in the Strater Hotel, 699 Main Avenue; 970-247-4431) presents a campy rendition of Victorian melodrama nightly during the summer season. Also in the Strater, the **Diamond Belle Saloon** has a ragtime piano player and is frequently a site for sing-alongs.

Farquahrts (725 Main Avenue, Durango; 970-247-9861), a student hangout, serves pizzas as well as drinks and features bluegrass or folk music early in the week and gutsy rock as the weekend draws near. **The Pelican's Nest** (656 Main Avenue, Durango), upstairs from the West Antique Shop, features live jazz nightly except Mondays.

The only gambling hall in southern Colorado today is the **Ute Mountain Casino** in Towaoc, the capital of the Ute Mountain Reservation. Although the gambling goes on seven days a week until 4 a.m., no alcoholic beverages are allowed to be served on tribal land. Shuttle buses run to the reservation; for information call 970-565-8800.

Telluride's most venerable drinking establishment is the **Sheridan Bar** (225 West Colorado Avenue; 970-728-3911), a dignified old hotel bar that harks back to the Victorian era but can become rowdy during ski season. For really loud fun, though, the place to go is the **Fly Me to the Moon Saloon** (132 East Colorado Avenue; 970-728-6666). It presents live rock, R & B or reggae bands nightly during the ski and festival seasons and has an underground dancefloor.

In Ouray, for an authentic Old West atmosphere complete with modern-day mountain men (and women), spend an hour or two in the **Silver Eagle Saloon**

(617 Main Street; 970-325-4161). A nonalcoholic alternative for a night out in Ouray is **San Juan Odyssey** (460 Main Street; 970-325-4228), a computerized multimedia show produced by Ouray's mayor, country singer C. W. McCall, and shown nightly during the summer months since 1976 in the old Ouray Opera House.

DURANGO AND SAN JUAN SKYWAY AREA PARKS

Navajo Lake State Park—Thirty-five-mile-long Navajo Lake wanders among pine-forested hills and reaches into a hundred hidden side canyons. The reservoir was created in 1962 when the San Juan River was dammed to provide irrigation for the Navajo Reservation. Most of the lake lies in New Mexico, where there is another state park of the same name. At the opposite end of the lake from the dam, Colorado's Navajo Lake State Park combines a wild, remote feel with a few modern conveniences such as an airstrip for fly-in campers and the largest boat ramp in the state (80 feet wide and a quarter-mile long). Fishing and waterskiing are the main water sports.

Facilities: Picnic area with tables and restrooms; visitors center; boat ramp; airstrip; marina with boat, ski and fishing tackle rentals and groceries; day-use fee, $3; information, 970-883-2208. Food and lodging are two miles away in Arboles. *Fishing:* Good for bluegill, catfish, crappie, largemouth bass, kokanee salmon and rainbow, brown and brook trout.

Camping: The 71-site campground is situated on a peninsula so that most sites have water frontage; $7 to $10 per night. There are showers, flush toilets and a dump station; four sites have electric hookups.

Getting there: Located two miles south of Arboles and Route 151. The park is 35 miles south of Pagosa Springs and 45 miles southeast of Durango.

San Juan National Forest—This two-million-acre forest includes a 130-mile expanse of mountains north of Pagosa Springs and Durango, from the Continental Divide on the east to the Dolores River on the west. Much of its boundary adjoins other public lands—Uncompahgre National Forest on the north, Rio Grande National Forest on the east and Bureau of Land Management grazing land on the west. San Juan National Forest includes the jagged, lofty Needle Mountains, which rise to the east of the San Juan Skyway and narrow-gauge railroad in the vast Weminuche Wilderness. Parts of the Lizard Head and South San Juan wilderness areas also lie within San Juan National Forest. The San Juan Mountains were a rich gold-mining district in the 1870s to 1920s, containing numerous mines, camps and wagon roads and narrow-gauge tracks; today, more than 2000 miles of unpaved forest roads, many of which require four-wheel-drive vehicles or are suitable for mountain biking, provide access to many areas of the forest. For serious backpackers, San Juan National Forest is one of the most popular playgrounds in the Rocky Mountains.

Facilities: There are picnic areas, all with tables, some with drinking water, and restrooms, as well as 1155 miles of hiking trails; information, 970-247-4874. *Fishing:* Primarily for trout in the Animas River, Vallecito Reservoir and Lemon Reservoir; also in more than 90 natural lakes and 280 streams.

Camping: There are 38 campgrounds with a total of 784 RV/tent sites. All have drinking water but no hookups. Among them are seven campgrounds on and near Vallecito Reservoir, six along the San Juan Skyway and three near Wolf Creek Pass; $7 to $14 per night.

Getting there: The best highway access is via the San Juan Skyway Scenic Byway—Route 145 between Dolores and Lizard Head Pass and Route 550 between Durango and Silverton. The southeastern part of the forest can be reached via Route 600 at Vallecito Reservoir and from Route 160 over Wolf Creek Pass.

Mancos State Park—A three-mile road winds into the mountains above Mancos to the reservoir that provides the small town with drinking and irrigation water. The lake is open to nonmotorized boating and fishing as well as windsurfing. A four-mile trail runs from the lake along slopes and ridgelines bright with wildflowers to join a larger trail network in the adjoining San Juan National Forest. The park is also open in the winter months for snowmobiling, cross-country skiing and ice skating.

Facilities: Picnic area with tables and restrooms, boat ramp; day-use fee, $3; information, 970-883-2208. *Fishing:* Good for rainbow and brown trout.

Camping: There are 33 RV/tent sites are scattered along the lakeshore; $6 per night (no hookups). Drinking water is available, but there's no dump station.

*Getting There:*Located in Arboles on County Road 982.

McPhee National Recreation Area—Completed in 1987, McPhee Reservoir flooded the lower portion of the Dolores River Canyon and a network of tributary canyons to create a long, narrow lake that provides almost boundless opportunities for backcountry boating and fishing. Before it was flooded, the canyon was the site of a number of Anasazi pueblo ruins and home to a wide assortment of wildlife. Archaeological surveys performed during the dam's construction yielded numerous artifacts, many of which are on exhibit at the Bureau of Land Management's Anasazi Heritage Center nearby. A "mitigation area" surrounding the lake protects habitat for birds and animals, including bobcats, coyotes, mountain lions, ospreys, beavers and mule deer, that previously lived in the canyons where the lake is today.

Facilities: Picnic areas with tables, drinking water, restrooms, boat ramps, hiking trails; information, 970-882-1435. *Fishing:* Good for rainbow, brown and cutthroat trout as well as largemouth bass.

Camping: McPhee campground, on the lake's western shore, and House Creek campground, on the eastern shore, have 133 RV/tent sites with drinking water and dumping stations but no hookups. Sites cost $6 per night.

Getting there: Located 12 miles west of Dolores off Route 184.

Ridgway State Park—Recreational facilities are located in two separate areas along the shoreline of 80,000-acre Ridgway Reservoir. The main recreational site, on a promontory at the lake's south shore, has a boat ramp, a public swimming beach, two campgrounds and four miles of hiking trails. The mile-long, paved main trail leads to the Dallas Creek Recreation Site, at the east end of the reservoir where both Dallas Creek and the Uncompahgre River flow in.

Facilities: Picnic areas with tables and restrooms, boat ramp, marina (970-626-5094) with boat rentals; information, 970-626-5822. *Swimming:* Permitted. *Fishing:* Good for rainbow and brown trout; ice fishing in winter.

Camping: The Dakota Terrace and Elk Ridge campgrounds offer a total of 177 RV/tent sites and 10 walk-in tent sites; $7 to $10 per night. Most have electric hookups. There are showers, flush toilets and laundry facilities as well as a dump station. Pa-co-chu-puk has 42 RV sites (full hookups), showers and flush toilets; $12 per night.

Getting there: Located five miles north of Ridgway on Route 550, about midway between Telluride and Ouray.

Uncompahgre National Forest (Southern Unit)—This part of Uncompahgre National Forest (see also "Grand Junction Area Parks") encompasses the mountains around Telluride and Ouray. Big Blue Wilderness contains Uncompahgre Peak (14,309 feet) and Wetterhorn Peak (14,015 feet) near Ouray. Other areas without roads include the Mount Sneffels and the Lizard Head wilderness areas, both near Telluride. All are destinations for serious mountain-climbing expeditions.

Facilities: Hiking trails. *Fishing:* Best in July and August for rainbow, brown and brook trout, especially in Owl Creek and Beaver Lake east of Ridgway; information, 970-327-4261.

Camping: Matterhorn and Sunshine campgrounds near Telluride offer 38 RV/tent sites with drinking water but no flush toilets or hookups; $8 per night. Amphitheater campground near Ouray has 30 RV/tent sites with drinking water but no flush toilets or hookups; $10 per night.

Getting there: Access is via the San Juan Skyway—Route 145 between Lizard Head Pass and Telluride and Route 550 between Ouray and Silverton.

The Sporting Life

FISHING

Hundreds of lakes, rivers and mountain streams throughout southwestern Colorado offer great fishing for several species of trout; most areas are stocked annually by the Colorado Division of Wildlife. Rainbow and brown trout are the most common, and some areas have kokanee (freshwater salmon). There is bass fishing on some of the larger reservoirs.

ALAMOSA AREA West of Antonito, at the southern end of the San Luis Valley, the **Conejos River** is highly regarded by fly-fishermen.

GUNNISON–CRESTED BUTTE AREA Between Gunnison and Crested Butte, the **Roaring Judy State Wildlife Area** permits flyfishing in the East River, both upstream and downstream from the state fish hatchery there. It is a catch-and-release area, so all fish under 12 inches long must be returned to the water. **Willowfly Anglers** (P.O. Box 339, Almont, CO 81229; 970-641-1303) offers trout-fishing float trips on the upper **Gunnison River**, while **Tenderfoot Guides** (P.O. Box 246, Gunnison, CO 81230; 970-641-0504) arranges fishing trips on Blue Mesa Reservoir in **Curecanti National Recreation Area**. The recreation area includes not only Blue Mesa and two other reservoirs on the Gunnison River that are stocked but also eight tributary creeks that offer good rainbow, brown, brook and cutthroat trout fishing.

The east and west forks of the **San Juan River** above Pagosa Springs are also known for especially good trout fishing, with rainbow and brown trout at lower elevations and cutthroat trout higher upstream.

DURANGO AND SAN JUAN SKYWAY AREA A broad spectrum of fishing options, from largemouth bass in the shallows to kokanee salmon in the deeps, can be found at **Navajo Lake State Park**, southeast of Durango. Directly east of Durango, another large fishing lake, **Vallecito Reservoir**, also offers bass fishing.

The **Dolores River** is reputed to be one of the finest dry flyfishing areas in the West. In particular, the stretch of river below **McPhee Reservoir** teems with large rainbow and brown trout and Snake River cutthroats. Guides for wading or horseback flyfishing expeditions on the Dolores River and its tributaries can be arranged through **West Fork Guide Service** (P.O. Box 300, Dolores, CO 81323; 970-882-7959).

They say 12- to 18-inch rainbow and brown trout are the norm in the San Miguel River near Telluride. Guided flyfishing trips on the river are available from **Telluride Flyfishers** (150 West Colorado Avenue, Telluride; 970-728-4477). They also offer combination flyfishing schools.

BOATING

ALAMOSA AREA Near Alamosa, the shallow, natural San Luis Lake (the largest of several lakes in San Luis Lakes State Park) is a locally popular spot for waterskiing, fishing, sailing and windsurfing. There are no boat rentals, though.

GUNNISON–CRESTED BUTTE AREA A few miles west of Gunnison, Curecanti National Recreation Area (Route 50; 970-641-0406) offers water sports on 20-mile-long Blue Mesa Reservoir. You can rent a fishing boat, pontoon boat or cruiser at **Elk Creek Marina** (Route 50; 970-641-0707) or **Lake Fork Marina** (Route 92; 970-641-3048); both are Curecanti National Recreation Area concessions, and rental rates are identical. A more secluded recreational lake is Taylor Park Reservoir, in the mountains east of Crested Butte. Boat rentals there are available through **Taylor Park Boat House** (Taylor Park; 970-641-2922).

DURANGO AND SAN JUAN SKYWAY AREA Vallecitos Reservoir, east of Durango, is the most popular lake in the Durango region for water sports. Boat rentals are available at **Angler's Wharf** (17250 County Road 501, Bayfield; 970-884-9477) and **Mountain Marina** (14810 County Road 501, Bayfield; 970-884-9450). On Navajo Lake, southeast of Durango, **San Juan Marina** (1526 County Road 982; 970-883-2343) has a full spectrum of rentals, from little fishing skiffs to 50-foot houseboats. Near Dolores, you can rent fishing boats, pontoon boats or jet skis on McPhee Reservoir at **McPhee Marina** (25021 Highway 184, Lewis; 970-882-2257).

RIVER RAFTING

GUNNISON–CRESTED BUTTE AREA **Scenic River Tours** (703 West Tomichi Avenue, Gunnison; 970-641-1830) runs the Gunnison and Upper Taylor rivers, with trips ranging from the gentle and sublime to fast-action whitewater thrills. Also offering Gunnison River trips, including expeditions through the Black Canyon of the Gunnison, is **Tenderfoot Guides & Outfitters** (P.O. Box 246, Gunnison, CO 81230; 970-641-0504); among their trips is a moonlight float trip complete with a fireside dinner.

GRAND JUNCTION AREA Near Fruita, the favorite stretch of the Colorado River for rafting runs through Ruby and Horse Thief canyons, where you may see ducks, beaver, coyote, mule deer and even eagles. **Rimrock Adventures** (P.O. Box 608, Fruita, CO 81521; 970-858-9555) offers full-day raft trips through the canyons, as well as shorter guided trips and raft, canoe and tube rentals.

DURANGO AND SAN JUAN SKYWAY AREA Durango rafting companies run the lower Animas River south from town past old mining ruins, down a series of wet-and-wild rapids and through the Southern Ute Reservation. Contact **Mountain Waters Rafting** (108 West 6th Street, Durango; 970-259-4191) or **Flexible Flyers Rafting** (2344 County Road 255, Durango; 970-247-4628). **Pagosa Rafting and Wilderness Journeys** (P.O. Box 222, Pagosa Springs, CO 81147; 970-731-4081) offers raft trips on the San Juan River as well as special two- and three-day expeditions.

BALLOONING AND GLIDING

For a truly unique perspective on the spectacular San Juan Mountains, try drifting silently on the updrafts above the mountain slopes in a glider or hot-air balloon. Both are among the pricier thrills to be found in the region; the cost of a glider ride—including glider rental, pilot and tow plane, is about the same as hot-air ballooning. Either way, you'll come away with an experience that's sure to remain a vivid memory.

GUNNISON–CRESTED BUTTE AREA **Big Horn Balloon Company** (P.O. Box 361, Crested Butte, CO 81224; 970-349-6335) takes passengers on flights among the mountain crags that surround the ski resort of Crested Butte. It bills itself as the world's highest-altitude balloon operation.

GRAND JUNCTION AREA **Grand Junction Balloon Port** (2210 1 Road, Grand Junction; 970-243-8553) organizes balloon flights over the Grand Valley.

DURANGO AND SAN JUAN SKYWAY AREA Scenic glider rides over Durango and the Animas Valley can be arranged through the **Durango Soaring Club** (Val-Air Gliderport, Route 550, Durango; 970-247-9037).

In Pagosa Springs, **Blue Horizon Balloon Adventures** (P.O. Box 4445, Pagosa Springs, CO 81147; 970-731-5468) offers hot-air balloon flights above lush meadows in the San Juan Mountains and champagne afterward. Advance reservations are essential; often, one day's notice is all that's necessary.

In Durango, champagne flights over the San Juans are available at **Mariah Balloon Company** (P.O. Box 2744, Durango, CO 81302; 970-385-4940) and **Air Durango Hot Air Balloon Company** (P.O. Box 2138, Durango, CO 81302; 970-385-1749).

Glider rides among the spectacular mountains that surround Telluride are offered by **Telluride Soaring** (Telluride airport, Telluride; 970-728-5424).

San Juan Balloon Adventures (P.O. Box 66, Ridgway, CO 81421; 970-626-5495) offers balloon flights every morning year-round (weather permitting) from Ridgway, between Telluride and Ouray on the San Juan Skyway route.

DOWNHILL SKIING

GUNNISON–CRESTED BUTTE AREA Located 28 miles north of Gunnison, **Crested Butte Ski Area** (Route 135; 970-349-2222), a midsize winter resort, offers excellent downhill skiing for beginners through experts. The total vertical drop is 2775 feet. There are eight chairlifts. Many consider the north face, where telemarking was invented, to be Colorado's ultimate "extreme skiing" run. The resort rents skis. Open Thanksgiving to early April.

Monarch Ski Area (Route 50, Monarch Pass; 970-539-3573), 43 miles east of Gunnison, is only about one-third the size of Crested Butte. Since the ski lifts start beside the summit of Monarch Pass (11,312 feet), you ski above timberline on the highest part of the mountain. The vertical drop is 1160 feet. The resort is used mainly by weekenders from Colorado Springs and Denver, but the four chairlifts run almost empty on winter weekdays. Half the trails are suitable for beginners; 25 percent are intermediate and 25 percent are expert. Ski rentals are available. Open Thanksgiving to late March.

GRAND JUNCTION AREA **Powderhorn Ski Area** (Route 65, Grand Mesa National Forest; 970-242-5637) is a small intermediate-level ski area with one chairlift and a 1650-foot vertical drop on the north slope of Grand Mesa. Located 40 miles east of Gunnison, the ski area has rentals and a ski school. Open December through March.

DURANGO AND SAN JUAN SKYWAY AREA What you see from the highway of **Purgatory Ski Area** (Route 550; 970-247-9000) is just a hint of the complex trail network that works its way around the broad side of the mountain, making this relatively small ski area, with its 2029-foot vertical drop, wider than it is high. There are nine chairlifts. Located 29 miles north of Durango, the ski area has rentals and a ski school. There are 20 percent beginners' runs, 50 percent intermediate, and 30 percent advanced or expert. Open Thanksgiving to late April.

Wolf Creek Ski Area (Route 160, Wolf Creek Pass; 970-731-5605) receives more snowfall than any other ski area in the state—over 400 inches a year. The small ski area near the Wolf Creek Pass summit is located 70 miles west of Alamosa and 80 miles east of Durango. It has a vertical drop of 1425 feet and four chairlifts. There are 20 percent beginners' runs, 50 percent intermediate, 30 percent advanced. Open Thanksgiving through April. There is a rental shop at the base.

Telluride Ski Area (Route 145, Telluride; 970-728-4424) has a reputation as an "experts only" ski mountain. Developers in the early 1970s ran into financial problems after completing only the incredibly steep runs on the front side of the mountain. Today, 75 percent of the runs are for beginning and intermediate skiers, but these runs are hidden on the back side of the mountain. The vertical drop is an awesome 3165 feet. There are nine chairlifts. The Plunge and Spiral Stairs running down the front face are the longest, steepest mogul runs in Colorado. There are ski rentals and a ski school. This ski resort offers the most spectacular mountain scenery in the state. Open from Thanksgiving through April.

SKI RENTALS In Mt. Crested Butte, **Flatiron Sports** (10 Crested Butte Way; 970-349-6656) rents downhill and cross-country skis. In Telluride, downhill and cross-country equipment can be rented at **Telluride Sports** (150 West Colorado Avenue; 970-728-4477) or **Paragon Sports** (213 West Colorado Avenue; 970-728-4525). The best place to rent cross-country skis is **Telluride Nordic Center** (Town Park; 970-728-3404).

CROSS-COUNTRY SKIING

GUNNISON–CRESTED BUTTE AREA More than 20 kilometers of groomed cross-country ski trails, maintained by the Crested Butte Nordic Council, start from the outskirts of Crested Butte. For equipment rentals, maps and information on other cross-country ski routes in the area, go to the **Crested Butte Nordic Ski Center** (512 2nd Street, Crested Butte; 970-349-6201). The center also offers group and individual lessons.

GRAND JUNCTION AREA Cross-country skiing is an incomparable experience among the lakes, Douglas-fir forests and lava hills atop Grand Mesa. The **Grand Mesa Nordic Council** (P.O. Box 3077, Grand Junction, CO 81501; 970-434-9753), a local nonprofit group of skinny-ski enthusiasts, grooms nearly 70 kilometers of trails each winter.

DURANGO AND SAN JUAN SKYWAY AREA **Purgatory Ski Touring Center** (Route 550, Purgatory; 970-247-9000 ext. 3196) offers rentals, cross-country ski lessons and more than 15 kilometers of groomed trails.

Telluride Nordic Center (136 Country Club Drive, Telluride, 970-728-5989) maintains 30 kilometers of groomed trails and offers rentals. In Ouray, cross-country ski rentals and information about groomed trails in the national forest can be obtained at **Big Horn Mercantile** (609 Main Street; 970-325-4257).

For more information on renting equipment, see the ski-rental section in "Downhill Skiing" above.

GOLF

ALAMOSA AREA Golfers visiting the Alamosa area have the unique opportunity to play the game on a buffalo ranch: the scenic **Great Sand Dunes Golf Course** (5303 Route 150, Mosca; 719-378-2357) is located at Zapata Ranch. Also in the region is the **Alamosa Golf Club** (6678 North River Road, Alamosa; 719-589-9515).

GUNNISON–CRESTED BUTTE AREA On the outskirts of Gunnison, the **Dos Rios Golf Club** (Route 50, Gunnison; 970-641-1482) is open to the public in the summer months. Near the foot of the ski slopes at Crested Butte, the golf course at **Skyland Resort** (385 Country Club Drive, Mount Crested Butte; 970-349-6131) is ranked as one of the best mountain golf courses in America.

GRAND JUNCTION AREA Grand Junction's main public golf course, **Tiara Rado Golf Course** (2063 South Broadway; 970-245-8085) is located near the entrance to Colorado National Monument. In the nearby community of Fruita is the **Adobe Creek National Golf Course** (876 18½ Road; 970-858-0521).

DURANGO AND SAN JUAN SKYWAY AREA Foremost among the golf courses in the Durango area is the **Pagosa Pines Golf Club** (1 Pines Club Place, Pagosa Springs; 970-731-4755). In Durango, the **Hillcrest Golf Course** (2300 Rim Drive; 970-247-1499) has spectacular mountain views. Also near Durango is the **Dalton Ranch & Golf Club** (435 County Road 252; 970-247-7921). The golf course at the prestigious **Tamarron Resort** (40292 Route 550 North, Durango; 970-259-2000) is open to nonguests on a standby basis—only guests can reserve tee times in advance.

TENNIS

Crested Butte has three municipal tennis courts in **Town Park**, open to the public at no charge on a first-come, first-served basis. In Grand Junction, there are eight public tennis courts at the municipal **Lincoln Park** (12th Street at Gunnison Avenue). Near Pagosa Springs, tennis courts and racquets are rented to the public at **Fairfield Pagosa Resort** (Route 160, Pagosa Springs; 970-731-4123 ext. 2078). In Durango, **Fort Lewis College** (College Heights; 970-247-7571) has 12 tennis courts, which are open to the public when they're not in use for school activities. Telluride, Ouray and Silverton each have two municipal tennis courts in their respective town parks.

HORSEBACK RIDING

GUNNISON–CRESTED BUTTE AREA Near Gunnison, guided private and group rides are available at **Monarch Valley Stables** (Route 50, Gunnison; 970-641-6177). In the Crested Butte area, one-hour to all-day guided trail rides on Crested Butte Mountain are offered by **Lazy F Bar Outfitters** (P.O. Box 383, Gunnison, CO 81230; 970-349-7593), located two miles past the Crested Butte Airport.

GRAND JUNCTION AREA **Rimrock Adventures** (P.O. Box 608, Fruita, CO 81521; 970-858-9555), near the Route 340 entrance to Colorado National

Monument, offers guided horseback trips into the back canyons of the national monument and the nearby Black Ridge Wilderness.

DURANGO AND SAN JUAN SKYWAY AREA **Wolf Creek Outfitters** (West Fork Road, Pagosa Springs; 970-264-5332) leads guided horseback rides into the high country around Wolf Creek Pass.

Vallecito Reservoir has several riding stables. **Outlaw West Livery/Elk Point Lodge** (County Road 501, Bayfield; 970-884-9631 or 970-884-2070 in the winter) offers guided rides.

Just north of Durango, **Red Mountain Ranch** (27846 Route 550, Durango; 970-247-9796) has hourly and daily rides, as does **Engine Creek Outfitters & Cascade Stables** (50827 Route 150, Durango; 970-259-2556).

Near the entrance of Mesa Verde National Park, the **Mesa Verde Riding Stable** (Route 160 West, Mancos; 970-533-7269) guides group tours. In Dolores, you can ride at **Circle K Ranch** (26913 Route 145; 970-562-3808).

Horses and tours are available in Telluride at **Many Ponies Outfit** (122 South Townsend Avenue; 970-728-6278) and **Telluride Horseback** (9025 Route 145; 970-728-9611). **Deep Creek Sleighs & Wagon Rides** (133 West Colorado Avenue; 970-728-3565) offers horse-drawn sleigh and wagon rides with dinner nightly.

Ouray Livery Barn (834 Main Street, Ouray; 970-325-4606) rents horses for independent riding. In Silverton, **Silverado Outfitters** (Mineral Street; 970-387-5668) leads breakfast and dinner rides.

PACK TRIPS AND LLAMA TREKKING

A pack trip into the southern Colorado Rockies can turn a vacation into an adventure. For those who want to hike long distances into the high country but don't want to be burdened with backpacks, llama trekking may be just the ticket. Besides being an extraordinary hiking companion, the llama carries your lunch, camera gear and fishing tackle—up to about a 40-pound load.

ALAMOSA AREA Near Rio Grande Reservoir on the Silver Thread Scenic Byway above Creede, **Lost Trails Ranch** (5224 East 3 South Road, Monte Vista; 719-852-2315) guides customized llama trips into elk country.

GUNNISON–CRESTED BUTTE AREA Multiday horse pack trips into the West Elk and Raggeds wilderness areas can be arranged at **Fantasy Ranch** (P.O. Box 236, Crested Butte, CO 81224; 970-349-5425), **Stormy Ridge Outfitters & Guides Ltd.** (P.O. Box 547, Crested Butte, CO 81224; 970-641-4648) or **Teocalli Outfitters** (P.O. Box 1425, Crested Butte, CO 81224; 970-641-6733). In the Gunnison area, **Gunnison Country Guide Service** (P.O. Box 1443, Gunnison, CO 81230; 970-641-2830) arranges half-day and full-day pack trips suited to various interests and abilities.

GRAND JUNCTION AREA For a true once-in-a-lifetime experience, join the **Uncompahgre Wagon Train** on its journey across the remote, timeless expanse of Grand Mesa. The wagon train, which operates continuously from April until mid-September, can accommodate 40 passengers at a time. A remuda of riding horses accompanies the wagon train, so guests have their choice of traveling horseback or in the wagon. You can join the wagon train for as many or few days as you wish—it's sort of like a horse-drawn bed and breakfast, except you sleep in tents with cots and sleeping bags. Reservations should be made far in advance by contacting Uncompahgre Wagon Train (21375 Route 550 South, Montrose, CO 81402; 970-249-3807).

DURANGO AND SAN JUAN SKYWAY AREA In Bayfield, **Outlaw West Livery** (County Road 501A; 970-884-9631) has guided rides of varying lengths, including seven-day full-service pack trips in the Weminuche Wilderness. Just north of Durango, **Red Mountain Ranch** (27846 Route 550, Durango; 970-247-9796) offers overnight pack trips, as does **Engine Creek Outfitters & Cascade Stables** (50827 Route 150, Durango; 970-259-2556). In Silverton, **Silverado Outfitters** (Mineral Street; 970-387-5668) lead pack trips on the Colorado and Continental Divide trails. Near Durango, the **Buckhorn Llama Company** (1834 County Road 207, Durango; 970-259-5965) takes visitors on trips into the high San Juans.

BICYCLING

ALAMOSA AREA The flat, straight roads of the **San Luis Valley** make the area ideal for bicycle touring. Besides the main highways, a grid of farm roads crisscrosses the valley with very little traffic. There are National Forest jeep roads suitable for mountain biking in the **Cumbres Pass** area west of Antonito (information, Rio Grande National Forest, Creede Ranger District, P.O. Box 270, Creede, CO 81130; 719-658-2556) and in the Creede area (information, Rio Grande National Forest Headquarters, 1803 West Route 160, Monte Vista; 719-852-5941).

GUNNISON–CRESTED BUTTE AREA Since the sport was invented in Crested Butte in the late 1970s, mountain biking has become Colorado's most popular summertime sport. World-class, organized events include Crested Butte's Fat Tire Bike Week in July. Some popular mountain-biking routes in the area are **Kebler Pass Road** and the roads from **Pitkin** to the west portal of the **Alpine Tunnel** and over Cumberland Pass to **Tincup** and **Taylor Park Reservoir**, all described elsewhere in this chapter. For details on these and many other forest roads that make good bike routes, get a Gunnison National Forest map from the ranger station at 216 North Colorado Street, Gunnison; 970-641-0471.

GRAND JUNCTION AREA One of the most ambitious and memorable mountain-biking trips to be found anywhere is **Kokopelli's Trail**, a route established in 1989 by the Colorado Plateau Mountain-Bike Trail Association (Grand Junction; 970-241-9561) in cooperation with the Bureau of Land Management. The trail begins at the Loma Boat Launch, off Route 70 near Fruita, and runs 128 miles along back roads and trails generally following the course of the Colorado River, all the way to Moab, Utah. Another ultimate mountain-bike route is the **Tabeguache Trail**, which goes south from Grand Junction for 142 miles along the Uncompahgre Plateau, climbing to 10,000-foot altitudes. For detailed information on both trails, contact the Bureau of Land Management

(2815 H Road, Grand Junction; 970-244-3000) or Colorado Plateau Mountain-Bike Trail Association (P.O. Box 4602, Grand Junction, CO 81501; 970-241-9561).

DURANGO AND SAN JUAN SKYWAY AREA An easy ride near Pagosa Springs, the **Turkey Springs Trail** (6 miles) offers views of Pagosa Peak. A more challenging route, the **Willow Draw Trail** (16 miles), starts at Pagosa Springs City Park and climbs high into the hills before the thrilling downhill run back into town.

In the Durango area, the chairlift at **Purgatory Ski Area** (Route 550, Durango; 970-247-9000); admission) is equipped in the summer to take riders and their bikes to the summit, where they can ride the four-mile **Harris Park Loop** across the alpine **Hermosa Creek Valley** on the back side of the mountain. A longer and more challenging ride, the **Hermosa Creek Trail** (23 miles) takes cyclists through high meadows and along the rim of the Hermosa Cliffs. Just up the highway from Purgatory, the graded **Lime Creek Road** (11 miles) makes for a gentle ride through aspen forests with sweeping panoramic views of the surrounding mountains.

Unpaved **Ilium Road** is a favorite among mountain bikers in the Telluride area. The eight-mile road takes you to historic mining sites and waterfalls in a deep canyon. For an ultimate all-terrain biking experience, the trail to **Bear Creek Falls** climbs 1100 feet in elevation on its way to one of the most beautiful canyons in the area. **Ingram Falls Road** is a steep three-mile ascent to Bridal Veil Falls, at the upper end of the canyon overlooking town. For a week-long mountain-bike trek, the **San Juan Hut System**, a series of six shelters along a 215-mile bike route between Telluride and Moab, Utah, crosses varied terrain from alpine tundra to slickrock desert.

Unpaved, rugged four-wheel-drive roads leading to abandoned mines in the San Juan Mountains make for challenging mountain-bike trips. Around Ouray, great mountain-bike routes include the jeep trail from near Amphitheater campground up to the Portland and Chief Ouray mines. Another starts above Lake Lenore on the way to the Bachelor Mine and runs past the Wedge Mine to the Bridge of Heaven.

BIKE RENTALS In the Alamosa area, **Kristi Mountain Sports** (Villa Mall, West Route 160, Alamosa; 719-589-6772) and **San Juan Sports** (Main Street, Creede; 719-589-9759) rent bikes. In Gunnison, rentals are at **Tomichi Cycles** (134 West Tomichi Avenue; 970-641-9069). Bicycling is a big industry in Crested Butte, where rentals are available at **Bicycles Etc.** (419 6th Street; 970-349-6286), **Flatiron Sports** (10 Crested Butte Way; 970-349-6656) and **Crested Butte Sports Ski & Bike Shop** (Evergreen Condominiums, 35 Emmons Loop Road; 970-349-7516). In Grand Junction, both road and mountain bikes can be rented at **The Bike Peddler** (710 North 1st Street; 970-243-5602). Rentals are also available at **The Cycle Center** (141 North 7th Street; 970-242-2541). In Pagosa Springs, you'll find bicycles at **Pedal the Peaks** (River Center; 970-264-4110). In Durango, try **Hassle Free Sports** (2615 Main Avenue; 970-259-3874) or **The Outdoorsman** (949 Main Avenue; 970-247-4066). Places to rent bicycles in Telluride include **Olympic Sports** (101 West Colorado Avenue;

970-728-4477) and **Paragon Ski and Sport** (217 West Colorado Avenue; 970-728-4525). In Ouray, there's **Downhill Biking** (722 Main Street; 970-325-4284).

HIKING

All distances listed for hiking trails are one-way unless otherwise noted.

ALAMOSA AREA Although no permanent trails mar the sands of **Great Sand Dunes National Monument**, it is virtually impossible to get lost. The dunes are so vast that hikers with plenty of water can explore the dune field for days (backcountry hiking permit required). Also in the national monument, the **Mosca Pass Trail** (3.5 miles) climbs to the crest of the Sangre de Cristo Range for spectacular views of the San Luis and Wet Mountain valleys.

Various trailheads in the vicinity of Creede provide access to the Weminuche Wilderness. They range from the fairly easy climb to Ruby Lake on the **Fern Creek Trail** (3.5 miles) to the 80-mile stretch of the **Continental Divide Trail** that crosses the wilderness area from Stony Pass to Wolf Creek Pass.

GUNNISON–CRESTED BUTTE AREA Curecanti National Recreation Area has hiking trails through a wide range of habitats: the lush streamside greenery of the five-mile **Neversink Trail**; the dry, rugged **Curecanti Needle Trail** (2.5 miles) to the base of the spirelike rock formation for which it is named; and the steep **Curecanti Creek Trail** (2 miles) down to Morrow Point Reservoir in the Black Canyon of the Gunnison. Within **Black Canyon of the Gunnison National Monument**, four trails, ranging in distance from one to three miles, descend from the rim to the river; a high-clearance vehicle is necessary to reach the trailheads.

Hikers can explore the West Elk Wilderness west of Gunnison and Crested Butte on the **Mill Creek Trail** (15 miles), which climbs to heights of over 12,000 feet. There is an extensive network of interconnecting trails from **Cement Creek**, seven miles south of Crested Butte. Perhaps the ultimate hike in the Crested Butte area is the **Conundrum Trail** (14 miles), which starts above the ghost town of Gothic and crosses the Continental Divide to Conundrum Hot Springs and, from there, descends toward Aspen.

GRAND JUNCTION AREA **Colorado National Monument** has about 44 miles of trails. The most remote and challenging hike in the park is **No Thoroughfare Canyon**, eight and a half miles long, studded with juniper and enclosed by sheer cliffs 400 feet high. Midway up the canyon, the intermittent stream at the bottom plunges over two waterfalls about three-quarters of a mile apart whenever the water is flowing—usually in late spring. Another great hike in Colorado National Monument is the **Liberty Cap Trail** (5.5 miles), a fairly level trail that follows a ridge to an "island in the sky" overlooking the Grand Valley. The park also has a number of shorter trails suited to hikes of a half-hour to four hours.

One of the best hikes in the Grand Junction area is **Rattlesnake Canyon**, where rock formations include a dozen large natural arches. Take Black Ridge Road, which exits from West Glade Park Road just outside the back entrance to Colorado National Monument. The 11-mile drive to Rattlesnake Canyon takes about an hour. Passenger cars can negotiate the first nine miles, but visitors without four-wheel-drive must walk the last two miles. From the road's end, a steep, edgy foot trail descends through the first arch, and you reach eight others on a two-mile loop hike.

On Grand Mesa, the main hiking trail is the **Crag Crest Trail** (10 miles). The trail keeps to the high ground as it winds among the lakes and through the fir-and-aspen forests, commanding sweeping views of the mesa, the valley below and the San Juan Mountains in the distance.

DURANGO AND SAN JUAN SKYWAY AREA Durango has an overwhelming number of hiking options. The ultimate trail in the area is the **Colorado Trail** (469 miles), which goes all the way from Durango to Denver, following the Continental Divide most of the way. The first segment of the trail goes from Durango to Silverton, a distance of about 70 miles through the rugged La Plata Mountains.

Another magnificently ambitious hike is the **Needle Creek Trail**, which starts at the ghost town of Needleton, a stop on the Durango & Silverton Narrow-Gauge Railroad route. The trail climbs into the jagged peaks of the Weminuche Wilderness to join a network of other trails, including the spectacular **Chicago Basin** route, which follows alpine valleys all the way to Creede—a 75-mile trip that takes about a week. Backpackers without train tickets use a longer route to reach the high wilderness, starting at Vallecito Reservoir and taking the **Vallecito Trail** or the **Pine River Trail**. Still other trails into the Weminuche Wilderness start from Route 550.

Among the many day-hike options in the Durango area are **Red Creek Trail** (6 miles), on Missionary Ridge above town, and **Twin Buttes Trail** (4 miles), overlooking town.

Telluride is hiker's heaven in the summertime. Short, challenging trails like the steep one-mile climb to **Bridal Veil Falls** start from the outskirts of town. For an all-day or overnight hike, the **Bear Creek Trail** passes another waterfall and climbs high in the mountains to join the **Wasatch Trail** for a descent to Bridal Veil Falls, making a strenuous ten-mile loop. For mountaintop vistas without the pain, hikers can ride the chairlift (which operates all year) up the Telluride ski slopes and hike along at 10,500-foot elevation alpine ridges.

In Ouray, short hikes include the **Lower Cascade Falls Trail** (.5 mile), which starts just a few blocks from the center of town, and the steep **Upper Cascade Falls Trail** (2.5 miles), which starts from the natural amphitheater south of town. For an all-day hike, try **Bear Creek Trail** (7.25 miles), which passes several old mining operations on its way to the summit of Engineer Pass.

Near Silverton, the **Highland Mary Lakes Trail** (2.5 miles) takes you through a landscape thoroughly probed by miners a century ago and leads up to a pair of alpine lakes. This trail joins the Canada-to-Mexico **Continental Divide Trail** as it passes through the Weminuche Wilderness. The **Molas Pass Trail** (3 miles) starts at Molas Lake on Route 550 and descends steeply to the Animas River and the Durango & Silverton train tracks a thousand feet below, offering breathtaking views and a hard climb back up to your car.

Transportation

BY CAR

Southern Colorado has two main east-west highways, each of which crosses the Continental Divide over a high switchback pass.

Route 50 exits from Route 25 at Pueblo and runs west through Cañon City before winding its way over Monarch Pass (11,312 feet) and then descending into the Gunnison–Crested Butte area. Route 50 continues westward to join Route 70 at Grand Junction.

Route 160 exits from Route 25 at Walsenburg and, after an easy climb over La Veta Pass (9413 feet), descends into the San Luis Valley and the Alamosa area. After crossing the valley, it goes over Wolf Creek Pass (10,850 feet) and down into the Durango area.

Several north-south highways connect Route 50 with Route 160. The straightest and fastest roads are **Route 285** and **Route 17**, both of which run the length of the San Luis Valley, meeting Route 50 at Poncha Springs and Route 160 at Salida. All three of the other north-south roads are among the most scenic mountain drives in this book, and all are discussed in detail earlier in this chapter. They are: **Route 149**, also known as the Scenic Thread Scenic Byway, which meets Route 50 at Gunnison, goes through Lake City and Creede and intersects Route 160 at Del Norte; and **Route 550** and **Route 145**, together known as the San Juan Skyway Scenic Byway. Route 550 leaves Route 160 at Durango and goes through Silverton and Ouray. Route 145 leaves Route 160 at Mancos, a short drive west of Durango, and goes through Dolores and Telluride. The two highways merge before reaching Route 50 at Montrose.

BY AIR

Mesa Airlines/United Express has flights between Denver and **Alamosa Municipal Airport**. Visitors arriving by air may wish to arrange shuttle service through their lodging; no public transportation is available in Alamosa.

Continental Express, Mesa Airlines/United Express and Skywest/Delta Connection fly into **Gunnison County Airport**. The airport, which serves both Gunnison and Crested Butte, also handles ski-trip flights from other parts of the United States during the winter months. Airport shuttle service is furnished by **Alpine Express** (970-641-5074).

Walker Field Public Airport, located in Grand Junction, has flights to and from Denver on Continental Airlines, Mesa Airlines/United Express and Sky West/Delta Connection. **Blondie's Limousine Service** (970-241-1400) and **Grand Junction Luxury Limousine Service** (970-434-1488) both operate ground transportation.

Daily commuter flights from Denver to **Durango–La Plata Airport** are provided by America West Express, Continental Express and Mesa Airlines/ United Express. Airport shuttles are operated by **Durango Transportation Inc.** (970-259-4818).

Continental Express, Mesa Airlines/United Express and Skywest/Delta Connection serve the **Telluride Regional Airport**; the Continental and Mesa flights also land at **Montrose Regional Airport**. Ground transportation at both airports is available from **Telluride Transit Company Airport Shuttle Service** (970-728-6000).

BY TRAIN

The "California Zephyr," operated by **Amtrak** (800-872-7245), stops in Grand Junction on its way from Denver and Glenwood Springs to Salt Lake City and San Francisco.

BY BUS

Greyhound Bus Lines has bus service to Gunnison (821 West Tomichi Avenue; 970-641-2912), Montrose (50 North Townsend Street; 970-249-6673), Grand Junction (230 South 5th Street; 970-242-6012) and Durango (275 East 8th Avenue; 970-247-2755).

CAR RENTALS

Rental cars are scarce in the Alamosa area. Try **L & M Auto Rentals** (Alamosa Municipal Airport, Alamosa; 719-589-4651) or **Freedom Rent-A-Car System** (1313 Route 160, Monte Vista; 719-852-5152).

Agencies at the Gunnison County Airport include **Avis Rent A Car** (800-331-1212), **Budget Rent A Car** (800-527-0700) and **Hertz Rent A Car** (800-654-3131). Four-wheel drives can be rented in Crested Butte at **Whetstone Automotive 4-Wheel-Drive Rental** (301 Belleview Avenue; 970-349-7374) or **Flatiron Sports** (10 Crested Butte Way; 800-821-4331) and in Lake City at **Rocky Mountain Jeep Rental** (549 South Gunnison Avenue, Wade's Addition; 970-944-2262) or **Lake City Auto & Jeep Rentals** (809 Route 149; 970-944-2311).

Grand Junction has a full complement of name-brand car-rental agencies. Most are located at Walker Field Airport, including **Avis Rent A Car** (800-331-1212), **Budget Rent A Car** (800-527-0700), **Hertz Rent A Car** (800-654-3131) and **National Interrent** (800-328-4567).

In Durango, too, most of the standard car-rental agencies have representatives at Durango–La Plata Airport. They include **Avis Rent A Car** (800-331-1212), **Budget Rent A Car** (800-527-0700), **Hertz Rent A Car** (800-654-3131) and **National Interrent** (800-328-4567). You can rent either a late-model used car or a four-wheel-drive vehicle at **Rent A Wreck** (21760 Route 160 West; 800-327-0116).

Along the San Juan Skyway, four-wheel-drives are for rent at **Telluride Outside 4 X 4 Rentals** (666 West Colorado Avenue, Telluride; 970-728-3895), **Switzerland of America Jeep Rentals** (226 7th Avenue, Ouray; 800-432-5332), **Colorado West Jeep Rentals** (332 5th Avenue, Ouray; 970-325-4014) and **Triangle Rent A Jeep** (864 Greene Street, Silverton; 970-387-9990).

PUBLIC TRANSPORTATION

The **Durango Lift** (949 East 2nd Avenue, Durango; 970-259-5438) provides in-town, fixed-route bus service during the summer months and shuttle service from Durango to the slopes at Purgatory during ski season.

TAXIS

Taxi service is provided in Gunnison by **Alpine Express** (Gunnison County Airport; 970-641-5074) and in Crested Butte by **Town Taxi** (226½ White Rock Avenue; 970-349-5543). In Grand Junction, call **Sunshine Taxi** (1331 Ute Avenue; 970-245-8294). In Durango, the taxi company is **Durango Transportation** (547½ East 2nd Avenue; 970-259-4818). In Telluride, it's **Skip's Taxi** (129 West San Juan Avenue; 970-728-9606).

CHAPTER FIVE

Utah Rockies

The Uinta Mountains are the only range in the Rockies that runs east and west, instead of north and south like Utah's other great range, the Wasatch Mountains. Forming a fortress wall along the L-shaped state line between Wyoming and Utah, the two ranges meet at right angles just east of Salt Lake City.

Dramatic contrasts characterize the region, from the raw, arid canyon country around Vernal to the steep, pyramidal Wasatch Mountains with their lush forests, to the stark desert on the north and west shores of Utah's single most unusual feature, the inland sea known simply as the Great Salt Lake.

The Ute tribe, for whom the state of Utah was named, has inhabited the area for many centuries—and many Ute still do, making their homes on the large reservation south of Vernal. But Anglo civilization came earlier to this part of Utah than to almost all other regions described in this book. The Mormons, a highly successful religious group of the early 19th century, came to the Cache, Salt Lake and Utah valleys at the dawn of the pioneer era, seeking isolation in a "New Zion" so remote that there was not another city within nearly 1000 miles, and transformed the land into a surprisingly rich agricultural area. The Mormon pioneer spirit lives on in contemporary Utah, creating an economy more prosperous than any other in the intermountain West.

Though industry and agriculture predominate in Utah, both the state government and private business have made a major effort to stimulate tourism during the past 20 years. The keystone of Utah's developing tourist industry has been skiing: With an incredible 500 inches of snowfall each winter, northern Utah boasts some of the finest snow conditions in the Rockies. A typical snow base in Utah's ski areas is more than 15 feet deep. Most of Utah's ski areas are within 40 minutes' drive from downtown Salt Lake City—closer, in fact, than *any* major Colorado ski area is to Denver and the other Front Range population centers. In fact, skiing in this area is considered world class—so much so that Salt Lake City has been selected to host the Winter Olympics in 2002.

The nearness of the mountains, which often appear to loom massively over Salt Lake City and its satellite communities, makes for an abundance of recreation in summer as well as winter. As the mountains provide habitat for deer, elk and even bears just a few minutes from the city, they also attract thousands of hikers, anglers, mountain bikers, campers and picnickers to the canyon scenery just beyond the city limits. A longer drive will bring serious trekkers to trailheads that can take them into some of the most pristine wilderness areas in the Rockies, high in the Wasatch and Uinta mountains.

Vernal Area

Perched in Utah's northeastern corner just 30 miles from the Colorado state line and 40 miles from Wyoming, the town of Vernal is surrounded by a diversity of landscapes—to the east, the rugged sandstone canyon country of Dinosaur National Monument; to the south, the arid farm and ranch lands of the Uinta and Ouray Indian Reservation; and to the north, the high, cool Uinta Mountains and, beyond them, Flaming Gorge Reservoir, one of the most scenic large recreational lakes in the Rockies.

Vernal seems to fancy itself a small-town version of Jurassic Park. The hub of an area that government tourism agencies have dubbed "Dinosaurland," Vernal is the home of places like the Dinosaur Inn, the Dina Drive-Inn, the Dinah Skate Center, the Dinaland Golf Course, Dinaland Aviation, Dinosaur Gifts-N-Things and the town's big summer festival, Dinosaur Days. Vernal's touristic centerpiece, the **Utah Field House of Natural History State Park and Dinosaur Gardens** (235 East Main Street; 801-759-0392; admission), contains museum exhibits on the history, prehistory and geology of the area, but its main feature is a collection of 14 life-size dinosaur replicas created by local sculptor Elbert Porter set amid lush landscaped gardens that contrast dramatically with the surrounding desert.

The dinosaur motif that pervades this community derives from nearby **Dinosaur National Monument** (Route 149; 801-789-2115; admission), where some of the first complete dinosaur skeletons ever assembled for museums were unearthed as early as 1909. Sixty-five million years ago, a sandy barrier island at the mouth of a river delta lush with tropical forest became the dinosaurs' final resting place when they drowned in a flood. Over the eons, thousands of them were entombed in sandy sediments that later hardened into sandstone. The fossil remains of prehistoric giants such as the vegetarian aptosaurus, diplodocus and stegosaurus as well as the meat-eating allosaurus have been shipped to museums around the world. Today paleontologists continue to expose dinosaur bones at the quarry but do not remove them. The sandstone face, with its still-emerging jigsaw puzzle of fossil skeletons, forms one wall of the **Dinosaur Quarry**, the main sightseeing attraction at this national monument. Although the park encompasses

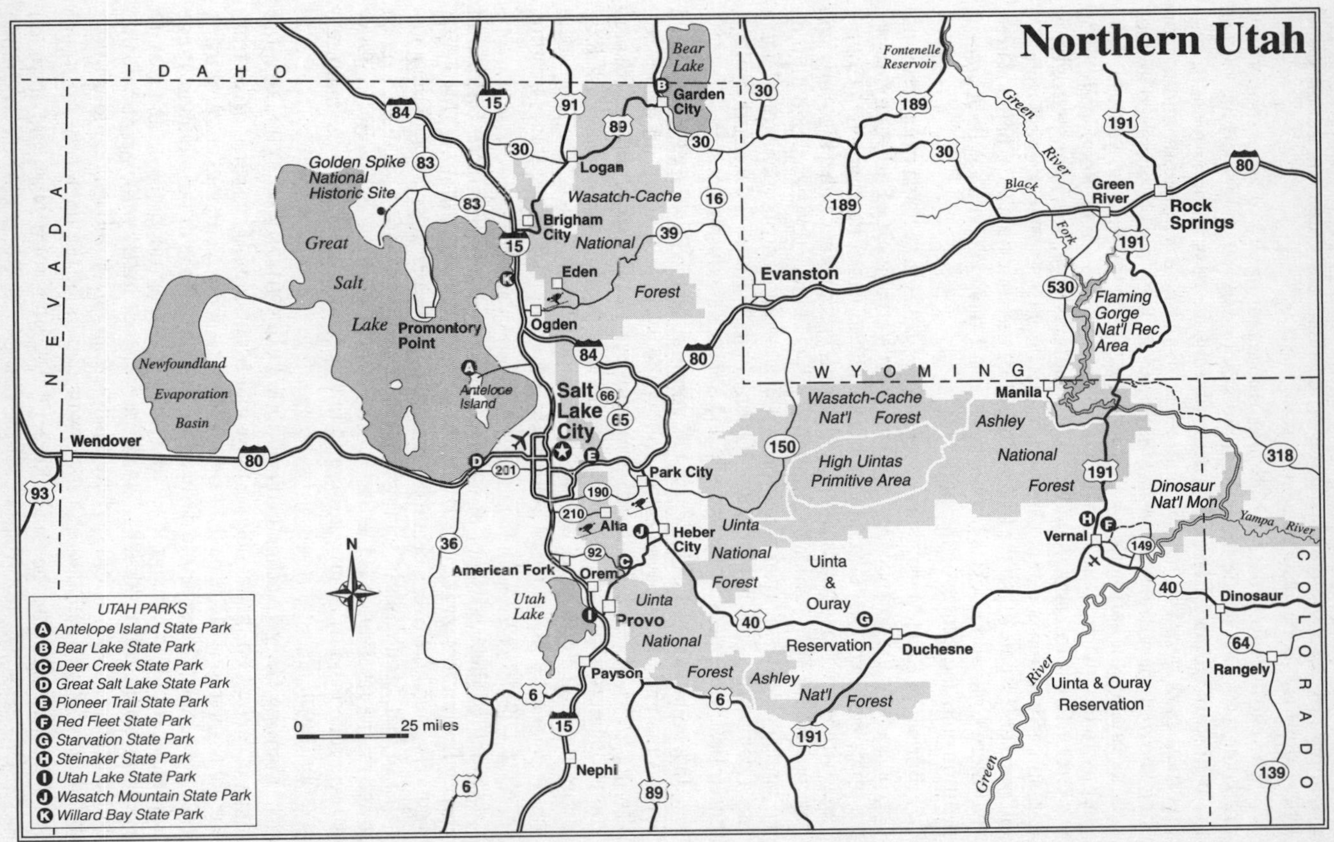
Northern Utah
UTAH PARKS
A Antelope Island State Park
B Bear Lake State Park
C Deer Creek State Park
D Great Salt Lake State Park
E Pioneer Trail State Park
F Red Fleet State Park
G Starvation State Park
H Steinaker State Park
I Utah Lake State Park
J Wasatch Mountain State Park
K Willard Bay State Park
0
25 miles
N
I D A H O
W Y O M I N G
C O L O R A D O
N E V A D A
Rock Springs
Green River
Evanston
Manila
Vernal
Dinosaur
Rangely
Duchesne
Heber City
Park City
Salt Lake City
Ogden
Eden
Brigham City
Logan
Garden City
Bear Lake
Provo
Orem
American Fork
Payson
Nephi
Alta
Wendover
Utah Lake
Great Salt Lake
Promontory Point
Antelope Island
Golden Spike National Historic Site
Newfoundland Evaporation Basin
Fontenelle Reservoir
Flaming Gorge Nat'l Rec Area
Dinosaur Nat'l Mon
Ashley National Forest
Wasatch-Cache Nat'l Forest
Wasatch-Cache National Forest
High Uintas Primitive Area
Uinta & Ouray Reservation
Uinta National Forest
Ashley Nat'l Forest
Green River
Black Fork
Yampa River

a vast area of desert canyon wilderness, the Dinosaur Quarry is the only spot where dinosaur bones can be seen.

The entrance to Dinosaur National Monument lies 12 miles east of Vernal off Route 149. Just inside the monument's boundary is a huge parking lot and the **Dinosaur Quarry Visitors Center**. During the busy summer months, visitors must park here and take a shuttle bus to the quarry; exhibits and a short slide show at the visitors center are designed to keep people occupied as they wait as much as a half hour for their shuttle. In the off-season, you can drive directly to the quarry. Past the visitors center, the Cub Creek Road leads along the Green River to campgrounds, hiking trails, Native American petroglyphs and an early settler's cabin. The two-hour Harper's Corner Scenic Drive (25 miles east off Route 40 on the Colorado side of the state line; see Chapter Three, "Northern Colorado Rockies") rounds out an all-day visit with a spectacular expedition into the center of the park.

Bureau of Land Management recreational lands in the area offer lots more canyon scenery and solitude. An easy tour from Vernal is **Dry Fork Canyon** (★), ten miles northwest of town on Dry Fork Canyon Road. Passing Uinta County Park, with its picnic grounds and children's playground beneath a big American flag and World War I–vintage "Remember the Maine" slogan painted high on the sandstone cliff, the road takes you to a spectacular array of prehistoric Native American petroglyphs at McConkie Ranch, then continues to Dry Fork Village, the earliest settlement in the valley, and several shady picnic areas.

In a high-clearance vehicle you can continue on the Dry Fork Canyon Road beyond the end of the pavement to follow the 74-mile **Red Cloud Loop** (★), offering views of the high Uintas' deep canyons and forests of pine and aspen. Points of interest along the scenic drive include picnic areas at Oak Park Reservoir and Iron Springs, as well as caves along Brush Creek. The loop route returns to Vernal at Steinaker State Park, a reservoir offering fishing, boating, camping and swimming.

Much of the land south of Vernal is part of the million-acre **Uinta and Ouray Indian Reservation** (801-722-5141). The ancestors of these Ute people were relocated here over a century ago from their former reservation in the gold-rich San Juan Mountains of southwestern Colorado. The only time there is much to see on the reservation is the first week of July, when the Northern Ute Pow-wow, a rodeo and tribal arts-and-crafts fair, is held at Duchesne, the main reservation town.

Flaming Gorge National Recreation Area (801-784-3445) lies 36 miles north of Vernal on the far side of the Uinta Mountains. The scenic drive from Vernal to the reservoir on paved Route 191 takes about an hour to drive, skirting 9722-foot Mount Lena before descending the north slope of the mountain range past several public campgrounds that nestle among the pines on the way to **Flaming Gorge Dam** (801-784-3445), the 502-foot-high hydroelectric dam that created the reservoir in 1964. There visitors can take a self-guided tour to see the electric power generators in the lower depths of the dam.

The dam backs up the Green River for 91 miles to the west and north, all the way to the stark, arid fringes of the Great Divide Basin near the Wyoming towns of Rock Springs and Green River. While the Wyoming portion of the reservoir is surrounded by a barren, brownish landscape that only a bass fisherman could love, the Utah portion offers such spectacular scenery that it may well qualify as the most beautiful artificial lake in the American West. The best way to see it is to rent a boat at either Cedar Springs Marina near the dam or Lucerne Valley Marina near the town of Manila. Motorists will find the best scenery along Route 44 westward toward Manila, especially at the **Red Canyon Visitors Center**, on the **Hideout Canyon–Carter Creek Hiking Trail**, on the paved scenic loop through the **Sheep Creek Canyon Geological Area** and at the **Canyon Gooseneck Overlook**. The road distance from the dam to Manila is only 36 miles, but you may want to allow several hours to explore the area.

VERNAL AREA HOTELS

Vernal has an abundance of motels, all on the main drag and all with room rates in the budget and moderate ranges. Advance reservations are rarely necessary.

The **Best Western Dinosaur Inn** (251 East Main Street, Vernal; 801-789-2660, fax 801-789-2467), one of the town's better motor inns, certainly has the best location—next door to the Utah Field House of Natural History State Park and Dinosaur Gardens. The two-story motel has 59 cheerful, contemporary rooms around a swimming pool, whirlpool and children's playground. Ask for a room with a view of the dinosaurs. Moderate.

You can spend the night far from the main highway by heading for the shore of Flaming Gorge Reservoir. Catering primarily to anglers, all Flaming Gorge lodgings require reservations well in advance for weekend nights and usually have plenty of room during the week. The most comfortable of them is the **Flaming Gorge Lodge** (Route 191, Dutch John; 801-889-3773), a family-run motel with 44 rooms plus a coffee shop, dining room, grocery store, bait-and-tackle shop and raft rentals. Modern, spacious guest rooms, most with lake views, make this the most attractive lodge in the Flaming Gorge area. Moderate.

Located on the rim of Red Canyon overlooking Flaming Gorge Reservoir, **Red Canyon Lodge** (Route 44, Flaming Gorge National Recreation Area; 801-889-3759) offers rustic log cabins dating back to the 1930s. The cabins have two rooms, each with a queen-size bed. There are outdoor picnic tables and a fire ring. Some cabins have private baths; others share a central restroom and showers. The lodge has also recently added several modern luxury cabins with covered porches, kitchenettes and full baths. The older cabins are budget-priced, and the luxury cabins are in the moderate range.

VERNAL AREA RESTAURANTS

Chain fast-food places aside, the options for dining out in Vernal are limited. The local favorite is the **Great American Cafe** (13 South Vernal Avenue; 801-789-1115), a plain, wholesome little place where the specialties are homemade cinnamon rolls for breakfast and catfish the rest of the time. Specialty salads, submarine sandwiches and steaks are also served. Budget.

Big Jim's BBQ Emporium (773 East Main Street, Vernal; 801-789-3932) serves up sizzling slabs of ribs, as well as chicken and steaks, in an extra-casual atmosphere. Budget.

The **Last Chance Bar and Restaurant** (3340 North Vernal Avenue, Vernal; 801-789-3151), an Old West–flavored saloon, is known around town for great breakfasts. The chef also serves up sandwiches and steak dinners. Budget.

The finest dining in this part of the state is at **Red Canyon Lodge** (Route 44, Flaming Gorge National Recreation Area; 801-889-3759). The steak-and-trout menu is about what you'd expect of a restaurant lost in the woods; it is the setting, at one of the most scenic segments of Flaming Gorge, that makes it worth the drive. Budget to moderate.

VERNAL AREA NIGHTLIFE

There's not much to do after dark in these parts. Travelers spending the night in Vernal are well advised to make sure their motel room has cable TV. Those who truly crave a night on the town might look for smoky, pool-shootin', country-and-western-on-the-jukebox fun at the **Last Chance Bar and Restaurant** (3340 North Vernal Avenue; 801-789-3151) and **Gateway Saloon & Social Club** (773 East Main Street; 801-789-5075).

VERNAL AREA PARKS

Steinaker State Park—Set in a desert oasis on the outskirts of Vernal, Steinaker Reservoir is overlooked by most boaters and fishermen, whose attention is diverted by the bigger, more scenic Flaming Gorge Reservoir, not far up the road.

Facilities: Restrooms, picnic areas, boat ramp; day-use fee, $3; information, 801-789-4432. *Swimming:* Permitted. *Fishing:* Good for both rainbow trout and largemouth bass.

Camping: There are 31 RV/tent sites (no hookups); $7 to $8 per night.

Getting there: Located five miles north of Vernal on Route 191.

Red Fleet State Park—Red Fleet Reservoir, a few miles north of Steinaker Reservoir, offers a pretty setting, its north shore flanked by the strangely sculpted red sandstone cliffs that give the lake its name.

Facilities: Restrooms, picnic areas, boat ramp; day-use fee, $3; information, 801-789-6614. *Swimming:* Permitted. *Fishing:* Good for trout, bass and bluegill.

Camping: There are 29 RV/tent sites (no hookups); $7 to $8 per night.

Getting there: Located ten miles north of Vernal on Route 191.

Starvation State Park—The name, a grim reminder of the hardships suffered by the Ute people who were relocated here from their southwestern Colorado homeland in the 1880s, belies the beauty of this long, narrow lake on the Strawberry River, surrounded by the lush forested hills of the Uinta and Ouray Indian Reservation.

Facilities: Restrooms, picnic areas, boat ramp, marina; day-use fee, $3; information, 801-738-2326. *Swimming:* Permitted. *Fishing:* Good for both bass and walleye.

Camping: There are 54 RV/tent sites (no hookups); $9 to $10 per night.

Getting there: Located four miles west of Duchesne off Route 40.

Ashley National Forest—Surrounding the Utah portion of Flaming Gorge National Recreation Area, this national forest contains the vast, 457,000-acre High Uintas Wilderness. Kings Peak (13,528 feet), the highest mountain in Utah, reigns in the heart of the wilderness, surrounded by five other peaks over 13,000 feet high. While there is unpaved road access to campgrounds on all four sides of the wilderness boundary, the only paved access is from Route 150 east of the Park City area. Mountain sheep, elk and moose are abundant in the wilderness.

Facilities: Hiking trails. *Fishing:* Good for rainbow and other trout species in many natural lakes and streams.

Camping: Twenty-one campgrounds offer a total of 420 RV/tent sites; $2 to $7 per night. There are also 608 RV/tent sites in 13 campgrounds within Flaming Gorge Recreation Area, with similar camping fees. No hookups are available.

Getting there: Highway access to the eastern edge of the national forest is via Route 191 north of Vernal; the western edge of the forest is reached via Route 150 east of Park City.

North of Salt Lake City

The steep wall of the Bear River Range flanks the Cache Valley, an enclave of rich farmland watered by rivers that pour from mountain canyons. Chief among them is the Logan River, which flows for 30 miles between the lofty limestone cliffs of **Logan Canyon**, a popular place for trout fishing, camping, hiking, kayaking and whitewater rafting. Exploring side roads in Wasatch-Cache National Forest can turn a drive through the canyon into a full-day expedition. The **Jardine Juniper** (★), reached by a short, steep trail, is said to be the world's oldest juniper tree—an estimated 3200 years old. A little farther down the canyon is the trailhead for the five-mile trek to **Old Ephraim's Grave** (★). Old Ephraim was the largest grizzly bear ever shot in Utah—over ten feet tall. In 1923, when the bear was killed, its skull was put on display in the Smithsonian Institution, where it remained for many years before being returned here to be made part of a small monument. If that's not enough sightseeing excitement for one day, **Wind Cave** (★) offers a chance to explore a series of small caverns and archways shaped by ice and wind erosion. Bring a flashlight.

At the mouth of the canyon is the hillside town of **Logan**, home of **Utah State University**. The main campus attraction is the **Nora Eccles Harrison Museum of Art** (650 North 1100 East Street; 801-750-1412). The free museum features an outstanding ceramics collection as well as changing exhibits of paintings and sculptures. The town of Logan is built around the **Mormon Temple and Tabernacle**, a smaller-scale replica of the Mormon Temple in Salt Lake City.

Six miles south of Logan on Route 89/91 is the **Ronald V. Jensen Living Historical Farm** (Route 89/91, Logan; 801-245-4064; admission), an open-air museum focusing on traditional farm life in the Mormon valleys. Thirteen farm buildings dating back to the early 1900s have been moved from various parts of the valley to this 120-acre farm. Staff members in period costume demonstrate seasonal farm activities such as wheat threshing and sheep shearing.

Between the Cache Valley and the north shore of the Great Salt Lake, the steep **Wellsville Mountains** rise like a wall nearly 5000 feet from the valley floor, taller relative to the width of their base than any other mountain range in the United States. Their western slope is a federally designated wilderness area.

Skirting the southern tip of the Wellsville Mountains, Route 89/91 brings you to **Brigham City**, where another highway, Route 83, continues 32 miles west to **Golden Spike National Historic Site** (Route 83; 801-471-2209; admission). Steam locomotives mark the spot where the westbound Union Pacific and eastbound Central Pacific railroads met in 1869 to complete the first transcontinental railroad. Near the historic site is the starting point of Promontory Road, which follows the shoreline of the Great Salt Lake around the peninsula known as **Promontory Point**. Although the pavement ends before the road reaches the tip of the peninsula, following the main road will bring you north through backcountry within the National Historic Site boundaries and eventually return you to the visitors center.

Traveling south on Route 15, you'll find yourself in **Ogden** before you realize you've left Brigham City. **Ogden Union Station** (2501 Wall Avenue; 801-629-8444; admission), the biggest visitors' attraction in town, no longer offers passenger train service but instead houses a collection of museums—the **Utah State Railroad Museum**, the **Browning Firearms Museum**, the **Browning-Kimball Car Museum**, the **Natural History Museum**, the **Myra Powell Art Gallery** and the **Japanese House of Peace**—a full afternoon's browsing for a single admission charge.

The **Ogden River Parkway**, a walking and jogging trail, follows the wooded riverbank for three miles through town, passing several parks along the way. The biggest spectacle along the route is the **George S. Eccles Dinosaur Park** (1544 East Park Boulevard, Ogden; 801-393-3466; admission), with 26 of the most realistic full-size dinosaur replicas this side of Jurassic Park, plus a fossil exhibit hall. Farther along the parkway is the **Utah State University Botanical Gardens** (1750 Monroe Boulevard, Ogden; 801-451-3204), a relatively small arboretum with both native and exotic trees and shrubs labeled for identification along short, easy nature trails.

Fort Buenaventura State Park (2450 A Avenue, Ogden; 801-621-4808) is the reconstruction of an early fort and trading post established by mountain man Miles Goodyear in 1846 to resupply pioneers bound for Oregon and California. Just a year after it was built, the fort was purchased from Goodyear by the Mormon Church and became the center of the community that became Ogden. Guides in period dress describe the fort's history, and exhibits tell of the mountain men and native peoples who lived there.

The **Great Salt Lake** lies a short distance west of Logan, Ogden and Salt Lake City. Saltier than the Pacific Ocean, it is the largest inland body of water in the United States (the Great Lakes, between the United States and Canada, don't count), measuring 92 miles north to south and 48 miles east to west. Snowmelt from the Wasatch Mountains fills the Great Salt Lake, but unlike other lakes in the Rockies, no river or stream drains water from it. The water simply evaporates in the arid desert climate, leaving an accumulation of water-soluble minerals that make the water salty. In fact, the Great Salt Lake is one of the saltiest bodies of water on earth, surpassed only by the Dead Sea.

Constantly changing, the Great Salt Lake seems to have a life of its own. Since scientists began recording measurements a century ago, the lake's salinity has ranged from 5.5 percent all the way to 27.3 percent, and there's no clear-cut explanation for the variance. Its water level also fluctuates dramatically. In the 1980s the lake inexplicably rose by up to 12 feet, threatening to flood portions of suburban Ogden and Salt Lake City. As mysteriously as it had risen, however, the lake began to fall again in 1987.

One effect of the lake's rising level was to cut off 75-square-mile **Antelope Island State Park** (801-451-3286; admission), the largest of ten islands in the Great Salt Lake, from the mainland. A century ago, herds of bison and elk were introduced to its grassy mountain slopes to make the island a private hunting preserve for Mormon elders. Eventually, a causeway was built from the lakeshore across the expanse of shallow water to Antelope Island, and it became a popular local picnicking and bathing spot. But in 1982, the rising lake destroyed the causeway, closing Antelope Island to visitors for more than a decade.

In a world without humans, the island's wildlife thrived. By the time the new causeway was built and the island was reopened in 1993, Antelope Island's original herd of ten bison had grown to 600, and deer, elk, coyotes and bobcats had also become abundant. Today, the northern half of the island, including its tallest mountain and sandiest beaches, is open to the public, while the southern half is completely fenced off as a wildlife refuge. Bison range freely in this rugged, huge area, but visitors rarely catch a glimpse of them, except perhaps for a few specimens that may be temporarily confined in enclosures for study. The best look at the herd comes during the annual bison roundup in November. Besides the refuge and beaches, the island offers a sailboat marina and many miles of trails for hiking and mountain biking. The causeway to Antelope Island is on Route 127, six miles east of the Layton exit (Exit 335) from Route 15.

NORTH OF SALT LAKE CITY HOTELS

Near Bear Lake are several small family-run motels in the lakefront town of Garden City as well as a charming bed and breakfast. The **Inn of the Three Bears Bed & Breakfast** (135 South Bear Lake Boulevard; 801-946-8590) offers three rustic Victorian-style guest rooms in country surroundings just an easy stroll from the lakeshore. Its moderate rates include a continental breakfast. In addition, one- to three-bedroom lakefront condominiums and townhouses are available for rent by the day or week. For details on availability, contact **Ideal Beach Resort Condominiums** (2176 South Bear Lake Boulevard; 801-946-3364) or **The Inn @ Harbor Village** (785 North Bear Lake Boulevard; 800-364-6480). Moderate to deluxe.

Logan boasts the **Center Street Bed & Breakfast Inn** (169 East Center Street; 801-752-3443), a red-brick mansion that dates back to 1879. Although the inn appears to be a typical antique-packed Victorian B & B, don't be fooled by the ornate period decor of the front parlor rooms: This place is a veritable theme park of accommodations. The mansion and carriage house contain 11 guest rooms and suites, each one individually—and flamboyantly—decorated. The Arabian Nights suite includes a bed disguised as a Bedouin tent, a sand-colored carpet and a red, heart-shaped sunken tub. Budget to moderate.

The **Snowberry Inn** (1315 North Highway 158, Eden; 801-745-2634), a five-unit bed and breakfast 15 minutes east of Ogden on the west shore of Pineview Reservoir in Ogden Canyon, has the feel of a rustic country inn with all the modern conveniences. Each guest room is individually decorated and has a private bath. The inn has an outdoor hot tub. Recreational facilities available at the lake include boating, windsurfing, golf, hiking, mountain biking and horseback riding. Moderate.

Ogden's premier in-town hostelry is the **Radisson Suite Hotel** (2510 Washington Boulevard; 801-627-1900, 800-333-3333, fax 801-394-5342). In a downtown historic-landmark building, the 144-room Radisson offers accommodations at various price levels, from studio suites with semidetached sitting areas and standard motel amenities to luxury two-bedroom suites with mountain views, whirlpool baths and kitchenettes with microwaves. Moderate to deluxe.

NORTH OF SALT LAKE CITY RESTAURANTS

For a home-cooked sit-down meal beside Bear Lake, try the **Greek Goddess Café** (205 North Bear Lake Boulevard, Garden City; 801-946-3333), at the motel of the same name. There's nothing particularly Greek about either the food or the decor, but the meat-and-potatoes fare certainly beats the fast-food drive-ins that make up most of the lakeshore's cuisine scene. Budget.

The local favorite eatery in Logan since 1923 is the **Bluebird Restaurant** (19 North Main Street; 801-752-3155). This place has a subtle, special quality that makes you feel as if you've slipped into an earlier, simpler era. Warm wood paneling, historic photos of Logan's early days and an old-fashioned marble soda fountain set the stage for home-cooked breakfasts, sandwiches and steak-and-seafood dinner fare. Budget.

Our favorite Chinese restaurant in Logan is the **Mandarin Garden** (432 North Main Street; 801-753-5789), offering a wide range of Mandarin and Szechuan selections, including sweet-and-sour pork tenderloin, stir-fry vegetables and tiny spicy chicken, served in a rather dark atmosphere bedecked with gold-and-red Chinese decor. Budget.

In Ogden, the **Gray Cliff Lodge** (508 Ogden Canyon Road; 801-392-6775) is synonymous with fine dining. Secluded in the canyon east of town, it presents trout, lamb, lobster, lamb and prime rib in a candlelight-and-crystal ambience. Prices are in the deluxe range.

Family dining fun seems to be behind the concept of **Prairie Schooner** (445 Park Boulevard, Ogden; 810-392-2712), where meal attendants in pioneer garb serve diners at tables designed to look like covered wagons amid a clutter of frontier memorabilia. The food—a conventional steak-and-seafood menu—is a cut above the dozen or so other family-oriented restaurants in town. Moderate.

For vegetarian and heart-healthy dining, the place to go is the plain-looking **Harvest Restaurant** (341 27th Street, Ogden; 801-621-1627), where specialties include fancy green salads, stir-fries and international vegetarian dishes. Budget.

NORTH OF SALT LAKE CITY SHOPPING

Perhaps the area's best bet for souvenir shopping is **Cox Honeyland** (1780 South Highway 91, Logan; 801-752-3234). Though the beehive symbol of Utah is said to represent industry, beekeeping has played a big part in Utah agriculture since the earliest pioneer times—especially in the Cache Valley. Cox Honeyland specializes in delicious fruited, creamed honeys in a wide range of flavors—including raspberry, boysenberry, orange, blueberry, apricot-pineapple, peanut butter and cinnamon—as well as honey cookies, honey candy and honey mustard.

NORTH OF SALT LAKE CITY NIGHTLIFE

Something of a cultural center for northern Utah, Logan has an outstanding opera company, the **Utah Festival Opera** (Eccles Theatre, 43 South Main Street; 801-752-0026), which performs Tuesday through Saturday nights during most of July, as well as the **Old Lyric Repertory Company** (801-750-1657), a professional company sponsored by the university's theater arts department, which presents contemporary dramas, comedies and musicals Wednesday through Saturday from late June through mid-August.

Thanks to its large college-student population, Logan has an active dance-club scene. One top hot spot is the **Retrix Dance Club** (97 East 1400 North; 801-753-7997), featuring deejay music for a full range of tastes on different evenings—progressive on Wednesdays, country on Thursdays and Saturdays, classic and contemporary rock on Fridays.

The Utah law that prohibits sale of liquor by the drink except with meals has been amended in recent years, authorizing low-profile bars, called "private clubs," to issue visitor memberships, valid for two weeks, at a low price comparable to a cover charge. Since this liberalization of Utah's notoriously strict drinking laws was intended mainly for the convenience of vacationers and business travelers, almost all private clubs are connected to motels.

One of the most popular private clubs in Ogden is **Club Nadir** (1500 West Riverdale Road; 801-399-3409), in the Motel 6. It offers dancing all night, with a comedy night every Wednesday. For those who prefer to watch TV while they drink, there's **Electric Alley** (247 24th Street; 801-627-1190), the only sports bar in town, in the Best Western Ogden Park Inn.

NORTH OF SALT LAKE CITY PARKS

Bear Lake State Park—This large natural lake, formed 8000 years ago by earthquakes, covers 112 square miles spanning the Utah-Idaho state line. It is a popular area for swimming, boating, fishing, mountain biking and camping. Bear Lake State Park consists of three separate units—Marina on the west shore, Rendezvous Beach on the south shore and Eastside/Cisco Beach on the east side—all of which provide public boat ramps and picnicking and camping areas. There are also several privately owned marinas, boat ramps and beaches around the lake. The lakeside tourist villages of Garden City and Laketown have food, lodging, groceries and gas, and paved roads encircle the lake. The 55-mile loop drive around the lake also goes to the Idaho towns of Fish Haven and St. Charles, Bear Lake National Wildlife Refuge and North Beach and Idaho Eastside state parks on the Idaho side of the state line. Keep an eye out for the Bear Lake Monster, a legend here since the 1860s.

Facilities: Picnic areas, restrooms, groceries, visitors center, hiking and mountain-bike trails, marinas, boat ramps; day-use fee, $3; information, 800-448-2327. *Swimming:* Permitted at state parks and several privately operated beaches. *Fishing:* Good for cutthroat and lake trout, whitefish and Bonneville cisco, one of at least four fish species found only in this lake.

Camping: The Utah state parks on Bear Lake have campgrounds with a total of 168 RV/tent sites (no hookups); $5 to $15 per night.

Getting there: Garden City, the small crossroads town on the lake's western shore, is 40 miles west of Logan at the upper end of Logan Canyon. Bear Lake State Park is one and a half miles north on Route 89. Rendezvous Beach State Park is 13 miles south on Route 30. Eastside/Cisco Beach is about 12 miles north of Laketown on the unnumbered road that follows the lake's eastern shore.

Wasatch-Cache National Forest—This 1,260,000-acre national forest extends from the Wyoming and Idaho boundaries to within four miles of downtown Salt Lake City. The long, narrow forest area encompasses some of the wildest mountain country in Utah, including the Mount Naomi Wilderness east of Logan, the Wellsville Mountains Wilderness west of Logan and the Mount Olympus Wilderness east of Salt Lake City. Logan Canyon and Ogden Canyon, the most popular recreation areas in the forest, provide easy forest access for hiking, fishing and camping.

Facilities: Hiking trails; boat ramp and marina at Pineview Reservoir; information, 801-524-5030. *Fishing:* Good for brown trout in the Logan and Ogden rivers; largemouth and smallmouth bass, crappie and perch are found in Pineview Reservoir.

Camping: Ten campgrounds in Logan Canyon have a total of 172 RV/tent sites (no hookups); $8 to $11 per night.

Getting there: Route 89 winds through Logan Canyon between Logan and Bear Lake. Route 39 climbs Ogden Canyon past Pineview Reservoir to the aspen-covered slopes of Monte Cristo Peak.

Willard Bay State Park—The park takes in the southern part of Willard Bay, a freshwater lake north of Ogden within the floodplain of the Great Salt Lake. Flood-control dikes separate the state park from the Bear River Migratory Bird Refuge, which encompasses the rest of Willard Bay and the contiguous South and North bays. The state park is popular for swimming and waterskiing as well as birdwatching.

Facilities: Picnic areas, restrooms, swimming beaches, boat ramps, marinas; $3 day-use fee; information, 801-734-9494. *Swimming:* Permitted. *Fishing:* Good for channel catfish, crappie, walleye and wiper fish.

Camping: There are 62 RV/tent sites (no hookups); $9 to $10 per night.

Getting there: Located eight miles north of Ogden. The South Marina is on a park access road off Route 15 Exit 354. The North Marina is off Route 15 at Exit 360.

Salt Lake City

Salt Lake City is the economic and spiritual center of Utah and the second-largest city in the Rocky Mountain West. Although the official census population of Salt Lake City is only 160,000, suburbs such as Jordan, Sandy and Bountiful merge together to create a metropolitan area of about three-quarters of a million people. Most of the sightseeing highlights are downtown around Temple Square and the State Capitol or along the base of the mountains on the east side of the city.

Temple Square (between North Temple, South Temple, West Temple and Main streets; 801-240-2534) is at the center of downtown Salt Lake City. Indeed, almost all downtown streets are named by their relationship to the square. For example, if you find yourself at the intersection of 2nd East and 4th South, you're two blocks east and four blocks south of Temple Square. The ten-acre plaza contains four main buildings and is bedecked with brilliant flower gardens, inspirational pioneer statues and the Seagull Monument—commemorating the birds that ate the hordes of locusts threatening the crops of the original Mormon colony during its first year in Utah and thereby saved the settlers from starvation.

The red-granite **Mormon Temple** (Temple Square), the Mormon Church's oldest extant temple, is impressive to say the least, with its spires towering to 210 feet and its angel rising above them. The temple, a replica of the ancient Temple of Solomon, was built between 1853 and 1893 according to specifications set forth in the Book of Mormon at a cost of $4 million. Although non–church members are prohibited from entering the temple, all are welcome at the huge, dome-shaped **Mormon Tabernacle** (Temple Square; 801-240-2530), a performance space acoustically designed for sacred choir music and housing one of the world's largest and finest pipe organs. Free organ recitals are presented daily at noon (2 p.m. on Sundays). The public is also invited to rehearsals of the Mormon Tabernacle Choir on Thursday evenings.

Temple Square also has two separate visitors centers on Temple Square, each truly monumental in scale. In addition to the huge *Christus* statue surrounded by a heavenly 360-degree mural at the North Visitors Center, the two centers exhibit oil paintings illustrating events from the Book of Mormon, often featuring familiar biblical figures in situations unique to the Mormon version of the Scriptures. A half-dozen theaters in the centers show films and multimedia presentations that explain various aspects of Mormon history and faith.

You can learn more about the early days of the Mormons at the **Museum of Church History and Art** (45 North West Temple Street; 801-240-3310), where exhibits include an original 1830 copy of the Book of Mormon, Utah's earliest log cabin, a scale model of Salt Lake City circa 1870 and a collection of gold coins minted by the Mormon Church in the days when Utahns considered themselves independent from the United States.

A block east of Temple Square stands the 26-story **Church of Jesus Christ of Latter-day Saints (LDS) Administration Building** (50 North Temple Street; 801-240-1000), international headquarters of the Mormon Church and one of the tallest skyscrapers in the Rocky Mountain states. The top-floor observation deck is open to the public. Next door, the grand former Hotel Utah has become the **Joseph Smith Memorial Building** (South Temple and Main streets; 801-292-1911). Besides administrative offices, the building contains FamilySearch Center, the world's largest genealogical library. The library contains microfilm and microfiche copies of family records from the United States, Canada, Great Britain, Scandinavia, Central Europe, Mexico, Central and South America, Australia, the South Pacific and South Africa.

On the same block, the **Beehive House** (67 East South Temple Street; 801-240-2671) was built in 1855 as the home of Mormon leader Brigham Young, who founded Salt Lake City. The house is open to the public and contains many of Young's personal effects as well as other furnishings and memorabilia of the pioneer era. **Eagle Gate**, which spans State Street just west of the house, was originally built as the entranceway to Young's plantation. **Brigham Young's Grave** is located about half a block northeast of Eagle Gate.

The **Brigham Young Monument**, one of the dozens of statues around downtown Salt Lake City depicting pioneer families (here accompanied by an Indian and a mountain man) is inscribed with the names of the first 148 Mormons to arrive in Utah. It stands in the middle of the street at Main and South Temple.

The **Salt Lake Art Center** (20 South West Temple Street; 801-328-4201), located between Temple Square and the Salt Palace convention center, features traveling art exhibitions, including many from the Smithsonian Institution. The center includes a sculpture garden and a small collection of work by local artists.

Near the capitol is the **Pioneer Memorial Museum** (300 North Main Street; 801-538-1050), operated by the Daughters of Utah. Emphasizing Mormon heritage, the museum contains an extensive collection of pioneer memorabilia including paintings, guns, dolls, quilts, flags, furniture, clothing, books and manuscripts. A separate carriage house, connected to the main museum by an underground passageway, contains a covered wagon, surreys, sleighs, a mule-drawn streetcar and a replica blacksmith shop.

Downhill to the west of the capitol is the **Marmalade historic district**, preserving a residential neighborhood that dates back to the late 19th century. Its name derives from the fact that the streets are named after fruits. Stroll through this quiet neighborhood and imagine yourself in an earlier era when Salt Lake was a peaceful frontier town.

The **Utah State Capitol** (Capitol Hill; 801-538-3000), with its classic architecture and colorful flower gardens, contains exhibits about the state's history and industry in the basement. The capitol dome is clad with copper, a symbol of secular, non-Mormon power. The copper came from the Kennecott Bingham Canyon Mine southwest of the city, the largest non-Mormon–owned business in the state in 1915, when the capitol was built.

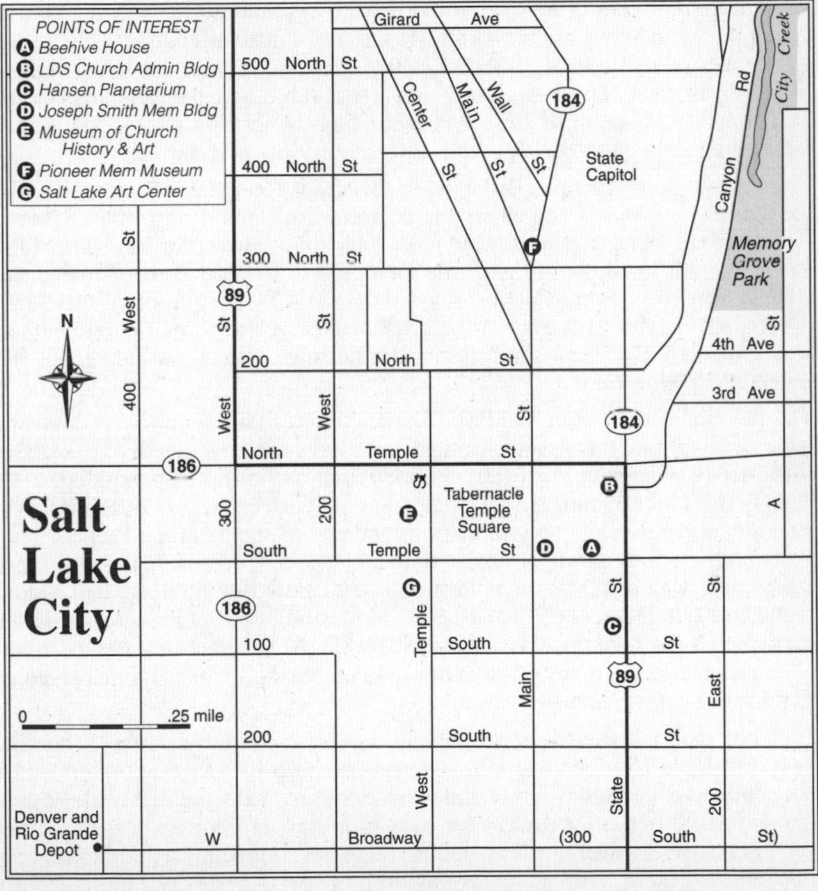

Hansen Planetarium (15 South State Street; 801-538-2098; admission) is unique in that its 50-foot star theater dome was constructed inside the former public library, filling the three-story square building. The staff produces educational shows that are presented in dozens of other planetariums around the United States, so the presentations here are among the most innovative in any planetarium in the nation. Besides conventional astronomy and laser light shows, the planetarium features audience-participation science-fiction shows where the audience votes on what happens next by pressing buttons on the armrests of their seats.

The **Utah Historical Society Museum** (300 Rio Grande Street; 801-533-3500), in the old Denver & Rio Grande Depot, features a standing collection of artifacts and historical photographs that trace Utahn culture from the ancient Anasazi through Mormon settlement and the coming of the transcontinental railroad and copper mining to modern technological devices, such as the Jarvik-7 artificial heart, invented in Utah.

Heading east from the downtown area on 300 South Street will take you through the **University of Utah** (801-581-5322) campus. The key sightseeing attractions on campus are the **Utah Museum of Natural History** (President's Circle at University Street; 801-581-4303; admission), with extensive displays of fossils, ancient Native American artifacts and biological specimens, and the nearby **Utah Museum of Fine Arts** (801-581-7332; admission), best known for its fine collection of 17th- and 18th-century art and decor.

Follow South Campus Drive, which becomes Hempstead Road as it leaves the university grounds and enters the adjacent Fort Douglas Military Reservation; the road changes names twice more, becoming Stover Street and then Red Butte Canyon Road, before reaching the university's **Red Butte Garden and Arboretum** (Red Butte Canyon Road; 801-581-4747; admission). Nestled in the foothills on the east edge of the city are 16 acres of formal public gardens and 150 acres of natural scrub oak and wildflower meadows containing four miles of walking trails.

Continue south from Red Butte Garden to return to Sunnyside Avenue, the main thoroughfare that leads to Emigration Canyon. At the mouth of the canyon is **Pioneer Trail State Park** (801-584-8391; admission). The park contains the **This Is the Place Monument**, a stone monolith with bronze statues of Brigham Young and other saints on top, marking the end of the Mormon Pioneer Trail. Wheel ruts of covered wagons are visible in the park. Costumed guides re-create the pioneer way of life at the collection of authentic old buildings and historic replicas at **Old Deseret** (801-584-8392; admission). Also at Pioneer Trail State Park, the **Hogle Zoological Gardens** (801-582-1631; admission) has more than a thousand animals, many of them housed in natural-like habitats that re-create rainforests, deserts and the African veldt.

You may not want to spend much time at the Great Salt Lake's shoreline near Salt Lake City because most of it is taken up by salt evaporators and is not conducive to outdoor sports. Indeed, the tons of "salt" yielded by these shallow industrial ponds are useless for culinary purposes because of the high percentages of other minerals they contain. Chemical companies refine such diverse minerals as potash, chlorine, gypsum and lithium from the crystalline deposits left behind as the water evaporates. Recreational use of the lake, particularly bathing and boating, are more appropriate at **Great Salt Lake State Park**, 16 miles west of Salt Lake City off Route 80 (see "Salt Lake City Parks" below).

SALT LAKE CITY HOTELS

Among Salt Lake City's most elegant accommodations is **The Inn at Temple Square** (71 West South Temple Street; 801-531-1000, 800-843-4668), a luxuriously refurbished downtown hotel built in 1930. The seven-story red-brick hotel has 90 individually designed, exceptionally spacious guest rooms and parlor suites done in period reproduction furnishings and soft-hued fabrics and wallpapers. Feather pillows, fluffy down comforters and fine linens grace the four-poster beds. The inn has the most central location in the city, adjoining Crossroads Mall and overlooking the Mormon Temple, the symphony hall and the Salt Palace convention center. Deluxe.

One of the few historic buildings to survive the urban renewal that turned much of downtown Salt Lake City into shopping malls is the **Peery Hotel** (110 West 300 South Street; 801-521-4300, 800-331-0073, fax 801-575-5014). The hotel, which has operated continuously since 1910, has an elegant lobby that features antique decor, stained glass and the kind of staircase that makes you feel like a movie star. Most of the 77 guest rooms and suites are unexceptionally furnished, and some are quite small, but the combination of central location, reasonable prices and old-time touches makes the Peery a bargain. Moderate.

The largest hostelry in town, the **Little America Hotel and Tower** (500 South Main Street; 801-363-6781, 800-453-9450, fax 801-322-1610) boasts 850 rooms and a 17-story tower surrounded by fountains and lavishly landscaped grounds. The spacious rooms feature bright, contemporary decor, and some have chandeliers and oversized sunken marble bathtubs. Hotel facilities include two swimming pools, sauna, whirlpool spa and exercise room. Moderate to ultra-deluxe.

The unabashedly romantic **Anniversary Inn** (678 East South Temple Street; 801-363-4900) was clearly designed with honeymooners in mind. The beautiful 1890s mansion offers 13 individually decorated suites such as the Opera House, with a balcony bed and a 52-inch television "stage"; the Lake Powell, with a river-raft bed, red rock walls and a waterfall; and the Hay Loft, with a luxury loft and a rustic bucket shower and jacuzzi. Deluxe rates include a continental breakfast.

The lowest-priced lodging in Salt Lake City is at the **Avenues Residential Center** (107 F Street; 801-363-8137). Accommodations at this unaffiliated hostel are in eight-bunk dormitory rooms. Guest share bathrooms as well as kitchen and laundry facilities, though unlike many youth hostels, sheets are provided. There are also a few very plain private rooms with double beds. Budget.

Across the street from the Governor's Mansion, the **Anton Boxrud Bed & Breakfast Inn** (57 South 600 East Street; 801-363-8035, 800-524-5511) has been restored with painstaking accuracy following the original architectural plans from its construction in 1901. While the exterior of the historic building is rather plain, the interior features beveled and stained glass, burled woodwork, hardwood floors and pocket doors. All six guest rooms and suites are furnished in turn-of-the-century antiques. Moderate.

The **Brigham Street Inn** (1135 East South Temple Street; 801-364-4461, fax 801-521-3201), near the University of Utah campus, presents a different concept in historical restoration. While the stately red-brick mansion with its pillared porches and curved bay windows has the look of a historical restoration from the outside, once you step through the front door there's hardly an antique in sight. Each of the nine guest rooms and three common rooms is a showcase of distinctive contemporary design. Deluxe.

SALT LAKE CITY RESTAURANTS

The **Carriage Court** (71 West South Temple Street; 801-536-7200) offers affordable dining elegance across the street from Temple Square. The menu at this white-linen-and-sterling-silver establishment features such selections as stuffed breast of chicken with red-currant piñon sauce and filet of halibut stuffed with tomatoes and wild mushrooms and served with a caviar *beurre blanc*. Prices are moderate.

The **Lion House** (63 East South Temple Street; 801-363-5466) offers fine dining in an 1856 residence that was originally part of Brigham Young's estate. The restaurant serves a set menu that changes daily and is posted two weeks in advance. The fare can be described as elegant home-style cooking. One typical weekday dinner might be cream of chicken noodle soup, an entrée choice of chicken enchiladas or lasagna, a poppyseed spinach salad and cream-cheese brownies. Dinner on weekends features a lavish seafood and prime-rib buffet. But it is the historic ambience that makes this place special. Deluxe.

One of the most spectacular views in Salt Lake City (rivaled only by the observation deck of the LDS church administration building) is the panoramic view of the Wasatch Mountains through the picture windows of **Nino's** (136 East South Temple Street; 801-359-0506), on the 24th floor of the University Club Building in downtown Salt Lake City. Overstuffed chairs, dark woods and brass railings set the stage for fine northern Italian cuisine, featuring such specialties as Italian veal with fresh pasta. Deluxe.

Possibly the best Middle Eastern restaurant in the entire Rocky Mountain region, **Cedars of Lebanon** (152 East 200 South Street; 801-364-4096) offers an impressive array of Lebanese, Armenian, Israeli, Moroccan, Greek and Turkish dishes, including a sublime lamb shish kebab. The ambience of this small, intimate restaurant is right out of the Arabian Nights. A belly dancer performs on weekends. Moderate.

Brewpubs, a staple throughout Colorado these days, are a rarity in Utah. Salt Lake City's first is **Squatter's Pub Brewery** (147 West Broadway; 801-363-2739), which makes several kinds of ale—from pale to cream stout—on the premises. Seating is in an outdoor beer garden in summer and around a big fireplace in winter. Because of Utah's stringent liquor laws, the brewery's ale can be served only with meals. Fortunately, the menu offers a lot of tempting soup, salad, sandwich and pizza choices, including good vegetarian options, as well as international house specialties like chicken stir-fry, beer-batter fish and chips and bratwurst with sauerkraut. Budget.

Given the Mormon abhorrence to such self-pollutants as alcohol, tobacco and caffeine, you might think health-conscious restaurant fare would be easy to find in Salt Lake City—but it isn't. The city's only vegetarian restaurant is the **Park Ivy Garden Cafe** (878 East 900 South Street; 801-328-1313). This sunny little restaurant with its cheerful garden decor features homemade croissants and imported cheeses as well as a creative menu of vegetarian meals, many of which use wheat-based meat substitutes. Try the chicken-style tacos, wheat meat stroganoff or tempeh ginger stir-fry. Budget.

In scenic Emigration Canyon just east of Hogle Zoological Gardens, the **Santa Fe Restaurant** (Emigration Canyon Road; 801-582-5888) offers New Mexico cooking plus Rocky Mountain favorites like rainbow trout and grilled buffalo, in the kind of self-conscious desert-pop ambience that seems more like Sedona than Santa Fe. There's outdoor deck dining for those who prefer all-natural surroundings. Moderate.

Adjoining the Santa Fe Restaurant and under the same ownership, **Ruth's Diner** (Emigration Canyon Road; 801-582-5888) has been operating in an old trolley car at this location since 1930. Ruth's offers a choice of Mexican dishes like *huevos rancheros* and *chile rellenos* as well as home-style cooking from cheeseburgers to fish filets. Budget.

SALT LAKE CITY SHOPPING

In Salt Lake City, a one-of-a-kind store is **Mormon Handicraft** (105 North Main Street; 801-355-2141), an LDS-sponsored crafts cooperative originally organized in the 1930s. Today, the store sells gift items on consignment for nearly 2000 Utahn crafters. There are shelves full of quilts, collector dolls, infants' clothing, toys, sewing supplies and stuffed animals.

Local artists and crafters display their work under the trees on the Art Center Plaza in front of the Salt Lake Art Center during the summertime **Saturday Art Markets**.

Most of the retail space in downtown Salt Lake City is contained in two covered shopping malls, each of which fills a city block between Temple Square and the Salt Palace. **ZCMI Center** (36 South State Street; 801-321-8743) is the latest incarnation of the Zions Cooperative Mercantile Institution founded by Brigham Young in 1868—the first department store in the United States.

For unique souvenirs, the place to start is **Deseret Book** (ZCMI Center, 36 South State Street; 801-328-8191), a huge bookstore one block from Temple Square with branch stores in virtually every shopping mall in the Salt Lake Valley. From inexpensive editions of the Book of Mormon itself to extra-wholesome children's books and strange esoterica about angels, Deseret Book brims with literature you won't find at your local shopping mall.

Crossroads Plaza (50 South Main Street; 801-531-1799) is another enclosed retail mall. Between the two you'll find every familiar shopping-mall chain store and enough local specialty shops to make the stroll worthwhile.

A more entertaining place for gift-shop browsing is **Trolley Square** (602 East 500 South Street; 801-521-9877), a historical restoration shopping mall that emphasizes cuteness. Among its greatest virtues: If you are visiting Salt Lake City for the day, you can park your car at Trolley Square and ride the restored turn-of-the-century motorized Utah Transit Authority Trolley to Temple Square for less than it costs to park downtown. Trolleys run every 15 minutes. Trolley Square has shops like **Clogg Corner** (801-322-4255), **Potions & Lotions** (801-355-1609) and **Eibo's Famous for Nothing** (801-531-7788).

A flour mill built by Mormon settlers in 1877 is the hub of a cluster of old-time storefronts that make up **Gardner Historic Village** (1095 West 7800 South Street; 801-566-8903). The village houses traditional gift and craft shops such as the **Village Quilt Shop** (801-566-1846), **Victorian Shoppe** (801-566-2881) and **Village Basket Junction** (801-566-1063), while the original mill contains the department store–size **Country Furniture & Gifts** (801-566-2842).

SALT LAKE CITY NIGHTLIFE

People who like to patronize strip joints soon discover that Salt Lake City is one of the few places in the non-Muslim world where exotic dancers remove everything *except* their leotards and tights. America's most family-oriented city, Salt Lake City has never believed much in nightlife. Prohibition lasted longer in Utah than in any other state and was repealed grudgingly. Except for 3.2 percent beer, alcoholic beverages can be sold only by state liquor stores, which are often hard to find. (Look in the phone book under Utah State Government.) Until recently, patrons had to bring their own bottles to bars and buy "setups," paying the price of a cocktail for the bartender to serve them their own booze. The law was recently changed with an eye toward boosting tourism. Now liquor can be served not only with meals in licensed restaurants but also at members-only "private clubs," to which anyone over the legal drinking age of 21 can purchase a two-week "temporary membership" for $5. Many private clubs do not offer live music or dancing, however, and many of the city's music and dance clubs (not to mention strip joints) are not licensed to serve anything stronger than 3.2 percent beer.

One of the city's most prestigious private clubs is the **Bella Vista** (136 East South Temple Street; 801-359-0501), atop downtown's 24-story University Club Building. The decor is Euro-tech in startling black and white, in dramatic contrast to the full-color scenery out the picture windows. This place is designed for conversation in elegant surroundings; there's no dancing or live music. **Club Max** (255 South West Temple Street; 801-328-2000), located in the Red Lion Hotel, features dancing to recorded pop and rock music seven nights a week and has a private-club liquor license. The **Ports O' Call Social Club** (400 South West Temple Street; 801-521-0589) is decorated like an Olde English pub, complete with a legendary resident ghost. Entertainment at this private club consists of a pool table, foosball, dartboard, video games and 17 TV sets, all tuned to sports. Another private club, **Green Street** (610 Trolley Square; 801-532-4200), offers a changing entertainment calendar throughout the week.

Salt Lake City's gay and lesbian community is very low profile, but it can be found by the persistent. The search starts practically in the shadow of the Mormon Temple at **Club D V8** (115 South West Temple Street; 801-539-8400). The tongue-in-cheek name says it all.

On the cultural side, the biggest performing arts draw in town is the **Mormon Tabernacle Choir**, which performs on Sunday mornings. There are also **organ recitals** in the Tabernacle on weekdays at noon, as well as **Concert Series** performances at Temple Square on Friday and Saturday evenings. All are sponsored by the LDS Church and are free. For current schedule information, call 801-240-2534.

The **Utah Symphony Orchestra**, ranked among the best in the United States, performs at the Salt Palace (123 West South Temple Street; 801-533-6407). Other municipal performing arts groups are the **Utah Opera Company** (801-533-6494) and **Ballet West** (801-533-5555). Both groups perform at the grand old restored Capitol Theatre (50 West 200 South Street).

SALT LAKE CITY PARKS

Great Salt Lake State Park—Bathing and boating are the main pursuits at this park, formerly called Saltair State Park after the grand beach resort that operated there from the 1890s until the Great Depression. The defunct hotel and pier at the Saltair resort were destroyed by fire in 1970. A reduced-scale modern replica of Saltair, located a few miles east of the state park, offers facilities for conferences and concerts.

Facilities: Restrooms, food stands, souvenir shops, a marina; information, 801-250-1822. *Swimming:* Permitted.

Camping: There's a camping area (no hookups); $7 per night.

Getting there: Located 16 miles west of Salt Lake City off Route 80.

South of Salt Lake City

The cities of **Provo** and **Orem**, along with the smaller towns of American Fork and Lehi, have grown together to form a single metropolitan area with a population of about 100,000 on the shore of **Utah Lake**, the largest freshwater lake in the state. Separated from Salt Lake City by a small, steep range called the Traverse Mountains, the greater Provo area is often referred to as the Utah Valley.

The cultural center of Provo is **Brigham Young University** (BYU) (University Hill; 801-378-4678). Owned and operated by the LDS Church, the school has 25,000 students, making it one of the largest nongovernment–owned universities in the United States. There are several museums on campus. The new **BYU Museum of Fine Arts** (801-378-4564) exhibits works by Utah artists as well as classic paintings by European artists including Rembrandt, Daumier and Dürer. Its permanent collection of more than 20,000 works makes this the largest art museum in the Rocky Mountain West. The **Bean Life Science Museum** (801-378-5051), near Marriot Center, contains research and display specimens of insects, plants, fish, shells, reptiles, mammals, birds and eggs. The **BYU Earth Science Museum** (1683 North Canyon Road; 801-378-3680), located near the football stadium north of the main campus, contains one of the largest fossil collections in the United States, including dinosaur skeletons. Also located off campus, the most unusual of the BYU museums is the **Museum of People and Cultures** (710 North 100 East Street; 801-378-6112), an anthropological museum emphasizing ancient peoples of the Southwest and Mexico. The museum shows how the early Mormons' beliefs about the biblical origins of Indians has fostered scholarly study of ancient American cultures, particularly at ancient Maya sites.

Farther south in the Wasatch Range, the paved **Mount Nebo Scenic Byway** starts at the town of Payson, 13 miles south of Provo on Route 15 (take Exit 252) and goes for 32 miles along the east side of the Mount Nebo Wilderness before returning to the interstate at Nephi. The road passes several campgrounds and trailheads and the **Devil's Kitchen Geologic Site**, an area of uniquely eroded red sandstone formations with paved trails and picnic areas.

Provo Canyon, the most popular mountain recreation area in Wasatch-Uinta National Forest, begins just west of Orem. Wide, paved Route 189 makes access to the canyon easy. The six-mile **Provo Canyon Parkway** recreation path parallels the highway, providing a quiet route for hikers, cyclists and picnickers. Following the course of the Provo River, it links a series of seven parks with scenic overlooks, picnic grounds and camping areas.

The most famous of Provo Canyon sights is **Bridal Veil Falls**, about four miles up the canyon. The double waterfall plunges more than 600 feet. While it is visible from the highway and the parkway, its best view point is from the **Skytram** (801-225-4461; admission), the world's steepest aerial tram, which rises 1228 vertical feet to a precipice above the falls. A network of hiking trails also starts near the base of the falls, and a visitors center provides information on Provo Canyon recreation spots.

Eight miles up Provo Canyon, the **Alpine Loop Scenic Byway** (Route 92) heads north around the east side of Mount Timpanogos (11,750 feet), providing access to the Timpanogos and Lone Peak wilderness areas. The paved road passes **Sundance**, Robert Redford's secluded mountain resort, ski area, outdoor theater and film institute, and then winds by switchbacks through aspen forests, passing several National Forest campgrounds and trailheads. Paved Forest Road 114 branches off the main route to take visitors to **Cascade Springs** (★), a dazzling chain of mountain springs, pools and streams that spill down a series of limestone terraces. The scenic backway route joins Route 44 and follows American Fork Creek down another scenic canyon to return to the Provo-area suburb of American Fork.

Shortly before returning to the city, the Alpine Loop brings you to **Timpanogos Cave National Monument** (Route 92, American Fork; 801-756-5238; admission). It is a steep one-and-a-half-mile hike from the visitors center to the cliffside cave entrance, which opens into a series of three caverns connected by manmade tunnels. You buy your tickets at the visitors center, make the climb on your own and meet a U.S. Park Service guide at the mouth of the cave. Inside, electric lighting reveals the subtle mineral hues of red, green and cream that paint the beautiful limestone formations. The national monument is also a major trailhead for pack trips into the Lone Peak Wilderness. Not far from the edge of town, the national monument is within ten miles of Route 15 Exit 287.

Continuing up Provo Canyon, instead of turning off on the Alpine Loop, will bring you to **Deer Creek Reservoir** (see "South of Salt Lake City Parks") and the Heber Valley, a high-altitude farming valley surrounding **Heber City**, where the star attraction is the **Heber Valley Scenic Railroad** (Heber City; 801-654-5601; admission). A steam locomotive pulling restored early-1900s coaches takes passengers on a choice of two scenic excursions—a ten-mile trip through Heber Valley and around Deer Creek Reservoir, or a longer journey into Provo Canyon. Continue north from Heber City on Route 40 for about 13 miles to reach the Park City area. (Park City can also be reached more directly from the Salt Lake City area via Route 80; Park City is less than ten miles south of Route 80 Exit 148.)

Park City is Utah's answer to Aspen: fast-track real estate development run amok in a picturesque old mining town that got its start in 1870 following the discovery of silver, lead, zinc and small amounts of gold in the area. Within two years, the town grew to 5000 people. Park City's silver mines were among the few that stayed open after the 1893 collapse of the silver market that destroyed so many mining towns in Colorado. Workers from closed mines elsewhere flocked to Park City in hopes of finding work, and by 1989 the population had doubled to 10,000 people. Despite terrible tragedies—including a fire that burned three-fourths of the town, fatal snowslides, typhoid and influenza epidemics and a disastrous mine explosion—Park City lived on long after other mining towns like Cripple Creek, Aspen and Telluride had become ghost towns and now has about 4500 residents.

Part of the secret of Park City's survival was illegal liquor. The rough-and-ready mining boom town had long held itself apart from the Mormon antivice attitudes that prevailed on the other side of Mount Olympus, and it became a local secret that many Salt Lake Citians would occasionally slip away to the mountains and break their antialcohol vows in the saloons of Park City. Officials turned a blind eye to Park City's sin scene even after Prohibition was imposed on the entire United States in 1921. Twenty-six saloons operated openly along Park City's main street throughout the Prohibition era, launching the town's tourist economy.

With the repeal of Prohibition, Park City's economy started a long, slow slide. World War II and its aftermath caused one mine after another to close down. By the 1950s, Park City was generally referred to as a ghost town, although a few more than a thousand people continued to live there. In 1963, the **Park City Ski Area** (801-649-8111) opened with a gondola, a chairlift and two J-bars. An old train took skiers up to the Silver King Mine, where they followed the mine shaft to the top of the mountain. Although the mine trip took too long and was quickly discontinued, the ski slopes were an immediate success. Today there are 14 lifts at Park City, plus satellite ski resorts at nearby ParkWest and Deer Valley, and the area attracts an estimated 850,000 skiers each winter. An **alpine slide** (801-649-7150; admission)—a twisting and turning chute that affords one the opportunity to scream down a mountain on a wheeled fiberglass sled—runs down the Park City ski slopes in summer.

Park City's four-block **Main Street Historic District** preserves 34 buildings from the old mining days, though a boom of reconstruction and new construction has made it a little tricky to identify the old edifices from the new. A guide to the historic district is distributed at the **Park City Historical Society & Museum** (528 Main Street; 801-649-6104, 800-453-1360). Formerly the city hall, the museum building has a dungeonlike jail in the basement. Visitors can walk through the old jail, which was used to lock up labor organizers in the mining days, and see mine-camp memorabilia and old photos on the main floor of the museum. Another showpiece of the historic district, two blocks down the street, is the **Egyptian Theatre** (328 Main Street; 801-649-9371), a replica of Warner Brothers' Egyptian Theatre in Hollywood, California. It was built as a vaudeville and silent movie theater in 1926 after an earlier theater on the site collapsed under heavy snow, just hours after a crowd of theater patrons had left. Today, the Egyptian Theatre presents contemporary plays, children's theater and opera performances.

SOUTH OF SALT LAKE CITY HOTELS

Provo has an abundance of brand-name motels and motor inns, most of them clustered around the University Avenue exit (Exit 266) from Route 15. A standout among them is **Horne's East Bay Inn** (1292 South University Avenue; 801-374-2500, 800-326-0025, fax 801-373-1146), a 116-room motor inn designed to accommodate conferences. Guest rooms are spacious and tastefully coordinated in pastel hues. Big potted plants, floral bedspreads and overstuffed chairs add touches of affordable elegance. The motel buildings surround a heated pool and an outdoor jacuzzi. Other facilities include volleyball, croquet and horseshoe courts and an exercise room. Budget to moderate.

The most luxurious lodgings in Provo are at the **Seven Peaks Resort** (101 West 100 North; 801-377-4700, 800-777-7144, fax 801-377-4708). The "resort" actually consists of two separate parts—the downtown Excelsior Hotel at Seven Peaks Resort, with 235 luxurious guest rooms and suites decorated in warm hues, and the Seven Peaks Resort Water Park, which also has a broad, grassy picnic area and an 18-hole golf course, about one and a half miles east on Center Street at the edge of town. A shuttle bus transports guests back and forth to the water park with its incredible winding water slide. Facilities at the hotel include an outdoor swimming pool, a sauna, a jacuzzi and a health club with exercise equipment. Moderate.

The **Whitney House** (415 South University Avenue, Provo; 801-377-3111), one of the few bed and breakfasts in the Provo area, offers four guest rooms furnished with country antiques in a Romanesque revival–style 1898 red-brick residence. Moderate rates include a full breakfast.

Secluded in a canyon adjacent to the Mount Timpanogos Wilderness on the narrow, paved Alpine Loop Road northeast of Provo, **Sundance** (Route 92; 801-225-4107, fax 801-226-1937) has emerged as one of the premier self-contained resorts in the Rockies. Built by actor-director-producer Robert Redford and named after one of his best-known movie roles, the resort has 72 magnificently appointed guest units (studio duplexes, one- to three-bedroom cottages and three- to five-bedroom residences, all in natural stone and wood) dispersed along the banks of a creek. Sundance is busy in winter, when its small but challenging ski slopes attract daytrippers. It is liveliest in January, when the Sundance Film Festival offers a prestigious showcase for new independent film productions. In summer, it offers an extensive network of hiking, mountain-biking and horseback-riding trails, as well as nightly theater performances of Broadway musicals. Ultra-deluxe.

Park City has more guest accommodations than any other community in Utah except Salt Lake City. Most are modern luxury ski lodges priced in the deluxe to ultra-deluxe range. Make reservations well in advance if you plan to stay during ski season. For assistance, call **Park City Reservations** (801-649-9598, 800-453-5789), **R & R Recreation & Resort Properties** (801-649-6175, 800-348-6759, fax 801-649-6225) or **ABC Reservations Central** (801-649-2223, 800-523-0666).

Park City always has a surplus of resort rooms in summer, and rates drop to practically nothing during the snowless months. A typical example is the **Edelweiss Haus** (1482 Empire Road; 801-649-9342, 800-438-3855), a modern complex of hotel rooms and rental condominiums located directly across the street from the Park City Resort Center and the ski slopes. Standard hotel rooms that rent for deluxe to ultra-deluxe rates in ski season cost as little as $35 during the summer months.

Midway between the ski area and the historic district, within easy strolling distance of everything in Park City, the **Silver Queen Hotel** (Heber Avenue at Main Street, Park City; 801-649-5986) was newly constructed in 1982 of red brick and sandstone blocks in a Victorian-revival style designed to blend with Park City's older buildings. The hotel offers 12 one- and two-bedroom luxury condominium suites with jacuzzis, fireplaces, kitchens and washer/dryers. Rooms are individually decorated in a European traditional style with warm, rich hues, floral accents and dark wood trim. Ultra-deluxe.

Several buildings in Park City's historic district have been converted into bed and breakfasts. The **Imperial Hotel** (221 Main Street; 801-649-1904, 800-669-8824, fax 801-645-7421) offers 12 rooms and suites in a cheerfully refurbished 1904 miners' boardinghouse. The decor throughout is brightly new-Victorian. Most rooms have private baths with clawfoot tubs or large Roman tubs. Deluxe.

The **Blue Church Lodge** (424 Park Avenue; 801-649-8009, 800-626-5467) was Park City's Mormon church from 1900 to 1962. Today, the building has been extensively renovated to house seven elegant condominium suites ranging in size from one to four bedrooms, paneled in rich wood and individually decorated with touches of country charm. There are four more suites in another

(Text continued on page 238.)

In the Land of Latter-Day Saints

The Mormon culture, built around the Church of Jesus Christ of Latter-day Saints (usually called "the LDS Church" or just "the LDS" by Utahns), permeates community life throughout the state of Utah. About 50 percent of Salt Lake City's population, more in satellite cities such as Provo and Ogden, and virtually everyone in rural areas belongs to the LDS Church and attends temple services every week.

While maintaining the thinnest veneer of separation of church and state, the LDS Church enjoys absolute political control in Utah. The result has been phenomenal economic development together with the toughest antivice laws in the United States restricting liquor, sex aids, R-rated movies and even cable television channels. Utah sees itself as one of the last bastions of "traditional family values" in the United States.

Utah's prosperous cities stand as living monuments to the most successful religious organization in U.S. history. The LDS Church was founded in upstate New York in 1830 by farmer Joseph Smith, who claimed that, seven years earlier, an angel named Moroni had shown him the location of 12 golden plates that the angel itself had buried in A.D. 421. The angel also gave Smith the power to read the ancient texts inscribed on the plates. As Smith translated and transcribed them, he realized that they were new books of the Bible. "Thou fool, that shall say: A Bible, we have got a Bible, and we need no more Bible," the new Scripture said. "Know ye not that there are more nations than one?" (2 Nephi 29:6)

The new books, collectively called the Book of Mormon, recount the fate of the Lost Tribes of Israel, whose disappearance in the Babylonian conquest of Jerusalem around 600 B.C. is documented in the Old Testament. In Mormon belief, the Lost Tribes escaped by boat and, with divine guidance, made their way to the Americas, where they gradually split into two rival tribes, the Nephites (the group to which Mormon, Moroni and the authors of the other books belonged) and the Lamanites. The Book of Mormon contains accounts of several appearances of Jesus Christ in the New World, spells out sacred laws for living in the American wilderness, tells how the two tribes became locked in a catastrophic war and ends with the annihilation of the Nephites. The LDS Church has traditionally held that Native Americans are descendants of the Lamanites. A new Bible for the New World, the Book of Mormon describes America as "a choice land/And whatsoever nation shall possess it shall be free from bondage and from captivity and from all other nations under the heavens, if they will but serve the God of the land."

After Joseph Smith had translated the plates, a three-year task, the angel reappeared and took them back. When he published the Book of Mormon, Smith and his followers met with such religious persecution that they fled

New York within a year, making their way west to seek the "New Zion," first in Ohio, then in Missouri and Illinois.

The Book of Mormon was first published in 1830, prefaced with affidavits of Smith's neighbors swearing that they had personally seen the gold plates. The sect grew rapidly. Non-Mormon scholars pointed out as early as 1833 that part of the Book of Mormon was plagiarized from a romantic novel by Reverend Solomon Spaulding about the origin of Native Americans, published a few years earlier; generations later, in 1977, handwriting experts concluded that parts of Smith's manuscript were in Spaulding's handwriting. Today, the church tends to downplay the book's allegedly miraculous origins along with other aspects of 19th-century Mormon beliefs. At the time, however, many frontier people eagerly accepted Smith's sequel to the Bible.

The group gained some credibility in 1839, when explorer John Lloyd Stephens published a best-selling account of his "discovery" of Central America's great Maya ruins. Many people saw the lost pyramids and cryptic hieroglyphs of the Maya as confirmation that the Nephites and Lamanites had actually inhabited ancient America. By 1841, Smith's spiritual community at Nauvoo had grown to more than 20,000 members, making it the second-largest city in Illinois. It lasted for three years.

An Illinois lynch mob killed Joseph Smith in 1844. Brigham Young took over leadership of the disarrayed Mormon community as its members fled in small groups to nearby Iowa. Smith and other elders began making plans for an exodus to the land west of the Rockies, and within three years the first Mormon wagon train, carrying 143 men, three women and two children, departed along an uncharted route that would later become the Oregon Trail. They reached the Great Salt Lake on July 24, 1847.

In the early years of their settlement, the Mormons prohibited others from entering the valleys along the Great Salt Lake, sometimes imprisoning or even attacking non-Mormon pioneers who strayed into their territory. But their isolation, a thousand miles from the nearest city, did not protect them for long. Hysterical stories about the excesses of Mormonism in the eastern press stirred anti-LDS sentiment on a national scale, and in 1858, the U.S. Army mounted the largest peacetime expeditionary force in its history to assert federal control over the Mormon communities. Soon after, the Supreme Court upheld the federal government's power to prohibit polygamy, a basic tenet of Mormon religion. The land of the Mormons was officially opened to the outside world with the arrival of the transcontinental railroad in 1870.

There are about 7.5 million Mormons today. About half live within a day's drive of Salt Lake City. The rest come from many ethnic and national backgrounds. The church maintains one of the world's largest international missionary efforts, with missions in almost every country.

building across the street. Each room has a fireplace, and the lodge has indoor and outdoor jacuzzis. Deluxe to ultra-deluxe.

The **Washington School Inn** (543 Park Avenue; 801-649-3800, 800-824-1672) served as Park City's public school from 1889 to 1931. After it closed, the stately limestone schoolhouse fell into disrepair and stood empty for 54 years before a complete renovation in 1985 turned it into one of Park City's finest bed and breakfasts. Though most of the 15 rooms and suites are on the small side compared to modern ski-lodge rooms in the same price range, all are richly decorated with extraordinary attention to detail, and some have fireplaces. Rates are ulltra-deluxe.

Celebrities who choose to vacation in the Park City area instead of at Sundance are most likely to stay at the **Stein Eriksen Lodge** (7700 Stein Way, Deer Valley; 801-649-3700, 800-453-1302). Owned and operated by an Olympic gold medalist skier, the lodge is located just above Deer Valley Ski Resort's mid-mountain village (accessible by car) at 8200 feet. Huge stone fireplaces warm the elegant Scandinavian-style lobby. The 118 rooms and suites feature amenities in abundance: bay windows and jacuzzis, fireplaces and armoires, down comforters and terrycloth robes. One entrance door opens directly onto the ski slopes, and groomed cross-country trails also start from the lodge. Other facilities include a heated pool, a spa and an exercise room. Ultra-deluxe year-round; seven-day minimum stay in peak ski season.

SOUTH OF SALT LAKE CITY RESTAURANTS

Mingles (101 West 100 North Street; 801-377-9074) ranks as Provo's classiest restaurant. Located downtown in the Seven Peaks Resort Hotel, Mingles serves breakfast, lunch and dinner daily in a sunny, contemporary setting decorated with plants. The menu offers a selection of steak and seafood entrées along with northern Italian pasta dishes. Moderate.

Like other Salt Lake–area cities, Provo has a sizable Chinese population and, consequently, excellent Asian food. The large, exotically decorated **Ling Ling Panda Chinese Restaurant** (138 West Center Street; 801-377-3323) features Hong Kong– and Mandarin-style food and offers a lunch buffet on weekdays and a dinner buffet on weekend evenings. Moderate.

People drive from Provo and Park City for fine dining at **Sundance** (Route 92; 801-225-4107), secluded in a side canyon that branches from Provo Canyon. The mountain resort has two restaurants, both open to the public. The more formal one is **The Tree Room**, decorated with Native American art and antiquities from owner Robert Redford's personal collection. You might try an appetizer of fried coconut shrimp followed by a Tree Room pepper steak with dijon mustard and homemade mango chutney and, for dessert, a chocolate truffle torte. Dinner only; deluxe. The more casual (and affordable) Sundance restaurant, **The Grill Room**, serves breakfast, lunch and dinner daily. Specialties include grilled vegetable pizza, tortilla soup and chicken breast stuffed with herbs and goat cheese. Moderate.

Park City is bursting with great restaurants, large enough to accommodate ski hordes with minimal waiting time and offering just about every kind of food imaginable. The stiff competition tends to keep prices reasonable and menus imaginative. In fact, one of the most popular restaurants in town, **The Bistro Royale** (U.S. Ski Team Building, Bonanza Street at Keams Boulevard; 801-649-1799), is known for the slogan "We Only Look Expensive." And they do, with lots of rich wood, white tablecloths and candlelight glow. You can dine in style on warm green asparagus tips, red pesto linguine with roasted almonds and black currants, and shrimp with raspberry-lime vinaigrette; or perhaps you'll want to simply savor the oyster bar or homemade pastries. Deluxe.

The family-style **El Cheepo Southwestern Grill** (225 Main Street, Park City; 801-649-0883), in the Treasure Mountain Inn, offers low-priced child portions and such kid-pleasers as hot dogs and really gooey quesadillas. For slightly more mature appetites there are fajitas, roast chicken, barbecued ribs and grilled trout in a spicy Tampico fruit salsa. Budget to moderate.

Evening Star Dining (268 Main Street, Park City; 801-649-5686), a homey little café, specializes in gourmet vegetarian fare such as sesame-ginger tofu with snow peas, tempeh satay, kebabs of vegetables and organic marinated tempeh with caramelized onions on a bed of brown Basmati rice and quinoa with a spicy peanut sauce. Moderate.

Park City seems to have far more than its share of northern Italian restaurants. One of the finest is **Mileti's** (412 Main Street; 801-649-8211). It's the sort of European-style contemporary restaurant where everything seems to flash and gleam. The menu of pastas, all made fresh daily, features such items as *capellini tutto mare*—a medley of clams, mussels, calamari and gulf shrimp steamed in a white-wine marinara broth and served over angel-hair pasta. Moderate.

Perhaps the ultimate fine-dining experience in the Park City area is out of town at **Glitretind** (Stein Eriksen Lodge, Deer Valley; 801-645-3700). This casually elegant European-style bistro serves international, highly original nouveau cuisine and offers outdoor-deck dining in a secluded alpine setting. Follow an appetizer such as gravlax or seafood strudel with a main course such as grilled Asian duck with bok choy, shiitake mushrooms, sour-cherry dumplings and ginger-plum sauce, or try the New Zealand red deer steak. Deluxe.

SOUTH OF SALT LAKE CITY SHOPPING

Provo is known for its antique shops. Among the shops featuring genuinely old collectibles, not always from Utah, are **L. H. Smoot & Company** (390 North University Avenue; 801-377-9369), **This-N-That** (1585 West Center Street; 801-375-3133) and **Antiques, Etc.** (260 North University Avenue; 801-375-1211).

One might expect a major ski-resort town like Park City to support a large number of art galleries and boutiques. To be sure, there *are* a few galleries and upscale boutiques. On the whole, however, retail in the Park City area is dominated by **The Factory Stores @ Park City** (Kimball Junction, Park City; 801-645-7078), a shopping center with 48 stores operated by Capezio, Guess, Nike, L'eggs/Hanes/Bali, American Tourister, Van Heusen and other famous-brand companies.

SOUTH OF SALT LAKE CITY NIGHTLIFE

Provo is a university town, so one would expect to find a rowdy beer-and-dancing club somewhere in town. But the university was founded by Brigham Young, and students are sworn to a strict code of dress and conduct that leaves little room for nightlife. As a result, Provo may well be America's quietest town after dark. If you spend the night here, make sure your hotel or motel has HBO, or, if you really want to go out, check the current events at **Brigham Young University** (801-378-7447), which sponsors a full calendar of stage performances and other cultural events, including world-renowned dance performances.

Park City is another story. It not only has its share of cultural events in summer, including stage plays at the **Egyptian Theatre** (328 Main Street; 801-649-9371), but it also supports a lively private-club scene. **Cisseros Bar and Grill** (306 Main Street; 801-649-6800) offers live bands and dancing nightly. The hottest spot in town is **"Z" Place** (427 Main Street; 801-645-9722), a large dance club and concert venue presenting both local and nationally known bands. The **Alamo Saloon** (447 Main Street; 801-649-2380) is a classic frontier-style tavern with pool tables, pinball and darts. **The Club** (449 Main Street; 801-649-6693) is a bar upstairs and has nightly dancing downstairs in the Island Bar.

SOUTH OF SALT LAKE CITY PARKS

Utah Lake State Park—On the eastern shore of Utah's largest freshwater lake, this park invites fishing, swimming and other water sports. The water tends to be chilly and murky, especially during spring runoff, but there's boundless room for boating, with tremendous views of the mountains surrounding the Utah Valley.

Facilities: Picnic areas, restrooms, boat ramps, marina, swimming area, visitors center; day-use fee, $3; information, 801-538-7220. *Swimming*: Permitted. *Fishing:* Fair for channel catfish, bullhead catfish and white bass.

Camping: There are 73 RV/tent sites (hookups available); $7 to $10 per night.

Getting there: Located at the west end of Center Street in Provo, three miles west of Route 15 Exit 268.

Uinta National Forest—This national forest encompasses almost one million acres. It surrounds the greater Provo area on three sides and contains the Lone Peak, Mount Timpanogos and Mount Nebo wilderness areas. Steep, pyramid-shaped peaks and lush canyons characterize the Uinta Mountains.

Facilities: Picnic areas; restrooms; hiking, bicycling and horseback trails; visitors center (at Bridal Veil Falls); information, 801-377-5780. *Fishing:* Good for trout in many streams, rivers and lakes.

Camping: Permitted in 40 campgrounds with a total of 930 RV/tent sites (no hookups); $10 to $11 per night.

Getting there: The major access routes to recreation areas in Uinta National Forest are American Fork Canyon (Route 44), Provo Canyon (Route 189) and the Aspen Loop Scenic Backway (Route 92), which connects the two canyons. Other areas are reached via the Mount Nebo Scenic Byway between Payson and Nephi.

Deer Creek State Park—At the upper end of Provo Canyon near Heber City, Deer Creek Reservoir is a popular place for sailboating and windsurfing because of the high winds created by Provo Canyon. Sailboard rentals are available at Deer Creek Island Resort on the east side of the lake.

Facilities: Picnic areas, restrooms, showers, marina, grocery store; day-use fee, $3; information, 801-654-0171. *Swimming:* Permitted in designated areas. *Fishing:* Good for smallmouth bass and walleye.

Camping: There are 23 RV sites and 10 tent sites; $9 to $10 per night. Camping is also permitted at two nearby National Forest campgrounds with a total of 84 RV/tent sites (no hookups); $4 to $5 per night.

Getting there: Located ten miles south of Heber City off Route 189.

Wasatch Mountain State Park—This 27,000-acre state park, the largest in Utah, is also the most developed. It has a 27-hole golf course, snowmobile trails and hunting and fishing areas, as well as vast expanses of undeveloped Douglas-fir and aspen forests.

Facilities: Picnic areas, restrooms, golf course, cross-country skiing and snowmobile trails, hiking trails, visitors center, snack bar; day-use fee, $3; information, 801-654-1791. *Fishing:* Good for rainbow trout in area streams.

Camping: Permitted in four campgrounds with a total of 152 RV/tent sites; 17 sites have hookups; $13 to $15 per night.

Getting there: Located five miles northwest of Heber City via Route 113 and Route 224.

The Sporting Life

RIVER RAFTING

Whitewater raft trips on the Green and Yampa rivers in Dinosaur National Monument are available through **Adrift Adventures** (P.O. Box 92, Jensen, UT 84035; 801-789-3600), **Arta River Trips** (P.O. Box 70, Jensen, UT 84035; 801-781-0528) and **Dinosaur River Expeditions** (540 East Main Street, Vernal; 801-649-8092, 800-342-8243). South of Salt Lake City, half-day and all-day raft trips down Provo Canyon are offered by **High Country Tours** (Provo; 801-645-7533).

BALLOONING

In Salt Lake City, hot-air balloon trips are organized by **Balloon Adventures** (2040 East Sunnyside Avenue; 801-583-3120). Provo has several hot-air balloon companies, including **Utah Balloons, Inc.** (709 South University Avenue; 801-377-8822) and **Stars & Stripes Inc.** (1675 North Freedom Boulevard; 801-756-2864). **Balloon the Rockies** (P.O. Box 399, Park City, UT 84060; 801-649-5551) offers balloon rides over Park City and several areas of northeastern Utah. Other Park City hot-air balloon operators include **Balloon Biz** (801-278-7208), **Balloon Affaire** (801-649-1217) and **Moon's Balloons** (801-645-9092).

SKIING

NORTH OF SALT LAKE CITY The road up Ogden Canyon forks at Pineview Reservoir at the upper end of the canyon. The north fork (Route 158) goes north to **Powder Mountain** (801-745-3772), while the south fork (Route 39 and Route 226) goes south to **Snowbasin** (801-399-1135).

SALT LAKE CITY **Snowbird** (800-453-3000) and **Alta** (801-742-3333) ski areas, with 3100-foot and 2045-foot vertical drops, and seven and eight chairlifts, respectively, are located 25 miles southeast of Salt Lake City in Little Cottonwood Canyon (Route 210), which receives over 500 inches of snow a year and is reputed to have some of the best and most consistent snow conditions in the world.

Brighton (800-873-5512) and **Solitude** (801-534-1400) ski areas are located just a few miles from Alta as the crow flies but are reached by a different route, through Big Cottonwood Canyon (Route 190). Eleven miles of the most scenic groomed cross-country ski trails in Utah are found at **Solitude Nordic Center** (adjoining Solitude Ski Area; 801-272-7613).

SOUTH OF SALT LAKE CITY The small but challenging ski area at **Sundance** (801-225-4107), with a 2150-foot vertical drop and four chairlifts, was designed as a centerpiece of Robert Redford's exclusive resort. There are also six miles of groomed cross-country trails here. **Park City** (801-649-0493) has 12 chairlifts, a gondola and a 3100-foot vertical drop, **ParkWest** (801-649-1000) has 7 chairlifts and a 2200-foot vertical drop, and **Deer Valley** (801-649-1000) has 11 chairlifts and a 2200-foot vertical drop. These three ski areas make up Utah's largest and busiest winter resort district. Park City is located 27 miles east of Salt Lake City via Route 80 and Route 224.

SKI RENTALS North of Salt Lake City, ski rentals are available at Powder Mountain and Snowbasin. In Ogden, **Fly Line Sports** (2943 Washington Boulevard; 801-394-1812) rents both alpine and nordic equipment.

In the Salt Lake City area, ski rentals are available at Alta and Brighton. Downhill and cross-country equipment are for rent in Salt Lake City at **Utah Ski Rental** (134 West 600 South Street; 801-355-9088) and **Canyon Sports Ltd.** (1844 East 7000 South Street; 801-942-3100).

GOLF

VERNAL AREA In Vernal, the **Vernal Municipal Golf Course** (675 South 2000 East Street; 801-781-1428) is commonly known as the Dinaland Golf Course.

NORTH OF SALT LAKE CITY Logan-area golf courses open to the public include the semiprivate **Logan Golf and Country Club** (710 North 1500 East Street, Logan; 801-753-6050), **Logan River Golf Course** (550 West 1000 South Street, Logan; 801-750-0123) and **Birch Creek Golf Course** (600 East Center Street, Smithfield; 801-563-6825). The **Barn Golf Club** (305 West Pleasant View Street, North Ogden; 801-782-7320), **Davis County Golf Course** (1074

Nicholls Road, Fruit Heights; 801-546-4154) and **Mount Ogden Golf Course** (1787 Constitution Way, Ogden; 801-629-8700) are three Ogden-area courses.

SALT LAKE CITY Greater Salt Lake City has no fewer than 16 public golf courses, including the **Bonneville Golf Course** (954 Conner Street, Salt Lake City; 801-583-9513), **Fore Lakes** (1285 West 4700 South Street, Murray; 801-266-8621), **Glendale** (1630 West 2100 South Street, Salt Lake City; 801-974-2403), **Glenmore** (9800 South 4800 West Street, South Jordan; 801-255-1742), **Meadowbrook** (4197 South 1300 West Street, Murray; 801-266-0971), **Mountain Dell** (Parley's Canyon, Salt Lake City; 801-582-3812), **Murray Parkway** (6345 South Riverside Drive, Murray; 801-262-4653), **Rose Park** (1386 North Redwood Road, Salt Lake City; 801-596-5030), **West Ridge** (Salt Lake City; 801-966-4653) and **Wingpointe** (3602 West 100 North Street, Salt Lake City; 801-575-2345).

SOUTH OF SALT LAKE CITY The Provo-Orem area has the **Seven Peaks Resort Golf Course** (East Center Street, Provo; 801-375-5155), **East Bay Golf Club** (434 East 1860 South Street, Provo; 801-379-6612) and **Cascade Fairways Golf Course** (1313 East 800 North Street, Orem; 801-225-6677). Park City's courses are the **Park City Golf Course** (Lower Park Avenue; 801-649-8701) and **Park Meadows Golf Club** (2000 Meadows Drive; 801-649-8701).

TENNIS

In the Logan area you'll find tennis courts at the **Community Recreation Center** (195 South 100 West Street; 801-752-3111). Salt Lake City has 16 tennis courts at **Liberty Park** (1300 South Street at 500 East Street, Salt Lake City; 801-596-5036) as well as smaller court complexes at 16 other city parks. Call the Parks and Recreation Department (801-972-7800) for locations. South of Salt Lake City, tennis and racquetball courts are open to the public for a fee at the **Park City Racquet Club** (1200 Little Kate Road, Park City; 801-649-8080) and the **Prospector Athletic Club** (2200 Sidewinder Drive, Park City; 801-649-6670).

PACK TRIPS

Guided trail rides and pack trips are available in the Ogden area at **Homestead Resort** (700 North Homestead Drive, Midway; 800-327-7220), in Provo at **Big Springs Riding Stable** (Wolf Mountain; 801-649-9023).

BICYCLING

VERNAL AREA In Flaming Gorge National Recreation Area, the 13-mile **Sheep Creek/Spirit Lake Loop** is a spectacular trip. It's best suited for mountain bikes but can be ridden on a ten-speed touring bike. Other mountain-bike trails at Flaming Gorge include the **Canyon Rim Trail** (5 miles), which passes through meadows and woodlands to an overlook above Red Canyon. **Dinosaur National Monument** has a 24-mile mountain-bike loop.

NORTH OF SALT LAKE CITY The 24-mile Little Pyrenees bike route, designed by a local bicycle club for ten-speed touring, loops through hilly pastoral lands and past a heron rookery in the marshes along the Little Bear River. Other great mountain-bike rides in the Logan area include the newly opened **River Trail** (8 miles) and the five-mile trail to **Old Ephraim's Grave**, both in Logan Canyon. A favorite ten-speed tour is the paved, nearly level 45-mile trail around **Bear Lake**.

At **Golden Spike National Historic Site**, mountain bikers can ride the original railroad bed where the Union Pacific and Central Pacific tracks met to form the first transcontinental railroad; the eight-mile trail starts at the visitors center. One of the most spectacular single-track mountain-bike trails in the region is the **Skyline Trail**, which runs both north and south from a trailhead in North Ogden Canyon for about 20 miles along the crest of the Wasatch Mountains. The paved roads that run around the north half of **Antelope Island** are quickly becoming favorite bike-touring routes, suitable to both mountain bikes and ten-speeds.

SALT LAKE CITY In Salt Lake City, the paved six-mile lower portion of the **City Creek Canyon Trail** runs from the State Capitol building to the foothills northeast of town. The trail is open to bicycles only on odd-numbered days.

SOUTH OF SALT LAKE CITY The paved **Provo Canyon Parkway** (6 miles) makes for a scenic ride on either a mountain bike or a ten-speed. The 26-mile **Squaw Peak Trail**, which leaves Route 189 at the mouth of Provo Canyon, makes for a high-altitude mountain-bike trip across the front of the Wasatch Mountains that affords spectacular views of the Utah Valley.

In the Park City area, **Deer Valley Resort**'s chairlifts carry mountain bikers to the top of Bald Mountain in summer to descend on a choice of trails ranging from easy to difficult. But the ultimate mountain-bike trail in the area is the **Historic Union Pacific Rail Trail**, which traces the route of an 1880 railroad that supplied coal to Park City through meadows and canyons and along the shore of Echo Reservoir. The spectacular 30-mile route has recently been converted into a bike trail.

BIKE RENTALS Bicycles can be rented in Vernal at **Basin Cycle** (450 North Vernal Avenue; 801-781-1226). In Logan, mountain and touring bikes are for rent at **Sunrise Cyclery** (138 North 100 East Street; 801-753-3294) and **Midnight Mountain Cycling** (780 East 275 North Street #1; 801-752-6251). In Ogden try **Miller Ski & Cycle Haus** (834 Washington Boulevard; 801-392-3911). In Salt Lake City, bicycle sales and repair shops abound but rental places are few and far between. One good place to rent a mountain bike is **Wild Rose Mountain Sports** (702 3rd Avenue; 801-533-8671). The best place to rent a bike for exploring Provo Canyon is Heber City's **Bike Shop** (160 South Main Street; 801-654-1143). Park City has a plethora of mountain-bike rental shops, including **White Pine Touring** (363 Main Street; 801-649-8710) and **Jans Mountain Outfitters** (1600 Park Avenue; 801-649-4949). The exclusive bike rental outlet for the Deer Valley slopes is **Cole Sport** (Deer Valley Resort; 801-649-4601).

HIKING

All distances listed for hiking trails are one-way unless otherwise noted.

VERNAL AREA Hiking trails in Flaming Gorge National Recreation Area include the easy, nearly level 2.5-mile **Canyon Rim Trail**, the steep ten-mile **Hideout-Carter Creek Trail** and the long but level seven-mile **Little Hole Trail**.

NORTH OF SALT LAKE CITY In Logan Canyon, the five-mile hike to **Old Ephraim's Grave** is a perennial favorite. A more ambitious hike is the **Birch Canyon Trail**, which starts from a trailhead five miles east of Logan's northern suburb of Smithfield; the challenging ten-mile trail climbs to the summit of 9566-foot Mount Jardine and provides access to a network of trails in the Mount Naomi Wilderness.

SALT LAKE CITY The **City Creek Canyon Trail** has two segments. The lower six miles of the trail is paved and runs from the State Capitol downtown northeast to Rotary Park through a lush creekside greenway. It is reserved for hikers on even-numbered days. The upper 4.5 miles climb from Rotary Park to City Creek Meadows near the crest of the Wasatch Mountains at an elevation of about 8000 feet. A reservation system designed to minimize impact on the trail and the watershed requires that you call 801-535-7911 a day in advance if you plan to hike the last mile of the trail above the city water-treatment plant. Near the Alta ski resort in Little Cottonwood Canyon, the two-mile **Mount Baldy Trail** makes a short, steep ascent to the mountain's 11,068-foot summit.

SOUTH OF SALT LAKE CITY There are networks of short, sometimes steep trails in the Provo Canyon area at **Bridal Veil Falls** and **Cascade Springs**. The three-mile **Sundance Nature Trail** at Sundance is open to the public; it winds through aspen forests to Stewart Falls, the location for the film *Jeremiah Johnson,* which first brought Robert Redford to the secluded valley where he built his resort. **Mount Timpanogos** rises 11,957 feet above sea level. A five-mile hiking trail starting from the Aspen Grove trailhead on the Alpine Loop Road, several miles north of Sundance, leads past a series of beautiful waterfalls and lakes and the mile-long Timpanogos Glacier on its way to the mountain's summit.

Transportation

BY CAR

Route 40 is the most direct route to the Vernal area. It exits Route 80 a short distance east of Salt Lake City, continues eastward from Vernal into Colorado and connects with **Route 70** near Winter Park. **Route 80** and **Route 15** intersect at Salt Lake City. Logan, Ogden and Provo are all near Route 15. Park City is near Route 80 east of Salt Lake City.

BY AIR

Salt Lake City International Airport is the only major commercial passenger terminal in the state. Air carriers here include America West, American Airlines, Continental, Delta, Northwest, Pan Am, United and several foreign international airlines.

Skywest Airlines (800-453-9417) provides commuter service to Vernal from Salt Lake City. All other destinations covered in this chapter use Salt Lake City International. Buses and limousine services—such as **Greyhound** (801-355-4684), **Lewis Brothers Stages** (801-649-2256) and **Utah Transit Authority** (801-287-4636)—run regularly from the airport to Logan, Ogden, Provo, Sundance and Park City.

BY BUS

Greyhound Bus Lines serves Salt Lake City (160 West South Temple Street; 801-355-4684) as well as Logan (18 East Center Street; 801-752-4921) and Provo (124 North 300 West Street; 801-373-4211).

BY TRAIN

Amtrak's "California Zephyr" provides passenger service to and from Los Angeles, Las Vegas, Oakland, Portland, Seattle, Denver and Chicago at the Denver & Rio Grande Depot (320 South Rio Grande; 801-364-8562) in Salt Lake City.

CAR RENTALS

Vernal's local car-rental agency, **Avis Rent A Car** (800-331-1212), is located at the municipal airport.

Car rentals are available in Logan at **Freedom Rent A Car** (1220 North Main Street; 801-752-2075) and in Ogden at several agencies including **National Interrent** (1135 West Riverdale Road; 800-328-4567) and **All American Rent A Car** (1764 Washington Boulevard; 801-394-3828).

The many agencies with desks at Salt Lake City International Airport include **Airways Rent A Car** (801-322-5055), **Budget Rent A Car** (801-363-1500), **Dollar Rent A Car** (800-800-4000), **Hertz Rent A Car** (800-654-3131), **Ready Car Rental** (801-596-2661) and **Thrifty Car Rental** (800-367-2277).

Provo car-rental agencies include **Payless Car Rental** (303 West 100 North Street; 800-237-2804) and **Freedom Rent A Car** (390 South State Street; 801-374-2144). Rentals are available in Park City from **Park City Rent A Car** (801-649-5499).

PUBLIC TRANSPORTATION

Utah Transit Authority provides regional bus service to Ogden (2500 Washington Boulevard, Ogden; 801-621-4636), to numerous transportation centers around Salt Lake City (801-287-4636) and to Provo (801-375-4636).

Park City Transit (801-649-6660) operates a ski-shuttle trolley between downtown and the ski areas during the winter season.

TAXIS

Local taxi service is provided in Logan by **Logan Cab** (801-753-3663) and in Ogden by **Yellow Cab** (801-394-9411). Salt Lake City has several cab companies, including **City Cab** (801-363-5014), **Ute Cab** (801-359-7788) and **Yellow Cab** (801-521-2100). In Provo, too, it's **Yellow Cab** (801-377-7070).

CHAPTER SIX

Southern Wyoming Rockies

Just about everyone on the highways of southern Wyoming is bound for someplace else—Yellowstone National Park, for instance, or Salt Lake City, or maybe the West Coast. It has been that way ever since the first pioneer wagon train set out for Oregon in 1846. Many have crossed the high, windblown plains of southern Wyoming, but few have stayed here. It remains one of the emptiest regions in the United States and just about the only part of the West where the present-day population is actually declining.

Winters are brutally cold, summers are as dry as dust and the wind never stops. Travelers are often heard to disparage southern Wyoming. As a cowboy saying goes, driving across Wyoming on Route 80 is more than a hassle; it's a career. Yet those who slow down for a closer look will discover some of the least-visited historic sites and natural areas in the Rockies—good places to stop for a break from the interstate.

In the southeastern part of the state, a short trip from the state capital, Cheyenne, and the exuberant university town of Laramie, the Medicine Bow Mountains and the Snowy Range offer craggy peaks, ice-cold alpine lakes, pine-and-aspen forests and meadows ablaze with wildflowers.

Following Route 80 (known in history as the Overland Trail) westward into the bleak desert of the Great Divide Basin takes you to the northern gateway of the spectacular Flaming Gorge National Recreation Area and onward into rugged, barren landscapes full of fossil evidence that life teemed here in prehistoric times.

Generally northbound, Route 25 veers west to follow the old Oregon Trail into Casper, commercial center for a huge area where oil drilling is the main business and pronghorn antelope outnumber humans. Yet even here alpine beauty can be found on the forested slopes of Mount Casper. Eagles nest in nearby canyons, and wetlands along the banks of the Platte River teem with bird and animal life. From Casper, travelers can continue along an empty two-lane highway that traces the old Oregon Trail westward to historic South Pass, at the southern tip of the Wind River Range, the tallest mountain range in Wyoming.

Most of the Wind River Range has been set aside as roadless wilderness area for the sole use of hikers and horseback riders. Just far enough off the beaten path to escape the high-powered tourist development that has come to characterize the Jackson area to the north, the pristine mountains have gained a reputation as a tree-huggers' heaven. They draw environmentally aware outdoors enthusiasts to the quiet little town of Lander, which is the best base camp for exploring the Wind River Range and, nearby, Wyoming's only Indian reservation.

Cheyenne-Laramie Area

Cheyenne, with its cowboy flair, and Laramie, with its college-town energy, lie an hour apart on opposite slopes of the low, gentle Laramie Mountains. West of Laramie rise the dramatic crags of the Snowy Range, and beyond them the forgotten old mining town of Encampment and the hot springs at Saratoga. All the areas described in this section can be visited in a one-day loop drive from Cheyenne, or as a series of detours from the interstate, or as a scenic, though time-consuming, alternative to the segment of Route 80 west of the Great Basin Desert.

Cheyenne is Wyoming's capital and (officially at least) largest city, with a population estimated at 50,008—exceeding the population estimate for Casper by eight residents. Approaching Cheyenne from the south via Route 25, travelers are struck by the small scale of the city in contrast to Denver, just 90 miles away. Cheyenne is a tourist town for only one week a year—the last week in July, when cowpersons and rodeo fans pack the streets for Frontier Days, the citywide festivities surrounding the world's largest outdoor rodeo. The rest of the time, this flat little one-story city barely within sight of the distant mountains offers little to inspire visitors to stay longer than the time it takes to stroll the capital district.

The 50-foot-diameter gold-leaf dome that tops the **Wyoming State Capitol** (Capitol Avenue between 24th and 25th streets; 307-777-7220), the tallest building in Cheyenne, is visible for miles across the plains. Stuffed bison and elk, as well as large murals that bring the state's history to life, adorn the interior of the capitol building.

Perhaps the capitol's most spectacular feature is the huge Tiffany stained-glass ceilings, floodlit from above, in the Senate and House of Representatives chambers and the interior of the capitol dome. Free guided tours of the capitol building are offered at regular intervals on weekdays.

The capitol's most striking artworks are those outside the building. On the west side is **The Spirit of Wyoming**, sculptor Ed Fraughton's dramatic bronze

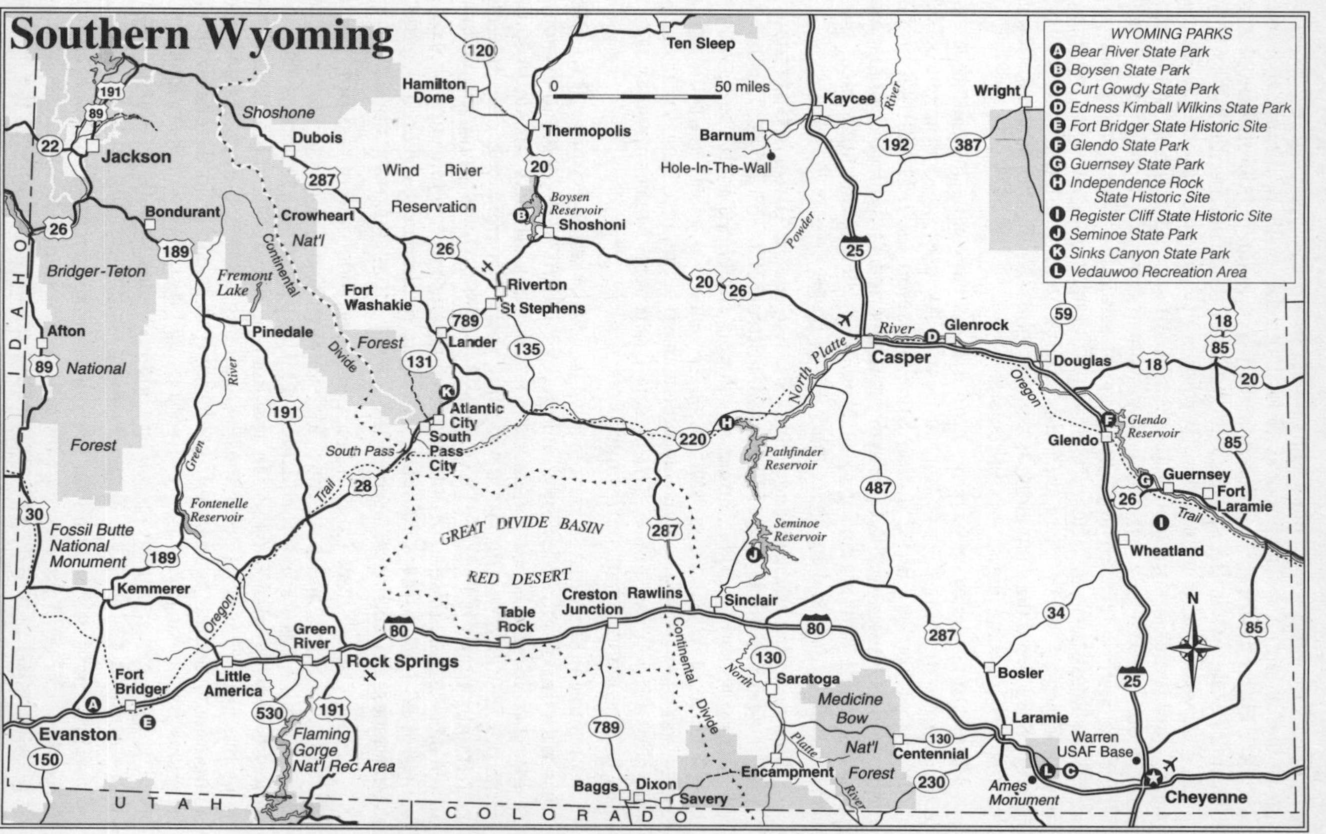

Southern Wyoming
WYOMING PARKS
A Bear River State Park
B Boysen State Park
C Curt Gowdy State Park
D Edness Kimball Wilkins State Park
E Fort Bridger State Historic Site
F Glendo State Park
G Guernsey State Park
H Independence Rock State Historic Site
I Register Cliff State Historic Site
J Seminoe State Park
K Sinks Canyon State Park
L Vedauwoo Recreation Area
0
50 miles
N
Jackson
Bondurant
Afton
Bridger-Teton
National
Forest
Fossil Butte National Monument
Kemmerer
Fort Bridger
Evanston
Shoshone
Dubois
Crowheart
Nat'l
Continental
Divide
Fremont Lake
Pinedale
Fontenelle Reservoir
Green
River
Oregon
Trail
Little America
Green River
Flaming Gorge Nat'l Rec Area
Rock Springs
South Pass
Fort Washakie
Forest
Lander
Atlantic City
South Pass City
Hamilton Dome
Wind River Reservation
Thermopolis
Boysen Reservoir
Shoshoni
Riverton
St Stephens
Ten Sleep
Barnum
Hole-In-The-Wall
Kaycee
Powder
River
Wright
Casper
North Platte
Glenrock
Douglas
Glendo
Glendo Reservoir
Guernsey
Fort Laramie
Wheatland
Pathfinder Reservoir
Seminoe Reservoir
GREAT DIVIDE BASIN
RED DESERT
Table Rock
Creston Junction
Rawlins
Sinclair
Saratoga
Encampment
Medicine Bow Nat'l Forest
Centennial
Bosler
Laramie
Ames Monument
Warren USAF Base
Cheyenne
Baggs
Dixon
Savery
I D A H O
U T A H
C O L O R A D O

rendition of the state's trademark, a bucking bronco and rider. On the opposite side of the building stands a horseless but slightly larger-than-life bronze statue of **Esther Hobart Morris**, who became the first woman public officeholder in the United States when she was elected justice of the peace in South Pass City in 1870. A year before her election, Wyoming had passed the first law in the country prohibiting discrimination on the basis of sex and granting women the right to vote. The state also elected the first woman governor in the United States (Nellie Taloe Ross, elected in 1924 to complete the last two years of her deceased husband's term in office; the state has not had another woman governor since) and seated the first woman jurors. The official state nickname is "The Equality State," and the state motto is "Equal rights." Well, almost equal: About one out of four state legislators is female.

After seeing the State Capitol, stroll a block east and a long block south to the Barrett Building (22nd Street at Central Avenue), a government office building that houses the **Wyoming State Museum** (307-777-7014) on the ground floor. Changing exhibits from the state's permanent collection of historic artifacts include clothing and gear of Native Americans, mountain men, pioneers, cavalry men, and ranchers, plus lots of guns.

Walk another block east and a block south to see the **Historic Governors' Mansion State Historic Site** (300 East 21st Street; 307-777-7778). This huge, redundantly named Georgian home, which was completed in 1905, served as the residence of Wyoming governors for 52 years. Take the free, self-guided tour to see rooms furnished and decorated in styles representing the decades when the mansion was in use. The present Governors' Mansion, which is not open to the public, fronts on Frontier Park.

The most interesting museum in town is the **Cheyenne Frontier Days Old West Museum** (North Carey Street at Frontier Park; 307-778-7920; admission). Besides a collection of Native American and cowboy artifacts similar in spirit to the one in the Wyoming State Museum, there is a small room displaying memorabilia from the Frontier Days rodeo, held at the rodeo grounds next door for ten days around the end of July. The main feature of this museum is its collection of 35 horse-drawn vehicles, including buckboards, covered wagons, stagecoaches and carriages, used in the annual Frontier Days Parade.

Across Carey Street from the Frontier Park rodeo grounds, **Lions Park** (North Carey Street at 8th Avenue) surrounds peaceful Sloans Lake and has broad, green lawns perfect for picnicking. The park's best feature is the **Botanical Garden** (307-637-6458). In addition to native trees and plants of Wyoming, the garden has solar greenhouses simulating desert and tropical rainforest environments, as well as vegetable gardens grown as part of local rehabilitation programs for physically challenged persons and disturbed youths. Lions Park also has bike paths, miniature golf, a children's playground, restrooms and a public swimming pool. The lake is used for boating, fishing and ice skating.

Aside from state government, Cheyenne's major employer is **Warren Air Force Base** (307-775-3381), where the federal government keeps intercontinental ballistic missiles at the ready. Some travelers may wish to visit the base to see the **Buffalo Soldier Monument**, which commemorates the African American soldiers who served in special (that is, segregated) U.S. cavalry and infantry units during the frontier era.

Cheyenne is in Laramie County, but the city of Laramie, 40 miles away, is in neighboring Albany County. The two cities are separated by the low **Laramie Mountains**, covered in ponderosa forest and studded with both large and small granite formations. Two paved routes cross the mountains between the two small cities. The faster highway, Route 80, whisks you over the mountains and down into Laramie in about 45 minutes. At the summit of Sherman Hill (8640 feet), a 12-foot-tall bronze bust of **Abraham Lincoln** mounted on a granite pedestal overlooks the highway. University of Wyoming art professor Robert Russin, Wyoming's leading sculptor, was commissioned to create it for Lincoln's 150th birthday in 1959. This route, built in 1923 and known as the Lincoln Highway, was the first transcontinental highway in America. Like present-day Route 80, it ran all the way from New York through Chicago to San Francisco. This summit is the highest point on the entire route.

The other way over the Laramie Mountains, Route 210 (known locally as Happy Jack Road), begins its climb into the high country soon after passing **Curt Gowdy State Park**. It is named after woodcutter Jack Hollingworth, who made the road in the 1880s to haul fuelwood and railroad ties down from the mountains. This paved two-lane route is just one mile shorter than going from Cheyenne to Laramie via Route 80; it's also somewhat slower and much more traffic-free, allowing you more opportunity to enjoy the scenery. It meets the interstate at the bust of Lincoln. The major point of interest in the Laramie Mountains, **Vedauwoo Recreation Area**, lies along a dirt road that runs between Route 80 and Happy Jack Road. Balanced rocks and myriad other weird granite formations sprout from the earth everywhere you look in this Medicine Bow National Forest recreation area. The major attraction of Vedauwoo is an area of sheer cliffs, overhanging in many spots, which rock climbers consider one of the great technical climbs. On most summer days and any weekend when the weather is sunny you can watch as dozens of rock climbers inch their way up the cliffs, clinging to the rock faces with fingers and toes.

The **Ames Monument**, a minor oddity, stands forlorn on a ridge about two miles south of Exit 329 on Route 80 (the same exit as for Vedauwoo but on the other side of the highway). The 60-foot sandstone pyramid was built in 1882 to immortalize Oakes and Oliver Ames, brothers who helped finance the Union Pacific Railroad. Their portraits in stone, now badly eroded and apparently used for target practice from time to time, are mounted high on opposite sides of the pyramid, which formerly marked the highest point on the transcontinental railroad. However, after the Ames brothers had been disgraced in a government scandal, the tracks were rerouted, bypassing the monument.

Laramie is one of numerous places in southeastern Wyoming (along with Laramie County, the Laramie Mountains, Laramie Peak, the Laramie River and Fort Laramie) named after Jacques La Remy, a French trapper believed to have been the first Anglo who ever set foot in Wyoming. He vanished in 1820; most historians believe he either went to live among the Arapaho people or died at their hands. Today, Wyoming's third-largest city is the site of the **University**

of Wyoming (Ivinson and 9th streets; 307-766-1121), which has about 10,000 students and is the only four-year college in the state. The most notable point of interest on campus is the **Geological Museum** (in the S. H. Knight Building; 307-766-4218), where exhibits include everything from fossilized skeletons of dinosaurs and prehistoric mammals to specimens of jade and uranium, as well as core samples from oil explorations. Other places worth visiting on the campus include the **Fine Arts Center** (307-766-6622), the **Anthropology Museum** (307-766-5136) and the **American Heritage Center** (in Coe Library; 307-766-4114).

History is also the focus at the **Laramie Plains Museum** (603 Ivinson Avenue, Laramie; 307-742-4448; admission), in the elegant 1892 mansion of banker Edward Ivinson. The rooms have been lavishly restored with antique furniture, turn-of-the-century kitchen appliances, handmade toys and historical photos and documents from Laramie's early days. Among the colorful gardens of the mansion's meticulously landscaped grounds are a cowboy line cabin and a one-room frontier schoolhouse. Guided tours only; call for current schedule.

Wyoming Territorial Park (975 Snowy Range Road, Laramie; 307-745-6161; admission), Laramie's major sightseeing highlight, is built around the Territorial Prison, used until 1901. Butch Cassidy served 18 months here for stealing horses early in his outlaw career—his only prison sentence. Legend has it that during his stay he learned the finer points of train robbery and met many of the men who would ride with him later. The prison was considered progressive in its day because it was the first one in the West to separate women inmates from the male prison population. Self-guided tours take you through restored cell blocks, the dining area and the chapel; the prison was converted to a livestock barn after a new penitentiary (now called the Old Frontier Prison) was built in Rawlins; later it was abandoned, so much of what visitors see today is modern restoration. The Territorial Park also has a so-far unimpressive "frontier town" of other old buildings gathered from around the state, as well as the U.S. Marshalls Museum, a dinner theater and a 19th-century steam-train exhibit.

The **Wyoming & Colorado Scenic Railroad** (2272 Snowy Range Road, Laramie; 307-742-9162) runs daily from May through mid-November, weather permitting. From Laramie it climbs to an altitude of over 9000 feet in the Snowy Range, stopping for lunch at the old mining town of Centennial. Despite the railroad's name and the fact that the tracks do indeed turn south and cross the state line, the portion of the trip covered by the 108-mile sightseeing trip takes place entirely in Wyoming.

West of Laramie, the **Snowy Range Scenic Byway** (Route 130) winds its way through Medicine Bow National Forest. At the foot of the Snowy Range, the old mining town of **Centennial** has been revived for tourists with restaurants, cabins, groceries, gift shops and several Old West saloons. The road climbs to an elevation of 10,800 feet, where alpine tundra surrounds a chain of mountain lakes whose dark waters mirror the awesome granite crags of 12,013-foot Medicine Bow Peak, so close you'll feel that you ought to be able to throw a stone and make a hole in the snow that clings to the north-facing slopes year-round. This 64-mile scenic route makes a spectacular alternative to Route 80.

The Snowy Range Scenic Byway descends from the mountains to **Saratoga**, an isolated resort community that owes its existence to **Saratoga Hot Springs** (Route 130). When they came to the area in 1878, the town's developers envisioned it as a western version of upstate New York's famed Saratoga Springs health spa, but it never really caught on. Today, the springs are open to the public for free. They include a large swimming pool, a smaller hot pool and several small, muddy 114°F springs along the bank of Spring Creek. The free **Saratoga Museum** (103 Constitution Avenue; 307-326-5511) contains prehistoric Native American artifacts, a replica of an old-time general store's interior, a sheep wagon, a blacksmith shop and a research library of family histories, diaries and old photographs.

Travelers may notice that local-history museums are more common than gas stations in southern Wyoming. Mining is the focus of the **Grand Encampment Museum** (Encampment; 307-327-5308), which recalls the glory days of the former mining town 19 miles south of Saratoga. Though the community of Encampment has fewer than 500 residents today, it was a boom town of 5000 between the years 1897, when a vein of copper ore was discovered there, and 1908, when it ran out. In those days Encampment had the largest smelter in the region, and a 16-mile-long tramway brought ore over the crest of the Sierra Madre from other mines farther west.

CHEYENNE-LARAMIE AREA HOTELS

Low-priced ma-and-pa motels line Lincolnway west of the downtown area, as well as Central Avenue on the south edge of town near Route 80. A good bet for the budget-conscious is the baby-blue, 16-room **Lariat Motel** (600 Central Avenue, Cheyenne; 307-635-8439). All rooms have bathtubs; four have kitchen facilities. Budget.

The only refurbished historic hotel in Cheyenne, and one of the few in the state, is the **Plains Hotel** (1600 Central Avenue; 307-638-3311). The location, across the street from the bus depot and train station, is convenient for strolling the downtown area and capital district. The lobby of this 1911 hotel is full of Old West atmosphere, while the 40 oversized guest rooms feature such amenities as queen-size beds and marble bathrooms. Moderate.

Cheyenne's finest accommodations are at **Holding's Little America** (2800 West Lincolnway; 307-634-2771), located at the crossroads of Routes 25 and 80. The sprawling 189-room complex boasts resort facilities including a nine-hole golf course, Olympic-size swimming pool and jogging track. The spacious rooms feature contemporary furnishings and warm color schemes. Moderate to deluxe.

Cheyenne has a number of attractive bed and breakfasts. One of the nicest is the **Rainsford Inn Bed & Breakfast** (219 East 18th Street; 307-638-2337), a stately, three-story Victorian mansion listed on the National Register of Historic Places. It's located in the quiet, residential Rainsford Historic District near downtown, on what was known as "Cattle Baron Row" in Cheyenne's early days. Common areas feature a fireplace, piano, sun porch and small art gallery, and the five suites are individually furnished with antiques. Deluxe.

Midway between Cheyenne and Laramie, the **Drummond's Ranch Bed and Breakfast** (39 Happy Jack Road, Cheyenne; 307-634-6042) adjoins Curt Gowdy State Park, just a few miles from Medicine Bow National Forest's Vedauwoo Recreation Area. The two-story ranch house has three guest rooms with four-poster beds and lots of horse pictures on the walls, and an indoor arena offers facilities for stabling horses and boarding pets. Human guests will enjoy the outdoor hot tub with its unobstructed mountain view. Deluxe.

In Laramie, most motels are found on the west side of town along 3rd Street (Route 287) or around the Snowy Range Road exit from Route 80. The 112-unit **Best Western Foster's Country Inn** (1561 Snowy Range Road; 307-742-8371), one of the largest motor inns in town, is conveniently located for visiting the Wyoming Territorial Park. Rooms in this white-brick building have a clean, new feeling and furnishings so standard you may feel that you've been there before. Moderate.

Accommodations with more character are found in the university district at **Annie Moore's Guest House** (819 University Avenue, Laramie; 307-721-4177). The six guest rooms in this 1912 residence, which formerly served as fraternity and sorority houses at different times, are bright, cheerful and accented with period antiques. Baths are shared. A continental breakfast is included in the rates, which are in the deluxe range.

Several guest ranches are located in the Snowy Range between Laramie and Saratoga. One of the best is **Brush Creek Ranch** (Route 130, Saratoga; 307-327-5241, 800-726-2499). The historic ranch was homesteaded in the 1880s and purchased in the early 1900s by heirs to the Schlitz Breweries fortune, who built a luxuriously rustic red-roofed, white-and-blue lodge on a ridge overlooking meadows and the creek for which the ranch is named. Guest accommodations are in private cabins with dark wood-paneled interiors and simple furnishings. Brush Creek is a working cattle ranch, and guests may participate in ranch chores if they wish. Recreational activities include horseback riding, fishing, bird-watching and, in winter, snowmobiling and cross-country skiing. Deluxe.

For a different kind of guest-ranch experience, check out the **Umbrella Ranch** (Star Route, Box 1100, Dixon; 307-383-2640). This family-owned ranch on the Little Snake River at the foot of the Sierra Madre offers rustic accommodations in a log cabin, bunkhouse or antique sheep wagon. Though there are no organized activities here, guests are welcome to help out with ranch chores or just explore the natural beauty of the surroundings. Meals are included. Moderate.

CHEYENNE-LARAMIE AREA RESTAURANTS

Many Cheyenne residents say that for fine dining and elegant ambience, they drive across the state line to Fort Collins. This may help explain why the **Victorian Rose** (1600 Central Avenue; 307-637-8701), a family-style restaurant in the Plains Hotel, tries to entice patrons with its slogan, "For An Enjoyable Dining Experience—In Cheyenne." It *is* an enjoyable place, too, with an old-fashioned feeling and a varied menu featuring pastas and daily specials as well as prime rib, trout and steaks. Moderate.

In truth, the Cheyenne restaurant scene is not as bleak as residents would have you believe. There are more than 80 restaurants (the majority of them fast-food franchises) to choose from. On the inexpensive end of the spectrum, a long-established local favorite is **Lexie's Cafe** (216 East 17th Street; 307-638-8712), where they serve hearty ranch-style breakfasts such as steak and eggs, and, for lunch, the biggest, juiciest hamburgers in town. The brick residence that houses Lexie's is the oldest building in Cheyenne. Budget.

International cuisine in Cheyenne generally means Mexican food, in which several restaurants around town excel. We recommend **Los Amigos Restaurant** (620 Central Avenue; 307-638-8591), where authentic south-of-the-border dishes surpass the standard piñatas-and-serapes ambience. Moderate.

Another notable Cheyenne restaurant is the **Owl Inn** (3919 Central Avenue; 307-638-8578), a casual, family-style place that has been in operation since 1935 and still serves great steak-and-potatoes-and-apple-pie fare. Moderate.

Terry Bison Ranch Chuckwagon Dinners (51 Route 25 Service Road East, Cheyenne; 307-634-4171) serves outdoor chuckwagon dinners featuring roast buffalo meat, followed by live western entertainment on Friday and Saturday evenings during the summer months. If you call for reservations and come early, you can take a wagon tour to see the captive buffalo herd—one of the largest ranch herds in the country—and other exotic livestock such as llamas and longhorn steers. Moderate.

If there were such a thing as Wyoming nouvelle cuisine, the place to sample it would be the **Café Jacques & 3rd St. Bar & Grill** (216 Grand Avenue, Laramie; 307-742-5522). A turn-of-the-century brick exterior conceals an eatery patterned after Parisian cafés. The inventive menu is far from Continental, though, offering such dishes as Hawaiian-style shrimp breaded with coconut and served on a bed of crushed pineapple. Moderate.

Jeffrey's Bistro (123 Ivinson Avenue, Laramie; 307-742-0744) appeals to students and travelers alike with natural foods and a good selection of vegetarian dishes. Moderate. Around the corner, **Jeffrey's Too** (116 South 2nd Street; 307-742-0744), the only espresso shop in Laramie—and one of only two in the entire state—serves baked goods, croissant sandwiches and gourmet deli fare in a pretty garden courtyard. Moderate.

CHEYENNE-LARAMIE AREA SHOPPING

If it's Levi's, Ropers or Stetsons you have in mind, you're in luck in downtown Cheyenne, where one of the largest selections of western wear in the state can be found at **Cheyenne Outfitters** (210 West 16th Street; 307-775-7550). The other largest selection in Wyoming is located across the street at **Wrangler** (1518 Capitol Avenue; 307-634-3048).

The most interesting place to shop in Laramie is the small downtown historic district along Ivinson and Grand avenues and 2nd and 3rd streets, where you'll find art galleries, bookstores and natural foods.

CHEYENNE-LARAMIE AREA NIGHTLIFE

You can two-step late into the night at the **Cheyenne Club** (1617 Capitol Avenue, Cheyenne; 307-635-7777), a great big barnlike dance hall right downtown where they feature live bands nightly and country-and-western dance lessons on some evenings. An even bigger country-and-western club is the **Cowboy South** (312 South Greeley Highway, Cheyenne; 307-637-3800). The **Mayflower Tavern** (112 West 17th Street, Cheyenne; 307-634-3684) is a famous spot in rodeo circles, where just about every rider worth his salt has tied one on after a Frontier Days event.

Laramie also has its share of saloons where you drink and dance with your hat on, notably the **Cowboy Grill** (309 South 3rd Street; 307-742-3141) and the **Cowboy Saloon** (108 South 2nd Street; 307-721-3165). Popular student hangouts are the **Draw Bridge Tavern** (1622 Grand Avenue; 307-745-3940) and the **Buckhorn Bar** (114 Ivinson Avenue; 307-742-3554).

CHEYENNE-LARAMIE AREA PARKS

Curt Gowdy State Park—Named for the Wyoming-born baseball star and sportscaster, this 1645-acre park in the foothills of the Laramie Mountains encompasses meadows, rolling pine-shaded hills and rugged granite rock formations surrounding two artificial lakes that provide Cheyenne's water supply. Unpaved roads almost completely encircle both lakes, providing access to 18 camping and picnic areas along the shores. Power boats dominate large Granite Reservoir, while anglers in hand-launched skiffs use the smaller Crystal Reservoir. The park is crowded on weekends and practically deserted during the week.

Facilities: Picnic areas, restrooms, playground, boat ramp, nature trail, archery range, amphitheater, group lodge; day-use fee, $3; information, 307-632-7946. *Fishing:* Good for rainbow trout.

Camping: Permitted in 280 RV/tent sites (no hookups); $4/night per vehicle.

Getting there: The park entrance is 23.5 miles west of Cheyenne and 24 miles east of Laramie on Route 210 (Happy Jack Road).

Medicine Bow National Forest—This 1,094,000-acre forest encompasses the Laramie Mountains, which lie between Cheyenne and Laramie and extend north as far as Casper, and the Medicine Bow Range west of Laramie. Most recreational use is in the Vedauwoo Recreation Area and along the Snowy Range Scenic Byway. The highest elevation is Medicine Bow Peak (12,013 feet), west of Laramie near the Snowy Range Scenic Byway. While unpaved roads provide access to most areas of the forest, there are four small, roadless wilderness areas. Most hiking trails in the forest are less than five miles long, except for a little-used 46-mile segment of the Continental Divide Trail that runs along a low ridge west of Encampment.

Facilities: Picnic areas, hiking trails; day-use fee, $3; information, 307-745-8971. *Fishing:* Good for trout in numerous lakes and streams. Winter ice fishing is especially popular.

Camping: The 39 campgrounds offer a total of 597 RV/tent sites (no hookups). Fees range from free to $8 per night.

Getting there: Major access routes are Route 210 (Happy Jack Road) between Cheyenne and Laramie, Route 130 (Snowy Range Scenic Byway) between Laramie and Saratoga, and Route 34 between Bosler and Wheatland.

Rock Springs–Green River Area

Route 80 traces the old Overland Trail, used by Pony Express mail carriers and stagecoaches carrying California-bound travelers beginning in the 1850s. Driving the modern interstate highway between Rawlins and Evanston, you can while away the long, dull trip by imagining the tedium and discomfort that travelers must have experienced in past times, when it took five days to cross Wyoming's Great Divide Basin. The advantage of the Overland Trail route was that it avoided a steep climb over the Rockies, crossing the Continental Divide unnoticeably at an elevation of less than 7000 feet; the disadvantage was that the route was hot, barren and waterless. This arid region is unique in that any water that falls here does not drain to either the Atlantic or the Pacific, but only into the lowest part of the basin, located north of Table Rock. If even a modest amount of rain fell here each year, the basin would fill up with water to form an inland sea larger than the Great Salt Lake. This does not happen because what little rain falls from the occasional passing cloud evaporates before reaching the ground.

At the eastern edge of the wasteland, the little town of **Sinclair** originated in 1923 as showpiece company town for Wyoming's first oil company, the Producers and Refiners Corporation. Remnants of the graceful Spanish mission–style architecture that set the "Wonder Town of Wyoming" apart from other communities in the region can still be seen. Sinclair was designed for 1500 residents but never reached that size. The town's name was changed when it was bought lock, stock and barrel in 1934 by Sinclair Oil, which is ubiquitous in Wyoming today.

Exit Route 80 at Sinclair to visit **Seminoe State Park**, a large, recreational reservoir flanked by sand dunes and sagebrush 35 miles to the north (see "Rock Springs–Green River Area Parks"). At **Fort Fred Steele State Historic Site**, just north of the interstate from the exit nine miles east of Sinclair, you'll find the poorly preserved remains of an army fort built in 1868 to protect the newly completed transcontinental Union Pacific Railroad from Indian attacks. Much of the abandoned fort was destroyed by fire in 1976. The site offers a pleasant stretch of riverbank along the North Platte.

Rawlins, the oldest community in the area, is the site of the **Old Frontier Prison** (5th Street at Walnut Street; 307-324-4422; admission), which replaced Laramie's Territorial Prison in 1901. The Old Frontier Prison was used for 80 years before a new penitentiary was opened south of town; the state prison continues to be Rawlins' largest employer. Regularly scheduled guided tours of the Old Frontier Prison let visitors enter the forbidding limestone walls to walk through the austere cell blocks, where graffiti drawn by inmates is still visible. Unlike Laramie's Territorial Prison, this one gives the impression that it was lived in until just yesterday—an impression preserved partly because it is used as a motion-picture location. The ultimate eerie sight on the tour is the gas chamber, where five prisoners were executed. Open only during the summer months.

It's a straight, fast 108-mile drive on Route 80 from Rawlins to Rock Springs across the Red Desert and the Great Divide Basin. Along most of this distance there are no settlements or inhabited ranches for 50 miles north or south of the interstate, and no roads except for a few jeep tracks leading to remote oil and gas wells. But this forbidding landscape is home to the largest remaining population of wild horses in the United States. On the west side of the basin, 15 miles apart, are the sister cities of **Rock Springs** and **Green River**; together, they boast the third-largest metropolitan population in the state.

Both towns owe their existence to mining. Rock Springs, now a center for oil and gas drilling, got its start in 1868 as the prime source of the coal used to fuel locomotives on the Union Pacific Railroad; Green River produces two-thirds of the world's supply of trona, or soda ash, from which baking soda is made. Both communities have downtown historic districts, and booklets describing building-by-building walking tours are widely available at truck stops, restaurants and motels.

Although on first impression Rock Springs and Green River do not seem to offer much of interest to pleasure travelers, both towns are gateways to **Flaming Gorge National Recreation Area**. Route 530 provides access to the west shore of the narrow, winding, 91-mile-long reservoir on the Green River; Route 191 from Rock Springs provides access to the east shore. From Route 191 a paved road that turns off to the west 13 miles south of Rock Springs goes ten miles between the bright orange walls of **Firehole Canyon** to the lakeshore; otherwise, the truly spectacular scenery of the gorge begins just over the state line in Utah (see Chapter Five, "Utah Rockies"). A 143-mile drive around the lake from Rock Springs to Green River takes all day and is well worth the trip.

Continuing westward from Green River on Route 80, a 40-mile drive through colorful badlands will bring you to the exit for **Fort Bridger State Historic Site** (Fort Bridger; 307-782-3842; admission); the fort is about a mile south of the highway. Mountain men Jim Bridger and Louis Vasquez started a trading post on this site in 1843. They operated the outpost for ten years, trading with the Shoshone for furs and soon becoming an important supply point on the Mormon Trail, a branch of the Oregon Trail leading to the new settlement of Salt Lake City. In 1853, in a dispute over who would be allowed to sell bullets to the Indians, Mormon leader Brigham Young sent a posse to burn the trading post and forced Bridger and Vasquez to flee. Two years later, when the U.S. Army moved in to assert federal control over the Mormon empire, they leased the site of the former trading post from Bridger and Vasquez and built a military base. Today, more than a dozen of the old fort buildings remain, scattered across a parklike area of green lawns and shade trees on the banks of Groshon Creek.

From Fort Bridger, Route 80 continues west for 35 miles to **Evanston**, an old railroad town with a brick historic district. **Depot Square**, a downtown restoration project, contains a replica of the Joss House, where Chinese immigrant railroad workers worshiped, alongside the restored Union Pacific depot. Today, Evanston still has a sizable Chinese population, and Chinese New Year's Day is one of the town's biggest events of the year. Evanston is best known for horseracing at **Wyoming Downs** (Route 89; 800-255-8238), where thoroughbred and quarterhorse races are held on weekends from Memorial Day to Labor Day and parimutuel off-track betting is offered year-round.

A detour north of the interstate, 41 miles from the Granger exit west of Little America via Route 30 or 35 miles north of Evanston via Route 189, brings you to **Kemmerer**, the unlikely little badlands town where retail entrepreneur James Cash Penney started the Golden Rule Store in 1902. It grew to become the nationwide JCPenney chain.

The area's big attraction, located 14 miles west of Kemmerer on Route 30, is **Fossil Butte National Monument** (Route 30; 307-877-3450; admission). The huge, white butte at the center of the park, a lakebed 50 million years ago, harbors billions of fossils in its layers of limestone, mudstone and volcanic ash: turtles, stingrays, five-foot garfish, schools of literally millions of herring and other lake inhabitants; leaves and seeds from palm, cypress and other trees that once covered the land in the area; and animals such as bats, crocodiles and diminutive horses that lived around the lake at the time. Some of the thousands of fossils discovered here are on display at the visitors center, and two loop trails, eleven-and-a-half and twenty-one-and-a-half miles long, go to a working fossil quarry and an older one used by scientists and collectors beginning in the late 1800s. Today, fossil collecting is prohibited within the national monument. A turnoff from the road into the national monument takes you to the privately owned **Ulrich's Fossil Quarries** (Route 30, Fossil Station; 307-877-6466; admission) where, for a $45 fee, you can hunt for fossils on a guided tour and keep all you find. Advance reservations are required.

ROCK SPRINGS–GREEN RIVER AREA HOTELS

The gingerbready three-story **Ferris Mansion Bed & Breakfast** (607 West Maple Street, Rawlins; 307-324-3961) was built in 1903 as the home of Rawlins copper tycoon George Ferris. Its current owners offer four guest rooms, all with private baths and period furnishings. Moderate.

Budget rates are found at a number of basic motels such as the **Cody Motel** (75 North Center Street, Rock Springs; 307-362-9490), whose 40 units have been recently remodeled. Some have kitchenette facilities including microwaves. Similar accommodations are available at the 17-unit **Flaming Gorge Motel** (316 Flaming Gorge Way, Green River; 307-875-4190).

The **Sha Hol Dee Bed & Breakfast** (1116 Pilot Butte; 307-362-7131) offers three large guest bedrooms in a remodeled 1901 homestead in downtown Rock Springs. The period furnishings are far more refined than anything that might have existed in turn-of-the-century Rock Springs, but whatever this place may lack in authenticity it makes up for in charm—a rare commodity along this stretch of interstate. Moderate.

Top of the line in Rock Springs is the 114-room **Holiday Inn** (1675 Sunset Drive; 307-382-9200), which has an indoor heated swimming pool and a jacuzzi. The guest rooms have that *déjà vu* atmosphere that makes you feel only slightly away from home as you spend a night in the vast wasteland of southwestern Wyoming. Moderate.

In a similar price range is **The Inn at Rock Springs** (2518 Foothill Boulevard, Rock Springs; 307-382-9600), an ultramodern 148-unit hotel with a sports pub, room service and the best exercise facilities in town, including an indoor swimming pool, whirlpool spa and weight-exercise area. Guest rooms are recently remodeled, spacious and stylish. Moderate.

Holding's Little America (Route 80 Exit 68, Little America; 307-875-2400) is the showplace motor inn of the Great Divide Basin and was one of the world's first motels. All alone in one of the West's most godforsaken locations, Little America was built in 1932 by a local rancher who envisioned it as a way station for travelers stranded by fierce blizzards. Earl Holding, who bought the motor inn in the 1960s, upscaled the facilities and created a luxury motor-inn chain. The grounds are landscaped with neat lawns and evergreen trees. The 131 guest rooms are spacious and well lit, with earth-tone decor that makes you feel like you fit right in. Moderate.

The only lodging in the Fort Bridger area is the pleasant, ordinary **Wagon Wheel Motel** (270 North Main Street, Fort Bridger; 307-782-6361). The 55 guest rooms have the standard amenities, from showers to bolted-down televisions. Moderate.

A standout in contrast to the dozen or so motel-style accommodations that cluster around the interstate exits in Evanston is the **Pine Gables Bed & Breakfast** (1049 Center Street; 307-789-2069), framed by tall pine trees in a quiet residential area. The six guest rooms are in a historic 1883 mansion furnished with Eastlake-style antiques. Moderate.

ROCK SPRINGS–GREEN RIVER AREA RESTAURANTS

The scent of barbecued ribs sizzling over an open-pit fire lures diners to **Pam's Bar-B-Cue** (2506 Foothill Boulevard, Rock Springs; 307-362-1043). The fare at this no-frills establishment also includes barbecued chicken and beef brisket. Budget.

Among the half-dozen Chinese restaurants in the area—all of which also serve American dishes—the **Sands Cafe** (1549 9th Street, Rock Springs; 307-362-5633), specializing in Cantonese, Szechuan and Mandarin dishes, offers the widest selection and most exotic decor. Moderate.

Although familiar fast-food emporiums dominate the interstate exits around Rock Springs and Green River, both towns also have an abundance of full-service restaurants. One of the finest is **Ted's Supper Club** (9 Purple Sage Road, Rock

Rock Springs; 307-362-7323), specializing in steak-and-lobster in a relatively elegant atmosphere—candlelight, white tablecloths and heavy chairs. Open for dinner only. Moderate to deluxe.

Mexican food is also easy to find. In Green River, **Trudel's Restaurante** (3 East Flaming Gorge Way; 307-875-8040) is a family restaurant with European touches owned and operated by a husband-and-wife team—he's Mexican, she's German. The menu is a mix of American standards and Mexican dishes prepared for the palates of gringos who don't like spicy food. German specials are sometimes offered, too. Moderate.

If you *do* like spicy Mexican food the **Santa Fe Trail** (1635 Elk Street, Rock Springs; 307-362-5427), located just off the interstate in the American Family Inn, features Mexican-American and Native American specialties "made from scratch with the finest ingredients." Moderate.

ROCK SPRINGS–GREEN RIVER AREA SHOPPING

At **Bridger Trading Post** (Fort Bridger State Historic Site, Fort Bridger; 307-782-3842), modern-day mountain men can tell you about black-powder shooting and the various mountain-man rendezvous gatherings around the state while you gaze at Native American beadwork, handmade brass lamps, antelope-horn oil vials and other old-fashioned treasures that you may not see for sale anywhere else.

ROCK SPRINGS–GREEN RIVER AREA NIGHTLIFE

Both Rock Springs and Green River have big, tough bar scenes that cater to the high-paid oil riggers and mineworkers who don't have many other places to spend their earnings. Prostitution, drugs and gambling are wide-open secrets out here.

Check out the saloons along Railroad Avenue in Green River for raunchy nightlife. **The Brewery** (50 West Railroad Avenue; 307-875-6143), the **Ponderosa Bar & Lounge** (41 East Railroad Avenue; 307-875-9948) and the **Embassy Bar** (77 East Railroad Avenue; 307-875-5552) have pool tables, sad country songs playing on the jukebox, tables in dark corners and an occasional drunken fistfight.

ROCK SPRINGS–GREEN RIVER AREA PARKS

Seminoe State Park—This remote, sprawling reservoir, surrounded by huge white sand dunes and sagebrush country teeming with pronghorn antelope, is known for excellent birdwatching as well as boating to wild backcountry shores. At the north end of the park is the "Miracle Mile" of the North Platte River, so called because of its reputation for incredible trout fishing.

Facilities: Restrooms, picnic area, playground, trails, boat ramp; day-use fee, $2; information, 307-328-0115. *Swimming:* Permitted. *Fishing:* Excellent for brown, rainbow and cutthroat trout as well as walleye.

Camping: Permitted in 96 RV/tent sites (no hookups); $4 per night.

Getting there: The entrance is located 34 miles north of Sinclair on paved Seminoe Road.

Seedskadee National Wildlife Refuge—This 13,500-acre expanse along the Green River north of Route 25 is one of the best birdwatching areas in Wyoming. More than 170 species of migratory birds, including sandhill cranes, Canada geese and many species of ducks, rest here on their fall migration and breed here in the spring. The river attracts an astonishing variety of wildlife, from golden eagles to deer, antelope and even moose, making it a popular area for rafting and canoeing.

Facilities: Restrooms; information, 307-875-2187. *Fishing:* Good for rainbow trout.

Getting there: Take Route 372 north from Green River for 27 miles and turn northeast on the marked road to the refuge headquarters.

Flaming Gorge National Recreation Area—Most recreational facilities—and most of the scenery—along 91-mile-long Flaming Gorge Reservoir lie on the Utah side of the state line (for more information, see Chapter Five, "Utah Rockies"). Most of the shoreline on the Wyoming side is flat, brown, rocky and less than spectacular, with the exception of Firehole Canyon, where a ten-mile paved road winds through colorful desert geology on its way to the lakeshore. There are also boat ramps at Upper Marsh Creek on the east shore and Squaw Hollow on the west shore. The only full-service marina on the Wyoming side of the state line is Buckboard Marina on the west shore. Mountain biking is a popular fall and spring sport in the backcountry of the recreation area.

Facilities: Picnic areas, restrooms, boat ramps, marina with boat rentals; information, 801-784-3445. *Swimming:* Permitted at Firehole Canyon. *Fishing:* Good for mackinaw and rainbow trout, smallmouth bass and kokanee salmon.

Camping: Permitted at Firehole Canyon (38 RV/tent sites) and Buckboard Crossing (68 RV/tent sites), neither with hookups; $9 per night.

Getting there: To reach Firehole Canyon, turn west on a paved road 13 miles south of Rock Springs off Route 191. To reach Buckboard Crossing, drive 25 miles south of Green River on Route 530. From both highways, dozens of primitive dirt roads lead to virtually every cove along the shoreline.

Bear River State Park—Probably the best rest area on Route 80, this park has hiking and biking trails along a marshy stretch of the Bear River, offering opportunities for fishing and birdwatching. There is a large state tourist information center. Day use only.

Facilities: Restrooms, picnic area, trails, visitors center; day-use fee, $3; information, 307-789-6547. *Fishing:* Permitted.

Getting there: The park is located at Exit 6 on Route 80, on the east edge of Evanston.

Casper Area

Two-thirds of the world's population of pronghorn antelope live in the grasslands that stretch out in every direction from Casper, Wyoming. They are not true antelope but the sole living species of a family of animals that had no relatives in Asia, Africa or Europe. Pronghorns were hunted to near-extinction during the pioneer migration and railroad era of the late 1800s; by 1903, there were fewer than 5000 left in the world. Pronghorns were one of the first animals to be legally protected as an endangered species. Today, they number more than 500,000 and are no longer on the endangered list. In fact, herds of wild pronghorn antelope are one of the Casper area's most interesting and frequent sights.

Casper itself would be of little interest to sightseers but for the fact that it is the largest city along the old **Oregon Trail**, perhaps the most important route in U.S. history. Today, more than 350,000 vacationers follow this route each summer, an interesting and occasionally beautiful shortcut from the Midwest to Yellowstone National Park.

Tracing the Oregon Trail across Wyoming takes two days with an overnight stop in Casper. The first bit of history along the route is found 125 miles to the east, on the banks of the Platte River just off Route 26, at **Fort Laramie National Historic Site** (307-837-2221; admission). Eleven buildings from the old fur trading post and cavalry fort have been restored and furnished with antiques from the pioneer era. In the summer months, Park Service personnel don period costumes and re-enact 19th-century frontier life.

Eleven miles west along Route 26, near the town of Guernsey, are two Oregon Trail points of interest. At **Oregon Trail Ruts National Historic Landmark**, a mile south of town following Wyoming Avenue, you can get a vivid idea of how many covered wagons passed this way in the days before pavement. Along the self-guided trail the 150-year-old wagon ruts worn into the sandstone are as much as six feet deep! Two miles farther south, at **Register Cliff State Historic Site**, thousands of pioneers etched their names in the lower reaches of a 150-foot-high sandstone cliff. Admission is free at both sites.

Thirteen miles west of Guernsey, the old Oregon Trail route joins Route 25 and veers north through a sagebrush landscape. Another 48 fast miles bring you to **Douglas**, which grew up around another historic fort. Only two buildings—officers' quarters and an ordnance warehouse—remain from the days when **Fort Fetterman State Historic Site** (307-684-7629) was a cavalry outpost established to protect pioneers from both Native Americans and outlaw gangs. The old officers' quarters now serves as a museum recounting the fort's history.

Douglas has been the site of the Wyoming State Fair since 1905. In addition to the fair, held annually in the third week of August, the fairgrounds draw visitors year-round to see the free **Wyoming Pioneer Museum** (State Fairgrounds; 307-358-9288). Extensive state-owned collections of Native American and frontier artifacts include a full-size teepee, pioneer clothing and weapons, and a re-creation of an old-time saloon.

(Text continued on page 268.)

Wagon Trains on the Oregon Trail

Between the first organized wagon train expedition in 1842 and the completion of the first transcontinental railroad in 1869, the period of the great westward migration, 350,000 pioneers traveled the Oregon Trail, more than on all other routes combined.

Wagon trains preferred the route partly because it followed the wide, flat bed of the Platte River for nearly half its distance, making it easy to navigate across the vast prairie of Nebraska all the way to Fort Caspar (the site of present-day Casper, Wyoming). Then, too, the Oregon Trail was the only possible way to get a wagon train across the Rocky Mountains. Colorado's mountains could not be scaled by wagons loaded with household goods. Farther south, hostile Apaches made skirting around the south end of the Rockies through New Mexico and Arizona unthinkable.

The Great Divide Basin route (the Overland Trail), south of the Oregon Trail, would later be used by the Pony Express, Overland Stage, the Union Pacific transcontinental railroad and modern-day Route 80 because it was more direct than the Oregon Trail and crossed the Continental Divide at its lowest point. In the early days, though, before there were trains to haul water to way stations in the desert, wagon teams of horses, mules or oxen could not survive the barren crossing.

The Oregon Trail saw three major migrations, all beginning within a few years of one another and overlapping. The first wagon trains were organized by land developers, whose exaggerated tales of rich farmland for the taking in Oregon's Willamette Valley enticed families by the thousands away from the rampant poverty of northeastern industrial cities. Around the same time, the Mormons, a newly formed religious group on the run from intolerance and frequent mob violence, migrated in search of a spot to build a "new Zion" in the unexplored West. They followed the Oregon Trail as far as South Pass in Wyoming, then turned southward to reach their promised land on the shores of the Great Salt Lake. Within three years after the Oregon Trail was opened, gold was discovered in northern California, swelling the traffic along the wagon train route with thousands of would-be prospectors hoping to get rich quick at the trail's end. In April 1849, when news of the first California gold discoveries reached the East, 20,000 people set out on the Oregon Trail in a single month—more than the total number who had migrated West up to that time.

Many people headed west alone on horseback with nothing but what could be carried behind their saddles. A covered wagon—needed to carry a family and basic household goods—was expensive. To buy a wagon, a team of horses, mules or oxen, and food and supplies for the 2000-mile journey cost about $1200. This was a sizable sum, more than an average American family earned in a year.

At Independence Rock and other Oregon Trail landmarks, modern travelers find crosses and bright wildflowers on the graves of pioneers who did not survive the rugged six-month trip. About 20,000 people—one out of every 18 who traveled the Oregon Trail—died along the way. Although traditional Hollywood westerns would have us believe that the greatest hazard the pioneers faced was hostile Indians, the truth is that Indian violence was rare until the 1860s. The biggest killer on the Oregon Trail was cholera from drinking water that had been inadvertently polluted by earlier travelers.

Today, a number of outfitters offer backcountry wagon train trips that let modern travelers re-create the pioneer experience for a few days. Among them are **Trails West, Inc.** (65 Main Street, South Pass City; 307-332-7801) and **Bar-T-Five Outfitters** (P.O. Box 2140, Jackson, WY 83001; 307-733-5386).

With a population of 50,000, **Casper** is tied with Cheyenne as the largest city in Wyoming. As you drive into this small city situated on a bend in the Platte River, you may well wonder what it's doing out here in the middle of nowhere. A visit to the free **Fort Caspar Museum** (4001 Fort Caspar Road; 307-235-8462), named after an army lieutenant killed by Indians on the site, makes it clear that the former trading post, stage stop, telegraph office and cavalry fortress was originally of minor importance compared to other frontier outposts like Fort Bridger and Fort Laramie. In fact, Casper—the spelling of the name was changed by a post office error—had hidden resources that the others did not: vast deposits of oil, natural gas, coal and uranium. Oil wildcatters turned Casper into a boom town in 1915. It was another ten years before the city achieved lasting fame, when Harry Sinclair leased exclusive rights to the oil-rich Teapot Dome formation (located along Route 25, just 21 miles north of the city) from the federal government—without public bidding, thanks to political connections in President Warren G. Harding's cabinet. The Teapot Dome deal mushroomed into the biggest corruption scandal to rock the U.S. presidency before Watergate. The secretary of the interior went to prison. As attested by the green brontosaurus signs that still mean gasoline in these parts, Mr. Sinclair did not lose his oil rights.

Casper has most of the motels and restaurants in central Wyoming but remarkably little else to entice travelers. The best bet for sightseeing around Casper is a half-day loop drive south of the city that takes you through a variety of habitats on the slopes of **Casper Mountain**, where wildlife is so abundant that the state game and fish department has posted signs with a binoculars symbol to mark the best viewing areas. Following Casper Mountain Road south from Wyoming Boulevard near the Casper College campus, you enter a mixed ponderosa pine and aspen forest in the area of **Rotary Park** and **Garden Creek Falls** that provides habitat for deer, elk, beavers and even black bears. The road continues to **Lookout Point**, near the summit of the mountain, for a grand view of the city, the prairie and the river. Farther along the same route, short unpaved side roads lead to **Casper Mountain Park** with its Braille Nature Trail and the dense, dark lodgepole pine forest of **Crimson Dawn Park**. The pavement ends in a valley between Casper Mountain and Muddy Mountain, where **Circle Drive Loop**, a hard-packed gravel road, leads west through sage and juniper country filled with flowers and songbirds, then joins paved Route 487. To return to Casper via Jackson Canyon, turn right (northeast) on Route 220. To resume a westward trip along the Oregon Trail, turn left (southwest).

West of Casper, the old Oregon Trail departs from Route 25 and becomes the two-lane blacktop Route 220. Ten miles south of the city on this route is the **Jackson Canyon Eagle Sanctuary** (★) (Route 220). The cliffs surrounding the canyon are inhabited by bald eagles during the winter months and golden eagles year-round, both of which range for up to 100 miles and may be spotted anywhere in the area. A side road crosses the Platte River at **Bessemer Bend** (County Road 308), where rich soil deposited by floods sustains thick shrubbery that provides habitat for a myriad of wildlife, including deer, antelope, songbirds and raccoons, and is a major stopover for millions of migrating waterfowl in the spring and fall.

A 48-mile drive southwest of Casper brings you to **Independence Rock State Historic Site** (Route 220). The huge granite dome bulging 193 feet up from the surrounding grasslands and covering 27 acres was one of the most familiar landmarks on the Oregon Trail. The names of more than 5000 Oregon Trail travelers were carved here, though only a few dozen are visible from the foot trail that leads around the base of the massive rock. Most of the inscriptions are high on the dome, so you have to climb to see them. Besides being a marker for pioneers to gauge their progress across the featureless high plains, Independence Rock became one of the first "tourist traps" in the Rockies: as early as 1855, Mormon entrepreneurs established a business there, charging pioneers five dollars each to inscribe their names on the rock and thus "insure their immortality."

A few miles farther along stands another Oregon Trail landmark, the **Devil's Gate**, 330-foot-high cliffs flanking the Sweetwater River. Although the original Oregon Trail ran through the gate, it was later rerouted because of the danger of Indian attacks from the top of the cliffs. The gate stands near the original ranch house of the Tom Sun Ranch, one of the first cattle ranches in Wyoming, which has operated continuously since 1872.

From Independence Rock, the Oregon Trail continues along Routes 220 and 287 for about 100 empty miles to the Lander and South Pass City area. If the trip seems endless, imagine what it must have been like in a wagon train traveling at a top speed of 15 miles a day.

CASPER AREA HOTELS

The one truly historic hotel in the area is the **Hotel Higgins** (416 West Birch, Glenrock; 307-436-9212), 22 miles east of Casper in the little town of Glenrock. This venerable railroad hotel, built in 1916, has been refurbished with period antiques. The eight guest rooms have brass beds, armoires and so much old-fashioned charm that it provides the perfect antidote to a long day on the interstate. Budget to moderate.

With more than 30 motels and motor inns, Casper has a near-monopoly on lodging in central Wyoming. Competition keeps room rates remarkably low. Even the classiest accommodations in town, such as the sprawling 225-unit **Casper Hilton Inn** (800 North Poplar; 307-266-6000) with its spacious guest rooms complete with indoor swimming pool, jacuzzi, restaurants and cocktail lounge, have moderate rates. This and other large motor inns cluster around Exit 188 on Route 25, while smaller, independently owned motels—nearly all of them with rates in the budget range—line East Yellowstone Highway (Route 20/26) through downtown. Typical of the breed is the **Sage and Sand Motel** (901 West Yellowstone Highway; 307-237-2088). The 35 nearly contemporary, blandly decorated guest rooms have double beds; a few have kitchenettes. Budget.

In Casper, the **Durbin Street Inn Bed & Breakfast** (843 South Durbin Street; 307-577-5774) offers four guest rooms with shared baths in an antique-furnished 1917 home within walking distance of downtown. The inn has fireplaces and a large porch and patio. Moderate.

The most intriguing lodging in the region is to be found at the **Bessemer Bend Bed & Breakfast** (6905 Speas Road, Casper; 307-265-6819). On the site of the historic Goose Egg Ranch, a setting used in Owen Wister's classic western novel *The Virginian*, this bed and breakfast has three large guest rooms with shared bath. Amenities include a hot tub. Reservations are essential, especially during spring and fall waterfowl migrations, when the inn's location near the Bessemer Bend wetlands and the Jackson Canyon Eagle Sanctuary makes it a favorite haunt of birdwatchers. Moderate.

CASPER AREA RESTAURANTS

Seafood is the specialty at the **Crazy Crab** (144 South Center Street, Casper; 307-266-3474), where you can enjoy fish, crab, shrimp, clams and a variety of chowders in casual surroundings. There is also a varied soup-and-salad bar. Budget prices.

For Mexican food, one of the best choices among several south-of-the-border restaurants is the unpretentious little **La Casacita Mexican Café** (633 West Collins Drive, Casper; 307-234-7633), where house specialties include fajitas, *chile rellenos* and corn-shucked tamales. Budget.

Bosco's Italian Restaurante (847 East A Street, Casper; 307-265-9658) features a wide selection of Italian dishes, from spaghettini with white clam sauce and gnocchi with meat sauce to shrimp scampi and veal scaloppine Marsala. Diners are invited to create their own fettuccine from a selection of fresh vegetables, meat and fish. The atmosphere is pure traditional Italian restaurant, complete with red checkerboard tablecloths and candles dripping wax down the sides of empty Chianti bottles. Moderate.

Perhaps the finest dining in the Casper area is five miles south of town at the **Goose Egg Inn** (Route 220, Casper; 307-473-8838). Prime rib, steaks, seafood and the house specialty, pan-fried chicken, are served in an Old West atmosphere at this picturesque inn, which was once part of the historic Goose Egg Ranch. Dinner only. Deluxe.

Armor's Restaurant (4800 Cy Avenue, Casper; 307-235-3000) serves a varied menu with Continental flair in a romantic atmosphere. The menu features Cajun entrées and veal specialties as well as the usual steak, chicken and seafood fare. Dinner nightly; lunch on weekdays only. Deluxe.

CASPER AREA SHOPPING

Your best shopping bet in Casper may be western wear. **Lou Taubert Ranch Outfitters** (125 East 2nd Street; 307-234-2500) is a complete cowboy department store with nine floors of western fashions for men, women and children, as well as gifts, western art, saddles, specialty foods and more than 10,000 pairs of cowboy boots in stock.

CASPER AREA NIGHTLIFE

The bar scene in Casper seems to consist almost entirely of small neighborhood bars, biker roadhouses and cocktail lounges in motor inns. The one really noteworthy nightspot in town is the **Beacon Club** (4100 West Yellowstone Highway; 307-577-1503), featuring live country-and-western bands and a young, lively crowd. South of town, the **Goose Egg Inn** (Route 220, Casper; 307-473-8838) starts the evening as a classy restaurant and stays open late as a dim cocktail lounge where the mood is as romantic as it gets out here on the frontier.

CASPER AREA PARKS

Guernsey State Park—This Platte River reservoir nestled among sheltering cliffs has sandy beaches and scenic side canyons. A collection of historic Civilian Conservation Corps buildings from the Great Depression era houses a museum of natural history and Native American and pioneer artifacts.

Facilities: Restrooms, groceries, picnic areas, boat ramp, marina, hiking trail; day-use fee, $3; information, 307-836-2334. *Swimming:* Permitted. *Fishing:* Walleye, largemouth bass, crappie, bluegill and catfish.

Camping: Permitted in 142 RV/tent sites (no hookups); $4 per night.

Getting there: Located off Route 26, just north of Guernsey.

Glendo State Park—This reservoir on the Platte River is one of Wyoming's prettiest lakes, with sandy beaches and crystal-clear water. High rock bluffs surround the reservoir, protecting it from the wind. It is a popular recreational site for boating, fishing, hiking, waterskiing and windsurfing.

Facilities: Restrooms, picnic area, playground, boat ramp, marina, hiking trails; day-use fee, $3; information, 307-735-4433. *Swimming:* Permitted. *Fishing:* Walleye and catfish.

Camping: Permitted in 165 RV/tent sites (no hookups); $4 per night.

Getting there: It's five miles east of the town of Glendo, off Route 25.

Edness Kimball Wilkins State Park—The cottonwood-lined banks of the Platte River form the setting for this day-use park designed for picnicking, fishing and birdwatching. Deer are frequently seen in the park. A walking trail following the river makes this a beautiful rest spot along Route 25. From the same highway exit, a short drive south on Hat Six Road leads to several marked wildlife-viewing areas on the sagebrush prairie where pronghorn antelope, sage grouse and prairie dogs are abundant. Day use only.

Facilities: Restrooms, picnic area, playground, beach, boat ramp; day-use fee, $3; information, 307-577-5150. *Swimming:* Permitted. *Fishing:* Good for catfish, pike and rainbow trout.

Getting there: Located off Route 20/26/87, eight miles east of Casper. Take Exit 182 on Route 25 north and turn east after crossing the railroad tracks.

Lander Area

The **Wind River Range**—a wall of granite spanning more than 90 miles from South Pass north to the Jackson area—is some of Wyoming's finest back-country for recreation. Only a few unpaved roads lead into these mountains; the higher reaches are designated as three vast wilderness areas: on the eastern slope, the Popo Agie Wilderness west of Lander and the Fitzpatrick Wilderness near Dubois; and on the western slope, the Bridger Wilderness, the largest federally designated wilderness area in Wyoming. A network of hiking and horse trails totaling more than 800 miles provides access to hundreds of lakes and streams. Much of the eastern slope of the mountains is part of the Wind River Indian Reservation and is off-limits to outsiders. The Wind River Range contains Gannett Peak, the highest in Wyoming (13,804 feet), and more than a dozen other mountains that rank among the state's highest.

The main town on the east side of the Wind River Range is **Lander**, one of the oldest towns in Wyoming. The town itself, far removed from major interstate routes as well as from the major tourism area surrounding Yellowstone and Jackson, retains the peaceful, amazingly ordinary character of 1950s small-town America despite its growing mystique as the spiritual home of environmentalism in Wyoming. It's a one-story town with a Norman Rockwell main street and neat, shady residential areas of modest turn-of-the-century frame houses. Lander's **Fremont County Pioneer Museum** (630 Lincoln Street; 307-332-4137; admission) has nine rooms full of everything from saddles and rock specimens to one of the best collections anywhere of old Shoshone and Arapaho artifacts.

A good place to start an exploration of the mountains around Lander is the **Scenic Loop Drive** to South Pass, which follows Route 131 (called Sinks Canyon Road, then Louis Lake Road as it enters the national forest and the pavement ends). To close the loop on this half-day scenic drive, return from South Pass City to Lander on the main highway, Route 28.

The loop drive takes you first to **Sinks Canyon State Park**, a limestone canyon six miles west of town, where an easy eleven-and-a-half-mile walking trail takes visitors past waterfalls, roaring whitewater torrents and riverbanks ablaze with wildflowers. The canyon is named for an odd phenomenon called "the sinks": midway down the canyon, the powerful Popo Agie River simply vanishes, plunging into an underground cavern from which it gushes back up to surface level a quarter-mile downhill.

The Oregon Trail's highest point, **South Pass** (7650 feet above sea level), on the Continental Divide, marked the halfway point on the pioneers' 2000-mile journey from the Missouri River to the West Coast. Here, at the southernmost tip of the rugged Wind River Range, wagon trains rendezvoused before descending steeply from the high plains into arid basin-and-range terrain that stretched for another thousand miles. In 1867, less than two years before the transcontinental railroad would divert the flow of settlers onto its more southerly route, a rich vein of gold was discovered at South Pass. As the Carissa Mine went into big-scale operation, hordes of prospectors flocked to South Pass to search for the mother lode from which the vein originated. Thirty more miles of the vein were opened. Within less than a year, South Pass City had grown into a community of more than 2000 people. But the South Pass gold boom was short-lived. The Carissa vein played out in just five years, and the mother lode was never found. By 1872, South Pass City was virtually a ghost town.

Today, 24 of the 250 buildings originally constructed in the boom town still stand at **South Pass City State Historic Site** (Route 28; 307-332-3684; admission), including the old South Pass Hotel, the Carissa Saloon, the South Pass jail, a Masonic lodge, a stamp mill, a livery stable, a butcher shop and miners' cabins. Free from touristy commercialism, South Park City is one of the best-preserved and most picturesque old mining boom towns in the Rocky Mountain West.

About four miles northeast of South Pass City on an unpaved back road, **Atlantic City** also survives from the same mining boom. In its heyday it was a suburb of South Pass City with a population of only about 500; unlike the larger town, Atlantic City was never completely abandoned. Some residents work in a still-operating gold mine and nearby iron strip mine, while others run small tourist shops in old miners' shacks.

To the north of Lander lies the vast, two-million-acre **Wind River Indian Reservation**. The only reservation in Wyoming, it is shared by the Shoshone and Arapaho people. The two tribes have never merged. They live in small towns along different roads through separate parts of the reservation. About three-fourths of the reservation is wild country encompassing about half the eastern slope of the Wind River Range as well as the Owl Creek Mountains to the north. One or another of the reservation towns hosts a powwow, rodeo or other event almost every weekend during the summer months. The events are open to the public. For current information, contact the **Northern Arapahoe Business Council** (P.O. Box 396, Fort Washakie, WY 82514; 307-332-6120) and the **Shoshone Business Council** (P.O. Box 538, Fort Washakie, WY 82514).

Heading northwest from Lander on Route 287 (the most direct route to the Yellowstone area) through the Shoshone part of the reservation, you pass **Fort Washakie**, named for the chief who signed the treaty granting the huge reservation to the Shoshone in 1868. Though Washakie is remembered as a friend of the white man, he was no wimp. The next village up the highway, **Crowheart**, marks the spot where in 1866, according to legend, Chief Washakie killed a Crow chief in single combat and ate his heart. Modern historians are quick to point out that the legend is not factual. In truth, Washakie did not eat his enemy's heart; he merely paraded it among his people on the tip of his lance. Upon his death in 1900 at the age of 96, Washakie became the first Native American ever buried in a U.S. Army cemetery with full military honors. **Chief Washakie's grave** can still be seen in the desolate, unlandscaped graveyard just outside the Fort Washakie compound. In a more remote location, about a mile down the road on the other side of the highway, is **Sacajawea's grave**. The renowned Sacajawea, a Shoshone woman by birth, was kidnapped by a rival tribe and sold to a French fur trader who married her. The couple signed on to guide the Lewis and Clark expedition 3000 miles from the Missouri River to the mouth of the Columbia River between Oregon and Washington. She returned to the Shoshone people many years later and died on the Wind River Indian Reservation in 1884 at an advanced age—78 years after the Lewis and Clark expedition.

The Arapaho people moved to the reservation ten years after the treaty, in 1878, after Shoshone warriors joined forces with the U.S. cavalry to conquer them. Legend has it that Washakie's tribe asked that the Arapaho, their traditional enemies, be confined nearby so that the victorious Shoshone could keep an eye on them. Today, the Arapaho live in the southeast part along Routes 132 and 138 around Ethete, Arapahoe and St. Stephens.

The oldest of several Christian missions on the reservation is **St. Stephen's Mission** (307-856-7806), three miles south of Riverton. Here, for three years, Jesuit missionaries held mass for Arapaho converts in tents before completing a convent and other mission buildings. The present church is brilliantly decorated with abstract Arapaho designs inside and out. The church has a museum with old photographs and antique beadwork, paintings and other creations on display. There are also a working art studio and a store where contemporary arts and crafts are offered for sale.

The federal government betrayed its promise to Chief Washakie in 1906, just six years after his death, when it "withdrew" a half-million-acre tract of farmland north of Riverton in the heart of the reservation, opening it to homesteaders. Today, the primarily Anglo population of **Riverton** (9200) exceeds the total population of the Wind River Indian Reservation (7500).

Continuing north on Route 287 beyond the reservation will bring you to **Dubois**, the midpoint on the trip from Lander to Jackson. Dubois has traditionally been a ranching community, so it's not surprising that as resort consciousness has radiated out from the Jackson area, dude ranching has become the main industry in these parts. As the gateway to the glacier-clad high country of the Fitzpatrick Wilderness in the northern Wind River Range, Dubois also attracts growing numbers of backpackers. The main sight worth stopping for is the **National Bighorn Sheep Interpretive Center** (907 West Ramshorn Road; 307-455-3429; admission).

You can also reach Jackson and the Yellowstone area by driving up the west side of the Wind River Range on Route 191, the shortest route from the Flaming Gorge and Rock Springs area. The only community of any size on this side of the mountains is **Pinedale**. Pinedale is too far off the beaten path to be included in the mainstream of northwestern Wyoming tourism, so its economy is based primarily on outfitters who guide hunting and fishing expeditions into the Bridger Wilderness, Wyoming's largest wilderness area.

LANDER AREA HOTELS

Lander doesn't have any of the sprawling name-brand motor inns that dominate almost all other southern Wyoming towns. Its motels are all of the independent ma-and-pa type, with inexpensive rates, but none is very large so they can fill up quickly. (For national-chain motels, visitors must go to the farming center of Riverton, 24 miles northeast across the Wind River Indian Reservation.)

The largest motel in town is the **Pronghorn Lodge** (150 East Main Street; 307-332-3940), with 42 spacious, comfortably furnished rooms and a whirlpool spa. Rates are moderate during the summer and budget in the off-season.

Another good bet is the two-story **Silver Spur Motel** (340 North 10th Street, Lander; 307-332-5189), which has 25 air-conditioned rooms with queen-size beds, including three two-bedroom family units, and a heated pool. Budget to moderate.

A number of small bed and breakfasts have sprung up in the Lander area. Right in town, the **Country Fare Bed & Breakfast** (904 Main Street; 307-332-5906) offers two guest rooms with shared bath in a Victorian home with unabashedly romantic decor. Open May through October only. Full breakfast is included in the moderate rates.

Five miles northwest of town, **Edna's Bed & Breakfast** (53 North Fork Road, Lander; 307-332-3175) offers two upstairs bedrooms with shared bath in the main house of a working cattle ranch. Children are welcome. Moderate rates include a full breakfast.

For a more authentic ranch stay, the **Cross Mill Iron Ranch** (Crowheart; 307-455-2414) accommodates guests whose main interest is horseback riding. Guests may participate in cowboy work on this 5000-acre cattle ranch, and a rodeo is held every Sunday afternoon. Accommodations are in pleasant but not lavish individual log cabins. Moderate.

The Dubois region has an abundance of guest ranches. Some family-oriented ranches offer a full roster of activities that may make you feel like you're at summer camp or Club Med. For instance, the **Double Bar J Ranch** (P.O. Box 1039, Dubois, WY 82513; 307-455-2681, fax 307-455-3360), situated 20 miles west of Dubois in Shoshone National Forest, offers horseback riding, mountain biking, pack trips, fishing, skeet shooting, bonfires, horseshoes, volleyball and, in the winter, snowmobiling, cross-country skiing and dog sledding. Accommodations are in log cabins with contemporary furnishings. Gourmet dinners are included in the deluxe rates.

Pinedale, too, is dude ranch country. In fact, ranch accommodations outnumber motels in the area. Many ranches in Bridger National Forest near Pinedale are especially geared toward fishing. The **Flying A Ranch** (Route 1, Box 7, Pinedale; 307-367-2385), for instance, features outstanding trout fishing at the ranch and on pack trips to mountain streams and lakes. Accommodations are in luxuriously appointed log cabins with private baths, separate living rooms, porches and fireplaces or woodburning stoves. Open mid-June through mid-October only. Deluxe.

Half Moon Lake Guest Ranch (P.O. Box 983, Pinedale, WY 82941; 307-367-2516, fax 307-367-6538), situated on Half Moon Lake ten miles north of Pinedale, has just five guest cabins. Unlike many of the area's guest ranches, the lodge accepts overnight and weekend guests and does not require a minimum stay. Boat rentals are available. Other activities at this year-round resort include horseback riding, waterskiing, cross-country skiing, ice fishing and snowshoeing. Moderate to deluxe.

LANDER AREA RESTAURANTS

A favorite restaurant in the town of Lander, **The Commons Restaurant** (170 East Main Street; 307-332-5149) serves breakfast, lunch and dinner in a family-oriented environment incongruously decorated in an English foxhunt motif. The menu features beef and seafood, and there is a salad bar. Moderate.

For the best salad bar in town, try **The Hitching Rack** (Route 287, Lander; 307-332-4322), another steak-and-seafood restaurant designed with family dining in mind. Moderate.

For something completely different in this all-American small town, try the **Big Noi Restaurant** (453 Main Street; 307-332-3102). Their Thai food may not quite rival the best you've ever tried, but it is unquestionably the best Thai food in Lander.

Improbable as it may seem, most of the fine dining in the Lander area is found in the near–ghost town of Atlantic City, about 20 miles south of Lander on a back road off Route 28 near South Pass. **Atlantic City Mercantile** (307-332-5145) serves dinner in an authentic mine camp setting with low ceilings and oil lanterns. Dinners feature rib-eye steaks smoke-grilled over aspen embers. Dinner only. Deluxe.

Also in Atlantic City, the **Miner's Delight Inn** (307-332-3513) features lavish six-course fixed-price dinners nightly. The well-publicized inn enjoys an international reputation, though many frontier gourmands contend that it no longer measures up to the competition. Deluxe.

For basic stick-to-your-ribs barbecue, burgers or pizza, greasy and good, try **Buckaroo Barbecue** (318 West Ramshorn Street, Dubois; 307-455-2021), a western-style diner with paintings by local artists on the walls. The local characters who tend to hang out here in the morning offer a people-watching experience along with your morning coffee. Budget.

The **Wild West Deli** (128 East Ramshorn Street, Dubois; 307-455-3354) has a good salad bar, along with a tasty array of homemade soups and sandwiches. Wooden booths, wood paneling and touches of ranch decor set the mood. Lunch only. Budget.

In Dubois, fine dining is found at the **Ramshorn Inn** (202 East Ramshorn Street; 307-455-2400), where the fare is the usual steaks, prime rib and seafood, and the ambience is candle-lit and rather rustic. Moderate.

For inexpensive eats in Pinedale, try **Calamity Jane's** (30 West Pine Street; 307-367-2469), a down-home café serving hamburgers, french fries, pizza and burritos. Budget.

Although dining options are somewhat limited in tiny Pinedale, you won't be disappointed with the fare at **McGregor's Pub** (25 North Franklin Avenue; 307-367-4443). Prime rib is the specialty, and there is a wider-than-usual selection of seafood, all served in a warm, contemporary western atmosphere. Seating is available on the large outdoor patio in the summer. Deluxe.

LANDER AREA SHOPPING

A number of western artists make their homes in the Lander area and show their work in studios and galleries here. Worth visiting are the **Tom Lucas Studio and Art Gallery** (245 North Fork Road, Lander; 307-332-3406), featuring wildlife and western themes in oil paintings and pen-and-ink drawings, and **Bar-Bar-A's Art Gallery** (555 Main Street, Lander; 307-332-7798), showing oils, acrylics, watercolors and photographs by local artists.

Probably the best prospect for souvenir hunting in the region is **St. Stephens Indian Mission** (St. Stephens; 307-332-9664), south of Riverton on the Wind River Indian Reservation. The church-operated store provides a way for local Arapaho artisans to sell their beadwork, carvings and other arts and crafts directly to the public. Contemporary and traditional Shoshone arts are exhibited at the **R. V. Greeves Art Gallery** (53 North Fork Road, Fort Washakie; 307-332-3557). Native American jewelry and beadwork can also be found in the **A & P Pawn Shop** (143 North 2nd Street, Lander; 307-332-7043).

LANDER AREA NIGHTLIFE

A few local bars in Lander have dancing on weekends. For country-and-western music, try **Nemo's Long Branch Saloon** (432 Route 287; 307-332-7742), also known as Barney's; for rock, the **One Shot Lounge** (695 Main Street; 307-332-2692).

In Dubois, you'll find live country-and-western at the **Ramshorn Inn** (202 East Ramshorn Street; 307-455-2444) and rock at the **Outlaw Saloon** (204 West Ramshorn Street; 307-455-2387).

There's live country music in Pinedale on weekends at the **Stockman's Bar** (16 North Maybell Avenue; 307-367-4562).

LANDER AREA PARKS

Boysen State Park—This large reservoir on the Wind River, flanking the eastern edge of the Wind River Indian Reservation, is a popular spot for boating, windsurfing, waterskiing and other water sports. The lake is nearly 20 miles long, with access at both ends, and the water is delightfully warm in the summer months. The upper end of the lake meets the mouth of the spectacular Wind River Canyon.

Facilities: Restrooms, picnic area, playground, hiking trails, swimming beach, boat ramp, marina, grocery store; information, 307-876-2796. *Swimming:* Permitted. *Fishing:* Good for brown and rainbow trout, walleye, sauger, smallmouth bass and crappie.

Camping: Permitted in 180 RV/tent sites (no hookups); $4 a night.

Getting there: Access is via any of several entrance roads off Route 20 north of Shoshoni.

Shoshone National Forest—This rugged 2,400,000-acre national forest spans the east side of the Wind River Range as well as all the forest land adjoining the eastern boundary of Yellowstone National Park. Its peaks and remote canyons are home to moose, elk, grizzly bears and a host of other wildlife. Two popular hiking areas in the Wind River Range, the Popo Agie Wilderness, south of the Wind River Indian Reservation, and the Fitzpatrick Wilderness, north of the reservation, contain glaciers, hundreds of natural lakes and Gannett Peak (13,804 feet), the highest mountain in Wyoming.

Facilities: Hiking trails; information, 307-527-6241. *Fishing:* Good for trout in many lakes and streams throughout the forest.

Camping: Permitted in four campgrounds with 66 RV/tent sites in the Lander area and three campgrounds with 48 RV/tent sites in the Dubois area (no hookups). Fees for developed sites are $6 to $8 a night.

Getting there: Access to the southern part of the Wind River Range is from Lander via the Sink Canyon and Louis Lake roads, and to the northern part from Dubois via Route 257 to Trail Lake.

Bridger-Teton National Forest—This 3,400,000-acre national forest encompasses the entire western slope of the Wind River Range. The west side of the mountains receives more rainfall than the east side, so streams and lakes are everywhere in the pine, spruce and fir forests that cling to the mountain slopes. Virtually the entire Wind River Range part of this national forest has been set aside as the roadless Bridger Wilderness, the largest federally designated wilderness area in Wyoming.

Facilities: Hiking trails; information, 307-739-5400. *Fishing:* Good for trout in hundreds of lakes and streams.

Camping: Ten campgrounds in the Pinedale area have a total of 158 RV/tent sites (no hookups), nearly all on lakeshores; $5 to $7 per night.

Getting there: The main forest access is from Pinedale via the Fremont Lake Road.

The Sporting Life

FISHING

Trout are by far the most common sport fish in almost all Wyoming lakes, river and streams. Rainbow trout are the favorite stocked variety; others include brown, brook and cutthroat. A few fishing areas in southern Wyoming boast rarer trout species such as the golden trout found in the Popo Agie River near Lander and the splake found in nearby Louis Lake. Some large, low-elevation reservoirs have warmwater species, particularly catfish, and walleye; Flaming Gorge Reservoir and a few other lakes are stocked with largemouth and smallmouth bass.

CHEYENNE-LARAMIE AREA In Saratoga, **Great Rocky Mountain Outfitters** (216 East Walnut Street; 307-326-8750) organizes guided fishing trips on the North Platte and Encampment rivers.

ROCK SPRINGS–GREEN RIVER AREA Although there are no fishing outfitters in the area, **Buckboard Marina** (Route 530, Green River; 307-875-6927) rents boats on Flaming Gorge Reservoir and can provide fishing tackle and bait.

CASPER AREA Fishing trips to several parts of the state can be arranged in Casper through **High Plains Angler** (1717 East Yellowstone Highway; 307-234-4700) and **Wyoming's Choice** (513 North Lennox Street; 307-234-3870).

LANDER AREA In Lander, fishing expeditions to backcountry lakes in the Wind River Range are available through **Lander Llama Company Wilderness Outfitting** (2024 Mortimer Lane; 307-332-5624). Llamas carry the backpacks, camping gear and fishing tackle while humans hike unencumbered.

SKIING

The **Snowy Range Ski Area** (Route 130; 307-745-5750), 32 miles west of Laramie, has downhill skiing. In the Rock Springs–Green River area, west along Route 80, you'll find downhill skiing at the small municipal **Eagle Rock Ski Area** (County Road 180, Evanston; 307-789-1770). In the Casper area, downhill slopes are found at the **Hogadon Ski Area** (Route 252; 307-235-8499) and on **Mount Casper**, where there are also good cross-country trails. As you might expect from Laramie's large student population, cross-country skiing is a very popular winter sport in the nearby Snowy Range as well as in the Pole Mountain area between Cheyenne and Laramie. In the Casper area, cross-country trails are found on **Mount Casper**.

SKI RENTALS In the Cheyenne-Laramie area, **Fine Edge** (1660-E North 4th Street, Laramie; 307-745-4499) rents downhill and cross-country skis, as well as snowboards. **Cross Country Connection** (1774 Snowy Range Road, Laramie; 307-721-2851) is your conncction for nordic equipment. The **Snowy Range Ski Area** (Route 130; 307-745-5750) offers downhill ski rentals. Cross-country skis are available at the **Green River Recreation Center** (1775 Hitching Post Drive, Green River; 307-875-4772). In Casper, try **Mountain Sports** (543 South Center; 307-266-1136), or the **Hogadon Ski Area** (Routc 252; 307-235-8499), south of Casper. In Lander, nordic skis can be rented at **Freewheel Sports** (149 Main Street; 307-332-6616).

GOLF

CHEYENNE-LARAMIE AREA Cheyenne's 18-hole **Municipal Golf Course** (4801 Central Avenue; 307-637-6418) is located north of town, adjacent to Lions Park. The nine-hole executive golf course at **Little America Hotel & Resort** (2800 West Lincolnway, Cheyenne; 307-775-8400) is also open to the public. In Laramie, there is the 18-hole **Jacoby Park Golf Course** (North 30th Street; 307-745-3111).

ROCK SPRINGS–GREEN RIVER AREA Both the **White Mountain Golf Course** (1820 Yellowstone Road, Rock Springs; 307-382-5030) and the golf course at the **Rolling Green Country Club** (west of Green River; 307-875-6200) are open to the public.

CASPER AREA Besides the **Casper Municipal Golf Course** (2120 Allendale Boulevard, Casper; 307-234-1037), there are municipal courses in other towns along Route 25 east of Casper: the **Douglas Community Club** (Douglas; 307-358-5099) and the **Glenrock Golf Course** (911 West Grove, Glenrock; 307-436-5560).

LANDER AREA The courses at the **Lander Golf & Country Club** (Capital Hill, Lander; 307-332-4653) and the **Riverton Country Club** (4275 Country Club Road, Riverton; 307-856-4779) are open to the public.

TENNIS

Tennis is a year-round sport at the **Cheyenne Frontier Days Indoor Tennis Center** (Frontier Park, Cheyenne; 307-778-7280). There are indoor tennis courts at the **Rock Springs Recreation Center** (3900 Sweetwater Drive, Rock Springs; 307-382-3265)

HORSEBACK RIDING

CHEYENNE-LARAMIE AREA In Cheyenne, **Blue Ribbon Horse Center** (406 North Fort Access Road; 307-634-5975) rents horses. At **Terry Bison Ranch** (51 Route 25 Service Road, Cheyenne; 307-638-0574) you can take guided dinner rides around the ranch. **Two Bars Seven Ranch** (Route 287, Tie Siding; 307-742-6072), a guest ranch south of Laramie near the Colorado state line, offers horseback rentals to non-guests.

LANDER AREA Contact **Great Divide Tours** (336 Focht Road, Lander; 307-332-3123) for guided horseback trips into the Wind River Range. All-day horseback tours of the South Pass area, following old trails past pioneer grave markers and settlers' cabins on the way to Sweetwater Canyon, are available from **Trails West, Inc.** (65 Main Street, South Pass City; 307-332-7801). Trails West also offers overnight wildlife photography trips into the backcountry of the Wind River Range and three-day covered wagon trips along the Oregon Trail.

PACK TRIPS

South of Laramie near the Colorado state line, **Two Bars Seven Ranch** (Route 287, Tie Siding; 307-742-6072), offers pack trips. In the Lander area, **Trails West, Inc.** (65 Main Street, South Pass City; 307-332-7801) has three-day covered wagon trips along the Oregon Trail.

BICYCLING

Mountain biking has not swept southern Wyoming the way it has more populous Colorado. Though the mountains, the prairies and even the Great Divide Basin desert have plenty of easy-riding back roads and trails, bicycle rentals are a rarity. An extensive network of forest roads and jeep trails makes the portion of Medicine Bow National Forest west of Laramie and south of the Snowy Range Scenic Byway a mountain bikers' paradise. The Casper Mountain area offers a diversity of cycling terrain, from open prairie to alpine forests and canyons. Lander, the center of the region's environmental movement, has more mountain bikers than anyplace else in the area. Bike shops in Lander and Riverton have maps of hundreds of miles of forest roads and trails that climb far into the Wind River Range.

BIKE RENTALS In Laramie, mountain bikes are for rent at **CycleFit Bicycle and Fitness Superstore** (3236 Grand Avenue; 307-721-4135) and in Casper at **Mountaineer's Mercantile** (8455 Casper Mountain Road; 307-577-6004). **Freewheel Sports** (149 Main Street; 307-332-6616) is the mountain-bike rental place in Lander. Rentals are also available at **Out Sportin'** (310 East Main, Riverton; 307-856-1373).

HIKING

All distances listed for hiking trails are one-way unless otherwise noted.

CHEYENNE-LARAMIE AREA Between Cheyenne and Laramie, the area around Vedauwoo is popular for hiking. The main artery is the **Headquarters National Recreation Trail** (5 miles), which runs around Pole Mountain from the Summit Rest Area east of Laramie. In the Snowy Range west of Laramie, the **Medicine Bow Peak Trail** (3 miles) ascends 1600 feet from the trailhead at Lake Marie to the 12,013-foot summit of the highest mountain in the area; the **Lost Lake Trail** (3.5 miles) branches off midway up the mountain and leads to another alpine lake.

LANDER AREA Hundreds of miles of wilderness hiking trails in the Wind River Range have given the mountains a reputation for the finest hiking in Wyoming. A spectacular short hike is the **Popo Agie Falls Trail** (1.5 miles), which leads from the trailhead a few miles above Sinks Canyon State Park to a series of roaring waterfalls that plunge as much as 60 feet. For long hikes along the Continental Divide, main access trails include the **Middle Fork Trail**, which also starts near the upper end of Popo Agie Canyon, and the easier **Sheeps Bridge Trail** from Worthen Meadow Reservoir on Louis Lake Road. The two trails merge after three miles and climb into the high country of the Popo Agie Wilderness, where various trails fork off to places like Ice Lakes (12 miles), Sweetwater Gap (16 miles) and the magnificent Cirque of the Towers (22 miles).

Farther north, at Trail Lake, 12 miles south of Dubois on gravel County Road 257, several trails lead into the Fitzpatrick Wilderness. Of these, the most dramatic is the difficult **Glacier Trail** (23 miles), which winds among cold mountain lakes to Dinwoody Glacier, high on the slope of Gannett Peak (13,804 feet), the highest mountain in Wyoming.

On the west side of the Wind River Range, 12 miles south of Pinedale, paved Boulder Lake Road leads to a trailhead on the eastern tip of the reservoir, where a network of trails meanders through an area of the Bridger Wilderness containing literally hundreds of lakes. **Horseshoe Lake** (11 miles from the trailhead) is among the most popular destinations. Other major trailheads for the Bridger Wilderness include those at the end of Fremont Lake Road and Willow Creek Road, both of which offer entry into a vast network of more than a dozen interconnecting trails that span the full 60-mile length of Wyoming's largest designated wilderness area.

Transportation

BY CAR

Cheyenne is at the intersection of **Route 25**, which follows the eastern edge of the Rockies from New Mexico to Canada, and **Route 80**, the most direct transcontinental truck route between Chicago and San Francisco. If you go west from Cheyenne, Route 80 will carry you past Laramie, Rock Springs and Green River.

Heading north on Route 25 will bring you to the Casper area. Between Cheyenne and Casper, Exit 92 from Route 25 puts you onto the eastern part of the Oregon Trail. West of Casper, **Route 20/26** is the most direct route to Grand Teton and Yellowstone national parks. History and light traffic combine to make the old Oregon Trail (**Route 220** from Casper to Three Rivers, then **Route 287** to Lander) an attractive alternative.

Following Route 287 north from Lander will bring you to Grand Teton and Yellowstone national parks by way of Dubois, the northern gateway to the Wind River Range.

There are two ways to reach Pinedale, the only settlement on the western slope of the Wind River Range. The faster one is north on **Route 191** from Exit 104 on Route 80 at Rock Springs. The slower one begins on **Route 28**, which skirts the southern tip of the Wind River Range from Lander via South Pass City, then joins **Route 191**, which travels up the western slope of the Wind River Range and offers a spectacle of nonstop mountain scenery all the way to Jackson.

BY AIR

There are no direct flights from most regions to anywhere in southern Wyoming. Commuter planes transport Wyoming air travelers to the international airport in Denver. Continental Express and United Express serve the **Cheyenne Airport** and Casper's **Natrona County International Airport**. Delta Airlines operates Sky West between Casper and Salt Lake City. The **Rock Springs Airport** is serviced by Continental Express. Continental Express and United Express fly into the **Riverton Regional Airport**.

BY BUS

Greyhound Bus Lines (1503 Capitol Avenue, Cheyenne; 307-634-7744) operates several buses a day in both directions on Route 80. Located at the same station, **Powder River Transportation** (307-635-1327) provides transportation to Casper and northern Wyoming destinations.

Greyhound Bus Lines also stops in Laramie (1559 McQue Street; 307-742-5188), Rawlins (301 West Cedar Street; 307-324-5496) and Rock Springs (1655 Sunset Boulevard; 307-362-2931).

Powder River Transportation services Casper (596 North Poplar Street; 307-266-1904) and Lander (206 East 2nd Street; 307-876-2466).

BY TRAIN

Amtrak (800-872-7245) offers east-west passenger service to Cheyenne and Laramie on the "Pioneer," which runs from Denver to Portland and Seattle and back. The Cheyenne station is about five miles south of town, and shuttle vans carry arriving travelers to the city center. The Laramie station is on the southern edge of town at 2272 Snowy Range Road.

CAR RENTALS

In Cheyenne, car-rental agencies operating from Cheyenne Airport include **Avis Rent A Car** (800-331-1212), **Dollar Rent A Car** (800-800-4000) and **Hertz Rent A Car** (800-654-3131).

The Rock Springs Municipal Airport has desks for **Avis Rent A Car** (800-331-1212) and **Hertz Rent A Car** (800-654-3131).

Car-rental agencies located at the Casper airport include **Avis Rent A Car** (800-331-1212), **Budget Rent A Car** (800-527-0700) and **Hertz Rent A Car** (800-654-3131).

The car-rental agencies nearest to the Lander area are at the Riverton Regional Airport. They include **Avis Rent A Car** (800-331-1212) and **Hertz Rent A Car** (800-654-3131).

TAXIS

Taxi service in Cheyenne is provided by **Yellow Cab Company** (307-638-3333) and in Laramie by **Laramie Taxi Service** (307-745-8294). The Rock Springs–Green River area is served by **Sweetwater Taxi** (307-362-3131) and **Downtown Taxi** (307-382-6161). In Casper, taxi service from the airport is provided by **RCCab** (307-235-5203). The only taxi service to Lander and other communities on the eastern slope of the Wind River Range is Riverton's **Cowboy Taxi** (307-856-7444).

CHAPTER SEVEN

Yellowstone and Jackson Hole

Recipe for a great trip:

Start with the world's oldest and best-known national park, Yellowstone. Add what may be North America's most spectacular mountain range, the Tetons. Throw in the dramatic scenery of hot springs, geysers and river gorges. Stir in generous portions of history and culture, from the Sioux and Shoshone Indians to President Teddy Roosevelt. Liberally season with fishing, hiking, skiing, rafting, horseback riding and other outdoor activities. Mix with the Old West flavor of the town of Jackson; add a dash of rodeo and guest ranches; garnish with some of the richest wildlife on the continent; and . . . *voila!* You have northwestern Wyoming's Rockies. Come prepared with an appetite for adventure.

The glories of this corner of the earth weren't lost on several thousand Teton and Wind River Shoshone Indians, who traditionally wintered in the Snake and Green river valleys but found a fertile hunting ground in Jackson Hole and other mountain valleys after the annual snowmelt.

The intrepid John Colter, who had gone to the Pacific with Lewis and Clark but soloed his return, was apparently the first white man to see Jackson Hole, the Tetons and the thermal phenomena of the Yellowstone basin in 1807. It wasn't long before mountain men and fur trappers penetrated the region in search of beaver and other pelts that were earning top dollar on the East Coast.

After 1845, the demand for furs diminished, the trappers moved out, and northwestern Wyoming briefly settled back into splendid isolation. The remoteness of the Teton country left it relatively un-pioneered until the end of the century, and even today its population remains sparse. Jackson, the "metropolis" of the region, has only about 5000 year-round residents.

Despite Jackson's relatively small size, no other community in the northern Rockies is as much of a tourist mecca. (There are some 2600 hotel rooms in

Jackson alone, with another 1000 in the surrounding valley and Grand Teton National Park. By contrast, Boise, Idaho, with a population 27 times greater than that of Jackson, has about the same number.)

Jackson is a perfect place to begin a vacation in the northwestern Rockies. Situated in the shadow of the Tetons at the southern gateway to Yellowstone National Park, it is surrounded by year-round recreational sites, including one of North America's leading ski resorts. The town itself is the very embodiment of an Old West town in the late 20th century, with mock gunfights in the streets, barstool saddles in the saloons and a seemingly endless choice of fine shops and restaurants.

North of Jackson are Grand Teton National Park, climaxed by the remarkable spire of the 13,772-foot Grand Teton itself, and the geothermal wonderland of Yellowstone National Park, the granddaddy of all natural preserves. From Old Faithful Geyser to the Grand Canyon of the Yellowstone, to the bison herds of the Hayden Valley and the elk that bed down in the Mammoth Hot Springs, this is a park that deserves days of exploration.

Jackson Hole

Let's start from the top: Jackson Hole is the valley. Jackson is the town.

Framed on the west by the Tetons and on the east by the Gros Ventre Range, Jackson Hole (a name bestowed by early-19th-century fur trappers to honor one of their own) encompasses about 400 square miles near the headwaters of the Snake River. Lying just west of the Continental Divide, it was created by the same faulting and geological upthrust that is still forcing the Teton Range ever heavenward.

The valley, about 48 miles long, includes the big lakes of Grand Teton National Park as well as Jackson and its smaller neighboring communities. Located at the convergence of trails from seven different passes and canyons, it is believed to have been near an important annual trade rendezvous site for mountain men, fur traders and Native Americans in the 1830s.

Jackson, with an elevation of about 6200 feet, is near the south end of the valley. Ironically, the town is one of the few places within Jackson Hole from which you *cannot* see the Tetons. Low-lying East Gros Ventre Butte effectively shields the community from that northwesterly perspective. Snow King Mountain anchors Jackson on the south; Jackson Peak, in the Gros Ventre Wilderness, rises to the east. It's only to the northeast, in the flats of the **National Elk Refuge** (Elk Refuge Road, Jackson; 307-733-8084), that there's a sense of the broader valley.

As many as 9000 American elk winter in the 24,700-acre refuge. In late spring they migrate to the higher alpine meadows of Grand Teton and Yellowstone national parks and adjacent Bridger-Teton National Forest, then return to Jackson Hole in mid-autumn. Although the refuge is open year-round, don't expect to see *Cervus canadensis* if you drive through in summer. (You will, on the other hand, be rewarded with sightings of a wide variety of bird life in the

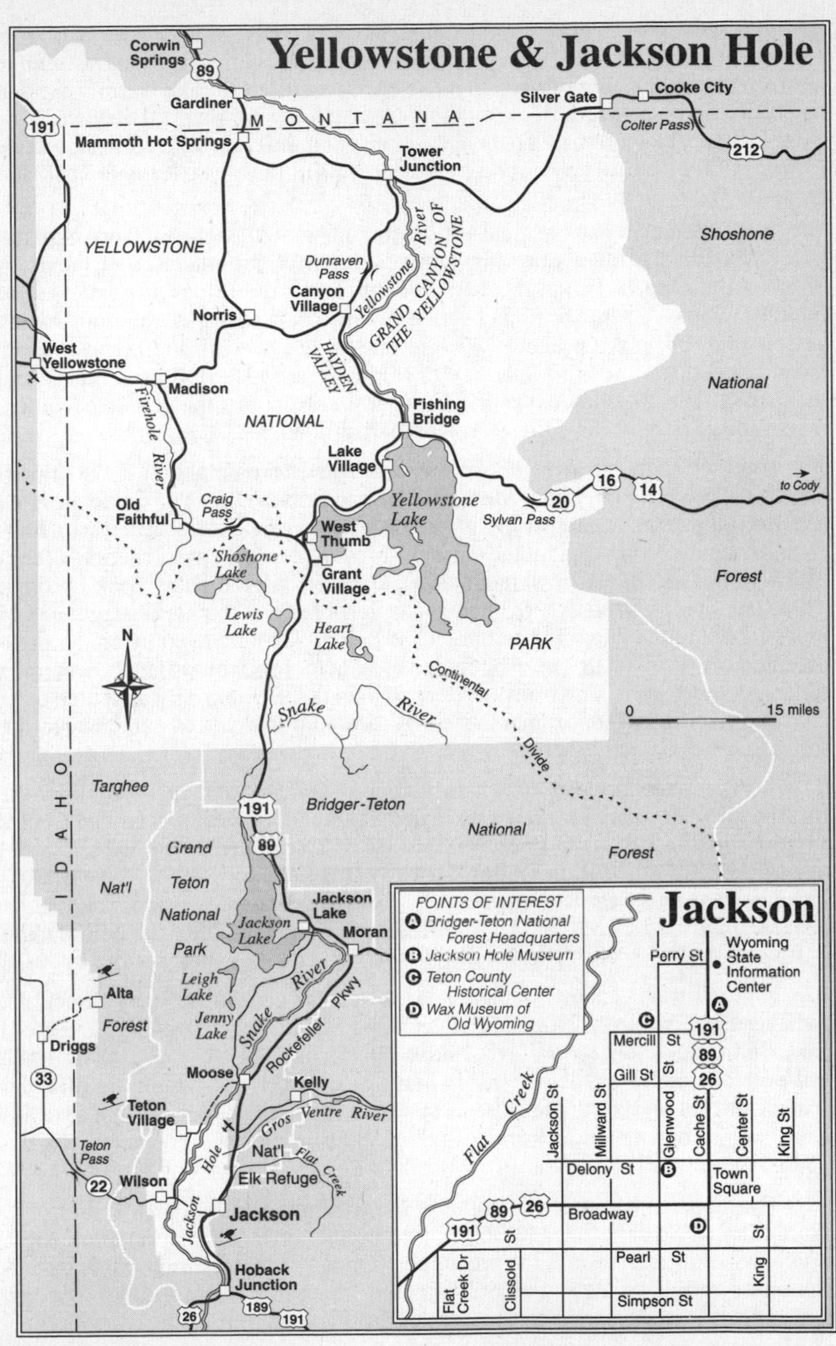
Yellowstone & Jackson Hole
Corwin Springs
Gardiner
MONTANA
Silver Gate
Cooke City
Colter Pass
Mammoth Hot Springs
Tower Junction
YELLOWSTONE
Dunraven Pass
Canyon Village
Yellowstone River
GRAND CANYON OF THE YELLOWSTONE
Norris
HAYDEN VALLEY
West Yellowstone
Madison
Firehole River
NATIONAL
Fishing Bridge
Lake Village
Shoshone
National
Forest
Yellowstone Lake
Sylvan Pass
to Cody
Old Faithful
Craig Pass
West Thumb
Shoshone Lake
Grant Village
Lewis Lake
Heart Lake
PARK
Continental Divide
N
Snake River
0
15 miles
IDAHO
Targhee
Bridger-Teton
National
Forest
Grand Teton National Park
Nat'l
Forest
Jackson Lake
Moran
Leigh Lake
Jenny Lake
Snake River
Rockefeller Pkwy
Alta
Driggs
Moose
Kelly
Gros Ventre River
Teton Village
Teton Pass
Wilson
Jackson Hole
Nat'l Elk Refuge
Flat Creek
Jackson
Hoback Junction
191
89
212
16
20
14
33
22
26
189
Jackson
POINTS OF INTEREST
A Bridger-Teton National Forest Headquarters
B Jackson Hole Museum
C Teton County Historical Center
D Wax Museum of Old Wyoming
Perry St
Wyoming State Information Center
Mercill St
Gill St
Jackson St
Millward St
Glenwood St
Cache St
Center St
King St
Delony St
Town Square
Broadway
Pearl St
Simpson St
Flat Creek Dr
Clissold St
King St
Flat Creek

wetlands, perhaps including trumpeter swans.) The best time to see elk is from Christmas through March, when the visitors center is open and guided 40-minute **sleigh rides** (Elk Refuge Road; 307-733-8084; admission) take warmly dressed nature lovers to a special viewing area. Get there by following Broadway east from Jackson Town Square about a mile to its end, just past refuge headquarters (307-733-8084; open year-round); then turn north onto Elk Refuge Road and continue for four miles.

It's no accident that the arches at the four corners of **Jackson Town Square**, in the heart of the town's bustling shopping district, are made up of hundreds of elk antlers. Each spring, local Boy Scouts scour the refuge for antlers shed by adult males . . . who promptly begin growing a new set for the autumn mating season (the elk, not the Scouts). White antlers are used in the arches; others are auctioned (on the third Saturday in May) to earn money for the refuge and the Scouts. The principal buyers are Chinese and Koreans; the powdered antlers are sold as an aphrodisiac in Asian herbalists' shops.

Another ritual, straight out of the Old West, takes place at the southeast corner of Town Square from Memorial Day to Labor Day. The **Jackson Hole Shootout** climaxes an almost-nightly confrontation (the gunfighters rest on Sundays) that may soon supplant the Hatfield-McCoy vendetta as the nation's longest running feud. Local merchants created the 20-minute show back in 1955. Then, as now, it involves a 6:30 stagecoach robbery, a female hostage, an old grudge, blazing six-guns and perhaps a bad haircut, all portrayed in highly melodramatic fashion by a troupe of about ten local actors and townspeople costumed in 19th-century garb. The irony here, of course, is that Jackson was settled *after* the rough-and-ready era romanticized by filmdom and never experienced the sort of action depicted here.

A good starting point for explorations of Jackson and Jackson Hole, the parklike Town Square (bounded by Broadway and Deloney, Cache and Center streets) is surrounded on all sides by false-fronted shops, restaurants and saloons—like the celebrated **Million Dollar Cowboy Bar** (25 North Cache Street; 307-733-2207) on the west side (of course). With saddles for barstools and silver dollars inlaid into its bar, it was a well-known watering hole long before Clint Eastwood filmed scenes from *Any Which Way You Can* here in the 1970s.

A block west of Town Square's northwest corner via Deloney Street, the **Jackson Hole Museum** (105 North Glenwood Street; 307-733-2414; admission) has exhibits depicting the valley's Native American prehistory and the fur trade and homesteader eras, as well as displays of early cowboy memorabilia and century-old photography. The museum sponsors summer walking tours of an eight-block area of downtown Jackson, including 19 historic buildings, every Tuesday, Thursday and Saturday.

The museum is associated with the **Teton County Historical Center** (105 West Mercill Street; 307-733-9605), two blocks farther north on Glenwood, where you can learn about the creation of Grand Teton National Park. A collection of trading beads and other Plains Indian artifacts is on display. The historical center is primarily an archive and research facility.

As you head north from Town Square on Cache Street, you pass on your right, after about two blocks, the **Bridger-Teton National Forest Headquarters** (340 North Cache Street; 307-739-5500). This is the place to learn about recreational opportunities in the 3.5 million acres of federal land that flank Jackson on the east and south. About two blocks farther is the modern **Wyoming State Information Center** (532 North Cache Street; 307-733-3316), operated by the Jackson Hole Chamber of Commerce. The center has some interesting displays on the region's natural attractions, as well as a lodging reservation service and more brochures than any traveler truly needs.

It's three miles from Town Square to the excellent **National Wildlife Art Museum** (★) (Rungius Road, Jackson; 307-733-5771; admission), which relocated from a corner of downtown to a rock castle overlooking the elk refuge in September 1994. Twelve galleries showcase original works by such noted American artists as George Catlin, John Clymer, Charles Russell, Carl Rungius, Conrad Schwiering and Ernest Thompson Seton.

A few miles farther, the northward highway enters the domain (but not the fee area) of Grand Teton National Park. Turn off the highway at Gros Ventre Junction (about seven miles from Jackson), to reach the tiny community of **Kelly**. The town, a ranching center established around the turn of the century, was vying with Jackson to become the Teton County seat until natural disaster played its hand in 1925. Just five miles east of Kelly in Bridger-Teton National Forest, the **Gros Ventre Slide** dumped 50 million cubic yards of sandstone—the entire north slope of Sheep Mountain—into the Gros Ventre River, damming the stream in minutes and creating five-mile-long Lower Slide Lake. Two years later, part of the natural dam collapsed, sending a wall of water, mud and rock upon Kelly and wiping the town off the map. Six people and hundreds of animals died.

Today, the partially reconstructed village is the home of the **Teton Science School** (1 Ditch Creek Road, Kelly; 307-733-4765), which offers educational programs. Its **Murie Memorial Museum** (★), which displays thousands of mammal, bird and plant specimens collected by field biologists, is open by appointment.

The Gros Ventre River—the name, incidentally, is pronounced "Grovont," and is a French trapper-ism meaning "big belly"—traces the northern boundary of the Gros Ventre Wilderness, one of three wilderness areas within Bridger-Teton National Forest.

Jackson Hole has two popular ski resorts and a third nearby. The **Snow King Resort** (400 East Snow King Avenue; 307-733-5200; admission for activities), established in 1939 as Wyoming's first ski resort, is actually right in Jackson, eight blocks southeast of Town Square. Summer visitors can take a 20-minute chairlift ride to the 7800-foot level of the mountain, then descend a half-mile through forest and meadow on an alpine slide.

Better known is the **Jackson Hole Ski Area** (Route 390, Teton Village; 307-733-4005; admission for activities), 12 miles west of Jackson. Its aerial tramway—two and a half miles long—ascends to the crest of 10,450-foot Rendezvous Peak in the Teton Range. Summer visitors can take the tram to the summit and ride or hike down.

At the foot of Rendezvous Peak is **Teton Village**, a community that came into its own with the resort's development in the 1960s. The 100-foot clock tower of the tramway's base facility, Valley Station, is surrounded by hotels and condominiums, restaurants and bars, shops and the Walk Festival Hall.

A third major resort, the **Grand Targhee Ski & Summer Resort** (Targhee Road, Alta; 307-353-2300), is almost directly over the back side of the Teton Range from Jackson Hole Ski Area. Though political boundaries place it in Wyoming, it can be reached only through Driggs, Idaho, and is therefore introduced in Chapter Ten, "Southeastern Idaho Rockies."

Those who do make the 42-mile trek from Jackson to Targhee must scale 8429-foot **Teton Pass**, the only road passage through the Teton Range. Route 22 switchbacks over the state line from the village of Wilson, affording spectacular panoramas of Jackson Hole if you can unclench your teeth long enough to find a roadside turnout from which to appreciate the views.

Wilson, named for "Uncle Nick" Wilson, patriarch of a very extended Mormon family that settled in Jackson Hole about 1889, lies about eight miles from Jackson and a mile west of the Teton Village junction. From here there is ready access to Bridger-Teton and the bordering **Targhee National Forest**; to the **Jedediah Smith Wilderness**, a parcel of Targhee that bounds Grand Teton National Park on its west side; and to the meandering ribbons of the **Snake River**'s upper portion.

The 1038-mile Snake, of course, is the main tributary of the Columbia River. Its source is in the Teton Wilderness, on the Continental Divide at the southeastern edge of Yellowstone National Park; the stream runs west and south through Jackson Lake and Grand Teton National Park, draining Jackson Hole, before rushing westward through the **Snake River Canyon**. Through the Hole, the Snake weaves a broad, flat plain that teems with wildflowers and wildlife through much of the year. Then it hits the canyon about 13 miles south of Jackson.

JACKSON HOLE HOTELS

Accommodation prices tend toward the high end in Jackson Hole, and with so many deluxe properties, it's hard to recommend one over another. The following list is merely a sampling of what's available in different lodging categories, different price ranges and different parts of the valley. Summer (June to mid-September) is the high season in Jackson, with winter (mid-December to March) priced somewhat lower. You'll get the best prices during spring and fall shoulder seasons.

In Jackson itself, the most elaborate hotel is the **Snow King Resort Hotel** (400 East Snow King Avenue; 307-733-5200, 800-522-5464, fax 307-733-4086), nine blocks southeast of Town Square. Located at the base of Snow King Mountain, the modern chalet-style hotel has 204 rather ordinary rooms and suites. The hotel's restaurants offer gourmet dining and more standard fare. Laundry facilities are available. Deluxe.

For historic flavor in Jackson, there's the **Wort Hotel** (50 North Glenwood Street; 307-733-2190, 800-322-2727, fax 307-733-2067). A downtown landmark at the corner of Broadway for more than a half-century, it was rebuilt after a 1980 fire, its gabled architecture intact. Its 60 bright, spacious rooms and suites have full baths. The Wort is perhaps best known for its bar, and its grill is among Jackson's best restaurants. Facilities include a hot tub and fitness center. Deluxe.

Bed and breakfasts are increasingly a part of the Jackson Hole scene. The **Nowlin Creek Inn** (660 East Broadway, Jackson; 307-733-0882, 800-542-2632, fax 307-733-0106), opposite Elk Refuge headquarters and six blocks east of Town Square, sets a tough standard for others to follow. The five rooms of this nonsmoking inn face either the refuge or Snow King Mountain. All have private baths with pedestal-style sinks and western-style furnishings. There's a sun deck, hot tub and library with a collection of regional literature. A gourmet breakfast is served each morning in the dining room. Deluxe.

The **Angler's Inn** (★) (265 North Millward Street, Jackson; 307-733-3682, 800-867-4667) is a small, family-run operation beside Flat Creek at the north end of downtown. Within the two-story wood-frame motel are 28 rooms with lodge-style furnishings, microwaves and refrigerators, as well as private baths. A bargain at low moderate.

There are several luxury resorts in the area, including Teton Pines and the Jackson Hole Racquet Club, both south of Teton Village on Route 390. But if we had to choose just one, it would be the **Spring Creek Resort** (Spring Gulch Road, Jackson; 307-733-8833, 800-443-6139, fax 307-733-1524), with a view across Jackson Hole to the high Tetons. Set on 1000 acres atop East Gros Ventre Butte, the modern rustic resort offers accommodations with handmade lodgepole furniture, vaulted ceilings and stone fireplaces. The resort has a restaurant, lounge, swimming pool and jacuzzi, a fitness center, tennis courts and riding stables. Ultra-deluxe.

Several lodges cluster in Teton Village beneath Rendezvous Peak. **The Inn at Jackson Hole** (3345 West McCollister Drive, Teton Village; 307-733-2311, 800-842-7666, fax 307-733-0844) is an elegant hotel just 100 yards from the aerial tramway terminal. It has 83 rooms, all with private baths and some with fireplaces and kitchenettes. The outdoor swimming pool is kept heated year-round; there's also a sauna and hot tubs, two restaurants and a bar. Moderate to deluxe.

The Hostel (★) (3315 McCollister Drive, Teton Village; 307-733-3415, fax 307-739-1142) attracts hard-core skiers who would rather spend extra days on the slopes than splurge on a hotel room. An old-time family-owned ski lodge at the foot of Jackson Hole's slopes, it has 54 rooms that sleep from two to four people in anything from double beds to single bunks. Rooms are extremely simple; all have private baths, dressers and bedside tables but little else. Guests share a fireside lounge, game rooms, a coin-op laundry, a ski-waxing room and an equipment storage area. Budget.

JACKSON HOLE RESTAURANTS

You can't go wrong at the delightful **Cadillac Grille** (55 North Cache Street, Jackson; 307-733-3279), which re-creates a 1940s art deco ambience opposite Town Square. A creative menu of fresh fish and game entrées is complemented by steaks, poultry and pasta. The list changes daily; recent selections included a stuffed leg of caribou in a pinot noir sauce and seared ahi tuna with a sauce of shiitake mushrooms, ginger and soy cream. Deluxe.

Diners at the **Snake River Grill** (84 East Broadway, Jackson; 307-733-0557) can survey Town Square from rooftop tables in summer or sit inside and gaze at Snow King Mountain's floodlit slopes in winter. Located upstairs in the Crabtree Corner complex, the restaurant serves American roasts and grills (such as fresh fish and free-range chicken) and Italian cuisine (pastas and pizzas from a wood-fired oven). There's a sophisticated wine list and a lighter bar menu. Dinner nightly; moderate.

It's well worth the short drive to **The Acadian House** (★) (1140 West Route 22; 307-739-1269), ensconced in a Louisiana-style gray-shingle house at the Wilson/Teton Village junction on the south side of Jackson. The Cajun and Creole dishes presented here, from étouffée and filé gumbo to blackened catfish and crawfish jambalaya, are as authentic as you'll find this far north of Bayou country. The wine list is short but enlightened. Moderate.

You can dine amid mash tubs, wort kettles and beer storage tanks at the **Jackson Hole Pub & Brewery** (265 South Millward Street, Jackson; 307-739-2337), where the emphasis is on custom ales, bitters, stouts, porters and other microbrews, as well as on stick-to-your-ribs meat dishes, pizzas baked in wood-burning ovens and pastas. An outside deck appeals to summer diners. Budget.

One of Jackson's original log cabins is an appropriate home for **Jedediah's Original House of Sourdough** (135 East Broadway; 307-733-5671), shaded by giant cottonwoods and located a block east of Town Square. Hearty home-style breakfasts (sourdough pancakes are a specialty), lunches (thick soups, buffalo burgers) and dinners (steaks, chops, trout) are served in a rustic atmosphere complete with old photographs and pioneer artifacts. Budget.

Some of the valley's finest dining is ten miles from town, out toward the Jackson Hole Ski Area. **The Grille at the Pines** (Teton Village Road, Wilson; 307-733-1005), in the Teton Pines Country Club & Resort clubhouse, specializes in mesquite-grilled meats, poultry and fresh fish, as well as homemade pastas, breads and desserts. The atmosphere is casual, yet the service is impeccable. On Sunday, there's a country brunch. Deluxe.

For a family night out, you can't top the **Bar-J Ranch** (Teton Village Road, Wilson; 307-733-3370). A cowboy musical revue featuring the ranch's own Bar J Wranglers follows an all-you-can-eat outdoor chuck-wagon dinner of barbecued beef or chicken served at 7:30 every night throughout the summer. A very moderate price tag includes dinner and show, tax and tip.

Jackson locals who want to avoid the tourist scene often drive ten minutes south to **Horse Creek Station** (★) (Route 89 South, Hoback Junction; 307-733-0810), a casual oasis where steaks and barbecue are the house specialties. A collection of antique fishing gear on the walls is a reminder that fresh seafood is also served. An adjacent saloon offers a sandwich menu. Budget to moderate.

JACKSON HOLE SHOPPING

Visitors who get a hankering to dress just a little more "cowboy," a little more Wyoming, can readily indulge themselves at a couple of dozen Jackson stores. Check out **Buckskin Mercantile** (125 North Cache Street; 307-733-3699) for traditional western wear and **Cattle Kate** (120 East Broadway; 307-733-7414) for 1990s clothing in 1890s designs.

Most of Jackson's two dozen or so art galleries specialize in western art and regional landscapes. Many are clustered around Town Square. Try **The Legacy Gallery** (20 West Broadway; 307-733-2353) for fine western art, the **Martin-Harris Gallery** (60 East Broadway; 307-733-0350) for contemporary art, **Sacred Trails** (81 King Street; 307-733-8874) for Native American art and the **Wilcox Gallery** (1975 North Route 89; 307-733-6450) for cowboy art and landscapes.

The **Bitterroot Trading Co.** (170 West Broadway; 307-733-4192) is a traditional trading post that sells antique firearms, hides, furs and Native American art and jewelry. The **Jackson Trading Company** (25 West Broadway; 307-733-5714) has more contemporary western furnishings and gifts. If you're looking for a good book, try **Valley Bookstore** (125 North Cache Street; 307-733-4533).

JACKSON HOLE NIGHTLIFE

Jackson is a summer mecca of the performing arts. Its best-known event is the **Grand Teton Music Festival** (P.O. Box 490, Teton Village, WY 83025; 307-733-1128, 800-959-4863, fax 307-733-7131; admission), held at Teton Village's Walk Festival Hall for eight weeks beginning in late June.

Jackson's live theater runs the gamut from serious musicals to tongue-in-cheek melodramas. The **Lighthouse Theatre** (49 West Broadway; 307-733-3670; admission), in Pink Garter Plaza, presents two different Broadway musicals throughout the summer. The **Jackson Hole Playhouse** (145 West Deloney Street; 307-733-6994; admission) presents classic musicals in an equally classic old-time theater, complete with popcorn and sarsaparilla concessions. **Dirty Jack's Wild West Theater** (140 North Cache Street; 307-733-4775; admission) dishes up slapstick musical comedy in heroes-and-villains tradition for the whole family.

Twice a week on summer evenings, the **JH Rodeo Company** (Snow King Avenue at Flat Creek Drive; 307-733-2805; admission) stages a rodeo—complete with bronco busting, bull riding and calf roping—at the Teton County Fair Grounds. Midway through the event, kids from 4 through 12 years are invited to enter a "calf scramble" on the arena floor.

Headquarters for two-steppers and Tennessee waltzers is the **Million Dollar Cowboy Bar** (25 North Cache Street, Jackson; 307-733-2207), on the west side of Town Square. Country bands play dance music nightly. Even if you don't dance, drop by for a beer and sit in a saddle-seated barstool.

Other spots heavy on C & W include **Rancher Spirits and Billiards** (20 East Broadway, Jackson; 307-733-3886), on the south side of Town Square, with nightly live music downstairs and nine very busy billiards tables upstairs; and the **Stagecoach Bar** (Route 22, Wilson; 307-733-4407), popular among locals especially on Sundays, when the venerable Stagecoach Band pumps out melodies.

The **Mangy Moose** (3285 West McCollister Drive, Teton Village; 307-733-4913) is the leading venue for live funk—blues, bluegrass, rockabilly and alternative rock. In town, the Snow King Resort's **Shady Lady Saloon** (400 East Snow King Avenue; 307-733-5200) presents low-key live jazz and contemporary rock for dancing and listening.

If it's Old West atmosphere you want, **JJ's Silverdollar Bar** (Wort Hotel; 50 North Glenwood Street, Jackson; 307-733-2190) will return you to those thrilling days of yesteryear at its historic bar inlaid with 2032 silver dollars. A ragtime pianist plays weeknights, a solo guitarist weekends. For drinks and conversation, try the **Log Cabin Saloon** (435 North Cache Street, Jackson; 307-733-7525), a rustic local favorite.

Cowboy country doesn't often embrace gay visitors, but the **Jackson Hole Gay & Lesbian Association** (P.O. Box 2424, Jackson, WY 83001; 307-733-5349) holds a social event once a week.

JACKSON HOLE PARKS

Bridger-Teton National Forest—Stretching south for 135 miles from Yellowstone National Park through five mountain ranges, this 3.4-million-acre forest is America's second largest outside of Alaska. It contains three wilderness areas, three national scenic byways, several hot springs, three ski areas (including Jackson Hole and Sun King) and the geologically intriguing Gros Ventre Slide.

Facilities: Picnic tables, restrooms, boat ramps, trails; information, 307-739-5500. *Swimming:* At the Granite Hot Springs pool, 27 miles southeast of Jackson; or at Fremont Lake and other lakes on the west slope of the Wind River Range near Pinedale. *Fishing:* Anglers can catch mountain whitefish, arctic grayling and six species of trout in lakes and streams.

Camping: There are 236 RV/tent sites and 42 for tents only in 26 campgrounds of the Teton National Forest (no hookups); no charge to $8 per night. Most of the 34 campgrounds are open only from June 1 to September 15.

Getting there: From Jackson, take Route 189 southeast for Pinedale and access to the Wind River Range; Route 89 South for Afton and the Salt Range; Route 26 North for Moran and the northern part of the national forest.

Targhee National Forest—Grand Teton National Park forms the eastern boundary of this 1.8-million-acre forest, most of which lies in Idaho. The Wyoming portion encompasses the western slope of the Teton Range (most of it in the Jedediah Smith Wilderness) from Yellowstone Park to Palisades Reservoir, on the Snake River at Alpine.

Facilities: In Wyoming, picnic tables, restrooms, boat ramp, trails; information, 208-624-3151. *Swimming:* In Palisades Reservoir. *Fishing:* Trout of all kinds and mountain whitefish are easily caught in the Snake River, Falls River and Teton Creek. Boaters can put in at Palisades Reservoir.

Camping: In Wyoming, 96 RV/tent units in four campgrounds (no hookups); $5 to $8 per night. Open from June to September.

Getting there: From Jackson, the westbound Teton Pass Highway (Route 22) passes through Targhee en route to Idaho. Several roads enter the forest from the Idaho side. Or take Route 26 southwest through Alpine to the Palisades Reservoir area.

Grand Teton National Park

Anyone who has ever laid eyes upon the stunning heights of the Teton Range has come away awestruck. Even people whose only glimpse of these dramatic mountains has been in photographs or paintings find themselves haunted by their beauty.

Climaxed by the 13,770-foot **Grand Teton**, this commanding range boasts 16 peaks of 11,000 feet or higher in a north-south stretch of less than 20 miles, towering over a string of conifer-shrouded lakes.

The geological forces that created the Tetons are still actively sculpting these peaks, which in Cenozoic terms might be considered teenagers. Some five million years ago, massive earthquakes began occurring (about every 1000 years) along a fault line where the mountains today meet the valley of Jackson Hole. Over the course of time, the mountain block on the west uplifted while the valley block dropped, so that today the Grand Teton rises about 6000 feet above Jenny Lake on the valley floor. Wind, water and late–Ice Age glaciation (only about 10,000 to 15,000 years ago) have continued to chisel the mountains' features.

The mountains and six piedmont lakes were within the national park's original boundaries in 1929. But extension of those borders to include the upper Jackson Hole, including the Snake River, induced a grim battle between conservationists and ranchers. A key player in the drama was philanthropist John D. Rockefeller, Jr., who bought up many of the ranch properties beginning in the late 1920s, then donated them to the National Park Service for a national monument that was created in 1943 and annexed to the national park in 1950. The highway corridor and adjacent lands that today connect Grand Teton and Yellowstone national parks have been named the **John D. Rockefeller, Jr., Memorial Parkway** in his honor.

Grand Teton National Park now covers an area of 485 square miles. Despite its close proximity to Yellowstone National Park, Grand Teton is very different from its famous sister. Yellowstone has premier attractions like Old Faithful Geyser and Mammoth Hot Springs, easily accessible either by car or by a short walk. Grand Teton's allure, on the other hand, is scenery that seems so close that you can reach out and touch it, but the park in fact demands active effort to fully appreciate it.

Teton Park Road skirts the shores of Jenny Lake, at the foot of the Grand Tetons, and Jackson Lake, a natural glacial lake whose size was increased significantly in 1911 by an earthen dam (since rebuilt) on the Snake River. Several park lodges are on or near the lakeshores. But rather than destinations in themselves, the lodges are best considered starting points for more energetic explorations of the park by foot, by boat, by horseback or by snowshoe.

Heading north from Jackson, the Rockefeller Parkway (Route 26/89/191) enters the national park about four miles north of Jackson. But you won't be charged a fee for passing through this area, the Antelope Flat corridor, unless you turn off onto the Teton Park Road at **Moose**, 12 miles north of Jackson, or Moran, 26 miles from Jackson. The former is the principal route for park explorers; the latter bypasses the Jackson Lake Lodge and heads more or less directly for the south entrance of Yellowstone Park.

At Moose, on the west side of the Snake River, are the park headquarters and **Moose Visitors Center** (Teton Park Road, Moose; 307-739-3399), with a variety of displays and information on park activities.

Moose, named for the ungainly looking creatures often seen browsing on willows beside the Snake, lies at the junction of Teton Park Road and **Moose-Wilson Road**, which winds through the national park's southwestern section. It passes trailheads for Phelps Lake and Death Canyon, then reaches Teton Village and the Jackson Hole Ski Area after about eight miles. Part of the road is unpaved.

Upriver from Moose, a half-mile north on Teton Park Road, then a half-mile east, is the log-built **Chapel of the Transfiguration**, whose altar window frames the Grand Teton. A short trail leads to **Menor's Ferry** (★), once the only crossing of the Snake for miles in either direction. The homestead cabin of Bill Menor contains a replica of his late-19th-century ferry; Bill's brother, Holiday, lived on the opposite side of the Snake. Like the "Grumpy Old Men" in the movie of the same name, the bachelor brothers were not on speaking terms.

Jenny Lake, eight miles north of Moose, is Teton Park's second-largest lake, filling a glacial trough a mile wide and a mile and a half long. There are two ways to approach the lake: from South Jenny Lake Junction or, for those with a bit more time, via the Jenny Lake Scenic Drive.

South Jenny Lake is the park's number-one focal point for backcountry hikers and mountaineers. The campground here is for tenters only. Ascents of the Grand Teton begin with registration at the Jenny Lake Ranger Station here; trails to a chain of lakes north (Leigh and String) and south (Bradley and Taggart) of Jenny Lake also begin at South Jenny.

Jenny Lake Scenic Drive begins as a two-way route from Teton Park Road, four miles north of South Jenny, to canoeing put-ins for String and Leigh lakes, but at the **Jenny Lake Lodge** (Jenny Lake Scenic Drive, Moran; 307-733-4647), a community of secluded log cottages that were once part of a dude ranch, it becomes a one-way southbound road, emerging back on Teton Park Road on the north side of South Jenny Lake Junction. The road offers serene views of Jenny Lake with the Grand Teton and its neighboring peaks rising behind.

It's eight miles from the Jenny Lake Scenic Drive junction (near the lake's north end) to **Signal Mountain Summit Road**, a steep and narrow byway that winds five miles to the top of Signal Mountain. From the summit, 800 feet above the surrounding country, visitors coming from the south can get their first glimpse of **Jackson Lake**, a natural lake formed by an immense Ice Age glacier that flowed out of Yellowstone Park. The 1911 damming of the Snake—a U.S. Bureau of Reclamation project that benefits eastern Idaho potato farmers—raised the lake's water level as much as 39 feet. The lake now extends 19 miles south, from the northern edge of Grand Teton National Park, and nine miles east and west at its widest.

Looming behind Jackson Lake is massive 12,605-foot **Mount Moran**, named for artist Thomas Moran, whose 1870s paintings immortalized the Teton Range on canvas for many Americans. Moran's close friend, photographer William Henry Jackson, did the same for the region on film. Many Jackson Holers lament that their valley was named not for William but for David Jackson, the trapper who passed through two generations earlier.

Teton Park Road rejoins the Rockefeller Parkway at **Jackson Lake Junction**. Northbound travelers can detour to the east here, following the Snake River downstream past **Oxbow Bend**, one of the park's richest wildlife-viewing areas, to **Moran**, where the park has its east entrance gate and a small community for park employees.

The **Colter Bay Indian Arts Museum** (Colter Bay Village, Moran; 307-543-3594), next to the ranger station and visitors center, houses a collection of Native American artifacts of artistic and religious significance.

It's about 17 miles from Colter Bay, or 23 miles from Jackson Lake Junction, to the south entrance of Yellowstone Park.

GRAND TETON NATIONAL PARK HOTELS

The **Grand Teton Lodge Company** (P.O. Box 240, Moran, WY 83013; 307-543-2855, 800-628-9988, fax 307-543-2869) is the principal concessionaire in Grand Teton National Park. It operates three separate properties: the **Jenny Lake Lodge** (Jenny Lake Scenic Drive, Moran; 307-733-4647), an ultra-deluxe former dude ranch whose 37 cabins are secluded in a conifer forest near the shores of Jenny Lake; the huge **Jackson Lake Lodge** (Rockefeller Parkway, Moran; 307-543-2811), with 385 rooms in multiplex cabins and the main hotel, starting in the moderate price range; and **Colter Bay Village** (Rockefeller Parkway, Moran; 307-543-2811), whose budget lodgings include 202 log cabins (some of them settlers' cottages remodeled and moved to their lakeside site), 72 tent cabins, 112 trailer sites and about 200 spaces for tents.

The **Signal Mountain Lodge** (Teton Park Road, Moran; 307-733-5470), on Jackson Lake at the foot of Signal Mountain, is one of the few privately owned and operated park properties. Its 79 units include 34 log cabins (many with refrigerators and microwaves) and 45 rooms in a two-story motel building, all overlooking the lake. Boat and canoe rentals are available from the lodge marina; there's also a beach and campground, two restaurants and a lounge. Moderate to deluxe.

Also within the park are **Dornan's Spur Ranch Log Cabins** (Moose Lane, Moose; 307-733-2522, fax 307-733-3544), 12 modern cottages overlooking the Snake River just west of the Moose junction. All have private baths, full kitchens, lodgepole furniture, porches and courtyards. One-bedroom cabins can sleep up to four; two-bedroom cabins can accommodate six. Dornan's also includes a highly regarded restaurant as well as a bar, grocery, gift shop, service station, sporting goods stores and rental outlets. Moderate to deluxe.

Jackson Hole offers more than a dozen guest ranches. One of the most popular is the **Gros Ventre River Ranch** (P.O. Box 151, Moose, WY 83012; 307-733-4138, fax 307-733-4272), 18 miles northeast of Jackson near Kelly. Guests stay in nine log cabins with ten-foot ceilings, fireplaces, kitchenettes and private baths. Gourmet meals are served with California wine in the main lodge, which also has a bar and a recreation room. Activities include horseback riding and flyfishing in summer, cross-country skiing and snowmobiling in winter. Moderate (American plan).

GRAND TETON NATIONAL PARK RESTAURANTS

Perhaps the best of the restaurants in the national-park lodges is **The Mural Room** (Jackson Lake Lodge, Rockefeller Parkway, Moran; 307-543-2811), whose walls are adorned with paintings that depict various episodes in the history of Jackson Hole. Three meals a day are served in smoke-free surroundings. Breakfast and lunch offer standard American fare; dinners are highlighted by a nightly outdoor barbecue. Moderate.

Seafood specialties are featured at the **Aspens Restaurant** (Signal Mountain Lodge, Teton Park Road, Moran; 307-543-2831), a few miles south down the lakeshore. Trout or other angler's takes from Jackson Lake itself may be offered, as well as steaks and other traditional American cuisine. Large windows look out upon the lake, and the smoke-free atmosphere is casual. Moderate.

There are few alternatives to lodge dining rooms and snack bars within the national park. An exception is **Leeks Restaurant Pizzeria** (Leeks Marina, Rockefeller Parkway, Moran; 307-543-2394). With an outdoor deck overlooking Jackson Lake opposite Mount Moran, this fully licensed summer-only eatery offers pizza, salad, burgers and other sandwiches. Budget.

GRAND TETON NATIONAL PARK NIGHTLIFE

Dornan's Spur Ranch (Moose Lane, Moose; 307-733-2415) has a weekly nighttime "hootenanny" of local writers and musicians that sometimes includes folk-rock legend Tom Rush.

GRAND TETON NATIONAL PARK

Grand Teton National Park—The spectacular Teton Range, the string of evergreen-ringed lakes at its eastern front and Jackson Hole itself are dominant features of this 485-square-mile park. Mountaineers are challenged by the Grand Teton and other peaks, while water-sports enthusiasts enjoy floating the upper Snake River and scanning its shores for wildlife.

Facilities: Lodges, restaurants, stores, picnic tables, restrooms, amphitheaters, visitors centers, marinas, boat ramps, boat and canoe rentals, hiking and horse trails; $10 weekly vehicle pass (includes Yellowstone National Park); information, 307-739-3399. *Swimming:* Permitted everywhere; designated beaches at Colter Bay and Signal Mountain Lodge. *Fishing:* The park's lakes and rivers yield mountain whitefish and brown, cutthroat and lake trout. Flyfishing for trout in the upper Snake River is an angler's dream.

Camping: There are 850 RV/tent sites at five park campgrounds (trailers allowed; no hookups); $10 per night; Jenny Lake has 49 tent sites; open from May to October. There are 334 units at three privately owned campgrounds; $14 to $22 per night: Colter Bay RV & Trailer Park (112 trailer sites with hookups; 307-543-2811); Colter Bay Tent Village (72 sites for tents only; 307-543-2811); Grand Teton Park KOA (36 tent sites, 114 RV sites with hookups; 307-733-1980). Reservations accepted; open from May to September.

Getting there: Take Route 26 north from Jackson or west from Dubois, or Route 89/191 north from Jackson or south from Yellowstone National Park.

Yellowstone National Park

The world's first national park remains first on nearly every visitor's list of Most Remarkable Places.

Nowhere else on earth is there as large and varied a collection of hydrothermal features—erupting geysers, bubbling mud caldrons, hissing fumaroles, gurgling mineral springs. The park is estimated to contain 10,000 thermal features, including more than 200 active geysers. Sites like Old Faithful Geyser and Mammoth Hot Springs have become part of the American lexicon, if not the American identity.

No other place in the contiguous 48 states has as great a concentration of mammals as does Yellowstone, or as extensive an interactive ecosystem. The park is home to an amazing five dozen species of mammals, including eight hoofed animals (bighorn sheep, pronghorn antelope, mountain goat, bison, elk, moose, mule deer and white-tailed deer) and two bears (black and grizzly).

Then there's the magnificent Grand Canyon of the Yellowstone, with its spectacular waterfalls; 136-square-mile Yellowstone Lake, the largest lake in North America at so high an elevation; rugged mountains reaching above 10,000 feet in all directions. It's no wonder city folk didn't believe the first stories they heard coming out of the West.

The park's 2.2 million acres were set aside by Congress as a national park on March 1, 1872. But convincing Washington had not been easy.

The heart of Yellowstone was once a giant volcanic caldera, 28 miles wide, 47 miles long and thousands of feet deep. Some geologists think the explosion that created this crater 600,000 years ago may have been 2000 times greater than Mount St. Helens' in 1980. Three ice ages sculpted the modern landscape, but they couldn't quiet the earth beneath. Nomadic tribes, who lived and hunted in the area for thousands of years thereafter, apparently avoided the most active geothermal areas, as did the Lewis and Clark expedition of 1804. Ever respectful of native superstition, William Clark noted that Indians who visited the region had "frequently heard a loud noise like thunder, which makes the earth tremble. . . . They conceive it possessed of spirits, who were adverse that men should be near them."

John Colter, a wayward member of the Lewis and Clark party, spent the winter of 1807 trapping and wandering throughout the area; he apparently was the first white man to observe the natural wonders of Yellowstone. But no one back East believed him. It didn't help when Jim Bridger, a mountain man as famous for his tall tales as for his knowledge of wilderness survival, claimed that "a fellow can catch a fish in an icy river, pull it into a boiling pool, and cook his fish without ever taking it off the hook."

Finally, in 1870, a group of respected Montana citizens set out to explore the area and put an end to rumor. Astonished by its discoveries (including Old Faithful), this Washburn-Langford-Doane party convinced Dr. Ferdinand Hayden, U.S. Geological Survey director, to investigate. In June 1871, Hayden took a survey party of 34 men, including painter Thomas Moran and photographer William Henry Jackson, to northwestern Wyoming. Their visuals and Hayden's 500-page report helped convince Congress to set aside this remarkable wilderness the following year. By the early 20th century, when rail access to the north entrance became possible, tourists were flooding in..

With 3472 square miles of terrain, Yellowstone—its name derives from the yellow rock cliffs of the Yellowstone River, which originates in the park—measures 54 miles east to west and 63 miles north to south, making it bigger than the state of Delaware. Its elevation ranges from 11,358 feet, atop Eagle Peak in the Absarokas, to 5314 feet, at the north entrance. The park has 370 miles of paved roads and more than 1200 miles of marked backcountry trails. In summer, when three million tourists visit, its population is greater than that of St. Louis or Cleveland. Its rainfall varies from 80 inches a year, in the southwestern Falls River Basin, to ten inches at Mammoth Hot Springs. Snow can fall in any month of the year.

Generally speaking, the park is open only from May through October, and many of its lodges and campgrounds have shorter seasons than that. But a second, winter season—running from mid-December to mid-March—attracts snowmobilers and cross-country skiers to the Old Faithful and Mammoth Hot Springs areas. Ironically, although 96 percent of the park is in Wyoming, only two of its five entrances—from Jackson (south) and Cody (east)—are in this state. Three entrances—West Yellowstone (west), Gardiner (north) and Cooke City (northeast)—are in Montana, which contains only 3 percent of the park. Idaho has the other 1 percent.

The following touring itinerary assumes that you're heading north from Jackson and Grand Teton National Park. From the West Thumb junction, on Yellowstone Lake, it proceeds clockwise around the park circuit for 141 miles and returns to West Thumb (which sits at six o'clock). The agenda can be easily picked up from any other gateway.

GRANT VILLAGE–WEST THUMB AREA Plan to spend about 90 minutes on the 64-mile drive from Jackson up Route 89/191 to **South Entrance**, even if you have already made your long detour through Grand Teton National Park. The **John D. Rockefeller, Jr., Memorial Parkway** is a busy highway with lots of junctions and turnouts. Once you're on Yellowstone National Park roads, you'll reduce your speed even more.

Just past the South Entrance ranger station, the road leaves the by-now slowly meandering Snake River and traces the steep-sided canyon rim of the tributary **Lewis River**, its black lava walls 600 feet high. Look for turnouts for **Moose Falls**, a split waterfall that enters the Lewis from Crawfish Creek, and **Lewis Falls**, a 37-foot drop.

Now you're on the east shore of **Lewis Lake**, a pretty three-mile-long, two-mile-wide favorite of fishermen. (The namesake of the lake is explorer Meriwether Lewis although he never set foot within 100 miles of it.) The lake lies just within the ancient Yellowstone caldera.

Six miles north of Lewis Lake, after crossing the Continental Divide for the first of three times in the next 15 miles, turn off a mile east to **Grant Village**, on the shore of **Yellowstone Lake**. The southernmost of numerous park communities you'll pass through on this park circuit, Grant Village was named for Ulysses S. Grant, who as president signed the bill that created Yellowstone National Park in 1872. It has a 299-room hotel, restaurants, campgrounds, boat ramps, several shops, service station, post office and other facilities.

Much of southern Yellowstone bears the scars of the terrible 1988 forest fires that ravaged about 36 percent (793,000 acres) of the park's vegetation and that took 25,000 firefighters about three months and $120 million to quell. But exhibits at the **Grant Village Visitors Center** (307-242-2650), beside the lakeshore amphitheater, explain fire's role not only as a destructive force but also as a creative one—clearing areas for the growth of new vegetation, which in turn nurtures a greater diversity of wildlife. Naturalists say major fires such as these occur once or twice a century when nature is allowed to take its course.

Grant Village lies on Yellowstone Lake's **West Thumb**, a bay so named because early surveyors thought the lake was shaped like a hand. (In our opinion, it's shaped more like a tired backpacker, and this bay is his or her head.) Measuring 20 miles from north to south, 14 miles from east to west, and with 110 miles of shoreline, this is the highest (7733 feet) large lake in the Western Hemisphere outside of South America's High Andes.

Less than two miles north of Grant Village, on the lakeshore, is the **West Thumb Geyser Basin**, noted for the vivid colors of its springs. A walkway winds past features like the Thumb Paint Pots, the intensity and hue of whose colors seem to change seasonally with the light; Abyss Pool, with a deep, cobalt blue crater of remarkably clear water; Fishing Cone, a spring whose volcanolike mound is surrounded by lake water; and Lakeshore Geyser, which spouts up to 60 feet high when it's not submerged by Yellowstone Lake.

West Thumb is at the south junction of the Grand Loop Road. You should take the westbound fork, which crosses the Continental Divide twice more—the first time at 8391 feet elevation—en route to Old Faithful.

(If you turn right here, you'll follow the north shore of Yellowstone Lake to its outlet near Lake Village. According to this itinerary, you will return from that direction 122 miles from here.)

OLD FAITHFUL AREA In a saddle between the crossings of the Divide, you can turn off at Shoshone Point for a view down Delacy Creek to Shoshone Lake, the park's second-largest body of water, three miles south. This is moose country. In the far distance, on clear days, you can see the towering spires of the Grand Tetons.

It's about 17 miles from West Thumb to the cloverleaf junction for **Old Faithful Geyser**, Yellowstone's best-known sight and the world's most famous geyser. While not the largest, the highest or the most regular geyser in the park, Old Faithful has demonstrated remarkably consistent behavior since its 1870 discovery. It erupts 19 to 21 times per day at intervals averaging about 75 minutes, varying by 30 minutes on either side. Eruptions, lasting from 90 seconds to five minutes, eject between 4000 and 8000 gallons of boiling water to heights of up to 180 feet. The **Old Faithful Visitors Center** (307-545-2750), next to the Old Faithful Inn by the west parking area, can tell you when to expect the next discharge. Normally, the shorter and smaller the last eruption, the less time you'll have to wait before for next one.

The park community of Old Faithful is one of Yellowstone's largest villages, with three overnight lodges; several restaurants, cafeterias and snack bars; numerous stores and shops; a full-service garage; a 24-hour medical clinic; a post office and other community facilities.

It's also the focal point of Yellowstone's spectacular **Upper Geyser Basin** (★), the world's single largest concentration of geysers. Weaving from the visitors center through the basin, on either side of the aptly named **Firehole River**, are about four miles of boardwalks and paved, wheelchair-accessible trails as well as many more miles of dirt paths. The geysers of Upper Geyser Basin are a motley group whose very *un*predictability makes Old Faithful's consistency seem all the more remarkable.

Directly opposite Old Faithful, overlooking the northeast bank of the river, is the Geyser Hill Group. It includes the **Anemone Geyser**, which bubbles explosively every seven to ten minutes; the **Plume Geyser**, which has erupted to 25 feet high every 30 to 50 minutes since 1942, when it first became active; the **Beehive Geyser**, which shoots water 180 feet or higher at irregular intervals of one to ten days; the four **Lion Geysers**, connected underground, which gush two or three times a day; and the **Giantess Geyser**, which erupts violently once or twice an hour, for 12 to 42 hours, two to six times a year, and then returns to dormancy.

Downstream is the **Castle Geyser**, probably the oldest in the park. Its ancient cone is 120 feet around. Castle's twice-daily explosions rise to 90 feet, last about 20 minutes and are followed by another 30 to 40 minutes of furious steaming. Nearby **Grand Geyser**, the world's tallest predictable geyser, erupts like a fountain up to 200 feet high every seven to 15 hours.

Upper Geyser Basin also includes several attractive springs and pools, the best known of which is **Morning Glory Pool**, reached by a one-and-a-half-mile stroll from the visitors center. Labeled in 1880 for its likeness to its namesake flower, the hot spring began to cloud because of vandalism (mainly trash thrown in the pool) and geological changes created by a 1959 earthquake, its epicenter just west of the park, that measured 7.1 on the Richter scale. Thanks to a harder line on park vandalism, the pool has begun to recover its original deep blue color. The vivid colors of these pools—yellow, orange, brown and green—are due to the presence of photosynthetic algae on the submerged earth. There are several more geyser basins along the Grand Loop Road as it proceeds north from Old Faithful toward the Madison junction.

The principal features of **Midway Geyser Basin** are **Excelsior Geyser** and **Grand Prismatic Spring**. Excelsior Geyser erupted in 1888 (to a height of 300 feet) and again in 1985 (nonstop for two days, to a height of 55 feet. If you missed it then, don't hold your breath). At all other times, it's like a pot of scalding water that continually boils over—at a rate of five million gallons *per day*. When the air cools at sunset, the geyser's steam fills the entire basin. Grand Prismatic Spring is Yellowstone's largest hot spring at 370 feet in diameter; it has azure blue water at its center, colorful algae around its edges.

Two miles past Midway, a turnoff down the three-mile, one-way **Firehole Lake Drive** marks the beginning of **Lower Geyser Basin**. This basin covers more ground than some of the others but its geysers are not as striking, with the exception of the **Great Fountain Geyser**, whose hour-long eruptions reach heights of 100 to 230 feet; intervals between eruptions vary from seven to 15 hours. Where the drive rejoins the Grand Loop Road you'll see the **Fountain Paint Pots**, a multicolored collection of gurgling mud pools that vary in size, color and intensity.

MADISON AREA–WEST ENTRANCE Grand Loop Road follows the Firehole River downstream another six and a half miles to Madison. Two miles before Madison, the river drops into a deep, dark canyon. Coming from the south, you must proceed to a turnoff for one-way **Firehole Canyon Drive**, about a half mile from Madison, and then backtrack. The two-mile route penetrates the 800-foot, black lava walls of the canyon, reaching its climax where the 40-foot **Firehole Falls** tumble and churn into the **Firehole Cascades**. Above the falls is a big swimming hole; the miles of geothermal activity upstream raise the river's temperature about 30 degrees higher than normally would be expected at this elevation and latitude.

Madison is one of the park's smaller communities. It doesn't offer overnight lodging, stores or service stations, but it does have a campground, a ranger station, an amphitheater and the **Explorer's Museum** (307-344-7381), with exhibits that tell the saga of the park's creation.

If you're ready for a sidetrip, a left turn at the junction will take you down the **West Entrance Road** 14 miles to the bustling town of West Yellowstone, Montana (see "Yellowstone Gateway Communities," later in this chapter). The route closely parallels the Madison River and is excellent for wildlife viewing.

To continue your tour, turn right at Madison and remain on the park's Grand Loop Road. About four and a half miles ahead, and right beside the highway, is **Gibbon Falls**, a veil-like 84-foot drop over a rock face. The route continues to ascend through the minor Monument and Gibbon geyser basins to Norris, 14 miles northeast of Madison.

NORRIS AREA For many visitors, Yellowstone's most intriguing thermal area is not the Upper Geyser Basin around Old Faithful but the **Norris Geyser Basin** (★). In a walk of less than two miles beginning just a few hundred yards west of the road junction, you can take in dozens of geysers, hot springs, mud pools and silica terraces in "one of the most extreme environments on earth," as it's called by some park publications. The basin is pervaded by the perpetually pungent smell of hydrogen sulfide.

Thermal activity seems to be on the increase here. After a moderate earthquake struck the area in March 1994, long-dormant geysers surged back to life, and geologists monitored dramatic increases in ground temperature in certain parts of the basin.

Start your visit at the rustic **Norris Geyser Basin Museum** (307-344-2812), where displays interpret hydrothermal geology. Then set out on the one-and-a-half-mile loop trail through patchily forested Back Basin (to the south) or the three-quarter-mile loop around the more open Porcelain Basin (to the north).

Back Basin has two highlights. **Steamboat Geyser** is the world's tallest active geyser—when it is, indeed, active. Its eruptions, though spectacular, are *highly* unpredictable. After its 1969 eruption, Steamboat lay dormant for nine years, until 1978; it spewed several times between then and 1991 but has again been dormant up to the time of this writing, in mid 1995. When the geyser does blast, it sends a shower of water 300 feet into the air for as long as 40 minutes.

Echinus Geyser is far more dependable. Its explosions come every 35 to 75 minutes, and they last anywhere from six minutes to an hour, with water rising skyward 40 to 60 feet. Small crowds gather on benches around its cone much as they do (on a larger scale!) around Old Faithful. Echinus is also the largest acid-water geyser known, with a pH level between 3.3 and 3.6—almost as high as vinegar. Acid-water geysers are extremely rare; most of those known to exist on earth are in the Norris Geyser Basin.

From an overlook northeast of the Norris museum you can get a good panorama of **Porcelain Basin**, which appears as a steaming sheet of whitish rock. Silica and clay are responsible for the milky color characteristic of this area's various springs and geysers; some are rimmed with orange, indicating the presence of iron compounds.

From Norris junction, the **Norris Canyon Road** proceeds 12 miles east to Canyon Village, effectively dividing the Grand Loop Road into two smaller loops. En route, about three miles east of Norris, it passes the pretty **Virginia Cascades**, where the Gibbon River slides through a narrow canyon and drops 60 feet. Most of the route is densely forested.

Less than a mile north of the junction, at the entrance to the Norris campground, is the **Museum of the National Park Ranger** (307-344-7353). Housed in a restored log cabin built in 1897 as a U.S. Army outpost, the museum contains exhibits explaining how park protection began as a domestic military function and evolved into the highly specialized occupation it is today.

The Grand Loop Road north from Norris to Mammoth Hot Springs, a distance of 21 miles, passes several interesting geothermal features. Vents in the slopes of **Roaring Mountain**, five miles from Norris, hiss and steam at the side of the road. A glossy black volcanic glass from which ancient Native Americans made utensils and tools forms 200-foot-high **Obsidian Cliff**, nine miles from Norris. **Sheepeater Cliff**, 14 miles from Norris, is composed of pentagonal and heptagonal columns of basalt, another volcanic byproduct.

This region of low-lying streams and small lakes is a favorite of moose, who feed on willow shrubs and underwater plants, and who often wander through the **Indian Creek campground**, located just to the southwest of Sheepeater Cliff.

MAMMOTH HOT SPRINGS AREA The Grand Loop Road begins its descent to Mammoth Hot Springs and the park's north entrance at **Golden Gate Canyon**, so named for the yellow lichen that paints its otherwise-barren rock walls.

The Mammoth Hot Springs, truly one of the park's highlights, are a spectacular series of steaming travertine terraces in a steady state of metamorphosis. Super-heated ground water rises to the surface as carbonic acid, dissolving great quantities of natural limestone. As it seeps through cracks in the earth, it deposits the limestone, which solidifies again as travertine (calcium carbonate). This white mineral provides a habitat for colorful bacterial algae (cyanobacteria), whose varying pastel hues reflect the temperature of the water they inhabit: White bacteria live in the hottest water, followed, in descending order, by yellow, orange, brown and, in the coolest, green.

The result of this thermal dynamism on the lower slopes of Terrace Mountain is a lopsided wedding cake of a hillside. About 500 gallons of water flow from the springs per minute; by some estimates, two tons of dissolved limestone are deposited each day. But the springs and terraces are constantly changing, new ones emerging while others become dormant.

Visitors coming from the south will get their first glimpse of Mammoth Hot Springs from the one-and-a-half-mile **Upper Terrace Loop Drive**, a narrow, one-way route that turns left off the Grand Loop Road about a mile and a half south of Mammoth village. The thermal landscape here is highly varied: Some terraces have been inactive for five centuries, others have come back to life after decades of dormancy, and still others have erupted from verdant forest in relatively recent times—even as park rangers and frequent visitors watched.

Probably the best place to view the entire Mammoth area is from the **Lower Terrace Overlook** off the Upper Terrace Loop Drive. Boardwalk trails lead a half mile downhill through the main terrace region to the village beyond. Features like **Minerva Spring** and **Jupiter Spring** go through cycles of activity and dormancy lasting years at a time. **Opal Terrace**, at the foot of the hill, deposits as much as a foot of travertine per year in its most active periods. **Liberty Cap**, a cone formed by a long-extinct hot spring, marks the north end of the Mammoth Hot Springs; it is 37 feet high and 20 feet in diameter at its base.

One of the most surprising aspects of these hot springs is their apparent allure to elk. Dozens of the magnificent antlered creatures bed down in the terraces, seemingly oblivious to tourists who pass within a few feet. They can be seen wandering throughout the village as well, more tame than wild.

Mammoth was the first settlement in Yellowstone National Park. Park headquarters (307-344-7381) are lodged in the gray stone buildings of the former **Fort Yellowstone**, a cavalry post during the three decades the park was administered by the U.S. Army, from 1886 to 1916. Also in the historic fort is the **Horace M. Albright Visitors Center** (307-344-2263), whose exhibits explain the army's role during those early years. There are also excellent wildlife displays and a slide program on park ecology, philosophy and history.

Other village facilities, open year-round, include a hotel, restaurants, a general store and other shops, a gas station with towing and repair services, a medical clinic, a post office, a campground and an amphitheater for evening programs. There's even a corral for trail riders. For park visitors planning to complete a circuit of the Grand Loop Road in two days, this is a good halfway point for food and lodging on the tour from Grant Village.

The **North Entrance Road**, which connects Mammoth Hot Springs with Gardiner, Montana (see "Yellowstone Gateway Communities," later in this chapter), five miles to the north, is the only route into the park that is open year-round. (The Northeast Entrance Road is open beyond the park boundary to Cooke City, Montana, but the Beartooth Highway beyond that point is closed from mid-October through May.)

The North Entrance Road passes through 600-foot-deep **Gardner Canyon** and swings by the steaming, subterranean outlet where the **Boiling River** flows into the Gardner River. At the north entrance, the route passes beneath the 30-foot stone **Roosevelt Arch**, dedicated in 1903 by President Theodore Roosevelt and inscribed, "For the Benefit and Enjoyment of the People."

East of Mammoth Hot Springs, the Grand Loop Road continues 18 miles to Tower Junction. En route, about four miles from Mammoth, it passes **Undine Falls**, which drop 60 feet between perpendicular cliff walls on Lava Creek.

TOWER-ROOSEVELT AREA About three and a half miles before Tower Junction you'll pass **Garnet Hill**. The rocks here are Precambrian granite gneiss estimated to be roughly 2.7 billion years old, formed before the first primitive lifeforms even began to appear on the planet. Imperfect garnets can be found in this ancient formation.

A short side road a little over a mile west of Tower Junction leads to a **petrified tree**, enclosed by a tall iron fence to prevent the vandalism that consumed its former neighbors. Petrified trees—like this upright 20-foot redwood stump—were fossilized 50 million years ago after falling volcanic ash covered them. They can be found in isolated locations throughout northern Yellowstone, especially nearby **Specimen Ridge** (★), where between nine and twelve separate petrified forests—one on top of another—have been identified. Rangers lead all-day hikes along the ridge trail southeast of Tower Junction.

Tower Junction takes its name from the unusual basalt pinnacles that rise above the Yellowstone River canyon just south of here. **Tower Fall** is about two miles south of the junction off the Grand Loop Road; it plummets 132 feet from the palisades into **The Narrows**, at 500 feet the deepest part of this section of the canyon, and its most confined. A trail that leads to the foot of the waterfall reveals more steam vents and hot springs, including **Calcite Springs**, where the geothermal waters deposit calcite, gypsum and sulfur.

At Tower Junction itself are a ranger station, a service station, horse corrals and the **Roosevelt Lodge**, a rustic 1920s log building (with cabins and a restaurant) named for Teddy Roosevelt. The environmentalist president favored this area's rolling hills for camping around the turn of the 20th century.

There are really two junctions at Tower Junction: that of the Grand Loop Road with the **Northeast Entrance Road**, and that of the **Lamar River** with the Yellowstone River. The Northeast Entrance Road follows the Lamar Valley upstream for the first half of its 29-mile run to the park's Northeast Entrance, closely paralleling an old Native American route, the Bannock Trail. Bison and elk winter in the broad, open meadows of this glacial valley. **Buffalo Ranch**, ten miles east of Tower Junction, was used as a breeding preserve for bison for a half century after its establishment in 1907, during which time it helped Yellowstone's once-rare bison population increase from 25 to a modern estimate of 2500. It's now home to the **Yellowstone Institute** (307-344-2294), a nonprofit academy specializing in wildlife and natural-history education for day or resident students. Some courses earn university credit.

There are two park campgrounds along this route: **Slough Creek campground** and **Pebble Creek campground**. Beyond are the isolated communities of Silver Gate and Cooke City (see "Yellowstone Gateway Communities," later in this chapter) and the rugged Beartooth Plateau.

South of Tower Junction, the Grand Loop Road passes Tower Fall, then begins a 12-mile ascent into the Washburn Range, a stretch that is Yellowstone's highest road. The area southeast of the highway, between Antelope Creek and the rim of the Yellowstone canyon, is a refuge for grizzly bears. Any human travel (even by foot) is prohibited in the area.

Trails from 8859-foot **Dunraven Pass** lead through groves of gnarled whitebark pine and subalpine fir to the fire lookout atop 10,243-foot **Mount Washburn**, a summer range for bighorn sheep. There are magnificent views from here across the Yellowstone caldera to the Red Mountains, 35 miles away, and on clear days to the Teton Range, 100 miles to the southwest.

CANYON AREA From Dunraven Pass the Grand Loop Road makes a five-mile descent through dense stands of lodgepole pine to **Canyon Village**.

The lodge here is among the park's newest; visitors also find dining facilities and a lounge, a campground and an amphitheater, riding stables and a general store, service station, post office and ranger station. Exhibits at the **Canyon Visitors Center** (307-242-2550) describe the creation of the Yellowstone River canyon by lava, glaciers and floods as well as other aspects of park geology.

While the **Grand Canyon of the Yellowstone** extends 24 miles to The Narrows, just past Tower Fall at its northern end, the truly "grand" part is its first couple of miles, which include the Upper and Lower Yellowstone Falls.

For your first view of the falls (you'll want more than one), take the two-and-a-half-mile, one-way North Rim Drive east and south from Canyon Village.

Your first stop is **Inspiration Point**, where you can park and descend several dozen steps to a lookout. To the southwest (about 1.4 miles) is the **Lower Falls**, at 308 feet Yellowstone's highest waterfall. (Around the corner to the south, out of view from this point, are the 109-foot **Upper Falls**.) The canyon is about 1000 feet deep at this point (it ranges from 800 to 1200), while the distance from here to the South Rim is about 1500 feet. Farther downriver are places where it widens out to about 4000 feet.

The vivid hues of the canyon walls—yellow, red, orange, brown and even blue—are proof of ancient hydrothermal action on rhyolite, a fine-grained volcanic rock heavy in silica, and its mineral oxides. Though the cliffs still exude steam and seem forbidding, they make a fine home for ospreys, which scan for fish from their huge summer nests built on rock porches high above the Yellowstone River, and violet-green swallows, which help keep down the populations of flying insects.

Less than a half mile south, after Grand Loop Road crosses Cascade Creek (whose own **Crystal Falls** empty into the Yellowstone just below this point), look for a turnout to the Upper Falls. The trail to the brink of these falls is almost a stairway, and it's only a couple of hundred yards in either direction.

Just over a half mile from the Upper Falls turnout, and about 2.3 miles south of Canyon Village, cross the Chittenden Bridge to Artist Point Road, which branches northeast along the canyon's South Rim. It ends 1.6 miles beyond at **Artist Point**, directly opposite Grandview Point but with a strikingly different perspective on the canyon.

The contrast between the reckless river that rushes through the Yellowstone canyon and the tranquil stream that meanders through the **Hayden Valley** is quite striking. Yet only about three miles separate these two opposite faces of the Yellowstone River. Whereas the canyon is hostile to most wildlife, the lush, six-mile valley between Alum and Trout creeks is a natural sanctuary.

Bison, moose, elk, bear and other large animals wander the former lakebed while trumpeter swans, sandhill cranes, great blue herons, white pelicans and other stately waterfowl abound in the marshes. Fishing is prohibited in the valley.

Numerous roadside parking areas have been created to accommodate wildlife viewing. Nevertheless, traffic jams are common. Park officials continually warn visitors to view large animals only from a distance, even if they're in their cars. The ferocity of grizzly bears is well documented, but bison, though they may seem docile, can be unpredictable and temperamental as well.

An intense thermal area beyond Elk Antler Creek marks the south end of the Hayden Valley, about 11 miles from Canyon Village. The varied features here are arguably the park's most foul smelling. The stench of hydrogen sulfide gas emanates from the constantly churning caldron of murky **Mud Volcano**. Rising volcanic gases continually bubble to the surface of **Black Dragon's Caldron**, which erupted in 1948 with such frenzy that it flung pitch-black mud dozens of feet around; Sour Lake, whose acid water has killed nearby trees;

Dragon's Mouth, whose bursts of steam roar and echo within its cavern; and **Sulphur Caldron**, its water yellow with sulfur.

YELLOWSTONE LAKE AREA Spawning cutthroat trout leap up the cascades at **Le Hardy Rapids** on the Yellowstone River in June and July, making their final approach to nearby Yellowstone Lake. **Lake Junction** is just three miles south from this point.

The first of three communities situated along the lake's northwest shore is **Fishing Bridge**, whose facilities (just east of Lake Junction) include a full-service garage, a general store, a ranger station and a park for hard-sided recreational vehicles. A camping restriction was imposed because of the area's popularity among park bears.

Despite its name, the bridge—which spans the Yellowstone River at its outlet from Yellowstone Lake—was closed to fishing in 1973. Visitors now use it primarily for watching the summer spawning spectacular of native cutthroat trout returning to the lake to lay their eggs. Pelicans, gulls and even bears are a part of the show. Exhibits at the **Fishing Bridge Visitors Center** (307-242-2450) focus on the geology and bird and fish life of the Yellowstone Lake area.

The turnoff from the Grand Loop Road to **Lake Village** is less than two miles south of Lake Junction. Lake Village is the home of the park's oldest lodging, the **Lake Yellowstone Hotel**, which opened to visitors in 1891. Though renovated, it has kept its historic flavor and is still going strong. Lake Village also has cabins, restaurants, stores, a ranger station and a hospital. Another two miles south is **Bridge Bay**, the lake's primary abode for tent campers and, with 420 sites, the park's largest campground.

West Thumb, at the junction of South Entrance Road, is where this tour route began. If you want to head out the park's **East Entrance Road** toward Cody, Wyoming, 77 miles from Lake Junction, you'll need to retrace your treadmarks to Fishing Bridge. It's 26 miles from there, through the dense evergreen forests surrounding 8530-foot Sylvan Pass in the Absaroka Range, to the East Entrance station.

For its first nine miles, the East Entrance Road traces the north shore of Yellowstone Lake. Moose often browse in the fens and sedge meadows of the **Pelican Creek Flats**, one to three miles east of Fishing Bridge. Although there's no immediate cause for alarm, the earth in this area is rising by as much as an inch per year—a warning of future volcanic activity, perhaps along the line of what exists in the Norris Geyser Basin today.

A short spur road climbs 600 feet to the **Lake Butte Overlook** for one last panoramic glimpse of Yellowstone Lake. Then it's back to the East Entrance Road and up the west side of the Absaroka Range. Look for marmots and pikas on the rocky slopes at higher elevations. Beyond **Sylvan Pass**, 20 miles from Fishing Bridge, the highway descends nearly 1600 feet in seven miles to **East Entrance**.

Several guest ranches, campgrounds and other tourist-oriented facilities are located just a few miles outside the park boundary in the Wapiti Valley, along the North Fork Shoshone River. This route is described in Chapter Eight "Northern Wyoming Rockies."

YELLOWSTONE NATIONAL PARK HOTELS

Yellowstone National Park probably offers more accommodations and more hotels of historic value than any other park. In all, Yellowstone boasts nine properties with 1043 hotel rooms and 1159 cabin units. *Note:* All accommodations must be booked through **TW Recreational Services** (Yellowstone National Park; 307-344-7311, fax 307-344-7456).

Grant Village (West Thumb; 307-242-3400), built in 1984, is the newest of the park hotels. Open late May to late September, it has 299 standard rooms, all with private bathrooms and showers. Facilities include a dining room and separate steakhouse, a lounge, a gift shop and a guest laundry. Moderate.

The massive yet rustic **Old Faithful Inn** (Old Faithful; 307-545-4600) was acclaimed a National Historic Landmark in 1987. Built of pine logs from the surrounding forests and volcanic rock from a nearby quarry, this 325-room hotel is said to be the largest log structure in the world. The gables on its steeply pitched roof were a trademark of architect Robert Reamer. In the enormous lobby are a stone fireplace and a clock handcrafted from copper, wood and wrought iron. The inn has deluxe suites, moderately priced rooms with private baths and budget-priced rooms with shared toilets and showers down the hall. Open early May to mid-October.

From the **Old Faithful Lodge and Cabins** (Old Faithful; 307-545-4900), just a couple of hundred yards south of the famous geyser, it seems as if you can reach out and touch the park landmark. The 130 rustic, budget-priced cabins include "frontier" units, with private toilets and showers, and "rough rider" units that share a common bathhouse. Open mid-May to mid-September.

Winter activities in this thermal basin center around the **Old Faithful Snow Lodge & Cabins** (Old Faithful; 307-545-4800), with 65 rooms. Most cabins have private baths; the lodge has shared toilets and showers. Open mid-December to mid-March and mid-May to early October. Budget and moderate.

The only other park accommodation open in both winter and summer is the **Mammoth Hot Springs Hotel** (Mammoth Hot Springs; 307-344-5400), built in 1937, which incorporates a wing of an earlier inn from 1911 (during the heyday of Fort Yellowstone). Its 223 rooms and cabin units come either with (moderate) or without (budget) private baths; four deluxe suite-style cabins have private hot tubs. Facilities include a dining room, fast-food outlet, lounge, gift shop and guest laundry. A decorative highlight is a huge United States map made of 15 woods from nine different countries. Open mid-May to late September and mid-December to early March.

The rustic **Roosevelt Lodge and Cabins** (Tower Junction; 307-344-5273), so named because of its proximity to President Teddy Roosevelt's favorite camping areas, has the feel of an earlier era. Its 69 cabins are of simple frame construction; some have electric heat and private baths, but most have wood-burning stoves and share a bathhouse. In the main lodge are two stone fireplaces, a family-style restaurant, a lounge and a gift shop. Open mid-June to late August. Budget and moderate.

Not far from the Grand Canyon of the Yellowstone is the 609-room **Canyon Lodge & Cabins** (Canyon Village; 307-242-3900). The new three-story lodge has hotel-style rooms with private baths; cabins are single-story four-plex units, all with private toilets and showers. In the main lodge are a dining room, cafeteria, snack shop, lounge and gift shop. Open early June to late August. Moderate.

The grande dame of Yellowstone hostelries is the **Lake Yellowstone Hotel & Cabins** (Lake Village; 307-242-3700). First opened in 1891 and listed on the National Register of Historic Places, the 296-room hotel has been fully renovated and again boasts its long-sequestered 1920s wicker furniture. The Sun Room, which has great lake views (especially at sunrise!), has evening cocktail service and frequent piano or chamber-music performances. Other facilities include a lakeside dining room, deli and gift shop. Guests choose between deluxe hotel rooms, less expensive annex rooms or cabins with private baths. Open mid-May to early October. Moderate to deluxe.

Relax in rocking chairs on the lodge porch of the **Lake Lodge and Cabins** (Lake Village; 307-242-3800) to take in a sweeping view of Yellowstone Lake to the east. The Lake Lodge has 186 cabins—some cozy, some spacious, all with private baths. In the classic log lodge are a big fireplace, a cafeteria, a lobby bar and a gift shop. There's also a guest laundry. Open mid-June to mid-September. Budget to moderate.

YELLOWSTONE NATIONAL PARK RESTAURANTS

Most restaurants within Yellowstone National Park are in the hotels and lodges themselves. Reservations are highly recommended at hotel dining rooms and the Old West Dinner Cookout.

The Steakhouse (Grant Village, West Thumb; 307-242-3400) serves up choice sirloins and filets mignon along with a sterling view across Yellowstone Lake. Seafood and chicken entrées are also on the dinner menu, and full breakfasts are served as well. Moderate.

The **Bear Pit Dining Room** (Old Faithful Inn, Old Faithful; 307-545-4600) offers a gourmet menu of prime rib, steak, seafood and poultry beneath the log beams and braces of this immense lodge. Etched glass panels are replicas of carved-wood murals. Three meals a day are served. Moderate. The hotel's **Pony Express** serves a take-out lunch and dinner menu. Budget.

Made-to-order deli sandwiches, homemade soup and other light fare are the specialties of the **Four Seasons Deli** (near Old Faithful Snow Lodge, Old Faithful). Budget.

Patrons of the **Mammoth Hotel Dining Room** (Mammoth Hot Springs; 307-344-5400) can enjoy three American-style meals a day amid the steaming travertine terraces for which the area is named. Moderate. In the same lodge, **The Terrace Grill** dishes up cafeteria-style fast food and snacks at budget prices.

For a taste of how things used to be, look no further than the **Old West Dinner Cookout** (Roosevelt Lodge, Tower Junction; 307-344-7311). Adventurous diners mount horses or clamber aboard a wagon and ride a short distance to Yancey's Hole, where they are served a hearty chuck-wagon dinner of steak, corn-on-the-cob, baked beans, corn muffins, cole slaw and more. Moderate.

The **Canyon Lodge Dining Room** (Canyon Village; 307-242-3900) offers American-style breakfasts and steak-and-seafood dinners daily in a forested setting just a half mile from the north rim of the Grand Canyon of the Yellowstone. Moderate prices.

Yellowstone's top-end culinary experience is at the **Lake Yellowstone Hotel Dining Room** (Lake Yellowstone Hotel, Lake Village; 307-242-7647). Prime rib, steak, seafood, chicken and vegetarian meals, as well as daily specials, are served in a classic lakeside setting of etched glass and wicker furniture. Breakfast and lunch are also available. Deluxe.

YELLOWSTONE NATIONAL PARK

Yellowstone National Park—Superlatives rule in Yellowstone's 2.2 million acres: the largest and most varied hydrothermal region on earth, the largest lake in North America at so high an elevation (7700 feet), the greatest diversity of wildlife in the Lower 48—the list goes on.

Facilities: Nine overnight lodges, 17 restaurants and snack shops, nine general stores and numerous other shops, 48 picnic areas, restrooms, five visitors centers, three museums, 11 amphitheaters, two marinas, boat ramps, boat and canoe rentals, 1200 miles of hiking and horse trails with 85 trailheads (permits required on some trails); $10 weekly vehicle pass (includes Grand Teton National Park); information, 307-344-7381. *Swimming:* Prohibited in thermal features; discouraged in Yellowstone and other lakes because of the risk of hypothermia from the cold waters. *Fishing:* Park permits ($5 for seven days) can be obtained at ranger stations, visitors centers and general stores. Regulations vary in park waters; for example, no fishing is allowed in a six-mile stretch of the Hayden Valley. Boating permits can be obtained at Grant or Lake villages. Cutthroat trout and mountain whitefish are native to Yellowstone waters, and rainbow trout have been introduced to all. There are brown trout in the Madison and Firehole rivers, mackinaw (lake trout) in Lewis and Shoshone lakes, brook trout in northeastern and western park streams, and arctic grayling in Wolf and Grebe lakes, between Norris and Canyon Village.

Camping: There are 2198 units (1853 for tents or RVs, 345 for RVs only) at 12 campgrounds (hookups at Fishing Bridge only), plus 330 backcountry campsites (tents only). Numbers of sites, open dates and fees are listed below. National Park Service campgrounds: *Lewis Lake* (85, early June to October 31, $6); *Norris* (116, mid-May to late September, $8); *Indian Creek* (75, early June to mid-September, $6); *Mammoth* (85, year-round, $8); *Tower Fall* (32, late May to mid-September, $6); *Slough Creek* (29, mid-May to October 31, $6); *Pebble Creek* (36, early June to early September, $6). TW Recreational Services campgrounds: *Grant Village* (414, late June to mid-October, $8); *Madison* (292, May 1 to October 31, $8); *Canyon* (280, early June to early September, $8); *Bridge Bay* (420, late May to late September, $10; reservations for stays from early June to Labor

Day through MISTIX, 800-365-2267); *Fishing Bridge* (345, RVs only, full hookups, mid-May to mid-September, $18).

Getting there: There are five park entrances: South (via Route 89/191 from Jackson and Route 287 from Dubois); West (via West Yellowstone, Route 20 from Idaho Falls, Route 191 from Bozeman and Route 287 from Ennis); North (via Gardiner, Route 89 from Livingston); Northeast (via Cooke City, Route 212 from Red Lodge and Billings); and East (Route 14/16/20 from Cody).

Yellowstone Gateway Communities

Just outside the three Montana entrances to Yellowstone National Park are a handful of small towns that serve a year-round coterie of tourists and outdoor-sports lovers. They are West Yellowstone, at the park's west entrance; Gardiner, at the north entrance; and Cooke City and Silver Gate, at the northeast entrance.

West Yellowstone, with about 900 full-time residents, is the park's primary "suburb," as it were. Founded in 1907 as a Union Pacific railroad terminus where Yellowstone visitors could transfer to stagecoaches for their tour of the national park, it gradually grew into the tourism-focused community it is today.

The train stopped running to West Yellowstone as private automobiles came into common use after World War II. The imposing stone Union Pacific Depot, damaged by the massive 7.1-magnitude 1959 earthquake but restored in 1972, is now the **Museum of the Yellowstone** (Yellowstone and Canyon avenues, West Yellowstone; 406-646-7814; admission). Permanent displays on regional history and wildlife are complemented by annually changing exhibits; there's also a bookstore and a theater showing documentary videos. Closed from November to April.

Almost across the street, the **Yellowstone IMAX Theatre** (Canyon Avenue, West Yellowstone; 406-646-4100; admission) presents *Grizzlies, Geysers, Grandeur* on its six-story screen with Dolby sound.

Next door to the theater, on the south side, is the **Grizzly Discovery Center** (Canyon Avenue, West Yellowstone; 406-646-7001; admission) where visitors can observe the natural behavior of grizzly bears in an outdoor viewing area constructed with minimal barriers. Several bears reside here; they have been orphaned, born in captivity or taken in as a habitual "problem" bear. The center also has museum displays and a gift shop.

The **West Yellowstone Visitor Information Center** (100 Yellowstone Avenue, West Yellowstone; 406-646-7701), open year-round, is one of the most comprehensive you'll find. Besides providing basic information on the town and the national park, chamber-of-commerce representatives locate lodging for tourists who arrive without reservations, and forest rangers advise on nearby camping when "Full" signs cover the campground board at Yellowstone's west entrance.

One of the most popular places to send campers is **Hebgen Lake**, less than five miles northwest of the town. Numerous recreation areas and campgrounds speckle the south and west shores of the 15-mile-long lake, created by the damming of the Madison River. The great earthquake of August 1959 had its epicenter just west of Hebgen Lake. The tremor dropped Hebgen's north shore 18 feet and caused a landslide that forged adjacent Quake Lake (see "Bozeman Area" in Chapter Thirteen). Twenty-eight campers died.

Gardiner, astride the Yellowstone River just five miles north of Mammoth Hot Springs, began life as an entertainment boom town for soldiers stationed at Mammoth in the late 19th century. By the time the army turned over its responsibilities to the National Park Service during World War I, the saloons, gambling halls and cigar factory were less important to Gardiner than its position as a terminus for the Yellowstone rail spur from Livingston.

Today, more than one million visitors a year stream through the Roosevelt Arch to the north entrance, the only park entrance open year-round. The town, while retaining some of its Wild West flavor, has a tidy tourist infrastructure of motels, restaurants, bars, a cinema and plenty of outfitters. For more information contact the **Chamber of Commerce** (P.O. Box 81, Gardiner, MT 59030; 406-848-7971).

Cooke City, four miles from Yellowstone's northeast entrance, goes about life in peaceful seclusion. Only a few hundred people live here and in the hamlet of **Silver Gate**, three miles west. In summer, the spectacular Beartooth Highway, which climbs to almost 11,000 feet atop the Beartooth Plateau, links the towns to Red Lodge, 66 miles northeast, and Cody, 77 miles southeast. But from mid-October through May, the towns are virtually isolated, reachable by only a 113-mile one-way road from Livingston, via Mammoth Hot Springs and Tower Junction.

Cooke City is perhaps best regarded as a stepping-off point for wilderness excursions. There's fishing, hunting and mountain climbing in the adjacent mountains, as well as horseback and backpacking trips. For more information, contact the **Cooke City Chamber of Commerce** (P.O. Box 1146, Cooke City, MT 59020; 406-838-2272, 406-838-2244).

Of particular note is the 14-mile trail to **Grasshopper Glacier** (★) in the Absaroka-Beartooth Wilderness Area. The glacier, one of the largest ice fields in the contiguous United States, takes its name from the millions of grasshoppers (of a now-extinct species) frozen in a sheer 80-foot cliff of glacial ice. Nearby is **Granite Peak**, at 12,799 feet Montana's tallest.

YELLOWSTONE GATEWAY COMMUNITIES HOTELS

Outside the west entrance, the **Stage Coach Inn** (209 Madison Avenue, West Yellowstone; 406-646-7381, 800-842-2882) is one of the nicest motels you'll find. A shingle-roofed lodging with a rock facade and a balcony that surrounds its large, knotty pine–paneled lobby and stone fireplace, it looks as if it came straight out of a storybook. The 86 guest rooms are cozy but nicely decorated. The inn has a dining room, coffee shop, casino-lounge, spa and sauna, game room for the kids and guest laundry. Moderate.

Six miles north of Mammoth Hot Springs, the two-story **Yellowstone Village Motel** (Route 89 North, Gardiner; 406-848-7417, 800-228-8158) is all rustic wood on the outside but virtually brand-new inside (it opened in 1992). The guest rooms include 40 standard-size units and two family condominium suites with full kitchens. The motel also has an indoor pool and sauna, a game arcade and a guest laundry. Budget to moderate.

In the Beartooth, the **All Seasons Mine Co. Hotel & Casino** (Route 212, Cooke City; 406-838-2251, 800-527-6462) has a little of everything. The 32 rooms have full baths and western-style decor. The hotel's restaurant is open for three meals daily, and there's a casino, hot tub and heated indoor pool. Moderate.

YELLOWSTONE GATEWAY COMMUNITIES RESTAURANTS

Regional game dishes—including elk and buffalo—are available outside the park's west entrance at the **Rustler's Roost** (234 Firehole Avenue, West Yellowstone; 406-646-7622), in the Best Western Pine Motel. Rainbow trout, chicken and prime rib are also on the menu at this family establishment, which offers a soup-and-salad bar and a children's menu as well. Three meals a day. Prices are moderate.

Alice's Restaurant (★) (1545 Targhee Pass Highway, West Yellowstone; 406-646-7296) is eight miles west of the park entrance on Route 20, but many folks find it worth the drive for its Bavarian atmosphere and excellent German-style cuisine. Schnitzels and grilled rainbow trout highlight the menu. The restaurant is located at the foot of the Continental Divide just east of the Idaho border. Moderate.

At the north entrance of the park, the **Yellowstone Mine Restaurant** (Route 89 at Hellroaring Street, Gardiner; 406-848-7336), in the Best Western by Mammoth Hot Springs, offers a fine steak-and-seafood menu amid the re-created ambience of a 19th-century mine. There's a children's menu, and breakfast is served as well. Moderate.

Beyond the park's remote northeast corner is **Joan & Bill's Restaurant** (Route 212; 406-838-2280), certainly a throwback to another era. Three meals are served daily in a relaxed and rustic family-style atmosphere in the heart of the old mining town of Cooke City. Budget.

YELLOWSTONE GATEWAY COMMUNITIES SHOPPING

Outside the park's west entrance in West Yellowstone, check out **Eagle's Store** (3 Canyon Avenue; 406-646-9300) for western wear, outdoor equipment and Native American crafts and the **Madison Gift Shop** (139 Yellowstone Avenue; 406-646-7745) for a large selection of souvenirs. **Kellem's Montana Saddlery** (222 Main Street, Gardiner; 406-848-7776) may be the most intriguing store outside the north entrance; its inventory runs from cowboy gear to clothing, silver jewelry and Montana-made gifts.

YELLOWSTONE GATEWAY COMMUNITIES NIGHTLIFE

Theater is growing in popularity in the gateway communities. West Yellowstone, in fact, has two stages. The **Musical Moose Playhouse** (124 Madison Avenue; 406-646-9710; admission) focuses on vaudeville revues presented "nearly year-round." The **Playmill Theatre** (29 Madison Avenue; 406-646-7757; admission) has presented a summer season of melodrama and musical comedy since 1964. Seven miles north of Gardiner, the professional **Paradise Players** (Route 89, Corwin Springs; 406-848-7891) present family-oriented dinner theater from June to September.

The Sporting Life

FISHING

Except within the boundaries of Yellowstone National Park, where all anglers regardless of residency must buy a seven-day park license, anyone fishing in Wyoming must obtain a state license. For more information, call the Jackson regional office of the **Wyoming Game and Fish Division** (307-733-2321).

Jackson Lake and other Grand Teton National Park lakes have excellent cutthroat and mackinaw (lake trout) fisheries. The Snake River is considered superb for cutthroat and brook trout.

Yellowstone Lake is renowned for its cutthroat trout, as is the upper portion of the Yellowstone River between Fishing Bridge and the Hayden Valley. Rainbow and brook trout and grayling are native to waters on the west side of the Continental Divide, including Shoshone and Lewis lakes, the Gallatin and Madison rivers and their tributaries, and Hebgen Lake, outside the park near West Yellowstone, Montana.

JACKSON HOLE Nearly two dozen fishing outfitters are based in Jackson Hole to guide anxious anglers to their limits of trout. **Joe Allen's Scenic Fishing** (300 Flat Creek Road, Jackson; 307-733-8025) has been leading guided trips for over 40 years; **Fort Jackson River Trips** (1000 South Route 89, Jackson; 307-733-2583) is the oldest float-trip operator in the valley.

YELLOWSTONE NATIONAL PARK Within the park, you can buy or rent complete fishing gear at marinas on Yellowstone Lake; guides are generally available at the marinas as well. Try the **Lake Yellowstone Hotel** (Lake Village; 307-242-3700) or **Grant Village** (West Thumb; 307-242-3400). Tackle is also available at **Hamilton Stores** located throughout the park (Mammoth Hot Springs; 307-344-7702).

YELLOWSTONE GATEWAY COMMUNITIES Outfitters in the gateway communities include **Bud Lilly's Trout Shop** (39 Madison Avenue, West Yellowstone; 406-646-7801), **Jacklin's Outfitters for the World of Fly Fishing** (105

Yellowstone Avenue, West Yellowstone; 406-646-7336) and **Parks' Fly Shop** (2nd Street, Gardiner; 406-848-7314).

BOATING

Marinas in Grand Teton National Park (on Jackson Lake) and Yellowstone National Park (on Yellowstone Lake) offer full boat-rental services and guided lake trips.

GRAND TETON NATIONAL PARK In Grand Teton, visit the **Colter Bay Marina** (Rockefeller Parkway, Moran; 307-543-3594), which is administered by the park and features twice-a-week dinner cruises, or the privately owned **Signal Mountain Lodge** (Teton Park Road, Moran; 307-733-5470). Shuttles across little Jenny Lake are operated by the **Teton Boating Co.** (South Jenny Lake, Moose; 307-733-2703).

YELLOWSTONE NATIONAL PARK In Yellowstone, 40-passenger excursion boats leave the **Bridge Bay Marina** (Bridge Bay; 307-344-7381) several times daily on lake cruises; there are also twilight trips and individual motorboat rentals. The marina at **Grant Village** (West Thumb; 307-242-3400) also has rentals. Ranger stations provide boat-operating permits on request.

RIVER RAFTING, CANOEING AND KAYAKING

The best rivers in the greater Yellowstone area for whitewater rafting and kayaking are the Snake, south of Jackson, and the Gallatin, north of Yellowstone in Montana. For tranquil float trips or easy canoeing with spectacular scenery and abundant wildlife, it is hard to top the upper Snake River through Grand Teton National Park.

JACKSON HOLE Whitewater enthusiasts love the eight-mile Snake River Canyon south of Jackson. It's a good half-day trip, exciting but not too strenuous, and it can be combined with some flatter portions of the river for a leisurely full-day excursion. **Barker-Ewing River Trips** (45 West Broadway, Jackson; 307-733-1000), **Mad River Boat Trips** (1060 South Route 89, Jackson; 307-733-6203) and a half-dozen other outfitters all run this stretch. The only rapid you *really* have to look out for is the one known as Lunch Counter!

The **Snake River Kayak & Canoe School** (155 West Gill Street, Jackson; 307-733-3127) introduces novice and intermediate paddlers to Snake River whitewater. Camping tours, by sea kayak, of the shores of Yellowstone Lake are also offered. **Far & Away Adventures** (Jackson; 307-733-9767) offer guided paddling trips on backcountry lakes in Yellowstone Park.

All manner of water craft and support gear can be rented or repaired at **Teton Aquatic Supplies** (145 West Gill Street, Jackson; 307-733-3127). Rentals of rafts and kayaks can also be made from **Leisure Sports** (1075 South Route 89, Jackson; 307-733-3040).

GRAND TETON NATIONAL PARK The **Grand Teton Lodge Company** (Jackson Lake Lodge, Moran; 307-543-2811) offers scenic float trips, including lunch and dinner voyages, along a ten-and-a-half-mile stretch of the upper Snake from mid-May through September. Numerous other outfitters, including **National Park Float Trips** (Moose; 307-733-6445), put in at Deadman's Bar, south of Moran, and take out at Moose Visitors Center.

YELLOWSTONE GATEWAY COMMUNITIES Most of the rafting outfitters that operate in the Montana rivers north of Yellowstone National Park are based in Bozeman, Livingston or Big Sky. An exception is the **Yellowstone Raft Company** (P.O. Box 46, Gardiner, MT 59030; 406-848-7777), which runs the Yellowstone, Gallatin and other rivers on the north side of the park. See Chapter Thirteen, "Southern Montana Rockies."

DOWNHILL SKIING

For die-hard skiers and snowboarders, there's no place like the **Jackson Hole Ski Area** (Route 390, Teton Village; 406-733-4005, 800-443-6931, fax 307-733-1286), 12 miles west of the town of Jackson. From the top of 10,450-foot Rendezvous Peak to the base lodge at Teton Village, the vertical drop is 4139 feet, the longest of any skiable mountain in the United States. About 33 feet of snow fall annually. Runs like Corbet's Couloir, a frightening mountaintop chute, and the Hobacks, a series of steep, ungroomed, backcountry glades, make this a mecca for expert skiers.

But only 50 percent of the area's 2500 acres are rated expert. There's plenty of intermediate terrain, and beginners are served by runs on adjoining Apres Vous Mountain. Lifts include seven chairlifts and a 2.4-mile-long aerial tramway that carries five dozen skiers to the summit every 12 minutes. Full alpine, telemark and snowboard rentals are available. The season extends from early December through early April.

The Jackson Hole Ski Area was not the first in the Hole. That honor belongs to the **Snow King Resort** (400 East Snow King Avenue, Jackson; 307-733-5200, 800-522-5464), established in 1939. The slopes drop 1571 feet right to the edge of town—just eight blocks southeast of Town Square, in fact. Three chairlifts and a surface tow serve 400 acres of skiable terrain, including 110 acres lit for night skiing. Snow King's season runs from Thanksgiving weekend to early April.

Also served by Jackson is the **Grand Targhee Ski & Summer Resort** (Targhee Road, Alta, Wyoming; 307-353-2300), on the west side of the Teton Range. The resort gets more than 500 inches of snow (more than 40 feet) a year, and is regarded as one of America's great getaways for powder hounds. Because it can only be reached through Idaho, it is detailed in Chapter Ten, "Southeastern Idaho Rockies."

Skiers who don't find the extremes they want at the formal ski areas can arrange to be dropped off in the Teton Range by helicopter. **High Mountain Heli-Skiing** (Teton Village Sports, Teton Village; 307-733-3274) offers packages.

SKI RENTALS For rentals outside the ski resorts themselves, try **Jack Dennis Sports** (50 East Broadway, Jackson, 307-733-3270; and Alpenhof Lodge, Teton Village, 307-733-6838) and **Teton Village Sports** (Crystal Springs Inn, Teton Village; 307-733-2181). Nordic specialists with rentals available include

Winter Wonderland

If anything, the natural wonders of Yellowstone National Park are more spectacular in winter than in summer. Imagine, for instance, the steam from hot springs and geysers filling the frigid Rocky Mountain air as snow falls all around.

From mid-December to mid-March, Yellowstone is a paradise for cross-country skiers, snowmobilers and snowshoers. Although the park is accessible by car only at its north entrance, via Gardiner, Montana—this route, through Mammoth Hot Springs to Tower Junction and Cooke City, Montana, on the Beartooth Plateau, is kept open year-round—there are other ways to get there.

Heated, ten-passenger snowcoaches (track vans) run from the south and west entrances as well as from Mammoth Hot Springs. Coaches operated by **TW Recreational Services** (Mammoth Hot Springs; 307-344-7311) depart from the south entrance for Old Faithful every afternoon, returning every morning. The journey takes three and a half hours. Similar trips connect Old Faithful and Canyon Village with West Yellowstone and Mammoth Hot Springs. Other snowcoaches are run by **Sno-Vans of Yellowstone** (530 Madison Avenue, West Yellowstone; 406-646-7276) and **Yellowstone Alpen Guides** (555 Yellowstone Avenue, West Yellowstone; 406-646-9591).

Mammoth Hot Springs Hotel and Old Faithful Snow Lodge are the only park accommodations open during winter, although warming huts throughout the park provide shelter. Old Faithful, like the rest of the park, can be reached only across snow. But like the Mammoth hotel, the Snow Lodge serves three good meals daily and offers both nordic skiing and snowshoeing equipment rentals and lessons. It's a good base for winter exploration of the park.

Hundreds of miles of cross-country ski trails are marked in Yellowstone, and the most popular are groomed. Those include the geyser basin trails at Old Faithful and the canyon rim trail at the Grand Canyon of the Yellowstone. Trail maps are available at visitors centers.

Snowmobiles are restricted to 300 miles of park roads, groomed daily. Expect a four-foot snowpack beside highways. TW Recreational Services rents snowmobiles with helmets and all appropriate clothing.

Within Grand Teton National Park, snowmobiling is permitted on ten miles of closed roads north of Moose and on Jackson Lake when it is sufficiently frozen. Ice fishing and ranger-led snowshoe hikes are other winter activities in that park.

Skinny Skis (65 West Deloney Street, Jackson; 307-733-6094) and **Wilson Backcountry Sports** (1230 Ida Drive, Wilson; 307-733-5228).

CROSS-COUNTRY SKIING

JACKSON HOLE The **Jackson Hole Nordic Center** (Teton Village; 307-739-2629) has 15 kilometers of groomed nordic trails along with full equipment rentals. There are also trails and rentals at the **Snow King Resort** (400 East Snow King Avenue, Jackson; 307-733-5200). And a pair of fair-weather golf courses are home to the **Spring Creek Nordic Center** (Spring Gulch Road, Jackson; 307-733-8833) and the **Teton Pines Nordic Ski Center** (3450 North Clubhouse Drive, Teton Village; 307-733-1005). Both have about 13 kilometers of groomed trails, rentals and instruction.

Hardy adventurers can learn winter mountaineering and join hut-to-hut skiing expeditions with **Jackson Hole Mountain Guides** (165 North Glenwood Street, Jackson; 307-733-4979).

GRAND TETON NATIONAL PARK Some 65 kilometers of marked but ungroomed trails are open to cross-country skiers in **Grand Teton National Park**; maps are available at the Moose Visitors Center (Moose; 307-733-2880), open daily in winter. Maps and information on nordic trails within **Bridger-Teton National Forest**—including the Cache Creek, Shadow Mountain, Teton Pass and Togwotee Mountain Lodge areas—are available from the National Forest office (340 North Cache Street, Jackson; 307-739-5500).

YELLOWSTONE NATIONAL PARK Yellowstone National Park has hundreds of miles of marked cross-country ski trails, including groomed tracks near Old Faithful and the Grand Canyon of the Yellowstone (see sidebar, "Winter Wonderland").

YELLOWSTONE GATEWAY COMMUNITIES Just outside the park boundaries, **The Rendezvous Ski Trails** (West Yellowstone; 406-646-7701) offer 26 kilometers of groomed trails, and another eight kilometers ungroomed, from November through April. The U.S. national cross-country and biathlon (skiing and shooting) teams train here each year.

For information on renting equipment, see the ski-rental section in "Downhill Skiing" above.

ICE SKATING

There's ice skating in Jackson at the **Snow King Center Ice Rink** (100 East Snow King Avenue, Jackson; 307-733-5200). The indoor rink at the foot of the Snow King Mountain ski slopes offers rentals and instruction. The rink is open to the public from November to April. There's also a free **outdoor rink** on Cache Street, two blocks south of Town Square, open daily in winter, weather permitting.

In Yellowstone National Park, the **Mammoth Hot Springs Hotel** (Mammoth Hot Springs; 307-344-5400) has an outdoor rink with skate rentals open throughout the winter.

GOLF

JACKSON HOLE Jackson Hole has some great 18-hole courses, but snow severely limits the season: It is typically May 1 to October 15.

The **Jackson Hole Golf & Tennis Club** (one mile west of Route 89 at Gros Ventre Junction; 307-733-3111), operated by the Grand Teton Lodging Company, has been rated by *Golf Digest* magazine as one of the top ten resort courses in the United States. Located eight miles north of Jackson, the course was redesigned by the renowned Robert Trent Jones, Jr.

The course at the **Teton Pines Country Club & Resort** (3450 North Clubhouse Drive, off Teton Village Road, Wilson; 307-733-1733), six miles west of Jackson, is every bit the equal of the Jackson Hole Golf & Tennis Club. Designed by Arnold Palmer and Ed Seay, it is rated the number-one course in Wyoming by *Golf Digest.* Though a private course, it's open to the public.

Playful putters will find an 18-hole miniature golf course at **Snow King Resort** (400 East Snow King Avenue, Jackson; 307-733-7680).

TENNIS

Both the **Jackson Hole Golf & Tennis Club** (off Route 89 at Gros Ventre Junction; 307-733-7787) and the **Teton Pines Tennis Center** (3450 North Clubhouse Drive, Wilson; 307-733-9248) have public courts available—six Plexicushion courts at the former, seven courts (plus indoor courts for winter play) at the latter. Call ahead for court times.

HORSEBACK RIDING

Three stables in Yellowstone National Park and two in Grand Teton offer park visitors ample opportunities for one- and two-hour guided rides in off-the-road wilderness. Private outfitters throughout the region provide many more options. Half-day, full-day and extended overnight trips are available. Some outfitters offer riding lessons; more commonly, novice riders will be matched with gentler horses.

JACKSON HOLE In Jackson Hole, for short daytrips and breakfast and dinner rides, check **Snow King Stables** (Snow King Resort, 400 East Snow King Avenue, Jackson; 307-733-5781), right in town; or the **A/OK Corral** (Route 191, Hoback Junction; 307-733-6556), a few miles south. At the latter, non-riders can travel in covered wagons to join their horse-borne friends at chuck wagon dinners. Horse rentals can be arranged through **Rocky Mountain Recreation** (Routes 26/89, Alpine Junction; 307-654-9900), 35 miles southwest of Jackson.

GRAND TETON NATIONAL PARK The Grand Teton Lodging Company offers all manner of trail rides from both the **Colter Bay Village Corral** (Rockefeller Parkway, Moran; 307-543-3594) and the **Jackson Bay Lodge Corral** (Rockefeller Parkway, Moran; 307-543-2811).

YELLOWSTONE NATIONAL PARK One- and two-hour guided trail rides depart from corrals at **Mammoth Hot Springs** (307-344-5400), **Roosevelt**

Lodge (307-344-5273) and **Canyon Village** (307-242-3900) throughout the day. Roosevelt visitors can also ride to Yancey's Hole for an Old West dinner cookout or hop aboard a horse-drawn stagecoach for half-hour rambles around the Tower Junction area. Schedules vary; the summer riding season is longest at lower-lying Mammoth than at the other two sites.

YELLOWSTONE GATEWAY COMMUNITIES Proficient riders can rent steeds for unguided trips from **Lone Rider Stables** (1111 Targhee Pass Highway, West Yellowstone; 406-646-7900).

PACK TRIPS

Backcountry horse trips are the forté of groups like **Bridger Teton Outfitters** (Star Route Box 347, Jackson, WY 83001; 307-733-7745), which ventures into the Gros Ventre Wilderness and Wind River Range, and **Peterson-Madsen-Taylor Outfitters** (Turpin Meadows, Moran; 307-543-2418), which focuses on the Teton Wilderness.

Guided pack trips through Yellowstone's backcountry and nearby wilderness are offered by **Diamond P Ranch** (2865 Targhee Pass Highway, West Yellowstone; 406-646-7246), **Hell's a Roarin' Outfitters** (Route 89 North, Gardiner; 406-848-7578), **Wilderness Connection** (Cinnabar Basin Road, Gardiner; 406-848-7287) and **Beartooth Plateau Outfitters** (Main Street, Cooke City; 406-838-2328).

LLAMA TREKKING

The llama is more a hiking companion than a mode of transportation; it carries all the gear while you proceed on foot. Guided four- and five-day llama treks through Yellowstone Park or the nearby Jedediah Smith Wilderness are the specialty of **Jackson Hole Llamas** (P.O. Box 7375, Jackson, WY 83001; 307-733-1617). Routes range from moderate to strenuous.

Treks into the Bridger-Teton National Forest and Gros Ventre Wilderness are the realm of **Black Diamond Llama Expeditions** (2150 East Barberry Road, Jackson; 307-733-2877). Llama rentals are offered by **Rendezvous Llamas** (P.O. Box 8459, Jackson, WY 83001; 307-739-1639); rates include a lesson.

BICYCLING

Mountain bikes have become a common sight in recent years, joining touring bikes on and off the roads of northwestern Wyoming. Many of the routes here are narrow and dangerous, so helmets and rear-view mirrors, small tool kits, first-aid kits and (if you're venturing into the backcountry) emergency survival kits are essential accessories.

JACKSON HOLE A broad, relatively flat valley surrounded on all sides by mountains, Jackson Hole is a natural for biking.

For a moderate day ride, locals recommend the **Cache Creek-Game Creek** loop trail, an 18-mile circuit around Snow King Mountain southeast of Jackson in Bridger-Teton National Forest.

One-day guided tours of the National Elk Refuge, lasting from three to nine hours, are offered by **Teton Mountain Bike Tours** (430 South Cache Street, Jackson; 307-733-0712).

GRAND TETON NATIONAL PARK Grand Teton National Park roads and other valley highways are great for touring; hundreds of miles of trails and dirt roads head into adjacent national forests. Wilderness areas are off-limits.

The 15-mile **RKO Road** in Grand Teton National Park, a dirt road along a bluff on the west side of the Snake River from Signal Mountain to Cottonwood Creek, is a good bet for a moderate day ride.

Teton Mountain Bike Tours (430 South Cache Street, Jackson; 307-733-0712) offers one-day guided tours, lasting from three to nine hours, through the national park.

YELLOWSTONE NATIONAL PARK Bicycling through Yellowstone can be an exhilarating experience but it is not without peril. There are no bicycle lanes along park roads, and because roads are narrow and winding, high-visibility clothing and helmets are recommended. Keep an eye out for campers and RVs passing you from behind; their projecting mirrors pose a particular safety threat. Though a few bike paths do exist around park communities, bicycles are not permitted on boardwalks or backcountry trails.

YELLOWSTONE GATEWAY COMMUNITIES Bicycle tours through Yellowstone are offered by **Yellowstone Eco Tours** (555 Yellowstone Avenue, West Yellowstone; 406-646-9009) and **Yellowstone Mountain Bike Tours and Rentals** (P.O. Box 840, Gardiner, MT 59030; 406-848-7600).

BIKE RENTALS Several Jackson Hole shops rent and repair bicycles and provide regional biking maps. For touring and mountain bikes in downtown Jackson try **Hoback Sports** (40 South Millward Street; 307-733-5335) and **Teton Cyclery** (175 North Glenwood Street; 307-733-4386). Near Grand Teton National Park, mountain-bike specialists are **Mountain Bike Outfitters** (10 Moose Lane, Moose; 307-733-3314), located at Dornan's at the south entrance to Grand Teton National Park, and **Wilson Backcountry Sports** (1230 Ida Drive, Wilson; 307-733-5288), at Fishcreek Center at the foot of Teton Pass. In the Yellowstone area, a good full-service bicycle shop is **Yellowstone Bicycles** (132 Madison Avenue, West Yellowstone; 406-646-7815).

HIKING

All distances listed for hiking trails are one-way unless otherwise noted.

JACKSON HOLE The moderate descent of **Rendezvous Peak** (4.2 miles) is made easier by the Jackson Hole Aerial Tramway. Take it to the top; then start down through Rock Springs Bowl. Wildflowers, small mammals and birds (including large raptors) are often seen.

Goodwin Lake-Cache Creek Trail (7.5 miles) is a moderately strenuous introduction to the Gros Ventre Wilderness Area east of Jackson. Starting at the end of Curtis Canyon Road, nine miles northeast of Jackson, the trail traverses a high plateau at 10,000 feet before dropping to the headwaters of Cache Creek. If you don't have a car waiting to pick you up at the trailhead, you'll have to walk an extra five miles downhill to Jackson. Guided interpretive hikes in the Bridger-Teton National Forest are offered by **The Hole Hiking Experience** (470 East Hanson Avenue, Jackson; 307-739-7155).

GRAND TETON NATIONAL PARK **Hidden Falls Trail** (2.5 miles) is an easy two-mile walk around the southwest shore of Jenny Lake from the South Jenny ranger station and a strenuous half-mile uphill scramble to the secluded cascade. If you want to continue, there's another half-mile climb to Inspiration Point and then six and a half more through Cascade Canyon to lovely Lake Solitude. Boat shuttles across Jenny Lake are available to return tired hikers from near Hidden Falls to the South Jenny ranger station.

Two Ocean Lake Trail (12.2 miles) circles the three-mile-long lake in the park's northeastern corner, skirts adjacent Emma Matilda Lake and climbs to a panoramic outlook toward Jackson Lake at Grand View Point. It's of moderate difficulty.

Teton Crest Trail (27 miles) has many feeder trails and many spurs. One popular if strenuous circuit of the Grand Teton begins at Jenny Lake Lodge (6900 feet), climbs west on the Paintbrush Canyon Trail to Lake Solitude, then turns south along the upper slopes of Mount Owen and the high Tetons. The trail crests at about 11,000 feet before descending again on switchbacks through Death Canyon to Phelps Lake and Teton Village (6300 feet).

All overnight backcountry camping requires a permit, which can be obtained free at ranger stations.

YELLOWSTONE NATIONAL PARK Yellowstone contains more than 1200 miles of marked hiking trails and 85 trailheads. Trails include the boardwalks and handicapped-accessible trails at **Upper Geyser Basin** (Old Faithful), **Norris Geyser Basin** and **Mammoth Hot Springs**, among others.

For youngsters, the **Fountain Paint Pot Nature Trail** (.5 mile) in the Lower Geyser Basin and the **Children's Fire Trail** (.5 mile) east of Mammoth Hot Springs have several interpretive stations to help teach about thermal activity and forest fires, respectively.

Backcountry permits are required for all overnight hikes and some day hikes in Yellowstone Park. They can be obtained at no charge from ranger stations within 48 hours before you start your hike. Topographic maps are sold at Hamilton Stores.

Avalanche Peak Trail (2.5 miles) is a strenuous ascent to a 10,566-foot summit, a mile west of Sylvan Pass on the East Entrance Road. Look for the unsigned trailhead opposite the Eleanor Lake picnic area. The trail transits several eco-zones before achieving the peak, which provides spectacular views across Yellowstone Lake to the Tetons and beyond.

Mount Washburn Trail (3 miles) leads to another panoramic point, but the climb isn't as steep as Avalanche Peak. Bighorn sheep are often seen on top. There are trailheads on the Grand Loop Road (north of Canyon Village) at the Dunraven Pass picnic area and the Chittenden Road parking area.

Seven Mile Hole Trail (5.5 miles) offers an impressive way to see the Grand Canyon of the Yellowstone . . . close up. Beginning on the Inspiration Point spur road a mile east of Canyon Village, it clings to the rim of the gorge for the first mile and a half, then swings into the pine forest and drops rapidly for three miles to the canyon floor near Sulphur Creek. Perhaps needless to say, the return climb is harder than the descent.

Bechler River Trail (32 miles) traverses the park's rarely visited southwest corner. It begins at Old Faithful, crosses the Continental Divide three times and then descends steep-sided Bechler Canyon, passing dazzling waterfalls and hot springs. The trail crosses Bechler Meadows, a low-lying haven for moose, black bear and trumpeter swans, and ends at Bechler River Ranger Station, off Cave Falls Road 25 miles east of Ashton, Idaho. Moderate.

YELLOWSTONE GATEWAY COMMUNITIES For guided hikes through the park, contact **Yellowstone Eco Tours** (555 Yellowstone Avenue, West Yellowstone; 406-646-9009).

MOUNTAINEERING

The Teton Range is considered one of the world's finest tests for experienced climbers. Yet even first-timers can master the apparently insurmountable 13,770-foot Grand Teton itself, given that they have good physical strength, determination and expert instruction.

The latter element can be provided by Jackson Hole's two internationally renowned climbing schools: **Exum Mountain Guides** (South Jenny Lake, Moose; 307-733-2297) and **Jackson Hole Mountain Guides** (165 North Glenwood Street, Jackson; 307-733-4979).

Teton Mountaineering (170 North Cache Street, Jackson; 307-733-3595) has the largest inventory of equipment and clothing in the area.

Transportation

BY CAR

Interstate highways surround, but don't invade, northwestern Wyoming. A broad choice of highways provide easy access from all directions, however. Five routes come together in Jackson Hole, seven in Yellowstone National Park.

To reach Jackson, take **Route 26** west off Route 25 at Casper; **Route 191** north at Rock Springs or **Route 189** north at Evanston off Route 80; or Route 26 east off Route 15 at Idaho Falls, Idaho.

To reach Yellowstone, take **Route 89/191** north from Jackson; **Route 14/16/20** west from Cody; **Route 212** southwest off Route 90 near Billings, Montana; **Route 89** south at Livingston, Montana, or **Route 191** south at Bozeman, Montana, off 90; **Route 287** southeast off 90 near Butte, Montana; or **Route 20** northeast off **Route 15** at Idaho Falls.

BY AIR

The region's primary airport is in Jackson. West Yellowstone is served by commuter airlines in summer.

Jackson Hole Airport has regular daily nonstop arrivals from and departures to Chicago, Denver and Salt Lake City, with connecting flights from many other cities. It is served by American Airlines, Continental Express, Delta Air Lines, SkyWest Airlines and United Express. Regional charters and scenic flights are available at the airport.

From May to September, the **West Yellowstone Airport** in West Yellowstone, at the west entrance to Yellowstone National Park, is served by regular SkyWest commuter flights and by charters. The airport closes during the winter.

Limousines and taxis take visitors to and from the airport. Try calling **Jackson Hole Transportation** (307-733-3135) or **All Star Transportation** (307-733-2888).

BY BUS

Greyhound Bus Lines (800-231-2222) serves West Yellowstone, Montana (between Idaho Falls, Idaho, and Bozeman, Montana), in summer.

Gray Line (800-733-2304) offers seasonal charter service and guided tours through Yellowstone Park from Jackson Hole (330 North Glenwood Street, Jackson; 307-733-4324) and West Yellowstone (633 Madison Avenue, West Yellowstone; 406-646-9374).

In addition, **Karst Stage** (406-586-8567) offers seasonal bus service into the park at its west (West Yellowstone) and north (Gardiner) entrances from Bozeman.

Backroads Tours and **Access Tours** (both at P.O. Box 2985, Jackson, WY 83001; 307-733-6664) offer multiday van tours of the northwestern Wyoming region and elsewhere in the Rockies for travelers with disabilities.

CAR RENTALS

Rental agencies at the Jackson Hole Airport are **Alamo Rent A Car** (800-327-9633), **Avis Rent A Car** (800-331-1212), **Budget Rent A Car** (800-527-0700) and **Hertz Rent A Car** (800-654-3131). A locally owned agency, worth checking out is **Jackson Hole Car Rental** (75 South Glenwood Street, Jackson; 307-733-6868, 800-722-2002).

In West Yellowstone, you'll find **Avis Rent A Car** (800-331-1212) at the Yellowstone Airport. **Big Sky** (415 Yellowstone Avenue; 406-646-9564) and **Budget Rent A Car** (131 Dunraven Street; 800-527-0700) are in town.

PUBLIC TRANSPORTATION

In Jackson, the **Southern Teton Area Rapid Transit** (307-733-4521), known as START, runs two routes—between Jackson and Teton Village, and Jackson and Hoback Junction, both extending to the Snow King Resort.

Guided all-day motorcoach tours of Yellowstone National Park are offered from various park lodgings by **BTW Recreational Services** (307-344-7311).

TAXIS

Jackson Hole Transportation (307-733-3135) and **All Star Transportation** (307-733-2888) provide taxi and limo service in Jackson Hole, meeting all incoming and departing flights.

In Jackson, quaint pedicabs, available for transportation and historical tours, are offered by the **Teton Carriage Company** (307-730-8705) within a four-block radius of the Town Square.

CHAPTER EIGHT

Northern Wyoming Rockies

Dramatic natural features like the Bighorn Canyon, Devils Tower and the Absaroka and Big Horn mountain ranges are what many visitors remember most about Wyoming's northern tier from Yellowstone Park east to the South Dakota border. But what really sets the region apart are its broad river basins and open grasslands. This is cowboy country, as true as true can be.

This is the land that fostered the legends of "Buffalo Bill" Cody and Butch Cassidy, of Crazy Horse and Sitting Bull. Cody's namesake town today proudly bears the label "Rodeo Capital of the World." Cassidy's Hole-in-the-Wall hideout is as remote as it ever was. Memories of Crazy Horse and Sitting Bull, whose proud Sioux warriors once rode the Powder River plains, live on at battlefield sites north and south of Sheridan. Throughout the region, guest ranches inspire horsemanship and campfire cooking.

Man has lived in the northern Wyoming Rockies for at least 10,000 years, white man for not much more than the last 150. Two major archaeological sites on the western slope of the Big Horn Mountains show that Native Americans were writing on cliff walls (at Medicine Lodge) and building astronomical monuments (at Medicine Wheel) long before the rise of any of the great Chinese, Egyptian or Mesoamerican civilizations.

It was the arrival of the horse some time around A.D. 1700 that marked the beginning of Wyoming's modern era. Brought by Spaniards to the New World, the horse revolutionized the lives of the Plains Indian. With the horse, the Lakota Sioux could hunt bison, win battles and dominate the area from the Black Hills to the Big Horn Basin.

The threat of Indian hostility against pioneers in the Big Horn region kept this part of the Wyoming territory largely unsettled by whites until the 1880s.

Then, army campaigns opened up more livestock range for cattlemen and sheepherders, who were moving north from the rail corridor in southern Wyoming.

Today, with just 18,000 people, the coal- and oil-boom town of Gillette is the largest community in Wyoming's north. Sheridan has about 14,000, Cody about 8000.

A center for ranching as well as tourism, Cody is on the western edge of the Big Horn Basin. The Bighorn River flows north through the basin from its headwaters in the Wind River Range, disappearing into Montana through the magnificent Bighorn Canyon and its encompassing national recreation area, near Lovell. Several highways scale the Big Horn Mountains east of the river, dropping on their eastern front to the prairies that stretch east from Sheridan, through the mineral-rich grasslands around Gillette, to the Black Hills of South Dakota.

Devils Tower National Monument, on Wyoming's northeasternmost corner, rises a quarter-mile straight up from surrounding pine forests, like a pillar that signals starships. (Remember Steven Spielberg's *Close Encounters of the Third Kind?* This was the place . . .)

Cody Area

Cody is Cowboy Country, with a capital C: it's the chosen home of Colonel William F. "Buffalo Bill" Cody and the self-proclaimed "Rodeo Capital of the World."

Located on the Shoshone River beneath the towering peaks of the Absaroka Range, at the western edge of the Big Horn Basin, Cody was founded in 1895 as a rail terminus of the Chicago, Burlington & Quincy line. A group of entrepreneurs, including Buffalo Bill himself, foresaw the commercial opportunities in tourism and recreation that such a location, 52 miles from the east entrance to Yellowstone National Park, might provide. Cody offered his name to the town, and his gracious partners concurred; he already had national name recognition.

Modern Cody has a battery of comfortable motels and restaurants serving travelers a short drive from Yellowstone—as well as considerable tourist attractions of its own.

Chief among them is the **Buffalo Bill Historical Center** (720 Sheridan Avenue, Cody; 307-587-4771; admission), certainly one of the finest museums in the Rocky Mountain region and, some say, in all of the United States. The large modern building, located at the west end of downtown Cody, is impossible to miss (not that you'd want to). Inside are four separate collections that comprise a sort of Smithsonian Institution of the American West.

The **Buffalo Bill Museum** is dedicated to Cody himself, a man who—probably more than any other—symbolized the emergence of the West from a primitive frontier to a vital and integral part of the United States. The vast assemblage includes "Lucretia Borgia," the rifle Cody used while earning the nickname "Buffalo Bill," shooting bison in the employ of the railroad; and a wide variety

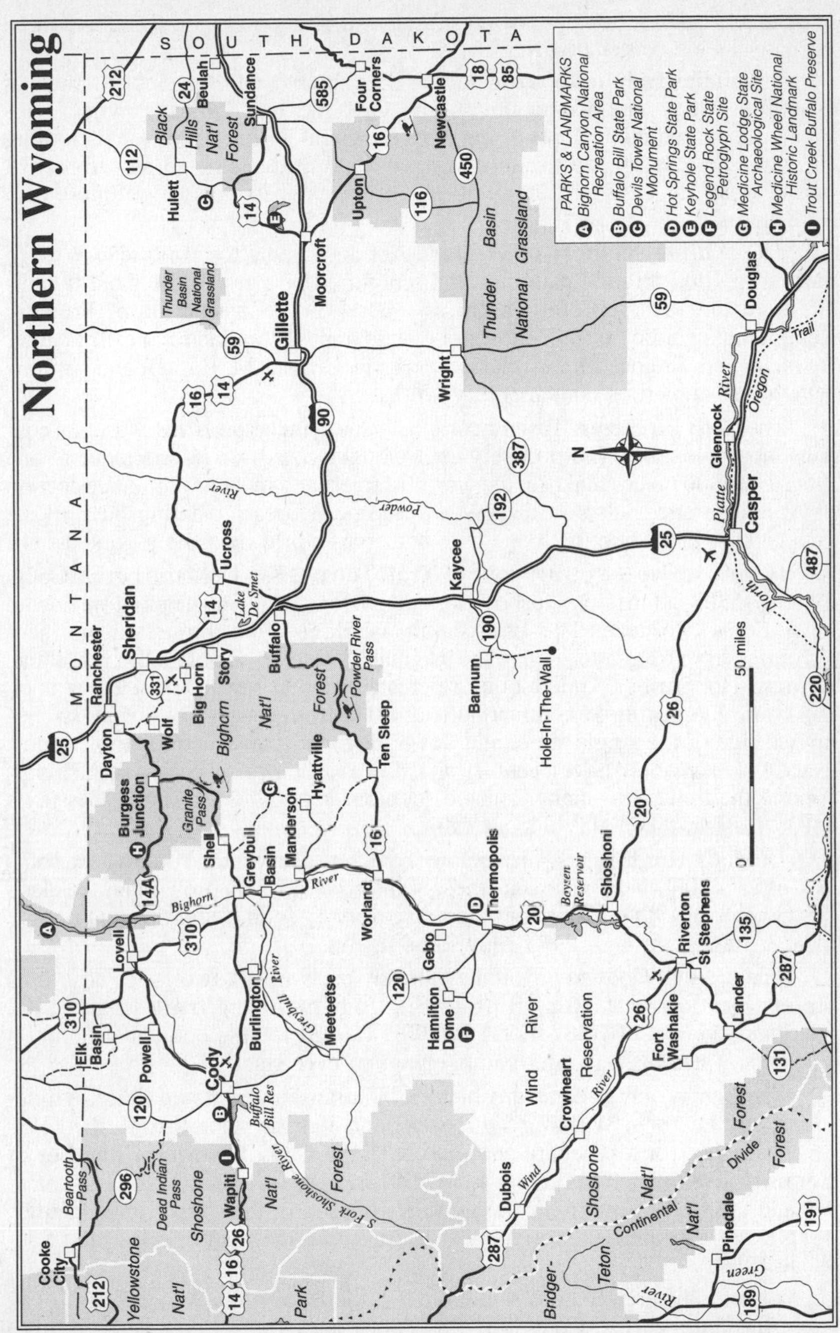
Northern Wyoming
MONTANA
SOUTH DAKOTA
PARKS & LANDMARKS
A Bighorn Canyon National Recreation Area
B Buffalo Bill State Park
C Devils Tower National Monument
D Hot Springs State Park
E Keyhole State Park
F Legend Rock State Petroglyph Site
G Medicine Lodge State Archaeological Site
H Medicine Wheel National Historic Landmark
I Trout Creek Buffalo Preserve
0 50 miles
N
Cooke City
Beartooth Pass
Yellowstone Nat'l Park
Dead Indian Pass
Shoshone Nat'l Forest
Wapiti
Elk Basin
Powell
Cody
Buffalo Bill Res
S Fork Shoshone River
Lovell
Bighorn River
Greybull
Shell
Burgess Junction
Granite Pass
Dayton
Ranchester
Sheridan
Wolf
Big Horn
Story
Bighorn Nat'l Forest
Basin
Manderson
Hyattsville
Burlington
Greybull River
Meeteetse
Worland
Ten Sleep
Powder River Pass
Buffalo
Lake De Smet
Ucross
Powder River
Gillette
Thunder Basin National Grassland
Moorcroft
Hulett
Black Hills Nat'l Forest
Beulah
Sundance
Four Corners
Upton
Newcastle
Wright
Kaycee
Barnum
Hole-In-The-Wall
Gebo
Hamilton Dome
Thermopolis
Boysen Reservoir
Shoshoni
Wind River Reservation
Riverton
St Stephens
Lander
Fort Washakie
Crowheart
Dubois
Wind River
Casper
Glenrock
Platte River
North Platte
Oregon Trail
Douglas
Bridger-Teton Nat'l Forest
Continental Divide
Pinedale
Green River
212
14
16
26
296
120
310
14A
25
331
24
112
14
16
59
90
585
18
85
450
116
387
192
190
20
26
120
287
131
135
287
191
189
487
220

of clothing, saddles, trophies and photographs recalling his colorful life and those of many of his contemporaries.

The **Plains Indian Museum** depicts the cultures and lifestyles of Arapaho, Blackfoot, Cheyenne, Comanche, Crow, Gros Ventre, Kiowa, Pawnee, Shoshone, Sioux and other tribes of the northern Great Plains. Traditional clothing (including beadwork and headdresses), spiritual artifacts (such as ceremonial pipes), weapons, tools and art are all part of the extensive display of more than 5000 items.

The **Whitney Gallery of Western Art** documents the American West in more than 1000 original paintings and sculptures by some of the most famous artists of the 19th and 20th centuries. There's a reconstruction of Frederic Remington's studio, early Yellowstone and Grand Teton landscapes by Albert Bierstadt and Thomas Moran, classic works by Charles M. Russell and Andrew Wyeth and numerous contemporary works.

The **Cody Firearms Museum**, originally the Winchester Arms Museum, contains more guns than you probably ever thought you'd see in one place at one time. The 4000 pieces make up the world's largest and most important collection of American arms; also on display are European firearms dating back to the 16th century and a hunting lodge with numerous world-record big-game heads.

History is also the cornerstone of **Trail Town** (1831 DeMaris Drive, Cody; 307-587-5302; admission), just off the Yellowstone Highway heading west from town. Some two dozen late-19th-century buildings from throughout northern Wyoming have been relocated to the original 1895 town site of Cody, just above DeMaris Hot Springs. Unlike other re-created frontier towns, Trail Town is almost entirely lacking in commercialism; aside from a boardwalk that extends up one side of the single street and down the other, the structures look almost exactly as they would have a century ago, down to their rustic period furnishings. Among the buildings (many donated by pioneer families) is Butch Cassidy's 1883 "Hole-in-the-Wall" hideout cabin.

DeMaris Hot Springs, just below Trail Town, are better known to some as **Colter's Hell**. Now dormant, these semiactive geysers drew health seekers throughout the 19th century after their discovery by John Colter during his 1807 pioneer travels through the Yellowstone region.

The original Cody town site had already been moved two miles east to its present location by the time Buffalo Bill Cody built **The Irma Hotel** (1192 Sheridan Avenue; 307-587-4221) in 1902. Named for the colonel's youngest daughter, it has been in continuous operation ever since.

The Irma is only one of many historic buildings in downtown Cody. A mile-long **Cody Historic Walking Tour** starts and ends near the Buffalo Bill Historical Center; for a brochure and map, visit the **Cody Country Chamber of Commerce** (836 Sheridan Avenue; 307-587-2297) next to City Park. The chamber and the Cody Country Art League are housed in the **Paul Stock Center**, a replica of Buffalo Bill's original T. E. Ranch on the South Fork of the Shoshone River.

Art of a different nature is exhibited at the **Harry Jackson Museum** (★) (602 Blackburn Street, Cody; 307-587-5508). Jackson, a Cody resident since his teens, is regarded as one of the leading living sculptors of the American West. Born in the early 1920s, he was a major player in both the abstract expressionism and realism movements and now focuses on painted sculpture.

Poignant is the word to describe the black-granite **Wyoming Vietnam Veterans Memorial** (Greybull Highway; 307-527-7511), southeast of Cody near Yellowstone Regional Airport. The memorial lists the names of 137 Wyoming citizens who were killed or missing in action in the Vietnam war.

ROUTES TO YELLOWSTONE Many consider the **Yellowstone Highway** (Route 14/16/20), west from Cody to Yellowstone National Park, to be among the most scenic roads in America. The 52-mile road, which follows the canyon of the North Fork of the Shoshone River through the Wapiti Valley to the park's east entrance, passes Buffalo Bill Dam and Reservoir and a circus of vivid rock formations.

The Yellowstone Highway tunnels through Rattlesnake Mountain six miles west of downtown Cody and emerges at the **Buffalo Bill Dam** (Yellowstone Highway, Cody; 307-527-6076), the first concrete-arch dam ever constructed. A modern visitors center affords spectacular views of the Shoshone River rushing toward Cody.

Behind the dam is the five-mile-long **Buffalo Bill Reservoir**, encompassed by 11,500-acre **Buffalo Bill State Park** (see "Cody Area Parks.")

Bison can be viewed from the highway as it proceeds west past the **Trout Creek Buffalo Preserve**, 14 miles out of Cody at the foot of Sheep Mountain.

About 20 miles from Cody, the road enters the community of Wapiti, spread along the highway for about five miles to the south of the towering Absaroka volcanic thrust. This valley takes its name—the Shoshone word for *elk*—from the **Wapiti District Ranger Station** (Yellowstone Highway, Wapiti; 307-527-6921), the first ever built in the United States (in 1903). Located 29 miles from Cody, it has interpretive displays not of elk but of grizzly bears.

The ranger station is just within the boundary of **Shoshone National Forest** (see "Cody Area Parks"), the direct result of more political finagling by Buffalo Bill. The colonel's influence led President Benjamin Harrison to proclaim the Yellowstone Park Timberland Reserve in 1891, protecting the timber on public domain; four years later, it became the first parcel of the new U.S. Forest Service. The territory's name was changed to Shoshone National Forest in 1945.

Such odd red-rock formations as the Playground of the Gods, the Chinese Wall, the Laughing Pig and the Holy City add fascination to the second half of the drive from Cody to Yellowstone. There are no fewer than 15 guest ranches along this route, many of them well worth a long stay. None, however, has the same history attached to it as **Pahaska Tepee Resort** (183 Yellowstone Highway, Cody; 307-527-7701), Buffalo Bill Cody's original 1904 hunting lodge.

Much less traveled than the Yellowstone Highway but certainly its scenic equal is the 46-mile **Chief Joseph Scenic Highway** (★) (Route 296). This road from Cody to the northeast entrance of Yellowstone Park skirts beautiful Sunlight Basin before connecting with the Beartooth Highway southeast of Cooke City, Montana. (In all, the distance from Cody to the northeast entrance is 81 miles.)

It could be argued that Route 296 is not really much of a highway. One seven-mile stretch—over 8071-foot **Dead Indian Pass**—is as yet unpaved, but the road is well maintained, and the drive as a whole is easily accomplished in most weather conditions.

Beginning off Route 120 (the principal Cody–Billings road) 17 miles north of Cody, Chief Joseph Highway crosses the Two Dot Ranch and winds to the top of Dead Indian Pass. Chief Joseph and his Nez Perce followers evaded the U.S. Army here in 1877 during their flight for freedom; the **Nez Perce (Nee-Me-Poo) National Historic Trail** retraces their escape route down the steep, nearly impassable slope of Clark's Fork Canyon.

Sunlight Basin, for many, is the highlight of this trip. The road from Dead Indian Pass descends about 2000 feet to the Sunlight Creek Bridge, suspended nearly a quarter-mile above spectacular **Sunlight Gorge**. The bridge is Wyoming's highest. Forest Road 101, an improved gravel road, follows Sunlight Creek about 15 miles upstream from here, past ranches, a ranger station and Shoshone National Forest campgrounds, to the foot of 11,950-foot Sunlight Peak.

The Chief Joseph Highway continues from the Sunlight Creek Bridge another 26 miles to its intersection with Route 212 (the Beartooth Highway), passing en route another area of dude ranches and a ranger station at Crandall Creek.

CODY AREA HOTELS

Cody hotel rates have enormous seasonal variance. High-season (June–August) rates can be more than twice what you'd pay for the same room during the long low season (October–April). Since most travelers visit during the high season, the following price designations reflect that rate level.

It's not the biggest, not the fanciest, certainly not the newest, but Buffalo Bill's very own hotel, **The Irma** (1192 Sheridan Avenue, Cody; 307-587-4221, 800-745-4762, fax 307-587-4221 ext. 21), still captures the imagination of guests with its turn-of-the-century spirit. Colonel Cody spent $80,000 to have this hotel in the heart of downtown Cody built of native wood and sandstone in 1902. Named for his youngest daughter, it has 40 rooms, including 15 restored Victorian chambers and 25 adjacent units, added later. The $100,000 cherrywood bar given to Buffalo Bill by England's Queen Victoria graces The Irma's restaurant; there are also two lounges. Moderate.

The **Parson's Pillow B & B** (1202 14th Street; 307-587-2382, 800-377-2348) occupies Cody's original Methodist-Episcopal house of worship, dedicated in 1902. Four guest rooms with private baths are individually decorated with Victorian antiques and lace. Full gourmet breakfasts are served in the dining room. Moderate.

Some of the 14 rooms at **The Lockhart Bed and Breakfast Inn** (109 West Yellowstone Avenue, Cody; 307-587-6074), on the west end of town, occupy the 1904 wood-frame home of western novelist Carolyn Lockhart (1870–1962). Others are in an adjoining motel annex. All room have antique furnishings, including old-fashioned double beds and private bathrooms with clawfoot tubs. A full breakfast is included. Moderate.

The Carriage House (1816 8th Street, Cody; phone/fax 307-587-2572, 800-531-2572) is a log-cabin village. Individual and duplex cabins contain 24 small wood-paneled units, including several with two or three bedrooms. There is no air-conditioning, but all rooms have full bathrooms. Moderate.

The biggest and the fanciest, if that's what you're looking for, is the **Holiday Inn Cody Convention Center** (1701 Sheridan Avenue, Cody; 307-587-5555, 800-465-4329, fax 307-527-7757). This is actually two properties under common management: the modern, 190-room Holiday Inn and the rustic, 83-cabin Buffalo Bill Village. The two-story Holiday Inn has standard, spacious motel units built around a central courtyard and swimming pool. The Village—open May through September only—consists of 1920s-vintage log cabins; the interiors have been completely remodeled. All rooms in Inn and Village have air-conditioning. Moderate to deluxe.

Buffalo Bill Cody's Rocky Mountain hunting lodge, built in 1905, is part and parcel of the **Pahaska Tepee Resort** (183 Yellowstone Highway, Wapiti; 307-527-7701, 800-628-7791, fax 307-527-4019), just two miles outside the east entrance to Yellowstone. The rough-hewn log lodge, nestled in pines near the North Fork of the Shoshone River, is surrounded by two- to six-room cabins with private baths. Rustic decor pervades the cabins, dining room and tavern. Moderate. (Closed October–November and March–April.)

Of all the guest ranches along the North Fork of the Shoshone River, the classiest may well be the **Rimrock Dude Ranch** (2728 Yellowstone Highway, Wapiti; 307-587-3970), almost exactly halfway between Cody and Yellowstone Park. Established in 1927, it lodges up to 35 guests in private log cabins with full baths. Several larger cabins have living rooms with stone fireplaces. Gourmet meals are served in the main ranch house, and evening entertainment ranges from billiards to square dancing. A horseback-riding program includes instruction, trail rides and wilderness pack trips; fishing and river rafting are among other activities. Open June–August for all-inclusive full-week packages. Deluxe.

CODY AREA RESTAURANTS

"Kickass cowboy cuisine" like steaks, prime rib and Rocky Mountain oysters is the fare at the rustic **Proud Cut Saloon & Restaurant** (1227 Sheridan Avenue; 307-527-6905), a longtime Cody stalwart in the heart of downtown. Prices are moderate.

Cody's finest dining experience may be at **Franca's** (1421 Rumsey Avenue; 307-587-5354), a small northern Italian spot a block off the main street. It serves exquisite four-course, set-menu dinners by reservation only, Thursday through Saturday. The carefully assembled wine list has more than 100 selections. Western and Italian art hang side by side on permanent display in a back gallery. Deluxe.

Pasta is the menu mainstay at **Maxwell's** (937 Sheridan Avenue, Cody; 307-527-7749), a handsome restaurant near the Buffalo Bill Historical Center with cut glass and wood decor inside, deck and patio seating outside. Soups, salads, sandwiches and pizza are also served. Budget.

Lovers of gourmet Mexican food won't be disappointed by **La Comida** (1385 Sheridan Avenue, Cody; 307-587-9556). The fajitas, the enchiladas and even the soups here are a couple of solid notches above the standard Tex-Mex hole in the wall. La Comida has outdoor patio seating. Budget.

On the North Fork guest-ranch strip, the **Elk & Ale** (Elephant Head Lodge, 1171 Yellowstone Highway, Wapiti; 307-587-3980) stands out. Cody residents have no problem driving 40 miles west to order rib-eye steak (marinated in garlic and sugar) or other home-style beef and seafood plates. Breakfast is offered, too. Moderate.

CODY AREA SHOPPING

If every store were like the **Cody Rodeo Company** (1291 Sheridan Avenue; 307-587-9783), shopping would always be a delight. From the mechanical bull near the entrance to the videos of live rodeo action playing nonstop on a screen on the far wall, this modest store is an attraction in itself. Western fashion clothing, books, household items, gifts and souvenirs—all with a cowboy theme—are the icing on the cake.

For traditional western duds, there are two good downtown stores: **Branding Iron Western Outfitters** (1131 Sheridan Avenue; 307-587-4582) and **Corral West Ranchwear** (1202 Sheridan Avenue; 307-587-2122). **The Plush Pony** (1350 Sheridan Avenue; 307-587-4677) is a western boutique for women. **Scary Mary's** (1209 Sheridan Avenue; 307-587-9933) has offbeat and vintage clothing and gifts.

Cody is becoming a regional art center of note, and a good place to start a gallery walk is at the **Cody Country Art League** (836 Sheridan Avenue; 307-587-3597). Located in the Paul Stock Center, it exhibits and sells paintings, sculptures and crafts by regional artists.

Among the many other fine galleries in Cody are the **Big Horn Gallery** (1167 Sheridan Avenue; 307-527-7587), offering classic and traditional western art; **Prairie Rose Northern Plains Indian Gallery** (1031 12th Street; 307-587-8181), featuring traditional reproductions by members of Sioux, Crow and other tribes; and **Raven Fine Art** (1318 Sheridan Avenue; 307-527-6468), which displays modern art. The **Harry Jackson Museum** (602 Blackburn Street; 307-587-5508) features the work of a major living sculptor of western themes.

The lodge-style furniture designs of Thomas Molesworth have been widely copied by modern craftspeople. **Sweet Water Ranch** (531 16th Street; 307-527-4044) is faithful to Molesworth's original designs in its hand-crafted products.

CODY AREA NIGHTLIFE

The first word in Cody evening entertainment, hands down, is the **Cody Nite Rodeo** (115 West Yellowstone Avenue; 307-587-2992; box office 307-587-5155; admission). Every night in June, July and August, battle-proven cowboys gather at Stampede Park, at the far west end of town, to test their mettle

Spirit of the Old West: "Buffalo Bill" Cody

Probably the single most remarkable character the Old West ever produced was William F. "Buffalo Bill" Cody.

Trapper, wrangler, Pony Express rider, army scout, buffalo hunter, wagonmaster, stagecoach driver, Indian fighter, actor and entrepreneur, Cody more than any other individual was responsible for giving the West the romantic image it held around the world at the turn of the 20th century.

Born in rural Iowa in 1846, Cody was forced at age 11, upon his father's death, to go to work as a mounted messenger. He rode for the Pony Express for 18 months, and after its demise in 1861 served in the Civil War. In 1867, Cody was hired by the Union Pacific Railroad to hunt buffalo to feed its construction crews. In eight months, he shot an average of 18 bison a day, over 4000 in all. He was bestowed the nickname "Buffalo Bill."

Through his 20s, Cody's frontier savvy—his horsemanship and marksmanship, his courage and stamina, his understanding of the wilderness, his understanding of Native American life—placed him in high esteem as a scout and guide. The Fifth Cavalry employed him almost continuously in its wars against the Plains Indians. Cody himself took part in 16 of those battles and was awarded a Congressional Medal of Honor for bravery.

Back East, sensationalist reporters and paperback novelists transformed this upstart frontiersman into a folk hero. When Cody was approached to play himself on stage, he proved to be a natural showman who substituted dash and humor for polish and experience. By 1883, Cody had put together his own Buffalo Bill's Wild West Show. For three decades—including ten years in Europe—this stage spectacular promoted the Old West with exhibitions of shooting and roping, a buffalo stampede, a stagecoach holdup and all manner of cowboy and Indian lore. Stars like riflewoman Annie Oakley and Sitting Bull, the Sioux chief, added to the myth.

Cody reveled in his personal fame—by some estimations, "the Colonel" was the world's best-known personality in 1900—but he used it as a vehicle to bring public attention to his favorite causes. In spite of his role in their decline, Cody championed both the integrity of Native American heritage and the recovery of the bison population. And he was an outspoken advocate of women's rights: "If a woman can do the same work that a man can do and do it just as well, she should have the same pay," he said.

A founder of the town of Cody in 1895, he held that preservation must go hand in hand with development. To that end, he invested his fortune in town planning, ranching, mining, irrigation and newspaper publishing.

Cody died in 1917 while visiting his sister in Denver.

in bull riding, calf roping, bulldogging and bareback and saddle bronco competition. Try to get a seat in Buzzard's Roost, above the chutes on the far side of the arena.

Look for western entertainment of a different kind at the **Sarsaparilla Melodrama Theatre** (Buffalo Bill Village, 1701 Sheridan Avenue, Cody; 307-587-5544; admission). Everything from vaudeville drama to cowboy poetry readings shows up on its stage. Call to inquire about the current schedule.

Elsewhere in Cody, there's live country-and-western music for dancing at **Cassie's** (214 Yellowstone Avenue; 307-527-5500) and classic rock in **Angie's Saloon at the Silver Dollar Bar** (1313 Sheridan Avenue; 307-587-3554). For belly-up-to-the-bar conversation and drinks, the local favorites are **The Irma** (1192 Sheridan Avenue; 307-587-4221) and the **Proud Cut Saloon** (1227 Sheridan Avenue; 307-527-6905).

CODY AREA PARKS

Buffalo Bill State Park—Encompassing five-mile-long Buffalo Bill Reservoir, which was created in 1910 by the Buffalo Bill Dam on the North and South forks of the Shoshone River, this 11,500-acre state park actually has four parcels—two for day use only (Sheep Mountain and Bartlett Lane) and two that welcome overnight campers (North Shore Bay and North Fork). The park is popular among boaters and anglers; *Outside* magazine has rated the reservoir as one of the ten best places for board sailing in the United States.

Facilities: Picnic tables, restrooms, boat ramps; day-use fee, $3; information, 307-587-9227. *Swimming:* No designated beaches; the water is cold, but swimming is permitted. *Fishing:* The reservoir is home to brown, rainbow, cutthroat and lake trout (mackinaw) as well as mountain whitefish.

Camping: There are 65 RV/tent units plus six for tents only at two campgrounds (no hookups); $4 per night. Open from May 1 to September 30.

Getting there: Take the Yellowstone Highway (Route 14/16/20) west eight miles from Cody to the reservoir. It's ten miles to North Shore Bay, 11 miles to park headquarters, 13 miles to North Fork and Sheep Mountain. To reach the Bartlett Lane area, take South Fork Road (Route 291) six miles south and west from Cody, opposite Trail Town; continue straight one mile at Bartlett Lane.

Shoshone National Forest—The nation's first protected forest when it was established in 1891 as the Yellowstone Park Timberland Reserve, Shoshone contains the first U.S. ranger station (at Wapiti). Today, the two and a half million acres of this preserve spread south for 170 miles from the Montana border, along the eastern border of Yellowstone National Park and the east slope of the Wind River Range.

Facilities: Picnic tables, restrooms, boat ramps, trails; information, 307-527-6921. *Swimming:* Cold but permitted in mountain lakes; beware of hypothermia. *Fishing:* Trout (rainbow, cutthroat, brook and brown) are common in lakes and streams, lake trout and arctic grayling less so.

Camping: There are 340 RV/tent units plus 201 for tents only in 35 campgrounds (no hookups), including ten campgrounds along the North Fork and ten campgrounds in the Sunlight Basin–Beartooth area; $8 per night.

Getting there: The Yellowstone Highway (Route 14/16/20), Chief Joseph Scenic Highway (Route 296), Beartooth Highway (Route 212) and South Fork Road (Route 291) all run through Shoshone National Forest.

Big Horn Country

East of Cody lies the Big Horn Basin—and beyond that, the Big Horn Mountains, their cloud-piercing passes penetrated by a trio of highways that drop to Sheridan and the eastern plains.

Surrounded on three sides by high mountain ranges (the 12,000-foot Absarokas to the west, the 13,000-foot Big Horns to the east and the 9600-foot Owl Creek Range to the south) and by rugged foothills to the north, the Big Horn Basin is like a fortress shielded by natural barriers. Measuring about 50 by 100 miles and averaging 4000 feet in elevation, it is drained by the northward-flowing Bighorn, which rises in the Wind River Range, enters the basin through the nearly impassable Wind River Canyon and disappears into Montana through the even more foreboding (but magnificent) Bighorn Canyon. Its numerous east- and west-flowing tributaries, including the Shoshone and Greybull rivers, allow an otherwise-arid climate to support large cattle and sheep ranches, which have thrived in the basin since 1879.

Yet the basin is not all agricultural. Scientists find its geology, fossil discoveries and ancient archaeological sites fascinating, and water-sports lovers have found paradise in the Bighorn Canyon National Recreation Area, near Lovell, and Hot Springs State Park, at Thermopolis.

The lofty Big Horn Mountains, which effectively split northern Wyoming into two equal parts, also separate the Bighorn and Powder river drainages. Route 16 (from Worland), 14 (from Greybull) and 14A (from Lovell) ascend its western slopes, the former two via interesting canyons, the latter past the unique Medicine Wheel National Historic Landmark, sacred ground to Native Americans. The mountains, a year-round recreational playground, are crowned by the Cloud Peak Wilderness Area.

THE SOUTHERN BIG HORN BASIN LOOP This 260-mile circuit hits the high points of the Big Horn Basin, including the cowboy flavor of Meeteetse, the renowned hot springs at Thermopolis and the Ten Sleep Canyon country east of Worland, before returning to Cody along the Greybull River.

Route 120 southeast from Cody skirts the Oregon Basin and Elk Butte oil fields before climbing the 6000-foot Meeteetse Rim into **Meeteetse**. Settled in the 1880s as a ranching center and given a Crow Indian name that means "meeting place," this town 32 miles southeast of Cody has stubbornly clung to a colorful

Old West ambience with century-old architecture including wooden sidewalks and hitching rails.

The Meeteetse Museums (1033 Park Avenue; 307-868-2423) tell the town's history in three separate buildings. The Hall Museum, in a 1900 Masonic hall, displays frontier artifacts. The Bank Archives, in a 1901 bank building, contain records and documents. The new Belden Museum of Western Photography exhibits both historic and modern work.

Though a little hard to find and well off the beaten path, the **Legend Rock State Petroglyph Site** (★) (Upper Cottonwood Creek Road, Hamilton Dome; 307-864-2176) is worth a detour. Some of the most impressive prehistoric rock carvings in America illustrate hundreds of yards of sandstone cliffs. Archaeologists have identified at least 283 pictures on 92 rock panels, some dating back to the time of Christ. Images range from identifiable animals, birds and humans to strange-looking figures wearing horned headdresses.

To reach the site, turn west off Route 120 on Upper Cottonwood Creek Road about 32 miles southeast of Meeteetse. Follow this road five miles to the Hamilton Dome junction, continuing west on BLM Road 1305. Turn left after the second cattle guard and left again at a Y intersection, continuing to a locked gate. Park here and walk a half mile downhill to the site, or obtain a key from Hot Springs State Park headquarters in Thermopolis during weekday business hours.

You were going to—or coming from—**Hot Springs State Park** (Route 20 and Park Street, Thermopolis; 307-864-2176) anyway. Big Spring, the world's largest single mineral hot spring, is located on the east bank of the Bighorn River at the north edge of the town of Thermopolis, 83 miles from Cody. Big Spring churns out 3.6 million gallons of 127°F water each day; at least 27 different minerals contained in the water have been identified, including large amounts of bicarbonate, sulfate, chloride and sodium. Some of the water is cooled and piped to a state-owned bath house (free) and two water parks (admission) open for public use; the balance flows over colorful **Rainbow Terrace**, reminiscent of the thermal features of Yellowstone Park, and into the Bighorn.

The town of **Thermopolis**, whose name is a combination of the Greek words for *heat* and *city*, was established around the springs after that 1896 government purchase. **Hot Springs Historical Museum** (700 Broadway; 307-864-5183; admission) recalls the town's early years with a re-created newspaper office, blacksmith shop, dentist's office and general store, as well as the original back bar from the Hole-in-the-Wall Saloon. An elk hide painted by Chief Washakie himself highlights an impressive collection of Native American artifacts.

South of Thermopolis, Route 2 follows the Wind River Canyon 32 miles to the small town of Shoshoni. Native Americans named the Wind River for the ever-present breeze funneling down the 2000-foot-deep gorge; yet as the river leaves the canyon about four miles above Thermopolis at the **Wedding of the Waters**, its name changes to the Bighorn. Highway signs placed throughout the canyon by the Wyoming Geological Association identify the eras of different rock strata.

Worland is 33 miles north of Thermopolis. Founded in 1903 on the west bank of the Bighorn, the entire town was moved two years later, building by building, to the east bank when residents learned that that was where the railroad would be built, making their move in the dead of winter when the river was completely frozen over. Today the town is the hub of a heavily irrigated agricultural district that produces malt barley, alfalfa hay, corn, beans, sugar beets and other crops.

Worland is also an important paleontological area. Remains of eohippus, the prehistoric ancestor of the modern horse, were discovered among the badlands of the **Gooseberry Formations** and **Painted Desert**, off Route 431 some 20 miles west of town. Fossil discoveries and geology are featured at the **Washakie County Museum and Cultural Center** (1115 Obie Sue Avenue, Worland; 307-347-4102), along with historical cowboy and ranch equipment.

Route 20 continues north, down the Bighorn River, from Worland. Route 16 heads due east 26 miles across arid plains to **Ten Sleep**, at the foot of the Big Horn Mountains. The community was built at a creek ford that was, in Native American parlance, 11 days' (ten sleeps') journey from . . . somewhere. Today it's the gateway to **Ten Sleep Canyon**, which begins about five miles east of town.

The sculpted limestone canyon is the southern of the three highway corridors through the Big Horn Mountains. Designated as the **Cloud Peak Skyway**, a national scenic byway, the route follows Ten Sleep Creek and transits 9666-foot **Powder River Pass** on its 65-mile run to Buffalo.

The route's summit offers the nearest highway access to the **Cloud Peak Wilderness**, a 195,000-acre primitive preserve capped by 13,165-foot Cloud Peak, the apex of the Big Horns. Hundreds of pristine mountain lakes speckle the slopes of the jagged peaks, both above and below timberline; they're remnants of the Ice Age glaciers that once covered the entire range. Wreckage of a 1943 U.S. Air Force B-17 crash that killed all ten crewmembers can still be seen on Bomber Mountain, just south of Cloud Peak.

After the detour up Ten Sleep Canyon, this loop trip heads north from the town of Ten Sleep, following Lower Nowood Road (Route 47) and Cold Springs Road (Route 31) to isolated **Hyattville**, at the confluence of Paintrock and Medicine Lodge creeks. Amid the rugged gulches of these Big Horn Mountain foothills is the **Medicine Lodge State Archaeological Site** (★) (Road 268A, Hyattville; 307-469-2234), six miles northeast of Hyattville, one of the most important sites in North America for the study of prehistoric man.

Though the prehistoric petroglyphs and pictographs on Medicine Lodge's red sandstone cliffs have long attracted visitors, it was not until 1969 that the full importance of the site was realized. A state archaeology team, digging through 26 feet of soil and rock, found more than 60 cultural levels spanning 10,000 years of human occupation. A visitors center now interprets some of the ongoing discoveries. The site offers trails, fishing and camping facilities and is open May to November 4. Nearby is the 12,127-acre **Medicine Lodge Wildlife Habitat Management Area**, ideal winter range for elk and mule deer.

From Hyattville, Route 31 travels 22 miles west to tiny **Manderson** on the Bighorn River. Here you can pick up Route 16/20 again, proceeding north to the town of **Basin**, surrounded by rich irrigated farmlands. Basin's place in

Old West history was affirmed in 1909 when the perpetrators of the final raid in the great range wars were convicted of murder here. The National Guard stood by to prevent further violence between the two vying factions: the open-range cattle ranchers and the homesteaders and sheepherders.

West from Basin, Route 30 crosses through the midriff of the Big Horn Basin's grain-producing and livestock-raising belt. It's 46 miles via Burlington and Lower Greybull Road to Route 120, just north of Meeteetse. Complete the loop by turning north on 120 and returning to Cody, a distance of about 24 miles.

THE NORTHERN BIG HORN MOUNTAIN LOOP A full-day, 207-mile loop trip from Cody on Routes 14A and 14 follows the agriculturally thriving Shoshone River valley to Bighorn Canyon National Recreation Area, climbs up and down the spectacular west-slope canyon country of the Big Horn Mountains and returns to Cody through semiarid grasslands.

The first quarter of the route traces the northern edge of the Big Horn Basin. Fifteen miles northeast of Cody, a half mile off Route 14A, is a memorial to the **Heart Mountain Relocation Center** (Road 19), where 11,000 Japanese Americans were interned during World War II. "May the injustices of the removal and incarceration of 120,000 persons of Japanese ancestry during World War II, two-thirds of whom were American citizens, never be repeated," reads the plaque, listed on the National Register of Historic Places.

The region's hub is the grain and sugar-beet farming community of **Powell**, 24 miles from Cody in the heart of the Shoshone Reclamation Project that owes its existence to water from Buffalo Bill Reservoir. Founded in 1909 and named for early Rocky Mountain river explorer John Wesley Powell, it is the home of the **Homesteader Museum** (1st and Clark streets; 307-754-9481), an impressive collection of early-20th-century Big Horn Basin settlers' memorabilia.

Twenty-five miles east of Powell is **Lovell**, a pleasant community that calls itself "The Rose Town of Wyoming." Private gardens and public parks throughout the town boast floral displays that demand a second look—a tribute to former Lovell parks director and community physician Dr. William Horsley, a 12-year director of the American Rose Society who died in 1971.

For travelers, Lovell is most notable as the gateway to the **Bighorn Canyon National Recreation Area** (406-666-2412). It took 64 million years of geological artistry for the Bighorn River to sculpt the 2200-foot-deep Bighorn Canyon. It took only a few years of engineering artistry for Montana's 525-foot Yellowtail Dam to fill the canyon in 1967 and create 71-mile-long Bighorn Lake. The result: 250,000 kilowatts of electricity, an important irrigation source for farmers of the eastern Rockies and Great Plains and a new playground for boaters and fishermen.

Begin your exploration of the national recreation area with a stop at the **Bighorn Canyon Visitors Center** (20 Route 14A East, Lovell; 307-548-2251), just east of town. The first National Park Service building to employ solar energy as its principal heating source (it opened in 1976), it offers geology, history, recreation and solar-energy displays.

The Marina at Horseshoe Bend (307-548-7326), located where the river emerges from the red-rock canyon to beget the broad southern section of Bighorn Lake, is 14 miles from Lovell. In summer, the 15-passenger *Canyon Queen* tour boat (307-548-7858; admission) offers excursions upstream and down.

The trip downriver is a good way to grasp the geological importance of this canyon, which slices deeply through the ancient Bighorn and Pryor anticlines. More than 500 million years of earth's history, dating back to early Paleozoic times (when shallow seas covered this part of the continent), can be read in these cliffs. Fossils of marine trilobites and of dinosaurs that inhabited tropical marshes or conifer forests have been found here. For road travelers, **Devil Canyon Overlook**, 18 miles north of Lovell in Montana, offers a 1000-foot-deep perspective on the Bighorn Canyon.

The TransPark Highway passes through a portion of the **Pryor Mountain Wild Horse Range** (see Chapter Thirteen, "Southern Montana Rockies"), a 47,000-acre Bureau of Land Management preserve established in 1968.

Route 37 ends 27 miles north of Lovell at **Barry's Landing**. In the vicinity are the remains of G. W. Barry's 1903 Cedarvale Dude Ranch at the ghost town of Hillsboro and the 1926 Lockhart Ranch of western novelist Carolyn Lockhart. North of Barry's Landing, for 35 miles downstream to the Ok-A-Beh area near the Yellowtail Dam, access is strictly by boat. The north end of Bighorn Canyon is reached from Fort Smith, south of Hardin, Montana.

But there's one more section of the national recreation area accessible from Lovell. Nine miles east of the visitors center, Route 14A crosses Bighorn Lake on Kane Bridge, one and a half miles long. This southern section of the recreation area embraces the **Yellowtail Wildlife Habitat Management Area** (307-527-7125). About two miles south of the Kane Bridge there's a turnoff to the 1883 **Mason-Lovell Ranch** on the lakeshore. The M-L Ranch, as it's usually called, was built as headquarters for a classic open-range cattle ranch operated by A. L. Mason and H. C. Lovell before the invention of barbed wire changed the West forever. A bunkhouse, blacksmith shop and married employees' cabin still stand.

From the Bighorn Canyon, Route 14A rapidly ascends the west slope of the Big Horn Mountains, climbing from about 3800 feet at the lake to about 9600 at Baldy Pass. About 12 miles from the M-L Ranch, it enters 1.1-million-acre **Bighorn National Forest**, which blankets the Big Horn Mountains from north to south. (For information on facilities, see "Sheridan Area Parks" later in this chapter.)

The national forest is home to one of the most remarkable places in Wyoming: the **Medicine Wheel National Historic Landmark** (★) (Forest Road 12; 307-548-6541). Located about 32 miles from Lovell, three miles off Route 14A via a steep, narrow, gravel Forest Service road and a one-and-a-half-mile trail, this ancient site near the summit of the Big Horns (at nearly 10,000 feet) is as much a mystery to modern archaeologists as to the Native Americans who consider it sacred ground. From a hub of rocks piled three feet high in a 12-foot circle, 28 spokes radiate to an outer circle of flat, white stones, 75 feet across and 245 feet in circumference. Outside this "Great Wheel," six small cairns stand beside a rock arrow that points toward Meeteetse, 70 miles southwest, where remnants of a similar wheel have been discovered.

There are many theories about what the Medicine Wheel might have been and about the long-forgotten peoples who may have built it between A.D. 1200 and 1700. Some say it was a monument to a great chief; others suggest its use in vision quests. Perhaps the most intriguing hypothesis is that it was an astronomical observatory along the lines of Stonehenge in England, used as a calendar to determine the summer solstice. Is it divine irony that the Federal Aviation Administration has a state-of-the-art radar facility in a geodesic dome overlooking the site from atop adjacent Medicine Mountain?

On the roof of the Big Horns, between 9000 and 10,000 feet in elevation, are mile after mile of undulating alpine meadows crisscrossed by Forest Service roads. It's ideal country for viewing deer, elk, sheep and other high-country wildlife. Then at Burgess Junction, 106 miles from Cody, Route 14A joins Route 14 for a twisting descent of the Big Horns' east slope to Dayton and Sheridan (49 miles).

To return to Cody via Route 14, turn southwest at this junction. Route 14 from Dayton to Shell is called the **Bighorn Scenic Byway**. For the first 12 miles south, it continues across the meadowlands, past campgrounds and fishing-access roads, to the South Tongue River. Route 14 then crosses 9033-foot **Granite Pass**, goes by the nearby **Antelope Butte Ski Area** (307-655-9530) and turns sharply west as it descends rapidly into **Shell Canyon**.

Millions of years of erosion by Shell Creek have carved this picturesque canyon, whose sedimentary deposits contain some of the earliest-known fossils of ammonites, hard-shelled marine creatures. About halfway through the canyon, the creek flows into a deep chasm through three-billion-year-old granite, out of which plummet **Shell Falls**. Most of the year, about 3600 gallons of water per second roar over these falls, among the highest in Wyoming outside of Yellowstone Park. An interpretive exhibit at the falls overlook describes canyon geology. By the time Shell Creek has reached the hamlet of **Shell**, at about 4200 feet, it has slowed to become a stream colored ruddy by the red sandstone through which it has swept.

Greybull, named for a legendary albino bison held sacred by Native Americans, was founded in 1905 as a railroad town at the confluence of the Greybull and Bighorn rivers. An important center for the mining of bentonite, a volcanic clay, Greybull is also an outfitting hub for the Big Horn Mountains and the gateway to a geologically intriguing badlands region. A giant allosaurus and 12 large sauropods are among the dinosaurs that have been dug from the clay and bedrock over six decades.

From Greybull, Route 14 joins with Routes 16 and 20 to cross 53 miles of dry creek and grassland back to Cody.

BIG HORN COUNTRY HOTELS

To stay in style at Hot Springs State Park, look no further than the **Holiday Inn of the Waters** (Park and Pioneer streets, Thermopolis; phone/fax 307-864-

3131, 800-465-4329). This two-story motor inn is within the park itself and offers a hot-spring pool, private mineral hot baths and a heated freshwater pool and wading pool, as well as a full health club, saunas and a whirlpool. The deluxe Safari Club restaurant and lounge (so named for their collection of big-game heads) are on premises. The rooms are spacious and tastefully decorated and are priced in the moderate range.

East of Worland near the summit of the Big Horn Mountains, **Meadowlark Lake Resort** (Route 16 East, Ten Sleep; 307-366-2424, 800-858-5672) offers lodge-style cabins (budget priced) and modern condo units (moderate priced) beside a lovely alpine lake at 8500-foot elevation. Three meals daily are served in the restaurant, and the saloon offers a full bar. Best of all, there's trout fishing and boating in the 300-acre lake and mountain biking in the Bighorn National Forest; in winter, there's downhill and nordic skiing, snowmobiling and ice fishing. The resort also has a convenience store and gas station.

Up in the Bighorn Canyon area, the **Horseshoe Bend Motel** (375 East Main Street, Lovell; 307-548-2221, fax 307-548-6837) offers year-round budget rates and 22 cozy rooms. Some rooms have refrigerators and microwaves; and there's a swimming pool.

The **Yellowstone Motel** (247 Greybull Avenue, Greybull; 307-765-4456, fax 307-765-2108) has lovely landscaped grounds—including a putting green and a heated outdoor swimming pool—at the foot of the Big Horns. The 35 standard rooms (including two family suites) have full baths. Room rates are in the low moderate range.

BIG HORN COUNTRY RESTAURANTS

Near Hot Springs State Park, **Pecos Bill's Pit Barbecue** (415 Park Street, Thermopolis; 307-864-5551) serves up generous portions of chicken, beef and pork ribs barbecued over natural wood, along with excellent salads and desserts. Prices are nonetheless budget.

PumperNicks (512 Broadway, Thermopolis; 307-864-5151) offers everything from crêpes and stuffed croissants for lunch to steak, chicken and seafood for dinner. Budget.

Elsewhere, the fare is heavily meat and potatoes. A pleasant exception is **Lisa's** (200 Greybull Avenue, Greybull; 307-765-4765), which adds a creative touch to home cookin' along the Bighorn River. Open for three meals daily in summer. Moderate.

BIG HORN COUNTRY SHOPPING

The historic **Meeteetse Mercantile Co.** (1946 State Street, Meeteetse; 307-868-2561) has been in continuous operation since 1899. This is a true old-time general store, selling everything from groceries and dry goods to clothing, hardware, antiques and sporting goods.

The **Stone School Gallery & Bookstore** (Route 14, six miles east of Greybull; 307-765-4384) occupies the old one-room Lower Shell Valley Stone

Schoolhouse, constructed in 1903 of locally quarried sandstone. The historic building, open seasonally, now sells more than 350 book titles of regional interest, as well as maps, paintings, prints, crafts and photography.

Also check out **The Hen's Nest** (505 Greybull Avenue, Greybull; 307-765-4647) for regional arts and crafts and **Center Stage** (608 Big Horn Avenue, Worland; 307-347-3817) for antiques and souvenirs.

BIG HORN COUNTRY PARKS

Hot Springs State Park—The park has several springs and terraces, but Big Spring (the largest mineral hot spring on earth) is the one that really matters to most visitors. Twenty-five thousand gallons of water per minute pour from this single 30-foot-wide spring at a temperature of 127°F, year after year. Some of the spring's water is cooled in retaining pools to 104°F and piped for public and private use—which is why visitors have made this the most popular park in Wyoming after Yellowstone and Grand Teton.

Facilities: Picnic tables, restrooms, playgrounds, trails, boat ramp; information, 307-864-2176. *Swimming:* State bath house (free), two water parks (admission). *Fishing:* A pier north of the park entrance extends into the Bighorn River, rich in brown, rainbow and cutthroat trout.

Getting there: From downtown Thermopolis take Park Street east off of Route 20.

Bighorn Canyon National Recreation Area—Seventy-one-mile-long Bighorn Lake, wedged between cliffs nearly one-half mile high, is the centerpiece of this paradise for boating and fishing enthusiasts. The Lovell visitors center directs travelers north, up the TransPark Highway, to The Marina at Horseshoe Bend, a camping resort at the south end of the canyon. The northern (Montana) end of the canyon can be reached only by boat or a roundabout road trip of more than 100 miles.

Facilities: Picnic tables, restrooms, visitors center, trails, boat ramps and rentals, marina, concessions, boat tours (admission); information, 307-548-2251. *Swimming:* Lifeguarded beach at The Marina at Horseshoe Bend. *Fishing:* Species in Bighorn Lake include brown, lake and rainbow trout; walleye; sauger; largemouth bass; channel catfish; yellow perch; sunfish; and ling. There's excellent ice fishing in winter.

Camping: There are 137 RV/tent sites plus seven for tents only in three campgrounds (one accessible only by boat) in southern (Wyoming) section; 126 hookups are available at Horseshoe Bend; open Memorial Day to Labor Day only ($4 per night). No charge at other sites or other dates.

Getting there: Take Route 37 north from Lovell to reach the canyon; Route 14A east from Lovell to the Mason-Lovell Ranch; Route 313 south from Hardin, Montana, to Fort Smith and the Yellowtail Dam.

Sheridan Area

Crow, Sioux and Cheyenne considered the Powder River Basin to be a sort of heaven on earth. Extending from the east slope of the Big Horn Mountains to the Black Hills, it had everything they could want: abundant shelter, mild winters, grass for their ponies and plenty of big game for their own sustenance.

It's no wonder that the tribes made their final stand here. The bloody Indian Wars of 1863–68 followed the blazing of the Bozeman Trail from southern Wyoming to the Montana goldfields; after treaties were signed, a Black Hills gold rush brought more whites to the region and another conflict erupted. This one culminated in the infamous Battle of Little Bighorn and "Custer's Last Stand," just north of Sheridan in southern Montana. Chiefs Red Cloud, Sitting Bull and Crazy Horse achieved their fame in these wars.

After the uprisings were quelled and the Native Americans were removed to reservations, the region quieted down for a few years—until the range wars. The 1892 Johnson County War, south of Sheridan, was the most famous of these. Wealthy cattle barons, fearing that homesteaders and sheep ranchers were rustling their livestock, sent two dozen hired guns from Texas to eliminate 70 "troublemakers." Two sheepmen were gunned down at the KC Ranch; but as the vigilantes moved in on the county seat of Buffalo, that city sent 200 citizens of its own to the cattlemen's TA Ranch headquarters. After a major shootout, and with the support of the U.S. cavalry, the Buffalo group made almost 50 arrests—but no one was ever convicted.

Today, cattle and sheep ranchers coexist peacefully, and seemingly endless hay fields provide feed for their livestock. Coal, oil, uranium and other natural resources are heavily mined in the region.

Sheridan was established in 1882 in the Goose Creek valley, at the foot of the Big Horns. Named for Civil War General Phillip Sheridan and located right on the Bozeman Trail, it quickly became the center of a thriving cattle-ranching district. Today it is a bustling city of 14,000. Sheridan's downtown **Main Street District** has more original late-19th- and early-20th-century buildings than any other community in Wyoming. Obtain a walking-tour map from the **Sheridan County Chamber of Commerce** (Exit 23 off Route 90; 307-672-2485).

Among the city's notable buildings is **The Sheridan Inn** (856 Broadway, Sheridan; 307-674-5440), once considered the finest hotel between Chicago and San Francisco. Built by the Burlington Railroad in 1893, it has hosted the likes of Will Rogers, Ernest Hemingway and three U.S. presidents; "Buffalo Bill" Cody often used its grounds to audition acts for his Wild West Show. Its unique design, with dormer windows extending from every room on the second and third floors, earned the inn recognition from *Ripley's Believe It or Not* as "the house of 69 gables." Despite being a national historic landmark, it was scheduled for demolition in the 1960s until an area rancher purchased and restored it. Today it has a luncheon restaurant, a saloon, a small museum and an art gallery. Self-guided tours are offered at a small admission charge, applied to continuing renovation.

The **Trail End Historic Center** (400 East Clarendon Avenue, Sheridan; 307-674-4589; admission), a beautiful brick hilltop mansion and carriage house adjacent to Kendrick Park, was the home of John B. Kendrick, a pioneer cattle rancher who became a Wyoming governor and U.S. senator. Kendrick built the three-story, Flemish-style home between 1908 and 1913 at a cost of $165,000. Beautifully carved and burnished woodwork highlights the period decor, which includes original furnishings. The three-and-a-half-acre grounds are planted with several hundred trees and shrubs indigenous to Wyoming, as well as many non-native species.

Also well worth a visit is the **Bradford Brinton Memorial** (Brinton Road, Big Horn; 307-672-3173), comprising the Quarter Circle A Ranch, 12 miles south of Sheridan via Routes 87 and 355. Brinton, an Illinois native, bought the ranch house (built in 1892 by two Scottish brothers) in 1923. Here, in the shadow of the Big Horns, he raised cattle and horses. He expanded the ranch house to 20 rooms and filled it with his vast collection of western art (including originals by Charles Russell, Frederic Remington and John James Audubon) and rare books (by Robert Louis Stevenson, Samuel Johnson and others).

Reminders of the Indian Wars of the 1860s are still evident at several sites within a half-hour's drive of modern Sheridan. Fifteen miles north up Route 90, on the south side of Ranchester, **Connor Battlefield State Historic Site** (City Park, off Route 14; 307-674-4589) commemorates the 1865 Battle of Tongue River. General Patrick Connor's 400 troops surprised a camp of Cheyenne and Arapaho, killing 65 and capturing 1000 horses at a loss of eight soldiers.

About a year later, **Fort Phil Kearny** (★) (Route 193, Story; 307-684-7629; admission) was built near the Bozeman Trail, 18 miles south of modern Sheridan. It had one of the shortest, and surely the bloodiest, histories of any outpost in the American West. The fort was constructed, in open violation of the treaty between the U.S. government and the Sioux, in an unprotected location in the heart of the Sioux's best buffalo-hunting territory. Sioux leaders Red Cloud and Crazy Horse vowed to drive the whites out. During Fort Kearny's first six months, 164 men—nearly two-thirds of the original garrison—were killed.

About half of the men were victims of the Fetterman Massacre of December 21, 1866. A stone monument on **Massacre Hill**, three miles north of the fort overlooking Route 87, marks the spot where Lieutenant Colonel William Fetterman and 80 troops were annihilated by some 2000 Sioux and Cheyenne warriors. In direct defiance of his commanding officer's orders, Fetterman had pursued the warriors after rescuing a wagon train from attack and rode directly into a classic ambush.

Two years later, after more battles with Red Cloud and Crazy Horse, the U.S. government decided to vacate the Powder River Basin and the Bozeman Trail. As soon as its garrison evacuated in August 1868, the Sioux burned Fort Kearny to the ground. No original structures remain to be seen today at this state historic site, but a modern museum and visitors center have exhibits and video programs describing the life and times of Fort Kearny, and offer information for self-guided tours of the fort grounds, battle sites and Bozeman Trail.

The smaller communities in the Big Horn foothills surrounding Sheridan are of interest for more than Indian Wars history. **Ranchester** and **Dayton**, twin ranching communities, 15 and 20 miles northwest of Sheridan, are gateways to the recreational opportunities of the northern Big Horn Mountains.

From Dayton, Route 14 weaves uphill for 27 miles on the **Bighorn Scenic Byway** to Burgess Junction, where the route sends separate forks through **Bighorn National Forest** (307-672-0751) to Lovell (Route 14A, via Medicine Wheel National Historic Landmark) and Greybull (Route 14, via Shell Canyon). (See "Big Horn Country," above.) A roadside lookout southwest of Dayton offers a striking panorama of the Tongue River country as well as a geological phenomenon known as **Fallen City**—boulders and columns, broken from a towering cliff, that give the appearance of ancient ruins.

Buffalo, the Johnson County seat 35 miles south of Sheridan, is the other major gateway to the Big Horns and a key transportation hub for the entire region. Downtown Buffalo's **Main Street Historic District**, built along a crooked old trail that forded Clear Creek, has buildings that have stood since 1884, the year the town was incorporated. Among them is the neoclassical **Johnson County Courthouse** (76 North Main Street; 307-684-7272). Walking-tour brochures can be obtained from the **Buffalo Chamber of Commerce** (55 North Main Street; 307-684-5544).

Of particular interest to visitors is the **Jim Gatchell Memorial Museum of the West** (110 Fort Street, Buffalo; 307-684-9331; admission), at the corner of North Main Street beside the courthouse. Beginning as a local pharmacist's private collection, the museum was moved into its own two-story home in 1956; it subsequently expanded into the adjacent 1909 Carnegie Library. The collection includes dioramas of the Wagon Box Fight, the Johnson County War and early Buffalo. More than 10,000 artifacts of Native Americans, soldiers, ranchers and other settlers are also on display.

Kaycee, 45 miles south of Buffalo off Route 25, was christened after the KC Ranch, the nearby 19th-century ranch where two sheep "rustlers" were killed to set off the Johnson County War of 1892. On the town's false-fronted Main Street (looking like something straight out of a TV oater), next door to the old log-cabin jail, is the **Hoofprints of the Past Museum** (Main Street; 307-738-2381), which preserves all manner of cowboy gear and other memorabilia from the history of southern Johnson County.

Butch Cassidy and the Sundance Kid knew this territory well. Kaycee was the nearest community to their notorious **Hole-in-the-Wall** (★) hideout, about 26 miles southwest. Despite its reputation, Hole-in-the-Wall was not a deep, dark cave nor a steep-sided canyon; it was (and is) a lush and spacious valley named after a London pub by two English brothers who established a cattle ranch at this remote location. Robert "Butch Cassidy" Parker may have chosen the hole as a place to train getaway horses for his "Wild Bunch" of outlaws—which also included Harry "Sundance Kid" Longabaugh and Harvey "Kid Curry" Logan. Other places may have been more secure, but few lawmen tried to penetrate the stronghold.

Modern travelers can visit the site by four-wheel-drive vehicle, horse or mountain bike. Take Route 190 west from Kaycee 17 miles to the townsite of Barnum, where the pavement ends. Turn left on dirt Arminto Road and follow a red-walled canyon four miles to the Bar C Ranch. Stop here to obtain permission to continue through Bureau of Land Management holdings to the Hole-in-the-Wall, five miles south of the Bar C. The closer you get, the more rugged the road. If you don't have an appropriate vehicle, you can book a trip with **Hole in the Wall Country Tours** (Kaycee; 307-738-2243).

SHERIDAN AREA HOTELS

A good choice in Sheridan for economy-minded visitors is the friendly **Rocktrim Motel** (449 Coffeen Avenue; 307-672-2464). The 18 wood-paneled guest rooms aren't particularly modern, but they're air-conditioned and spacious, and all have coffeemakers and mini-refrigerators. Full kitchenettes are available. Budget.

Just off Route 90 at the south end of town is the intriguing **Mill Inn** (2161 Coffeen Avenue, Sheridan; 307-672-6401), which occupies a former flour mill. (The grain elevator still stands next door.) It's been entirely altered, of course, and has become a pleasant motel with 45 standard rooms. There's no pool here, but there is an exercise room, and continental breakfast is included in the room rate. Moderate.

Top of the line in Sheridan is the five-story **Holiday Inn** (1809 Sugarland Drive; 307-672-8931, 800-465-4329, fax 307-672-6388), also at the south end. Within its "HoliDome" indoor recreation center are a swimming pool, sauna, hot tub and workout room, not to mention a putting green, racquetball court and game room. The 212 rooms are pretty much standard issue. Hotel facilities include a restaurant, coffee shop, lounge, gift shop and coin laundry. Children under 19 accompanied by their parents stay for free. Moderate to deluxe.

Downtown is the Best **Western Sheridan Center Motor Inn** (612 North Main Street, Sheridan; 307-674-7421, 800-528-1234, fax 307-672-3018), whose 138 guest rooms are contained in four separate buildings (two of them connected by a skybridge) on three facing corners at Main and 2nd. Continental breakfasts are free to guests. On site are a coffee shop, a restaurant and an adjoining lounge. The inn has both indoor and outdoor pools, a sauna and hot tub. Moderate.

The granddaddy of all dude ranches is **Eatons' Ranch** (County Road 89, Wolf; 307-655-9285), 15 miles west of Sheridan in the Big Horn foothills via Route 331. When the three Eaton brothers earned more money by taking in visitors on their North Dakota hay ranch than they did by selling grain, they relocated in 1904 to this site because it offered better riding country. Today the ranch has 54 rustic cabins, most with twin beds, all with private baths. After guests are fitted with saddles, they ride under the supervision of wranglers until they're ready to ride unescorted and then have free rein throughout the ranch's 7000-acre spread. There's also fishing, hiking, swimming in a heated outdoor pool and weekly square dances. Deluxe.

Considerably more sedate is Spahn's **Big Horn Mountain Bed & Breakfast** (★) (70 Upper Hideaway, P.O. Box 579, Big Horn, WY 82833; 307-674-8150), not far from the Bradford Brinton Memorial. From the front porch of this four-story log home on the Big Horn slope you can gaze across 100 miles of Powder River country. Binoculars are served with the country breakfast. There are two rooms with Victorian antiques in the solar-powered lodge, and two outlying cabins, one with its own wood stove and kitchen. All have private bathrooms. Hiking, cross-country skiing and wildlife watching are the activities of choice. Moderate.

Parklike grounds accented by spruce and apple trees surround the **Z Bar Motel** (626 Fort Street, Buffalo; 307-684-5535, 800-341-8000), a half-dozen blocks west of Buffalo's historic downtown. The motel consists of 20 quaint individual log cabins with modern western decor. Each unit has a refrigerator and private bath; some kitchen units and king-size beds are available. Budget.

SHERIDAN AREA RESTAURANTS

In Sheridan it's not hard to find a place to eat that maintains the atmosphere of northern Wyoming during the days of Buffalo Bill. Certainly, the aforementioned **Sheridan Inn** (856 Broadway; 307-674-5440), where Cody once auditioned Wild West Show acts, is one. Healthy, creative lunches are served daily in the pleasant if nondescript restaurant; the Buffalo Bill Saloon is adjacent.

Almost across the street, in the old Chicago, Burlington & Quincy Railroad depot, is the **California Zephyr Restaurant & Caboose Lounge** (841 Broadway, Sheridan; 307-674-5066). A spacious art deco ambience dominates here. Italian, Mexican and American cuisine—including an excellent prime rib—share the menu. There's dancing on weekends. Moderate.

Generous portions of cowboy home cookin' are what you'll get at **The Silver Spur** (832 North Main Street, Sheridan; 307-672-2749). This is just a good ol' family café and bar—but the breakfasts and lunches (no dinners) are tasty and filling. Budget.

The cozy **Ciao Bistro** (120 North Main Street, Sheridan; 307-672-2838) offers a distinctly different choice. Though located right in the heart of the historic district, this restaurant has more in common with big-city nouvelle cafés than with The Mint Bar, Sheridan's landmark watering hole, across the street. The bistro serves croissant sandwiches, pastas, cappuccinos and daily gourmet specials. Moderate.

A Korean restaurant in cowboy country is an oxymoron, to be sure. But the **Ae Suk Family Restaurant & Teriyaki House** (2004 North Main Street, Sheridan; 307-672-0357) holds its own. In addition to traditional Korean cuisine the menu features excellent sushi and tempura dinners, making this good-sized eatery an obligatory stop for Japanese tour groups traveling between Yellowstone National Park and Mount Rushmore. American-style breakfasts and lunches are also available. Budget to moderate.

A half-hour's drive south of Sheridan, between Routes 25 and 90, is the surprising sight of an antique (1925) carousel with 36 horses modeled after famous steeds of the American West. **Colonel Bozeman's Restaurant & Tavern** (675 East Hart Street, Buffalo; 307-684-5555) is an integral part of The Carousel Park. Situated on the Bozeman Trail crossing of Clear Creek, this Old West–style tavern is open for breakfast pancakes, lunch sandwiches, dinner steaks and bedtime desserts. Moderate.

The menu at the **Clear Creek Café** (820 North Main Street, Buffalo; 307-684-7755) appeals to a wide range of gourmet diners by combining favorite foods in creative preparations such as veal piccata, Bavarian chicken and rainbow trout almandine. Beef, lamb, pork and vegetarian selections also are offered in this elegant restaurant on the north side of downtown. Moderate.

SHERIDAN AREA SHOPPING

The truest "cowboy store" you're ever likely to find is **King's Saddlery and Ropes** (184 North Main Street; 307-672-2702) in historic downtown Sheridan. All manner of ranch gear, from saddles and ropes to tack, stirrups and leather gear, are sold here along with gift items for curious visitors. If you wish, you can take a look at 150 years' worth of Old West equipment, including more than 500 antique saddles and early leather-working tools, in saddlemaker-owner Don King's personal museum.

If you're looking to get outfitted for a week at a dude ranch, check out **Dan's Western Wear** (226 North Main Street, Sheridan; 307-672-9378), which has been serving the city since 1919. This is the place to find your Levi's jeans, Tony Lama boots and Stetson hat, as well as Native American turquoise and other jewelry. If the gear here is too traditional for you, head down the street to the **Custom Cowboy Shop** (321 North Main Street, Sheridan; 307-672-7733) where you can buy one-of-a-kind designs or have your own conceptions tailor-made.

For regional art in Sheridan, visit the **Foothills Gallery** (134 North Main Street; 307-672-2068) to see T. D. Kelsey's bronze sculptures. Prints of works by Charles Russell and Frederic Remington and etchings by Hans Kleiber are for sale at the **Hangin' Tree Gallery** (142 North Main Street; 307-674-9869). A superb collection of western history and literature by Wyoming and other western authors can be found at **The Book Shop** (117 North Main Street; 307-684-2939). Ask about the monthly poetry readings.

SHERIDAN AREA NIGHTLIFE

Sheridan is home to one of the great playhouses in the Rockies, the **WYO Theater** (42 North Main Street; 307-672-9083). Built in 1923 as a vaudeville theater called The Lotus, it was fully renovated in art deco style in 1989 and now stages resident and touring professional productions of all kinds. In summer, hero-and-villain melodramas or musical revues play nightly except Tuesdays, with matinee performances on Saturdays. Call for a current schedule.

When the cowboys aren't wrestling bulls or roping calves, you may find them during the afternoon at the **Buffalo Bill Saloon** (Sheridan Inn, 856 Broadway; 307-674-5440), sipping on a Wyoming Slug, a powerful mix of champagne and whiskey. At night, they may be knocking back a Black Dog Ale at **The**

Mint Bar (151 North Main Street; 307-674-9696). A Sheridan landmark, The Mint is worth a visit if only to check out its collection of Old West memorabilia.

Carousers not into the country-and-western scene prefer the **Beaver Creek Saloon** (112 North Main Street; 307-674-8181), a spacious watering hole with pool tables and live rock bands on weekends.

For nondrinkers and nonsmokers, **The Coffee House** (123 North Main Street; 307-674-8619) has live acoustic music in the early evenings Thursdays and Fridays, and pastries and sandwiches always.

SHERIDAN AREA PARKS

Bighorn National Forest—The Big Horn Mountains rise rapidly on both the east and west to a central plateau of alpine meadows and pine forests at 9000-to-10,000–foot elevation. The entire region—over 1.1 million acres from the Montana border south to the headwaters of the Powder River—belongs to the national forest.

Facilities: Picnic tables, restrooms, boat ramps, trails, ski areas; resort complex at Meadowlark Lake, gas and store at Burgess Junction; information, 307-672-0751. *Swimming:* Meadowlark Lake, on Route 16 west of Powder River Pass, is a good spot. There are many alpine lakes, all very cold. *Fishing:* Brook, rainbow and brown trout are prolific in the streams and lakes of the Big Horns, cutthroat trout somewhat less so.

Camping: There are 311 RV/tent sites plus 98 for tents only at 36 campgrounds (no hookups); no charge to $10 per night (most $8 to $9). Eight campgrounds can be reserved (800-280-2267). Most campgrounds open from May through October; higher-altitude sites may be open from June to mid-September.

Getting there: Routes 14 (to Greybull) and 14A (to Lovell) cross the Big Horns from Dayton, north of Sheridan. Route 16 (to Worland) crosses the range from Buffalo, south of Sheridan.

Northeastern Wyoming

The famed Black Hills of South Dakota lap over into Wyoming's northeastern corner, providing the state with such sites of keen recreational interest as Black Hills National Forest, Keystone State Park and the unmistakable Devils Tower National Monument. But there's more to this region than first meets the eye. Gillette, Wyoming's fastest-growing city, is at the heart of one of the richest mineral deposits in North America, and the Thunder Basin National Grassland is an immense tract of wildlife-rich high plains.

Gillette, is a modern-day boom town. Though established more than a century ago as a railroad depot, it grew only modestly (as a shipping center for livestock, grain and coal) until oil and uranium were discovered in the 1950s. The area's mineral wealth is staggering. The 16 open-pit mines surrounding Gillette produce 90 percent of Wyoming's coal, more than all the mines in either

West Virginia or Kentucky. About 25 million barrels of crude oil are pumped annually from 200 wells in the county. Tours can be scheduled at several Gillette-area coal mines. The **Gillette Convention & Visitors Bureau** (314 South Gillette Avenue, Gillette, 307-682-3673) will also make tour arrangements.

For a survey of Campbell County's natural-resource base, drop by the **High Plains Energy and Technology Center** (Cam-plex, Garner Lake Road and Windmill Drive, Gillette; 307-683-8802). At this outdoor exhibit visitors are encouraged to develop a close personal relationship with heavy mining equipment, including coal drills, oil rigs, locomotives and bulldozers. This small science museum is only one of several elements of the **Cam-plex** (Garner Lake Road and Indian Paintbrush Drive, Gillette; 307-682-0552), Wyoming's largest multipurpose events center.

The largest private bison herd in existence makes its home about 30 miles south of Gillette at the **Durham Buffalo Ranch** (★) (Route 59, Wright; 307-939-1271). More than 3500 bison roam the ranch's 55,000 acres. Tours are available by appointment year-round.

Gillette is also a gateway to **Thunder Basin National Grassland** (Routes 59 and 450; 307-358-4690), the nation's largest national grassland, a 1.8-million-acre tract of high plains and plateaus shared by five counties. Sheep and cattle share the acreage with one of the world's largest herds of pronghorn antelope.

At the eastern edge of Thunder Basin, 70 miles from Wright, is **Newcastle**. Named for the English coal port of Newcastle upon Tyne when it was founded in 1890, it has since developed into an oil-refining center astride Route 85, the principal route from Cheyenne to Deadwood in South Dakota's Black Hills. It is of interest to visitors mainly for its **Anna Miller Museum** (401 Delaware Avenue; 307-746-4188), whose focal point is the Jenny Stockade—a combination fort, hotel, store, telegraph office, blacksmith shop and stagecoach way station for a U.S. government–sponsored gold camp in the 1870s.

Some folks think **Sundance**, 50 miles north of Newcastle off Route 90, was named for the Sundance Kid. That may be true of a town of the same name in Utah, but here exactly the opposite was the case. In 1889, after serving 18 months in the Sundance jail for horse stealing, Harry Longabaugh simply began calling himself "The Sundance Kid."

The town, in fact, was named for nearby **Sundance Mountain**, the Temple of the Sioux *(Wi Wacippi Paha)*. At the base of this rocky mountain, warriors once undertook their mystical (and often self-torturing) sun dances to restore harmony to their world. There are plans to develop a ski area here.

The **Vore Buffalo Jump** (★) (Route 14, Beulah; 307-283-1192), 16 miles east of Sundance, is a work in progress. Discovered during the construction of Route 90 in the 1970s, the site revealed layer upon layer of bison bones—from perhaps as many as 20,000 animals that were stampeded over the rim of a ridge and into a deep natural sinkhole at various times between A.D. 1500 and 1800.

Northeastern Wyoming's No. 1 attraction is 33 miles north of Moorcroft. Although it was the site of *Close Encounters of the Third Kind*, visitors should *not* expect to see UFOs hovering over **Devils Tower National Monument** (Route 110, Devils Tower; 307-467-5501; admission). America's first national monument (established by President Theodore Roosevelt in 1906) is, rather, a site of geological fascination and a place to enjoy wildlife and numerous outdoor activities, including swimming, fishing and camping. Rock climbers also come to test their skills on the tower's nearly vertical walls.

Visible for many miles around, Devils Tower looms like a giant tree stump above the Belle Fourche River, where the pine forests of the Black Hills meet the grasslands of the Powder River Basin. Its formation began about 60 million years ago, when molten magma surged near the earth's surface and cooled underground as igneous rock. Sedimentary rocks eroded away around it, exposing this harder plug. Today, the monolith—the tallest rock formation of its kind in the United States—rises 867 feet above its base, 1267 feet above the river and 5117 feet above sea level. It is 1000 feet around at its base, an acre and a half on its sagebrush-and-grass-topped summit.

Kiowa Indians, who called the monolith *Mateo Tipi* (Bear Lodge), had their own explanation for how the Tower came to be. In their legend, seven sisters at play were threatened by a great bear. Fleeing in terror, they came to the stump of a huge tree, which they climbed. As they did so, the stump began to grow toward the heavens. The bear couldn't reach them, although its claws made long gouges on all sides of the tree. The sisters were carried into the sky, where they became the stars of the constellation Ursa Major, the "Big Dipper," or "Great Bear."

The "gouges" are still the most striking feature of Devils Tower. At close range, the nearly vertical walls appear as a mass of fluted, polygonal columns. Where the columns have broken off, they lie as a talus of boulders at the Tower's foot. Adventurous visitors may scramble through the boulder field for a closer look at even more adventurous rock climbers, who bring all their technical skills to bear in scaling the Tower.

The first recorded ascent of the Tower took place on July 4, 1893. Today, more than 1000 people climb the tower every year by some 80 specified routes. Climbers must register before and after their ascents at the **museum and visitors center** (open April through October) at the foot of the Tower. The rough-hewn log structure offers displays on the Tower's history, geology and wildlife. More than 90 species of birds have been recorded in the 1347-acre national monument, and whitetail deer are among the most commonly observed mammals.

Most common of all, however, is the blacktail prairie dog. A **prairie-dog colony**, or "town," flourishes beside the Belle Fourche River about a half mile from the entrance station, not far from the campground and amphitheater. Visitors should avoid getting too close to them, as they can bite and their old burrows may be occupied by rattlesnakes. But it is a delight to watch their clan behavior from a distance.

NORTHEASTERN WYOMING HOTELS

Gillette is a haven for national chain motels and motor inns that cluster around interstate highway exchanges. One of the best is the **Best Western Tower West Lodge** (109 North Highway 14-16; 307-686-2210, 800-528-1234, fax 307-682-5105), at Exit 124 on the west side of the city. A heated outdoor swimming pool is the focal point of this two-story, 190-room inn. Children under 18 accompanied by a parent stay free. Moderate.

A good base for exploring Devils Tower and the Black Hills is the **Bear Lodge Motel** (218 Cleveland Avenue, Sundance; 307-283-1611, 800-341-8000). A big fireplace surrounded by trophy mounts welcomes visitors to the spacious lobby of this two-story, 32-room motel. There's a large spa for all guests. Budget to moderate.

NORTHEASTERN WYOMING RESTAURANTS

A Gillette favorite is **The Prime Rib Restaurant** (1205 South Douglas Highway; 307-682-2944), which serves up hefty helpings of steak, seafood and (of course) prime rib. The restaurant, which sits just north of the downtown freeway interchange, has been honored in recent years by both American Express and *Wine Spectator* magazine. The piano bar lures diners for before- or after-dinner drinks. Moderate.

The turn-of-the-century atmosphere of **Bailey's Bar & Grill** (301 South Gillette Avenue, Gillette; 307-686-7678) perpetuates the mood of the old downtown post office building in which it's lodged. The menu here runs the gamut from hamburger lunches to gourmet chicken dinners. The restaurant features a fresh salad bar and delectable homemade pies. Budget to moderate.

Worth a stop if you're in the neighborhood is the **Flying V Cambria Inn** (★) (Route 85 North near Salt Creek Road, Newcastle; 307-746-2096). This historic stone building, eight miles north of Newcastle on the road to Sundance, is all that remains of the gold-mining ghost town of Cambria. Dinners feature steaks, prime rib, seafood and Italian cuisine. Moderate.

NORTHEASTERN WYOMING SHOPPING

The largest western store in northeastern Wyoming is **Corral West Ranchwear** (2610 South Douglas Highway, Gillette; 307-682-6200), which carries every sort of men's and women's clothing you might be seeking—and then some. It also offers a selection of Native American jewelry, Navajo blankets and novelty gifts ranging from rattlesnake eggs to jackalopes.

Old-time general stores are always fun to visit, but in cities—even in the West—they've invariably been replaced by supermarkets and strip malls. Off the beaten track in the Black Hills of northeastern Wyoming are two good ones. You'll recognize the **Four Corners Country Store** (Route 85, Four Corners; 307-746-4776)—18 miles north of Newcastle and 27 miles southeast of Sundance—by the old-fashioned gas pumps outside. Inside, beneath antique lighting fixtures, you'll find an amazingly wide variety of modern and not-so-modern goods.

The **Aladdin General Store** (★) (Routes 111 and 24; 307-896-2226) is probably the *only* reason to visit the village of Aladdin unless you're taking the back route from Devils Tower to the Black Hills. Located 20 miles northeast of Sundance, the store was built as a saloon in 1896 and has been in continuous operation since. It sells (alphabetically, to name but a few) antiques, art, books, clothing, fishing and hunting supplies, gasoline, groceries, liquor, outdoor equipment and souvenirs of all sorts.

NORTHEASTERN WYOMING NIGHTLIFE

Gillette's main entertainment venue is the **Cam-plex** (Garner Lake Road and Indian Paintbrush Drive; 307-682-0552). Within the 100-acre grounds of this multipurpose events center are the 960-seat **Heritage Center Theater** for concerts and live theater, two convention pavilions, a horseracing track and a rodeo arena where the National High School Finals Rodeo, the world's largest rodeo, takes place over ten days in July.

Gillette's hot spot, though, is the **Boot Hill Nightclub** (910 North Gurley Avenue; 307-682-1600), which boasts live country entertainment nightly and Wyoming's largest dancefloor. It's also a popular prime-rib and seafood restaurant before the music begins.

NORTHEASTERN WYOMING PARKS

Black Hills National Forest—The Wyoming portion (175,000 acres) of this 1.25-million-acre forest is small compared to what's across the border in South Dakota. But there are nice stretches of pine-covered hills north and south of Sundance, featuring such attractions as Cook Lake, Inyan Kara Mountain and Cold Springs Creek canyon. The Lakota Sioux called the hills *Paha Sapa* (hills that are black) because the forests of ponderosa pine covering them appeared dark from the plains.

Facilities: Picnic tables, restrooms, trails; summer day-use fees at Sheridan, Pecola and Deerfield lakes only, $2; information, 307-283-1361. *Swimming:* At your own risk in Cook Lake. *Fishing:* Trout in Cook Lake, Sand Creek and Cold Springs Creek.

Camping: There are 66 RV/tent sites at three Wyoming campgrounds (no hookups); $6 to $8 per night. Sites at two of the campgrounds (Cook Lake and Reuter Camp) can be reserved by calling 800-280-2267.

Getting there: To Cook Lake, take Forest Roads 838 (Warren Peak Road) and 830 (Bear Lodge Road) north from Sundance 18 miles. To Inyan Kara Mountain, take Route 585 south from Sundance 17 miles to Schlup Road; then turn west and continue for three and a half miles. To Cold Springs Creek, take Route 90 east from Sundance four miles to Exit 191, turn southeast on Moskee Road and continue for eight miles, and then turn north on Forest Road 863, which runs about 18 miles to Beulah.

Keyhole State Park—There aren't many places to engage in water sports in semiarid northeastern Wyoming. In fact, Keyhole Reservoir is just about it. Created by a Bureau of Reclamation dam on the Belle Fourche River, the lake is completely encircled by the 15,674-acre park. Most facilities—including a swimming beach and boat launches for boaters, anglers and waterskiers—are on the southeastern shore. Board sailors appreciate the breezes that blow down the western flank of the Black Hills. The nearby hamlet of Pine Haven offers a marina, motel and café.

Facilities: Picnic tables, restrooms, amphitheater, marina, boat ramp, playground, motel and café; day-use fee, $3; information, 307-756-3596. *Swimming:* Designated beach. *Fishing:* Excellent for northern pike, walleye, catfish, perch and smallmouth bass.

Camping: There are 140 RV/tent sites at three campgrounds (no hookups); $4 per night.

Getting there: From Route 90 between Moorcroft and Sundance, take Exit 165 (Pine Ridge Road) north six miles to the main park complex. Or follow Route 14 north five miles from Moorcroft; turn right on Route 113 and continue another five miles; and turn north on Pine Haven Road and continue two and a half miles to Pine Haven.

The Sporting Life

FISHING

The streams and lakes of northern Wyoming are renowned for their trout fishing. Fly-fishermen in their waders, thigh-deep in a rushing mountain river, choose hand-tied flies that match the caddis and mayfly hatches to bring in trophy-size rainbow, cutthroat, brown and brook trout. Spin anglers cast their lures for grayling and mountain whitefish. At a lower elevation, trollers drag live bait behind their boats to capture walleye, bass, northern pike, yellow perch and channel catfish from lakes and reservoirs.

CODY AREA The North and South forks of the Shoshone River, west of Cody, have sizable populations of rainbow, brown and cutthroat trout as well as whitefish. Buffalo Bill Reservoir also has lake trout. Fly-fishermen try the wild and scenic Clark's Fork for cutthroat, rainbow and brook trout. In the alpine lakes of the Absaroka and Beartooth ranges, the rare golden trout is a diamond among other species.

The yields of bluegills and crappies in Deaver Reservoir, 16 miles northeast of Powell, will put smiles on the faces of both youngsters and parents.

North Fork Anglers (937 Sheridan Avenue, Cody; 307-527-7274) and **Yellowstone Outfitters** (239A Yellowstone Avenue, Cody; 307-587-8240) offer guided fishing trips. **Aune's Absaroka Angler** (1390 Sheridan Avenue, Cody; 307-587-5105) specializes in flyfishing trips.

BIG HORN COUNTRY Bighorn Lake has both cold- and warm-water species: brown, lake and rainbow trout; walleye, sauger, ling, perch, catfish and largemouth bass. It's an angler's grab bag. Streams on the west slope of the Big Horn Mountains, produce brook, brown and rainbow trout.

Get boat and equipment rentals at **The Marina at Horseshoe Bend** (Route 37, Lovell; 307-548-7230) in Bighorn Canyon National Recreation Area.

SHERIDAN AREA On the east slope of the Big Horn Mountains you'll catch brown and rainbow trout in the Tongue River, Clear and Piney creeks and the Middle Fork of the Powder River. Higher-elevation lakes like Cloud Peak and Willow Park reservoirs, west of Buffalo, offer brook and cutthroat as well as rainbow trout. Lake De Smet, in the Powder River Basin north of Buffalo, has crappie, yellow perch and rock bass as well as rainbow and brown trout.

Good places to shop for tackle and to line up outfitters are **The Ritz** (135 North Main Street, Sheridan; 307-674-4101) and the **Fly Shop of the Big Horns** (377 Coffeen Avenue, Sheridan; 307-672-5866). Both **The Sports Lure** (66 South Main Street, Buffalo; 307-684-7682) and **Paul Wallop Mountain Fly Fishing** (P.O. Box 11, Big Horn, WY 82833; 307-674-6239) offer equipment rentals and guided trips.

NORTHEASTERN WYOMING In the far northeast, try Keyhole Reservoir for walleye, northern pike, yellow perch, smallmouth bass and channel catfish. Brown trout populate Sand Creek in Black Hills National Forest, just inside the South Dakota border.

Sportsmans Gun Center (202-A Kendrick Street, Gillette; 307-682-5868) is a good place to inquire about fishing guide services.

BOATING, BOARD SAILING AND WATERSKIING

The region's three principal venues for water sports in this semiarid land are manmade: Buffalo Bill Reservoir, near Cody; Bighorn Lake, near Lovell; and Keyhole Reservoir, not far from Moorcroft.

There are several boat launches, but no rentals, at both **Buffalo Bill State Park** (Yellowstone Highway, Cody; 307-587-9227) and **Keyhole State Park** (Route 113, Pine Haven; 307-756-3596). *Outside* magazine considers Buffalo Bill to be one of the ten best places for board sailing in the United States. Keyhole is also a popular location for board sailing and waterskiing.

Bighorn Lake supports the **Bighorn Canyon National Recreation Area** (Lovell; 307-548-2251). A variety of boats can be rented at **The Marina at Horseshoe Bend** (Route 37, Lovell; 307-548-7230). Boat tours are also offered from The Marina.

RIVER RAFTING AND KAYAKING

CODY AREA Rafting the Shoshone can mean very different experiences depending on which section of the river you choose. For example, the rapids on the 38-mile stretch of the North Fork that follows Route 14/16/20 from Sleeping Giant campground, near Pahaska Tepee, to Buffalo Bill Reservoir offer excitement but little risk to novice rafters on commercial trips.

Immediately below the Buffalo Bill Dam, a four-mile stretch of the main Shoshone offers severe drops like Iron Curtain that delight experienced kayakers and thrill-seeking rafters. At DeMaris Hot Springs, near Trail Town, the river levels out and quiets down.

The Clark's Fork of the Yellowstone is for experts only. No commercial trips are offered.

Cody's Shoshone River outfitters include **Cody Rapid Transit** (1370 Sheridan Avenue; 307-587-3535), **River Runners** (1491 Sheridan Avenue; 307-527-7238) and **Wyoming River Trips** (1701 Sheridan Avenue; 307-587-6661).

BIG HORN COUNTRY From Thermopolis, **Wind River Canyon Whitewater** (907 Shoshoni Street, Thermopolis; 307-864-9343) takes river enthusiasts on half-day, full-day and overnight excursions on the Wind River.

DOWNHILL SKIING

Three small ski hills—one in the Absarokas, two in the Big Horns—offer family recreation without the glitz of major resorts.

CODY AREA **Sleeping Giant Ski Area** (349 Yellowstone Highway, Wapiti; 307-587-4044), located 48 miles west of Cody and just four miles from Yellowstone Park's east entrance, is owned and operated by the Shoshone Lodge. Recently opened, the area has a day lodge, one chairlift and a surface lift. Vertical drop is 500 feet.

BIG HORN COUNTRY **Antelope Butte Ski Area** (Route 14, Shell; 307-655-9530), in Bighorn National Forest, has a chairlift, two surface lifts and 1000 feet of vertical. Located on the west side of 9000-foot Granite Pass, at the head of Shell Canyon, it is open Fridays through Sundays from December to April. There's a shop with full alpine, nordic and snowboard rentals.

High Park Ski Area (Route 16, Ten Sleep; 307-347-4480), 50 miles east of Worland and 41 miles west of Buffalo, also in Bighorn National Forest, has two poma lifts that service five runs on 600 vertical feet of terrain. Overlooking Meadowlark Lake on the west side of Powder River Pass, it also has equipment rentals. Open weekends and holidays from Thanksgiving to mid-April.

SKI RENTALS Full rental packages are available for downhill and cross-country skiers, snowboarders and snowshoers at **The Sports Lure** (66 South Main Street, Buffalo; 307-684-7682). Topographical maps, as well as full nordic equipment rentals, are found at **Sunlight Sports** (1251 Sheridan Avenue, Cody; 307-587-9517).

CROSS-COUNTRY SKIING

CODY AREA Cross-country ski opportunities in the area—especially in Shoshone National Forest (307-527-6241)—are almost limitless. From **Pahaska Tepee Resort** (183 Yellowstone Highway, Wapiti; 307-527-7701), for instance, some 12 kilometers of groomed track connect with Sleeping Giant Ski Area base facilities and extend into the national forest, where there are another 40 kilometers of marked (but ungroomed) nordic trails. Rentals are available at the resort.

There are more groomed trails in the Sunlight Basin area off Route 296, but without special facilities.

BIG HORN COUNTRY AND SHERIDAN AREA **Wood River Valley Ski Touring Park** (Wood River Road, Meeteetse; 307-868-2603), the largest cross-country area in northern Wyoming, is 22 miles southwest of Meeteetse. There are 25 kilometers of groomed novice and intermediate trails here, as well as a back-country trail system, a warming hut and an overnight tent available by reservation.

In the Big Horn Mountains, the **Willow Park Ski Touring Area** (Route 16, Ten Sleep; 307-672-0751), 45 miles east of Worland near Meadowlark Lake, offers 37 kilometers of groomed trails.

Bighorn National Forest (307-672-0751) also boasts the **Pole Creek Ski Touring Area** (Route 16, Buffalo), with 23 kilometers of groomed marked trails and a warming hut about 22 miles southwest of Buffalo, and the **Sibley Lake Ski Touring Area** (Route 14, Burgess Junction), with 13 kilometers of trails about 19 miles southwest of Dayton. Both are open to the public at no charge.

NORTHEASTERN WYOMING In Black Hills National Forest (307-283-1361), there's a system of novice and intermediate trails emanating from the **Reuter campground**, six miles northwest of Sundance.

For information on renting equipment, see the ski-rental section in "Downhill Skiing" above.

ICE SKATING

Skating takes place from December through February at **Homesteader Park** (Route 14A; 307-754-5106) at the east edge of Powell. The ice arena, open days and lit for night skating, has a warming house, skate rentals and concessions. There's no admission charge.

GOLF

The leading courses are **Olive Glenn Golf & Country Club** (802 Meadow Lane Drive, Cody; 307-587-5551) and the **Kendrick Golf Course** (Route 331, Sheridan; 307-674-8148). Municipal 18-hole links are the **Buffalo Golf Course** (West Hart Street and De Smet Avenue, Buffalo; 307-684-5266) and **Bell Knob Golf Course** (1316 Overdale Drive, Gillette; 307-686-7609).

TENNIS

Three of Cody's 17 city parks have outdoor courts, including lighted courts near downtown at **Paul Stock Park** (Beck Avenue and 9th Street). Other courts are at **Glendale Park** (Meadow Lane Avenue and 15th Street) and **Highland Manor Park** (Carter Avenue and 24th Street). For information, call the Cody Parks Department (307-527-7511).

There are public courts in Sheridan at **Kendrick Park** (Loucks Street at Big Goose Creek; 307-672-2485) and **Thorne-Rider Park** (Val Vista and 11th Street; 307-674-6421), and in Gillette at **Bicentennial Park** (300 West Warlow Drive; 307-686-3757) and the **Campbell County Recreation Center** (1000 South Douglas Highway; 307-682-7406).

HORSEBACK RIDING

Serious riders probably want to book a stay of a week or longer at one of the dozens of guest (or "dude") ranches throughout northern Wyoming. This book recommends only a few. For a more complete listing, contact local visitors bureaus or chambers of commerce, or the **Wyoming Division of Tourism** (Route 25 at College Drive, Cheyenne; 307-777-7777, 800-225-5996). There are also several books that list guest ranches; a favorite is Gene Kilgore's *Ranch Vacations*, 3rd edition (Santa Fe, New Mexico: John Muir Publications, 1994).

CODY AREA Many of the 23 guest ranches in the Cody area make horses available to day guests for guided trail rides. Perhaps your best bet, just two miles from Yellowstone Park's east entrance, is Buffalo Bill's own 1905 hunting lodge, the **Pahaska Tepee Resort** (183 Yellowstone Highway, Wapiti; 307-527-7701).

SHERIDAN AREA Riding the Big Horns is the realm of several outfitters based along the east flank of the range. Guided day and evening rides, as well as horse rentals for self-guided trips, can be booked through the **Wagon Box Horse Corral** (North Piney Road, Story; 307-683-2301), 20 miles south of Sheridan, or **Clear Creek Corrals** (280 South Williams Street, Buffalo; 307-684-7684), 35 miles south of Sheridan. Show riders will be pleased to discover the 65-acre **Big Horn Equestrian Center** (Bird Farm Road, Big Horn; 307-674-5179), about 12 miles south of Sheridan off Route 335.

PACK TRIPS AND LLAMA TREKKING

Ron Dube's Wilderness Adventure (P.O. Box 637, Cody, WY 82414; 307-527-7815) offers deluxe expeditions into the high country of the Absaroka Range, including the Washakie and Teton wilderness areas. In the Sheridan area, **Trails West Outfitters** (P.O. Box 111, Buffalo, WY 82834; 307-684-5233) has a summer base camp (with a full-time cook!) at the edge of the Cloud Peak Wilderness for its guided backcountry pack trips.

Llama excursions into the Bighorn National Forest can be booked with **Cloud Peak Llama Treks** (Story; 307-683-2732).

BICYCLING

CODY AREA Favorite excursions in Buffalo Bill country are **Rattlesnake Mountain**, a 17-mile climb (mainly through BLM land) to this bluff that overlooks Buffalo Bill Reservoir on the west side of Cody, and side trips off **South Fork Road**, which extends into Shoshone National Forest southwest of Cody.

SHERIDAN AREA On the west slope of the Big Horn Mountains, there's great biking on Bighorn National Forest roads, especially on **Forest Roads 10** and **15**—on either side of Route 14A between Medicine Wheel and Burgess Junction.

The roads and trails south and east of Burgess Junction are especially recommended, including **Forest Road 26** from Owen Creek campground (on Route 14) past the Sawmill Lakes to Red Grade Spring, near the town of Big Horn.

The 32-mile-long road, which skirts the north edge of the Cloud Peak Wilderness, descends from 9400 feet to 5100 feet.

In Buffalo, the **Clear Creek Trail System** extends 8.5 miles through town, traversing areas rich in both human and natural history. The trail is alternately paved, graveled and unsurfaced.

NORTHEASTERN WYOMING Gillette, an old community with the new face of a modern boom town, has installed a system of citywide bike paths.

BIKE RENTALS **Olde Faithful Bicycles** (1362 Sheridan Avenue, Cody; 307-527-5110) offers rentals and repairs of mountain and touring bikes. Three-hour guided mountain-bike tours are also available. **Back Country Bicycles** (241 North Main Street, Sheridan; 307-672-2453) and **The Sports Lure** (66 South Main Street, Buffalo; 307-684-7682) have full information on local trails as well as rentals. In Northeastern Wyoming, maps and vehicles are available from **Spoke & Edge Sports** (900 Carmel Drive, Gillette; 682-9343), and mountain bikes for negotiating the roads and trails of Devils Tower National Monument and the nearby Black Hills National Forest are available for rent from **Sky's the Limit** (Devils Tower; 307-467-5659), just outside the park entrance.

HIKING

The Absaroka and Big Horn ranges provide prime terrain for both day hikers and backcountry adventurers. All distances listed for hiking trails are one-way unless otherwise noted.

CODY AREA West of Cody, off the Yellowstone Highway, numerous long trails (and shorter segments thereof) lead from campgrounds, picnic areas and guest ranches into the adjacent Washakie and North Absaroka wilderness areas.

The strenuous **South Fork Trail** (36 miles) begins at the end of South Fork Road 43 miles southwest of Cody, follows the South Fork of the Shoshone River upstream to its Washakie Wilderness headwaters near Shoshone Pass, at 9800 feet, and then descends to Trail Lake north of Dubois.

The moderate **Pahaska-Sunlight Trail** (18 miles) is best accomplished from the top down. Arrange a drop-off in the Silvertip Basin at the end of the Sunlight Basin Road off Route 296, about 65 miles northwest of Cody. Descend 3700 feet along the North Fork of the Shoshone River to the Pahaska Tepee Resort on the Yellowstone Highway. Tent one night at Camp Monaco, seven miles downstream, where Buffalo Bill hosted Albert I, prince of Monaco, on Cody's final big-game hunt in 1913.

The **Beartooth Loop National Recreation Trail** (18 miles) begins and ends at Gardner Lake off Route 212, about 85 miles north of Cody between Cooke City and Red Lodge, Montana. The trail passes lakes, meadows and gentle river canyons on the Beartooth Plateau, varying in elevation from about 10,500 feet down to about 9000 feet. This is a Shoshone National Forest trail; expect to share it with motorized vehicles. Moderate.

Consult the rangers at **Shoshone National Forest** (P.O. Box 2140, Cody, WY 82414; 307-527-6241) for full information on regional trails.

BIG HORN COUNTRY **Bucking Mule Falls National Recreation Trail** (11 miles), in the northern Big Horn Mountains, rewards hikers with the sight of Bucking Mule Falls plunging 600 feet into Devil Canyon. The upper trailhead is at the end of Devil Canyon Road (Forest Road 14), off Route 14A east of Medicine Wheel. The well-marked, moderate but often-steep trail descends Bucking Mule Creek, crosses Devil Canyon and then follows Porcupine Creek downstream to Porcupine campground in Bighorn National Forest.

Mistymoon Trail (6.5 miles) leads to a string of beautiful alpine lakes on the western slope of the Cloud Peak Wilderness. Beginning at West Tensleep Lake, eight miles north of Meadowlark Lake off Route 16, the trail climbs steadily about 1200 feet (to above 10,000 feet) to Lakes Helen, Marion and Mistymoon. Ascents of 13,165-foot Cloud Peak often begin here. Backcountry permits are not required, but hikers are asked to fill out registration cards at trailheads.

SHERIDAN AREA Most of the best hikes are in Bighorn National Forest (1969 Sheridan Avenue, Sheridan; 307-672-0751), whose ranger stations have maps and information on hikes in the Big Horns, including Cloud Peak Wilderness.

Tongue River Canyon Loop Trail (14 miles) climbs between towering 1000-foot walls west of Dayton, off Tongue Canyon Road, and returns down Horse Creek. This was where Crazy Horse had hoped to make his final home. There's an elevation gain of about 4300 feet to 7300 feet on this moderate hike. Keep an eye out for wildlife and an old log flume.

The **Stull Lakes–Coney Lake Trail** (2 miles) leaves from the Twin Lakes picnic area on Red Grade Road (Forest Road 26), about 23 miles west of Big Horn. The moderate hike winds uphill into the Cloud Peak Wilderness, through lodgepole and spruce forests to the three Stull Lakes and, a mile farther, to little Coney Lake, nestled between mountains at 9300 feet. There's an elevation gain of about 900 feet from the trailhead.

NORTHEASTERN WYOMING In Black Hills National Forest, **Cook Lake Trail** (1 mile) circles the shoreline of a pretty, pine-shrouded lake that provides the only trout fishing in this part of Wyoming. This easy hike begins and ends at the Cook Lake campground, 18 miles north of Sundance off Bear Lodge Road. Contact Black Hills National Forest (Highway 14 East, Sundance; 307-283-1361) for complete trail information and maps.

At Devils Tower National Monument, the **Tower Trail** (1.25 miles), which loops around the base of Devils Tower, is by far the most popular hike. Starting and ending at the visitors center, this easy paved trail with benches en route is accessible to the elderly and the moderately disabled. Interpretive markers describe various aspects of geology and natural history.

The **Joyner Ridge Trail** (1.5 miles) is a moderate-level loop trail that begins and ends in the northern section of Devils Tower National Monument, about a mile from the visitors center. Park officials consider it "the gem of the monument." The trail traverses several ecosystems, including a ridgetop forest, sandstone cliffs and secluded meadow and prairie. Interpretive plaques are placed en route.

Transportation

BY CAR

Cody is slightly off the beaten track as far as interstate highways go, but it's at a junction of several major U.S. and state highways. To reach Buffalo Bill country, take **Route 14/16/20**, east from Yellowstone; **Route 120** northwest from Thermopolis or south from Red Lodge, Montana; **Route 16** west off Route 25 at Buffalo; or **Route 14** west off Route 25 near Sheridan.

By contrast, interstate highways make access to northeastern Wyoming quite simple. East-west **Route 90** and north-south **Route 25** join at Buffalo, a half-hour's drive south of Sheridan. Route 90 continues north and west to Sheridan, Billings and Seattle; east to Gillette, Sundance and Boston. Route 25 connects south to Casper, Cheyenne, Denver and El Paso, Texas.

BY AIR

Yellowstone Regional Airport has daily service year-round to and from Denver with Continental Express and Mesa Airlines/United Express, and summer service to and from Salt Lake City with SkyWest (for Delta).

Sheridan County Airport and Gillette's **Campbell County Airport** both offer daily connections to Denver—and with each other—via United Express.

BY BUS

Powder River Transportation (580 East 5th Street, Sheridan; 307-674-6188) is the regional line, connecting with national Greyhound routes from Casper and from Billings, Montana.

Besides the central depot in Sheridan, bus stations are located in Cody (1452 Sheridan Avenue; 307-527-7658), Gillette (1700 East Route 14/16; 307-682-1888) and most other sizable northern Wyoming towns.

CAR RENTALS

Avis Rent A Car (800-831-2847) and **Hertz Rent A Car** (800-654-3131) are represented at the airports in Cody, Sheridan and Gillette.

PUBLIC TRANSPORTATION

None of the cities of northern Wyoming has public transit, although Cody—whose privately operated, hourly trolley service ceased in 1994—hopes to re-establish some form of cross-town transportation.

TAXIS

In the absence of public bus systems, **Cody Taxi** (Cody; 307-587-9327), **Sheridan Transportation** (Sheridan; 307-674-6814) and **Yellow Checker Cab** (Gillette; 307-686-4090) do yeoman's work.

CHAPTER NINE

Southwestern Idaho Rockies

Southwestern Idaho is the cornerstone of the northern Rocky Mountains. Here is Boise (pronounced "BOY-see"), the largest city between Portland and Minneapolis, between Salt Lake and the Canadian border. Idaho's state capital, established in the 1860s after a gold-mining boom in the nearby Boise Basin, is a curious blend of sophistication and conservatism. The university town of 135,000 has its head in the future and its attendant growing pains (high-technology computer and engineering industries pad the local economy), but its heart is in the country. While Boiseans appreciate their burgeoning cultural scene, you're more likely to find them casting hand-tied caddis flies for rainbow trout in the Boise River than offering polite applause at a theater performance.

West of Boise, the Boise and Payette rivers empty into the Snake at the Oregon border. Their combined waters have created the fertile Treasure Valley, one of Idaho's richest agricultural regions, with broad fields of corn, alfalfa, sugar beets and potatoes, as well as vineyards and fruit orchards.

To the northwest is Hells Canyon, the deepest gorge on the North American continent, deeper even than Arizona's famed Grand Canyon. To the north are the alpine lakes and resort communities of the McCall area, gateway to the massive Frank Church–River of No Return Wilderness surrounding the Salmon River. Northeast and east is the Boise Basin, center of Idaho's most important gold rush, now a region better known for its whitewater rafting and its climactic Sawtooth Wilderness.

To the southeast are the Mountain Home Air Force Base, where the United States has its only air intervention wing, and the Bruneau Dunes, America's tallest sand dunes. Beyond them, to the south of Boise, are the Snake River Birds of Prey National Conservation Area, home of the continent's largest concentration of raptors, and the forbidding near-badlands of the Owyhee region.

Boise Area

Boise was named by French Canadian trappers in the early 19th century. According to local legend, the men crested a nearby hill after a hot, dry crossing of the desert and, gazing down upon the vegetation surrounding the Boise River, exclaimed: *"Les bois! Les bois!"* ("Woods! Woods!"). The city, established in 1863 as a service center for miners in the Rocky Mountain foothills, takes its name seriously: Its founders turned the banks of the river into a verdant greenbelt and planted so many species around their community that today Boise is known as "the City of Trees."

Within a year of its establishment, Boise was made the territorial capital. The seat of government remained here when Idaho achieved statehood in 1890. The **State Capitol** (700 West Jefferson Street; 208-334-2470), built between 1905 and 1920, was constructed of native sandstone quarried at nearby Table Rock; the marble in its interior comes from Alaska, Georgia, Vermont and Italy. Patterned after the U.S. Capitol in Washington, D.C., this neoclassical building is America's only geothermally heated statehouse. Tours of the 200,000-square-foot building take in four floors of fine art and historical exhibits, as well as the Senate and House chambers.

In the heart of Boise is **The Grove**, a broad public plaza and pedestrian mall built around an open fountain at 8th and Grove streets. Every week from mid-May to mid-September, this plaza attracts thousands of Boiseans to a Wednesday-evening musical bash called "Alive After Five." At the plaza's southwest corner is **Boise Centre on the Grove** (850 Front Street; 208-336-8900), the city's primary convention hall. In late 1995 construction is to begin at the southeast corner on what is to become the city's first luxury hotel, a $32 million, 250-room property. The WestCoast Hotel will include an ice rink—the only one in Boise—for a promised professional franchise in the Western Hockey League. A **Visitor Information Center** (South 8th Street; 208-344-5338) adjoining the convention hall offers city maps and other information.

Two blocks east of The Grove is the **Basque Museum and Cultural Center** (★) (607–611 Grove Street; 208-343-2671), a tribute to the colorful heritage and unique language of one of America's most invisible ethnic minorities. An anomaly even in their traditional homeland along the Atlantic coast of Spain and France, the Basques (who call themselves *Euskaldunak*) found the northern Great Basin region conducive to raising sheep and other livestock more than a century ago. Today Boise is home to the largest Basque community outside of Europe. The museum—the only one devoted to the Basque culture in the United States—occupies the city's oldest brick building (the 1864 Cyrus Jacobs-Uberuaga House, which was once a boarding house for Basque immigrants). The adjacent cultural center sponsors performances by the Oinkari Basque Dancers and other events.

South of The Grove is the **8th Street Market Place** (405 South 8th Street; 208-344-0641), a turn-of-the-century warehouse block that has been renovated

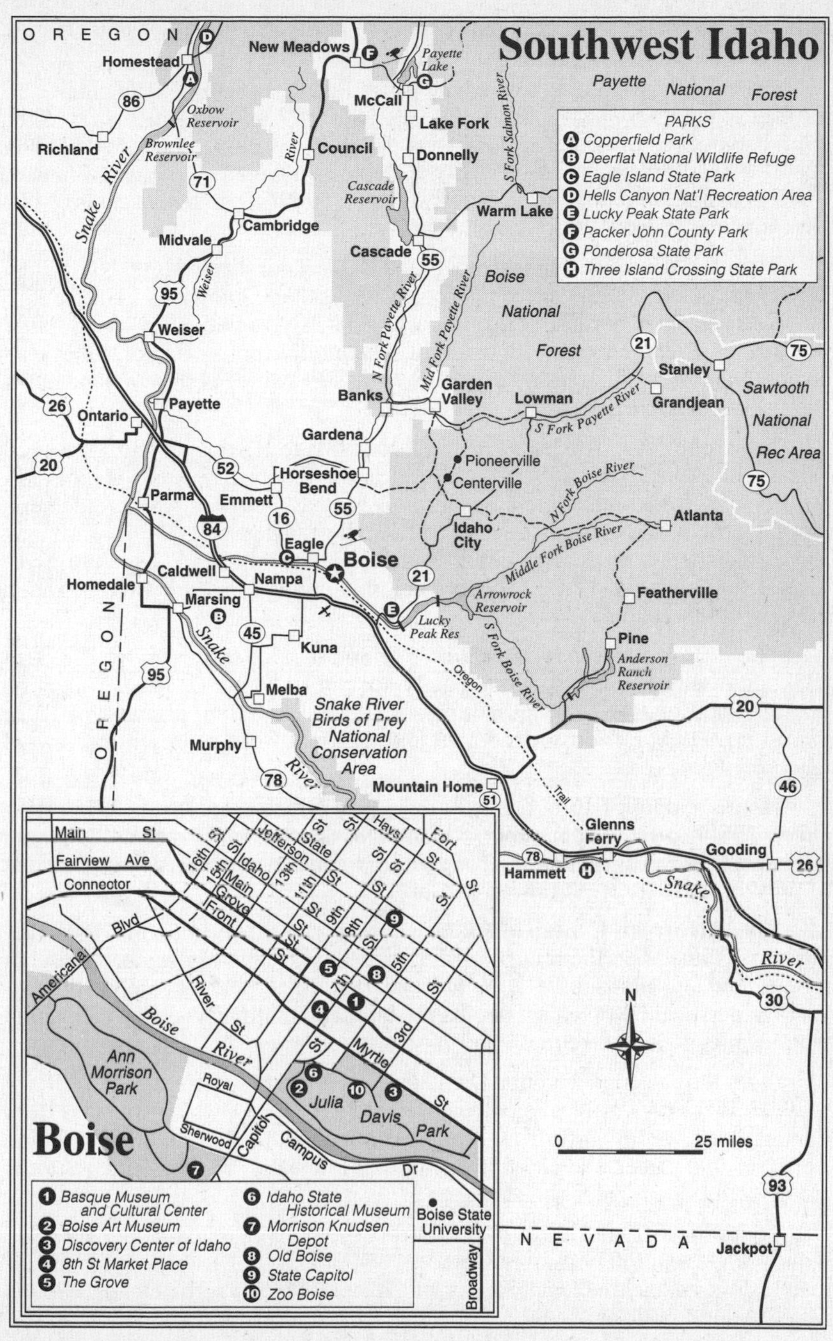
Southwest Idaho
Payette National Forest
PARKS
A Copperfield Park
B Deerflat National Wildlife Refuge
C Eagle Island State Park
D Hells Canyon Nat'l Recreation Area
E Lucky Peak State Park
F Packer John County Park
G Ponderosa State Park
H Three Island Crossing State Park
OREGON
Homestead
New Meadows
Payette Lake
McCall
Lake Fork
Donnelly
Richland
Oxbow Reservoir
Brownlee Reservoir
Council
Cascade Reservoir
Warm Lake
Cambridge
Midvale
Cascade
Boise National Forest
Weiser
Stanley
Sawtooth National Rec Area
Payette
Ontario
Banks
Garden Valley
Lowman
Grandjean
Gardena
Pioneerville
Centerville
Horseshoe Bend
Emmett
Parma
Idaho City
Atlanta
Eagle
Boise
Caldwell
Nampa
Homedale
Marsing
Featherville
Kuna
Lucky Peak Res
Arrowrock Reservoir
Pine
Anderson Ranch Reservoir
Melba
Snake River Birds of Prey National Conservation Area
Murphy
Mountain Home
Glenns Ferry
Hammett
Gooding
Oregon Trail
NEVADA
Jackpot
0 25 miles
Boise
1 Basque Museum and Cultural Center
2 Boise Art Museum
3 Discovery Center of Idaho
4 8th St Market Place
5 The Grove
6 Idaho State Historical Museum
7 Morrison Knudsen Depot
8 Old Boise
9 State Capitol
10 Zoo Boise
Boise State University
Ann Morrison Park
Julia Davis Park
Boise River

for shops, restaurants, offices and a cinema. There's a popular farmers' market here on Saturday mornings in summer.

Just past the Market Place and the **Boise Public Library** (715 South Capitol Boulevard; 208-384-4238), on the east side of Capitol Boulevard and the north bank of the Boise River, is 90-acre **Julia Davis Park** (Julia Davis Drive; 208-384-4240), the centerpiece of Boise's splendid Greenbelt system. Many of Boise's visitor attractions are concentrated here, with separate museums of history, art and science, as well as the city zoo.

The park also contains the depot of the **Boise Tour Trains** (600 North Julia Davis Drive; 208-342-4796; admission). One of them, known as "The Tootin' Tater," is so named because of its horn, which its drivers frequently use to startle pedestrians. Each motorized 1890s-replica locomotive pulls a pair of trolley cars on one-hour tours of the streets of historic Boise as a guide points out landmarks and tells punny stories.

The trolley stop is adjacent to the **Idaho State Historical Museum** (610 North Julia Davis Drive; 208-334-2120; admission), which recounts Idaho's colorful history from prehistoric times through the early days of white settlement. Displays focus on Native American culture, the fur-trading and gold-rush eras and establishment of modern cities. A neighboring Pioneer Village preserves several log, adobe and wood-frame dwellings dating from the 1860s through the early 20th century.

The nearby **Boise Art Museum** (670 South Julia Davis Drive; 208-345-8330; admission) contains the nationally acclaimed Glenn C. Janss Collection of American Realism. The museum also features a rotating calendar of 15 or more touring exhibitions of regional and national work representing a wide range of themes.

In the middle of Julia Davis Park is **Zoo Boise** (355 North Julia Davis Drive; 208-384-4260; admission), which focuses on regional species: elk, deer, moose, bighorn sheep and birds. The zoo has the most extensive display of birds of prey in the Pacific Northwest region.

The Discovery Center of Idaho (131 Myrtle Street; 208-343-9895; admission) is at the northern edge of the park. A participatory science museum for children and adults alike, it contains nearly 100 permanent exhibits that encourage personal involvement and hands-on manipulation. Visitors learn about motion, magnetism, electricity and much, much more.

A footbridge connects Julia Davis Park with the 110-acre campus of **Boise State University** (1910 University Drive; 208-385-1011), which stretches from Capitol Boulevard to Broadway Avenue on the south side of the Boise River. About 15,000 students attend this institution, the state's largest. Campus tours are offered on a regular schedule.

South of BSU via Capitol Boulevard is the 1925 Mission-style **Morrison Knudsen Depot** (2603 Eastover Terrace; 208-336-7500). Displays on Idaho railroad history occupy the Great Hall of this former Union Pacific Depot, through which Amtrak still operates.

BSU and Julia Davis Park are an integral part of the **Boise River Greenbelt** (1104 Royal Boulevard; 208-384-4240), a network of walking and biking paths, mostly paved, that extends 19 miles through the heart of the city, from southeast to northwest. A focal point for the city, the Greenbelt links parks and community facilities and provides access to the river for everyone from businessmen-anglers (some of whom spend their lunch hours flyfishing for trout) to summer floaters.

Traveling west, the Greenbelt passes through Boise's largest park, **Ann Morrison Memorial Park** (Ann Morrison Park Drive; 208-384-4240), with sports fields and extensive facilities, and tranquil **Kathryn Albertson Park** (Americana Boulevard; 208-384-4240), an urban wildlife refuge. Two miles farther northwest is **Veterans Memorial State Park** (960 Veterans Way; 208-384-2812), dedicated to Idahoans who gave their lives in Vietnam, Korea and the World Wars.

Traveling east along the Greenbelt, just past Julia Davis Park on the north bank of the Boise River, you'll see the world headquarters of the **Morrison-Knudsen Co**. (1 Morrison-Knudsen Plaza; 208-386-5000), one of the most prominent construction firms in North America. Morrison Knudsen's projects have included the Manned Spacecraft Center in Houston, the locks on the St. Lawrence Seaway, the old Defense Early Warning (DEW) radar system and some 100 dams around the world, including those on Hells Canyon.

Virtually next door to the east is the **Morrison-Knudsen Nature Center** (★) (600 South Walnut Street; 208-334-2225). This unique exhibit re-creates, in compact scale, the life cycle of a mountain stream. Through underwater windows, visitors can observe the growth and behavior of trout and other fish from developing eggs to full-size adults. The stream is fed by a wetland pond where such species as mink and muskrat find a wild home in an urban environment. Interpretive signs assist self-guided tours. A new natural-history museum and visitors center describe riparian ecology and stream hydraulics. The Nature Center is located behind the state **Department of Fish & Game** headquarters (600 South Walnut Street; 208-334-3700); both are adjacent to **Municipal Park** (South Walnut Street and Park Boulevard; 208-384-4240), a popular site for group picnics.

Municipal Park is just a quarter mile south of **Warm Springs Avenue**, old Boise's original upper-class residential district. This neighborhood's Victorian mansions were beneficiaries of the modern world's first urban geothermal heating system. Since 1892, 700,000 gallons of 172°F water have been pumped each day from a rhyolite aquifer beneath **Quarry View Park** (Bacon Drive and Old Penitentiary Road; 208-384-4240). The park's restored pump house can still be viewed. About 400 homes—including the Warm Springs district's oldest residence, the 1868 **G. W. Russell House** (1035 Warm Springs Avenue)—and eight government buildings, the State Capitol among them, are still heated in this way, at about half the cost of natural-gas heating.

Quarry View Park nestles at the foot of Castle Rock at the east end of the Warm Springs residential district, beside the **Old Idaho Penitentiary** (2445 Old Penitentiary Road; 208-334-2844; admission) about two miles east of downtown. More than 13,000 prisoners did time here between 1870, when the prison was built as a single cellhouse, and 1973, when it was replaced after a series of riots that helped convince state authorities to open a new facility (on Pleasant Valley Road in south Boise).

The Old Pen, as locals know it, was placed on the National Register of Historic Places in 1974. Today this foreboding complex—whose sandstone buildings and high turreted stone walls were quarried, hand-cut and constructed by the prisoners themselves—is an intriguing museum. Visitors can experience the claustrophobic women's ward and the desperation of solitary confinement, meditate in the inmates' rose garden and view the gallows that performed Idaho's only hanging (in 1957). Museum exhibits include displays of contraband weapons and prison tattoo art (the only one of its kind, featuring photos of inmates' own skin designs).

Housed within the Old Pen complex are the **History of Electricity in Idaho Museum**, a "current" display with hands-on exhibits, and the **Idaho Transportation Museum**, featuring numerous turn-of-the-century vehicles. Adjacent are the historic **Bishops' House** (2420 Old Penitentiary Road; 208-342-3279), moved from downtown Boise in 1975 and now used for public receptions, and the new **Museum of Mining & Geology** (2455 Old Penitentiary Road; 208-368-9876).

On the south side of the Old Pen, the **Idaho Botanical Garden** (2355 Old Penitentiary Road; 208-343-8649; admission) comprises nine separate theme and display gardens in bloom from late April through mid-October: gardens of heirloom roses and historical irises, gardens to inspire meditation and to attract butterflies and hummingbirds, Basque and Chinese gardens, an herb garden and a garden planted especially for children. A three-quarter-mile trail winds through Nature's Garden and along a nearby hillside.

Warm Springs Avenue continues southeast some three and a half miles to its junction with Route 21 outside the Boise city limits. One-half mile south of the junction is **Barber Park** (Healy Road, Boise; 208-343-1328), the "put-in" point for most of the quarter-million rafters and inner-tubers who float the Boise River each year.

North from downtown Boise, parallel routes extend up stately **Harrison Boulevard**, lined with early-20th-century manors of many architectural styles, and through the hip **Hyde Park** neighborhood, five blocks to its east. They come together near the intersection of Bogus Basin Road, which wends its way past Boise's best-known private residence—the palatial hilltop estate of industrialist J. R. Simplot (4000 North Simplot Lane), its giant Stars and Stripes always waving in the wind—to the **Bogus Basin Recreational Area** (2405 Bogus Basin Road, Boise; 208-332-5100). This midsize ski resort is located just 16 miles and not quite a mile above downtown Boise. **Bogus Creek Outfitters** (2405 Bogus Basin Road; 208-336-3130) offers winter sleigh rides here; in summer, the runners are replaced by wheels for horse-drawn wagon trips.

On the south side of Boise, near the bustling Boise Municipal Airport, is the **National Interagency Fire Center** (★) (3833 South Development Avenue, Boise; 208-387-5512)—the logistics support center for the thousands of firefighters who battle forest fires, grassland blazes and other wildfires in the United

States each year. Tours, arranged in advance, take in an infrared mapping system, an automatic lightning detection system, radio communication systems and other high-technology equipment.

Southwest of the airport is the **World Center for Birds of Prey** (5666 West Flying Hawk Lane, Boise; 208-362-8687; admission), six miles off Route 84 via South Cole Road. (See "An Eagle's-Eye View of the Snake River" in this chapter.) The World Center provides a perfect introduction to raptors for travelers continuing to the **Snake River Birds of Prey National Conservation Area** (Swan Falls Road, Kuna; 208-384-3300), 15 miles southwest of the capital.

BOISE AREA HOTELS

Downtown's most upscale lodging, pending the 1996 opening of the West-Coast Hotel on The Grove, is the **Owyhee Plaza Hotel** (1109 West Main Street; 208-343-4611, 800-233-4611, fax 208-336-3860). The 100-room property (an expansion is planned) is the home of an elegant restaurant as well as a piano lounge and coffee shop. Standard rooms are small but pleasant; executive-level third-floor rooms are considerably more spacious and cost only a few dollars more. Amenities include a swimming pool and workout room. Moderate.

Just four blocks from the capitol, the two-story **Sands Motel** (1111 West State Street; 208-343-2533) is quite modest, but it's clean and centrally located. The 18 air-conditioned guest rooms have private baths. Budget.

Boise's most centrally located bed and breakfast is the **Idaho Heritage Inn** (109 West Idaho Street; 208-342-8066, fax 208-343-2325), built in 1904 and listed on the National Register of Historic Places. The former residence of Governor Chase Clark (1941–43) and Senator Frank Church (1957–81), the geothermally heated mansion was sold in 1987 and restored as a six-bedroom B & B. There's a sunroom off the living room, which is large enough to have hosted many a political reception, and a dining room with an outdoor patio where breakfast is served in summer. Each guest room is decorated with antique furnishings and has a private bath. Moderate.

South of downtown, bordering the Boise State University campus, the two-story **University Inn** (2360 University Drive; 208-345-7170, 800-345-7170, fax 208-345-5118) has 80 cozy but nicely decorated rooms with wood furnishings and botanical-print decor. All rooms have spacious private baths. Located at the corner of Capitol Boulevard, the motel has a large swimming pool, a deck with hot tub, a lounge and a coffee shop. A continental breakfast is included in the room rate. Low moderate.

Business travelers guarantee high occupancy and high weekday rates at the six-story **Doubletree Club Hotel at Park Center** (475 Park Center Boulevard; 208-345-2002, 800-222-8733, fax 208-345-8354). But on Friday through Sunday nights the rates are cut by half and drop almost into the budget price range—making it a real bargain for nonbusiness travelers. On the ground floor are an elegant café and lounge, a large outdoor swimming pool and deck, and a workout room with adjoining spa. Moderate to deluxe.

Boise's largest hostelry, and presently its most deluxe, is the **Red Lion Hotel–Boise Riverside** (2900 Chinden Boulevard; 208-343-1871, 800-547-8010, fax 208-344-1079), located on the Greenbelt beside the Boise River one and a half miles west of downtown (and three-quarters of a mile west of its sister Red Lion–Downtowner). The 304 spacious and brightly decorated guest rooms have oversized bathtubs and double vanities. Facilities include two restaurants, two lounges, an outdoor swimming pool, a large fitness center with a jacuzzi beside the Greenbelt and a gift shop. Deluxe.

Economy-minded visitors planning to stay for seven days or more will find it difficult, if not impossible, to find less expensive accommodations than those at the **Ustick Inn** (★) (8050 Ustick Road; 208-322-6277). A "residence hotel" on the west side of town, this circa-1900 country farmhouse—long since absorbed by the Boise metropolis—offers 42 bunks for men and women travelers in private rooms and small dormitories. Unlike some hostels, however, there's no community kitchen. Rates run less than $100 weekly.

BOISE AREA RESTAURANTS

The largest city in the northern U.S. Rockies, Boise is the region's culinary capital, offering a wide variety of excellent restaurants (685 of them, according to the chamber of commerce) in all price ranges.

The **Bangkok House** (624 West Idaho Street, Boise; 208-336-0018) serves excellent Thai soups and spicy curries just two blocks from the State Capitol. Decor is minimal but uniquely Thai, including the Buddhist altar behind the cashier. Low moderate.

An Old Boise favorite is **Neville & Neville** (501 West Main Street; 208-345-8888), where great Jamaican jerk chicken and Hungarian mushroom soup are served in the casual atmosphere of a British sporting pub. There are deli sandwiches, too, as well as English draught beer and wines by the glass. Prices fall in the budget range.

The **Renaissance Ristorante Italiano** (★) (110 South 5th Street; 208-344-6776), in the basement of The Belgravia building, is a romantic northern Italian hideaway that many locals consider Boise's best restaurant. Veal, pork, chicken and shellfish dishes are done to perfection and served within two-foot-thick sandstone walls. Deluxe.

Lunch-hour lines often extend from The Grove into the front door of the **Brick Oven Beanery** (North 8th and West Main streets, Boise; 208-342-3456), where generous portions of soups, salads, sandwiches and "blue-ribbon specials" like shepherd's pie and salmon loaf are dished up cafeteria-style. Seating is in a homey dining room or outside on the plaza. Budget.

The old Idanha Hotel houses **Peter Schott's** (928 West Main Street, Boise; 208-336-9100), whose menu features Continental dishes with an imaginative new American flair. Don't miss the brie soup; all entrees (seafood, poultry and meats) are excellent. Service in the European-style dining room can be hoity-toity, though. Deluxe.

Angell's (999 West Main Street, Boise; 208-342-4900), an upscale steak-and-seafood establishment on the ground floor of J. R. Simplot's One Capital Center building, is consistently among the best in Boise for food, service and atmosphere. Light eaters have a choice of excellent salads; there's also a full-service lounge. Moderate to deluxe.

Yen Ching (305 North 9th Street; 208-384-0384), Boise's preeminent Chinese restaurant, specializes in the cuisine of northern China. You won't find chop suey on the menu here, but you *will* find good Mandarin spicy beef, kung pao chicken and moo shu pork. Moderate.

Downtown Boise's funkiest diner is **Moon's Kitchen** (815 West Bannock Street; 208-385-0472), at the rear of a gift shop a block and a half from the capitol. Moon's is like an old-time soda fountain, with malts and milkshakes "to die for" and a wide choice of hearty sandwiches. Budget.

Pasta, pizza and a popular wine bar are the best reasons to visit **Noodles** (North 8th and West Idaho streets, Boise; 208-342-9300), which spreads around the mezzanine of the historic Mode Building downtown. There's a smaller outlet at Boise Towne Square Mall. Moderate.

Shige Japanese Cuisine (150 North 8th Street, Boise; 208-338-8423) has a fine sushi bar on the second floor of the Capital Terrace shopping complex. You can also get noodle and tempura dishes here, but the deft work and sharp blade of the resident raw-fish expert is the reason most folks visit. Moderate.

Boise's widest selection of fresh seafood is offered by **Milford's Fish House** (405 South 8th Street; 208-342-8382), adjacent to the 8th Street Market Place. The handsome restaurant, whose decor features dark wood with brass accents, has Northwest salmon and halibut, Gulf snapper and prawns as well as the city's only full-fledged oyster bar. Moderate to deluxe.

Rick's Cafe Americain (646 Fulton Street; 208-342-4288) is located at The Flicks, Boise's only theater showing foreign and "art" films. This pleasant restaurant serves everything from hamburgers to gourmet pastas and fresh fish. An arbor-covered patio is especially popular in summer. Moderate. Gay-friendly.

There aren't many Basque restaurants in the United States, but **Oñati** (3544 Chinden Boulevard, Garden City; 208-343-6464) is one of the best. A variety of lamb, pork, chicken and fish dishes—heavy in garlic and olive oil, as is the norm in the Spanish–French coastal region of their origin—are served family-style in a warm and friendly atmosphere. Moderate.

Chapala II (3447 Chinden Boulevard, Garden City; 208-342-5648) may be the most traditional Mexican café in town. Jaliscan regional specialties such as *sopitos* and *chile verde* highlight the menu, although tacos and enchiladas still get more takers. Budget.

At the **Earth Food Cafe** (2907 West State Street, Boise; 208-342-7169), on the highway toward Eagle, vegetarian cooking is a fine art. Specialties include organic smoothies and macrobiotic dishes. Three meals a day are served, and there's a Sunday brunch. Budget.

BOISE AREA SHOPPING

In downtown Boise, two small but intriguing shopping complexes are the historic **8th Street Market Place** (405 South 8th Street; 208-344-0641)—galleries, gift shops, restaurants, theaters and offices housed in a pair of turn-of-the-century former warehouses—and the modern **Capital Terrace** (150 North 8th Street; 208-338-1600), with numerous retail outlets, offices, salons, restaurants and lounges. The **Old Boise Shopping District** (West Main Street between Capitol Boulevard and North 4th Street) is heavy in art galleries and fashion outlets, bistros and bars.

For gift and souvenir shopping in Boise, **Taters** (249 South 8th Street; 208-338-1062), on The Grove, boasts such unique-to-the-state products as potato novelty items, huckleberry gift packs and trout ties and T-shirts. **Made in Idaho** (90 Boise Towne Square; 208-378-1188) features handcrafted items, foods and wines exclusively produced within the state.

Art lovers will want their first stop in Boise to be at the **Boise Art Museum Store** (670 South Julia Davis Drive; 208-345-8330), which sells arts, crafts, books, jewelry and prints of noted masterpieces. **Gallery 601** (850 West Main Street; 208-336-5899) features the nationally acclaimed work of Idaho's Jane Wooster Smith, a modern American folk artist. Other leading fine-art exhibitors include **Brown's Gallery** (1022 West Main Street; 208-342-6661) and **Fritchman Galleries** (112 North 6th Street; 208-385-0279). Boise galleries get together for a "First Thursday" event each month; call 208-336-2631 for information.

Of special interest eight miles west of Boise is the **Orville Jackson Drug Co.** (50 East State Street, Eagle; 208-939-6511), the nearest thing to an old-time general store in the Boise area. You'll find everything from old medicine bottles, ax handles, kerosene lanterns and early-20th-century Coca Cola canisters to Crackerjacks and cow- and pig-shaped cookie cutters.

BOISE AREA NIGHTLIFE

Ever since Idahoans Paul Revere and the Raiders busted the pop charts in the mid '60s with "Kicks" and "Hungry," Boise has been an active if under-recognized player in the national entertainment scene. But today, although Boise has an active core of local rock, blues and country bands, it is better known for more sophisticated culture. Tickets for most events can be obtained from **Select-A-Seat** (208-385-3535), which operates outlets in all Albertson's stores.

The **Morrison Center for the Performing Arts** (2201 Campus Lane, Boise State University; 208-385-1110) is widely recognized as one of the finest civic concert theaters in the United States, hosting numerous performances every month by musicians, actors and dance troupes.

Several resident companies also make use of the Morrison Center. Heading the list is the **Boise Philharmonic** (516 South 9th Street; 208-344-7849), which performs a concert season from September to May. The city supports the nationally acclaimed **Ballet Idaho** (516 South 9th Street; 208-343-0556), whose performances (including a Christmas-season *Nutcracker*) extend from September to March, and the **Boise Opera Company** (516 South 9th Street; 208-345-3531), which presents operas by Mozart, Puccini and other classical composers.

The **Idaho Shakespeare Festival** (412 South 9th Street; 208-336-9221) features a quartet of works from mid-June to Labor Day. The theater is scheduled to move in 1996 from Park Center Boulevard; call for information.

Other local troupes perform in regular September-to-May seasons. The **Boise Actors Guild** (3820 Cassia Street; 208-344-2089) and **Boise Little Theater** (100 East Fort Street; 208-342-5104) tend toward serious theater; the **Stage Coach Theatre** (2000 Kootenai Street; 208-342-2000) leans toward comedy; the **Knock 'em Dead Dinner Theater** (807 West Idaho Street; 208-385-0021) focuses on musicals.

For up-to-date information on all major arts events in the greater Boise area, call **ArtsLine** (208-376-2787).

The *Idaho Statesman*'s Friday "Scene" section lists five dozen different venues that feature live popular music on a weekly basis.

For alternative rock there's **Neurolux** (111 North 11th Street; 208-343-0886), which hosts some of the region's most popular bands—including Boise's own Built to Spill—on a nightly basis. Bands from heavy metal to hip-hop and techno-rock appear at **Bogie's** (1124 Front Street; 208-342-9663). Local rock bands perform at such Old Boise bars as **Humpin' Hannah's** (621 West Main Street; 208-345-7557) and **Tom Grainey's** (107 South 6th Street; 208-345-2505), both popular with college students. One of the Rockies' finest blues clubs is the **Blues Bouquet** (1010 West Main Street; 208-345-6605), which draws touring acts from Chicago to Los Angeles. The **Boise Blues Society** (208-344-2583) has information on other events.

The jazz scene is slow, however. There are Wednesday-night sessions at **The Sandpiper** (1100 West Jefferson Street; 208-344-8911), but most jazz fans stay alert for news of performances by internationally renowned jazz pianist Gene Harris, a local resident.

For country music, **Shorty's Saloon** (5467 Glenwood Street; 208-323-0555), in Garden City near the Western Idaho Fairgrounds, is a mecca for cowboys from far and wide. However, if you're just learning how to line dance, check out the dance lessons offered nightly at the **Rock 'n' Rodeo** (1005 South Capitol Boulevard, Boise; 208-338-5555) before taking to the floor with the rest of the posse.

Everyone is welcome to dance at **Alive After Five** (The Grove; 208-336-2631), featuring different musical entertainers from 5 to 7 p.m. every Wednesday from May through September.

Boise has two excellent brewpubs—the **TableRock Brewpub/Grill** (705 Fulton Street; 208-342-0944), between the university and downtown, and the **Harrison Hollow Brew House** (2455 Harrison Hollow; 208-343-6820), just off Bogus Basin Road.

The **Piper Pub & Grill** (150 North 8th Street; 208-343-2444), with a Capital Terrace balcony overlooking West Main Street, is Boise's leading singles bar, attracting after-work throngs of 30-something lawyers and legislative aides.

Partners (2210 West Main Street; 208-331-3551) is the city's most popular gathering place for gays.

Coffee houses are big in Boise as well. **Dreamwalker** (1015 West Main Street; 208-343-4196) features local songwriters and poets; **Flying M Espresso** (500 West Idaho Street; 208-345-4320) has acoustic performers.

Boise's first full-time comedy club opened in late 1994 in the 8th Street Market Place: **The Funny Bone** (404 South 8th Street; 208-331-2663), which hosts up-and-coming comics working the national circuit.

BOISE AREA PARKS

Lucky Peak State Park—Extending 11 miles along the Boise River between the Lucky Peak and Arrowrock dams, Lucky Peak Reservoir is the city's favorite getaway for water sports and is an important water resource. Two of the state park's three units are below Lucky Peak Dam. The Discovery unit, just below the outflow from the dam, is a popular fishing and picnic spot. Sandy Point Beach, at the foot of the towering dam, is a great place for children with water-dog tendencies to frolic while their parents watch from a manicured lawn. Spring Shores' 285-slip marina is the largest in the state parks system; this is a base for boating, sailing, waterskiing and board sailing. There is dining at Spring Shores and Sandy Point. Most facilities are open from mid-May through October only.

Facilities: Picnic tables, restrooms, trails, boat ramps, boat rentals, marina, concessions; day-use fee, $2; information, 208-334-3360. *Swimming:* Outstanding beach at Sandy Point; designated beach area at Spring Shores. Both have lifeguards. Swimming at Discovery is very hazardous and not recommended. *Fishing:* Trout, kokanee salmon, smallmouth bass and channel catfish in Lucky Peak Reservoir; all but kokanee below the dam.

Getting there: Four miles east of downtown Boise, Warm Springs Avenue joins Route 21. Continue east five miles from here to the Discovery unit; six miles to Sandy Point; 12 miles via Middle Fork Road to Spring Shores.

Eagle Island State Park—Area families come in droves on hot summer weekends to the park's 11-acre artificial lake. A special attraction is a waterslide extending down a hillside above a long, sandy beach. Located between two channels of the Boise River, the 546-acre park—on the site of a former state-prison honor farm—is mostly undeveloped, making it ideal habitat for deer, raptors and other wildlife. Park facilities are open Memorial Day through Labor Day only.

Facilities: Picnic tables, restrooms, concessions, playground; day-use fee, $2; information, 208-939-0696. *Swimming:* Designated beach with waterslide and lifeguards. *Fishing:* There's trout in the Boise River.

Getting there: Take State Street (Route 44) west 13 miles from downtown Boise; turn south and continue one-half mile on Linden Road, then turn east and proceed one-half mile on Hatchery Road. Or take Chinden Boulevard (Route 20/26) west 12 miles from downtown; at Linden Road, turn north and continue one and a half miles to Hatchery Road, which leads into the park.

An Eagle's-Eye View of the Snake River

South of Boise, the Snake River has scoured a deep trough through the Owyhee Plateau. Basalt cliffs tower hundreds of feet above the river. Prevailing canyon winds create updrafts for the world's largest concentration of nesting eagles, hawks, owls and falcons. In 1993, Congress designated this Bureau of Land Management (BLM) area the **Snake River Birds of Prey National Conservation Area**. Encompassing 483,000 acres of public land for 81 miles along the Snake River, the preserve is home to more than 800 pairs of raptors.

Canyon crevices and ledges provide ideal shelter for the birds' nests, which they build each spring when they mate and raise their young. From their aeries, the birds soar on warm canyon winds over the surrounding plateau, feeding on ground squirrels, jackrabbits and other rodents.

Fifteen species of raptors call this section of the Snake River their home, including the golden eagle, prairie falcon, northern harrier, turkey vulture and American kestrel, as well as three hawks and seven owls. Nine migratory species also make lengthy visits, among them the bald eagle, osprey and peregrine falcon.

The preserve's nearest boundary to Boise is 15 miles southwest of the capital. By road, there are good viewing spots at **Dedication Point** (Swan Falls Road), 23 miles from Boise via Route 84 Exit 44, and at **Celebration Park** (Can-Ada Road), 36 miles from Boise via Route 84 Exit 38. You'll see the greatest number of birds between mid-March and the end of June, especially in late spring.

The best way to view the Birds of Prey Area is by boat or raft down the Snake. Floaters can put in at the Swan Falls Dam and take out ten miles later at Celebration Park after a midway stop to study ancient petroglyphs on 70 boulders at Wees Bar, accessible only by river.

A good introduction to the national conservation area, though administratively unrelated, is the **World Center for Birds of Prey** (5666 West Flying Hawk Lane, Boise; 208-362-8687), six miles south of Boise off Route 84 via South Cole Road. Operated by the conservationist Peregrine Fund, the center is the world's largest and most sophisticated private facility for raptor breeding, research and education. More than 4000 falcons, hawks, eagles and owls of 22 species have been hatched, nurtured and released worldwide by the center since its establishment in 1984. Guided tours begin in the interpretive center and take in the incubation process, a Tropical Raptor Building with birds from around the world and a demonstration with live birds on an outdoor stage.

Treasure Valley

The principal highway through the 50-mile-long Treasure Valley is Route 84, which runs west from the capital through Canyon County, past the large towns of Nampa and Caldwell, en route to Oregon. To the north, Route 52 follows the lower Payette River through Emmett and Payette.

Though sometimes passed off as a suburb of Boise, **Nampa** is an important city in its own right: It is Idaho's fourth largest with nearly 30,000 people, including the state's largest Hispanic population. One of the biggest rodeos in America, the **Snake River Stampede** (Stampede Grounds, Cavalry Street and Garrity Boulevard; 208-466-4641), takes place in Nampa every July.

The city, located15 miles from Boise, is the home of the **Canyon County Historical Museum** (1200 Front Street; 208-467-7611). Housed in the 1902 Oregon Short Line Depot beside the train tracks in downtown Nampa, it has an interesting collection of railroad memorabilia and other exhibits on the county's past.

Five miles southwest of Nampa, a visitors center at **Deerflat National Wildlife Refuge** (13751 Upper Embankment Road, Nampa; 208-462-9278) describes some of the 200 species of birds sighted at the sanctuary's Lake Lowell. Nature trails offer access to both fishing and birdwatching at the ponds.

Before leaving Nampa, stop by the **Nampa Chamber of Commerce** (1305 3rd Street South; 208-466-4641) and pick up a brochure for a "Farm to Market Tour," a self-guided driving tour of the surrounding farmlands. The tour takes you to ten roadside fruit and vegetable stands, "u-pick" orchards, a cheese factory and three wineries south and west of town.

Many of the activities in Nampa's sister city of **Caldwell**, nine miles up Route 84, are centered around **Albertson College of Idaho** (2112 Cleveland Boulevard; 208-459-5011). One of the West's most highly regarded private liberal-arts schools, it was founded as The College of Idaho in 1891 and changed its name upon its centennial to honor alumnus Joe Albertson, the Boise supermarket magnate who bequeathed much of his fortune to the school.

Caldwell's annual June air show, which creates quite a buzz locally, is a function of the city's **Warhawk Air Museum** (4917 Aviation Way; 208-454-2854; admission), at Caldwell Industrial Airport. Several World War II aircraft are on permanent display along with wartime photographs and artifacts.

The small town of **Parma**, 14 miles northwest of Caldwell via Route 20/26, is the home of **Old Fort Boise** (East Main Avenue; 208-722-5138), a replica of a Hudson's Bay Company trading post built at the mouth of the Boise River, five miles northwest of here, in 1834. The adobe fort was an important Oregon Trail oasis until it washed away during a flood of the Boise River in 1853. The replica contains a museum and a pioneer cabin; it's open summer afternoons and by appointment.

Emmett sits on the south bank of the Payette River surrounded by hillside fruit orchards, 31 miles northwest of Boise and 29 miles northeast of Caldwell at the junction of Routes 16 and 52.

Payette, which lies at the mouth of the Payette River 29 miles downstream from Emmett (55 miles northwest of Boise via Routes 80 and 95), boasts a turn-of-the-century downtown with 80 historic buildings. The **Payette County Historical Museum** (90 South 9th Street; 208-642-2362), open Sunday afternoons in summer, will suggest a walking tour and offers displays of vintage clothing and furniture; a special feature is memorabilia of Baseball Hall of Famer Harmon Killebrew, a Payette native.

TREASURE VALLEY HOTELS

The area's nicest accommodations are the **Shilo Inn Nampa Suites** (1401 Shilo Drive, Nampa; 208-465-3250, 800-222-2244, fax 208-465-5929). The four-story motor inn has 83 suites, including eight with efficiency kitchens; others have mini-refrigerators. Facilities include an indoor swimming pool, a whirlpool, a sauna, a steam room and an exercise room. There's also a restaurant, deli and lounge. Moderate.

In downtown Nampa, the **Desert Inn Motel** (115 9th Avenue South; 208-467-1161, fax 208-467-5268) has 40 comfortable rooms, some with refrigerators and microwave ovens. All have private baths; a swimming pool is an inviting diversion on hot summer days. Budget.

Just off the 10th Avenue freeway exit in Caldwell is the **Sundowner Motel** (1002 Arthur Street; 208-459-1585, 800-459-1585, fax 208-454-9487). Some of the 66 rooms in the two-story motel have refrigerators and microwaves. There's a swimming pool. Budget rates include a continental breakfast.

TREASURE VALLEY RESTAURANTS

The Ranch House Steak House & Saloon (1809 Karcher Road, Nampa; 208-466-7020) keeps the spirit of the annual Snake River Stampede alive year-round with its Old West atmosphere and hand-cut steaks. Besides beef, the menu offers pork ribs, chicken and seafood. Moderate.

In an area with a sizable Hispanic population you can expect some good Mexican restaurants. One of the best here is **El Charro Café** (1701 1st Street North, Nampa; 208-467-5804), a southwest Idaho mainstay since 1954. You can get the standard enchiladas and burritos for lunch and dinner every day, as well as a uniquely south-of-the-border stew: *menudo*. Budget.

Texas barbecue—beef brisket, pork ribs and chicken—is the specialty of the **Armadillo Restaurant** (4808 East Cleveland Boulevard, Caldwell; 208-459-1226). Full meals come with baked beans and potato salad or cole slaw. At lunch, check out the menu for chili burgers and batter-fried finger steaks. Low moderate.

TREASURE VALLEY NIGHTLIFE

The **Nampa Civic Center** (311 3rd Street South, Nampa; 208-465-2252) is an important venue for the performing arts, including touring dance troupes and theater companies.

The new $6 million **Langroise Center for the Performing and Fine Arts** (Albertson College, Caldwell; 208-459-5836) boasts a 192-seat music recital hall and a 120-seat theater. The **Jewett Auditorium** (Albertson College, Caldwell; 208-459-5836) has another 850 seats for major concerts.

There's live country or rock music weekends at the **New Country Twi-Lite Lounge** (453 Caldwell Boulevard, Nampa; 208-466-9890), **Victor's** (211 21st Street South, Caldwell; 208-454-1497) and the **Eagle's Nest** (1st Street, Emmett; 208-365-1101).

Jazz fans wait with baited breath for **Jazz at the Winery** (19348 Lowell Road, Sunnyslope; 208-459-7222), served up on Sunday afternoons from mid-June to early August at the Ste. Chapelle Winery southwest of Caldwell.

TREASURE VALLEY PARKS

Deerflat National Wildlife Refuge—Five miles southwest of Nampa, this 11,430-acre refuge—one of the nation's first—was established in 1909 around seven-and-a-half-mile-long Lake Lowell. Nearly 200 species of resident and migrant waterfowl, shorebirds, upland game birds and raptors have been counted at the refuge, and in late fall, as many as 100,000 ducks make their homes here. Mule deer and coyotes are among resident mammals.

Facilities: Visitors center, picnic tables, restrooms, boat ramps, trails; information, 208-467-9278. *Swimming:* Two designated swimming areas; no lifeguards. *Fishing:* Year-round angling for largemouth and smallmouth bass, trout, perch, crappie, bluegill, bullhead and channel catfish.

Getting there: To reach the upper dam, take Route 45 (12th Avenue Road) south one and a half miles from downtown Nampa; then turn west on Lake Lowell Avenue and continue for three and a half miles. The visitors center is located at 13751 Upper Embankment Road.

Hells Canyon and the McCall Area

Hells Canyon dominates the Oregon-Idaho border region north of the Treasure Valley. The mile-and-a-half abyss of North America's deepest gorge is surrounded by a national recreation area and wilderness area; upstream (south) on the Snake River, a series of hydroelectric dams have created three long, narrow reservoirs that delight boaters and anglers. East of the canyon, vast woodlands speckled with mountain lakes extend 100 miles to the Middle Fork of the

Salmon River and the Frank Church–River of No Return Wilderness. In the heart of this scenic landscape is the year-round resort community of McCall, a gateway for fishing, skiing, horseback riding and other outdoor pursuits.

Located 14 miles north of Payette on Route 95, **Weiser** is Idaho's gateway to the upper reaches of Hells Canyon and to the Brownlee, Oxbow and Hells Canyon dams upriver from the gorge. It's also the home of the National Oldtime Fiddlers' Contest, held every June since 1953 in the Weiser High School gymnasium. In case you miss the event, you can relive its excitement at the **National Old-Time Fiddlers' Hall of Fame** (8 East Idaho Street; 208-549-0450) in the Weiser Chamber of Commerce.

The village of **Cambridge**, 32 miles north of Weiser, is the junction for Hells Canyon travelers and their last chance to purchase supplies or to grab a motel bed or café meal. A small local museum marks the intersection of Route 71, which branches northwest off Route 95 toward Brownlee Dam, 29 miles distant. The dam has created long, narrow **Brownlee Reservoir**, noted among anglers for its giant catfish, bass and crappie.

Route 71 crosses the Snake into Oregon just below Brownlee Dam, proceeding up the west bank of the river 12 miles to the Idaho Power Company's Copperfield Park site before crossing back into Idaho below the Oxbow Dam. The paved Snake River Road (Forest Road 454) enters Payette National Forest and traces the east bank of the Snake to Hells Canyon Dam, 22 miles from Copperfield Park.

Cross the dam to enter the **Hells Canyon National Recreation Area** (headquarters located at 88401 Route 82, Enterprise, Oregon; 503-426-4978). The 652,000-acre recreation area protects a vast and colorful canyon that is deeper by 2000 feet, and narrower by a mile, than Arizona's exalted Grand Canyon of the Colorado. From the summit of Idaho's He Devil Mountain (9393 feet) to the surface of the Snake River at its foot (1350 feet), Hells Canyon has a depth of 8043 feet.

The incredible scope of the gorge is apparent even to those who end their exploration at Hells Canyon Dam. But visitors who continue farther into the canyon, either by water or by land, discover more than stark and spectacular scenery. Hells Canyon was well known to prehistoric Native Americans and early white settlers alike, as evidenced by 8000-year-old petroglyphs, artifacts from Chief Joseph's Nez Perce, remnants of 1860s gold mines and 1890s homesteads. The natural history is equally impressive: The canyon is home to a plethora of unique botanical species and to a diverse wildlife that ranges from deer, elk, bighorn sheep and mountain goats to cougars, black bears, coyotes and a dazzling variety of bird life.

McCALL AREA **McCall** may not be Idaho's best-known resort community—that honor falls to Sun Valley, with Coeur d'Alene running a strong second—but it is a favorite of many Idahoans.

Located 37 miles northwest of Council and 106 miles north of Boise on the **Payette River Scenic Route** (Route 55), the mountain town of 2600 permanent residents nestles at the south end of **Payette Lake**, a glove-shaped, six-mile-long crystal gem surrounded by timbered 7000-foot peaks. Besides its beautiful setting, the town has a score of pleasant lodgings and restaurants, several art galleries and gift shops.

McCall is a town with two very distinct tourist seasons. Summer brings boaters, fishermen and other water-sports lovers to Payette Lake. Hunters, horseback riders and mountain bikers head into the remote reaches of adjacent **Payette National Forest** (106 West Park Street, McCall; 208-634-0700), while river rafters and kayakers may be diverted by the whitewater of the **North Fork of the Payette River**. Originating at Upper Payette Lake, only about 16 miles north of McCall, the stream runs south for the entire 75-mile length of Valley County, nurturing the **Long Valley** as it passes through Payette Lake and Cascade Reservoir.

In winter, alpine skiers frequent **Brundage Mountain Ski Area** (Brundage Mountain Road; 208-634-4151), which ranks among Idaho's leading resorts. The McCall area also offers excellent nordic skiing and snowmobiling as well as the **McCall Winter Carnival** in late January. Continuously scenic through the seasons is **Ponderosa State Park** (East Lake Drive; 208-634-2164), one of Idaho's prettiest parks. Its main unit occupies a two-mile peninsula just northeast of McCall; a second unit is at the head of Payette Lake.

On Route 55 northwest from McCall, just past Brundage Mountain Road, is tiny **Packer John County Park** (New Meadows; 208-253-4561), a former Idaho state park that preserves a replica of the cabin where Idaho's first territorial convention was held in 1863. The park offers camping and fishing. At **New Meadows**, 12 miles from McCall, the highway connects with Route 95 (linking Weiser and Grangeville). New Meadows features a 1911 train depot, long abandoned for that purpose and now serving as a museum and library, and **Zim's Hot Springs** (★) (Route 95, New Meadows; 208-347-2686), four miles north, with a mineral pool beside the Little Salmon River open to swimmers and soakers year-round.

South of McCall, Route 55 follows the Payette Valley in the direction of Boise. **Lake Fork**, six miles from McCall, got its start as a turn-of-the-century Finnish community; the 1917 **Finnish Evangelical Lutheran Church** (Farm to Market Road, Lake Fork), on a hilltop one and a half miles east of the village, is still a valley landmark and has been listed on the National Register of Historic Places. **Donnelly**, another seven miles south, is at the junction of Roseberry Road. The old townsite of **Roseberry** is one and a half miles east. Most of its remains—several circa-1890s buildings, including the community's original general store and Methodist Episcopal church—make up the **Valley County Museum** (Farm to Market Road; 208-325-8871). The museum is open weekend afternoons in the summer and by appointment.

Cascade Reservoir, more than 20 miles long and four and a half miles wide, extends from Donnelly to south of Cascade. It boasts 110 miles of shoreline, a rich bird life (including bald eagles and white pelicans) and thriving schools of rainbow and brown trout, kokanee salmon and perch. The BOR's **Sugarloaf Recreation Area** (★) (Sugarloaf Road; 208-382-4258), located on a treeless peninsula midway along the lake's eastern shore, is a wonderful place for birdwatching.

Cascade, 29 miles south of McCall on Route 55, is a recreational hub, with a Boise National Forest district ranger station, several motels and restaurants and a disproportionate number of sporting goods stores.

A fishing resort at **Warm Lake**, 25 miles east of Cascade in Boise National Forest, draws many outdoor-sports lovers to the area. Warm Lake boasts two overnight lodges with restaurants, three campgrounds, boat ramps and rentals, a swimming beach, gas and phones.

HELLS CANYON AND McCALL AREA HOTELS

The handful of small motels in the Hells Canyon gateway area includes the **State Street Motel** (1279 State Street, Weiser; 208-549-1390). The inn's 13 cozy rooms have private baths, and a café is attached to the motel. Rooms are priced in the budget range.

The **Hunters Inn** (10 Superior Street, Cambridge; 208-257-3325), poised at the junction of Route 95 to McCall and Route 71 to Hells Canyon, was a favorite hangout of the Civilian Conservation Corps after it opened in 1927. Today the restored hotel has five rustic bed-and-breakfast rooms with shared baths upstairs, pine walls with mounted hunting trophies downstairs, and a gourmet coffee and pastry shop. Low moderate.

Among the nicest accommodations in McCall are the 116 rooms at the **Shore Lodge** (501 West Lake Street; 208-634-2244, 800-657-6464, fax 208-634-7504). Spread along the south shore of Lake Payette, this handsome lodge has a fine restaurant and lounge, a swimming pool, a hot tub and sauna and a fitness center with racquetball courts. Moderate to deluxe.

Since the early 20th century, the **Hotel McCall** (★) (1101 North 3rd Street, McCall; 208-634-8105, fax 208-634-4425) has welcomed guests to its lakefront location on Route 55. All 22 rooms are decorated with country ambience, with handsome quilts and fresh flowers. A full continental breakfast is served each morning, complimentary wine or tea in the early evening. The hotel has a garden patio, sun deck and recreation room. Bicycles are available for guests' use. Prices are moderate.

The cast and crew of the 1938 Spencer Tracy classic *Northwest Passage* stayed in a beautiful pine inn and spent many of their evenings around a pair of stone fireplaces. That inn is now known as **Northwest Passage Bed & Breakfast** (201 Rio Vista, McCall; 208-634-5349, 800-597-6658, fax 208-634-4977). Five wood-paneled rooms feature '30s furnishings; a gourmet breakfast is served each morning. A separate guest apartment has a private kitchen, dorm facilities for a dozen people and a fireplace. Moderate.

One of Idaho's most remote yet luxurious guest ranches is **Wapiti Meadow Ranch** (Forest Road 412, Cascade; radio phone 208-382-4336, 208-382-3217 in winter), 60 miles east of McCall in the Salmon River Mountains near Yellow Pine. The ranch was homesteaded during a 1905 gold rush; the lodge was built in 1926 and became Idaho's first "dude ranch." Pack trips, flyfishing and cross-country skiing are the favored activities at the ranch, which has four cabins and a handful of lodge rooms nestled against the 8000-foot peaks of the Frank Church–River of No Return Wilderness. The ranch features a gourmet restaurant and a hot tub. Moderate and deluxe.

HELLS CANYON AND McCALL AREA RESTAURANTS

After days of sparse rations in Hells Canyon's backcountry, many outdoor-sports lovers on the way back to Boise stop at **The Grub Steak** (103 Illinois Avenue, Council; 208-253-6002). Rancher-sized steaks and prime rib with baked potatoes are served in a rustic atmosphere. Moderate.

A Lake Payette classic is **Lardo's** (600 West Lake Street, McCall; 208-634-8191), named not for a culinary additive but for a former mining town. A rustic saloon on the west side of town, it is noted for its Italian dishes and for its charcoal-grilled burgers and steaks. Budget and moderate.

The Huckleberry (402 North 3rd Street, McCall; 208-634-8477), on the west side of Route 55 about a half-mile south of the lake, hosts performances by acoustic musicians during the dinner hour most weekend evenings. You can get three meals a day here: Try the huckleberry pancakes at breakfast, the home-made soups at lunch, and steak and seafood for dinner. Moderate.

A new addition to the Lake Payette dining scene is the **McCall Brewing Co.** (807 North 3rd Street, McCall; 208-634-2333), where hearty pastas, fresh seafood, grilled chicken and sausage sandwiches and other brewpub preparations are offered up with the brewery's own ales and stouts. Happy hour is often celebrated on a spacious deck that looks toward the lake. Moderate.

HELLS CANYON AND McCALL AREA SHOPPING

McCall is the region's shopping center. **Mountain Monkey Business** (501 Pine Street; 208-634-8268) has an eclectic selection of fashions and souvenir items. **On the Wild Side** (302 East Lake Street; 208-634-2704) focuses on wild-life themes in its limited-edition prints, sculptures and gift items. The **Blue Grouse Bookshop** (1001 North 2nd Street; 208-634-2434), in the McCall Drug Store, has a good selection of regional-interest titles.

HELLS CANYON AND McCALL AREA NIGHTLIFE

In the Hells Canyon area, the **Athena Club** (35 East Idaho Street, Weiser; 208-549-9931) features live rock performances by Boise-area bands on Friday and Saturday nights.

Near the shores of Payette Lake, the **Alpine Playhouse** (1210 Roosevelt Street, McCall; 208-634-7631) hosts a variety of musical and theatrical events throughout the year, mainly on weekends.

Locals visit the lounge at the **Shore Lodge** (501 West Lake Street, McCall; 208-634-2244) to dance to live rock or country bands on weekends.

HELLS CANYON AND McCALL AREA PARKS

Idaho Power Company Parks—Four sites in the Hells Canyon area are maintained year-round by Idaho Power. Three of the parks are on the Idaho shore of long, narrow reservoirs: Woodhead Park on Brownlee Reservoir, McCormick Park on Oxbow Reservoir and Hells Canyon Park on Hells Canyon Reservoir. Copperfield Park is located just below Oxbow Dam on the Oregon side of the Snake River.

Facilities: Picnic tables, restrooms, boat ramps, trails; information, 208-383-2422. *Swimming:* Okay in the reservoirs but not in the river. *Fishing:* Excellent for a wide variety of species, including steelhead, trout, catfish and white sturgeon (catch and release only).

Camping: There are ten tent sites and 34 RV sites at McCormick Park; ten tent sites and 62 RV sites at Copperfield Park; 30 tent sites and 23 RV sites at Hells Canyon Park; tent and RV sites at Woodhead Park are under construction in 1995. Tent sites are $4 per night, RV sites are $7.

Getting there: Woodhead and McCormick parks are both on Route 71 north of Cambridge. Copperfield Park is on Oregon Route 86 just past the Route 71 junction. Hells Canyon Park is seven miles north of Copperfield Park on Snake River Road.

Hells Canyon National Recreation Area—The Snake River's colorful Hells Canyon, deeper by 2000 feet than Arizona's Grand Canyon, is the centerpiece of a 652,488-acre parcel, much of it wilderness, most of it in Oregon. In addition to the canyon, the Idaho portion includes the lofty (9000-foot) Seven Devils Mountains. Whitewater rafters, kayakers and drift boaters put in at the mouth of Hells Canyon Creek, just below Hells Canyon Dam, for trips down the "national wild and scenic" portion of the Snake that extends 32 miles to Pittsburg Landing, Idaho; 51 miles to Dug Bar, Oregon; and 79 miles to Grande Ronde, Washington. In the fall, steelhead fishing trips are popular. For non-boaters, a boardwalk nature trail extends from the Hells Canyon Creek Information Station. Primary overland routes to Pittsburg Landing and the Seven Devils Mountains start from Riggins and White Bird. (See Chapter Eleven, "Northern Idaho Rockies.")

Facilities: Picnic tables (21 locations), pit toilets or restrooms, boat ramps (four locations), hiking and horse trails; information, 208-628-3916 (Riggins) or 503-426-4978 (Enterprise, Oregon). *Swimming:* The Snake River is very swift, and swimming is discouraged. *Fishing:* Access from 18 sites.

Camping: Primitive camping along the river for rafters and backpackers. Unimproved campgrounds in the Seven Devils high country.

Getting there: Take Route 95 off Route 84 at Idaho Exit 3, traveling north 54 miles to Cambridge. Turn northwest on Route 71 and continue 25 miles to Brownlee Dam; then follow the Snake River Road 38 miles via Copperfield Park, Oregon, to Hells Canyon Dam. Cross the dam to enter the recreation area. There's also four-wheel-drive access via Council and Black Lake.

Payette National Forest—Some of the largest blocks of undeveloped wilderness remaining in the contiguous United States can be found in the 2.3 million acres of this forest, only a third of which is accessible by road (2800 miles) and trail (2125 miles). Payette National Forest covers much of west-central Idaho between the wild and scenic Snake and Salmon rivers and Boise National Forest.

Facilities: Picnic tables, restrooms, boat ramps, trails, ski area (Brundage Mountain); information, 208-634-0400. *Swimming:* No designated areas, but there are many small lakes. *Fishing:* Trout in mountain lakes and streams; steelhead on the South Fork of the Salmon River.

Camping: There are 215 RV/tent units plus 41 for tents only in 21 campgrounds (no hookups); $3 to $6 per night.

Getting there: Best access is via Forest Service roads emanating from McCall (on Route 55), Council (on Route 95) and New Meadows (at the junction of Routes 55 and 95).

Frank Church–River of No Return Wilderness Area—The biggest designated federal wilderness outside of Alaska is slightly larger than Yellowstone National Park. It extends 97 miles along the Salmon River and covers 2,353,739 acres in six national forests, including large parts of Payette and Challis, and portions of Boise, Salmon, Nez Perce and Bitterroot national forests. The Salmon River's main and middle forks are considered to offer the nation's premier whitewater experience.

Facilities: Trails; information, 208-634-0600. *Swimming:* Possible only in a few alpine lakes. *Fishing:* Steelhead, trout and whitefish.

Camping: Primitive only.

Getting there: Trailheads are near Yellow Pine and Stanley. Most visitors fly to airstrips on the Salmon River's main or middle forks.

Ponderosa State Park—Covering 840 acres on a heavily wooded peninsula extending into Payette Lake at the edge of McCall, this stately park is one of Idaho's finest. Rich in bird and animal life—from beaver to deer and even bear—the park attracts campers and water-sports lovers in summer, cross-country skiers in winter. A second unit of the park, the 630-acre North Beach Area at the head of Payette Lake, is open for day use only; it has a large sandy beach where the Payette River (a favorite of canoeists) enters the lake.

Facilities: Picnic tables, restrooms, boat ramps, trails, playground; day-use fee, $2; information, 208-634-2164. *Swimming:* Designated beaches at both units. *Fishing:* Payette Lake offers excellent trout fishing.

Camping: There are 170 sites (117 with RV hookups, ten for tents only), all in the main unit, open May 20 to October 15; tent sites are $9 per night, RV sites are $12.

Getting there: To reach the main unit from downtown McCall, take Lake Drive (Route 48) northeast two miles from Route 55. To North Beach, take Warren Wagon Road (Route 21) north seven miles from McCall up the west shore of Payette Lake.

Boise County and the Boise Basin

The city of Boise is not in Boise County, nor is much of the Boise River. But miners and loggers in this region laid much of the foundation of southwestern Idaho's social and economic history well over a century ago. Their energy and ingenuity can still be seen in the county's small towns, rugged hills and creek and river valleys.

Excellent highways make the exploration of Boise County an easy daytrip from Boise. Route 55 heading toward McCall joins the Payette River at Horseshoe Bend, 28 miles from Boise. Fourteen miles farther, Route 17 (South Fork Road) heads east up the South Fork of the Payette River 33 miles to Lowman, where it joins Route 21. Travelers here can choose to turn north across the Sawtooth Range to Stanley, 58 miles distant, or return to Boise, 72 miles southwest, via Idaho City. The full 147-mile loop can easily be covered in four hours without stops.

Horseshoe Bend, with 700 people the largest town on the west side of the county, is another Boise Cascade mill town. Its name comes from its position at a huge curve in the Payette River, where the southward-flowing stream swings west toward the Snake River.

Tiny **Banks**, situated at the confluence of the North and South forks of the Payette, is important mainly as a whitewater rafting center. Whereas the North Fork, falling steeply from the Long Valley, may appeal mainly to expert kayakers, the South Fork, flowing westerly from the summit of the Sawtooths, is one of the most popular rafting rivers in the United States. Several whitewater outfitters make their headquarters either here or at **Garden Valley**, upriver ten miles via Route 17.

During the early mining-boom days of the 1860s and 1870s, homesteads along the South Fork of the Payette grew vegetables for the gold and silver seekers in the mountains—thus, the name "Garden Valley." Natural hot springs warm numerous greenhouses that thrive year-round, providing this valley with a longer growing season than that in most other parts of the state.

Lowman, in the heart of Boise National Forest, is the western gateway to the Sawtooth Range and the hub of a vacation-home community. East from here, Route 21—the **Ponderosa Pine Scenic Route**—climbs to nearly 8000 feet before dropping into the exquisite mountain village of Stanley (see Chapter Ten, "Southeastern Idaho Rockies").

On the western flank of the Sawtooths, just within the **Sawtooth National Recreation Area**, is the remote outfitting center of **Grandjean**. Located at the end of six-and-a-half mile Grandjean Road off Route 21 is the Sawtooth Lodge providing a base for horseback riders and hikers who tackle the craggy peaks overlooking the hamlet. The boundary of the Sawtooth Wilderness is just a mile by trail from the lodge.

Turning south from Lowman on Route 21 brings travelers to **Idaho City**, the center of southern Idaho's biggest mining boom. For a short time in the early 1860s, in fact, Idaho City was the largest community in the Pacific Northwest and Idaho's first territorial capital. Between 1862 and the early 1880s, more than $250 million in gold was recovered by sluicing and placer mining from the surrounding hills. Although the gold ran out and its peak population of some 6200 (one-third of them Chinese, 91 percent of them adult males) dwindled to a present-day 300, the town has persisted. Located 38 miles northeast of the state capital, it remains the seat of Boise County and a shining example of historic preservation.

The **Boise Basin Mercantile Co.** (313 Main Street; 208-392-4443), better known as "The Merc," has been in continuous operation at its present location since 1865. The 1867 **Boise Basin Historical Museum** (402 Montgomery Street; 208-392-4550; admission), open summers and by appointment, recalls 19th-century life in the town through photographs and artifacts, and steers visitors on walking tours of the historic township, from its planked boardwalks to its **Pioneer Cemetery** (Centerville Road).

Another survivor of the gold-mining era is isolated **Atlanta** (★), on the Middle Fork of the Boise River about 60 miles east of Idaho City. The home of 500 people in the 1870s, it now has about 40 full-time residents and offers basic facilities for hunters, fishermen, snowmobilers and cross-country skiers. Located at the southern edge of the Sawtooth Wilderness, Atlanta is reached off Route 21 south of Lowman via well-maintained National Forest roads.

There are numerous other tiny communities in the Boise Mountains. **Rocky Bar**, 14 miles southwest of Atlanta (via James Creek Road 126) and seven miles north of Featherville, is a ghost town with a trove of mining ruins. **Featherville** and **Pine**, located on the South Fork of the Boise River and reached via Route 61, 59 and 49 miles northeast of Mountain Home, respectively, have campsites and resort facilities.

Pine is at the head of **Anderson Ranch Reservoir Recreational Area** (2180 American Legion Boulevard, Mountain Home; 208-587-7961), which surrounds a popular, 17-mile-long fishing and waterskiing lake. There are plenty of boat ramps at Pine; at Fall Creek, halfway down the lake's north shore; and at **Anderson Dam**, which has created this reservoir on the South Fork of the Boise 24 miles above Mountain Home.

BOISE COUNTY AND BOISE BASIN HOTELS

Five miles north of Route 17, amid evergreens and mountain wildflowers, is the **Warm Springs Creek Bed & Breakfast** (Terrace Lakes, Middle Fork Road, Garden Valley; 208-462-3516), a modern pine home with hardwood floors and a carousel fireplace. Five guest rooms are decorated with country collectibles and handmade quilts; one suite has a private bath; the other four rooms share two baths. Moderate.

In Idaho City, the **Idaho City Hotel** (215 Montgomery Street; 208-392-4290) offers year-round 19th-century ambience in a two-story country inn. Situated in the heart of the old mining town, the hotel has five quaint rooms with antique furnishings and not-so-antique private bathrooms. Budget.

The **Fall Creek Resort** (Fall Creek Road, Pine; 208-653-2242), on Anderson Ranch Reservoir 31 miles from Mountain Home, is a getaway for watersports enthusiasts. The resort has ten motel units with private baths and a 30-space RV park with hookups and a dump station. Also at the resort are a marina with boat rentals, restaurant and lounge, mini-mart, hot tub and workout area. Moderate.

BOISE COUNTY AND BOISE BASIN RESTAURANTS

The **Long Branch Saloon** (Route 55, Horseshoe Bend; 208-793-2762), near the Payette River on the main highway from Boise to McCall, offers hearty steaks and fried chicken in the evening, juicy burgers and other sandwiches at midday, in a ranch-style atmosphere. Budget to moderate.

Calamity Jayne's (Main Street and Route 21, Idaho City; 208-392-4453) is one of the Boise Basin's better dining options. Re-creating the atmosphere of a miners' cookhouse opposite the visitors center, the small café serves big helpings of steak and eggs in the morning, burgers and deli-style sandwiches (including several vegetarian choices) in the afternoon. Budget.

BOISE COUNTY AND BOISE BASIN SHOPPING

A few miles north of Horseshoe Bend, **Cooper's Wood Wildlife** (★) (Route 55, Gardena; 208-793-2387) features the work of master woodcarver Jon Cooper, from chainsaw art down to finely detailed carvings. This is also a good place to look for paintings, sculptures and Native American crafts.

You can relive some of the rough-and-ready mining days of the 1860s at the **Happy Burro Trad'n Post** (200 Main Street, Idaho City; 208-392-6668), where mine artifacts, silver and gold jewelry and T-shirts are among the souvenirs and gifts available.

BOISE COUNTY AND BOISE BASIN PARKS

Boise National Forest—Rugged mountains, covered with forests of pine, fir and spruce and sliced by deep river canyons, make up most of this 2.6-million-acre plot of federal land north and east of Boise. Ranging in elevation from 2600 feet to more than 9800 feet, the national forest has more than 850 miles of backcountry trails, more than 250 lakes and reservoirs, and some 7600 miles of rivers and streams.

Facilities: Picnic tables, restrooms, boat ramps, boat rentals, marinas, trails, several resorts; information, 208-364-4100. *Swimming:* Designated beaches at some reservoirs and lakes. *Fishing:* Good trout fishing, especially in the south and middle forks of the Boise and Payette rivers, and in Anderson Ranch and Arrowrock reservoirs.

Camping: There are 471 RV/tent units plus 118 for tents only in 38 campgrounds (no hookups); no charge to $6 per night. Most campgrounds are open mid-May through September. In addition, 12 wilderness cabins—some summer only, some winter only—accommodate from two to six people for $15 to $30 per night.

Getting there: The most direct route is Route 21 northeast from Boise through Idaho City and Lowman. To reach Arrowrock Reservoir, take Forest Road 268 (Middle Fork Road) east off Route 21, east of Boise. To reach Anderson Ranch Reservoir, take Forest Road 134 (Anderson Dam Road) or Route 61 (Louise Creek Road) north off Route 20, northeast of Mountain Home. To Warm Lake, take Forest Road 22 (Warm Lake Road) east off Route 55 from Cascade.

Mountain Home and Owyhee County

Mountain Home may seemed misnamed. Indeed, the city of 7500 people spreads across a flat tract of high desert, between the Rocky Mountain foothills and the Snake River but not actually a part of either. For Idaho visitors, it's of special interest as the gateway to the middle Snake River, with its unique state parks of historical and geological fascination, and the vast open spaces of Owyhee County that stretch beyond.

Mountain Home, located 48 miles southeast of Boise via Route 84, is of principal importance for its **Mountain Home Air Force Base** (Route 67, Mountain Home; 208-828-6800), where the United States has its first and only air intervention composite wing—which can be deployed anywhere in the world on a moment's notice. Tours of the base, located 11 miles southwest of the city, are available by prior arrangement.

For history buffs, the **Elmore County Historical Society Museum** (180 South 3rd Street East, Mountain Home; 208-587-2104) displays artifacts of Chinese miners and early Native American residents, as well as farming tools and other memorabilia of turn-of-the-century pioneers.

Mountain Home lies near the original route of the Oregon Trail. **Glenns Ferry**, 29 miles east off Route 84, is directly on it. In fact, early pioneers established their main ford of the Snake River here, where three islets broke the river's flow into smaller, more fordable channels. Each August, that frequently made crossing is reenacted at **Three Island Crossing State Park** (Madison Avenue, Glenns Ferry; 208-366-2394). There's an Oregon Trail interpretive center (you can still see the wagon ruts behind the building) as well as a campground and a pasture for bison and longhorn cattle.

West of Glenns Ferry and south of Mountain Home, on the south side of the Snake River, is one of Idaho's unique scenic attractions: **Bruneau Dunes State Park** (Route 78, Bruneau; 208-366-7919). Flanked by the **Snake River Birds of Prey National Conservation Area** (see "An Eagle's-Eye View of the Snake River," above), this park preserves the tallest freestanding sand dunes (470 feet) in North America.

The village of Bruneau, seven miles southwest of the dunes on Route 51/78, is a gateway to two more scenic attractions. Eighteen miles southeast of the community, an overlook on the Bruneau River gives a dramatic look at the north end of **Bruneau Canyon**, a 60-mile-long gorge whose sheer walls drop between 800 and 1200 feet down to the river's surface. Reach the overlook via Hot Springs and Clover Three Creek roads, both unsurfaced.

Bruneau is a good launch pad for exploring **Owyhee County**. Named for three natives of the Hawaiian Islands (then sometimes known as "Owyhee") who were lost in this wild region during an 1819 fur-trapping expedition, this southwesternmost Idaho county covers five million acres but has only about 7000 residents. Expect to see vast ranchlands, mining ghost towns and plenty of rugged and barren mountain and canyon land. Paved roads and tourist services are few and far between.

Northwest of Bruneau, Route 78 follows the Snake River through the county's population belt, such as it is. The county seat of **Murphy** 47 miles from Bruneau and 45 miles south of Boise, was once the largest livestock-shipping point in the Pacific Northwest. Its excellent **Owyhee County Historical Society** (190 Basey Street, Murphy; 208-495-2319) features a homesteader's cabin with its kitchen still intact, an old schoolhouse and a railroad depot, a reconstructed mining stamp mill with mine equipment, farm machinery and a research library.

The county's highlight is **Silver City** (★), Idaho's best-preserved ghost town. The 23-mile dirt Silver City Road turns west off Route 78 about five miles southeast of Murphy; it is normally open from late May through mid-October but is subject to closure because of bad weather. Inquire locally before tackling this route.

Between 1863, when the first gold was mined here, and 1942, when World War II mining restrictions put the final whammy on a dying community, some $40 million in gold and silver was taken from the Silver City district. Forty wood-frame buildings, in various stages of disrepair, still stand for curious visitors to explore. Before entering any, however, inquire at the two-story, 1892 **Old Schoolhouse Museum** (Morning Star Mill Road); all buildings are privately owned. Of special note are the 1866 Idaho Hotel and the 1898 Our Lady of Tears Catholic Church.

The most northwesterly corner of Owyhee County boasts its densest population around the Treasure Valley farming communities of Marsing and Homedale. Highways head back to Boise from here, via Caldwell and Nampa.

MOUNTAIN HOME AND OWYHEE COUNTY HOTELS

Where the road to Mountain Home Air Force Base meets Route 30 East, you'll find the **Hi Lander Motel & Steak House** (615 South 3rd Street West, Mountain Home; 208-587-3311). This two-story motel has 34 rooms with full baths, including four kitchen units and seven family suites. Amenities include a swimming pool and a workout room. Budget.

A 1907 Queen Anne–style home with distinctive stonework is now the **RoseStone Inn** (495 North 3rd Street East, Mountain Home; 208-587-8866, 800-717-7673). All five guest rooms at this bed and breakfast, redecorated in Basque antiques, have private baths and queen-size beds. Guests can choose between a continental or full gourmet breakfast. Moderate.

The Idaho Hotel (P.O. Box 75, Murphy, ID 83650; 208-495-2520) is one of the few signs of life in the ghost town of Silver City. Its 20 rooms share baths and have minimal furnishings, but it has a restaurant and lounge on the ground floor. The road to Silver City, 28 miles southwest of Murphy, is normally open from late May to mid-October. Budget.

MOUNTAIN HOME AND OWYHEE COUNTY RESTAURANTS

With air force personnel from all over the nation based in Mountain Home, the town offers all manner of cuisine, from Italian to Korean. But for old-fashioned American cooking, the **Top Hat** (145 North 2nd Street East; 208-587-9223) is a city favorite. The menu delivers everything from southern fried chicken and catfish to steaks and prawns. Moderate.

A benefit of stopping for a meal at **The Gear Jammer Travel Plaza** (Route 20 at Route 84 Exit 95, Mountain Home; 208-587-3400) is the chance to choose from a soup-and-salad bar and a hot buffet table. This truck stop also offers a 24-hour menu to satisfy any hungry traveler. Budget to moderate.

One of the Treasure Valley's finest restaurants seems lost on the edge of the Owyhee County desert. But **The Blue Canoe** (★) (Route 78, Melba; 208-495-2269), a nine-table café eight miles north of Murphy, has a growing reputation for outstanding gourmet cuisine. The menu features steaks, seafoods and daily specials in the Continental mold. Closed Monday, Tuesday and January. Prices are moderate.

Another outpost of fine dining is the **Sandbar River House** (18 East 1st Avenue, Marsing; 208-896-4124), with a deck overlooking the Snake River 15 miles southwest of Caldwell. Steak and seafood dishes dominate at this casual spot. Moderate.

MOUNTAIN HOME AND OWYHEE COUNTY NIGHTLIFE

Several lounges in Mountain Home offer entertainment for service personnel and local residents. One of the most popular is **Joe's Club** (185 South 2nd Street East; 208-587-5055), which features live country-and-western bands on Friday and Saturday nights.

MOUNTAIN HOME AND OWYHEE COUNTY PARKS

Three Island Crossing State Park—One of the principal Snake River crossings on the Oregon Trail is commemorated here. Wagon ruts, 150 years old, still help identify the pioneers' route across three gravel bars that broke the river's flow into channels. The crossing was a risky but preferable alternative to continuing on a longer, drier route along the edge of the Owyhee Plateau. It wasn't abandoned until a ferry was built two miles upriver in 1869. Bison and longhorn cattle are pastured on the riverside today.

Facilities: Picnic tables, restrooms, trails, interpretive center; day-use fee, $2; information, 208-366-2394. *Fishing:* Trout, catfish and other species in the Snake River.

Camping: There are 50 sites, all with full hookups for RVs. Tent sites are $9 per night, and RV sites are $12.

Getting there: From downtown Glenns Ferry, one mile off Route 84 southeast of Mountain Home, take Commercial Street south about a mile, then Madison Avenue west for about two miles.

Bruneau Dunes State Park—This unique desert environment includes the largest single-structured sand dunes in North America: 470 feet high and about one square mile at their base. Estimated to have been created by the Bonneville Flood of 15,000 years ago, the dunes form at the center of a semicircular natural basin just south of the Snake River; all other dunes on this continent form at the edge of basins. Reptiles, raptors and waterfowl inhabit the park. Trails circle the two main dunes and the interconnected ponds at their base.

Facilities: Picnic tables, restrooms, visitors center, hiking and horseback trails; day-use fee, $2; information, 208-366-7919. *Swimming:* Tubing is popular. *Fishing:* Bass and bluegill in the park lakes.

Camping: There are 48 RV/tent sites, 32 of them with full RV hookups. Tent sites are $9 per night, RV sites $12.

Getting there: From Route 84 at Mountain Home, take Route 51 south 16 miles, then Route 78 east four miles. From Route 84 at Hammett (20 miles east of Mountain Home), take Route 78 west 18 miles.

The Sporting Life

FISHING

Trout—rainbow, brown, brook and cutthroat—are the primary species sought in Idaho, particularly in the southwest. The Snake River and its tributaries, including the Boise, the Payette and the Weiser, are prime waters.

BOISE AREA In the middle Snake south of Boise, **Birds of Prey Expeditions** (252 North Meridian Road, Kuna; 208-922-5285) offers float fishing between C. J. Strike and Swan Falls dams. Tackle shops include **Streamside Adventures** (6907 Overland Road, Boise; 208-853-8704) and **The Ultimate Angler** (1033 West Bannock Street, Boise; 208-389-9957), both of them fly-fishing specialists, and **Rocky Mountain Anglers** (832 Vista Avenue, Boise; 208-336-3336).

TREASURE VALLEY Lake Lowell, south of Nampa, is a favorite destination for anglers seeking rainbow trout, smallmouth and largemouth bass, crappie, perch, bluegill and catfish. For information and equipment, visit **Howard's Tackle Shop** (1707 Garrity Boulevard, Nampa; 208-465-0946).

HELLS CANYON AND McCALL AREA October–November steelhead-fishing expeditions originating from Hells Canyon Dam are offered by numerous outfitters including **Hughes River Expeditions** (Route 71, Cambridge; 208-257-3477) and **Hells Canyon Adventures II** (Route 86, Oxbow, Oregon; 503-785-3352).

On the Snake River above Hells Canyon, Brownlee, Oxbow and Hells Canyon reservoirs are prime locations; some of the best catfishing in Idaho is at Brownlee. On the Weiser River system, trout, bass and bluegill are denizens of Crane Creek, Mann Creek and Lost Valley reservoirs.

Cascade Reservoir, on the North Fork of the Payette River, is regarded as one of the finest fisheries in the state, with rainbow, brook and brown trout; chinook, coho and kokanee salmon; yellow perch and mountain whitefish. Other good fishing lakes on the Payette River system are Payette Lake, Upper Payette Lake, and Black Canyon, Paddock Valley and Deadwood reservoirs. **The Sports Marina** (1300 East Lake Drive, McCall; 208-634-8361) on Payette Lake has full equipment and information.

BOISE COUNTY AND BOISE BASIN On the Boise River system, Lucky Peak, Arrowrock and Anderson Ranch reservoirs are likely venues for rainbow and brown trout, smallmouth bass and (at Anderson Ranch) kokanee.

MOUNTAIN HOME AND OWYHEE COUNTY C. J. Strike Reservoir near Mountain Home is excellent for trout. The Bruneau and Owyhee rivers boast trophy-size rainbow trout. There are largemouth bass and bluegill in the Bruneau Lakes at Bruneau Dunes State Park.

RIVER RAFTING AND KAYAKING

Some of America's greatest whitewater rafting rivers—Hells Canyon of the Snake, the Middle Fork of the Salmon and the South Fork of the Payette—are located in southwestern Idaho. South of the Snake, the infrequently visited Owyhee and Bruneau desert rivers promise steep canyon vistas, thrilling whitewater and excellent wildlife viewing.

For information on guided trips in southwestern Idaho and elsewhere in the state, contact the **Idaho Outfitters and Guides Association** (711 North 5th Street, Boise; 208-342-1438). **Birds of Prey Expeditions** (252 North Meridian Road, Runa; 208-922-5285) offers trips through the Snake River and the Birds of Prey National Conservation Area.

BOISE AREA **Idaho River Sports** (1521 North 13th Street, Boise; 208-336-4844) and **Boise Water Sports** (3204 Overland Road, Boise; 208-342-1378) are good places to arrange rentals of rafts, kayaks and essential gear.

HELLS CANYON AND McCALL AREA Certainly the best way to experience Hells Canyon, North America's deepest gorge, is by raft down the Snake River. (The return trip is often by jet boat back up the river to the put-in point.) The most frequently traveled stretch is the 30 miles of moderately challenging rapids between Hells Canyon Dam, north of Cambridge, and Pittsburg Landing, west of White Bird. The season extends from April to October. Contact **Canyon Outfitters** (Route 86, Halfway, Oregon; 503-742-4110) or **Hells Canyon Adventures** (Route 86, Oxbow, Oregon; 503-785-3352) for guided trips.

Although most trips on the Middle Fork of the Salmon, ranked as one of the top-ten whitewater rivers in the world, begin from Challis or Salmon (see Chapter Ten, "Southeastern Idaho Rockies"), at least one southwest Idaho outfitter extends its territory for five-day, 96-mile trips on this challenging stream. That's **Epley's Whitewater Adventures** (1107 North Davis Street, McCall; 208-634-5173), which also offers a variety of shorter trips on the Salmon and North Fork of the Payette.

BOISE COUNTY AND BOISE BASIN Payette River trips, less than an hour's drive north of Boise, draw hundreds of rafters on any given weekend day from May through September. Families enjoy riding the gentle rapids of the main Payette below Banks; experienced rafters tackle the tough rapids of the South Fork canyon, which includes a portage around a 40-foot waterfall. Largest of several outfitters is the **Cascade Raft Company** (Route 55, Horseshoe Bend; 208-462-3292), with 16 full-time river guides and special wine-tasting trips. Other outfitters include **Idaho Whitewater Unlimited** (Route 55, Banks; 208-793-2512) and the **Headwaters River Company** (Route 55, Banks; 208-793-2348).

Cascade and Headwaters also offer kayaking trips. Indeed, the North Fork of the Payette immediately above Banks is ranked among the world's finest advanced kayak runs.

BOATING

The region's most popular destinations for boating and other water sports are Lucky Peak and Arrowrock reservoirs, east of Boise; Payette Lake and Cascade Reservoir, in the McCall area; and Anderson Ranch Reservoir, northeast of Mountain Home. Lucky Peak has eight boat launch sites and a marina at the Spring Shores unit of Lucky Peak State Park; Arrowrock, just up the Boise River, an additional boat ramp. Cascade has 24 launch sites and a marina at the town of Cascade; Anderson Ranch has seven ramps. There's also a public marina, **The Sports Marina** (1300 East Lake Drive, McCall; 208-634-8361), with boat rentals on Payette Lake.

The trio of Snake River reservoirs upriver of Hells Canyon Dam—Hells Canyon, Oxbow and Brownlee reservoirs—draw water-sports enthusiasts from Oregon as well as Idaho. Farther south and east up the Snake, there are good launch sites at Homedale, Marsing, Walter's Ferry, Grand View and Glenns Ferry. You can rent boats from **Idaho River Sports** (1521 North 13th Street, Boise; 208-336-4844).

DOWNHILL SKIING

BOISE AREA **Bogus Basin** (2405 Bogus Basin Road, Boise; 208-332-5100) may be a "local" area, just 16 road miles north of downtown Boise in Boise National Forest, but it's been called "one of the 12 best-kept secrets in skiing" by no less an authority than *Ski* magazine. From the summit of 7590-foot Shafer Butte there's a vertical drop of 1800 feet to the base of the Superior Chair—not enormous by major resort standards, but sufficient to guarantee a wide range of challenges on its 45 runs, served by six chairlifts and four rope tows. The mountain offers 2000 acres of night skiing. Snow permitting, Bogus keeps its lifts operating from Thanksgiving through Easter.

HELLS CANYON AND McCALL AREA A decidedly local area is tiny **Hitt Mountain** (Jackson Road, Midvale; 208-355-2256), east of Brownlee Reservoir in Payette National Forest. It has four runs served by a T-bar and rope tow, and a 500-foot vertical.

Brundage Mountain (Brundage Mountain Road, McCall; 208-634-4151), eight miles northwest of McCall, is located in the heart of a snow belt that brings it huge quantities of "champagne powder." With four chairlifts and two surface tows, 1300 acres of terrain and an 1800-foot vertical drop, it is regarded as an intermediate mountain with several expert runs and forested glades. For powder hounds who don't get enough at Brundage, Sno-cat ski trips extend to two other nearby peaks, with the opportunity to stay overnight in a Mongolian yurt.

SKI RENTALS For downhill and cross-country equipment rentals in the Boise area, check out **Greenwood's Ski Haus** (2400 Bogus Basin Road, Boise; 208-342-6808) or **McU Sports** (2314 Bogus Basin Road, Boise; 208-336-2300). Snowboarding specialists include **Pedersen's Ski & Sport** (Boise Towne Square Mall, Boise; 208-377-2701) and **Action Sports** (15th and Front streets, Boise; 208-383-0073). **Idaho Mountain Touring** (915 West Jefferson Street, Boise; 208-336-3854) specializes in cross-country rentals. Near Brundage Mountain in the Hells Canyon and McCall Area, visit **Home Town Sports** (402 West Lake Street, McCall; 208-634-2302).

CROSS-COUNTRY SKIING

Bogus Basin (2405 Bogus Basin Road, Boise; 208-332-5100) has 27 kilometers of cross-country trails from a lodge at the foot of the alpine slopes. The McCall area also has excellent nordic skiing, especially at **Ponderosa State Park** (East Lake Drive, McCall; 208-634-2164).

Other popular "park 'n' ski" cross-country areas include **Crawford** and **Scott Valley**, four and eight miles, respectively, east of Cascade on Warm Springs Road (Forest Road 22); and **Whoop-Um-Up**, **Gold Fork** and **Banner Ridge**, 15, 17 and 20 miles northeast of Idaho City on Route 21. Banner Ridge has the longest network of trails, 25 kilometers.

For information on renting equipment, see the ski-rental section in "Downhill Skiing" above.

GOLF

Public links in the Boise area include the **Boise Ranch Golf Course** (6501 South Cloverdale Road; 208-362-6501), **Quail Hollow Golf Course** (4520 North 36th Street; 208-344-7807), **Shadow Valley Golf Course** (15711 Route 55 North; 208-939-6699), **Warm Springs Golf Course** (2495 Warm Springs Avenue; 208-343-5661) and **Eagle Hills Golf Course** (605 North Edgewood Lane, Eagle; 208-939-0402). Elsewhere in southwestern Idaho, check out the **Centennial Golf Course** (Centennial Drive, Nampa; 208-467-3011), **Purple Sage Golf Course** (Caldwell; 208-459-2223), **Scotch Pines Golf Course** (10610 Scotch Pines Road, Payette; 208-642-1829), **McCall Golf Course** (East Lake Drive, McCall; 208-634-7200), **Terrace Lakes Golf Course** (Middle Fork Road, Garden Valley; 208-462-3250) and **Silver Sage Golf Course** (Air Base Road, Mountain Home; 208-828-6151).

TENNIS

In Boise, no fewer than 17 city parks have public courts, among them **Ann Morrison Memorial Park** (Ann Morrison Park Drive west of Capitol Boulevard), **Julia Davis Park** (Julia Davis Drive east of Capitol Boulevard) and **Fort Boise Park** (Fort and Reserve streets), which is lighted for night play. Contact Boise Parks & Recreation Department (1104 Royal Boulevard; 208-384-4240) for more information. In Nampa, contact Nampa Parks & Recreation (411 3rd Street South; 208-465-2215); in Caldwell, Caldwell Parks & Recreation (618 Irving Street; 208-455-3060).

HORSEBACK RIDING

Bogus Creek Outfitters (2405 Bogus Basin Road, Boise; 208-336-3130) and **Towle Outfitters** (4155 North Columbine Street, Boise; 208-378-4386) offer summer trail rides by the hour or day into Boise National Forest from the Bogus Basin ski area. Towle specializes in photo trips; Bogus Creek offers wagon rides in summer and winter sleigh rides at the ski area.

PACK TRIPS AND LLAMA TREKKING

The trails of Hells Canyon National Recreation Area and the Snake River Birds of Prey National Conservation Area are popular places for horseback expeditions of one to several days. Contact **Snake River Adventure Outfitters** (8241 Butte Road, Melba; 208-495-2170) for information.

On the edge of the Frank Church–River of No Return Wilderness east of McCall, **Gillihan's Guide Service** (Forest Road 371, Big Creek; 208-327-0907) offers trail rides and pack trips. And on the west side of the Sawtooth National Recreation Area, **Sawtooth Wilderness Outfitters** (P.O. Box 81, Garden Valley, ID 83622; 208-462-3416 in winter, 208-259-3408 in summer) plans guided pack trips of three to ten days.

High Llama Wilderness Tours (2500 Millway, Boise; 208-323-0868) offers an alternative to horse packing. The Andean beasts of burden carry the load as you hike alongside on photo, fishing or sightseeing trips.

BICYCLING

The **Boise River Greenbelt** (1104 Royal Boulevard, Boise; 208-384-4240) is one of the finest urban biking systems you'll find anywhere. The mostly paved network of paths extends 19 miles through the heart of the city, linking parks from Willow Lane, in the northwest, to Lucky Peak State Park, some ten miles southeast.

Popular off-the-pavement trails for Boise-area bikers include the **8th Street Extension** to Hulls Gulch (3 to 6 miles) and Boise Ridge (8 miles), a mile north of Fort Street via North 8th Street, and the **Swan Falls Dam** road through a corner of the Snake River Birds of Prey National Conservation Area, a 45-minute drive from Boise south of Kuna.

Additionally, the ski runs at **Bogus Basin** (2405 Bogus Basin Road, Boise; 208-332-5100) and **Brundage Mountain** (Brundage Mountain Road, McCall; 208-634-4151) are used on summer weekends by mountain bikers, who can take the chairlifts to the summit and ride back down again.

There's seemingly endless biking on the trails of **Boise National Forest** (1750 Front Street, Boise; 208-364-4100) and **Payette National Forest** (106 West Park Street, McCall; 208-634-0700).

BIKE RENTALS Mountain and touring bikes are available from **Wheels R Fun** (South 13th Street at the Greenbelt, Boise; 208-343-8228). You can rent mountain bikes from **Action Sports** (15th and Front streets, Boise; 208-383-0073) or **Idaho Mountain Touring** (915 West Jefferson Street, Boise; 208-336-3854).

HIKING

Greenbelt aside, Boise is a gateway to a wide choice of trails. Following are some of the most popular. All distances listed are one-way unless otherwise noted.

BOISE AREA **Hulls Gulch National Recreation Trail** (3.5 miles) is a Bureau of Land Management interpretive trail, complete with signs describing natural features, just outside the northern city limits. To reach the upper trailhead, take North 8th Street to the end of the pavement and continue six and a half miles. En route, you'll pass the lower trailhead three and a half miles from the end of the pavement.

Mores Mountain Trail (2 miles) is an easy nature hike for kids and families, offering spectacular views from the Treasure Valley to the Sawtooth Range. It begins and ends at the Shafer Butte picnic area, 20 miles from Boise (four miles past the Bogus Basin Recreation Area) on Bogus Basin Road.

HELLS CANYON AND VALLEY COUNTY See Chapter Eleven, "Northern Idaho Rockies," for information on the **Snake River National Recreation Trail** and the **Seven Devils Trail**.

Loon Lake Trail (15 miles) follows the meandering Secesh River, a tributary of the South Fork of the Salmon, upstream along a segment of the Idaho State Centennial Trail. The gently ascending trail begins at the Ponderosa campground on Lick Creek Road (Route 48) between McCall and Yellow Pine; it ends at the Chinook campground off Warren Wagon Road (Route 21) between McCall and Warren.

Needles Route Trail (9.5 miles) follows a long ridge of the Salmon River Mountains between Cascade and Warm Lake, providing spectacular scenic views. This moderately strenuous and not particularly well marked Boise National Forest hike begins off Forest Road 497 just north of Warm Lake Road (Route 22).

BOISE COUNTY AND BOISE BASIN **Crooked River Trail** (9.5 miles) descends for six and a half miles into the steep and narrow river canyon, then ascends rapidly. This Boise National Forest hike is moderately difficult. The trailhead is on Forest Road 384 (Crooked River Road), just off Route 21 between Idaho City and Lowman; it ends on Forest Road 327 (North Fork Road).

Clear Creek Trail (2 miles) climbs a ridge northeast of Lowman (off Forest Roads 582 and 515) through fir forest and meadows woven with streams. The ascent is gradual, so this is a good one for kids.

Camp Creek Trail (5.7 miles) offers wonderful views across Anderson Ranch Reservoir and the hamlets of Pine and Featherville on the South Fork of the Boise River. This moderately difficult trail, which is open to motorized vehicles, climbs a steep ridge off Lester Creek Road (Forest Road 128) in the Anderson Ranch Reservoir Recreation Area.

Trinity Lakes Trail (3 miles) takes in a dozen or more small alpine lakes nestled at the foot of 9451-foot Trinity Mountain, itself topped by a lookout accessible by four-wheel-drive vehicle. Take Fall Creek Road (Forest Road 129) north from Anderson Dam, off Route 20.

MOUNTAIN HOME AND OWYHEE COUNTY **Bruneau Dunes Trail** (5 miles) in Bruneau Dunes State Park begins and ends at the park visitors center, looping around the ancient 470-foot dunes and the ponds at their base.

Transportation

BY CAR

Route 84 between Portland, Oregon, and Salt Lake City crosses southwestern Idaho diagonally from west to east, providing the major thoroughfare of travel. **Route 20**, extending east from Mountain Home to Idaho Falls, provides the quickest route to Sun Valley from Boise. **Route 21** heads northeast from Boise around the edge of the Sawtooth Mountains, then loops back south into Stanley in the Sawtooth National Recreation Area. **Route 55** is the primary northbound route from Boise, following the Payette River through Cascade and McCall to join Route 95 at New Meadows. **Route 95** travels south from Coeur d'Alene and Lewiston, following Idaho's western border and crossing Route 84 south of Payette. In western Owyhee County it passes into Oregon.

BY AIR

Delta, Northwest, Southwest and United, as well as regional carriers Empire, Horizon and SkyWest, fly into **Boise Municipal Airport**.

Airway Taxicab (208-866-3767) serves Boise Municipal Airport.

BY BUS

Boise's intercity bus depot is located downtown at 1212 West Bannock Street. It is served by **Greyhound Bus Lines** (208-343-3681), which makes daily stops in Boise, and by **Boise-Winnemucca/Northwestern Stage Lines** (208-336-3302), a regional coach line that operates daily northbound routes to McCall, Grangeville, Lewiston and Spokane, and southbound routes to Nampa and Caldwell, Winnemucca and Reno, Nevada.

Elsewhere in southwestern Idaho there are bus terminals in Nampa (315 12th Avenue South; 208-467-5122), Caldwell (1017 Arthur Street; 208-459-2816) and McCall (147 North 3rd Street; 208-634-2340).

Sun Valley Stages (815 Ann Morrison Park Drive, Boise; 208-336-4038) operates charter service to the Sun Valley resort community from Boise, including airport pickups. **Mile High Shuttle & Tour** (McCall; 208-634-3495) runs between Boise and the resort town of McCall.

BY TRAIN

Amtrak (1701 Eastover Terrace, Boise; 208-336-5992) runs through Boise on a regular eastbound and westbound schedule between Chicago and Portland, Oregon. Arrivals and departures have a tendency to occur in the middle of the night, which is why there's someone on hand here between 10:30 p.m. and 5 a.m. from Sunday to Friday.

CAR RENTALS

Boise has 18 automobile rental agencies. At the airport are **Avis Rent A Car** (800-331-1212), **Budget Rent A Car** (800-527-0700), **Dollar Rent A Car** (800-800-4000), **Hertz Rent A Car** (800-654-3131), **National Interrent** (800-227-7368) and **Payless Car Rental** (800-634-6539).

Another option, with three outlets and low prices, is **U-Save Auto Rental** (4195 Chinden Boulevard, Garden City, 800-999-9404; 225 East Fairview Avenue, Meridian, 800-272-8728; 1655 Garrity Boulevard, Nampa, 800-272-8728).

Disabled visitors may want to make reservations with **Wheelchair Access Van Rentals** (2605 North Dalton Lane, Boise; 208-939-0617).

PUBLIC TRANSPORTATION

Boise-area bus service is provided by **Boise Urban Stages** (208-336-1010), known locally as "The BUS."

TAXIS

At least a half-dozen cab companies operate in the city, including **Boise City Taxi** (208-377-3333) and **Kwik Yellow Orange Cab** (208-345-8880). In Nampa and Caldwell, try **A-1 Stop-n-Go Taxicab** (Nampa, 208-466-4999; Caldwell, 208-459-4999).

CHAPTER TEN

Southeastern Idaho Rockies

The story of southeastern Idaho is inseparable from that of the Snake River. Here, where the desert ends and the mountains begin, the Snake cuts a swath across Idaho from east to west and brings life to a parched land.

Rising on the Continental Divide near Wyoming's Yellowstone and Grand Teton national parks, the Snake rushes toward Idaho with a whitewater roar. Then, slowed by a series of dams, it patiently irrigates the state's famous fields of potatoes and forage crops before sprinting northwesterly toward the Oregon border and Hells Canyon.

En route, like a master illusionist, the river manifests its own magic. Here are a broad waterfall, higher than Niagara . . . sand dunes taller than those of Death Valley . . . thousands of underground springs bursting from sheer canyon walls.

And the river is nature's history book. There are fossil remains of the Hagerman horse, a zebralike Pliocene ancestor of the modern steed; wagon ruts from the mid-19th-century Oregon Trail, which traced the banks of the Snake for hundreds of miles; and on every rooftop a TV antenna, a reminder that an eastern Idaho farm boy named Philo Taylor Farnsworth III was plowing a field in 1920 when he envisioned a way to send pictures through the air—and who, before he was 22, invented electronic television.

South of the Snake, the semiarid Great Basin extends for hundreds of miles across Nevada and Utah. In southeastern Idaho, it gives rise to hot springs, geysers, deep caves and towering monoliths.

To the north, the component ranges of the Rocky Mountains soar above the Snake River Plain, climaxing at 12,662-foot Borah Peak, the state's highest summit. Rivers like the Salmon and the Wood flow from this rugged, forested region that includes the largest wilderness area in the United States outside of Alaska.

In modern geologic times (until only about 2000 years ago) the southern fringe of the Idaho Rockies was a volcanic region of spatter cones and lava flows. Craters of the Moon National Monument preserves the starkest features of this era just 25 miles from the first and largest concentration of nuclear reactors on earth. Lava beds cloak thousands of square miles south and east from Craters of the Moon to the Snake River. Though the surface of this "empty quarter" is stark and barren, there's plenty of activity underground: Two mountain rivers disappear into the aquifer, only to filter through canyon walls thousands of years and 100 miles later.

The vast Snake River Plain owes its fertility ("just add water") to prehistoric Lakes Idaho and Bonneville, both of them enormous inland seas. Lake Idaho, geologists say, covered this region between eight million and two and a half million years ago; it left behind rich silt deposits and a meandering Snake River. Lake Bonneville, which stretched across western Utah and neighboring states beginning about one and a half million years ago, burst its walls south of modern Pocatello toward the end of the Pleistocene era (about 15,000 years ago) and created a flood of biblical scale. Discharging waters like a faster-flowing Amazon (at 15 million cubic feet per second), the Bonneville Flood—estimated to have been 300 feet deep in places—swept across the river bed of old Lake Idaho, scouring the Snake River Canyon and Hells Canyon nearly to their present depths and eventually finding its way down the Columbia River Gorge to the Pacific Ocean.

Twin Falls Area

Through the basalt of south-central Idaho, the Bonneville Flood carved the stark, winding, 105-mile **Snake River Canyon,** with sheer cliffs as high as 600 feet. There's no better place to grasp its magnitude than Twin Falls, the small-town metropolis of the so-called Magic Valley. Just upriver the Shoshone Falls, the "Niagara of the West," drop in a broad arc. Downriver the Thousand Springs weep from a canyon wall near Hagerman Fossil Beds National Monument. South and north are such phenomena as the Shoshone Ice Caves and the striking City of Rocks.

With a population of about 30,000, **Twin Falls** is poised a stone's throw from the south rim of the canyon. Most folks approach the town from the north off Route 84, via Route 93 across the 933-foot-long **Perrine Bridge**. The world's highest bridge when it opened in 1927, it has been rebuilt and strengthened but still offers a breathtaking view from 486 feet above the Snake River Canyon.

At the south end of the bridge is the **Buzz Langdon Visitors Center** (Route 93 North; 208-733-3974). Pedestrian walkways and overlooks afford bird's-eye scrutiny of the lush canyon floor, including golf courses and a ramp from which daredevil Evel Knievel attempted to jump the canyon on a rocket-powered motorcycle in 1974. (He failed but parachuted to safety.)

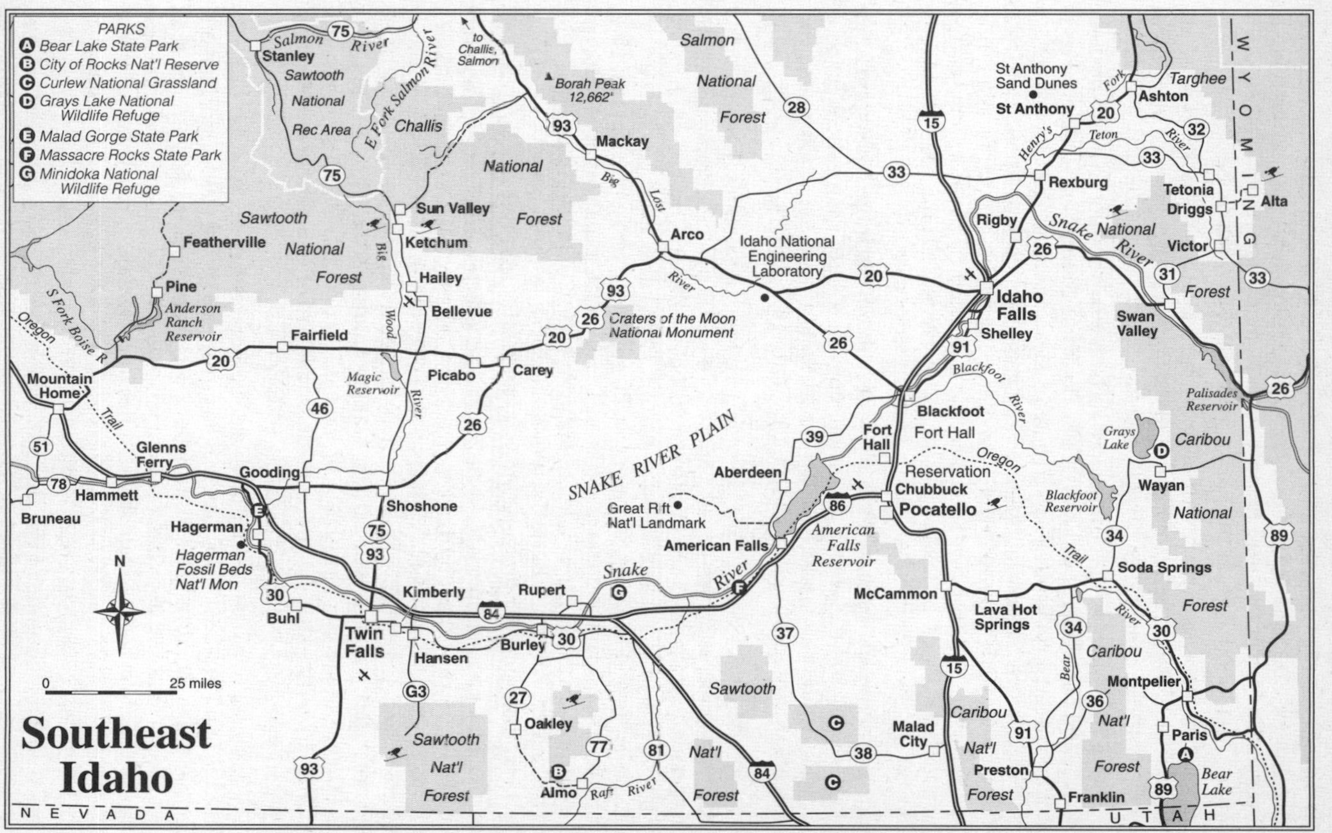
Southeast Idaho
PARKS
A Bear Lake State Park
B City of Rocks Nat'l Reserve
C Curlew National Grassland
D Grays Lake National Wildlife Refuge
E Malad Gorge State Park
F Massacre Rocks State Park
G Minidoka National Wildlife Refuge
0
25 miles
N
W Y O M I N G
U T A H
N E V A D A
Stanley
Salmon River
Sawtooth National Rec Area
E Fork Salmon River
to Challis, Salmon
Challis National Forest
Borah Peak 12,662'
Mackay
Big Lost River
Arco
Salmon National Forest
Targhee National Forest
Ashton
St Anthony Sand Dunes
St Anthony
Henry's Fork
Teton River
Rexburg
Rigby
Idaho Falls
Shelley
Tetonia
Driggs
Victor
Alta
Swan Valley
Snake River
Palisades Reservoir
Caribou National Forest
Grays Lake
Wayan
Blackfoot Reservoir
Soda Springs
Bear River
Montpelier
Paris
Bear Lake
Franklin
Preston
Caribou Nat'l Forest
Lava Hot Springs
McCammon
Malad City
Pocatello
Chubbuck
Fort Hall Reservation
Fort Hall
Blackfoot
Blackfoot River
Oregon Trail
American Falls Reservoir
American Falls
Aberdeen
Idaho National Engineering Laboratory
Craters of the Moon National Monument
SNAKE RIVER PLAIN
Great Rift Nat'l Landmark
Sawtooth Nat'l Forest
Raft River
Almo
Oakley
Burley
Rupert
Hansen
Kimberly
Twin Falls
Buhl
Shoshone
Picabo
Carey
Bellevue
Hailey
Ketchum
Sun Valley
Big Wood River
Magic Reservoir
Sawtooth National Forest
Fairfield
Gooding
Hagerman
Hagerman Fossil Beds Nat'l Mon
Featherville
Pine
Anderson Ranch Reservoir
S Fork Boise R
Mountain Home
Glenns Ferry
Hammett
Bruneau

An interesting museum in Twin Falls is the **Norman and Lilly Herrett Museum** (★) (315 Falls Avenue West; 208-733-9554 ext. 356). Located at the two-year College of Southern Idaho, it exhibits more than 10,000 Native American artifacts ranging from pre-Columbian Maya to modern Hopi.

The city took its name from the impressive but often overlooked **Twin Falls** on the Snake River about six miles east of the Perrine Bridge. There's an overlook a mile north of Falls Avenue East (3500 East Road, Kimberly; 208-423-4223).

The Twin Falls might be due more acclaim were they not so near **Shoshone Falls** (3300 East Road, Twin Falls; 208-736-2265; admission), among the most impressive cataracts in the western United States. Plummeting 212 feet—52 feet more than famed Niagara Falls—Shoshone Falls pour massive amounts of Snake River water over a 1000-foot-wide, horseshoe-shaped basalt rock face in spring. At other times, when irrigation canals have diverted the river's flow, visitors may see only a trickle of water passing the powerhouse at the head of the falls. But the lava-walled canyon scene remains spectacular.

Twenty miles south of Twin Falls, the **Idaho Heritage Museum** (Route 93, Hollister; 208-655-4444; admission) boasts the state's largest collection of mounted wildlife as well as Native American artifacts. The 7000-square-foot museum is closed Mondays and January through February.

THE MINI-CASSIA AREA Minidoka and Cassia counties, known to most Idahoans simply as "Mini-Cassia," make up a well-irrigated farming and ranching region that flanks the Snake River. Its hub is **Burley**, located on the south shore of Milner Reservoir 40 miles east of Twin Falls. Burley is best known as a power-boating center: The reservoir, 20 miles long and a few hundred yards wide, hosts the Idaho Regatta every June. The town's **Cassia County Historical Museum** (East Main Street and Highland Avenue; 208-678-7172), open April to November, describes Burley's 19th-century role as the focus of five pioneer byways, including the Oregon, Mormon and California trails.

Oakley (★), which boasts Idaho's highest concentration of late-19th-century buildings, most of them intricate stone and wood structures, is 20 miles south of Burley in the Goose Creek Mountains. The entire town of 660—laid out by Mormon leaders in 1882—is listed on the National Register of Historic Places. Visitors start walking tours at the **Oakley Cooperative Mercantile** (Main and Center streets), built in 1883, or the old Worthington Hotel, which houses exhibits of early settlers' artifacts in the **Daughters of Utah Pioneers Museum** (Main Street and Blaine Avenue; 208-678-7172).

The granite pillars of **City of Rocks National Reserve** (★) (City of Rocks Road, Almo; 208-824-5519) marked the crossroads of the California Trail and Kelton Stage Road for pioneer travelers. Their inscriptions can still be seen scrawled in axle grease on the rock columns towering 60 stories above the desert sage. Take a gravel road southeast 18 miles from Oakley, or reach City of Rocks via Route 77 southeast from Burley. A visitors center is open daily, although winter snowstorms may close the park's gravel roads.

Rupert, eight miles from Burley on the north side of the Snake, boomed as an agricultural center after the completion in 1906 of the nearby **Minidoka**

Dam, the Pacific Northwest's first hydroelectric power house. Today, Rupert has perhaps the most traditional town square in Idaho, with downtown businesses facing the lively plaza and its bandstand on all sides.

The dam holds back **Lake Walcott**, a reservoir popular among boaters, waterskiers and anglers. Along with 11 miles of the Snake River to its east, the lake is encompassed by the 25,000-acre **Minidoka National Wildlife Refuge** (Minidoka Dam Road, Rupert; 208-436-3589). Famous for the 250,000-plus ducks and geese that cluster here each fall, this refuge is home to 208 species of resident and migratory birds, including swans, herons and egrets. There's a fall-winter hunting season along the lake's southern shore and around Tule Island in the Snake. Campsites with hookups are administered by the Bureau of Reclamation (208-436-6117).

THE HAGERMAN VALLEY Probably the most interesting daytrip in the Twin Falls area is a loop that takes drivers west and north on Route 30 through the lush Hagerman Valley.

Buhl, 17 miles west of Twin Falls, is surrounded by picturesque barns and rich farmland. Southwest of the community is one of Idaho's geological oddities: **Balanced Rock**, a 40-foot, mushroom-shaped boulder perched upon a pedestal only a few feet in diameter. Geologists say it's been that way since prehistoric times. (Take Castleford Road south four miles from Buhl, then Orchard Drive nine miles west.)

Buhl is also home to the world's largest commercial trout farm: **Clear Springs Foods** (1500 East 4424 North, Clear Lakes Road; 208-543-4316). Self-guided tours of aquaculture operations are offered from a new visitors center. Don't miss the display of live white sturgeon, one of them ten feet long and more than 70 years old. Clear Springs is in the heart of a 30-mile stretch, between Twin Falls and Hagerman, from which come more than 70 percent of all commercially raised trout in the United States.

West of Buhl, Route 30 curves north to return to the Snake River and the **Thousand Springs Scenic Route**. From the roadway along the river's southwest bank, you can look to the black cliffs on the opposite canyon wall and see dozens of apparently sourceless waterfalls cascading from what seems sheer rock. (There once may have been several hundred of these springs, but most have been diverted for irrigation or fish farming.) The spectacular springs are the outflow from the Snake River Plain Aquifer, a porous lava basin into which the Big and Little Lost rivers disappear, only to reemerge from these palisades. One of the largest and most accessible of the Thousand Springs can be seen at **Niagara Springs State Park** (Niagara Springs Road, Wendell; 208-837-4505; admission), where the springs' icy blue waters pour down a cliffside at 250 cubic feet per second. To reach the park from Wendell, take Route 46 (Rex Leland Highway) south five miles to Niagara Springs Road, continuing another three and a half miles to the park. The final descent is narrow and steep, not recommended in a large RV or with a trailer.

Route 30 continues north past several commercial hot springs and enters an agricultural area carpeted with grassy pastures and melon fields. This is the

Hagerman Valley, where pioneers along the Oregon Trail traded with the native peoples for fresh trout.

Today a much more distant history attracts visitors to the **Hagerman Fossil Beds National Monument** (West 2700 South Road, Hagerman; 208-837-4793). In the 1930s, a Smithsonian Institution expedition unearthed a partial skeleton of *Equus simplicidens,* a zebralike Pliocene horse extinct for more than three million years, above the west bank of the Snake. More than 150 individual horse fossils have been excavated since, as well as fossils of mastodons and sabertooth tigers. The Hagerman Fossil Beds are the richest known deposit of terrestrial fossils from the Upper Pliocene era, when this region was marshy and semitropical. To reach the national monument grounds, turn west on Route 30 just south of the Snake River bridge, south of Hagerman. There's an overlook above Upper Salmon Falls Reservoir, two miles from the junction. The main fossil quarry is about nine miles northwest via unmarked and unsurfaced roads.

Although there are no visitor facilities in the monument itself, a temporary center (221 North State Street; 208-837-4793) is in downtown Hagerman. **Tours** (★) are frequently organized on summer Saturday afternoons and during Hagerman Fossil Days in May. Collection and removal of fossils are prohibited.

About three miles north off Route 30 is **Malad Gorge State Park** (1074 East 2350 Road South, Hagerman; 208-837-4505; admission), another example of the dramatic hand of nature in southern Idaho. Here, the Big Wood River tumbles over a 60-foot waterfall into the Devil's Washbowl, where the Malad River begins its two-and-a-half-mile run to the Snake. A steel footbridge spans the 250-foot-deep gorge, offering striking glimpses of million-year-old geology. The 651-acre park includes two miles of trails.

Route 30 climbs out of the Hagerman Valley at Bliss. Turn east here on Route 26 and cross beneath Route 84. Proceed through Gooding to **Shoshone**, an old railroad town still of importance as the sole Amtrak station for Twin Falls (26 miles south) and Sun Valley (56 miles north).

Shoshone has several intriguing cave systems that beckon spelunkers. Most important are the **Shoshone Indian Ice Caves** (Route 75 North; 208-886-2058; admission), where Native Americans once found relief from desert heat. Forty-minute guided tours descend into the longest of the caves, a lava tube 1000 feet long with a floor of ice that ranges up to 30 feet deep. Air currents, never warmer than 33°F, have formed fantastic shapes. Located 17 miles north of Shoshone, the cave is open from May to October.

TWIN FALLS AREA HOTELS

Twin Falls is big on chain properties and franchises, but for a smaller, well-kept motel, check out the **Monterey Motor Inn** (433 Addison Avenue West; 208-733-5151). Located on westbound Route 30/93, this single-story motel has 28 rooms—cozy except for a couple of two-bedroom units—with standard amenities plus a swimming pool, hot tub and coin laundry. Budget.

Up the price ladder is the **Best Western Canyon Springs Inn** (1357 Blue Lakes Boulevard North, Twin Falls; 208-734-5000, 800-727-5003, fax 208-734-

5000 ext. 5000) at the north end of the city. Two stories and 112 rooms face a central swimming pool, an exercise room and a meeting area. All of the warmly decorated, carpeted rooms have king- or queen-size beds and spacious baths. Children under 18 stay free with a parent. Hotel facilities include a restaurant, a lounge and an espresso shop. Moderate.

A great place for families is the **Best Western Burley Inn & Convention Center** (800 North Overland Avenue, Burley; 208-678-3501, 800-528-1234, fax 208-678-9532). Sitting on the north bank of the Snake River at Route 84 Exit 208, it has separate swimming and wading pools, a playground, a volleyball net and a coin laundry; what's more, children 18 and under stay free with parents. Hotel facilities include a fine-dining restaurant, a coffee shop and a cocktail lounge. Low moderate.

The **Hagerman Valley Inn** (State Street and Hagerman Avenue, Hagerman; 208-837-6196) is the preferred choice along the Thousand Springs Scenic Route. With but ten clean and comfortable rooms, it's not a big place, but it's new and it's near the Rose Creek Winery and Frog's Lilypad Restaurant at the south end of town. Guests can share the inn's jacuzzi. Budget.

One of the region's few backpacker-oriented lodgings is the **Gooding Hotel Bed & Breakfast and AYH Hostel** (112 Main Street, Gooding; 208-934-4374). This historic downtown hotel has eight dormitory beds (low, low budget rates) and four private rooms (budget to moderate). Guests share washrooms, showers, a kitchen, a laundry, a TV room, an equipment storage area and off-street parking. A full breakfast is served to those who want it. The hotel dates from 1906, a year before the town was even founded.

TWIN FALLS AREA RESTAURANTS

Since 1927, Twin Falls' **Depot Grill** (545 Shoshone Street South; 208-733-0710) has been dishing up three meals a day from the railroad station. The passenger depot is gone now, but the restaurant lives on, open 24 hours daily to keep hungry farm boys fed. This is all-American food, and lots of it. Budget.

The small yellow house just south of the railroad tracks wouldn't attract much attention were it not an outstanding Mexican restaurant. **La Casita** (111 South Park Avenue West, Twin Falls; 208-734-7974) features all-homemade cuisine in a simple, alcohol-free atmosphere. Budget.

A'roma Italian Cuisine (147 Shoshone Street North, Twin Falls; 208-733-0167) serves innovative pastas and such northern Italian specialties as veal piccata and Venetian prawns in a casual café climate. Moderate.

The delightful **Uptown Bistro** (117 Main Avenue East, Twin Falls; 208-733-0900) in pedestrian-friendly midtown is the city's most innovative café. Changing exhibits of area artists' works make it a gallery. Deli sandwiches and daily specials are on the lunch menu; dinners are casual from Monday to Wednesday, gourmet Continental on Thursday, Friday and Saturday. Moderate to deluxe.

The Sandpiper (1309 Blue Lakes Boulevard North, Twin Falls; 208-734-7000) is the region's most elegant restaurant, serving prime rib, fresh seafood and pastas in a nautical atmosphere next door to the Best Western Canyon Springs Inn. Moderate to deluxe.

In Mini-Cassia, **Price's Cafe** (2444 Overland Avenue, Burley; 208-678-5149) is a four-generation favorite (it's been around since 1932) that offers breakfasts, lunches, steaks and seafood dinners, as well as homemade pies for dessert. Budget to moderate.

It's no surprise that the **Snake River Grill** (State Street and Hagerman Avenue, Hagerman; 208-837-6227), located in the heart of the nation's premier fish-farming region, specializes in Idaho rainbow trout. Rib steaks and prawns, accompanied by Hagerman's own Rose Creek wine, are popular dinner choices. Breakfast and lunch are also served amid light-wood decor. Moderate.

TWIN FALLS AREA SHOPPING

The Black Sheep Gallery (830 Blue Lakes Boulevard North, Twin Falls; 208-733-9971) carries handmade crafts by 40 artisans, from clothing to furniture. **Larson Arts** (132 Main Avenue North, Twin Falls; 208-733-0813) offers paintings, sculptures, ceramics and jewelry by Rocky Mountain artists.

Art lovers won't want to miss **Snake River Pottery** (River Road, Bliss; 208-837-6527), Idaho's oldest ceramics studio, which exhibits wheel-turned earthenware and other works of art.

TWIN FALLS AREA NIGHTLIFE

To find out what's happening in the cultural realm in south-central Idaho, contact the **Magic Valley Arts Council** (401 2nd Street North, Twin Falls; 208-734-2787). The association represents the **Magic Valley Symphony**, which presents four seasonal concerts a year, and the **Magic Valley Community Concert Association**, which brings touring performers to local stages. Call its 24-hour Artsline (208-733-1000 ext. 2787) for recorded information on current events.

Several community theater groups perform regular schedules, most frequently at Twin Falls' finest stage, the **College of Southern Idaho Fine Arts Auditorium** (315 Falls Avenue West; 208-733-9554).

Country-and-western is the preferred genre for live music in Twin Falls. **Honker's Place** (121 4th Avenue South; 208-733-4613) has weekend bands, as does **The Windbreak** (1749 Kimberly Road; 208-734-3446). **The Sandpiper** (1309 Blue Lakes Boulevard North; 208-734-7000) features live acoustic music Wednesday through Saturday nights. For a good pint of beer, look no further than **Dunken's Draught House** (102 Main Avenue North; 208-733-8114), which boasts 21 handcrafted Northwest beers on tap.

For most folks in the Twin Falls area, a big night out means making the 50-mile drive to Jackpot, Nevada. The town's four casinos are all in a quarter-mile stretch of Route 93. **Cactus Pete's** (702-755-2321) is the largest, with 30,000 square feet of gaming tables, slot machines and other devices designed to separate gamblers from their nest eggs. The showroom here brings in a wide range of entertainers.

TWIN FALLS AREA PARKS

Shoshone Falls/Dierkes Lake Park—This city park offers two recreation areas in one: a ten-acre plot with picnic grounds beside a scenic overlook of the "Niagara of the West," and a larger area surrounding the small reservoir on a bench above the river. Shoshone Falls are at their fullest in the early spring, before irrigation water is diverted.

Facilities: Picnic tables, restrooms, boat ramp, hiking trails, playground, concession; day-use fee (summer only), $2; information, 208-736-2265. *Swimming:* Designated beach at Dierkes Lake. *Fishing:* At Dierkes Lake and in the Snake below the falls.

Getting there: From Blue Lakes Boulevard (Route 93) in Twin Falls, take Falls Avenue East three miles to 3300 East Road; then turn north and continue for two miles.

Sawtooth National Forest—Comprising six parcels from the City of Rocks to the summits of the Sawtooth Range, this 2.1-million-acre national forest includes several districts south and southeast of Twin Falls. Most frequently used trails and rivers are north and west of Ketchum, overlapping the Sawtooth National Recreation Area. There are 1100 lakes—the largest of which is Redfish Lake, south of Stanley—and 193 recreational sites.

Facilities: Picnic tables, restrooms, boat ramps, marina (at Redfish Lake), trails, four alpine ski areas; information, 208-737-3200. *Swimming:* Beaches at Redfish, Stanley and Alturas lakes. *Fishing:* Trout and steelhead in the upper Salmon and Big Wood rivers, some two dozen species in all.

Camping: There are 830 RV/tent sites (no hookups) plus 230 for tents only at 73 campgrounds; $3 to $8 per night. Most sites are open from June to October only.

Getting there: Most of the national forest is north (via Route 75) and west (via Forest Road 227) of Ketchum. In south-central Idaho, major parcels are the South Hills, south of Hansen via Route G3; the Albion Mountains, south of Albion via Route 77 and Howell Canyon or Cottley Road; and the Black Pine Mountains, between Routes 81 and 84 southeast of Malta.

City of Rocks National Reserve—Rock climbers from around the world visit this park to scale its lofty granite columns. Some of the formations overlook the desert landscape by 500 feet or more. Oregon Trail wagon ruts and pioneer graffiti can still be seen.

Facilities: Picnic tables, restrooms, hiking trails, visitors center; wheelchair accessible; information, 208-824-5519.

Camping: There are 100 primitive sites (no hookups); $6 per night. Water and firewood are limited; it's best to bring your own.

Getting there: From Burley, take Route 81 east nine miles to Declo, Route 77 south 20 miles via Albion to Connor, the Elba-Almo Highway southwest 16 miles to Almo, and City of Rocks Road west two miles to the reserve. Or take Route 27 south 20 miles from Burley to Oakley, the gravel Birch Creek Road southeast 14 miles, then Emery Canyon Road east four miles.

Sun Valley Area

East of the Sawtooth Range and north of the lava beds is the famed summer-winter resort of Sun Valley, established in the Wood River Valley in 1936. Besides its own attributes, Sun Valley is a great starting point to discover Craters of the Moon National Monument, whose eerie landscape trained moon-walking astronauts, as well as the Sawtooth National Recreation Area and the fishing and challenging whitewater of the upper Salmon River (see next section).

The story of **Sun Valley** began after the 1932 Winter Olympic Games in Lake Placid, New York. The Games made an enormous impression upon avid skier W. Averell Harriman, the future New York governor and international diplomat who was then chief executive of Union Pacific Railroad. Harriman beseeched Austrian Count Felix Schaffgotsch to search the West for a place to build a winter resort "of the same character as the Swiss and Austrian Alps." Schaffgotsch's exploration ended at the old mining and ranching center of Ketchum.

Within weeks, an ecstatic Harriman had purchased a 4000-acre ranch in the name of the Union Pacific and had begun building a handsome lodge. Then he enlisted marketing genius Steve Hannagan, who coined the name *Sun Valley,* encouraged the haute couture orientation of the complex and flew in a bevy of Hollywood stars to promote its official opening in 1936. Clark Gable, Errol Flynn and Claudette Colbert were among the film notables who came for the debut. You can see many of the luminaries' black-and-white photos today on the "Wall of Fame" in the **Sun Valley Lodge**. (The flood of celebrities has never ceased; today such notables as actors Arnold Schwarzenegger, Bruce Willis, Demi Moore, Jamie Lee Curtis and Mariel Hemingway call the valley home.)

With luxury accommodations, fine dining and entertainment in place, Harriman set about creating the world's finest ski area. He instructed Union Pacific engineers to construct a chairlift (modeled after a maritime banana hoist); when unveiled on Dollar Mountain, it became the prototype for what is now standard issue at all alpine resorts. Today, Sun Valley has 18 chairs on its two ski mountains. Fourteen are on Bald Mountain ("Baldy"), one of North America's largest ski mountains with a vertical drop of 3400 feet from its 9150-foot summit.

Union Pacific sold Sun Valley in 1964, but the resort has continued to expand, improve and modernize under its current owner, Little America. Today, **Sun Valley Resort** (208-622-4111) is like a European village with two elegant 1930s lodges (both fully renovated), hundreds of condominiums, multiple sports facilities, upscale restaurants and shops.

Sun Valley's four 18-hole golf courses and 85 tennis courts make it one of America's leading sports resorts. There's also swimming, hiking, horseback riding, bicycling and year-round skating, plus world-class trout fishing in nearby streams. On summer weekend evenings, the Sun Valley Lodge hosts world-class ice shows featuring many former Olympic medalists.

If the furs-and-pearls crowd are attracted to the venerable Sun Valley village and neighboring **Elkhorn Resort** (a smaller and younger clone two miles southeast), the slightly less affluent congregate in gentrified **Ketchum**, two miles west of Sun Valley village. Founded as a silver- and lead-mining camp around 1880, Ketchum evolved into the largest sheep-shipping center in the western United States in the early 20th century. That boom was in decline when along came Mr. Harriman and new prosperity.

Whereas Sun Valley has an alpine feel, downtown Ketchum is strictly western. Restaurants, bars, galleries and specialty shops are housed in late-19th-century brick buildings along Main Street (Route 75), while the ski lifts of Baldy rise to the west of town, just across the Big Wood River. Hotels and condominiums cluster around the two main access areas to the mountain at River Run and Warm Springs.

Hailey, 12 miles south of Ketchum, was the richest town in Idaho in the 1880s and the first to have a telephone exchange and electric lighting. It was the birthplace of poet Ezra Pound (1885–1972), one of the most important and controversial figures in 20th-century literature. Town history is recounted at the **Blaine County Museum** (North Main Street; 208-788-2809; admission). Modern history is being rewritten by resident movie star Bruce Willis *(Die Hard, Pulp Fiction),* who has bought up a half-dozen downtown buildings, including the Hailey theater and newspaper, with plans for a retail and entertainment complex.

Perhaps the Wood River Valley's most famous resident ever was Nobel Prize–winning author Ernest Hemingway (1899–1961). An ardent fly-fisherman, "Papa" Hemingway spent the last years of his globetrotting life in Ketchum. He is buried among four pine trees in the heart of **Ketchum Cemetery** (★) (Route 75 North at 10th Street East; 208-726-9201). The **Ernest Hemingway Memorial**—a bust and an epitaph—stands beside Trail Creek, a mile northeast of the Sun Valley Lodge via Trail Creek Road.

THE SNAKE RIVER PLAIN Hemingway's favorite fishing hole was Silver Creek, now protected by the preservationist Nature Conservancy as the **Silver Creek Preserve** (Kilpatrick Road, Picabo; 208-788-2203). A short jog off Route 20, 14 miles south of Hailey and another dozen miles east, this natural area has a catch-and-release policy for fly-fishermen pursuing its native trout. Canoeists and birdwatchers are other regular visitors.

Silver Creek is an easy detour for any traveler heading east on Route 20 along the northern edge of the volcanic Snake River Plain. The region's highlight is **Craters of the Moon National Monument** (Route 20/26/93, Arco; 208-527-3257; admission), 33 miles east of Silver Creek and 71 miles from Ketchum. Landscapes here are so alien that American astronauts have used it as a training ground. Volcanic eruptions and lava flows that began 15,000 years ago, and continued until only about 2000 years ago, created a 60-mile-long Great Rift Zone of fissure vents and spatter cones.

The park's seven-mile Loop Road is open from May to October. Plan at least two hours, leaving time for short walks. There are lava flows, volcanic vents, basaltic cinder cones, spatter cones, tree molds, lava-tube caverns and other weird and wonderful features.

Arco sits at the junction of five highways directly between Craters of the Moon (19 miles southwest) and the world's first nuclear power plant (18 miles southeast). That healthy glow in the faces of the townspeople is a reminder that Arco was the first city in the world to be lighted by nuclear-generated electricity.

Some scientists estimate the depth of the porous Snake River Plain lava to be a mile or more. On this sturdy foundation stands the **Idaho National Engineering Laboratory** (Route 20 West, Idaho Falls; 208-526-0050). Covering 890 square miles of desert, the facility is dedicated to peacetime uses of nuclear power. Fifty-two reactors (the most on the planet) have been built at INEL since it was established in 1949, and 13 are still in operation.

Visitors are welcomed at **Experimental Breeder Reactor No. 1** (EBR-I), a national historic landmark housed in a red-brick building off Route 20. In December 1951, this reactor was the world's first to produce electric power with atomic energy. It ceased operation in 1964, but today guides show off the inner sanctum, including four nuclear reactors (two of them nuclear-propulsion prototypes), turbines, a control room and a hot cell used to inspect and repair radioactive materials. Free tours are offered daily in summer.

One of North America's most powerful earthquakes of recent decades occurred along a fault line at the foot of Borah Peak on October 28, 1983. Registering 7.3 on the Richter scale, it dropped the valley floor five feet, raised Borah Peak's summit two feet and rattled cities up to 500 miles away. An escarpment 21 miles long and up to 14 feet high can be seen outside the **Earthquake Visitors Information Center** (Double Springs Pass Road, Mackay; 208-588-2274), a mile east of the highway.

SUN VALLEY AREA HOTELS

Because Sun Valley is a major resort, the average price of lodging in the area is higher than anywhere else in the northern Rockies. The best times to seek bargains are the spring and fall "shoulder seasons," between the skiers and the golfers, or even in the early (pre-Christmas) or late (April) ski seasons. Winter peak-season rates are the highest.

Heading the slate of luxury accommodations are the venerable **Sun Valley Lodge** and **The Sun Valley Inn** (1 Sun Valley Road, Sun Valley; 208-622-4111, 800-786-8259, fax 208-622-3700). The stately and historic four-story lodge, which opened in 1936, has 150 rooms; the two-story chalet-style inn, a year younger, has 112. Both have handsome, spacious rooms and suites with views of golf courses, ski runs and/or an outdoor ice skating rink. More than 100 apartment and condominium units with full kitchens are also available. Village facilities include 12 restaurants, four lounges and a plethora of posh shops. There are indoor and outdoor heated pools at each hotel, saunas, hot tubs, fitness rooms, a bowling alley and movie theater, trap and skeet shooting, golf courses and tennis courts. In winter, besides alpine skiing, there's a nordic center and sleigh rides. Moderate to ultra-deluxe.

Two miles south of Sun Valley Village, you'll find the **Radisson Sun Valley Resort** (Elkhorn Road, Sun Valley; 208-622-4511, 800-355-4676, fax 208-

622-3261) anchoring modern, European-style Elkhorn Village. Included in this four-story hotel's 220 rooms are 46 two-bedroom and ten three-bedroom suites. The resort has five restaurants, cocktail lounges and a nightclub; four swimming pools, jacuzzis, a sauna, a steam room and a workout room; and facilities for golf, tennis, bicycling, horseback riding, alpine and nordic skiing and more. Moderate to ultra-deluxe.

Several charming bed-and-breakfast inns are located in and around Ketchum. Among the most unforgettable is the **Idaho Country Inn** (134 Latigo Lane, Ketchum; 208-726-1019, fax 208-726-5039), built atop Saddle Hill of stone and logs. The ten guest rooms are individually themed to Idaho history, wildlife or outdoor sport. A river-rock fireplace faces a living room and library, and there's a ski-storage area and hot tub. Deluxe.

Halfway between downtown Ketchum and Baldy's Warm Springs village is the **Heidelberg Inn** (1908 Warm Springs Road, Ketchum; 208-726-5361, 800-284-4863, fax 208-726-2084). A pleasant motel with a Tyrolean exterior, it has 30 rooms with microwave ovens, refrigerators and down comforters. Kitchen and fireplace units are available. There's a swimming pool, hot tub, sauna, barbecue area and laundry. Moderate.

Some of the oldest accommodations are the least expensive. Take, for example, **The Ketchum Korral** (310 Main Street South, Ketchum; 208-726-3510, 800-657-2657, fax 208-726-5287). Eight historic log cabins have stone fireplaces, full kitchens, private patios and bathrooms; nine more-modern motel units retain similar ambience. The spacious grounds, close to downtown, include a volleyball area and a 14-person hot tub. Low moderate.

If a 12-mile commute isn't a problem, look in Hailey for the best lodging rates in the Sun Valley area. The two-story **Airport Inn** (820 4th Avenue South, Hailey; 208-788-2477, fax 208-788-3195), a block off Route 75 at Cedar Street, has 29 plain but clean and comfortable rooms. Some kitchen units and fireplace suites are available. There's an outdoor hot tub, a coin laundry and bicycle rentals. Low moderate.

SUN VALLEY AREA RESTAURANTS

Every European-style ski resort must have its **Konditorei** (Sun Valley Village Mall, Sun Valley; 208-622-2235). Breakfast pastries, open-faced lunch sandwiches and light dinners, as well as ice-cream specialties, are served in an Austrian-coffeehouse atmosphere. Low moderate.

The top-of-the-line choice is the **Lodge Dining Room** (1 Sun Valley Road, Sun Valley; 208-622-2150), with elegant French and Continental cuisine served by tuxedoed waiters beneath crystal chandeliers at the historic Sun Valley Lodge. Orchestral combos nightly play music for dancing at the foot of a marble staircase. Reservations are requested for dinner but are not accepted for the outstanding Sunday buffet brunch. Ultra-deluxe.

In winter, there's no more charming evening out than to take a horse-drawn sleigh to the **Trail Creek Cabin** (Trail Creek Road, Sun Valley; 208-622-2135). Book two days in advance for the trip to this rustic cabin in the woods. A roaring fire and hearty homemade soup greet guests; a robust four-course dinner—complete with accordion music—follows. You can also sleigh or cross-country ski to the cabin for lunch. Deluxe.

In Ketchum, **The Kneadery** (260 Leadville Avenue North; 208-726-9462) is worth a visit just to see the life-size animal carvings ("The Ketchum Zoo") and lovely flower arrangements on its deck. But do plan to eat here. The pleasant, casual restaurant serves omelettes for breakfast and healthy soups and salads at lunch. Budget.

Local diners have voted **The Sawtooth Club** (209 Main Street North, Ketchum; 208-726-5233) the valley's most popular restaurant for three years running. The creative cuisine, much of it prepared on a mesquite grill, varies from the expected (steaks, fresh seafood) to the serendipitous (chicken Senegalese in an apple brandy curry, Cajun shellfish pasta). A big stone fireplace anchors the ground-floor lounge. Moderate.

If you're a lover of hot and spicy foods, look no further than **China Pepper** (511 Leadville Avenue North, Ketchum; 208-726-0959). Szechuan, Hunan and Thai specialties are featured here, including green papaya salad, tiger rolls (with crab and black-tiger prawns in a *chile serrano* dip) and some unusual pork, seafood and vegetarian dishes. Moderate.

Desperate for familiar food? The **Pioneer Saloon** (308 Main Street North, Ketchum; 208-726-3139) is the place for steaks, prime rib and nightly fish specials. One of Ketchum's oldest businesses (and looking like it), the Pioneer also boasts shrimp teriyaki, pork chops and a classic cheeseburger. Moderate.

Innovative "pub grub" is the claim of **The Cafe at the Brewery** (202 North Main Street, Hailey; 208-788-0805) in the Sun Valley Brewing Co. building. Sure, you'll get the standard steaks and chops, but how about garlic-rosemary sausage? homemade chicken pot pie? roasted-vegetable quesadillas? The soups, pizzas and homemade desserts are excellent. Budget to moderate.

SUN VALLEY AREA SHOPPING

Sun Valley and Ketchum have become important centers for art collectors. There are at least two dozen fine-art galleries in Ketchum and a couple more in Sun Valley Village. A good way to see a wide variety is to join a guided tour offered by the **Sun Valley Gallery Association** (208-726-2602).

You might want to start at the **Sun Valley Center for the Arts and Humanities** (620 Sun Valley Road East, Ketchum; 208-726-9491) for a good sampling of contemporary regional artists. The work of Jane Wooster Scott, a nationally renowned modern folk artist who lives locally, is prominently displayed at the **Sun Valley Art Gallery** (Sun Valley Village Mall, Sun Valley; 208-622-2269). The **Valley Artists Guild Gallery** (4th Street East and Main Street North, Ketchum; 208-726-0955) is an artisans' cooperative in Town Square.

Idahoans are represented in many other major galleries in Ketchum, including the **Stonington Gallery** (220 East Avenue North; 208-726-4826), **Friesen Gallery** (511 Leadville Avenue North; 208-726-4174) and **Kneeland Gallery** (271 1st Avenue North; 208-726-5512).

Galleries aside, the best places to browse and buy in the Sun Valley area may be the **Sun Valley Village Mall**, near the lodges; **Giacobbi Square** (4th Avenue East and Leadville Avenue North, Ketchum), the area's largest indoor mall; and **Main Street North** in downtown Ketchum.

There are some excellent bookshops. In Ketchum, the **Main Street Bookcafe** (211 Main Street North; 208-726-3700) and **Chapter One** (191 Main Street North; 208-726-5425) combine shelf space with espresso bars; the **Different Drummer** (120 Main Street North; 208-788-4403) has a small café. At the resort village is **Ex Libris** (Sun Valley Village Mall, Sun Valley; 208-622-8174). Guidebooks, maps and travel accessories can be purchased at the **Travel Smart Shoppe** (601 Sun Valley Road East, Ketchum; 208-726-4884).

SUN VALLEY AREA NIGHTLIFE

Like any major resort, Sun Valley has a lively evening scene. And it's far from restricted to bar activities.

The weekly **Sun Valley Ice Shows** (208-622-2231) fill the 600-seat Sun Valley Lodge Terrace to capacity from mid-June to mid-September. The world's best skaters—including Scott Hamilton, Brian Boitano, Oksana Baiul, Katarina Witt, Nancy Kerrigan and Kristi Yamaguchi—perform under starry skies each Saturday night. Tickets include a buffet dinner; book well in advance.

The clearinghouse for Wood River Valley culture is the **Sun Valley Center for the Arts and Humanities** (620 Sun Valley Road East, Ketchum; 208-726-9491), which sponsors a series of year-round events.

The 42-member **Sun Valley Summer Symphony** (208-622-5607) performs a series of 12 free outdoor concerts in a large tent at the Sun Valley Lodge Esplanade from the first through the third weekend of August.

The **Sun Valley Repertory Company** (208-726-3706) offers summer and winter stage seasons at the nexStage Theatre (120 Main Street South, Ketchum). A typical summer season features a Shakespearean tragedy and a trio of 20th-century comedies, performed from late June to mid-September. A second thespian group, the **Laughing Stock Theatre Company** (208-726-3576), offers one production each in fall, winter and spring.

For live music, the **Duchin Lounge** at the Sun Valley Lodge (1 Sun Valley Road, Sun Valley; 208-622-2145) has light jazz trios performing traditional dance music nightly during the peak summer and winter seasons.

If your ear is more attuned to rock, blues and reggae, there's plenty to suit you in Ketchum. **Whiskey Jacques** (209 Main Street North; 208-726-5297) has live music and dancing Wednesday through Sunday nights. **X's Taphouse and Brew Pub** (271 Main Street North; 208-726-2267) presents local rock Friday through Sunday, while **Buckwheat's** (160 5th Street West; 208-726-2887) focuses on alternative rock. A cover may be charged depending upon entertainment. For country-and-western, try **Slavey's Saloon** (Main Street North and Sun Valley Road East; 208-726-3852), where bands play weekends.

SUN VALLEY AREA PARKS

Craters of the Moon National Monument—Fifteen thousand years of volcanic history created this 83-square-mile landscape of lava flows and cinder cones, fissure vents and tubelike caverns on the northern fringe of the Snake River Plain. Some geologists predict the earth here will erupt again; others maintain that the subterranean hot spot has moved east to Yellowstone National Park. Ranger-led walks and evening programs begin from the visitors center.

Facilities: Picnic tables, restrooms, hiking and cross-country ski trails (one wheelchair accessible), visitors center; day-use fee, $4; information, 208-527-3257 or 208-532-1412.

Camping: There are 40 RV/tent sites (no hookups) plus ten for tents only; $10 per night. Open from late May to early October.

Getting there: The park entrance is 19 miles southwest of Arco and 71 miles southeast of Sun Valley, on the south side of Route 20/26/93.

The Sawtooths and Upper Salmon

North of Sun Valley, Routes 75 and 93 meander through some of Idaho's wildest areas, places so isolated they've earned nicknames like "America's Alps" and "The River of No Return."

The Sawtooth National Recreation Area, whose craggy "alps" exceed 10,000 feet, covers 1180 square miles beginning just eight miles north of Ketchum. The Salmon River, renowned worldwide for its remote trout fishing and whitewater rafting, originates in the Sawtooth before rushing nearly 425 miles to the Snake River.

The **Sawtooth National Recreation Area** (SNRA) encompasses the highest peaks of Idaho's central Rockies—the striking Sawtooth, White Cloud and Boulder ranges—and more than 300 alpine lakes. It contains the headwaters not only of the Salmon but also of the Big Wood, Boise and Payette rivers. Hundreds of campsites, several secluded guest ranches and a handful of motels, cabin complexes and small resort lodges are within the recreation area. The 339-square-mile **Sawtooth Wilderness Area**, which adjoins it to the west, provides a more primitive experience for backpackers and horse packers.

Swing by the **SNRA Visitors Center** (Route 75 North, Ketchum; 208-726-7672) or the U.S. Forest Service's **Ketchum Ranger District Office** (206 Sun Valley Road, Ketchum; 208-622-5371) to pick up a free audio cassette (★) (and a tape player if your vehicle doesn't have one) describing the 61-mile drive from Ketchum to Stanley. You can return the loaned items at the Redfish Lake or Stanley ranger stations.

Thirty miles from Ketchum, the drive takes you over the 8701-foot **Galena Summit**, from which the Big Wood River begins. The summit offers impressive views of the Sawtooth and White Cloud ranges and the headwaters of the Salmon River between them.

As Route 75 switchbacks down to the Sawtooth Valley at about 7000 feet elevation, it skirts a series of opaline mountain lakes to its west. Largest are **Alturas Lake** (Forest Road 205), 24 miles south of Stanley (41 miles north of Ketchum), and **Redfish Lake** (Forest Road 214), seven miles south of Stanley. Alturas Lake is popular with swimmers, sailors and anglers.

Redfish Lake is the crown jewel of the Sawtooth. Some 300 feet deep, nestled at the foot of craggy 10,000-foot mountains and skirted by sandy beaches, it's a major recreation center offering swimming, boating, waterskiing, fishing, hiking and horseback riding. A **Forest Service visitors center** (Redfish Lake Road, Stanley; 208-774-3376) includes exhibits and audio-visual displays; lake tours begin from the **Redfish Lake Lodge marina** (Redfish Lake Road, Stanley; 208-774-3536).

In the heart of the SNRA is the village of **Stanley**, where Route 21 from Boise (135 miles southwest) joins Route 75 from Ketchum and Salmon. An all-seasons outfitting center with an Old West facade, Stanley still has the same dirt roads and log cabins it must have had in the 1890s, when it was settled. The **Stanley Museum** (Route 75; 208-774-3517), in the 1934 Valley Creek Ranger Station a half-mile north of the Route 21 junction, tells the story of historic logging and mining in photographs and artifacts.

SALMON RIVER COUNTRY Between its source in the high Sawtooth and its mid-river outfitting center at the town of Salmon—the largest community in this part of Idaho—the Salmon River courses northeastward about 150 miles through the SNRA and the Challis and Salmon national forests. It curves sharply west at North Fork, 20 miles north of Salmon, and proceeds about 250 miles more, dividing Idaho neatly in two and joining the Snake River just south of the Washington-Oregon border. Nicknamed "The River of No Return" because no boat was able to travel upriver until after World War II, the Salmon drains 14,000 square miles of central Idaho, more than any river in any single state outside of Alaska.

Route 75 follows the Salmon 55 miles east from Stanley to Challis. **Sunbeam**, a hot-springs hamlet 13 miles from Stanley, offers road access to the **Land of the Yankee Fork Historic Area**. A century ago, the Yankee Fork of the Salmon River was favored by placer gold miners. If you follow the Custer Motorway, a 36-mile gravel road through the **Challis National Forest** (208-879-2285), from Sunbeam to Challis, you'll see communities and artifacts from that rich mining past. Four-wheel-drive is recommended; high-clearance vehicles are essential.

A highlight, at the mouth of Jordan Creek eight miles from Sunbeam, is the **Yankee Fork Gold Dredge** (Custer Motorway, Custer; admission), just beyond the ghost-town site of Bonanza. From 1940 to 1953 the Snake River Mining Company operated this unwieldy-looking dredge that dug gravel from the Yankee Fork riverbank, separated the gold out and spewed tailings behind. Modern environmentalism would have banned it. Measuring 112 feet long and weighing 988 tons, the diesel-powered dredge recovered more than $1 million in gold and silver. It has been restored as a museum and is open for tours from July 1 through Labor Day.

Custer, two miles farther, still has a few buildings from the 1880s and 1890s, including the **Custer Museum** (208-838-2201) in a one-room schoolhouse. Mining equipment, gambling tables and old weapons are displayed in summer. You can pan for gold or walk a self-guided trail past the General Custer stamp mill, which processed $12 million in gold between 1881 and 1904. A general store and cemetery are worth visits.

The **Land of the Yankee Fork Historic Area Interpretive Center** (Route 75 South, Challis; 208-879-5244), open year-round, is located at the junction of Route 93 just south of Challis. A 60-foot cliff that rises behind the building was a **Shoshone Indian Buffalo Jump** used from the 13th to 19th centuries to slaughter bison, which were herded off the precipice. Founded in 1878 as a supply center for area miners, **Challis** has thrived as a ranching town.

Route 93 follows the banks of the main Salmon River for 60 miles from Challis to Salmon. Although its economy is based on timber and cattle ranching, **Salmon** is regarded far and wide as the "whitewater capital of the world." The Lemhi River joins the Salmon River here, and the number of rafting, fishing and horse-packing outfitters based in the town are prominent reminders that you're at the edge of the wilderness.

That wilderness is the **Frank Church–River of No Return Wilderness**, the largest single wilderness area in the lower 48 states, located about 25 miles west as the eagle flies. (See Chapter Nine, "Southwestern Idaho Rockies.") To get there from Salmon, you must first pass through the **Salmon National Forest** (208-756-2215), which surrounds the town on all sides.

A trip down the main Salmon or its remote Middle Fork is not for the timorous. Deer, elk, black bear, mountain goats and wolves are among the hundreds of species that thrive in the rugged mountains and grassy pine meadows along the river. If you look closely in the deep river gorges, you'll see Native American bivouacs containing cave paintings and petroglyphs as old as 8000 years.

THE SAWTOOTHS AND UPPER SALMON HOTELS

In the heart of the Sawtooth National Recreation Area is the **Idaho Rocky Mountain Ranch** (Route 75, Stanley; 208-774-3544), a 1000-acre spread founded in 1930 as a private club for wealthy easterners nine miles south of Stanley. Today, all nine log cabins (with rock fireplaces) and four cozy lodge rooms welcome summer guests. All units have handcrafted pine furniture and private baths. Breakfasts and full dinners are served in the lodge from June 1 to September 15. Moderate to deluxe.

The **Mountain Village Resort** (Route 21 at Route 75, Stanley; 208-774-3661, 800-843-5475, fax 208-774-3761) is located at the main intersection of Stanley near the Salmon River and is one of the few year-round lodgings in the Sawtooth area. Sixty renovated log-style motel rooms have private baths; there are some kitchen units. Within the complex are a restaurant and a natural hot-springs tub. Low moderate.

The **Twin Peaks Ranch** (Route 93 South, Salmon; 208-894-2290, 800-659-4899, fax 208-894-2429), overlooking the Salmon River some 20 miles south of Salmon, has nothing to do with the weird TV series of the same name. Built in 1923 by the renowned du Pont family, it features a stately lodge and 13 rustic one- to three-bedroom cabins beside an old barn as well as a large swimming pool. Deluxe.

THE SAWTOOTHS AND UPPER SALMON RESTAURANTS

The **Stanley Kasino Club** (21 Ace of Diamonds Avenue, Stanley; 208-774-3516) is a year-round can't-miss on the dirt main street of this Sawtooth mountain town. The rustic restaurant offers a salad bar, nightly pasta specials and a menu of beef, lamb, pork, poultry and fresh seafood when it's available. Moderate.

In Challis, midway between Stanley and Salmon, the **Challis House & Y-Inn Cafe** (Main Street; 208-879-4426) serves three meals a day, 362 days a year. The café serves everything from apple dumplings to steaks in a country atmosphere amid polished log walls. The Challis House, open for dinner Friday and Saturday, boasts a prime-rib buffet and salad bar. Budget to moderate.

Fishermen and rafters dive into the steak-and-seafood fare of the **Shady Nook Restaurant** (Route 93; 208-756-4182), just north of downtown Salmon. Those meek of heart may not want to study the restaurant's big-game trophy collection too closely before cutting into their prime rib. Moderate.

THE SAWTOOTHS AND UPPER SALMON PARKS

Sawtooth National Recreation Area (SNRA) and Wilderness—Spread across three-quarters of a million acres and three national forests—the Sawtooth, Challis and Boise—the SNRA is a year-round playground for mountain recreation lovers. No vehicular travel is permitted on the trails of the Sawtooth Wilderness, which borders the SNRA on its west and includes the craggy and dramatic summit of the Sawtooth Range.

Facilities: Picnic tables, restrooms, boat ramps, marina, trails, visitors center; information, 208-726-7672. *Swimming:* Beaches at Redfish and Alturas lakes. *Fishing:* Outstanding trout and steelhead fishing in the Salmon, Big Wood, Boise and South Fork of the Payette rivers; trout and kokanee in major lakes.

Camping: There are 492 RV/tent sites (no hookups) at 36 developed campgrounds; $6 to $8 per night. Eight campgrounds are available by reservation (800-280-2267). Most sites are open from June to October only.

Getting there: The national recreation area is focused around the town of Stanley. Best access to the wilderness is from Redfish Lake, seven miles south of Stanley, or from Grandjean, 44 miles west of Stanley.

Land of the Yankee Fork Historic Area—A tribute to Idaho's mining heritage created for the state's 1990 centennial, this district—along the Yankee Fork of the Salmon River—preserves the ghost towns of Bonanza and Custer and the Yankee Fork Gold Dredge, among other historical sites.

Facilities: Picnic tables, restrooms, trails, visitors center; information, 208-879-5244. *Fishing:* Trout in the Yankee Fork.

Camping: There are 47 RV/tent sites (no hookups) at six campgrounds; $6 per night.

Getting there: From Challis, take Garden Creek Road west into the Custer Motorway. From Sunbeam (13 miles east of Stanley and 42 miles southwest of Challis on Route 75), take the Custer Motorway (Yankee Fork Road) north eight miles to Bonanza and ten miles to Custer; then continue to Challis.

Challis National Forest—Covering two and a half million acres of central Idaho from the Middle Fork of the Salmon River to the Lost River Sinks, the Challis forest includes the state's tallest mountain, Borah Peak. It contains more than 1600 miles of trails in the Salmon River, Pioneer, Lost River and Lemhi ranges of the Rockies, as well as the Land of the Yankee Fork Historic Area and a large part of the Frank Church–River of No Return Wilderness.

Facilities: Picnic tables, restrooms, boat ramps, trails; information, 208-879-2285. *Swimming:* At Mosquito Flat Reservoir west of Challis and other small mountain lakes. *Fishing:* Excellent trout fishing in streams and lakes, with an important fall steelhead run in the Middle Fork of the Salmon.

Camping: There are 252 RV/tent sites (no hookups), plus 44 for tents only, at 28 campgrounds; $4 to $6 per night. Five wilderness cabins near Mackay and one near Clayton are open from December to April, lodging four to six people at $15 to $30 per night.

Getting there: Forest roads extend north and west off Routes 75 and 21 from Challis and Stanley, east and west off Route 93 between Challis and Mackay.

Salmon National Forest—Comprising 1.8 million acres of east-central Idaho from the Frank Church–River of No Return Wilderness to the Bitterroot Range along the Montana border, this national forest is one of Idaho's least developed. The emphasis is on Salmon River boating and rafting, fishing and big-game hunting, backcountry hiking and horseback riding (over 1200 miles of trails) and, in winter, cross-country skiing and snowmobiling.

Facilities: Picnic tables, restrooms, boat ramps, trails; information, 208-756-2215. *Swimming:* No designated beaches. *Fishing:* The Middle Fork and main Salmon rivers have renowned steelhead and salmon runs; trout thrive in streams and lakes.

Camping: There are 167 RV/tent sites (no hookups), plus 15 for tents only, at 17 campgrounds; $4 to $6 per night. Four A-frame cabins, open year-round for hikers, horse riders and snowmobilers, accommodate six; $15 per night.

Getting there: A network of roads extends west from Route 93 north and south of Salmon; principal among them are the Salmon River Road (Forest Road 030) from North Fork, 21 miles north, and Moccasin Creek Road (Forest Road 021) from Williams Creek, five miles south. A few roads extend off Route 28 southeast of Salmon.

Pocatello Area

Idaho's second-largest city, Pocatello is a transportation hub in the heart of a rich agricultural and phosphate-mining region. Located on the Portneuf River ten miles upstream from American Falls Reservoir, a water-sports mecca on the Snake River, the city of 46,000 is close to the Fort Hall Indian Reservation, the geological wonders of Massacre Rocks State Park and the Great Rift National Landmark, and the expansive potato fields near Blackfoot.

Named for a Shoshone chief who granted the Union Pacific a right-of-way through the Fort Hall reservation, Pocatello in the early 20th century was America's largest rail center west of the Mississippi River. The **Oregon Short Line Depot** (Union Pacific Avenue at Bonneville Street), a three-story station dedicated in 1915 by former U.S. President William Howard Taft, is in the heart of its 12-square-block **Downtown Historic District**. Today the hotel is closed but restoration is planned. The 1902 **Stanrod Mansion** (648 North Garfield Street; 208-234-6184) is regarded as the finest Victorian building in Idaho. Stop by the **Greater Pocatello Chamber of Commerce** (343 West Center Street; 208-233-1525) for walking-tour maps and other information.

East of downtown is **Idaho State University** (ISU) (741 South 7th Avenue; 208-236-0211). On campus, the **Idaho Museum of Natural History** (Hutchinson Quadrangle; 208-236-3168) has fine exhibits on fossil and archaeological prehistory, including the Wah'-Muza site on the Fort Hall reservation. There are also displays on threatened and endangered animal and plant species, a children's discovery area and a gift shop.

Pocatello's "don't-miss" attraction is **Ross Park** (Avenue of the Chiefs; 208-234-6232). Within this urban oasis are the Bannock County Historical Museum; the Fort Hall Replica; a re-created 19th-century Pocatello townsite; a Union Pacific display; the **Ross Park Zoo** (208-234-6196; admission), specializing in creatures native to the northern Rockies; a rose garden and bandstand; and a swimming pool, water slide, picnic tables, ball fields and volleyball courts. It's on the south side of the city between 2nd and 4th avenues.

Bannock County Historical Museum (★) (Ross Park; 208-233-0434; admission) is an outstanding, well-presented small museum with exhibits spanning prehistory to modern times. Of unusual interest is the muralized Donor Wall, an illustrated county history. The museum is open daily in summer, closed Sunday and Monday the rest of the year.

The nearby **Fort Hall Replica** (Ross Park; 208-234-6233; admission) is a full-scale historic reconstruction of the Portneuf River trading post that served Oregon Trail travelers from 1843 to 1865. Created from original Hudson's Bay Company plans, it includes a guardhouse, blacksmith shop, tack shop, living quarters and museum with pioneer, military and Native American artifacts. Open from April through September.

NORTH AND WEST OF POCATELLO The original site of Fort Hall is 20 miles north of Ross Park on the **Fort Hall Indian Reservation** (Route 91, Fort Hall; 208-237-9791). A small obelisk marks the site beside Oregon Trail ruts on Sheepskin Road about six miles west of Route 91 at Spring Creek; permission to visit must be obtained from Shoshone-Bannock officials. A tribal guide may take you to the **Wah'-Muza** site, where ISU archaeologists have uncovered three house floors, a large midden and numerous fire hearths that indicate four periods of occupation dating back 2000 years.

The 820-square-mile reservation, created in 1869, is home to 3000 Shoshone-Bannocks. Once separate tribes with similar seminomadic cultures but different languages, Shoshones and Bannocks were forced into alliance by white settlement. Intermarriage predictably followed. Today they have a phosphate mine and extensive Snake River fishing rights; their tribal festival and rodeo each August is one of the West's major native celebrations. The small but interesting **Shoshone-Bannock Tribal Museum** (Gay Mine Road, Fort Hall; 208-237-9791) is west of Route 15 Exit 80.

The drive to Fort Hall is a good beginning for a 125-mile daytrip loop around American Falls Reservoir and back to Pocatello. Continue up Route 15 to Blackfoot. Cross the Snake River and take secondary Route 39 through potato country to the town of American Falls. After a side trip to Massacre Rocks State Park, return to Pocatello via Route 86.

Blackfoot, halfway between Pocatello and Idaho Falls, is in the heart of the state's leading potato region. Eastern Idaho's high elevation, its light and moist volcanic soil, its hot days and cool nights are ideal for the russet Burbank potato. More than 300,000 acres are devoted to this tuber, whose yellow flowers and viney leaves are especially evident in late spring and early summer. Digging takes place in autumn.

Idaho's World Potato Exposition (★) (130 Northwest Main Street, Blackfoot; 208-785-2517) is located in a 1913 train depot. Museum exhibits and videos place the Idaho potato in international context with information on its history, growth, production and processing, nutritional value, economic importance and more. There's a farm machinery display and a gift shop/café with "free baked 'taters for out-of-staters." Open from May through September; call for winter hours.

From Blackfoot, follow Route 39 west through the farming communities of Rockford, Pingree and Springfield. This region owes its agricultural prowess to 86 miles of canals emanating from the Snake River and American Falls Reservoir.

A side trip leads to the captivating volcanic terrain of the **Great Rift National Landmark**, the longest-exposed rift in North America, and its **Crystal Ice Cave** (★) (Crystal Ice Cave Road, American Falls; 208-236-6860; admission). A short, steep path drops 150 feet to the opening of the cave, whose ice formations are created by water trickling through a fissure into a constant 31°F temperature. Just south of the cave's parking lot is the **King's Bowl**, a dramatic crater—150 feet deep and 100 feet across—formed by a violent explosion about 2100 years ago.

The Great Rift, on Bureau of Land Management public lands, extends north to Craters of the Moon National Monument. To reach it, leave Route 39 seven miles south of Aberdeen or five miles north of American Falls, taking North Pleasant Valley Road west. After 11 miles, follow signs north on Winter Road for four miles, then west again another 13 miles on a gravel BLM road.

The Bureau of Reclamation's 1927 **American Falls Dam** (Route 39, American Falls; 208-226-2434), on the Snake River, created **American Falls Reservoir** for irrigation storage and obliterated the 50-foot falls for which it is named. The current $46 million dam, built in 1976 by the Idaho Power Company, is 86 feet high and 2900 feet long. Free tours are offered weekday afternoons.

There are several day-use parks along the shore of American Falls Reservoir, the largest reservoir on the Snake with 935 square miles of water surface when full. Most of the parks are near the town of **American Falls**, a potato processing and shipping center that was moved to its present site when the reservoir was created.

At **Massacre Rocks State Park** (3592 North Park Lane, American Falls; 208-548-2672; admission), 11 miles west of American Falls, the Oregon Trail passed through a break in the high rock walls lining the Snake River. A visitors center has displays and interpretive programs on Shoshone and pioneer history, geology and the area's prolific plant and animal life. Three miles downstream is 20-foot-high **Register Rock**, where pioneers carved their names or scrawled them in axle grease. Look for the Indian's head carving made in 1866 by J. J. Hansen, then seven years old. He came back in 1913 as a 54-year-old sculptor and dated the rock again.

POCATELLO AREA HOTELS

Of the few bed-and-breakfast homes in southeastern Idaho, **The Liberty Inn** (404 South Garfield Street; 208-232-3825) in Pocatello is particularly charming. Dating from 1893 and displaying original Victorian furnishings, it has four guest rooms with private baths. Coffee and gourmet breakfasts are delivered to the rooms each morning. The inn is a few blocks' walk from the historic district. Low moderate.

The **Sundial Inn** (835 South 5th Avenue; 208-233-0451, 800-377-0451) suits budget watchers. Located across the street from the Idaho State University campus, the two-story motel has 53 nicely appointed guest rooms, all with private baths. A coffee shop is adjacent.

The **Best Western Cottontree Inn** (1415 Bench Road; 208-237-7650, 800-662-6886, fax 208-238-1355) is a three-story property with 147 spacious rooms just off Route 15. Rooms have standard furnishings and about 40 rooms have kitchens, though no utensils are provided. The motel includes a restaurant and lounge, a coin laundry, an indoor pool, a whirlpool, tennis and racquetball courts and a playground for the kids (who stay free). Moderate.

POCATELLO AREA RESTAURANTS

Eduardo's Mexican Restaurant (612 Yellowstone Avenue, Pocatello; 208-233-9440) is as friendly a place as you'll find anywhere. Even the host greets you as a long-lost "amigo." The decor is casual and the fare traditional—generous portions of burritos, enchiladas, chimichangas and the like. Budget.

The Continental Bistro (140 South Main Street; 208-233-4433) is a pleasant addition to Pocatello's historic district: French and northern Italian cooking and European service in a spacious room that features light jazz music for atmosphere. There's outdoor dining in the summer and as weather permits. A popular and upbeat lounge adjoins. Moderate.

Remo's (160 West Cedar Street, Pocatello; 208-233-1710) is a great place to take the family or to have a pleasant meal in garden surroundings on the outdoor patio in summer. Specializing in steaks, prime rib and fresh fish, Remo's is also noted for its outstanding Italian cuisine, including ravioli and fettuccine, chicken cacciatore and veal piccata. The wine list is the most extensive in southeastern Idaho. Moderate.

One of Pocatello's best is at the airport, six miles west of town. The **Blue Ribbon Restaurant** (Pocatello Airport; 208-233-8002) serves up steak, seafood and chicken specialties in a country atmosphere, complete with fresh flowers and gurgling fountains. Try the Idaho potato bread or a flambéed dessert. There's a children's menu and a full lounge. Moderate.

The world's potato capital isn't the place you'd expect to find good Chinese-American food, but the **Cathay Cafe** (45 Northwest Main Street, Blackfoot; 208-785-1750) has been serving up hefty portions of chop suey and egg foo yung to eastern Idahoans since 1951. An all-you-can-eat smorgasbord is offered on Thursdays and Sundays. There's a full lounge, too. Low moderate.

POCATELLO AREA SHOPPING

Worth a visit is **Chocolate Soup** (150 South Main Street, Pocatello; 208-233-4041), whose custom-design gift baskets are a work of art in themselves.

Art lovers in Pocatello can check out the **Cinnamon Tree Collectible Gallery** (9th Avenue and Oak Street; 208-232-6371), the **Pocatello Art Center** (401½ North Main Street; 208-232-0970) and the **Tara-James Gallery** (200 South Main Street; 208-232-2925).

Pocatello bookstores of note include **Walrus & Carpenter Books** (121 South Main Street; 208-233-0821) and the **Idaho State University Bookstore** (Red Hill Road and South 8th Avenue; 208-236-3237).

POCATELLO AREA NIGHTLIFE

Cultural life in Pocatello revolves around Idaho State University (ISU) (741 South 7th Avenue; 208-236-0211). The **ISU Department of Music** (208-236-3636) has regular student and faculty performances at Goranson Hall. The **Idaho State Civic Symphony** (208-236-3479) performs an October-to-May schedule in the same facility. **Theatre ISU** (208-236-3595) offers six plays—two each in the fall, winter and spring—at Frazier Hall.

For more information about performing arts in Pocatello, contact the **Pocatello Arts Council** (208-234-6292).

Rock-music enthusiasts in Pocatello are served by **The Network** (1435 North Main Street; 208-234-7054), which sometimes books touring national acts, and **The First National Bar** (232 West Center Street; 208-233-1516), which presents bands Thursday through Saturday evenings in an old bank building in the historic district. The college crowd gathers at the **Bull & Bear** (320 West Center Street; 208-232-2814), while sports fans love **Dudley's Sports Bar & Grill** (150 South Arthur Street; 208-238-3539).

Greater Pocatello claims Idaho's largest country-and-western nightclub: **The Green Triangle** (4010 Yellowstone Avenue, Chubbuck; 208-237-0354). The club has music nightly, classes in western swing and line dancing, even a mechanical bull. **Bobby Joe's Five Mile Inn** (4828 Yellowstone Avenue, Chubbuck; 208-237-9950) also has live country-and-western music and dancing most nights.

POCATELLO AREA PARKS

Willow Bay Recreation Area—The largest park on American Falls Reservoir, Willow Bay is popular for its fishing access and its sandy beach, where sailboats and paddleboats can be rented and board-sailing lessons are offered. There's also a lakeview café and other facilities.

Facilities: Picnic tables, restrooms, boat ramps, playground, concessions; information, 208-226-2688. *Swimming:* Lifeguards keep an eye on the beach in summer. *Fishing:* American Falls Reservoir has an outstanding rainbow trout fishery and numerous other species.

Camping: There are 26 RV/tent sites (all with hookups), plus an undeveloped overflow area; $8 to $13 per night, depending upon hookups required. Open from April through October; reservations accepted.

Getting there: From the town of American Falls, take Marina Road north two miles across Route 39.

Massacre Rocks State Park—This scenic 1000-acre park on the Snake River was well known to mid-19th-century travelers on the Oregon Trail, who feared attack by hostile Shoshones from the high rock walls that line the river. Ten pioneers were ambushed and killed in 1862; otherwise, the location was peaceful. Look for wagon ruts and for migrants' names scrawled on 20-foot-high Register Rock, three miles downstream from the visitors center. Unusual geology (it was gouged by the prehistoric Bonneville Flood), a prolific natural history (300 species of desert plants, more than 200 kinds of birds), hiking, water sports and an interpretive program attract many visitors.

Facilities: Picnic areas, restrooms, boat ramp, hiking trails; visitors center; day-use fee, $2; information, 208-548-2672. *Swimming:* None designated. *Fishing:* Good trout fishing in the Snake River.

Camping: There are 52 RV/tent sites (all with hookups); $9 to $12 per night in summer, $6 to $9 in winter, depending upon hookups required.

Getting there: From American Falls, take Route 86 west 11 miles to well-marked Exit 28.

Bear River Country

History takes a front seat in southeasternmost Idaho's Bear River country, from the ruts of the Oregon Trail to the earliest white settlement in the state. The varied region also contains Lava Hot Springs, Idaho's leading hot-springs resort; the phosphate-mining center of Soda Springs, with the world's largest captive geyser; and Minnetonka Cave, its ice-crystal walls preserving prehistoric marine fossils, overlooking turquoise-blue Bear Lake.

The Bear River provides a common theme. The only major stream in Idaho that is *not* a tributary (directly or indirectly) of the Snake or Columbia river, it rises in Utah's Uinta Mountains and—after a meandering, 350-mile course through parts of Wyoming and Idaho—flows into the Great Salt Lake. In Idaho, the slow-flowing Bear passes through or near the region's three major towns, Montpelier, Soda Springs and Preston. Below Montpelier, it is joined by the waters flowing from huge Bear Lake, adding to its importance as an irrigation resource.

The first permanent non-Native American communities in Idaho were founded in this region in the 1860s by settlers of the Mormon faith. Drifting north from their Salt Lake City base, the Mormons sought respect for their doctrines, particularly polygamy but also economic and social tenets. Today they are the largest religious group in Idaho, about 400,000 strong; in southeastern Idaho, a non-Mormon is an exception.

Plan two days to explore Bear River country, on a loop drive beginning southeast of Pocatello off Route 15. From McCammon, take Route 30 east through Lava Hot Springs and Soda Springs to Montpelier. Follow Route 89 south past Bear Lake to Logan, Utah; then return through Idaho via Franklin and Preston to Route 15 and Pocatello. The full circuit, minus almost-obligatory detours, is 245 miles.

Before Oregon Trail pioneers arrived, Bannock and Shoshone tribes had declared **Lava Hot Springs** to be a truce zone. Hydrogeologists say the mineral pools, at the base of lava cliffs along the Portneuf River, have remained at 104 to 110°F for 50 million years. Today the hot springs are promoted as **Idaho's World Famous Hot Pools & Swim Complex** (430 East Main Street; 208-776-5221; admission). There are six swimming pools and four mineral-rich but sulfur-free soaking pools, two of them with whirlpools (open year-round). The Sunken Gardens bloom on the lava walls near the pools.

The phosphate-mining center of **Soda Springs** is 27 miles east on Route 30. What is claimed as the world's only "captive geyser" shoots a stream of water 150 feet into the air at **Geyser Park** (1st Street South at 1st Street West; 208-547-2600). Unleashed in 1937 when a drill crew inadvertently struck an underground chamber of carbon dioxide at a depth of 315 feet, the geyser has been capped and now erupts by timer: every half hour in summer, on the hour the rest of the year.

Two designated scenic byways meet at Soda Springs. Route 34, the **Pioneer Historic Route**, runs 49 miles south to Preston (discussed later in this tour) and 47 miles northeast to the village of Freedom in Wyoming's Star Valley. En route it skirts the **Grays Lake National Wildlife Refuge** (74 Grays Lake Road, Wayan; 208-574-2755) in a mountain valley at 6400 feet. The world's largest nesting population of greater sandhill cranes (about 200 pairs) makes its home at this 32,000-acre lake. Trails, open from October through March (the non-nesting season), attract nordic skiers and hardy hikers. A visitors center is open April to mid-November.

Southeast of Soda Springs, the **Bear Lake–Caribou Scenic Route** follows Route 30 to **Montpelier**, then Route 89 down the western shore of Bear Lake and into Utah. Butch Cassidy and his Wild Bunch got away with $7000 when they robbed the Montpelier bank in 1896; today, Montpelier is the hub of the Bear Lake area.

As it approaches Bear Lake, Route 89 enters the charming farming village of **Paris**, Idaho's second-oldest settlement (1863). Paris is best known for its **Paris Idaho Stake Tabernacle** (Main Street; 208-945-2112). The Mormon house of worship was built in 1889 in Gothic style from red sandstone, sledded to Paris from a quarry on the east side of Bear Lake.

Follow Route 89 south to the village of St. Charles, where it reaches **Bear Lake**. Unique for its brilliant aquamarine color caused by a high concentration of limestone particles, this lake—seven miles across and 20 miles long, half of it across the border in Utah—contains several species of fish found nowhere else on earth. The annual spawning runs of the Bonneville cisco, a swift, sardine-like whitefish, begin with the winter frost; ice fishermen dip nets and buckets for them. **Bear Lake State Park** (181 South Main Street, Paris; 208-945-2790; admission) has two units, both of them white-sand swimmers' delights. A sandbar divides Bear Lake from marshy Mud Lake and the **Bear Lake National Wildlife Refuge** (Merkley Lake Road, Montpelier; 208-847-1757), to its north. Encompassing Mud Lake and the Dingle Swamp, this boggy 17,600-acre preserve is home to one of the largest Canada geese populations in the West, as well as large numbers of ducks (mallard, canvasback, pintail, redhead, teal and widgeon), herons, egrets, white pelicans and white-faced ibises.

St. Charles was the birthplace of Gutzon Borglum (1867–1941), sculptor of Mount Rushmore. A monument on the church grounds, beside Route 93 in the heart of town, commemorates his life. The Utah state border is eight miles south; the **Bear Lake Convention and Visitors Bureau** (Fish Haven; 208-945-2072) has its headquarters just two miles north of the border.

West of Bear Lake, gravel roads climb creek canyons to the 9000-foot heights of the Wasatch Range and **Caribou National Forest** (208-236-7500). Of particular interest is **Minnetonka Cave** (Forest Road 412, St. Charles; 208-945-2407; admission). The half-mile-long limestone cavern is noted for its stalagmites and stalactites, ice-crystal walls, banded travertine rock and even fossils of prehistoric plants and marine mammals. Guided tours through its nine chilly rooms are offered from mid-June to Labor Day. Expect a workout: You'll climb or descend 448 steps at 7700-foot elevation.

From Bear Lake you can return north up Route 89 to its junction with secondary Route 36, four miles north of Paris, and continue west to Franklin, a 65-mile drive from Fish Haven. Or you can continue west on Route 89 from

Garden City, surmounting scenic Sunrise Summit and descending the Logan Canyon to bustling Logan (see Chapter Five, "Utah Rockies"). Just past the Utah State University campus, turn north on Route 91 and cross the border to Franklin, 66 miles from Fish Haven.

Franklin is one and a quarter miles north of the Utah border. When founded in 1860 as the first white settlement in what is now Idaho, it was believed to be south of the 42nd parallel and thus in Brigham Young's Utah. An 1872 survey gave townspeople a big surprise. The National Register of Historic Places today lists the **Lorenzo Hatch Home** (127 East Main Street), built in 1870 in Greek revival style, and the **Pioneer Relic Hall** (East Main Street and 1st Street East), a small early settlers' museum in a two-story stone store built in 1895.

Northwest of Franklin, Route 91 proceeds through **Preston**—a farming town whose 3800 people make it the largest community in Bear River country—to **Red Rock Pass**. It was here that Lake Bonneville burst its banks some 15,000 years ago (22 miles from modern Preston) and began the catastrophic Bonneville Flood. The highway joins Route 15 at Virginia, 33 miles from Preston and 35 miles south of Pocatello.

BEAR RIVER COUNTRY HOTELS

The private hot mineral pools at the European-style **Lava Hot Springs Inn** (5 Portneuf Street, Lava Hot Springs; 208-776-5830) are open 24 hours a day to guests. Built as a hospital on the banks of the Portneuf River in the 1920s, the inn has 17 rooms with an art deco–era decor. Four jacuzzi suites have private baths; other rooms share facilities. A full gourmet breakfast is served to all guests. Moderate.

Hot mineral pools are also an amenity at the **Riverside Inn & Hot Springs** (255 Portneuf Street, Lava Hot Springs; 208-776-5504, 800-733-5504). This old three-story bed-and-breakfast hotel beside the Portneuf River has 16 rooms; some low-cost rooms share bathrooms while others have private facilities. Budget to moderate.

Oregon Trail wagon ruts can still be seen at the **Bar H Bar Ranch** (1501 Eight Mile Creek Road, Soda Springs; 208-547-3082, 800-743-9505), eight miles southeast of Soda Springs off Route 30. The historic, 9000-acre working ranch in the foothills of the Bear River Range runs 2000 head of beef cattle; guests are invited to assist in branding and calving, repairing fences and other day-to-day chores. Eight guests stay in four private rooms in a rustic bunkhouse with lodge-style furnishings and eat three hearty meals a day with their hosts. In summer there's horseback riding, fishing and hiking; in winter, cross-country skiing and snowmobiling. Moderate.

Bear Lake Bed & Breakfast (500 Loveland Lane, Fish Haven; 208-945-2688) overlooks the shimmering aquamarine lake from a hillside just off Route 89, two miles north of the Utah border. Four of the seven bedrooms in the log home are rented to guests; there's an outdoor hot tub; a full breakfast is served. A deluxe room has a fireplace and private bath; others share bathrooms. Moderate.

BEAR RIVER COUNTRY RESTAURANTS

For Old West flavor, try **The Lazy 'A' Ranch** (Route 30 West, Lava Hot Springs; 208-776-5035). Not only do adults and kids get a hearty chuckwagon-style meal of barbecued beef or chicken with all the fixin's; they also take in a dinner show that includes cowboy songs and stories, followed by dancing to a live band. Dinners are served Thursday to Saturday. Moderate.

For good, solid home cooking, **Betty's Cafe** (Route 30 West, Soda Springs; 208-547-4802) hits the spot. Come for biscuits and gravy in the morning, great soups at midday, robust helpings of meats and chicken in the evening. Look for a brown house along the highway a couple of miles west of downtown Soda Springs. Budget.

The outlaw gang that once robbed a bank in Montpelier lives on at **Butch Cassidy's Restaurant and Saloon** (260 North 4th Street, Montpelier; 208-847-3501). Steak, prime rib and seafood are the evening bill of fare at this popular dining spot, which serves three meals daily. Moderate.

BEAR RIVER COUNTRY PARKS

Caribou National Forest—The tall tales of Canadian miner Jesse "Cariboo Jack" Fairchild, who in 1870 discovered gold on the slopes of 9600-foot Caribou Mountain, gave this region its name. The 1,087,000-acre forest has six parcels in Idaho and bits in Wyoming and Utah; the largest part extends from Palisades Reservoir south to Montpelier. Additional sections are south of Soda Springs to the Utah border and on either side of Route 15 south of Pocatello. The forest's timbered and sage-covered slopes contain 1200 miles of trails for hiking, horseback riding, cross-country skiing and snowmobiling.

Facilities: Picnic areas, restrooms, boat ramps, trails, ski area (Pebble Creek); information, 208-236-7500. *Swimming:* Possible in mountain lakes. *Fishing:* There's rainbow, brook, brown and cutthroat trout, bluegill and bass.

Camping: There are 188 RV/tent sites (no hookups), plus 182 sites for tents only, at 28 campgrounds; $9 per night for RVs, $5 for tents. Four guard stations are available for rental in the Soda Springs Ranger District for $20 per night; reservations, 208-547-4356.

Getting there: Major access points off Route 15 south of Pocatello are from Exits 63 west, 58 east, 22 west, 17 and 13 east. From Soda Springs, take Route 34 north or Eight Mile Canyon Road 425 south; from Montpelier, take Route 36 west or Crow Creek Road 111 north; from Bear Lake, take Paris Canyon Road 421, Bloomington Canyon Road 409 or St. Charles Creek Road 412 west. The headquarters are located at 250 South 4th Avenue, Pocatello.

Bear Lake State Park—Spanning the border of Idaho and Utah, Bear Lake is noted for its remarkable turquoise color caused by suspended limestone particles. Known in the 1820s as the site of an annual mountain men's rendezvous, the seven-by-twenty-mile lake contains several species of fish found nowhere else. The 52-acre state park consists of two parcels: one-and-a-half-mile-long

East Beach, site of a campground, and two-mile-long North Beach, whose white sands are a swimmer's delight.

Facilities: Picnic tables, restrooms, trails, boat ramps; day-use fee, $2; information; 208-945-2790. *Swimming:* Lifeguarded beaches at North Beach and East Beach. *Fishing:* Excellent for cutthroat and native lake trout, as well as other species; ice fishing for the unique Bonneville cisco in winter.

Camping: There are 48 RV/tent sites at East Beach (all with hookups); $12 per night for RVs, $9 for tents. Open from mid-May through September.

Getting there: From St. Charles, 18 miles south of Montpelier on Route 89, take Turnpike Road five miles east to North Beach, then Merkley Lake and Eastside Lake roads another eight miles east and south to East Beach.

Curlew National Grassland—Caribou National Forest administers the three parcels of this 47,000-acre grassland along Rock Creek and Deep Creek west of Malad City. Open to homestead settlement in the 1920s and 1930s, this land was quickly overgrazed and laid to waste; it is now a federal sustained-yield management area open for grazing, fall game-bird hunting and year-round recreation, mainly at three-mile-long Stone Reservoir.

Facilities: Picnic tables, restrooms; information, 208-766-4743. *Swimming:* Beach at Stone Reservoir. *Fishing:* Stone Reservoir is noted for crappie fishing; trout have also been stocked.

Camping: There are 18 RV/tent sites (no hookups) at two campgrounds; $5 per night.

Getting there: From Malad City, 58 miles south of Pocatello on Route 15, take Route 38 west 23 miles to Holbrook. The Stone Reservoir parcel of the grassland is immediately south, the two Rock Creek parcels just to the north.

Idaho Falls

Idaho Falls, the state's major eastern gateway, marks a place of transition from the Snake River Plain to the Rocky Mountain wilderness. Part of the fertile region that made Idaho potatoes world famous, this city of 44,000 is within a two-hour drive of Yellowstone and Grand Teton national parks. Above Idaho Falls, the Snake flows out of the high Tetons, their crests visible for miles around. This area lures outdoors lovers with its rich wildlife and scenic beauty.

Idaho Falls, originally known as Eagle Rock, was established in 1865 at the site of an early bridge across a narrow stretch of the Snake. The village name was changed to Idaho Falls in 1891 to attract settlers, but there were no falls until 1911, when a power diversion weir created a 20-foot drop to validate the name. The falls can be viewed from the bridge where Broadway crosses the Snake between downtown Idaho Falls and Route 15. They mark the southern end of the city's new **Snake River Greenbelt**, one of 39 parks administered by Idaho Falls City Parks (208-529-1478). Extending along both sides of the river for two and a half miles north to the Route 20 bridge, it includes a biking path and the Rotary International Peace Park, whose granite lanterns were a gift from Idaho Falls' sister city in Japan.

The Greater Idaho Falls Chamber of Commerce (505 Lindsay Boulevard; 208-523-1010) shares a visitors center with the U.S. Forest Service and Bureau of Land Management on the west side of the Greenbelt, while a city architectural landmark, the impressive **Idaho Falls Temple** (1000 Memorial Drive; 208-523-4504) of the Church of Jesus Christ of Latter-day Saints (Mormons), bounds the Greenbelt to the east.

The 75-acre **Russell Freeman Park** (Science Center Drive; 208-529-1478) is connected to the Greenbelt along the Snake; reached via Fremont Avenue north of Route 20, it contains the **Idaho State Vietnam Veterans Memorial**, an inverted steel V accompanied by the names of all Idaho fatalities and MIAs from the Southeast Asian war. It was dedicated in 1990.

With 80 acres south of downtown, **Tautphaus Park** (Rollandet Avenue at 25th Street; 208-529-1470) is the city's largest, and includes an aquatic center, an ice skating rink, a small amusement park and picnic grounds. It also features the **Idaho Falls Zoo** (admission), with 250 animals of more than 50 species, including several large cats and a giant tortoise exhibit.

To discover Idaho Falls' history, stop at the **Bonneville County Historical Museum** (200 Eastern Street; 208-522-1400; admission) in a 1916 Carnegie Library building. Its permanent exhibits range from natural history and early agriculture and mining to the atomic era.

North of Idaho Falls, Route 15 makes a virtual beeline for the Montana border, 77 miles north, and 6823-foot Monida Pass on the Continental Divide. Other than scenic beauty, there's not a whole lot to see along this route. **Camas National Wildlife Refuge** (Refuge Road, Hamer; 208-523-1010) is immediately to the west of the interstate, 30 miles north of Idaho Falls. A wide variety of waterfowl are attracted to this marshy 10,578-acre refuge on the northern fringe of the porous Snake River Plain. Camas Creek meanders through the preserve. Besides geese, swans, herons, cranes and other waterfowl, many of which nest here from spring to fall, look for ospreys and eagles, deer and antelope, beaver and smaller mammals. Gravel roads, open daily, extend through the refuge.

Sixty miles from Idaho Falls is the **Spencer Opal Mine** (Idmon Road, Spencer; 208-374-5476), the only commercial opal mine in North America. Discovered in 1948 by hunters, it is noted for its plentiful star opals, red, green, pink, yellow or blue in color. Rockhounds can obtain a permit and directions to the open-pit mine at the Opal Shop in tiny Spencer; the mine is seven miles east on a south-facing hillside at 7000 feet.

IDAHO FALLS HOTELS

One of eastern Idaho's better lodging bargains is the **Littletree Inn** (888 North Holmes Avenue; 208-523-5993, 800-521-5993, fax 208-523-7104). Located near the Pinecrest golf course off Route 26 on the northeast side of Idaho Falls, it's a hit with business travelers. Its nicely kept rooms include some cooking units with refrigerators and microwave ovens. Facilities include a swimming pool, hot tub, fitness center, coin laundry, restaurant and lounge with live dance music most nights. Low moderate.

Motel West (1540 West Broadway; 208-522-1112, 800-582-1063, fax 208-524-1144) is one of those privately run motels you wish every city had. A step above the standard "ma and pa" label, it retains the friendly feel of a smaller lodging. Each pleasant, comfortable room has nice wood decor. There's an indoor pool, a hot tub, a coin laundry and an adjacent café. The motel is on the west side of Idaho Falls, on Route 20 toward Arco. Budget to moderate.

Many major hotel chains are represented in Idaho Falls, including Holiday Inn, Quality Inn, Shilo Inn, Comfort Inn and Super 8, all on the west side of the Snake just off Route 15. Largest is the **Best Western Stardust Motor Lodge** (700 Lindsay Boulevard; 208-522-2910, 800-527-0274, fax 208-529-8361), a 249-unit structure spread across five buildings beside the Snake River Greenbelt. Facilities include a swimming pool, hot tub, sauna and fitness room, coffee shop, barbecue restaurant and lounge. Moderate.

IDAHO FALLS RESTAURANTS

If you enjoy great "greasy spoons," you can't go wrong at the **North Highway Cafe** (460 Northgate Mile; 208-522-6212). Huge portions of chicken, seafood and hickory-smoked beef are served up for lunch and dinner; breakfast starts at 5 a.m. There are kids' menus as well. Budget.

Mama Inez (344 Park Avenue; 208-525-8968), behind an unimposing storefront in the downtown historic district, offers authentic Mexican food at budget prices.

Jake's Steak and Fish House (851 Lindsay Boulevard; 208-524-5240) is a classy dining spot with a family emphasis. Rich wood decor with brass trim and Idaho Falls' best oyster bar make it an after-work choice for many. Moderate.

IDAHO FALLS SHOPPING

Gallery crawlers can start their exploration at the **Idaho Falls Arts Council Gallery** (241 Cliff Street; 208-522-0471), which features exhibits of local and regional artists, and then visit the nearby **Willowtree Gallery** (210 Cliff Street; 208-524-4464), offering limited-edition collector prints, and the **Navajo Spirit Gallery** (545 Shoup Avenue; 208-528-2809), with a good selection of southwestern items, custom furniture, pottery and metal art.

The city's best bookstore is **Books & Co.** (435 A Street; 208-522 4300) in the downtown historic district.

IDAHO FALLS NIGHTLIFE

The **Idaho Falls Arts Council** (241 Cliff Street; 208-522-0471) coordinates a wide choice of activities.

The **Idaho Falls Symphony Orchestra and Chorale** (208-529-1080) and the **Idaho Falls Opera Theater** (208-523-0620) offer frequent performances at the Idaho Falls Civic Auditorium (501 South Holmes Avenue; 208-529-1396).

The **Actors' Repertory Theater of Idaho** (208-524-1489), known locally as ARTI, stages fall and spring performances at University Place (1776 Science Center Drive; 208-526-1385) and a dinner theater at the Peppertree Restaurant (888 North Holmes Avenue; 208-524-6226) in the Littletree Inn.

There's a lively country music scene at the **Stardust Lounge** at the Best Western Stardust Motor Lodge (700 Lindsay Boulevard; 208-522-2910) and the **Rockin' Horse** (1560 Lindsay Boulevard; 208-524-7201), where free dance lessons are offered Tuesday and Thursday evenings.

The **Peppertree Lounge** at the Littletree Inn (888 North Holmes Avenue; 208-524-6226) offers Top-40 rock, comedy (Thursdays) and karaoke (Saturdays). **Chic's** (840 Northgate Mile; 208-525-9976) has live rock-and-roll Wednesday through Saturday nights. **Decades** (2096 North Yellowstone Highway; 208-529-2964) has the area's largest selection of microbrews.

The Swan and Teton Valleys

There are two routes from Idaho Falls to Jackson, Wyoming, and Grand Teton National Park, both via the upper Snake River. Route 26 runs southeasterly through the lovely Swan Valley and along the shore of Palisades Reservoir to Jackson. Route 31 branches northeasterly at Swan Valley and offers a slower but spectacular detour through the isolated Teton Valley. It also provides a back door to Wyoming's Grand Targhee resort area on the west slope of the Teton Range.

The road to the Swan Valley passes near **Heise Hot Springs** (Heise Road, Ririe; 208-538-7312; admission), a popular weekend getaway for eastern Idahoans 23 miles northeast of Idaho Falls on the bank of the Snake. The resort's hand-hewn, three-story log hotel was built in 1898; today it has two commercial pools and a golf course.

Above Heise, Route 26 follows the Snake 35 miles to the Palisades Dam, a stretch considered one of Idaho's most pristine wildlife habitats. The gently rippling river is known for huge trout and birds, including bald eagles and great blue herons.

Palisades Dam (Route 26, Irwin; 208-483-2392) is at the northwest end of 17-mile-long **Palisades Reservoir**, which extends to the Wyoming border at Alpine. The Bureau of Reclamation dam was the largest earth dam yet built when it was completed in 1959 at a cost of $76 million. Interpretive tours of the facility can be arranged. North and east of the reservoir and the Snake River is **Targhee National Forest** (208-624-3151); south and west is Caribou National Forest (see "Bear River Country Parks," above).

The village of **Swan Valley**, 11 miles west of the dam, has limited tourist facilities; it is more a junction than a town, the point from which Route 31 traverses 6764-foot Pine Creek Pass in the Big Hole Range to the **Teton Valley**.

The 13,000-foot crest of the Teton Range stands sentinel over a valley that has adopted its name. Thirty miles long and 15 miles wide, the valley was known as Pierre's Hole when it hosted mountain men's gatherings in the 1830s. Local residents who revel in the rustic re-enact the rendezvous in August.

Most of the year, cattle ranching and hay farming sustain the economy of **Driggs**, the valley's main town; **Victor**, six miles to its south; and **Tetonia**, eight miles north. Some younger residents have brought ecotourism to the region with businesses geared to outdoor recreation, guest ranches, bed-and-breakfast inns and small restaurants.

This trend has largely followed the development of the **Grand Targhee Ski & Summer Resort** (Ski Hill Road, Alta, Wyoming; 307-353-2300), which opened in 1970. The Wyoming resort—which can be reached only through Driggs, 12 miles away—has lodges, condominiums, restaurants and some of the finest powder skiing in the Rocky Mountains during its November-to-April ski season.

At Tetonia, Route 33 turns sharply west to Rexburg. Travelers to Jackson return to Victor and take the highway southeast across 8429-foot **Teton Pass**. This spectacular route, first pioneered in 1811 and opened as a Forest Service road in 1913, is steep and winding—not for the faint-hearted—but is paved and well maintained. Its views on either side of the Teton Range are worth the drive.

THE SWAN AND TETON VALLEYS HOTELS

There's charming lodging on the Snake River at **Swan Valley Bed & Breakfast** (Swan Valley Highway, Irwin; 208-483-4663, 800-241-7926). The modern log lodge has five guest rooms with private baths and bright country decor; a common area with a big-screen TV and fireplace; a riverside deck with a hot tub; and a barbecue area. A full breakfast is served each morning. Rates are in the moderate range.

A hideaway for lovers of luxury is the 1600-acre **Teton Ridge Ranch** (200 Valley View Road, Tetonia; 208-456-2650). It has one two-bedroom cottage and five suites with private whirlpools, steam showers and wood-burning stoves. There are fireplaces in the living and dining rooms and library, a bar, a game room with a TV and stereo, and live country-and-western music twice weekly. Winter and summer wilderness programs are offered. Open from mid-December through March and from June through September, with a one-week minimum stay in midsummer. Deluxe.

Grand Targhee Ski & Summer Resort (Ski Hill Road, Alta, Wyoming; 307-353-2300, 800-443-8146, fax 307-353-8148) has rooms in three alpine lodges at 8000 feet. All have southwestern decor with handcrafted lodgepole furnishings and private baths. The Targhee Lodge has moderate motel-style rooms; the Teewinot Lodge has deluxe hotel-style rooms; the condo-style Sioux Lodge features bunk beds, kiva fireplaces and kitchenettes. All are an easy walk from restaurants, lounges, shops and sports facilities. Costs vary from moderate to ultra-deluxe, with rates lowest in summer, highest on holidays in the peak ski season.

THE SWAN AND TETON VALLEYS RESTAURANTS

The **Painted Apple Café** (55 North Main Street, Victor; 208-787-2039) combines a gallery for craftspeople with a stage for area musicians and a dining room with the decor and home cooking of Grandma's house. Moderate.

Vegetarians are happy to find **Table Mountain Natural Foods** (285 North Main Street, Driggs; 208-354-8663). Healthy soups, salads and sandwiches are served in a café and espresso bar; a small grocery is attached. Budget.

Skadi's Fine Dining (Grand Targhee Resort, Alta, Wyoming; 307-353-2300) is a favorite of skiers and summer sports enthusiasts. Located in the Rendezvous Base Lodge, Skadi's offers wholesome breakfasts, energizing lunches and gourmet Continental cuisine for dinner. Moderate to deluxe.

THE SWAN AND TETON VALLEYS NIGHTLIFE

Pierre's Playhouse (Main Street, Victor; 208-787-2249), at the foot of the Teton Valley, has been presenting old-fashioned melodrama to summer visitors since 1964.

THE SWAN AND TETON VALLEYS PARKS

Targhee National Forest—Palisades and Island Park reservoirs, Henry's Lake and Lower Mesa Falls are among the highlights of this 1.8-million-acre forest, which extends from the Tetons west to the Lemhi Range, and which follows the Continental Divide from Montana to the edge of Yellowstone and Grand Teton national parks in Wyoming. There are more than 1200 miles of trails.

Facilities: Picnic tables, restrooms, boat ramps, trails, ski areas, resort stores, restaurants; information, 208-624-3151. *Swimming:* Beaches at Island Park and Palisades reservoirs. *Fishing:* Henry's Fork of the Snake River and the Island Park area are world renowned. Palisades Reservoir and other streams are also excellent. Game fish include rainbow, brook, brown and cutthroat trout, kokanee salmon and mountain whitefish.

Camping: There are 670 RV/tent sites (no hookups) at 33 campgrounds; no charge to $10 per night. All but 58 of the sites are in Idaho. Reservations are available at some campgrounds; call 800-280-2267. Five wilderness cabins—three near Island Park and two near Palisades Reservoir, accommodating two to ten people—are available year-round for $15 to $30 per night.

Getting there: Routes 20 (Ashton to West Yellowstone, Montana) and 26 (Idaho Falls to Jackson, Wyoming) pass through large segments of the forest, and there is access from numerous other roads.

Henry's Fork

Fewer than 20 miles north of Idaho Falls, the northwest-flowing Snake makes a 120-degree turn south and begins a long, arcing run through southern Idaho's heavily irrigated lava plain. Just before the dogleg, it is joined by Henry's Fork, perhaps the single finest trout stream in the United States. The river rises on the Continental Divide near West Yellowstone, Montana, and flows about 100 miles southwest to the main Snake.

Route 20 from Idaho Falls more or less follows the stream to its source. Before crossing the main Snake, Route 20 passes through **Rigby**, a childhood home of Philo Taylor Farnsworth III. Farnsworth lived in Idaho from age 12 to 16. His science classes and fascination with electronics inspired him to daydream as he plowed the fields after school. He was just 14 (in 1920) when he conceived the idea of a dissector that could reduce pictures to their basic electrons, transmit them to a receiver and reassemble them into a visual image. By the time he was 22, Farnsworth had created the first cathode-ray tube and the first electronic television.

The architectural highlight of fast-growing **Rexburg**, 12 miles northeast of Rigby, is the twin-towered **Upper Snake River Valley Historical Museum** (51 North Center Street; 208-356-9101). Built in Italianate style as a Mormon tabernacle in 1911, the gray stone church, listed on the National Register of Historic Places, was sold to the city in 1978. Most visitors are particularly interested in its exhibits about the June 5, 1976, Teton Dam collapse, which caused one of the worst floods in American history.

The dam was 23 miles up the Teton River from Rexburg. An observation post today overlooks the **Teton Dam Site** (Teton Dam Road, Newdale; 208-356-5700), a mile north of Route 33 between Sugar City and Tetonia. The ill-conceived Bureau of Reclamation project was approaching completion, its reservoir nearly filled, when it collapsed at midday, sending 80 billion gallons of water downstream at 15 miles per hour. Flood waters were contained three days later by American Falls Reservoir. Remarkably, only six people drowned, but 25,000 were driven from their homes, 18,000 head of stock were lost and $800 million damage was suffered by the residents of eastern Idaho.

St. Anthony, 12 miles northeast of Rexburg, is gateway to the **St. Anthony Sand Dunes** (Red Road, St. Anthony; 208-523-1012), eight miles northwest. The band of dunes, 35 miles long and up to five miles wide, has individual peaks as high as 1300 feet, taller than those of Death Valley. The white-quartz dunes have been deposited by alluvial action and blown by prevailing winds to the northeastern end of the Snake River Plain over millions of years.

Ashton, 14 miles from St. Anthony, marks the north end of the 108-mile **Teton National Scenic Byway**. Travelers can detour from here onto Route 47, the **Mesa Falls Scenic Byway**. The circuit skirts two undisturbed waterfalls on Henry's Fork and accesses the remote southwest corner of Yellowstone National Park. The Yellowstone route begins six miles east of Ashton off Route 47 (as Marysville Road) and extends 19 miles to Cave Falls on Wyoming's Falls River.

You can backpack the Belcher River Trail from here to Old Faithful, a hike of probably four days.

More spectacular are the **Upper and Lower Mesa Falls** (★). From an overlook at Targhee National Forest's Grandview campground you can see Lower Mesa Falls thunder 65 feet through a narrow gorge. Upriver three-fourths of a mile, Upper Mesa Falls drop 114 feet to a frothy pool. Boardwalk trails lead from a paved parking area, past a historic forest lodge, to viewing platforms.

The falls mark the edge of the **Island Park Caldera**, 18 by 23 miles in diameter, first identified by geologists in 1939 and now regarded as the world's largest crater. This collapsed prehistoric volcano, identified by the 1200-foot scarp on its south and west sides, is now covered with dense pine forest and extensive meadows.

Mesa Falls Scenic Byway rejoins Route 20 just north of the entrance to **Harriman State Park** (Green Canyon Road, Island Park; 208-558-7368; admission), 18 miles from Ashton. Established as a private Union Pacific Railroad retreat by the wealthy Harriman family in 1902, this 4330-acre park—Idaho's second largest—became a state park in 1977. Daily tours of the 27 original buildings of the working cattle ranch are offered in summer, and the visitors center becomes a warming hut for cross-country skiers in winter. A 16,000-acre wildlife refuge surrounds the park, which lies along nine miles of Henry's Fork. **Island Park Reservoir**, created by a dam on Henry's Fork six miles from the park, fills the crater of the old caldera. The resort community of **Island Park** is on Route 20 at its eastern end, and five boat launches provide access for water sports.

Henry's Lake, 19 miles north of Island Park, occupies a mountain bowl four miles long, three miles wide and 6470 feet above sea level. Several trout-fishing resorts are around its shores, as well as **Henry's Lake State Park** (Goose Bay Road, Island Park; 208-558-7532).

It's five miles from Henry's Lake to the 7072-foot summit of **Targhee Pass**, which crosses the Continental Divide into Montana. West Yellowstone, at the western entrance to Yellowstone National Park, is 12 miles farther east.

HENRY'S FORK HOTELS

Rexburg's **Calaway Motel** (361 South 2nd Street West; 208-356-3217), a block west of the Ricks College campus, is a fine place for the wallet watcher. The 16 rooms are clean, spacious and comfortable, with double beds, but the bathrooms have no baths, only showers. Budget.

Sawtelle Mountain Resort (Route 20, Island Park; 208-558-9366, 800-574-0404) is the newest of a proliferation of lodges in the Island Park area. It's geared to fishing and snowmobiling, with rentals nearby and direct access to 600 miles of trails. Lodging is in motel rooms, all with private baths. There are two outdoor hot tubs; a continental breakfast is included. Rates run in the low end of the moderate range.

HENRY'S FORK RESTAURANTS

Me 'n Stan's Restaurant (167 West Main Street, Rexburg; 208-356-7330) is a family-style place just a block from the Porter Park carousel. Steak and seafood highlight the menu, and a big salad bar is a big hit with many. Special menus are available for kids and seniors. Moderate.

Up on Henry's Fork, the **Bar A Supper Club** (Route 26, Island Park; 208-558-7358), near the north edge of Harriman State Park by the Last Chance Lodge, serves hearty ranch-style portions of chili, Texas burgers and the like 'til midnight daily. It's right on the riverbank. Budget to moderate.

HENRY'S FORK PARKS

Henry's Lake State Park—A quiet mountain oasis just 15 miles from Yellowstone National Park's west entrance, sheltered on three sides by the Continental Divide just south of the Montana border, Henry's Lake fills an alpine valley of about 12 square miles. The 585-acre park, on the southeast shore near its outlet to Henry's Fork, is ideal for fishing enthusiasts.

Facilities: Picnic tables, restrooms, hiking trails, boat ramp; day-use fee, $2; information, 208-558-7532. *Swimming:* No designated beach. *Fishing:* Excellent angling for cutthroat and brook trout and cutthroat-rainbow hybrids.

Camping: There are 50 RV/tent sites (all with hookups); $12 per night for RVs, $6 for tents. Open Memorial Day weekend through September.

Getting there: From Idaho Falls, take Route 20 northeast 87 miles to Goose Bay Road; turn west two miles to the park entrance.

The Sporting Life

FISHING

TWIN FALLS AREA It's no accident that fishing the middle Snake River and surrounding waters is so rewarding: More than two million rainbow and steelhead trout, as well as catfish and tilapia, are produced each year in hatcheries and "fish farms" along this stretch of the river. Between Hagerman and Twin Falls, the five Oster Lakes feature bass and bluegill fishing that begins in March, two months earlier than the general season (which runs from Memorial Day through November). Salmon Falls Reservoir, 39 miles southwest of Twin Falls, offers rainbow and brown trout, kokanee salmon and trophy-size walleye, crappie, bass and perch.

SUN VALLEY AREA Author Ernest Hemingway made the trout waters of the Sun Valley area—particularly those of Silver Creek and the Big Wood River—famous through his writings. Southwest of Sun Valley, near Fairfield, Magic Reservoir and Mormon Reservoir are great places to troll for rainbow and brown trout. Area guides include **Bill Mason Outfitters** (Sun Valley Mall,

Heaven for Fly-Fishermen

The prospect of laying a hand-tied lure on a placid stretch of river and reeling in a giant trout has a romance shared by few outdoor recreations. And few places are better suited to flyfishing than southeastern Idaho.

Author Ernest Hemingway made Silver Creek, southeast of Sun Valley, famous as his favorite fishing hole. Henry's Fork of the Snake River, northeast of Idaho Falls, is considered to be among the best trout streams on earth. Many other streams, from the Big Wood River to the Big Lost River, the Salmon River to Salmon Falls Creek, are equally enticing.

The roots of flyfishing date back at least 2000 years to the Roman Empire. But flyfishing as it's known in the 1990s did not become possible until a century ago, when the horsehair line was reinvented. The modern flycasting line—typically nylon with a plastic covering, tapered to a monofilament leader—provides the weight for casting the virtually weightless fly; it can float atop the water or sink below the surface. A flexible fiberglass or graphite rod, usually about eight feet long, is whipped in an often individualized motion that sends the line and lure to a precise location in the water.

Artificial flies may be made from silk, fur, feathers or other material, but they usually represent a natural food source for the fish: aquatic or terrestrial insects, freshwater shrimp or snails, for instance. Most commonly imitated are mayflies, caddis flies and midges, all of which begin their lives in the water as nymphs before emerging as winged insects. Females return to the water to lay eggs.

It is the angler's challenge to simulate the insect's natural behavior and outwit the fish—either by "wet-fly" fishing with the lure underwater, or "dry-fly" fishing on the surface of the water. Dry-fly anglers try to cast a slack line, allowing their lure to remain naturally on the surface as long as possible before it is caught in the current.

Lodges throughout southeastern Idaho provide flyfishing guides and instruction. For visitors with money to burn and a powerful passion to catch trophy-size cutthroat, rainbow and German brown trout, it's hard to top **The Lodge at Palisades Creek** (Irwin; 208-483-2222). From June to October, experienced guides take visitors out fishing on the upper Snake.

Hemingway's Silver Creek fishing hole is now owned and monitored by the preservationist Nature Conservancy as the **Silver Creek Preserve** (Picabo; 208-788-2203). The water temperature of the spring-fed stream stays near 40 degrees year-round; its rainbow, brown and brook trout are big and smart. A strict catch-and-release policy applies, enabling the fish to get older, bigger and smarter.

Sun Valley; 208-622-9305) and **Silver Creek Outfitters** (507 Main Street North, Ketchum; 208-726-5282).

SAWTOOTHS AND UPPER SALMON North of Sun Valley, the Salmon River, its Middle Fork and their tributaries, beginning in the Sawtooth National Recreation Area, are rich in native cutthroat trout and steelhead (which run from late February through April). You can take bull trout from Redfish and Alturas lakes, giant mackinaw from Stanley Lake. **Sawtooth Guide Service** (Ace of Diamonds Street, Stanley; 208-774-9947) and **Triangle C Ranch** (Benner Street, Stanley; 208-774-2266) take anglers down the Salmon River and into the high lakes of the Sawtooth Range.

POCATELLO AREA Anglers pursue rainbow trout in American Falls Reservoir, cutthroat trout in Blackfoot Reservoir. **Anderson Outfitting** (5027 North Yellowstone Avenue, Pocatello; 208-237-6544) leads guided trips.

BEAR RIVER COUNTRY Idaho's most unique fishery is at Bear Lake, which has four species of fish found nowhere else on earth. The winter run of the swift, sardinelike Bonneville cisco thrills ice fishermen. Bear Lake also draws anglers with its five species of trout, including huge mackinaw, as well as the Bear Lake and Bonneville whitefish and the Bear Lake sculpin. Guides include **Bear River Outfitters** (8989 Route 30, Montpelier; 208-847-0263).

SWAN AND TETON VALLEYS The main Snake (sometimes called the South Fork), upstream from its confluence with Henry's Fork, and Palisades Reservoir have giant trout. There are coho salmon in Ririe Reservoir. Check with **Mountain Stream Fishing & Outfitters** (3378 Highway 26, Irwin; 208-483-3332), near Palisades Reservoir, for guided expeditions.

HENRY'S FORK Henry's Fork of the Snake boasts native cutthroat trout that may weigh over ten pounds. There are coho salmon in Island Park Reservoir, rainbow and hybrid cutthroat trout in Henry's Lake. **Henry's Fork Anglers** (Route 26, Last Chance, Island Park; 208-558-7525), south of Island Park Reservoir, provides specialized guide service.

BOATING, BOARD SAILING AND WATERSKIING

Snake River reservoirs are the most popular places for boating. Marinas at American Falls Reservoir and Gem Lake (Idaho Falls) are the busiest, with rentals available at each location. You can rent boats in Pocatello and Idaho Falls from **American Marine** (1175 Alameda Street, Pocatello, 208-237-7039; or 1710 West Broadway, Idaho Falls, 208-523-7487).

RIVER RAFTING AND KAYAKING

The Middle Fork of the Salmon River is Idaho's most famous stream for whitewater lovers and is ranked as one of the ten best in the world. With 100 rapids in 100 miles, it is federally protected as a "wild and scenic river," entirely surrounded by the Frank Church–River of No Return Wilderness.

The main Salmon River—from Stanley to Challis to Salmon, and all the way downstream to Riggins—is also a popular float. Many outfitters specialize in the Salmon; they include the **Middle Fork River Company** (401 Lewis Street, Ketchum; 208-726-8888), **The River Company** (Route 21, Stanley; 208-774-2244) and **Aggipah River Trips** (Route 93, Salmon; 208-756-4167).

The Snake River can be docile for long stretches, but it can also be deceivingly dangerous. The "Hagerman Run," a six-and-a-half-mile stretch past Malad Gorge from the Lower Salmon Dam to the Bliss Bridge, draws raves from beginning rafters with experienced guides. **High Adventure River Tours** (136 Maxwell Avenue, Twin Falls; 208-733-0123) and **Idaho Guide Service** (492 Robbins Avenue, Twin Falls; 208-734-8872) operate on this stretch.

South Fork Expeditions (Route 20, Swan Valley; 208-483-2722) rafts the upper Snake. **Canyon Whitewater Supply** (450 South Yellowstone Highway, Idaho Falls; 208-522-3932) has rentals.

Other popular rivers include the Big Wood and Little Wood, near Sun Valley; the Raft, east of Burley; the Portneuf, through Lava Hot Springs and Pocatello; the Blackfoot, east of Blackfoot; the Bear, through Montpelier and Soda Springs; the Teton, between Driggs and Rexburg; and Henry's Fork, above Rexburg.

DOWNHILL SKIING

Sun Valley (Sun Valley Road, Sun Valley; 208-622-4111, 800-635-8261) is one of the world's most famous winter resorts. Opened in 1936, it encompasses massive, 9150-foot Bald Mountain ("Baldy"), its 3400-foot vertical drop appealing to Olympic medalists and intermediate skiers alike, and little Dollar Mountain, geared toward beginners and intermediates. Eighteen chairlifts (14 of them on Baldy) serve 77 runs and have a total uphill capacity of 21,580 skiers per hour, making long lift lines virtually nonexistent. The resort, which usually opens Thanksgiving weekend and operates until May 1, has 2067 skiable acres. Make arrangements for wilderness helicopter ski trips with **Sun Valley Heli-Ski** (260 1st Avenue North, Ketchum; 208-622-3108). For current snow reports, call 208-622-2093 or 800-635-4150.

Swan and Teton valleys boast the other leading ski area. **Grand Targhee** (Targhee Road, Alta, Wyoming; 307-353-2300 or 800-827-4433) is nestled on the west slope of the Grand Tetons. Although technically in Wyoming, it can be reached only via Driggs, 12 miles west. Each winter, Targhee is blessed with 500 inches of snow, more than 40 feet, making it a favorite of powder skiers. One of its two mountains, 10,230-foot Peaked Mountain, is perpetually ungroomed: Skiers are ferried there by Sno-Cat in groups of eight, accompanied by two guides. Fred's Mountain, only slightly smaller at 10,200 feet, has three chairlifts, one rope tow and 46 runs. Both mountains have 1500 acres of skiable terrain; the vertical drop is 2822 feet.

Smaller family-oriented alpine destinations, none with overnight accommodations, include these:

TWIN FALLS AREA **Magic Mountain** (Route G3, Kimberly; 208-423-6221), 38 miles southeast of Twin Falls via Route 84 Exit 182. Located in Sawtooth National Forest, the area has two chairs, one poma lift, one rope tow and 20 runs on a 800-foot vertical.

Pomerelle Ski Area (Howell Canyon Road, Albion; 208-638-5599), 32 miles southeast of Burley via Route 84 Exit 216. On the eastern slope of 9265-foot Mount Harrison in the Albion Mountains, the resort has two chairlifts, a rope tow and 22 runs on a 1000-foot vertical. Night skiing is available, but the area is closed Sundays and Mondays.

SUN VALLEY AREA **Soldier Mountain** (Soldier Creek Road, Fairfield; 208-764-2300), 60 miles southwest of Sun Valley via Route 20 and 12 miles north of Fairfield. The Sawtooth National Forest area has a 1400-foot vertical with two chairlifts and 36 runs.

POCATELLO AREA **Pebble Creek** (Green Canyon Road, Inkom; 208-775-4452), 19 miles southeast of Pocatello via Route 15 Exit 58. On the west side of 9271-foot Mount Bonneville in Caribou National Forest, the resort boasts a 2000-foot vertical drop and 24 runs served by four chairlifts.

IDAHO FALLS **Kelly Canyon** (Kelly Canyon Road, Heise; 208-538-6261), 25 miles northeast of Idaho Falls via Route 26. Overlooking the Snake River's south fork in Targhee National Forest, the area has four chairlifts and 20 runs with a 938-foot vertical drop.

SKI RENTALS Aside from the resort facilities themselves, there are many places to rent skiing and snowboarding equipment. In the Twin Falls area, try **Pinetree Sports** (2165 Overland Avenue, Burley; 208-678-5869) for ski equipment and **Pedersen's Ski & Sports** (Magic Valley Mall, 1485 Pole Line Road East, Twin Falls; 208-733-0367) for snowboard rentals. In the Sun Valley area, the leaders in downhill ski rentals include **Sturtevant's Alpine Sports** (314 Main Street North, Ketchum; 208-726-4502) and **Formula Sports** (460 Main Street North, Ketchum; 208-726-3194), while **Elephant's Perch** (280 East Avenue North, Ketchum; 208-726-3497) is a cross-country specialty shop. **Scotts Ski & Sports** (218 North Main Street, Pocatello; 208-232-1449) and **Solitude Sports** (393 Park Avenue, Idaho Falls; 208-523-7000) also offer equipment rentals.

CROSS-COUNTRY SKIING

There are nordic tracks near most of the ski areas of southern Idaho, including Sun Valley, Grand Targhee, Magic Mountain, Pomerelle and Pebble Creek. The Sun Valley area, in fact, has three: **Sun Valley Nordic Center** (Old Dollar Road, Sun Valley; 208-622-2150), **Warm Springs Nordic Center** (1801 Warm Springs Road, Ketchum; 208-726-3322) and **Skiers Country Club** (Radisson Elkhorn Resort, Sun Valley; 208-622-4511). Contact the **Sun Valley Cross Country Ski Association** (P.O. Box 2420, Sun Valley, ID 83353; 208-726-3423) for information and a free map and guide.

Backcountry touring is especially popular in the Sawtooth National Recreation Area (mainly around Galena Summit and in the Stanley area) and in the Teton Range (accessed from Grand Targhee Resort). For information, contact **Sawtooth Mountain Guides** (Route 21, Stanley; 208-774-3324) or **Rendezvous Ski Tours** (219 Highland Way, Victor; 208-787-2906).

Park 'n' Ski areas in southeastern Idaho include **Mink Creek** (24 kilometers, intermediate), on the Bannock Highway 15 miles south of Pocatello, and **Trail Canyon** (16 kilometers, all abilities), on Trail Canyon Road 12 miles northeast of Soda Springs, both in Caribou National Forest; **Bear Gulch/Mesa Falls** (15 kilometers, intermediate and advanced), on Route 47 seven miles northeast of Ashton, **Fall River Edge** (11 kilometers, beginner and intermediate), on Cave Falls Road ten miles east of Ashton, and **Brimstone/Buffalo River** (4 kilometers, beginner), on Route 20, a quarter-mile north of the Island Park Ranger Station, all in Targhee National Forest; and **Harriman State Park** (33 kilometers, all abilities), on Route 20, twenty miles north of Ashton.

For information on renting equipment, see the ski-rental section in "Downhill Skiing" above.

ICE SKATING

The famous outdoor ice skating rink at the **Sun Valley Lodge** (1 Sun Valley Road, Sun Valley, 208-622-2194) has rentals available; there's plenty of free-skating time allotted, but some hours are reserved for hockey or private groups. Idaho Falls' **Tautphaus Park** (Rollandet Avenue at 25th Street; 208-529-1470) also has a rink and rentals.

GOLF

Twin Falls' beautiful **Canyon Springs Golf Course** (Canyon Springs Road; 208-734-7609) is located beneath the Perrine Bridge in the Snake River Canyon. Other area courses are **Twin Falls Municipal Golf Course** (Route 30 West, Twin Falls; 208-733-3326), **Clear Lake Country Club** (403 Clear Lake Lane, Buhl; 208-543-4849) and **Burley Municipal Golf Course** (Route 81, Burley; 208-678-9807).

The Sun Valley area boasts two 18-hole layouts designed by Robert Trent Jones, Jr.: **Sun Valley Resort Golf Course** (Sun Valley Road, Sun Valley; 208-622-2251) and **Elkhorn Resort Golf Course** (Elkhorn Road, Sun Valley; 208-622-3309).

In Pocatello, try **Highland Golf Course** (201 Von Elm Lane; 208-237-9922) and **Riverside Golf Course** (3500 Bannock Highway; 208-232-9515). There's a good municipal course in Blackfoot—**Blackfoot Golf Course** (3115 Teeples Drive; 208-785-9960).

Idaho Falls has **Pinecrest Golf Course** (701 East Elva Street; 208-529-1485), **Sage Lakes Golf Course** (100 East 65 Street North; 208-528-5535) and **Sand Creek Golf Course** (5200 South Hackman Road; 208-529-1115). Other courses in the area are **Rexburg Municipal Golf Course** (South Airport Road, Rexburg; 208-359-3037), **Teton Lakes Golf Course** (1014 North Hibbard Highway, Rexburg; 208-359-3036) and the pitch-and-putt **Aspen Acres Golf Club** (4179 East 1100 North, Ashton; 800-845-2374).

TENNIS

Sun Valley has been rated by *Tennis* magazine as one of the top 50 tennis resorts in the United States. The **Sun Valley Resort Tennis Club** (Old Dollar Road, Sun Valley; 208-622-2156) has 18 courts and a pro shop open daily in summer. The nearby **Radisson Sun Valley Resort** (Elkhorn Road, Sun Valley; 208-622-4511 ext. 1054) has 17 courts. For information on Sun Valley–area public courts, contact the City of Ketchum Park Department (480 East Avenue North, Ketchum; 208-726-7820).

Twin Falls has 15 public courts, including six at **Twin Falls High School** (Locust Street and Stadium Boulevard); contact the City of Twin Falls Parks & Recreation Department (208-736-2265). In Pocatello, **Idaho State University** has six outdoor and four indoor courts, and there are 25 more courts in the city and suburbs; contact the Pocatello Parks and Recreation Department (208-234-6232). In Idaho Falls, the best place to find courts is **Tautphaus Park** (Rollandet Avenue and 25th Street); contact the Idaho Falls Parks and Recreation Division (208-529-1480).

HORSEBACK RIDING

In Twin Falls, **Pioneer Mountain Outfitters** (3321 Michigan Avenue; 208-734-3679) has year-round stables, offering everything from trail rides to winter sleigh rides.

At the Sun Valley resort, one- and two-hour rides are offered daily by **The Horsemen's Center** (Sun Valley Road, Sun Valley; 208-622-2391), while expeditions of up to a full day are available at **Elkhorn Village Stables** (Elkhorn Road, Sun Valley; 208-622-8503).

In far-eastern Idaho, **Bustle Creek Outfitters** (Grand Targhee Resort, Alta, Wyoming; 307-353-2300), just inside the Wyoming border via Driggs, Idaho, offers one-hour trips from Grand Targhee and full-day expeditions into the nearby Jedediah Smith Wilderness.

PACK TRIPS AND LLAMA TREKKING

The Sawtooth National Recreation Area is the single most popular destination for those who enjoy pack trips into the Sawtooth and White Cloud ranges. Outfitters include **Sawtooth Wilderness Outfitters** (Grandjean; 208-259-3408), **Galena Stage Stop Corrals** (Route 75, Galena Summit; 208-726-1735) and the **Mystic Saddle Ranch** (Stanley; 208-774-3591).

Challis and Salmon are gateways to the Frank Church–River of No Return Wilderness Area. Contact **Mile Hi Outfitters** (Route 93, Challis; 208-879-4403) or **Rawhide Outfitters** (204 Larson Street, Salmon; 208-756-4276).

For the Tetons and adjacent wilderness, try **Outfitters Pack Station** (1462 West Broadway, Idaho Falls; 208-522-3446).

A popular option is llama trekking. In the Sun Valley area, **Venture Outdoors** (408 North 6th Street, Hailey; 208-788-5049) lets you do everything from "taking a llama to lunch" on a three-hour midday walk to making five-day trips into the Sawtooth and other mountains.

BICYCLING

TWIN FALLS AREA Popular destinations are south of Burley in the Mount Harrison/Lake Cleveland area of Sawtooth National Forest and in the City of Rocks National Reserve, as well as in some of the Bureau of Land Management–administered lava lands of the Snake River Plain near Shoshone. For information, contact the **Magic Valley Cyclists** (1841 Addison Avenue East, Twin Falls; 208-733-0671).

SUN VALLEY AREA The pride of the resort community is the paved **Wood River Trail System**, which extends the length of the Wood River Valley for 21 miles from Lake Creek (four miles north of Ketchum) to Bellevue (17 miles south), mainly on a former railroad right-of-way. Administered by the Blaine County Recreation District (Hailey; 208-788-2117), it is linked to the ten-mile **Sun Valley Trails** by a pedestrian underpass. Runners, walkers and in-line skaters share the trails with cyclists.

SAWTOOTHS AND UPPER SALMON Numerous off-road trails are also available to cyclists in the adjacent Sawtooth National Forest and the nearby Sawtooth National Recreation Area. Farther north, biking is growing in popularity in the Challis and Salmon national forests, particularly in the Land of the Yankee Fork Historic Area near Challis. **Venture Outdoors** (408 North 6th Street, Hailey; 208-788-5049) offers guided mountain-biking trips in the Sawtooth National Forest, ranging in length from three hours to five days.

POCATELLO AREA Massacre Rocks State Park (west of American Falls) and the trails of Caribou National Forest are popular destinations. **Crystal Summit Cyclists** (2201 North Jana Street, Pocatello; 208-232-7510) can point you in the right direction, or you can join **Silent Sports Common Adventures** (208-232-3711) for a weekend or Wednesday- or Thursday-night ride.

IDAHO FALLS Popular biking areas include the city's own five-mile Snake River Greenbelt and Mount Taylor, south of Idaho Falls. The city's **Alpine Club** (1100 Cranmer Avenue, Idaho Falls; 208-522-8135) shares biking information with visiting cyclists.

SWAN AND TETON VALLEYS Targhee National Forest near Swan Valley and Driggs has numerous single-track trails. **Big Hole Mountain Bike Tours** (12 East Little Avenue, Driggs; 208-354-2828) offers guided downhill runs on the west side of the Tetons near Grand Targhee Resort.

HENRY'S FORK The Mesa Falls and Island Park areas north of Ashton, as well as Harriman State Park, feature fine trails for bicycling.

BIKE RENTALS Rentals and repairs are offered by such shops as **Rock's Cycling and Fitness** (334 East Main Street, Burley; 208-678-3764), **Pete Lane's** (Sun Valley Village Mall, Sun Valley; 208-622-2279), **Sturtevant's Alpine Sports** (314 North Main Street, Ketchum; 208-726-4502), **Scott's Bike Shop** (230 North Main Street, Pocatello; 208-232-4964) and **Crossroads Bike Shop** (337 River Parkway, Idaho Falls; 208-522-1600).

HIKING

Southeastern Idaho has five national forests, two federal wilderness areas, two national monuments, a national recreation area, a national reserve and seven state parks, so it's no surprise that the region offers a surplus of hiking trails. Following are just a few recommended jaunts. All distances listed are one-way unless otherwise noted.

TWIN FALLS AREA **Malad Gorge Trail** (2 miles), in Malad Gorge State Park, crosses a steel footbridge over the 250-foot chasm, then follows the canyon rim for additional overlooks of the river and the 60-foot waterfall that tumbles into the Devil's Washbowl.

Independence Lakes Trail (4 miles) ascends a saddle of 10,339-foot Cache Peak, in Sawtooth National Forest north of the City of Rocks National Reserve, to a lovely group of trout-rich alpine ponds at the 9000-foot level of the mountain. The trailhead is off Cottley Road, west of Elba and southeast of Burley via Route 77.

SUN VALLEY AREA **Bald Mountain Trail** (3.8 miles) offers a summer ascent of the ski resort's primary peak without the aid of chairlifts. The trail, which begins at the River Run parking lot in Ketchum and climaxes at a fire lookout, gains 3331 feet.

Craters of the Moon National Monument's **Echo Crater Trail** (3.5 miles) crosses ancient lava flows and passes cinder cones and petrified trees. There are campsites at the crater (bring water); a trail continues beyond. Pick up a free backcountry permit at the visitors center and stay on established trails. The smooth, ropy *pahoehoe* lava may be inviting, but *a'a* flows are fiercely sharp and make fast work of footwear.

The **Borah Peak Trail** (6 miles) is really a series of unimproved paths established by others who have climbed Idaho's highest mountain (12,655 feet). The west ridge is the route preferred by most. The Challis National Forest trailhead, on Birch Springs Road north of Mackay, is at an elevation of 7215 feet.

SAWTOOTHS AND UPPER SALMON **Sawtooth Lake Trail** (4.5 miles) begins five miles west of Stanley, off Iron Creek Road in the Sawtooth National Recreation Area, and rises to beautiful mile-long Sawtooth Lake, the largest lake in the Sawtooth Wilderness Area. It's a fairly gentle trail until the last three-quarters of a mile, when there's a steep ridge ascent to the lake.

Bench Lakes Trail (8 miles) begins at the Redfish Lake Visitors Center and climbs to a series of small alpine lakes that stairstep down the upper slopes of 10,229-foot Heyburn Peak. There's a 1200-foot elevation gain to the first of the four lakes, 2100 feet to the uppermost.

POCATELLO AREA The **West Fork of Mink Creek Trail** (6.6 miles) follows an old jeep road up a stream in Caribou National Forest, only 13 miles south of downtown Pocatello. The creek contains numerous beaver ponds; you'll have to watch closely to spot the rodents themselves. The trailhead is one mile south of the ranger station on Bannock Highway.

BEAR RIVER COUNTRY **Petticoat Peak Trail** (2 miles) climbs to the summit of the 8000-foot-plus Fish Creek Range, just four miles northeast of Lava Hot Springs. The hike, very steep in places, is worthwhile for the marvelous views from the summit.

SWAN AND TETON VALLEYS **Upper Palisades Lake Trail** (14 miles) is closed to all vehicles, which makes it a pleasant overnight camping excursion for backpackers. Three miles above the pretty, mile-long lake, located at about 7200-foot elevation, is an impressive waterfall. The trailhead is at the end of Upper Palisades Lake Road, southeast of Irwin.

Darby Canyon Trail (2.7 miles) climbs into Wyoming's Jedediah Smith Wilderness, on the west slope of the Tetons, to the Wind and Ice Cave on 10,966-foot Mount Bannon. The climb begins in woods and passes through alpine meadows accented by waterfalls. The trailhead is at the east end of eight-mile Darby Canyon Road, off Route 33 between Driggs and Victor.

HENRY'S FORK The **Coffee Pot Rapids Trail** (2.5 miles) follows Henry's Fork of the Snake River downstream from placid waters to boiling rapids. The easy walk begins at the Upper Coffeepot campground in Targhee National Forest, six miles north of Island Park.

The best way to hike the **Sawtell Peak–Rock Creek Basin Trail** (6 miles) is from the top down. Get a drop-off where steep, winding, 11-mile Forest Road 024 (off Route 20) ends at the Federal Aviation Administration radar installation atop 9866-foot Sawtell Peak. The view from here extends across three states and the entire Island Park Caldera. Then descend to the Rock Creek Basin near Henry's Lake State Park.

Transportation

BY CAR

An interstate freeway system of three separate routes is the primary connecting network through southeastern Idaho, linking the region with Boise and Portland (Oregon) to the west, Salt Lake City (Utah) to the south and Butte (Montana) to the north.

Eastbound **Route 84** from Portland and Boise skirts Twin Falls and Burley before turning southeast into Utah.

Southbound **Route 15** from Butte climbs over the Continental Divide to Idaho Falls and Pocatello, proceeding south into Utah, where it is joined by Route 84. The highway continues to Salt Lake City, Las Vegas (Nevada) and southern California.

Routes 15 and 84 are linked between Burley and Pocatello by **Route 86**, which follows the Snake River through American Falls.

BY AIR

Each of southeastern Idaho's major communities has a regional airport.

Twin Falls–Sun Valley Regional Airport, ten miles south of downtown Twin Falls, and Sun Valley's **Friedman Memorial Airport**, on Route 75 in Hailey, are served by Horizon commuter aircraft from Boise and SkyWest from Salt Lake City.

Pocatello Municipal Airport, six miles west of Pocatello at Exit 56 on Route 86 West, has SkyWest flights from Salt Lake. **Idaho Falls Municipal Airport–Fanning Field** is served by American Airlines, Horizon and SkyWest. Local buses and taxis provide ground transportation.

BY BUS

Greyhound Bus Lines follow the interstate corridor from Boise to Salt Lake City or West Yellowstone, Montana. Major depots are in Twin Falls (461 2nd Avenue South; 208-733-3002), Pocatello (215 West Bonneville Street; 208-232-5365) and Idaho Falls (2874 North Holmes Avenue; 208-522-0912). Other stops are made (from west to east) in Bliss, Hagerman, Buhl, Burley, Rupert, Blackfoot and Rexburg.

C.A.R.T. ("Community and Rural Transportation") serves eastern Idaho from Idaho Falls (850 Denver Street; 208-522-2278). Other main depots are in Driggs, Rexburg and Salmon.

Charter bus service is available to Sun Valley from Boise and Twin Falls via **Sun Valley Stages** (815 Ann Morrison Park Drive, Boise; 208-336-4038); from Idaho Falls, Pocatello and Salt Lake City via **Teton Stage Lines** (1425 Lindsay Boulevard, Idaho Falls; 208-529-8036).

BY TRAIN

Amtrak's (800-872-7245) "Pioneer" runs a route across southern Idaho from Boise en route to and from Salt Lake City and Chicago. The train stops at Union Pacific depots in Shoshone (304 North Rail Street; 208-886-2231), for Twin Falls and Sun Valley, and in Pocatello (300 South Harrison Avenue; 208-236-5555), for eastern Idaho.

CAR RENTALS

Four national agencies are ubiquitous in the regional centers. **Avis Rent A Car** (800-331-1212), **Budget Rent A Car** (800-527-0700), **Hertz Rent A Car** (800-654-3131) and **National Interrent** (800-328-4567) have outlets at the Twin Falls, Sun Valley (Hailey), Pocatello and Idaho Falls airports. **U-Save Auto Rental** (800-272-8728) has downtown locations in all four cities.

PUBLIC TRANSPORTATION

In Sun Valley, **Ketchum Area Rapid Transit** (800 1st Avenue North, Ketchum; 208-726-7576), known as KART, provides free year-round service that links downtown Ketchum with Sun Valley resort, as well as Elkhorn Village and the Warm Springs and River Run communities at the foot of the ski slopes.

Pocatello Urban Transit (215 West Bonneville Street; 208-234-2287) and Idaho Falls' **C.A.R.T. Transit** (850 Denver Street; 208-522-2278) have extensive routes through those cities. Fares are nominal. Twin Falls does not have a public bus network, but **Trans IV Buses** (496 Madrona Street; 208-736-2133) offers scheduled charter service.

TAXIS

Every city has its taxis. In southeastern Idaho, they include **Yellow Cab** (Twin Falls; 208-733-9101), **A-1 Taxicab** (Ketchum; 208-726-9351), **Mulligan Sun Valley Limousine** (Ketchum; 208-726-9137), **Taxi Dispatching** (Pocatello; 208-232-1115) and **Dial a Taxi** (Idaho Falls; 208-521-5133).

CHAPTER ELEVEN

Northern Idaho Rockies

Idaho's Panhandle is a land quite different from the vast, arid stretches of the south, so dependent upon the Snake River and its tributaries. Northern Idaho has dense forests, mineral-laden slopes and huge lakes whose waters are as pristine as any in North America. Where the Snake does cut a course, it does so in dramatic fashion, carving the deepest canyon on the continent, then slackening out to give Idaho a seaport 470 miles from the Pacific Ocean, at Lewiston.

Social and geographical differences have bred a strong sectionalism in the state that persists to the present day. Only one highway links northern and southern Idaho, and its final segment was paved only in 1938. Coeur d'Alene, Moscow, Lewiston and other towns of the north look more to Spokane, Washington, as their market center than they do to Boise. And Idaho's ten northern counties are the only part of the Rocky Mountain region in the Pacific time zone; southern Idaho, like all of Montana, Wyoming, Colorado and Utah, is on Mountain time.

The time-zone rift closely follows the Salmon River from the Bitterroot Range, on the Montana border, to its confluence with the Snake south of Lewiston. Nicknamed the "River of No Return" because it was long a one-way stream—no one succeeded in taking a boat upriver until after World War II—the Salmon drains 14,000 square miles of central Idaho, more than any river in any single state outside of Alaska. It is one of two major Snake River tributaries (the other is the Clearwater) in Idaho's Panhandle.

Engulfed by wilderness for much of its course, with few primitive roads approaching its banks, the Salmon is a stunning underscore for the northern Idaho Rockies. The river's main access point is Riggins, located where the Little Salmon pours into the Salmon about halfway between Boise and Lewiston. Travelers from the south climb out of the Salmon River canyon at the crest of White Bird Hill, where a stunning new panorama unfolds before them. The Camas Prairie, long the happy hunting ground of the Nez Perce, is now a fertile patchwork of wheat, alfalfa and rapeseed fields flanked on the east and north by the Clearwater River. Farther east are the wild rivers, mountains and forests through which Lewis and Clark descended from the Continental Divide in the early 19th century. The forests include giant old-growth cedar and one of the nation's largest virgin stands of white pine.

Where the Clearwater empties into the Snake is Lewiston, Idaho's fourth-largest city with a population of about 28,000. More than one million tons of grain and lumber are shipped from this port each year; the blue-collar city also supports a huge timber mill and a recreational munitions factory.

Forty-five minutes' drive north of Lewiston in Moscow, the University of Idaho is an island of academia in the center of the agriculturally unique Palouse Hills. The ripple and wave of wheat and barley in the continental breezes are almost hypnotic to drivers traveling through the seemingly endless sea of steep, round-topped hills.

Two great lakes support the largest towns of the northern Panhandle region, Coeur d'Alene (on Coeur d'Alene Lake) and Sandpoint (on Lake Pend Oreille). The two communities and their environs have distinct characters.

Boating and other water sports are big in Coeur d'Alene, a burgeoning resort town with a nationally acclaimed resort hotel (The Coeur d'Alene), upscale restaurants, outlet malls and theme parks. When snow falls, Coeur d'Alene turns its attention to winter sports: *Ski* magazine in 1994 called it America's most livable ski town. Silver Mountain, about 45 miles east at Kellogg, has America's longest gondola, and Schweitzer Mountain, just outside Sandpoint, has a new lodge and spectacular views of Lake Pend Oreille.

Pend Oreille is a mammoth body of water, 43 miles long, with record-size trout and northern pike and water so deep that the U.S. Navy conducts top-secret sonar experiments more than 1000 feet beneath the lake's surface. Sandpoint, located where the Pend Oreille River flows from the lake, supports a small but growing community of artists. The wood-products industry dominates the Idaho economy from here to the Canadian border 60 miles away, but secluded Priest Lake, an hour's drive west and north, is one of Idaho's more beautiful spots to consort with nature.

Lewiston-Moscow Area

Located at the confluence of the Clearwater and Snake rivers, Lewiston is an attractive town noted for its trees (hundreds of species, say urban foresters) and its mild "banana belt" climate. Connected via two Snake River bridges with its twin city of Clarkston, Washington, it has both Idaho's lowest point (740 feet) and its longest growing season (200 days).

From the visitor's standpoint, Lewiston's chief virtue is as a gateway to **Hells Canyon National Recreation Area**. Jet boats depart the Lewiston-Clarkston slackwater every morning for day-long and overnight excursions up the Snake to America's deepest canyon. (At 7600 feet, Hells Canyon is about 2300 feet deeper than Arizona's Grand Canyon.) The canyon's northern limit is about 30 miles south of Lewiston, but the area is all but inaccessible except by boat.

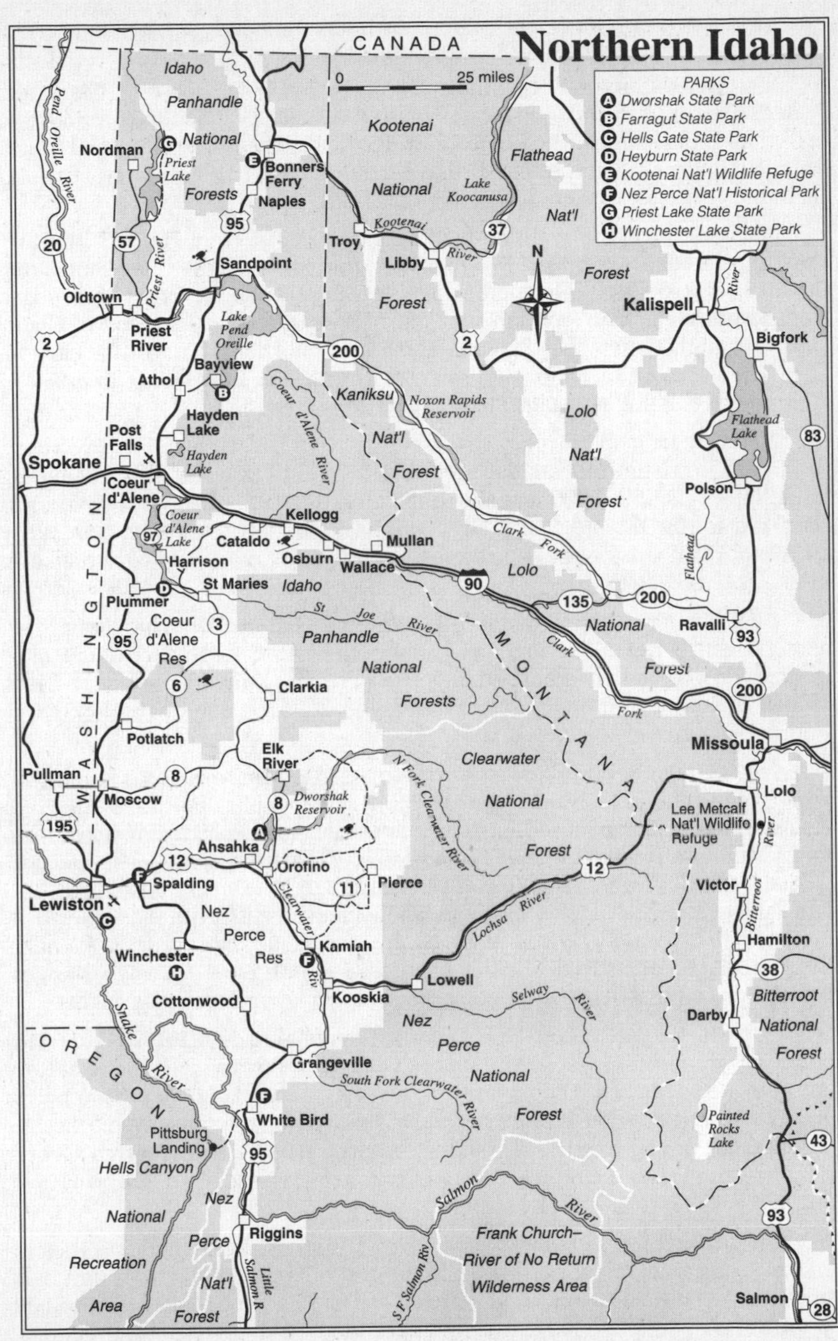

Northern Idaho
CANADA
0 25 miles
PARKS
A Dworshak State Park
B Farragut State Park
C Hells Gate State Park
D Heyburn State Park
E Kootenai Nat'l Wildlife Refuge
F Nez Perce Nat'l Historical Park
G Priest Lake State Park
H Winchester Lake State Park
Idaho Panhandle National Forests
Kootenai National Forest
Flathead Nat'l Forest
Kaniksu Nat'l Forest
Lolo Nat'l Forest
Lolo National Forest
Idaho Panhandle National Forests
Clearwater National Forest
Nez Perce National Forest
Bitterroot National Forest
Frank Church–River of No Return Wilderness Area
Hells Canyon National Recreation Area
Nez Perce Nat'l Forest
Coeur d'Alene Res
Nez Perce Res
WASHINGTON
MONTANA
OREGON
Nordman
Priest Lake
Bonners Ferry
Naples
Troy
Libby
Sandpoint
Oldtown
Priest River
Kalispell
Bigfork
Lake Pend Oreille
Bayview
Athol
Hayden Lake
Post Falls
Spokane
Coeur d'Alene
Coeur d'Alene Lake
Kellogg
Cataldo
Mullan
Osburn
Wallace
Harrison
St Maries
Plummer
Polson
Ravalli
Flathead Lake
Clarkia
Potlatch
Elk River
Pullman
Moscow
Dworshak Reservoir
Ahsahka
Orofino
Pierce
Lewiston
Spalding
Winchester
Kamiah
Lowell
Kooskia
Cottonwood
Grangeville
White Bird
Pittsburg Landing
Riggins
Missoula
Lolo
Lee Metcalf Nat'l Wildlife Refuge
Victor
Hamilton
Darby
Painted Rocks Lake
Salmon
Lake Koocanusa
Kootenai River
Noxon Rapids Reservoir
Coeur d'Alene River
Clark Fork
Flathead River
St Joe River
N Fork Clearwater River
Clearwater River
Lochsa River
Selway River
Snake River
South Fork Clearwater River
Salmon River
S F Salmon Riv
Little Salmon R
Bitterroot River
Pend Oreille River
Priest River
20
57
95
2
200
37
83
90
135
93
3
6
8
195
12
11
97
38
43
28
N

Spectacular geology, abundant wildlife, artifacts from early settlers and prehistoric pictographs are among the attractions that await visitors.

The **Hells Canyon NRA Snake River Office** (P.O. Box 699, Clarkston, WA 99403; 509-758-0616) is located on the west bank of the Snake, about two and a half miles south of the Route 12 bridge that connects Lewiston and Clarkston. There are no interpretive displays here, but you'll find plenty of useful literature and park rangers to answer questions.

Many of the area's eight jet-boat operators depart from **Hells Gate State Park** (Snake River Avenue; 208-743-2363), four miles south of Lewiston along the Snake's east shore. There are campsites for tents and RVers. Others leave from **Swallow Park** on the Clarkston side of the river or from the port of Clarkston. Overnighters typically stay in guest-ranch bunkhouses below the canyon. See "The Sporting Life" for outfitters, or contact the **Lewiston Chamber of Commerce** (2207 East Main Street, Lewiston; 208-743-3531).

You can get a spectacular, bird's-eye view of Lewiston and its two rivers from atop **Lewiston Hill** on the north side of the Clearwater. Take Route 95 to the top of the hill, 2000 feet above the city; turn off at the Vista House gift shop and follow the old Spiral Highway back down for panoramas at every switchback. This route, an engineering marvel of its time, was constructed in 1917. The round-trip drive takes less than an hour.

Lewiston has a nicely renewed **Downtown Historic District** along Main and D streets between 5th Street and Snake River Avenue. History aficionados can learn about the city's background as a port city at the '30s art deco **Luna House Museum** (3rd and C streets; 208-743-2535), home of the Nez Perce County Historical Society.

Just 28 miles north of Lewiston via Route 95 is **Moscow**, home of the **University of Idaho** (UI). Named not for the Russian capital but for a village in Pennsylvania, and pronounced not "MOS-cow" but "MOS-koh," this cultured town forms half of the Palouse Country's college row. UI students (sports teams are nicknamed "Vandals," which should not be taken as a reflection on student behavior) share many activities, including social and athletic events, with those of Washington State University (WSU), just ten miles across the state border in Pullman. Before Idaho raised its legal drinking age from 19 to 21 a few years ago, Moscow was the place for WSU students to spend their Friday and Saturday nights.

Of particular interest on the 450-acre UI campus are the **Kibbie Dome Athletic Center**, a 17,500-seat indoor stadium and arena on Perimeter Drive at Rayburn Street; **Shadduck Arboretum**, which offers picnicking among more than 200 kinds of vegetation on Nez Perce Drive; and geology displays at the Department of Mining Engineering and Metallurgy. The **UI Information Center** (208-885-6111) is on campus at 3rd and Line streets, just south of Pullman Road, a few blocks west of the city center.

Arterial highways circumvent Moscow's **Main Street**, which has thus remained quaint and friendly to pedestrians and buskers. Restaurants and bars, small shops, bookstores and art galleries like **The Prichard Gallery** (414 South Main Street; 208-882-6000) attract students and other townspeople alike.

The **McConnell Mansion** (110 South Adams Street; 208-882-1004), three blocks east of Main, gives a glimpse of what Moscow was like a century ago. Built in 1886 by an Idaho governor, it now houses the Latah County Historical Society and recalls a late-Victorian lifestyle in its furnishings and decor.

Horse lovers won't want to miss the **Appaloosa Horse Club Museum and Heritage Center** (5070 Route 8 West; 208-882-5578), three miles west of Moscow at the Washington state line. Exhibits describe the evolution of the appaloosa, its importance to the Nez Perce and its role today.

Surrounding Moscow for many miles in all directions are the rolling hills of the Palouse. In addition to wheat and barley, farmers here produce more dry peas and lentils than in any other part of the United States—about 500 million pounds annually.

Proceed north on Route 95 toward Coeur d'Alene, and you'll climb to **Mary Minerva McCroskey State Park** (★) (208-686-1308), on the Latah-Benewah county line. There are no signs announcing the primitive park, but turn left at a sign for "Skyline Drive" and you'll encounter miles of spectacular views from an unpaved road. Hiking, cross-country skiing and nature walking are the main pursuits of the 5300-acre park.

If you turn east off 95 onto Route 6 at the historic company lumber town of **Potlatch**, you'll find yourself on the **White Pine Scenic Route**, a marvelous wooded drive through the Idaho Panhandle National Forests to St. Maries. Farther southeast, via **Clarkia** on Route 3, is the **Emerald Creek Garnet Area** (★) one of only two places in the world (the other is India) where star garnets are found. Because the area is on National Forest land, anyone is welcome to dig for the precious stones between Memorial Day and Labor Day. Properly equipped diggers can take Forest Road 447 eight miles off the highway, then hike another half-mile to the garnet site. The St. Maries Ranger District (P.O. Box 407, St. Maries, ID 83861; 208-245-2531) will provide information.

SOUTHBOUND ROUTE 95 In the other direction, from Lewiston toward Boise, Route 95 follows the Clearwater River east for about eight miles. Then it crosses the stream and ascends a small hill to the **Nez Perce National Historical Park Visitors Center** (Route 95, Spalding; 208-843-2261). A film and museum exhibits provide an orientation to the park's 38 sites in four states, but primarily those in Idaho.

A worthwhile side trip at **Cottonwood** is the Benedictine **Monastery of St. Gertrude** (★) (Keuterville Road; 208-962-3224), high atop a hill overlooking the Camas Prairie. The building is easily visible from Route 95, two and a half miles away. Its striking twin 97-foot towers rise above the monastery, which was built of blue porphyry quarried from a nearby hill. A convent and priory when it was built in 1925, it now welcomes both men and women monks. The chapel, whose hand-carved high altar was constructed without the use of a single nail, is open to visitors, as is the St. Gertrude's Museum, which displays a potpourri of religious and pioneer artifacts and quirky personal collections of the sisters.

Grangeville is the seat of Idaho County, which stretches from Oregon to Montana and encompasses 5.4 million acres, much of it wilderness. The town of 3200 is today a lumber and agricultural center and an outfitting hub for trips into the Selway-Bitterroot, Frank Church–River of No Return and Gospel Hump wilderness areas of the **Nez Perce National Forest** (208-983-1950). Grangeville is also the home of the Ray Holes saddle, one of the most venerated names in western horsemanship.

It's ten highway miles from Grangeville to the apex of 4245-foot **White Bird Hill**, and eight miles of continual downhill grade on the south side. About halfway down the descent, at a panoramic overview, a Nez Perce National Historical Park display describes the initial battle of the 1877 Nez Perce war. The Indians routed two cavalry companies on the rambling plains below this viewpoint, but four months later they were forever subjugated.

Cottonwoods hang over White Bird Creek as it flows through the pretty village of **White Bird**, 3000 feet below the hill's summit. The creek enters the Salmon River about a mile from the hamlet. Just upriver, Forest Road 493—often too wet or icy for any but four-wheel-drive vehicles—provides Idaho's only road access to the heart of Hells Canyon. The winding, 17-mile climb and descent to **Pittsburg Landing**, on the Snake River, is appreciated by whitewater rafters (many of whom take out here after the frightening 32-mile run from Hells Canyon Dam) and backpackers (who can begin or end their trek on the Snake River National Recreation Trail here).

Riggins, the Salmon River rafting capital, marks the southern limit of northern Idaho; it's still a full three-hour drive from here to the state capital at Boise. A handful of small motels, cafés and bars trumpet their appeal to outdoors enthusiasts.

The **Hells Canyon NRA Riggins Office** (P.O. Box 832, Riggins, ID 83549; 208-628-3916), about a half-mile south of town on Route 95, provides full information on trails and campsites in the recreation area. **Heavens Gate Overlook**, 19 miles from Riggins via rugged, steep, unpaved Forest Road 517, affords a spectacular late-summer vista of Hells Canyon, four and a half miles west and one and a half miles down, and the adjacent **Seven Devils Mountains**.

THE CLEARWATER VALLEY Route 12 spans north-central Idaho from west to east. From Lewiston, the highway follows the Clearwater River upstream for 93 miles to Lowell. It then turns up the Lochsa River—a designated "wild and scenic river corridor"—to Lolo Pass, on the Rockies' crest.

For much of its distance, Route 12 traces the **Lolo Trail**, an ancient Native American trade and hunting route also followed by explorers Lewis and Clark in 1805 and 1806. Roadside historical markers describe many points of interest; for more information, contact **Clearwater National Forest** (12730 Route 12, Orofino; 208-476-4541).

With about 2800 people, the logging town of **Orofino**, 40 miles upstream from Lewiston, is the largest community along Route 12 in Idaho. Its **Clearwater Historical Society Museum** (315 College Avenue; 208-476-5033) is worth a look for pioneer artifacts.

More significantly, Orofino is the gateway to the **Dworshak Dam** project, completed in 1973 on the North Fork of the Clearwater River. The 717-foot-high

I Will Fight No More, Forever

In the mythology of the Nez Perce people, the ancient hero Coyote slew and dismembered a monster and flung its body parts to the four winds. The different peoples of the world sprang up in all directions, but none in the land where Coyote stood. Realizing this, Coyote squeezed the blood from the monster's heart, thereby giving birth to the Nee-me-poo, "The People." History has proven them to be a people with tremendous heart.

Named *nez percé,* "pierced noses," by French Canadian fur trappers—erroneously, because nose jewelry has never been a tribal tradition—the Nee-me-poo lived for centuries in the valleys of the Clearwater and Snake rivers and their tributaries. They fished, hunted and harvested the edible root of the camas lily from the prairies and plateaus. The tribe's mobility and lifestyle changed in the early 1700s with their acquisition of appaloosa horses, which they successfully bred, but they remained gracious and peaceful, as the Lewis and Clark expedition a century later would testify.

When Christian missionaries arrived in the 1840s in advance of later westward expansion, many Nez Perce adopted the white man's religion and culture. Two tribal factions emerged. Pro-American Christians acquiesced to the growing U.S. territorial presence. When gold was discovered on Nez Perce land in 1860, they agreed to restrict themselves to a reservation only one-tenth the size of their traditional tribal lands.

A "non-treaty" faction led by young Chief Joseph of Oregon's Wallowa Valley resisted being moved onto the new reservation. Although tribe members were philosophically opposed to violence, when attempts were made to forcibly relocate them, they struck back, delivering a crushing defeat to U.S. cavalry forces near White Bird, Idaho, in June 1877. Joseph's 130 Nez Perce renegades were then pursued across Idaho and Montana before surrendering four months later, just 42 miles short of Canadian refuge. "I will fight no more, forever," Joseph said. He and many of the other Nez Perce leaders were forced to live out their lives in exile from their homeland.

Idaho's Nez Perce have been a self-governing tribe under U.S. law since 1948. **Nez Perce National Historical Park**, established in 1965, now encompasses 38 separate sites, 29 of them in Idaho and the remainder in Oregon, Washington and Montana. Visitors who wish to tour the sites should start at the park headquarters and **visitors center**, on Route 95 about 11 miles east of Lewiston. Other sites of interest include the **White Bird Battlefield**, ten to 15 miles south of Grangeville; the purported location of the **Heart of the Monster** myth, three miles south of Kamiah; and the **Lolo Trail**, followed by the fleeing non-treaty Nez Perce in 1877.

dam (the largest ever constructed by the U.S. Army Corps of Engineers) creates 54-mile-long **Dworshak Reservoir**, on the western shore of which lies **Dworshak State Park** (Freeman Creek Road, Cavendish; 208-476-5994). Ninety-minute guided tours of the Dworshak Dam are offered from its **visitors center** (Dworshak Dam Road, Ahsahka; 208-476-1255), located at the top of the dam six miles west of Orofino.

From Orofino, Route 12 proceeds up the gentle Clearwater River Valley. The citizens of **Kamiah**, responding to economic disaster when a big lumber mill closed its doors in the early 1980s, gave their downtown business district a Victorian West facelift to attract tourism. If you're driving by, it's certainly worth a few extra minutes to admire the work put into its city hall, fire station, library, and virtually every privately owned building along a three-block stretch. A couple of miles southeast on Route 12, Nez Perce National Historical Park markers indicate the **Heart of the Monster** site where, according to tribal legend, Coyote created the Nez Perce.

Not far south of here, Route 12 turns east at Kooskia and follows the Clearwater to **Lowell**, where the wild Lochsa and Selway rivers join to form the Middle Fork. There are few services from here to Lolo Pass on the Montana border, although numerous fine U.S. Forest Service campsites are located along both the Lochsa and (especially) the Selway. Before crossing into Montana, stop to learn about human and natural history at the **Lolo Pass Visitors Center** (208-942-3113) atop Lolo Pass.

(Note: Forest Road 500, the Lolo Motorway, more exactly re-creates the original Lolo Trail than Route 12—but this is a primitive dirt road with virtually no facilities en route. It takes a sturdy four-wheel-drive vehicle about two days to cover its 90 miles.)

LEWISTON-MOSCOW AREA HOTELS

The **Sacajawea Motor Inn** (1824 Main Street, Lewiston; 208-746-1393, 800-333-1393, fax 208-743-3620) is a friendly, two-story accommodation near the Clearwater River bridge east of downtown. Its 90 rooms are comfortable and well kept. There are some suites with whirlpools and microwave ovens. Facilities include a restaurant and lounge, an outdoor swimming pool and a hot tub, a fitness room and a coin laundry. Moderate.

Lewiston's finest is the **Ramada Inn** (621 21st Street; phone/fax 208-799-1000, 800-232-6730), on a hillside with a view toward the Clearwater River bridge. The city's only microbrewery opened in the hotel in 1994; casual meals are served in this pub, upscale cuisine at a restaurant. A swimming pool, jacuzzi and full-service athletic and racquetball club are in the suites wing. Moderate to deluxe.

In Moscow, the top accommodation is the **University Inn** (1516 Pullman Road; 208-882-0550, 800-325-8765, fax 208-883-3050), a Best Western property two miles from downtown near the west end of the University of Idaho campus. With three indoor pools, putting greens on a landscaped courtyard, a 24-hour coffee shop, a gourmet restaurant and two lounges, it offers more than enough to guests in its 173 rooms. Moderate to deluxe.

A remote getaway is the **Huckleberry Heaven Lodge** (★) (Elk River; 208-826-3405), on little Elk Creek Reservoir 54 miles east of Moscow via Route 8. The lodge is rustic and room guests must walk down the hallway to find a bathroom, but the price is unbeatable, and everything from fishing poles and mountain bikes to horses and canoes is available for daily rental. Home-cooked meals are served by reservation. Budget.

Nestled on the Middle Fork of the Clearwater River, just off the Lolo Pass Highway (Route 12), the **Looking Glass Guest Ranch** (HC-75, Box 32, Kooskia; 208-926-0855) offers horseback riding, river rafting, hiking, fishing and other outdoor pursuits. There are seven rooms, each with rustic decor and a private bathroom. Moderate.

For a directory of 14 B & Bs in the greater Lewiston-Moscow area, contact **Heart of the Inland Northwest Bed & Breakfast** (702 Public Avenue, Moscow; 208-882-4061).

LEWISTON-MOSCOW AREA RESTAURANTS

For cheap eats in Lewiston, both **Effie's Burgers** (1120 Main Street; 208-746-1889) and the **Anytime Tavern and Grill** (1350 Main Street; 208-746-6230) offer giant-size hamburgers. The latter has only four tables and a half-dozen barstools, but it is open 24 hours daily. Budget.

Zany Graze (2006 19th Avenue, Lewiston; 208-746-8131) is the place to head for light-hearted family fun. One of several local eateries owned by the Happy Day Corporation, Zany's perpetuates a '50s diner theme in its cuisine and decor; expect good service and hearty American food. Budget to moderate.

For upscale dining in downtown Lewiston, try **Jonathan's** (301 D Street; 208-746-3438). A formal menu of steak and seafood, Continental and Cajun specialties is served in the low-lit basement dining room of the historic Bollinger Plaza building; there's a more casual lounge on the first floor. Moderate to deluxe.

For an elegant evening out, many locals head for the **Three Mile Inn** (Snake River Highway, Asotin; 509-243-4158), a 20-mile drive south of downtown Lewiston on the Washington side of the Snake River near Asotin. The inn takes reservations Tuesday through Saturday nights for its gourmet steak and seafood specialties, including prime rib and lobster. Picture windows afford a marvelous view of the Snake as it crawls out of Hells Canyon. Moderate to deluxe.

In Moscow, light meals like sandwiches and pastas, wine and microbeers are offered at **The Beanery** (602 South Main Street; 208-882-7646), a literature-littered coffeehouse that has assumed a larger role in the off-campus community. Budget prices.

The **West 4th Bar & Grill** (313 South Main Street, Moscow; 208-882-0743) has a wide-ranging and creative menu of steaks, chicken, seafood and pasta in the simple, high-ceilinged atmosphere of the old Hotel Moscow downtown. Moderate. At the same address, the **Main Street Deli & Bakery** serves counter-order breakfasts and deli-style luncheon sandwiches. Outdoor seating is available. Budget.

Outside of the two main cities, you can't go wrong in the Clearwater valley at the **Ponderosa Restaurant** (220 Michigan Avenue, Orofino; 208-476-4818). This is hearty meat-and-potatoes food for hard-working loggers, who may finish up the night at the Ponderosa's Brass Rail lounge. Budget.

LEWISTON-MOSCOW AREA SHOPPING

Urban renewal in Lewiston's downtown historical district has made it perhaps the busiest and most interesting place to shop in the region. Check out **Morgans' Alley** (301 Main Street; 208-743-8593): 22 businesses, including gift and craft stores and restaurants, are contained in four early-20th-century buildings linked by brick arches, stairways and passageways.

In Moscow, **Northwest Showcase** (520 South Main Street; 208-883-1128) displays and sells regional crafts and foods.

If you're an equestrian looking for the finest for your horse, don't fail to stop at the **Ray Holes Saddle Company** (213 West Main Street, Grangeville; 208-983-1460). Holes' custom riding and pack saddles have been renowned since the 1930s. But don't be surprised if you have to wait a year or more for your order: There are hundreds of others in line ahead of you.

LEWISTON-MOSCOW AREA NIGHTLIFE

The pickings are slim for a lively nightlife in working-class Lewiston. Try **Curley's Alibi** (1702 Main Street; 208-743-0317) for country-and-western dancing, and **TomFoolery** (1st and C streets; 208-746-2005) for live rock music and comedy acts. **M. J. Barleyhopper's** (Ramada Inn, 621 21st Street; 208-799-1000), a microbrewery and pub, is a good place to find a designer draft and a conversation.

Nightlife in Moscow, though smaller than Lewiston, benefits from its campus influence. The **Hartung Theatre** (6th Street and Stadium Road; 208-885-6484), on the University of Idaho campus, presents a mix of drama, comedy and musicals during the school year; in summer, the **Idaho Repertory** makes its home for five weeks in this 419-seat theater.

Among student-oriented pubs in Moscow, **John's Alley** (114 East 6th Street; 208-882-7531) is a favorite. **Chasers** (University Inn, 1516 Pullman Road; 208-882-0550), has dancing most nights. Check local newspapers as well as bulletin boards along Main Street to see who has live music and when.

LEWISTON-MOSCOW AREA PARKS

Hells Canyon National Recreation Area—The Snake River muscles through North America's deepest gorge (as much as 7600 feet from mountaintop to canyon floor) on the Idaho-Oregon border, creating a thrilling experience for whitewater-rafting enthusiasts and other river adventurers. There's also great fishing, hiking and horseback riding. Pictographs and native artifacts indicate that man has inhabited or visited this chasm for thousands of years.

Facilities: Picnic tables (21 sites), pit toilets or restrooms, boat ramps (four sites), hiking and horse trails; information, 509-628-3916 (Riggins) or 509-758-0616 (Clarkston). *Swimming:* The Snake River is unsafe. *Fishing:* Access from 18 sites; species include trout, steelhead and catfish.

Camping: Primitive camping along the river for rafters and backpackers. There are unimproved campgrounds in the Seven Devils high country and developed tent and RV sites on Idaho Power Company and National Forest lands adjacent to the recreation area in Idaho and Oregon.

Getting there: The only paved road access is at Hells Canyon Dam—the primary rafting put-in point—from Cambridge, Idaho, or Homestead, Oregon, via Copperfield Park. There is four-wheel drive access from Route 95 near Riggins to Pittsburg Landing, and jet-boat access upriver from Lewiston.

Hells Gate State Park—Snake River frontage makes this refuge a prime playground for Lewiston-area residents. It's also a great departure point for boat excursions up the river into Hells Canyon, 30 miles south.

Facilities: Picnic tables, restrooms, marina and boat launch, bike path, playground, hiking and horse trails (horses for rent); day-use fee, $2; information, 208-799-5015. *Swimming:* Designated beach in day-use area. *Fishing:* Especially popular when steelhead run in November and December.

Camping: There are 64 RV sites with hookups and 29 tent sites, open March 1 to November 1; $12 per night for RV hookups, $9 for tents.

Getting there: The park is four miles south of Lewiston at the end of Snake River Avenue.

Winchester Lake State Park—Fishermen and nature lovers enjoy this pine-enveloped lake with five miles of shoreline at the edge of the Camas Prairie. With 418 acres, the park is larger than the adjacent village of Winchester.

Facilities: Picnic tables, restrooms, boat ramp, hiking and cross-country skiing trails; day-use fee, $2; information, 208-924-7563. *Swimming:* No formal area. *Fishing:* Trout and bass; ice fishing popular in winter.

Camping: There are 49 RV hookups plus 29 for tents only; $5 per night.

Getting there: It's southwest of Winchester, three miles off Route 95.

Clearwater National Forest—Extending west from the Bitterroot Range on the Montana border, down the tributary systems of the Lochsa River and the North Fork of the Clearwater River (with an additional parcel in the Palouse Hills), this 1.8-million-acre national forest encompasses much of the Idaho that explorers Lewis and Clark first saw nearly 200 years ago. There are 1700 miles of hiking trails in the forest, which includes a portion of the Selway-Bitterroot Wilderness south of the Lochsa.

Facilities: Picnic tables, restrooms, trails, resort store (at Powell, near Lolo Pass); information, 208-476-4541. *Swimming:* At Laird Park (on the Palouse River near Harvard) and isolated small mountain lakes. *Fishing:* Cutthroat, brook and rainbow trout and mountain whitefish are native to the streams.

Camping: There are 324 RV/tent sites and six for RVs only (no hookups) plus 26 for tents only at 21 campgrounds. Seasons vary, but most are open late May through September; $5 to $6 per night.

Getting there: Routes 6 and 8 northeast of Moscow, Route 11 east of Orofino and Route 12 east of Kooskia are the principal access highways.

Nez Perce National Forest—One complete federal wilderness area (Gospel Hump) and parts of three others (Selway-Bitterroot, Frank Church–River of No Return and Hells Canyon)— together comprising one million acres—make this rugged, 2.2-million-acre national forest one of Idaho's least accessible. Stretching across the middle Panhandle from Montana to Oregon in a belt broken only by the Route 95 corridor through Riggins, it's noted for its deep canyons, its fall steelhead runs and its Nez Perce and early gold-mining history. It's bordered on the south by the main Salmon River, on the west by Hells Canyon of the Snake River; the Selway and South Fork of the Clearwater River are other major streams.

Facilities: Picnic tables, restrooms, boat ramps, trails; information, 208-983-1950. *Swimming:* Not recommended in whitewater rivers. *Fishing:* This area's rivers are noted for their annual late-fall run of steelhead trout.

Camping: There are 162 RV/tent sites (no hookups) plus 35 for tents only at 24 campgrounds. Seasons vary, but most are open from June to October; $4 to $5 per night.

Getting there: Route 14 east of Grangeville provides the best road access, serving the forest communities of Elk City and Red River Hot Springs. Another primary route is Forest Road 223 up the Selway River from Lowell, on Route 12.

Dworshak State Park—This 1300-acre park is spread along the western shore of serpentine, 54-mile-long Dworshak Reservoir, created by the 1973 damming of the North Fork of the Clearwater River.

Facilities: Picnic shelter, restrooms, amphitheater, boat ramps, playground; day-use fee, $2; information, 208-476-5994. *Swimming:* Beach at Freeman Creek campground when reservoir is full. *Fishing:* Reservoir has record bass, kokanee and trout; fish cleaning station available.

Camping: There are 50 RV/tent sites with hookups, 55 tent-only sites, plus group sites, open May 1 to October 15; $12 per night for hookups, $9 for tents.

Getting there: It's 24 miles north of Orofino by road, via Route P1 through Cavendish; or six miles north of Ahsahka by boat from Dworshak Dam.

Coeur d'Alene Area

Coeur d'Alene didn't make a good first impression on white visitors. Early 19th-century French Canadian fur traders, frustrated by their inability to trade cheap trinkets to indigenous tribes in exchange for valuable pelts, said the natives had "*les coeurs d'alênes*"—"the hearts of awls."

In modern Coeur d'Alene, by contrast, you *can* get something for nothing. You can get spectacular scenery and ready access to a wide variety of recreational opportunities and historic sites. Put something down, and you can stay in fine resort hotels and dine in excellent restaurants. In short, it now makes a *very* good first impression . . . and then some.

Located on the northern shore of 23-mile-long **Coeur d'Alene Lake,** the city of Coeur d'Alene (now pronounced "CORE-duh-LANE") is smack on the Route 90 corridor, just a half-hour's drive east of Spokane, Washington. The centerpiece of the town of 27,000 is its widely acclaimed resort, **The Coeur d'Alene** (115 South 2nd Street; 208-765-4000). Even non–hotel guests can enjoy a walk on the world's longest floating boardwalk (3300 feet), which surrounds the resort's bustling marina, or play a round of golf on a waterfront course that includes the world's first and only floating green.

The long, narrow lake itself, most of it nestled in dense evergreen forest, was once listed among the world's five most beautiful by *National Geographic.* Home to the largest population of osprey in the western United States, the lake attracts fishermen and other water-sports enthusiasts from hundreds of miles away. **Lake Coeur d'Alene Cruises** (208-765-4000; fare) depart in summer from Independence Point, just west of the resort. There are 90-minute afternoon cruises three times daily, as well as Sunday brunch and Monday dinner cruises. On Sundays and Wednesdays, six-hour length-of-the-lake cruises head up the tributary **St. Joe River**, which at 2200-foot elevation is said to be the highest navigable stream in the United States.

Sherman Avenue is the quaint main street of downtown Coeur d'Alene. A good way to explore it, and the rest of the city, is on a double-decker London bus tour (fare), which departs twice daily from the **Coeur d'Alene Visitors Center** (1st Street and Sherman Avenue; 208-664-0587).

Opposite the visitors center, at City Park, is the **Museum of North Idaho** (115 Northwest Boulevard; 208-664-3448; admission), with extensive exhibits on the region's mining and logging history and native culture. A few blocks farther west, on the campus of North Idaho College, the **Fort Sherman Museum** (College Drive and River Avenue; 208-664-3448; admission), in the powderhouse of a late-19th-century military fort, has displays that depict life in Coeur d'Alene in that era. Nearby, now owned by the college, are the former Fort Sherman officers' quarters and chapel.

There are great places for cheap recreation on either side of the resort: **City Park** (West Lakeshore Drive), with a lifeguarded swimming beach and broad grassy tracts for sunbathing, picnicking and Frisbee playing; and **Tubbs Hill**, a 150-acre natural park that juts into the lake and offers, among other trails, a three-mile loop beginning from the 3rd Street boat launch on the resort's east side.

A pleasant half-day's drive is the **Lake Coeur d'Alene Scenic Byway**, a 95-mile loop along the eastern shore of Coeur d'Alene Lake (via Route 97) and back on Route 3, past a chain of nine small lakes, to the interstate. The byway exits Route 90 about ten miles east of Coeur d'Alene at **Wolf Lodge Bay**, noted for its November gathering of bald eagles. It meanders down the photogenic shoreline to **Harrison**, an old lumber and shipping town with several structures still standing from the 1800s, then turns north on Route 3 past Black, Care, Medicine, Rose and other lakes whose surrounding wetlands delight birdwatchers.

An alternative route back to Coeur d'Alene follows Route 3 south to the lumber town of **St. Maries** on the winding St. Joe River. West of St. Maries on Route 5 is **Heyburn State Park** (Route 5, Plummer; 208-686-1308), Idaho's second largest; it encompasses the channel of the St. Joe and several lakes created by its silt deposits as it flows toward Coeur d'Alene Lake. Route 5 joins Route 95 at Plummer, in the heart of the **Coeur d'Alene Indian Reservation**. The city of Coeur d'Alene is 34 miles north.

West from Coeur d'Alene on Route 90 toward Spokane is the town of **Post Falls**, built around a Spokane River sawmill in 1880. A huge Louisiana-Pacific lumber mill now stands beside **Falls Park**, which overlooks a narrow canyon that provided a spillway for that early mill. Nearby **Treaty Rock Park** preserves pictographs said to have sealed an 1871 treaty between a Coeur d'Alene Indian chief and Post Falls founder Frederick Post. The two parks are connected by **Centennial Trail**, a paved path for walkers, runners and bicyclists that when completed will extend for 63 miles and link Coeur d'Alene with Spokane.

THE SILVER VALLEY Traveling east along the Route 90 corridor, you enter the Silver Valley region. As you approach the historic mining area 24 miles east of Coeur d'Alene, look for a hilltop church near the town of **Cataldo**. The Mission of the Sacred Heart, the oldest standing building in Idaho, is preserved within **Old Mission State Park** (Route 90 Exit 39, Cataldo; 208-682-3814; admission). Erected in 1850–53 by members of the Coeur d'Alene tribe under the direction of Jesuit Father Antonio Ravalli, the Greek revival–style structure still contains its original artwork, which has been restored. The neighboring parish house and nearby cemetery are also open. The mission's significance is interpreted by a park visitors center. Services are held here on high holy days, highlighted by an annual Feast of Assumption pilgrimage by Coeur d'Alene Indians on August 15.

The **Silver Valley** is the largest silver-producing area in the world (more than one billion troy ounces in its century of activity), as well as a major player in the mining and smelting of lead and zinc. Though an 1882 gold rush first brought miners scurrying to this western slope of the Rockies, it was the other elements that made their fortunes, three violent labor strikes in the 1890s notwithstanding.

Kellogg was always a company town whose heart and soul belonged to Bunker Hill, one of the world's largest lead-mining firms. When the company downscaled and laid off hundreds of workers in the 1970s, city fathers promoted a Bavarian theme in Kellogg's downtown architecture, without a lot of success. But in 1990 they opened the world's longest gondola (3.1 miles up 6295-foot Kellogg Peak) and, suddenly, the once-tiny Silverhorn ski hill put on a whole different face as Silver Mountain.

Silver Mountain (610 Bunker Avenue; 208-783-1111) cannot yet be called a world-class resort, but a lodging and dining infrastructure is already developing around it. In summer, when there's no snow for skiers, bikers can rent two-wheelers at the gondola and enjoy the mountain trails. A concert series in July and August attracts some of the top contemporary names in popular music and jazz to an open-air amphitheater near the gondola's upper terminal, and sightseers can ride the gondola any winter or summer day just to enjoy the view.

Elsewhere in Kellogg, the **Staff House Museum** (820 McKinley Avenue; 208-786-4141) houses the collection of the Shoshone County Mining and Smelting Museum, open daily in summer.

The best preserved of the Silver Valley mining towns is **Wallace**, deservedly a designated national historic district. A tour of the **Sierra Silver Mine** (420 5th Street; 208-752-5151; admission) is not to be missed. A 16-passenger trolley takes visitors from the downtown ticket office on a narrated journey to the entrance of the depleted mine, where they are fitted with hardhats. A guide discusses mining history and techniques during the one-hour walking tour through a 1000-foot, descending U-shaped tunnel. Tours are offered seven days a week, June through September.

Wallace is a town of museums. The **Wallace District Mining Museum** (509 Bank Street; 208-556-1592; admission) recalls the history of the Silver Valley in artifacts, photographs and a video presentation. The elegant and historic **Northern Pacific Depot Railroad Museum** (219 6th Street; 208-752-0111; admission), with its chateau-style architecture, was moved to its present location in 1986 to make room for completion of the freeway through town; it recounts the district's railroading past. The **Oasis Bordello Museum** (605 Cedar Street; 208-753-0801; admission) offers tours of a brothel that operated in Wallace—along with three others—until federal officers finally closed it down in 1988. Wallace had been the last U.S. city outside of Nevada to allow bordellos.

THE NORTHERN PANHANDLE The drive north up Route 95 from Coeur d'Alene to Sandpoint, normally about 45 minutes, can easily stretch into hours with side trips.

Hayden Lake, about five miles north of Coeur d'Alene, is often misleadingly portrayed as a stronghold of the white supremacist Aryan Nation; while the neo-Nazi group does have a headquarters near here, the overwhelming majority of area residents, many of whom live in secluded lakeside estates, repudiate its activities.

The **Silverwood Theme Park** (North 26225 Route 95, Athol; 208-772-0513; admission) is a worthy destination for families and airplane enthusiasts. Located about halfway between Coeur d'Alene and Sandpoint, it combines carnival rides (20 of them) with a Victorian main street, family-oriented entertainment and a transportation theme. The park is open daily from the second weekend of June through Labor Day, weekends for a month before and after those dates.

Deep, writhing **Lake Pend Oreille** (pronounced "pond-or-RAY")—about 1200 feet deep and with 111 miles of shoreline—is the monster of the north. (It was named by early French Canadian trappers, who found native tribes wearing pendant ornaments in their earlobes.) At its southern end, four miles off Route 95 near Athol, is **Farragut State Park** (Route 54, Bayview; 208-683-2425). The U.S. Navy had a major training base here during World War II, and the huge park later became a popular venue for Scout jamborees. The navy still operates a deep-water acoustic testing facility for electronically controlled submarines at the little fishing-resort town of **Bayview**, just north of Farragut.

Sandpoint is on the lake's north shore where the Pend Oreille River leaves the lake. Route 95's two-mile **Long Bridge**, which enters the town from the south, crosses between the two, flanked by a bicycle path. The town of 5500 is a magnet for artisans; their creations include the **Cedar Street Bridge Public**

Market (1st and Cedar streets; 208-263-0502), with two stories of covered galleries, restaurants and offices on a public bridge over Sand Creek.

The town's leading attraction may be the burgeoning **Schweitzer Mountain Resort** (Schweitzer Mountain Road, Sandpoint; 208-263-9555). Just 11 miles uphill off Route 95, the three-decade-old ski resort is Idaho's second largest (after Sun Valley). It's not an exaggeration to say that the view from here across Lake Pend Oreille is truly magnificent.

A good portion of Lake Pend Oreille's shoreline is inaccessible by road. But an interesting stretch of highway for campers and boaters is the 34 miles of Route 200 along Pend Oreille's northeastern shore, between Sandpoint and the Montana border. The **Hope Peninsula**, a large promontory extending into the lake about halfway to the state line, has several resorts, campgrounds and boat launches around its shores. **Clark Fork**, located where the river of the same name empties into Lake Pend Oreille, is a fishing and lumbering center on the main Northern Pacific Railroad line.

West from Sandpoint, Route 2 follows the Pend Oreille River for 29 miles to the Washington border town of Newport. Six miles east of the boundary is **Priest River**. In summer 1996, a tourist train is scheduled to follow this same route twice daily; for information, contact the **Sandpoint Chamber of Commerce** (Route 95 North, Sandpoint; 208-263-2161). The train will pass the **Albeni Falls Dam** (Old Priest River Road, Oldtown; 208-437-3133), which offers public tours and has an adjacent recreation area.

The Priest River flows out of **Priest Lake**, Idaho's least developed and most pristine large lake. Including scenic Upper Priest Lake, it is 25 miles long; its southern end is 30 miles north of the town of Priest River via Route 57. Only two tiny hamlets lie near its shores, and National Forest and other federal and state lands surround more than 75 percent of it. Most casual visitors approach the lake through the three separate units of **Priest Lake State Park** (Coolin Road, Coolin; 208-443-2200). The Indian Creek site, halfway up its eastern shore, has the widest range of facilities.

Fourteen miles northwest of **Nordman**, one of those Priest Lake hamlets, and close to the Washington state line is a unique old-growth forest area, the **Roosevelt Grove of Ancient Cedars** (★) (Priest Lake Ranger District; 208-443-2512). Some of the giant trees in the 20-acre upper grove are estimated to be at least 2000 years old. This has been a protected area since 1943. The cedars, in Idaho Panhandle National Forests, are two miles off Forest Road 302 via the Granite Falls Trail.

North from Sandpoint toward the Canadian border is the lumber town of **Bonners Ferry**. About ten miles east, where Route 2 crosses the Moyie River, an overlook affords a memorable view of powerful **Moyie Falls** and the Big Moyie Canyon Bridge, 600 feet above the river. **Kootenai National Wildlife Refuge** (★) (West Side Road; 208-267-3888), five miles west of Bonners Ferry on the south shore of the Kootenai River, provides 3000 acres of wetland wilderness for migratory birds and a variety of native mammals. There are well-maintained trails for hiking.

COEUR D'ALENE AREA HOTELS

In 1990, just four years after the resort opened, readers of *Condé Nast Traveler* voted **The Coeur d'Alene** (115 South 2nd Street; 208-765-4000, 800-688-5253, fax 208-667-2707) their favorite resort in the continental United States. There's no question that the 18-story hotel is something special. Its lakefront location in downtown Coeur d'Alene and high standard of friendly service deserve their reputation. The resort has 338 rooms and suites that range from standard to luxury penthouse in style, as well as three restaurants, three lounges, a shopping plaza, a large indoor fitness center, a marina, lake cruises and a golf course—the latter featuring a floating green on the 14th hole. Deluxe to ultra-deluxe.

There are now 28 bed-and-breakfast homes in Coeur d'Alene, but first there was **The Greenbriar Inn** (315 Wallace Street; 208-667-9660). This historic brick house, constructed in Colonial revival style in 1908, is on the National Register of Historic Places. It has handsome mahogany woodwork and eight guest rooms, some with private baths, all with period antiques that differ from room to room. Gourmet breakfasts are included. Moderate.

Looking for a "city slicker" opportunity at a guest ranch? The **Hidden Creek Ranch** (7600 East Blue Lake Road, Harrison; 208-689-3209, 800-446-3833, fax 208-689-9115), near Coeur d'Alene Lake, may fill the bill. Horseback riding, fishing, mountain biking and other activities fill the days, campfires and cookouts the evenings. Up to 40 guests stay in the main lodge, where gourmet meals are served daily, or six log cabins, all with traditional lodgepole furnishings and private baths. Open from May to November with a three-day minimum stay, a week preferred. Moderate to deluxe.

On the banks of the Spokane River about eight miles west of Coeur d'Alene is **Templin's Resort Hotel** (414 East 1st Avenue, Post Falls; 208-773-1611, 800-528-1234, fax 208-773-4192). This Best Western property has a marina and offers cruises aboard the *Spokane River Queen.* The hotel has 167 rooms with standard amenities and river view, a restaurant and lounge, a fitness center, shops and more. Moderate.

Backpackers en route through the Silver Valley can find a bunk at the **Kellogg AYH Hostel** (834 West McKinley Avenue, Kellogg; 208-783-4171). Many of the 36 beds are scooped up by skiers and mountain bikers; most are in dorms, but a couple of private rooms are available. As at most hostels, guests share toilets and shower facilities, a kitchen and a laundry. The hostel occupies an 80-year-old building once used by the former Bunker Hill Mining Company. Budget.

Near Lake Pend Oreille in downtown Sandpoint, **Connie's Motor Inn** (323 Cedar Street; 208-263-9581, 800-528-1234, fax 208-263-3395), a three-story Best Western hotel, has 53 comfortable and well-maintained rooms. Motel facilities include a restaurant-lounge, a swimming pool and a hot tub. Moderate.

Skiers will enjoy Schweitzer Mountain's **Green Gables Lodge** (Schweitzer Mountain Road, Sandpoint; 208-265-0257, 800-831-8810, fax 208-263-7961). Built in elegant alpine style at the foot of two chairlifts and the top of another, the lodge has 82 rooms with private baths and modern wood decor, fine dining in a bar and grill, stone fireplaces in the wood-appointed lobby area, even outdoor hot tubs. Deluxe.

On Priest Lake, **Hill's Resort** (Luby Bay Road, Nordman; 208-443-2551, fax 208-443-2363) has 50 housekeeping units—all with kitchens and private baths—that range from rustic cabins to luxury chalets. The latter boast picture windows that look out upon the pristine lake and the Selkirk Mountains beyond. A year-round family resort with 12 acres of lakefront, it also has an award-winning restaurant and a lounge. A wide range of outdoor activities are offered, with water-sports rentals and tennis courts on site. There's a one-week minimum stay in July and August. Moderate.

The **Naples AYH Hostel** (Route 2, Naples; 208-267-2947), 11 miles south of Bonners Ferry in northernmost Idaho, is lodged in an old dance hall with beautiful hardwood floors. There are 23 beds, mainly in dormitories but some private rooms are available; guests share a kitchen and toilet and shower facilities. Located a block west of Route 95, the hostel features its own old-fashioned general store and laundromat. Budget.

COEUR D'ALENE AREA RESTAURANTS

For true Mexican food prepared by a Mexican family, skip the chain joints and drop in at **Toro Viejo** (117 North 2nd Street, Coeur d'Alene; 208-667-7676). The menu for the most part looks familiar, with tacos and enchiladas, but the preparation is way beyond Tex-Mex. Decor is festive and colorful. Budget.

Generous portions of home-cooked Italian pastas are served amidst family portraits and other heirlooms at **Papino's** (★) (315 Walnut Street, Coeur d'Alene; 208-765-2348). Located in a little white house with red shutters, between 3rd and 4th streets about a mile north of downtown, this one's hard to find but it's worth the effort. Budget to moderate.

Jimmy D's (320 Sherman Avenue, Coeur d'Alene; 208-664-9774) serves creative Continental cuisine, including good fresh seafood and pasta, in a casual "speakeasy" atmosphere. Jazz plays on tape here, but it's live across the street at Jimmy D's Wine Cellar, which you can see through the restaurant's full windows on Sherman Avenue. Moderate.

For a romantic night out, the place to go is **Beverly's**, overlooking Coeur d'Alene Lake from picture windows on the seventh floor of The Coeur d'Alene resort (115 South 2nd Street, Coeur d'Alene; 208-765-4000). Try to be there for the sunset view. The menu features Continental dishes and wild game, and service is impeccable. Deluxe.

In the Silver Valley, a good dining choice—one in tune with the turn-of-the-century mining flavor of the district—is **The Historic Jameson** (304 6th Street, Wallace; 208-556-1554). It occupies a 19th-century hotel and saloon and perpetuates its original Victorian ambience. Burgers, deli sandwiches and Mexican dishes highlight the lunch menu, while dinners are strictly of the steak-and-seafood variety. Budget to moderate.

In the Pend Oreille district, there's good Italian food at **Ivano's** (124 South 2nd Avenue, Sandpoint; 208-263-0211). The emphasis here is on classic Northern

Italian styles, including veal, chicken and fresh seafood. Many diners enjoy the outdoor deck of the renovated home, located two blocks west of Route 95. Moderate.

Swans Landing (Lakeshore Drive at Route 95, Sandpoint; 208-265-2000) is a delightful alternative at the south end of the Long Bridge over Lake Pend Oreille. Sweeping views combined with steak, seafood and wild game specialties make this modern log building a favorite waterfront hangout. All soups and desserts are homemade. Moderate.

Every table in the fine dining room at **Hill's Resort** (Luby Bay Road, Nordman; 208-443-2551) has a view of Priest Lake and the Selkirk Mountains beyond. Nature's bounty, from morel mushrooms to wild huckleberries, are combined in many of the recipes, which feature chicken, beef and native trout. Open daily in summer, weekends the rest of the year. Moderate.

COEUR D'ALENE AREA SHOPPING

Coeur d'Alene visitors can find most of what they want in the shops that line **Sherman Avenue** between 2nd and 8th streets. The Coeur d'Alene resort operates **The Shops**, a two-story mall, between 2nd and 3rd. Look also for **Northwest Artists** (217 Sherman Avenue; 208-667-1464), a cooperative venture of 31 regional artisans, and **The Bookseller** (311 Sherman Avenue; 208-664-8811).

In the Silver Valley, the **Wallace District Art Center** (515 Cedar Street, Wallace; 208-752-8381) displays painting, sculpture and crafts from area artisans.

A must in Sandpoint is the **Cedar Street Bridge Public Market** (1st and Cedar streets; 208-263-0502), two floors of covered arts and crafts galleries and clothing and souvenir shops on a solar-heated bridge over Sand Creek, akin to the famed Ponte Vecchio in Florence, Italy.

COEUR D'ALENE AREA NIGHTLIFE

Summer theater is popular in Coeur d'Alene. The professional **Northwest Summer Playhouse** (14th and Garden streets; 208-667-1323) performs musical comedies and other plays during a July–August season and the **Carousel Players** of the Coeur d'Alene Summer Theatre (208-667-0254) offer a similar July–August program of musicals.

When Coeur d'Alene residents want to dance or listen to contemporary bands, they head to the **Shore Lounge** (The Coeur d'Alene resort, 115 South 2nd Street; 208-765-4000) or **Foxy's Lounge** (Holiday Inn, 414 West Appleway Avenue; 208-765-3200). **Celebrities Night Club** (524 Sherman Avenue; 208-664-9100) draws a younger crowd with louder rock. Jazz lovers can get their fill on a nightly basis at **Jimmy D's Wine Cellar** (313 Sherman Avenue; 208-664-9463).

The beverage of choice at many northern Idaho bars is T. W. Fisher's Centennial Pale Ale. The brew is manufactured right at the Coeur d'Alene Brewing Company and served at its adjoining **T. W. Fisher's: A Brew Pub** (204 North 2nd Street; 208-664-2739). Brewery tours are offered daily.

You can boo the villain and applaud the hero in summer performances by **Sixth Street Melodrama** (212 6th Street, Wallace; 208-752-3081 or 208-752-

8871). The mining-town ensemble, which play in a delightful little Victorian theater, offers more serious productions in fall, winter and spring.

Sandpoint's **Panida Theater** (300 North 1st Avenue; 208-263-9191), a historic Spanish mission–style landmark, presents a wide range of plays, concerts, dance events and films to Lake Pend Oreille–area folks.

COEUR D'ALENE AREA PARKS

Heyburn State Park—Idaho's second-largest state park (created in 1908) embraces three smaller lakes and the bayou of the St. Joe River as it flows into Coeur d'Alene Lake. Heyburn's 7800 acres offer fishing, camping and nature watching along the forested shores of Chatcolet, Benewah and Hidden lakes. Hawley's Landing is the most modern of several use areas.

Facilities: Picnic tables, restrooms, amphitheater, boat ramps, hiking trails, lodging, dining, store; information, 208-686-1308. *Swimming:* Beaches at Plummer Point and Rocky Point. *Fishing:* Year-round for bass and panfish.

Camping: There are 85 RV/tent sites and 15 for RVs only (57 hookups) plus 33 for tents only in three campgrounds, open from mid-April through October. $12 per night for RV hookups, $9 per night for tents.

Getting there: The park is located below the south end of Coeur d'Alene Lake, 10 to 14 miles west of St. Maries on Route 5.

Idaho Panhandle National Forests—About half the land in the upper Panhandle is contained within this 2.5-million-acre forest, consisting of the former St. Joe, Coeur d'Alene and Kaniksu national forests, and extending into neighboring Washington and Montana. Most of Pend Oreille, Priest and Hayden lakes, and part of Coeur d'Alene Lake, are included in the forest.

Facilities: Picnic tables, restrooms, boat ramps, trails, four ski areas; information, 208-765-7223. *Swimming:* Beaches at Pend Oreille and Priest lakes. *Fishing:* Kokanee salmon, northern pike and many species of trout in Coeur d'Alene, Pend Oreille and Priest lakes and their tributary rivers.

Camping: There are 473 RV/tent sites and 61 for RVs only (no hookups) plus 98 sites for tents only at 42 campgrounds (eight accessible by trail or boat only); no charge to $8 per night. Most campgrounds are open from May to October. Reservations available for Samowen campground at Hope, 800-283-2267.

Getting there: Numerous roads extend into the national forest, including Route 50 east of St. Maries, Route 268 (Fernan Lake Road) east of Coeur d'Alene, Route 9 north of Cataldo, Route 278 (Johnson Creek Road) south of Clark Fork, Route 57 north of Priest River and the Moyie River Road north of Bonners Ferry.

Farragut State Park—Established in 1942 as an inland U.S. naval training station, this 4000-acre park was decommissioned in 1946 but later gained fame as a venue for national and world Scout jamborees. The park has more than three miles of Lake Pend Oreille shoreline and offers many recreational opportunities.

Facilities: Picnic tables, restrooms, visitors center, amphitheater, boat ramp, rifle range; more than 20 miles of trails for hiking, mountain biking, horseback riding and cross-country skiing; day-use fee, $2; information, 208-683-2425.

Swimming: Beach with lifeguards at Beaver Bay. *Fishing:* Year-round for trophy-size game fish, including trout, kokanee and northern pike.

Camping: There are 45 RV sites (all with hookups) in one campground, 93 tent sites in another; five group camps by reservation. $12 per night for RV hookups, $9 for tents.

Getting there: Take Route 95 north from Coeur d'Alene for 20 miles; then turn east on Route 54. It's about four miles to the park entrance.

Round Lake State Park—This 142-acre gem is a great place for families. Nature trails weave through the evergreen forest that surrounds a small lake carved by an Ice Age glacier. Campfire programs describe the lush plant, bird and animal life found here. The handsome visitors center dates from 1926.

Facilities: Picnic tables, restrooms, visitors center, amphitheater, boat ramp, trails; day-use fee, $2; information, 208-263-3489. *Swimming:* Designated beach. *Fishing:* Year-round for trout, bass and panfish; fishing dock for non-boaters.

Camping: There are 53 RV/tent sites (no hookups); $9 per night.

Getting there: Located two miles west of Route 95 on Dufort Road, ten miles south of Sandpoint.

Priest Lake State Park—Three separate units offer myriad recreational opportunities along the shore of Idaho's most pristine large lake. Dickensheet, 46 acres on the banks of the north-flowing Priest River just south of the lake, is popular with whitewater rafters and river anglers. Indian Creek, 295 acres on Priest Lake's eastern shore, is the most developed site; open year-round (and attracting winter snowmobilers and nordic skiers), it has a small store as well as the park headquarters. Lionhead, 415 acres at the lake's north end, draws nature lovers. Lionhead and Dickensheet are open May through September only.

Facilities: Picnic tables, restrooms, boat ramps, trails, store (at Indian Creek); day-use fee, $2; information, 208-443-2200. *Swimming:* Sandy beaches at Indian Creek and Lionhead. *Fishing:* Excellent trout fishing in lake and river.

Camping: There are 11 RV/tent sites (no hookups or water) at Dickensheet; 92 RV/tent sites (11 full hookups) at Indian Creek; 47 RV/tent sites (no hookups) at Lionhead. $9 to $13 per night for RVs, $9 for tents.

Getting there: Take Route 57 north from the town of Priest River for 30 miles; then turn east on Coolin Road. It's one mile to Dickensheet, 16 miles to Indian Creek, 28 miles to Lionhead.

The Sporting Life

FISHING

The large lakes of the far north—Coeur d'Alene, Pend Oreille and Priest—are home to trophy-class kamloops, cutthroat, Dolly Varden and rainbow trout, kokanee salmon and northern pike. Spirit and Hayden lakes, near Coeur d'Alene, and Dworshak Reservoir, north of Orofino on the North Fork of the Clearwater River, are also outstanding for kokanee.

The lower Snake, from Hells Canyon to its confluence with the Columbia in Washington, is the only place in the world where steelhead trout, catfish and ancient sturgeon—prehistoric, boneless fish that can grow to 14 feet or longer—share the same waters.

Other rivers share November-to-January steelhead runs and host rainbow trout throughout the year. In many smaller lakes, rainbow trout share the waters with bass and panfish like bluegills, perch and crappies.

Among the many reputable outfitters are **Barker River Trips** (2124 Grelle Street, Lewiston; 208-743-7459), **Hells Canyon Fishing Charters** (Route 95, Riggins; 208-628-3714), **Clearwater Outfitters** (4088 Canyon Creek Road, Orofino; 208-476-5971), **Priest Lake Guide Service** (Route 57, Nordman; 208-443-2956) and **Diamond Jim's Charter Fishing** (Route 200, Hope; 208-263-5746). Ask at marinas about lake charters, or at the **Fins & Feathers** tackle shop (1816½ Sherman Avenue, Coeur d'Alene; 208-667-9304).

BOATING

Two of the biggest Snake River jet-boat outfitters, both of which leave from Hells Gate State Park in Lewiston, are **Beamer's Hells Canyon Tours** (1451 Bridge Street, Clarkston, Washington; 509-758-4800, 208-743-4800, 800-522-6966) and **Snake River Adventures** (227 Snake River Avenue, Lewiston; 208-746-6276, 800-262-8874).

Motorboats are easily rented at the northern lakes, especially in Coeur d'Alene and Sandpoint and on Priest Lake. Try **Skyview Boat Rentals** (Lakeshore Drive, Coeur d'Alene; 208-772-7587), **Sandpoint Marina** (East Lake, Sandpoint; 208-263-1493) and **Templin's Resort** (414 East 1st Avenue, Post Falls; 208-773-1611). **Dock Holidays** (P.O. Box 665, Coeur d'Alene, ID; 208-772-5415) also has houseboats for longer-term use.

WATERSKIING, BOARD SAILING AND JET SKIING

Water sports of all kinds are very popular at Lewiston's "slackwater" confluence of the Snake and Clearwater rivers. No boat rentals are available for waterskiers, sailors or even board sailors, but there are jet-ski rentals from **Macs Cycle** (700 Bridge Street, Clarkston, Washington; 509-758-5343), just across the river from Lewiston. In Coeur d'Alene, **North Shore Rentals at City Beach** (Independence Point; 208-664-1175) rents sailboards, paddleboats, canoes, kayaks and aqua-cycles for use along the lake's northwestern shore. Private concessionaires here may also offer waterskiing and parasailing. On Lake Pend Oreille, **Windbag Marina** (City Beach, Bridge Street, Sandpoint; 208-263-7811) also rents sailboards, sailboats, paddleboats, canoes and other seaworthy vessels.

SCUBA DIVING

Here's a surprise: Scuba divers *love* Coeur d'Alene Lake. No fewer than 28 wrecks of old steamships can be found beneath the lake's surface. Consult the Yellow Pages for equipment rentals and information on where to dive.

RIVER RAFTING AND KAYAKING

Whitewater rafting is big here, and there is no shortage of expeditioners. The most popular streams are the Snake River, through Hells Canyon; the Salmon River, through its entire course but especially around Riggins; and the Lochsa and Selway rivers, tributaries of the Clearwater.

River outfitters include **Northwest Dories** (1127-B Airway Avenue, Lewiston; 208-743-4201); **Salmon River Experience** (812 Truman Street, Moscow; 208-882-2385, 800-892-9223); **Northwest Voyageurs** (Route 95, Lucile; 208-628-3022), 11 miles north of Riggins; **Exodus** (Route 95, Riggins; 208-628-3484); **Salmon River Challenge** (Route 95, Riggins; 208-628-3264); and **River Odysseys West** (P.O. Box 579, Coeur d'Alene, ID 83814; 208-765-0841). Some of them, including Northwest Voyageurs, may also offer whitewater kayaking trips. Check with the Lewiston Chamber of Commerce's **Whitewater Center** (2207 East Main Street, Lewiston; 208-743-3531) or the **Idaho Outfitters and Guides Association** (711 North 5th Street, Boise; 208-342-1438) for an exhaustive listing.

(Hells Canyon rafters put in below the Hells Canyon Dam, accessible only from the south via Cambridge. For information, see Chapter Nine, "Southwestern Idaho Rockies.")

SKIING

Northern Idaho has two major destination resorts, both in the Coeur d'Alene area, and a handful of smaller day areas.

Schweitzer Mountain Resort (Schweitzer Mountain Road, Sandpoint; 208-263-9555), in the Selkirk Mountains 11 miles northwest of Sandpoint, has a vertical drop of 2400 feet, the second longest in Idaho, and 2350 acres of skiable terrain. The 6400-foot peak has distinct north and south faces—a guarantee against blustery winds from one direction or the other—and is served by six chairlifts. Cross-country trails are available. Open Thanksgiving through April, snow conditions permitting. Average annual snowfall is 300 inches.

Silver Mountain (610 Bunker Avenue, Kellogg; 208-734-2556), in the Silver Valley 35 miles east of Coeur d'Alene, has blossomed since the world's longest single-stage gondola (3.1 miles) opened in 1990. The vertical drop here is 2200 feet to the Mountain Haus at 5700 feet; five chairlifts serve the rest of the mountain, which peaks at 6300. Skiable terrain is 2000 acres including nordic skiing trails. Silver Mountain's season is similar in length to Schweitzer's.

Here are other, smaller northern Idaho ski areas:

In the Lewiston–Moscow area, **Cottonwood Butte** (Radar Road, Cottonwood; 208-962-3631), seven miles west of Cottonwood via West Lake Road, has a T-bar and a rope tow that carry skiers up an 875-foot vertical. **Snowhaven** (Fish Creek Road, Grangeville; 208-983-2851), has a T-bar, a rope tow and a 400-foot vertical. It's located about five miles south of Grangeville. **Bald Mountain** (Bald Mountain Road, Pierce; 208-464-2311), off Route 11 seven miles north of Pierce in Clearwater County, has a T-bar and a rope tow to serve a 975-foot vertical. **North-South Ski Bowl** (Route 6, Emida; 208-245-4222), a favorite of University of Idaho students, is on the White Pine Scenic Route about 25 miles south of St. Maries and 42 miles northeast of Moscow. A 500-foot vertical is served by a chairlift and a rope tow.

In the Coeur d'Alene area, 15 miles east of Wallace on the Idaho-Montana state line, **Lookout Pass** (Route 90 Exit 0, Wallace; 208-744-1301) has a chairlift, a rope tow and an 850-foot vertical. Cross-country skiing is available. **Fourth of July Pass** (Route 90 Exit 28, Coeur d'Alene; 208-765-7381), 14 miles east of Coeur d'Alene in the Idaho Panhandle National Forests, has groomed cross-country trails for all ability levels.

SKI RENTALS In the Lewiston-Moscow area, **Follett's Mountain Sports** (1019 21st Street, Lewiston, 208-743-4200; and 421 West 3rd Street, Moscow, 208-882-6735), **Gart Sports** (625-A 21st Street, Lewiston; 208-746-8040) and **Northwestern Mountain Sports** (1016 Pullman Road, Moscow; 208-882-0133) rent both alpine and nordic equipment. Skis and boards are also available at the foot of Snowhaven ski area. In Coeur d'Alene, **Bitterroot Bike & Ski** (296 Sunset Avenue; 208-664-9470) and **Great Escape Ski & Sport** (317 Sherman Avenue; 208-667-1342) rent downhill and cross-country skis. Skis and snowboards are available close to Silver Mountain at **Loulou's** (610 Bunker Avenue, Kellogg; 208-783-1123) and in the lodge of Schweitzer Mountain at **The Alpine Shop** (800-831-8810). Grangeville's **Holiday Sports** (126 West Main Street; 208-983-2299) specializes in cross-country skis.

GOLF

There's no shortage of public and private golf courses in northern Idaho. The most famous is **The Coeur d'Alene Resort Golf Course** (900 Floating Green Drive, Coeur d'Alene; 208-667-4653), voted "America's most beautiful resort course" by *Golf Digest*. Its signature hole, the 14th, has the world's only floating (and movable) green.

Other 18-hole public links are **Bryden Canyon Golf Course** (445 O'Connor Road, Lewiston; 208-746-0863), the **University of Idaho Golf Course** (1215 Nez Perce Drive, Moscow; 208-885-6171), **Coeur d'Alene Golf Club** (2201 Fairway Drive, Coeur d'Alene; 208-765-0218), **The Highlands Golf & Country Club** (North Inverness Drive, Post Falls; 208-773-3673), **Avondale-on-Hayden Golf & Tennis Club** (10745 Avondale Loop, Hayden Lake; 208-772-5963) and **Hidden Lakes Country Club** (8840 Lower Pack River Road, Sandpoint; 208-263-1642).

TENNIS

In Lewiston, look for free outdoor courts at **Lewiston High School** (1114 9th Avenue) and **Sacajawea Junior High School** (3610 12th Street), or call Lewiston Parks & Recreation (208-746-2313). In Moscow, check out **Ghormley Park** (6th and Lilly streets) and **Moscow Junior High School** (1410 East D Street), or call the Moscow Parks and Recreation Department (208-882-0240). The **University of Idaho** has 15 courts available, some of them lighted, for a small fee.

In Coeur d'Alene, there are courts at **McEuen Field** (Front Avenue) and **North Idaho College** (West Lakeshore Drive); in Sandpoint, at **City Beach** (Bridge Street). Or call city parks departments in Coeur d'Alene (208-667-9533) or Sandpoint (208-263-3158).

HORSEBACK RIDING

Pleasant trail rides along the Snake River start at **Hells Gate State Park** (Snake River Avenue, Lewiston; 208-743-2363), and in the Palouse Hills at the **Appaloosa Horse Club** (5070 Route 8 West, Moscow; 208-882-5578).

Many guest ranches in the region offer rides as part of lodging packages or rent horses to day visitors. Try the **Rider Ranch** (4199 South Wolf Lodge Creek Drive, Coeur d'Alene; 208-667-3373), **Hidden Creek Ranch** (7600 East Blue Lake Road, Harrison; 208-689-3209) or **Canary Creek Guest Ranch** (Rose Lake; 208-689-3566), all on or near Coeur d'Alene Lake; or **Western Pleasures** (2050 East Seile Road, Sandpoint; 208-263-9066), near Lake Pend Oreille.

PACK TRIPS

Lochsa River Outfitters (Route 12, Lowell; 208-926-4149) takes riders into the Selway-Bitterroot Wilderness on the Idaho-Montana border. Other outfitters offering backcountry adventures include **Four Seasons Outfitting** (1st Street and Sherman Avenue, Coeur d'Alene; 208-765-2863) and **Idaho Outdoor Experience** (Cabinet Gorge Road, Clark Fork; 208-266-1216).

BICYCLING

LEWISTON–MOSCOW AREA Lewiston's 16-mile **Clearwater & Snake River National Recreation Trail**, built by the U.S. Army Corps of Engineers, follows dikes and levees to connect a series of riverfront parks with the city center.

COEUR D'ALENE AREA **Centennial Trail**, which follows the Spokane River from Wolf Lodge Bay, east of Coeur d'Alene, to Spokane, Washington, eventually will extend for 63 miles; several links are still under construction. In Sandpoint, the **Long Bridge** south on Route 2 across Lake Pend Oreille is flanked by a two-mile bicycle and jogging track.

The ski areas of **Silver Mountain** (610 Bunker Avenue, Kellogg; 208-734-2556) and **Schweitzer Mountain Resort** (Schweitzer Mountain Road, Sandpoint; 208-263-9555) turn their slopes into biking trails by summer. Biking opportunities are almost limitless in other mountain areas such as **Lookout Pass** (Route 90 Exit 0, Wallace; 208-744-1301) on the Idaho-Montana border, where rentals and guided tours are available. **Farragut State Park** (Route 54, Bayview; 208-683-2425), at the south end of Lake Pend Oreille, also has a series of marked bike trails.

BIKE RENTALS In Lewiston, **Pedals-N-Spokes** (829 D Street; 208-743-6567) rents bikes. In the Coeur d'Alene area, rentals and repairs are offered by **Mountain Outfitters** (509 Sherman Avenue, Coeur d'Alene; 208-765-6386) and **The Bicycle Depot** (100 East Railroad Avenue, Post Falls; 208-773-8081).

In Sandpoint, **Fifth Avenue Bike, Board & Ski** (512 Larch Street; 208-263-5821) has rentals.

HIKING

A widely varied choice of trails is available to visitors to the northern Idaho Rockies. The following list is but a sampling. All distances listed are one-way unless otherwise noted.

LEWISTON–MOSCOW AREA **Hobo Cedar Grove Nature Trail** (1.5 miles) loops through a 240-acre grove of old-growth western red cedar. Brochures in a registration box at the trailhead have interpretive passages that coincide with numbered signposts along the trail, which is accessible to the moderately disabled. The trailhead is reached from Clarkia, on Route 3; the grove is 12 miles northeast via Forest Roads 321 and 3357.

Snake River National Recreation Trail (27.9 miles) follows the Snake River through Hells Canyon from Granite Creek (with access by boat from Hells Canyon Dam, about six miles upriver) to Pittsburg Landing (accessible by road from White Bird and Riggins). Hikers pass old mining sites and native petroglyphs, and wave at whitewater rafters churning past.

Seven Devils Trail (15.7 miles) penetrates the highest and most rugged mountains (up to 8500 feet) in the Hells Canyon National Recreation Area. The panoramic views to the canyon floor are sensational. The trailhead is near the Heavens Gate Lookout, 17 miles from Riggins via Forest Road 517.

COEUR D'ALENE AREA **Tubbs Hill Trail** (3.4 miles) loops around the circumference of a 150-acre city park that juts into Coeur d'Alene Lake. En route are three-story high caves, sandy beaches and scenic overlooks.

Caribou Ridge Trail (4.6 miles) descends 1800 feet from a lookout and picnic area atop 4000-foot Mount Coeur d'Alene to a National Forest campground at Beauty Bay, one of the easternmost spurs of Coeur d'Alene Lake. The upper trailhead is on Forest Road 439, off Route 97.

Navigation Trail (10 miles) begins at Beaver Creek campground at the north end of Priest Lake, 12 miles north of Nordman via Forest Road 2512. It passes through forest, meadow and bog, beaver ponds and an old trapper's cabin, with many scenic views of Upper Priest Lake, before ending at Forest Road 1013.

Transportation

BY CAR

Route 95, the only north-south highway connecting Idaho's Panhandle with the Snake River Valley, is the principal artery. If you're coming from Boise, take **Route 55** north to New Meadows and there pick up Route 95, which proceeds through Riggins, Grangeville, Lewiston, Moscow, Coeur d'Alene and Sandpoint en route to Canada. The main east-west highways in the Panhandle are

Route 90, the interstate that runs east from Seattle and Spokane through Coeur d'Alene and on through Montana to Chicago and Boston; and **Route 12**, which extends from Washington to Minnesota via Lewiston and the Lolo Pass.

BY AIR

The **Lewiston–Nez Perce County Airport** and **Coeur d'Alene Airport** handle regional traffic. Empire Airlines flies round-trip from Boise to Coeur d'Alene via Lewiston four times every weekday. Empire also flies to both cities from Spokane. Horizon Air connects Lewiston with Seattle, Spokane, Portland and Boise. Horizon also flies into the **Pullman–Moscow Regional Airport**.

In addition, **Spokane International Airport** is served by Alaska, Continental, Delta, Horizon and United. **Shields Industries** (509-535-6979) offers shuttle service between the airport and Coeur d'Alene. **Link Transportation** (208-882-1223) provides ground service from the Spokane airport to the University of Idaho in Moscow after a stop at Washington State University in Pullman.

BY BUS

Northwestern Trailways (800-366-3830) serves cities throughout the region, including Lewiston (3120 North-South Highway; 208-746-8108), Moscow (102 West 6th Street; 208-882-5521), Riggins (100 South Main Street; 208-628-3718), Grangeville (Route 95 North; 208-983-0721), Coeur d'Alene (1923½ North 4th Street; 208-664-3343) and Sandpoint (402 5th Avenue; 208-263-7721).

BY TRAIN

Sandpoint has the only passenger rail service in northern Idaho. **Amtrak**'s (800-872-7245) northernmost line, the "Empire Builder," cuts across the Panhandle here, providing daily westbound service to Seattle and Portland, Oregon; eastbound to Chicago. The depot is on Railroad Avenue.

CAR RENTALS

At the Lewiston and Coeur d'Alene airports, look for **Budget Rent A Car** (800-527-0700), **Hertz Rent A Car** (800-654-3131) and **National Interrent** (800-328-4567).

PUBLIC TRANSPORTATION

Valley Transit (1424 Main Street, Lewiston; 208-743-2545), **Moscow Public Transit** (124 East 3rd Street, Moscow; 208-882-8313), **Panhandle Area Transit** (137 Spruce Avenue, Coeur d'Alene; 208-334-9769) and **Sandpoint Area Transit** (Sandpoint; 208-263-7287) provide service in their respective communities.

TAXIS

In Lewiston, call **Black & White Cab** (208-743-3223); in Moscow, **Richard's Taxi** (208-882-1881); in Coeur d'Alene, **Sunset Taxi** (208-664-2424); in Sandpoint, **Bonner Cab** (208-263-7626).

CHAPTER TWELVE

Western Montana Rockies

Western Montana is a child of the last Ice Age.

Glacial icecaps and inland seas receded from the Rockies only about 12,000 years ago. Their legacy—a wonderland of steep-sided mountains and broad valleys, of deep blue lakes and racing rivers—can be enjoyed by all who visit the region today.

Spectacular Glacier National Park, on the Canadian border, is the crowning achievement of this glacial age. Among its chiseled peaks, several of which exceed 10,000 feet, are 250 lakes and more than 700 miles of hiking and horseback trails. Glacier is indeed at the roof of the Rockies. Its watershed, on both sides of the Continental Divide, flows in not two but three directions: to the Pacific Ocean, the Gulf of Mexico and Hudson Bay.

South and west of Glacier Park, waves of mountain ranges enclose myriad river valleys and lakes—including Flathead Lake, the largest natural freshwater lake west of the Mississippi River.

Native Americans, of course, were the first permanent residents of western Montana. Nomadic tribes hunted Montana's plains and foraged its valleys for thousands of years before the Flathead settled west of the Continental Divide around A.D. 1500. About a century later, Plains tribes like the Blackfoot migrated to the east side of the mountains, where vast herds of bison provided them with a steady supply of food and hides for clothing and shelter.

French and British trappers may have preceded American explorers Meriwether Lewis and William Clark (in 1805 and 1806) as the first whites to penetrate the region. In 1841, the first permanent white settlement—a Jesuit mission—was established in the Bitterroot Valley. Gold and silver rushes in the 1850s and 1860s soon led to Montana statehood (in 1864).

Today the economy of Montana's western portion depends heavily upon mining and logging, pursuits increasingly supported by a network of hydroelectric dams on the Missouri, Flathead, Kootenai, Clark Fork and other rivers on both sides of the Continental Divide. But the environmental ethic is especially strong in this mountainous region. That sentiment is particularly evident among the liberal thinkers in the university town of Missoula and in the tourist-oriented communities along the west flank of Glacier Park.

Aside from the obvious scenic treasures of Glacier, the tourist economy of western Montana is tied closely to outdoor sports and wildlife viewing. Fishing and hunting, hiking and horseback riding, skiing and river rafting are some of the more popular pastimes. Five national forests and eight designated wilderness areas provide ample opportunities.

Author Norman Maclean wrote his classic *A River Runs Through It* about life on the Blackfoot River, which runs through the Garnet Range and Lolo National Forest just east of Missoula. The spirit of a people in love with their natural environment, as portrayed in the book and 1993 movie, is typical of the entire region.

Missoula

Sitting on the Clark Fork River at the intersection of five river valleys, surrounded by mountains on all sides, the university town of **Missoula**, with a population of 43,000, is unquestionably one of Montana's most attractive communities. It's an intellectually and artistically oriented city, perhaps Montana's most cultured; yet its proximity to outdoor recreation—the Rattlesnake Wilderness, which bans motorized travel, begins just a mile from the city limits—makes it a mecca for backpackers, river rafters and fishermen alike.

Missoula got its name from British explorer David Thompson, who mapped the area in 1812 and dubbed it *Ne-missoola-takoo*, meaning "at the cold chilling waters" in the native Salish language. The first settlement here was in 1860, but the town grew quickly as a regional center for mining, logging and the railroad industry.

Twenty-seven city buildings are today on the National Register of Historic Places, including the old **Northern Pacific Depot** (100 West Railroad Avenue), at the north end of Higgins Avenue, downtown Missoula's main street. The station now houses a brewery and restaurant; the biweekly Farmers Market spreads around its portals; and city trolley tours begin at the circle in front. Inquire at the **Missoula Convention & Visitors Bureau** (825 East Front Street; 406-543-6623) for details on this and other organized tours.

Just three blocks southeast of the depot is the west end of the **East Pine Street Historic District**. Beginning at Pattee Street and extending five blocks east to Monroe, the thoroughfare boasts fine Queen Anne houses facing a central park strip. Turrets and asymmetrical features interspersed with more neoclassical styles make this a "must-see" for architecture buffs.

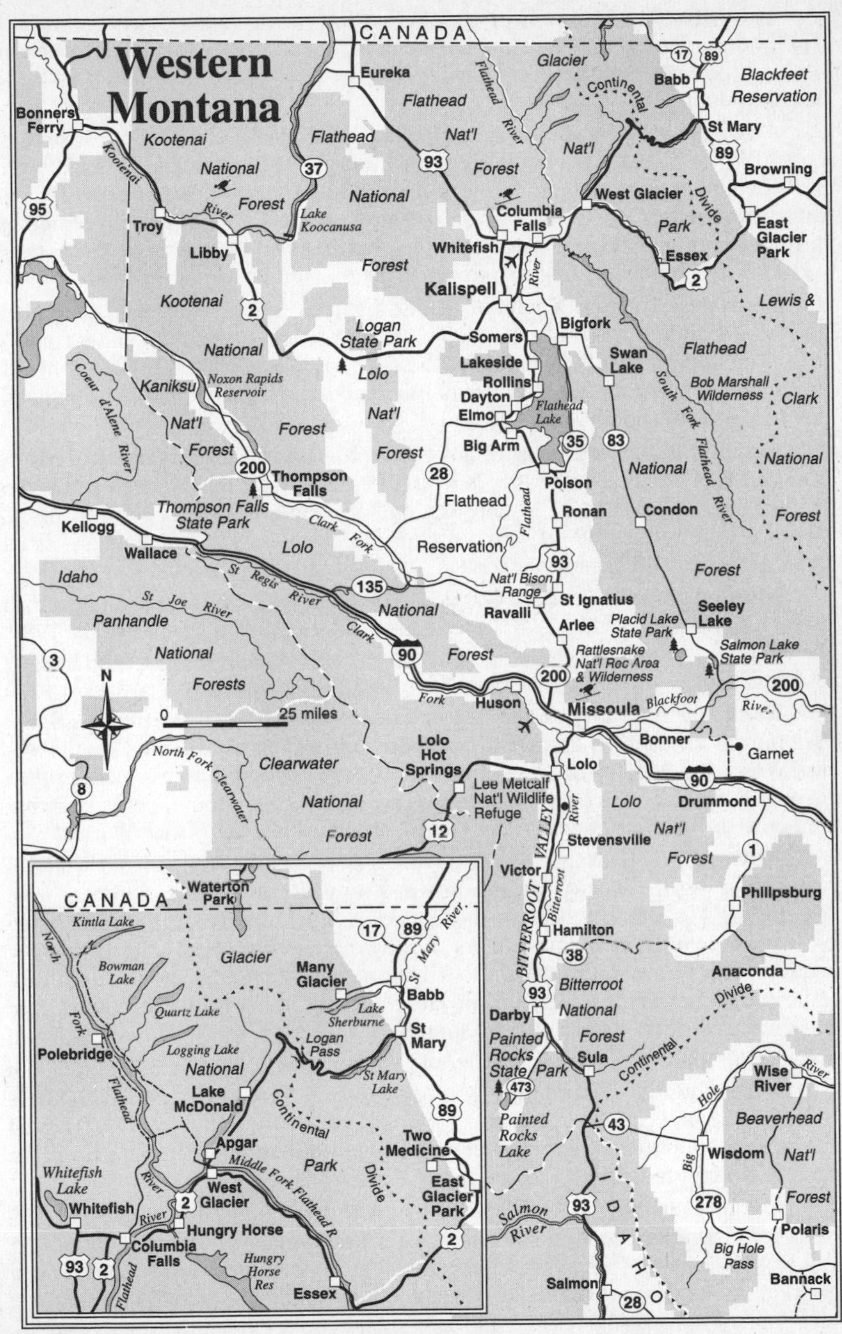
Western Montana
CANADA
Eureka
Glacier
Flathead
Nat'l
Forest
Babb
Blackfeet Reservation
St Mary
Browning
Bonners Ferry
Kootenai
National
Forest
Troy
Libby
Lake Koocanusa
Columbia Falls
Whitefish
West Glacier
Park
Essex
East Glacier Park
Kalispell
Logan State Park
Somers
Bigfork
Lakeside
Rollins
Dayton
Elmo
Big Arm
Flathead Lake
Polson
Swan Lake
Condon
Bob Marshall Wilderness
Lewis & Clark National Forest
Kaniksu Nat'l Forest
Noxon Rapids Reservoir
Lolo Nat'l Forest
Thompson Falls
Thompson Falls State Park
Kellogg
Wallace
Idaho Panhandle National Forests
Flathead Reservation
Ronan
Nat'l Bison Range
St Ignatius
Ravalli
Arlee
Placid Lake State Park
Seeley Lake
Salmon Lake State Park
Rattlesnake Nat'l Rec Area & Wilderness
Huson
Missoula
Bonner
Garnet
Drummond
0 25 miles
Clearwater National Forest
Lolo Hot Springs
Lee Metcalf Nat'l Wildlife Refuge
Lolo
Stevensville
Victor
Hamilton
Philipsburg
Anaconda
Bitterroot National Forest
Darby
Painted Rocks State Park
Sula
Painted Rocks Lake
Wise River
Beaverhead Nat'l Forest
Wisdom
Polaris
Big Hole Pass
Bannack
Salmon
IDAHO
Salmon River
Waterton Park
Kintla Lake
Bowman Lake
Quartz Lake
Logging Lake
Polebridge
Lake McDonald
Apgar
Many Glacier
Lake Sherburne
Logan Pass
St Mary Lake
Two Medicine
Whitefish Lake
Hungry Horse
Hungry Horse Res
Continental Divide
Middle Fork Flathead R

The **Missoula Museum of the Arts** (335 North Pattee Street; 406-728-0447; admission), a half block south of Pine, specializes in art of the western states. A permanent collection includes works by such local luminaries as Kendahl Jan Jubb and Monte Dolack.

Three blocks west is the **Missoula County Courthouse** (220 West Broadway; 406-721-5700), a 1910 building with a distinctive copper-domed clock tower that contains a two-ton bell. Painter Edgar Samuel Paxson, best known for his 1899 painting of *Custer's Last Stand*, created a series of eight murals depicting different eras of Montana history for the courthouse. Completed in 1914, they surround the upper landing of the main inside staircase.

Nearby **St. Francis Xavier Catholic Church** (420 West Pine Street) also boasts outstanding artistry in its steeple, its stained-glass windows and its paintings. The church was built in 1891; the 66 early Renaissance–style murals in its sanctuary were the work of Jesuit Brother Joseph Carignano, who created them in just 18 months of 1901 and 1902.

A short distance southeast of downtown Missoula, the **University of Montana** (UM) (Campus Drive; 406-243-0211) spreads across 150 acres and some 50 buildings at the foot of Mount Sentinel, characterized by a giant *M* on its slopes. Chartered in 1893, UM has an enrollment of 10,600 students and is an integral part of life in Missoula.

Missoula Memorial Rose Garden (700 block of Brooks Street at Bickford Street) was established in 1946 to remember World War II casualties. In 1989, the Montana Vietnam Veterans Memorial—a 12-foot-tall bronze sculpture by Deborah Copenhaver—was dedicated in the park's northeast corner.

If you leave the city center area and head west of Reserve Street on South Avenue, you'll come to **The Historical Museum at Fort Missoula** (South Avenue West; 406-728-3476). A complex of 12 historical structures, including an early U.S. Forest Service lookout and a one-room schoolhouse, spreads across 32 acres in the core of what was once Fort Missoula (1877–1947).

As Broadway (Business Route 90) extends northwest from downtown Missoula, it passes the **Rocky Mountain Elk Foundation** (2291 West Broadway; 406-523-4545), which appeals to those who like their animals stuffed. A couple of dozen creatures, including hunters' trophy elk, are exhibited in the taxidermy section. There's also an art gallery with original paintings and bronze sculptures, a theater that presents wildlife films and a gift shop that sells everything from books and T-shirts to racks of elk antlers.

About four miles north of downtown, off Rattlesnake Drive, Sawmill Gulch Road leads into the **Rattlesnake National Recreation Area and Wilderness** (406-329-3814). Tiny lakes and craggy peaks speckle the 61,000 acres of rugged mountain country. Camping and fishing are permitted, and there are trails for hiking, biking and skiing.

About seven miles from downtown, next to Johnson Bell International Airport, is the **Smokejumper Training Center and Aerial Fire Depot** (★) (5765 Route 93 West; 406-329-4934; admission). Throughout the summer, U.S. Forest Service smokejumpers, trained to parachute into remote areas to fight wild fires, give guided tours of the largest smokejumper base in the United States and describe their jobs firsthand. Historical photographs and dioramas explain how fires are detected and squelched, sometimes (as in July 1994) at a cost of firefighters' lives. The adjacent Intermountain Sciences Laboratory continues research into new firefighting technologies.

DETOURS FROM ROUTE 90 From 1930 to 1953, **Ninemile Remount Depot** (Ninemile Road, Huson; 406-626-5201) was a Forest Service dispatch center that supplied pack animals for firefighting and other backcountry work. The Civilian Conservation Corps constructed the Cape Cod–style ranger station in the 1930s; today, it is a working ranch open all summer long. Scheduled guided tours are available; you can also take a self-guided tour of the saddle shop, blacksmith shop and corrals at any time. To reach Ninemile from Route 90, take Exit 82, 22 miles northwest of Missoula, then follow the signs four miles north.

A detour from Route 90 East leads to **Garnet** (★) (Bear Creek Road; 406-329-3914), one of the best preserved of Montana's myriad ghost towns. Located about 45 miles east of Missoula—the final ten miles via a narrow, steep and decidedly backcountry byway—it was home to about 1000 men, women and children after an 1897 gold strike. Four hotels, 13 saloons and a school were among its buildings. But after the claims were mined out, the population dwindled and disappeared.

Today the Bureau of Land Management and the nonprofit Garnet Preservation Association operate a small visitors center and maintain a couple of dozen log structures. Two of these cabins can be rented in winter by snowmobilers or cross-country skiers, and some mining still continues in the area. A trail leads about 300 yards to the townsite from the picnic ground near the parking area. Exit Route 90 at Bearmouth; follow the frontage road about six miles east; then turn north on Bear Creek Road.

MISSOULA HOTELS

The largest of four bed and breakfasts in Missoula is **Goldsmith's Inn** (809 East Front Street; 406-721-6732), with seven rooms. A 1911 manse that was home to an early University of Montana president, it was moved to its present site on the Clark Fork and restored in 1989. There's reproduction Victorian antique decor throughout, from the beds to the wallpaper to the hand-painted tiles in the private baths (yes, every room has its own). Gourmet breakfasts are served at the restaurant next door. Moderate.

For wallet watchers, the **4B's Inn South** (3803 Brooks Street; 406-251-2665) is a leading example of a regional chain. This motel has 91 rather sterile-looking guest rooms. There's a large hot tub in a solarium and an adjacent restaurant. If this one's full, check out **4B's Inn North** (4953 North Reserve Street; 406-542-7550). Budget.

Ruby's Reserve Street Inn (4825 North Reserve Street; 406-721-0990), just off Route 90 at the north end of Missoula, is a new entrant in the upscale sweepstakes. Its 128 units are smaller than the Holiday Inn's or Red Lion's (see below) but have similar facilities and are neat and clean. In addition to a swimming pool, hot tub, sauna and workout room available to all guests, the motel has some guest rooms with waterbeds and private hot tubs, as well as larger family units and a children's playground. A complimentary continental breakfast is served. Moderate.

Missoula's foremost property may be the **Holiday Inn Missoula-Parkside** (200 South Pattee Street; 406-721-8550), beside the Higgins Avenue Bridge overlooking the Clark Fork River. Every one of the hotel's 200 rooms has either a mountain view or a balcony overhanging its spacious atrium lobby, which resembles a Midwest town square with its brickwork, trees, benches and gaslight lamps. Rooms have queen- or king-size beds, air-conditioning and desks. Within the inn are a restaurant, a lounge (featuring live contemporary rock music and casino machines), an indoor swimming pool and a hot tub, sauna, workout room and game room. Moderate to deluxe.

MISSOULA RESTAURANTS

The **Black Dog Cafe** (138 West Broadway; 406-542-1138) is Missoula's only 100 percent vegetarian eatery. A pleasant café across Ryman Street from the county courthouse, it has a full lunch and dinner menu and an outdoor seating area. Budget to moderate.

At **Santorno's Italian Restaurant** (120 West Front Street; 406-542-1963) everything is Roma, *bella* Roma. Authentic Old World dinners are served by candlelight on handmade Italian dishes; you can almost imagine the strains of violin music beside your table. Standard pastas, meats, seafood and vegetarian items fill the menu, and there's full bar service. Moderate.

At two Missoula outlets of **The Mustard Seed** (Southgate Mall, 406-542-7333; and 419 West Front Street, 406-728-7825), traditional Chinese dishes, from subtle Cantonese to tangy Szechuan, are given a contemporary American treatment in original recipes with fresh ingredients. The restaurants are low-lit, modern and efficient. Wine and beer are served. Moderate.

Locals never seem to have any trouble finding Missoula's **Alley Cat Grill** (125½ Main Street; 406-728-3535), but visitors sometimes do: It's tucked back in an alley off Ryman Street near West Front Street. For an alley hideaway, though, this candlelit dinner house sets a very high standard. The focus is on creative fresh seafood and meat entrées, including fresh steamed clams, grilled swordfish, rack of lamb, and filet mignon in a green peppercorn sauce. Desserts are homemade, and there's a good list of wines, beers and espresso drinks. Moderate to deluxe.

One flight above the historic Crystal Theatre, in a former dime-a-dance hall, **The Lily Restaurant** (131 South Higgins Avenue; 406-542-0002) aspires to contemporary elegance. An international menu, ranging from saucy French to spicy Cajun and Thai cuisine, is presented with white-tablecloth service beneath high skylit ceilings. Dinner only is served Tuesday through Saturday nights. An in-house baker prepares elaborate desserts, and the wine and beer list is extensive. Moderate to deluxe.

MISSOULA SHOPPING

Missoula's largest selection of handicrafts, art and food items made or produced within the state is sold at the **Montana Craft Connection** (1605 Stephens Street; 406-549-4486). The **Sutton West Gallery** (121 West Broadway; 406-721-5460) has rotating monthly exhibits of current work by many of the region's leading contemporary painters, sculptors, potters and jewelers. The **Monte Dolack Gallery** (139 West Front Street; 406-549-3248) offers the work of a nationally known poster artist who lives and works in Missoula.

The leading local bookstore is **Fact & Fiction** (216 West Main Street; 406-721-2881), which often highlights Montana authors with readings and signings. **Garden City News** (329 North Higgins Avenue; 406-543-3470) has more than 800 magazines on its racks, as well as a variety of national newspapers and detailed maps.

Some 90 vendors take to the streets every Saturday morning and Tuesday evening in summer for the **Missoula Farmers Market** (Circle Square, north end of Higgins Avenue; 406-777-2636). For a quarter-century now, gardeners and produce growers, bakers and coffee roasters, tinkers and tailors and all manner of artists have offered their goods for sale in the area fronting the Northern Pacific Depot, now usually overflowing onto Alder Street between North Higgins Avenue and Pattee Street.

Just as the street market is an age-old international tradition, the trading post is a trademark of the American West. The **Three Rivers Trading Post** (1124 Cedar Street; 406-721-2406) is a repository of Native American crafts: hand-beaded buckskin and moccasins, quillwork, carved arrowheads and many other collectibles and gifts.

MISSOULA NIGHTLIFE

As Montana's undeclared "cultural capital," Missoula has a wider choice of sophisticated entertainment than anywhere else in the state.

For stage aficionados, there is the **Montana Repertory Theatre** (UM Performing Arts Center; 406-243-4481), a top-notch professional company that tours regionally. The **Missoula Children's Theatre** (200 North Adams Street; 406-728-1911), which visits nearly 300 communities a year, making it one of the largest touring children's theaters in America, and its associated **MCT Community Theatre**, which presents a fall-spring season, both perform at the Front Street Theatre (221 East Front Street; 406-728-1911).

Music lovers have the **Missoula Symphony Orchestra & Chorale** (Wilma Theatre, 131 South Higgins Avenue; 406-721-3194), whose five-concert subscription series features outstanding guest artists October and May; its integral ensemble, the **String Orchestra of the Rockies**, which performs throughout Montana; and a dance troupe, the **Garden City Ballet Company** (406-721-3675). Consult entertainment listings in the daily *Missoulian* or the weekly *Missoula Independent* for schedules, prices and venues.

You can find live music of all kinds around the city. Try **Jay's Bar** (119 West Main Street; 406-728-9915; cover) for contemporary rock bands on tour; the **Union Club** (208 East Main Street; 406-728-7980) for rhythm-and-blues; the **Old Post Pub** (103 West Spruce Street; 406-721-7399) for jazz; and **The Top Hat** (134 West Front Street; 406-728-9865; occasional cover) for blues and folk.

The **Iron Horse Brew Pub** (100 West Railroad Street; 406-728-8866) in the Northern Pacific Depot serves up old-style German pilsners and ambers produced next door at the Bayern Brewing Co. (406-721-8704). The pub has a full bar, a beer garden and live music; Thursdays are smoke-free.

MISSOULA PARKS

Lolo National Forest—Based in Missoula, this forest encompasses much of four counties from the Idaho border (east of Sandpoint) to the Continental Divide, excluding the Flathead Indian Reservation. It surrounds or borders five wilderness areas and numerous lakes and rivers, including the Blackfoot, Clark Fork, Clearwater, St. Regis and Thompson.

Facilities: Picnic tables, restrooms, boat ramps, trails; information, 406-329-3750. *Swimming:* There are many lakes to choose from. *Fishing:* At one place or another in the national forest you can catch brook, cutthroat, brown, rainbow, bull and lake trout; kokanee salmon; mountain and lake whitefish; largemouth and smallmouth bass; northern pike; and yellow perch.

Camping: There are 416 RV/tent sites (no hookups) and 80 for tents only at 21 campgrounds; no charge to $9 per night.

Getting there: Starting in Missoula, you can reach the forest by traveling southwest on Route 12, west on Route 90, northwest on Route 200, or northeast via Route 200 to Route 83.

Bitterroot Valley

The Bitterroot River flows almost due north for 100 miles from the Continental Divide to enter the Clark Fork River just west of Missoula. The lovely valley it has carved, between the Bitterroot and Sapphire Mountains, was the site of the first pioneer settlement in Montana. In 1841, Jesuit Father Pierre De Smet established a Roman Catholic mission at what is now Stevensville. A nearby fort soon followed, and the onrush of settlers wasn't far behind. Today the valley is a thriving grain-growing region close by numerous historical locations and outdoor recreation.

Route 93 follows the Bitterroot Valley south from Missoula to Lost Trail Pass, where it enters Idaho.

Many Missoula workers commute daily from Lolo, 11 miles south at the junction of Route 12, which continues to Lewiston, Idaho. **Lolo Hot Springs**, 26 miles west of Lolo, has been a popular getaway for area residents for more than a century.

The **Lolo Pass Visitor Information Center** (Route 12; 208-942-3113), seven miles farther west on the Montana-Idaho border, is located at 5235 feet at the intersection of ancient Native American trade routes coming from the north, south, east and west. The center, staffed by Clearwater National Forest in summer (closed in winter), contains displays describing the natural and human history of the pass, including Lewis and Clark's passage along the Lolo Trail.

Twenty-eight miles south of Missoula, and just over a mile east of Route 93, is historic **Stevensville**, site of the first permanent white settlement in Montana. Father De Smet's **St. Mary's Mission** (De Smet Park, West 4th Street, Stevensville; 406-777-5734) was the first Catholic mission in the American Northwest. The grounds of the restored Italianate mission include the chapel and priest's residence, a log-house pharmacy, a Native American museum, a cemetery, a gift shop, the mission's original apple orchard and a picnic area. Tours are offered daily in summer.

Major John Owen built **Fort Owen** (Route 269; 406-542-5500) of adobe and logs in 1850, and it soon became a regional trade center. Brochures and interpretive displays lend themselves to self-guided tours of the fort, which is a free state park located one-half mile east of the Stevensville junction.

The **Lee Metcalf National Wildlife Refuge** (Route 203; 406-777-5552) encompasses 2700 acres of wetland along the east bank of the Bitterroot River, two miles north of Stevensville. Named for the late Senator Metcalf, a Stevensville native, the refuge is home to many deer and birds, including osprey, tundra swans and a wide variety of other migratory waterfowl. Dirt roads, interpretive trails and a picnic area are open year-round.

Twelve miles farther, north of **Hamilton**, hub of the Bitterroot Valley, is the valley's preeminent manmade attraction: the **Marcus Daly Mansion** (Eastside Highway; 406-363-6004; admission). "Copper King" Daly, an Irish immigrant, and his family used the Georgian revival–style estate as a summer escape from Butte between 1890, when it was built, and 1941, when Mrs. Daly died. The three-story mansion—which contains 42 rooms, 24 bedrooms, 15 baths and seven Italian marble fireplaces in its 24,000-plus square feet—is now owned by the state. Tours are offered daily in summer and by appointment the rest of the year.

The **Selway-Bitterroot Wilderness** (406-363-7161), straddling the Bitterroot Range on Montana's western border with Idaho, extends about 60 miles from 9075-foot Lolo Peak to 10,157-foot Trapper Peak. No motorized travel is allowed in the wilderness area itself, but several roads offer trailhead access.

Little Darby, 17 miles south of Hamilton, boasts the **Darby Historic Ranger Station** (Main Street; 406-821-3913), which displays early-20th-century U.S. Forest Service memorabilia and offers current information on recreation in the **Bitterroot National Forest** (see "Bitterroot Valley Parks.")

About four miles south of Darby, consider turning off Route 93 onto Route 473. The road, mostly paved for 28 miles, winds past **Painted Rocks State Park** (West Fork Road, Conner; 406-542-5500), which offers hiking, camping, fishing and other water recreation. Five miles south of the state park, look for the **Alta Ranger Station** (★), the first Forest Service ranger station in the United States.

It was built in 1899 by two men using cross-cut saws and axes. Though only traces remain, Alta was then a tent city inhabited by more than 500 gold miners.

BITTERROOT VALLEY HOTELS

The Fort at Lolo Hot Springs (Route 12, Lolo Hot Springs; 406-273-2201) creates a wilderness feeling while providing a thimbleful of luxury. The main attraction is its natural hot-spring pools. Standard rooms have twin or double beds; deluxe rooms have queen beds, dinettes and sleeper sofas. The resort includes a restaurant, saloon with casino machines and gift shops. Horses are available for summer rides, snowmobiles for winter excursions. Moderate.

In the heart of the Bitterroot Valley, the newly renovated **Best Western Hamilton Inn** (409 South 1st Street, Hamilton; 406-363-2142, 800-426-4586, fax 406-363-2142) has 36 spacious rooms, some with kitchenettes. The two-story motel has a large outdoor hot tub, and it offers free morning coffee. Moderate.

Nestled against the Selway-Bitterroot Wilderness near the foot of lofty Trapper Peak, the **Triple Creek Ranch** (West Fork Road, Darby; 406-821-4664, fax 406-821-4666) combines outdoor activity programs with luxury accommodations. The adults-only ranch has plush cabins and poolside suites for up to 16 couples and 23 single visitors, all with kitchenettes, fully stocked refrigerators, complimentary liquor and private hot tubs. Full gourmet meals are served in the lodge. Open May through October for a full range of summer programs, December through February for winter activities. Ultra-deluxe.

BITTERROOT VALLEY RESTAURANTS

The Hamilton (104 Main Street, Victor; 406-642-6644) is a throwback to the traditional pubs of the British Isles. Between games of darts you can enjoy fish and chips or fresh fruit cobbler and sip on imported and microbrewed ales and stouts. Budget.

The Bitterroot Valley's leading restaurant may well be **The Banque Club** (225 West Main Street, Hamilton; 406-363-1955), located in an old downtown bank building on two floors. On the ground floor, creative Continental cuisine is served in elegant ambience for moderate to deluxe prices; upstairs, The Exchange Bar & Grill offers more casual chowing and drinking at somewhat lower cost.

Isolated but worth a detour is the **Black Horse Inn** (Route 473 south of Darby in the West Fork Meadows Ranch; 406-349-2468, 800-800-1437). Wild game and German cuisine are the featured courses on an adventuresome menu served in a large, rustic dwelling in the upper Bitterroot Valley. A five-course menu special changes daily. Dinner and Sunday brunch only. Moderate.

BITTERROOT VALLEY SHOPPING

Art lovers traveling south through the Bitterroot Valley won't want to miss the **Bronze Horse Foundry and Gallery** (Eastside Highway, Victor; 406-777-3957), the oldest foundry in the Northwest, located about six miles south of Stevensville. The gallery offers collectible sculptures and limited-edition bronze and silver castings.

BITTERROOT VALLEY PARKS

Bitterroot National Forest—The forest cloaks most of the Sapphire Mountains and the lower slopes of the Bitterroots (below the boundary of the Selway-Bitterroot Wilderness) on either side of the well-populated Bitterroot Valley. It also shrouds the upper East and West forks of the Bitterroot River. Headquarters are in Hamilton.

Facilities: Picnic tables, restrooms, boat ramps, trails; information, 406-363-3131. *Swimming:* Dive where you dare, but beware the current of the Bitterroot. *Fishing:* The Bitterroot River and its tributaries are famed for trout (brook, cutthroat, brown and rainbow) and mountain whitefish. The East Fork also has bull trout.

Camping: There are 144 RV/tent sites (no hookups) and 16 for tents only in 15 campgrounds; no charge to $8 per night.

Getting there: Most recreational sites are a short distance off Route 93 between Stevensville and Lost Trail Pass.

Lake Como Recreation Area—Rock Creek rushes from the Bitterroots to feed this small reservoir, a favorite of area water-sports lovers. Open June 1 to September 15.

Facilities: Picnic tables, restrooms, boat ramps, trails; information, 406-363-3131. *Swimming:* Designated beach. *Fishing:* Brook, cutthroat and rainbow trout live in the lake's waters.

Camping: There are 11 RV/tent sites (no hookups); $8 per night.

Getting there: Take Route 93 south from Hamilton 12 miles, then Lake Como Road two miles west.

Painted Rocks State Park—Built along the shore of pretty Painted Rocks Reservoir, deep in the southern Bitterroot Range, this park offers high mountain trails through dense forest. The reservoir is popular for boating and waterskiing from May to mid-August (the water level is too low in other months). Open year-round.

Facilities: Picnic tables, restrooms, boat ramps, hiking trails; information, 406-542-5500. *Swimming:* No beach. *Fishing:* The best fishing in the park is at Slate Creek, which has several trout species.

Camping: There 25 primitive sites (no hookups or potable water).

Getting there: The park is 44 miles south of Hamilton, the first 20 on Route 93, the final 24 on mostly paved West Fork Road (Route 473).

Flathead Indian Reservation and Lake

Spanning 1942 square miles of land surrounding the meandering Flathead River and broad Flathead Lake between Missoula and Kalispell, the Flathead Indian Reservation is the home of the Confederated Salish and Kootenai Tribes.

Within this vast and scenic swath of landscape are located the impressive National Bison Range, the charming St. Ignatius Mission, several units of Flathead Lake State Park and other attractions, not the least of which is the foreboding Mission Range that marks the reservation's eastern boundary.

Most travelers cross the reservation via Route 93 between Missoula and Kalispell. Probably the most intriguing detour along the way—for nature lovers, at least—is the **National Bison Range** (Route 212, Moiese; 406-644-2211; admission). When it was established by President Theodore Roosevelt in 1908, only about 20 wild bison survived from an estimated 50 million a century earlier; most had been wantonly slaughtered during the four decades between 1840 and 1880. Today up to 500 of the great beasts, each of which can weigh a ton or more, roam this reserve's 19,000 acres of natural grassland and scattered woods. A 19-mile scenic drive begins and ends at the visitors center; it climbs a well-maintained dirt road over Red Sleep Mountain, enabling observation of bison herds (including, in the spring and early summer, many calves). Allow at least 90 minutes. The reserve also harbors significant herds of elk, mule deer, white-tail deer, bighorn sheep and pronghorn antelope. To reach the main entrance, turn west off Route 93 on Route 200 at Ravalli, 37 miles north of Missoula; after six miles, turn north again on Route 212, and proceed about four miles to the bison range.

If you stay on Route 93 through Ravalli, you'll surmount a saddle and find yourself staring into the spectacular **Mission Range** of the Rockies. Sheer, glacier-carved cliffs drop dramatically from the stark, snow-specked, 8000-to-9000-foot climes of Mount Harding, Mountaineer Peak and Daughter of the Sun Mountain, presenting a stunning backdrop for the farms and communities of the Mission Valley below its western flank.

Perhaps no view of the Mission Range is more spiritually uplifting than one taking in the **St. Ignatius Mission** (off Route 93; 406-745-2768). A designated national historic site, the mission was established by the wide-ranging Jesuit Father Pierre De Smet in 1854, 13 years after he founded St. Mary's Mission at modern Stevensville. Flathead and other tribes erected the current church in 1891 from lumber and a million kiln-baked bricks. Brother Joseph Carignano, whose work also adorns St. Francis Xavier Church in Missoula, painted the mission's 58 wall and ceiling murals. Nineteenth-century artifacts and Native American crafts are exhibited in the original log chapel and priest's residence, located next to the current church.

The **Four Winds Historic Village and Trading Post** (★) (Route 93; 406-745-4336), three miles north of St. Ignatius, is a private venture featuring several 19th-century buildings from around the Mission Valley that were reassembled at this site. Among them is an 1885 train depot that now houses antique toy and train collections (toured by appointment only). The active trading post, which re-creates a store of a similar era, is almost a museum in its own right.

Beyond St. Ignatius, you're deep in the heart of the **Flathead Indian Reservation** (P.O. Box 278, Pablo MT 59855; 406-675-2700) on which more than half of the 6700 enrolled tribal members live. Pow-wows, open to the public, are held in July at opposite ends of the reserve in the villages of Arlee and Elmo. The southeasternmost and northwesternmost corners of the reservation are primitive areas open to tribal members only; but most of the eastern flank of the reservation, from Flathead Lake to the Jocko River, makes up the **Mission Mountains Tribal Wilderness**, with nine public trailheads providing access to high-country lakes and peaks.

A mile north of Pablo, where tribal headquarters are located, the new **Sqélix'w-Aqsmakni'k Cultural Center** (Route 93; 406-675-0160), "The People's Center," includes an exhibit gallery of Salish, Kootenai and Pend Oreille tribal life. Ten miles southwest of Ravalli at the foot of Hewolf Mountain, the **Agnes Vanderburg Cultural Camp** (★) (South Valley Creek Road; 406-745-4572), open summers, offers free classes in Salish and Pend Oreille language, crafts and customs to tribal and nontribal members alike.

On either side of Pablo are the **Ninepipe National Wildlife Refuge** (Dellwo Road; 406-644-2211) and the **Pablo National Wildlife Refuge** (Minersinger Trail; 406-644-2211), which together contain more than 4500 acres of pond-and-wetland habitat for waterfowl. The refuges are also available for the day use of curious visitors.

At the town of Polson, seven miles north of Pablo and just over halfway from Missoula to Kalispell, Route 93 meets **Flathead Lake**, the largest natural freshwater lake west of the Mississippi River. Twenty-eight miles long and 15 miles at its widest, the lake boasts 185 miles of shoreline. A driving loop of the lake is 86 miles by paved highway.

With 3300 residents, **Polson** is the largest town on the lakeshore and has a thriving resort business heavily oriented toward boating and fishing. Fishermen come from all over North America to test the deep waters of Flathead Lake, gouged by the last glaciers, and it's likewise popular with other boating enthusiasts, from motorboaters to sailboaters. A good way to explore is aboard the 41-foot tour boat **Port Polson Princess** (Polson; 406-883-2448).

Around the lakeshore northeast and northwest of Polson are six separate units of Flathead Lake State Park (see "Flathead Indian Reservation and Lake Parks" for information). The park has primitive campsites and facilities.

The hamlet of Dayton, 23 miles northwest of Polson with a view toward Wild Horse Island, is the site of Montana's only winery: **Mission Mountain Winery** (Route 93; 406-849-5524). Because the winter climate is too harsh for viticulture, most grapes are imported from Washington's Columbia Valley, then blended here. The cabernet sauvignon and Johannesburg riesling are surprisingly good. The tasting room is open daily, May through October. Dayton is also the junction for **Lake Mary Ronan State Park** (Lake Mary Ronan Highway; 406-849-5082; admission), seven miles northwest off Route 93. Shrouded in a forest of Douglas fir and western larch west of Flathead Lake, this pleasant lakefront park is a favorite of birdwatchers, huckleberry pickers and mushroom hunters.

North from Dayton along Route 93, around the western lakeshore, you'll spot numerous residences overlooking Flathead Lake, often spectacularly situated in beautiful communities like Rollins and Lakeside. On the way, the highway passes the **West Shore Unit** (Route 93; 406-844-3901) of Flathead Lake State Park. West Shore's rock formations attract hikers and photographers.

At **Somers**, Route 93 breaks away from Flathead Lake and continues to Kalispell, only eight miles farther north. Lower Valley Road (Route 82) continues east, along the north end of the lake and across the Flathead River, to Route 35. The town of **Bigfork** is two miles south of this junction.

Located where the Swan River enters Flathead Lake, Bigfork blossoms with the spring flowers that line its main street and hang outside its sidewalk cafés and restaurants. The village is rapidly gaining a statewide reputation as a center for the fine and performing arts with its **Bigfork Art & Cultural Center** (525 Electric Avenue; 406-837-6927) and the new, million-dollar **Bigfork Summer Playhouse** (526 Electric Avenue; 406-837-4886). Also at Bigfork is Flathead Lake State Park's **Wayfarers Unit** (Route 35; 406-837-4196).

Boat tours are a great way to see Flathead Lake. One option: the 51-foot racing sloop **Questa** (Bigfork; 800-332-7148), which won the 1930 America's Cup for financier J. P. Morgan.

The **Swan Lake Road** (Route 83), which tucks itself behind the Mission Range and takes the 124-mile back-door route to Missoula, begins near Bigfork, follows the Swan River south nearly to its source, crosses a saddle and proceeds down the Clearwater River to its confluence with the Blackfoot. The principal resort communities along this route are **Swan Lake**, at the southern end of the 12-mile-long lake of the same name, and **Seeley Lake**.

FLATHEAD INDIAN RESERVATION AND LAKE HOTELS

Mandorla Ranch Bed & Breakfast (★) (6873 Allard Road, St. Ignatius; 406-745-4500), at the foot of the Mission Range on the Flathead Indian Reservation, couldn't ask for a more beautiful setting. Five guest rooms, three with private baths, share a log home with oak antiques, Native American motifs, original western art and mounted game. A deluxe suite even has a fireplace and private entrance to a hot-tub solarium. A 25-foot sunken fireplace and sofa sit beneath the cathedral ceiling of the "great room," and there's a TV room and library adjacent. The 35-acre ranch is home to a host of animals, including horses, and there are riding trails directly behind it. Moderate.

On Flathead Lake, you can't do better than the tribe-owned **KwaTaqNuk Resort at Flathead Bay** (303 Route 93 East, Polson; 406-883-3636, 800-882-6363, fax 406-883-5392), where you can get lakefront accommodation and a hefty helping of Native American culture along with it. The 112 high-ceilinged guest rooms have Salish-Kootenai motifs and all standard amenities, including private baths. The resort offers a restaurant, a lounge and casino, a gift shop and an art gallery, two swimming pools (one indoor) and a whirlpool; it also features a native crafts pavilion. Moderate to deluxe.

Swan Hill Bed and Breakfast (460 Kings Point Road, Polson; 406-883-5292, 800-537-9489), a large and luxurious redwood country home on ten acres overlooking Flathead Lake, features an indoor pool with a skylit cathedral ceiling. The four guest rooms have Queen Anne, wicker or whitewashed pine furnishings; three have private baths. A full breakfast is served on an outdoor deck that is frequently visited by deer in the evening. Moderate.

Budget accommodations are hard to come by in this region, especially during the peak summer tourist season, so the two-story **Timbers Motel** (8540 Route 35, Bigfork; 406-837-6200, 800-321-4546) is a pleasant surprise. Located at the south end of town, this inn has 40 nicely furnished units, all with full baths and in-room coffee; facilities include an outdoor swimming pool, a whirlpool and a sauna.

FLATHEAD INDIAN RESERVATION AND LAKE RESTAURANTS

It would be hard to find a setting more peaceful than at the **Allentown Restaurant** (41000 Route 93, Charlo; 406-644-2588), which sits at the edge of the Ninepipe National Wildlife Refuge at the foot of the striking Mission Range. Dinner entrées here focus on steaks, seafood and pasta; soups and sandwiches are popular at lunch. Big picture windows offer a fine view of the refuge's ducks and other waterfowl. Moderate.

The **China Garden** (Routes 93 and 35, Polson; 406-883-4048) is one of Montana's better Asian restaurants, at least if you like Americanized dishes like chop suey and egg foo yung. They're accompanied by a pleasant view across Flathead Lake. Low moderate.

One of the Flathead's best places for fine dining in a beautiful setting is the **Montana Grill on Flathead Lake** (5480 Route 93 South, Somers; 406-857-3889). A large, modern log cabin facing a small lakefront park, just west of the point where the highway from Kalispell hits Flathead Lake's north shore, it draws raves for its mesquite broiler and its summer Sunday brunches. Steaks, chicken, seafood (including lake fish, of course) and pasta are the bill of fare. Moderate to deluxe.

There's more dining by the lake at the **Bridge Street Gallery & Restaurant** (408 Bridge Street, Bigfork; 406-837-5825). Contemporary American cuisine is served in a gallery of international art and on an outside deck surrounded by herb and flower boxes. The café also has one of the area's best wine lists, from which you can order by the bottle or the glass. Moderate.

The **Bigfork Inn** (604 Electric Avenue, Bigfork; 406-837-6680) offers a country-style Swiss-chalet atmosphere and outdoor dining just down the block from the Bigfork Summer Playhouse, so it's a hit with theatergoers. Fresh seafood, chicken and steaks are the year-round dinner fare, along with hearty sandwiches at lunch (served summers only). Budget to moderate.

FLATHEAD INDIAN RESERVATION AND LAKE SHOPPING

Col. Doug Allard's Flathead Indian Museum and Trading Post (Route 93, St. Ignatius; 406-745-2951) displays exquisite traditional beadwork and sells replicas, as well as a wide range of souvenirs and regional art. It also has a huckleberry factory where outstanding jams, syrups, ice cream and milkshakes (to name just a few items) are sold.

The **Four Winds Trading Post** (Route 93, St. Ignatius; 406-745-4336), about three miles farther north, has everything from Nez Perce cornhusk bags, beaded moccasins, cedar-bark baskets and porcupine-quill headdresses to T-shirts and cassette tapes of traditional Native American music.

On the south side of Flathead Lake, **Three Dog Down** (61543 Route 93, Polson; 406-883-3696) has been rated "best in the world" by *Glamour* magazine for its sheepskin coats, bedding, pillows and comforters.

The Great Montana Mercantile and Trading Post (469 Electric Avenue, Bigfork; 406-837-3001) has a fine selection of local and regional crafts.

FLATHEAD INDIAN RESERVATION AND LAKE NIGHTLIFE

The **Bigfork Summer Playhouse** (526 Electric Avenue, Bigfork; 406-837-4886) is the area's most acclaimed theater company, offering live productions of a variety of popular shows every summer night except Sundays.

FLATHEAD INDIAN RESERVATION AND LAKE PARKS

Thompson Falls State Park—Nature walks and birdwatching along the Clark Fork River and boating access to Noxon Rapids Reservoir are the highlights of this park, open from May through September.

Facilities: Picnic tables, restrooms, boat ramps, trails; day-use fee, $3; information, 406-827-3636 in summer, 406-752-5501 in winter. *Swimming:* Designated beach. *Fishing:* The reservoir is a fisherman's delight with mountain and lake whitefish; cutthroat, brown, rainbow and bull trout; largemouth and smallmouth bass; northern pike; and yellow perch.

Camping: There are 20 primitive sites (no hookups); $5 per night for state residents, $8 to $9 per night for nonresidents.

Getting there: Two miles north of the town of Thompson Falls off Route 200, 103 miles northwest of Missoula.

Flathead Lake State Park—Comprising six separate units around the circumference of huge Flathead Lake—two on the west shore, three on the east, plus Wild Horse Island—this park is used primarily for summer recreation. Gouged by glaciers more than 10,000 years ago, Flathead Lake has a surface area of 188 square miles and a maximum depth of 339 feet. Traveling clockwise around the lake from Polson, the park units are: *Big Arm* (Elmo; 406-849-5255), with boat access to Wild Horse Island; *Wild Horse Island* (Elmo; 406-849-5255), a 2163-acre wilderness in the lake's west arm that is indeed home to a handful of wild horses, as well as bighorn sheep and bald eagles, restricted to day use only; *West Shore* (Lakeside; 406-844-3901), known for its intriguing rock formations; *Wayfarers* (Bigfork; 406-837-4196), a day-use area; *Yellow Bay* (south of Bigfork; 406-982-3291), in the heart of the cherry-orchard country; and *Finley Point* (near Polson; 406-887-2715), set on a forested peninsula at the south end of the lake.

Facilities: Picnic tables, restrooms, amphitheater (Big Arm), marina (Finley Point), boat ramps, boat rentals (Big Arm), hiking, interpretive trails (Big Arm and Yellow Bay); day-use fee, $3; information, 406-752-5501. *Swimming:* Beaches at each unit. *Fishing:* Trophy-size lake trout, lake whitefish and yellow perch are caught in the lake, as well as cutthroat and bull trout.

Camping: There are 120 RV/tent sites at five campgrounds, including 16 hookups at Finley Point; $8 to $9 per night. Reservations, 406-755-7275.

Getting there: On Route 93 on the lake's west side, Big Arm is two miles east of Elmo and West Shore is four miles south of Lakeside; take a boat from Big Arm to Wild Horse Island. On Route 35 along the east shore, Wayfarers is at Bigfork; Yellow Bay is 13 miles south of Bigfork; Finley Point is six miles northeast of Polson, then three miles north via Finley Point Road.

Placid Lake and **Salmon Lake State Parks**—Located four miles apart, just a few miles from Seeley Lake in the Clearwater Valley, these parks are popular with water-sports enthusiasts. Snowfall keeps both closed from December through April.

Facilities: Picnic tables, restrooms, boat ramps, nature trail (Salmon Lake); day-use fee, $3; information, 406-542-5500. *Swimming:* At designated beaches. *Fishing:* Both lakes have mountain whitefish; cutthroat, brown and rainbow trout; kokanee salmon; largemouth bass; and yellow perch. Salmon Lake also has brown trout.

Camping: There are 40 RV/tent sites at Placid Lake, 25 RV/tent sites at Salmon Lake (no hookups); $8 to $9 per night.

Getting there: Salmon Lake is five miles south of Seeley Lake on Route 83. Placid Lake is three miles south of Seeley Lake via Route 83 and three miles west on North Placid Lake Road.

Flathead Valley

Stretching about 40 miles north from the top end of Flathead Lake, flanked on the east by the lofty peaks of Glacier National Park and on the west by the evergreen-shrouded Salish Mountains, the Flathead Valley nestles around the meandering Flathead River. A bustling tourist region with lumber and fruit-growing industries (especially cherries), it has not one but three regional centers, all situated within 15 miles of one another: Kalispell, Whitefish and Columbia Falls.

As the largest town for more than 100 miles in any direction, **Kalispell** is a good place to begin an exploration of the region to the west and south of Glacier Park. The town of 12,000 people is 32 miles from West Glacier and only eight miles north of Flathead Lake.

Founding father Charles Conrad made a fortune as a Missouri River trader after his family lost their Virginia plantation during the Civil War. In 1895 he built a new estate, now known as **The Conrad Mansion** (Woodland Avenue between 3rd and 4th Streets East; 406-755-2166). The three-story, 26-room Norman-style home, set amid three acres of gardens, still contains most of its original Victorian decor: oak woodwork in the Great Hall, sleigh-style beds, imported marble in the bathrooms. One-hour tours are offered daily from mid-May to mid-October.

Worth a look is Kalispell's art museum, the **Hockaday Center for the Arts** (2nd Avenue and 3rd Street East; 406-755-5268). The work of regional and national artists is exhibited in three galleries; there's also a permanent collection of western art and a sales gallery.

Two nice parks stand out. **Woodland Park** (Woodland Park Drive; 406-752-6600), at the east end of 2nd Street, is built around a lagoon and contains Kalispell's municipal swimming-pool complex. **Lone Pine State Park** (300 Lone Pine Road; 406-755-2706), five miles southwest of downtown, has a nature education center.

Whitefish, 15 miles north of Kalispell via Route 93, is a lure for younger adults who like to play hard day and night. **Whitefish Lake State Park** (West Lakeshore Drive; 406-862-3991), a mile and a half northwest, is located on the south shore of a six-mile-long lake popular for fishing and boating. **The Big Mountain** (Big Mountain Road; 406-862-3511), a long-established winter ski resort, eight miles north of Whitefish, operates a chairlift (admission) to a mid-mountain viewing station and restaurant in summer.

Aluminum and timber are the economic mainstays in **Columbia Falls**, but the town's position as western gateway to Glacier National Park is almost equally as important. In the 15 miles from here to West Glacier, Route 2 skirts such attractions as the **Big Sky Waterslide & Miniature Greens** (Columbia Falls; 406-892-5025; admission), a water park with nine slides; the **House of Mystery** (Hungry Horse; 406-892-1210; admission), said to be situated on a vortex; the **Great Bear Adventure** (Coram; 406-387-4099; admission), a drive-through park for *ursus* lovers; and the **Glacier Maze** (Coram; 406-387-5902; admission), with bumper boats, miniature golf and two levels of puzzling passageways.

If you need some serenity after all that action, inhale the view from **Hungry Horse Dam** (West Side Road, Hungry Horse; 406-387-5241). The reservoir formed by this 564-foot dam, four miles off Route 2, extends snakelike for 33 miles between the rugged Swan and Flathead ranges of the Rockies.

The South, Middle and North forks of the Flathead form the **Flathead National Wild and Scenic River** system (West Glacier; 406-755-5401), the nation's longest. Between them the three forks stretch 219 miles across spectacular wilderness and near-wilderness. The North and Middle forks define the western boundary of Glacier National Park. Whitewater rafters, kayakers and fly-fishermen are regular visitors.

At **West Glacier**, where many of the Flathead River rafting companies are headquartered, is the west entrance to the national park. But nontourists who want to avoid the twisty-turviness of Going-to-the-Sun Road can stay on Route 2, crossing the Continental Divide at mile-high Marias Pass and reaching East Glacier, 55 miles away, in less than 90 minutes.

MONTANA'S NORTHWEST CORNER The region west of Kalispell is a land of dense, Pacific Northwest–like conifer forests, rich in timber and silver ore, and rivers harnessed for hydroelectric power.

Libby, the regional center, is located 89 miles from Kalispell and 83 miles from Sandpoint, Idaho. It is the home of **Libby Dam** (Route 37; 406-293-5577), 17 miles east on the Kootenai River, and the gateway to serpentine, 90-mile-long **Lake Koocanusa**, which extends north into Canada's British Columbia province. Along its shores are several recreation areas and campgrounds.

West of Libby 18 miles is **Troy**, where Asarco Corp. operates the largest silver mine in the United States, removing four million ounces of the precious ore annually. The **Ross Creek Cedar Grove Scenic Area** (Route 56; 406-295-4693) is 25 miles south of Troy near Bull Lake; it boasts an interpretive trail, less than a mile long, that leads among giant old-growth cedar trees, some estimated at more than 500 years old.

FLATHEAD VALLEY HOTELS

You can get off the Route 93 motel strip and stay downtown at the **Kalispell Grand Hotel** (100 Main Street, Kalispell; 406-755-8100). The refurbished 1909 hotel has two restaurants, a casino and a lounge. Guest rooms, on the second and third floors, are comfortably spacious. A complimentary continental breakfast is served. Moderate.

A favored bed and breakfast in Kalispell is the **Switzer House Inn** (205 5th Avenue East; 406-257-5837, 800-257-5837), a 1910 Queen Anne revival home between downtown and Woodland Park. Three of the four bedrooms, all decorated in country English style, have queen-size beds; the other has twins. There's also a library/TV room. Full breakfasts feature homemade granola and fruit compotes. Moderate.

Kalispell's leading lodging is the **Best Western Outlaw Inn** (1701 Route 93 South; 406-755-6100), which comes with all the bells and whistles: indoor swimming pools, jacuzzis, sauna, tennis and racquetball courts, fine-dining restaurant, lounge with live music and casino. The 225 rooms are sufficiently spacious but otherwise standard motel fare. Moderate to deluxe.

In Whitefish, the **Mountain Holiday Motel** (6595 Route 93 South; 406-862-2548, 800-543-8064, fax 406-862-3103) offers bang for your buck. The property offers indoor and outdoor swimming pools, a hot tub, a sauna and a guest laundry. The 34 rooms are neat and comfortable, with private patios and some refrigerators. Coffee is always on in the lobby. Budget to moderate.

Among many fine B & Bs—there are at least 40 in the Flathead Valley area—the **Bad Rock Country B & B** (480 Bad Rock Drive, Columbia Falls; 406-892-2829) stands out. Old West antiques and majestic mountain views typify the seven guest rooms (all with private baths) in this elegant country house, set on 30 acres near the west entrance to Glacier National Park. Four rooms in new log cabins have fireplaces and patios. Guests enjoy gourmet breakfasts and hot-tub relaxation. Deluxe.

The **Izaak Walton Inn** (★) (Route 2, Essex; 406-888-5700) is just across the Middle Fork of the Flathead from the national park. Diesel helper engines that idle in a railyard 100 feet from the inn's front door and hilltop cabooses that shelter overnight hikers and nordic skiers on the edge of the adjacent Great Bear Wilderness are testimony to its railroad heritage: The Izaak Walton was built in 1939 to lodge Great Northern Railroad service crews. Today it is a National Historic Register property surrounded by trestles and tunnels. The rustic lobby, simple wood-paneled rooms and country-style restaurant hold a museum's worth of memorabilia. Deluxe.

For a full listing of accommodations or assistance in finding a room, contact the **Flathead Convention & Visitor Association** (15 Depot Loop, Kalispell; 406-756-9091).

FLATHEAD VALLEY RESTAURANTS

You may not find cheaper meals anywhere than at **Sykes' Grocery, Market & Restaurant** (★) (202 2nd Avenue West, Kalispell; 406-257-4304). In business since 1905, Sykes' serves three meals a day, seven days a week, at its lunch counter. Coffee is still ten cents a cup, quarter-pound burgers cost $1.50, pork chop dinners run $3.50. Besides a deli and an ice-cream counter, Sykes' sells fresh produce and camping gear, and operates a pharmacy, all in the same shop. Budget.

The **Bulldog Pub & Steakhouse** (208 1st Avenue East, Kalispell; 406-752-7522) is at the head of the pack for Old World ambience and hearty steaks. The shrimp, chicken and prime rib are good, too. Enter off a parking lot around the corner from Kalispell City Hall; expect an intriguing weapons collection mounted on the walls, smoky air and loud blues. Moderate.

Located midway between Kalispell and Whitefish, **Fenders Restaurant & Lounge** (4090 Route 93 North, Kalispell; 406-752-3000) is built around a classic-automobile theme. Antique vehicles, like a '41 Ford and a '56 Chevy, have been remodeled into restaurant booths, and other period memorabilia decorate the walls. The menu is heavy on steak and seafood, as well as barbecued ribs and Cajun-style chicken. Moderate.

Drawing raves on the east side of the Flathead Valley is **Tracy's Restaurant at Meadow Lake** (100 St. Andrews Drive, Columbia Falls; 406-862-7580). Located within a resort condominium community by an 18-hole championship golf course, Tracy's offers creative "new American" preparations of wild game, as well as seafood and prime rib. Deluxe.

FLATHEAD VALLEY SHOPPING

The emphasis here, from the visitor's standpoint, is on vacation souvenirs and outdoor recreational gear.

For the former, try **The Huckleberry Patch** (Route 2, Hungry Horse; 406-387-5670). Apart from a very wide selection of T-shirts and other reasonably priced gifts and native artifacts, the store includes a wildlife display and a restaurant famous for its huckleberry pancakes. For local and regional crafts and products, visit **Mostly Montana**, in the 40-store Gateway West Mall (Route 2 West, Kalispell; 406-752-6662).

Thirty different dealers are represented at the **Kalispell Antiques Market** (1st and Main streets, Kalispell; 406-257-2800).

FLATHEAD VALLEY NIGHTLIFE

The **Glacier Orchestra & Chorale** (140 1st Avenue East, Kalispell; 406-257-3241) presents 11 concerts in an October-to-May season, often with guest conductors and performers.

On an everyday basis, locals frequent **Moose's** (173 North Main Street, Kalispell; 406-755-2337) for darts and lively conversation; the **Blue Moon** (6105 Route 2, Columbia Falls; 406-892-9925), at the Whitefish-Kalispell junction, for country-and-western music and dancing; and any of several saloons along a two-block stretch in downtown Whitefish for loud music and general rowdiness.

The **Whitefish Theatre Company** (P.O. Box 1463, Whitefish, MT 59937; 406-862-5371), a community troupe, offers everything from musicals to dramas in a year-round season, including summer Shakespeare.

FLATHEAD VALLEY PARKS

Whitefish Lake State Park—Providing water-sports access to the seven-mile-long lake, this state park is one of Montana's most popular.

Facilities: Picnic tables, restrooms, boat ramps, boat rentals, snack bar; day use fee, $3; information, 406-862-3991 or 406-752-5501 (winter). *Swimming:* City Beach at park, with designated children's area; other sandy beaches along lakeshore. *Fishing:* Lake, bull and cutthroat trout; lake whitefish and northern pike.

Camping: There are 25 RV/tent sites (no hookups); $8 to $9 per night.

Getting there: One-half mile west of downtown Whitefish on Route 93, turn north one mile on West Lakeshore Drive.

Flathead National Forest—Covering more than two million mountainous acres south and west of Glacier National Park, this forest encompasses Hungry Horse Reservoir, the Jewel Basin Hiking Area, The Big Mountain ski resort and many other important recreational sites, including the Great Bear Wilderness Area.

Facilities: Picnic tables, restrooms, boat ramps, trails; information, 406-755-5401. *Swimming:* At selected sites. *Fishing:* The three forks of the Flathead River and Hungry Horse Reservoir are well known for their cutthroat and bull trout and mountain whitefish. Ashley Lake has kokanee salmon; Handkerchief Lake, arctic grayling.

Camping: There are 243 RV/tent sites (no hookups) and nine for tents only in 12 campgrounds; $4 to $7 per night.

Getting there: Most highways and secondary roads that lead out from the Flathead Valley penetrate the forest. The greatest concentration of sites is off the East Side and West Side roads that flank Hungry Horse Reservoir, joining near the Spotted Bear Ranger Station.

Logan (Thompson Chain of Lakes) State Park—Located near the source of the Thompson River, this park is the focal point of a necklace of small lakes and ponds.

Facilities: Picnic tables, restrooms, boat ramps, trails; day-use fee, $3; information, 406-293-7190. *Swimming:* Designated beach. *Fishing:* Brown and rainbow trout, kokanee salmon, largemouth and smallmouth bass, yellow perch and northern pike.

Camping: There are 50 RV/tent sites (no hookups); $8 to $9 per night.

Getting there: Off Route 2, 50 miles west of Kalispell.

Kootenai National Forest—Kootenai occupies Montana's densely forested northwestern corner, a center of the logging and mining industries. The national forest encompasses 90-mile-long Lake Koocanusa and the Cabinet Mountains Wilderness.

Facilities: Picnic tables, restrooms, boat ramps, trails; information, 406-293-8861. *Swimming:* Mainly at campgrounds on Lake Koocanusa. *Fishing:* The Kootenai River has rainbow and bull trout, mountain whitefish and kokanee salmon; Lake Koocanusa also has cutthroat trout and burbot, the Tobacco River bull trout and the Yaak River brook trout.

Camping: There are 531 RV/tent sites (no hookups) and 18 for tents only at 15 campgrounds; no charge to $7 per night.

Getting there: Route 37, which follows the Lake Koocanusa shoreline, connects Route 2 at Libby (89 miles west of Kalispell) with Route 93 at Eureka (67 miles north of Kalispell).

Glacier National Park

Certainly the crowning attraction of the northern Montana Rockies is **Glacier National Park** (West Glacier; 406-888-5441), which embraces about 1600 square miles of spectacular mountain scenery on the Canadian border. **Going-to-the-Sun Road**, the lone highway to cross the park, has been termed "the most beautiful 50 miles in the world." More than 730 miles of foot and horse trails—the most of any national park in America—grace Glacier's terrain, and more than 900 drive-in campsites are available. Wildlife—elk, deer, mountain goats and bighorn sheep—is everywhere abundant. Several hundred grizzly bears also make their home in the park.

Entering the park at West Glacier, stop at **Glacier Park Headquarters** (West Glacier; 406-888-5441) for maps and information. Nearby is the splendid new **Travel Alberta Visitors Center** (West Glacier; 406-888-5743). A replica *Tyrannosaurus rex* skeleton greets you at the door, and elsewhere there are impressive displays and detailed information for motorists who plan to continue north of the international border after their visit to Glacier. Contiguous with Glacier in Canada's Alberta province is Waterton Lakes National Park; together, the two parks form Waterton-Glacier International Peace Park.

Apgar Village (406-888-5484), located two miles from West Glacier where the McDonald River flows out of **Lake McDonald**, has a visitors center as well as a lodge and motel, a campground, a restaurant and deli, a general store, three gift shops and boat and bicycle rentals. Apgar Village is at the junction of the park's two principal roads: the 40-mile **Inside North Fork Road**, which goes to Bowman and Kintla lakes and other sites in the park's rarely visited western boundary region, and Going-to-the-Sun Road.

For its first ten miles, the highway traces the southeastern shore of Lake McDonald, the park's longest and deepest (472 feet) body of water, through forests of larch and lodgepole pines. Going-to-the-Sun Road is normally kept open year-round as far as Lake McDonald, which is at 3153-foot elevation. (Larger trailers and recreational vehicles—those longer than 21 feet and wider than eight feet—may be restricted from traveling the road.) As the road begins to climb beyond Lake McDonald, the mountains' western slopes come into view. The increased precipitation on this side of the mountains has yielded occasional groves of old-growth cedar and hemlock.

About eight miles from Lake McDonald, Going-to-the-Sun Road makes a 90-degree turn to the northwest and begins a rapid climb (with but a single hairpin switchback) to subalpine meadows and 6646-foot **Logan Pass**. It traverses the precipitous **Garden Wall**, passes the **Weeping Wall** (where springs pour from the side of the cliff) and affords unparalleled panoramas of mountains, glaciers, waterfalls and the McDonald River valley.

Surrounded by snow drifts as late as August, Logan Pass sits on the Continental Divide. Its visitors center offers a variety of interpretive programs, guided hikes and other activities, many of them focusing on the natural history of the high country.

Descending the east side of the Divide, the road offers several views south toward 10,052-foot Mount Jackson and **Jackson Glacier**, a source of the St. Mary River. Though there are many small glaciers on its higher peaks, Glacier Park was named for the geologic glaciation that carved its features, rather than for its rivers of ice.

The descent ends at **St. Mary Lake**, another long, narrow body of water. The **St. Mary River** flows north from here, making its way to Hudson Bay in northern Ontario.

Another visitors center with activities and interpretive programs is located at **St. Mary** (406-732-4431), where Going-to-the-Sun Road terminates at its junction with Route 89 outside the park entrance. Here also you'll find a campground and other lodging, restaurants, a garage, a general store and a historic ranger station.

Two of Glacier Park's most scenic locations—Many Glacier and Two Medicine—aren't accessible from Going-to-the-Sun Road; instead, there are separate approaches to each from the east side of the park.

To get to **Many Glacier**, head north on Route 89 from St. Mary, as if you were proceeding to Canada's Waterton Lakes. After nine miles, turn left at Babb junction; then follow Many Glacier Road 12 miles west, along the Swiftcurrent River and Lake Sherburne, to the **Many Glacier Hotel** (406-732-4480). Surrounded by some of the park's most starkly magnificent summits—one of whose cliffs drops 4200 feet, farther than any in California's renowned Yosemite National Park—the hotel sits on turquoise **Swiftcurrent Lake**, one of a series of small lakes fed by Grinnell Glacier.

Two Medicine is the name given to three lakes, a river and a park community in the southeastern section of Glacier. It's reached by traveling 20 miles south from St. Mary on Route 89, another nine miles west and south toward East Glacier on Route 49, and then nine miles west past Lower Two Medicine Lake on Two Medicine Road. A historic chalet near the shore of Two Medicine Lake has a general store and snack bar (but no lodging), and there are lake cruises and boat rentals as well as a campground. Some of Glacier's finest hiking is among the colorful foliage and through the twisting valleys of this corner of the park.

BLACKFEET INDIAN RESERVATION Spread across one and a half million acres, the shield-shaped **Blackfeet Indian Reservation** (P.O. Box 850, Browning, MT 59417; 406-338-7276) is larger than Glacier National Park, which it borders on the east. This land of sharp geographical contrast, extending from the dramatic Rocky Mountain Front across some 50 miles of sparse prairies, is the home of the Blackfoot tribe, Montana's largest. Of its 9000 members, 7000 live on the reservation.

St. Mary, located where Going-to-the-Sun Road meets Route 89, is one of about ten communities on the reservation. **East Glacier Park**, at the southeastern corner of the national park, 31 miles from St. Mary, is another. It is most notable for its historic **Glacier Park Lodge** (Route 49, East Glacier Park; 406-226-5551). The adjacent community of East Glacier Park that has grown up nearby has an Old West facade and a keen orientation toward outdoor recreation.

Browning is the seat of tribal government and the site of the North American Indian Days celebration in mid-July. Located 13 miles northeast of East Glacier Park, it is the focus of most visitor interest in the reservation.

The **Museum of the Plains Indian** (Route 89 opposite Route 2 junction, Browning; 406-338-2230) is one of Montana's finest small museums. Its galleries include an interpretive collection of traditional clothing and artifacts of the Blackfoot and other northern Great Plains tribes, contemporary paintings and sculptures by tribal artists, an audio-visual presentation and changing exhibits. The museum shop is a good place to find authentic arts and crafts. Half-day and full-day tours of the reservation's **historic sites** (★) (406-338-7406) begin at the museum.

Nearby, the **Bob Scriver Museum of Montana Wildlife & Hall of Bronze** (Routes 2 and 89, Browning; 406-338-5425; admission) presents the work of one of Montana's best-known wildlife sculptors.

GLACIER NATIONAL PARK HOTELS

The **Lake McDonald Lodge** (Going-to-the-Sun Road, Glacier National Park; 406-888-5431), built in 1913, is one of several impressive historic lodges in or adjacent to the national park. Set on the west side of the park, at the north end of Lake McDonald in a grove of giant cedars, the lodge has 100 guest units—individual cabins and double rooms in the main lodge and motel annex—all with private bathrooms. Its huge lobby contains a big stone fireplace and collection of big-game trophies. Facilities include a fine-dining restaurant, a coffee shop, a lounge and a camp store. Open early June to late September. Moderate to deluxe.

The **Many Glacier Hotel** (Many Glacier Road, Glacier National Park; 406-732-4411) offers unquestionably the most awesome view of any lodge in the park: across Swiftcurrent Lake toward spectacular Grinnell Glacier, which tumbles down the east face of the Continental Divide from 9500 feet. The hotel has 200 guest rooms—small, basic, but with private baths—and a spacious lobby and dining area. Request a lakeside room. Open early June to mid-September. High moderate.

A favorite is the **Glacier Park Lodge** (Route 49, East Glacier Park; 406-226-5551). The huge structure, built of fir and cedar logs at the end of World War I, is a tourist attraction in itself with its four-story atrium, supported by tree trunks, and a brilliant wildflower garden in front of its entrance. All 155 guest rooms are clean and well maintained. Facilities include a restaurant, coffee shop and lounge and game room as well as a swimming pool, a nine-hole golf course and horse stables. Open early June to mid-September. Deluxe.

Glacier Park, Inc., Lodging is the operator of six National Park inns, with a common reservation line for all: 406-226-5551 from mid-May to mid-September, 602-207-6000 the rest of the year. Aside from the three noted above, they include the **Village Inn Motel** (Camas Road, Apgar Village, Glacier National Park; 406-888-5632), with 36 moderately priced rooms at the south end of Lake McDonald; the **Rising Sun Motor Inn** (Going-to-the-Sun Road, Glacier National Park; 406-732-5523), with 72 cabins and rooms in the low-moderate price range on the northern shore of St. Mary Lake; and the **Swiftcurrent Motor Inn** (Many Glacier Road, Glacier National Park; 406-732-5531), with 88 motel rooms and rustic cabins priced from budget to moderate.

For the budget backpacker, there's **Brownie's Grocery and AYH-Hostel** (1020 Route 49, East Glacier Park; 406-226-4426). Open May 1 to October 15, this two-story log hostel has 31 beds in male and female dormitories and a couple of private rooms. A community kitchen, showers, laundry and equipment storage are available.

GLACIER NATIONAL PARK RESTAURANTS

Eddie's Restaurant (Camas Road, Apgar Village, Glacier National Park; 406-888-5361) is a good choice on the west side of the park. Families enjoy a wide-ranging menu—everything from burgers, spaghetti and fresh salads to steak and seafood entrées—in a casual atmosphere near Lake McDonald. Three meals a day are served. Open late May to mid-September. Moderate.

The Goat Lick Dining Room (Glacier Park Lodge, Route 49, East Glacier Park; 406-226-5551) is the place to bring big appetites on the east side of the park. Rocky Mountain trout, steaks and finger-lickin' favorites like barbecued chicken and ribs are served up in a room with the ambience of the Old West. Don't forget your bib. Open early June to mid-September. Moderate.

Nearby, the **Glacier Village Restaurant** (Route 2 East at Route 49, East Glacier Park; 406-226-4464) offers sit-down pancake-and-egg breakfasts and cafeteria service for lunch and dinner. Open early May to mid-September. Budget to moderate.

For those who can't go long without Mexican food, **Serrano's** (29 Dawson Avenue, East Glacier Park; 406-226-9392) offers generous portions of enchiladas and tacos. The restaurant, open evenings only, occupies a historic log home. Open May 1 to mid-October. Moderate.

GLACIER NATIONAL PARK SHOPPING

Every lodge and store in the park has a souvenir outlet. The best of the bunch—and the one with the longest season, open from the second week of May through October—may be the **Montana House of Gifts** (Going-to-the-Sun Road, Glacier National Park; 406-888-5393), a regional craft shop at Apgar Village, on the west side of the park.

In Browning on the Blackfeet Indian Reservation, don't miss the excellent gift shop at the **Museum of the Plains Indian** (Route 89 opposite the Route 2 junction, Browning; 406-338-2230), offering authentic Plains Indian arts and crafts.

GLACIER NATIONAL PARK

Glacier National Park—Rugged mountains and deep glacial lakes, as well as the longest system of hiking trails in any national park, are the highlights of this wildlife-rich, 1600-square-mile preserve that crowns the Continental Divide. The 52-mile Going-to-the-Sun Road connects its green western boundary with the striking Rocky Mountain Front that marks its eastern flank.

Facilities: Lodges, restaurants, stores, picnic tables, restrooms, amphitheaters, visitors centers, boat ramps and rentals, hiking and horse trails; day-use fee, $5; information, 406-888-5441. *Swimming:* Cold but possible in most lakes. *Fishing:* Trout and whitefish in most streams and lakes.

Camping: There are 1001 RV/tent sites in ten campgrounds, including 215 sites with RV hookups in nine campgrounds; $8 to $10 per night. No reservations. Opening dates vary from early May to mid-June, closing dates from early Sep-

Beware the Bear

Of all the great mammals of the Rocky Mountains, none is as feared or as respected as the grizzly bear. Once numbering at about 50,000 in the lower 48 states, ranging from the Mississippi River west to the Pacific Ocean, this great bear was reduced by white settlement to fewer than 1000 on 2 percent of its former range. Today, most grizzlies—protected as a threatened species under the federal Endangered Species Act—inhabit the national parks and wilderness areas running down the spine of the Rockies from the Canadian border through Yellowstone National Park.

In western Montana, Glacier National Park and the adjacent Great Bear Wilderness are two of its strongholds. Biologists estimate there are several hundred resident grizzlies.

Ursus arctos horribilis is the second largest omnivore (that is, meat and plant eater) in North America, superseded only by the polar bear. Males can weigh more than 1000 pounds, females 600. Though nocturnal, an adult can be aggressive if intruders disturb it . . . or its cubs.

The grizzly is easily distinguished from the more docile American black bear (*Ursus americanus*) by its broad head; a well-defined shoulder muscle, which helps it dig for rodents, insects and roots; and its frequently silver-tipped, or "grizzled," fur coat. Grizzlies don't climb trees as well as black bears, but they can outrun horses in a sprint.

Only occasionally do backcountry visitors see grizzlies today. Even in Yellowstone Park, once renowned for its begging roadside bears, they have been removed to the wilderness. Wildlife watchers who want to observe grizzlies should look during the dawn and dusk hours around the fringes of woodlands and meadows, near water . . . from a distance.

To avoid grizzly encounters, travel in numbers, make plenty of noise (by talking, singing or even wearing bells) and avoid hiking at night. Clean cooking gear immediately after use, and store food in airtight containers away from your campsite. Don't bury your garbage; pack it out.

If confronted by a grizzly while hiking, do *not* turn your back and run. Move slowly away, avoiding eye contact. If the grizzly charges, stand your ground: Bears often feign a charge or run past you. As a last resort, curl into a ball and play dead, covering your neck and head with your hands and arms. If a grizzly invades your camp, find a tree or boulder to climb as high as you can. If you are attacked, fight back with any weapon, including your fists. Playing dead will *not* work here.

Grizzlies kill humans only infrequently; more often they die at the hands of man. But like the wise Scout, it's best to be prepared.

tember to mid-October. Primitive camping is permitted at Apgar Village and St. Mary through the winter.

Getting there: Enter from the west at West Glacier, 32 miles northeast of Kalispell on Route 2; from the east at St. Mary, 155 miles northwest of Great Falls on Route 89.

The Sporting Life

FISHING

Robert Redford's 1992 movie *A River Runs Through It* may have brought Montana flyfishing to the awareness of a nation of anglers, but the richness of Montana's fishing life has never been a secret to anyone who lives in the state. That's especially true in western Montana.

Huge populations of trout—rainbow, brook, cutthroat and brown, in particular—inhabit the creeks and rivers that flow from the Continental Divide. In the Missoula and Flathead Valley areas, this is the predominant fish. Mountain whitefish and bull trout are also widely found in rivers and lakes, and many lakes have yellow perch.

Other species may not be as widely distributed. Huge Flathead Lake and nearby Whitefish Lake are known for their lake trout and lake whitefish. Whitefish Lake also has northern pike, as do several lakes in the Seeley-Swan region. You'll find kokanee salmon, a favorite of gourmets, in Lakes Koocanusa and Mary Ronan, among others. Noxon Rapids Reservoir, on the Clark Fork near the Idaho border, boasts ten different species of fish, more than anywhere else on the west side of the Continental Divide.

Many fishing equipment companies operate guided tours to area rivers and lakes as an adjunct service. Contact **Grizzly Hackle Fishing Co.** (215 West Front Street, Missoula; 406-721-8996) or **Tom's Tackle** (108 First Street East, Polson; 406-883-6209). Flyfishing specialists include **Streamside Anglers** (317 South Orange Street, Missoula; 406-728-1085) and the **Lakestream Flyshop** (15 Central Avenue, Whitefish; 406-862-1298). Leading outfitters include **Wilderness Outfitters** (3800 Rattlesnake Drive, Missoula; 406-549-2820) and **Glacier Fishing Charters** (375 Jensen Road, Columbia Falls; 406-892-2377).

BOATING

On Flathead Lake, numerous marinas rent boats of all sizes for fishing or pleasure boating. They include **Flathead Surf & Ski** (303 Route 93, Polson; 406-883-3900), the **Big Arm Resort and Marina** (Route 93, Elmo; 406-849-5622) and the **Bigfork Marina & Boat Center** (100 Parkway Avenue, Bigfork; 406-837-5556).

In Glacier National Park, the **Glacier Park Boat Company** (406-752-5488) rents a variety of vessels—including rowboats, canoes and boats with six-horsepower motors—on several lakes. Scenic launch tours are also offered. In summer, contact the various rental outlets directly: on Lake McDonald at **Apgar Village** (406-888-5609) and the **Lake McDonald Lodge** (406-888-5727); on Swiftcurrent and Josephine lakes at the **Many Glacier Hotel** (406-732-4480); and on Two Medicine Lake at the **Two Medicine Lake Boat Dock** (406-226-4467).

RIVER RAFTING, KAYAKING AND CANOEING

There are floating opportunities of all kinds available across western Montana. That goes for kayakers and canoeists as well as rafters.

In the Missoula area, popular trips are through Hellgate Canyon and Alberton Gorge on the Clark Fork River, and down the Blackfoot. **Pangaea Expeditions** (P.O. Box 5753, Missoula, MT 59801; 406-721-7719) is among the outfitters who run these streams.

Western Montana's most popular area for rafting is on the various forks of the Flathead River, on the west side of Glacier National Park. If you're not an experienced rafter, the best and safest way to go is with an outfitter. At least four different outfitters have their headquarters in West Glacier, including the **Montana Raft Company** (Route 2, West Glacier; 406-888-5466), which runs the Middle and North forks on trips ranging from three hours to three days.

Kayakers enjoy the same rivers as rafters. But if you prefer lake water to whitewater, **Glacier Sea Kayaking** (Route 93, Rollins; 406-862-9010) allows you to explore Flathead Lake's coastline and islands by day or by moonlight.

The region's best canoeing is in the Seeley-Swan area and at the Thompson Chain of Lakes. On Route 83, the **Clearwater Canoe Trail** has a put-in four miles north of Seeley; canoeists can glide down the Clearwater River for an hour or two to the north end of Seeley Lake, then take a footpath back along the stream. An hour's drive west of Kalispell at **Logan State Park**, the ten-mile Thompson Chain of Lakes beside Route 2 demands only a few very short portages.

For rentals of river equipment, check out **The Trailhead** (Higgins Avenue and Pine Street, Missoula; 406-543-6966). The **Blackfoot River Kayak School** (11780 Route 200 East, Bonner; 406-258-5254), east of Missoula, rents kayaks on a daily and weekly basis.

DOWNHILL SKIING

Montana's largest destination ski resort, and one of its oldest, is **The Big Mountain** (Big Mountain Road, Whitefish; 406-862-3511), overlooking Whitefish Lake about 12 miles (as the eagle flies) west of Glacier National Park. Established in the 1960s, The Big Mountain is just that: It has more than 3000 acres of skiing terrain and some 60 runs served by seven chairlifts and two surface lifts. The vertical drop is 2300 feet from a summit elevation of 7000 feet. There are gentle groomed slopes for beginning skiers, steep and deep powder for experts. Base facilities include lodge and condominium accommodations, restaurants and bars, and ski shops with full rentals.

Day-use ski areas (with no on-site lodging) in western Montana include the following:

Montana Snowbowl (1700 Snowbowl Road, Missoula; 406-549-9777), 12 miles northwest of Missoula. Advanced skiers appreciate the steep-sided bowls, but there are also beginners' slopes. Two chairlifts and two surface tows service 30 runs; vertical drop is 2600 feet from a summit elevation of 7600 feet.

Lost Trail Powder Mountain (Route 93, Conner; 406-821-3211) straddles the Montana-Idaho border above the Bitterroot Valley, 91 miles south of Missoula. The snow arrives here early in the season and stays late. Two chairlifts and two rope tows serve 18 runs in the Bitterroot National Forest. There's a 1200-foot vertical drop from a top elevation of 7800 feet.

Turner Mountain (Route 508, Libby; 406-293-4317) is in the Purcell Mountains west of Lake Koocanusa, in northwesternmost Montana. A single tow climbs to the top of the 5952-foot peak; more than half of the 14 runs that descend 2117 feet of vertical to the base area are deemed expert.

SKI RENTALS In Whitefish, you can find downhill and cross-country skis at **Silvertip** (33 Baker Avenue; 406-862-2600) and the **Sportsman & Ski House** (40 East Idaho Street; 406-755-6484), while **Ski Mountain Sports** (200 Wisconsin Avenue; 406-862-7471) carries both types of skis as well as snowboards. Missoula has many ski-rental shops renting downhill and cross-country skis including **Open Road Bicycles & Nordic Equipment** (218 East Main Street; 406-549-2453), **The Trail Head** (110 East Pine Street; 406-543-6966) and **Shamrock Sports & Outdoors** (130 West Broadway; 406-721-5456), which also rents snowboards.

CROSS-COUNTRY SKIING

The Big Mountain (Big Mountain Road, Whitefish; 406-862-3511) boasts an excellent 15-kilometer track for cross-country skiers; in fact, it's a training center for U.S. Olympic biathletes and nordic racers. Other major destinations for cross-country skiers in winter include **Nightingale Nordic** (Graves Creek Road, Lolo; 406-273-2415), 25 miles southwest of Missoula, a complete nordic resort; and **Holland Lake Lodge** (Route 83, Condon; 800-648-8859), with a 25-kilometer trail system and full lodging and rental packages in the Swan River Valley.

At Chief Joseph Pass (Route 43, Conner), near Lost Trail Pass, a 24-kilometer network of rated trails, groomed weekly, has been developed by the Bitterroot Cross Country Ski Club. The **Izaak Walton Inn** (Route 2, Essex; 406-888-5700) has 35 kilometers of groomed cross-country ski trails on its grounds and offers several extensive backcountry packages into nearby Glacier National Park.

For information on renting equipment, see the ski-rental section in "Downhill Skiing" above.

GOLF

When the snow disappears, the golf courses flourish. Among the leading public courses in western Montana are the **Buffalo Hill Municipal Golf Club** (north end of Main Street, Kalispell; 406-755-5902), a 27-hole championship course with views from The Big Mountain to Flathead Lake; and the **Larchmont Municipal Golf Course** (3200 Old Fort Road, Missoula; 406-721-4416), an 18-hole course that hosts the Montana Open golf tournament.

In the Glacier Park area, the **Flathead Valley Golf Association** (15 Depot Loop, Kalispell; 800-392-9795) will make advance tee-time reservations for visiting golfers at any of the area's nine 18-hole courses.

TENNIS

Local parks and recreation offices are happy to share the locations and open hours of municipal courts. Call for information (Missoula, 406-721-7275; Kalispell, 406-752-6600 ext. 274). Or try **McCormick Park** (Cregg Lane at the Orange Street Bridge, Missoula) or **Northridge Park** (Northridge Drive, Kalispell).

HORSEBACK RIDING

For trail rides of a few hours to all day, check out **East Fork Outfitters** (at the Camp Creek Inn guest ranch, 7674 Route 93 South, Sula; 406-821-3508) or **L-Diamond-E Ranch Outfitters** (Rock Creek Road, Clinton; 406-825-6295), both in the Bitterroots south of Missoula. The latter will take you by horse to sapphire mines.

Big Sky Rides (750 Foys Lake Road, Kalispell; 406-755-7433), near Lone Pine State Park, specializes in family adventure with gentle trail rides and week-long horsemanship camps for kids.

In Glacier National Park, **Mule Shoe Outfitters** operate small corrals at Many Glacier (406-732-4203) and Lake McDonald (406-888-5121) for guided rides through the park. Beginning July 1 and continuing through Labor Day, they range from two hours to all day. First-timers are welcome.

PACK TRIPS AND LLAMA TREKKING

While many horse-packing outfitters serve hunters in particular, others prefer riders who simply enjoy the outdoors. They'll take you anywhere, even through the most remote reaches of the Great Bear Wilderness. Try **Rocky Mountain Adventures** (756 Little Sleeping Child Road, Hamilton; 406-363-0200), **Babcock Creek Outfitters** (280 Twin Lakes Road, Whitefish; 406-862-7813) or **Great Divide Guiding & Outfitters** (P.O. Box 315, East Glacier Park, MT 59434; 406-226-4487).

Guided llama pack trips—you walk, but the llama carries your load—are offered in the Missoula area by **Tranquility Base Llamas** (Route 263, Frenchtown; 406-626-4207); in the Bitterroot Valley by **Allaman's Montana Adventure Trips** (West Fork Road, Darby; 406-821-3763); and in the Glacier National Park area by the **Great Northern Llama Co.** (600 Blackmer Lane, Columbia Falls; 406-755-9044).

BICYCLING

Missoula has been called "one of the top ten bicycling cities in the United States" by *Bicycling* magazine. The sentiment clearly carries north into the Flathead Valley area and Glacier National Park.

So important is bicycling to western Montana that the **Adventure Cycling Association** (ACA) (150 East Pine Street, Missoula; 406-721-1776), formerly known as BikeCentennial and regarded as America's leading bike-touring organization, has established its national headquarters there. The ACA publishes touring maps and supports a national network of cycling routes.

Bike touring is encouraged through **Glacier National Park**, and several tour operators lead groups across the Continental Divide on Going-to-the-Sun Road. But because of the increased danger of accidents during the peak travel season—mid-June to Labor Day—bicyclists are restricted from hazardous sections of the narrow, winding highway between 11 a.m. and 4 p.m. Bicycles are not permitted on park trails or off-road.

Local bicycle shops have information on planned activities and mountain-biking routes. Favorite locations for the latter include the **Rattlesnake National Recreation Area** (Sawmill Gulch Road, Missoula; 406-329-3814) and **The Big Mountain Ski and Summer Resort** (Big Mountain Road, Whitefish; 406-858-5439). Another popular area is **Kreis Pond** (Lolo National Forest, Huson; 406-626-5201), with 35 miles of designated mountain-bike trails near the Ninemile Ranger Station and Remount Depot, 27 miles northwest of Missoula.

BIKE RENTALS Leading bike shops for rentals and repairs include **New Era Bicycles** (741 South Higgins Avenue, Missoula; 406-728-2080) and **All Season Sport & Cycle** (615 Nucleus Avenue, Columbia Falls; 406-892-2755). You can also rent bicycles in Glacier National Park at the **Village Inn Motel** (Camas Road, Apgar Village; 406-888-5632).

HIKING

Western Montana is one of the greatest places on earth for hiking, backpacking and mountaineering. Glacier National Park itself has 730 miles of trails, more than any other national park. All distances listed for hiking trails are one-way unless otherwise noted.

MISSOULA AREA **Crazy Canyon Trail** (3.4 miles), in the Pattee Canyon Recreation Area near Missoula's southeastern city limits, presents a moderate climb to the top of 5158-foot Mount Sentinel, overlooking Missoula from the south side of the Clark Fork River. You can descend from here via the **Hellgate Canyon Trail** (2.1 miles) to the banks of the Clark Fork or via the **"M" Trail** (1.8 miles) to the University of Montana campus.

Stuart Peak Trail (12 miles) is a strenuous ascent through the Rattlesnake National Recreation Area and Wilderness. Beginning at the Sawmill Gulch Road trailhead, it traverses Spring Gulch and then rises above the timberline for great views from the upper slopes of 7960-foot Stuart Peak. The loop trail returns past Twin Lakes and Lake Creek. The elevation gain is more than 3800 feet from the trailhead.

BITTERROOT VALLEY **Lake Como Trail** (7 miles) circles a reservoir popular among water-sports enthusiasts, 14 miles south of Hamilton at the foot of the Bitterroot Mountains. With virtually no elevation gain, it's an easy walk. A trailhead is at Lake Como Recreation Area; from the trail's end, a one-mile walk along the road beside the dam will return you to your starting point.

The best way to hike the **South Lost Horse Creek Trail** (13 miles) is from the top down. The trailhead is on the Idaho border at the west end of 18-mile-long Lost Horse Road (Forest Road 429), nine-and-a-half miles south of Hamilton off Route 93. From Bear Creek, cross a 6100-foot Bitterroot Mountain pass to Fish Lake; then descend 1700 feet down the steep-sided canyon of South Lost Horse Creek. Moderate.

FLATHEAD INDIAN RESERVATION AND LAKE Numerous trails penetrate the Mission Mountains Wilderness. One of the shortest and most spectacular is the **Turquoise Lake Trail** (4.6 miles), which climbs to a sparkling glacial lake nestled beneath a sheer cliff at the 5800-foot-level of Daughter of the Sun Mountain. The moderately strenuous trail begins at the end of 12-mile-long Forest Road 561 southwest of Condon, about halfway between Swan and Seeley lakes.

The **Jewel Basin Hiking Area** (★) has been set aside by the U.S. Forest Service and Flathead National Forest for foot travel only. Located 15 miles from Kalispell and about five miles from Bigfork, it has 35 miles of trails. Access is from West Side Road (Hungry Horse Reservoir) or from Jewel Basin Road, off Foothill Road (northeast of Bigfork). There's fishing and camping at 25 alpine lakes, wildlife and seasonal floral displays.

FLATHEAD VALLEY The **Danny On Memorial Trail** (5.6 miles) climbs The Big Mountain, seven miles north of Whitefish, from the lodge at the foot of the slopes. Named after a noted botanist and photographer of the region, the trail passes through beautiful meadows with views across the Flathead Valley. For a shorter (3.8-mile) one-way downhill hike, take the chairlift up the mountain.

Guided day and weekend hikes through the western Montana backcountry are organized by the **Montana Wilderness Association** (43 Woodland Park Drive, Kalispell; 406-755-6304). Each trip is limited to a few hikers, though, so advance reservations are necessary.

GLACIER NATIONAL PARK The **Avalanche Lake Trail** (2 miles) begins at the Avalanche Creek campground, four miles from Lake McDonald. Its first section—the broad and paved 300-yard **Trail of the Cedars**—is a wheelchair-accessible route that loops through an old-growth forest of western red cedars. Then it rambles up the churning gorge of Avalanche Creek to the lake itself, fed by a series of waterfalls that tumble down 2000-foot cliffs on its far side.

The Garden Wall (11.8 miles) features a traverse from the Logan Pass Visitors Center to the Granite Park Chalet, then a rapid descent to "The Loop"—a 150-degree switchback on Going-to-the-Sun Road. The trail negotiates the precipitous slope of the ice-sculpted Garden Wall, often more appropriate for mountain goats than people.

The **Hidden Lake Nature Trail** (3 miles) is among the park's most popular. Starting from the Logan Pass Visitors Center, it begins with a one-and-a-half-mile boardwalk across a fragile alpine meadow, a natural amphitheater of wildflowers called the Hanging Gardens of Logan Pass. You can return to the visitors center from a scenic overlook, where the boardwalk ends, or continue another mile and a half on a rough trail that drops rapidly to Hidden Lake.

The **Grinnell Glacier Trail** (5.5 miles) leaves from the Many Glacier Hotel, climbing slowly past Lake Josephine, then rapidly (about 1500 feet) to Upper Grinnell Lake and the glacier. The scenery is spectacular, and if you've never been close to a glacier before, you can get a close-up look at crevasses, bergschrunds and nunataks.

The official park hiking and backpacking concessionaire, **Glacier Wilderness Guides** (Route 2, West Glacier; 406-888-5466), has been hiking the backcountry for 12 years. Trips range from one to six days. Experienced guides carry all the group equipment and most of the food; participants handle only their personal gear and some food. Among the trails explored: **Belly River** (12 miles), **Cut Bank Creek** (14 miles), **Stoney Indian Pass** (56 miles), **Two Medicine** (7 miles) and **Waterton Lake–Bowman Lake** (26 miles).

Transportation

BY CAR

Route 90, the main east-west interstate highway through Montana, connects Missoula with Seattle and Coeur d'Alene, Idaho, to the west; with Butte, Bozeman, Billings and Sheridan, Wyoming, to the east.

The primary north-south artery through western Montana is **Route 93**; from the Idaho border at Lost Trail Pass, it runs north through the Bitterroot Valley to Missoula, where it crosses Route 90. It then continues north to the Canadian border via Flathead Lake, Kalispell and Eureka.

Route 2, which runs east from Sandpoint, Idaho, through Libby, Kalispell, Columbia Falls and around the south side of Glacier National Park to Browning and eastern Montana, is the other important route in western Montana.

BY AIR

Missoula's **Johnson Bell International Airport** is served by Continental, Delta and Northwest, as well as the regional carrier Horizon. Kalispell's **Glacier Park International Airport** is served by Delta and Horizon.

BY BUS

Greyhound Bus Lines (800-231-2222) runs east and west through Montana from Seattle to Missoula, Billings and points east. **Intermountain Transportation** (403 2nd Street East, Whitefish; 406-862-6700) provides regional bus service. Major bus stations are in Missoula (1660 West Broadway; 406-549-2339) and in Kalispell (1301 Route 93 South; 406-755-4011).

BY TRAIN

Amtrak's (800-872-7245) Seattle-Chicago "Empire Builder" cuts across northern Montana, making scheduled stops at Whitefish (North Central Avenue; 406-862-2268), West Glacier and East Glacier en route from Idaho to North Dakota.

CAR RENTALS

Missoula has ten agencies; the Flathead Valley has 12 in Kalispell and Whitefish. They include airport outlets for **Avis Rent A Car** (800-331-1242), **Budget Rent A Car** (800-527-0700), **Hertz Rent A Car** (800-654-3131) and **National Interrent** (800-328-4567).

PUBLIC TRANSPORTATION

Missoula's **Mountain Line** (406-721-3333) is an extensive citywide bus system with reasonable fares. Glacier National Park provides scheduled transportation between its various lodges on historic **red buses** (406-226-5551); also within the park, **Rocky Mountains Transportation** (406-862-2539) runs daily shuttle service on Going-to-the-Sun Road between West Glacier and St. Mary.

TAXIS

Transportation in the Missoula area is provided by **Yellow Cab** (406-543-6644). In the Flathead Valley, where there is no public bus line, **Kalispell Taxi & Airport Shuttle** (406-752-4022) offers 24-hour service.

CHAPTER THIRTEEN

Southern Montana Rockies

Mining discoveries near the crest of the Continental Divide provided the initial impetus for Montana's growth. More than a quarter of a century later, that mining heritage remains the unifying theme throughout southern Montana.

The Montana Territory was established in 1862 after major gold discoveries at Bannack and Virginia City—the former now a ghost town, the latter saved from that fate by tourism. Statehood was granted in 1889; the capitol has remained for more than 100 years in another gold-boom town, Helena. Its main street is still called Last Chance Gulch, and nearby Victorian mansions attest to its former affluence.

Soon after Montana became a state, world demand for copper turned Butte into "the richest hill on earth." At the turn of the century, more than 100,000 people lived in the city. Today, its population is barely a third that large. But Butte's stately and historic downtown (more properly referred to as "Uptown" for its hillside location) is more reminiscent of 19th-century San Francisco than of any other town in the Rockies. Butte's copper mines continue to be America's most productive.

Bozeman, the other main population center of southern Montana, is a university town (home of Montana State) that has burgeoned in recent years as a tourist gateway: It is less than two hours' drive north of Yellowstone National Park and within an hour of two major ski resorts.

In addition to the historical value of the region's cities, ghost towns and battlefields, southern Montana offers sterling natural features (such as the Gates of the Mountains on the Missouri River near Helena and Lewis and Clark Caverns between Butte and Bozeman), manmade attractions (including Bozeman's Museum of the Rockies and Butte's World Museum of Mining), wildlife viewing and outdoor-sports opportunities (not just in Yellowstone, but in numerous national forests and wilderness areas as well).

Helena Area

An 1864 gold strike in Last Chance Gulch led to the founding of **Helena**, nestled between the Continental Divide and the Missouri River. Dubbed the "Queen City of the Rockies" because of its grand architecture and cultural sophistication, Helena became the capital of the Montana Territory within a year of its founding and ultimately was chosen as the state capital.

Aside from its urban enticements, the city is an access point to numerous ghost towns and scenic attractions, including Helena National Forest and the Gates of the Mountains Wilderness, where the Missouri River leaves the mountains and heads into the northeastern plains.

Helena's gold rush lasted for about two decades, a period during which, in today's dollars, an estimated $3.6 billion worth of the mineral was taken from Last Chance Gulch. Today, **Last Chance Gulch** is the historic main street of this colorful town of 25,000, and the three-block stretch from 6th Avenue to Wong Street is a pedestrian mall. Markers describe buildings of historical and architectural significance, including an old bordello, and statues.

Self-guided walks of Last Chance Gulch and the surrounding **Capital City Historic District** are described in brochures available from the Helena Chamber of Commerce (201 East Lyndale Street; 406-442-4120). Or take the **Last Chance Tour Train** (6th Avenue and Roberts Street; 406-442-4120; fee), a four-car trolley that offers one-hour city tours from mid-May through September. Trips begin more or less hourly from outside the Montana Historical Society, opposite the State Capitol.

Within the historic district, more distinctive even than the capitol, is the **St. Helena Cathedral** (530 North Ewing Street; 406-442-5825), its two gothic spires towering high above Last Chance Gulch. Modeled after the famous cathedral of Cologne, Germany, and the Votive Church of Vienna, Austria, the cathedral was completed in 1913. Its $66-million stained-glass windows (by F. X. Zettler of Munich) represent the second most expensive art collection in Montana. Interior furnishings, including pews, are of hand-carved oak; the lighting fixtures are bronze; and marble statues stand throughout the cathedral.

The **Montana State Capitol** (6th Avenue at Washington Drive; 406-444-2511) and the surrounding capital district lie about a mile east of Last Chance Gulch. Completed in 1902 and expanded ten years later, the imposing neoclassical capitol building features a copper-faced dome that rises 165 feet above its 14-acre grounds. Its exterior is of Montana sandstone and granite; the interior is decorated in French Renaissance style. Of particular note are panels by noted painters depicting themes from the state's past. A mural by Charles M. Russell is among the artist's masterpieces: *Lewis and Clark Meeting the Flathead Indians at Ross' Hole* covers the wall above the rostrum of the House of Representatives. Hourly tours are offered every day in summer; self-guided tours are encouraged at other times.

Opposite the capitol is the excellent museum of the **Montana Historical Society** (225 North Roberts Street; 406-444-2694). Its largest permanent gallery

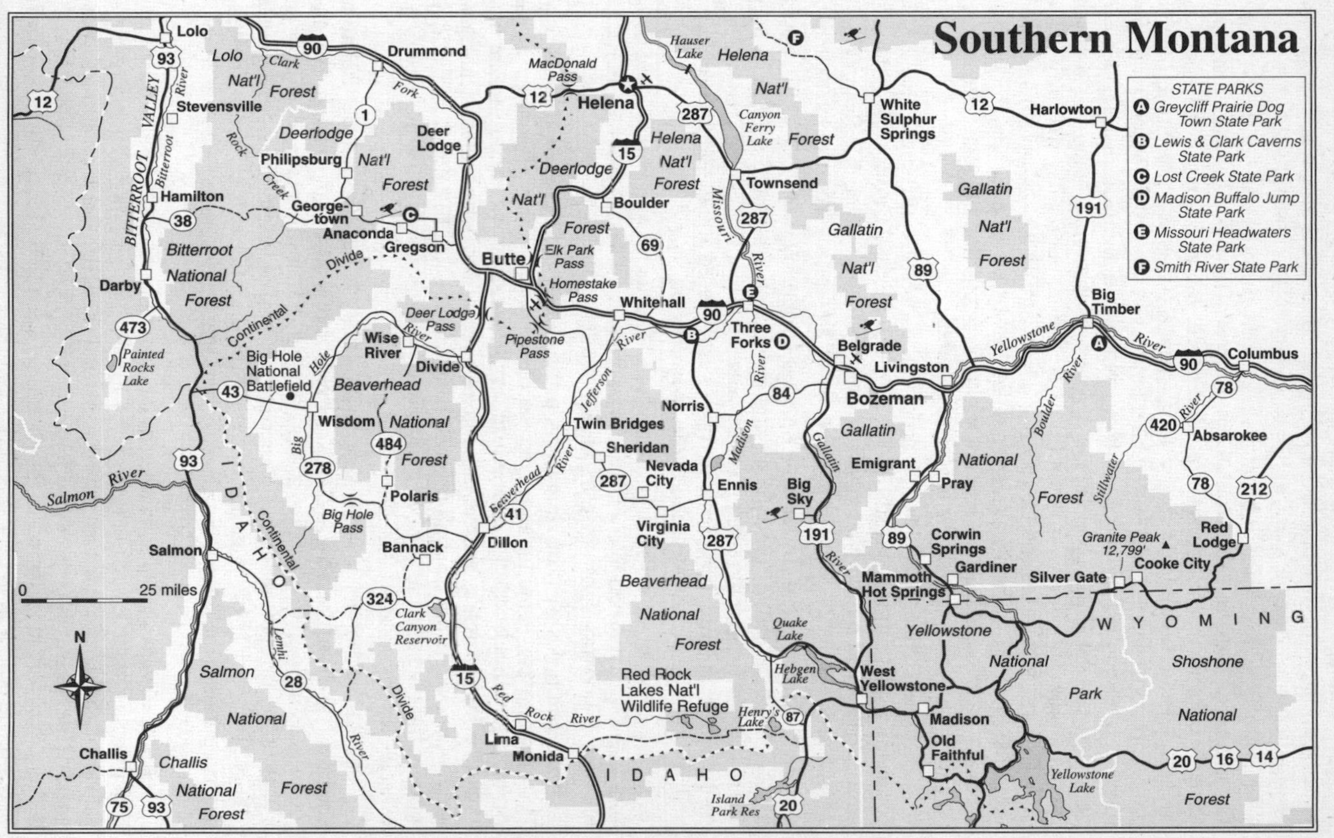
Southern Montana
STATE PARKS
A Greycliff Prairie Dog Town State Park
B Lewis & Clark Caverns State Park
C Lost Creek State Park
D Madison Buffalo Jump State Park
E Missouri Headwaters State Park
F Smith River State Park
Lolo
Stevensville
Hamilton
Darby
BITTERROOT VALLEY
Bitterroot River
Painted Rocks Lake
Drummond
Philipsburg
Georgetown
Anaconda
Gregson
Deer Lodge
Butte
Helena
MacDonald Pass
Hauser Lake
Canyon Ferry Lake
Townsend
White Sulphur Springs
Harlowton
Big Timber
Columbus
Absarokee
Red Lodge
Cooke City
Granite Peak 12,799'
Silver Gate
Gardiner
Corwin Springs
Mammoth Hot Springs
Pray
Emigrant
Livingston
Bozeman
Belgrade
Three Forks
Big Sky
West Yellowstone
Madison
Old Faithful
Yellowstone Lake
Yellowstone National Park
Ennis
Norris
Virginia City
Nevada City
Sheridan
Twin Bridges
Whitehall
Boulder
Elk Park Pass
Homestake Pass
Pipestone Pass
Deer Lodge Pass
Divide
Wise River
Wisdom
Polaris
Bannack
Big Hole Pass
Big Hole National Battlefield
Dillon
Lima
Monida
Clark Canyon Reservoir
Red Rock Lakes Nat'l Wildlife Refuge
Henry's Lake
Hebgen Lake
Quake Lake
Island Park Res
Salmon
Challis
Continental Divide
Lolo Nat'l Forest
Deerlodge Nat'l Forest
Helena Nat'l Forest
Gallatin Nat'l Forest
Beaverhead National Forest
Bitterroot National Forest
Salmon National Forest
Challis National Forest
Shoshone National Forest
Gallatin National Forest
Missouri River
Yellowstone River
Madison River
Jefferson River
Beaverhead River
Gallatin River
Boulder River
Stillwater River
Red Rock River
Lemhi River
Salmon River
Clark Fork
Rock Creek
Big Hole River
IDAHO
WYOMING
25 miles
0
N
90
15
93
12
191
89
287
212
78
420
84
41
43
278
484
324
28
38
473
1
69
87
20
16
14
75

traces the history of the state, from prehistory through World War II; there are also galleries of Russell's art and F. Jay Haynes' photography.

The official residence of Montana's governor has moved, but the **Original Governor's Mansion** (304 North Ewing Street; 406-442-3115) is open April through December afternoons for guided hourly tours. Built in 1888, the Victorian mansion three blocks above Last Chance Gulch was the home of nine governors between 1913 and 1959. Other impressive late-19th-century mansions can be glimpsed on a driving or walking tour of the **mansion district**, located northwest of Last Chance Gulch, mainly west of Benton Avenue and south of Hauser Boulevard. Noteworthy not for its elevation, but for its proximity to the State Capitol, **Mount Helena City Park** (Adams Street; 406-442-4120) has seven trails rising to the summit, a quarter mile above Last Chance Gulch. Nearest access is west six blocks on Lawrence Street, south three blocks on Harrison Avenue, then west on Adams Street to its end.

South of Helena, a half-hour's drive in the direction of Butte on Route 15, is the town of **Boulder**. Worth a look is the **Jefferson County Courthouse**, built in 1889 and on the National Register of Historic Places: It features gargoyles perched on 24-inch-thick stone walls above its three-story entrance.

Just east are the **Boulder Hot Springs** (Route 69; 406-225-4339), noted for their high content of radon, a mining byproduct considered helpful by sufferers of arthritis, emphysema and other ailments. Hot (104°F) and cold soaking pools, salt scrubs and therapeutic massages are offered at the health resort here, built in 1888 and currently undergoing restoration.

One of Montana's finest ghost towns is **Elkhorn** (★) (Forest Road 258; 406-444-4720), reached by traveling seven miles southeast of Boulder on Route 69, then following signs north another 11 miles.

Sixteen miles west of Helena, atop the Continental Divide at 6320-foot MacDonald Pass, is an authentic replica of a pioneer village. **Frontier Town** (Route 12; 406-442-4560) was built of hand-hewn logs beginning in the late 1940s by John Quigley, a direct descendant of early Montana settlers. Unfortunately, new owners have put more energy into a gift shop, restaurant and unique western bar than into the neglected town itself, which seems full of possibilities. Closed November to March.

A real-life frontier town is **Marysville** (Marysville Road), about 22 miles northwest of Helena off Route 279. At its zenith, this boom town near the Drumlummon Mine (said to have produced as much as $50 million in gold) supported a population of 2000 with six hotels, four general stores, two churches and a school. Today, only the presence of the nearby Great Divide ski area and other sports options in the surrounding Helena National Forest preserve it as a "living" ghost town.

Route 279 crosses the Continental Divide at Flesher Pass, then follows the upper reaches of the Blackfoot River into **Lincoln**. The ranching community is the gateway to National Forest recreation at several small lakes as well as the **Scapegoat Wilderness**, which borders the south end of the famed Bob Marshall Wilderness. No road, in fact, crosses the Divide between Lincoln and Route 2, which traces the southern boundary of Glacier National Park 100 miles to the north.

A series of Missouri River reservoirs, created by early-20th-century dams, provide wide recreational opportunities east of Helena. **Holter Lake**, **Hauser Lake** and **Canyon Ferry Lake** attract walleye, trout, kokanee salmon and perch fishermen, as well as boaters, waterskiers and board sailors.

Holter Lake offers access to one of the Helena area's preeminent attractions: the **Gates of the Mountains**. Narrated commercial **tour boats** (★) (Route 15 Exit 109; 406-458-5241; fee) that depart from the Upper Holter Lake marina, 20 miles north of Helena, ply a steep canyon whose quarter-mile-high limestone walls seemed to open and close before the eyes of the advancing Lewis and Clark expedition in 1805. Beyond these "gates," as the explorers dubbed them, were the Missouri River headwaters and the crest of the Rockies. Tours operate from Memorial Day through September.

The canyon's western slopes make up the **Gates of the Mountains Game Preserve**; to the east lies the **Gates of the Mountains Wilderness**. Both are vehicle-free parcels of **Helena National Forest** (2800 Skyway Drive, Helena; 406-449-5201). Rocky Mountain goats, deer, bighorn sheep, osprey, eagles and occasional bear—as well as ancient Native American petroglyphs—can be seen from the tour boat.

Due east of Helena is 25-mile-long, four-mile-wide Canyon Ferry Lake, whose **Canyon Ferry Recreation Area** (Canyon Ferry Road; 406-444-4475; admission), is the state's most popular for water-sports enthusiasts.

Route 12 proceeds southeast from Helena to **Townsend**, at the head of Canyon Ferry Lake, then turns sharply east across the Big Belt Mountains to the town of **White Sulphur Springs**. The hot springs from which the community takes its name have been compared to Germany's famed Baden-Baden spa: They have high levels of chloride, sulfate, sodium, potassium and bicarbonate, as well as calcium, silica and magnesium. Though known for centuries by Native Americans, the springs today are enclosed by the **Spa Hot Springs Motel** (202 West Main Street; 406-547-3366; admission).

The casual visitor to White Sulphur Springs is more likely to spot the cut-granite Victorian mansion, looming high on a hill over the town, than the springs themselves. This is **The Castle** (310 2nd Avenue Northeast; 406-547-3370; admission), built in 1892 as a private home and now housing the Meagher County Museum. Open summers, the museum displays period furnishings and memorabilia of regional history; an adjacent carriage house exhibits antique buggies.

HELENA AREA HOTELS

The Sanders—Helena's Bed & Breakfast (328 North Ewing Street, Helena; 406-442-3309) occupies a three-story 1875 mansion overlooking Last Chance Gulch and the cathedral, just a block from the Original Governor's Mansion. The home has seven restored bedrooms, all with period antiques, private baths and air-conditioning. Gourmet breakfasts are served in a lovely dining room. Moderate.

Within hailing distance of the Last Chance Gulch pedestrian mall is the **King's Carriage Inn** (910 North Last Chance Gulch, Helena; 406-442-6080, fax 406-449-4131). Its 125 comfortable rooms all have standard amenities. There's a 24-hour restaurant here, a casino-lounge, an outdoor swimming pool, steambaths and saunas. A good value at budget to moderate rates.

The **Park Plaza Hotel** (22 North Last Chance Gulch, Helena; 406-449-7583, fax 406-442-4030) is in the heart of historic downtown. It doesn't have a pool, but it *does* have a restaurant, nightclub and lounge. Its 71 rooms are standard issue with queen-size beds and air-conditioning. Moderate.

Helena's largest and most luxurious lodging is the **Best Western Colonial Inn** (2301 Colonial Drive; 406-443-2100, 800-442-1002, fax 406-443-2100), just off Route 15. This two-story motel's 149 spacious rooms have just what you'd expect from an upscale property, including king- or queen-size beds and air-conditioning: some have microwaves and refrigerators. A restaurant and lounge are located off the elegant atrium lobby, and the motel contains two swimming pools, a hot tub, a sauna and a coin laundry. Moderate.

Native Americans called them "wampum waters." Today, two year-round pools at the **Spa Hot Springs Motel** (202 West Main Street, White Sulphur Springs; 406-547-3366) contain the healing mineral waters of White Sulphur Springs. The motel's 21 rooms aren't fancy, but they offer free access to the pools (nonguests must pay an admission fee). Budget.

HELENA AREA RESTAURANTS

For atmosphere, it's hard to outdo **The Stonehouse Restaurant** (120 Reeder's Alley at South Park Avenue, Helena; 406-449-2552) in a restored 19th-century brick building at the entrance to a historic shopping and artisans' mall. The staff even dresses as they might have 100 years ago. The menu focuses on steak and seafood dinners at moderate to deluxe prices.

The **Queen City Cafe** (42 South Park Avenue, Helena; 406-442-3354) has a relaxing garden atmosphere and an interesting daily menu of Continental and international cuisine, from chicken Parisienne and fresh grilled seafood to jambalaya and lasagna. Moderate.

Northern Italian cuisine is the menu mainstay at **On Broadway** (106 Broadway, Helena; 406-443-1929), lodged in an 1889 grocery store refurbished in art deco style. A wide choice of chicken, seafood and vegetarian dishes—as well as a handful of meat dishes—share the spotlight with one of the city's best wine lists. Moderate.

You can get two pounds of beef ribs for $12.95 at **The Windbag Saloon** (19 South Last Chance Gulch, Helena; 406-443-9669). This is steak lover's paradise, and there are lots of chicken and fish dishes as well. The desserts are local legend. The rustic building, so it is claimed, was "one of the cleanest, most respected bordellos in all of Montana" until "Big Dorothy" was closed down in 1973. Budget to moderate.

Bert & Ernie's Saloon and Eatery (361 North Last Chance Gulch, Helena; 406-443-5680) offers a wide variety of sandwiches and salads, and a handful of nightly dinners. The best things here are the eclectic antique decor and the extensive list of microbrews and wines by the glass. Budget.

An hour and a half west of Helena near the banks of the Blackfoot River, the atmosphere is even more rustic, the food even more meat-and-potatoes. Behind log-cabin walls, the **Seven-Up Ranch Supper Club** (Route 200, Lincoln; 406-362-4255) prepares what some swear is the best prime rib between Great Falls and Missoula. Moderate.

HELENA AREA SHOPPING

Perhaps the most interesting shopping, from a visitor's standpoint, is at **Reeder's Alley** (100 South Park Avenue, Helena), a short block west of Last Chance Gulch at Wong Street. Built as an inn for miners and laborers during the early gold-rush era, it was largely constructed of brick freighted up the Missouri River from St. Louis. Until recently an arts center, it has undergone extensive and authentic restoration and has reopened as a block of arts and crafts galleries and retail specialty shops.

Potters from all over the world come to work and study at the **Archie Bray Foundation** (★) (2915 Country Club Avenue, Helena; 406-443-3502). The public gallery offers outstanding traditional and contemporary pottery, sculpture and ceramics, at prices to match. Studio tours are by appointment.

Two Bears Gifts (511 North Sanders Street, Helena; 406-442-8241), in Capital Plaza, though a good mile removed from the Last Chance Gulch pedestrian mall, may be the best option for made-in-Montana souvenirs. Look for jewelry and other artwork, glassware, shirts and hats, books and huckleberry products.

State legislators peruse the racks at the **Main News Smoke Shop** (9 North Last Chance Gulch, Helena; 406-442-6424). Local and national newspapers and more than 800 magazine titles are sold here.

Certainly one of the Helena area's most intriguing stores is **The Prospector's Shop** (★) (6312 Route 12 West; 406-442-1872), five miles west on the MacDonald Pass highway. On display are all manner of mining equipment and supplies, from metal detectors to sluice boxes and gold dredges. It's fascinating just to stop and browse a while.

HELENA AREA NIGHTLIFE

Since its earliest days of gold-rush affluence, Helena has been a magnet for performing artists of national renown. Today the **Myrna Loy Center for the Performing Arts** (15 North Ewing Street; 406-443-0287), occupying the renovated Lewis and Clark County Jail, showcases music, theater and dance, as well as films, conferences and festivals.

Local thespians perform Thursday through Saturday nights in the historic brownstone **Grandstreet Theater** (325 North Park Street; 406-443-3311), close by Last Chance Gulch. And the **Helena Orchestra and Symphony Chorale** (406-442-1860) makes its home beneath the exotic minaret of the Moorish-style Helena Civic Center (Benton and Neill avenues).

For late-night revelers in Helena, **JD's** (22 North Last Chance Gulch; 406-443-2200) is a disco-nightclub in the Park Plaza Hotel that attracts a mostly mid-to-late-20s crowd. **Jeff's Joint** (101 North Last Chance Gulch; 406-443-2200), though cozy, features live rock bands, and **The Windbag Saloon** (19 South Last Chance Gulch; 406-443-9669), lodged in a former brothel, offers a rustic atmosphere for conversation and acoustic music.

HELENA AREA PARKS

Helena National Forest—Three principal units make up this 975,000-acre national forest, one of ten in the state. The largest segment takes in both sides of the Continental Divide west of Helena, from the Scapegoat Wilderness nearly to Boulder. Smaller parcels include the Big Belt Mountains, east of Canyon Ferry Lake, and the Elkhorn Mountains, south of the capital. The forest includes 730 miles of trails and 1600 miles of backroads.

Facilities: Picnic tables, restrooms, trails; information, 406-449-5201. *Swimming:* At your own risk. *Fishing:* Rainbow and brown trout are plentiful throughout. The Dearborn River also has cutthroat trout and mountain whitefish, the Blackfoot River both of those plus bull trout. Anglers can find brook trout in the Elkhorn Mountains' alpine lakes, arctic grayling in tiny Park Lake, southwest of Helena.

Camping: There are 135 RV/tent sites (no hookups) plus seven tents-only sites in nine campgrounds; no charge to $6 per night. Four recreational cabins within the forest are available by reservation for $20 per night.

Getting there: Principal highways are Route 200, through Lincoln; Route 12, west of Helena and east of Townsend; York Road and several connecting roads, east of Hauser and Canyon Ferry lakes. Consult the National Forest office for specific routes.

Holter Lake Recreation Area—Located at the lower (north) end of the Missouri River reservoir that flows between the lofty limestone cliffs of the Gates of the Mountains, this area is especially popular with boating and fishing enthusiasts.

Facilities: Picnic tables, restrooms, boat ramp; wheelchair accessible; day-use fee, $2; information, 406-494-5059. *Swimming:* Designated beach. *Fishing:* Excellent for walleye, kokanee salmon, brown and rainbow trout and yellow perch.

Camping: There are 50 RV/tent sites (no hookups); $6 per night. Nearby Log Gulch, administered by the Bureau of Land Management, has 100 RV/tent sites available on the same basis.

Getting there: Take Route 15 north from Helena for 33 miles to Wolf Creek Exit 226, east three miles on Recreation Road to Wolf Creek Bridge, then south three miles on Beartooth Road.

Canyon Ferry Recreation Area—The most popular and largest of Montana's 46 state recreation areas consists of 24 units around the 76-mile shoreline of Canyon Ferry Lake. All but six of the sites are within a few miles of the Canyon Ferry Dam (tours available) at the reservoir's north end; the park visitors center is located in adjacent Canyon Ferry Village, along with lodging and RV resorts, restaurants, a grocery store and other facilities.

Facilities: Picnic tables, restrooms, showers, three marinas, boat rentals, boat ramps, concessions; wheelchair accessible; information, 406-475-3310. *Swimming:* Several sites have designated beaches. *Fishing:* Good for kokanee salmon, rainbow and brown trout, yellow perch and burbot.

Camping: There are 383 RV/tent sites (no hookups) in eight developed and three undeveloped campgrounds; largest is Hellgate (130 RV/tent sites), nine miles southeast of Canyon Ferry Village on Hellgate Gulch Road. No charge to $6 per night.

Getting there: For park headquarters, take Route 12/287 ten miles east from Helena; then turn north on Route 284 (Canyon Ferry Road) and continue eight miles to Canyon Ferry Village.

Smith River State Park—At this unique state park, a 61-mile stretch of the remote Smith River canyon, is set aside for rafters and fishermen on float trips. River enthusiasts put in at Camp Baker, 23 miles northwest of White Sulphur Springs, and take out at Eden Bridge, about 20 miles south of Great Falls. Rafters pay a $15 application fee, plus a per-person fee, to use the river route.

Facilities: Picnic tables, toilets, hand-launch access; information, 406-454-3441. *Fishing:* Trout, mountain whitefish and burbot.

Camping: There are 22 primitive riverside camps for boaters and rafters.

Getting there: To the put-in, take Route 360 northwest from White Sulphur Springs 16 miles toward Fort Logan and then follow signs north seven miles on Smith River Road to Camp Baker.

Butte Area

Butte is the center of a rich mining district on the crest of the Rockies, including the various copper and silver towns on the Pintler Scenic Route. It's also the gateway to the beauty of the Anaconda-Pintler Wilderness and the historical attractions of Deer Lodge, including Grant-Kohrs Ranch National Historic Site and the old Montana Territorial Prison.

At the turn of the 20th century, few cities in western North America were larger than Butte, which stretches down a long slope on the west side of the Continental Divide. Urbane and cosmopolitan, "the richest hill on earth" had a population of more than 100,000, a powerful position in the national labor movement and a cast of millionaires.

Though the city was founded on gold in the 1860s and thrived on silver in the 1870s, copper was king. During the 1880s, Butte became the world's greatest copper producer. In succeeding decades, some 19 *billion* pounds of the ore were taken from underground by hard-rock miners, and state-of-the-art smelters extracted the metal for shipment around the nation and overseas.

"Copper kings" like Marcus Daly and William Andrews Clark fought for control of the city's wealth. (Daly's Anaconda Copper Mining Company amalgamated with John Rockefeller's Standard Oil and dominated Butte into the

1970s.) Irish and Cornish miners, followed by dozens of other nationalities—among them Italians, Finns, Serbians, Croatians, Germans, Chinese and Mexicans—came to Butte and created their own distinctive ethnic communities.

After the First World War, demand for copper decreased and an exodus from Butte began. The population declined further after 1955, when labor-intensive hard-rock mining was abandoned in favor of more cost-efficient open-pit mining, changing the face of Butte forever. Whole neighborhoods on the city's east side were evacuated and razed to allow the hillside to be excavated. The first hole, the Berkeley Pit, was exhausted and closed in 1982; other adjacent mines are currently being worked.

Today, Butte is a city in transition. Though only about 33,000 people now make their homes here, its history is evident everywhere.

Uptown Butte is the city's downtown. It is reminiscent of parts of San Francisco without its cable cars; built on a hillside at about 5700 feet, it has preserved an eclectic turn-of-the-century architecture and clings to a big-city ambience in a small-town environment. Black headframes that once towered over the entrances to hard-rock mines are a unique accent on the city skyline. About six square miles, encompassing 4500 buildings, have been designated a national historic landmark district—one of the largest such districts in the United States.

The hillsides that surround Butte, wasted of vegetation in an era when copper smelters spewed toxic sulfurous fumes into the atmosphere, are finally recovering. The city, meanwhile, is diversifying its economy to include medical and energy research, education and tourism.

A 90-minute introductory tour of the city on **Old No. 1**, a motorized replica of an open electric trolley, is offered several times daily throughout the summer (admission) from the **Butte-Silver Bow Chamber of Commerce** (2950 Harrison Street; 406-494-5595). The chamber also provides free brochures for a walking tour of the mansions, churches and other buildings of historic Uptown.

Start a self-guided tour of Butte at the **Berkeley Pit** (200 Shields Street; 406-782-8117), 7000 feet wide, more than a mile long and 1800 feet deep. The pit has been filling with ground water since its pumping system was shut down with the mining operation; it is the deepest body of water in Montana, but its chemical content is an ecological hell for the Environmental Protection Agency and the mine's owner, the Atlantic Richfield Company (ARCO). A public tunnel leads to a viewing stand with taped narrations, open March through November; a visitors center/gift shop outside the tunnel is open daily in summer.

For a more thorough look at Butte's mining history, head west two miles on Park Street to the **World Museum of Mining** (West Park and Granite streets; 406-723-7211). The free 12-acre museum, open April to November, re-creates a circa-1899 mining camp complete with mine entrances, machinery and a fully furnished, three-square-block village (known as "Hell Roarin' Gulch") where miners and their families lived, shopped and enjoyed various services and entertainments. The museum headquarters building has two floors of exhibits and a gift shop. From a platform behind the Hell Roarin' Gulch schoolhouse, the **Neversweat and Washoe Railroad** (406-723-8343; admission) takes passengers on a one-hour guided tour to the defunct Anselmo Mine Yard, Wednesdays through Sundays in summer.

Two blocks away, another mansion, this one built in 1898 for William Clark's son Charles, has been converted to a heritage museum. The four-story **Arts Chateau** (★) (321 West Broadway; 406-723-7600; admission), designed in the style of France's Loire River chateaus, houses permanent and changing exhibits of regional art and the George Grant collection of 700 handwoven fishing flies.

High above Butte, overlooking the city from an elevation of 8510 feet on the crest of the Continental Divide, a 90-foot statue of **Our Lady of the Rockies** is said to represent all women "regardless of religion." It was built by volunteers in 1985 and is maintained by a nonprofit organization. Daily summer bus tours (admission) begin from an information center and gift shop in the former St. Mary's Church (434 North Main Street; 406-782-1221).

Two small museums sit in the heart of the historic district. **The Mai Wah Society** (★) (17 West Mercury Street; 406-494-5595; admission), open Memorial Day to Labor Day, displays artifacts and photographs from Butte's once-bustling community of Chinese miners. The **Dumas Red Light Antique Mall** (45 East Mercury Street; 406-782-3808) preserves the last of the city's "Venus Alley" brothels that operated from the late 19th century until 1982.

THE PINTLER SCENIC ROUTE West of Butte, the **Pintler Scenic Route**, which follows Route 1 through historic mining towns and the Deerlodge National Forest, combines with Route 90 through Deer Lodge to make a 150-mile driving loop that can easily take up a full day.

The Pintler Route begins 18 miles northwest of Butte at the Anaconda exit from Route 90. It's nine miles from the interstate into **Anaconda**, a city of 10,000 founded by Marcus Daly when he erected a copper smelter and reduction works in 1883. Though it ceased operating in 1980, the 585-foot **Anaconda Smelter Stack**, on a hill south of town, remains the city's landmark and a state historic park. Once known as the Washoe Stack, it is one of the world's tallest freestanding brick structures, taller even than the Washington Monument. A Jack Nicklaus–designed golf course is scheduled to open around the old smelter works in 1996.

The downtown **Anaconda Historic District** is worthy of exploration. Vintage tour buses (admission) depart twice daily from the **Anaconda Visitors Center** (306 East Park Street; 406-563-2400), housed in a replica of an old train depot that once served the Anaconda Copper Mining Company. Brochures describing a self-guided walking tour are available here.

Among the district's significant buildings is the **Washoe Theater** (★) (305 Main Street; 406-563-6161), a 1000-seat art deco theater built in 1937. The Smithsonian Institution rates the theater's elaborate interior as one of the most beautiful in the nation.

The 10,000-foot-high peaks of the Anaconda-Pintler Wilderness rise to the south as Route 1 follows Warm Springs Creek west from Anaconda to **Georgetown Lake**, a year-round recreation area in Deerlodge National Forest. At Georgetown Lake, the Pintler Scenic Route turns north and follows Flint Creek to the Clark Fork River. About ten miles north of the lake, it's a short detour into **Philipsburg**, an 1860s silver-mining town and now (in its entirety) a national historic district. The many circa-1890s brick businesses along Broadway, the town's colorful main street, have been restored and now house a variety of shops and restaurants.

Twenty-one ghost towns are located within 40 miles of Philipsburg, so it's appropriate that the town's **Granite County Museum and Cultural Center** (135 South Sansome Street; 406-859-3388; admission) is the home of the Ghost Town Hall of Fame. Open mid-May through December.

Route 1 rejoins the interstate at **Drummond**, 26 scenic miles north of Philipsburg. Missoula is 48 miles northwest. But turn southeast (right) instead and follow Route 90 about 31 miles to **Deer Lodge**, home of several important tourist attractions.

Chief among them is the **Grant-Kohrs Ranch National Historic Site** (Route 10 North, Deer Lodge; 406-846-2070; admission). For more than a century the headquarters of a cattle empire that once controlled one million acres of the northern Rockies, the ranch was set aside by the federal government in 1972 to illustrate the history of the ranching industry. Half-hour guided tours of the elegant 23-room Kohrs home, built in 1862 and expanded in 1890, begin at the visitors center. Guests may take themselves through interpretive displays in a bunkhouse row and buggy shed, tack room, blacksmith shop and more. Cattle graze and draft horses still work the remaining 1500 acres of the ranch.

Within the walls of the **Montana Territorial Prison** (1106 Main Street, Deer Lodge; 406-846-3111; admission) are three separate museums: the **Old Montana Prison**, the Towe Ford Museum and the Montana Law Enforcement Museum. Massive gray stone walls and crenelated guard towers earmark the foreboding prison, which was in active use for 108 years until 1979. Guided and self-guided tours give glimpses of the cellblocks and maximum-security corridors. The **Towe Ford Museum** features more than 100 perfectly restored Ford automobiles from 1903 to the 1960s; the **Law Enforcement Museum** is a memorial to Montana officers who have died in the line of duty. The prison and Ford museum are open February through November; the law-enforcement museum is open mid-May through October.

From Deer Lodge, Butte is 41 miles southeast via Route 90.

BUTTE AREA HOTELS

For a taste of Victorian luxury without modern amenities, William A. Clark's **Copper King Mansion** (★) (219 West Granite Street, Butte; 406-782-7580) is a real find. Five exquisite bedrooms (two with private baths, the others with shared baths) display the likes of hand-painted fresco ceilings, sycamore and walnut woodwork and other turn-of-the-century touches. A gourmet breakfast is served in a dining room whose cupboards brim with the finest crystal and silver. The mansion is entirely deserving of its listing as a national historic site. Moderate.

The ten-story **Finlen Hotel and Motor Inn** (100 East Broadway, Butte; 406-723-5461, 800-729-5461), with its mansard roof, is a massive presence in the Uptown skyline. Modeled after New York's Astor, it opened in 1924 and was long the favored hotel in this mining city. The Finlen fell on hard times and was turned into senior residential housing but has since undergone renovation: 16 cozy rooms on the tower's second and third floors have been reopened to travelers. Another 34 are in an adjoining two-story motor inn. Budget.

Butte's finest is the **Best Western Copper King Inn** (4655 Harrison Avenue; 406-494-6666, 800-543-5814, fax 406-494-7611). Though its 150 rooms are four miles south of the Uptown historic district, opposite the airport on Route 2, they are spacious and tastefully furnished. There are separate restaurants for fine dining and casual meals. Beneath a two-story atrium roof are a swimming pool, a hot tub, a sauna and an exercise room. Adjoining is the CopperDome, a 24,000-square-foot facility beneath an inflated roof used for indoor tennis, major concerts, trade shows and conferences. Moderate to deluxe.

Eighteen miles west of Butte, just three miles off Route 90 near Anaconda, is the **Fairmont Hot Springs Resort** (1500 Fairmont Road, Gregson; 406-797-3241, 800-443-2381, fax 406-797-3337). Set in picturesque surroundings at the foot of 10,600-foot Mount Haggin, the resort attracts hot-spring soakers and swimmers with four indoor and outdoor pools and golfers with its 18-hole golf course, one of Montana's best. There's even a petting zoo for the kids. There are 158 spacious rooms and suites with standard furnishings and amenities. Moderate to deluxe.

Scharf's Motor Inn (819 Main Street, Deer Lodge; 406-846-2810, 800-341-8000) meets basic requirements for travelers who want to spend a night near the Grant-Kohrs Ranch and Montana Territorial Prison. Rooms are clean and comfortable if nothing fancy, and the motel has its own family restaurant and lounge. A couple of kitchens are available for families. Budget.

BUTTE AREA RESTAURANTS

Creative Continental dining in an old mining town? That's what you get at the **Uptown Café** (47 East Broadway, Butte; 406-723-4735). There's a heavy emphasis on seafood (from cioppino to coquilles Saint-Jacques) at this elegant gallery-style eatery, but look for chicken, beef, veal and pasta dishes as well. The wine list is small but enlightened. Lunch Monday through Friday, dinner Tuesday through Saturday. Deluxe.

At the **Metals Banque Restaurant** (8 West Park Street, Butte; 406-723-6160), you can actually eat in the vault of a restored bank tower. In an atmosphere of Italian marble, African mahogany and solid copper window frames, choose from steak, seafood or Mexican specialties. Full bar and microbrews; budget to moderate prices.

If the **Pekin Noodle Parlor** (★) (117 South Main Street; 406-782-2217) isn't Butte's oldest restaurant, it's close. Established a century ago in what was then a bustling Chinatown, it remains a "hole in the wall." Guests are served heaping helpings of chow mein, chop suey and egg foo yung. Budget.

Just around the corner is a veritable Butte institution, **Pork Chop John's** (★) (18 West Mercury Street; 406-782-0812). Though John's has since extended its little empire to Billings and Bozeman, this tiny chop shop—a streetside take-out window and a half-dozen counter stools inside—is the original. Budget.

The place to go in Deer Lodge is the **Broken Arrow Casino & Steakhouse** (317 Main Street; 406-846-3400). This candlelit steakhouse in the heart of downtown, between the Territorial Prison and the Grant-Kohrs Ranch, serves up dinners in a rustic ambience. The casino-lounge adjoins. Moderate.

BUTTE AREA SHOPPING

Right in the Copper City itself, the **Butte Copper Co.** (3015 Harrison Avenue; 406-494-2070) boasts that it has "anything and everything in copper." Its stock includes copper jewelry, other semiprecious metals and gems, and various less pricey souvenirs.

Art lovers are well served at the gift shop and sales gallery at the **Arts Chateau** (321 West Broadway, Butte; 406-723-7600). Paintings, prints, pottery, jewelry, crafts and books are among the items available for purchase.

Butte's premier bookstore is **Books and Books** (205 West Park Street; 406-782-9520), which offers an extensive selection of current and classic literature and occasional appearances by authors.

On the Pintler Scenic Route, the shop at the **Sapphire Gallery** (★) (119 East Broadway, Philipsburg; 406-859-3236) displays and sells an intriguing variety of international artworks, as well as framed fossils-as-art.

BUTTE AREA NIGHTLIFE

The focus of the arts in Butte, and the home of the Butte-Silver Bow Arts Foundation, is the striking **Arts Chateau** (321 West Broadway; 406-723-7600). In addition to its permanent art collection, the Chateau sponsors year-round performances by visiting chamber orchestras and ballet troupes.

At this writing, visiting classical artists typically perform at the **Butte Civic Center** (1340 Harrison Avenue; 406-723-8262). Restoration of the old Fox Theater (315 West Park Street) is nearing completion, at which point the **Butte Center for the Performing Arts** will take over the magnificent art deco theater in the heart of Uptown Butte.

Popular concert entertainers on tour often appear at south Butte's **Copper-Dome**, adjoining the Best Western Copper King Inn (4655 Harrison Avenue; 406-494-6666). The inn's lounge, **Jox**, has established itself as the city's most upscale nightclub with live rock bands on weekends, comedy nights midweek. Occasional cover.

Bands also perform at the **Cavalier Lounge** (Finlen Hotel, 100 East Broadway; 406-723-5171) and the **Silver Dollar Saloon** (133 South Main Street; 406-782-7367), the latter discreetly frequented by gays and lesbians. For atmosphere and colorful drinking companionship, check out **Charlie's New Deal Bar** (333 South Arizona Street; 406-723-9968), the **M & M Bar** (9 North Main Street; 406-

723-7612) or the **Helsinki Bar & Steam Bath** (402 East Broadway; 406-723-9004), one of two surviving businesses left over from Butte's once-thriving Finntown.

In Deer Lodge, the **Old Prison Players** perform musical comedies and melodramas Wednesday through Sunday evenings, late June through late August, behind the walls of Montana Territorial Prison (1106 Main Street; 406-846-3111; admission).

BUTTE AREA PARKS

Lost Creek State Park (★)—A short nature trail leads to the base of Lost Creek Falls, which makes a spectacular drop from the 1200-foot-high limestone cliffs of the Flint Creek Range north of Anaconda. Rocky Mountain goats and bighorn sheep are frequently seen here; bring binoculars.

Facilities: Picnic tables, restrooms, wheelchair-accessible trails; information, 406-542-5500. *Fishing:* Mountain whitefish and trout.

Camping: There are 25 primitive sites (no hookups).

Getting there: From Anaconda, take Route 1 east for one and a half miles, Route 273 north for two miles, then Forest Road 635 west for six miles.

Deerlodge National Forest—Straddling the Continental Divide and eight separate mountain ranges, this 1.2-million-acre national forest surrounds Butte on all sides. Ranging over 10,000-foot peaks and rolling grasslands, the forest includes 140 lakes, 630 miles of trails and the Discovery Basin ski area. The Sheepshead Mountain Recreation Area, on Maney Lake 19 miles north of Butte via Route 15 and Forest Road 442, has a campground, picnic area, fishing pier and sports fields designed specifically for the disabled.

Facilities: Picnic tables, restrooms, trails, boat ramps; information, 406-496-3400. *Swimming:* Designated beaches at Delmoe, Echo, Georgetown, Homestake and Moose lakes. *Fishing:* Four species of trout, three kinds of char, mountain whitefish and arctic grayling live in more than a thousand miles of streams. Rock Creek and Georgetown Lake are especially popular.

Camping: There are 266 RV/tent sites (no hookups) plus 80 for tents only at 22 campgrounds; no charge to $6 per night. The national forest also has four recreational cabins that can be reserved at $15 to $20 a night.

Getting there: Forest areas can be reached from interstate freeway exits in all directions from Butte, as well as Route 2 (Harrison Avenue South) through Pipestone Pass and Route 1 (the Pintler Scenic Route) to Georgetown Lake.

Dillon Area

Montana's largest county, Beaverhead, stretches from just south of Butte all the way to the Idaho border, covering 5550 square miles. Within the county are Bannack State Park, an authentic 1860s ghost town; the scenic beauties of the sparsely populated Big Hole Valley and Pioneer Mountains; and the Big Hole National Battlefield, just east of Chief Joseph Pass.

Dillon, which sits just off Route 15 an hour's drive south of Butte, is a good base from which to explore the region. Established as a Union Pacific railroad town, it has become a center for ranching and summer recreation.

The **Dillon Visitor Information Center** (125 South Montana Street; 406-683-5511), housed in an old train depot, offers a brochure for a walking tour of the historic late-19th-century downtown. The most intriguing building is the **Beaverhead County Courthouse** (Pacific and Bannock streets; 406-683-2383), whose four-faced Seth Thomas clock looks in all directions from a 60-foot tower.

Next door to the visitors center is the **Beaverhead County Museum** (15 South Montana Street; 406-683-5027), a log building that boasts an impressive and well-organized collection of artifacts and memorabilia from native (mainly Shoshone) and pioneer history. A quarter-mile-long boardwalk leads past a homesteader's cabin and Dillon's first flush toilet (in an outhouse, of course).

Western Montana College (710 South Atlantic Street; 406-683-7011) has a Victorian main hall built in 1896. But the highlight is the campus art gallery/museum (406-683-7126), featuring the Seidensticker Wildlife Collection of trophy game from Africa, Asia and North America. Open Monday through Thursday.

Bannack State Park (4200 Bannack Road, Bannack; 406-834-3413; admission), 25 miles west of Dillon via Route 278, is an 1860s ghost town at its authentic best—preserved but mostly unrestored, except to ward off Mother Nature and Father Time. Its 60-odd hand-fashioned buildings of rough-hewn logs and brick masonry contain little more than the memories and shattered dreams of their former owners.

The town was founded in 1862 on Grasshopper Creek, site of the first major gold strike in the future Montana. Bannack was briefly the territory's first capital (before Virginia City) and claimed its first school, first hotel and first jail.

As Bannack grew to 3000, so did its reputation for lawlessness. But one of the West's most remarkable chapters was written here and in Virginia City by a league of law-abiding vigilantes in 1864. When the vigilantes realized that their sheriff, Henry Plummer, was secretly the leader of a gang of murderous "road agents" known as The Innocents, they hunted the gang down, administered hasty trials and hung them on gallows built by Plummer himself.

The gallows can still be seen on a walking tour of Bannack, as well as the imposing Meade Hotel and courthouse, Skinner's Saloon, the Methodist church, the Masonic temple, Bachelor's Row and other sites. Rings for leg irons remain in the floor of the Bannack jail. Guided tours are offered three times daily, on weekends and holidays.

Continuing west for seven miles past the Bannack junction, Route 278 conjuncts the **Pioneer Mountains National Scenic Byway** (Route 484). This 40-mile backcountry drive through **Beaverhead National Forest** (406-683-3900) extends north 40 miles to Wise River on Route 43.

The first 12 miles of the road, open year-round, extend to **Elk Horn Hot Springs** (Route 484, Polaris; 406-834-3434), a resort with a mineral pool, restaurant and rustic lodge; and **Maverick Mountain** (Route 484, Polaris; 406-834-3454), a popular local ski resort. Beyond the hot springs, car travel is recommended between July and October only, as snow comes early and stays late. (The route is open to snowmobiles in winter.)

Drivers who skip the Pioneer Mountains and remain on Route 278 soon cross 7360-foot Big Hole Pass and descend to the valley of the **Big Hole River** near its headwaters at the foot of the Bitterroot Range. The remote, often-snowbound Big Hole Valley is most famous for its trout fishing, big-game hunting and hay-fattened cattle.

The largest settlement in this sparsely populated valley is **Wisdom**, which has only 180 people. Here Route 278 ends at its junction with Route 43, offering you two options: Turn west toward Idaho (it's just 26 miles to Lost Trail Pass, at the head of the Bitterroot Valley south of Missoula), or continue north and east down the Big Hole Valley and complete your loop back to Dillon.

If you choose the westbound route, you're 11 miles from **Big Hole National Battlefield** (Route 43, Wisdom; 406-689-3155; admission in summer), just beneath 7264-foot Chief Joseph Pass. The pass was named for the Nez Perce Indian leader who in 1877 took his people on an ill-fated exodus from their tribal lands in northeastern Oregon and central Idaho. The tragedy of the Nez Perce is related in displays and a video program at the national battlefield's visitors center and museum. Several trails begin at a picnic area and wind through the battleground, which is one of Montana's three units of the Nez Perce National Historical Park. (See "I Will Fight No More, Forever" in Chapter Eleven, Northern Idaho Rockies.)

DILLON AREA HOTELS

The **Metlen Hotel** (5 South Railroad Avenue, Dillon; 406-683-2335) may be on "the other side of the tracks," and it has definitely seen better days, but it's a magnet for the true budget traveler. Built in 1897, this three-story white elephant has survived nearly a century as a residential hotel. Most of the 20-some rooms share down-the-hall bathrooms; a handful of rooms have private baths but minimal furnishings.

The **Sundowner Motel** (500 North Montana Street; 406-683-2375, 800-524-9746) is a friendly property at the edge of downtown Dillon with 32 spacious rooms, queen-size beds, a swimming pool and a playground. Refrigerators are available by request. Budget.

The most upscale property in Beaverhead County is the **Best Western Paradise Inn** (650 North Montana Street; 406-683-4214, 800-528-1234, fax 406-683-4216), located at Dillon's north end at Route 15 Exit 63. The two-story motor inn has 65 rooms with queen-size beds and air-conditioning. A restaurant serves three meals daily, and there's a lounge and casino, an indoor swimming pool, a whirlpool and an exercise room. Moderate.

DILLON AREA RESTAURANTS

Dillon was never a mining town per se, but **The Mine Shaft** (26 South Montana Street; 406-683-6611) has captured a smidgen of that atmosphere, with antique mining equipment displayed on rough-hewn walls in the basement of a historic building opposite the Beaverhead County Museum. Steaks and chicken are popular at lunch and dinner. Moderate.

Located opposite Western Montana College is the **Crosswinds Restaurant** (1008 South Atlantic Street, Dillon; 406-683-6370). A family-style eatery open from early till late, it serves breakfast anytime, offers an expansive salad bar and has special menus for the kids. Budget to moderate.

DILLON AREA SHOPPING

The **Southwest Montana Artists Gallery** (125 North Idaho Street, Dillon; 406-683-4245) is a cooperative run by regional artisans. Located on the second floor of the city hall building, it presents paintings, sculptures and crafts in a range of artistic media.

DILLON AREA NIGHTLIFE

The Short Line Players/Wapiti Theatre (406-683-6402) offers dinner-theater performances ranging from comedy to drama on select weekend nights between Memorial Day and mid-September at the Dillon Elks Lodge (27 East Center Street; 406-683-5552; admission). **The Old Depot Theatre** presents vaudeville nightly except Mondays at the old Union Pacific Depot (125 South Montana Street; 406-683-5511; admission).

DILLON AREA PARKS

Clark Canyon Recreation Area—Waterskiing and fishing (in winter, ice fishing) are the most popular pursuits on 6600-acre Clark Canyon Reservoir. Traces of Lewis and Clark's Camp Fortunate can be found on the northwest shore.

Facilities: Picnic tables, restrooms, boat ramps, marina; wheelchair accessible; information, 406-683-6472. *Swimming:* No designated beaches or lifeguards, but there are several sandy spots that people swim beside. *Fishing:* Renowned rainbow trout fishery; also mountain whitefish, brown trout and burbot.

Camping: Nine campgrounds, most without designated sites (no charge); 38 hookups at Beaverhead Marina and RV Park (406-683-5556) with fees from $8 to $15 per night.

Getting there: The reservoir is located 20 miles south of Dillon on Routes 15 and 324.

Red Rock Lakes National Wildlife Refuge (★)—Framed on two sides by the Continental Divide, this remote refuge is a crucial nesting area for the rare trumpeter swan. Located more than 15 miles in any direction from paved roads, it is also ideal haven for waterfowl, songbirds, raptors, moose, elk and antelope. About three-quarters of the preserve's 43,500 acres is designated wilderness.

Facilities: Restrooms, boat ramps, trails; information, 406-276-3536. *Fishing:* Rainbow and brown trout and mountain whitefish inhabit the lakes.

Camping: Primitive only.

Getting there: From Dillon, take Route 15 south 63 miles to Monida on the Idaho state border; then turn east for 20 miles on gravel Centennial Valley Road (formerly Red Rock Pass Road).

Bannack State Park—This restoration of a true ghost town preserves the main street and more than 60 buildings of Montana's first territorial capital.

Facilities: Picnic tables, restrooms, visitors center; wheelchair accessible; day-use fee, $3; information, 406-834-3413. *Fishing:* Brown and rainbow trout and mountain whitefish in Grasshopper Creek.

Camping: There are 30 RV/tent sites (no hookups); $7 to $8 per night May to September, $7 per night October to April.

Getting there: Take Route 278 west from Dillon 21 miles; then turn south on Route 5 and continue for four miles to Bannack Road.

Beaverhead National Forest—Cloaking 2.1 million acres of southwestern Montana from the Bitterroots to the Madison Range, the Beaverhead forest has more than 1500 miles of hiking trails and well over 100 lakes. It is readily explored on the Pioneer Mountains National Scenic Byway, a 40-mile backcountry drive from Wise River to Polaris, and on the Gravelly Range Road, which climbs to elevations of nearly 10,000 feet south of Virginia City.

Facilities: Picnic tables, restrooms, trails, boat ramps, ski area; information, 406-683-3900. *Swimming:* Designated beaches at some lakes. *Fishing:* The Big Hole River is famous for mountain whitefish and brook, brown and rainbow trout. Lakes on the east slope of the Bitterroots have golden, cutthroat and lake trout, arctic grayling and burbot.

Camping: There are 197 RV/tent sites (no hookups) plus 94 for tents only at 33 campgrounds; no charge to $6 per night. Within the forest are 12 recreational cabins, which can be reserved for $15 to $20 per night.

Getting there: Routes 43 (through the Big Hole Valley), 278 (Dillon to Wisdom) and 287 (through Virginia City), as well as the Pioneer Mountains and Gravelly Range roads, provide the most direct access.

Humbug Spires Primitive Area—White granite outcroppings, 70 million years old, rise like steeples 600 feet into the sky at this 8000-acre Bureau of Land Management preserve. Backpackers and rock climbers are drawn to the scenic location.

Facilities: Trails; information, 406-494-5059.

Camping: Primitive only. There are 20 RV/tent sites (no hookups) at the Divide Bridge campground, six miles west off Route 15 Exit 99; $4 per night.

Getting there: Take Route 15 north from Dillon 37 miles to Exit 99 at Moose Creek; then drive three miles northeast on Moose Creek Road to the Humbug Spires trailhead.

Alder Gulch

The discovery of the richest deposit of placer gold on earth took place in the valley of a tiny creek 70 road miles southeast of Butte.

The **Alder Gulch** mining district yielded some $130 million in gold nuggets, gold flakes and gold dust in the decades that followed the original strike in 1863. After the gold ran out, Virginia City persisted, first as Montana's territorial capital, today as the tourism-oriented seat of Madison County. Nearly 100 buildings in nearby Nevada City have been completely restored, while the roads surrounding Alder Gulch offer myriad reminders of the boom era.

The area is an almost essential detour on the road from Butte to Bozeman. Follow Butte's Harrison Avenue south past the airport, where it becomes Route 2 and climbs across the Continental Divide at 6453-foot Pipestone Pass. Turn south again on Route 41 and continue to Twin Bridges, a small town on the Jefferson River 42 miles from Butte; then bear left (southeast) on Route 287.

On the banks of the Ruby River halfway between Twin Bridges and Nevada City, look for a large brown building with a historical marker sign nearby. **Robber's Roost** (2841 Route 287, Sheridan; 406-842-5936) was a roadhouse (read *saloon-bordello*) where villains and ne'er-do-wells gathered in the 1860s and 1870s when stagecoaches that ran between Virginia City and Bannack were subject to regular holdups.

Nevada City, 29 miles from Twin Bridges, and Virginia City, little more than another mile up Alder Gulch, grew up around that 1863 gold strike in the Tobacco Root Mountains. When President Abraham Lincoln created the Montana Territory the following year, Virginia City was chosen as its capital and remained so until Helena wrested that status away in 1875. But long after that—long after other mining towns were abandoned—Alder Gulch continued to produce gold.

By World War II, though, Nevada City was a ghost town and Virginia City was getting decidedly long in the tooth. A team of historic preservationists headed by Charles and Sue Bovey restored and furnished original buildings wherever possible; in the case of Nevada City, they moved several complete structures in from other areas.

Today, **Nevada City** has the authentic flavor of an early-day mining camp. Officially known as the **Nevada City Museum** (Route 287; 406-843-5377; admission), it consists of five streets with nearly 100 buildings, including homes, shops and schoolhouses. A music hall contains a remarkable collection of machines that produce music ranging from the harmonic to the cacophonic. There's also a cozy hotel, cabins and a restaurant. Mock gunfights occur on the streets of the town, hearkening back to an era when desperadoes used real bullets. It's open only from mid-May to mid-September.

While Nevada City is a re-creation, **Virginia City**, a national historic landmark district, remains very much alive. Every building along the three-block stretch of Wallace Street west of Broadway is of original construction. No other main street in the American West can make that claim. Walking-tour brochures are available from numerous merchants as well as the **Virginia City Area Chamber of Commerce** (302 West Wallace Street; 406-843-5377).

In Virginia City, both the **Thompson-Hickman Memorial Museum** (218 East Wallace Street; 406-843-5346) and the **Madison County Museum** (219 West Wallace Street; 406-843-5321) display pioneer artifacts and historical photographs and documents.

The **Alder Gulch Shortline** railroad (West Wallace and Main streets; 406-843-5377; admission) runs all summer long between the **Steam Railroad Museum**, lodged in restored railcars at Virginia City's west end, and Nevada City. Wallace Street itself has several restaurants and numerous fine shops worth visiting to browse or buy.

To proceed to Bozeman after leaving Virginia City, continue 13 miles east to Ennis, on the Madison River. Take Route 287 north 16 miles to Norris; then turn east on Route 84 for the final 38 miles into Bozeman.

ALDER GULCH HOTELS

A variety of lodgings, all with the rustic flavor of a 19th-century mining camp, are available in the Alder Gulch area. When you book with the **Fairweather Inn** (305 West Wallace Street, Virginia City; 406-843-5377, 800-648-7588, fax 406-843-5377), you can opt for Victorian hotel rooms with private or shared baths, upscale suites with period antiques or 125-year-old cabins (Virginia City's Daylight Village, Nevada City's Miners' Cabins) whose interiors have been restored but whose exteriors have hardly been touched. Budget.

An alternative is the **Virginia City Country Inn** (115 Idaho Street, Virginia City; 406-843-5515), a pleasant bed-and-breakfast establishment just a block south and uphill from the highway through town. A quaint wood-frame Victorian house built in 1879, it has five spacious bedrooms with antique furnishings and a separate efficiency cabin. A full breakfast is served in the dining room, and guests can relax on three porches, in the TV room or beside a fireplace. Bathrooms are shared. Moderate.

ALDER GULCH RESTAURANTS

En route to Alder Gulch, the family-oriented **Blue Anchor Restaurant** (102 North Main Street, Twin Bridges; 406-684-5655) offers three meals a day, seven days a week. Lunch and dinner specials frequently include Cajun-style barbecues. Budget to moderate.

Virginia City's **Bale of Hay Saloon** (330 West Wallace Street; 406-843-5510) was a grocery during the town's boom years, but it was restored as this saloon in 1945. Always rustic and often lively, with live music and antique music machines, it has summer patio dining and a mesquite grill to which area fishermen often bring their fresh catches. Budget to moderate.

ALDER GULCH SHOPPING

There are plenty of souvenir shops in the restored mining towns of Alder Gulch, but the **Vigilante Gift Shop** (115 West Wallace Street, Virginia City; 406-843-5345) may be the biggest and friendliest of the bunch.

ALDER GULCH NIGHTLIFE

From June to mid-September, the **Virginia City Players**—Montana's oldest summer-stock troupe—act out 19th-century melodramas nightly except Mondays at the Virginia City Opera House (350 West Wallace Street; 406-843-5377; admission). The **Brewery Players** offer cabaret-style follies every night but Tuesday at the Gilbert Brewery (Hamilton and Jefferson streets, Virginia City; 406-843-5377; admission).

Bozeman Area

Bozeman is an oasis of sophistication in the heart of a region rich in recreation. Located at the center of a thriving agricultural area, at the foot of the Bridger Range in the Gallatin River Valley, this city of 25,000 has become a darling of affluent young (or young-at-heart) visitors.

Bozeman is wedged between two good-size ski areas—the destination resort of Big Sky and the nearby Bridger Bowl, a day resort that has a condominium development at its base. River enthusiasts raft and kayak the Gallatin, golfers have a choice of numerous area courses and fly-fishermen bubble about several streams.

The city is the northern gateway to Yellowstone National Park and the Absaroka-Beartooth and Lee Metcalf wilderness areas, a region most easily explored on a 200-mile loop trip through the Gallatin and Madison valleys. And it is only a 45-minute drive from the spectacular Lewis and Clark Caverns and Three Forks, where the Jefferson, Madison and Gallatin rivers join to form the Missouri River headwaters.

Named for John Bozeman, a 19th-century wagon master, **Bozeman** is Montana's "yuppie" city. The home of Montana State University (MSU) and a hangout for such Hollywood luminaries as actress Meryl Streep, its prices are higher than those in other Montana cities.

The one attraction in Bozeman that no visitor should miss is the **Museum of the Rockies** (600 West Kagy Boulevard; 406-994-2251; admission), at the edge of the MSU campus. The museum's dinosaur exhibit is world class; paleontologists offer summer field courses at Egg Mountain (northwest of Great Falls), where the first known dinosaur eggs were discovered in recent years. Exhibits focus on Native American culture, contemporary western art, American history with a Rockies perspective and scientific discoveries. The museum operates a pioneer homestead and a nature center, and has an excellent gift shop.

Ghost Towns

The thing about mining boom towns is, as soon as the ore is worked out of the hills or streams, there's nothing left to hold a town there. Thus it has been throughout the Rocky Mountain foothills of southern Montana, where settlements that thrived with thousands of people in the latter half of the 19th century dwindled to nearly nothing by the early 20th.

A visit to one of these abandoned communities can be a poignant experience. You can almost see the miners carrying their gold dust to the assay office, almost hear the rowdy shouts and raucous music as you stroll by the old saloon.

The two most accessible ghost towns are Bannack and Nevada City, both gold-mining communities dating from the 1860s. They are very different. **Bannack**, a Montana state park, has been left mostly unrestored, except to prevent the ravages of time and nature from taking their course too quickly. **Nevada City**, a privately owned museum, has been fully and carefully restored as it probably appeared in its heyday, right down to the interior furnishings of its 100-or-so buildings.

Hidden treasures await backroad explorers with time and perhaps a four-wheel drive vehicle.

Elkhorn (★) (Forest Road 258, south of Helena) was an 1880s silver-mining town whose smelter produced as much as $30,000 worth of ore in a single month. Its ruins, some still scarred with bullet holes, contain fine examples of frontier architecture. To get there, take Route 69 seven miles southeast from Boulder; then follow signs east and north another 11 miles.

Situated east of Missoula, **Garnet** (★) was home to about 1000 men, women and children after an 1897 gold strike. Four hotels, 13 saloons and a school were among its buildings. A couple of dozen of the town's vacated log structures are preserved today. Exit Route 90 at Bearmouth; follow the frontage road about six miles east; then turn north on steep and narrow Bear Creek Road.

Castle (★) (southeast of White Sulphur Springs) was a silver boom town of the 1880s. Today all that remain are weathered homes and various outbuildings. To get there, take Route 89 south from White Sulphur Springs for 17 miles; follow Route 294 east for 15 miles; turn north and continue eight miles on Forest Road 581.

For an overview of Montana's ghost towns, stop to see the **Ghost Town Hall of Fame** at the Granite County Museum and Cultural Center (135 South Sansome Street, Philipsburg; 406-859-3388) on the Pintler Scenic Route west of Butte. In the Sapphire, Flint Creek and other ranges surrounding Philipsburg are no fewer than 21 ghost towns with names like Granite, Princeton, Red Lion and Southern Cross.

Montana State University (south of College Street and west of South 7th Avenue; 406-994-0211), with an enrollment of about 10,800, is a national leader in agricultural research and education, physical science and technology.

East of the campus is the **South Willson Historic District** (South Willson Avenue). Four dozen houses in this residential area, from small cottages to large mansions, can be viewed with the help of a walking-tour brochure, available from the Museum of the Rockies or the **Bozeman Area Chamber of Commerce** (1205 East Main Street; 406-586-5421). Some of the large homes, which date back to the 1880s, are now fraternity and sorority houses.

There's more early Bozeman history at the **Gallatin County Pioneer Museum** (317 West Main Street; 406-585-1311). A county jail from 1911 to 1982, the building now holds audiences captive with displays of agricultural implements, Native American artifacts and the jail's original gallows room (complete with noose and drop floor).

The **American Computer Museum** (234 East Babcock Street; 406-587-7545; admission), on the ground floor of a downtown office building, claims to be the "world's second museum of its type." Visitors can trace the computer's history from the abacus and early mechanical calculators through the development of the microchip. Guided tours and videos are geared for all ages and levels of computer knowledge.

Northeast of Bozeman, Bridger Canyon Road (Route 86) climbs gradually through a short, rocky canyon to a mountain valley surrounded by the peaks of the Bridger Range. A smattering of ranches and new homes have been built in this valley, reminiscent of some in Switzerland. Sixteen miles from Bozeman at the head of the valley is **Bridger Bowl** (15795 Bridger Canyon Road; 406-587-2111), a popular local ski resort within Gallatin National Forest.

GALLATIN-MADISON LOOP **Gallatin National Forest** (601 Nickles Drive; 406-587-6920) dominates Gallatin County south of Bozeman. Route 191 follows the Gallatin River, one of the three headwater streams of the Missouri, upstream nearly to its source in Yellowstone National Park. Through much of its course, the Gallatin, a favorite of whitewater rafters and kayakers, follows a narrow gorge between the Spanish Peaks on its west and the Gallatin Range on its east. The magnificent 82-mile drive to West Yellowstone passes two parcels of the **Lee Metcalf Wilderness** and a turnoff to the Big Sky resort before entering the northwest corner of Yellowstone Park. (See Chapter Seven.)

On the south side of the 10,000-foot Spanish Peaks, 48 miles from Bozeman, is the **Big Sky Ski & Summer Resort** (Big Sky Road, Big Sky; 406-995-4211). Established in the 1970s by a group of investors including Montana native Chet Huntley, the late network newscaster, Big Sky has grown into two separate year-round villages. Both Meadow Village and Mountain Village, six miles apart, have lodging and dining facilities as well as shopping. Visitors can take a **gondola** (admission) from Mountain Village to the 9500-foot level of the mountain.

From Big Sky, you can continue up the Gallatin River on Route 191, skirting the corner of Yellowstone National Park. The park's west entrance is at West Yellowstone, 39 miles south of Big Sky. (See Chapter Seven.)

To complete the loop back to Bozeman, turn west on Route 287 at **Hebgen Lake**, eight miles north of West Yellowstone. Hebgen is a reservoir created by the manmade damming of the Madison River; immediately west of the Hebgen Dam is **Quake Lake**, created, as its name implies, by an earthquake.

The **Madison Canyon Earthquake Area and Visitor Center** (Route 287; 406-646-7369), at the west end of Quake Lake, commemorates the epicenter of an August 17, 1959, earthquake that measured 7.1 on the Richter scale. The temblor dropped the north shore of Hebgen Lake by 18 feet and caused a landslide that blocked the Madison River canyon, thereby creating Quake Lake. Tragically, 28 people died at a nearby campground as a direct result.

Route 287 follows the **Madison Valley** north 119 miles from West Yellowstone to Three Forks. Flanked on the east by the 11,000-foot peaks of the Madison Range and on the west by the 10,000-foot Tobacco Root and Gravelly ranges, the route offers ready access to the Beaverhead National Forest and several parcels of the Metcalf Wilderness.

Ennis, in the heart of the Madison Valley, is an hour's drive north of Quake Lake on Route 287. Located on the east side of the Tobacco Root Mountains just 13 miles from the historic mining town of Virginia City (see "Alder Gulch," above), Ennis is a hunting and fishing center whose three blocks of downtown businesses boast Old West–style facades.

THREE FORKS AREA Traveling west from Bozeman, Route 90 bypasses a series of small Gallatin Valley towns whose names speak of founders from a variety of backgrounds: Belgrade (Serbian), Churchill (British), Amsterdam (Dutch), Manhattan (New Yorker!).

At Route 90 Exit 283, 25 miles west of Bozeman, a secondary road leads seven miles south to **Madison Buffalo Jump State Park** (Buffalo Jump Road, Logan; 406-994-4042; admission). This site preserves a cliff over which Native Americans stampeded bison as long as 2000 years ago. Interpretive displays describe how buffalo meat and hides were thus obtained on a mass scale before the mid-16th century, when horses altered the Plains Indians' hunting practices.

At the valley's west end, located near the point where three rivers come together to form the Missouri River 30 miles from Bozeman, is the town of **Three Forks**. Three Forks' colorful history as a tribal crossroads, trading post and rail center is related in exhibits at its **Headwaters Heritage Museum** (Main Street; 406-285-3495), which dates from 1910.

Five miles from town, **Missouri Headwaters State Park** (Trident Road, Three Forks; 406-994-4042; admission) is located at the convergence of the Gallatin, Madison and Jefferson rivers. "All of them run with great velocity and throw out large bodies of water," wrote Captain Meriwether Lewis in 1805.

Lewis and Clark Caverns State Park (Route 2, Cardwell; 406-287-3541 or 406-287-5424 in summer; admission), 18 miles west of Three Forks, comprises what may be the most impressive limestone caves in the northwestern United States. A fairyland of ancient stalactites, stalagmites and other wonders of the underground, created over millions of years, highlights the 90-minute guided tour (offered May through September). Visitors should be modestly fit.

The route includes more than 600 steps leading through hands-and-knees crawl space, narrow rock slides and cathedral-size chambers inhabited by bats.

BOZEMAN AREA HOTELS

In the heart of the South Willson Historic District, three blocks from downtown Bozeman, is the **Voss Inn** (319 South Willson Avenue; 406-587-0982), a restored 1883 Victorian with elegant hardwood floors. Its six rooms contain such period antiques as clawfoot tubs, carved armoires, and brass or iron beds. Rooms are air-conditioned or have fans. Gourmet breakfasts are delivered to the rooms each morning; afternoon tea and evening sherry are served in the parlor, which has a piano and small library. Moderate.

Several budget motels are located along Main Street in Bozeman. We like the **Alpine Lodge** (1017 East Main Street; 406-586-0356), which has 14 units in the Tyrolean-style, yellow-and-brown main building and adjacent cabins. All have full kitchens, private baths and standard motel amenities.

The **Sacajawea Hostel** (105 West Olive Street, Bozeman; 406-586-4659) is a find for backpackers. It has a dozen bunk beds in three dorm rooms; hostellers share toilets, showers and kitchen facilities. Unlike many hostels, this one is open year-round and doesn't have a curfew. Budget.

The chateau-like tower of the **Best Western GranTree Inn** (1325 North 7th Avenue, Bozeman; 406-587-5261, 800-624-5865, fax 406-587-9437) is a landmark for visitors arriving off Route 90. This pleasant two-story property has a restaurant and coffee shop, a lounge and casino, an indoor pool, a jacuzzi and a coin laundry. Moderate to deluxe.

For a taste of old-time luxury, visit the **Gallatin Gateway Inn** (76405 Route 191 South, Gallatin Gateway; 406-763-4672, fax 406-763-4672 ext. 313), a restored railroad hotel listed on the National Register of Historic Places. Built in Spanish Colonial–style in 1927, the inn has a cavernous lobby with a huge fireplace and a grand piano beneath mahogany ceiling beams. Its 35 rooms are cozy but comfortable; most have full private baths, but some must share. The 15-acre grounds include a year-round swimming pool, a hot tub, a tennis court, a fly-casting pond and mountain-bike rentals and trails. Moderate to deluxe.

The most prestigious place to stay at the Big Sky resort complex is **The Huntley Lodge at Big Sky** (1 Lone Mountain Trail; 406-995-4211, 800-548-4486, fax 406-995-4860). A three-story granite fireplace greets guests to the lobby of the seven-story slopeside ski lodge, which also has a fine restaurant and a lounge with live entertainment. The 300 rooms are modern and spacious. On-site recreation includes golf, tennis, horseback riding, mountain biking and fishing; the lodge has two swimming pools, saunas, whirlpools, a steam room and an exercise room. Deluxe.

Montana's Yellowstone country has many friendly guest ranches. One of the longest established is the **Lone Mountain Ranch** (P.O. Box 69, Big Sky, MT 59716; 406-995-4644, fax 406-995-4670), homesteaded as a cattle ranch in 1915 and attracting paying guests since the 1940s. Guests stay in 23 log cabins with full baths and fireplaces; gourmet meals are served family-style in an elaborate log-and-stone dining hall. Activities on the 4000-acre ranch include horseback riding, trout fishing and hiking in summer, cross-country skiing in winter. Closed in spring and fall. Deluxe.

A historic railroad hotel built in 1910, the **Sacajawea Inn** (5 North Main Street, Three Forks; 406-285-6515, 800-821-7326, fax 406-285-6515), is a pleasant place to lay one's head on the road west from Bozeman. Its 33 restored guest rooms are small but clean, each with a private bath. The hotel has a restaurant and small espresso bar; smoking is not permitted. Rates include a continental breakfast. Moderate.

BOZEMAN AREA RESTAURANTS

The Rocky Mountain Pasta Company (105 West Main Street, Bozeman; 406-586-1314) is much more a classic northern Italian restaurant than a noodle dispensary. Located on the ground floor of the 1929 Baxter Hotel in the heart of downtown, it serves fine food and wines in a warm, elegant atmosphere. Moderate. The adjoining Bacchus Pub offers salads, sandwiches and other light fare at budget prices.

John Bozeman's Bistro (242 East Main Street, Bozeman; 406-587-4100) boasts "world cuisine with Montana style," and it delivers on that promise. Housed in a historic downtown brewery building, it offers up innovative preparations of steaks, seafoods and other popular dishes, often with Asian culinary twists. Lunch and dinner are offered Tuesday through Sunday, breakfasts on weekends only. Moderate to deluxe.

Asian food lovers are delighted with the hard-to-find **New Asia Kitchen** (★) (1533 West Babcock Street, Bozeman; 406-586-0522). Just one block south of Main Street opposite McDonald's, this unassuming yellow house is shrouded from view by trees and other buildings. Spicy Chinese and Thai dinners are prepared here with a macrobiotic touch: They're different from what you'd find in a large West Coast city, but the ingredients are fresh and free of monosodium glutamate. Moderate.

Fred's Mesquite Diner (451 East Main Street, Bozeman; 406-585-8558) is just what its name implies: a small downtown diner with a mesquite charcoal grill. The result: steaks, chicken, ribs and other foods with gourmet taste and low price tags. The patio is a great place for people watching. Budget.

Order hearty soups and healthy salads at **Community Food Co-op** (908 West Main Street, Bozeman; 406-587-4039). This small, casual deli also features a menu board of sandwiches and entrées, as well as daily ethnic specials such as sweet potato *quesadillas*, Anasazi eggplant stew and tempeh stir-fry. A great deal at low-budget prices.

South of Bozeman, a mile south of the Big Sky junction in a Best Western motel, **Buck's T-4** (Route 191, Big Sky; 406-995-4111) offers two attractive alternatives to resort restaurants. Buck's dining room specializes in wild game, from pheasant to wild boar, moose to antelope, at deluxe prices; steaks and seafood are also available. The **Gameroom Grill** serves budget-priced pizzas and lighter fare.

Perhaps the fine French, Cajun and Creole cuisine dished up at the **Continental Divide Restaurant** (★) (Yellowstone Highway, Ennis; 406-682-7600) is a legacy of the Louisiana Purchase. Otherwise, it's hard to explain how a place this good could have found itself behind an Old West facade in an area that caters mainly to outdoor sportsmen and tourists. It's worth driving the 13 miles from Virginia City to dine here. Deluxe.

BOZEMAN AREA SHOPPING

It's fun to browse downtown Bozeman's 100-or-so retail stores, including eight galleries and five antique shops. Among the newest shopping meccas is the **Emerson Cultural Center** (111 South Grand Avenue; 406-587-9797), a nonprofit arts center whose tenants include craftspeople (jewelers, ceramicists, woodworkers and clothiers) and cultural organizations. Some three dozen artisans have their studios in this former school, built in 1919; many of them welcome visitors.

To see the work of noted regional artists like Gary Carter and Russell Chatham, check out the **Beall Park Art Center** (409 North Bozeman Street, Bozeman; 406-586-3970), four blocks north of Main Street. For true 19th- and 20th-century western classics, you can't beat the top-of-the-line selection (with prices to match) at **Thomas Nygard Inc.** (127 East Main Street, Bozeman; 406-586-3636). If you've ever had a hankering for a Charles Russell or an Albert Bierstadt, Nygard can help you out.

The Antique Mall (612 East Main Street, Bozeman; 406-587-5281) claims to be Montana's largest antique mall, with 14,000 square feet of furniture, glassware, art and memorabilia.

Readings by celebrated authors are regular features of **The Country Bookshelf** (28 West Main Street; 406-587-0166), an excellent, comprehensive bookstore in Bozeman.

BOZEMAN AREA NIGHTLIFE

In large part because of Montana State University, Bozeman is a very culturally active city.

The **Bozeman Symphony Orchestra and Symphonic Choir** (104 East Main Street; 406-585-9774), **Intermountain Opera Association** (104 East Main Street; 406-587-2889) and **Montana Ballet Company** (221 East Main Street; 406-587-7192) all perform at the Willson School auditorium (404 West Main Street). The symphony has a fall-through-spring season; the opera mounts two productions each year; and every Christmas season the dance troupe performs Tchaikovsky's *Nutcracker*.

The summer **Bozeman Stage Company** and spring-to-fall **Vigilante Theatre Company** (111 South Grand Avenue; 406-586-3897), both based in the Emerson Cultural Center, offer several shows throughout the year, including dramas, comedies and musicals.

Popular nightlife hot spots in Bozeman are **Rock's Bar** (321 East Main Street; 406-585-8851), which features a variety of rock, reggae and rhythm-and-blues bands most nights; and **Little John's Bar** (515 West Aspen Street; 406-587-1652), where free dance lessons precede appearances by country-and-western bands. The **Cat's Paw** (721 North 7th Avenue; 406-586-3542) hosts comedians on Thursday and live bands on Friday and Saturday.

For a quiet drink, there's the **Spanish Peaks Brewery** (120 North 19th Avenue; 406-585-2296), a restaurant and microbrewery that has developed a solid regional reputation with its Black Dog Ale. Coffeehouses have gotten big among nondrinkers here; **The Leaf and Bean** (35 West Main Street; 406-587-1580) often hosts acoustic musicians, poets and other throwbacks to the early beat days of Greenwich Village.

BOZEMAN AREA PARKS

East Gallatin State Recreation Area—A local park that surrounds little Glen Lake near the confluence of Bridger and Bozeman creeks, East Gallatin owes its existence to community volunteers. Water-sports lovers, including swimmers, fishermen, board sailors, kayakers and canoeists, appreciate their efforts.

Facilities: Picnic tables, restrooms; day-use fee, $2; information, 406-994-4042. *Swimming:* 300-foot beachfront on Glen Lake. *Fishing:* Lake stocked with trout, perch and sunfish.

Getting there: Located on Manley Road, off Griffin Drive (between 7th and Rouse avenues) north of the Bozeman city limits.

Hyalite Canyon Recreation Area—Covering 34,000 acres of Gallatin National Forest southeast of Bozeman, this wheelchair-accessible park area is popular among anglers, hikers and mountain bikers. The reservoir, created in the 1940s, has a "no-wake" rule that restricts motorboaters to low speeds.

Facilities: Picnic tables, restrooms, boat ramps, trails, rental cabin; wheelchair accessible; information, 406-587-6920. *Swimming:* No designated beaches. *Fishing:* Good for cutthroat trout and arctic grayling.

Camping: There are 39 RV/tent sites at three campgrounds (no hookups); $8 per night.

Getting there: From downtown Bozeman, take South 19th Avenue seven miles south to Hyalite Canyon Road (Route 62), an extension of Fowler Lane. It's ten miles from here to Hyalite Reservoir, twelve to the Palisade Falls trailhead.

Gallatin National Forest—Stretching east and west across the Absaroka, Gallatin and Madison ranges, this 1.7-million-acre forest includes large parts of two wilderness areas (the Absaroka-Beartooth and the Lee Metcalf), the upper reaches of four important trout rivers (the Yellowstone, Gallatin, Madison and Boulder), and the Big Sky and Bridger Bowl ski resorts.

Facilities: Picnic tables, restrooms, boat ramps, trails; wheelchair accessible at Hyalite Canyon; information, 406-587-6791. *Swimming:* In some lakes. *Fishing:* Brown and rainbow trout and mountain whitefish are in major rivers; many also have brook and cutthroat trout. Golden trout are found in alpine lakes of the Gallatin and Crazy ranges, arctic grayling in the Gallatins, walleye and yellow perch in Dailey Lake.

Camping: There are 558 RV/tent sites (no hookups) plus 89 for tents only at 30 campgrounds; no charge to $8 per night. Reservations (800-283-2267) are accepted at four summer-only campgrounds near West Yellowstone. Also, 23 recreational cabins can be reserved for use by hikers or cross-country skiers at $20 per night.

Getting there: Route 191, south of Bozeman, and Route 89, south of Livingston, traverse the forest, and numerous other spur roads provide access.

Missouri Headwaters State Park—Located where the Gallatin, Madison and Jefferson rivers flow together to create the Missouri River, this park offers fishing and hiking, wildlife viewing, camping and picnicking. Exhibits discuss the site's importance as a gathering place for Native Americans long before the Lewis and Clark expedition stumbled upon it in 1805.

Facilities: Picnic tables, restrooms, boat ramp, trails; day-use fee, $3; information, 406-994-4042. *Swimming:* Not advised. *Fishing:* Many anglers swear by the confluence, where brown and rainbow trout and mountain whitefish from all three rivers enter the Missouri.

Camping: There are 21 primitive sites (no hookups); $4 to $5 per night for Montana residents, $7 to $8 for nonresidents.

Getting there: Take Exit 278 from Route 90 at Three Forks; follow Route 205 east for two miles and then Route 286 (Trident Road) north for three miles.

Lewis and Clark Caverns State Park—Deep limestone caves, some of the most impressive in North America, are the highlight of Montana's first state park. The park is open year-round, but cavern tours operate from May through September only. Bats inhabit the caves, while deer and other animals live on the nearby slopes.

Facilities: Picnic tables, restrooms, showers, visitors center, amphitheater, restaurant, trails; day-use fee, $3; information, 406-287-3541 or 406-287-5424 in summer. *Fishing:* Brown and rainbow trout and mountain whitefish can be caught in the adjacent Jefferson River.

Camping: There are 50 RV/tent sites (no hookups); $9 per night. Three primitive cabins are available for $25 to $39 per night depending upon season.

Getting there: Take Route 2 (off Route 90) from Three Forks (18 miles east of the park) or from Cardwell (ten miles west).

Park and Sweet Grass Counties

East of Bozeman, the interstate highway crosses a low pass in the Bridger Range and descends to the Yellowstone River valley. The first two counties through which it passes—Park (with its seat in Livingston) and Sweet Grass (with its seat in Big Timber)—exemplify the transitional nature of Montana's landscape as they stretch from the 10,000-foot heights of the Absaroka Range to the vastness of the Great Plains.

The historic rail town of Livingston is the hub of the upper Yellowstone valley, a place where wilderness meets the Wild West. From here, Route 90 continues past the Crazy Mountains, the ranching center of Big Timber and Greycliff Prairie Dog Town State Park, through the Rocky Mountain foothills to Billings and beyond.

Founded in 1882 by the Northern Pacific Railroad and named for a former director of that line, **Livingston** was the original gateway to Yellowstone National Park. Tourists changed trains here from the main east-west line to a spur line that followed the Yellowstone River upstream to Gardiner at the park's north entrance.

The community quickly became a trading center for farmers, ranchers and miners of the Yellowstone valley, and by 1905 a thriving city of about 5000 people had emerged. Since then, growth has been modest: Modern Livingston's population hovers around 6700. But 436 buildings from that turn-of-the-century boom era are preserved in its downtown historic district and three residential districts on the National Register of Historic Places. Among them is a log cabin that once was the home of notorious frontierswoman Martha "Calamity Jane" Canary.

The place to begin a walking tour, or to gather information on area attractions, is the **Livingston Chamber of Commerce** (212 West Park Street; 406-222-0850). The chamber and adjoining **Livingston Depot Center** (200 West Park Street; 406-222-2300; admission) are located in the 1902 Northern Pacific station, designed in Italian villa–style by the same architectural firm that created New York's Grand Central Station. The Depot Center is a satellite museum for the Buffalo Bill Historical Center in Cody, Wyoming; exhibits include rail history, Yellowstone exploration, western art and more. It's open daily from mid-May to mid-October and doubles as a performing-arts center.

There are more history exhibits across the tracks and two blocks north at the **Park County Museum** (118 West Chinook Street; 406-222-3506). Located in an early-20th-century schoolhouse, it's open daily in summer and by appointment. Taxidermy enthusiasts will appreciate the **Lone Wolf Wildlife Museum** (Sleeping Giant Trade Center, Route 89; 406-222-6140), a mile south of the city center.

PARADISE VALLEY The Route 89 corridor upriver to Yellowstone Park, 53 driving miles south of Livingston, follows the scenic **Paradise Valley** beneath the constant gaze of the Absaroka Range. The Yellowstone River—the longest free-flowing (undammed) river in the United States—is considered a blue-ribbon trout stream through this portion, which is also popular among whitewater rafters.

Twenty miles south, near the small towns of Emigrant and Pray, are the **Chico Hot Springs** (Chico Road, Pray; 406-333-4933). A resort here provides access to natural mineral hot springs and other health therapies.

Climbing the Yellowstone valley from Emigrant, Route 89 circles 8600-foot Dome Mountain, home of a historic winter elk range. West of the hamlet of Miner (38 miles from Livingston), Rock Creek Road extends nine miles to a trailhead for the **Gallatin Petrified Forest**, whose fossilized specimens include still-upright tree trunks estimated to be between 35 and 55 million years old. Another nine miles past Miner, near the small tourist center of **Corwin Springs**, bright-red **Devils Slide** is an unmistakable geological feature: The exposed sedimentary rocks at the base of Cinnabar Mountain are about 200 million years old.

Gardiner, at the north entrance to Yellowstone Park, is about five miles from the Mammoth Hot Springs resort center. (See Chapter Seven, "Yellowstone and Jackson Hole.")

SWEET GRASS COUNTY **Big Timber** is 33 miles east of Livingston (an hour's drive from Bozeman) at the foot of the Crazy Mountains. A livestock-producing and recreational center surrounded by Gallatin National Forest, the town has several sites of interest.

A historical museum—the **Crazy Mountain Museum** (Frontage Road, Route 90 Exit 367; 406-932-5126)—features a miniature reproduction of Big Timber as it appeared in 1907, when it was known as Cobblestone City. Exact down to the finest architectural details, it covers more than 12 blocks of the old town at a scale of 1/16 inch to one foot. Fewer than 20 percent of the 184 buildings represented in the model still stand in downtown Big Timber. Open summers only.

Nearby is the **Victorian Village** (Frontage Road, Route 90 Exit 367; 406-932-4378; admission), a museum and antique store. Exhibits include a complete hot-metal print shop, millinery and dry-goods shops, a harness barn, a carpenter's shop and a chapel. Open summers only.

Sheep and cattle ranchers have waged a successful war against the prairie dog, whose burrows create dangerous holes and which compete with stock for grasses and forage: The prairie dog's range is now less than 20 percent its original size. The **Greycliff Prairie Dog Town State Park** (Route 90 Exit 377, Greycliff; 406-252-4654; admission), nine miles east of Big Timber, is a 98-acre park that preserves a traditional prairie-dog colony, albeit tiny compared to the huge cities of these ground squirrels that once spread across the plains.

PARK AND SWEET GRASS COUNTIES HOTELS

It seems only natural to stay in historic hotels in historic communities. The **Murray Hotel** (201 West Park Street, Livingston; 406-222-1350, fax 406-222-6547) has 43 recently renovated rooms with simple decor in the heart of town; all have private baths and standard amenities. There's also a restaurant and bar. Budget to moderate.

The two-story red-brick **Grand Hotel** (McLeod Street, Big Timber; 406-932-4459), built in 1890, has high-ceilinged Victorian rooms with period furnishings and modern conveniences. Rates include breakfast in the hotel restaurant; there's a bar as well. Budget.

PARK AND SWEET GRASS COUNTIES RESTAURANTS

The **Winchester Cafe** (201 West Park Street, Livingston; 406-222-2708), in the 19th-century Murray Hotel, is the region's best fine-dining experience. Though the Victorian atmosphere is casual, you'll be treated to dinners of steaks and seafood, chicken and prime rib at moderate prices. Breakfast and lunch are also served. Moderate.

Calamity Jane's Steakhouse (106 East Park Street; 406-222-2255), in the heart of Livingston's historic district, pays tribute to the rowdy late-19th-century frontierswoman who moved into a log cabin in this old rail town but found the sedentary lifestyle too tame. Buffalo steaks, chicken and seafood are hits at dinner here; soups and sandwiches are served at lunch, both inside and on the patio. Prices are moderate.

PARK AND SWEET GRASS COUNTIES SHOPPING

Art galleries include the **Paradise Gallery** (East River Road, Livingston; 406-222-6297), where the art of Carol Newbury Howe and other wildlife artists is presented; and the **Zemsky-Hines Gallery** (108 East 3rd Street, Big Timber; 406-932-5307), which features the works of resident western artists Jessica Zemsky and Jack Hines along with other regional artists.

Books Etc. (106 South Main Street, Livington; 406-222-7766) is the leading book dealer in the two-county region.

PARK AND SWEET GRASS COUNTIES NIGHTLIFE

Livingston has a pair of noteworthy stage groups. The **Firehouse 5 Playhouse** (Sleeping Giant Trade Center, Route 89; 406-222-1420) presents melodrama and vaudeville Tuesday through Saturday nights and Sunday afternoons through the summer, and a variety of community musicals and holiday specials during the winter. The **Blue Slipper Theatre** (113 East Callender Street; 406-222-7720), now in its fourth decade as a community theater, serves up comedies, mysteries, dramas and other more serious productions in a season lasting from fall through spring.

PARK AND SWEET GRASS COUNTIES PARKS

Absaroka-Beartooth Wilderness Area—Abutting Yellowstone National Park on its northern edge, and nearly half as large as the park itself, this 944,000-acre wilderness comprises two distinctly different mountain ranges: in its western half, the rugged, forested Absarokas; in the east, near Red Lodge, the alpine meadows and plateaus of the Beartooths. Several Absaroka peaks top 11,000 feet, but more than two dozen Beartooth summits exceed 12,000, including Granite Peak, Montana's highest mountain at 12,799 feet. A unique feature is the Grasshopper Glacier, a remote ice field named for the millions of ancient grasshoppers frozen into the face of a sheer 80-foot ice cliff.

Facilities: Trails; information, 406-587-6747. *Swimming:* At your own risk in frigid alpine lakes. *Fishing:* Seven species of trout (brook, brown, bull, cutthroat, golden, lake and rainbow) inhabit small lakes on the Beartooth Plateau. All but golden, plus mountain whitefish, can be taken elsewhere in major streams.

Camping: Primitive only.

Getting there: The Absaroka-Beartooth has many gateways, including Mill Creek Road, off Route 89 south of Livingston; the Boulder River road from McLeod, south of Big Timber; East and West Rosebud roads, off Route 78 south of Absarokee; and Route 212 (the Beartooth Highway) southwest of Red Lodge.

The Sporting Life

FISHING

Fishing is not just a sport in Montana. To many, it's a religion.

Cold-water species such as trout, whitefish and arctic grayling thrive in the high-elevation streams and lakes on either side of the Continental Divide in southern Montana. In nationally famous streams like the Big Hole, Beaverhead, Madison, Gallatin and Boulder, anglers cast for three species of trout—brook, brown and rainbow—as well as mountain whitefish. Many also have the rarer cutthroat trout; a few may have bull trout. Georgetown Lake, west of Anaconda, offers kokanee salmon.

A few high-elevation lakes, such as Holter and Dailey, have walleye and yellow perch. But these are mainly low-elevation species, joining largemouth and smallmouth bass, sauger, northern pike, channel catfish and black crappie in lakes and rivers across the southeast.

For fishing tackle or information on guided expeditions, try **Fran Johnson's Sport Shop** (1957 Harrison Avenue, Butte; 406-782-3322), **Fishing Headquarters** (610 North Montana Street, Dillon; 406-683-6660) or **Montana Troutfitters Orvis Shop** (1716 West Main Street, Bozeman; 406-587-4707). Among regional flyfishing specialists are **Fish-On Fly & Tackle** (3346 Harrison Avenue, Butte; 406-494-4218), **The Rivers Edge** (2012 North 7th Avenue, Bozeman; 406-586-5373) and **Big Sky Flies & Guides** (Route 89, Emigrant; 406-333-4401).

RIVER RAFTING, CANOEING AND KAYAKING

Southern Montana river trips come in two varieties: whitewater and flatwater.

For whitewater rafters and kayakers, top streams are the Smith River, east of Helena, and the upper Madison, Gallatin and Yellowstone rivers, south of Bozeman. A 61-mile stretch of the Smith, extending from Fort Logan to Eden Bridge, has been set aside as a state park with 22 riverside campsites. The Madison boasts Beartrap Canyon, with alternating calm water and rapids through the Lee Metcalf Wilderness below Ennis Lake. The Gallatin, squeezed into a narrow canyon above Big Sky, has the region's most challenging whitewater. The Yellowstone, above Emigrant, appeals to families with wildlife viewing, hot springs and a handful of exciting-but-not-too-exciting rapids. The Boulder and Stillwater rivers are also popular.

Flatwater paddlers, especially canoeists, appreciate the tranquility and wildlife-watching opportunities of the region. The Big Hole River (from Wisdom to Wise River), Jefferson River (Twin Bridges to Three Forks) and Yellowstone River (Pray to Livingston), as well as the remote Red Rock Lakes, west of West Yellowstone on Montana's southern border with Idaho, are among the most appealing stretches.

Keep in mind that rivers are higher in June, when snow is still melting in the summits, than in August. That means the water is usually colder and more wild in spring, but rocks pose more of a hazard in late summer.

Leading outfitters in the region include **Montana Whitewater** (P.O. Box 1552, Bozeman, MT 59715; 406-763-4465) and the **Yellowstone Raft Company** (P.O. Box 160262, Big Sky, MT 59716; 406-995-4613). Many outfitters also offer guided kayaking expeditions.

DOWNHILL SKIING

HELENA AREA **Great Divide** (Marysville Road, Marysville; 406-449-3746), 22 miles northwest of Helena off Route 279, is a midsize day area with 50 runs and a 1520-foot vertical drop from the rim of the Continental Divide. Facilities include three chairlifts and a surface tow. Cross-country and snowmobile trails also extend from the base area into Helena National Forest.

BUTTE AREA For sheer scenic beauty, it's hard to top **Discovery Basin** (Forest Road 65, Georgetown; 406-563-2184). Looking across Georgetown Lake toward the Anaconda Range, 20 miles west of Anaconda and 45 miles from Butte, it has three chairlifts and two surface tows running from just below the summit of 8187-foot Rumsey Mountain. There are 30 runs with a 1300-foot vertical.

DILLON AREA **Maverick Mountain** (Route 484, Polaris; 406-834-3454) is among the most isolated of Montana's ski areas. Located in Beaverhead National Forest near Elk Horn Hot Springs on the Pioneer Mountains National Scenic Byway, 35 miles west of Dillon and about 100 miles southwest of Butte, it appeals to committed skiers with 15 trails, averaging more than a mile in length, and a 2120-foot vertical drop. There's one chairlift; a surface tow serves a beginner's bowl.

BOZEMAN AREA Just 16 miles from Bozeman, an easy distance for a day destination, is **Bridger Bowl** (15795 Bridger Canyon Road, Bozeman; 406-586-2389, 800-223-9609). The resort's "mogul-cutter" grooming equipment and its steep Bridger Ridge—looming 500 feet above the upper lifts, for those willing to hike a bit—make it a favorite mountain for expert skiers and snowboarders. But there are plenty of groomed bowls and powder glades for novice and intermediate skiers. The Gallatin National Forest resort has 2000 acres of terrain and a 2000-foot vertical drop from its 8100-foot summit. Fifty runs are served by five chairlifts and one surface tow.

The **Big Sky Ski & Summer Resort** (Big Sky Road, Big Sky; 406-995-4211, 800-548-4486), in the Madison Range less than an hour's drive south of Bozeman, is beginning to get its due as a major national destination for winter-sports lovers. Established in the 1970s, the ski resort boasts a vertical drop of more than 3000 feet (the state's longest) from the 10,000-foot level of Lone Mountain to the Mountain Village complex at its base. Two gondolas, five chairlifts and three surface tows serve 55 runs that weave across 2100 acres of skiable terrain. All levels of skiing ability are well served.

SKI RENTALS Many stores throughout the region offer equipment rentals and information. **The Outdoorsman** (2700 Harrison Avenue, Butte; 406-494-7700) and **Chalet Sports** (108 West Main Street, Bozeman; 406-587-4595) offer both downhill and cross-country rentals. **World Boards Inc.** (601 West Main Street, Bozeman; 406-587-1707) is the place for snowboarders. Cross-country equipment specialists include **Montana Outdoor Sports** (708 North Main Street, Helena; 406-443-4119), **Pipestone Mountaineering** (829 South Montana Street, Butte; 406-782-4994) and **Cache Creek Outdoor Shoppe** (131 West Main Street, Bozeman; 406-587-0975).

CROSS-COUNTRY SKIING

West of Butte, the **Mt. Haggin Nordic Ski Area** (★) (Route 274, Anaconda; 406-782-0316), created by the Mile High Nordic Ski Club, offers groomed trails at the foot of the Anaconda Range; it operates by donation and volunteer energy. The region's leading nordic center is the **Bohart Ranch Cross-Country Ski Center** (16621 Bridger Canyon Road, Bozeman; 406-586-9070), just up the road from the Bridger Bowl downhill area. Bohart Ranch has 30 kilometers of groomed and tracked trails, as well as a year-round biathlon training range and a warming cabin. At Big Sky, the **Lone Mountain Ranch** (Big Sky; 406-995-4644) caters to cross-country skiers with 75 kilometers of groomed and tracked trails for all ability levels.

For information on renting equipment, see the ski-rental section in "Downhill Skiing" above.

GOLF

Among Montana's best 18-hole public golf courses are **Bill Roberts Municipal Golf Course** (Benton and Cole avenues, Helena; 406-442-2191), **Bridger Creek Golf Club** (2710 McIlhattan Road, Bozeman; 406-586-2333) and the Arnold Palmer–designed **Big Sky Golf Course** (Meadow Village, Big Sky; 406-995-4706).

Wild elk can be a hazard when they graze on the greens at **Fairmont Hot Springs Resort** (1500 Fairmont Road, Gregson; 406-797-3241). The 649-yard fifth hole of this course is regarded as one of the most challenging in the state.

TENNIS

Perhaps the most intriguing place to charge a Montana net is within **The CopperDome Racquet Club** (4655 Harrison Avenue; 406-494-6666). The inflated CopperDome is attached to the Best Western Copper King Inn opposite the Butte airport. Elsewhere, city parks and recreation offices have exhaustive listings of municipal courts. In Helena, call 406-447-8463; in Bozeman, try **Bogart Park** (325 South Church Avenue) or call 406-587-4724.

HORSEBACK RIDING

For daytrippers, **Peterson's Fairmont Corral** (Star Route East, Anaconda; 406-797-3377), located a mile south of the Fairmont Hot Springs resort outside of Butte, emphasizes guided breakfast and dinner trail trips; riders can also rent horses for backcountry expeditions. **Rush's Lakeview Guest Ranch** (Red Rock Lakes, Lima; 406-276-3300) has a summer horsemanship school, photography workshops and other year-round programs on the edge of the remote Red Rock Lakes National Wildlife Refuge. The **Grace Meadows Equestrian Center** (1021 Cobb Hill Road, Bozeman; 406-585-9345) also has horses available for country canters.

PACK TRIPS AND LLAMA TREKKING

Overnight pack trips from a night to a week or longer can be set up for fishermen, hunters, photographers or nature lovers. Most trips are guided, but some outfitters can arrange "wilderness drop trips": They'll pack you in and out, but you're on your own during the interim.

Among dozens of outfitters in the region are **Red Mountain Outfitters** (P.O. Box 24, Lincoln, MT 59639; 406-362-4360), which specializes in the Scapegoat and Bob Marshall wildernesses; **Cayuse Outfitters** (P.O. Box 1218, Livingston, MT 59047; 406-222-2100), which offers Absaroka tours that focus on archaeology; **Jake's Horses** (Doe Creek Road, Big Sky; 406-995-4630), which climbs into the Madison Range near the Big Sky resort complex, off Route 191; and **Medicine Lake Outfitters** (3246 Linney Road, Belgrade; 406-388-4938), which offers pack trips into Yellowstone National Park. The Absaroka-Beartooth and Lee Metcalf wildernesses—between Bozeman/Livingston and Yellowstone National Park—are extremely popular for pack trips. Visitors centers can offer extensive lists of outfitters.

Wilderness llama-trekking expeditions are offered by **Yellowstone Llamas** (P.O. Box 5042, Bozeman, MT 59717; 406-586-6872).

BICYCLING

Bozeman is the biking center of the southern Montana region. Bicyclists and runners share numerous urban trails, chief among them the one-and-a-half-mile **Gallagator Linear**, which connects the Museum of the Rockies, on Kagy Boulevard near South 3rd Avenue, with Bogart Park, at South Church Avenue and Story Street. An extension of the Gallagator is under construction at this writing. Also popular is the **Painted Hills Trail**, off Kagy Boulevard in the southeast corner of Bozeman. (In winter, cross-country skiers enjoy the same trails that bikers do when there's no snow.) Inquire locally for the "Bozeman Area Bike Trail Map."

Mountain bikers enjoy roads and trails in national forests throughout southern Montana. Among the most popular areas are the seasonal alpine and nordic ski trails at the **Big Sky Ski & Summer Resort** (Big Sky Road, Big Sky; 406-995-4211), south of Bozeman. Guided mountain-bike tours are offered by **Dave Willborn Outfitter** (775 Medicine Lodge Road, Dillon; 406-681-3117). Vehicles are not permitted in wilderness areas.

BIKE RENTALS Among the region's leading bike shops are **Great Divide Cyclery** (827 South Montana Street, Butte; 406-782-4726), **Bangtail Bikes** (508 West Main Street, Bozeman; 406-587-4905) and **Livingston Cycle** (117 West Callender Street, Livingston; 406-222-2628).

HIKING

The national forests, wilderness areas and other public lands of southern Montana contain literally thousands of miles of trails that offer an astounding range of choices for hikers of all experience and ability levels. From the Bitterroot Range, along the Idaho border, across the frontiers of Yellowstone National Park to the prairies, there's something for everyone. Adding to hikers' enjoyment are 50 recreational cabins available (by reservation) from the U.S. Forest Service at a cost of $15 to $30 per night. Contact specific National Forest offices.

Following are a few of the region's more popular trails. All distances listed are one-way unless otherwise noted.

HELENA AREA Mount Helena is a 900-acre city park that has seven separate trails to its 5468-foot peak. The reward for climbers is a bird's-eye view of the capital's Last Chance Gulch, a quarter-mile below the summit. Many hikers take the easy **1906 Trail** (2 miles) to the summit and descend on a steeper path, like the **Prospect Shafts Trail** (1.5 miles) past old mining sites or the **Prairie Trail** (2.5 miles), which is especially colorful during the spring and early-summer wildflower seasons. Nearest trailhead to downtown Helena is at the west end of Adams Street.

Refrigerator Canyon Trail (2 miles) offers access into the eastern part of the Gates of the Mountains Wilderness. After climbing dramatically through a narrow limestone canyon, the trail levels out to several excellent viewing points. The trailhead is on Beaver Creek Road north of Hauser Lake.

Hanging Valley National Recreation Trail (6 miles) in Helena National Forest northeast of Hauser Lake, climbs rapidly through limestone cliffs on the west side of the Big Belt Mountains before dropping into a valley of giant Douglas fir. The trail, which involves a 2260-foot elevation gain, begins at the Vigilante campground near York.

BUTTE AREA The **Sheepshead Trail System** (5 miles) is a system of paved paths that provide handicapped access to the outdoors. These Deerlodge

National Forest trails traverse meadows and wooded hills, and loop around a small lake. Trails begin at the Sheepshead Mountain Recreation Area, 19 miles north of Butte via Route 15 to Elk Park.

The **Continental Divide National Scenic Trail** (45 miles) is actually part of a 3100-mile Canada-to-Mexico trek; the segment through the Anaconda-Pintler Wilderness from Storm Lake, south of Georgetown Lake, to East Fork Road, east of Sula, offers a challenging backpack and spectacular views along the boundaries of Beaverhead, Deerlodge and Bitterroot national forests.

DILLON AREA **Lion Creek Trail** (9 miles) is one of the most attractive routes into the Pioneer Mountains. The path winds through meadows and forests to alpine lakes surrounded by 9800-foot peaks. The trailhead is in the Beaverhead National Forest west of Melrose, 30 miles north of Dillon.

Big Hole Battlefield National Recreation Trail (3.8 miles) traces the route along the Continental Divide by which Chief Joseph is thought to have led his Nez Perce warriors after they fled this 1877 battleground.

Humbug Spires Trail (2 miles) enters a fascinating geological preserve of 600-foot Mesozoic granite columns. Rock climbers often gather at this Bureau of Land Management sanctuary, 40 miles north of Dillon.

ALDER GULCH AREA **Louise Lake National Recreation Trail** (1.7 miles) switchbacks 3000 feet up two steep ridges to a shimmering lake cradled between the sheer cliffs of the Tobacco Root Mountains. Wildlife viewers often spot mountain goats. The trailhead is in Deerlodge National Forest at the end of South Boulder Road, south of Whitehall.

BOZEMAN AREA **Bridger Foothills National Recreation Trail** (20.8 miles) begins at the foot of Montana State University's hillside *"M,"* at Bozeman's northern city limits, and follows the rim of the Bridger Range through Gallatin National Forest. It ends after a 2640-foot elevation gain at Fairy Lake campground, at the foot of 9665-foot Sacajawea Peak, highest summit in the Bridgers.

Palisades Falls National Recreation Trail (.6 mile) is designed for visually impaired hikers. Beginning about 20 miles south of Bozeman off East Fork Road, above Hyalite Canyon, the hard-surfaced Gallatin National Forest trail climbs just over 500 feet to the 900-foot waterfall. There are descriptive signs in both English and Braille.

Hyalite Peak Trail (7.2 miles) ascends to the peak of 10,299-foot Hyalite Peak, high point of the Gallatin Range south of Bozeman. The trailhead for this strenuous climb is at 7000 feet, three miles south of Hyalite Reservoir at the end of Hyalite Canyon Road.

PARK AND SWEET GRASS COUNTIES **Pine Creek Trail** (5 miles) follows steep, rocky Pine Creek from the Pine Creek campground, 14 miles south of Livingston, past Pine Creek Falls to glacial Jewell Lake. The alpine gem lies at 9032 feet in the Absaroka-Beartooth Wilderness. There's a 3400-foot elevation gain on this trail.

Rock Creek North Trail (4 miles) climbs 2000 feet into the Crazy Mountains from a Gallatin National Forest trailhead off Rock Creek Road North, northeast of Livingston. It ends at Rock Lake, resting in a saddle between 11,214-foot Crazy Mountain and 10,737-foot Conical Peak, the highest points in the stark, craggy range.

Transportation

BY CAR

Route 90 runs 548 miles east and west across Montana, connecting many of its largest cities (Missoula, Butte, Bozeman and Billings) with points west (Seattle) and east (Chicago and Boston). **Route 15** runs 385 miles north and south, from the Canadian border through Great Falls, Helena and Butte to Pocatello, Idaho, and points south (Salt Lake City and San Diego). The two routes cross and briefly converge at Butte.

BY AIR

Bozeman's **Gallatin Field Airport** is served by Continental, Delta, Horizon, Northwest and SkyWest; Butte's **Bert Mooney Airport** by Horizon and SkyWest; the **Helena Airport** by Delta, Horizon and SkyWest.

BY BUS

Greyhound Bus Lines (800-231-2222) offers service to the larger towns along the Route 90/94 corridor. In summer, it also stops at West Yellowstone, on a spur route south from Bozeman to Idaho Falls.

Intermountain Transportation Co. (406-563-3841) connects Butte, Dillon and other towns of southwestern Montana. **Karst Stage** (406-586-8567) and the **Montana Motor Coach Ltd.** (406-586-6121) offer seasonal service between Bozeman, Livingston and Yellowstone National Park.

The central bus terminal in Helena is at 5 West 15th Street (406-442-5860), in Butte at 105 West Broadway (406-723-3287), and in Bozeman at 625 North 7th Avenue (406-587-3110).

CAR RENTALS

Helena has eight car-rental agencies, Butte has six and Bozeman has twelve. At the airports, each town has **Avis Rent A Car** (800-331-1212), **Budget Rent A Car** (800-527-0700) and **Hertz Rent A Car** (800-654-3131). Rentals can also be found in Anaconda, Dillon and Livingston.

PUBLIC TRANSPORTATION

The **Butte-Silver Bow Transit System** (406-723-8262) runs an extensive route system through Butte and surrounding areas, with nominal fares. No other southern Montana town has a public transportation system.

TAXIS

All cities and larger towns in southern Montana have taxi services. In Butte, call **City Taxi** (406-723-6511). In the Bozeman area, a different **City Taxi** (406-586-2341) provides cabs.

CHAPTER FOURTEEN

Montana East of the Rockies

Montana is known as "Big Sky" country, and nowhere is that more evident than in the sweep of real estate that extends east from the Rocky Mountains to the Dakotas.

Only three states (Alaska, Texas and California) are larger than Montana. Yet only 800,000 Montanans live on 147,000 square miles of land—about 5.4 people per square mile. Only Alaska and Wyoming have a lower population density.

Quite literally, eastern Montanans have a home "where the buffalo roam, where the deer and the antelope play." Two centuries ago, tens of millions of American bison, in herds of thousands, cavorted through these mountains and prairies, across the headwater streams of the Missouri River and down the Yellowstone River valley. Deer and pronghorn antelope remain in large numbers, but the bison were hunted to near-extinction in the 19th century and have made only a modest comeback in the 20th.

The bison nearly met the same fate as their Jurassic predecessors, whose bones and other fossil remains have been found en masse from the Rockies' eastern slope to the Makoshika Badlands near Montana's boundary with North Dakota. In fact, more skeletons of *Tyrannosaurus rex,* believed to have been the largest dinosaur ever to walk the earth, have been found in Montana than in all other discovery areas put together.

As far as human habitation goes, this has always been a land more suited to outdoors lovers and implacable individualists than to genteel urbanites. The Native Americans—primarily Blackfoot, Crow (Sioux) and Cheyenne—who lived in this region before the arrival of whites were horsemen and hunters who relied heavily on bison to provide food and hides for clothing and shelter.

The geographical magnitude of eastern Montana can be most clearly grasped from the eastern flank of Glacier National Park. Here, the Rocky Mountain Front drops dramatically to the northern Great Plains. Stark, undulating prairies march hundreds of miles eastward to the Dakotas, broken only by occasional highland rills and by the valley of the Missouri River. This broad, slow-flowing stream provides water for the arid farmland, habitat for waterfowl and other wildlife, recreation for the sportsman and sportswoman.

Despite the paucity of population in the eastern plains, Montana's two largest cities are located here. Billings, a thriving community of 90,000 in the southeastern part of the state, owes its existence to railroads and ranching. Through it flows the Yellowstone River, the longest undammed river in the contiguous 48 states. Great Falls, with 55,000 people, is a trade and industrial center on the Missouri River below the Rockies' eastern fringe. Only two other cities in the region—Havre, with a population of 10,200, and Miles City, with 8500—have more than 6000 people.

Billings Area

Montana's largest city nestles between sandstone cliffs in the valley of the Yellowstone River, within the shadow of the Rockies but with an outlook toward the Great Plains. **Billings** is the urban hub for a vast and sparsely populated region that includes eastern Montana, northern Wyoming and the western Dakotas.

Called "The Magic City" because it sprang up almost overnight after its founding as a railroad town in 1882, Billings grew as an agricultural, trade and transportation center. Now oil and medicine are major industries as well, and two colleges (Eastern Montana University and Rocky Mountain College) attract a young population and enliven the city's cultural life.

For Rocky Mountain travelers, Billings is a gateway to such attractions as Little Bighorn Battlefield National Monument, the Bighorn Canyon National Recreation Area, the mountain town of Red Lodge and its spectacular Beartooth Highway, which travels past Montana's highest peaks to Yellowstone National Park. The Yellowstone, Musselshell and Bighorn rivers are acclaimed fishing streams, and there are unique geological and cultural features throughout southeastern Montana's "Custer Country."

Many visitors get their first impression of Billings at the **Visitors Center and Cattle Drive Monument** (815 South 27th Street; 406-252-4016), a few blocks off Route 90 Exit 450. The bronze sculpture in front of the modern building was commissioned to commemorate Montana's centennial cattle drive of 1989 to Billings from Roundup, 50 miles north.

Perhaps the most notable of Billings' downtown attractions is the **Moss Mansion** (914 Division Street; 406-256-5100; admission). Built in 1902 by famed architect Henry Janeway Hardenbergh for bank president Preston B. Moss, this elegant three-story mansion features a Moorish entryway (inspired by Spain's

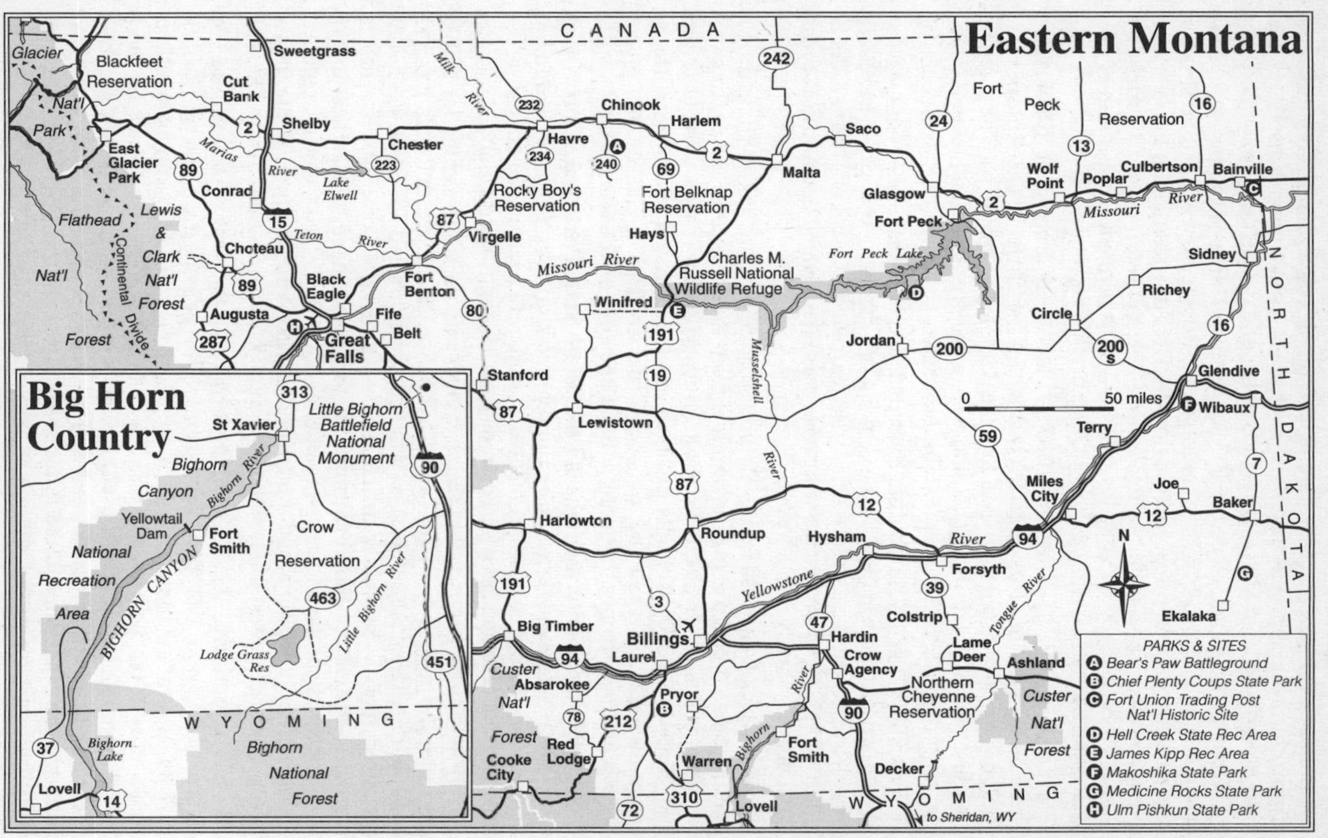
Eastern Montana
CANADA
NORTH DAKOTA
WYOMING
Glacier Nat'l Park
Blackfeet Reservation
Flathead Nat'l Forest
Lewis & Clark Nat'l Forest
Continental Divide
East Glacier Park
Cut Bank
Sweetgrass
Shelby
Conrad
Marias River
Teton River
Lake Elwell
Chester
Choteau
Augusta
Black Eagle
Great Falls
Fife
Belt
Fort Benton
Milk River
Virgelle
Rocky Boy's Reservation
Havre
Chinook
Harlem
Fort Belknap Reservation
Hays
Winifred
Missouri River
Charles M. Russell National Wildlife Refuge
Malta
Saco
Glasgow
Fort Peck
Fort Peck Lake
Fort Peck Reservation
Wolf Point
Poplar
Culbertson
Bainville
Sidney
Richey
Circle
Jordan
Musselshell River
Stanford
Lewistown
Harlowton
Roundup
Big Timber
Billings
Laurel
Absarokee
Red Lodge
Cooke City
Custer Nat'l Forest
Pryor
Warren
Lovell
Fort Smith
Bighorn River
Hardin
Crow Agency
Hysham
Yellowstone River
Forsyth
Colstrip
Lame Deer
Northern Cheyenne Reservation
Decker
to Sheridan, WY
Ashland
Tongue River
Miles City
Terry
Glendive
Wibaux
Joe
Baker
Ekalaka
0 50 miles
N
PARKS & SITES
A Bear's Paw Battleground
B Chief Plenty Coups State Park
C Fort Union Trading Post Nat'l Historic Site
D Hell Creek State Rec Area
E James Kipp Rec Area
F Makoshika State Park
G Medicine Rocks State Park
H Ulm Pishkun State Park
Big Horn Country
St Xavier
Little Bighorn Battlefield National Monument
Bighorn Canyon National Recreation Area
BIGHORN CANYON
Yellowtail Dam
Fort Smith
Crow Reservation
Little Bighorn River
Lodge Grass Res
Bighorn Lake
Bighorn National Forest
Lovell
2
89
15
89
287
223
87
80
232
234
240
69
191
19
242
24
2
13
16
16
200
200 S
59
87
12
12
94
39
47
90
3
191
94
212
78
72
310
7
313
90
463
451
37
14

Alhambra), a formal French parlor and an English Tudor dining room. Elaborate original furnishings provide a glimpse of the Mosses' Victorian lifestyle. Guided tours are offered from March through October and during the Christmas season.

Two museums are worth a visit. The **Western Heritage Center** (2822 Montana Avenue; 406-256-6809), in an imposing Romanesque sandstone structure at the corner of 29th Street, focuses on Native American and pioneer history throughout the Yellowstone valley region. The **Yellowstone Art Center** (401 North 27th Street; 406-256-6804; admission) has a permanent collection of work by regional artists, from the days of exploration to modern times.

You can get a good feel for Billings' layout by driving the **Black Otter Trail** along the rim of its overlooking sandstone cliffs—"The Rimrocks"—north of downtown, carefully avoiding the potholes as you do so. The route begins just west of Main Street (Route 87) in the Billings Heights area, above the grounds of the MetraPark exhibition center.

Boothill Cemetery, in **Boothill Swords Park**, is all that remains of the short-lived town of Coulson (1877–85). Among the graves is that of H. M. "Muggins" Taylor, who as an army scout first carried the news of Custer's defeat at Little Bighorn to the outside world. He was later gunned down while serving as Coulson's sheriff.

The Black Otter Trail rejoins Airport Road just before busy Billings-Logan International Airport. Facing the terminal from the city side of the parking area is the **Peter Yegen, Jr., Yellowstone County Museum** (Airport Road at North 27th Street; 406-256-6811). Its displays include a diorama of pioneer life, an authentic roundup wagon and, outside, a life-size statue, *The Range Rider of the Yellowstone*, facing the metropolis at the foot of the Rimrocks.

On Billings' north city limits is **Lake Elmo State Park** (Lake Elmo Drive; 406-252-4654). The 64-acre Lake Elmo attracts city residents for swimming, fishing, non-motorized boating and board sailing. Boat rentals, board-sailing lessons and concessions are offered from June through August only.

If the *Range Rider* could see far enough into the bluffs on the far side of the valley, he might spot **Pictograph Cave State Park** (Coburn Road; 406-252-4654; admission) just southeast of Billings. An estimated 4500 years ago, prehistoric hunters lived in three different caves at this site; some 30,000 artifacts, including distinctive rock paintings (pictographs), have told archaeologists a great deal about the hunters' way of life. Short trails lead to the caves; there are also interpretive signs and a picnic area. Take Exit 452 from Route 90 and follow Coburn Road six miles south. Open daily from mid-April to mid-October.

There's more history in southwest Billings at **Oscar's Dreamland** (★) (Storey Road; 406-656-0966; admission). This pioneer town and agricultural museum is a tribute to the efforts of one man, Oscar Cooke, to preserve Montana's early-1900s homesteading era. An old train circles the 19-acre grounds that also include an early carousel and Ferris wheel, a garage full of Model-T Fords and hundreds more rare and antique vehicles and farm machines. Take the South Frontage Road three miles along Route 90 from Exit 446; then turn south one mile on Wise Lane. Open daily from May through October.

THE BEARTOOTH FACE An hour's drive southwest of Billings on Route 212 brings travelers to the foot of Montana's loftiest mountains. Granite Peak, at 12,799 feet the highest of the high, crowns the plateau that towers above the historic mining town of Red Lodge. It and numerous smaller communities provide access to the lakes and streams of Custer National Forest and the Absaroka-Beartooth Wilderness.

Red Lodge, which lists its elevation as 5555 feet, is the logical portal to the region. Its 2000 residents live in a lovely town whose appearance may not be a lot different from what it was during its coal-mining boom of 1890–1910.

Six blocks of Broadway (the main street) from 8th to 14th streets and numerous side streets make up the **Red Lodge Historic District** (406-446-1718). Nearly all the buildings date from the boom period. Among them are the Theatorium, decorated with imported Italian marble statues; the 1889 railroad station; the 1893 Spofford (now Pollard) Hotel, which hosted such historical figures as "Buffalo Bill" Cody, "Calamity Jane" Canary and John "Liver Eatin'" Johnston; the 1899 Carbon County Courthouse; and the 1897 Finnish Opera House.

Much of the region's history is retold through artifacts and memorabilia south of town at the **Carbon County Museum** (Route 212, Red Lodge; 406-446-3914). The old homestead cabin of "Liver Eatin'" Johnston, upon whose life the Robert Redford movie *Jeremiah Johnson* was based, stands intact on the grounds.

The hills around Red Lodge were always rich in coal, but perhaps none more so than those flanking **Bear Creek**, over the hill to the east. In 1943, though, the mining industry—already on the wane—heard its death knell. An underground explosion in the Smith Mine killed 74 men near Washoe, four miles from Red Lodge. A tipple and several outbuildings still stand as sober reminders of Montana's worst coal-mining disaster.

Red Lodge's coal industry never recovered from the Smith Mine tragedy. Since World War II, tourism has been the economic mainstay of the area. In summer, Red Lodge is a northeastern gateway to Yellowstone National Park; in winter, the **Red Lodge Mountain Ski Area** (Forest Road 1478; 406-446-2610), with 2000 feet of vertical terrain just six miles west of town, is a popular destination.

The Yellowstone gateway route is the **Beartooth Highway** (Route 212 West). Officially opened in 1936, this 70-mile designated scenic byway through Custer and Shoshone national forests has been called "the most beautiful drive in America" by CBS television correspondent Charles Kuralt. The trip through isolated Cooke City to the park entrance (see "Yellowstone Gateway Communities" in Chapter Seven) may take up to three hours because of the highway's elevation (nearly 11,000 feet at its high point) and its prodigious number of switchbacks. For more information, contact the Chamber of Commerce (406-446-1718) or the U.S. Forest Service (406-446-2103).

But *breathtaking* is not the only descriptive word that applies here. Numerous trails leave the highway to enter the Beartooth Plateau portion of the **Absaroka-Beartooth Wilderness**. Nearly a million acres in size, this wilderness area includes some two dozen mountains over 12,000 feet in elevation. (See

"Park and Sweet Grass Counties Parks" in Chapter Thirteen for details on facilities.) Traveling around the rim and over the top of the Beartooth Plateau, visitors get spectacular vistas across magnificent glaciated peaks and pristine alpine lakes. (*Note:* Because snow stays late and returns early, the Beartooth Highway normally is open only from June to the middle of October.)

BILLINGS AREA HOTELS

The **Josephine Bed & Breakfast** (514 North 29th Street, Billings; 406-248-5898) is one of only two B & Bs in greater Billings, and the other is in a country cornfield. The Josephine offers three bright, antique-filled bedrooms in a 1915 home a short walk from the downtown hub. It *is* old-fashioned, however: None of the rooms has air-conditioning and all share bathrooms. Smoking is not permitted inside the house. Moderate.

North of downtown en route to the airport and Eastern Montana University, the **Rimrock Inn** (1203 North 27th Street, Billings; 406-252-7107, 800-624-9770, fax 406-252-7107 ext. 305) has all the basics and more, such as a free continental breakfast, a fitness area with a hot tub and a restaurant and lounge. Rooms are no-frills. Budget.

Downtown Billings' finest accommodations are at the **Radisson Northern Hotel** (19 North Broadway; 406-245-5121, 800-822-3384, fax 406-259-9862). More than five decades old, the ten-story, 160-room hotel has been fully remodeled with a contemporary western flair. Some rooms have refrigerators. There's a restaurant, a lounge and an exercise room; guests get golf privileges at a nearby course. Deluxe.

Also in downtown Billings, a step down in price, is the **Best Western Ponderosa Inn** (2511 1st Avenue North; 406-259-5511, 800-628-9081, fax 506-245-8004). This motel has 130 guest rooms in a pair of two-story buildings. One building faces an outdoor courtyard with a swimming pool; the other looks toward a 24-hour restaurant and cellar lounge. In addition to the pool, the Ponderosa has a sauna, fitness room and coin laundry. Moderate.

Conveniently located off Route 90 for travelers arriving from the west, the **Holiday Inn Billings Plaza** (5500 Midland Road, Billings; 406-248-7701, 800-637-3670, fax 406-248-8954) is the region's largest. With 316 rooms in seven stories adjoining the biggest exposition hall in the northern Great Plains, it has everything you'd expect a convention hotel to have, like a full-service restaurant, room service and a lounge-casino with live entertainment and dancing. A waterfall tumbles past twin glass elevators in the atrium lobby. Softly lit, tastefully decorated rooms have all amenities. Moderate to deluxe.

One of the region's classiest resorts is undoubtedly the **Rock Creek Resort** (Route 212 South, Red Lodge; 406-446-1111, fax 406-446-3688), five miles south of Red Lodge at the foot of the Beartooth Highway. The handsome Beartooth Lodge and adjacent Grizzly Condos have 75 rooms, 32 with kitchens, designed in contemporary rustic style with balconies. The restaurant serves exquisite American and Continental cuisine. The resort offers tennis and mountain biking; golf, horseback riding and skiing are available nearby. Kids have a playground and game room. Deluxe.

Red Lodge's **Pollard Hotel** (★) (2 North Broadway; 406-446-0001, 800-765-5273, fax 406-446-3733), built in 1893, once hosted the likes of "Buffalo Bill" Cody and William Jennings Bryan. Now a century old, it's undergone a total facelift and is the only hotel in the northern Rockies to be accepted as a member of the select Historic Hotels of America. Entirely nonsmoking, the Pollard has 36 rooms and suites, some with indoor balconies, others with parlors and hot tubs. There's a full fitness club with saunas and a racquetball court. Moderate to deluxe.

BILLINGS AREA RESTAURANTS

Top of the line in southeastern Montana is **Juliano's** (2912 7th Avenue North, Billings; 406-248-6400), which serves up generous portions of fresh game and Continental cuisine in a converted turn-of-the-century livery stable behind The Castle, a medieval-looking sandstone manor, and on an outdoor patio. The restaurant does its own baking and has an extensive wine list. Deluxe.

Also atmospheric, but in a more judicial sort of way, is **Walkers Grill** (301 North 27th Street; 406-245-9291), which occupies the ground floor of Billings' renovated Old Chamber Building opposite the Yellowstone County Court House. Dinner is a creative affair, with Italian, Mexican, Cajun and Asian influences in various seafood and meat dishes; lunch is simpler, with a focus on soups, salads and pastas. Moderate.

For straight beef and seafood, it's hard to top **Jake's Steak & Fish House** (2701 1st Avenue North; 406-259-9375) in the heart of downtown Billings. A large salad bar complements meals amid the garden decor of the main restaurant, and a lighter menu is served in the wood-and-brass Good Time Bar. Moderate.

The Granary (1500 Poly Drive; 406-259-3488) serves prime rib, Alaskan king crab and Cajun cuisine in a building constructed as a mill by the former Billings Polytechnic Institute in 1935. The original machinery is still on display. There's an outdoor patio lounge. Moderate.

The **Great Wall Restaurant** (1309 Grand Avenue; 406-245-8601) boasts the best Chinese food in Montana, and few are they who argue. A wide variety of pork, beef, chicken and shrimp dishes, in varied Cantonese, Mandarin and Szechuan styles, are prepared at this west Billings restaurant. Budget to moderate.

Next door to the Great Wall is a surprise: **Khanthaly's Eggrolls** (★) (1301 Grand Avenue; 406-259-7252), a Laotian fast-food restaurant in the middle of the prairie. Because Laos is wedged between Thailand, Vietnam and China, its food bears influences from all three traditions. Budget.

On the Beartooth Face, in Red Lodge, **Pius & Karin** (115 South Broadway; 406-446-3333) is an elegant Continental restaurant that serves gourmet food and sophisticated wine in rustic surroundings. This is fine dining, priced to match. There's a pleasant bar as well. Deluxe.

Just a block away, **17 Broadway: The Restaurant** (17 South Broadway, Red Lodge; 406-446-1717) has a lunch and dinner menu of new American cuisine in the casual setting of a late-19th-century Victorian library. Sunday brunch is popular here. Moderate.

Two miles north, **The Round Barn** (Route 212, Red Lodge; 406-446-1197) is a bargain for big eaters. Nightly except Tuesday it offers a smorgasbord of salads, main courses and desserts to hungry families. The 64-foot-diameter brick barn was once a milking parlor for a dairy farm; today, the upper story is a dinner theater where vaudeville, family musicals and visiting instrumentalists appear throughout the summer. Budget.

BILLINGS AREA SHOPPING

The shops at the **Yellowstone Art Center** (401 North 27th Street, Billings; 406-256-6804) and the **Western Heritage Center** (2822 Montana Avenue, Billings; 406-256-6809) are excellent places to find regional arts and crafts.

Other spots of special interest downtown include **Collector's Emporium** (114 North 29th Street; 406-259-2338), an antique mall of 14,000 square feet; **Billings Army/Navy Surplus** (15 North 29th Street; 406-259-8528), the largest of its kind in the northwestern United States; **Stillwater Traders** (2nd Avenue North and North 29th Street; 406-252-6211), featuring all manner of cowboy kitsch; and **Center Lodge Native Arts** (121 North 29th Street; 406-252-9994), with modern and traditional Native American arts and crafts.

BILLINGS AREA NIGHTLIFE

The **Alberta Bair Theater for the Performing Arts** (2801 3rd Avenue North, Billings; 406-256-6052) is Montana's largest concert hall. A renovated former Fox theater on the corner of Broadway downtown, it has been acoustically redesigned and is now in use more than 110 nights a year. Touring professional ballet, opera, theater and symphony companies appear here, as do **The Billings Symphony Orchestra and Chorale** (401 North 31st Avenue; 406-252-3610), which presents concerts monthly in a September-to-April season, and the **Billings Community Concert Association** (1603 Grand Avenue; 406-245-0460).

The city's other major venue is the **Babcock Theater** (2812 2nd Avenue North; 406-256-5543), where nonprofit Starfire Productions hosts concerts of acoustic music, live theater and children's theater, cultural exchanges and silver-screen film presentations.

Big-name concerts of country and popular musical artists usually are held at **MetraPark Arena** (308 6th Avenue North, Billings; 406-256-2422). The greatest concentrations take place in mid-August during the Montana Fair.

The mainstay of community theater is the **Billings Studio Theatre** (1500 Rimrock Road; 406-248-1141), which performs at Rocky Mountain College. The troupe stages five plays of different genres (often including a musical, a comedy, a drama and a Shakespearean classic) during a September-to-May season.

Billings' rock-and-rollers appreciate **The Bungalow** (925 South 27th Street; 406-248-4656), which boasts live music nightly except Monday, a huge dance-floor, an outdoor patio and casino gaming. **Casey's Golden Pheasant** (109 North

Broadway; 406-256-5200) brings blues, bluegrass and zydeco to downtown Billings, while country-and-western dancers prefer to head out to **Drifters Tavern** (3953 Montana Avenue; 406-259-8619) or the **Corral Bar** (5005 Route 312 East; 406-373-5345) to do their two-stepping. Gays are welcomed at the Corral.

A popular downtown gathering place is **The Billings Club** (2702 1st Avenue North; 406-245-2262), with microbrews on tap in an outdoor beer garden and satellite TV in every corner of the indoor sports bar.

Down in the Beartooth area, Red Lodge locals spend a lot of time at the **Snow Creek Saloon** (124 South Broadway; 406-446-2542). On weekends, they often travel eight miles east to the **Bear Creek Saloon** (Route 308, Bearcreek; 406-446-3481), where pig races and enchiladas are the big events on hot summer nights.

BILLINGS AREA PARKS

Cooney Reservoir State Park—Fishing, boating, swimming and wildlife watching are the hobbies of choice at this irrigation reservoir, south of the Yellowstone River in the shadow of the Beartooth Range.

Facilities: Picnic tables, restrooms, boat ramp, groceries; day-use fee, $3; information, 406-445-2326. *Swimming:* Designated beach. *Fishing:* Good for walleye pike and rainbow trout.

Camping: There are 75 RV/tent sites (no hookups); $7 per night.

Getting there: From Boyd, on Route 212 halfway between Laurel and Red Lodge, travel eight miles west on Cooney Dam Road.

Custer National Forest—Montana's most diverse national forest extends across nearly 2.5 million acres of the southern part of the state, in seven different parcels reaching from the Stillwater River, west of Red Lodge, to Capitol Rock, southeast of Ekalaka on the border of South Dakota. In between, it includes a large chunk of the Absaroka-Beartooth Wilderness as well as the Pryor Mountains, west of Bighorn Canyon, and the Ashland District lands, east of the Tongue River.

Facilities: Picnic tables, restrooms, trails, ski area (Red Lodge Mountain); information, 406-657-6361. *Swimming:* In a few lakes. *Fishing:* The rivers and lakes of the Beartooth Face boast mountain whitefish and brook, brown and rainbow trout; a few lakes also have cutthroat trout. Otter Creek, east of Ashland, may have bass or catfish.

Camping: There are 277 RV/tent sites (no hookups) plus 91 for tents only at 20 campgrounds; no charge to $7 per night. A recreational cabin, available at $15 per night, is located at Beaver Creek in the Ashland District.

Getting there: Main approach roads for the Beartooth region are Routes 212 and 78 from Red Lodge, or Route 419 from Absarokee. Enter the Pryor Mountains via Crow Reservation Road 11, off Route 5 between Pryor and Warren; the Ashland District from Route 212 or Otter Creek Road; and the Ekalaka District from county roads south and east of Ekalaka, at the end of Route 7.

The Big Horns and Beyond

Route 90 connecting Billings with Sheridan, Wyoming, 130 miles southeast, is an avenue to many of the leading attractions of southeastern Montana. Traversing the Crow Indian Reservation, it passes directly by the Little Bighorn Battlefield of "Custer's Last Stand" fame and comes within a short drive of Bighorn Canyon National Recreation Area.

At the northwest corner of the Crow Reservation is **Hardin**, a farming and ranching center of 3000 people. Twelve months a year, the best reason to visit Hardin is to see its **Big Horn County Historical Museum** (★) at the **State Visitor Center** (Route 90 Exit 497; 406-665-1671). Located at the east end of town, the free museum preserves more than a dozen homestead-era buildings from all over Big Horn County. Picnic grounds surround the 24-acre "village," which includes a farm home and outbuildings, railroad depot, service station, mercantile shop, school and church (still used for services on summer Sundays). Antique farm implements and machinery are on display.

Hardin lives hard by its memories of Little Bighorn. While the battlefield is 18 miles southeast of here, the Custer's Last Stand Reenactment takes place five times each year during Little Big Horn Days, the last full weekend of June. Advance tickets can be purchased from the **Hardin Area Chamber of Commerce** (200 North Center Avenue; 406-665-1672).

Little Bighorn Battlefield National Monument (Battlefield Road, Crow Agency; 406-638-2621; admission) is where the *real* action took place, however, and there's no better way to understand the maneuvers and tactics of the best known of all Native American battles than to spend some time here. The clash, which took place on June 25 and 26, 1876, memorializes one of the Plains Indians' last armed attempts to defend their traditional life against the intrusion of white civilization.

Museum displays and dioramas in the visitors center and ranger-led talks and tours describe the chain of events that led Sioux and Cheyenne warriors to vanquish a corps of 260 U.S. Army cavalrymen. Not a soldier survived the massacre; among the dead was their leader, Lieutenant Colonel George Armstrong Custer.

The national monument, reached off Route 212 at Exit 510 from Route 90, includes the **Custer National Cemetery** (for veterans of the armed services) and a four-and-a-half-mile tour road that winds through the sage-covered hills overlooking the Little Bighorn River.

Given that the Indians were fighting for their ultimate freedom, it's ironic that the national monument is now within the **Crow Indian Reservation** (Crow Agency; 406-638-2601). The vast (2.3-million-acre) reservation is home to about 5200 Apsalooké ("Children of the Large-Beaked Bird"), or Crow, a Sioux tribe. Stretching 55 miles north and south, from Billings to the Wyoming border, and 83 miles east and west, from West Pryor Mountain to Rosebud Creek, the tribe leans upon tourism for its economic wherewithal.

After Little Bighorn Battlefield, the Crow Reservation's second ace-in-the-tourism-hole is the **Bighorn Canyon National Recreation Area** (Fort Smith; 406-666-2412). The park spans two states, stretching south well into Wyoming, but it is from Hardin that most Montana visitors reach it. Its central feature is 71-mile-long Bighorn Lake, which fills a dramatic desert canyon whose limestone walls rise a half mile high on either side, revealing millions of years of geologic history. See "Big Horns and Beyond Parks," below, for more information.

Bighorn Lake was created in 1965 by 525-foot-high Yellowtail Dam. Today, the **Yellowtail Dam Visitor Center** (Route 313, Fort Smith; 406-666-3234), open summers only, describes the construction and operation of the dam. The **Fort Smith Visitor Center** (Afterbay Road, Fort Smith; 406-666-2339) has displays that focus on wildlife and geography and sponsors evening programs at a nearby campground.

The best vista of the meandering reservoir and gorge is from the **Devil Canyon Overlook** (Route 37; 406-548-2251), a course that requires drivers to backtrack more than 100 miles through Lovell, Wyoming. Those who do are rewarded with a magnificent view where Bighorn Canyon cuts through the Pryor Mountains. (For more on this side of the recreation area, see Chapter Eight, "Northern Wyoming Rockies.")

Those same Pryor Mountains, on the west side of Bighorn Canyon, are the site of the 44,000-acre **Pryor Mountain National Wild Horse Range** (Route 37 via Lovell, Wyoming; 406-657-6262). About 130 mustangs, believed to be descended from a herd that has lived in this area for more than two centuries, freely roam this rugged desert land administered by the Bureau of Land Management. Backcountry roads penetrate the range from Route 310 east of Warren.

Just inside the Crow Reservation's western boundary is **Chief Plenty Coups State Park** (Route 416, Pryor; 406-252-1289; fee), which preserves the log home, store and grave of the last Crow chief. Plenty Coups deeded the land, 35 miles south of Billings, to the Crow nation in 1928. It is now an interpretive center for Crow tribal history as well as a memorial to the chief himself.

The Crow Reservation is bordered on the east by the wooded mesas and creek beds of the **Northern Cheyenne Indian Reservation** (Lame Deer; 406-477-6253). Covering 445,000 acres west of the Tongue River, the reservation is home to 5600 Northern Cheyenne, who call themselves the "People of the Morning Star." Reservation headquarters are in Lame Deer, as well as the **Northern Cheyenne Arts and Crafts Center** (Route 212; 406-477-6284), which displays beadwork and other handicrafts.

More impressive is the **Plains Indian Museum at St. Labre Indian School** (★) (Tongue River Road, Ashland; 406-784-2200), on the reservation's eastern frontier 21 miles from Lame Deer. The modern museum has a colorful and varied collection of clothing and artifacts from Cheyenne, Sioux and other Plains tribes. The school, founded as a mission in 1884, is notable for its stylized stone church, built in the shape of a teepee but with a metal cross protruding in place of the center supporting pole.

Rosebud Battlefield State Park (Route 314, Decker; 406-232-4365), 44 miles southwest of Lame Deer, marks the spot where Sioux warriors took on a cavalry division in June 1876, setting the stage for the Battle of the Little Bighorn eight days later.

The little town of **Broadus**, a 44-mile drive east from Ashland on Route 212, has one of the most memorable local museums to be found in the northern Rockies. **The Powder River Historical Museum** (102 West Wilson Street; 406-436-2276) is actually two museums in one. The main building, two blocks off the highway, displays a well-organized homestead-era collection including a complete general store, a ranch's chuck wagon, the original Powder River jail and many antique vehicles.

If those don't grab you, ask to see **Mac's Museum** (★) in a rear building. Until his death in 1986, pioneer resident R. D. "Mac" McCurdy devoted most of his waking hours to his personal collection of arrowheads, fossils, rocks, insects, birds' eggs and more. But those pale in comparison to his 200,000 seashells from throughout the world. Many of them are no larger than pinheads, but McCurdy identified all by their exact genera and species. Scientists visit from all over North America to study McCurdy's collection. Open from Memorial Day to Labor Day or by appointment.

BIG HORNS AND BEYOND HOTELS

Near the Little Bighorn Battlefield, in downtown Hardin, an early-20th-century boarding house has been restored as a bed-and-breakfast home. The **Kendrick House Inn** (206 North Custer Avenue; 406-665-3035) is a handsome Georgian with seven guest rooms decorated in late-Victorian style. Each room has a pedestal sink, but the bathrooms (two of them) must be shared. There are full breakfasts in the dining room and TV in the library. Moderate.

The **Western Motel** (830 West 3rd Street, Hardin; 406-665-2296, fax 406-665-2298) isn't flashy, but the price tag is right. The two-story property has 28 rooms (four of them two-bedroom family suites) with outdated furnishings but private baths in every unit. Budget.

A unique experience for cultural adventurers is offered by the **Sacred Ground Camp** (★) (P.O. Box 78, Pryor, MT 59066; phone/fax 406-245-7673) on the Crow Indian Reservation. Participants spend a full week living Indian-style in teepees in the remote Pryor Mountains, west of Bighorn Canyon. They learn tribal wisdom from Crow elders, study native cooking and crafts, consort with plants and wildlife during hikes and horseback rides through the mountains, and immerse themselves in traditional singing, dancing and (if they wish) sacred ceremonies. Open June through September. Moderate.

BIG HORNS AND BEYOND RESTAURANTS

Once you get away from Billings, culinary choices are pretty much limited to steak and potatoes. **The Merry Mixer Restaurant & Lounge** (317 North Center Avenue, Hardin; 208-665-3735) is a prime example. You can get a good steak or a big slab of prime rib accompanied by a baked potato, a basic iceberg-lettuce salad and a hearty cup of coffee. The atmosphere is strictly red vinyl and low lights, but the service is friendly. Low moderate.

For Native American fast food, the **Shake & Burger Hut** (Crow Agency; 406-638-2921) is worth a visit. Ask for a Navajo taco and you'll get ground beef, cheese and other fixings folded within tasty, pan-fried bread. Budget.

BIG HORNS AND BEYOND SHOPPING

Native American culture vultures might seek out the **Jailhouse Gallery** (812 North Center Street, Hardin; 406-665-3239) for modern Indian paintings and craftwork, or the **Little Coyote Gallery** (St. Labre Indian School, Tongue River Road, Ashland; 406-784-2200), on the Crow Indian Reservation, for more traditional handicrafts as well as contemporary works.

BIG HORNS AND BEYOND NIGHTLIFE

Montana's largest gambling establishment is the **Little Bighorn Casino** (Route 212, Crow Agency; 406-638-4444), a stone's throw from the Little Bighorn Battlefield at the same exit off Route 90.

BIG HORNS AND BEYOND PARKS

Bighorn Canyon National Recreation Area—Prior to 1965 the Bighorn River cut a deep gorge through the Pryor and Big Horn mountain ranges. Since the construction of 525-foot-high Yellowtail Dam, in 1965, Bighorn Lake has stretched 71 miles through the canyon. But the half-mile-high cliffs remain, and boating and fishing enthusiasts have a new playground. Visitors centers at Fort Smith, Montana, and Lovell, Wyoming, relate the canyon's geological and natural history.

Facilities: Picnic tables, restrooms, visitors centers, amphitheaters, trails, boat ramps, two marinas, concessions; some sites are wheelchair accessible; information, 406-666-2412. *Swimming:* Designated beach at Horseshoe Bend, Wyoming; elsewhere at your own risk. *Fishing:* In Bighorn Lake: trout, walleye pike, burbot, largemouth bass, sauger, channel catfish, yellow perch and crappie. In the Bighorn River below the dam: mountain whitefish, burbot, smallmouth bass and catfish.

Camping: There are 30 RV/tent sites (no hookups) plus 27 for tents only at four campgrounds; two campgrounds are accessible only by boat; no charge.

Getting there: From Hardin, take Route 313 south 43 miles to the visitors center at Fort Smith. From the visitors center at Lovell, Wyoming, on Route 14A east of Cody, take Route 37 north to Devil Canyon and Barry's Landing.

Tongue River Reservoir State Park—Fishing, boating and other water sports are popular on this 12-mile-long lake, set in the prairies amid red shale cliffs and juniper canyons just north of the Wyoming border.

Facilities: Picnic tables, restrooms, boat ramp, concession, groceries; day-use fee, $3; information, 406-232-4365. *Swimming:* Designated beach. *Fishing:* Good for walleye, northern pike, bass and crappie.

Camping: There are 20 RV/tent sites (no hookups); $7 per night.

Getting there: From Decker, 20 miles north of Sheridan, Wyoming, take Route 314 six miles north, then Route 382 (the Tongue River Dam Road) two miles northeast.

The Lower Yellowstone Valley

Northeast from Billings, Route 94 follows the Yellowstone River downstream some 223 miles to Glendive, not far from the river's confluence with the Missouri, before turning abruptly east through North Dakota toward Minneapolis and Chicago.

The longest undammed river in the lower 48 states, the Yellowstone—which runs 671 miles from its source in Wyoming's Absaroka Range to the Missouri—in its lower portion is a broad, gently flowing stream. Along with its principal tributaries, the northward flowing Bighorn, Tongue and Powder rivers, it irrigates tens of thousands of square miles of ranchland used in livestock and grain production.

Along the south bank of the Yellowstone, stretching 27 miles from Huntley (11 miles east of Billings) to Bull Mountain, the Huntley Irrigation Project embraces 35,000 acres of lush cropland set aside as a federal homesteading project in 1907 and three other small communities. The townsite of Osborn, three miles east of Huntley, is now the location of the **Huntley Project Museum of Irrigated Agriculture** (Route 312, Huntley; 406-967-2680), which preserves 18 buildings and more than 5000 agricultural and household items from the early 20th century.

Near the east end of the Huntley project is **Pompeys Pillar** (Route 312, Pompeys Pillar; 406-875-2233), a sandstone butte on whose face Captain William Clark carved his name in 1806. That signature is the only direct physical evidence remaining from the Lewis and Clark expedition of 1803–1806, making the 150-foot-high butte a national historic landmark. Take Exit 23 off Route 94.

Other than Billings, **Miles City** is the largest community in eastern Montana. Located 145 miles east of the "Magic City," and 94 miles west of the North Dakota border, the town of 8500 people lays claim to the moniker "Montana's Cowboy Capital."

Founded in 1877 near old Fort Keogh at the confluence of the Tongue and Yellowstone rivers, and named (as so many Montana towns were) for an army officer, Miles City became headquarters for the Montana Stockgrowers' Association within three years after the arrival of the Northern Pacific Railroad in 1881. It remains a major ranching and farming center.

Fort Keogh (Main Street West; 406-232-4970), once the largest army post in Montana, opened in 1877 following the Little Bighorn uprising and remained of major importance through 1908, when it closed. Several of its original buildings have been incorporated into the Livestock and Range Research Station at Fort Keogh, an applied agricultural science facility two miles from downtown that focuses on genetics, reproduction and nutrition of beef cattle. Tours are offered weekdays by appointment.

A miniature replica of old Fort Keogh is displayed at the **Range Riders Museum** (Main Street West; 406-232-6146; admission), an impressive nine-building complex whose collection also includes a re-creation of the main street of 19th-century Miles City, the Charles M. Russell Art Gallery and a Memorial Hall with hundreds of portraits and plaques remembering pioneer Custer County residents. There's also the Heritage Center, with early photography and Native American artifacts; a one-room school and log house; and displays of manifold antique vehicles, guns and hats. Open April to October or by appointment.

The Custer County Art Center (Water Plant Road; 406-232-0635), downriver from the Range Riders Museum where the Tongue enters the Yellowstone, may be the world's only gallery housed in historic water-storage tanks. It features a permanent collection of western art, changing exhibitions of local and regional works, and a gift shop with a wide range of art and books.

Miles City, by the way, got rid of parking meters years ago. It's a lot more fun to browse the quaint downtown historic district without them. Besides, quarters are essential to poker machines —and like every Montana town, Miles City has its quotient of casinos.

Terry, equidistant from Miles City and Glendive, boasts the dubious distinction of having "the tallest sign in eastern Montana" at a beside-the-interstate convenience store. Certainly more important, it was the home of British photographer Lady Evelyn Cameron, who moved to Terry in 1894 with her naturalist husband and her 5 x 7 Graflex camera and recorded the lifestyle of eastern Montana homesteaders for the next 34 years. When a Time-Life editor discovered a stash of thousands of Cameron's photos in the basement of a private home, her previously unknown work quickly rocketed to fame. The new Cameron Gallery in the **Prairie County Museum** (★) (Terry; 406-637-5782) has an extensive collection of her work.

A few miles northwest of town via Scenic View Road are the **Terry Badlands** (406-232-7000), a 44,000-acre Bureau of Land Management tract containing sandstone spires, buttes, natural bridges and other colorful geological phenomena. There's a scenic overlook, wildlife watching and hiking trails.

But badlands lovers will be yet more impressed by the pine-and-juniper-studded terrain at **Makoshika State Park** (Makoshika Park Road, Glendive; 406-365-6256; admission), located southeast of Glendive, 78 miles northeast of Miles City. In Sioux, *makoshika* means "bad earth"; but to paleontologists, this rippled earth has been very good, yielding the complete fossil remains of such great dinosaurs as triceratops and tyrannosaurus. A new visitors center opened in 1994 at the 8123-acre park.

Anglers call **Glendive** "the paddlefishing capital of the world." Found only in the Yellowstone and Missouri rivers and in China's Yangtze River, paddlefish are prehistoric bottom feeders with two-foot-long, paddle-shaped snouts. See the fishing section in "The Sporting Life" at the end of this chapter.

Route 90 turns away from the Yellowstone River at Glendive and makes a beeline for the North Dakota border. Eight miles from the frontier is the small community of **Wibaux**, founded in 1889 by French-born cattle baron Pierre Wibaux. The town office building he constructed in 1892 has been restored and is now the **Pierre Wibaux House Museum** (Orgain and Wibaux streets; 406-795-2427). Besides memorabilia of the cattleman himself, it includes a wide variety of turn-of-the-century pioneer items, Native American artifacts and a classic car display. Open May to September. A state travel information center is across Orgain Street.

A twice-life-size statue of Pierre Wibaux stands atop a hill at the west end of Orgain Street, overlooking **St. Peter's Catholic Church**, which Wibaux built in 1885 with money donated by his father in France. The church has beautiful stained-glass windows and a lava-rock exterior that is covered in summer by climbing vines.

Baker is 45 miles south of Wibaux via Route 7. This pleasant town of 1800 sits at the crossroads of Route 12, 80 miles east of Miles City. Baker Lake, surrounded by parks and recreational facilities, is right in town. Baker also boasts the **O'Fallon Historical Museum** (1st Street West and Fallon Avenue; 406-778-3265), which displays the "world's largest steer"—almost six feet high and just under two tons in weight—and a variety of vintage clothing and homestead-era items.

Thirty miles west of Baker and five miles north of Route 12 via Ismay Road is a hamlet that wouldn't attract interest had it not changed its name in 1993. **Joe** (formerly Ismay), Montana, now goes by the same name as star professional football quarterback Joe Montana. The community of 22 people said it wanted to raise a couple of thousand dollars to cover the annual operating costs of its volunteer fire department, but within a year the promotion had earned nearly $70,000. So the entire population traveled to Kansas City to watch their namesake play for the Chiefs—and to have their photo taken together, of course. Montana (the quarterback) retired in 1995, but you can still buy caps, T-shirts and other souvenirs by calling 1-800-HELP JOE.

Medicine Rocks State Park (Route 7, Ekalaka; 406-232-4365), 25 miles south of Baker, commemorates a place of unusual sandstone rock formations that Sioux hunting parties once visited to conjure sacred spirits and other "big medicine." Wind and water erosion have created a Swiss-cheese landscape where many species of wildlife find a haven.

LOWER YELLOWSTONE VALLEY HOTELS

The Buckboard Inn (1006 Haynes Avenue, Miles City; 406-232-3550, 800-525-6303), in the heart of the Yellowstone valley, is a likely stop for travelers headed east on Route 94. The motel's 58 cozy ground-floor guest rooms, spread ranch-style around an outdoor swimming pool, have queen-size beds, and there's always coffee and doughnuts in the lobby. Budget.

Approaching the Dakotas, the three-story **Jordon Motor Inn** (223 North Merrill Avenue, Glendive; 406-365-3371) is an upscale property that offers respite from summer heat in an indoor swimming pool and warm haven from winter's chill in a sauna. All rooms have combination baths; there's also a dining room, separate coffee shop and full lounge. Low moderate.

LOWER YELLOWSTONE VALLEY RESTAURANTS

A popular local hangout on the eastern plains for more than a century has been Miles City's **Hole in the Wall** (602 Main Street; 406-232-9887). An Old West atmosphere still pervades this steak-and-seafood house; prime rib is a house specialty while a salad bar is a concession to changing tastes. Moderate.

LOWER YELLOWSTONE VALLEY NIGHTLIFE

If you're traveling east across the prairies, you won't want to miss Miles City's venerable **Montana Bar** (612 Main Street; 406-232-5809). First opened in 1902, it has a classic back bar with beveled leaded glass. Locals will urge you to drink Milestown Draught, brewed just down the street.

LOWER YELLOWSTONE VALLEY PARKS

Makoshika State Park—Skeletons of the greatest dinosaurs to walk the earth have been discovered amid the deep, barren gullies of these badlands, a few miles southeast of Glendive near the North Dakota border. Grotesquely eroded limestone and sandstone columns are other geological features.

Facilities: Picnic tables, restrooms, visitors center, trails, shooting and archery ranges; day-use fee, $3; information, 406-232-4365.

Camping: There are 16 RV/tent sites (no hookups); $7 to $8 per night.

Getting there: From Glendive, travel southeast on Snyder Avenue to Makoshika Park Road.

Great Falls Area

Great Falls is Montana's heartland. Not a "mountain town," not a "cowboy town," the state's second-largest city is near enough to the Rocky Mountain crest to be a recreational gateway, near enough to eastern Montana's semiarid ranch country to be an agricultural center. It's a place in between, straddling history as it does the Missouri River, mindful of its roots as a 19th-century trade hub but also a thoroughly modern center of national air defense and a hydroelectric power industry.

Great Falls is best known, in fact, as "The Electric City." The series of dams on the Missouri just below the community provide power to a huge area, and the river's water supports a thriving wheat and barley industry in the rolling hills north of here.

When explorers Lewis and Clark first ventured into this stretch of the Missouri in 1805, they discovered a different river from the one visitors see today. Over a ten-mile stretch there were five cataracts, which they called the "Great Falls of the Missouri": "A sublimely grand specticle," Lewis wrote in his journal. He quickly noted that "the river was one continued sene of rappids and cascades which I readily perceive could not be encountered with our canoes." The party was forced to portage their equipment around the falls; the 18-mile ordeal took 15 days to complete.

Today, as a result of five hydro projects, the falls are not the spectacles that Lewis observed. The feature usually called the Great Falls—the farthest downstream (ten miles from downtown) and, at 80 feet, the largest of the five falls—is now controlled by Ryan Dam, built in 1915. **Broadwater Overlook Park** (10th Avenue South and 2nd Street; 406-761-4434) features a heroic bronze sculpture by Montana artist Bob Scriver that commemorates the portage and has a visitors center with interpretive displays.

Undoubtedly the best place to experience the river locally is **Giant Springs/ Heritage State Park** (4600 Giant Springs Road; 406-454-3441), three miles east of the city off River Drive. "The largest fountain I ever saw" is how Lewis described the springs, which bubble from the earth at a rate of nearly eight million gallons per hour and flow 201 feet to the Missouri. (The spring is one of the world's largest; the *Guinness Book of World Records* lists the outflow, named the Roe River, as the world's shortest river.)

Great Falls was also the home of C. M. Russell (1864–1926), the nation's most acclaimed frontier artist. (See "Charles M. Russell: The Cowboy Artist" in this chapter.) The **Charles M. Russell Museum Complex** (400 13th Street North; 406-727-8787; admission) includes his home, his original log-cabin studio and an outstanding art museum. The world's most extensive collection of Russell's original works is here: oils, watercolors, pen-and-ink sketches, metal and wood sculptures, even some accompanying poetry. All of it focuses on the cowboys, Native Americans and wildlife of the northern prairies and Rocky Mountain slopes. Also displayed are works by Russell's contemporaries and other artists of the American West, as well as the John Browning Firearms Collection. There is an excellent gift shop.

Another center for the arts is **Paris Gibson Square** (1400 1st Avenue North; 406-727-8255), an imposing stone building constructed in 1895. Its galleries include the Center for Contemporary Arts, a fine-art shop and a café. And the **Montana Cowboys Association Museum** (311 3rd Street Northwest; 406-761-9299) has a log-cabin display of Old West memorabilia at the fairgrounds.

West of the Russell Museum and Paris Gibson Square is Great Falls' most architecturally interesting neighborhood, the **Northside Residential Historic District**, dating from 1885. Thirty-nine homes on 3rd and 4th Avenues North, between Park Drive and 10th Street, are described in a one-hour walking tour that begins at the **Cascade County Historical Archives** (301 2nd Avenue North; 406-452-3462).

Ulm Pishkun State Park (Ulm-Vaughn Road at Goetz Road; 406-454-3441; admission) represents some violent history of the ancient world. Thousands of years ago, Native Americans drove herds of bison up this mile-long *pishkun*, or buffalo jump, from which the beasts plunged to their deaths. Arrowheads, knives, hammers, hide scrapers and other tools have been discovered at this site, believed to be the largest of its kind in the United States. To reach it, take Route 15 south ten miles from Great Falls to Ulm (Exit 270); then follow signs four miles north.

THE ROCKY MOUNTAIN FRONT Route 89 north, connecting Great Falls with Glacier National Park's eastern portals, draws ever closer to the dramatic Rocky Mountain Front, where the range's craggy peaks drop suddenly to the prairies, unbuffered by the waves of lower mountains found to the west.

The largest town in these environs is **Choteau**, a center for outdoor recreation and dinosaur digging, with a population of about 1800. Choteau (pronounced "SHO-toe") is the gateway to the nation's best-known wilderness area, several wildlife refuges and a paleontological reserve.

Displays of fossils and artifacts in the town's **Old Trail Museum** (Route 89; 406-466-5332; admission) interpret some of these regional attractions. Attached to the museum, located at the north edge of town, is a block of frontier-style craft shops, as well as an ice-cream parlor and the log-cabin studio of artist Jesse Gleason.

Several roads head west from Choteau into **Lewis and Clark National Forest** and the fringe of the **Bob Marshall Wilderness** (406-466-5341). "The Bob," as it is known to wilderness lovers, preserves more than a million acres of rugged mountains, rivers and lakes. Neither motorized vehicles nor bicycles are permitted in this land of grizzly bears and mountain lions.

At the foot of the Rocky Mountain Front, the Teton River flows through a wetland that is a spring feeding ground for grizzlies and home to the largest population of bighorn sheep in the United States. The Nature Conservancy purchased and set aside 18,000 acres as the **Pine Butte Swamp Preserve** (Bellview Road; 406-466-5526), 17 miles west of Choteau, to protect the flora and fauna of this unique region. Tours from the interpretive center here are offered by appointment only.

The conservancy also owns the adjoining **Egg Mountain** (★) fossil field (Bellview Road; 406-994-6618). This site on the Willow Creek Anticline, 12 miles west of Choteau, is where the first dinosaur eggs (42 of them, in 14 nests) were discovered in North America. Beginning the last week of June and running through the third week of August, one-hour guided tours of the site are offered daily.

There are federal wildlife management areas near Choteau at Pishkun Reservoir, Willow Creek Reservoir, Ear Mountain, Sun River, Blackleaf Creek and elsewhere. The most accessible—because the highway to Great Falls runs right through its heart—is the **Freezout Lake Wildlife Management Area** (Route 89,

Fairfield; 406-454-3441). A birdwatcher's checklist of 187 species spotted here is available from reserve headquarters.

FORT BENTON Historic **Fort Benton**, 42 miles northeast of Great Falls via Route 87, has been called "the birthplace of Montana." Established as a Missouri River trading post for buffalo robes by the American Fur Company in 1846, it was named for Missouri senator Thomas Hart Benton. Its importance mushroomed in 1860, when steamboats began docking here after journeying from St. Louis or New Orleans; no port in the world was farther (3485 miles) from an ocean.

For the next 27 years, until the Northern Pacific Railroad arrived in 1887, effectively ending river trade, Fort Benton was the most important city in Montana. The **Riverfront Steamboat Levee** (Front Street between 14th and 18th streets; 406-622-5494), now a national historic landmark, became the rowdiest four blocks in the West after gold was discovered in the nearby hills in 1862. Saloons and brothels were open 24 hours a day, and gunfights were more common than royal flushes. Many of the buildings facing the levee date from the steamboat era, including the Grand Union Hotel, Stockman's National Bank, the mercantile T. C. Power & Co. and the city's first firehouse.

The only building still standing on the site of **Old Fort Benton** (Old Fort Park, Front Street) is an adobe blockhouse, believed to be the oldest standing building in Montana. Interpretive signs describe the layout of the rest of the fort, some ruins of which remain. Artifacts from the fort and the town's heyday are on display next to the fort in the **Museum of the Upper Missouri** (Front and 19th streets; 406-622-5494; admission), open summers only. About four blocks north, the **Museum of the Northern Great Plains** (1205 20th Street; 406-622-5316; admission) is Montana's state agricultural museum, with exhibits that trace a century of farm history as well as a veritable outdoor park of antique machinery. It's open summers only.

Fort Benton's position on the Missouri River has not been forgotten in modern times: It is the departure point for commercial boat tours and float trips down the **Upper Missouri National Wild and Scenic River**. Contact the Bureau of Land Management (P.O. Box 1160, Lewistown, MT 59457; 406-538-7461) for information.

From Fort Benton to the James Kipp Recreation Area northeast of Lewistown, the broad, slow-flowing Missouri winds through the scenic White Cliffs, Citadel Rock State Monument, Hole-in-the-Wall and other geological curiosities, offering sightings of abandoned homesteads and a great deal of wildlife. The **Upper Missouri River Visitors Center** (1718 Front Street, Fort Benton; 406-622-5185), open daily in summer, has full information for prospective river travelers.

There's a shuttle service for floaters and canoeists about 30 miles northeast of Fort Benton at Virgelle. After Virgelle, the Missouri turns east while Route 87 proceeds north.

GREAT FALLS AREA HOTELS

The four-story **Great Falls Inn** (1400 28th Street South; 406-453-6000) only opened in February 1994, but it has already convinced many that it can deliver quality for price. Its 45 spacious rooms have queen-size beds and wood furnishings; 16 are equipped with refrigerators and microwaves. A continental breakfast comes with the room price. There's a laundry on the third floor and a fireplace in the lobby. Budget.

Downtown, **The Rainbow Hotel** (20 3rd Street North; 406-727-8200) is one of Great Falls' older properties and one of the city's most elegant. Its 91 nicely restored rooms may not be fancy, but they're clean and comfortable, with private baths, and are just upstairs from a restaurant and lounge. The historic hotel is one and a half blocks from the Civic Center. Moderate.

The **Best Western Heritage Inn** (1700 Fox Farm Road; 406-761-1900, 800-548-0361, fax 406-761-0136) is at the head of the class in Great Falls. Its central atrium/courtyard, designed in a loose French Quarter style, has an indoor swimming pool, hot tubs, saunas, a video arcade and a sidewalk café. The two-story motor inn—near the south freeway entrance to Great Falls—has 240 spacious and modern rooms with queen beds and desks. Moderate.

One especially good guest ranch, not far from the Bob Marshall Wilderness, is the **Seven Lazy P Ranch** (Canyon Road, Choteau; 406-466-2044). Located 30 miles west of Choteau on the North Fork of the Teton River, it focuses on horse pack trips into The Bob and seasonal fishing and hunting. Guests stay in six rustic cabins, five with private baths; most socializing is around the large stone fireplace in the main lodge. Meals are hearty and ranch-style. Three-day minimum stay, American plan. Moderate.

GREAT FALLS AREA RESTAURANTS

At **Mama Cassie's Italian Ristorante** (319 1st Avenue North, Great Falls; 406-454-3354), the emphasis is on pasta. But Mama also dishes out generous portions of chicken cacciatore, Italian submarines and New York cheesecake. This is a homey sort of place open for three meals a day. Budget.

For Mexican food, **El Comedor** (1120 25th Street South, Great Falls; 406-761-5500) is a pleasant, off-the-main-drag establishment operated by a family from south of the border. There's nothing too gourmet here—you'll get the standard enchiladas, burritos and tostadas amid a decor of sombreros, serapes and piñatas—but it works when you're in the mood for something spicy. Budget.

Eddie's Supper Club (3725 2nd Avenue North, Great Falls; 406-453-1616) is a long-established local favorite. Eddie's pioneered the "campfire" steak; some argue that it's the best steak in Montana. Three meals a day are served in the coffee shop, furnished with formica-topped tables, and the low-lit, vinyl-upholstered dining room. Budget to moderate.

The **Broker Restaurant & Lounge** (Rainbow Hotel, 20 3rd Street North, Great Falls; 406-727-8200) is perhaps the finest the city has to offer. Subdued lighting and a historic downtown atmosphere lend it a feeling of casual elegance. The menu features steaks, poultry and seafood. Moderate.

Whole families enjoy **Borrie's** (★) (1800 Smelter Avenue, Black Eagle; 406-761-0300), on the north side of the Missouri River opposite downtown Great Falls. Established in 1939, the hard-to-find restaurant serves up traditional

Italian (lasagna, ravioli, spaghetti) and American (steaks, seafood, chicken) fare with an ebullient ambience. Dinner nightly. Moderate.

GREAT FALLS AREA SHOPPING

Perhaps the best place to claim memories of Great Falls is the shop at the **Charles M. Russell Museum Complex** (400 13th Street North; 406-727-8787). The museum shop specializes in reproductions of western art but has a good selection of books and various quality souvenirs.

For Montana-made merchandise, visit **Fantastik Baskets** (2110 10th Avenue South; 406-727-9760). Its wares include pottery and other crafts, food baskets and elk- and buffalo-hide accessories.

Great Falls' Farmers Market takes place throughout the summer, 5 to 6:30 p.m. Wednesdays and 8 a.m. to noon Saturdays. Fruit, vegetables, baked goods and craft items are sold at **Whittier Park** on the south side of the Civic Center (Central Avenue and 1st Street).

GREAT FALLS AREA NIGHTLIFE

As befits a city of 55,000, Great Falls has an active music scene. It's headed by the **Great Falls Symphony** (Civic Center; 406-453-4102), which plays an October-to-May classical season and a late-June pops concert at the Gibson Park bandshell (Park Drive). Between October and April, the **Great Falls Community Concert Series** (Civic Center; 406-453-9854) stages six musical events with guest artists.

For drinks and dancing, **Philly's** (400 10th Avenue South; 406-727-7200), in the Holiday Inn Great Falls, has as many regulars as any lounge in town. **Club Cigar** (208 Central Avenue; 406-727-8011) wins kudos for its historic downtown atmosphere, while **The Max** (1700 Fox Farm Road; 406-761-1900), in the Best Western Heritage Inn, is clearly Great Falls' number-one casino.

GREAT FALLS AREA PARKS

Lewis and Clark National Forest—The eastern edge of the Rocky Mountain Front, below the Bob Marshall Wilderness, and a handful of small mountain ranges southeast of Great Falls—the Little Belt, Big Snowy, Highwood and Castle mountains—are encompassed by this national forest.

Facilities: Picnic tables, restrooms, boat ramps, trails, two ski areas; information, 406-791-7700. *Swimming:* Gibson Reservoir, few other places. *Fishing:* Brook, brown and rainbow trout (the Teton River also has cutthroat); mountain whitefish; burbot (in the Smith River).

Camping: There are 241 RV/tent sites (no hookups) plus 29 for tents only at 15 campgrounds; no charge to $6 per night.

Getting there: Reach the Rocky Mountain Front section of the forest via various secondary roads that lead west off Routes 89 and 287 from Choteau and

Charles M. Russell: The Cowboy Artist

Perhaps no artist more exemplified the American West than Charles Marion Russell, a hard-drinking, tough-talking, whimsical whisper of a man who learned to punch cows and ride with the Indians, but who attracted a circle of friends that included presidents and movie stars.

Born in St. Louis, Missouri, in 1864, Russell was never cut out for his parents' high-society lifestyle. When Charles was 16, his father shipped him off to Montana to what was hoped would be a "school of hard knocks" for the rebellious youth . . . but the lad thrived on it.

Initially a failure as a sheepherder, Russell was befriended by a mountain man, Jake Hoover, who taught him how to survive in the Wild West. The pair shared a tiny sod-roofed cabin in the Little Belt Mountains until Russell got a job as a night wrangler at a cattle ranch. That left his days open to paint, draw and sculpt.

One of the reasons that Russell's works stand out from those of other western artists is that he lived what he put on canvas. Even though his vivid depictions of the West began to earn him a profit, he continued to wrangle cattle for another decade. He also spent a full winter with the Blackfeet, learning their spoken language as well as a sign language that any Plains Indian tribe could understand.

Eventually, Russell found it expedient for his artistic career to move from the prairie. He relocated to Great Falls in 1897, married, and three years later built a home in a fashionable neighborhood near downtown. In 1903, he constructed a separate log studio—"a cabin just like I used to live in," he said.

For the rest of his life, until his death in 1926, this was Russell's sanctuary, a place where he surrounded himself with his personal collections of cowboy and Native American lifestyles, and where he produced every last work he painted or sculpted. Both the house and the studio are now a part of the C. M. Russell Museum Complex, donated by Russell's widow, Nancy, to the city of Great Falls.

Russell's works—more than 4500 oils and watercolors, pen-and-ink drawings, clay and wax sculptures and illustrated letters (he was a renowned storyteller)—symbolize the adventure and the freedom of the West as he knew and loved it. For many easterners, the work of "America's Cowboy Artist" was their principal link to the romance of the Old West.

Russell was a lifelong defender of the pre-20th-century West, and he decried the rapid changes he saw during his lifetime.

"I liked it better when it belonged to God," he said.

Augusta. Route 89 (Kings Hill Scenic Byway) also cuts through the Little Belt Mountains between Great Falls and White Sulphur Springs.

Bob Marshall Wilderness Area—The second-largest wilderness in the lower 48 states, The Bob and its adjoining preserves (the Great Bear and Scapegoat wilderness areas) occupy more than one and a half million very wild, rugged and mountainous acres on the Continental Divide. Some 1800 miles of trails crisscross the region.

Facilities: Trails; information, 406-791-7700. *Fishing:* Mountain whitefish; brook, cutthroat and rainbow trout; bull trout in alpine lakes.

Camping: Primitive only.

Getting there: From the east, main access to The Bob is via Canyon Road (off Route 89 near Choteau), which follows the Teton River nearly to its headwaters; Sun River Road (off Route 287 in Augusta), which ends at Gibson Reservoir; and Augusta Ranger Station Road (also from Augusta), which extends up Wood Creek. There are major trailheads at the terminus of each. You can also approach the wilderness from the west (off Route 83) or from the north (at Spotted Bear Ranger Station southeast of Hungry Horse).

The Hi-Line

Route 2, running east about 400 miles along the Canadian border from the Blackfeet Indian Reservation to Williston, North Dakota, and paralleled by the Great Northern Railway line, is known to Montanans as "the Hi-Line." Cattle ranching and grain production, notably wheat, sustain the economy of this northernmost tier of the state, which extends more than one-eighth of the way across the United States. The Missouri River draws most of the region's southern boundary.

At the eastern edge of the Blackfeet Reservation, still within the shadow of the high peaks of Glacier National Park, is **Cut Bank**, a major grain-storage center that marks the western corner of Montana's Golden Triangle. This region, which stretches from Great Falls (100 miles southeast of Cut Bank) to Canada, from the Rocky Mountain Front to the Missouri River, is literally one of the breadbaskets of the nation. Farms between Havre and Cut Bank produce more than half of the wheat and barley grown in Montana, one of the top five states in those commodities.

Routes 2 and 15 intersect at the grain and railroad town of **Shelby**, 23 miles east of Cut Bank. **Shelby's Marias Museum of History and Art** (206 12th Avenue; 406-434-2551) recalls such snippets of past glory as the 1923 world heavyweight championship fight here between Jack Dempsey and Tommy Gibbons. In all, the ten-room museum displays 10,000 items, including several recreated early-20th-century rooms.

Shelby is just 35 miles south (via Route 15) of the Canadian border at Sweetgrass, the busiest international port of entry between Blaine, Washington (connecting Seattle and Vancouver) and Pembina, North Dakota (connecting

Minneapolis and Winnipeg). Between Shelby and the border, the Kevin-Sunburst Oil Field is Montana's largest: It has pumped some 80 million barrels of oil since its discovery in 1922.

Havre, with 10,200 people the largest town on the Hi-Line (and the home of Montana State University–Northern), benefits economically from both the 100 miles of grain fields to its west and the 300 miles of ranch country to its east. The city hopes to attract history buffs with **Havre Beneath the Streets** (★) (100 3rd Avenue; 406-265-8888; admission), a four-year project (completed in 1994) that restored long-dormant tunnels and underground corridors beneath the community. Developed around 1900 in the early days of the Great Northern Railway and last put to serious use by Prohibition-era bootleggers, they now welcome visitors. Public tours include a saloon, drugstore, meat market, bakery, barber shop, laundry, tack shop, hardware store and even a brothel and Chinese opium den.

Havre got its start in 1879 when **Fort Assiniboine** (Route 87, six miles southwest of the current town site) was constructed; it was then the largest military fort west of the Mississippi River. Guided tours are offered through the **H. Earl Clack Memorial Museum** (Route 2 at the Hill County Fairgrounds; 406-265-9913; admission). Open daily in summer, it features archaeological and area history displays. The museum also organizes one-hour guided tours of the **Wahkpa Chug'n** archaeology site (behind Holiday Village Shopping Center, Route 2 West; 406-265-6417), a prehistoric campsite and bison kill ground on the banks of the Milk River, believed to have been used as long as 2000 years ago.

Twenty miles south of Havre is the **Rocky Boy's Indian Reservation** (Box Elder; 406-395-4282). Located in the foothills of the Bears Paw Mountains, the reservation is home to about 2500 Chippewas and Crees.

Though the Route 2 corridor that follows the Milk River east from Havre (for 175 miles, to its confluence with the Missouri at Fort Peck) may be bleak to the undiscerning eye, there are plenty of interesting sights along the route or a short detour away.

The small farming town of **Chinook**, 21 miles from Havre, was named not for salmon but for the warm winter winds that can raise temperatures from 0° to 50°F in a matter of minutes. Sixteen miles south is the **Bear's Paw Battleground** (Route 240; 406-357-2590), the northeasternmost of 38 Nez Perce National Historical Park sites and one of three units in Montana. This is where Chief Joseph and his band of renegade Nez Perce surrendered to U.S. government forces on October 5, 1877, and where Joseph is said to have uttered his famous words: "From where the sun now stands, I will fight no more, forever."

Route 2 enters the **Fort Belknap Indian Reservation** at Harlem, about 42 miles from Havre. About 2800 Assiniboine and Gros Ventre tribespeople live on the 700,000-acre reservation. Tours focus on the historic Hays district; arrangements can be made through the **Fort Belknap Tourism Office and Information Center** (Route 2, Harlem; 406-353-2205).

The tiny town of **Saco**, almost midway from Havre to the Dakota border, is an unlikely place for a nationally acclaimed broadcast journalist to have begun his childhood education, but it is indeed where late newsman Chet Huntley learned his ABCs (or was that NBCs?) in the early 20th century. In fact, the one-room **Huntley School** has been restored and is open for visits. Inquire locally.

Glasgow was once best known for its U.S. Air Force base. Today there are only memories. Many of them are displayed in the **Valley County Pioneer Museum** (Klein Road; 406-228-8692), along with a wildlife collection, fossils, Native American artifacts and items from railroad and engineering history.

Engineering is, indeed, important to the area: **Fort Peck Dam** (Route 24; 406-526-3411), on the Missouri River, is just 18 miles south of Glasgow. **Fort Peck Museum** (Powerhouse 1) interprets for visitors the dam's hydroelectric, irrigation and flood-control functions and offers exhibits on geology and paleontology.

Fort Peck Lake—the reservoir created by the dam—is 134 miles long with 1520 miles of shoreline. Thirteen recreation areas with boat launch sites and campgrounds surround its shores; the vast majority of adjacent land belongs to the **Charles M. Russell National Wildlife Refuge** (headquarters in Lewistown; 406-538-8706). Hundreds of species of birds as well as elk, deer, pronghorn antelope and smaller animals make their homes in this million-acre preserve of wetlands, prairies and badlands (see "Heartland Parks," below). Within the Russell refuge is another, more primitive reserve: the **UL Bend National Wildlife Refuge** (406-538-8706), located on a prairie peninsula about 75 miles west of the dam. Elk needn't migrate from this native prairie; it supports them year-round.

Fort Peck is still a good two-hour drive (in the best of conditions) from North Dakota. This northeasternmost region of Montana is dominated by the two-million-acre (550-square-mile) **Fort Peck Indian Reservation**, home to 10,700 mainly Assiniboine and Sioux tribespeople. Tribal headquarters are in Poplar, 21 miles east of Wolf Point. Its **Fort Peck Assiniboine and Sioux Culture Center and Museum** (Route 2 East; 406-768-5155) has permanent exhibits of arts and crafts.

Resting almost exactly on the Montana–North Dakota border, 13 miles southeast of Bainville, is the **Fort Union Trading Post National Historic Site** (Route 327, Bainville-Snowden Road; 701-572-9083; admission). The Missouri River's principal fur-trading post from the 1830s until the Civil War has been restored to depict that era of America's westward expansion. A visitors center is open daily, and there are picnic tables and hiking trails.

HI-LINE HOTELS

How could you go wrong with a motel that lists its location as "next to a 27-foot-tall Talking Penguin"? That Chilly Willy–looking fellow standing outside **Glacier Gateway Inn** (1121 East Railroad Street, Cut Bank; 406-873-5544) trumpets the town's distinction as the "coldest spot in the nation," which it has been on occasion. The motel is not so ostentatious; its 18 rooms have queen-size beds and air-conditioning (the latter presumedly for summers). There's also an exercise room. Breakfasts are complimentary. Budget.

TownHouse Inns of Havre (629½ West 1st Street, Havre; 406-265-2728) boasts the most full-service accommodation on Montana's northern plains. A modern café overlooks an atrium swimming pool and spa; there's also a fitness room and sauna. The casino claims to be "Havre's most liberal." Wood furnishings are a nice touch in the otherwise-ordinary rooms. Moderate.

On the Fort Peck Indian Reservation, less than an hour's drive east of Fort Peck Dam and Lake, the **Sherman Motor Inn** (200 East Main Street, Wolf Point; 406-653-1100, fax 406-653-3456) is a clean and comfortable three-story property. Its 46 ample rooms have queen-size beds and desks; there's also a lounge and a restaurant open for three meals daily. Budget.

HI-LINE RESTAURANTS

Boxcars (619 1st Street, Havre; 406-265-2233) appeals to the northern palate with its menu of barbecued ribs, fried chicken and the like. The restaurant, done up in the decor of an old railroad station, also serves a hearty Sunday buffet. A lounge and casino adjoin. Budget.

Sam's Supper Club (307 Klein Road, Glasgow; 406-228-4614) specializes in charbroiled steaks from the surrounding cattle country and filets of walleye pike from nearby Fort Peck Lake. The low-lit restaurant, just off Route 2, also makes its own ice cream and other desserts. Lunch is served Monday to Friday, dinner Tuesday to Saturday. Low moderate.

HI-LINE NIGHTLIFE

The back bar at the **Palace Bar** (228 1st Street, Havre; 406-265-7584) was built in St. Louis in 1883 and carried up the Missouri River on a steamboat. Towering and ornate, it is worth a visit just to see it.

The most prominent stage association between the Rocky Mountain Front and the border of the Dakotas is the **Fort Peck Theatre Company** (Missouri Avenue, Fort Peck; 406-228-9219). The summer repertory presents musicals and dramas every weekend of summer at its historic theater near the eastern Montana dam.

HI-LINE PARKS

Beaver Creek County Park—Extending for 16 miles along Beaver Creek Road south of Havre, this is the nation's largest county park, covering approximately 10,000 acres. There's fishing in two lakes and many fine scenic views.

Facilities: Picnic tables, restrooms, trails; information, 406-395-4565. *Swimming:* Designated beach. *Fishing:* Various trout species.

Camping: There are 100 RV/tent sites (no hookups) plus eight for tents only; no charge.

Getting there: Take Route 234 (Beaver Creek Road) south from Havre toward Rocky Boy's Indian Reservation.

The Heartland

Route 200 spans Montana's "Heartland," the state's geographical center, more or less paralleling the Hi-Line. Running east from Great Falls between 50 and 110 miles south of Route 2, it crosses the Judith Basin to Lewistown, the region's largest town; drops to the Musselshell River valley; then races through a couple of hundred miles of "great wide open" before hitting another town with a population of more than a thousand: Sidney, on the Yellowstone River at the North Dakota border.

Many of the small towns en route—including Belt, Stanford, Windham, Utica, Circle and Richey—have their local historical museums, but few are worth a stop for any but the most diehard regional-history lovers. An exception is **Mehmke's Steam Engine Museum** (Route 87/89/200, Fife; 406-452-6571). Located just ten miles east of Great Falls, this is the world's largest privately owned collection of steam engines, all of them still operational. It's a mechanic's dream . . . or nightmare.

Near Belt, 23 miles from Great Falls, Route 89—the **Kings Hill National Scenic Byway** (406-547-3361)—turns south off Route 200, crossing the Little Belt Mountains to White Sulphur Springs. This 71-mile Lewis and Clark National Forest highway follows Belt Creek past **Sluice Boxes State Park** (Evans-Riceville Road, Belt; 406-454-3441), located at an abandoned railroad grade; through the historic mining and ranching communities of Neihart and Monarch; to 7393-foot Kings Hill Pass, on the south side of which is the **Showdown Ski Area** (Route 89, Neihart; 406-236-5522), Montana's oldest.

Lewistown, whose 6000 people live in the exact center of Montana, 105 miles east of Great Falls, is a ranching and wheat-farming center. The town is rich in late-19th-century pioneer history: Its downtown, Courthouse Square and Silk Stocking District are listed on the National Register of Historic Places. Self-guided tour brochures can be obtained at the **Central Montana Museum** (408 East Main Street; 406-538-5436), which chronicles the area.

Perhaps most interesting to visitors, Lewistown is the headquarters of the **Charles M. Russell National Wildlife Refuge** (Airport Road; 406-538-8706). The million-acre refuge, which surrounds Fort Peck Lake, supports a rich variety of wildlife and such recreational activities as camping, boating and fishing. The primary access point is at the **James Kipp Recreation Area** (Route 191; 406-538-7461), 65 miles northeast of Lewistown; the site is also the takeout point for boat tours and floats of the Upper Missouri National Wild and Scenic River from Fort Benton.

For a scenic backcountry driving tour of a small portion of the Russell wildlife refuge, depart east from Route 191 on the north side of the river from James Kipp Recreation Area. About ten miles south of the recreation area, Knox Coulee Road leads west to the **Missouri Breaks National Back Country Byway** (call the Bureau of Land Management at 406-538-7461 for information), a 73-mile loop through badlands along the edge of the refuge to Winifred, a near ghost town on Route 236, 37 miles north of Lewistown.

East from Lewistown on Route 200, it's 130 miles to **Jordan**, once called "the lonesomest town in the world" by a New York radio station. Another 26 miles north is the lone state park on Fort Peck Lake: **Hell Creek State Recreation Area** (Hell Creek Road; 406-232-4365; fee). Despite its isolation, this is a popular area, especially for boaters. It has a marina and offers camping and motel lodging.

HEARTLAND HOTELS

The Heartland's finest lodging is the **Park Inn International** (211 East Main Street, Lewistown; 406-538-8721, 800-437-7275, fax 406-538-8969). Occupying most of a city block in the downtown hub, the two-story inn has 124 guest rooms, their spaciousness accented by high ceilings. Facilities include indoor and outdoor swimming pools, a whirlpool, a dining room, a coffee shop and a lounge. Moderate.

A stone's throw from North Dakota, the two-story **Richland Motor Inn** (1200 South Central Street, Sidney; 406-482-6400, fax 406-482-4743) has comfortable rooms, all with standard motel furnishings. There's a game room for the kids, and a continental breakfast is included in the budget rate.

HEARTLAND RESTAURANTS

You can take the whole family to **Whole Fandamily** (206½ West Main Street, Lewistown; 406-538-5161) for healthy home cooking. Soup, giant sandwiches and "international" dinner specials are presented in a home-style atmosphere. Don't miss the rich desserts. Budget.

Eastern Montana ranchers may not be anxious to ride out to their own south 40 (acres), but they'll make a beeline for Sidney's **South 40** (207 2nd Avenue Northwest; 406-482-4999). Huge cuts of prime rib are served, along with hearty homemade soups and a salad bar. Moderate.

HEARTLAND SHOPPING

Take a look at the **Lewistown Art Center** (801 8th Avenue North; 406-538-8278) for work by regional artisans.

HEARTLAND NIGHTLIFE

Bar Nineteen (Fairgrounds Road, Lewiston; 406-538-3250), combines a steak house with the dancingest country-and-western bar for 100 miles in any direction.

HEARTLAND PARKS

Ackley Lake State Park—Named for an early settler, this lake, at the northern foot of the Little Belt Mountains, is one of the most popular destinations for Heartland water-sports lovers.

Facilities: Picnic tables, restrooms, boat ramps; information, 406-454-3441. *Swimming:* Designated beach. *Fishing:* Rainbow trout.

Camping: There are 23 primitive sites (no hookups).

Getting there: Take Route 87 from Great Falls 82 miles east to Hobson; turn south on Route 400 for five miles, then southwest on gravel-surfaced Ackley Lake Road for two miles.

Charles M. Russell National Wildlife Refuge—Encompassing one million acres of wetland, prairie and badland surrounding 134-mile-long Fort Peck Lake, this refuge provides a home for hundreds of species of birds and a great many large animals. Thirteen recreation areas along its shores have boat launch sites and campgrounds.

Facilities: Picnic tables, restrooms, boat ramps, trails; information, 406-538-8706. *Swimming:* Generally okay. *Fishing:* Mountain whitefish, brook and rainbow trout, burbot, smallmouth bass, walleye, northern pike, sauger, sturgeon, channel catfish and paddlefish.

Camping: There are 72 RV/tent sites (no hookups) plus 69 for tents only at 13 campgrounds; no charge to $8 per night.

Getting there: Headquarters are in Lewistown; easiest road access, besides Fort Peck Dam, is at the James Kipp Recreation Area on Route 191, 65 miles northeast of Lewistown.

Hell Creek State Recreation Area—The only state park on huge Fort Peck Lake, Hell Creek is located about midway down its southern shore. Probably as many visitors arrive by motorboat as by car.

Facilities: Picnic tables, restrooms, marina, boat ramps, boat rentals, store and concessions; day-use fee, $3; information, 406-232-4365. *Swimming:* Yes. *Fishing:* Walleye, northern pike, smallmouth bass, burbot, sauger, channel catfish, sturgeon, paddlefish, whitefish, brook and rainbow trout.

Camping: There are 40 RV/tent sites (no hookups); $7 per night.

Getting there: Take Hell Creek Road north from Jordan 26 miles to the Hell Creek Arm of Fort Peck Lake.

The Sporting Life

FISHING

Warm-water fish like bass, walleye, northern pike, catfish and perch do well in the Yellowstone River below Billings and in the Missouri River (below Fort Benton) and Fort Peck Lake.

The region's most unusual species is the paddlefish, an enormous bottom feeder with a two-foot snout that hasn't changed much during 70 million years of evolution. Sought for their delicious meat and caviar-like roe, these fish, which weigh well over 100 pounds at full maturity, must be snagged with huge treble hooks and stout casting gear. The paddlefish season extends from May to July; a popular fishing hole is the Yellowstone Intake Diversion Dam, 17 miles north of Glendive via Route 16.

Elsewhere in the southeast, the Musselshell River is famous for both trout and catfish; Bighorn Lake is home to walleye, catfish and perch as well as brown and rainbow trout and burbot. Cold-water species such as trout and whitefish thrive on the Beartooth Plateau; rare golden trout inhabit some of the higher elevation lakes; there are bull trout in Rock Creek, which flows through Red Lodge.

In the north, the Milk and Marias rivers carry trout, catfish and perch; the Teton River and other streams flowing from the Rocky Mountain Front are excellent for several species of trout.

Good tackle shops in Billings include **The Classic Angler** (1091 Broadwater Avenue; 406-652-2001) and **Rainbow Run Fly Shop** (2244 Grand Avenue; 406-656-3455). In Great Falls, try **Mountain Bait & Tackle** (414 9th Street South; 406-453-2551) or **Wolverton's Fly Shop** (210 5th Street South; 406-454-0254). Inquire at any shop about guided expeditions, or contact **Montana River Outfitters** (1401 5th Avenue South, Great Falls; 406-761-1677).

BOATING

The Upper Missouri National Wild and Scenic River is a major draw for river lovers who don't need whitewater to enjoy the scenery. For 149 miles, from Fort Benton to the James Kipp Recreation Area on Fort Peck Lake, this broad, slow-flowing stream meanders past striking geological features and abandoned homesteads, and through the Charles M. Russell National Wildlife Refuge.

Ask about commercial boat tours, or get information about renting a vessel and navigating downstream, at the **Upper Missouri River Visitors Center** (1718 Front Street, Fort Benton; 406-622-5185) or the wild and scenic river headquarters north of Lewistown (Route 191; 406-538-7461). Among the leading commercial operators is **Missouri River Outfitters** (P.O. Box 762, Fort Benton, MT 59442; 406-622-3295).

The 13 boat launch sites around the 1520-mile shoreline of vast Fort Peck Lake are administered by the Russell wildlife refuge. Contact the refuge office for information (Airport Road, Lewistown; 406-538-8706).

RIVER RAFTING AND CANOEING

Most of the rivers of eastern Montana are too slow for whitewater rafting, and many of them are quite muddy. Exceptions are the Stillwater River, which flows off the Beartooth Plateau west of Billings, and the Smith River south of Great Falls, a 61-mile stretch administered by Montana State Parks.

Beartooth Whitewater (601 North Broadway, Red Lodge; 406-446-3142) runs the Stillwater. **Lewis & Clark Expeditions** (4085 Cheff Lane, Ronan; 406-644-2446) runs the Smith.

For independent Missouri River floaters, **Virgelle Mercantile** (Big Sandy; 406-378-3110), at the Virgelle river-ferry landing on the Missouri about 30 miles northeast of Fort Benton off Route 87, rents rafts and canoes and operates a shuttle service. **Montana River Outfitters** (25th Avenue Northeast and Old Havre Highway, Great Falls; 406-761-1677) also rents rafts and offers guided voyages.

Canoeists are served with both rentals and guided trips by the **Flowing Rivers Guide Service** (1809 Darlene Street, Billings; 406-252-5859) and the **Missouri River Canoe Co.** (HC 67 Box 50, Loma, MT 59460; 406-378-3110, 800-426-2926).

SKIING

None of the ski areas in eastern Montana has on-site lodging, but there are several excellent day resorts.

Nearest to Billings is **Red Lodge Mountain** (Red Lodge Mountain Road, Red Lodge; 406-446-2610, 800-444-8977), at the edge of the Beartooth Plateau just outside the old coal-mining town of Red Lodge. It's little more than an hour's drive from Montana's largest city. Five chairlifts ascend to the summit of 9416-foot Grizzly Peak, from which 35 runs drop 2016 feet to the base lodge. The ski resort is in Custer National Forest. Lodging is in Red Lodge.

Showdown Ski Area (Route 89, Neihart; 406-236-5522, 800-433-0022), on the Kings Hill Scenic Byway 60 miles south of Great Falls, is Montana's oldest ski area. The resort in the Little Belt Mountains has two chairlifts and two tows serving 34 runs and 1400 feet of vertical from an 8200-foot summit. The **Kings Hill Winter Sports Complex** (Route 89, Neihart; 406-236-5522, 800-433-0022) here has 18 kilometers of groomed trails for all abilities in Lewis and Clark National Forest.

Rocky Mountain Hi (South Fork Teton River Road, Conrad; 406-278-5308) is in Lewis and Clark National Forest on the fringe of the Bob Marshall Wilderness, 28 miles west of Choteau. The area boasts 25 trails served by a chairlift and a rope tow; vertical drop is 1000 feet from a 7400-foot summit.

Bear Paw Ski Bowl (Rocky Boy's Indian Reservation, Box Elder; 406-265-8404) draws its clientele from the Havre area. It has one chairlift, one tow and nine runs on a 900-foot vertical drop from a summit elevation of 5280 feet.

SKI RENTALS In Billings, you can check out **Reiter's Ski Outfit** (450 Main Street; 406-252-9341) for downhill skis and **The Base Camp** (1730 Grand Avenue; 406-248-4555) for cross-country skis. In Red Lodge, **Sir Michael's Sport Shoppe** (21 North Broadway; 406-446-1613) rents both alpine and nordic equipment. In Great Falls, **Scheels All Sports** (#3 Holiday Village Mall, 1200 10th Avenue South; 406-453-7666) carries downhill and cross-country rentals, while **Bighorn Wilderness** (600 Central Avenue, Great Falls, 406-453-2841) specializes in cross-country skis.

GOLF

Among the leading 18-hole courses in eastern Montana are the **Briarwood Country Club** (3429 Briarwood Boulevard, Billings; 406-245-2966), acclaimed by *USA Today* as one of Montana's best; **Lake Hills Golf Club** (1930 Club House Way, Billings Heights; 406-252-9244); **Red Lodge Mountain Golf**

Course (828 Upper Continental Drive, Red Lodge; 406-446-3344); and **R. O. Speck Golf Course** (River Road, Great Falls; 406-761-1078).

TENNIS

In Billings, look for municipal courts at **North Park** (6th Avenue North and North 21st Street); the Billings Parks Division (510 North Broadway; 406-657-8372) has a full listing of city courts. In Great Falls, **Montana Park** (18th Street Southwest and Fox Farm Road) has a number of courts; contact Great Falls Recreation & Park Activities (2 South Park Drive; 406-771-1265) for more information.

HORSEBACK RIDING

Beartooth Mountain Wagon Trains & Cattle Drives (P.O. Box 63, Red Lodge, MT 59068; 406-446-2179) climb into high country along the Meeteetse Trail in the foothills of the Beartooth Range.

Trips with **Powder River Wagon Train and Cattle Drive** (P.O. Box 483, Broadus, MT 59016; 406-427-5317) involve a full week on the trail with real-life cowboys: riding, caring for horses and performing camp chores, as well as sightseeing and enjoying campfire entertainment.

For a complete listing of cattle-drive outfitters, contact the **Custer Country Tourism Region** (Route 1, Box 1206, Hardin, MT 59034; 406-665-1671).

For standard trail riding, **Miller Outfitters** (663 Vaughn South Frontage Road, Great Falls; 406-761-5184) offers a stable of Tennessee walking horses. **Bonanza Creek Country** (Lennep Route, Martinsdale; 800-476-6045), a guest ranch east of White Sulphur Springs, offers rides into the Crazy and Little Belt mountains.

PACK TRIPS

For trips into the Bob Marshall Wilderness and adjacent wildernesses, reputable outfitters include **A Lazy H Outfitters** (P.O. Box 729, Choteau, MT 59422; 406-466-5564) and the **JJJ Wilderness Ranch** (P.O. Box 310, Augusta, MT 59410; 406-562-3653).

BICYCLING

National Forest roads and trails are generally open to mountain biking, but wheeled vehicles—motorized or not—are not allowed in designated wilderness areas. Local bicycle shops have information on planned activities and mountain-biking routes.

Among the most popular areas for mountain bikers are **Kings Hill** (Route 89, Neihart; 406-547-3361), with 212 miles of trails from the Showdown Ski Area; and in far eastern Montana, the eight-mile route through the badlands of **Makoshika State Park** (Makoshika Park Road, Glendive; 406-365-8596).

Great Falls' River Road, which follows the Missouri River downstream for five miles from downtown's 10th Avenue Bridge to Giant Springs/Heritage State Park, is paralleled by the **River's Edge Trail**, an immensely popular urban bike route.

BIKE RENTALS Shops offering rentals, repairs and information include **Beartooth Bicycle & Sports** (2160 Central Avenue, Billings; 406-656-2453), **Wacky's Spoke & Hackle** (1500 South Broadway, Red Lodge; 406-556-2138) and **Central Bike** (705 Central Avenue, Great Falls; 406-453-8702).

HIKING

While the rolling prairies of Montana's southeast don't excite many hikers, there are interesting trails in adjacent mountains, state parks and riverfront areas. All distances listed for hiking trails are one-way unless otherwise noted.

BILLINGS AREA **Lake Fork Trail** (18 miles) offers a good glimpse of the Absaroka-Beartooth Wilderness. The trail begins at about 8000-foot elevation, one and a half miles west of Route 212, 14 miles south of Red Lodge; proceeds upstream past alpine lakes to Sundance Pass, at about 10,500 feet; then drops rapidly to the West Fork of Rock Creek, ending at about 7600 feet at the end of Route 71.

Granite Peak Trail (12 miles) is one of the three most often used routes to the summit of Montana's highest mountain, 12,799-foot Granite Peak in the Absaroka-Beartooth Wilderness. The trail begins at East Rosebud Lake and circles Froze to Death Mountain; from there, narrow rock ledges, glacial snow bridges and vertical climbs make this one for experienced mountaineers.

GREAT FALLS AREA **River's Edge Trail** (5 miles) follows an abandoned railway bed through Great Falls, along the east and south shores of the Missouri River. The trail begins at Oddfellows Park, just under the Warden Street Bridge, and continues to Giant Springs/Heritage State Park. It connects with several other parks along the way, and draws bicyclists, in-line skaters and runners as well as day hikers.

Clary Coulee Trail (6 miles), which begins 26 miles west of Choteau off Canyon Road, climbs more than 1200 feet above the North Fork of the Teton River and along the eastern ridge of Choteau Mountain, yielding far-reaching, panoramic views of the Great Plains.

Windy Mountain/Briggs Creek Trail (7 miles) is a loop trek through the Highwood Mountains, 42 miles east of Great Falls in Lewis and Clark National Forest. The trail climbs gradually up a creek bed and descends a mountain slope.

HEARTLAND **Crystal Lake/Crystal Cascades Trail** (6.2 miles) combines an easy 1.7-mile loop around a wooded lakeshore with a moderate climb up a small creek into the Big Snowy Mountains. The cascades flow from a cave and gurgle over a stairstep ledge for nearly 100 feet. The trailhead is 30 miles south of Lewistown on Forest Road 275.

Transportation

BY CAR

Billings is immediately west of the junction of two interstate highways: **Route 90**, which runs southeast 98 miles to the Wyoming border, continuing east to Chicago and Boston; and **Route 94**, a spur that follows the Yellowstone River northeast (via Miles City) 247 miles to the North Dakota border at Wibaux, and on to Chicago.

Great Falls is at the easternmost point of **Route 15**, which extends south from the Canadian border to Helena, Butte, Idaho Falls, Salt Lake City and southern California.

Route 87, though not a freeway, directly connects Billings with Great Falls, 230 miles northwest, via Roundup and Lewistown.

Other major east-west routes are **Route 2**, the Hi-Line, from Glacier National Park through Havre and Glasgow to North Dakota; **Route 12**, from Helena down the Musselshell Valley to Miles City and the Dakotas; **Route 200**, from Lewistown through the Heartland to Sidney; and **Route 212**, which approaches Billings from the west via Yellowstone National Park and Red Lodge, then travels east off Route 94 at Little Bighorn Battlefield, continuing to South Dakota's Black Hills and beyond.

North-south routes include **Route 59**, which extends from Jordan through Miles City and Broadus to northeastern Wyoming; **Route 89**, which connects Great Falls with Glacier and Yellowstone national parks; and **Route 191**, which runs from Malta (on the Hi-Line) via Lewistown to Big Timber (on Route 94).

BY AIR

Billings-Logan International Airport is Montana's largest. Four national airlines—Continental, Delta, Northwest and United—and three regional carriers—Big Sky, Horizon and SkyWest—schedule regular arrivals and departures.

Great Falls International Airport is served by Delta, Northwest and Horizon Airlines.

Big Sky Airlines provides commuter service between Billings and seven other eastern Montana cities: Miles City, Glendive, Havre, Lewistown, Glasgow, Wolf Point and Sidney.

BY BUS

Billings-based **Rimrock Trailways** (800-255-7655) serves all of Montana's major cities and many of its smaller ones. Its home depot is at 1206 Cordova Street (406-245-5392); in Great Falls, it arrives and departs from the Union Bus Depot (326 1st Avenue South; 406-453-1541).

Larger towns along the Route 90/94 corridor also greet buses of the nationwide **Greyhound Bus Lines** (800-231-2222). In Billings, catch it at 2502 1st Avenue North (406-245-5116). Greyhound does not serve Great Falls.

BY TRAIN

Amtrak's (800-872-7245) Seattle-Chicago "Empire Builder" makes several stops on the Hi-Line east of Glacier National Park: Cut Bank (1029 East Railroad Street; 406-873-2171), Shelby (198½ Burlington Street; 406-434-5031), Havre (235 Main Street; 406-265-5381) and Malta (51 South 1st Street; 406-654-1622).

CAR RENTALS

Avis Rent A Car (800-331-1212), **Budget Rent A Car** (800-527-0700), **Hertz Rent A Car** (800-654-3131) and **National Interrent** (800-328-4567) service both the Billings and Great Falls airports.

PUBLIC TRANSPORTATION

Billings Metropolitan Transit (406-657-8218), better known as "The MET," and **Great Falls Transit** (406-727-0382), known by the acronym GFT, have extensive bus networks through their respective cities.

TAXIS

For taxi service and airport shuttle service in Billings, call **City Cab** (2713 1st Avenue North; 406-252-8700) or **Yellow Cab** (3940 1st Avenue South; 406-245-3033). In Great Falls, dial **Diamond Cab** (1005 11th Street North; 406-453-3241), which also operates wheelchair-accessible vans.

Index

Hotel, restaurant and trail names are not indexed unless cited as a sightseeing or historical attraction. Regional chapters include: (Colorado) Denver and the Front Range, Northern Colorado Rockies, Southern Colorado Rockies; (Idaho) Northern Idaho Rockies, Southeastern Idaho Rockies, Southwestern Idaho Rockies; (Montana) Montana East of the Rockies, Southern Montana Rockies, Western Montana Rockies; (Utah) Utah Rockies; and (Wyoming) Northern Wyoming Rockies, Southern Wyoming Rockies, Yellowstone and Jackson Hole.

Absaroka-Beartooth Wilderness Area, 551–52, 565–66
Ackley Lake State Park, 589–90
Adolph Coors Company, 60
Aerial Tramway, 67
Agnes Vanderburg Cultural Camp, 495
Air Force Academy, 77
Air travel. *See* Transportation *in regional chapters*
Aladdin: shopping, 356–57
Alamosa area, 158–63; hotels, 159–61; nightlife, 162; parks, 162–63; restaurants, 161; shopping, 162; sightseeing, 158–59
Alamosa Municipal Airport, 207
Albeni Falls Dam, 470
Albertson College of Idaho, 380
Alder Gulch, 538–40; hotels, 539; nightlife, 540; restaurants, 539; shopping, 540; sightseeing, 538–39
Alder Gulch Shortline (railroad), 539
Alice: sightseeing, 57
Almo: sightseeing, 408
Alpine Loop Backcountry Byway, 165, 185
Alpine Loop Scenic Byway, 184, 232
Alpine Tunnel, 166
Alta: hotels, 438–39; restaurants, 439; sightseeing, 290, 438
Alta Ranger Station, 491–92
Alturas Lake, 421
Amaze'n Breckenridge (maze), 112
American Computer Museum, 542
American Falls (town): sightseeing, 426–27
American Falls Dam and Reservoir, 427
American Fork: sightseeing, 232–33
American Heritage Center, 254
Ames Monument, 243
Amtrak. *See* Transportation *in regional chapters*
Anaconda: sightseeing, 529; visitor information, 529
Anaconda Smelter Stack, 529
Anasazi Heritage Center, 182
Anderson Dam, 390
Anderson Ranch Reservoir Recreational Area, 390
Anheuser Busch Brewery, 67
Animals, 11, 14–16. *See also* Bears
Animas: sightseeing, 165
Animas Forks, 185
Ann Morrison Memorial Park, 371
Anna Miller Museum, 354
Antelope Butte Ski Area, 344
Antelope Island State Park, 219
Anthropology Museum, 254
Antonito: sightseeing, 159
Appaloosa Horse Club Museum and Heritage Center, 459
Arapaho National Recreation Area, 111
Arapaho National Wildlife Refuge, 108
Arapahoe Basin, 111
Arco: sightseeing, 415–16
Argo Mill and Museum, 57
Art Castings, 65
Arts Chateau, 529
Ashcroft: restaurants, 130; sightseeing, 128
Ashland: shopping, 573; sightseeing, 571
Ashley National Forest, 217
Ashton: sightseeing, 440
Asotin: restaurants, 463

Aspen area, 126–32; hotels, 128–29; nightlife, 131–32; parks, 132; restaurants, 129–30; shopping, 131; sightseeing, 126–28
Aspen Art Museum, 127
Aspen County Historical Archives, 127
Athol: sightseeing, 469
Atlanta: sightseeing, 390
Atlantic City: restaurants, 276; sightseeing, 273
Auraria Higher Education Center, 46
Avery House, 66
Avon: restaurants, 123; sightseeing, 117

Bachelor-Syracuse Mine, 184
Baker: sightseeing, 576
Balanced Rock, 409
Baldpate Inn Key Room, 68
Ballooning, 97, 142–43, 198–99, 241
Bank of Telluride, 183
Banks: sightseeing, 389
Bannack: sightseeing, 534
Bannack State Park, 534, 537, 541
Bannock County Historical Museum, 425
Barber Park, 372
Barr Lake State Park, 48
Barry's Landing, 343
Basin: sightseeing, 341–42
Basque Museum and Cultural Center, 368
Bayfield: hotels, 186
Bayview: sightseeing, 469
Bean Life Science Museum, 232
Bear Creek (town): nightlife, 569; sightseeing, 565
Bear Creek Canyon Park, 82
Bear Creek Regional Park and Nature Center, 79, 82
Bear Lake, 69
Bear Lake (town): sightseeing, 431; visitor information, 431
Bear Lake–Caribou Scenic Route, 431
Bear Lake National Wildlife Refuge, 431
Bear Lake State Park, 222, 431, 433–34
Bear River Country, 430–34; hotels, 432; parks, 433–34; restaurants, 433; sightseeing, 430–32
Bear River State Park, 264
Bears, 15, 509
Bear's Paw Battlefield, 585
Beartooth Face, 565–66
Beartooth Highway, 565
Beaver Creek: restaurants, 123; sightseeing, 117
Beaver Creek County Park, 586
Beaverhead County Courthouse, 534
Beaverhead County Museum, 534
Beaverhead National Forest, 534, 537
Bed and breakfasts. *See* Hotels
Beehive House, 224
Belt: sightseeing, 588
Benson Park Sculpture Garden, 65
Bergen Park: sightseeing, 56
Berkeley Pit, 528
Berthoud Pass, 106
Betty Ford Alpine Gardens, 118
Beulah: sightseeing, 354
Big Hole National Battlefield, 535
Big Hole River, 535
Big Horn (Wyoming): hotels, 351; sightseeing, 348
Big Horn area (Montana), 570–74; hotels, 572; nightlife, 573; parks, 573–74; restaurants, 572–73; shopping, 573; sightseeing, 570; visitor information, 570
Big Horn Country (Wyoming), 339–46; hotels, 344–45; parks, 346; restaurants, 345; shopping, 345–46; sightseeing, 339–44
Big Horn County Historical Museum, 570
Big Sky: hotels, 544–45; restaurants, 545; sightseeing, 542
Big Sky Ski & Summer Resort, 542
Big Sky Waterslide & Miniature Greens, 500
Big Thompson Canyon, 66
Big Timber: hotels, 550; shopping, 551; sightseeing, 550
Bigfork: hotels, 497; nightlife, 498; restaurants, 497; shopping, 498; sightseeing, 496
Bigfork Art & Cultural Center, 496
Bigfork Summer Playhouse, 496
Bighorn Canyon National Recreation Area, 342, 346, 571, 573
Bighorn Scenic Byway, 344, 349
Billings area, 562–69; hotels, 566–67; nightlife, 568–69; parks, 569; restaurants, 567–68; shopping, 568; sightseeing, 562–66
Billings-Logan International Airport, 595
Bishops' House, 372

Bitterroot National Forest, 493
Bitterroot Valley, 490–93; hotels, 492; parks, 493; restaurants, 492; shopping, 492–93; sightseeing, 490–92
Black American West Museum, 47
Black Canyon of the Gunnison National Monument, 164
Black Eagle: restaurants, 581–82
Black Hawk: hotels, 61; nightlife, 63; restaurants, 62; sightseeing, 60
Black Hills National Forest, 357
Black Otter Trail, 564
Blackfeet Indian Reservation, 506–507
Blackfoot: restaurants, 428; sightseeing, 426
Blaine County Museum, 415
Bliss: shopping, 412
Board sailing, 359, 444, 476
Boating, 39. *See also* Sports *in regional chapters*
Bob Marshall Wilderness Area, 579, 584
Bob Scriver Museum of Montana Wildlife & Hall of Bronze, 507
Bogus Basin Recreational Area, 372
Boise area, 368–79; hotels, 373–74; map, 369; nightlife, 376–78; parks, 378; restaurants, 374–75; shopping, 376; sightseeing, 368–73, 379; visitor information, 368
Boise Art Museum, 370
Boise Basin. *See* Basin County and Boise Basin
Boise Basin Historical Museum, 390
Boise Basin Mercantile Co., 390
Boise Centre on the Grove, 368
Boise County and Boise Basin, 389–92; hotels, 390–91; parks, 391–92; restaurants, 391; shopping, 391; sightseeing, 389–90
Boise Municipal Airport, 402
Boise National Forest, 391–92
Boise Public Library, 370
Boise River Greenbelt, 371
Boise State University (BSU), 370
Boise Tour Trains, 370
Bonners Ferry: sightseeing, 470
Bonneville County Historical Museum, 435
Boothill Swords Park, 564
Boreas Pass Road, 112–13
Botanical Garden, 252
Boulder (Colorado): hotels, 69–70; nightlife, 73; restaurants, 70–71; shopping, 72; sightseeing, 64–65
Boulder (Montana): sightseeing, 522
Boulder Canyon and Falls, 65
Boulder Hot Springs, 522
Boulder Mountain Park, 74
Box Canyon Falls and Park, 184
Box Elder: sightseeing, 585
Boysen State Park, 277
Bozeman area, 540, 542–48; hotels, 544–45; nightlife, 546–47; parks, 547–48; restaurants, 545–46; shopping, 546; sightseeing, 540, 542–44; visitor information, 542
Bradford Brinton Memorial, 348
Breckenridge–South Park area, 111–17; hotels, 113–15; nightlife, 116; parks, 116–17; restaurants, 115–16; shopping, 116; sightseeing, 111–13
Bridal Veil Falls, 183, 232
Bridger Bowl, 542
Bridger-Teton National Forest, 278, 294
Brigham City: sightseeing, 218
Brigham Young Monument, 224
Brigham Young University (BYU), 231–32
Brigham Young's Grave, 224
Bristlecone Pine Scenic Area, 113
Broadmoor Hotel, 78
Broadus: sightseeing, 572
Broadwater Overlook Park, 578
Browning: shopping, 508; sightseeing, 506–507
Browning Firearms Museum, 218
Browning-Kimball Car Museum, 218
Brownlee Reservoir, 383
Brundage Mountain Ski Area, 384
Bruneau: sightseeing, 392–93
Bruneau Canyon, 393
Bruneau Dunes State Park, 392, 395
Buckskin Joe, 89
Buena Vista: hotels, 114; restaurants, 115; sightseeing, 113
Buffalo: hotels, 351; restaurants, 352; sightseeing, 349; visitor information, 349
Buffalo Bill Dam, 333
Buffalo Bill Historical Center, 330, 332
Buffalo Bill Museum, 330, 332
Buffalo Bill State Park, 333, 338
Buffalo Bill's Grave and Memorial Museum, 60

Buffalo Soldier Monument, 252–53
Buhl: sightseeing, 409
Burley: hotels, 411; restaurants, 412; sightseeing, 408
Bus travel. *See* Transportation *in regional chapters*
Butte area, 527–33; hotels, 530–31; nightlife, 532–33; parks, 533; restaurants, 531–32; shopping, 532; sightseeing, 527–30; visitor information, 528
Buzz Langdon Visitors Center, 406
Byers-Evans House, 46
BYU (Brigham Young University), 231–32
BYU Earth Science Museum, 232
BYU Museum of Fine Arts, 231–32

Caldwell: hotels, 381; nightlife, 382; restaurants, 381; sightseeing, 380
Calendar of events, 21–28
Camas National Wildlife Refuge, 435
Cambridge: hotels, 385; sightseeing, 383
Cameron Pass, 67
Campbell County Airport, 365
Camping, 37–38. *See also* Parks *in area and city entries*
Cam-plex, 354
Canoeing, 142, 317–18, 511, 552–53, 591–92
Cañon City: hotels, 90; restaurants, 91; sightseeing, 89
Canyon area (Yellowstone): hotels, 311; restaurants, 312; sightseeing, 307–309; visitor information, 307
Canyon County Historical Museum, 380
Canyon Ferry Recreation Area, 523, 526–27
Capitol City: sightseeing, 165
Car rentals. *See* Transportation *in regional chapters*
Car travel, 32–33. *See also* Transportation *in regional chapters*
Carbon County Museum, 565
Carbondale: sightseeing, 126
Cardwell: sightseeing, 543–44
Caribou National Forest, 431
Cascade: hotels, 385–86; sightseeing, 385
Cascade Reservoir, 384–85
Cascade Springs, 232
Casper area, 265–71; hotels, 269–70; nightlife, 271; parks, 271; restaurants, 270; shopping, 270; sightseeing, 265–69
Casper Mountain, 268
Casper Mountain Park, 268
Cassia County Historical Museum, 408
Castle: sightseeing, 541
The Castle, 523
Castlewood Canyon State Park, 55
Cataldo: sightseeing, 468
Cave of the Winds, 84
Cavendish: sightseeing, 462
Cedar Street Bridge Public Market, 469–70
Celestial Seasonings, 65
Centennial: sightseeing, 254
Centennial Trail, 468
Centennial Village, 66
Central City: hotels, 61; nightlife, 63; restaurants, 62; sightseeing, 57–58, 60, 86
Central Montana Museum, 588
Challis: restaurants, 423; sightseeing, 422
Challis National Forest, 421, 424
Chapel of the Transfiguration, 296
Charles M. Russell Museum Complex, 578
Charles M. Russell National Wildlife Refuge, 586, 588, 590
Charlo: restaurants, 497
Chatfield State Recreation Area, 54–55
Chautauqua Park, 65
Cheesman Park, 48
Cherry Creek, 86
Cherry Creek State Recreation Area, 55
Cheyenne Airport, 282
Cheyenne Frontier Days Old West Museum, 252
Cheyenne-Laramie area, 250–59; hotels, 255–56; map, 251; nightlife, 258; parks, 258–59; restaurants, 256–57; shopping, 257; sightseeing, 250–55
Cheyenne Mountain Zoo, 78
Chico Hot Springs, 549
Chief Joseph Scenic Highway, 333–34
Chief Plenty Coups State Park, 571
Chief Washakie's grave, 273
Children, traveling with, 33–34
Children's Museum of Denver, 47
Chimney Rock Archaeological Area, 178
Chinook: sightseeing, 585
Choteau: hotels, 581; sightseeing, 579
Chubbuck: nightlife, 429

Church of Jesus Christ of Latter-day Saints (LDS) Administration Building, 224
City of Rocks National Reserve, 408, 413
Clark: hotels, 139
Clark Canyon Recreation Area, 536
Clark Fork, 470
Clarkia: sightseeing, 459
Clarkston (Washington): sightseeing, 456, 458
Clear Springs Foods, 409
Clearwater Historical Society Museum, 460
Clearwater National Forest, 460, 465–66
Clearwater Valley, 460, 461
Cleveholm Manor (Redstone Castle), 134
Climax Molybdenum Mine, 118
Cloud Peak Wilderness, 341
Cody area, 330–36, 338–39; hotels, 334–35; map, 330; nightlife, 336, 338; parks, 338–39; restaurants, 335–36; shopping, 336; sightseeing, 330–34; visitor information, 332
Cody, "Buffalo Bill," 60, 337
Cody Firearms Museum, 332
The Coeur d'Alene (resort), 467
Coeur d'Alene Airport, 481
Coeur d'Alene area, 466–75; hotels, 471–72; nightlife, 473–74; parks, 474–75; restaurants, 472–73; shopping, 473; sightseeing, 466–70; visitor information, 467
Coeur d'Alene Indian Reservation, 468
Coeur d'Alene Lake, 467
Collegiate Peaks, 113
Colorado. *See* Denver and the Front Range; Northern Colorado Rockies; Southern Colorado Rockies
Colorado History Museum, 46
Colorado National Monument, 173
Colorado Railroad Museum, 60
Colorado School of Mines Geology Museum, 60
Colorado Ski Museum and Ski Hall of Fame, 118
Colorado Springs Airport, 102
Colorado Springs area, 75–82; hotels, 79–81; map, 45; nightlife, 82; parks, 82; restaurants, 81; shopping, 81–82; sightseeing, 75–79, 89
Colorado Springs Fine Arts Center, 76
Colorado Springs Pioneers Museum, 76
Colorado State Capitol, 43
Colorado Territorial Prison Museum, 89
Colter Bay Indian Arts Museum, 297
Colter's Hell, 332
Columbia Falls: hotels, 501–502; nightlife, 503; restaurants, 502; sightseeing, 500
Como: sightseeing, 113
Conner: sightseeing, 491
Connor Battlefield State Historic Site, 348
Conrad Mansion, 500
Conundrum Hot Springs, 128
Cooke City: hotels, 315; restaurants, 315; sightseeing, 314
Cooney Reservoir State Park, 569
Copper Mountain Ski Area: hotels, 122; sightseeing, 118
Coram: sightseeing, 500
Corazon de Trinidad National Historic District, 94
Corwin Springs: nightlife, 316; sightseeing, 550
Cottonwood: sightseeing, 459
Council: restaurants, 386
Craters of the Moon National Monument, 415, 420
Crazy Mountain Museum, 550
Creede: hotels, 160–61; nightlife, 162; restaurants, 161; shopping, 162; sightseeing, 159
Crested Butte. *See* Gunnison–Crested Butte area
Crimson Dawn Park, 268
Cripple Creek: hotels, 90; nightlife, 92; restaurants, 91; sightseeing, 85, 87, 88
Cripple Creek and Victory Narrow Gauge Railroad, 88
Cripple Creek District Museum, 88
Cross-country skiing. *See* Sports *in regional chapters*
Cross Orchards Historic Site, 172
Crow Agency: nightlife, 573; restaurants, 573; sightseeing, 570
Crow Indian Reservation, 570
Crowheart: hotels, 275; sightseeing, 273
Crystal Ice Cave, 426
Cumbres and Toltec Scenic Railroad, 159
Cumbres Pass, 159
Curecanti National Recreation Area, 164, 171

Curlew National Grassland, 434
Curt Gowdy State Park, 243, 258
Custer: sightseeing, 421–22
Custer County Art Center, 575
Custer Museum, 422
Custer National Cemetery, 570
Custer National Forest, 569
Cut Bank: hotels, 586; sightseeing, 584

D & F Tower, 47
Darby: hotels, 492; restaurants, 491; sightseeing, 491
Darby Historic Ranger Station, 491
Daughters of Utah Pioneers Museum, 408
Dayton (Montana): sightseeing, 495–96
Dayton (Wyoming): sightseeing, 349
Dead Indian Pass, 334
Decker: sightseeing, 571–72
Dedisse Park, 63
Deer Creek State Park and Reservoir, 233, 241
Deer Valley: hotels, 238; restaurants, 239
Deerflat National Wildlife Refuge, 380, 382
Deerlodge National Forest, 533
Del Norte: sightseeing, 159
Denver, 44, 46–55; hotels, 48–50; map, 49; nightlife, 53–54; parks, 54–55; restaurants, 50–52; shopping, 52–53; sightseeing, 44, 46–48
Denver and the Front Range, 16, 43–103; calendar of events, 21–28; Colorado Springs area, 75–82; Denver, 44, 46–55; introduction, 43–44; maps, 45, 49, 59; north of Denver, 64–75; Pikes Peak area, 83–92; Pueblo-Walsenburg-Trinidad area, 93–96; sports, 96–101; transportation, 102–103; weather, 44; west of Denver, 55–64
Denver Art Museum, 46
Denver Botanic Gardens, 48
Denver Civic Center, 46
Denver Firefighters Museum, 46
Denver International Airport, 102
Denver Museum of Miniatures, Dolls and Toys, 48
Denver Museum of Natural History, 48
Denver Zoo, 48
Devil's Gate, 269
Devil's Kitchen Geologic Site, 232
Devils Slide, 550
Devils Tower National Monument, 354–55
Dillon area, 533–37; hotels, 535; nightlife, 536; parks, 536–37; restaurants, 535–36; shopping, 536; sightseeing, 533–35; visitor information, 534
Dillon Reservoir, 112, 116–17
Dinosaur National Monument, 138, 212, 214
Dinosaur Ridge, 56
Dinosaur Valley, 172
Disabled travelers, 35–36
Discovery Center of Idaho, 370
Dixon: hotels, 256
Doc Holliday's Grave, 133
Dolores: restaurants, 191; sightseeing, 182
Dominguez Canyon, 173–74
Donnelly: sightseeing, 384
Douglas: sightseeing, 265
Downhill skiing. *See* Sports *in regional chapters*
Driggs: restaurants, 439; sightseeing, 438
Drummond: sightseeing, 530
Dry Fork Canyon, 214
Dubois: hotels, 275; nightlife, 277; restaurants, 276; sightseeing, 274
Dumas Red Light Antique Mall, 529
Durango and San Juan Skyway area, 178–96; hotels, 185–90; nightlife, 193–94; parks, 194–96; restaurants, 191–92; shopping, 192–93; sightseeing, 178–85
Durango & Silverton Narrow-Gauge Railroad, 179
Durango–La Plata Airport, 207
Durham Buffalo Ranch, 354
Dutch John: hotels, 215
Dworshak Dam and Reservoir, 460–61
Dworshak State Park, 462, 466; visitor information, 462

Eagle: shopping, 376
Eagle Gate, 224
Eagle Island State Park, 378
Earthquake Visitors Information Center, 416
East Gallatin State Recreation Area, 547
Eastern Montana, 19, 561–96; Big Horn area, 570–74; Billings area, 562–69; calendar of events, 21–28;

Great Falls area, 577–82, 584; Heartland, 588–90; Hi-Line, 584–87; introduction, 561–62; Lower Yellowstone Valley, 574–77; map, 563; sports, 590–94; transportation, 595–96
Echo Lake, 56
Echo Park, 138
Eden: hotels, 220
Edgar Mine, 57
Edness Kimball Wilkins State Park, 271
Egg Mountain, 579
Egyptian Theatre, 234
8th Street Market Place (Boise), 368, 370
Eisenhower Memorial Tunnel, 111
Eldorado Canyon State Park, 74
Elk Horn Hot Springs, 534
Elk Meadows County Park, 63
Elk River: hotels, 463
Elkhorn: sightseeing, 522, 541
Elkhorn Resort, 414–15
Elmore County Historical Society Museum, 392
Emerald Creek Garnet Area, 459
Emmett: sightseeing, 381
Empire: hotels, 61; shopping, 62; sightseeing, 57
Encampment: sightseeing, 255
Engineer Pass Road, 184
Ennis: restaurants, 544; sightseeing, 543
Enos Mills Cabin and Nature Study Area, 68
Ernest Hemingway Memorial, 415
Essex: hotels, 502
Estes Park: hotels, 70; nightlife, 73; restaurants, 71–72; shopping, 72; sightseeing, 67–68
Estes Park Area Historical Museum, 67–68
Evanston: hotels, 262; sightseeing, 261
Evergreen: sightseeing, 56
Explorer's Museum, 303

Fallen City, 349
Falls Park, 468
Farragut State Park, 469, 474–75
Fauna, 11, 14–16. *See also* Bears
Featherville: sightseeing, 390
Fife: sightseeing, 588
Fine Arts Center, 254
Finnish Evangelical Lutheran Church (Lake Fork), 384
Firehole Canyon, 260
Fish and fishing, 39–40, 443. *See also* Sports *in regional chapters*
Fish Creek Falls, 137
Fish Haven: hotels, 432; visitor information, 431
Fiske Planetarium, 64
Flaming Gorge Dam, 214–15
Flaming Gorge National Recreation Area: hotels, 215; parks, 264; restaurants, 216; sightseeing, 214–15, 260
Flat Tops Trail Scenic Byway, 138
Flat Tops Wilderness, 138
Flathead Indian Reservation and Lake, 494–99; hotels, 496–97; nightlife, 498; parks, 498–99; restaurants, 497; shopping, 498; sightseeing, 494–96
Flathead Lake State Park, 498–99
Flathead National Forest, 503–504
Flathead National Wild and Scenic River, 500
Flathead Valley, 499–504; hotels, 501–502; nightlife, 503; parks, 503–504; restaurants, 502; shopping, 502–503; sightseeing, 499–501; visitor information, 502
Flora, 10–11
Florissant Fossil Beds National Monument, 88
Foreign travelers, 36
Fort Assiniboine, 585
Fort Belknap Indian Reservation, 585
Fort Benton: sightseeing, 580
Fort Bridger: hotels, 262; shopping, 263; sightseeing, 260
Fort Bridger State Historic Site, 260
Fort Buenaventura State Park, 218–19
Fort Caspar Museum, 268
Fort Collins: hotels, 70; nightlife, 73; restaurants, 71; shopping, 72; sightseeing, 66–67
Fort Collins–Loveland Municipal Airport, 102
Fort Collins Municipal Railway, 67
Fort Collins Museum, 66
Fort Fetterman State Historic Site, 265
Fort Fred Steele State Historic Site, 259
Fort Garland: sightseeing, 158
Fort Garland Museum, 158
Fort Hall Indian Reservation, 425–26
Fort Hall Replica, 425
Fort Keogh, 575
Fort Laramie National Historic Site, 265

Fort Owen, 491
Fort Peck: nightlife, 587; sightseeing, 586
Fort Peck Assiniboine and Sioux Culture Center and Museum, 586
Fort Peck Dam and Museum, 586
Fort Peck Indian Reservation, 586
Fort Peck Lake, 586
Fort Phil Kearny, 348
Fort Sherman Museum, 467
Fort Smith: sightseeing, 571
Fort Union Trading Post National Historic Site, 586
Fort Washakie: shopping, 277; sightseeing, 273
Fort Yellowstone, 306
Fossil Butte National Monument, 261
Fossil Station: sightseeing, 261
Four Corners: shopping, 356
Four-Mile Historic Park, 48
Four Winds Historic Village and Trading Post, 494–95
Frank Church–River of No Return Wilderness Area, 388, 422
Franklin: sightseeing, 432
Fraser: nightlife, 111; sightseeing, 108
Fred Harman Art Museum, 178
Freezout Lake Wildlife Management Area, 579–80
Fremont County Pioneer Museum, 272
Friedman Memorial Airport, 452
The Front Range. *See* Denver and the Front Range
Frontier Historical Museum, 133–34
Frontier Town, 522

G. W. Russell House, 371
Galena Summit, 420–21
Gallatin County Pioneer Museum, 542
Gallatin Field Airport, 558
Gallatin Gateway: hotels, 544
Gallatin-Madison Loop, 542–43
Gallatin National Forest, 542, 547–48
Gallatin Petrified Forest, 550
Galloping Goose #5, 182
Garden City (Idaho): nightlife, 377; restaurants, 375
Garden City (Utah): hotels, 219–20; restaurants, 220
Garden of the Gods, 76–77
Garden Valley: hotels, 390; sightseeing, 389
Gardena: shopping, 391
Gardiner: hotels, 315; restaurants, 315; shopping, 315; sightseeing, 314, 550
Garnet: sightseeing, 487, 541
Gates of Lodore, 138
Gates of the Mountains, 523
Gates of the Mountains Fame Preserve and Wilderness, 523
Gates Planetarium, 48
Gay- and lesbian-friendly establishments: hotels, 80–81; nightlife, 54, 82, 231, 294, 378, 532, 569
Genessee Park, 56
Geological Museum, 254
Geology, 4–5
George S. Eccles Dinosaur Park, 218
Georgetown: hotels, 61; sightseeing, 57, 86
Georgetown Lake, 529–30
Geyser Park, 430
Ghost Town Hall of Fame, 541
Ghost Town Museum, 78
Ghost towns, 541. *See also specific ghost towns*
Giant Springs/Heritage State Park, 578
Gillette: hotels, 355–56; nightlife, 357; restaurants, 356; shopping, 356; sightseeing, 353–54; visitor information, 354
Glacier Maze, 500
Glacier National Park, 504–508, 510; hotels, 507; map, 486; park, 508, 510; restaurants, 508; shopping, 508; sightseeing, 504–507; visitor information, 504–505
Glacier Park International Airport, 516
Glade Park, 173
Glasgow: restaurants, 587; sightseeing, 586
Glen Eyrie, 77
Glendive: hotels, 577; sightseeing, 575–76
Glendo State Park, 271
Glenns Ferry: sightseeing, 392
Glenrock: hotels, 269
Glenwood Canyon, 132–33
Glenwood Canyon Trail, 133
Glenwood Springs area, 132–37; hotels, 134–35; nightlife, 136; parks, 136–37; restaurants, 135–36; sightseeing, 132–34
Gliding, 142–43, 198–99
Going-to-the-Sun Road, 504–505
Gold, 86–87
Gold Camp Road, 79

Golden: hotels, 61; restaurants, 62; shopping, 63; sightseeing, 60
Golden Gate Canyon State Park, 63–64
Golden Spike National Historical Site, 218
Gooding: hotels, 411
Gooseberry Formations, 341
Gothic: sightseeing, 166
Granby: hotels, 109; sightseeing, 108
Grand Canyon of the Yellowstone, 307–309
Grand Encampment Museum, 255
Grand Junction area, 172–77; hotels, 174–75; nightlife, 176; parks, 176–77; restaurants, 175; shopping, 175; sightseeing, 172–74
Grand Lake. *See* Winter Park–Grand Lake area
Grand Mesa: hotels, 174–75; sightseeing, 174
Grand Mesa National Forest, 176
Grand Mesa Scenic Byway, 174
Grand National Forest, 295–99; hotels, 297–98; nightlife, 298; parks, 298–99; restaurants, 298; sightseeing, 295–97; visitor information, 296
Grand Targhee Ski & Summer Resort, 290, 438
Grand Teton, 295
Grand Teton National Park, 295–99; hotels, 297–98; nightlife, 298; parks, 298–99; restaurants, 298; sightseeing, 295–97; visitor information, 296
Grandjean: sightseeing, 389
Grangeville: shopping, 464; sightseeing, 459–60
Granite County Museum and Cultural Center, 530
Granite Peak, 314
Grant-Kohrs Ranch National Historic Site, 530
Grant Village–West Thumb area (Yellowstone): hotels, 310; restaurants, 311; sightseeing, 301–302; visitor information, 301
Grasshopper Glacier, 314
Grays Lake National Refuge, 431
Great Bear Adventure, 500
Great Dikes, 94
Great Falls area, 577–82, 584; hotels, 580–81; nightlife, 582; parks, 582, 584; restaurants, 581–82; shopping, 582; sightseeing, 577–80
Great Falls International Airport, 595
Great Pagosa Hot Springs, 178
Great Rift National Landmark, 426
Great Salt Lake, 219
Great Salt Lake State Park, 231
Great Sand Dunes National Monument, 158
Greeley: sightseeing, 66
Greeley Municipal Museum, 66
Green Mountain Falls: hotels, 80
Green River. *See* Rock Springs–Green River area
Gregson: hotels, 531
Greybull: hotels, 345; restaurants, 345; shopping, 345–46; sightseeing, 344
Greycliff: sightseeing, 550
Greycliff Prairie Dog Town State Park, 550
Grizzly bears, 15, 509
Grizzly Discovery Center, 313
Gros Ventre Slide, 289
Gros Ventre Wilderness, 289
The Grove (Boise), 368
Guernsey: sightseeing, 265
Guernsey State Park, 271
Guides and outfitters, 40–41. *See also* Sports *in regional chapters*
Gunnison County Airport, 207
Gunnison–Crested Butte area, 163–71; hotels, 166–68; nightlife, 170–71; parks, 171; restaurants, 168–70; shopping, 170; sightseeing, 163–66; visitor information, 168
Gunnison National Forest, 163, 171

H. Earl Clack Memorial Museum, 585
Hagerman: hotels, 411; restaurants, 412; sightseeing, 410
Hagerman Fossil Beds National Monument, 410
Hagerman Valley, 409–10
Hailey: hotels, 417; restaurants, 418; sightseeing, 415
Hall of Presidents Wax Museum, 78
Hamer: sightseeing, 435
Hamilton: hotels, 492; restaurants, 492; sightseeing, 491
Hamilton Dome: sightseeing, 340
Hanging Lake, 133
Hansen Planetarium, 226
Hardin: hotels, 572; restaurants, 572–73; shopping, 573; sightseeing, 570; visitor information, 570

Harlem: sightseeing, 585; visitor information, 585
Harriman State Park, 441
Harrison: hotels, 471; sightseeing, 467
Harry Jackson Museum, 332–33
Havre: hotels, 586–87; nightlife, 587; restaurants, 587; sightseeing, 585
Havre Beneath the Streets, 585
Hayden Lake, 469
Headwaters Heritage Museum, 543
Healy House and Dexter Cabin, 119
Heart Mountain Relocation Center, 342
Heartland (Montana), 588–90; hotels, 589; nightlife, 589; parks, 589–90; restaurants, 589; shopping, 589; sightseeing, 588–89
Heber City: sightseeing, 233
Heber Valley Scenic Railroad, 233
Hebgen Lake, 313–14
Heise Hot Springs, 437
Helen Hunt Falls, 79
Helena Airport, 558
Helena area, 520–27; hotels, 523–24; nightlife, 525–26; parks, 526–27; restaurants, 524–25; shopping, 525; sightseeing, 520–23
Helena National Forest, 523, 526
Hell Creek State Recreation Area, 589, 590
Hells Canyon and McCall area, 382–88; hotels, 385–86; nightlife, 386; parks, 387–88; restaurants, 386; shopping, 386; sightseeing, 382–85
Hells Canyon National Recreation Area, 383, 387, 456, 458, 469, 464–65; visitor information, 458, 460
Hells Gate State Park, 458, 465
Hemingway Memorial, 415
Henry's Fork, 440–42; hotels, 441; parks, 442; restaurants, 442; sightseeing, 440–41
Henry's Lake, 441
Henry's Lake State Park, 441, 442
Heritage Museum, 119
Heyburn State Park, 467–68, 474
High Plains Energy and Technology Center, 354
Highline Lake State Park, 177
Highway of Legends Scenic Byway, 94
Hi-Line, 584–87; hotels, 586–87; nightlife, 587; parks, 587; restaurants, 587; sightseeing, 584-86
Historic Governors' Mansion State Historic Site, 252
Historical Museum of Fort Missoula, 486
History, 5–10
History of Electricity in Idaho Museum, 372
Hiwan Homestead Museum, 56
Hoback Junction: restaurants, 292
Hockaday Center for the Arts, 500
Hogle Zoological Gardens, 226
Hole-in-the-Wall, 349–50
Hollister: sightseeing, 408
Holter Lake Recreation Area, 523, 526
Homesteader Museum, 342
Hoofprints of the Past Museum, 349
Hope Peninsula, 470
Horseshoe Bend: restaurants, 391; sightseeing, 389
Horsetooth Mountain Park, 74
Horsetooth Reservoir, 74
Hostels. *See* Hotels
Hot Springs Historical Museum, 340
Hot Springs State Park, 340, 346
Hot Sulphur Springs, 108
Hotels, 30–31. *See also* Hotels *in area and city entries*
House of Mystery, 500
Humbug Spires Primitive Area, 537
Hungry Horse: shopping, 503; sightseeing, 500
Hungry Horse Dam, 500
Huntley: sightseeing, 574
Huntley Project Museum of Irrigated Agriculture, 574
Huntley School, 586
Huson: sightseeing, 487
Hyalite Canyon Recreation Area, 547
Hyatville: sightseeing, 341

Ice skating, 98, 320, 361, 447
Idaho. *See* Northern Idaho Rockies; Southeastern Idaho Rockies; Southwestern Idaho Rockies
Idaho Botanical Garden, 372
Idaho City: hotels, 390; restaurants, 391; shopping, 391; sightseeing, 389–90
Idaho Falls, 435
Idaho Falls (town), 434–37; hotels, 435–36; nightlife, 436–37; restaurants, 436; shopping, 436; sightseeing, 416, 434–35; visitor information, 435

Idaho Falls Municipal Airport–Fanning Field, 452
Idaho Falls Temple, 435
Idaho Heritage Museum, 408
Idaho Museum of Natural History, 425
Idaho National Engineering Laboratory, 416
Idaho Panhandle National Forests, 474
Idaho Power Company Parks, 387
Idaho Springs: restaurants, 62; sightseeing, 56–57, 86
Idaho State Capitol, 368
Idaho State Historical Museum, 370
Idaho State University (ISU), 425
Idaho State Vietnam Veterans Memorial, 435
Idaho Transportation Museum, 372
Idaho's World Famous Hot Pools & Swim Complex, 430
Idaho's World Potato Exposition, 426
Idalaka: sightseeing, 576
Idarado Mine and Mill, 183
Ignacio: sightseeing, 178
IMAX Theaters, 48, 313
Independence Pass, 126
Independence Rock State Historic Site, 269
Indian Springs Spa, 56–57
Irma Hotel, 332
Irwin: hotels, 438; sightseeing, 437
Island Acres State Park, 177
Island Park: hotels, 441; restaurants, 442; sightseeing, 441
Island Park Caldera, 441

Jack Dempsey Museum, 158
Jackpot (Nevada): nightlife, 412
Jackson. *See* Jackson Hole area
Jackson Canyon Eagle Sanctuary, 268
Jackson Hole Airport, 326
Jackson Hole area, 286–95; hotels, 290–91; map, 287; nightlife, 293–94; parks, 294–95; restaurants, 291–92; shopping, 293; sightseeing, 286–90; visitor information, 289
Jackson Hole Museum, 288
Jackson Hole Shootout, 288
Jackson Hole Ski Area, 289
Jackson Lake, 296–97
James Kipp Recreation Area, 588
Japanese House of Peace, 218
Jardine Juniper, 217
Jefferson County Courthouse, 522
Jenny Lake, 296
Jenny Lake Scenic Drive, 296
Jet skiing, 476
Jim Gatchell Memorial Museum of the West, 349
Joe: sightseeing, 576
Johnson Bell International Airport, 516
Johnson County Courthouse, 349
Jordan: sightseeing, 589
Joseph Smith Memorial Building, 224
Julia David Park, 370

Kalispell: hotels, 501; nightlife, 503; restaurants, 502; shopping, 503; sightseeing, 499–500; visitor information, 502
Kamiah: sightseeing, 462
Kathryn Albertson Park, 371
Kaycee: sightseeing, 349–50
Kebler Pass Road, 165–66
Kellogg: hotels, 471; sightseeing, 468
Kelly: sightseeing, 289
Kemmerer: sightseeing, 261
Ketchum: hotels, 417; nightlife, 419; restaurants, 418; shopping, 418–19; sightseeing, 415, 420
Ketchum Cemetery, 415
Keystone Resort: nightlife, 116; sightseeing, 111–12
Keyhole State Park, 357–58
Kimberly: sightseeing, 408
Kings Hill National Scenic Byway, 588
Kooskia: hotels, 463
Kootenai National Forest, 504
Kootenai National Wildlife Refuge, 470
Kuna: sightseeing, 373, 379

La Garita: shopping, 162
Lace House, 60
Lake City: hotels, 167; sightseeing, 164
Lake Coeur d'Alene Scenic Byway, 467
Lake Como Recreation Area, 493
Lake Elmo State Park, 564
Lake Fork: sightseeing, 384
Lake Koocanusa, 501
Lake Mary Ronan State Park, 495–96
Lake Pend Oreille, 469
Lake Pueblo State Recreation Area, 95
Lake San Cristobal, 165
Lake Walcott, 409
Lame Deer: sightseeing, 571
Land of the Yankee Fork Historic Area, 421–22, 423–24

Lander area, 272–78; hotels, 274–75; nightlife, 277; parks, 277–78; restaurants, 276; shopping, 277; sightseeing, 272–74; visitor information, 273
Laramie. *See* Cheyenne-Laramie area
Laramie Mountains, 253
Laramie Plains Museum, 243
Larimer Square, 47
Last Chance Tour Train, 520
Lathrop State Park, 95
Lava Hot Springs: hotels, 432; restaurants, 433; sightseeing, 430
Leadville. *See* Vail-Leadville area
Leadville, Colorado & Southern Railroad, 119
Leadville Ice Palace, 120
Leanin' Tree Museum, 65
Lee Metcalf National Wildlife Refuge, 491
Lee Metcalf Wilderness, 542
Legend Rock State Petroglyph Site, 340
Lesbian- and gay-friendly establishments: hotels, 80–81; nightlife, 54, 82, 231, 294, 378, 532, 569
Lewis and Clark Caverns State Park, 543–44, 548
Lewis and Clark National Forest, 579, 582, 584
Lewis Lake, 301
Lewiston: hotels, 589; nightlife, 589; restaurants, 589; shopping, 589; sightseeing, 588
Lewiston Hill, 458
Lewiston-Moscow area, 456–66; hotels, 462–63; nightlife, 464; parks, 464–66; restaurants, 463–64; shopping, 464; sightseeing, 456–62; visitor information, 458
Lewiston–Nez Perce County Airport, 481
Libby: sightseeing, 501
Libby Dam, 501
Lincoln: restaurants, 525; sightseeing, 522
Lions Park, 252
Liquor laws, 221, 230
Little America: hotels, 262
Little Bighorn Battlefield National Monument, 570
Little Dolores Falls, 173
Little Park Desert Preserve, 173
Living History Site, 77
Livingston: hotels, 550; nightlife, 551; restaurants, 551; shopping, 551; sightseeing, 549; visitor information, 549
Livingston Depot Center, 549
Lizard Head Pass, 182
Llama trekking. *See* Sports *in regional chapters*
Logan (Montana): sightseeing, 543
Logan (Utah): hotels, 220; nightlife, 221; restaurants, 220; shopping, 221; sightseeing, 217–18
Logan Canyon, 217
Logan (Thompson Chain of Lakes) State Park, 504
Lolo Hot Springs: hotels, 492; sightseeing, 490
Lolo National Forest, 490
Lolo Pass, 462, 491
Lolo Trail, 460, 461
Lone Pine State Park, 500
Lone Wolf Wildlife Museum, 549
Long Bridge, 469
Longs Peak, 68
Lookout Mountain, 60
Lorenzo Hatch Home, 432
Lory State Park, 74
Lost Creek State Park, 533
Loveland: sightseeing, 65–66
Loveland Basin–Loveland Valley, 111
Loveland Museum and Gallery, 65–66
Loveland Pass, 111
Loveland Sculpture Works, 65
Lovell: hotels, 345; sightseeing, 342
Lowell: sightseeing, 462
Lower Cascade Falls, 184
Lower Yellowstone Valley, 574–77; hotels, 576–77; nightlife, 577; parks, 577; restaurants, 577; sightseeing, 574–76
Lowman: sightseeing, 389
Lucky Peak State Park, 378
Luna House Museum, 458

Ma Wah Society, 529
MacGregor Ranch Museum, 68
Mackay: sightseeing, 416
Mac's Museum, 572
Madison Area–West Entrance (Yellowstone): sightseeing, 303–304
Madison Buffalo Jump State Park, 543
Madison Canyon Earthquake Area and Visitors Center, 543
Madison County Museum, 539

Madison Valley, 543
Makoshika State Park, 575, 577
Malad Gorge State Park, 410
Mammoth Hot Springs, 305
Mammoth Hot Springs area (Yellowstone): hotels, 310; restaurants, 311; sightseeing, 305–306
Manassa: sightseeing, 158
Mancos: restaurants, 191; sightseeing, 182
Mancos State Park, 195
Manderson: sightseeing, 341
Manitou Cliff Dwellings Museum, 84
Manitou Springs: hotels, 89–90; nightlife, 92; restaurants, 90–91; shopping, 91; sightseeing, 84–85
Marble: sightseeing, 134
Marcus Daly Mansion, 491
Marina at Horseshoe Bend, 343
Maroon Bells–Snowmass Wilderness, 128
Maroon Lake, 128
Marsing: restaurants, 394
Marysville: sightseeing, 522
Mason-Lovell Ranch, 343
Massacre Hill, 348
Massacre Rocks State Park, 427, 429
Matchless Mine, 118
Maverick Mountain, 534
May Minerva McCroskey State Park, 459
May Natural History Museum, 89
McCall area. *See* Hells Canyon and McCall area
McCall Winter Carnival, 384
McConnell Mansion, 459
McPhee National Recreation Area, 195
McPhee Reservoir, 182
Medicine Bow National Forest, 258–59
Medicine Lodge State Archaeological Site, 341
Medicine Lodge Wildlife Management Area, 341
Medicine Rocks State Park, 576
Medicine Wheel National Historic Landmark, 343–44
Meeker House Museum, 66
Meeteetse: shopping, 345; sightseeing, 339–40
Meeteetse Museums, 340
Mehmke's Steam Engine Museum, 588
Melba: restaurants, 394
Menor's Ferry, 296
Mesa Falls Scenic Byway, 440–41
Mesa Verde National Park: hotels, 188; sightseeing, 182
Meuller State Park and Wildlife Area, 92
Middle Park, 106, 108
Miles City: hotels, 576–77; nightlife, 577; restaurants, 577; sightseeing, 574–75
Million Dollar Cowboy Bar, 288
Million Dollar Highway, 184
Mineral Point: sightseeing, 165
Mini-Cassia area: sightseeing, 408–409
Minidoka Dam, 408–409
Minidoka National Wildlife Refuge, 409
Minnetonka Cave, 431
Miracle Rock, 173
Miramont Castle, 84
Mission Mountain Winery, 495
Mission Mountains Tribal Wilderness, 495
Mission Range, 494
Missoula, 484–90; hotels, 487–88; nightlife, 489–90; parks, 490; restaurants, 488; shopping, 489; sightseeing, 484–87; visitor information, 484
Missoula County Courthouse, 486
Missoula Memorial Rose Garden, 486
Missoula Museum of the Arts, 486
Missouri Breaks National Back Country Byway, 588
Missouri Headwaters State Park, 543, 548
Moiese: sightseeing, 494
Molly Brown House, 44, 46
Molly Kathleen Gold Mine, 88
Monarch Pass, 163
Monastery of St. Gertrude, 459
Montana. *See* Eastern Montana; Southern Montana Rockies; Western Montana Rockies
Montana Cowboys Association Museum, 578
Montana East of the Rockies. *See* Eastern Montana
Montana Historical Society Museum, 520, 522
Montana State Capitol, 520
Montana State University (MSU), 542
Montana Territorial Prison, 530
Monte Vista: hotels, 160; sightseeing, 159

Monte Vista National Wildlife Refuge, 159
Montpelier: restaurants, 433; sightseeing, 431
Montrose: sightseeing, 164
Moose: hotels, 297–98; nightlife, 298; sightseeing, 296
Moraine Park and Museum, 68–69
Moran: hotels, 297; restaurants, 298; sightseeing, 296, 297
Mormon Tabernacle, 223–24
Mormon Temple, 223
Mormon Temple and Tabernacle (Logan), 218
Mormons, 236
Morrison: restaurants, 61–62; sightseeing, 56
Morrison-Knudsen Co., 371
Morrison Knudsen Depot, 370
Morrison-Knudsen Nature Center, 371
Mosca: hotels, 160; restaurants, 161; sightseeing, 158
Moscow. *See* Lewiston-Moscow area
Mosquito Pass Road, 113
Moss Mansion, 562, 564
Mount Crested Butte: hotels, 168; nightlife, 170–71; sightseeing, 165
Mount Helena City Park, 522
Mount Meeker, 68
Mount Moran, 297
Mount Nebo Scenic Byway, 232
Mount Washburn, 307
Mountain Home Air Force Base, 392
Mountain Home and Owyhee County, 392–95; hotels, 393–94; nightlife, 394; parks, 394–95; restaurants, 394; sightseeing, 392–93
Mountaineering, 325
Mountains, meaning of, 12–13
Moyie Falls, 470
Murie Memorial Museum, 289
Murphy: sightseeing, 393
Museum of Church History and Art, 224
Museum of Mining & Geology, 372
Museum of North Idaho, 467
Museum of People and Cultures, 232
Museum of the National Park Ranger, 304
Museum of the Northern Great Plains, 580
Museum of the Plains Indian, 506
Museum of the Rockies, 540
Museum of the Upper Missouri, 580
Museum of the Yellowstone, 313
Museum of Western Art, 46–47
Museum of Western Colorado, 172
Myra Powell Art Gallery, 218

Nampa: hotels, 381; nightlife, 382; restaurants, 381; sightseeing, 380; visitor information, 380
Naples: hotels, 472
Nathrop: hotels, 114; sightseeing, 113
National Bighorn Sheep Interpretive Center, 274
National Bison Range, 494
National Center for Atmospheric Research, 65
National Elk Refuge, 286, 288
National Interagency Fire Center, 372–73
National Mining Hall of Fame and Museum, 119
National Old-Time Fiddlers' Hall of Fame, 383
National Wildlife Art Museum, 289
Native Americans (Colorado), 180–81
Natrona County International Airport, 282
Natural History Museum, 218
Navajo Lake, 178
Navajo Lake State Park, 194
Neihart: sightseeing, 588
Nevada City Museum, 538, 541
Neversweat and Washoe Railroad, 528–29
New Meadows: sightseeing, 384
Newcastle: restaurants, 356; sightseeing, 354
Newdale: sightseeing, 440
Nez Perce (Native American tribe), 461
Nez Perce National Forest, 460, 466
Nez Perce (Nee-Me-Poo) National Historic Trail, 334
Nez Perce National Historical Park, 459, 461; visitor information, 461
Niagara Springs State Park, 409
Ninemile Remount Depot, 487
Ninepipe National Wildlife Refuge, 495
Ninth Street Historic Park, 46
Niwot: shopping, 72
Nokhu Crags, 67
Nora Eccles Harrison Museum of Art, 217–18

Nordman: hotels, 472; restaurants, 473; sightseeing, 470
Norman and Lilly Herrett Museum, 408
Norris area (Yellowstone): sightseeing, 304–305
Norris Geyser Basin Museum, 304
North Cheyenne Canyon, 79
North Fork of Payette River, 384
North of Denver, 64–75; hotels, 69–70; map, 59; nightlife, 73; parks, 73–75; restaurants, 70–72; shopping, 72; sightseeing, 64–69
North of Salt Lake City, 217–23; hotels, 219–20; nightlife, 221–22; parks, 222–23; restaurants, 220–21; shopping, 221; sightseeing, 217–19
North Park, 106, 108
Northeastern Wyoming, 353–58; hotels, 355–56; nightlife, 357; parks, 357–58; restaurants, 356; shopping, 356–57; sightseeing, 353–55
Northern Cheyenne Arts and Crafts Center, 571
Northern Cheyenne Indian Reservation, 571
Northern Colorado Rockies, 16–17, 105–53; Aspen area, 126–32; Breckenridge–South Park area, 111–17; calendar of events, 21–28; Glenwood Springs area, 132–37; introduction, 105–106; map, 107; sports, 142–51; Steamboat Springs area, 137–41; transportation, 151–53; Vail-Leadville area, 117–26; weather, 105; Winter Park–Grand Lake area, 106–11
Northern Idaho Rockies, 18, 455–81; calendar of events, 21–28; Coeur d'Alene area, 466–75; introduction, 455–56; Lewiston-Moscow area, 456–66; map, 457; sports, 475–80; transportation, 480–81
Northern Pacific Depot, 484
Northern Pacific Depot Railroad Museum, 469
Northern Panhandle (Idaho), 469–70
Northern Wyoming Rockies, 17–18, 329–65; Big Horn Country, 339–46; calendar of events, 21–28; Cody area, 330–36, 338–39; introduction, 329–30; map, 331; Northeastern Wyoming, 353–58; Sheridan area, 347–53; sports, 358–64; transportation, 365
Oakley: sightseeing, 408
Oasis Bordello Museum, 469
O'Fallon Historical Museum, 576
Ogden: hotels, 220; nightlife, 221–22; restaurants, 221; sightseeing, 218–19
Ogden River Parkway, 218
Ogden Union Station, 218
Oh My God Road, 57
Ohio City: sightseeing, 166
Old Colorado City: hotels, 80; shopping, 81–82; sightseeing, 76
Old Deseret, 226
Old Ephraim's Grave, 217
Old Faithful area (Yellowstone): hotels, 310; restaurants, 311; sightseeing, 302–303; visitor information, 302
Old Faithful Geyser, 302
Old Fort Benton, 580
Old Fort Boise, 380
Old Frontier Prison, 259–60
Old Idaho Penitentiary, 371–72
Old Mission State Park, 468
Old Schoolhouse Museum, 393
Old Trail Museum, 579
Older travelers, 34–35
Oldtown: sightseeing, 470
Opera House (Central City), 58
Oregon Short Line Depot, 425
Oregon Trail, 265, 266–67, 268–69, 272
Oregon Trail Ruts National Historic Landmark, 265
Original Governor's Mansion, 522
Orofino: restaurants, 464; sightseeing, 460, 462
Orvis Hot Springs, 184
Oscar's Dreamland, 564
Our Lady of the Rockies statue, 529
Ouray: hotels, 189–90; nightlife, 193–94; restaurants, 192; shopping, 193; sightseeing, 183–84
Ouray Hot Springs Pool, 184
Outfitters and guides, 40–41. *See also* Sports *in regional chapters*
Owyhee County. *See* Mountain Home and Owyhee County
Owyhee County Historical Society, 393
Oxbow Bend, 297

Pablo: sightseeing, 495
Pablo National Wildlife Refuge, 495
Packer John County Park, 384
Packing, 29–30

Pagosa Springs: hotels, 185–86; sightseeing, 178
Pahaska Tepee Resort, 333
Painted Desert, 341
Painted Rocks State Park, 491, 493
Palisades Dam and Reservoir, 437
Paradise Valley, 549
Paramount Theatre, 47
Paris: sightseeing, 431
Paris Gibson Square, 578
Paris Idaho Stake Tabernacle, 431
Park and Sweet Grass counties, 548–52; hotels, 550; nightlife, 551; parks, 551–52; restaurants, 551; shopping, 551; sightseeing, 548–50; visitor information, 549
Park City (Colorado): sightseeing, 113
Park City (Utah): hotels, 235, 238; nightlife, 240; restaurants, 239; shopping, 239; sightseeing, 233–34
Park City Historical Society & Museum, 234
Park City Ski Area, 233–34
Park County Museum, 549
Parma: sightseeing, 380
Payette: sightseeing, 381
Payette County Historical Museum, 381
Payette Lake, 383–84
Payette National Forest, 384, 388
Payette River Scenic Route, 383–84
Peak to Peak Highway, 65
Pearl Lake State Park, 141
Pearl Street Mall, 64–65
Perrine Bridge, 406
Peter Yegen, Jr., Yellowstone County Museum, 564
Pets, traveling with, 34
Phantom Canyon, 88–89
Philipsburg: shopping, 532; sightseeing, 530, 541
Phoenix Gold Mine, 57
Picabo: sightseeing, 415
Pictograph Cave State Park, 564
Pierre Wibaux House Museum, 576
Pike National Forest, 92
Pikes Peak, 83, 84
Pikes Peak area, 83–92; hotels, 89–90; nightlife, 92; parks, 92; restaurants, 90–91; shopping, 91; sightseeing, 83–89
Pikes Peak Auto Hill Climb Race Car Museum, 85
Pikes Peak Cog Railway, 84–85
Pikes Peak Highway, 83–84
Pikes Peak Museum, 85
Pine: hotels, 391; sightseeing, 390
Pine Butte Swamp Preserve, 579
Pinedale: hotels, 275; nightlife, 277; restaurants, 276; sightseeing, 274
Pintler Scenic Route, 529–30
Pioneer Historic Route, 430–31
Pioneer Memorial Museum, 224–25
Pioneer Mountains National Scenic Byway, 534–35
Pioneer Museum, 163–64
Pioneer Relic Hall, 432
Pioneer Trail State Park, 226
Pitkin: sightseeing, 166
Pitkin County Airport, 151
Pittsburg Landing, 460
Placid Lake State Park, 499
Plains Indian Museum, 332
Plants, 10–11
Plummer: sightseeing, 467–68
Pocatello area, 425–29; hotels, 427; nightlife, 428–29; parks, 429; restaurants, 427–28; shopping, 428; sightseeing, 425–27; visitor information, 425
Pocatello Municipal Airport, 452
Polaris: sightseeing, 534
Polson: hotels, 496–97; restaurants, 497; shopping, 498; sightseeing, 495
Pompeys Pillar, 574
Ponderosa Pine Scenic Route, 389
Ponderosa State Park, 384, 388
Post Falls: hotels, 471; sightseeing, 468
Potlach: sightseeing, 459
Poudre River Canyon, 67
Powder River Historical Museum, 572
Powell: sightseeing, 342
Prairie County Museum, 575
Pray: sightseeing, 549
Preston: sightseeing, 432
Prichard Gallery, 458
Priest Lake, 470
Priest Lake State Park, 470, 475
Priest River, 470
Primitive camping. *See* Camping
Pro Rodeo Hall of Fame and American Cowboy Museum, 77
Promontory Point, 218
Provo: hotels, 234; nightlife, 240; restaurants, 238; shopping, 239; sightseeing, 231–32
Provo Canyon, 232
Pryor: hotels, 572; sightseeing, 571

Pryor Mountains National Wild Horse Range, 343, 571
Public transportation. *See* Transportation *in regional chapters*
Pueblo Levee Mural Project, 93
Pueblo Memorial Airport, 102
Pueblo-Walsenburg-Trinidad area, 93–96; hotels, 94; nightlife, 95; parks, 95–96; restaurants, 94–95; sightseeing, 93–94
Pullman-Moscow Regional Airport, 481
Purgatory: hotels, 190; sightseeing, 185

Quake Lake, 543
Quarry View Park, 371

Rafting, 39. *See also* Sports *in regional chapters*
Ranchester: sightseeing, 348, 349
Range Riders Museum, 575
Rattlesnake Canyon, 173, 174
Rattlesnake National Recreation Area and Wilderness, 486
Rawlings: hotels, 261; sightseeing, 259–60
Red Butte Garden and Arboretum, 226
Red Cloud Loop, 214
Red Fleet State Park, 216
Red Lodge: hotels, 566–67; nightlife, 569; restaurants, 567–68; sightseeing, 565
Red Lodge Mountain Ski Area, 565
Red Mountain Pass, 184
Red Rock Lakes National Wildlife Refuge, 536–37
Red Rock Pass, 432
Red Rocks Park and Amphitheater, 56, 63
Redfish Lake, 421
Redstone: hotels, 135; sightseeing, 134
Redstone Castle (Cleveholm Manor), 134
Register Cliff State Historic Site, 265
Register Rock, 427
Restaurants, 31–32. *See also* Restaurants *in area and city entries*
Rexbury: hotels, 441; restaurants, 442; sightseeing, 440
Ridgway: shopping, 193; sightseeing, 184
Ridgway State Park, 195–96
Rifle Falls State Park, 136–37
Rigby: sightseeing, 440
Riggins: sightseeing, 460
Rim Rock Drive, 173
Rio Grande County Museum, 159
Rio Grande National Forest, 163
Ririe: sightseeing, 437
River rafting, 39. *See also* Sports *in regional chapters*
Riverfront Steamboat Levee, 580
Riverton: sightseeing, 274
Riverton Regional Airport, 282
Robber's Roost, 538
Rock Springs Airport, 282
Rock Springs–Green River area, 259–64; hotels, 261–62; nightlife, 263; parks, 263–64; restaurants, 262–63; shopping, 263; sightseeing, 259–61
The Rockies. *See* Rocky Mountains
Rocky Bar: sightseeing, 390
Rocky Boy's Indian Reservation, 585
Rocky Mountain Biological Laboratory, 166
Rocky Mountain Elk Foundation, 486
Rocky Mountain National Park, 68, 73
Rocky Mountains, 1–41; areas, 16–19; calendar of events, 21–28; economy, 120–21; fauna, 11, 14–16; flora, 10–11; geology, 4–5; history, 5–10; map, 3; seasons, 19–21; sports, 37–41; visitor information, 29
Ronald V. Jensen Living Historical Farm, 218
Roosevelt Grove of Ancient Cedars, 470
Roosevelt National Forest, 75
Roseberry: sightseeing, 384
Rosebud Battlefield State Park, 571–72
Rosemont, 93
Ross Creek Cedar Grove Scenic Area, 501
Ross Park and Zoo, 425
Round Lake State Park, 475
Routt National Forest, 141
Roxborough State Park, 55
Royal Gorge, 89
Rupert: sightseeing, 408–409
Russell, Charles M., 578, 583
Russell Freeman Park, 435
Russell Gulch: sightseeing, 57

Sacajawea's grave, 273–74
Saco: sightseeing, 585–86
St. Anthony: sightseeing, 440
St. Anthony Sand Dunes, 440

St. Charles: sightseeing, 431
St. Francis Xavier Catholic Church (Missoula), 486
St. Helena Cathedral, 520
St. Ignatius: hotels, 496; shopping, 498; sightseeing, 494
St. Joe River, 467
St. Maries: sightseeing, 467
St. Mary's Lake and Glacier, 57
St. Mary's Mission, 491
St. Peter's Catholic Church (Wibaux), 576
St. Stephen's Mission: shopping, 277; sightseeing, 274
Salida: hotels, 115; restaurants, 115–16; sightseeing, 113
Salmon: hotels, 423; restaurants, 423; sightseeing, 422
Salmon National Forest, 422, 424
Salmon River Country, 421–22
Salt Lake Art Center, 224
Salt Lake City, 223–31; hotels, 227–28; map, 225; nightlife, 230–31; parks, 231; restaurants, 228–29; shopping, 229–30; sightseeing, 223–27
Salt Lake City International Airport, 246
San Isabel National Forest, 95
San Juan Historical Society Pioneer Museum, 178
San Juan Mountains, 86
San Juan National Forest, 194–95
San Juan Skyway area. *See* Durango and San Juan Skyway area
San Luis: hotels, 160; restaurants, 161; shopping, 162; sightseeing, 158
San Luis Lakes State Park, 162–63
San Luis Museum, Cultural and Commercial Center, 158
San Luis Valley, 158
San Miguel County Historical Museum, 183
Sandpoint: hotels, 471–72; nightlife, 474; restaurants, 472–73; shopping, 473; sightseeing, 469–70; visitor information, 470
Sangre de Cristo Arts and Conference Center, 93
Saratoga: hotels, 245; sightseeing, 255
Saratoga Hot Springs, 255
Saratoga Museum, 255
Sawtooth National Forest, 413
Sawtooth National Recreation Area (SNRA) and Wilderness, 389, 420, 423; visitor information, 420
The Sawtooths and Upper Salmon, 420–24; hotels, 422–23; parks, 423–24; restaurants, 423; sightseeing, 420–22; visitor information, 420, 421
Scapegoat Wilderness, 522
Schweitzer Mountain Resort, 470
Scuba diving, 476
Seasons, 19–21, 105
Seedskadee National Wildlife Refuge, 264
Seeley Lake, 496
Selway-Bitterroot Wilderness, 491
Seminoe State Park, 259, 263–64
Seven Devils Mountains, 460
Seven Falls, 79
Shadow Mountain Lake, 108
Shelby: sightseeing, 584–85
Shelby's Marias Museum of History and Art, 584
Shell: sightseeing, 344
Shell Falls and Canyon, 344
Sheridan (Montana): sightseeing, 538
Sheridan area (Wyoming), 347–53; hotels, 350–51; nightlife, 352–53; parks, 353; restaurants, 351–52; shopping, 352; sightseeing, 347–50; visitor information, 347
Sheridan County Airport, 365
Sheridan Inn, 347
Sheridan Opera House, 182
Sherman: sightseeing, 165
Shoshone: sightseeing, 410
Shoshone–Bannock Tribal Museum, 426
Shoshone Falls, 408, 413
Shoshone Falls/Dierkes Lake Park, 413
Shoshone Indian Buffalo Jump, 422
Shoshone Indian Ice Caves, 410
Shoshone National Forest, 277–78, 333, 338–39
Showdown Ski Area, 588
Shrine Pass Road, 117
Sidney: hotels, 589; restaurants, 589
Sierra Silver Mine, 469
Silver City: hotels, 394; sightseeing, 393
Silver Creek Preserve, 415, 443
Silver Gate: sightseeing, 314
Silver Mountain, 468
Silver Queen Gondola, 127–28
Silver Thread Scenic Byway, 159, 164
Silver Valley, 468–69
Silverthorne: hotels, 113
Silverton: hotels, 190; restaurants, 192; shopping, 193; sightseeing, 184–85

Silverwood Theme Park, 469
Sinks Canyon State Park, 272
16th Street Mall, 47
Skiing, 40. *See also* Sports *in regional chapters*
Skyline Drive, 89
Skytram, 232
Sluice Boxes State Park, 588
Smith River State Park, 527
Smokejumper Training Center and Aerial Fire Depot, 486–87
Snake River, 290
Snake River Birds of Prey National Conservation Area, 373, 379
Snake River Canyon, 290, 406
Snake River Greenbelt, 434–35
Snake River Plain, 415–16
Snake River Stampede, 380
Snow King Resort, 289
Snowmass: hotels, 129
Snowy Range Scenic Byway, 254
Soda Springs: hotels, 432; restaurants, 433; sightseeing, 430
Somers: restaurants, 497; sightseeing, 496
South Jenny Lake, 296
South of Salt Lake City, 231–35, 238–41; hotels, 234–35, 238; nightlife, 240; parks, 240–41; restaurants, 238–39; shopping, 239; sightseeing, 231–34
South Park, 108. *See also* Breckenridge–South Park area
South Park City (museum), 113
South Pass, 272–73
South Pass City State Historic Site, 273
Southeastern Idaho Rockies, 18, 405–53; Bear River Country, 430–34; calendar of events, 21–28; Henry's Fork, 440–42; Idaho Falls, 434–37; introduction, 405–406; map, 407; Pocatello area, 425–29; Sawtooths and Upper Salmon, 420–24; sports, 442–51; Sun Valley area, 414–20; Swan and Teton Valleys, 437–39; transportation, 451–53; Twin Falls area, 406–13
Southern Colorado Rockies, 17, 155–209; Alamosa area, 158–63; calendar of events, 21–28; Durango and San Juan Skyway area, 178–96; Grand Junction area, 172–77; Gunnison–Crested Butte area, 163–71; introduction, 155–56; map, 157; sports, 196–206; transportation, 207–209
Southern Montana Rockies, 19, 519–59; Alder Gulch, 538–40; Bozeman area, 540, 542–48; Butte area, 527–33; calendar of events, 21–28; Dillon area, 533–37; Helena area, 520–27; introduction, 519; map, 221; Park and Sweet Grass counties, 548–52; sports, 552–58; transportation, 558–59
Southern Ute Indian Cultural Center, 178
Southern Wyoming Rockies, 17, 249–83; calendar of events, 21–28; Casper area, 265–71; Cheyenne-Laramie area, 250–59; introduction, 249–50; Lander area, 272–78; map, 251; Rock Springs–Green River area, 259–64; sports, 278–81; transportation, 282–83
Southwestern Idaho Rockies, 18, 367–403; Boise area, 368–79; Boise County and Boise Basin, 389–92; calendar of events, 21–28; Hells Canyon and McCall area, 382–88; introduction, 367; map, 369; Mountain Home and Owyhee County, 392–95; sports, 395–401; transportation, 401–403; Treasure Valley, 380–82
Spanish Peaks, 94
Spaulding: sightseeing, 459
Spencer: sightseeing, 435
Spencer Opal Mine, 435
Spokane International Airport, 481
Sports, 37–41. *See also* Sports *in regional chapters*
Sqélix'w-Aqsmakni'k Cultural Center, 495
Staff House Museum, 468
Stagecoach State Park, 141
Stanley: hotels, 422; restaurants, 423; sightseeing, 421
Stanley Hotel, 67
Stanley Museum, 421
Stanrod Mansion, 429
Starvation State Park, 216–17
Stations of the Cross, 158
Steam Railroad Museum, 539
Steamboat Lake State Park, 141
Steamboat Ski Area, 137
Steamboat Springs area, 137–41; hotels, 138–39; nightlife, 140; parks,

141; restaurants, 139–40; shopping, 140; sightseeing, 137–38
Steinaker State Park, 216
Stevensville: sightseeing, 491
Story: sightseeing, 348
Strawberry Park Hot Springs, 137
Stringtown: restaurants, 124
Sugarloaf Recreation Area, 384–85
Summit Lake, 56
Sun Valley area, 414–20; hotels, 416–17; nightlife, 419; parks, 420; restaurants, 417–18; shopping, 418–19; sightseeing, 414–16
Sun Valley Resort, 414
Sunbeam: sightseeing, 421
Sundance (resort) (Utah): hotels, 235; restaurants, 238; sightseeing, 232
Sundance (Wyoming): hotels, 356; sightseeing, 354
Sundance Mountain, 354
Sunlight Basin, 334
Sunnyslope: nightlife, 382
Super Slide, 112
Swallow Park, 458
Swan and Teton Valleys, 437–39; hotels, 438–39; nightlife, 439; parks, 439; restaurants, 439; sightseeing, 437–38
Swan Lake, 496
Swan Valley (town): sightseeing, 438
Sweet Grass County. *See* Park and Sweet Grass counties
Swetsville Zoo, 67

Tabor Opera House, 119
Targhee National Forest, 294–95, 437, 439
Targhee Pass, 441
Tautphaus Park, 435
Taxis. *See* Transportation *in regional chapters*
Taylor Park Reservoir, 171
Teller House, 58
Telluride: hotels, 188–89; nightlife, 193; restaurants, 191–92; shopping, 193; sightseeing, 182–83
Telluride Regional Airport, 208
Temple Square, 223–24
Ten Sleep: hotels, 345; sightseeing, 341
Terry: sightseeing, 575
Terry Badlands, 575
Tesla Museum, 76
Teton County Historical Center, 288
Teton Dam Site, 440
Teton National Scenic Byway, 440
Teton Pass, 290, 438
Teton Science School, 289
Teton Valley. *See* Swan and Teton Valleys
Teton Village: hotels, 291; nightlife, 293, 294; sightseeing, 289–90
Tetonia: hotels, 438; sightseeing, 438
Thermopolis: hotels, 344–45; restaurants, 345; sightseeing, 340
This Is the Place Monument, 226
Thomas-Billings Home, 58, 60
Thompson Falls State Park, 498
Thompson-Hickman Memorial Museum, 539
Thousand Springs Scenic Route, 409–10
Three Forks: hotels, 545; sightseeing, 543
Three Island Crossing State Park, 392, 394–95
Thunder Basin National Grassland, 354
Timpanogos Cave National Monument, 232–33
Tincup: sightseeing, 166
Tongue River Reservoir State Park, 573–74
Towaoc: nightlife, 193; sightseeing, 178
Tower-Roosevelt area (Yellowstone): hotels, 310; restaurants, 311–12; sightseeing, 306–307
Townsend: sightseeing, 522
Trail End Historic Center, 348
Trail Ridge Road, 69
Trail Town, 332
Train travel. *See* Transportation *in regional chapters*
Treasure Valley, 380–82; hotels, 381; parks, 382; restaurants, 381; nightlife, 382; sightseeing, 380–81; visitor information, 380
Treaty Rock Park, 468
Trianon Museum of Art Gallery, 47
Trimble Hot Springs, 185
Trinidad. *See* Pueblo-Walsenburg-Trinidad area
Trinidad State Recreation Area, 96
Trout Creek Buffalo Preserve, 333
Troy: sightseeing, 501
Tubbs Hill, 467
Turner Museum, 47
Turquoise Lake, 125
Twin Bridges: restaurants, 539

Twin Falls, 408
Twin Falls area, 406–13; hotels, 410–11; nightlife, 412; parks, 413; restaurants, 411–12; shopping, 412; sightseeing, 406–10
Twin Falls–Sun Valley Regional Airport, 452

Uinta and Ouray Indian Reservation, 214
Uinta National Forest, 240
UL Bend National Wildlife Refuge, 586
Ulm Pishkun State Park, 579
Ulrich's Fossil Quarries, 261
Uncompahgre National Forest, 176–77
Uncompahgre National Forest (Southern Unit), 196
Union Station (Denver), 47
United States Air Force Academy, 77
U.S. Geological Survey National Earthquake Information Center, 60
United States Mint, 46
U.S. Olympic Training Center, 76
University of Colorado, 64
University of Colorado Museum, 64
University of Idaho (UI), 458
University of Montana (UM), 486
University of Utah, 226
University of Wyoming, 253–54
Upper Cascade Falls, 184
Upper and Lower Mesa Falls, 441
Upper Missouri National Wild and Scenic River, 580
Upper Snake River Valley Historical Museum, 440
Utah Field House of Natural History State Park and Dinosaur Gardens, 212
Utah Historical Society Museum, 226
Utah Lake, 231
Utah Lake State Park, 240
Utah Museum of Fine Arts, 226
Utah Museum of Natural History, 226
Utah Rockies, 17, 211–47; calendar of events, 21–28; introduction, 211–12; maps, 213, 225; north of Salt Lake City, 217–23; Salt Lake City, 223–31; south of Salt Lake City, 231–35, 238–41; sports, 241–45; transportation, 245–47; Vernal area, 212–17
Utah State Capitol, 225
Utah State Railroad Museum, 218
Utah State University, 217–18
Utah State University Botanical Gardens, 218
Ute Indian Museum, 164
Ute Mountain Casino, 178
Ute Mountain Tribal Park, 178

Vail–Beaver Creek Jet Center, 151
Vail-Leadville area, 117–26; hotels, 119, 122–23; nightlife, 125; parks, 125–26; restaurants, 123–24; shopping, 124; sightseeing, 86, 117–19
Vail Nature Center, 118
Vail Pass, 117
Vail Valley, 117
Vail Village. *See* Vail-Leadville area
Valley County Museum, 384
Valley County Pioneer Museum, 586
Van Briggle Art Pottery, 78
Vedauwoo Recreation Area, 253
Vega State Park, 177
Vernal area, 212–17; hotels, 215; nightlife, 216; parks, 216–17; restaurants, 215–16; sightseeing, 212–15
Veterans Memorial State Park, 371
Victor (Colorado): hotels, 90; restaurants, 91; sightseeing, 88
Victor (Idaho): nightlife, 439; restaurants, 439; sightseeing, 438
Victor (Montana): restaurants, 492; shopping, 492–93
Victor–Lowell Thomas Museum, 88
Victorian Village, 550
Virginia City: hotels, 539; nightlife, 540; restaurants, 539; shopping, 540; sightseeing, 538–39; visitor information, 539
Visitor information, 29. *See also* Visitor information *in area and city entries*
Visitors Center and Cattle Drive Monument, 562
Vore Buffalo Jump, 354

Wahkpa Chug'n, 585
Wah'-Muza, 426
Walden: sightseeing, 108
Walker Field Public Airport, 207
Wallace: nightlife, 473–74; restaurants, 472; shopping, 473; sightseeing, 469
Wallace District Mining Museum, 469
Walsenburg. *See* Pueblo-Walsenburg-Trinidad area

Wapiti: hotels, 335; restaurants, 336; sightseeing, 333
Warhawk Air Museum, 380
Warm Lake: sightseeing, 385
Warren Air Force Base, 252–53
Wasatch-Cache National Forest, 222–23
Wasatch Mountain State Park, 241
Washakie County Museum and Cultural Center, 341
Washoe Theater, 529
Waterskiing, 96, 359, 444, 476
Wayan: sightseeing, 431
Weather, 19–21, 105
Wedding of the Waters, 340
Weiser: hotels, 385; nightlife, 386; sightseeing, 383
Wellsville Mountains, 218
Wendell: sightseeing, 409
West Glacier: sightseeing, 500, 504–505
West of Denver, 55–64; hotels, 61; map, 59; nightlife, 63; parks, 63–64; restaurants, 61–62; shopping, 62–63; sightseeing, 55–60
West Thumb. *See* Grant Village–West Thumb area
West Vail: hotels, 122; nightlife, 125
West Yellowstone: hotels, 314; nightlife, 316; restaurants, 315; shopping, 315; sightseeing, 313; visitor information, 313
West Yellowstone Airport, 326
Western Heritage Center, 564
Western Montana College, 534
Western Montana Rockies, 18–19, 483–517; Bitterroot Valley, 490–93; calendar of events, 21–28; Flathead Indian Reservation and Lake, 494–99; Flathead Valley, 499–504; Glacier National Park, 504–508, 510; introduction, 483–84; map, 485; Missoula, 484–90; sports, 510–16; transportation, 516–17
Western Museum of Mining & Industry, 77–78
Wheeler Opera House, 127
Wheeler-Stallard House Museum, 127
White Bird: sightseeing, 460
White Bird Battlefield, 461
White Bird Hill, 460
White House Ranch, 77
White Pine Scenic Route, 459
White River National Forest, 125-26, 132
White Sulphur Springs: hotels, 524; sightseeing, 523
Whitefish: hotels, 501; nightlife, 503; sightseeing, 500
Whitefish Lake State Park, 500, 503
Whitney Gallery of Western Art, 332
Wibaux: sightseeing, 576
Wiesbaden Hot Springs Spa, 184
Wilderness areas and permits, 38
Will Rogers Shrine of the Sun, 78–79
Willard Bay State Park, 223
Willow Bay Recreation Area, 429
Wilson: nightlife, 294; restaurants, 292; sightseeing, 290
Winchester Lake State Park, 465
Wind Cave, 217
Wind River Indian Reservation, 273
Wind River Range, 272
Windsurfing, 96
Winter Park–Grand Lake area, 106–11; hotels, 108–10; nightlife, 111; parks, 111; restaurants, 110; shopping, 110; sightseeing, 106–108
Winter Park Ski Train, 106
Winter sports, 40. *See also* Sports *in regional chapters*
Wisdom: sightseeing, 535
Wolf: hotels, 350
Wolf Creek Pass, 178
Wolf Lodge Bay, 467
Woodland Park, 500
Woodland Park: sightseeing, 85
Woody Creek: restaurants, 130
Worland: shopping, 346; sightseeing, 340–41
World Center for Birds of Prey, 373, 379
World Figure Skating Hall of Fame & Museum, 78
World Museum of Mining, 528–29
Wright: sightseeing, 354
Wyoming. *See* Northern Wyoming Rockies; Southern Wyoming Rockies; Yellowstone and Jackson Hole
Wyoming & Colorado Scenic Railroad, 254
Wyoming Downs, 261
Wyoming Pioneer Museum, 265
Wyoming State Capitol, 250, 252
Wyoming State Museum, 252
Wyoming Territorial Park, 254
Wyoming Vietnam Veterans Memorial, 333

Yampa Valley Regional Airport, 151
Yampah Vapor Caves, 134
Yankee Fork Gold Dredge, 421
Yellowstone and Jackson Hole, 17, 285-327; calendar of events, 21–28; Grand Teton National Park, 295–99; introduction, 285–86; Jackson Hole area, 286–95; map, 287; sports, 316–25; transportation, 325–27; Yellowstone Gateway Communities, 313–16
Yellowstone Art Center, 564
Yellowstone Gateway Communities, 313–16; hotels, 314–15; nightlife, 316; restaurants, 315; shopping, 315; sightseeing, 313–14; visitor information, 313, 314
Yellowstone Highway, 333
Yellowstone IMAX Theatre, 313
Yellowstone Institute, 307
Yellowstone Lake, 301
Yellowstone Lake area: hotels, 311; restaurants, 312; sightseeing, 309; visitor information, 309
Yellowstone National Park, 299–313; hotels, 310–11; parks, 312–13; restaurants, 311–12; sightseeing, 299–309
Yellowstone Regional Airport, 365
Yellowtail Dam, 571
Yellowtail Wildlife Habitat Management Area, 343

Zim's Hot Springs, 384
Zoo Boise, 370

HIDDEN GUIDES

Adventure travel or a relaxing vacation?—"Hidden" guidebooks are the only travel books in the business to provide detailed information on both. Aimed at environmentally aware travelers, our motto is "Adventure Travel Plus." These books combine details on unique hotels, restaurants and sightseeing with information on camping, sports and hiking for the outdoor enthusiast.

ULTIMATE GUIDES

These innovative guides present the best and most unique features of a destination. Quality is the keynote. They are as likely to cover a mom-and-pop café as a gourmet restaurant, a quaint bed and breakfast as a five-star tennis resort. In addition to thoroughly covering each destination, they feature short articles and one-line "teasers" that are both fun and informative.

THE NEW KEY GUIDES

Based on the concept of ecotourism, The New Key Guides are dedicated to the preservation of Central America's rare and endangered species, architecture and archaeology. Filled with helpful tips, they give travelers everything they need to know about these exotic destinations.

About the Authors

Richard Harris is co-author of Ulysses Press' bestselling *Hidden Southwest* and has written or co-written eight other guidebooks including *The New Key to Cancún and the Yucatán*. He has also served as contributing editor on guides to Mexico, New Mexico and other ports of call for John Muir Publications, Fodor's, Birnbaum and Access guides. He is president of PEN New Mexico. When not traveling, Richard writes and lives in Santa Fe, New Mexico with his shaggy 150-pound dog Oso (that's "bear" in Spanish).

John Gottberg, co-author of Ulysses Press' *Hidden Pacific Northwest* and *Ultimate Washington*, has traveled and worked all over the world. The former chief editor of the Insight Guide series and the travel news and graphics editor for the *Los Angeles Times*, he has written eight travel books and been published in *Travel & Leisure* and *Islands* magazines. He is presently a contributing editor for *International Living* magazine and a restaurant critic for the *Idaho Statesman* in Boise where he lives.

About the Illustrator

Doug McCarthy is a graduate of San Francisco's Academy of Art and the co-owner of Graphic Detail, a specialty graphics company. A native New Yorker, he lives in the San Francisco Bay area with his family.